STRATEGIC HUMAN RESOURCE MANAGEMENT

SECOND 2 EDITION

STRATEGIC HUMAN RESOURCE MANAGEMENT

SECOND 2 EDITION

Jeffrey A. Mello
Towson University

THOMSON
™
SOUTH-WESTERN

Australia · Canada · Mexico · Singapore · Spain · United Kingdom · United States

THOMSON

SOUTH-WESTERN™

Strategic Human Resource Management

Second Edition

Jeffrey A. Mello

VP/Editorial Director:
Jack W. Calhoun

VP/Editor-in-Chief:
Dave Shaut

Sr. Publisher:
Melissa Acuña

Acquisitions Editor:
Joe Sabatino

Sr. Developmental Editor:
Mardell Toomey

Marketing Manager:
Jacquelyn Carrillo

Production Editor:
Cliff Kallemeyn

Technology Project Editor:
Kristen Meere

Media Editor:
Karen Schaffer

Manufacturing Coordinator:
Diane Lohman

Art Director:
Mike Stratton

Production House:
Stratford Publishing Services, Inc.

Printer:
Courier
Westford, MA

DEDICATION

To my daughter and inspiration,
Logan Simone Mello

ABOUT THE AUTHOR

Jeffrey A. Mello is Professor and Chair of the Management Department in the School of Business and Economics at Towson University. He previously was a faculty member at George Washington University, the University of California at Berkeley, and Northeastern University, from where he received his Ph.D. He has been a recipient of the David L. Bradford Outstanding Educator Award, presented by the Organizational Behavior Teaching Society, and has received international, national, and institutional awards for his research. He has authored three books and published more than one hundred book chapters, journal articles, and conference papers in journals such as the *Journal of Business Ethics, Business Horizons, International Journal of Public Administration, Business & Society Review, Journal of Employment Discrimination Law, Seton Hall Legislative Journal, Journal of Individual Employment Rights, Public Personnel Management, Employee Responsibilities and Rights Journal, Labor Law Journal, Journal of Law and Business* and the *Journal of Management Education.* He currently serves as an editor of *Employee Responsibilities and Rights Journal* and on the editorial review boards of four leading management journals. He has also served as an editor for the *Journal of Management Education.* He is a member of the national and regional divisions of the Academy of Legal Studies in Business, Organizational Behavior Teaching Society, Decision Sciences Institute, Society for Human Resource Management and the Academy of Management.

BRIEF CONTENTS

CONTENTS

7 Employment Law 297

PART 2: IMPLEMENTATION OF STRATEGIC HUMAN RESOURCE MANAGEMENT

8 Staffing 343

PART 3: HARVARD BUSINESS SCHOOL CASES

PREFACE

Several years ago, while teaching at the Haas School of Business at the University of California at Berkeley, I was asked to develop a new graduate-level (MBA) course in strategic human resource management. I was not able to find an appropriate text. Although I found the market flooded with a variety of HR texts, none was a true text in *strategic* HR. Certain texts had the word "strategic" in their titles, but none provided a truly integrative framework that linked HR practices and programs with the process of strategic management. At best, these books contained a cursory chapter that addressed strategic HR and then abandoned the concept in subsequent chapters in favor of more traditional coverage of HR from the perspective of "personnel administration." At worst, they had no content that related to strategy at all.

Shortly thereafter, I attended the Human Resources/Industrial Relations Teaching Conference in Atlanta. At that conference, various "interest groups" convened to discuss HR subject matter. I attended the strategic HR group, along with approximately two dozen other faculty members from business schools on several continents. When the leader of the group opened the discussion, the first question that was immediately raised was whether anyone knew of a good text in strategic HR. Everyone in the room broke into laughter as the central focus of the next hour became the shared perception that there was not a single good text in strategic HR. The question became, "Why won't someone write one?!" Needless to say, I was pleased to find my perceptions of the market confirmed and excited about the possibility of writing a text in strategic HR. However, that still left me with a course to teach and no suitable text.

Frustrated, I decided against using a conventional text and compiled a collection of published articles, including some of my own writings, to use as readings that were centered around a conceptual model of strategic HR I had developed. Student reaction to the course framework and readings was extremely positive. I subsequently taught the course as a capstone offering to a group of graduate students who were enrolled in a specialized HR degree program. Many of these students were middle- and even senior-level HR managers employed in a variety of organizations. The fact that they also found the course and course materials so relevant and applicable to their job responsibilities led me to believe that I had developed something of value for both academic and practitioner audiences.

The result of these experiences is this text. *Strategic Human Resource Management* is designed for both graduate students enrolled in a survey course in human resource management who would benefit from a general management approach to strategic HR as well as for working professionals enrolled in specialized HR and executive programs as a capstone offering. The materials within the book, including text, readings and exercises, have also been utilized successfully at the advanced undergraduate level.

Since the printing of the first edition much has changed in human resource management. It is virtually impossible to pick up any practitioner-oriented publication on HR and not read about the need for HR to be strategic. In the academic domain, there has been a significant increase in the number of published articles in the management literature related to HR. No longer is HR simply relegated to specialized journals that deal with HR. Indeed both the academic and practitioner literature show a significant movement toward the publication of HR-oriented articles, illustrating clearly the fact the HR is a general management responsibility and its effective practice a key to successful operating results.

ORGANIZATION AND CONTENT

The text is organized into two sections. The first section, Chapters 1-7, examines the context of strategic HR and develops a framework and conceptual model for the practice of strategic HR. The chapters in this section examine employees as "investments;" explore trends that are affecting human resource management practice; describe what strategic HR is, particularly in contrast to more traditional approaches to HR; and look at how both the design of work systems and relevant employment laws influence the practice of managing people in organizations. The second section, Chapters 8-14, examines the actual practice and implementation of strategic HR through a discussion of strategic issues that need to be addressed while developing specific programs and policies related to the traditional functional areas of HR (staffing, training, performance management, etc.). Covered within this section are strategic issues related to staffing, training, performance management, compensation, labor relations, employee separation, and managing a global workforce. Both the integrative framework that requires linkage between and consistency among these functional HR activities and the approach toward writing about these traditional functional areas from a strategic perspective distinguish the text from what is currently on the market.

CHAPTER FEATURES

All chapters contain the following:

- an opening vignette featuring a well-known organization to introduce chapter topic as well as several additional vignettes within each chapter that illustrate pertinent chapter concepts
- very current research

- intermittent notes appearing at the bottom of the page alert the reader to pertinent readings found later in each chapter
- three carefully selected readings that are integrated within the text discussion

Strong pedagogical features appear at the end of each reading and at the end of each chapter that are designed to foster the learning experience individually, in the classroom, as a group, and on the Internet. These include:

- end-of-chapter discussion questions
- experiential exercises to aid in student learning
- innovative Internet exercises
- recommended discussion questions for each of the readings

NEW TO THE SECOND EDITION

In keeping with the most pertinent issues within human resource management there are significant additions to this second edition. A full 50% of the readings are new to this edition. The readings provide a balance between those articles that have become "classics" and those that represent the latest in thinking and practice relative to human resource management. There are also 18 new original exhibits that explain chapter concepts, 44 new "in practice" vignettes, which describe strategic HR practices in a wide variety of organizations and 161 new references.

There is also significant new chapter content. Chapter 1 has new sections on the valuation of human assets and measurement of the human capital and HR value chain. Chapter 2 has a greatly expanded discusion of technology now with three sub-components: telecommuting, employee surveillance and e-HR. It also has a greatly expanded discussion of diversity, which includes extended coverage of generational diversity and disabilities. Finally, it has a new section on ethics, which includes off-duty behavior, non-compete clauses, Sarbanes-Oxley Act and codes of ethics. Chapter 4 has new sections on Ulrich's HR roles, Lengnick-Halls' HR roles, HR competencies, and Lepak and Snell's employment models. Chapter 5 has greatly expanded coverage of succession planning as well as a new section on CEO succession. Chapter 6 has expanded coverage of rotation program, teams and mergers and acquisitions as well as a new section on outsourcing and offshoring. Chapter 7 has an updated section on EEOC activities as well as an enhanced discussion of the Americans With Disabilities Act and a new section on employment practices liability insurance. Chapter 8 has expanded coverage of online recruiting as well as new sections on behavioral interviewing and the Big Five personality traits. Chapter 10 has enhanced coverage of multi-rater feedback and forced rankings as well as a new section on competencies. Chapter 11 has updated coverage of the Fair Labor Standards Act, enhanced coverage of performance-based pay systems and a new section on executive compensation. Chapter 12 has a new section on the rights of non-unionized employees under the NLRA as well as an update on new union organizing strategies. Chapter 13 has expanded sections on challenges associated with downsizing, the strategic management of retention and retirement. Finally, Chapter 14 has new sections on terrorism and the European Union.

Also new to this edition is a set of recommended cases published by Harvard Business School Publishing (HBSP). Thomson Higher Education is an authorized distributor of customized cases from HBSP and, for those instructors who prefer to teach using the case method, two cases have been recommended for each chapter that closely parallel the subject matter of each chapter and the context and framework in which it is presented in the text. Many of these cases apply material that cuts across several chapters and topics and hence, are truly strategic in nature. The organizations described in the cases are intentionally diverse. They represent a variety of industries and also vary in size, ownership and stage of development. Many of them are organizations with which students have direct experience; others are those that few, if any, students have ever heard of. All of the cases, however, provide rich, practical, hands-on illustration of challenges that real organizations face relative to the strategic management of human resources.

INSTRUCTOR RESOURCES

We provide an instructor's resource CD-ROM (ISBN: 0324290446) to accompany this text that includes an instructor's manual, prepared by Tamela D. Ferguson of The University of Louisiana at Lafayette, that includes chapter outlines, answers to end-of-chapter content, and suggested topics for student papers. Additionally, the IRCD contains a PowerPoint slide presentation prepared by Nancy Day of The University of Missouri that covers all main text concepts, including slides that will encourage classroom discussion of the main text content and readings.

ANCILLARY PRODUCTS

The accompanying instructor's manual with test bank (ISBN 0-324-06585-X) provides suggestions as to how to use each of these various activities as well as how to create an integrated and stimulating learning environment that incorporates a variety of learning approaches. PowerPoint® presentation slides have been created to accompany chapter material and enliven presentation of text material in the classroom. Our Web site, http://mello.swcollege.com also provides additional resources for students and instructors.

Thomson Business & Professional Publishing is an authorized distributor of **Harvard Business School Publishing case studies** and **Harvard Business Review article reprints**. This unique opportunity offers:

Convenience for You: Work with one source instead of multiple vendors, allowing your local Thomson representative to manage the prompt delivery of your teaching resources and student materials.

Convenience for Your Students: Students get everything they need in one affordable package on the bookstore shelf—with less hassle for them and less concern for you that they get everything they need.

Affordable Resources: We are able to provide printed articles and cases at very affordable and competitive prices. If you package your coursepack with a Thomson textbook, you can be assured you are providing your students the best possible price. To learn more, contact your Thomson representative.

Access to our Business & Company Resource Center (BCRC): A complete business library at your fingertips, BCRC is an online business research tool that allows students to search thousands of periodicals, journals, references, financial information, industry reports, company histories and more. To learn more visit: http://bcrc.swlearning.com

If you are interested in ordering or learning more about Harvard Business School Publishing cases and articles—including those recommended in the case map provided with this text—please contact your local Thomson sales representative.

ACKNOWLEDGMENTS

Numerous individuals were instrumental in ensuring the success of the first edition of this text as well as with the development of this second edition. The staff at South-Western / Thomson has displayed support and unbridled enthusiasm for this project since its inception. Thanks to Charles McCormack, original Acquisitions Editor, Joe Sabatino, Acquisitions Editor for the second edition, and Senior Developmental Editor *extra ordinaire* (emphasis added by me) Mardell Toomey for their contributions. Thanks to my colleagues who provided support, encouragement and advice through their use of and/or comments on the first edition including

David Balkin
University of Colorado

Regina Bento
University of Baltimore

David DeCenzo
Coastal Carolina University

Beth Crockford
Colby-Sawyer College

Jason Harris-Boundy
University of Washington

Louise Lemieux-Charles
University of Toronto

Mark Lengnick-Hall
University of Texas at San Antonio

Kathleen Montgomery
University of California at Riverside

Andre Petit
Universite de Sherbrooke

Robert Preziosi
Nova Southeastern University

Sheila Puffer
Northeastern University

Paul Shibelski
American University

Margaret Vickers
University of Western Sydney

A very humble thanks is extended to the individuals below who provided a formal review of the first edition and for the valuable recommendations they provided that greatly assisted me in the development of the second edition.

Zoe Barsness
University of Washington

Nancy Day
University of Missouri—Kansas City

Melinda Drake
Limestone College

Mary Graham
Clarkson University

Todd Jones
Mountainstate University

Robert Metchick
University of New Haven

Donald Otto
Lindenwood University

Parbudyal Singh
University of New Haven

Jon Werner
University of Wisconsin at Whitewater

Ellen Whitener
University of Virginia

Finally, a heartfelt thanks to my family, the Mellos, Cotes and Costas, for their love and support. A special thanks goes to my nieces and nephews, Jasmine, Blake, Grant, Emma, and new to this edition, Ben and Ricky, for continuing to bring happiness and sunshine into my life every day. And last, but not least, also new to this edition, thanks to my beloved daughter, Logan Simone, for taking me places I never knew existed.

Jeffrey A. Mello

PART 1

THE CONTEXT OF STRATEGIC HUMAN RESOURCE MANAGEMENT

CHAPTER 1

AN INVESTMENT PERSPECTIVE OF HUMAN RESOURCE MANAGEMENT

How can a retailer gain a competitive advantage in a cutthroat marketplace? Middle- and high-end retailers generally locate in close proximity to each other and often carry similar, but not identical, merchandise. Consequently, their sales and profit margins are usually in tandem. Nordstrom, however, has consistently produced above-industry-average profits and continued to be profitable when its competitors' profits were falling or flat.

The key to Nordstrom's success lies with the different way it manages its employees. Sales employees are known as "associates" and considered the organization's most valuable asset. The company's success is rooted in its strategy of providing superlative customer service. Associates are encouraged to act as entrepreneurs and build strong personal relationships with customers, or "clients." In fact, many clients will shop only with a particular Nordstrom associate and call in advance to determine associate schedules or to make appointments.

Nordstrom's strategy involves a heavy investment in the organization's sales force. Nordstrom provides associates with extensive training on merchandising and product lines and offers high compensation. Its commitment to its employees is evident from the fact that the company organization chart is depicted inverse from that of a traditional retailer. Associates are at the highest level on the chart, followed by department and merchandise managers and, finally, executives. This depiction cements the organization's philosophy that the customer is king. All efforts of senior, middle and lower-level managers should support the efforts of the sales force.

Effective organizations are increasingly realizing that, of the varied factors that contribute to performance, the human element is clearly the most critical. Regardless of the size or nature of an organization, the activities it undertakes, and the environment in which it operates, its success is determined by the decisions its employees make and the behaviors in which they engage. Managers at all levels in organizations are becoming increasingly aware that a critical source of competitive advantage often comes not from having the most ingenious product design or service, the best marketing strategy, state-of-the-art technology, or the most savvy financial management but from having the appropriate systems for attracting, motivating, and managing the organizations' human resources (HR).

Adopting a strategic view of HR, in large part, involves considering employees as human "assets" and developing appropriate policies and programs as investments in these assets to increase their value to the organization and the marketplace. The characterization of employees as human assets can have a chilling effect on those who find the term derogatory due to its connotation that employees are to be considered "property." However, the characterization of employees as assets is fitting, considering what an asset actually is: something of value and worth. Effective organizations realize that their employees do have value, much as the organization's physical and capital assets have value. Exhibit 1-1 illustrates some of the value employees bring to an organization.

EXHIBIT 1-1: SOURCES OF EMPLOYEE VALUE

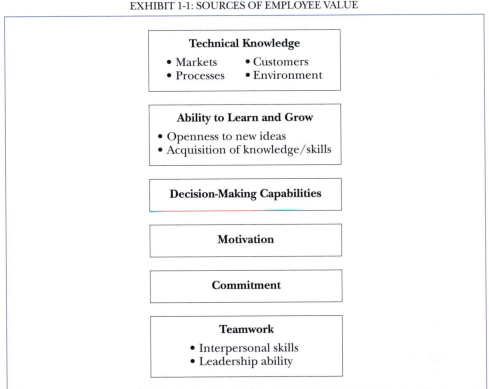

ADOPTING AN INVESTMENT PERSPECTIVE

The characterization of employees as human assets has important implications for the strategic management of human resources in that it allows us to consider HR from an investment perspective. Physical and capital assets in organizations such as plant, property, machinery, and technology are acquired and subsequently managed most effectively by treating them as investments; the organization determines the optimal mix of high-performance, high-return assets to its strategic objectives. Analyses are made of the costs and benefits of certain expenditures, with judgments made concerning the riskiness and potential returns of such expenditures. Viewing human resources from an investment perspective, much as physical assets are viewed, rather than as variable costs of production, allows an organization to determine how to best invest in its people. Further, considering the risk and return on possible expenditures related to the acquisition or development of human assets allows an organization to consider how current expenditures can best be allocated to meet long-term performance goals.

In considering whether to undertake the expense of a new training program, for example, an organization needs to consider not only the out-of-pocket costs for the training but also the related opportunity costs, such as lost time on the job, and weigh these costs against the potential benefits of the training, such as enhanced performance, potential increased loyalty, and motivation. The training also needs to be assessed relative to risk because the enhanced marketability of employees makes them more desirable to competitors. Similarly, in considering compensation programs as an investment, an organization needs to consider what it is "investing" in when it pays someone (knowledge, commitment, new ideas, retention of employees from competitors). The potential return on the organization's financial outlay in compensation will determine whether its compensation system is a viable investment strategy.

Taking an investment perspective toward human resources/assets is critical considering that other physical assets such as facilities, products and services, technologies, and markets can be readily cloned or imitated by competitors.[1] Human assets cannot be duplicated and therefore become the *competitive advantage* that an organization enjoys in its market(s). This is becoming increasingly important as the skills required for most jobs become less manual and more cerebral and knowledge-based in nature.[2] Rapid and ongoing advances in technology have created a workplace where laborers are being replaced by knowledge workers. An organization's "technology" is becoming more invested in people than in capital. Thought and decision-making processes as well as skills in analyzing complex data are not "owned" by an organization but by individual employees. This is in stark contrast to traditional manufacturing organizations where the employer usually owns or leases the machinery and production processes, and duplication of the organization's "capital" is restricted primarily by cost considerations.

Managing Employees at United Parcel Service

Although taking a strategic approach to human resource management usually involves looking at employees as assets and considering them as investments, this does not always mean that an organization will adopt a "human relations" approach to HR.

A few successful organizations still utilize principles of scientific management, where worker needs and interests are subordinate to efficiency. United Parcel Service (UPS) is a prime example of this. At UPS, all jobs from truck loaders to drivers to customer service representatives are designed around measures of efficiency. Wages are relatively high, but performance expectations are high as well. This approach toward managing people is still "strategic" in nature because the systems for managing people are designed around the company's strategic objectives of efficiency. Consequently, all employee training, performance management, compensation, and work design systems are developed to promote this strategic objective of efficiency.

Managing an organization's employees as investments mandates the development of an appropriate and integrated approach to managing human resources that is consistent with the organization's strategy. As an example, consider an organization whose primary strategic objective involves innovation. An organization pursuing an innovation strategy cannot afford high levels of turnover within its ranks. It needs to retain employees, and transfer, among employees, the new knowledge being developed in-house. It cannot afford to have its employees develop innovative products, services, and processes and then take this knowledge to a competitor for implementation. The significant investment in research and development ends up having no return. Because the outcome of this expenditure (research and development) is knowledge that employees have developed, it is critical as part of the organization's overall strategy for the organization to devise strategies to retain its employees and their knowledge bases until the "new knowledge" becomes "owned" by the organization itself (through diffusion throughout the organization) rather than by the employee.

This leads to a dilemma involving investing in human assets. An organization that does not invest in its employees may be less attractive to prospective employees and may have a more difficult time retaining current employees; this causes inefficiency (downtime to recruit, hire, and train new employees) and a weakening of the organization's competitive position. However, an organization that does invest in its people needs to ensure that these investments are not lost. Well-trained employees, for example, become more attractive in the marketplace, particularly to competitors who may be able to pay the employee more because they have not had to invest in the training that the employee has already received. Although an organization's physical assets can't "walk," its human assets can, making the latter a much more risky investment. An organization can certainly buy or sell its physical assets because it has "ownership" of them, but it does not own its human assets. Consequently, organizations need to develop strategies to ensure that employees stay on long enough for the organization to realize an acceptable return on its investment relative to the employees' acquired skills and knowledge, particularly when the organization has subsidized the acquisition. This requires the organization to determine the actual "value" of each employee. Valuation of human assets has implications for compensation, advancement opportunities, and retention strategies as well as how much should be invested in each area for each employee.

VALUATION OF ASSETS

There are five major kinds of assets or capital that organizations can leverage to aid in performance and add value to operations. These categories are financial assets/capital, physical assets/capital, market assets/capital, operational assets/capital, and human assets/capital, as shown in Exhibit 1-2. Financial assets/capital include

EXHIBIT 1-2: TYPES OF ORGANIZATIONAL ASSETS/CAPITAL

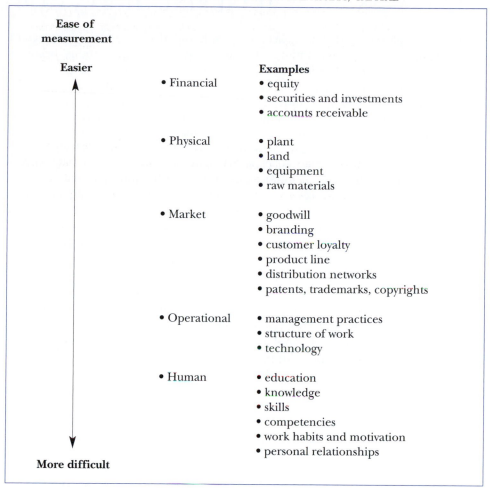

equity, securities and investments, and accounts receivable. Physical assets/capital include plant, land, equipment, and raw materials. Market assets/capital include goodwill, branding, customer loyalty, distribution networks, product lines and patents, trademarks, and copyrights. Operational assets/capital include management practices, the structure of work, and the use of technology. Human assets/capital include employee education levels, knowledge, skills, competencies, work habits and motivation, and relationships with coworkers, customers, suppliers, regulators, and lenders.

Financial and physical assets/capital are relatively easy to measure via accounting practices. Most of these assets are tangible and have some clear market value. Market and operational assets/capital are a bit more challenging to measure, but accounting practices have been developed that generally can place a subjective value on such assets. Human assets/capital, however, are very difficult to measure; attempts to do so are at the forefront of current research being conducted in human resource management. ▼

▶ Reading 1.1, "The Hidden Leverage of Human Capital," illustrates how human assets/capital can provide a significant financial return to organizations. It explains the distinguishing features of human capital management and provides a call for an enhanced understanding among organizational leaders of the role of human capital in organizations.

Given that employees and their collective skills, knowledge, and abilities represent a significant asset for organizations, a critical issue for organizations becomes measuring this value as well as its contribution to the organization's bottom line. One of the first studies that successfully demonstrated this relationship was conducted by Huselid in the mid-1990s. This study identified what were called "high performance work systems" (HPWS) and demonstrated that integrated, strategically focused HR practices were directly related to profitability and market value.[3] A recent study by Watson Wyatt Worldwide found that the primary reason for organizational profitability is the effective management of human capital. This involves, in part, providing employees with rewards that are commensurate with their contributions and ensuring that investments in employees are not lost to competitors by actively managing employee retention.[4] Another study found that effective, integrated management of human capital can result in up to a 47 percent increase in market value.[5] A landmark study conducted by Becker, Huselid, and Ulrich that examined a variety of human resource management quality indices found that the top 10 percent of organizations studied enjoyed a 391 percent return on investment in the management of their human capital.[6]

Extending these findings, Dyer and Reeves attempted to define what can be called the HR "value chain."[7] They argued that performance could be measured via four different sets of outcomes: employee, organizational, financial and accounting, and market-based. More important, they proposed that these sets of outcomes had a sequential cause-and-effect relationship, as indicated in Exhibit 1-3. Each outcome fueled success in a subsequent outcome, establishing a causal link between HR practices and an organization's market value. ▼▼

EXHIBIT 1-3: HR VALUE CHAIN

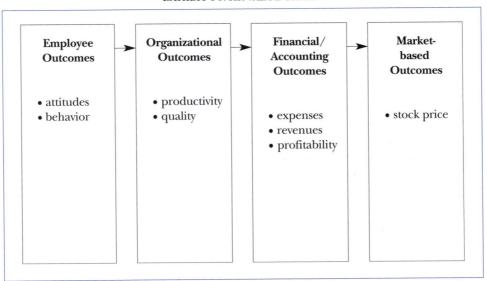

▶▶ Much of the research that has the potential to move HR practice and corresponding organizational performance forward has not been acted on and applied because it hasn't been effectively disseminated. Reading 1.2, "Seven Common Misconceptions about Human Resource Practices: Research Findings versus Practitioner Beliefs," addresses this void and illustrates that organizations whose HR professionals remain abreast of the latest academic research have superior financial performance relative to those that fail to do so.

Given this proven link between integrated and strategic HR practices and bottom-line performance, HR practitioners have been faced with the task of developing appropriate HR metrics, which specifically illustrate the value of HR practices and activities, particularly relative to accounting profits and market valuation of the organization. This task has proved to be far more complex than anticipated, given the difficulties of measuring human assets/capital. One study concluded that 90 percent of *Fortune 500* organizations in the United States, Canada, and Europe evaluate their HR operations on the basis of three rather limited metrics: employee retention and turnover, corporate morale and employee satisfaction, and HR expense as a percentage of operational expenses.[8] Such "staffing metrics" simply document the extent to which HR performs traditional job functions without necessarily illustrating how HR impacts company profits and shareholder value. Moreover, a focus on such staffing metrics involves a demonstration of how employees can be treated as expenses, rather than as assets that can be managed, invested in, and leveraged for profit.

Senior HR executives in these organizations stressed that they lacked accurate and meaningful methods that measured performance, despite the fact that human assets/capital can account for as much as 80 percent of the value of an organization.[9] One reason is that most accounting valuation methods stress the past and current value of assets. Much of the value of human assets/capital rests with the value of an organization and its ability to proactively meet challenges that lie ahead, relative to responsiveness to changing economic, political, and market conditions. As a result, valuation of human assets/capital and analysis of human capital investments can be value-laden, subjective, expensive—and hence, ignored.

Measuring Human Assets/Capital at Dow Chemical

Dow Chemical has been a leader in forging the frontiers of measuring human capital. Dow has attempted to develop a reliable measure to help calculate each employee's current and anticipated future contribution to the financial goals of the business. A pilot project currently is being tested in a single business unit; it examines employee performance on project assignments using two specific metrics: expected human capital return (EHCR) and actual human capital return (AHCR). EHCR involves a calculation of the break-even point of investment in an employee, above salary and additional outlays such as recruiting and training expenses. AHCR involves a calculation of the "value created" by the employee based on the projects she or he was worked on. This metric considers the skills and knowledge of each employee relative to the net present value of a specific project. The desired outcomes of these measures are assisting managers with matching employee talents and project needs, identifying employee development opportunities, and creating a more efficient and effective means for project team staffing. Although the program is still in the pilot stage, with validation studies in progress, Dow anticipates rolling out the metrics to other business units in the very near future.[10]

Given the complex nature of measuring human assets/capital and return on such investments, where does an organization begin in assuming such an undertaking? One helpful model has been developed by Mercer that can allow those concerned with measuring HR performance and documenting the value added of specific initiative to demonstrate to senior management the value added and bottom-line impact.[11] This model involves six steps: (1) identify a specific business problem that HR can impact; (2) calculate the actual cost of the problem to the organization; (3) choose a HR solution that addresses all or part of the problem; (4) calculate the cost of the solution; (5) six to 24 months after implementation, calculate the value of the improvement for the organization; (6) calculate the specific return on investment (ROI) metric.

One caveat should be obvious from not only Mercer's approach but also that currently being employed at Dow Chemical. Unlike the returns on other types of assets/capital, the returns on investments in human assets/capital are often not realized until some point in the future. Key decision makers need to be patient in waiting for these results and HR also needs to subsequently take interim measures and provide status reports to senior management that illustrate preliminary beneficial results. HR needs to move away from mere data collection, however, and perform more comprehensive analysis of performance measures that relate to the critical metrics for which operating divisions are held accountable. Toward this end, HR needs to partner with chief financial officers to understand the language of investment and asset management. If HR continues to be seen as a cost center, it will be the primary target during cost-cutting operations, given that labor is the primary cost incurred in the service and information-intensive sectors that are fueling the growth in our economy. One study places the relative expenses for human capital as high as 70 percent of overall expenditures.[12] Hence, the challenge for HR is to provide senior management with value-added human capital investments backed by solid and meaningful financial metrics.

FACTORS INFLUENCING HOW "INVESTMENT ORIENTED" AN ORGANIZATION IS

Not all organizations realize that human assets can be strategically managed from an investment perspective. As shown in Exhibit 1-4, five major factors affect how "investment oriented" a company is in its management of human resources. The first of these is management values.[13] Management may or may not have an appreciation of the value of its human assets relative to other capital assets such as brand names, distribution channels, real estate, facilities and equipment, and information

EXHIBIT 1-4: FACTORS INFLUENCING AN ORGANIZATION'S INVESTMENT ORIENTATION

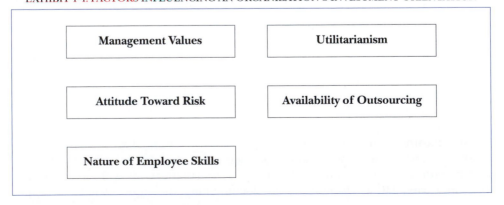

Management Values	Utilitarianism
Attitude Toward Risk	Availability of Outsourcing
Nature of Employee Skills	

systems. The extent to which an organization can be characterized as investment oriented may be revealed through answers to the following questions:

- Does the organization see its people as being central to its mission/strategy?
- Do the company's mission statement and strategic objectives, both company-wide and within individual business units, espouse the value of or even mention human assets and their role in achieving goals?
- More important, does the management philosophy of the organization encourage the development of any strategy to prevent the depreciation of its human assets, or are they considered replicable and amortizable, like physical assets?

Senior management values and actions will determine organizational investment in assets. It is critical to understand how the organization's strategy mandates the investment in particular assets relative to others. Whether management values its people will be a critical factor in its willingness to invest in them.

The second factor is attitude toward risk. The most fundamental lesson in financial management is that a trade-off exists between risk and return. Higher risk investments generally are expected to have a greater potential return; lower risk, safer investments generally are expected to have a more modest return. For example, in financial markets, bonds are considered less risky investments than stocks but have a limited, fixed return. Stocks, on the other hand, are considered higher risk but have no limit as to their potential return.

Both personal and institutional investment strategies can be highly conservative (risk averse) or pursue unlimited returns with reckless abandon. Investments in human assets are generally far more risky for an organization than investments in physical assets: Unlike physical assets, human assets are not *owned* by the organization. An organization with risk-averse management philosophies is far less likely to make significant investments in people. Other organizations see investments in employees as necessary for their success and develop strategies to minimize the potential risk of losing their investments. An organization can attempt to gain some "ownership" of employee services through long-term employment contracts or by offering employees financial incentives, such as stock-ownership programs, as well as additional professional development opportunities.

The third factor is the nature of the skills needed by employees. Certain organizations will require employees to develop and utilize very specialized skills that might not be applicable in another organization; another employer might have employees utilize and develop skills that are highly marketable. For example, if an employer has a custom-made information system to handle administrative HR functions, employees using that system might not transfer those skills to another employer. However, if an employer uses a popular software program for which there is high demand for skilled employees among competitors, the investment in employees becomes more risky.

As a result, an organization that decides to provide its employees with specialized training in skills that can be utilized by others in the marketplace has a much stronger need to develop a strong retention strategy than an organization that teaches employees skills that are less marketable. Employees with skills demanded in the marketplace become more valuable and sought-after assets by companies that choose not to make expenditures or invest in training and skill development.

The fourth factor affecting the investment orientation is the "utilitarian" mentality of the organization. Organizations that take a utilitarian or "bottom line" perspective evaluate investments by using utility analysis, also known as *cost-benefit analysis*. Here, the costs of any investment are weighted against its benefits to determine whether the prospective investment is either profitable or, more commonly, achieves the target rate of return the organization has set for its investments. A highly utilitarian approach attempts to quantify all costs and benefits. For example, rather than just considering direct cash expenditures, this approach would also consider costs such as the time involved to develop and administer an innovative performance measurement system (by considering how much people are being paid for the time involved in the process), the cost of having larger applicant pools (by considering how much longer it would take to screen applicants), and the cost of employing more extensive employee selection procedures (again, by considering time and its monetary value).

The distinct problem many utilitarian organizations run into regarding investments in people involves the fact that many benefits of HR programs and policies are extremely difficult to quantify. If these programs and policies can be assessed quantitatively, subjectivity as to the actual value of the benefit may make consensus on the overall value difficult. This is especially true for programs that attempt to enhance performance in service organizations. Consider, as an example, the customer service division of your local Internet service provider. Measures of effective service are not only difficult to assess objectively, but the organization may not be able to determine how much service is necessary to prevent customers from jumping to competitors and maintain their loyalty. Additional investments in service may not have any direct financial benefit.

Similarly, a government organization or public utility that attempts to develop a program to enhance efficiency may have a difficult time in finding the cost justifiable. Given that no market mechanisms exist for government agencies or legal monopolies, customers have no choice among competitors. Customers may complain to regulators or officials, but there may be no incentive or benefit for the organization to enhance its efficiency from an investment perspective. On a more basic level, a program that is designed to improve employee morale can have benefits that may be very difficult to measure and quantify. A utilitarian organization is likely to reject such "soft" programs that have no quantifiable return. Hence, the more utilitarian an organization, the more likely it is to see HR programs as investments, creating a challenge for those advocating for such HR programs to find a means to show their impact on the bottom lime. Some very recent studies have begun to address this issue by attempting to establish a link between HR strategies and systems and an organization's financial performance. Initial results have shown a significant impact of HR systems on both market-based and accounting-based measures of performance.[14]

The final factor impacting an organization's willingness to invest in its people is the availability of cost-effective outsourcing. An investment-oriented approach to managing an organization will attempt to determine whether its investments produce a *sustainable* competitive advantage over time. When specialists who may perform certain functions much more efficiently exist outside of the organization, any internal programs will be challenged and have to be evaluated relative to such a standard. This is true for virtually any organizational function including, but not limited to, customer service, accounting, manufacturing, and human resource management functions.

The organization is further likely to invest its resources where key decision makers perceive they will have the greatest potential return. This may result in few investments in people at the expense of investment in market and product development, physical expansion, or acquisition of new technology. As an example, employers in the fast-food industry, such as McDonald's, invest little in their people; they require minimal experience, provide little training, pay low wages, and expect high turnover because the supply of workers is excessive relative to demand. Organizations in this industry tend to invest much more in new product development, physical expansion, and marketing through competitive advertising.

CONCLUSION

Developing an effective strategy to manage an organization's human assets requires considering employees as investments. Such an approach helps to ensure that HR practices and principles are clearly in sync with the organization's overall strategy, forces the organization to invest in its best opportunities, and ensures that performance standards are met. As an example, employee stock-ownership programs attempt to strategically invest in the organization and its people by making employees owners of the company. Instead of having a conflict as to how profits should be allocated (bonuses to employees or reinvested in the business), both can be achieved simultaneously. This, in turn, has the goal of gaining more commitment from employees and encouraging them to adopt a long-term focus toward the organization; this is often a shortcoming/deficiency of American organizations that are concerned with short-run indicators of performance. Employees who now intend to stay with the organization longer, given their vested ownership rights, provide organizations with an incentive to incur the short-term costs involved with investing in human assets for the long-term financial gains that can result from such investments.

An investment perspective of HR is often not adopted because it involves making a longer term commitment to employees. Because employees can "walk" and because American organizations are so infused with short-term measures of performance, investments in human assets, which tend to be longer-term investments, are often ignored. Organizations performing well financially may feel no need to change their investment strategies. Those not doing well usually need a quick fix to turn things around and therefore ignore longer-term investments in people.

However, while investments in HR are longer term, once an organization gains a competitive advantage through its employees, the outcomes associated with the strategy are likely to be enduring and difficult to duplicate by competitors as such programs and values become more firmly entrenched in the organization's culture. The commitment that an organization makes to its employees through its investments in them is often rewarded with the return of employees making a longer-term commitment to the organization. Although investments in human assets may be risky and the return may take a long time to materialize, investment in people continues to be the main source of sustainable competitive advantage for organizations. ▼▼▼

CRITICAL THINKING

1. Why do senior managers often fail to realize the value of human assets vis-à-vis other assets?

2. Why do line managers often fail to realize the value of human assets vis-à-vis other assets?

▶▶▶ Reading 1.3, "Producing Sustainable Competitive Advantage Through the Effective Management of People," illustrates how financially successful companies employ and implement an investment perspective of HR to gain such an advantage.

3. What can HR do to make senior and line managers take more of an investment approach to human assets?

4. Why is a competitive advantage based on a heavy investment in human assets more sustainable than investments in other types of assets?

5. Why can some organizations that fail to invest heavily in human assets still be financially successful? Why can some organizations that do invest heavily in human assets still be financially unsuccessful?

6. What challenges exist relative to valuation of human assets and measuring human capital?

Reading 1.1

7. List all of the various expenses and costs generally associated with employing workers. For each of these costs, devise strategies to leverage this expenditure into some kind of return on investment. How might you attempt to sell senior management to adopt these strategies for investing in human capital?

Reading 1.2

8. Investigate at least two pieces of HR-related research that have recently been published in academic journals. If the authors have not already done so, determine the specific implications of this research for human resource practice and then determine how these implications might be best implemented.

Reading 1.3

9. Consider your current or most recent employer. Describe how investment oriented its approach to managing human resources appears to be by applying the "thirteen principles for managing people" presented in this article. Where does this organization invest the majority of its resources? Do such investments make sense in light of the organization's goals and strategy?

EXPERIENTIAL EXERCISES

1. Obtain the annual report for a *Fortune 500* company of your choice. Review the material presented and the language used in the text. Write a one-page memo that assesses how investment oriented the organization appears to be toward its human assets.

2. Arrange yourselves in small groups of four or five students and compare and contrast the similarities and differences among the organizations you investigated. Can you isolate any factors that appear to influence how an organization perceives the value of its employees?

INTERNET EXERCISES

1. Repeat the previous exercise for a small, privately held technology company. Do these new e-commerce businesses take a similar approach in how they perceive their human assets? Does this approach differ from those of the *Fortune 500* companies?

CHAPTER REFERENCES

1. Quinn, J. B., Doorley, T. L. and Paquette, P. C. "Beyond Products: Services-Based Strategy," *Harvard Business Review*, 90, (2), pp. 59–67.
2. Lawler, E. III. *The Ultimate Advantage: Creating the High Involvement Organization*, San Francisco: Jossey-Bass, 1992, p. 21.
3. Huselid, M. A. "The Impact of Human Resource Management Practices on Turnover, Productivity, Corporate Financial Performance," *Academy of Management Journal*, 38, (3), pp. 635–672.
4. Bates, S. "Study Links HR Practices with the Bottom Line," *HR Magazine*, December 2001, 46, (12), p. 14.
5. Gachman, I. and Luss, R. "Building the Business Case for HR in Today's Climate," *Strategic HR Review*, 1, (4), pp. 26–29.
6. Becker, B. E., Huselid, M.A. and Ulrich, D. *The HR Scorecard: Linking People, Strategy and Performance*. Boston: Harvard Business School Press, 2001.
7. Dyer, L. and Reeves, T. "HR Strategies and Firm Performance: What Do We Know and Where Do We Need to Go?" *International Journal of Human Resource Management*, 6, (3), pp. 656–670.
8. Bates, S. "Executives Judge HR Based on Poor Metrics, Study Finds," *HR Magazine*, September 2003, 48, (9), p. 12.
9. Ibid.
10. Bates, S. "The Metrics Maze," *HR Magazine*, December 2003, pp. 51–60.
11. Mercer, M. *Turning Your Human Resources Department into a Profit Center*. New York: AMACOM, 1989.
12. Weatherly, L. A. "Human Capital—The Elusive Assets," Society for Human Resource Management, *Research Quarterly*, 2003.
13. Greer, C. R. *Strategy and Human Resources: A General Manager's Perspective*, Englewood Cliffs, NJ: Prentice-Hall, 1995.
14. Becker, B. E. and Huselid, M. A. "High Performance Work Systems and Firm Performance: A Synthesis of Research and Managerial Implications," *Research in Personnel and Human Resource Management*, 16, 1998, pp. 53–101.

The Hidden Leverage of Human Capital

Jeffrey A. Oxman, *Sloan Management Review*

A down economy is not the time to "slash-and-burn," but rather to ensure growth potential during the ensuing rebound. This requires a focus on strengthening key relationships, capitalizing on underutilized staff, clarifying strategic roles and forging stronger links between compensation and results.

More than 20,000 times last year in the United States, according to the Bureau of Labor Statistics, midsize and large companies responded to adversity by slashing on average about 100 staff members at a time. Considering all the news coverage about the economic downturn and the poor job market, that might, at first glance, seem like a dog-bites-man story. But that is a lot of jobs. Did circumstances always merit the drastic actions? If so, were the actions taken deliberately and carefully, with all appropriate respect toward the people involved? What sorts of provisions were made to ensure that key talent was protected? These questions are important because they go to the heart of how companies avoid lasting damage in the marketplace and build long-term value.

Trying to get a handle on the answers from publicly available data is problematic, as even a broad-based research effort would be brought to a halt at the gates of internal company performance information and organizational dynamics. But it is a safe assumption that many of these 20,000 organizations did destroy value somewhere along the way by cutting capacity that they soon had to replace, by making poor choices as to who should go and who should stay, by being careless in communicating the rationale for change and protecting the motivation levels of surviving employees, and by missing the opportunity to rethink their business model to optimize their positioning for the recovery ahead.

Organizations such as Wal-Mart Stores, Cisco, Charles Schwab and even American Airlines have recently tried to rehire laid-off employees.[1] But in so doing, the churn they generate often serves to demoralize employees and create an environmental uncertainly that compromises staff engagement,

loyalty, customer service—and ultimately, company performance.

The broader issues here go well beyond layoffs. Is there a right way to manage a company through a time of challenge or tepid economic growth? What general guidelines can be discerned from the lessons of the past? And what sorts of decisions can managers make today to improve the odds that their companies will emerge as the winners of tomorrow?

Slash and Burn: Re-Engineering and Core Competencies

It used to be an article of faith that re-engineering initiatives, analytically evaluated and quickly implemented into an organization's operations, could serve as a magic bullet by helping companies realize previously unimagined efficiencies. In concert with operational streamlining, the conventional wisdom of a decade ago also advocated a devolutionary focus, whereby organizations, while earmarking core competencies for attention, at the same time took drastic steps to move outside the company those areas that didn't fall within the core.

Perhaps the exemplar of the era was the former head of Scott Paper Co., "Chainsaw" Al Dunlap. Starting in May 1994, in an effort to rebuild shareholder value, he let go more than 11,000 employees and shrank the company by selling off and outsourcing various business units and functions. Wall Street loved it for a while, as market value tripled, but ultimately it became clear that the way the restructuring had been handled rendered it difficult for the company to deliver sustained performance, and Scott Paper had to realistically evaluate its ability to survive as an independent entity. In 1995, it reached a conclusion—the company was sold to Kimberly-Clark, a longtime rival.

In this vein, while many "ruthless" organizations achieved notable efficiencies, the best re-engineering success stories—as measured by long-term company sustainability achieved—came to be viewed as those that not only emphasized a tough focus on business drivers, but also combined it with a more human touch. Jack Welch at General Electric Co., for example, while restructuring and selling underperforming units, made significant investments in management development and training, and communicated to employees the logical and rallying message that GE should be number one or two in any business in which it competed.

Similarly, Archie Norman at Asda, the U.K. supermarket group, averted bankruptcy by both flattening the organizational structure and articulating a clear long-term strategy based on everyday low pricing. In so doing, he embarked on creating an atmosphere of trust and openness.

It seemed paradoxical, but the qualities of what came to be viewed as superlative corporate leadership were best captured in a headline in the *Financial Times* that read "Wanted: Ruthless Axeman with People Skills."[2]

This context is useful as the starting point for articulating a broad-based model for management success in the current economic environment.

A Broader Leadership Model for the New Millennium

There is a sailing proverb that says, "Races are won at night and in a light wind." A quiet time, after all, is the one in which the boat can be best prepared. It's appealing to think of this quasirecessionary time as the light night wind, with people training to work better as an effective team, loads balanced, equipment optimized, communications tested to be crystal clear.

Four broad areas of preparation are critical: strengthening key relationships across customers, employees and shareholders; leveraging downtime by capitalizing on underutilized staff for innovation initiatives; refocusing staff on what's important at the company by prioritizing strategic roles and clarifying individual goals; and building return on compensation by forging stronger links between the pay people get and the results they achieve.

Strengthening Key Relationships While strategic models of company stakeholders almost universally focus on customers, employees and shareholders, there is widespread disagreement as to where

priorities lie within this list. The strongest strategies focus on all three groups of stakeholders and follow through with this approach in tough times as well as easier ones.[3]

Strengthening key relationships starts with keeping a finger on the pulse of frequently changing customer and employee needs. A good way to embark upon pulse taking is executing well-designed, customized surveys to better track the unique requirements of different customer and employee groups and how those requirements change over time. The real value of customized surveys is to help focus company resources on those customers and employees for whom company efforts yield the highest returns—whether they be key customer groups or high-performing employees whose perspectives are often obscured in more traditional, broad-based, generic questionnaires.

That said, in a challenging environment, follow-through on relationships means doing more than just surveying. Since customers and employees believe that companies reveal their true colors at a time of crisis, poor survey follow-up, or indeed any perceived mistreatment, can alienate those stakeholders permanently. Thus, what comes to the fore in relationship building—more than the newfangled concept of management—is its trusty cousin, leadership.

Leaders from Winston Churchill to Rudolph Giuliani, John F. Kennedy to Warren Buffett have a lot to impart to businesspeople with regard to building effective relationships in a crisis environment. They stood up and were visible. They didn't anticipate failure yet stuck to the facts even when the facts were dire. And for the most part, they didn't overreach. Winston Churchill's brutal honesty was combined with optimism—"blood, toil, tears and sweat" but always an upbeat feeling that England would survive "however long and hard the road may be." Former New York City Mayor Giuliani's comment that the World Trade Center death toll would be "more than we can bear" was interspersed at the same time with his steady campaign to rally a city's spirits. Mobilizing a fatigued group through a difficult time, after all, has its own historical best practices.[4]

Finally, together with leadership (perhaps, indeed, component parts of it), communication and engagement are critical to strengthening relationships. Communications across, and proactive engagement of, customers, employees and shareholders in helping to solve specific business problems go a long way toward smoothing the implementation of effective solutions.

Leveraging Downtime In challenging times, managers are often faced with employees who suddenly find themselves with too much free time on their hands. In the old days, when this situation persisted, some of these folks would have had to be let go, due to onerous fixed-cost structures. But today's managers have a tool their predecessors lacked: variable pay.

In the last decade, many companies have been able to significantly leverage their costs by migrating to a variable-pay model, in which compensation kicks in only if company, division and/or team results dictate. The result has been increased flexibility, in a tough business environment, to keep what might in the past have been at-risk employees on staff, albeit sometimes less busy, at reduced pay levels.

Across the nation, despite the large layoff figures cited at the outset, this phenomenon has had a dramatic ameliorative effect on unemployment rates. One estimate puts the benefit at a full percentage point of employment nationally; that is, what was a 5.5% unemployment rate in fall 2001 would have been 6.5% had it not been for the new prevalence of variable pay nationwide.[5]

What does this mean for successful management in a business downturn? For starters, managers should be attuned to the risk that the good news about being able to preserve years of individual experience within company knowledge banks could be offset by unproductive employee downtime.

Almost every company, especially if it is coming out of particularly heady times, has a few areas of relative neglect to which it can now profitably allocate that downtime. These areas—most often infrastructure, marketing and operations—are ones for which experienced staff, in particular, are well positioned to offer unique insights to help the company build for the future.

Organizations should be asking some broad, basic questions and involving not just senior management, but cross-functional staff groups at all levels. Are internal company tools and procedures adding sufficient value? Have we done enough to ensure our customers fully understand how our products and services can help them be more successful? Are we optimally aligned, organizationally, to serve the customers, market segments and geographies we serve today? Strategic initiatives undertaken to tackle

questions like these serve a double purpose: In leveraging the wisdom of key staff, they prepare the company optimally for the future and harvest most people's enthusiasm to play more diverse organizational roles and develop their own capabilities.

Refocusing Staff on What's Important The question "What's most important in an organization?" can elicit surprising responses. BEA Systems, which in 2001 reached $1 billion in sales faster than any software company had previously (surpassing even Microsoft's 1980s pace), has a new CEO, Alfred Chuang, who has what some might call a ruthless perspective. "We focus on two things," he says. "Building product and selling product. I know that a lot of other functions are involved in that process, including marketing, servicing and infrastructure. But if you are not within the line of sight between the inception of the idea and delivering it to customers and making them happy, your job is not that important."[6]

BEA has a track record of success it's hard to quibble with, but it is critical for companies to go through an examination of not just employee roles, but also their people. Just as there are more strategic roles (for example, R&D in pharmaceuticals) and less strategic roles (tellers in retail banking), so there are also key people in organizations whose impact on performance can be significant, regardless of role.

How do companies determine who these people are and focus them adroitly? The key is to transform performance management from perfunctory end-of-year paper pushing to a disciplined, strategic and value-added process.

Elevating performance management starts with clearly defining and differentiating between core competencies and results—and balancing them appropriately. Some law firms, for example, rate partners exclusively on project sales and reward them for those sales through base and incentive pay. More-sophisticated law firms blend other considerations into the evaluations of a partner's results delivered—for example, sales in conjunction with profitability. But best-practice firms, when looking at a partner's longer-term contribution to the firm's sustained success, consider the extent to which he or she demonstrates competencies such as attracting and retaining an enthusiastic team of junior people, broadening firm offerings into new clients and practice areas, and enhancing client satisfaction.

The "A" partners in those firms are the ones who deliver high performance on both long-term competencies (people development, new practice areas, client satisfaction) and current results (sales, profits). This competencies/scorecard framework—viewed pictorially with competency results on one axis and scorecard results on another, with people graphically positioned at their approximate performance levels—provides a roadmap for people development that is much better supported by the long-term economics of the business.

For unfortunate cases in which job cuts are absolutely required, this methodical framework for identifying critical resources stands an organization in good stead. It makes possible a matrixed analysis of strategic jobs against priority people, which in turn yields a valuable blueprint as to what cuts should be targeted.[7]

Building Return on Compensation If what is sometimes called "talent management," as outlined earlier, is done correctly, the foundation for wise compensation decision making is already laid. Base-pay progression can be readily and sensibly linked to competency achievement, and incentive pay to annual (or semiannual or quarterly) results. To the extent that it is tied closely to drivers of business success, built upon commonly understood criteria, and applied consistently over time, compensation—frequently viewed by managers as a sunk cost—can instead be considered an investment with a quantifiable return.

Some years ago, my colleagues and I had a team working with a subsidiary of Kodak—a photofinisher called Qualex Inc. Qualex provided overnight wholesale photofinishing services predominantly to large stores (at which retail customers had dropped off their film for developing). Every evening, Qualex would receive drop shipments of large quantities of film from the stores and (using predominantly low-wage employees) splice the film together, run rolls of negatives through the photo-development process, and by morning redistribute the pictures to the stores from which the film had come.

Across its approximately 50 locations, though, the company had a problem—significant turnover, averaging nearly 60% annually, with the added problem of spikes in turnover during the summer, just when its sales volume tended to be highest. (To make matters even worse, the company was losing the very people it could least afford to lose—the most technically

proficient—as these were the people whose pay was least competitive with pay in comparable companies.) The visible business effects were shaky productivity and quality results, which, above and beyond the inherent costs, often had the secondary cost of forgone revenue because of the company's inability to meet productivity levels contractually specified in service-level agreements.

Implementation of customized rewards helped solve the problem. Rather than bring Qualex's compensation to market levels with traditional base-salary increases (historically, this had been done for years, with little operational effect), the company designed and offered to its employees generous summertime pay premiums. These premiums constituted significant rewards for employees' productivity during the period and their perseverance in the role all the way through to summer's end. Later on, new, annual group incentives tied to specific productivity and quality goals were layered into employees' pay. Because all of the new variable-pay components represented meaningful amounts, they garnered significant employee attention and had quite a noticeable effect on reducing turnover and improving operational performance.

While the costs of the new programs were significantly higher than previously awarded salary increases (about $20 million vs. $8 million), regression models linking pay to turnover to results predicted that the higher investment would demonstrate a $20 million operational return through improved productivity and quality. The historical $8 million annual salary increases, on the other hand, would have had no discernible return, because that practice would have perpetuated the old turnover, productivity and quality problems. Qualex got its expected return and wound up with more satisfied and motivated employees, working in a more positive environment and doing a better job for customers at a net lower cost.[8]

Admittedly, this type of solution is not always as straightforward to implement in environments where metrics like productivity and quality are less readily available or less appropriately measured at the individual and team level than they might be in a manufacturing or processing setting—environments such as IT architecture. However, it is safe to say that improved alignment between the value drivers in the business and the manner in which employees are rewarded is almost always possible. And given the dominance of pay as an expense-line item, such action, if implemented well, usually has a substantial, quantifiable, bottom-line effect.

Broad compensation overhauls like the one at Qualex are not always necessary to enhance return on an organization's compensation dollar. Since variable-pay plans do already exist in many companies, they often can be amended to ensure that plan payouts awarded to employees will generate return. One way to accomplish this is to ensure that plans are driven by goals over which, as closely as possible, employees have some line of sight (for example, cost management, rather than company profitability).

There are several other considerations in tailoring variable-pay programs for higher return. Shortening plan-performance periods can be helpful, especially for cases in which substandard performance occurred some time ago but within the current performance period—demotivating employees to perform now because no matter what they accomplish, they still won't receive incentives. In addition, payments for achieving stretch goals may be enhanced, and supplementing semiannual or annual payouts with spot awards can more swiftly recognize employees for special contributions.

The Real Value of Human Assets

It's become a cliché to say that the service economy revolves around human assets, but even in manufacturing and production environments, wherein traditional machinery and equipment assets loom large, the caliber of people makes an enormous difference to the inherent value of an enterprise.

It's impossible to overstate the contribution of people—especially when they are aligned with corporate goals, fully engaged in making the enterprise effective, and well suited for their individual roles. Consider that in the past 20 years the market-value-to-book-value ratio of the S&P 500 has gone from around 1:1 to around 6:1. That increase has caused many academics to begin to develop new models of company value that include human-capital components to better account for a corporation's true worth.

In good times and bad, it is critical that companies play their cards right with all their key stakeholders—including employees. The costs of failing to do so are high. A 1999 survey of more than 1,000 companies in Britain showed results that for many observers at least partially explained that country's slight lag in the marketplace. The responses of about 1,000 human-resource directors in Britain indicated that more than 60% of staff are so poorly engaged that most employers would not rehire them. And nearly a quarter of survey respondents didn't believe that their work force gave their companies a competitive edge.[9]

Whether this is a result of hiring poorly or of a failure to develop good people into appropriate roles, managers in this situation have to overcome significant obstacles to success. And managers not in that situation need to make sure they avoid it.

After all, in the United States at least, there have been nine recessions since World War II and nine recoveries: a perfect record. It's foolish not to think of this period as an opportunity to lay the groundwork for an exciting future.

Source: Reprinted from "The Hidden Leverage of Human Capital" by Jeffrey A. Oxman, *MIT Sloan Management Review* (Summer 2002, 43, 4, p. 79), by permission of Massachusetts Institute of Technology. All rights reserved.

Endnotes

1. S. Armour, "Sorry We Cut Your Job—Want It Back?" *USA Today*, Wednesday, Aug. 29, 2001, sec. B, p. 1; and I. P. Cordle, "American Back to Business in Miami," *Miami Herald*, Sunday, Feb. 3, 2002, sec. E, p. 1.

2. S. London, "Wanted: Ruthless Axeman With People Skills," *Financial Times*, Nov. 14, 2001, p. 17.

3. S. Maranjian, "Employees vs. Customers vs. Shareholders," Fool.com, Jan. 31, 2002, www.fool.com/news/foth/2002/foth020131.htm.

4. J. Useem, "What it Takes," *Fortune*, Nov. 12, 2001, 128–132.

5. D. Eisenberg, "Paying To Keep Your Job," *Time*, Oct. 15, 2001, 80–83.

6. G. Anders, "BEA Systems: A Study in Sustainability," Fast Company, March 2002: www.fastcompany.com/build/build_feature/churchill3.html.

7. "The Road to Recovery," white paper, Sibson Consulting Group, New York, November 2001, p. 2.

8. P. V. LeBlanc, J. P. Gonzalez and J. A. Oxman, "Maximize Your Compensation ROI With High-Yield Investments in Human Capital," *Compensation & Benefits Review* 30 (March–April 1998): 59–68.

9. "We Like 40% of Our Staff," Automotive Management, Aug. 13, 1999: www.mtselect.co.uk/articles/40staff.html.

Seven Common Misconceptions about Human Resource Practices: Research Findings versus Practitioner Beliefs

Sara L. Rynes, Kenneth G. Brown, and Amy E. Colbert, *Academy of Management Executive*

Managers as a class are anything but stupid. But there is evidence that the job-specific knowledge bases of many, and perhaps most, executives are quite substandard. In turn, low knowledge bases may lead executives to make decisions that are less than optimal—and sometimes not even satisfactory.[1]

Considerable research demonstrates that most organizations do not employ state-of-the-art human resource (HR) practices.[2] One reason for the gap between research and practice is that very few practicing HR managers read the research literature.[3] Two major explanations have been offered as to why this is the case. The first is that HR research has become excessively technical, thus discouraging practitioners from attempting to keep up with the latest research findings.[4] This view assumes that practicing HR managers regard research findings as potentially useful, but inaccessible. The less sanguine view is that HR practitioners do not read the research because they see it as irrelevant or impractical for their needs.[5]

Whatever HR managers may feel about academic research findings, evidence is accumulating that certain HR practices are consistently related to higher individual performance, organizational productivity, and firm financial performance.[6] At least two research trends over the past two decades have increased our ability to detect relationships between HR practices and performance. The first is the development of statistical techniques which allow aggregation of many studies in order to reach more reliable conclusions about both average effects and contextual moderators.[7] The second is the emergence of the Strategic HR literature, which has stimulated much more research into the relationships between HR practices and performance at the level of the *firm* rather than the individual.[8] This last step means that we no longer have to wonder about the degree to which relationships found at the individual level are mirrored at higher levels of aggregation.

As one example of such firm-level research, a study by Welbourne and Andrews found that new companies that placed a high value on HR (as assessed by content of their prospectuses) and that included high levels of organizationally based pay-for-performance had a five-year survival rate of 92 percent as compared with 34 percent for companies that were low on both dimensions.[9] As another example, Huselid found that an increase of one standard deviation in scores on a "high-performance HR practices" scale (which included such practices as employee attitude surveying, paying for performance, formal communication programs, and use of employment tests) was associated with a 23 percent increase in accounting profits and an 8 percent increase in economic value.[10]

With research showing bottom-line effects of certain HR practices, the lack of research knowledge can clearly be costly to HR managers and their organizations. Indeed, although a direct causal link cannot be drawn, Terpstra and Rozell found that companies whose HR professionals read the academic research literature have higher financial performance than those that do not.[11]

Although the results of HR research are clearly relevant to practicing managers, not so clear is the extent to which HR managers' current beliefs are consistent (or inconsistent) with the latest findings. The areas of greatest inconsistency should dominate efforts to inform managers about HR research. We therefore conducted a survey to determine which particular areas of research findings most need more effective dissemination to practicing HR managers.

Research Findings versus Managerial Beliefs: Assessing the Gap

HR professionals are most directly responsible for acquiring and disseminating knowledge about best practices in "people management" throughout the organization. Although much of the day-to-day implementation of HR practices resides with line managers, it is the HR function's role to help executives develop a human resource strategy that is at once consistent with both the organizational business strategy and with best practices revealed by empirical research.[12]

To examine the extent to which the beliefs of HR professionals are consistent with established research findings, a 35-item questionnaire was constructed.[13] Content of the questionnaire was based on the major categories contained in the Human Resource Certification Institute's (HRCI) Professional in Human Resources (PHR) certification exam. However, in contrast to the certification exam (which focuses heavily on definitional, legal, and procedural issues), the present survey focused on *research* findings regarding the effectiveness of particular HR practices. Items were constructed that were based on up-to-date research results. Respondents indicated whether they agreed, disagreed, or were uncertain about each item, allowing us to determine where practitioner beliefs diverge most sharply from research findings.

The survey was sent to a stratified random sample of 5,000 Society for Human Resource Management members whose titles were at the manager level and above. This sampling strategy was designed to ensure that respondents would be among the most seasoned HR professionals, with significant responsibilities for HR policy and implementation. Responses were received from 959 recipients before the cutoff date, for a response rate of 19 percent. Nearly half the respondents (49 percent) were HR managers, while 26 percent were directors, 18 percent vice presidents, and 7 percent from other functional areas. The average respondent had 14 years of experience in HR. These high levels of experience and job responsibility suggested that our respondents should be relatively well-informed members of the HR profession.

The Seven Most Common Misconceptions

For the remainder of this article, we discuss the seven HR research findings that were least believed by our responding group of HR managers. The first four of these findings pertain primarily to issues of selection (i.e., employee traits that are most strongly associated with performance and effective means of assessing them). The next two pertain to issues of effective performance management—performance appraisal and performance improvement. The final item concerns problems with relying on survey data to determine the importance of pay (and other potential motivators) in people's behavior.

1. On average, conscientiousness is a better predictor of employee performance than intelligence.
Although 72 percent of participants agreed with this statement, a substantial amount of research suggests that it is incorrect. A recent meta-analytic summary of nineteen different selection methods reported a predictive validity coefficient of .51 for tests of intelligence (or general mental ability, GMA), as compared with an average validity of .31 for measures of conscientiousness.[14] This means that on average, GMA explains roughly 25 percent of the variance in employee performance, while conscientiousness explains only 9 percent. The authors conclude.

> Research evidence for the validity of GMA measures for predicting job performance is stronger than that for any other method . . . literally thousands of studies have been conducted over the last nine decades. . . . Because of its special status, GMA can be considered the primary personnel measure for hiring decisions.[15]

Not only is GMA the single best overall predictor of likely performance, but the positive economic effects of assessing it in selection can be very substantial. For example, based on estimates derived from comparing the productivity of the most- and least-productive workers, Jack Hunter estimated that the use of rank-ordered ability scores in the federal government would increase productivity by more than $13 billion relative to simply using a minimum cutoff score at the 20th percentile. Similarly, he estimated an increase of $12 million per year for a much smaller unit, the Philadelphia police department.[16]

Given the strength of these findings, why do so many managers—especially ones trained in HR management—assume the opposite? Although many explanations are possible, we think two are particularly likely.

First, as a culture, Americans have long held negative stereotypes about highly intelligent people.[17] One such stereotype is that intelligent people are brilliant but impractical ("ivory tower intellectuals"), while a second views them as capable, but socially inept ("nerd, geek, egghead"). A third stereotype likens intelligent people to the hare in Aesop's fable—erratic performers who are brilliant on occasion but who generally underperform the "slow and steady" in the long run.[18] A final stereotype portrays intelligent people as rude, arrogant, and difficult to manage. For example, in his recent book *Working with Emotional Intelligence*, Daniel Goleman repeatedly gives examples of intelligent people with extremely negative social traits, such as being "unbelievably arrogant" or "brutally acerbic, socially awkward, with no social graces or even a social life."[19]

The resilience of such stereotypes suggests that many people hold implicit theories of intelligence that associate high levels of GMA with a variety of unattractive personal characteristics. Conscientiousness, on the other hand, is viewed positively by most people, and the stereotype of a conscientious person is nearly always good. In reality, however, intelligence is virtually uncorrelated with such personality traits as conscientiousness, agreeableness, and emotional stability.[20] Thus, for every highly intelligent introvert there is a highly intelligent extrovert; for every brilliant neurotic, there is someone who is both highly intelligent and emotionally stable.

A second (but probably less likely) reason that managers may underestimate the importance of intelligence to job performance is that people may not believe that employee intelligence varies much *within* particular job categories. For example, Goleman has argued that "in professional and technical fields the threshold for entry is typically an IQ of 110 to 120. . . . Since everyone [in these fields] is in the top 10 percent or so of intelligence, IQ itself offers relatively little competitive advantage."[21] However, in a very-large-sample study designed explicitly to test this narrow-variability-in-IQ hypothesis, the average variability of intelligence within each of 80 applicant pools for specific job categories was found to be only 10 percent less than the full variability exemplified in national norms.[22] Thus, very substantial differences in intelligence still exist among applicants for any given type of job.

There are several implications of these findings (see Table 1). The first is that because both GMA and conscientiousness are important predictors of performance in virtually all jobs, both characteristics should be assessed as thoroughly as possible in the employee selection process.[23] A second implication is that the higher the level of job complexity, the more selection should be weighted toward GMA (see Endnote 14). How might this be done?

Research suggests that the best way to assess GMA is through paper-and-pencil testing.[24] Several good paper-and-pencil tests are available for such purposes, such as the Wonderlic Personnel Test, which only takes 12 minutes to administer and which correlates very highly with more intensive methods of assessing intelligence.[25] Another point in its favor is that its items are not exotic or highly abstract but rather look like typical items from a junior high or high school exam. In addition, considerable research suggests that applicants typically view ability tests as valid means of assessment and therefore are not likely to be put off by companies that require them.[26]

Although direct assessment of ability thus has two important features to recommend it (high validity and low cost), it also has some liabilities. For example, cognitive ability tests do produce adverse impact against certain groups and, rightly or wrongly, receive a considerable amount of negative press.[27] Thus, companies that are trying to balance a number of outcomes (e.g., applicant reactions, workforce diversity) in addition to achieving validity may choose to assess GMA in less direct ways, but in ways that also have substantial validity.

For example, research has shown that structured interviews, work samples, and simulations that assess job knowledge are likely to be moderately correlated with GMA, as well as being good predictors of job performance.[28] Assessing job knowledge in these ways has the additional advantages of having very high face validity to applicants and lower levels of adverse impact against minorities, while still retaining considerable validity. The most important implication, however, is that deliberate attempts to assess and use GMA as a basis for hiring should be made for *all* jobs. Failure to do so leaves money on the table.

2. *Companies that screen job applicants for values have higher performance than those that screen for intelligence.* A large majority of our responding SHRM managers agreed with this statement (57 percent), although available research evidence does not support it. At the outset, it should be said that there is far less research on the effects of selecting for

Research-Inconsistent Beliefs	What Research Shows	Ways to Implement Research Findings
1. Conscientiousness is a better predictor of employee performance than intelligence.	The average validity coefficient is .51 for intelligence, .31 for conscientiousness. They are *both* important predictors of performance, but intelligence is relatively more important. At the very lowest levels of job complexity (unskilled work), their importance is about equal. However, as jobs increase in complexity, intelligence becomes more and more important.	• Select new employees on both intelligence (general mental ability, GMA) and conscientiousness. Well-validated measures of both constructs are available. • In addition to pencil-and-paper tests, GMA can also be assessed through job-knowledge tests, work samples, or simulation interview questions.
2. Companies that screen job applicants for values have higher performance than those that screen for intelligence.	Intelligence is the best single predictor of performance. Although values fit does predict employee satisfaction and retention, little evidence exists of a direct link to performance. Even if a link is shown some time in the future, it is unlikely to approach the magnitude of the effect size for intelligence.	• Even if you are interested in people's values, assess GMA and conscientiousness first. • Define what values are important to you. Then, assess them through procedures such as behavioral description interviews or accomplishment records to see whether people actually behave in ways consistent with the desired values. • Consider which personality constructs are likely to reflect the values you want; then measure personality using well-validated instruments.
3. Integrity tests don't work well in practice because so many people lie on them.	People try to make themselves look a little more ethical than they actually are. This does not seem to affect the usefulness of these tests as predictors of performance.	• Integrity tests can be used in combination with ability tests to yield very high overall predictability of job performance.
4. Integrity tests have adverse impact on racial minorities.	Racial and ethnic differences on integrity test scores are trivial. Hispanics have been found to score .14 standard deviations higher than whites, ; Asians, .04 standard deviations higher; Native Americans, .08 standard deviations higher, and African-Americans, .04 lower.	• Combining integrity tests with tests of GMA may reduce the amount of adverse impact in overall selection systems because minorities and whites have nearly equivalent scores on integrity tests.
5. Encouraging employees to participate in decision making is more effective for improving organizational performance than setting performance goals.	On average, performance improves 16 percent when goal-setting is implemented. The average effect from employee participation is < 1 percent. Participation can produce both positive and negative outcomes. Employees must have a clear picture of *what* they are participating *for*—that is, what they are trying to achieve—in order for participation to be successful.	• Develop goals that are inspiring, challenging, and that stretch people's capabilities. • Once goals are clearly communicated and accepted enlist broad participation, and do not shut down ideas. • Support participation and goal attainment through the reward system, such as with gain sharing or other group incentive programs.

| 6. Most errors in performance appraisal can be eliminated by providing training that describes the kinds of errors managers tend to make and suggesting ways to avoid them. | Performance-appraisal errors are extremely difficult to eliminate Training to eliminate certain types of errors often introduces other types of errors and sometimes even decreases accuracy. The most common appraisal error is leniency, and managers often realize they are committing it. Mere training is insufficient to eliminate these kinds of errors; more systemic action is required such as intensive monitoring or forced rankings. | • Training, practice, and feedback about how to avoid appraisal errors are necessary, but insufficient, for eliminating errors.
• Eliminating errors may require alternative approaches to evaluation, such as forced distribution (e.g., General Electric).
• Top managers should serve as strong role models for the performance evaluation process and attach managerial consequences to the quality of performance reviews. |
| 7. If employees are asked how important pay is to them, they are likely to overestimate its true importance. | People tend to *understate* the importance of pay to their decisions due to social desirability considerations and lack of self-insight. Research that examines people's *behaviors* in response to pay (rather than their attitudes) tends to show very strong motivational effects. | • Recognize that employee attitude surveys are subject to a variety of cognitive biases such as social desirability and lack of self-insight.
• Wherever possible, study employee *behaviors* in addition to attitudes; the two will not always converge. |

values than there is about selecting for GMA or personality. Still, much evidence suggests that selecting for GMA leads to higher performance, and very little evidence suggests the same for values.

The available research comes in two forms. One stream focuses on values *congruence* or values *fit*. The importance of employee values has frequently been conceptualized in terms of compatibility between organizational and applicant values, rather than as a matter of positive versus negative values in an absolute sense.[29] For example, some companies focus very strongly on assessing and rewarding individual performance (e.g., Lincoln Electric or General Electric), while others motivate and reward almost entirely on the basis of group efforts and results (e.g., Southwest Airlines, Nucor). Thus, the logic goes that individualistic values would be an asset at Lincoln or GE, but a serious detriment at Southwest or Nucor.

Research has generally shown that values fit has positive consequences for employee attitudes and length of service.[30] However, there is much less evidence of a positive relationship between values fit and *performance*.[31] For example, one study found that workers who had congruent values received higher supervisory ratings when work tasks were interde-

pendent, but *lower* evaluations when work was not interdependent.[32] Another found that workers who believed their values were congruent with the organization's displayed more citizenship behaviors but not higher task performance.[33] Thus, in distinct contrast to the research on intelligence, the limited evidence on values congruence suggests rather small and inconsistent effects on performance.

Although researchers have primarily studied the relationship between values and performance in terms of values *fit*, a second stream of research focuses on the effect of values on performance *indirectly* through research on employee personality. For example, research suggests that when managers and recruiters talk about the kinds of values they are looking for, they most often mention such characteristics as "work ethic, teamwork values, desire for improvement, liking pressure, and liking variety and change."[34] Although managers tend to describe these traits as *values*, many researchers have studied them as *personality* traits. Thus, for example, the values of "work ethic" and "desire for improvement" can be translated into the personality trait of conscientiousness, while the value of "liking variety and change" translates into openness to experience.

From this perspective, we have already seen that although some values (or personality traits) such as "work ethic" are assets to performance, they are not as important as intelligence. Thus, from either perspective (values fit or values per se), the idea that values are more important predictors of performance than intelligence is not supported by the research evidence. We would suggest, however, that more research should be done to assess this question, both at the individual and the organizational level.

3. Although there are "integrity tests" that try to predict whether someone will steal, be absent, or otherwise take advantage of an employer, they don't work well in practice because so many people lie on them.[35]

Only 32 percent of our responding HR managers realized that this was an inaccurate statement. Because the statement seems highly plausible on its face, analysis of the evidence concerning integrity tests requires breaking the statement into pieces.

First, research shows that applicants *can* distort their answers on integrity tests (and other selection devices such as resumes) in order to make themselves look better to employers.[36] In addition, many applicants probably *do* distort their answers to some extent, particularly when they believe the scores will be used for selection or promotion purposes.[37] Interestingly, however, the fact that applicants can (and probably do) distort their responses to integrity tests does *not* make them ineffective as predictors of performance.[38] In fact, the average corrected validity coefficient for integrity tests is a very respectable .41, with counterproductive behaviors such as theft, absenteeism, or violence being somewhat better predicted (.47) than overall job performance (.34).[39]

These findings raise the interesting question of why integrity tests maintain their validity, despite the potential for deliberate response distortion. One possibility is that most people distort their responses to roughly the same degree, so that the "faking factor" becomes more or less a constant (and thus a non-differentiator) in the prediction equation. Another possibility is that the extent of response distortion may be correlated with valid predictors such as conscientiousness or emotional stability.[40] Whatever the reason, to the extent that distortion is occurring, it does not appear to destroy the usefulness of integrity tests as selection devices.

It should also be noted that integrity tests work very well in conjunction with tests of GMA. This is because cognitive ability is essentially uncorrelated with the underlying dimensions tapped by integrity tests, particularly conscientiousness. Because highly intelligent people are no more (or no less) likely to be honest or conscientious than those with lesser ability, using integrity tests along with ability tests yields completely unique incremental information. In fact, the highest overall validity for any combination of two selection methods appears to be obtained by using integrity tests in conjunction with tests of GMA.[41]

4. One problem with using integrity tests is that they have high degrees of adverse impact on racial minorities.

Despite their validity, managers may nevertheless be nervous about using integrity tests for a variety of other reasons. One possibility is that integrity tests, while valid, may eliminate larger proportions of minority than majority candidates. Although nearly 70 percent of our respondents thought that this might be true, it is not the case.

Recent large-sample research evidence reveals that differences in integrity test scores across racial and ethnic groups are trivial (although gender differences are not).[42] Thus, another potential advantage of using integrity tests in conjunction with cognitive ability tests is that, unlike ability tests, integrity tests are unlikely to produce adverse impact. Furthermore, although evidence suggests that integrity tests are not among the best-liked selection devices, they generally are seen by applicants as an appropriate means of differentiating among candidates.[43]

5. On average, encouraging employees to participate in decision making is more effective for improving organizational performance than setting performance goals.

Although considerable research has shown this statement to be false, only 17 percent of respondents clearly disagreed with it. Evidence regarding this issue comes from a number of sources.

First, meta-analysis has been used by Ed Locke and his colleagues to examine the comparative effectiveness of various performance-improvement interventions.[44] This research suggests that on average, performance improves by 16 percent following goal-setting interventions, as compared with less than 1 percent for employee participation. Moreover, the effects of goal-setting appear to be positive in virtually all cases, whereas increased participation actually leads to decreases in performance in a substantial minority of cases.

The weak results for participation seem puzzling, given the number of corporate success stories that seem to have employee participation at their core (e.g., Southwest Airlines, Rosenbluth Travel, or Springfield Remanufacturing). However, other research suggests that the success of participation programs may depend on the order in which performance interventions are introduced. Specifically, it appears that in order for participative management to succeed, employees must first know *what* they are attempting to achieve through participation. In other words, goal-setting or some other means of conveying performance expectations may have to precede employee participation in order for it to be effective. As Cusumano and Selby wrote after studying Microsoft for several years: "Although having creative people in a high-tech company is important, it is often more important to *direct* their creativity."[45] For this reason, Microsoft work assignments are characterized by strong emphasis on project deadlines, multiple milestones on the path to project completion, and frequent merging of different employees' pieces of code to see how well the project is moving toward completion.

Research by McKinsey and Company on high-performing work teams also suggests the value of challenging goals for increasing the effectiveness of participation.[46] In their study of factors that distinguish high-performing teams from mediocre ones, they were surprised to find that the typical emphasis on building "teamwork" and "teamwork values" was ineffective for producing peak levels of team performance. Rather, the true distinguishing factor was the existence of a challenging, meaningful task that inspired team members and stretched their capacities. Although the concept of teamwork is different from that of participation, the pre-eminent role of a challenging goal in focusing employee efforts appears to be common to both.

In summary, participative management strategies are unlikely to be effective unless employees are clear about performance goals and objectives. However, for most employees, the major source of information about what is expected and how they are performing is the annual performance review. This is unfortunate because previous research suggests that when performance appraisal is the major vehicle for communicating information about performance, confusion about goals and objectives appears to be more common than not.[47] Therefore, other performance management strategies that incorporate both objective targets and supra-individual goals (e.g., project milestones or group incentive systems) would appear to provide a better chance of producing coordinated, effective participation (see Table 1).

6. Most errors in performance appraisals can be eliminated by providing training that describes the kinds of errors managers tend to make and suggesting ways to avoid them.

Although 70 percent of our HR respondents agreed with the preceding sentence, research clearly shows it to be false. A long line of research shows that performance appraisal is one of the most problematic HR practices, as well as one of the most difficult to improve.[48] In particular, rater training of the type described above (simply describing errors and suggesting ways to eliminate them) has been found to be notoriously ineffective for improving appraisal accuracy.[49] For one thing, many managers do not believe that they, personally, make the errors described by the trainer.[50] In addition, research has shown that training to reduce certain kinds of errors can actually *increase* inaccuracy by introducing other types of errors.[51]

Rather, improvement of performance appraisal appears to require a fairly intensive set of activities. These include active participation in rating videotaped performers against performance specifications, providing written justifications of their ratings, (usually) making several errors in relation to "correct" appraisal ratings, having group discussions of ways to overcome the errors, and providing further practice sessions, spaced over time.[52] Even so, it should be emphasized that studies that have shown rating improvements as a result of these methods have assessed rater accuracy by using carefully constructed videotape scenarios, where the correct rating can be known and where raters are not personally involved with the "picture-people" they are rating. Thus, it is still unclear whether managers who are able to correctly evaluate videotaped performances by unknown actors actually transfer this learnings to subsequent ratings of their own employees.

When dealing with "real employees," it is generally believed that getting rid of appraisal errors—particularly leniency—requires very substantial monitoring of appraisals and clear statements by top management that leniency or other forms of inaccuracy are not acceptable.[53] For example, General Electric found that they were unable to eliminate excessive leniency from performance appraisals until they began to insist that managers rank employees on a bell curve and attached substantial penalties to managers for failure to do so. Although this system appears to be working well at GE, it should be noted that this strong ratings differentiation is accompanied by many other supportive actions, such as three thorough performance reviews of managers each year, very aggressive career planning, highly differentiated monetary rewards linked to appraisal distributions, and refusal to promote managers who will not make the distinctions. Although one can certainly debate whether you can truly have accurate appraisals when every unit is required to rate on the same bell curve (this recently became a major issue at the Ford Motor Company), one positive feature is that measurement studies have shown that it is in fact easier to make accurate *rankings* than accurate *ratings*.[54]

7. *Surveys that directly ask employees how important pay is to them are likely to overestimate pay's true importance in employees' actual decisions.*

Although 56 percent of the HR managers responding agreed with this statement, the fact is that people are more likely to *under*-report the importance of pay than to over-report it. Moreover, this tendency has been known for quite some time. As far back as 1966, researchers cautioned that self-reports of pay importance are likely to provide underestimates due to people's tendency to answer surveys in socially desirable ways.[55] That is, people are likely to understate the importance of pay due to norms that view money as a somewhat crass source of motivation.

Evidence that people under-report pay importance comes from two different types of studies. One type compares individuals' direct self-reports of pay importance with importance as inferred from their preferences for various job descriptions. By measuring each job in terms of its underlying characteristics (i.e., different levels of pay, promotion potential, work duties, job security, and the like) and then comparing jobs with subjects' overall assessments of job attractiveness, the importance of each underlying job characteristic to overall assessments can be inferred without asking direct questions about importance. In such studies, pay has generally been found to be a substantially more important factor when inferred from participants' overall evaluations of job attractiveness than from their direct reports of pay importance.[56]

A second type of study uses the psychological principle of projection to infer how people evaluate characteristics that are heavily laden with social desirability. In the largest study of this kind, a Midwestern utility assessed the relative importance of ten job characteristics (including pay) to 50,000 applicants over a thirty-year period.[57] Based on applicants' self-reports, pay appeared to be the fifth most important characteristic to men and seventh to women. However, when asked to rate the importance of those same ten attributes to "someone just like yourself—same age, education, and gender," pay jumped to first place among both men and women.[58] In other words, people seem to believe that pay is the most important motivator to everyone except themselves.

Recognizing that employees are likely to understate the significance of pay is important, so that managers are not lulled into a false sense of complacency about their pay policies. More generally, this survey item calls attention to the broader need for managers to understand the limitations of rating and ranking survey methodologies. Although such surveys are not entirely useless as a basis for managerial decision making, they do have very serious limitations in terms of designing HR policies. For example, survey findings are likely to be highly unstable across minor variations in method, such as the number of job characteristics included, specific terminology used to describe the various characteristics (e.g., "high pay" versus "fair pay"), purpose of the survey (pure research versus policy making), and whether or not respondents are assured anonymity.[59]

For these reasons, managers are likely to benefit more from research that examines how employees actually *behave* differently under alternative employment practices than from studies of perceived importance. Studies of this type in the compensation area suggest that pay is indeed an important motivator of behavior.[60] For example, Locke and colleagues' meta-analysis found the introduction of monetary incentives to produce the largest and most reliable increases in job performance (median = 30 percent)—almost twice as large as the effects of goal setting or job enrichment. Thus, Locke et al. concluded, "Money is the crucial incentive . . . no other incentive or motivational technique comes even close to money with respect to its instrumental value."[61]

Putting Research into Practice

Previous academics and practitioners have documented a variety of reasons why research findings are not implemented in organizations.[62] However, our survey of HR managers suggests that one of the main reasons is lack of knowledge. Although this might seem unsurprising, some argue that improved mechanisms of information dissemination have made lack of knowledge a trivial problem. For example, Pfeffer and Sutton argue: "We now live in a world where knowledge transfer and information exchange are tremendously efficient, and where there are numerous organizations in the business of collecting and transferring best practices. So, there are fewer and smaller differences in what firms know than in their ability to act on that knowledge."[63]

Our results belie the assertion that knowledge transfer is "tremendously efficient." Indeed, what is particularly striking about our results is that with the exception of the research on integrity tests and values, all the other findings (i.e., regarding goal-setting, performance appraisal, intelligence, and conscientiousness) have been known for at least a decade and, in some cases, considerably longer than that. Moreover, our respondents are HR practitioners who have the most to gain from knowing this research: mid- to high-level HR managers and executives. In addition, our results also suggest that differences in knowledge across firms are likely to be large rather than small; some executives in our sample believed only 9 of the 35 research findings (26 percent), while others believed 30 of the 35 (86 percent).

One obvious solution to this problem would be for practitioners to read more of the research literature. Indeed, in our sample, practitioners who usually read academic research journals tended to agree with 23 of the research findings, as compared with the sample mean of 20—an improvement of 15 percent. However, the problem with this strategy is that very few practitioners appear to read this literature. Specifically, fewer than 1 percent of our sample indicated that they usually read the academic literature, while 75 percent reported that they *never* do so.

Thus, it appears that outlets such as *The Executive* and other efforts to disseminate research knowledge[64] to practitioners are sorely needed. In addition, very explicit attempts to turn findings into "maps for action"[65] may prove useful in helping practitioners to translate research into action. Then, as they conduct their implementation attempts, researchers can document the successes and failures via "action research."[66]

In closing, we remind the reader that what we know from a large and growing body of HR research has become considerably clearer over the past two decades. Failure to be aware of the findings from this research is likely to put one (and one's company) at a competitive disadvantage. At the same time, although enhanced knowledge can be an important asset for improving organizational performance, it is not by itself enough. Rather, improved knowledge acquisition must be paired with effective implementation. Results from our SHRM managers suggest that the transfer of knowledge from research to practice remains imperfect, even in this world of increasingly efficient markets for information.

Source: *Academy of Management Executive: The Thinking Manager's Source* by Rynes. Copyright © 2002 with permission of Academy of Management in the format Textbook via Copyright Clearance Center.

Endnotes

1. Gannon, M. J. 1983. Managerial ignorance. *Business Horizons*, May–June: 26(3).
2. Johns, G. 1993. Constraints on the adoption of psychology-based personnel practices: Lessons from organizational innovation. *Personnel Psychology*, 46(3): 569–592.
3. Terpstra, D. E., & Rozell, E. J. 1997. Attitudes of practitioners in human resource management toward information from academic research. *Psychological Reports*, 80(2): 403–412.
4. Campbell, J. P., Daft, R. L. & Hulin, C. L. 1982. *What to study: Generating and developing research questions.* Beverly Hills: Sage.
5. Oviatt, B. M., & Miller, W. D. 1989. Irrelevance, intransigence, and business professors. *The Academy of Management Executive.* 3(4): 304–312.

6. Becker, B., & Gerhart, B. 1996. The impact of human resource management on organizational performance. *Academy of Management Journal*, 39(4): 779–801.

7. Hunter, J. E., & Schmidt, F. L. 1995. *Methods of meta-analysis: Correcting error and bias in research findings.* Thousand Oaks: Sage.

8. For a good overview of this research, see the 1996 special issue of *Academy of Management Journal* edited by Becker & Gerhart, op. cit.

9. Welbourne, T. M., & Andrews, A. O. 1996. Predicting the performance of initial public offerings: Should human resource management be in the equation? *Academy of Management Journal*, 39(4): 891–919.

10. Huselid, M. A. 1995. The impact of human resource management practices on turnover, productivity, and corporate financial performance. *Academy of Management Journal*, 38(3): 635–672.

11. Terpstra, D. E., & Rozell, E. J. 1997. Sources of human resource information and the link to organizational profitability. *Journal of Applied Behavioral Science*, 33(1): 66–83.

12. Ulrich, D. 1997, *Human resource champions: The next agenda for adding value and delivering results*, Boston: Harvard Business School Press.

13. The original questionnaire had 39 items, but four items were later eliminated due to ambiguous wording or new research findings.

14. Validities are higher than .51 for more complex jobs (e.g., .58 for professional and managerial jobs) and lower for less complex jobs (e.g., .40 for semi-skilled jobs). Schmidt, F. L., & Hunter, J. E. 1998. The validity and utility of selection methods in personnel psychology: Practical and theoretical implications of 85 years of research findings. *Psychological Bulletin*, 124(2): 262–274.

15. Ibid., 264–266.

16. These figures are in 1980 dollars and thus would be considerably larger now. See Schmidt, F. L., & Hunter, J. E. 1981. Employment testing: Old theories and new research findings. *The American Psychologist*, 36(Special Issue): 1128–1137.

17. Hofstadter, R. 1996. *Anti-intellectualism in American life.* New York: Alfred A. Knopf; and Whyte, W. H. 1956. *The organization man.* New York: Touchstone Books.

18. An example can be seen in this quote from 120 years ago: "A great many of the most 'precocious' youths have dropped out of memory, while some of the plodding, but untiring and persevering ones, are holding the reins of government or guiding the counsels of school and senate." Thayer, 1882, quoted in Stross, R. E. 1997. *The Microsoft way.* Reading, MA: Addison-Wesley: 32.

19. Goleman, D. 1998. *Working with emotional intelligence.* New York: Bantam Books: 22, 35, 40.

20. Goff, M., & Ackerman, P. L. 1992. Personality-intelligence relations: Assessment of typical intellectual engagement. *Journal of Educational Psychology*, 84(4): 537–552.

21. Goleman, op. cit., 20.

22. Sackett, P. R., & Ostgaard, D. J. 1994. Job-specific applicant pools and national norms for cognitive ability tests: Implications for range restriction corrections in validation research. *Journal of Applied Psychology*, 79(5): 680–684.

23. See also Behling, O. 1998. Employee selection: Will intelligence and conscientiousness do the job? *The Academy of Management Executive.* 12(1): 77–85.

24. Huffcutt, A. I., Conway, J. M., Roth, P. L., & Stone, N. J. 2001. Identification and meta-analytic assessment of psychological constructs measured in employment interviews. *Journal of Applied Psychology*, 96(5): 897–913.

25. The Wonderlic is available via *www.wonderlic.com*. For a review, see Murphy, K. 1984. The Wonderlic Personnel Test. In J. Hogan & R. Hogan (Eds.). *Business and industry testing: Current practices and test reviews.* Austin: Pro-Ed: 191–197.

26. Ryan, A. M., & Ployhart, R. E. 2000. Applicants' perceptions of selection procedures and decisions: A critical review and agenda for the future. *Journal of Management*, 26(3): 565–606.

27. These factors, in combination with the complexity of legal requirements, suggest that most if not all companies should get legal advice about the defensibility of their overall selection systems.

28. For example, John Hunter found job knowledge to be correlated .80 with GMA and .80 with job performance as assessed by the highly valid method of work sampling. See Hunter, J. E. 1986. Cognitive ability, cognitive aptitudes, job knowledge, and job performance. *Journal of Vocational Behavior*, 29(3): 340–362.

29. Adkins, C. L., Ravlin, E. C., & Meglino, B. M. 1996. Value congruence between co-workers and its relationship to work outcomes. *Group and Organization Management*, 21(4): 439–460; Adkins, C. L., Russell, C. J., & Werbel, J. D. 1994. Judgments of fit in the selection process: The role of work-value congruence. *Personnel Psychology*, 47(3): 605–623: and Welch, J. 2001. *Jack: Straight from the gut.* New York: Warner Business Books.

30. Chatman, J. 1991. Matching people and organizations: Selection and socialization in public accounting firms. *Administrative Science Quarterly*, 36(3): 459–484; and Meglino, B. M., & Ravlin, E. C. 1998. Individual values in organizations: Concepts, controversies, and research. *Journal of Management*, 24(3): 351–389.

31. Lauver, K., & Kristof-Brown, A. 2001. Distinguishing between employees' perceptions of person-job and person-organization fit. *Journal of Vocational Behavior* 59(3): 454–470; and Meglino & Ravlin, ibid.

32. Adkins, Ravlin, & Meglino, op. cit.

33. Lauver & Kristof-Brown, op. cit.

34. Bretz, R. D., Rynes, S. L., & Gerhart, B. 1993. Recruiter perceptions of applicant fit: Implications for individual career preparation and job search behavior. *Journal of Vocational Behavior*, 43(2): 310–327; and Kristof-Brown, A. L. 2000. Perceived applicant fit: Distinguishing between recruiters' perceptions of person-job and person-organization fit. *Personnel Psychology*, 53(3): 643–671.

35. Integrity tests (sometimes called "honesty tests") were initially designed to predict applicant propensities to steal. Over time, they have been used to predict an increasingly broader range of behaviors, including counterproductive behaviors (e.g., absenteeism, tardiness, or violence) and even general job performance. Evidence suggests that integrity tests tap three of the "big five" personality dimensions—mostly Conscientiousness, but also Agreeableness and Emotional Stability.

36. Ryan, A. M., & Sackett, P. R. 1987. Pre-employment honesty testing: Fakability, reactions of test takers and company image. *Journal of Business and Psychology*, 1(2): 248–258.

37. Cunningham. M. R., Wong, D. T., & Barbee, A. P. 1994. Self-presentation dynamics on overt integrity tests: Experimental studies of the Reid Report. *Journal of Applied Psychology*, 79(5): 643–658.

38. Hough, L. M., Eaton, N. K., Dunnette, M. D., Kamp, J. D., & McCloy, R. A. 1990. Criterion-related validities of personality constructs and the effect of response distortion on those validities. *Personnel Psychology*, 75(5): 581–595; and Ones, D. S., Viswesvaran, C., & Reiss, A. D. 1996. Role of social desirability in personality testing for personnel selection: The red herring. *Journal of Applied Psychology*, 81(6): 660–679.

39. Ones et al., 1993, op. cit.

40. Ones et al., 1996, op. cit.

41. Schmidt & Hunter, op. cit.

42. Ones, D. S., & Viswesvaran, C. 1998. Gender, age, and race differences on overt integrity tests: Results across four large-scale job applicant data sets. *Journal of Applied Psychology*, 83(1): 35–42. Although racial and ethnic differences are trivial, women score significantly higher than men.

43. Ryan & Sackett, op. cit.

44. Locke, E. A., Feren, D. B., McCaleb, V. N., Shaw, K. N., & Denny, A. T. 1980. The relative effectiveness of four methods of motivating employee performance. In K. D. Duncan, M. M. Gruneberg, & D. Wallis (Eds.). *Changes in working life*. New York: John Wiley & Sons: 363–388.

45. Cusumano, M. A., & Selby, R. W. 1995. *Microsoft secrets*. New York: The Free Press: 10.

46. Kaizenbach, J. R., & Smith, D. K. 1994. *The wisdom of teams: Creating the high-performance organization*. New York: Harper Business.

47. Beer, M. 1997. Conducting a performance appraisal interview. Harvard Business School Case 9–497–058. Boston: Harvard Business School Press.

48. Kluger, A. N., & DeNisi, A. 1996. The effects of feedback interventions on performance. *Psychological Bulletin*, 119(2): 254–284; and Longenecker, C. O., Sims, H. P., & Gioia, D. A. 1987. Behind the mask: The politics of employee appraisal. *The Academy of Management Executive*, 1(3): 183–193.

49. Latham, G. P., & Wexley, K. N. 1980. *Increasing productivity through performance appraisal*. Reading, MA: Addison-Wesley; and Levine, J., & Butler, J. 1952. Lecture versus group decision in changing behavior. *Journal of Applied Psychology*, 36(1): 29–33.

50. Latham & Wexley, ibid.; and Wexley, K. N., Sanders, R. E., & Yuki, G. A. 1973. Training interviewers to eliminate contrast effects in employment interviews. *Journal of Applied Psychology*, 57(2): 233–236.

51. Bernardin, H. J., & Buckley, M. R. 1981. Strategies in rater training. *Academy of Management Review*, 6(2): 205–212; and

Bernardin, H. J., & Pence, E. G. 1980. The effects of rater training: Creating new response sets and decreasing accuracy. *Journal of Applied Psychology*, 65(7): 60–66.

52. Latham, G. P., & Latham, S. D. 2000. Overlooking theory and research in performance appraisal at one's peril: Much done, more to do. In Cooper, C. L., & Locke, E. A. (Eds.). *Industrial and organizational psychology: Linking theory with practice*. Oxford: Blackwell: 199–215.

53. Longenecker, et al., op. cit.; and Welch, op. cit.

54. Cronbach, L. J., et al. 1972. *The dependability of behavioral measurements: Theory of generalizability of scores and profiles*, NY: John Wiley.

55. Opsahl, R. L., & Dunnette, M. D. 1966. The role of financial compensation in industrial motivation. *Psychological Bulletin*, 66(1): 94–118.

56. Feldman, D. C., & Arnold, H. J. 1978. Position choice: Comparing the importance of organizational and job factors. *Journal of Applied Psychology*, 63(6): 706–710; and Rynes, S. L., Schwab, D. P., & Heneman, H. G. 1983. The role of pay and market pay variability in job application decisions, *Organizational Behavior and Human Performance*, 31(3): 353–364.

57. Jurgensen, C. E. 1978. Job preferences (what makes a job good or bad?). *Journal of Applied Psychology*, 63(2): 267–276.

58. Jurgensen, ibid.

59. Lawler, E. E. III. 1971. *Pay and organizational effectiveness: A psychological view*. New York: McGraw-Hill.

60. Gerhart, B., & Milkovich, G. T. 1990. Organizational differences in managerial compensation and financial performance. *Academy of Management Journal*. 33(4): 663–691; and Locke et al., op. cit.

61. Ibid., 379.

62. Johns, op. cit.; and LaPointe, J. B. 1990. Industrial-organizational psychology: A view from the field. In Murphy, K. R., & Saal, F. E. (Eds.). *Psychology in organizations; Integrating science and practice*. Hillsdale, NJ: Erlbaum: 7–24.

63. Pfeffer, J., & Sutton, R. I. 2000. *The knowing-doing gap*. Boston: Harvard Business School Press: 243.

64. Examples include Locke. E. A. 2000. *The Blackwell handbook of organizational behavior*. Oxford: Blackwell; and Cooper & Locke, op. cit.

65. Argyris, C. 1985. Making knowledge more relevant to practice: Maps for action. In Lawler, E. E., Mohrman, A. M., Mohrman, S. A., Ledford, G. E., & Cummings, T. G. (Eds.). *Doing research that is useful for theory and practice*. San Francisco: Jossey-Bass.

66. Susman, G. I., & Evered, R. D. 1978. An assessment of the scientific merits of action research. *Administrative Science Quarterly*, 23(4): 582–603.

Producing Sustainable Competitive Advantage Through the Effective Management of People

Jeffrey Pfeffer, *Academy of Management Executive*

Suppose that in 1972, someone asked you to pick the five companies that would provide the greatest return to stockholders over the next 20 years. And suppose that you had access to books on competitive success that were not even written. How would you approach your assignment? In order to earn tremendous economic returns, the companies you picked should have some sustainable competitive advantage, something that 1) distinguishes them from their competitors, 2) provides positive economic benefits, and 3) is not readily duplicated.

Conventional wisdom then (and even now) would have you begin by selecting the right industries. After all, "not all industries offer equal opportunity for sustained profitability, and the inherent profitability of its industry is one essential ingredient in determining the profitability of a firm."[1] According to Michael Porter's now famous framework, the five fundamental competitive forces that determine the ability of firms in an industry to earn above-normal returns are "the entry of new competitors, the threat of substitutes, the bargaining power of buyers, the bargaining power of suppliers, and the rivalry among existing competitors."[2] You should find industries with barriers to entry, low supplier and buyer bargaining power, few ready substitutes, and a limited threat of new entrants to compete away economic returns. Within such industries, other conventional analyses would urge you to select firms with the largest market share, which can realize the cost benefits of economies of scale. In short you would probably look to industries in which patent protection of important product or service technology could be achieved and select the dominant firms in those industries.

You would have been very successful in selecting the five top performing firms from 1972 to 1992 if you took this conventional wisdom and turned it on its head. The top five stocks, and their percentage returns, were (in reverse order): Plenum Publishing (with a return of 15,689%), Circuit City (a video and appliance retailer; 16,410%), Tyson Foods (a poultry producer; 18,118%), Wal-Mart (a discount chain; 19,807%), and Southwest Airlines (21,775%).[3] Yet during this period, these industries (retailing, airlines, publishing, and food processing) were characterized by massive competitive and horrendous losses, widespread bankruptcy, virtually no barriers to entry (for airlines after 1978), little unique or proprietary technology, and many substitute products or services. And in 1972, none of these firms was (and some still are not) the market-share leader, enjoying economies of scale or moving down the learning curve.

The point here is not to throw out conventional strategic analysis based on industrial economics but simply to note that the source of competitive advantage has always shifted over time. What these five successful firms tend to have in common is that for their sustained advantage, they rely not on technology, patents, or strategic position, but on how they manage their workforce.

The Importance of the Workforce and How It Is Managed

As other sources of competitive success have become less important, what remains as a crucial, differentiating factor is the organization, its employees, and how they work. Consider, for instance, Southwest Airlines, whose stock had the best return from 1972 to 1992. It certainly did not achieve that success from economies of scale. In 1992, Southwest had revenues of $1.31 billion and a mere 2.6% of the U.S. passenger market.[4] People Express, by contrast, achieved $1 billion in revenues after only 3 years of operation, not the almost 20 it took Southwest. Southwest exists not because of regulated or protected markets but in spite of them. "During the first three years of its history, no Southwest planes were flown."[5] Southwest waged a battle for its very existence with competitors who sought to keep it from flying at all and, failing that, made sure it did not fly out of the newly constructed

Dallas–Fort Worth international airport. Instead, it was restricted to operating out of the close-in Love Field, and thus was born its first advertising slogan, "Make Love, Not War." Southwest became the "love" airline out of necessity, not choice.

In 1978, competitors sought to bar flights from Love Field to anywhere outside Texas. The compromise Southwest wrangled permitted it to fly from Love to the four states contiguous to Texas.[6] Its competitive strategy of short-haul, point-to-point flights to close-in airports (it now flies into Chicago's Midway and Houston's Hobby airports) was more a product of its need to adapt to what it was being permitted to do than a conscious, planned move—although, in retrospect, the strategy has succeeded brilliantly. Nor has Southwest succeeded because it has had more access to lower-cost capital—indeed, it is one of the least leveraged airlines in the United States. Southwest's planes, Boeing 737s, are obviously available to all its competitors. It isn't a member of any of the big computerized reservation systems; it uses no unique process technology and sells essentially a commodity product—low-cost, low frills airline service at prices its competitors have difficulty matching.

Much of its cost advantage comes from its very productive, very motivated, and by the way, unionized workforce. Compared to the U.S. airline industry, according to 1991 statistics, Southwest has fewer employees per aircraft (79 versus 131), flies more passengers per employee (2,318 versus 848), and has more available seat miles per employee (1,891,082 versus 1,339,995).[7] It turns around some 80% of its flights in 15 minutes or less, while other airlines on average need 45 minutes, giving it an enormous productivity advantage in terms of equipment utilization.[8] It also provides an exceptional level of passenger service. Southwest has won the airlines' so-called triple crown (best on-time performance, fewest lost bags, and fewest passenger complaints—in the same month) *nine* times. No competitor has achieved that even once.[9]

What is important to recognize is why success, such as that achieved at Southwest, can be sustained and cannot readily be imitated by competitors. There are two fundamental reasons. First, the success that comes from managing people effectively is often not as visible or transparent as to its source. We can see a computerized information system, a particular semiconductor, a numerically controlled machine tool. The culture and practices that enable Southwest to achieve its success are less

obvious. Even when they are described, as they have been in numerous newspaper articles and even a segment of "60 Minutes," they are difficult to really understand. Culture, how people are managed, and the effects of this on their behavior and skills are sometimes seen as the "soft" side of business, occasionally dismissed. Even when they are not dismissed, it is often hard to comprehend the dynamics of a particular company and how it operates because the way people are managed often fits together in a system. It is easy to copy one thing but much more difficult to copy numerous things. This is because the change needs to be more comprehensive and also because the ability to understand the system of management practices is hindered by its very extensiveness.

Thus, for example, Nordstrom, the department store chain, has enjoyed substantial success both in customer service and in sales and profitability growth over the years. Nordstrom compensates its employees in part with commissions. Not surprisingly, many of its competitors, after finally acknowledging Nordstrom's success, and the fact that it was attributable to the behavior of its employees, instituted commission systems. By itself, changing the compensation system did not fully capture what Nordstrom had done, nor did it provide many benefits to the competition. Indeed, in some cases, changing the compensation system produced employee grievances and attempts to unionize when the new system was viewed as unfair or arbitrary.

Thirteen Practices for Managing People

Contrary to some academic writing and to popular belief, there is little evidence that effective management practices are 1) particularly faddish (although their implementation may well be), 2) difficult to understand or to comprehend why they work, or 3) necessarily contingent on an organization's particular competitive strategy. There are interrelated practices—I enumerate 13, but the exact number and how they are defined are somewhat arbitrary—that seem to characterize companies that are effective in achieving competitive success through how they manage people.

The following policies and practices emerge from extensive reading of both the popular and academic literature, talking to numerous people in firms in a variety of industries, and the application of some simple common sense. The particular way of subdividing the terrain is less important than considering the entire landscape, so the reader should realize that the division into categories is somewhat arbitrary. The themes, however, recur repeatedly in studies of organizations. It is important to recognize that the practices are interrelated—it is difficult to do one thing by itself with much positive result.

EMPLOYMENT SECURITY

Security of employment signals a long-standing commitment by the organization to its workforce. Norms of reciprocity tend to guarantee that this commitment is repaid. However, conversely, an employer that signals through word and deed that its employees are dispensable is not likely to generate much loyalty, commitment, or willingness to expend extra effort for the organization's benefit. New United Motor Manufacturing (NUMMI), the Toyota-GM joint venture in California, guaranteed workers' jobs as part of the formal labor contract in return for a reduction in the number of job classifications and an agreement not to strike over work standards. This commitment was met even in the face of temporarily slow demand, and many observers believe that as a result, trust between employees and the organization increased substantially.

Taking on people not readily eliminated exerts pressure to be careful and selective in hiring. Moreover, "employment security enhances employee involvement because employees are more willing to contribute to the work process when they need not fear losing their own or their coworkers' jobs. Employment security contributes to training as both employer and employee have greater incentives to invest in training,"[10] because there is some assurance that the employment relationship will be of sufficient duration to earn a return on the time and resources expended in skill development.

SELECTIVITY IN RECRUITING

Security in employment and reliance on the workforce for competitive success mean that one must be careful to choose the right people, in the right way. Studies covering populations ranging from machine operators, typists, and welders to assembly workers—all in self-paced jobs so that individual differences mattered—indicate that the most productive employees were about twice as good as the least

productive.[11] Southwest Airlines worries a lot about hiring the right people. In fact, it flies some of its best customers to Dallas and involves them in the flight attendant hiring process, believing that those who are in contact with the frontline employees probably know best what makes a good employee. At Lincoln Electric, hiring is done very carefully based on the desire to succeed and the capacity for growth.[12]

One of the practices of many of the Japanese automobile-manufacturing plants opened in the United States that proved especially newsworthy was their extensive screening of employees. Some of this was undoubtedly done to weed out those who were likely to be pro-union, but much of the screening was to find those people who could work best in the new environment, could learn and develop, and needed less supervision. There was little screening for particular skills, under the assumption that these could be readily learned. Nordstrom, the very effective specialty retailer whose sales per square foot are about double the industry average, tends to recruit sales clerks who are young and college-educated, seeking a career in retailing.[13]

Besides getting the right people in the door, recruiting has an important symbolic aspect. If someone goes through a rigorous selection process, the person feels that he or she is joining an elite organization. High expectations for performance are created, and the message sent is that people matter.

HIGH WAGES

If you want to recruit outstanding people, and want them to stay with the organization, paying more is helpful, although not absolutely necessary. High wages tend to attract more applicants, permitting the organization to be more selective in finding people who are going to be trainable and who will be committed to the organization. Perhaps the most important, higher wages send a message that the organization values its people. Particularly if these wages are higher than required by the market, employees can perceive the extra income as a gift and work more diligently as a result.[14] Nordstrom typically pays its people an hourly wage higher than the prevailing rate for retail clerks at comparable stores. Coupled with incentive pay for outstanding work, Nordstrom salespeople often earn twice the average retail income.

Companies sometimes believe that lowering labor costs is essential for competitive success. This is not invariably the case, even in cost-competitive businesses, because in many organizations, labor costs are a small fraction of the total costs. Furthermore, even if labor costs (let alone labor rates) are higher, it may be that enhanced service, skill, and innovation more than compensate by increasing the level of overall profit. For instance, the CEO of Wendy's, facing declining company profitability, decided that the best way to become the customer's restaurant of choice was to become the employer of choice.[15] This entailed improving both benefits and base compensation, instituting a quarterly bonus, and creating an employee stock option plan. The results were dramatic: "Our turnover rate for general managers fell to 20% in 1991 from 39% in 1989, while turnover among co- and assistant managers dropped to 37% from 60%—among the lowest in the business. With a stable—and able—workforce, sales began to pick up as well."[16]

INCENTIVE PAY

There has been a tendency to overuse money in an effort to solve myriad organizational problems. People are motivated by more than money—things like recognition, security, and fair treatment matter a great deal. Nevertheless, if people are responsible for enhanced levels of performance and profitability, they will want to share in the benefits. Consider the alternative—if all the gains from extra ingenuity and effort go just to top management or to shareholders (unless these are also employees), people will soon view the situation as unfair, become discouraged, and abandon their efforts. Thus, many organizations seek to reward performance with some form of contingent compensation.

Lincoln Electric is deservedly famous for its piecework and incentive bonus plan. Contrary to first impressions, the plan does much more than merely reward individual productivity. Although the factory workforce is paid on a piecework basis, it is paid only for good pieces—workers correct quality problems on their own time. Moreover, defects can be traced to the individual who produced them. Quality is emphasized as well as productivity. Additionally, piecework is only a part of the employee's compensation. Bonuses, which often constitute 100% of regular salary, are based on the company's profitability—encouraging employees to identify with the whole firm. They are also based on the individual's merit rating, and that rating is, in turn based on four equally important aspects of performance: dependability, quality, output, and ideas and cooperation.[17] This broader evaluation mitigates the pernicious tendencies of simplistic incentive systems to go awry.

EMPLOYEE OWNERSHIP

Employee ownership offers two advantages. Employees who have ownership interests in the organizations for which they work have less conflict between capital and labor—to some degree they are both capital and labor. Employee ownership, effectively implemented, can align the interests of employees with those of shareholders by making employees shareholders, too. Second, employee ownership puts stock in the hands of people, employees, who are more inclined to take a long-term view of the organization, its strategy, and its investment policies and less likely to support hostile takeovers, leveraged buyouts, and other financial maneuvers. Of course, to the extent that one believes this reduced risk of capital market discipline inhibits efficiency, significant employee shareholding is a disadvantage. However, the existing evidence largely contradicts this negative view.

It is probably no coincidence that all five of the companies mentioned as providing the best shareholder returns from 1972 to 1992 appear on The Employee Ownership 1000, a listing of "1000 companies in which employees own more than 4% of the stock of a corporation" traded on the New York or American stock exchanges or the over-the-counter market.[18] Although employee ownership is no panacea, and its effects depend largely on how it is implemented, the existing evidence is consistent with the view that employee ownership has positive effects on firm performance.[19]

INFORMATION SHARING

If people are to be a source of competitive advantage, clearly they must have the information necessary to do what is required to be successful. At the Advanced Micro Devices submicron development center, there are computer terminals throughout the plant that every employee has been trained to use in order to obtain information about product yields, development progress, production rates, or any other aspect of the operation. One reason sometimes given for not disclosing information to large numbers of employees is that it may leak to competitors. When

Robert Beck was head of human resources for the Bank of America, he perceptively told the management committee, reluctant to disclose the bank's strategy and other information to its employees, that the competitors almost certainly knew the information already; typically, the only people in the dark are the firm's own employees.

PARTICIPATION AND EMPOWERMENT

Sharing information is a necessary precondition to another important feature found in many successful work systems: encouraging the decentralization of decision making and broader worker participation and empowerment in controlling their own work process. At Nordstrom, the written philosophy states:

> We also encourage you to present your own ideas. Your buyers have a great deal of autonomy, and are encouraged to seek out and promote new fashion directions at all times. . . . Nordstrom has a strong open-door policy and we encourage you to share your concerns, suggestions and ideas . . .
>
> *Nordstrom Rules*:
>
> Rule #1: Use your good judgment in all situations. There will be no additional rules.[20]

The evidence is that participation increases both satisfaction and employee productivity.[21] Autonomy is one of the most important dimensions of jobs and was the focus of many job-redesign efforts undertaken as part of the quality of working life movement in the 1960s and 1970s.[22] The fundamental change involves moving from a system of hierarchical control and coordination of activity to one in which lower-level employees, who may have more or better information, are permitted to do things to enhance performance. At a Levi Strauss jeans factory, when it was time to purchase new forklift trucks, the drivers themselves got involved. They determined specifications, negotiated with suppliers, and made the final purchase decision, in the process saving the company money as well as obtaining equipment more appropriate for that plant. At Eaton, a unionized manufacturer, workers tired of fixing equipment that broke down and suggested that they build two new automated machines themselves. They did it for less than a third of what outside vendors would have charged

and doubled the output of the department in the first year.[23]

SELF-MANAGED TEAMS

Organizations that have tapped the power of teams have often experienced excellent results. Monsanto, a large chemical company, implemented work organization based on self-managed teams at its chemical and nylon complex near Pensacola, Florida. Teams of workers were responsible for hiring, purchasing, job assignments, and production.[24] Management was reduced from seven levels to four, and the plant experienced increases in both profitability and safety. At a 318-person submarine systems plant owned by AT&T, costs were reduced more than 30% through the use of teams.[25] Federal Express uses teams in its back-office operation with great success—service problems fell 13% in 1989 after the company's 1,000 clerical workers were organized in teams and given additional training and authority.[26] One of the more dramatic examples of the benefits of using teams occurred at Johnsonville Sausage. In 1986, a manufacturer asked Johnsonville to produce private-label sausage. The president was about to decline the new business, because he believed that the plant was already at capacity and could not handle the additional workload. However,

> before deciding, he assembled his 200 production workers, who are organized in teams of five to 20, and asked them to decide. . . . After . . . ten days, they came back with an answer: "We can do it." . . . The teams decided how much new machinery they would need and how many new people; they also made a schedule of how much to produce per day. Since Johnsonville took on the new project, productivity has risen over 50% in the factory.[27]

Teams work because of the peer monitoring and expectations of coworkers that are brought to bear to both coordinate and monitor work. Indeed, even critics of the team concept often argue that the problem with teams as a substitute for hierarchy is not that this approach doesn't work but that it works too well. Thus, a dissident union leader in the NUMMI plant noted: "[W]hen the team's under pressure, people try to meet the team's expectations and under peer pressure, they end up pushing themselves too hard. . . . The team concept is a nice idea, but when you put the teams under pressure, it becomes a damn effective way to divide workers."[28]

TRAINING AND SKILL DEVELOPMENT

An integral part of most new work systems is a greater commitment to training and skill development. Note, however, that this training will produce positive returns only if the trained workers are then permitted to employ their skills. One mistake many organizations make is to upgrade the skills of both managers and workers but not change the structure for work in ways that permit people to do anything different. Under such circumstances, it is little wonder that training has no apparent effect.

At Advanced Micro Devices' submicron development facility, some 70% of the technicians came from older facilities at AMD. In keeping with AMD's emphasis on employment stability, as old facilities were closed, people were evaluated with respect to their basic skills. If accepted, they were put through a seven-month program at Mission College—at full pay and at company expense—and then went to work in the new facility. This training not only demonstrated the firm's commitment to its employees, which was then reciprocated, but also ensured that the facility would be staffed with highly qualified people who had been specifically trained for their new jobs.

At a Collins and Aikman carpet plant in Georgia, more than a third of the employees were high school dropouts, and some could neither read nor write. When the firm introduced computers to increase productive efficiency, however, it chose not to replace its existing workforce but to upgrade its skills. After spending about $1,200 per employee on training, including lost job time, the company found that the amount of carpet stitched increased 10%. Moreover, quality problems declined by half. The employees, with more skills and better morale, submitted some 1,230 suggestions, and absenteeism fell by almost half.[29]

CROSS-UTILIZATION AND CROSS-TRAINING

Having people do multiple jobs has a number of potential benefits. The most obvious is that doing more things can make work more interesting—variety is one of the core job dimensions that affect how people respond to their work. Variety in jobs permits a change in pace, a change in activity, and potentially even a change in the people with whom one comes in contact, and each of these forms of variety can make work life more challenging. Beyond its motivational effects, having people do multiple jobs has other important benefits. One is keeping the work process both transparent and as simple as possible. If people are expected to shift to new tasks readily, the design of those tasks has to be straightforward enough so they can be learned quickly. A second, somewhat related benefit is the potential for newcomers to a job to see things that can be improved that experienced people don't see, simply because they have come to take the work process so much for granted.

Multiskilling is also a useful adjunct to policies that promise employment security. After all, it is easier to keep people at work if they have multiple skills and can do different things. By the same token, maintaining employment levels sometimes compels organizations to find new tasks for people, often with surprising results. When Mazda, the Japanese automobile manufacturer, suffered a decline in business in the 1980s, rather than laying off factory workers, it put them to work selling cars, which, in Japan, are often sold door to door. At the end of the year, when awards were presented to the best salespeople, the company discovered that the top ten were all former factory workers. They could explain the product effectively, and of course, when business picked up, the fact that factory workers had experience talking to customers yielded useful ideas about product characteristics.

At Lechmere, a retail chain owned by Dayton-Hudson, the company experimented with cross-training and utilization of employees at a new store in Sarasota, Florida. The store offered the workers raises based on the number of jobs they learned to perform, a variant of a pay-for-skill plan. The workforce, composed of 60% full-time employees rather than the 30% typical for the chain, was substantially more productive than in other stores. "Cashiers are encouraged to sell records and tapes. Sporting goods salesmen get tutoring in forklifts. That way Lechmere can quickly adjust to changes in staffing needs simply by redeploying existing workers. The pay incentives, along with the prospect of a more varied and interesting workday, proved valuable lures in recruiting."[30]

SYMBOLIC EGALITARIANISM

One important barrier to decentralizing decision making, using self-managed teams, and eliciting employee commitment and cooperation is the symbols that separate people from each other. Consequently, it is not surprising that many of the firms that are known for achieving competitive advantage through people have various forms of symbolic egalitarianism—ways of signaling to both insiders and outsiders that there is comparative equality and it is not the case that some think and others do. At NUMMI, the executive dining room was eliminated, and everyone eats in the same cafeteria. Everyone wears a blue smock. There are no reserved places in the employee parking lot.

Communication across levels is greatly enhanced by the opportunity to interact and meet in less formal settings. This means that senior management is more likely to know what is actually going on and be able to communicate its ideas more directly to everyone in the facility. The reduction in the number of social categories tends to decrease the salience of various subdivisions in the organization, diminishes "us" versus "them" thinking, and provides more of a sense of everyone working toward a common goal. This egalitarianism makes cross-movement easier because there are fewer status distinctions to be overcome. At NUMMI, there is only one classification for Division 1 personnel compared to more than 80 previously. The number of skilled trades classifications shrank from 18 under the old General Motors systems to 2.[31]

Egalitarian symbols come in many forms. In some organizations, it is dress—few who have worked in a manufacturing facility have not heard the phrase "the suits are coming" when people from headquarters, typically more formally dressed, arrive. Physical space is another way in which common fate can be signaled, or not. The CEO at Solectron, a contract manufacturer that won the Malcolm Baldrige award, does not have a private office, and neither does the chairman. In contrast, John DeLorean's graphic description of the fourteenth-floor headquarters for General Motors is one of hushed, quiet offices reached by a private elevator that was secured—in other words, executives cut off from the rest of the organization.[32]

Although symbolic egalitarianism would seem easy to implement, the elimination of status symbols is often one of the most difficult things for a company to do. A friend bemoaned the fact that just as he had reached a managerial level that entitled him to use a private dining room, have preferential parking, and occupy a larger office, his employer embarked on a total quality movement and eliminated all of these perquisites.

WAGE COMPRESSION

Although issues of wage compression are most often considered in terms of hierarchical compression, and particularly CEO pay relative to that of others, there is a horizontal aspect to wage compression as well. It can have a number of efficiency-enhancing properties for organizations.

It is important to remember that wage compression is distinct from incentive pay. Incentive pay simply means that people are rewarded, either individually or in groups, for their performance. These rewards can be large, producing wide variation in salaries, or small, producing substantially less variation. It is also important to recognize that incentive pay—particularly when applied to larger units such as work groups, departments, or the entire organization—can either reduce or increase the wage dispersion that would otherwise exist. Most gain-sharing and profit-sharing programs actually reduce pay dispersion, although they need not do so.

When tasks are somewhat interdependent and cooperation is helpful for accomplishing work, pay compression, by reducing interpersonal competition and enhancing cooperation, can lead to efficiency gains.[33] Furthermore, large differences in the allocation of organizational rewards can motivate people to achieve these rewards. Although increased motivation can produce greater efforts, large differences in rewards can as readily result in excessive time and energy spent on ingratiating oneself with one's supervisor or trying to affect the criteria for reward allocation.[34] By this reasoning, a more compressed distribution of salaries can actually produce higher overall performance, as there is less incentive for individuals to waste their time on gaming the system.

To the extent that wages are compressed, pay is likely to be deemphasized in the reward system and in the organization's culture. This has some obvious economic benefits—people are not constantly worrying about whether they are compensated appropriately and attempting to rebargain their salaries. A de-emphasis on pay can also focus attention on the other advantages of organizational membership such as good colleagues and work that is interesting and meaningful. There is a literature in psychology that suggests we attempt to figure out why we are doing what we are by looking at ourselves as an outside observer would.[35] If we see we are very well paid, perhaps on a contingent basis, for what we do, we are likely to attribute our behavior to the economic rewards. If, however, we are not particularly well paid, or if pay is less salient, and if it is distributed on a less contingent basis (which will make it less salient), then we are likely to attribute our behavior to other, more intrinsic factors such as the inherent enjoyment of the work. In other words, being paid in a contingent fashion for what we do can actually undermine our intrinsic interest in and satisfaction with that activity.[36] Thus, pay compression, by helping to de-emphasize pay, can enhance other bases of satisfaction with work and build a culture that is less calculative in nature.

PROMOTION FROM WITHIN

Promotion from within is a useful adjunct to many of the practices described. It encourages training and skill development because the availability of promotion opportunities within the firm binds workers to employers and vice versa. It facilitates decentralization, participation, and delegation because it helps promote trust across hierarchical levels; promotion from within means that supervisors are responsible for coordinating the efforts of people whom they probably know quite well. By the same token, those being coordinated personally know managers in higher positions. This contact provides social bases of influence so that formal position can loom less important. Promotion from within also offers an incentive for performing well, and although tied to monetary rewards, promotion is a reward that also has a status-based, nonmonetary component. Perhaps more important, it provides a sense of fairness and justice in the workplace. If people do an outstanding job but outsiders are being brought in over them, there will be a sense of alienation from the organization. One other advantage of promotion from within is that it tends to ensure that people in management positions actually know something about the business, the technology, and the operations they are managing. There are numerous tales of firms managed by those with little understanding of the basic operations, often with miserable results. David Halberstam's history of Ford Motor tells how finance took control of the company. Not only were these people not "car men," they knew little about automobiles, technology, production processes, or the market—anything that could not be conveyed via statistics—and had little interest in learning.[37] The problem with managing only through statistics is that without some understanding of the underlying processes that produce the measures, it is likely that managers will either focus on inappropriate measures or fail to fully comprehend what they mean.

By contrast, at Lincoln Electric, almost everyone who joins the company learns to weld—Lincoln's main product is, after all, arc welding equipment. Graduation from the welding program requires coming up with some innovation to the product. At Nordstrom, even those with advanced degrees start on the sales floor. Promotion is strictly from within, and when Nordstrom opens a new store, its key people are recruited from other stores around the country. This helps perpetuate the Nordstrom culture and values but also provides assurance that those running the store know what they are doing and have experience doing it the Nordstrom way.

Taking the Long View

The bad news about achieving some competitive advantage through the workforce is that it inevitably takes time to accomplish. By contrast, a new piece of equipment can be quickly installed; a new product technology can be acquired through a licensing agreement in the time it takes to negotiate the agreement; and acquiring capital only requires the successful conclusion of negotiations. The good news, however, is that once achieved, competitive advantage obtained through employment practices is likely to be substantially more enduring and more difficult to duplicate. Nevertheless, the time required to implement these practices and start seeing results means that a long-term perspective is needed. It also takes a long time horizon to execute many of these approaches. In the short term, laying off people is probably more profitable compared to trying to maintain employment security; cutting training is a quick way to maintain short-term profits; and cross-training and cross-utilization may provide insights and innovation in time, but initially, the organization foregoes the advantages of more narrow specialization and the immediate proficiency achieved thereby.

What determines an organization's time horizon is an important issue, but one outside the scope of this article. In general, however, there is some evidence that family ownership, employee ownership, or other forms of organization that lessen the immediate pressures for quick earnings to please the securities market are probably helpful. Lincoln Electric is closely held, and the Nordstrom family retains a substantial fraction of the ownership of that retailer. NUMMI has Toyota as one of the joint venture partners, and Toyota's own plans for the facility virtually dictate that it can take a long-term view, which is consistent with its culture and tradition. Again, the Walton family's ownership position in Wal-Mart helps ensure that the organization takes a long view of its business processes.

It is almost inconceivable that a firm facing immediate short-term pressure would embark on activities that are apparently necessary to achieve some competitive advantage through people. This provides one explanation for the limited diffusions of these practices. If the organization is doing well, it may feel no need to worry about its competitive position. By the same token, if the organization is in financial distress, the immediate pressures may be too severe to embark on activities that provide productivity and profit advantages, but only after a longer, and unknown period of time.

Measurement of the Practices

Measurement is a critical component in any management process, and this is true for the process of managing the organization's workforce. Measurement serves several functions. First, it provides feedback as to how well the organization is implementing various policies. For example, many organizations espouse a promotion from within policy but don't fulfill this objective. Often, this is because there is no systematic collection and reporting of information such as what percentage of the positions at given levels have been filled internally. A commitment to a high-wage policy obviously requires information as to where in the relevant labor market the organization's wages fall. A commitment to training is more likely to be fulfilled if data are collected, not only on the total amount spent on training but also on what types of employees have received training and what sorts of training are being delivered.

Second, measurement ensures that what is measured will be noticed. "Out of sight, out of mind" is a principle that applies to organizational goals and practices as well as to people. One of the most consistent findings in the organizational literature is that measures affect behavior.[38] Most people will try to succeed on the measures even if there are no direct, immediate consequences. Things that are measured get talked about, and things that are not don't.

It is no accident that companies seriously committed to achieving competitive advantage through people make measurement of their efforts a critical component of the overall process. Thus, for example, at Advanced Micro Devices' submicron development facility, management made how people were managed a priority and measured employee attitudes regularly to see whether they were "achieving the vision." One survey asked questions such as: How many teams are you on in your own department and with members of other departments? How many hours per week do you spend receiving training and training others? The survey also asked the extent to which people agreed or disagreed with statements such as: there is problem solving at all levels in my work group; people in my work group are encouraged to take the initiative; a spirit of teamwork exists in our work group.

In a world in which financial results are measured, a failure to measure human resource policy and practice implementation dooms this to second-class status, oversight, neglect, and potential failure. The feedback from the measurements is essential to refine and further develop implementation ideas as well as to learn how well the practices are actually achieving their intended results.

Overarching Philosophy

Having an overarching philosophy or view of management is essential. It provides a way of connecting the various individual practices into a coherent whole and also enables people in the organization to persist and experiment when things don't work out immediately. Moreover, such a philosophy makes it easier to explain what the organization is doing, justify it, and mobilize support from internal and external constituencies. Most simply put, it is hard to get somewhere if you don't know where you are going. In a similar fashion, practices adopted without a deeper understanding of what they represent and why they are important to the organization

TABLE 1: NEW VERSUS OLD PARADIGMS AT LEVI STRAUSS

Old Paradigm	New Paradigm
Economy of scale as basis for improvement logic	Economy of time as basis for improvement logic
Quality involves trade-offs	Quality is a "religion"; no compromise
Doers are separate from thinkers	Doers must also be thinkers
Assets are things	Assets are people
Profit is the primary business goal	Customer satisfaction is the primary business goal
Hierarchical organization: goal is to please the boss	Problem-solving network organization: goal is to please the internal or external customer
Measure to judge operational results	Measure to help people make operational improvements

Source: Presentation by Peter Thigpen at the Stanford School of Business, February 26, 1991.

may not add up to much, may be unable to survive internal or external problems, and are likely to produce less than stellar results.

Many companies that seek competitive success through their people and practice a number of approaches really began with some underlying principles or else developed them early in the process. Levi Strauss's quality enhancement process began with the understanding that "manufacturing for quality and speed meant breaking the old paradigms," turning the culture upside down and completely reorienting the parameters of the business.[39] The company and its manufacturing senior vice president explicitly articulated the underlying assumptions of the old way of thinking and the new, as illustrated in Table 1.

Some Words of Caution

It would be difficult to find a single company that does all of these things or that does them all equally well. Some successful firms have tended to do a higher percentage, and it is useful to grade one's own company against the overall list. Nevertheless, there are few companies that do everything. Which practice is most critical does depend in part on the company's particular technology and market strategy.

A second important caution is to recognize that it is possible for a company to do all of these things and be unprofitable and unsuccessful, or to do few or none of them and be quite successful. How? These factors are almost certainly related to a company's ability to achieve competitive success through its workforce. But although that may be an

important basis of success, and one that is even increasing in importance, it is clearly not the *only* basis of success.

IBM, for instance, has done many of these things and has built a skilled and dedicated workforce. That in and of itself, however, could not overcome a product strategy that overemphasized large, mainframe computers. People Express, now defunct, also built a strong culture, selectively recruited, and used innovative compensation and work organization strategies to build flexibility and productivity in its operations. Indeed, it was one of the lowest-cost providers of airline services. But this cost advantage could not overcome other problems, such as the founder's edifice complex, which resulted in too-rapid expansion, acquisition of Frontier Airlines and becoming seriously financially overleveraged, and a growth rate that was not sustainable given the firm's fundamental human resource policies. In focusing on managing the workforce, I highlight only *one* dimension of the several that determine corporate performance.

By the same token, it is possible to be successful, particularly for a while, doing none of these things or even their opposite. Frank Lorenzo took over Continental Airlines and put it into bankruptcy in 1983 to break its union contracts. To say he played hardball with his employees was an understatement. Lorenzo's strategy was founded on financial and negotiating skills, not on his workforce. For a while, these strategies worked—although Continental lost $161 million in 1983, by 1985 it earned about $60 million, a very rapid turnaround. Similarly, Carl Icahn at Trans World

Airlines made money, for a while, taking strikes and fighting with his workforce, seeking success through financial strategies. Neither airline succeeded in the long run, but in the short run, cutting wages and benefits, cutting employment levels, and managing through fear can produce temporary results.

A third word of caution is that these practices have potential downsides as well as benefits and are not necessarily easy to implement, particularly in a one-at-a-time fashion. One obvious problem is that they all necessarily entail more involvement and responsibility on the part of the workforce. There are many employees who would rather work only with their bodies and check their minds at the door—particularly if that is what they have become accustomed to—and instituting work practices that entail more effort and involvement may force turnover. These practices may be resisted by others in the company as well. The reader is cautioned that implementation issues loom large, regardless of how sensible the practices may be.

Endnotes

1. Michael E. Porter, *Competitive Advantage* (New York, NY: Free Press, 1985), 1.
2. *Ibid.*, 4.
3. "Investment Winners and Losers," *Money*, October 1992, 133.
4. Bridget O'Brian, "Southwest Airlines is a Rare Air Carrier: It Still Makes Money," *The Wall Street Journal*, October 26, 1992, A1.
5. James Campbell Quick, "Crafting an Organizational Culture: Herb's Hand at Southwest Airlines," *Organizational Dynamics* 21, Autumn 1992, A7.
6. O'Brian, *op. cit.*, A7.
7. Quick, *op. cit.*, 50.
8. O'Brian, *op. cit.*, A1.
9. Ibid., A7.
10. Clair Brown, Michael Reich, and David Stern, "Becoming a High Performance Work Organization: The Role of Security, Employee Involvement, and Training," Working Paper 45, Institute of Industrial Relations (Berkeley, CA: University of California Press, 1992), 3.
11. Frank I., Schmidt and John E. Hunter, "Individual Differences in Productivity: An Empirical Test of Estimates Derived from Studies of Selection Procedure Utility," *Journal of Applied Psychology* 68, 1983, 407–414.
12. Harry C. Handlin, "The Company Built upon the Golden Rule: Lincoln Electric," in Bill L. Hopkins and Thomas C. Mawhinney (eds.), *Pay for Performance: History, Controversy, and Evidence* (New York, NY: Haworth Press, 1992), 157.
13. "Nordstorm: Dissension in the Ranks?" Case 8-191-002 (Boston, MA: Harvard Business School, 1990), 7.
14. George Akerlof, "Gift Exchange and Efficiency Wage Theory," *American Economic Review* 74, 1984, 79–83.
15. James W. Near. "Wendy's Successful 'Mop Bucket Attitude'," *The Wall Street Journal*, April 27, 1992, A16.
16. *Ibid.*
17. Handlin, *op. cit.*, 159.
18. Joseph R. Blasi and Douglas L. Kruse, *The New Owners* (New York, NY: Harper Business, 1991), 257.
19. Corey M. Rosen, Katherine J. Klein, and Karen M. Young, *Employee Ownership in America* (Lexington, MA: Lexington Books, 1996).
20. Richard T. Pascale, "Nordstrom, Inc.," unpublished case (San Francisco, CA: 1991), Exhibits 7 and 8.
21. David I. Levine and Laura D'Andrea Tyson, "Participation, Productivity, and the Firm's Environment," in Alan S. Blinder (ed.), *Paying for Productivity: A Look at the Evidence* (Washington, DC: The Brookings Institution, 1990), 183–243.
22. J. Richard Hackman and Greg R. Oldham, *Work Redesign* (Reading MA: Addison-Wesley, 1980).
23. Thomas F. O'Boyle, "Working Together: A Manufacturer Grows Efficient by Soliciting Ideas from Employees," *The Wall Street Journal*, June 5, 1992. A4.
24. Barnaby Feder, "At Monsanto, Teamwork Works," *New York Times*, June 25, 1991, C1.
25. Barbara Presley Noble, "An Approach with Staying Power," *New York Times*, March 8, 1992, 23.
26. Brian Dumaine, "Who Needs a Boss?" *Fortune*, May 7, 1990, 54.
27. *Ibid.*, 55.
28. Paul S. Adler, "The Learning Bureaucracy: New United Motor Manufacturing, Inc.," in Barry M. Staw and Larry L. Cummings (eds.), *Research in Organizational Behavior* (Greenwich, CT: JAI Press, in press), 32.
29. Helene Cooper, "Carpet Firm Sets Up an In-House School to Stay Competitive," *The Wall Street Journal*, October 5, 1992, A1, A6.
30. Norm Alster, "What Flexible Workers Can Do," *Fortune*, February 13, 1989, 62.
31. Adler, *op. cit.*, 17.
32. J. Patrick Wright, *On a Clear Day You Can See General Motors* (Grosse Pointe, MI: Wright Enterprises, 1979).
33. Edward P. Lazear, "Pay Equality and Industrial Policies," *Journal of Political Economy* 97, 1989, 561–580.
34. Paul Milgrom and John Roberts, "An Economic Approach to Influence Activities in Organizations," *American Journal of Sociology* 94, 1988, S154–S179.

35. Daryl J. Bem, "Self-Perception Theory," in Leonard Berkowitz (ed.), *Advances in Experimental Social Psychology*, vol. 3 (New York, NY: Academic Press, 1982), 1–62.

36. Mark R. Lepper and David Greene, "Turning Play into Work: Effects of Adult Surveillance and Extrinsic Rewards on Children's Intrinsic Motivation," *Journal of Personality and Social Psychology* 31, 1975, 479–486.

37. David Halberstam, *The Reckoning* (New York, NY: William Morrow, 1986).

38. See, for example, Peter M. Blau, *The Dynamics of Bureaucracy* (Chicago, IL: University of Chicago Press, 1955); and V. F. Ridgway, "Dysfunctional Consequences of Performance Measurement," *Administrative Science Quarterly* 1, 1956, 240–247.

39. Presentation by Peter Thigpen at Stanford Graduate School of Business, February 26, 1991.

CHAPTER

2

CHALLENGES IN STRATEGIC HUMAN RESOURCE MANAGEMENT

IBM has utilized technology to not only improve the delivery of its HR programs to its employees but also to significantly reduce administrative costs. In 1997, IBM created its Human Resource Service Center (HRSC), based in Raleigh, North Carolina. The HRSC utilizes networking technologies to deliver HR information and service to more than 500,000 active and retired employees ("customers") in the United States. The Center handles more than 1.5 million calls and processes more than 2.5 million transactions annually.

The Center services over 20 separate IBM business units in areas including benefits, retirement planning, compensation, employee suggestions, staffing, job posting, orientation, performance management, EEO compliance, employee separations, leaves of absence, and skill development. It is staffed by 80 customer services representatives who act as generalists in helping employees with a wide range of HR-related issues. In addition, 80 "program specialists" handle more complex issues pertaining to particular HR programs (i.e., compensation, tuition reimbursement, short-term foreign service assignments, etc.). In addition, a number of functions are fully automated; for example, employees can set up their own flexible benefit program without even talking to another person. These employees and automated functions are supported by an in-house intranet of more than 5,000 pages.

In establishing the HRSC, IBM sought to capitalize on its belief in the importance of combining people, technology, and customer service, much as it does with its external customers. IBM's strategy to improve employee service and reduce the costs of human resource administration has led to impressive results. Employees seem to value the HRSC; the Center has a customer satisfaction rate that exceeds 90 percent. The Center also allowed IBM to reduce the costs of providing HR services by 40 percent during its initial year, and additional cost efficiencies are gained each year as new services are added.

Adapted from Gonsalves, B., Ellis Y. M., Riffel, P. J. and Yager, D. "Training at IBM's Human Resource Service Center; Linking People, Technology, and HR Processes," *Human Resource Management*, Summer 1999, Vol. 38, No. 2, pp. 135–142.

In addition to the many challenges organizations face in abandoning traditional approaches to managing people as part of adopting an investment perspective to human resources (HR), there are a number of critical trends affecting the employment relationship that further affect how organizations need to manage their employees. Some of these trends pertain to changes taking place in the external environment of the organization; others pertain to some of the ways organizations are responding internally to such trends. The four major arenas of change are technological advancement, increasing attention to ethical behavior, demographics and diversity, and globalization. Globalization will be discussed separately in Chapter 14.

IMPACT OF TECHNOLOGY

One of the most significant trends affecting HR and people in organizations is technology. Simply defined, an organization's technology is the process by which inputs from an organization's environment are transformed into outputs.[1] Technology includes tools, machinery, equipment, work procedures, and employee knowledge and skills. All organizations, be they manufacturing or service, public or private, large or small, employ some form of technology to produce something for the open marketplace or for a specific group of constituents.

With constant advances in technology and work processes, organizations are under increased competitive pressure to implement, if not develop on their own, more efficient means of operations. However, the financial considerations of whether to adopt a new technology must be balanced with a number of strategic issues and, more specifically, a number of specific strategic HR issues, as shown in Exhibit 2-1. The specifics of these issues will be discussed in greater detail in Chapter 6 but are presented here to give the reader a sense of how technological initiatives need to be considered from a holistic perspective that transcends the

EXHIBIT 2-1: ISSUES FOR INTEGRATING NEW TECHNOLOGIES

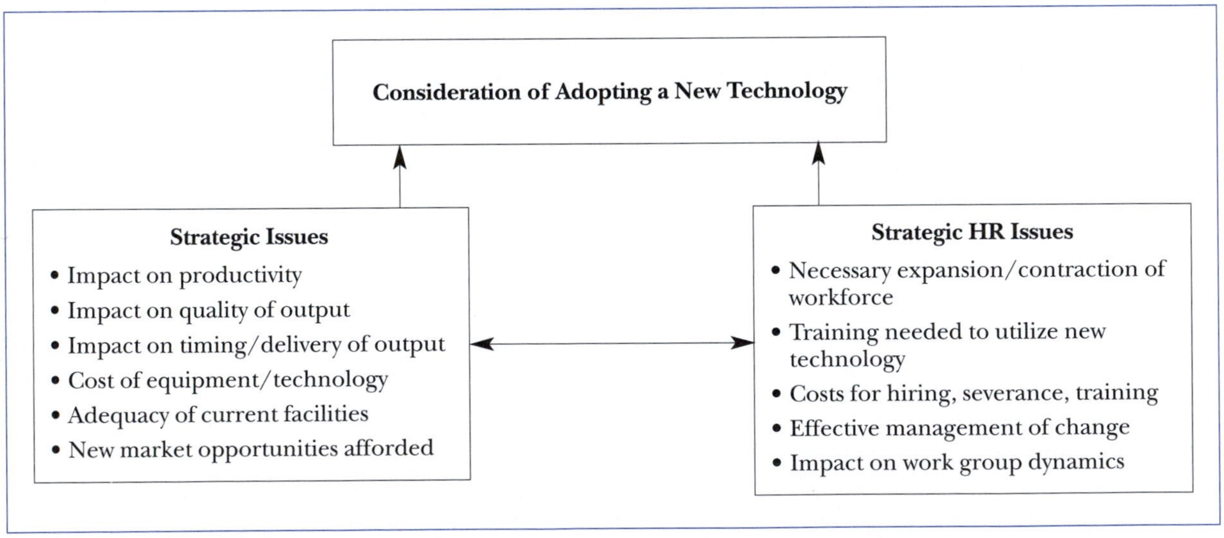

Consideration of Adopting a New Technology

Strategic Issues
- Impact on productivity
- Impact on quality of output
- Impact on timing/delivery of output
- Cost of equipment/technology
- Adequacy of current facilities
- New market opportunities afforded

Strategic HR Issues
- Necessary expansion/contraction of workforce
- Training needed to utilize new technology
- Costs for hiring, severance, training
- Effective management of change
- Impact on work group dynamics

EXHIBIT 2-2: IMPACT OF TECHNOLOGY ON ORGANIZATIONS

- Requires changes in skills and work habits of employees

- Elimination of some lower-level positions and layers of management

- Less hierarchy, more collaboration

sole consideration of economic costs. At this juncture, we will address three ways in which work is changing, as illustrated in Exhibit 2-2.

As newer technologies are developed and implemented, the skills and work habits required of employees change as well. There is a much greater need to continue to upgrade existing employee skills today than there has ever been at any time in the past. Gone are the days when employees utilized the same skills and equipment to perform their jobs for decades at a time.

At the same time that technological change is creating demand for workers with more sophisticated training and skills, a significant number of new workforce entrants have limited technical skills and, in some cases, little or no training beyond basic literacy. For at least the first decade of the 21st century, immigrants will represent the largest increase in the workforce in the United States.[2] This is compounded by the fact that the growth in our economy and the greatest number of jobs being created are in the service sector, particularly services related to information processing. Service organizations are relatively easy to establish and expand, and they provide significant entrepreneurial opportunities. However, service sector employees need different skills than those utilized in manufacturing.[3] Rather than manual dexterity, service sector employees need strong interpersonal and communication skills as well as the ability to be flexible in handling a variety of problems relating to serving clients. Customers of service organizations need much more "customized" or individualized output. For example, the clients of a real estate brokerage do not all wish to purchase the same kind of housing. However, many organizations are finding it quite challenging to bridge the gap between the skills new workforce entrants possess and those required in the marketplace in an expedious, efficacious manner.

The implementation of advanced technologies has also resulted in many organizations eliminating lower-level positions held by employees who performed tasks that can now be accomplished through automation. This has resulted in reduced employee headcounts with those remaining employees having higher levels of training and skills. Automated technologies require more technically trained employees who act as troubleshooters to repair, adjust, or improve existing processes.[4] Consequently, organizations have been able to reduce and, in some cases, eliminate layers of management and move toward "flatter" organization structures with fewer levels in the hierarchy. At the same time, because these technical workers have advanced training, the power bases in many organizations have been rearranged from management to technical workers. It is not uncommon today for managers to have limited understanding of the technical dimensions of their subordinates' work. This is a dramatic departure from traditional supervision and creates unprecedented challenges for managers.

Technological change has resulted in hierarchical distinctions being blurred and more collaborative teamwork where managers, technicians, and analysts work together on projects. This, in part, is reflected in the growing trend for organizations to offer total quality management (TQM) initiatives for employees that focus on collaborative attempts to improve organizational processes to ensure continual improvement in the quality of the organization's product or service. Similarly, technology has created more flexible, dynamic organization structures that facilitate change and adaptation to changes in the organization's environment. These alternative structures take the form of unbundled corporations, autonomous groupings or subsidiaries, or smaller, streamlined units designed to be more responsive to changing customer needs and competitive pressures.[5]

HR ISSUES AND CHALLENGES RELATED TO TECHNOLOGY

In addition to impacting how work is organized and organization structure, technology has created three new areas of concern for HR and organizations: telecommuting, workplace monitoring and surveillance, and e-HR.

Telecommuting

Telecommuting, the process by which employees work from home, is increasing dramatically in popularity in both small and large organizations. The key factors that have facilitated this trend are the advances taking place in information processing and telecommunications technologies. Telecommuting involves more than merely an agreement between employees and supervisors that the subordinate can work at home. It involves a management system that allows employees a tremendous amount of discretion as to how they fulfill their job responsibilities.

The number of Americans working from their home at least part of the workweek grew dramatically, from 3.4 million in 1990 to 19.6 million by the beginning of 2000. Two thirds of *Fortune 100* companies currently have telecommuting programs, half of which were implemented over the past three years. Of the remaining *Fortune 100* organizations, 60 percent are planning to implement a telecommuting program.

Telecommuting programs can provide a number of benefits. Stringent environmental regulations, such as the Clean Air Act, have put pressure on many urban areas to reduce employee commuting on roadways. It is estimated that if 5 percent of Los Angeles commuters worked from home once a week, 9.5 million gallons of gasoline would be saved annually, and 94 million fewer tons of pollutants would be dumped into the atmosphere. Telecommuting can be used as a retention aid, as a more flexible work environment can allow an employee to balance multiple roles. Telecommuting can help employers to retain their investment in employees in situations where the employee needs to relocate for personal reasons, as well as when the organization needs to relocate and the employee is unable to do so. Telecommuting also creates flexibility in recruiting, and allows employers to hire from a broader prospective applicant pool. Organizations can gain significant savings relative to real estate costs, which are often high in larger urban areas. Additional studies also show that telecommuting can significantly increase productivity.

Despite these benefits, there is often strong resistance to telecommuting from direct supervisors of workers who would telecommute, primarily over the issue of measuring performance and monitoring progress of employees who are working remotely. Although the criteria for performance and accountability standards need not be different for those who telecommute vis-à-vis those employees who do not, the fact that there is no face-to-face contact is disconcerting to many supervisors.

A clear performance measurement system is the key component of a successful telecommuting program. The telecommuting employee should have a clearly defined set of measurable objectives, which can be integrated into a telecommuting agreement. Organizations such as Hewlett-Packard and Cisco Systems have successfully implemented objectives-based performance management programs that have facilitated telecommuting arrangements.

A second issue is deciding how many, and which, employees will be offered participation in the telecommuting program. Care has to be exercised to avoid creating resentment or morale problems among nonparticipants. A key factor to be considered is the extent to which an individual's job responsibilities can be performed effectively away from the office. Attention also must be paid to individual employee characteristics. Telecommuting generally requires employees to have strong organizational and time management skills, as well as to be self-motivated.

Another consideration is the expense of purchasing equipment for the employee's home office. Similarly, liability for injuries incurred while working at home must be factored in. Because the home workspace is considered an extension of the company's, the liability for job-related injuries continues to rest with the employer.

A final issue is that many managers are just not comfortable having their direct reports away from the office. Unfortunately, this is due to the fact that many managers have had no prior telecommuting experience themselves. Training programs aimed at both telecommuters and those who supervise such employees that cover issues such as goal setting, time management, and project reporting could help mitigate some of these concerns.

Attention also needs to be paid to the investment that a networking system will require and the capacity of that system to support the volume of remote access from telecommuters. A technological feasibility assessment is as important as ensuring that the appropriate employees are allowed to participate in the program.

One study has shown that a well-designed and implemented telework program can reduce turnover by an average of 20 percent, boost productivity by up to 22 percent, and reduce absenteeism by nearly 60 percent.[6] ▼

Telecommuting at Merrill Lynch

Financial services giant Merrill Lynch did not rush into the decision to offer its employees the option to telecommute. The program was the product of four years of study, research, and planning that resulted in a well-designed, strategized approach to telecommuting that fits the organization's strategic objectives and culture. A 21-page manager's guide was developed that explained the nature and benefits of alternative work arrangements. Workshops are required in which employees and managers confront issues that could be affected by telecommuting, including productivity

▶Reading 2.1, While telework provides numerous benefits to employers and employees alike, it has presented one unique and unprecedented challenge with which organizations are wrestling. This challenge, managing virtual work teams, is addressed in Reading 1.1, "Five Challenges to Virtual Team Success: Lessons from Sabre, Inc."

measurement, time management, coworker communication, and career planning. Prior to allowing an employee to start telecommuting, a two-week "simulation lab" experience is required, during which prospective telecommuters work in isolation from their managers and coworkers. During that time, communication is allowed by phone or e-mail only as it would be if the employee were working at home. Employees also receive training in troubleshooting problems with computer hardware and software that will be used at home. During the first year of the program, productivity among telecommuters increased 15 to 20 percent, turnover declined by 6 percent, and fewer sick days were used by telecommuters. The program has also been used effectively as a recruiting tool and allowed the organization to retain many workers it would have lost when it moved its headquarters.[7]

Employee Surveillance and Monitoring

Most employers and employees agree that technology, particularly access to the Internet, has enhanced employees' abilities to do their jobs. The dizzying array of information available on demand on the Internet allows more comprehensive and faster data collection when addressing issues and problems at work. Online technology also makes it far easier for employees to work at home via either telecommuting or on the employee's own time. As employees perform more of their job responsibilities on "nonwork" time, they may feel much more free to take care of their personal needs during work hours, as long as their job responsibilities are being fulfilled. One study found that 90 percent of employees admitted to visiting nonwork-related Web sites while at work, spending an average of more than 2 hours per week taking care of personal work and needs.[8] Much of this activity centers around banking, bill paying, and shopping, but there is also significant employee visits to adult Web sites, chat rooms, dating sites, and gaming sites during the working day.

In response, an increasing number of employers have implemented electronic monitoring of their employees, using software to track employee Internet use. More than 80 percent of large employers are now utilizing such technology, which can monitor not only Internet usage but also e-mails, computer files, and voice-mail and telephone usage. Such monitoring raises serious concerns about employee rights to privacy and can also have a detrimental effect on employee morale and loyalty. As heightened job demands require employees to spend more and more time at the office and to do work-related business at home, the line between work and personal life blurs. Hence, employers have to balance the need for employee productivity with employees' rights to privacy and their need to maintain a balance between work and personal life.

Employees actually have very limited privacy rights in the area of workplace monitoring. The Electronic Communications Privacy Act (ECPA), passed in 1986, is the only federal law that addresses employer monitoring of electronic communications in the workplace. While ECPA prohibits the intentional interception of employees' oral, wire, and electronic communications, it contains two important workplace exceptions. The first is the "business purpose exception," which allows the monitoring and interception of employee communications as long as the employer can show a legitimate business reason for doing so. The second is the "consent exception," which allows for monitoring of employee communications when employees have provided the employer with their permission to do so, thereby relinquishing employee claims for invasion of privacy.

ECPA also provides that employers may monitor oral telephone communications if they normally do so within the course of their business. This is important for telemarketing and customer service operations where employers have particular concerns related to professionalism, productivity, and quality control. However, ECPA requires that employers refrain from listening to employee telephone conversations the moment they determine that such calls are personal in nature.

Because many employers have taken punitive action against employees for their use of technology for personal purposes during working hours, there is the potential for increased tension between employees and employers surrounding the use of telecommunications technology. Employers who chose to monitor employee use of telecommunications equipment should implement a clear and succinct policy and communicate this policy to all employees. Monitoring should be kept to a minimum and be consistent with "business necessity" or with performance problems or deficiencies dealt with as part of the employer's performance management system. As employee loyalty continues to decline, employers need to ensure that their policies do not create additional distrust on the part of their employees.

e-HR

Technological advances have also provided HR with an incredible opportunity to deliver many of its transactional types of services online, freeing HR staff to work on more strategic issues. Payroll, employee benefits, scheduling, recruiting, training, and career development are just some of the areas that are being delivered in a self-service format to employees. While there are many examples of how various employers are using e-HR to benefit both employees and the organization, the examples provided here illustrate the range of HR activities that are being delivered electronically, as well as the scope of how "deep" such delivery can go.

Time Warner Cable, Inc., in Houston has more than 1,660 employees, spread out over 27 locations. The majority of these employees work a great distance from any HR office or staff. In response to the mandate for better delivery of HR services, Time Warner installed kiosks at its remote locations to provide better service to installers and service center personnel in these locations. Initially designed to facilitate the delivery of HR programs and services, many other departments in the organization soon wanted to become a part of the communications vehicle. Employees can now do everything from participate in open enrollment for benefits to learn about the activities of the public affairs department via the kiosks.[9]

In 2003, the city of Dallas stopped issuing paychecks to its employees. This was not due to the inability of the city to pay its employees but rather was a result of the full elimination of paper paychecks. Many employees had been receiving their pay through direct deposit, but for those without bank accounts, the city began issuing debit cards. The distribution of paper paychecks was expensive and time-consuming for the city; the move to "electronic pay" resulted in a $150,00 annual savings, in addition to the freed-up time of human resource staff. Payroll debit cards can be used to obtain cash at automated teller machines as well as to purchase goods from most retailers. In addition to the Dallas city government, employers such as Little Caesars pizza, Sears, Office Depot, and Chicago's public school system have eliminated the use of paper paychecks in lieu of plastic.[10]

American Airlines, Inc., was one of the early pioneers in using the Internet for customer service. It has since expanded its use of online technology for managing its more than 100,000 employees worldwide. American has a highly mobile workforce, with more than 25 percent in the air at any time and more than 50 percent with no office. Consequently, it needed an effective means to communicate with employees at a time and place that was convenient for each employee. A program was launched to assist employees with the purchase of low-cost personal computers to facilitate the implementation of American's "Jetnet" program. Under this program, employees and retirees can complete benefits enrollment and book travel. Pilots and flight attendants, who bid for monthly flight schedules through a preference system, saw the time required for this activity reduced from four to five hours monthly to less than 30 minutes. Jetnet has allowed American not only to greatly reduce costs but also to provide its mobile workforce with a tremendous added time-saving convenience.[11]

One of the most comprehensive examples of electronic delivery of human resource services can be seen at General Motors. GM sees itself not as the world's largest manufacturer of automobiles but rather as an e-commerce organization that just happens to manufacture cars. A special unit of GM, e-GM, has been created to produce consumer Web sites and business-to-business portals, and to deliver e-HR services. The delivery of e-HR, through GM's "Employee Service Center," is designed to allow HR to move away from transactional issues and focus more on strategic issues. The ESC allows different information to be displayed to different employee groups, in line with each group's needs. Access to the center is not limited to the workplace; employees can access it anywhere through the Internet. The site receives more than 15 million hits per month and allows employees to enroll in classes online, develop a career development plan that can be reviewed with their supervisor, view job postings, manage their benefits, and review their employment history. GM has rolled out its ESC to its international divisions and sees the project as continuous, with an updated re-release of the site planned every six months.[12]

ETHICAL BEHAVIOR

The recent series of corporate bankruptcies, scandals, and business meltdowns has reinvigorated the discussion and debate about ethical behavior in organizations. Ethics, however, go far beyond issues related to financial reporting and disclosure. Many areas of operations, as well as aspects of how employees are treated, leave a tremendous amount of discretion for employers relative to their practices and policies. Many executives report that an organization's reputation is a paramount concern in deciding whether to accept an offer of employment. A recent survey found that 65 percent of executives reported that they would thoroughly investigate the culture and value system of any prospective employer.[13] This same survey found that 40 percent of executives had resigned from an organization at least once because of the employer's perceived unethical business practices. Of this group, 75 percent reported that they did not expose the behavior at the time but 33 percent stated that, given recent corporate scandals, they would disclose and report the behavior if faced with the situation again.

There are numerous dimensions of the employment relationship where ethical decisions need to be made by senior management. The challenge faced by these individuals rests with the fact that ethics are not universally defined but rather subject to personal values and convictions. Ethical behavior is subjectively assessed as right or wrong, appropriate or inappropriate, and, in some cases, moral or immoral.

One area of ethical concern for HR is employee off-duty behavior. Winn-Dixie Stores, Inc., faced a very challenging situation when it terminated a truck driver with a 20-year history of exemplary service and performance when it was discovered he was a cross-dresser in his private life. The truck driver, dressed as a woman and assuming a female identity, accompanied his wife and family in public. Concerns about the company image caused Winn-Dixie to terminate his employment.

He sued on the grounds that he was terminated for something that had nothing to do with his employment and job performance, but there is no law that universally protects employee's off-duty behavior. Winn-Dixie did win in court, but may have lost significantly in the court of public opinion. The story generated tremendous media attention that provided a good deal of support for the driver, from both the general public and his Winn-Dixie coworkers.[14]

The Winn-Dixie's example pertains to only one area of off-duty conduct. Employers also face dilemmas about off-duty behavior involving tobacco, alcohol and drug use, political and religious activity, and prior arrests and/or convictions. The majority of jobs are considered to be "at-will," which will be discussed in depth in Chapter 7, and employees have very limited protection at the federal level from arbitrary dismissal from their jobs. However, there has been a movement toward providing greater protection for employees in regard to their off-duty behavior. At this juncture, four states—New York, California, North Dakota, and Colorado—protect all off-duty, legal activity of employees.

Another increasingly important area of ethical consideration for employers is ownership of work. Given that a good deal of employee work in a knowledge economy involves the application of knowledge and skills in the development of new and improved products, services, and processes, conflicts have arisen concerning intellectual property rights. Employers have used nondisclosure and noncompete agreements to ensure that the work developed by its employees stays with the employer when employees leave. This is serious business for large and small employers alike. It is estimated that *Fortune 1000* organizations incur losses exceeding $45 billion annually from trade-secret theft.[15] Technology has made it much easier for such confidential information to be transmitted. No longer are documents stored in locked file cabinets in secure rooms; now they are contained on hard drives and diskettes that can be accessed more easily.

A related ethical dilemma is the "fairness" of noncompete clauses, which may address the employee going to work for a competitor or starting her or his own business. When accountants, consultants, attorneys, physicians, or other trained professionals decide to start their own business, do they have a right to bring clients with them and/or actively recruit former clients? Noncompete agreements have received mixed reviews in the courts. Some courts have found them to be binding legal contracts and hold former employees to their obligations. Other courts have found them to be invalid and unnecessarily restrictive of free enterprise and the right to compete. The ethical concern involves balancing the rights of employers to "own" work that was done for compensation by employees versus the rights of individuals to work for whom they chose, including themselves.

Intrapreneurship at Intel

One very unique approach to balancing ownership rights has been developed by Intel. Given the demand for services and products provided in Intel's markets, many employees have opted to start their own businesses, which then have competed against Intel. In lieu of requiring that employees sign noncompete agreements, Intel created a New Business Initiative (NBI) division that actively solicits new business proposals from its employees. The NBI functions as a kind of internal venture capital operation. It operates autonomously: Its staff receives proposals from employees and makes recommendations for start-up funding for those ventures it deems worthy. NBI has proven to be a highly successful retention tool and has afforded Intel the opportunity to avoid the often antagonistic work environment that results from noncompete agreements.[16]

In response to the accounting scandals that rocked the U.S. economy in the early part of the decade, Congress passed the Sarbanes-Oxley Act of 2002. The act was passed to eliminate both deception in accounting and management practices by increasing government oversight of financial reporting and holding senior executives more directly responsible for violations. As a result, organizations need to respond seriously to, and investigate, employee complaints of possible wrongdoing or fraud. Much of the responsibility will fall with HR to create policies and procedures to communicate anonymous, confidential concerns and to establish a review mechanism for such reports.[17]

An important provision of Sarbanes-Oxley is the protection it provides to "whistle-blowers," employees who provide information and/or assistance to investigators that assists in the review of potential violations of federal laws related to fraud against shareholders. Such whistle-blowers are protected only when information is provided to one of three sources: a federal regulatory or law enforcement agency; any member or committee of Congress; and a person with supervisory authority over the employee who has the authority to investigate such allegations. Reporting such activity to the media or even an HR manager may fall outside of the protection offered by the act. An employee is protected as long as he or she "reasonably believes" that the reported conduct is a violation, regardless of the outcome of any investigation. ▼▼

Given the increased concern for ethical behavior and accountability, it is clearly in an organization's best interest to establish some kind of Code of Ethics. Currently, more than 90 percent of Forbes 500 organizations have such codes and more than 82 percent have recently revised them.[18] Exhibit 2-3 presents the Code of Ethical and Professional Standards in Human Resource Management developed by the Society for Human Resource Management for its members and profession. Such industry-specific standards can greatly assist executives in developing an in-house code, but an organization's formal code needs to address a variety of issues specific to the organization. Frank Ashen, executive vice president for Human Resources at the New York Stock Exchange, has developed some guidelines for an organization's Code of Ethics that are presented in Exhibit 2-4.[19]

EXHIBIT 2-3: SOCIETY FOR HUMAN RESOURCE MANAGEMENT CODE OF ETHICAL AND PROFESSIONAL STANDARDS IN HUMAN RESOURCE MANAGEMENT

Society for Human Resource Management
CODE PROVISIONS

Professional Responsibility

Core Principle

As HR professionals, we are responsible for adding value to the organizations we serve and contributing to the ethical success of those organizations. We accept professional responsibility for our individual decisions and actions. We are also advocates for the profession by engaging in activities that enhance its credibility and value.

Intent
- To build respect, credibility and strategic importance for the HR profession within our organizations, the business community, and the communities in which we work.
- To assist the organizations we serve in achieving their objectives and goals.

▶▶Reading 2.2, "The Employment Law Impact of the Sarbanes-Oxley Act," provides a more complete discussion of the affect the act will have on employment law.

- To inform and educate current and future practitioners, the organizations we serve, and the general public about principles and practices that help the profession.
- To positively influence workplace and recruitment practices.
- To encourage professional decision-making and responsibility.
- To encourage social responsibility.

Guidelines
1. Adhere to the highest standards of ethical and professional behavior.
2. Measure the effectiveness of HR in contributing to or achieving organizational goals.
3. Comply with the law.
4. Work consistent with the values of the profession.
5. Strive to achieve the highest levels of service, performance, and social responsibility.
6. Advocate for the appropriate use and appreciation of human beings as employees.
7. Advocate openly and within the established forums for debate in order to influence decision-making and results.

PROFESSIONAL DEVELOPMENT

Core Principle
As professionals we must strive to meet the highest standards of competence and commit to strengthen our competencies on a continuous basis.

Intent
- To expand our knowledge of human resource management to further our understanding of how our organizations function.
- To advance our understanding of how organizations work ("the business of the business").

Guidelines
1. Pursue formal academic opportunities.
2. Commit to continuous learning, skills development and application of new knowledge related to both human resource management and the organizations we serve.
3. Contribute to the body of knowledge, the evolution of the profession and the growth of individuals through teaching, research, and dissemination of knowledge.
4. Pursue certification such as CCP, CEBS, PHR, SPHR, etc. where available, or comparable measures of competencies and knowledge.

ETHICAL LEADERSHIP

Core Principle
HR professionals are expected to exhibit individual leadership as a role model for maintaining the highest standards of ethical conduct.

Intent
- To set the standard and be an example for others.
- To earn individual respect and increase our credibility with those we serve.

Guidelines
1. Be ethical; act ethically in every professional interaction.
2. Question pending individual and group actions when necessary to ensure that decisions are ethical and are implemented in an ethical manner.
3. Seek expert guidance if ever in doubt about the ethical propriety of a situation.
4. Through teaching and mentoring, champion the development of others as ethical leaders in the profession and in organizations.

FAIRNESS AND JUSTICE

Core Principle
As human resource professionals, we are ethically responsible for promoting and fostering fairness and justice for all employees and their organizations.

Intent

To create and sustain an environment that encourages all individuals and the organization to reach their fullest potential in a positive and productive manner.

Guidelines

1. Respect the uniqueness and intrinsic worth of every individual.
2. Treat people with dignity, respect, and compassion to foster a trusting work environment free of harassment, intimidation, and unlawful discrimination.
3. Ensure that everyone has the opportunity to develop their skills and new competencies.
4. Assure an environment of inclusiveness and a commitment to diversity in the organizations we serve.
5. Develop, administer, and advocate policies and procedures that foster fair, consistent, and equitable treatment for all.
6. Regardless of personal interests, support decisions made by our organizations that are both ethical and legal.
7. Act in a responsible manner and practice sound management in the country(ies) in which the organizations we serve operate.

CONFLICTS OF INTEREST

Core Principle

As HR professionals, we must maintain a high level of trust with our stakeholders. We must protect the interests of our stakeholders as well as our professional integrity and should not engage in activities that create actual, apparent, or potential conflicts of interest.

Intent

To avoid activities that are in conflict or may appear to be in conflict with any of the provisions of this Code of Ethical and Professional Standards in Human Resource Management or with one's responsibilities and duties as a member of the human resource profession and/or as an employee of any organization.

Guidelines

1. Adhere to and advocate the use of published policies on conflicts of interest within your organization.
2. Refrain from using your position for personal, material, or financial gain or the appearance of such.
3. Refrain from giving or seeking preferential treatment in the human resources processes.
4. Prioritize your obligations to identify conflicts of interest or the appearance thereof; when conflicts arise, disclose them to relevant stakeholders.

USE OF INFORMATION

Core Principle

HR professionals consider and protect the rights of individuals, especially in the acquisition and dissemination of information while ensuring truthful communications and facilitating informed decision-making.

Intent

To build trust among all organization constituents by maximizing the open exchange of information, while eliminating anxieties about inappropriate and/or inaccurate acquisition and sharing of information.

Guidelines

1. Acquire and disseminate information through ethical and responsible means.
2. Ensure only appropriate information is used in decisions affecting the employment relationship.
3. Investigate the accuracy and source of information before allowing it to be used in employment-related decisions.
4. Maintain current and accurate HR information.
5. Safeguard restricted or confidential information.
6. Take appropriate steps to ensure the accuracy and completeness of all communicated information about HR policies and practices.
7. Take appropriate steps to ensure the accuracy and completeness of all communicated information used in HR-related training.

EXHIBIT 2-4: GUIDELINES FOR DEVELOPING A CODE OF ETHICS/CONDUCT

- Need for Personal Integrity—a statement about dealing with individuals both inside and outside of the organization
- Compliance and Laws—addressing intolerance for violating employment, labor, or any other laws that affect the organization
- Political Contributions and Activity—a statement concerning the employer's policy in this domain, including solicitation of personal and/or financial support
- Confidential Information—a statement that identifies what is considered confidential and how such information should be treated, including a statement on employee expectations of privacy
- Conflicts of Interest—a statement that employees are expected to act in the employer's interests in carrying out their job duties along with disclosure requirements
- Books and Records—a statement stressing the practice of using accurate and accepted standards for financial reporting, as well as a prohibition against falsification
- Employment Policies—a general statement on how employees are to be treated, including issues of fairness, discrimination, and safety
- Securities Transactions—a statement on any restrictions that might exist relative to the purchase or sale of stock, as well as a statement and policy directed at insider trading
- Use of Company Assets—a statement that assets will be used only for business, rather than personal interests and needs
- Gifts, Gratuities, and Entertainment—a statement about such relationships and exchanges with clients, with further guidance provided for employees who deal with individuals from other countries where customs, laws, and business practices may differ from those domestically
- The Environment—a statement about the organization's relationship to its environment, if the area of business has an impact on the environment
- Compliance—a statement concerning how the Code of Ethics is to be communicated, certified, implemented, and enforced

Codes of ethics/conduct can be effective only if communicated to all employees and reinforced through the behaviors of senior managers and the organization's reward system. Codes that are developed, then exist, isolated from specific business practices and rewards are likely to have little impact on employees' behavior. Senior managers need to lead by example, modeling the kinds of behaviors expected of employees at all levels of the organization. Finally, such codes can succeed only if a mechanism exists to enforce compliance with their terms, including follow-up and corrective action.

WORKFORCE DEMOGRAPHIC CHANGES AND DIVERSITY

Demographic changes in society and the composition of the workforce are also creating a number of challenges for management of human resources. Diversity has become and continues to be one of the principal buzzwords for both public and private organizations, as recognizing and promoting diversity is seen as critical for organizational success. The motivation behind diversity initiatives can vary from organization to organization. Some employers have a commitment to understanding and appreciating diversity, whereas others implement diversity initiatives simply to ensure compliance with federal, state, and local employment laws.

Congress has passed numerous laws that prohibit discrimination in employment in both private and public sector organizations. Title VII of the Civil Rights Act of 1964 prohibits discrimination based on race, color, religion, gender, and national origin. Subsequently, numerous federal laws such as the Pregnancy Discrimination Act, Age Discrimination in Employment Act, and Americans with Disabilities Act have been passed that protect employees. Each of these federal laws will be discussed in Chapter 7. In addition, many individual states and municipalities have passed additional laws that protect certain groups of employees. The processes and

	Compliance with EEO laws	Managing Diversity
Impetus	Mandatory, forced, external	Voluntary, internal
Focus	Productivity, compliance	Understanding
Elements	Usually limited to race, gender, ethnicity	All elements of diversity
Company Culture	Fitting employees into existing culture	Creating a culture that is fluid, adaptive
Outcomes	Preferences, quotas	Equality
Time Frame	Short-term, one-shot	Continuous and ongoing
Scope	Independent of other HR activities and company strategy	Fully integrated with other HR activities and company strategy

outcomes associated with diversity initiatives that are rooted in compliance differ greatly from those that truly embrace diversity. These differences are presented in Exhibit 2-5.

Generational Diversity

Advances in health care are allowing us, as a society, to live longer, remain healthier longer, and remain in the workplace longer. Census data show 13 percent of the United States population is age 65 or older, with that percentage expected to grow to 20 percent, or 70 million individuals, by 2030.[20] As baby boomers continue to live longer and remain healthy, 80 percent of this group plan to continue working past the age of 65.[21] Such "working retirements" suggests a very different type of employment relationship and a very different kind of lifestyle than that chosen by previous generations. A benefit to society is that these individuals' continued self-sufficiency may result in their being far less dependant on cash-strapped government pensions and health care programs. Organizations clearly benefit through the knowledge and contacts these individuals have developed through their years of professional experience.

This "graying of the workforce" can create a number of challenges, both real and perceived. Older workers are often perceived to be more resistant to change, particularly in implementing radically new programs and utilizing new technology that break from long-established ways of doing things. They may also have increased health care costs relative to their younger counterparts. As older workers remain in the workplace longer, fewer advancement opportunities are made available for younger workers and, in many instances, older workers command higher salaries despite the fact that they may have skills and training that are less current than those of younger workers, particularly relative to technology.

At the same time, it is important to remember that older workers can be as productive, if not more productive, than younger employees. The United States is a society that tends to devalue its older citizens and such biases and predispositions are often found in organizational settings. However, older workers may have much more loyalty to their employers than their younger counterparts. They also can provide significant knowledge of the organization and industry, as well as key contacts within their professional networks.

A number of employers have developed incentive programs for early retirement and then, in many cases, hired retirees back on a part-time basis or as consultants to take advantage of their knowledge and experience. Such programs need to be implemented carefully, however, as federal laws prohibit the setting of a mandatory retirement age in the overwhelming majority of occupations as well as using coercion to "encourage" older workers to retire.

Baby boomers, or those born between 1945 and approximately 1962, are now in their midcareer years and employers are finding that the supply of workers in this age bracket exceeds the demand for them in the middle and senior management-level ranks. As one moves up the management hierarchy, there are fewer and fewer positions available and the competition for senior management positions among boomers has become intense. Ironically, technology often plays a role here, as many middle and senior-level management positions have been eliminated because of flatter organizational structures and the increased use of information technology to perform functions previously done by middle managers. Many of these individuals will never progress beyond middle management. This can be greatly disconcerting for those who have been long-term employees of an organization and seen their pre-boomer predecessors and coworkers rewarded and promoted for performance. Consequently, this creates a new HR challenge in managing these "plateaued" workers. Organizations need to find ways to retain them and keep them motivated despite the fact that they may have mastered their current responsibilities and aspire to advance in their careers. Slower and alternative career paths have become the norm for many of these workers. An increasing number are choosing to go out and start their own businesses.

Consequently, baby busters, those born during the declining birthrate years from approximately 1963 to the mid-1970s, also need to have lower expectations relative to the pace of their careers. The baby boomers of the previous generation have essentially created a bottleneck in the management hierarchy that busters find themselves behind. Until the baby boom generation has retired, there may be fewer opportunities in larger organizations for baby busters.

At the same time, this baby bust generation, which is assuming low- and some mid-level management positions, often receives higher wages than some of the baby boomers due to the forces of supply and demand. There are far fewer individuals in this lower age bracket and in many industries, particularly rapidly growing ones like multimedia and the Internet, these workers have skills and training that the previous generation lacks and therefore command significant incomes in their early career years. In many organizations workers in their thirties may be making as much as or more than coworkers twenty and thirty years their senior. The combination of limited supply of younger workers, high illiteracy among many new workforce entrants, and demand for skills fueled by technological change has resulted in a whole new workplace dynamic for this generation.

A different workplace dynamic is being created by what are known as "Generation X" employees. "Generation X" was born from the mid-1960s to the late 1970s. Many of these individuals were raised in families of divorce and may have developed a tolerance for upheaval and readjustment. They witnessed firings and layoffs of family members, which may greatly influence their limited loyalty to an employer. They also have been using computers and other advanced technologies all of their lives and, since birth, have been exposed to near-constant change in their everyday lives. More important, they bring attitudes and perceptions about work that differ significantly from those of preceding generations. These include an expectation of increased employee self-control; perceptions of themselves as independent contractors or consultants, rather than as employees; less interest in job security; no expectations of long-term employment; and a demand for opportunities for personal growth and creativity.[22]

"Generation Y" employees, sometimes called the "Baby Boom Echo," are those born after 1979. They are just beginning to enter the workforce and represent a cohort that is as large as the baby boom generation. Like the Generation X cohort, they have high comfort levels with technology, but also tend to bring a more global and tolerant outlook on life to the workplace, having been raised in more culturally diverse environments and been exposed to cultural differences through the media. Twenty-five percent live in a single-parent household.[23] They often are very entrepreneurial in nature and, on average, have shorter attention spans. They also may fail to see the need to work from an office or for a particular employer, opting for more transient and variable project work.[24]

Sexual orientation has been an area of diversity that increasingly has been embraced by both large and small and public and private employers. Nine of the 10 largest corporations in the United States, as well as nearly 400 of the *Fortune 500* employers, now prohibit discrimination on the basis of sexual orientation.[25] More than 200 of these employers offer full benefits for domestic partners of employees regardless of sexual orientation, although extension of benefits to domestic partners was prompted by demands from gay and lesbian employees for equality in benefits. While there is no federal law that prohibits discrimination in employment based on sexual orientation, a number of states and municipalities have passed nondiscrimination laws and ordinances. Canadian organizations and employers those that are members of European Union countries are prohibited by statute from discriminating in employment on the basis of sexual orientation. In addition to feelings about equality, some organizations are motivated to address sexual orientation issues because of the bottom line. Surveys have shown 70 percent of gay and lesbian consumers to be brand-loyal to those companies that have progressive employment policies regarding sexual orientation. This gay and lesbian consumer market is estimated at $500 billion annually.[26]

Individuals with disabilities are protected from discrimination in employment under the Americans with Disabilities Act of 1990, as will be discussed in Chapter 7. Nonetheless, individuals with disabilities often are not included in diversity initiatives, nor have they experienced full eradication of employment discrimination. There are 54 million Americans with disabilities; of those nearly 70 percent who are capable of working are unemployed, making individuals with disabilities the demographic group with the highest rate of unemployment in the United States.[27] Many technological innovations are increasing the ability for individuals were severe disabilities to be employed, closing the gap between physical limitations and productivity. However, the lack of employment opportunities for individuals with disabilities has less to do with ability than with the fact that many supervisors do not understand the needs of employees with disabilities, and stereotypes about disabilities believed by supervisors and coworkers prevent individuals with disabilities from being fully integrated into the workplace.[28] Hence, diversity initiatives need to pay particular attention to misperceptions surrounding individuals with disabilities.

Diversity at Hasbro

Several years ago, Pawtucket, Rhode Island–based toy manufacturer Hasbro, Inc., rolled out a diversity initiative that was offered as a half-day workshop to all of its 8,000 employees. Called "D@H = p3," which stands for "diversity at Hasbro equals people, products and productivity," the program received an award from the Society for Human Resource Management. The program involves a series of three exercises related to diver-

sity. The first, a variation of the game show "Who Wants to Be a Millionaire," focuses on the benefits diversity can have for a business. The second, an adaptation of Hasbro's Pokeman trading card game, facilitates an understanding of how cultural and individual differences impact an organization. The third uses Hasbro-manufactured toys, such as Lincoln Logs, to illustrate community-building and an individual's place as a responsible member of her or his community. The program was designed to allow participants to better understand diversity as a business and competitive issue for Hasbro, understand each individual's frame of reference relative to diversity, and identify opportunities for development and increased effectiveness that can be achieved through diversity. The response to the program was overwhelming, with individuals asking to be involved with future workshops about diversity.[29]

Diversity at Texas Instruments

In approaching diversity, Texas instruments (TI) eschewed the conventional strategy of bringing in external consultants for mandatory training and instead focused on an approach that attempted to embed the ideals of inclusion throughout the organization. This approach involved the establishment of "business resource groups," which include groups formed on the basis of religion, race, gender, sexual orientation, and single-parent status. These groups' distinctions relative to traditional "affinity groups" supported by other employers, is that the primary function of business resource groups at TI is business, rather than social. All business resource groups are open to all employees, regardless of background. The diversity within these groups helps to make them unique relative to those found in other organizations. Under the mentorship of an executive-level sponsor, the groups focus not only on career issues but also on business issues as each group is required to contribute to the company's success in some measurable way.[30]

One of the most notable consequences of these new workplace dynamics is that there is now an increased emphasis on the management of professionals. With fewer and fewer nonprofessional employees in organizations, situations often arise where a highly skilled/trained employee reports to a direct supervisor who is not familiar with the nature of the work being performed by subordinates. These technical workers need and want more autonomy in their responsibilities and seek greater input and participation in their work activities. In response to this, some organizations have established two separate career tracks: technical/professional and managerial/administrative. However, managers who have oversight of technical areas in which their skills are not as well developed as those of their subordinates require us to reevaluate the nature of supervision and develop alternative strategies for managing employees.

The use of project teams helps to address this issue. Here, a technical employee often reports to a technical supervisor yet is assigned to a project team, overseen by a project or engagement manager. This model, which has been used for many years in accounting, management consulting, and advertising, often involves technical workers being responsible to both the technical and project managers and can provide enhanced opportunities for employee skill and career development. This dual reporting relationship, however, can be extremely frustrating for the technical employee who may receive conflicting requests from technical and project supervisors as well as for those supervisors who do not have full authority over their subordinates.

The employees of today, both younger workers and their older peers, have values and attitudes that stress less loyalty to the company and more loyalty to oneself and one's career than those exhibited by employees in the past. This is not surprising in light of the waves of corporate downsizing and layoffs and the manner in which they have eroded employee loyalty and commitment. Workers are generally staying with employers for far shorter periods than they did previously and are moving on to other opportunities, particularly those with smaller start-up organizations in the same industry or with clients. Employees with higher levels of training, education, and skills demand more meaningful work and more involvement in organizational decisions that affect them. Employees are becoming much more proactive and taking their career management into their own hands rather than leaving this responsibility with their employer. Larger employers who wish to retain the experience and skills of their employees need to develop creative retention strategies to prevent the flight of employees who may be attractive to competitors. For example, both Charles Schwab and Solectron provide employees with stock options that vest only after the employee has been with the company for a given number of years. Both of these organizations have employees who have experiences that make them highly marketable. Requiring a certain length of service in order to receive full vesting benefits allows not only better retention but facilitates human resource planning efforts; both Schwab and Solectron can anticipate dates key employees might be more likely to consider separation.

Personal and family life dynamics continue to evolve and create challenges for organizations as well. The increased incidence of single-parent families and dual-career couples creates issues around child and elder care, relocation, and "parental stigma" where employees, particularly managerial employees, who devote significant time to family issues are seen as less promotable and less committed to their careers and employers. This stigma has presented particular challenges for women. Nontraditional family arrangements, where opposite or same-sex partners share their lives and living expenses, place increased pressure on organizations to offer domestic partner benefits to employees equal to those that the organization provides to employees with legal spouses. Although the provision of domestic partner benefits has increased dramatically in both large and small organizations, political and religious groups continue to lobby against and fight such efforts and to call for boycotts of companies that provide benefits to nonmarried couples.

An increasing number of employees are opting for nontraditional work relationships, often in the form of part-time work, independent consulting, or contingent or temporary employment. Workers opting for such arrangements often seek to enjoy more flexibility in their lives as well as the opportunity to have time to pursue other endeavors. Organizations encourage these arrangements, which allow them to enjoy lower costs in employing these workers and the added ease of being able to expand or contract their workforce as necessary. These workers, however, generally receive few or no benefits and obviously have little job security. Consequently, they tend to be less loyal to their employers than permanent, full-time employees. There is a growing trend for organizations to outsource or contract certain functions or activities outside of the organization, which simultaneously creates numerous entrepreneurial opportunities for individuals. Many plateaued baby boomers have, in fact, left their organizations and then taken their former employers on as clients.

Given the changes that have been taking place in the composition of the workforce and employee values and attitudes, it is not surprising that in recent years organizations have become much more concerned about managing diversity.

Understanding and appreciating diversity is critical for organizations as the increasing proportions of various ethnic and minority groups in the American consumer population make it imperative for organizations to understand the needs and wants of these groups if they hope to effectively market goods and services to them. Consider the following United States Census Bureau predictions:

- By 2050, close to 50 percent of the United States population will be non-Caucasian.
- By 2005, the ethnic minority share of the workforce will be 28 percent, up from 22 percent in 1990 and 18 percent in 1980.
- By 2025, African-Americans will represent 14 percent of the population, up from 12 percent in 1994.
- By 2025, Hispanics will represent 17 percent of the population, up from 10 percent in 1994.
- By 2025, Asians and Pacific Islanders will represent 8 percent of the population, more than doubling from 3 percent in 1994.[31]

Diversity Initiatives at Intel

Intel, one of the world's leading manufacturers of computer chips, understands the importance of diversity in the workplace. In an industry where demand for trained professionals greatly exceeds supply, Intel has developed a creative program for recruiting and developing minority employees.

To assist with recruiting, Intel hired a leading consulting firm to assist it in identifying the ten colleges and universities with the highest minority enrollments in the field of circuitry design. Intel has also established an undergraduate minority scholarship fund that awards in excess of $1 million annually to undergraduate students. Though recipients are not required to work for Intel after graduation, a significant number of them opt to do so.

Intel has also established a college internship program whereby students are identified as high-potential employees as early as their sophomore year. Interns receive employment and are matched with mentors for their entire college careers. Those who choose to stay on board after graduation are assigned to supervisors who provide specific training that will allow their proteges to develop a variety of skills that can be applied to different jobs within the organization and will willingly allow employees to transfer within the company in order to retain their services. As a result, Intel has seen the proportion of ethnic minorities in management positions jump from 13 percent to 17 percent in a four-year period, despite efforts by its competitors to recruit its talent away.[32]

There is probably no better way to understand and market to these groups than to have them represented as employees at all levels of the organization. In addition to this, diversity initiatives help to ensure that personal differences that have nothing to do with job performance are less likely to impact hiring, promotion, and retention decisions. Intense competition and tight labor market conditions make it imperative that such decisions result in the hiring and promotion of the most qualified individuals.

As a result, diversity management programs have become quite popular. In fact, an entire industry has developed around helping organizations manage diversity. However, many diversity initiatives are ill-conceived, not integrated with the organization's mission and objectives, and can create additional challenges above those for which

EXHIBIT 2-6: INDIVIDUAL DIMENSIONS OF DIVERSITY

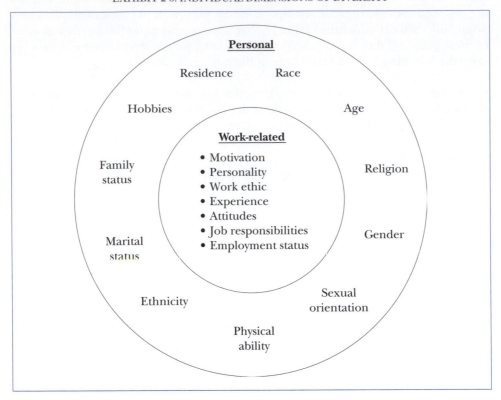

they were designed to respond. Key decision makers in organizations need to ask themselves what benefits diversity specifically provides their organization. There are numerous ways to implement diversity initiatives and different levels on which to understand diversity. There is no one best way to manage diversity in organizations; the optimal way is contingent upon the organization, its people, its mission, and its culture. Diversity initiatives also have to make the critical decision about where to draw the line, meaning which elements of diversity will be incorporated into the initiative and which will be excluded.

Diversity initiatives can present organizations with a complicated mosaic. Exhibit 2-6 presents a model of some of the individual dimensions of diversity. Both work-related and personal sources of diversity are presented. While most diversity initiatives cover some combination of personal dimensions, managers must remain cognizant of the work-related dimensions of diversity in ensuring that workers are managed and given job assignments that allow for both maximum satisfaction and productivity. ▼▼▼

An understanding of and appreciation for diversity is both necessary and desirable for all organizations. However, it is important that those responsible for diversity initiatives realize that diversity can be a double-edged sword. Prior to undertaking any diversity issues, an organization needs to strategize its approach in dealing with diversity. This involves consideration of six issues, as illustrated in Exhibit 2-7.

▶▶▶Reading 2.3, "Employee Satisfaction," addresses how demographic changes and diversity are requiring more attention to the complexities surrounding job satisfaction.

EXHIBIT 2-7: THE STRATEGIC MANAGEMENT OF DIVERSITY

1) Determine why diversity is important for the organization
2) Articulate how diversity relates to the mission and strategic objectives of the organization
3) Define diversity and determine how inclusive its efforts will be
4) Make a decision as to whether special efforts should be extended to attract a diverse workforce
5) Assess how existing employees, customers, and other constituencies feel about diversity
6) Determine specific types of diversity initiatives that will be undertaken

CONCLUSION

The contexts in which human resources are managed in today's organizations are constantly changing. The larger environments in which organizations operate can be in a state of constant change. Nowhere is this more evident than in the areas of technology, ethics, workforce composition, and globalization. Organizations of the 21st century cannot expect to be successful without an understanding of and response to these trends and changes. No longer do organizations utilize one set of manufacturing processes, employ a homogeneous group of loyal employees for long periods of time, or develop one set way of structuring how work is done and supervisory responsibility is assigned. Constant, if not continuous, changes in who organizations employ and what these employees do require HR practices and systems that are well-conceived and effectively implemented to ensure high performance and continued success.

More important, HR practices must constantly be reviewed and evaluated to allow an organization to respond to changes taking place in its environment. Nothing should be accepted as a "given." Failure to allow HR to assess and drive change initiatives can greatly compromise an organization's ability to remain competitive in an everchanging marketplace and society.

CRITICAL THINKING

1. What are the most important societal trends affecting HR today?

2. What are the most important workplace trends affecting HR today?

3. How well do you feel HR as a profession responds to these trends?

4. Predict societal changes that you believe might take place within the next ten years. What challenges will these changes present to organizations?

5. Predict workplace changes that you believe might take place within the next ten years. What challenges will these changes present to organizations?

6. How will HR be impacted by these changes? How can HR help organizations become more effective in meeting the challenges these changes present?

Reading 2.1

7. Select an industry outside of the travel industry and apply Sabre's model for managing virtual teams to an organization in this industry. What aspects of

Sabre's program are generic to all industries? What other kinds of challenges in managing virtual teams manifest themselves in other industries?

Reading 2.2

8. What specific policies would you recommend that an organization implement in-line with the Sarbanes-Oxley Act of 2002? What areas of the law might be ambiguous and could present challenges to organizations as they try to develop compliance guidelines?

Reading 2.3

9. Identify different employee groups and discuss the ways each might seek to gain satisfaction from their employment. What particular challenges does this present for human resource management?

EXPERIENTIAL EXERCISES

1. In small groups, identify and discuss the significant trends related to technology, ethics, and diversity that impact your college, university, or employer. What challenges do these trends present? What initiatives have been established thus far to meet these challenges?

INTERNET EXERCISES

1. Visit the Web site of the United States Bureau of Labor Statistics (http://www.bls.gov). What trends do you see taking place in the data presented? What information at the site is most useful for organizations in assessing workforce trends?

CHAPTER REFERENCES

1. Perrow, C. "A Framework for the Comparative Analysis of Organizations," *American Sociological Review*, 32 (1967), pp. 194–208; Rousseau, D. M. "Assessment of Technology in Organizations: Closed versus Open Systems Approaches," *Academy of Management Review*, 4, (1979), pp. 531–542.
2. Harvey, B. H. "Technology, Diversity and Work Culture—Key Trends in the Next Millennium," *HR Magazine*, 45, (7), July 2000, p. 59.
3. Bowen, D. E. and Lawler, E. III. "The Empowerment of Service Workers; What, Why, How and When," *Sloan Management Review*, Spring 1992, pp. 31–39.
4. Daft, R. L. *Organization Theory and Design*, 6th ed. Cincinnati: South-Western College Publishing, 1998, pp. 126–130.
5. Ibid.
6. Wells, S. J. "Two Sides to the Story," *HR Magazine*, October 2001, p. 41.
7. Wells, S. J. "Making Telecommuting Work," *HR Magazine*, October 2001, pp. 34–45.
8. Society for Human Resource Management, *Workplace Visions*, No. 5, 2001, p. 5.
9. Robb, D. "Kiosks Bring HR Services to All Employees," *HR Magazine*, October 2002, pp. 109–114.
10. Demby, E. R. "Plastic Paychecks," *HR Magazine*, April 2003, pp. 89–94.
11. Roberts, B. "Portal Takes Off," *HR Magazine*, February 2003, pp. 95–99.
12. Jossi, F. "Taking the E-HR Plunge," *HR Magazine*, September 2001, pp. 96–103.

13. Leonard, B. "Corporate Scandals Will Slow the Pace of Executive Recruitment," *HR Magazine*, October 2002, pp. 27–28.
14. Hirschman, C. "Off Duty, Out of Work," *HR Magazine*, February 2003, pp. 51–56.
15. Society for Human Resource Management, *Workplace Visions*, No. 5, 2001, p. 4.
16. Ibid.
17. Fitzgerald, P. W., Warren, S., Bergman, J., Teeple, M. and Elrod, G. B. "Employment Law Implications of the Sarbanes-Oxley Act of 2002: What Should Human Resource Managers Do Now?" Paper presented at the Academy of Legal Studies in Business Annual Meeting. Nashville, TN, 2003.
18. Ashen, F. Z. "Corporate Ethics—Who Is Minding the Store?" Society for Human Resource Management White Paper. www.shrm.org/hrresources/whitepapers_published/CMS_00248.asp
19. Ibid.
20. Society for Human Resource Management, *Workplace Visions*, No. 4, 2001.
21. Ibid.
22. Harvey, B. H. "Technology, Diversity and Work Culture—Key Trends in the Next Millennium," *HR Magazine*, 45, (7), July, 2000, p. 59.
23. Society for Human Resource Management, *Workplace Visions*, No. 2, 2001.
24. Robinson, K. "Get Ready to Mediate among Generations, Speakers Advise," *HR News*, December 2002.
25. Human Rights Campaign Workplace Project. www.hrc.org
26. Cadrain, D. "Equality's Last Frontier," *HR Magazine*, 48, (3), March 2003, pp. 64–68.
27. Cohen, S. "High-Tech Tools Lower Barriers for the Disabled," *HR Magazine*, October 2002, pp. 60–65.
28. Gray, C. "Employees A-Plenty: The Emerging Workforce of People with Disabilities," Society for Human Resource Management, *Mosaics*, 8, (1), 2002.
29. Leonard, B. "Reflecting the Wide World of HR," *HR Magazine*, July 2002, pp. 50–56.
30. Frase-Blunt, M. "Thwarting the Diversity Backlash," *HR Magazine*, June 2003, pp. 137–143.
31. Minehan, M. "The Fastest Growing U.S. Ethnic Groups," *HR Magazine*, 42, (5), May 1997.
32. Adams, M. "Diversity: Building a Rainbow One Stripe at a Time," *HR Magazine*, 43, (8), August 1998.

Five Challenges to Virtual Team Success: Lessons from Sabre, Inc.

Bradley L. Kirkman, Benson Rosen, Cristina B. Gibson, Paul E. Tesluk, and Simon O. McPherson,
Academy of Management Executive

Off the coast of Mexico, a team of five people struggles to stay afloat on a raft they assembled on shore. Waves crash around them, their raft begins to tip over, and two members fall into the sea. A third member helps the submerged members back onto the raft. Finally, the raft is righted and the team paddles furiously onward.

While this might sound like a scene from a reality TV show, these events are actually part of team-building at Sabre, Inc. for its virtual teams. The crashing waves symbolize unanticipated and rapid change, the construction of the raft from everyday materials demonstrates creativity and resourcefulness, and the entire exercise shows that you either sink or swim as a team. Just one year earlier, virtual team members at Sabre had spent three days in face-to-face team-building activities designed to launch a division-wide virtual teams initiative. This raft exercise reinforced the knowledge and skills learned in earlier teambuilding. We examine the challenges of building and managing virtual teams and present five important lessons learned from Sabre's experience.

Virtual Teams: Origins and Trends

While work teams were used in the U.S. as early as the 1960s, the widespread use of teams and quality circles began in the Total Quality Management movement of the 1980s. In the late 1980s and early 1990s, many companies implemented self-managing or empowered work teams. To cut bureaucracy, reduce cycle time, and improve service, line-level employees took on decision-making and problem-solving responsibilities traditionally reserved for management. By the mid-1990s, increasing numbers of companies such as Goodyear, Motorola, Texas Instruments, and General Electric had begun

exporting the team concept to their foreign affiliates in Asia, Europe, and Latin America to integrate global human resource practices.[1] Now, due to communication technology improvements and continued globalization, virtual teams have increased rapidly worldwide.

Virtual teams are groups of people who work interdependently with shared purpose across space, time, and organization boundaries using technology to communicate and collaborate.[2] Virtual team members may be located across a country or across the world, rarely meet face-to-face, and include members from different cultures.[3] Many virtual teams are cross-functional and emphasize solving customer problems or generating new work processes.[4] Virtual work allows organizations to combine the best expertise regardless of geographic location.[5]

Due to employee travel restrictions resulting from the 2001–2002 recession and the events of September 11, 2001, virtual teaming will likely increase exponentially. This increase will parallel that of telecommuters, or employees who work from remote locations and communicate electronically.[6] Two out of three Fortune 500 companies currently employ telecommuters.[7] The United States Labor Department reported that 19 million people worked from home online or from another location in 2001,[8] and the GartnerGroup estimated that by 2002 over 100 million people worldwide will be working outside traditional offices.[9] While many organizations have embraced virtual teaming, little is known, beyond anecdotal evidence and conventional wisdom, about what makes virtual teams work or even how they differ from face-to-face teams.

Anthony Townsend and colleagues (August 1998) first discussed in detail the concept of virtual teams for *The Executive*.[10] The authors defined virtual teams, specified why they have become popular, discussed communication technologies, and provided preliminary guidelines for building virtual teams. More recently in *The Executive* (August 2000), Wayne Cascio examined virtual workplaces more generally, discussing the disadvantages of virtual teaming and methods for training team members and leaders.[11] Building on and extending this work, we examined specific challenges encountered by virtual team leaders and members. Much of the previous virtual-teams research emanated from anecdotal evidence or case studies.[12] We comprehensively studied a large number of cross-functional virtual teams in a high-technology company to challenge the prevailing conventional wisdom regarding virtual teams. To extract important lessons, we drew on our experiences with 65 cross-functional virtual teams at Sabre.

Sabre, Inc.: Business at Internet Speed

In 1960, Sabre began as the computerized reservation system of American Airlines and is the inventor of electronic commerce for the travel industry. In March 2000, Sabre spun off from AMR (the parent company of American Airlines) and became 100 percent publicly traded. Headquartered in Dallas/Fort Worth, the company currently employs over 6,000 employees in 45 countries. Sabre processes over 400 million travel bookings annually (40 percent of the world's travel reservations) and is used by over 60,000 travel agents in 114 countries. Sabre also owns Travelocity.com, the world's leading online business-to-customer travel site; and it owns GetThere, the world's leading supplier of Web-based business-to-business travel reservation systems. Sabre's competitors include: Galileo (owned by Cendant Corporation), Worldspan (owned by Delta, Northwest, and TWA), and Amadeus (majority owned by Air France, Iberia, and Lufthansa). Major competitors of Sabre's Travelocity.com include Expedia.com and Orbitz.com.

Our research focused on executives, vice presidents, and virtual team leaders and members in Sabre's North American Sales and Service, Operations, and Financial Services Division. Sabre's 65 virtual teams are cross-functional, based in the U.S. and Canada, and often span several states or provinces. With over 500 members, they average about eight members per team. Virtual team members are located in both field and employee home offices and in the company's Texas headquarters. On each team, account executives sell reservation systems, field service technicians install systems, training representatives teach travel agents how to use the systems, installation operations coordinators schedule installation and training appointments, account management specialists handle customer billing and collection, and customer service representatives field inquires throughout the process. Clearly, Sabre's virtual teams are highly interdependent. To coordinate activities, members communicate using e-mail, telephone, video conferencing, and Web-based conferencing.

Sabre switched from functionally based work teams to market-based, cross-functional virtual teams in 1999 to integrate different functions to improve customer responsiveness. Functional silos were limiting Sabre's ability to satisfy customers. For instance, from 1996 to 1998, Sabre's North American customer satisfaction ratings fell from a 79 percent satisfaction rate to 68 percent, while competitor ratings remained unchanged. The purpose of virtual teams was to strengthen customer focus to increase productivity, market share, and profitability.

Cross-functional virtual teams represent a specific, albeit common, type of virtual team. Indeed, there are many types of virtual teams, each presenting unique management challenges. For example, global virtual teams must overcome cultural and communication barriers.[13] Virtual teams assigned to accomplish specific projects often have high start-up costs. Some research on cross-functional teams has shown that as teams become more cross-functional, both positive team processes (e.g., information sharing, team task and strategy agreement, and flexibility) and outcomes such as unit performance decrease.[14] The challenge for Sabre was to recognize obstacles confronting teams that are both cross-functional and virtual. Lessons learned from Sabre should apply to cross-functional virtual teams and other virtual teams that create synergies based on the special expertise of members in distant locations.

The Dimensions of Virtuality

Sabre's virtual teams are only moderately, and not completely, virtual. A virtual relationship is one that is primarily conducted using technology, but virtual teams vary in the degree to which this is the case.[15] In fact, degree of virtuality is a complex multidimensional construct.[16] One dimension of virtuality is the proportion of time that team members work face-to-face compared to virtually. A second dimension is the proportion of team members at any one location. Along this dimension, the highest degree of virtuality would be when all members work at distant locations. A third dimension is the proportion of time members devote to a virtual team compared to time spent on other duties. In some instances, individuals may work only a few hours a month on a virtual team project, while devoting most of their time to activities unrelated to virtual work.

Sabre's virtual teams meet face-to-face only once a year. While about 15 percent of the members work at the same location, most teammates work at distant locations. Virtual team activity is the primary focus of each member. Accordingly, our findings could apply to other cross-functional virtual teams.

Five Challenges of Virtual Teams

From our interviews with over 75 executives, team leaders, and team members, we uncovered some surprising insights about meeting the challenges of managing and working in virtual teams (we summarize our interview methodology in the Appendix). For each of the five challenges, we first present the conventional wisdom (i.e., what consultants and researchers are saying), we then highlight Sabre's innovative responses, and finally we extract the lessons learned from Sabre that should help other organizations using virtual teams. Table 1 presents

TABLE 1: CONVENTIONAL WISDOM, VIRTUAL TEAM CHALLENGES, AND LESSONS LEARNED FROM SABRE

Conventional Wisdom	Virtual Team Challenge	Lessons Learned from Sabre
Building trust in virtual teams is extremely difficult, given the limited face-to-face interaction.	Establishing trust based on performance consistency rather than social bonds.	• Rapid responses to virtual teammates foster trust. • Establishing norms around communication patterns is key. • Team leaders play important roles in reinforcing timeliness and consistency of team interaction. • Levels of trust based on performance compensate for lack of social interaction.
Virtual teams will struggle with creating synergy.	Overcoming group-process losses associated with virtual teams.	• Extensive training in virtual teamwork helps overcome process loss. Training in virtual team leadership, conflict management, and meetings management is particularly valuable for overcoming process loss. • Adaptation of decision-making software facilitates problem solving and decision-making.
Virtual team members experience isolation and detachment.	Creating a virtual environment of inclusiveness and involvement.	• Consider individual differences in preferences for working virtually when selecting virtual team members. • Give virtual team members a realistic preview of the potential for feeling detached. • Team leaders play a critical role in maintaining continuous contact with remotely situated virtual team members. • Redesign job assignments to provide virtual team members with occasional face-to-face customer contact to reduce isolation. • Convene face-to-face meetings for virtual team members at company-sponsored conferences.

TABLE 1: CONVENTIONAL WISDOM, VIRTUAL TEAM CHALLENGES, AND LESSONS LEARNED FROM SABRE

Because of the need to communicate via information technology, selection of virtual team members overemphasizes technical skills and underemphasizes interpersonal and teamwork skills.	Identifying virtual team members who have a healthy balance of technical and interpersonal skills.	• Use behavioral interviewing techniques and simulations as part of the selection process. • Use panels of current virtual team members to help recruit and select new team members and ensure the appropriate balance of technical and interpersonal skills. The panel approach has the additional benefit of building support and facilitating socialization of the newly selected virtual team member.
Assessment and development of virtual team members is very limited in the virtual team environment.	Establishing the appropriate quantitative and qualitative data for accurate assessment of virtual team members.	• Use of a comprehensive "balanced scorecard" approach provides valuable quantitative data on team performance. • Monitor group communication archives to assess subjective factors, including idea generation, leadership, and problem-solving skills.
	Developing creative approaches for providing feedback, coaching, and support for virtual team members.	• Use team-member peer reviews to assess contributions to team effectiveness. • Use "richer" communication media, including video conferencing, for performance evaluation feedback. • Identify on-line training and development resources to address virtual team members' knowledge, skills, and abilities in need of further improvement.

a summary of conventional wisdom, virtual team challenges, and lessons learned.

CHALLENGE 1: BUILDING TRUST WITHIN VIRTUAL TEAMS

Conventional wisdom: Most consultants and researchers agree that building trust is the greatest challenge in creating successful virtual teams and organizations.[17] Trust has been called the glue of the global workplace.[18] As Charles Handy, author of "Trust and the Virtual Organization," stated,

> Most of our organizations tend to be arranged on the assumption that people cannot be trusted or relied upon, even in tiny matters. . . . It is unwise to trust people whom you do not know well, whom you have not observed in action over time, and who are not committed to the same goals. . . . Trust needs touch . . . high tech has to be balanced by high touch to build high-trust organizations. Paradoxically, the more virtual an

organization becomes, the more its people need to meet in person.[19]

In Wayne Cascio's *Executive* article on working virtually, he stated, "Lack of trust can undermine every other precaution taken to ensure successful virtual work arrangements."[20] Furthermore, Sirkka Jarvenpaa and her colleagues have stated, "In virtual organizations, trust requires constant face-to-face interaction—the very activity the virtual form eliminates."[21] The conclusion from conventional wisdom is that trust is very difficult to build and requires frequent face-to-face interaction. Thus, a specific challenge for virtual teams, compared to face-to-face teams, is the difficulty of building trust between team members who rarely, or never, see each other.

Our findings at Sabre, however, question this conventional thinking. Consider the following interview quotes about trust:

> When you are working with people you never see, you can develop trust, but you must respond to that person. Follow through. If

you tell them you are going to get back to a customer, get back to them.

(Dallas/Fort Worth team member)

I think trusting someone in a virtual team is linked directly to their work ethic. It is task first. The trust has been built through the task-based relationship that has evolved.

(Account executive)

You gain the trust in people when they deliver what they promise, when all are contributing to the same idea and goal. I think that on a virtual team you start trusting each other when you start meeting those results and everybody has their role within the team and knows what their responsibility is and takes ownership to achieve results.

(Canadian team member)

We concluded that trust can be built virtually and does not require face-to-face interaction. The key issue is the type of trust developed. For example, in face-to-face teams, members trust their teammates after spending time with them, sharing meals, discussing personal matters, or socializing outside work. People trust others when important information they share stays confidential. Researchers call this type of trust benevolent or interpersonal trust.[22] In contrast, we found that trust in virtual teams grows through team member reliability, consistency, and responsiveness when dealing with teammates and customers, or what is known as ability-based or task-based trust.[23]

Lessons learned: One lesson learned is that building trust requires rapid responses to electronic communications from team members, reliable performance, and consistent follow-through. Unlike face-to-face teams, where trust develops based on social bonds formed by informal chats around the water cooler, impromptu meetings, or after-work gatherings, virtual team members establish trust based on predictable performance.[24] Accordingly, team leaders should coach virtual team members to avoid long lags in responding, unilateral priority shifts, and failure to follow up on commitments.[25] A team charter that explicitly identifies important types of team member behaviors (e.g., responding to all e-mails from team members within 24 hours) is a complementary strategy that leaders may use to develop trust among virtual team members. These

actions will build strong team norms about types of behavior that foster trust.[26]

Upon first glance, the challenge of building trust may seem typical for any team or organization. However, building trust is a unique challenge for virtual teams because managers cannot rely on past methods of trust-building based on social interaction, face-to-face meetings, and direct observations of fellow team member commitment. Working virtually magnifies and exacerbates trust issues confronting almost all teams. The need for a proactive approach to identifying and facilitating trust based on speed, consistency, and responsiveness of virtual team members is the first important lesson learned from Sabre.

CHALLENGE 2: MAXIMIZING PROCESS GAINS AND MINIMIZING PROCESS LOSSES ON VIRTUAL TEAMS

Conventional wisdom: Many researchers and consultants believe that the group-process gains (positive synergy) produced in face-to-face teams are more difficult to obtain in virtual teams and that process losses (negative synergy) are more likely.[27] Cascio stated, "The major disadvantages of virtual teams are . . . [that] the synergies that often accompany face-to-face communication [are lost]."[28] In discussing telecommuting, Nancy Kurland and Dianne Bailey said, "Managers may find it difficult to create team synergy and to overcome the absence of informal, interactive learning."[29] Beverly Geber stated that in order to convince executives to incur the expense of getting virtual team members face-to-face, "It's best to use the synergy ploy. Remind executives that often a company's best ideas are born out of chance encounters in a hallway or around a water cooler. Letting virtual team members get together sometimes for extended water cooler discussions improves the chances for serendipity."[30] Steve Alexander quotes a manager as saying, "I think virtual teams are less productive in the sense that you're missing out on those corridor talks between the sales and the technical people that sometimes bring about very good results . . . it's not as perfect as having everyone sit in the same building."[31]

This conventional wisdom suggests that generating synergy (and avoiding process losses) is difficult in virtual teams because members rarely interact face-to-face. Thus, another challenge specific to virtual, but not face-to-face, teams is creating synergy without daily physical encounters. In response to this challenge, Sabre invested in teambuilding as part of its virtual team launch. Pre-launch classroom activities included developing team mission statements and core values to help members set objectives, clarify roles, build personal relationships, develop team norms, and establish group identity. Sabre also encourages virtual team members to assemble once or twice yearly. While pre-launch teambuilding and scheduled face-to-face meetings cannot fully compensate for the lack of daily informal interaction, these interventions do help team members establish a common set of goals, expectations, and operating principles.

To further instill shared purposes and goals, every team must complete a business plan outlining its annual goals and objectives. One team member commented, "Virtual teams need to understand much more so than co-located teams what goal they are working towards because you are working in such different areas and, in our case, in different countries. It plays a much stronger role if you know what your ultimate target is going to be. Everyone is working toward the same thing." To help teams run effective virtual meetings, brainstorm solutions, resolve conflicts, and take action, Sabre relies on continuous virtual team training. Each team completes a series of CD-ROM training modules developed by the Hillsboro, Oregon consulting firm The Belgard Group. Nicknamed Tour de Teams by Sabre, the 15 training modules contain exercises and scenarios such as developing a team charter, managing a team meeting, resolving conflicts, and selecting new team members. One team member commented, "When we complete the team training modules, we have a conference call and go over all of the points. We take them very seriously. So when we have virtual meetings, we now have tools to help us stay on track and communicate effectively."

Sabre's experience also shows that working virtually can reduce team process losses associated with stereotyping, personality conflicts, power, politics, and cliques commonly experienced by face-to-face teams. Diversity research shows that visual cues such as race/ethnicity and gender can decrease team integration and performance in highly diverse teams.[32] Virtual team members may be unaffected by potentially divisive demographic differences when there is minimal face-to-face contact. And, while the research is still relatively new, some researchers have found that electronic collaboration generates more minority participation, which might increase overall integration and level of attachment of minority members.[33] Other studies show that electronic group decision support systems help virtual teams make higher quality decisions than face-to-face teams.[34]

Lessons learned: A critical priority for virtual team leaders is helping their virtual teams maximize process gains and minimize process losses. Sabre's well-trained virtual teams overcome process losses. Sabre's training begins with teambuilding and continues with efforts to help virtual teams create charters and mission statements, clarity goals, and develop operating norms. Sabre sustains virtual team effectiveness with an ongoing virtual training program to build new skills in meetings management, problem solving, decision-making, and other team processes. Sabre's comprehensive training efforts allow virtual teams to create synergy by bridging barriers of time and space and collaborating effectively. Moreover, stereotyping, gossip, politics, and conflict are often minimized in virtual teams like Sabre's.

CHALLENGE 3: OVERCOMING FEELINGS OF ISOLATION AND DETACHMENT ASSOCIATED WITH VIRTUAL TEAMWORK

Conventional wisdom: Regarding isolation in virtual teams, Cascio stated, "The major disadvantages of virtual teams are the lack of physical interaction—with its associated verbal and nonverbal cues," and "Some level of social interaction with supervisors and coworkers is essential in almost all jobs. Without it, workers feel isolated and out of the loop."[35] Charles Handy has stated, "The loneliness of the long-distance executive is well documented. Few are going to be eager advocates of virtuality when it really means that work is what you do, not where you go."[36] Telecommuting researchers Kurland and Bailey stated, "Probably the most commonly expressed challenge of telecommuting is overcoming the isolation caused by the separation of the telecommuter from the social network of the traditional work space."[37] In a separate article, Kurland and Terry Egan said, "Employees' primary reluctance about telecommuting rests on concerns about isolation," and "Employees comment that they miss the informal interaction they garner by being in the presence of colleagues and friends."[38] Finally, Paula Caproni warned, "Many researchers and practitioners are concerned that high-quality relationships may be particularly difficult to achieve in teams in which team members are geographically dispersed."[39]

This conventional wisdom suggests that virtual team members will be less productive and satisfied than people working face-to-face due to feelings of isolation and detachment. Thus, a specific challenge for virtual team leaders that does not confront face-to-face team leaders is overcoming member feelings of isolation. Researchers have long held that people are motivated and satisfied at work, in part, as a result of interactions with coworkers.[40] Colleagues share stories and pictures, have lunch or take breaks together, and celebrate promotions or the birth of children. In face-to-face teams, these activities occur naturally and frequently and build esprit de corps. Team leaders use team-building activities like ropes courses, bowling nights, or barbeques to solidify team cohesion and spirit. In virtual teams, most of these possibilities are lost.

Indeed, some virtual team members have reported feelings of alienation.[41] Consider these comments from Sabre team members:

We get left off a lot of things because there are meetings we can't go to for cost reasons. We miss out on those opportunities to get together and bond as a group, and that is tough sometimes. And you do feel like stepchildren sometimes.

(Dallas/Fort Worth team member)

I find that by working at home, my work is my home and I miss that interaction. I don't have as many people to network with on issues or successes. Sometimes I can't reach anyone by phone and it's frustrating. When you work in an office, you just look over their cube and there they are.

(Account executive)

As much as we want to go and run the world from our bedrooms, in our slippers, we are humans, we have to be touched, seen, and heard.

(Account executive)

Sabre counteracts feelings of virtual team member isolation first by recognizing individual needs for social interaction or lack of it. While individuals with strong social needs may find virtual teamwork difficult, others desire independent, virtual work. Some Sabre employees welcome minimal social interaction and reductions in gossip, politics, and minor disruptions that often accompany face-to-face work. Others tout the advantages of working from home including reduced travel time, proximity to young children, and flexibility. In selection interviews, Sabre questions candidates on their suitability for virtual teamwork. Sabre uses realistic job previews[42] to counter team-member isolation, which allows candidates to select out of isolating positions. Some virtual team members interact with customers, partially satisfying social needs. Sabre also gives employees options for working from home or an office where they have opportunities to interact with other Sabre employees who may, or may not, be virtual teammates.

Sabre's team-building and training sessions help overcome team-member isolation. Most consultants and researchers believe initial face-to-face meetings are critical for all team members to build personal relationships with teammates.[43] Annual company meetings and occasional special events provide additional opportunities for face-to-face meetings. General managers frequently communicate with individual team members to reduce feelings of isolation. Since regular face-to-face interaction is not feasible, managers communicate with routine phone calls or e-mails to keep isolated team members in the loop. One Canadian manager encourages the most isolated team members to build networks of contacts within the company and to stay in close communication with headquarters. Other general managers have established mentor-protégé relationships giving isolated team members a sense of inclusion. As one manager noted, "I work constantly to counteract the out-of-sight, out-of-mind problems with virtual team members. My goal is to keep everyone fully involved."

Lessons learned: General managers admitted that it took some time to recognize how to deal with virtual team member isolation. Initially, these managers interpreted minimal communication as a signal that all was well. Over time, however, managers recognized that some virtual team members needed more frequent and some almost daily communication. Sabre's experience with isolated virtual team members is that feelings of detachment and alienation, while possible, can be overcome with careful attention to social needs. Psychological testing identifies members with strong social needs, realistic job previews shape expectations of prospective employees, increased client contact and teambuilding meet social needs, and virtual team leaders proactively reach out to far-flung team members. While isolation can hamper team functioning, Sabre uses a variety of techniques to minimize potential problems.

CHALLENGE 4: BALANCING TECHNICAL AND INTERPERSONAL SKILLS AMONG VIRTUAL TEAM MEMBERS

Conventional wisdom: Since face-to-face interaction is minimal, some managers assume that interpersonal skills for virtual team members are less important than for face-to-face teams. For example, Beverly Geber suggests that managers should "select people who are comfortable sharing information and working with computers."[44] Anthony Townsend and colleagues note, "What is different about the virtual team is the amount of technical training that is required to empower the team member to function in the virtual environment. Training to maintain technical proficiency will be an important component of any virtual team member's continuing education program."[45] A manager in Martha Haywood's book *Managing Virtual Teams: Practical Techniques for High-Technology Managers* stated, "I don't care about this guy's feelings. I want to know when he's going to call me back."[46] Such sentiments illustrate the lack of emphasis on interpersonal relations.

Conventional wisdom assumes that virtual team members should be selected almost exclusively for their technical skills. After climbing a steep learning curve, Sabre's experience has been quite different. A divisional vice president captured the importance of striking a balance between technical and interpersonal skills by stating, "In our hiring in the past, we were guided by the level of technical skill, but now we are more sensitive to the level of interpersonal skills an individual brings to the equation, because this is a very key element in how these teams interact. We are more sensitive to a well-rounded person. If the work ethic is there and their ability to work with others is there, we can train them to be very effective at their jobs."

We asked team leaders and members to discuss ideal virtual team member skills. An overwhelming majority mentioned ability to communicate as most important. A close second was desire to support a team and teamwork in general. Team members also listed flexibility and adaptability in playing many different team roles. Other members discussed the importance of giving and receiving feedback. Others mentioned a sense of humor. One Canadian team member commented, "Technical job skills are important, but I tend to look at their ability to be part of a team, how they adjust to working with others, and their people skills." Managers often mentioned working independently, being a self-starter, thinking outside of the box, and taking initiative. Task-relevant skills were low on their lists. One manager commented, "It is not what the job is about. We can teach them the job. It is the right personality and the ability to get along with other team members. I don't care if they know twenty different kinds of software or not. I am more interested in how that person is going to fit into that team."

A significant challenge for virtual team leaders is recruiting, selecting, and retaining team members who have a good balance of technical and interpersonal skills. Clearly, virtual team members must have financial, marketing, or technology skills to carry out specific tasks. Moreover, all employees must be well versed in using the communications technology necessary to coordinate the efforts of a cross-functional virtual team. However, Sabre's experience suggests that virtual team members must also possess excellent interpersonal skills. In response to challenges of recruiting and selecting virtual team members with the right balance of technical and interpersonal skills, managers at Sabre have adjusted their selection procedures. Many use behavioral interviewing and scenario-based questions to assess communication and teamwork skills. For example, a Canadian manager presents this situation: "I will say, 'You haven't seen me for a month. You have been flying around the Northwest Territories. You are out of touch. How are you going to stay connected to us?'"

A second approach to selecting virtual team members is panel interviews. Using teleconferences, prospective future virtual teammates interview job candidates, and virtual team members assess interpersonal skills and team fit. A secondary benefit is the extra effort teammates make to welcome and socialize candidates they have selected. In future years, managers may develop a variety of simulations to aid virtual team candidate assessment.

Lessons learned: At Sabre, clearly the selection of virtual team members involves assessments of both task and interpersonal skills. Contrary to conventional wisdom, just because team members seldom interact face-to-face does not mean inter-personal skills will be less important than task-relevant skills. Indeed, interpersonal skills may be more important as team members attempt to com-municate effectively without relying on traditional non-verbal cues.

CHALLENGE 5: ASSESSMENT AND RECOGNITION OF VIRTUAL TEAM PERFORMANCE

Conventional wisdom: Again, Charles Handy put it best when he asked, "How do you manage people whom you do not see?" and "We will . . . have to get accustomed to working with and managing those whom we do not see. . . . That is harder than it sounds."[47] Kurland and Bailey stated. "A major challenge for managers is their inability to physically observe their employees' performance. They ques-tion, 'How do you measure productivity, build trust, and manage people who are physically out of sight?' If a manager can't see her subordinates in action, then she can't note where the employee is struggling and where he is strong . . . monitoring and measur-ing [employee] performance remain problematic and a source of concern."[48] Cascio said, "By far the biggest challenge is performance management."[49]

Conventional wisdom suggests that it is extraor-dinarily difficult for virtual team leaders to assess member performance and ensure fairness for mem-bers they rarely see. At Sabre, however, virtual team evaluations and rewards are a priority. Accordingly, Sabre developed a comprehensive, multi-tiered ass-essment process. First, Sabre developed a balanced scorecard[50] for each team. At the organizational level, balanced scorecards typically elevate non-financial measures such as employee or customer sat-isfaction to the level of importance typically held by financial measures such as stock price or return on equity. At the team level, Sabre's balanced scorecard consists of:

- Growth (share of the market);
- Profitability (costs versus revenue generated for each travel booking);
- Process improvement (cycle time, or the time required to order and install customer hard-ware); and
- Customer satisfaction (assessed with survey data collected from actual customers).

Sabre makes extraordinary efforts to monitor each team's customer satisfaction including setting annual customer service goals. Managers collect survey data quarterly from each team's external customers. Sabre posts team customer service scores on its intranet. Members know exactly where their team stands rela-tive to other teams. Closely monitoring client satisfac-tion helps Sabre create intense customer service focus. Moreover, virtual team leaders have an exter-nal, albeit subjective, basis for evaluating and reward-ing virtual teams. One developmental need for virtual teaming at Sabre is allowing more team-member input in setting customer service goals. Presently, management still controls this decision-making aspect.

Another important element of the balanced scorecard is process improvement (i.e., cycle time) or the extent to which team members reduce the time from the placement of an order to the installa-tion of, and training on, a reservation system. Process improvement is an objective measure of team learn-ing at Sabre. Thus, Sabre's teams are responsible for both day-to-day work and continuous improvement of their processes and cycle time.

Managers also assess individual team member performance. Sabre tracks objective individual per-formance measures such as number of installations, development of new business, number of individuals trained to use a system, accuracy of financial con-tracts, and customer retention. Because these mea-sures are objective and quantifiable, evaluations are much less susceptible to stereotyping, favoritism, or other contaminating perceptual biases. Ironically, virtual team member evaluations may be more accu-rate than evaluations of face-to-face team members.[51] Biases induced by demographic differences such as race, gender, and age can lower both individual per-formance ratings.[52] and team ratings.[53] Contamina-tion of evaluations by perceptual biases is less likely when team leaders have extensive objective data.

In addition to objective measures, general man-agers track subtle virtual team member behavior such as taking leadership roles during virtual team meet-ings, suggesting internal quality improvement strate-gies, coaching new team members off-line, and other intangible actions that enhance team effectiveness. General managers monitor electronic discussions, team e-mails, and other team activities. Managers often have more accurate records of individual con-tributions to virtual teams than they do from informal observations of face-to-face teams. They also supple-ment their own evaluations with peer evaluations. Using modified 360-degree performance evaluations, general managers collect peer and even customer input electronically.

General managers also provide timely feedback and resolve performance problems quickly. Some managers emphasize choosing appropriate communications media to deliver constructive feedback. They recommend using two-way communication channels such as teleconferences so feedback delivery can be followed immediately by interactive problem-solving or counseling sessions. Communicating constructive feedback from a distance forces managers to do more research, collect and analyze all of the relevant facts, and carefully craft messages. Knowing that their ability to resolve misunderstandings is constrained, managers emphasize careful preparation. Moreover, managers identify ahead of time resources that teams can tap in responding to problems. Other managers hold regularly scheduled monthly virtual meetings with each team member. One manager said, "It has to be a two-way street. They have to feel comfortable being honest and straightforward with me even with the bad stuff. I find that communicating electronically overcomes some of the interpersonal issues that might have made me hold back in the past."

Lessons learned: Sabre has built a comprehensive performance review system. The balanced scorecard provides an excellent approach for measuring team effectiveness. Sabre assesses individual contributions to team effectiveness by monitoring electronic communications and systematically collecting data from peers and direct reports using 360-degree assessments. Performance data provide a solid foundation for recognizing and rewarding team and individual performance, developing new training programs to assist virtual teams, and identifying individual team members who can benefit from off-line mentoring and coaching. Managers have developed effective techniques to deliver feedback. As one manager stated, "Most everyone's work is measured in the results they produce and through statistics, and it can all be pulled out systematically for each individual." In the virtual workplace, team members can be judged more on what they actually do rather than on what they appear to be doing.

Continuous Improvement at Sabre

While we have focused on positive aspects of Sabre's virtual teams, some lessons were learned only after trial and error. For example, managers said that

recognizing the sense of isolation among virtual team members took time. Similarly, some general managers reported initial reluctance to provide strong negative feedback virtually, preferring face-to-face meetings.

Our research identified a variety of other problems associated with managing and supporting virtual teams at Sabre. General managers still struggle with finding effective strategies for empowering virtual teams. Human Resources continues to fine-tune the content and delivery of virtual team training. Lastly, Sabre still struggles with the appropriate mix of rewards for individual contributions and team performance. While we have emphasized Sabre's positive lessons learned, these lessons were learned after false starts, stumbles, and reassessments. Moreover, new problems require continuous fine-tuning. Working with similar organizations, we found that this ongoing process of adaptation and adjustment is crucial to maximize virtual team effectiveness. Permanent, inflexible programs or policies such as a rigid structure or one-shot training do not provide adequate support for collaboration such as virtual teaming, in which members themselves are expected to grapple with uncertainty, innovate, and remain flexible.

One key to promoting ongoing adaptation at Sabre is communities of practice[54] (or what Sabre calls Centers for Excellence) where virtual team members in the North American division and beyond (including Sabre employees in Latin America, Europe, and Asia) share best practices. The Centers for Excellence, started in 2001 in the areas of sales, technology, training, and operations, are designed to provide innovative process solutions from Sabre's global operations. An excellent example is Sabre's 24/7 Learning Café. Developed by the technology Center for Excellence, the Café is an on-line training scheduler that allows Sabre employees worldwide to schedule and access virtual training modules such as "Coaching and Developing Others" and "New Product Training." More recently, the operations Center for Excellence developed a standardized product-demonstration tool that allows account executives, regardless of their experience level or location, to provide consistent demonstrations to customers of state-of-the-art reservation systems. The Centers for Excellence allow learning to occur within and across Sabre's virtual teams despite the conventional wisdom that process improvements occur in serendipitous face-to-face encounters in traditional work

Have Virtual Teams Improved Sabre's Bottom-Line Results?

Most of the interviewees at Sabre agreed that the transition from traditional, functional, face-to-face teams to cross-functional, virtual teams improved customer service. Regarding objective measures, after Sabre introduced cross-functional virtual teams, customer satisfaction ratings improved each year from a low of 68 percent in 1997 to 85 percent in 2000. In addition, North American market share increased from 43 percent in 1997 to 50 percent in 2000. Also during this period, Sabre's number of travel bookings increased significantly each year. While we cannot attribute all of these improvements solely to Sabre's implementation of virtual teams, clearly customers have responded positively to the changes at Sabre, which include using virtual teams.

However, benefits such as improved customer service are only half of the equation needed to assess virtual teaming effectiveness. In determining any return on investment, managers must also assess costs of implementing organizational designs. A central issue for virtual teams is the difficulty of assigning monetary values to costs that are not easily quantified.[55] These may include opportunity costs associated with internal resources devoted to the team. Several researchers have suggested calculating costs of team-member time and support-person time based on average salary and time spent with virtual teams.[56] Data regarding costs and benefits of virtual teaming can then be used to compare different virtual efforts using the same metric. The goal of such an analysis is determining if a virtual team's charter is consistent with a company's bottom-line objectives. Given the substantial resources necessary to support virtual teams, these are important questions to address in designing virtual teams and setting them up for success.

Virtual Teams: The Way Business Is Evolving

Using Sabre's experiences, we have highlighted five critical challenges that organizations face when implementing and using virtual teams. As organizations expand globally, the need to tap the talents, experience, and special skills of employees working in distant locations will increase. Most corporate executives predict that technology-mediated communication and virtual teaming will increasingly replace physical travel. However, creating and supporting virtual teams is a very difficult assignment. Identifying challenges ahead and learning from the Sabre experience represent a good place to start. In the words of one Sabre executive, "I think that virtual teams is inevitably the way business is evolving. We are working hard to get ahead of the curve."

Appendix
Summary of Methodology Used to Study Virtual Teams at Sabre

We selected Sabre's North American Sales and Service, Operations, and Financial Services Division based on its extensive use of virtual teams. Our work with other organizations using virtual teams suggests that Sabre's use is representative and comparable to that of the typical organization. From Sabre's 65 cross-functional virtual teams, members of a representative subset of 18 teams (i.e., varying by division, region, size of customer, and country) were selected to participate in face-to-face interviews. From those 18 teams, a representative subset of 58 teams members (34 percent of the total of 169 members) was interviewed based on variance in job function, demographics, and organizational tenure. We also interviewed the 11 team leaders of these 18 teams (some team leaders led more than one team), six divisional vice presidents who supervised the team leaders, and the executive vice president of the North American Division (for a total of 76 interviews). No team members or leaders declined to be interviewed.

Separate interview protocols were developed for each of the three organizational levels, and all interviewees within each level were asked identical questions. Each of the researchers (i.e., the first four coauthors of this paper) interviewed a roughly equal number of team members and leaders. The researchers had no prior relationship with Sabre or any virtual team members before the two entities entered into a research partnership. The researchers traveled from New York to California and from Quebec to British Columbia to meet virtual team members and leaders. Each interview lasted for one hour. The interviews were tape recorded and in some cases videotape recorded. Full transcriptions of each interview were prepared. All of the researchers participated in the divisional and executive vice president interviews via conference call. The interviewees were told that Sabre and the researchers had formed a partnership to examine the key drivers of, and significant obstacles to, virtual team effectiveness. All respondents were assured that their interview and survey responses were the property of the researchers and that only summary data would be returned to Sabre. Thus, their responses were confidential. Total time to conduct and analyze the interviews was six months. Sample virtual team member interview questions included:

- Describe the main differences between the teams you have worked on before in this company and your current virtual team.
- Describe the special challenges you have encountered working virtually.

- If you were involved in the hiring of a new member of your virtual team, what characteristics would you look for?
- What specific behaviors has your team leader (general manager) demonstrated that particularly help the functioning of your virtual team?

Regarding data analysis, all researchers read each interview transcript and created their own categories and themes. Each researcher then collected representative comments under each category. The researchers then met face-to-face to compare the categories. Discrepancies were resolved, and the researchers agreed upon a consensus set of categories. Representative comments were then collated by category. This process allowed us to retain only those themes that were represented by a large number of respondent comments.

Endnotes

1. For more information about global work team implementation, see Kirkman, B. L., Gibson, C. B., & Shapiro, D. L. 2001. "Exporting" teams: Enhancing the implementation and effectiveness of work teams in global affiliates. *Organizational Dynamics*, 30(1): 12–29.

2. Lipnack, J., & Stamps, J. 2000. *Virtual teams: People working across boundaries with technology.* 2nd ed. New York: Wiley. See also, Duarte, D. L., & Snyder, N. T. 2001. *Mastering virtual teams.* 2nd ed. San Francisco: Jossey-Bass.

3. Maznevski, M. L., & Chudoba, K. M. 2000. Bridging space over time: Global virtual-team dynamics and effectiveness. *Organization Science*, 11(5): 473–492; and Montoya-Weiss, M. M., Massey. A. P., & Song, M. 2001. Getting it together: Temporal coordination and conflict management in global virtual teams. *Academy of Management Journal*, 44(6): 1251–1262, for issues involving virtual teams composed of members from different countries.

4. Chase, N. 1999. Learning to lead a virtual team. *Quality*, 38(9): 76; and Geber, B. 1995, Virtual teams. *Training*, 32(4): 36–40; and Bell, B. S., & Kozlowski, S. W. J. 2002. A typology of virtual teams: Implications for effective leadership. *Group & Organization Management*, 27(1): 14–49.

5. Gibson, C. B., & Cohen, S. G., forthcoming. *Virtual teams that work: Creating the conditions for virtual team effectiveness.* San Francisco: Jossey-Bass.

6. See Cooper, R. C. 1997, Telecommuting: The good, the bad, and the particulars. *Supervision*, 57(2): 10–12; McCune, J. C. 1998. Telecommuting revisited. *Management Review*, 87(2): 10–16; and Pearlson, K. E., & Saunders, C. S. 2001. There's no place like home: Managing telecommuting paradoxes. *The Academy of Management Executive*, 15(2): 117–128, for more information on telecommuting.

7. Cascio, W. F. 2000. Managing a virtual workplace. *The Academy of Management Executive*, 14(3): 81–90; Kurland, N. B., & Bailey, D. E. 1999. Telework: The advantages and challenges of working here, there, anywhere, and anytime. *Organizational Dynamics*, 28(2): 53–67; and Kurland, N. B., & Egan, T. D. 1999. Telecommuting: Justice and control in the virtual organization. *Organization Science*, 10(4): 500–513.

8. Pearlson & Saunders, op. cit.

9. Elkins, T. 2000. Virtual teams: Connect and collaborate. *IIE Solutions*, 32(4): 26–32.

10. Townsend, A. M., DeMarie, S. M., & Hendrickson, A. R. 1998. Virtual teams: Technology and the workplace of the future. *The Academy of Management Executive*, 12(3): 17–29.

11. Cascio, op. cit.

12. Maznevski & Chudoba, op. cit.

13. Boudreau, M. C., Loch, K. D., Robey, D., & Straud, D. 1998. Going global: Using information technology to advance the competitiveness of the virtual transactional organization. *The Academy of Management Executive*, 12(4): 120–128: and Maznevski & Chudoba, op. cit.

14. Bunderson J. S., & Sutcliffe, K. M., in press. Comparing alternative conceptualizations of functional diversity in management teams: Process and performance effects. *Academy of Management Journal;* Dougherty, D. 1992. Interpretive barriers to successful product innovation in large firms. *Organization*

Science, 3(2): 179–202; Lovelace, K. Shapiro, D. L., & Weingart, L. R. 2001. Maximizing cross-functional new product teams' innovativeness and constraint adherence: A conflict communication perspective. *Academy of Management Journal*, 44(4): 779–793; Ancona, D. G., & Caldwell, D. F. 1992, Demography and design: Predictors of new product team performance. *Organization Science*, 3(3): 321–341; and Parker, G. M. 1994. *Cross-functional teams: Working with allies, enemies, and other strangers*, San Francisco: Jossey-Bass.

15. Maznevski & Chudoba, op. cit.

16. Gibson & Cohen, op. cit.

17. See, for example, Coutu, D. 1998. Trust in virtual teams. *Harvard Business Review*, 76(3): 20–21; Jarvenpaa, S., & Leidner, D. 1999. Communication and trust in global virtual teams. *Organization Science*, 10(6): 791–815; Jarvenpaa, S. L., Knoll, K., & Leidner, D. E. 1998. Is anybody out there? Antecedents of trust in global virtual teams. *Journal of Management Information Systems*. 14(4): 29–64; Platt, L. 1999. Virtual teaming: Where is everyone? *Journal of Quality & Participation*, September/October: 41–43; Cascio, op. cit.; and Townsend, op. cit.

18. O'Hara-Devereaux, M., & Johansen. B. 1994. *Global work: Bridging distance, culture, and time*. San Francisco: Jossey-Bass; Hart, P., & Saunders, C. 1997. Power and trust: Critical factors in the adoption and use of electronic data interface. *Organization Science*, 8(1): 23–42; and Sheppard, B. H., & Sherman, D. M. 1998. The grammars of trust: A model and general implications. *Academy of Management Review*, 23(3): 422–437.

19. Handy, C. 1995. Trust and the virtual organization. *Harvard Business Review*, 73(9): 40–48.

20. Cascio, op. cit., 83.

21. Jarvenpaa et al., op. cit., 30.

22. For a more complete discussion of trust, see Mayer, R. C., Davis, J. H., & Schoorman, F. D. 1995. An integrative model of organizational trust. *Academy of Management Review*, 20(3): 709–734. For a discussion about the impact of trust on cooperation and teamwork, see Jones, G. R., & George, J. M. 1998. The experience and evolution of trust: Implications for cooperation and teamwork. *Academy of Management Review*, 23(3): 531–546.

23. Mayer et al., op. cit.

24. Geber, op. cit., 39.

25. Gibson, C. B., & Manuel, J., forthcoming. Building trust: Effective multicultural communication processes in virtual teams. In C. B. Gibson & S. G. Cohen (Eds.), *Virtual teams that work: Creating the conditions for virtual team effectiveness*. San Francisco: Jossey-Bass.

26. For more on creating team charters and other team-development tools and interventions, see Fisher, K., Rayner, S., & Belgard, W. 1995. *Tips for teams*. New York: McGraw-Hill.

27. The notion of process gains and losses is explained in more detail in J. R. Hackman's work. See Hackman, J. R. 1987. The design of effective work teams. In J. W. Lorsch (Ed.), *Handbook of organizational behavior*. Englewood Cliffs, NJ: Prentice-Hall: 315–345; and Hackman, J. R. (Ed.), 1990. *Groups that work (and those that don't)*. San Francisco: Jossey-Bass.

28. Cascio, op. cit., 84.

29. Kurland & Bailey, op. cit., 59.

30. Geber, op. cit., 39.

31. Alexander, S. 2000. Virtual teams going global. *Infoworld*, 22(46): 55–56.

32. Ancona & Caldwell, op. cit. See also, Lichtenstein, R., Alexander, J. A., Jinnett, K., & Ullman. E. 1997. Embedded intergroup relations in interdisciplinary teams: Effects on perceptions of level of team integration. *Journal of Applied Behavioral Science*, 33(4): 413–434; and Timmerman, T. A. 2000. Racial diversity, age diversity, interdependence, and team performance. *Small Group Research*, 31(5): 592–606.

33. McLeod, P., Baron, R., Marti, M., & Yoon, K. 1997. The eyes have it: Minority influence in face-to-face and computer-mediated group discussion. *Journal of Applied Psychology*, 82(5): 706–718.

34. Gallupe, R. B., Bastianutti, L., & Cooper, W. H. 1991. Unblocking brainstorms. *Journal of Applied Psychology*, 76(1): 137–142. See also, Lam, S. S. K., & Shaubroeck, J. 2000. Improving group decisions by better pooling information: A comparative advantage of group decision support systems. *Journal of Applied Psychology*, 85(4): 565–573.

35. Cascio, op. cit., 82, 84.

36. Handy, op. cit., 4.

37. Kurland & Bailey, op. cit., 61.

38. Kurland & Egan, op. cit., 502.

39. See Caproni, P. J. 2001. *The practical coach: Management skills for everyday life*. Upper Saddle River, NJ: Prentice-Hall (see specifically Chapter 8, entitled "Diverse teams and virtual teams: Managing differences and distances": 247–287).

40. Emery, F. E. 1959. *Characteristics of sociotechnical systems*. London: Tavistock.

41. Geber, op. cit., 36; and Cascio, op. cit., 82.

42. Philips, J. M. 1998. Effects of realistic job previews on multiple organizational outcomes: A meta-analysis. *Academy of Management Journal*, 41(6): 673–690.

43. Joinson, C. 2002. Managing virtual teams. *HR Magazine*, 47(6): 69–73.

44. Geber, op. cit., 40.

45. Townsend et al., op. cit., 26.

46. Haywood, M. 1998. *Managing virtual teams: Practical techniques for high-technology managers*. Boston: Artech House.

47. Handy, op. cit., 3, 4.

48. Kurland & Bailey, op. cit., 59.

49. Cascio, op. cit., 87.

50. For more information on the balanced scorecard, see: Kaplan, R. S., & Norton, D. P. 1996. Using the balanced scorecard as a strategic management system. *Harvard Business Review*, 74(1): 75–85.

51. Alexander, op. cit.

52. See, for example, Kraiger, K., & Ford, J. K. 1985. A meta-analysis of rater race effects in performance ratings. *Journal of Applied Psychology*, 70(1): 56–65. See also, Pulakos. E. D., Oppler, S. H., White, L. A., & Borman, W. C. 1989. Examination of race and sex effects on performance ratings. *Journal of Applied Psychology*, 74(5): 770–780.

53. Baugh, S. G., Graen, G. B. 1997. Effects of team gender and racial composition on perceptions of team performance in cross-functional teams. *Group & Organization Management*, 22(3): 366–383. See also, Kirkman, B. L., Tesluk, P. E., & Rosen, B., in press. The impact of demographic heterogeneity and team leader-team member demographic fit on team empowerment and effectiveness. *Group & Organization Management*.

54. Brown, J. S., & Duguid, P. 1991. Organizational learning and communities of practice: Toward a unified view of working, learning, and innovation. *Organization Science*, 2(1): 40–57.

55. See Levenson, A., & Cohen, S. G., forthcoming. Meeting the performance challenge: Calculating ROI for virtual teams. In C. B. Gibson & S. G. Cohen (Eds.), *Virtual teams that work: Creating the conditions for virtual team effectiveness*. San Francisco: Jossey-Bass; and Levenson, A., forthcoming. ROI and strategy for teams and collaborative work systems. In M. Beyerlein, C. McGee, G. Klein, L. Broedling, & J. Nemiro (Eds.), *The collaborative work systems field book*. San Francisco: Jossey-Bass/Pfeiffer, for more information about assessing the costs and benefits of virtual teaming.

56. Levenson and Cohen, op. cit.

The Employment Law Impact of the Sarbanes-Oxley Act

Paul E. Starkman, *Employee Relations Law Journal*

The Sarbanes-Oxley Act (Act) contains some of the most important provisions relating to employment, executive compensation, and corporate ethics to be enacted in recent years. The Act directly applies to publicly traded companies and their executives but its reverberations will be far broader. This article discusses how the Act changes the employment landscape for corporate America. It also examines how executives and other employees will be affected by the Act, both on the job and in their pocketbooks. The article provides practical pointers on how publicly traded companies and those who work for them can meet the challenges presented by this new government mandate.

The Sarbanes-Oxley Act of 2002 (Act), which was signed into law by President Bush on July 30, 2002, and went into effect immediately, contains sweeping provisions affecting employment and executive compensation. The Act directly applies to publicly traded companies and their executives but it also impacts companies that do business with public corporations as "contractors" and "subcontractors" (i.e., outside auditors, accountants, human resources consultants, and legal counsel). Its reverberations also will be felt by nonpublicly traded companies, such as privately owned subsidiaries and related entities, whose financial activities are included in or may affect the financial statements and consolidated tax returns of public companies. This article examines the Act's dramatic employment-related changes, including the creation of new whistleblower protections.

The Sarbanes-Oxley Act's effect on the employment, compensation, and duties of executives and attorneys employed by publicly traded companies and their related entities also is discussed. Although the full impact of the Act may not become clear for many years to come, corporate America must begin grappling with it now or risk substantial civil and criminal liability.

The Act Creates New Whistleblower Protections

The Act's most significant employment-related change is that it contains increased protections for whistleblowers. It not only creates new civil statutory whistleblower causes of action but also criminalizes retaliation against government informants. As more fully discussed below, the provisions of the Act creating the new civil causes of action are contained in two subsections. No public company (i.e., a company with a class of securities registered under Section 12 of the Securities Exchange Act of 1934 (codified at 15 U.S.C. Section 78l) or that is required to file reports under Section 15(d) of the same act (15 U.S.C. Section 78o(d)) or any "officer, employee, contractors, subcontractors or agents" of such company may discharge, demote, suspend, threaten, harass, or in any other manner discriminate against an employee in the terms and conditions of employment because of any lawful act done by the employee[1]. Under one subsection, the employee must have filed cause for, testified in, participated in, or otherwise assisted in a "proceeding" relating to an alleged violation of federal securities or anti-fraud laws.[2] Under a second subsection, the employee must have reported conduct that he or she "reasonably believes" violated federal securities and anti-fraud laws internally to supervisors or others within the company with authority to deal with the misconduct or externally to federal or congressional authorities.[3] A third, separate subsection of the Act, discussed more fully below, criminalizes retaliation against government informants.[4] All in all, the Act's new whistleblower protections significantly change the legal landscape for public corporations and their employees.

THE ACT CREATES A CAUSE OF ACTION FOR THOSE WHO ASSIST IN A GOVERNMENT "PROCEEDING"

Under Section 1514A(a)(2), the Act bars retaliation against an employee because of any lawful act done by the employee to identify or cause, testify in, participate in, or otherwise assist in a proceeding underway or about to be underway (with "any knowledge of the employer") relating to an alleged violation of federal securities laws, Securities and Exchange Commission (SEC) rules, or any federal law relating to fraud against shareholders (which may or may not cover all the Sarbanes-Oxley Act's provisions).[5] Unlike the other civil causes of action created by the Act, an employee need not have a reasonable belief that a violation of the designated federal laws has occurred to have a claim under Section 1514A(a)(2).[6] The employee must, however, assist in a "proceeding" that has been "filed or [is] about to be filed (with any knowledge of the employer)" before a cause of action under this subsection of the Act will arise.[7] Although the Act does not define a "proceeding," courts interpreting the meaning of that term in other statutes, such as the Fair Labor Standards Act, 29 U.S.C. Section 215(a)(3)(1988), have held that a "proceeding" requires the initiation of an adjudicatory action by a court or administrative agency and does not include investigations, audits, and other non-adjudicatory action by an agency.[8] Moreover, regardless of the exact scope of the term "proceeding" as used in the Act, it appears that no claim will arise under subsection 1514A(a)(2) if an employee is discharged for providing information on possible securities law violations to a government agency before a "proceeding" is filed or about to be filed; however, the employee may have a claim under some other part of the Act.

THE ACT ALSO PROTECTS WHISTLEBLOWERS WHO REPORT CONDUCT THEY "REASONABLY BELIEVE" VIOLATES FEDERAL LAWS

Under the Act, a cause of action also will arise for retaliation because of any lawful act done by the employee "to provide information, cause information to be provided, or otherwise assist in an investigation" regarding any conduct that the employee reasonably believes constitutes a violation of federal securities laws, SEC rules, or any federal law pertaining to fraud against shareholders.[9] An employee is protected, however, only if he or she provides information or assistance to:

- A federal regulatory or law enforcement agency;
- A member of Congress or congressional committee; or
- A person with supervisory authority over the employee or any other person "working for" the employer who has the authority to investigate, discover, or terminate the misconduct.[10]

Giving information to persons or entities who are not listed in this subsection may not be protected, so that employees who "go public" to the media or leak information to state or local authorities may find themselves without a claim under the Act.

The Act contains an extensive list of federal and congressional authorities to whom reports can be made (thereby triggering the Act's protections under subsection 1514A(a)(1)). The Bush Administration, however, has proposed a narrow interpretation of the Act's language on making reports to members of Congress as referring only to "investigations authorized by the rules of the Senate or the House of Representatives and conducted for a proper legislative purpose." Until the dust settles concerning the interpretation of this provision, not every report to a member of Congress or person on their staff will necessarily trigger the Act's protections.

The Act also broadly defines the other non-governmental persons to whom internal reports can be made. It remains to be seen whether persons "with supervisory authority over the employee" includes those within only a "dotted line" reporting relationship. Likewise, it is unclear who within a covered entity will be deemed to be an "other person working for the employer who has the authority to investigate, discover, or terminate the misconduct."[11] At a minimum, this latter category seems to include in-house legal departments, audit committees, human resources departments, and corporate compliance personnel. Whether this provision will be broadly defined to encompass persons with apparent authority, but no actual authority to remedy misconduct of the kind covered by the Act, is an open issue. Companies that may fall within the scope of the Act would be wise to designate who within the organization has the authority to investigate, discover, or terminate financial misconduct and then disseminate the list of designated persons to let employees know to whom such reports should be made and to forestall claims that reports to non-designated persons triggered the Act's protections.

Subsection 1514A(a)(1)'s use of the term "reasonable" to qualify "belief" means that although the employee's suspicions need not be correct, a mere subjective belief probably will not be enough if a reasonable person would not believe that the conduct violated federal law. It will be interesting to see whether courts interpreting this subsection will infer a requirement of a "bona fide" or good faith (i.e., honest) belief, similar to that required to state a retaliation claim under most employment statutes, to preclude claims under the Act by employees who act for "bad" reasons (such as to get even against their employer for perceived slights) or who may have ignored, tolerated, or even participated in the misconduct until it suited their purposes to report it.[12]

The requirement under both subsections 1514A(a)(1) and (2) that the retaliation was because of "any lawful act by the employee" appears to incorporate case law under other employment statutes that holds that employees who engage in wrongful or criminal conduct in connection with their protected activity may be precluded from bringing claims.[13] Thus, employees who steal confidential company documents, illegally record conversations, or otherwise act improperly in gathering information or assisting in an investigation or proceeding may find themselves without a remedy. In any event, the requirement that the adverse employment action has been "because of the designated protected activity means that the Act does not prevent public companies from taking adverse action against an employee for legitimate reasons unrelated to activity protected by the Act.

THE LIST OF ENTITIES AND INDIVIDUALS COVERED BY THE ACT IS BROAD

Even though Section 1514A is titled "Whistleblower Protection for Employees of Publicly Traded Companies," the Act covers not only publicly traded companies but also "any officer, employee, contractor, subcontractor, or agent of such company."[14] The Act's whistleblower provisions thus potentially cover companies that do business with publicly traded companies, such as outside auditors, accountants, and law firms, depending on how the terms "contractor" and "subcontractor" are ulti-

mately interpreted. Likewise, the liability of a wholly owned subsidiary of a publicly traded company when, for example, the subsidiary has retaliated against one of its employees for reporting wrongdoing involving or affecting the financial condition of the publicly traded parent, is an open question.

The Act's inclusion of "officer, employee . . . or agent" suggests that officers and managers employed by covered entities may be subject to liability in their individual capacities if they are involved in a prohibited employment action against employees protected by the Act. Moreover, if officers and managers can be liable, it appears to follow that such liability also may fall on coworkers who, for example, harass a fellow employee who has made a protected report. The extent to which nonemployee directors will be personally liable under the Act may depend on how the term "agent" is defined.

Although other federal employment statutes contain references to "employees" and "agents" when describing covered entities, courts have refused to find officers, managers, and other nonemployers individually liable under those laws.[15] Thus the full reach of the Act's civil causes of action remains to be seen, but the list of potentially liable entities and individuals is broad indeed.

THE ACT PROVIDES ACCESS TO FEDERAL COURT FOR WHISTLEBLOWERS

Actions brought under the Act must follow, at least initially, the procedures set forth in the Whistleblower Protection Program, which were enacted in 2000 to afford protection to airline industry employees providing air safety information (airline whistleblower protection provision).[16] An employee who alleges discharge or other discrimination in violation of the Act must file a complaint with the Department of Labor (DOL) within 90 days of the alleged retaliation.[17] Unlike the airline whistleblower protection provision and most federal whistleblower laws, however, if the DOL does not issue a final decision within 180 days of the filing of the complaint and there is no showing that such delay is because of the bad faith of the claimant, an employee may bring an action for de novo review in an appropriate federal district court.[18] The district court will have jurisdiction without regard to any amount in controversy.[19] The access to federal court (if the DOL does not act within 180 days) that is built into the Act increases the potential significance of a whistleblower claim under the Act in terms of expanded discovery, added expense, and an increased risk of adverse publicity.

THE ACT'S BURDEN OF PROOF ALLOCATIONS TRACK FEDERAL DISCRIMINATION LAWS

The Act expressly adopts the burden of proof allocation from the airline whistleblower protection provision.[20] To avoid dismissal, a complainant must make a prima facie showing that the prohibited conduct was a "contributing factor" in the unfavorable employment decision.[21] If the complainant under the Act meets this requirement, an investigation will be conducted unless the employer can demonstrate, by "clear and convincing evidence," that it would have taken the same unfavorable employment action in the absence of that behavior.[22] This provision imposes a relatively light burden on employees to initiate a DOL investigation and a heavy burden on employers to forestall one.

REMEDIES AVAILABLE UNDER THE ACT DIFFER FROM OTHER WHISTLEBLOWER PROVISIONS

By incorporating the airline whistleblower protection provision, the Act seems to provide that if, after an investigation, the DOL determines that a violation has occurred, the employer may be ordered to reinstate the employee and provide compensatory damages.[23] Moreover, an appeal of the DOL's initial determination by the employer (to the federal appellate court) will not automatically stay the DOL's order.[24] Thus, under the Act, an employee may be able to obtain reinstatement with the same seniority status that he or she would have had but for the discrimination and also may recover back pay with interest and special damages including attorneys' fees and litigation costs;[25] however, the Act does not provide for either punitive damages or jury trials.

In contrast, for example, the anti-retaliation provision of the False Claims Act (discussed below) allows for the same remedies as the Act, except that the False Claims Act allows the recovery of "two times the amount of back pay."[26] Further, even though the Act does not allow punitive damages, state-law whistleblower protections (which are not preempted by the Act) often do.[27]

An open question under the Act is whether an employee can be penalized for bringing a frivolous whistleblower discrimination claim. The Act itself does not provide any penalties against an employee for bringing such a claim, but it arguably adopts the section from the airline whistleblower protection provision that provides that if the DOL finds that an employee filed a frivolous or bad faith complaint, the employee may be ordered to pay the first $1,000 of the employer's attorneys' fees in defending against the claim.[28] This penalty has not yet been applied in an airline case, however, and may not be used to any extent under the Act.

THE ACT EXPANDS WHISTLEBLOWER PROTECTIONS UNDER FEDERAL LAW

The new civil causes of action created by the Act expand the avenues of relief available to whistleblowers under federal law.[29] The Act does not contain procedural requirements or burdens of proof that often bar whistleblower actions under other statutes. For example, qui tam actions brought pursuant to the False Claims Act allow a private citizen to sue in the name of the United States against those who submit false or fraudulent claims for payment or approval to an agent of the United States.[30] To maintain a qui tam action, however, the complainant must be an "original source of the information."[31] An "original source" is defined as "an individual who has direct and independent knowledge of the information on which the allegations are based and has voluntarily provided the information to the Government before filing an action. . . ."[32] A qui tam action will be barred if an employee has not reported the allegedly illegal conduct to the authorities before bringing suit, unlike the Act, which allows an employee to bring an action after reporting misconduct either externally (to federal or congressional authorities) or internally (to a person with supervisory authority over the employee or such other person working for the employer who has the authority to investigate, discover, or terminate the misconduct).[33]

Likewise, the federal Whistleblower Protection Act (WPA) affords protection to federal employees and federal contractors who have been discharged based on the disclosure of information that evidences "a violation of any law, rule, or regulation," "gross mismanagement," or a "substantial and specific danger to public health or safety." Disclosures of impropriety are not protected by the federal WPA, however, unless a disinterested observer with knowledge of the essential facts known to be readily ascertainable by a whistleblowing employee reasonably could conclude that the actions of the government evidenced gross mismanagement.[34] Moreover, the pool of potential plaintiffs under the Act is far broader than under the WPA because it includes all employees of private sector, publicly traded companies and their "contractors, subcontractors, and agents," rather than the federal employees and contractors protected by the WPA.[35]

STATE LAW RETALIATORY DISCHARGE CLAIMS ARE NOT SUPPLANTED BY THE ACT

The Act's new federal causes of action for whistleblowers are in addition to, but do not supplant, the often-inconsistent whistleblower protections provided by state law. Many states provide statutory causes of action that may protect whistleblowers who are discharged in retaliation for reporting violations of federal or state law.[36] A few states, however, limit retaliatory discharge actions to claims involving violations that create a substantial and specific danger to public health or safety.[37] Other states have used the common law as a basis to create a tort cause of action to protect whistleblowers who are terminated in contravention of a clearly mandated public policy of the state;[38] however, not every discharge for reporting financial improprieties and similar white-collar crimes has been found to be in contravention of a clearly mandated state public policy.[39] Moreover, some states recognize a cause of action only for retaliatory discharges and do not provide relief for demotions, constructive discharges, and refusals to rehire allegedly in retaliation for whistleblower activities, unlike the Act, which encompasses all types of employment actions.[40] Whistleblowers thus often find that state laws provide only scant protection indeed.

Because the Act does not supplant or preempt rights that an employee has under state law, other federal laws, or collective bargaining agreements, the Act's new civil causes of action will add new arrows to the quivers of plaintiffs' attorneys.[41] For example, if an employee is able to bring a claim under the Act in federal court, nothing prevents him or her from also seeking in the same proceeding a jury trial and punitive damages under a state-law whistleblower cause of action.

THE ACT IMPOSES CRIMINAL PENALTIES FOR RETALIATION AGAINST GOVERNMENT INFORMANTS AND DOCUMENT DESTRUCTION

In addition to the creation of a civil cause of action, the Act, at 18 U.S.C. Section 1513(e) amends the obstruction of justice statute to clearly criminalize retaliation against government informants in the following manner:

Whoever knowingly, with the intent to retaliate, takes any action harmful to any person, including interference with the lawful employment or livelihood of any person, for providing to a law enforcement officer any truthful information relating to the commission or possible commission of any Federal offense, shall be fined under this title or imprisoned not more than 10 years, or both.

This criminal provision of the Act covers disclosures of any violations of federal law, not just employee reports of securities law and corporate fraud violations, which are the subject of the Act's civil causes of action. Moreover, informants are protected even if the information they provide does not show that a violation of federal law actually occurred—it is enough that the information was "truthful." Individuals protected by this provision apparently need not be employees who have been subjected to a retaliatory employment action (discharge, demotion, etc.) because the Act prohibits "any action harmful to any person, including interference with the lawful employment or livelihood of any person."[42] This would seem to include independent contractors and other third parties who provide law enforcement officers with truthful information about the possible commission of a federal offense. This new criminal provision may provide many whistleblowers and government informants with potential coverage under the civil RICO statute.[43] It remains to be seen whether Section 1513(e) will expose officers and managers to criminal prosecution for intentionally retaliating against informants.

The Act also states that anyone who intentionally "alters, destroys, mutilates, conceals, covers up [or] falsifies" any record or document to "impede, obstruct or influence the investigation or proper administration" of an investigation is subject to criminal fines and up to 20 years imprisonment.[44] This prohibition applies to any document relevant to the "investigation of any matter within the jurisdiction of any department or agency of the United States or any bankruptcy cases or in relation or contemplation of any such matter or case."[45] Among other things, this provision closes a loophole in existing law by prohibiting acts of destruction by an individual acting alone.[46] Although the full reach of the Act is unclear, it would certainly cover the destruction of documents relevant to an investigation into violations of the Act itself, but it arguably also could cover the destruction or falsification of documents relevant to an Equal Employment Opportunity Commission (EEOC) charge, a wage and hour investigation, or a similar matter. The possibility of spending 10 or 20 years in jail for violating the Act substantially "ups the ante" for those officers responsible for bringing their employees into compliance.

The Act Dramatically Affects Officer Compensation Programs

The Sarbanes-Oxley Act redefines executive compensation, removing, redefining, and re-creating various benefits executives may have taken for granted.

EXECUTIVE BONUSES ARE SUBJECT TO FORFEITURE UNDER THE ACT

The chief executive officer and the chief financial officer of a publicly traded company may be required to forfeit any bonuses or incentive-based compensation, including any equity-based compensation and profits from the sale of their company's securities, that they have received in the previous 12 months if there has been a restatement of the company's financial reports because of any "material noncompliance" with the SEC's financial reporting requirements.[47] The SEC is authorized to grant exemptions when "necessary and appropriate."[48] Companies should incorporate the Act's forfeiture provision into their bonus policies and compensation programs.

PERSONAL LOANS TO EXECUTIVES ARE REGULATED BY THE ACT

The Act in broad language also prohibits covered companies from directly or indirectly extending credit or arranging for extensions of credit to any director or executive officer "(or the equivalent thereof)," other than certain specified broker/dealer margin loans or other loans made in the ordinary course of business.[49] Home improvement loans and consumer credit loans provided by a company in that business as well as margin loans by SEC-registered broker-dealers are allowed, but margin loans to non-employee directors or to executive officers employed only by affiliated companies may not be permitted.[50] Advances for valid business expenses do not appear to be covered, but many loans that are typically part of compensation programs probably are covered. The Act also may cover relocation loans, securities acquisition loans, the extension of credit as part of split-dollar life insurance, and company guarantees for third-party loans.

This portion of the Act has a grandfather provision excluding credit that already had been provided prior to the date of enactment (July 30, 2002), but material modification or renewal of the terms would bring the financing within the scope of the Act.[51] The general rule is that future loans or loan extensions by publicly traded companies to their directors and/or executives may not be made on terms that are more favorable than those offered to the general public.[52] Companies that do not offer loans or financing to the general public may find themselves unable to offer incoming or current executives loans or financing at below market rates. This grandfather provision does not address loans to an employee who is later promoted to an executive officer position and raises questions about loan arrangements that involve future payouts pursuant to a binding commitment in effect on July 30, 2002, such as split-dollar life insurance, which typically involves the payment over time by employers of premiums under initial split-dollar insurance policies on behalf of directors and executive officers.[53]

This portion of the Act undoubtedly will affect executive compensation programs and corporate recruitment and hiring strategies because companies now may not be able to offer loans and other financing incentives that heretofore were made available to executives for recruitment and retention purposes.

SEC CAN REMOVE OR TEMPORARILY FREEZE PAYMENTS TO EXECUTIVES AND DIRECTORS

The Act gives the SEC the authority to prevent individuals from servicing as directors or officers of public companies if they have violated anti-fraud provisions of the Securities Exchange Act.[54] This is a change from prior law in that the SEC no longer is required to obtain a court order before an individual can be removed or disqualified from serving as an officer or director of a public company.

Any "extraordinary payments" proposed to be made by a public company to any of its executive officers or directors during the course of an investigation of the company for possible securities law violations can be temporarily frozen.[55] On petition by the SEC, a federal court is authorized to freeze such payments for up to 45 days (with a possible 45-day extension) in an interest-bearing account.[56] If the individual is charged with a securities law violation during this period, the escrow can continue, subject to court approval, until the conclusion of any legal proceedings.[57]

THE ACT'S CONFLICTS OF INTEREST PROVISIONS MAY PRECLUDE HIRING

The Act precludes registered public accounting firms from auditing a company if a highly placed executive (such as a CEO, CFO, chief accounting officer, comptroller, or equivalent officer) was employed by the auditing firm and participated in the company's prior year's audit.[58] The Act also makes it unlawful for such an accounting firm to provide human resources consulting services to a public company contemporaneously with an audit.[59] Companies will need to implement hiring procedures to make sure they do not recruit executives who are barred from employment by the Act. Covered entities also will want to have executive candidates confirm during the recruitment process that their employment would not violate the Act.

ATTORNEYS HAVE NEW RESPONSIBILITIES UNDER THE ACT

The SEC has promulgated rules of professional responsibility for attorneys appearing and practicing before that body.[60] These rules include a requirement that attorneys, including in-house attorneys, report evidence of material violations of securities laws or breaches of fiduciary duty to the company's chief legal counsel or CEO.[61] If the chief counsel or CEO does not respond appropriately, the attorney must report any evidence obtained to the audit committee or the company's board of directors.[62]

The SEC also may sanction any person appearing or practicing before it who is lacking of character or integrity or has engaged in improper conduct.[63] This could include a single instance of highly negligent conduct.

The Act requires "attorneys appearing and practicing before the [SEC]" to "report evidence of a material violation of securities law or breach of fiduciary duty or similar violation by the company or any agent thereof.[65] Thus, in-house attorneys

and even some outside legal counsel may have a statutory obligation to become whistleblowers under the Act.

The Act Requires New Employment Policies and Procedures

Unlike most whistleblower laws, the Act mandates that publicly traded corporations, acting through their audit committees, establish procedures for "the receipt, retention and treatment of complaints received by the [public company] regarding accounting, internal accounting controls or auditing matters."[66] The Act further requires publicly traded companies to establish procedures for receiving "the confidential, anonymous submissions of employees of the [public company] of concerns regarding questionable accounting or auditing matters."[67] As a result, covered companies will need to review their personnel policies, implement codes of conduct, establish hotlines and other avenues for employees to make confidential anonymous complaints, provide training for supervisors and affected employees, and implement procedures to handle such complaints and the investigations that may result from them.

At a minimum, companies should also re-examine their Directors and Officers liability insurance and other types of insurance to make sure they will provide coverage for claims arising from the Act. For example, the definition of "Wrongful Acts" in such policies must be read in conjunction with policy exclusions and conditions and applicable law to see if coverage will extend beyond negligence or carelessness to encompass alleged intentional violations of the Act.

Companies also would be wise to expressly prohibit retaliation for raising concerns about accounting and financial practices. At a minimum, this policy must be communicated in writing and through training. Personnel manuals and supervisors' guidelines should be revised to emphasize that employees who complain about corporate fraud are to be protected from retaliation in the same manner as those who complain about discrimination and harassment. As noted above, the policy should designate and disseminate who within the organization has "authority to investigate, discover, or terminate misconduct" because reports to such individuals can trigger liability unde the Act.

As noted above, the Act requires the establishment of procedures for receiving and handling complaints of corporate fraud. Companies thus must address who within the organization will be designated to receive and investigate these complaints. Although the human resources department is an obvious choice, consideration also should be given to whether others should be designated, such as the audit committee, given the potentially technical nature of corporate fraud complaints. Moreover, protocols and procedures should be set up to address how investigations should be conducted. Although the complaint-intake and investigation protocols may track those used with respect to harassment complaints, special care must be exercised to ensure that investigators do not create "smoking guns" or elicit corporate admissions that violations of the Act have occured, given the significant criminal and civil penalties that exist under the Act.

Compensation program bonus policies and stock option plans will have to be amended to take account of the Act's new forfeiture provisions. Hiring and recruitment strategies and background check procedures will have to be revamped to avoid hiring executives whose employment is precluded by the Act.

Training will be required to properly implement all the Act's mandates. Supervisors and managers as well as higher-level executives must be trained on how to recognize complaints of corporate fraud (which may be difficult to differentiate from internal gripes about nonactionable management practices), how to respond to them, and the need to avoid taking actions that might be retaliatory. It is likely that training will be viewed, as it is under discrimination statutes, as strong evidence of effective, good faith attempts to comply with the Act.[68]

Public companies now are required to disclose in their filings with the SEC whether they have a code of ethics for senior financial officers and, if not, they must describe why not.[69] This code of ethics must promote: (1) honest and ethical conduct and handling of conflicts of interest; (2) full, fair, accurate, timely, and understandable disclosure of SEC filings; and (3) compliance with applicable government rules and regulations.[70] The code of ethics, along with any changes or waivers of that code, must be filed with the SEC and posted on the company's web site.[71] The code of ethics should make clear that violations of the Act and the employer's guidelines regarding it are cause for immediate discharge.

Conclusion

The Sarbanes-Oxley Act imposes new, important risks and responsibilities on publicly traded companies, their executives, and those that do business with them. Companies covered by the Act must be cognizant of its accounting, ethical, and whistleblower protections and other employment-related provisions to conform their policies and procedures to meet the requirements imposed. Only by confronting the Act now will public companies and those who work for them be able to shield themselves from the substantial potential liability presented by the Act.

Source: Reprinted/Adapted with permission from *Employee Relations Law Journal* (Spring, 2003, 28, 4), "The Employment Law Impact of the Sarbanes-Oxley Act," by Paul E. Starkman.

Endnotes

1. 18 U.S.C. Section 1514(a).
2. 18 U.S.C. Section 1514(a)(2).
3. 18 U.S.C. Section 1514(a)(1).
4. 18 U.S.C. Section 1514(e).
5. 18 U.S.C. Section 1514A(a)(2). The reference in the Act to "sections 1341, 1343, 1344, or 1348" refers to Title 18 of the United States Code, which addresses mail fraud; wire, radio, or television fraud; bank fraud; and securities fraud.
6. Compare 18 U.S.C. Section 1514A(a)(2) with 18 U.S.C. Section 1514A(a)(1).
7. 18 U.S.C. Section 1514A(a)(2).
8. Ball v. Memphis Bar-B-Q Co. Inc., 228 EM 360 (4th Cir. Sept. 14, 2000) (after an employee was fired from his job when he told the company's president that, if he were deposed in a yet-to-be-filed lawsuit under the Fair Labor Standards Act (FLSA) that was threatened against the company, he would not testify to a version of events suggested by the president, the Fourth Circuit affirmed the court's grant of Memphis Bar-B-Q's motion to dismiss for failure to state a claim, finding that the FLSA's anti-retaliation provision was not sufficiently broad to protect Ball. Although the circuit court found that Ball's allegations described morally unacceptable retaliatory conduct, the court stated that it would not be faithful to the language of the testimony clause of the FLSA's anti-retaliation provision if it were to expand that provision to cover intracompany complaints or to potential testimony in a future–but-not-yet-filed court proceeding; but see Valerio v. Putman Associates Inc., 173 F.3d 35 (1st Cir. 1999) (internal complaint triggers protection under

FLSA's retaliation provision, which protects any employee who "has filed any complaints or instituted or caused to be instituted any proceeding" under the act); Lambert v. Ackerly, 169 F.3d 666 (9th Cir. Oct. 1, 1998) (when employee complained to company officials about discontinuation of automatic overtime payments, called the DOL, told her supervisor about the call to the DOL, and had her lawyer send an unfiled lawsuit to her employer, the Ninth Circuit held that the FLSA retaliation claim survived summary judgment, even though plaintiff never actually filed a formal complaint or instituted or testified in an FLSA proceeding).

9. 18 U.S.C. Section 1514A(a)(1).

10. 18 U.S.C. Section 1514A(e)(1) (A), (B), and (C).

11. 18 U.S.C. Section 1514A(a)(1)(c).

12. Lipphardt v. Durango Steakhouse of Brandon, Inc., 267 F.3d 1183 (11th Cir. Sept. 28, 2001) (to establish that she engaged in protected activity; the plaintiff must have had a good faith, reasonable belief that she had been sexually harassed, and this requires that she subjectively held this belief and that her belief was objectively reasonable).

13. Kiel v. Select Artificials, Inc., 169 F.3d 1131 (8th Cir. 1999) (when the plaintiff shouted at the co-owner that she was selfish, slammed his desk drawer, and made a remark about the co-owner's new car, stating that the ADA "confers no right to be rude"); Laughlin v. Metropolitan Washington Airports Authority, 149 EM 253 (4th Cir. 1998) (taking document from boss's desk was not protected activity); Douglas v. Dyn McDermitt Petroleum Operations Co., 144 F.3d 36, 376 (5th Cir. 1998) (the Fifth Circuit found that an in-house counsel's "opposition" to alleged discriminatory practices by her employer was not protected because she breached legal ethics when she gave a copy of her internal letter complaining of discrimination to a whistleblower officer from the U.S. government); Hernandez v. McDonald's Corp., 975 F. Supp. 1418 (D. Kan. 1997) (employee's secret taping of meeting with manager after having been instructed not to tape the meeting was held to be a clearly valid reason for discharge); Bodoy v. North Arundel Hospital, 945 F. Supp. 890 (D. Md. Jan. 20, 1996) (summary judgment for employer because secret taping of meeting with supervisor was a valid reason for discharge despite claim that taping related to EEOC charges, because taping was illegal in Maryland); see also Hubert v. Consolidated Medical Laboratories, 306 Ill. App. 3d. 1118 (2d Dist. 1999) (employee who initially followed doctor's illegal instructions to switch tissue samples, but then reported the incident, could not bring retaliatory discharge action because of her own part in the wrongdoing).

14. 18 U.S.C. Section 1514A(a). Frobose v. American Savings and Loan Association of Danville, 152 F.3d 602 (7th Cir. 1998) (summary judgment for employer reversed because in Title VII whistleblower retaliation case employer must rebut prima facie case with clear and convincing evidence and must carry burden of persuasion, unlike Title VII discrimination case).

15. Sattar v. Motorola, Inc., 138 F.3d 1164 (7th Cir. 1998) (affirming the dismissal of Title VII religious discrimination claim against two supervisors used "individually and in their corporate capacity" because "a supervisor does not, in his individual capacity, fall within Title VII's definitions of employer" and because plaintiff did not allege that the supervisors were the sole owners of the company, the court did not have to consider whether they had any corporate capacity separate from the company). Supervisors can, however, be individually liable under the FLSA and the Family and Medical Leave Act (FMLA). O'Brien P. Dekalb-Clinton Counties Ambulance District, 1996 U.S. Dist. LEXIS 14636 (W.D. Mo. June 24, 1996); Donovan v. Schoolhouse Four Inc., 573 F. Supp. 185, 190 (W.D. Va. 1983); Freemon v. Foley, 911 F. Supp. 326 (N.D. 111. Nov. 8, 1995) (the FMLA tracks the definition of "employer" found in the FLSA, not that found in Title VII or the Americans with Disabilities Act; hence, supervisor may be held individually liable for FMLA violation); Beyer v. Elkay Manufacturing Co., 1997 U.S. Dist. LEXIS 14459 (N.D. 111. 1997) (finding supervisor liable under FMLA). But see Frizzell P. Southwest Motor Freight Inc., 906 F. Supp. 441 (E.D. Tenn. 1996) (refusing to find individual liability under FMLA).

16. 18 U.S.C. Section 1514A(b)(2)(A).

17. 49 U.S.C. Section 42121(b)(1). The Act's 90-day statute of limitations is shorter than the 180- to 300-day limitations period for filing charges of retaliation under other federal employment discrimination statutes, such as Title VII (42 U.S.C. Section 2000e et seq.) and the Age Discrimination in Employment Act (ADEA, 29 U.S.C. Section 610–621).

18. 18 U.S.C. Section 1514A(b)(1)(B). Some of the other federal statutes that prohibit retaliatory discharge and grant whistleblowers a private cause of action include: Federal Deposit Insurance Corporation Improvement Act, 12 U.S.C. Section 1831] (2002); Vessels and Seamen Act, 46 U.S.C. Section 2114 (2002). Other statutes that prohibit retaliatory discharge of whistleblowers and provide a procedure for investigating and punishing violations of the statute, but do not grant the employee a private cause of action under federal law, include: Clean Air Act, Section 42 U.S.C. 7622 (2002); Comprehensive Environmental Response, Compensation and Liability Act, 42 U.S.C. Section 9610(b) (2002); Energy Reorganization Act, 42 U.S.C. Section 5851 (2002); Federal Surface Mining Act, 30 U.S.C. 1293(b) (2002); Migrant and Seasonal Agricultural Workers Protection Act, 29 U.S.C. Section 1855(b) (2002); Occupational Safety and Health Act, 29 U.S.C. Section 660 (2002); Safe Drinking Water Act, 42 U.S.C. Section 300(i)-9(i)–(iii) (2002); Solid Waste Disposal Act, 42 U.S.C. Section 6971(b) (2002); Surface Transportation Act, 49 U.S.C. Section 31105(b) (2002); Toxic Substances Control Act, 15 U.S.C. Section 2622 (2002); Water Pollution Control Act, 33 U.S.C. Section 1367 (2002); Whistleblower Protection Act, 5 U.S.C. Section 2302(b) (2002) (see Braun v. U.S., 707 F.2d 922, 925 (6th Cir. 1983)).

19. 18 U.S.C. Section 1514A(b)(1)(B).

20. 18 U.S.C. Section 1514(b)(2)(C) incorporating the procedures set forth in 49 U.S.C. Section 42121(b).

21. 49 U.S.C. Section 42121(b)(2)(B)(i).

22. 49 U.S.C. Section 42121(b)(2)(B)(ii). This is consistent with the affirmative defense in employment discrimination actions (i.e., that even if an improper motive existed, the plaintiff cannot recover if the employer would have taken the same action for a legitimate reason) first recognized by the U.S. Supreme Court in Price Waterhouse v. Hopkins, 490 U.S. 228 (1986), and later modified by the Civil Rights Act of 1991 at 42 U.S.C. Section 2000e-5(g)(2)(B).

23. 49 U.S.C. Section 42121(b)(3)(b)(ii) and (iii).

24. See Senate Rep. No. 107–146.

25. 18 U.S.C. Section 1524A(c)(2).

26. 31 U.S.C. Section 3730(h).

27. See notes 36 to 38 and accompanying text.

28. 49 U.S.C. Section 4212(b)(3)(C).

29. Examples of federal statutes providing protection for whistleblowers include: Whistleblower Protection Act of 1989, Pub. L. No. 101–12, 103 stat. 16 (1989) (codified as amended in scattered sections of 5 U.S.C.); Age Discrimination in Employment Act (ADEA), 29 U.S.C. Section 621 (1988); Asbestos Hazard Emergency Response Act of 1986, 15 U.S.C. Section 2641 (1988); Asbestos School Hazard Detection Act of 1980, 20 U.S.C. Section 3601 (1988); Clean Air Act (CAA), 42 U.S.C. Section 7401 (1988); Comprehensive Environmental Response, Compensation and Liability Act of 1980 (CERCLA), 42 U.S.C. Section 9601 (1988); Department of Defense Authorization Act of 1984, 10 U.S.C. Section 1587 (1988); Department of Defense Authorization of 1987, 10 U.S.C. Section 2409 (1988); Employee Retirement Income Security Act (ERISA), 29 U.S.C. Section 1001 (1988); Energy Reorganization Act of 1974 (ERA), 42 U.S.C. Section 5801 (1988); Equal Employment Opportunity Act (Title VII), 42 U.S.C. Section 2000e (1988); Fair Labor Standards Act (FLSA), 29 U.S.C. Section 215(a)(3) (1988); Federal Employers' Liability Act (FELA), 45 U.S.C. Section 51 (1988); Federal Mine Safety and Health Act (FMSHA), 30 U.S.C. Section 801 (1988); Federal Water Pollution Control Act of 1972, 33 U.S.C. 1251 (1988); Hazardous Substances Release Act, 46 U.S.C. Section 9601 (1988); International Safe Containers Act, 46 U.S.C. Section 1501 (1988); Jurors' Employment Protection Act, 28 U.S.C. Section 1861 (1988); Longshoremen's and Harbor Workers' Compensation Act, 33 U.S.C. Section 901 (1988); Migrant Seasonal and Agricultural Worker Protection Act, 29 U.S.C. Section 1801 (1988); Occupation Safety and Health Act, 29 U.S.C. Section 651 (1988); Public Health Service Act, 42 U.S.C. Section 201 (1988); Safe Drinking Water Act, 42 U.S.C. Section 300f (1988); Solid Waste Disposal Act, 42 U.S.C. Section 6901 (1988); Surface Mining Control and Reclamation Act, 30 U.S.C. Section 1201 (1988); Surface Transportation Assistance Act of 1978, 49 U.S.C. Section 2301 (1988); Toxic Substance Control Act, 15 U.S.C. Section 2601 (1988); Vessels and Seamen Act, 46 U.S.C. Section 2114 (2002); Water Pollution Control Act, 33 U.S.C. Section 1367(a) (2002).

30. 31 U.S.C. Section 3730(b).

31. 31 U.S.C. Section 3730(e)(4)(A).

32. 31 U.S.C. Section 3730(e)(4)(B).

33. See Brandon v. Anesthesia and Pain Mgmt. Assoc. Ltd., 277 RM 936, 944 (7th Cir. 2002); United States ex rel Aflatooni v. Kistap Physicians Servs., 163 F.3d 516, 521 (9th Cir. 1998).

34. LaChance v. White, 174 F.3d 1378 (Fed. Cir. 1999) (purely subjective perspective of the employee is not sufficient even if shared by coworkers).

35. 49 U.S.C. Section 42121(b)(2)(B)(i). The Act's articulation of the claimant's burden of proof is similar to other federal employment discrimination laws in which the term "because of" has been interpreted to mean the protected activity was a "motivating factor" in the employment decision. Foster v. Arthur Anderson, LLP., 168 F.3d 1029, 1033 (7th Cir. 1999). It remains to be seen whether the Act's use of the term "contributing factor" will be interpreted differently from "motivating factor."

36. State whistleblower statutes include: Code of Ala. 25-8-57 (1988); Alaska Stat. Section 39.90.100 (1992); Ariz. Rev. Star. Ann. Section 28-531 (West Supp. 1992); Cal. Lab. Code Section 1102.5 (West Supp. 1994); Colo. Rev. Stat. Ann. Section 24-50.5-101 (West 1990); Conn. Gen. Stat. Ann Section 31-51n (West 1987); Del. Code Ann. Tit. 29, Section 5115 (1991); Fla. Stat. Ann Section 112.3187 (West 1992); O.C.G.A. Section 34-9-24 (1998); Haw. Rev. Stat. Section 378-61 to 69 (Supp. 1992); 5 ILCS 395/0.01 (West 1999); Ind. Code Ann. Section 36-1-8-8 (Burns Supp. 1992); Iowa Code Ann. Section 79.28 (West 1991); Kan. Star. Ann. Section 75-2973 (Supp. 1998); Ky. Rev. Stat. Ann. Section 61.101 (Michie/Bobbs-Merrill 1986); La. Rev. Stat. Ann. 30-2027; Me. Rev. Stat. Ann. Tit. 26, Section 831–840 (West 1988); Miss. Code Ann. Section 7-5-307 (1998); Md. Code Ann. Art, Section 64A, Section 12F (Supp. 1992); Mich. Comp. Law Section 15.361–389 (1981); Minn. Stat. Section 181.932–935 (1994); Mo. Ann. Stat. Section 105.55 (Vernon Supp. 1992); N.C. Gen. Stat. Section 126–84 (1997); N.H. Rev. Stat. Ann. 275:E-1 to E-9 (Supp. 1993); N.J. Stat. Ann. Section 34:19-1 to 19-8 (West Supp. 1993); N.M. Stat. Ann. 60-9-25 (1998); N.Y. Lab. Law Section 740 (McKinney); Ohio Rev. Code Ann. 41113.51–53 (Baldwin 1992); 74 Okla. Stat. Ann. Section 840-2.5 (1994); Or. Rev. Stat. Section 654.062 (1993); 43 Pa. Cons. Stat. Ann. Section 1421 (1991); R–I. Gen. Laws Section 28-50-1-28-50-9 (1995); S.C. Code Ann. Section 8-27-10 (Law. Co-op Supp. 1992); Tenn. Code Ann. Section Section 50-1-304 (1991); Tex. Govt., Section 554.001-009 (1993); Utah Code Section 67-21-1 (Supp. 1992); Wash. Rev. Code Ann. Section 42.40.010; W. Va. Code 6c-1-1; Wis. Stat. Ann. Section 230.80–89 (West 1987).

37. See Colo. Rev. Stat. Ann. Section 24-50.5-101 (2002) (prohibiting retaliation based on information given about state agency actions that are not in the "public interest"); Fla. Stat. Ann. Section 112.3187 (2002); N.Y. Lab. Law Section 740 (2002); Ohio Rev. Code Ann. Section 4113.52(A)(1)(a)(2002); Or. Rev. Star. Section 654.062 (2001).

38. See, e.g., Milton v. IITResearch Institute, 138 F.3d 519, 522 (4th Cir. 1998) (the Fourth Circuit found that pursuant to Maryland law, a cause of action would arise when (1) the employee was fired for refusing to violate the law, or (2) the employee was fired for exercising a specific right or duty); Leudtke v. Nabors Alaska Drilling, Inc., 768 P.2d 1123, 1130 (Alaska 1989); Wagenseller v. Scottsdale Mem'l Hosp., 710 P.2d 1025, 1033 (Ariz. 1985); Tameny v. Ad. Richfield Co., 610 P.2d 1330, 1333 (Cal. 1980); Sheets v. Teddy's Frosted Foods, Inc., 427 A.2d 385, 387 (Conn. 1980); Palmateer v. Intl Harvester Co., 421 N.E.2d 876, 878 (1981) (the Illinois Supreme Court explained that for a retaliatory discharge cause of action to arise, "a matter must strike at the heart of a citizen's social rights, duties and responsibilities before the tort will be allowed"); Frampton v. Central Indiana Gas Co., 297 N.E.2d 425, 428 (Ind. 1973); Firestone Textile Co. v. Meadows, 666 S.W.2d 730, 732 (Ky. 1983); Leuthans v. Washington Univ., 894 S.W.2d 169, 171 n.2 (Mo. 1995); Ambroz v. Cornhusker Square Ltd., 416 N.W.2d 510, 514–15 (Neb. 1987); Coman v. Thomas Mg. Co., Inc., 381 S.E.2d 445,447 (N.C. 1989); Geary v. United States Steel Corp., 319 A.2d 174, 180 (Pa. 1974); Payne v. Rozendaal, 520 A.2d 586, 589–90 (Vt. 1986); Brockmeyer v. Dun & Bradstreet,

335 N.W.2d 834, 840 (Wis. 1983). A few states, including Alabama, Mississippi, and Georgia, do not recognize common law wrongful termination claims. See Salter v. Alfa Inc. Co., Inc., 561 So. 2d 1050, 1051–53 (Ala. 1990); Perry v. Sears, Roebuck & Co., 508 So. 2d 1086, 1089–90 (Miss. 1987); Evans v. Bibb Co., 342 S.E.2d 484, 484–86 (Ga. App. 1986).

39. Milton v. HIT Research Institute, 138 F.3d 519 (4th Cir. 1998) (rejecting claim based on plaintiffs' refusal to participate in the employer's alleged abuse of its tax-exempt status); Adler v. American Standard Corp., 291 Md. 31, 432 A2d 464 (1981), 830 F.2d 1303 (4th Cir. 1987) (rejecting claim because the plaintiff could not establish a securities laws violation); Reich v. Holiday Inn, 454 So. 2d 982 (Ala. 1984) (rejecting a claim that the plaintiff was fired in retaliation for refusing to pay invoices that allegedly were from a dummy corporation set up by the defendants to defraud stockholders and the IRS); Doherty P. Kahn, 289 Ill. App. 3d 544, 559 (Ist Dist. 1997) (a refusal to assist in a conspiracy to restrain trade and engage in unfair competition was not a sufficient violation of Illinois public policy to give rise to a retaliatory discharge claim); Martin v. Platt, 386 N.E.2d 1026 (Ind. App. 1979) (no cause of action for accusing superior of receiving illegal kickbacks); Suchodolski v. Michigan Consol. Gas Co., 412 Mich. 692, 694 (Mich. 1982) (corporate management dispute and complaints about internal accounting practices were not a violation of a clearly mandated public policy supporting an action for retaliatory discharge); Remba v. Federation Employment & Guidance Serv., 149 App. Div. 2d 131, 134 (N.Y. Sup. Ct. 1989) (rejecting retaliatory discharge claim under New York law based on plaintiff's alleged refusal to participate in employer's purportedly fraudulent billing of city); Bergstein v. Jordache Enterprises, Inc., 767 F. Supp. 535 (S.D.N.Y. 1991) (applying Pennsylvania law) (discharge for complaining about unlawful pricing practices was held to involve mere objections to employer's policies); but see McNulty v. Borden, Inc., 474 F5 1111 (E.D. Pa. 1979) (antitrust price-fixing gave rise to retaliatory discharge claim under Pennsylvania law); Thompson v. St. Regis Paper Co., 102 Wash. 2d 219, 685 P.2d 1081 (1984) (Washington state law cause of action recognized for reporting noncompliance with accounting requirements of Foreign Corrupt Practice Act); Moskaf v. 1st Tennessee Bank, 815 S.W.2d 509 (Tenn. App. 1991) (upholding cause of action for bank employee who refused to continue practice of falsifying records to show compliance with federal laws and to continue to forge loan documents); Haigh v. Matsushita Elect. Corp., 676 F. Supp. 1332 (E.D. Va. 1987) (recognizing cause of action for refusal to participate in alleged illegal price-fixing scheme).

40. See e.g., Hartlein v. Illinois Power Co., 151 Ill. 2d 142 (1992); Graham v. Commonwealth Edison Co., 318 Ill. App. 3d 736 (1st Dist. 2000) (in a divided decision, the First District held that a cause of action for retaliatory discharge is not available to redress any employer conduct short of actual discharge, and there is no cause of action for retaliatory demotion); Welsh v. Commonwealth Edison Co., 306 Ill. App. 3d 148 (1st. Dist. 1999) (Illinois does not recognize a cause of action for retaliatory demo-

tion or retaliatory constructive discharge in violation of public policy).

41. 18 U.S.C. Section 1514A(d).

42. 18 U.S.C. Section 1513(e).

43. Racketeer Influenced and Corrupt Organizations Act, 18 U.S.C. Section 1961–1968.

44. 18 U.S.C. Section 1519.

45. 18 U.S.C. Section 1519.

46. 18 U.S.C. Section 1510 currently prohibits individuals from persuading others to engage in "obstructive conduct."

47. 16 U.S.C. Section 7243(a)(1) and (2).

48. 15 U.S.C. Section 7243(b).

49. 15 U.S.C. Section 78m(k)(1) and (2)(a).

50. 15 U.S.C. Section 78m(k)(2).

51. 15 U.S.C. Section 78m(k)(1).

52. 15 U.S.C. Section 78m(k)(2)(C).

53. The IRS has proposed Treasury Regulations under which the loan treatment to be given to a split-dollar arrangement for tax purposes would depend on the form of ownership (i.e., whether policy is owned by the executive or the employer), but it is unclear whether the form of ownership will govern the treatment of split-dollar arrangements under the Act.

54. 15 U.S.C. Section 78u-3(f).

55. 15 U.S.C. Section 78u-3(c)(A)(A)(i).

56. 15 U.S.C. Section 78u-3(e)(3)(A)(i).

57. 15 U.S.C. Section 78j-l(1).

59. 15 U.S.C. Section 78j-l(g)(6).

60. 15 U.S.C. Section 7245.

61. 15 U.S.C. Section 7245(1).

62. 15 U.S.C. Section 7245(2).

63. 15 U.S.C. Section 78d-3(a)(1)-(3).

64. 15 U.S.C. Section 78d-3(b)(2)(A).

65. 15 U.S.C. Section 7245.

66. HH. 3763 Section 301(m)(4)(A), to be codified as 15 U.S.C. Section 78f(m)(4)(4).

67. 15 U.S.C. Section 78f(m)(4)(B).

68. The courts and legislatures are increasingly expecting employers to provide supervisors and management-level employees with training concerning employment law basics in general and anti-harassment policies in particular. Matthis v. Phillips Chevrolet, Inc., 269 EM 771 (7th Cir. 2001) (holding that it was an "extraordinary mistake" for an employer to fail to train its hiring managers on employment law basics); Shaw v. Auto-Zone, Inc., 180 EM 806 (7th Cir. 1999) (noting with approval that "in addition to distributing this policy to its employees, AutoZone regularly conducted training sessions on sexual harassment"); Kohler v. Inter-Tel Technologies, 244 F.3d 1167 (9th Cir. Apr. 11, 2001) (citing with approval that "Inter-Tel also conducted mandatory sexual harassment training seminars for the entire Emeryville work force"). See Cal. Gov't Code Sections 12950(b); Me. Rev. Star. Ann. tit. 26, Sections 806–807; Mass. Gen. Law ch. 151(B), Sections 34 (requiring harassment training). Other courts have held that a formal training program on equal employment opportunity matters will enable an employer to take advantage of the affirmative defense recognized by the U.S. Supreme Court in Kolstad v. American Dental Association, 527 U.S. 526 (1999), which allows an employer to avoid liability for punitive damages arising out of the discriminatory employment decisions of mana-

gerial agents when those decisions were contrary to the employer's "good faith efforts" to comply with federal employment laws. EEOC v. Wal-mart Stores, 187 F. Supp 1241 (Both Cir. 1999) (holding that the employer's written policy against discrimination and its ADA Compliance Manual were insufficient to constitute a "good faith effort" to prevent discrimination when the personnel manager at the store testified that during her seven years as a manager she had never received any ADA or employment discrimination training); Romano v. U-Haul International, 235 F.3rd 655 (1st Cir. 2000) (finding a lack of "good-faith effort" when U-Haul "did not put forth evidence of an active mechanism for renewing employees; awareness of the policies through specific education programs or periodic redissemination or revision of their written materials").

69. 15 U.S.C. Section 7264(a).
70. 15 U.S.C. Section 7264(c)(1)-(3).
71. 15 U.S.C. Section 7264(b). The SEC is proposing to extend the scope of this section to include a company's principal executive officer. The SEC also is proposing to broaden the definition of the term "code of ethics" as used in Section 406 to include the following three additional factors: (1) avoidance of conflicts of interest, including disclosure to an appropriate person or persons identified in the code of any material transaction or relationship that reasonably could be expected to give rise to such a conflict; (2) the prompt internal reporting to an appropriate person or persons identified in the code of violations of the code; and (3) accountability for adherence to the code. In addition to providing the required disclosure, a company also would have to file a copy of its ethics code as an exhibit to its annual report. All companies that file a Form 10-K report (see 17 C.F.R. Section 249.310) or a form 10-KSB report (see 17 CFR 249.310b) would be subject to the proposed disclosure requirement.

Employee Satisfaction

Jennifer Schramm, *Workplace Visions*

Changes in demographics and a shifting industrial base will have a considerable impact on job satisfaction in the future. This is because many factors that determine job satisfaction vary depending on age, industry, gender and other characteristics. Based on what we know now about factors that lead to job satisfaction in today's workforce, we can estimate which issues could have the biggest impact on job satisfaction in the future. Unfortunately, many of the factors employees will cherish most in the coming decades will be the very things employers will find increasingly difficult to offer to them. Though there are no easy answers, planning ahead and focusing on addressing the issues that *can* be changed will go a long way in maintaining and improving employee job satisfaction.

The Potential Impact of Demographic Changes on Job Satisfaction

An aging population will increase the emphasis on health care benefits, retirement planning and job security. However, due to high costs and market fluctuations, these are the very areas where employers are finding it more and more difficult to give employees what they want. Women are attaining a higher proportion of professional qualifications and degrees than men—many professions currently dominated by men will eventually have proportionally more women. With a skills shortage potentially unfolding in the not too distant future, more companies will need to address the job satisfaction factors that women value in order to attract skilled professionals. And industrialized countries may start to compete with each other for skilled immigrant labor as a way to address the imbalance of old to young workers. Learning what attracts this kind of skilled labor will become an important endeavor.

A Shifting Industrial Base

The shift from a manufacturing to a service economy will also continue to have implications for employee satisfaction. Some fast-growing sectors appear to have higher levels of job satisfaction than the declining manufacturing industry, but by no means all of them. Most worrying is that the service and health care sectors both show low levels of job satisfaction, though the growing fields of education, financial services and nonprofits all show high levels of satisfaction.

What Does This Mean for Employers?

Employers may find it increasingly difficult to deliver some of the key factors that will be most important in determining employee job satisfaction. However, HR practitioners can meet this challenge by preparing for the future and by focusing on areas where they can make a difference.

Job Satisfaction and Wider Political and Economic Trends

Though employers and HR practitioners can do a lot to raise levels of job satisfaction, there are several issues such as health care costs, job security and pensions that will be partially dependent on wider political and economic trends. HR practitioners will need to be aware of these issues and be ready to play an active role in the political response to these challenges.

Introduction

Broader changes in demographics and the economy could mean that for a growing proportion of the U.S. workforce, the very factors that are most important to them in determining their levels of job satisfaction are the ones most likely to decrease in the future. Could this mean a rise in dissatisfied employees in the years to come?

The whole issue of employee satisfaction is not always easy to get a handle on. Much of the available data is conflicting, which could reflect how quickly the field is changing. The vagaries of the economy could also play a role. Within the span of just a few years we have seen reports indicating that job satisfaction is low and getting worse, while a recently conducted SHRM study indicated that most employees are fairly satisfied with their work. For many right now, simply having a job is satisfaction enough.

The ever-shifting state of job satisfaction could be why many HR practitioners are having difficulty pinpointing exactly what kinds of issues to focus on. But even if employee expectations were obvious, meeting them would still be an entirely different matter. External pressures, cost cutting measures and a slow economy have meant cuts to some of employees' most prized benefits. And continuing economic difficulties could create a further erosion of some of the key factors that promote job satisfaction. How then will organizations attract and retain talented people in this environment?

This is a question that will become more and more relevant in the next decades, as the war for talent heats up once again. With this in mind, it is useful to look at some of the current key components to employee satisfaction and to see how these might be affected as a result of future developments in society and the economy.

One of the more interesting aspects that SHRM research highlights is that job satisfaction means different things to different people depending upon their age, gender or other demographic differences. This certainly makes sense and the awareness of these differences can help companies to create policies that maximize job satisfaction for most of its people. This knowledge, coupled with demographic projections can also help us to identify some of the key areas of conflict that may develop over the next decades.

The Potential Impact of Demographic Changes on Job Satisfaction

Changing demographics will have a large impact on job satisfaction in many ways. The most obvious is different demographic groups prize different factors when it comes to their levels of job satisfaction. Demographic groups that will represent an increasing proportion of the workforce are seeing the things that are most important to them in terms of job satisfaction decline. This will put pressure on employers to find ways to maintain these offerings; employers in turn are likely to look to the government to take

some of this pressure off—particularly in the areas of health care and pensions.

What are the more important demographic issues that will determine job satisfaction in the future?

AGE

In the last two decades the number of Americans past retirement age who are still in the job market has risen by half according to the U.S. Census Bureau. This trend is likely to continue into the future. According to the AARP, baby boomers, who will be the next large generation to retire, plan to do so at a later age than current retirees.

What kinds of factors lead to job satisfaction for older workers? Unsurprisingly, benefits top the list, followed by job security. As they prepare for retirement, older workers will continue to want security and, unless credible alternatives are presented, they will continue to look to their employers to provide it. But increasingly, employers are finding it difficult to provide such benefits—largely for reasons of costs. The convergence of disappointing earnings and a slow economy has meant that employers are, some for the first time, being forced to support underfunded pension plans. This is making them rethink how much they can offer employees upon retirement. According to recent research from Hewitt Associates, around 32 percent of the companies they surveyed are planning to make changes to pension investment allocations. The costs are likely to get even higher as a larger proportion of the population retires, putting further pressure on companies' pension funds. Health insurance benefits for retirees are also facing cutbacks. Another survey from Hewitt Associates and the Kaiser Family Foundation showed that 22 percent of large companies surveyed were likely to eliminate subsidized benefits for retirees.

There is some evidence that if employers begin to associate older workers too much with costly benefits this could give rise to age discrimination. Recent SHRM research on older workers showed that one of the few disadvantages employers saw in hiring older workers was the belief that older employees cause expenses such as health care and pension costs to rise. It is no surprise that many of today's age discrimination cases focus on the issue of retirement benefits.

Organizations are beginning to realize how important this age shift will be. But most have yet to take specific actions to address the issue. For example, few organizations have established phased retirement programs. Equally, eldercare provisions remains extremely rare as an employee benefit, though employees caring for elderly relatives are expected to grow rapidly over the next few decades; according to the National Council on Aging around 40 percent of the workforce may be caring for older parents by 2020. These responsibilities are likely to reinforce in the minds of older workers the importance of security in their retirement—hence strengthening the value they place on benefits and job security as factors in job satisfaction.

Another factor that is likely to increase in importance for this demographic is work/life balance. Though many baby boomers report that they want to work longer than the current retirement age, and though workers are currently staying on the job longer than in the past, many people will be forced to retire earlier than planned due to an unexpected disability. Some who are no longer able or willing to work full-time, however, may wish to continue working on a part-time basis. The baby boomer generation was also the first in which women entered the workforce in high numbers bringing with them a greater awareness of work/life balance. For this reason, unlike previous generations, baby boomer pre-retirement workers may be more comfortable with the whole idea of work/life balance and are likely to be more vocal advocates of flexible working lives.

Though there may be difficulties in meeting older workers' expectations in terms of benefit offerings, there is some justification for optimism. Generally older workers describe themselves as more satisfied with their working lives than younger workers. It will be critical to continue to observe levels of job satisfaction among older workers to see if a decline in the kinds of benefits they value brings about any decline in job satisfaction for this age group.

GENDER

Because women have traditionally assumed the role of caregiver, both for children and for elderly or disabled dependents, the whole issue of work/life balance is closely related to gender issues. This is borne out in the findings of the SHRM job satisfaction research, which showed a clear gender difference in the value placed on work/life balance as a factor in determining job satisfaction. For women, work/life balance was the most important factor in determining job satisfaction, whereas for men this was also important but only after issues such as benefits, job security, compensation/pay and communication with management. As gender roles become more fluid this could change; it is unlikely, however, to mean a decrease in the emphasis on work/life balance among women. Instead, it is more likely that the issue will become more significant for men.

Paying attention to what drives job satisfaction for women is important for several reasons. First, women will continue to make up a growing proportion of the workforce. Even if levels of female labor participation plateau, they are already nearly level with male participation rates and are likely to grow within skilled professions because young women are now surpassing men in diploma/professional degree acquisition rates. These high levels of educational attainment mean that, increasingly, companies looking for skilled workers will need to attract women. Additionally, the factors driving job satisfaction for women may also be a precursor to what will eventually drive job satisfaction for both women and men.

We can see this in studies like the SHRM research that showed that younger generations of men currently working their way up through the workforce place more value on work/life balance than older men do. Men in Generations X and Y report more interest in and place more value on flexible working schedules. Men are also likely to have more caring responsibilities in the future than they may currently have—this includes both childcare and eldercare. Fathers taking on the childcare role is becoming more accepted, particularly among younger workers. According to a recent *Newsweek* poll, 34 percent of men say that if their wives earned more money, they would consider quitting their jobs or reducing their hours in order to become the primary caregiver. Researchers estimate that this percentage is even higher among younger men. In addition, the impact of an aging population and resulting increased caring responsibilities will not only affect women. Already today out of the estimated 54 million Americans who are involved in care giving, 44 percent are men, according to the National Family Caregivers Association. With both men and women pushing for more flexibility, companies will be under much more pressure to provide it in an equitable way.

IMMIGRATION

One final demographic trend worth nothing is the expected increase in immigration as a response to fewer workers replacing those retiring. Attracting skilled employees from abroad could begin to influence the benefits some industries that rely heavily on imported skilled labor start to offer their employees. Little research has been done into what attracts highly skilled immigrants to particular employers. This is not surprising since up to now most employers in industrialized nations could rely on the high living standards of their countries to attract skilled immigrants on this basis alone.

But if, as predicted, a labor shortage due to an aging population begins to manifest itself in industrialized countries within the next decade or so, there may be much more competition between these countries for young, skilled (and in many cases unskilled) immigrant labor. Eventually more research will probably be done into what kinds of work environments attract immigrant labor and lead to high job satisfaction. We can guess that some immigrant employees may have slightly different criteria for job satisfaction than their native-born counterparts, but at this stage there is insufficient information to make it really clear how this trend could impact employee satisfaction.

A Shifting Industrial Base

Apart from demographics, one key shift over the coming years will be in the economy's emphasis on different types of industries. We know already that different industries have different levels of job satisfaction. Will industries that currently enjoy high levels of job satisfaction grow or decline over the next decades?

So far, the indications are that many of them are set to grow while many of the industries with lower levels of job satisfaction will decline. In the SHRM research, employees in the nonprofit, financial and education industries all reported higher levels of job satisfaction. According to the Bureau of Labor Statistics (BLS) these are all some of the fastest-growing industries. At the same time employees in the manufacturing industry, where lower levels of growth are expected, were among the least satisfied.

There are a few significant exceptions to this trend. Employees in the service sector—not including nonprofits—were found in the SHRM research to be the most dissatisfied with their work; according to the BLS the largest and fastest-growing major industry group is the service sector. High levels of job dissatisfaction in this sector will inevitably translate into high levels of job dissatisfaction overall. The health industry is another job sector that is predicted to grow but here again, health workers were among the most dissatisfied.

Identifying what factors are most important to people in these industries can help employers to produce a more satisfying work environment for employees now and in the years to come. Interestingly, for workers in the services sector, work/life balance is the most important factor, with communication and job security nearly tied for second place. Clearly, employers in the services sector will need to take work/life balance issues into account for the foreseeable future. This may be because many women work in the services sector but there could be other reasons for its predominance. Many women also work in the health sector but the critical job satisfaction factors for this industry look very different. Here the most important factor was benefits followed by career development and job security tied for second place and career advancement and communication tied for third place.

COMPANY SIZE

Another aspect that seems to play an important role in job satisfaction is company size. People appear to grow less satisfied with their jobs as the size of the organization increases. It would appear that small employers are better able to offer more of the key factors their employees value than larger organizations. Employees in small businesses name these as work/life balance, job security, benefits and communication. Whereas it is not difficult to imagine that small employers are able to accommodate their employees' work/life balance requirements, they cannot always offer job security and benefits to the same degree that larger employers are able to. It is unclear what is causing this apparent contradiction. What it could mean is that smaller employers are offering enough of some factors such as work/life balance to make up for those that they are not able to offer.

What Does This Mean for Employers?

Obviously the differences in criteria considered necessary for high levels of job satisfaction are not

Industry	First	Second	Third	Fourth	Fifth
Education	Communication (71%)	Job Security (69%)	Benefits (66%)	Career Development (63%)	The Work Itself (63%)
Finance	Job Security (71%)	Work/Life Balance (67%)	Communication (66%)	Benefits (64%)	Compensation/ Pay (59%)
Government	Benefits (66%)	Communication (61%)	Work/Life Balance (59%)	Job Security (58%)	The Work Itself (56%)
Health	Benefits (74%)	Career Development (68%)	Job Security (68%)	Career Advancement (65%)	Communication (65%)
High Tech	Work/Life Balance (67%)	Compensation/ Pay (62%)	Job Security (57%)	Benefits (56%)	The Work Itself (56%)
Manufacturing (Durable Goods)	Job Security (75%)	Communication (75%)	Benefits (72%)	Compensation/ Pay (72%)	Recognition by Management (69%)
Manufacturing (Nondurable Goods)	Job Security (73%)	Communication (67%)	Benefits (67%)	Compensation/ Pay (60%)	Career Advancement (53%)
Services (Nonprofit)	Compensation/ Pay (83%)	Career Advancement (75%)	Job Security (75%)	Benefits (75%)	Career Development (67%)
Services (Profit)	Work/Life Balance (75%)	Communication (69%)	Job Security (66%)	Compensation/ Pay (63%)	Recognition by Management (56%)

Source: SHRM/USATODAY.com Job Satisfaction Poll

TABLE 2: TOP FIVE "VERY IMPORTANT" ASPECTS FOR EMPLOYEES BY GENDER

Gender	First	Second	Third	Fourth	Fifth
Male	Benefits (62%)	Job Security (61%)	Compensation/Pay (58%)	Communication (55%)	Work/Life Balance (53%)
Female	Work/Life Balance (72%)	Communication (71%)	Job Security (70%)	Benefits (67%)	Compensation/ Pay (61%)

Source: SHRM/USATODAY.com. Job Satisfaction Poll

only divided along demographic (i.e., age, gender, etc.) lines, but also along professional interests and career paths, It is critical, therefore, that employers get as good an understanding of the unique attributes of their workforce as possible so that they can put their limited resources into the areas that will produce the best outcomes.

The complexity of all of the different competing factors that go into job satisfaction, many of which cannot always be controlled, can seem overwhelming for employers and it can be difficult to know where to start when attempting to address some of these issues. As already mentioned, an important first step is to understand in detail what factors most drive the levels of job satisfaction in your workforce. Findings from job satisfaction surveys and other research can act as a background. But as the differences between the health and services industries illustrate, making assumptions based on just a few factors such as gender or age may not be revealing the whole picture and could be misleading. Ideally, carrying out an internal audit and using the findings to direct priorities can make a real difference.

In addition to this research on existing priorities and concerns, it is important to be able to project what your business's workforce is likely to look like in the future and to use what is known today to try to prepare for tomorrow. If you know that the older workers in your organization currently share certain preferences, you may be able to use this existing data to prepare for a time when older workers will make up a larger proportion of your workforce. If, based on current degree attainment levels, you know your profession will soon be made up of a much higher proportion of women, you may be able to project and prepare for the future based on what you know about women in your organization today.

JOB SATISFACTION FACTORS SHARED BY MOST OR ALL GROUPS

Another approach is to look at job satisfaction factors that seem to span across demographics, industry size and employer type. Chances are if you can get these shared factors right you can go quite some way in increasing job satisfaction in your workforce. These issues can be divided into two groups—those, like benefits, wages and job security, that to a large extent depend on the financial position of the company and in this way to the economy overall, and those that are less dependent and may be easier, or at least less costly, to shape to meet employee preferences by changing practices and processes and perhaps to at least some degree the organizational culture.

The most important of these latter issues are communication with management, work/life balance, the employee's relationship with his/her immediate supervisor and career development. These four issues tend to come up frequently in studies on job satisfaction. In the SHRM research they appeared again and again regardless of the age, gender, industry or company size of the respondents.

In particular, work/life balance and communication showed up in the top five factors for all age groups. This means that however you look at it, employees are likely to highly prize these factors in the future. If, for example, these preferences are cohort specific—that is Generation Xers will always value work/life balance no matter how old they get—these issues will be of critical importance. But even if these issues are age specific—that is they are characteristic of certain life stages such as the child-rearing or pre-retirement years—they continue to be of critical importance because *every* age group values these factors highly. Therefore, investment in these areas is likely to go a long way in promoting job satisfaction among all employees.

COMMUNICATION

Communication is valued highly by employees in every age group and most particularly by women. The value of being able to communicate effectively with employees will only increase as teams become more virtual in nature. One danger, however, is that employees are becoming immune to organizational communication as they are inundated with information. E-mails and other electronic forms of communication have added to the "information fatigue" many workers are experiencing.

A key way of ensuring that communication is effective is to measure its impact. Though most organizations rely on informal, ad hoc feedback, more structured rigorous methods are needed if truly reliable, usable data is to be collected and if key communications priorities are to be established. Establishing these goals will help to shape how measurement methods are developed.

Though supporting effective communication may not be as financially burdensome as some other factors leading to high levels of employee satisfaction such as health care or pensions, it does require an investment of time and money, but done well could more than make up for its costs in higher levels of job satisfaction and reduced turnover.

WORK/LIFE BALANCE

Though many employers have done a great deal to promote a workplace that helps employees balance the needs of their work and personal lives, the demographic trends outlined earlier suggest that in the decades to come there will be even more emphasis on this issue. Most of the people who employers will be trying to attract fall into demographic and professional groups that highly prize work/life balance—in some cases more than any other factor. For example, employees surveyed by SHRM in the high-tech sector rate work/life balance as the most important factor in job satisfaction. Remember, this is the high-tech sector, which as we all know, is not exactly dominated by women. This emphasis on work/life balance is evidenced in a recent story on top technology managers who are now avoiding the CEO suite. And the primary reason? The excessively long hours.

Employers will be competing on this measure not only with other employers but also the lure of self-employment. This may be especially true in the case of women, who are starting their own businesses in record numbers. The number of female-owned companies is growing twice as fast as all other businesses. A recent study by the Rochester Institute of Technology (RIT) found that the main reason that women start their own companies is to better balance their work and family lives. Clearly women are trying to create something for themselves that they do not feel they can get from employers. But trends suggest this frustration will be or already is shared by most other employee groups. Developing workable, effective and fair policies for work/life balance will continue to be one of the very top priorities for employers if they are to attract talented employees in the years ahead.

RELATIONSHIP WITH SUPERVISOR

This issue appears to be especially important for younger workers and is closely related to career development and communication. This may be generational, in which case it will continue to be an important factor as Generations X and Y age. Of course the most important way to deal with this issue is in the recruitment and promotion of line managers. Making sure that managers have the information and skills necessary to meet this need is crucial. There are also indications that a slightly different, less traditional, management style will be most successful, one that involves employees in decisions by actively seeking contributions, and provides challenging and meaningful work that makes as much use as possible of employees' key skills and interests. Trust has also emerged as an important issue in this regard. Unfortunately, overall, levels of trust—at least in senior management—are currently low. If this trend continues, it is likely to have a noticeably depressive effect on job satisfaction levels.

CAREER DEVELOPMENT AND OPPORTUNITIES

Successful organizations in the future will offer many different kinds of employment as a way to attract people at different stages in life. But most employees regardless of where they are at in their lives will continue to want opportunities to develop their careers and themselves. For obvious reasons this is an issue that younger employees are more focused on. But with fewer workers, retaining and developing younger workers so that they can move through to higher levels in the organization could take on even more importance than it does today.

Today's working life can mean that a career path can change drastically even when the job remains the same, or alternatively that a career can stall even when jobs are changed frequently. The balance of responsibility for career management is certainly shifting with much more individual responsibility for career planning. At the same time detailed planning of a career over a lifetime is almost impossible since so many future jobs and opportunities do not even exist yet.

But though the individual may need to take more responsibility for his/her own career development, organizations that can offer an environment where this self-directed career management can take place within the context of the current work situation will be highly attractive to potential employees. They will expect the focus to be on developing their employability overall by offering learning opportunities and collaborative work that exposes them to wider professional networks, while at the same time enabling them to fully develop their abilities and technical skills through their everyday tasks and projects.

Job Satisfaction and Wider Political and Economic Trends

Though most job satisfaction factors are largely dependent upon the employer, some of the most important factors are closely linked to broader economic and political considerations. Probably the two most critical are job security and benefits. While job security is closely tied to economic conditions, trends in benefits—while also largely tied to the economy—can be strongly influenced by government policies.

JOB SECURITY

Only a few years ago, it appeared that we were making our way toward a free agent world of work where individual freedom to pick and choose temporary work projects and short-term employment relationships with a wide variety of employers, or "clients," had triumphed over stable employment with a single employer. Perhaps at the time it made sense, and certainly most people's career paths are not what they were 30 years ago. However, the stability and security of a permanent position continues to be what most workers seem to want right now.

According to new SHRM research on job security, HR practitioners and employees differ in their assessment of employment satisfaction with the level of job security in their current position. Employees are actually more satisfied with this aspect of their work than HR professionals believe them to be. This is good news because the more satisfied employees are with their levels of job security, the higher their levels of overall job satisfaction tend to be. The reasons for this feeling of security were for most people confidence in their own skills and abilities, the importance of their jobs to the organizations's success and their tenure at the organization.

So though financial conditions obviously have a major role to play in job security, it is not foremost in employees' minds when considering their own situation. One reason HR professionals might have a slightly different view on this is that they may have access to more information about potential job losses than the average employee does. Perhaps because of this, HR professionals are more likely to cite the financial standing of the company as one of the key determinants of a sense of job security than employees. An awareness of this dichotomy can help HR practitioners to focus on improving areas that help employees feel more secure such as providing training and learning opportunities that enable employees to feel more in control of their own skills development. These kinds of initiatives can go some way in alleviating concerns about job security even in tough economic times.

Another employment and economic trend that may have an impact on employees' sense of job security both now and in the future is the continuing decline of unions. Employees in the SHRM research felt that not being unionized was the top factor that made them feel their sense of job security was lessened. This finding may surprise most HR practitioners and it is important to be aware of. However, the relative importance of this factor may well change over time depending on how labor trends develop.

Of course, the main issue in determining job security is the labor supply overall. Here the assumption is that with the decline in available workers as the population ages, people have a greater sense of job security because there will be fewer people competing for jobs. But a severe skills shortage could have such a detrimental impact on national competitiveness that it could cause slower job growth. So though a labor shortage appears to strengthen the position of at least skilled employees, this is not a guarantee. For this reason education and skills policies are of vital importance. A largely unskilled labor force unable to meet the challenges of a global economy and to support a large cohort of retirees would severely threaten job security levels of all workers due to declining competitiveness and global market shares.

Though several of the key issues around job security are tied closely to broader external trends, there is still much that HR practitioners working closely with managers can do to raise levels of job satisfaction in relation to job security. Keeping lines of communication open between employees and management was found to be an extremely critical factor in improving employees' sense of job security. This may be one reason why employees in smaller companies have a better sense of security and hence higher job satisfaction levels. Their ability to more easily communicate with managers may make it easier for them to get accurate information. After all, feelings of insecurity frequently stem from not knowing; when employees feel as though they have reliable information, even if the news is not good they are more likely to feel a sense of control. Ultimately, it may be that a sense of control is the truly decisive issue when it comes to feeling secure in one's job.

BENEFITS AND COMPENSATION

It is no surprise that benefits and compensation play a major role in determining job satisfaction. But as everyone knows, increasingly the costs of benefits are spiraling out of control. Many companies are running large corporate pension deficits which could worsen if markets are slow to recover. A small but rising number of companies are suspending 401(k) matches. And rising health care costs are a concern for everyone. Many employers are already making adjustments in employee co-pays and many more are likely to follow. Even with these cost cutting measures, the costs of benefits are changing the makeup of compensation. Though compensation costs have remained fairly stable overall, benefits increases are around double those of wages.

Though companies are beginning to cut back on many benefits, most are mindful that they are among the most important factors in determining employee job satisfaction. If the situation remains largely as it is today, the value employees place on benefits is unlikely to decrease. If anything, the issue will become even more critical given what we know about the demographic trends outlined earlier. No one can be sure exactly how this problem will play itself out, though there will certainly be pressure from employers put on the government to produce some answers. In the meantime learning as much about how benefits and compensation impact employees' overall levels of job satisfaction is vital. For this reason, over the next year SHRM will be conducting further research into these two areas as part of its job satisfaction series of research.

Conclusion

Though many of the factors that determine job satisfaction levels are related to broader trends HR practitioners have little control over, there is still much that can be done to address the challenges brought about by a changing workforce, industrial shifts and changing working practices. Take the first step by learning about which trends and factors are most likely to impact your workforce now and in the future and moving to address those issues as much as possible. The findings of SHRM's continuing research on job satisfaction indicate that successfully addressing even a few of these issues could make a real difference in job satisfaction in your organization.

Selected Bibliography

"Americans Express Little Trust in CEOs of Large Corporations or Stockbrokers" Gallup Poll, July 2002. www.gallup.com

Baby Boomers Envision Their Retirement: An AARP Segmentation Analysis American Association of Retired Persons (AARP) & Roper Starch Worldwide, Inc., February 1999. http://research.aarp.org/econ/boomer_seg.html

Bureau of Labor Statistics (BLS) National Compensation Survey U.S. Department of Labor www.bls.gov/opub/cwc/articles.htm

Bureau of Labor Statistics (BLS) Occupational Outlook Handbook http://stats.bis.gov/oco/home.htm

Burke, Mary Elizabeth, Esen, Evren and Collison, Jessica. *SHRM® 2003 Benefits Survey*. SHRM, June 2003. www.shrm.org/surveys

Collison, Jessica. *Older Workers Survey*, SHRM/NOWCC/CED, June 2003. www.shrm.org/surveys

Esen, Evren. *Job Satisfaction Research Series: Job Satisfaction Poll.* SHRM/USA Today, December 2002. www.shrm.org/surveys

Esen, Evren. *Job Satisfaction Research Series: Job Security Survey.* SHRM, June 2003. www.shrm.org/surveys

Galther, Chris. "On the sidelines," *Boston Globe*, June 2, 2003.

Henry J. Kalser Family Foundation www.kff.org

Hewitt Associates www.hewitt.com

Hopkins, Jim. "Mars vs. Venus extends to entrepreneurs too," *USA Today*, May 19, 2003.

National Council on Aging www.ncoa.org

National Family Caregivers Association www.nfcacares.org

Tyre, Peg, McGinn, Daniel. "She Works, He Doesn't." *Newsweek*, May 12, 2003.

CHAPTER

3

STRATEGIC MANAGEMENT

Costco is an international chain of membership retail warehouse stores that offers brand-name merchandise at prices lower than those of other retailers. Costco has effectively utilized a strategy that has allowed it to produce stellar financial results relative to competitors. Although Sam's Club, another warehouse retailer and chief competitor, has 42 percent more members and 70 percent more stores, Costco's annual sales exceed those at Sam's by $1 billion. This is particularly impressive, given that Sam's is affiliated with Wal-Mart Stores.

Costco's strategy involves having a lower overhead by utilizing warehouse space and buying in bulk, both of which drive their costs down. Perhaps more important, Costco only carries approximately 4,000 SKUs (stock-keeping units) of inventory as opposed to the typical supermarket, which carries about 30,000 SKUs, or the typical discount retailer, which carriers about 40,000 SKUs. Consequently, the consumer is not overwhelmed at Costco as the organization does the comparison shopping for its customers through its buying

process and selection of merchandise. Costco also employs very limited staff outside of the functions of buying and merchandising products, further eliminating unnecessary overhead.

Costco realizes a need among busy consumers who not only want value but also want convenience. Costco's streamlined operations and willingness to accept lower profit margins on merchandise than its competitors allow them to offer goods at very competitive prices. Costco also offers convenience to time-sensitive customers by offering a variety of products including but not limited to electronics, clothing, food, furniture, jewelry, and appliances under one roof. Clearly, Costco knows its customers' needs, and its strategy is effective as it has been rewarded with increased sales and customer loyalty, reflected in its 97 percent member renewal rate.

Source: Hitt, M. A., Ireland, R. D. and Hoskisson, R. E. "Costco Companies, Inc.: The Retail Warehouse Store Revolution," *Strategic Management*, 3d ed., Cincinnati: South-Western College Publishing, 1999.

The central idea behind strategic human resource management is that all initiatives involving how people are managed need to be aligned with and in support of the organization's overall strategy. No organization can expect to be successful if it has people management systems that are at odds with its vision and mission. Many organizations suffer from the syndrome of seeking certain types of behaviors and performance from employees but have human resource management programs, particularly those related to performance feedback and compensation, that reward the opposite behaviors.[1] As a prerequisite for understanding how to strategically manage human resources (HR), it is necessary to understand the process of strategic management.

Strategic management is the process by which organizations attempt to determine what needs to be done to achieve corporate objectives and, more important, *how* these objectives are to be met. Ideally, it is a process by which senior management examines the organization and the environment in which it operates and attempts to establish an appropriate and optimal "fit" between the two to ensure the organization's success. Strategic planning is usually done over three- to five-year time horizons by senior management, with a major review of the strategic plan on an annual basis or when some significant change impacts the organization, such as a merger or acquisition, or its environment.

MODELS OF STRATEGY

There are two major models that outline the process of what strategy is and how it should be developed. The first is the industrial organization (I/O) model. This "traditional" model formed the basis of strategic management through the 1980s.[2] The I/O model argues that the primary determinant of an organization's strategy should be the external environment in which the organization operates and that such considerations have a greater influence on performance than internal decisions made by managers.[3] The I/O model assumes that the environment presents threats and opportunities to organizations, that organizations within an industry control or have equal access to resources, and that these resources are highly mobile between firms.[4] The I/O model argues that organizations should choose to locate themselves in industries that present the greatest opportunities and learn to utilize their resources to suit the needs of the environment.[5] The model further suggests that an organization can be most successful by offering goods and services at a lower cost than its competitors or by differentiating its products from those of competitors such that consumers are willing to pay a premium price.

The second major model is the resource-based model, sometimes referred to as the resource-based view (RBV) of the firm. The resource-based model argues that the organization's resources and capabilities, rather than environmental conditions, should be the basis for organizational decisions.[6] Included among these resources are an organization's human resources.[7] Organizations hence gain competitive advantage through the acquisition and value of their resources. This approach is consistent with the investment perspective of human resource management. ▼

▶ Reading 3.1, "Human Resource and the Resource Based View of the Firm," further illustrates how the resource-based view of the firm has formed the foundation for strategic human resource management. An understanding of this theoretical foundation is indispensable when attempting to implement the concepts of strategic human resource management in the workplace.

The RBV challenges the assumptions of the I/O model. The resource-based view assumes that an organization will identify and locate key valuable resources and, over time, acquire them.[8] Hence, under this model, resources may not be highly mobile across organizations as once they are acquired by a particular organization, that organization will attempt to retain those resources that are of value.[9] However, resources are only of value to an organization when they are costly to imitate and nonsubstitutable.[10]

In contrasting the two approaches, the I/O model suggests that an organization's strategy is driven by external considerations; the RBV argues that strategy should be driven by internal considerations. The I/O model argues that strategy will drive resource acquisition; the RBV argues that strategy is determined by resources. Interestingly enough, research has provided support for both positions.[11]

Sarasota Memorial Hospital

Why would a nurse pass up a job paying $2 more per hour than her current position with an employer whose facility she drives past on her way to work? For nurses at Florida's Sarasota Hospital, the answer is simple. Sarasota Hospital's strategic plan centers around a "pillars of excellence" concept, adopted after a benchmarking study that included hospitals from across the United States. Sarasota developed its five pillars of excellence—service, people, quality, finance, and growth—then did all strategic planning around them. A performance management system was designed to support the pillars; HR was given the directive to establish a strategic plan under the "people" pillar. It created a set of cross-functional teams leadership development; service recovery; measurement; reward and recognition; inpatient, outpatient, and ER patient satisfaction; and physician satisfaction. Each team engaged in process mapping and eliminated duplicated steps. Next to be cut were steps that didn't add value, followed by nonessential, "sacred cow" steps. The outcome? Both customer and employee satisfaction have increased dramatically and operations have become far more efficient. Customer satisfaction rose from the 43rd to the 97th percentile in one year. During this time, staff turnover decreased from 24 to 16 percent, with the current rate this year further reduced to 9 percent. The culture of the organization—and the ability of each employee to see her or his contribution to it—helps explain why employees are willing to drive further to work for lower pay at Sarasota Memorial.[12]

THE PROCESS OF STRATEGIC MANAGEMENT

Our examination of strategy, for the purposes of understanding the relationship between HR and strategy, will consider the premises of both the I/O and RBV models. In line with this, the process of strategic management is presented as a series of five distinct steps, as outlined in Exhibit 3-1.

Mission Statement

The first stage of strategic management is for the organization to establish or examine, if it currently has one, its mission statement. Virtually all organizations have a mission statement that, in very simple terms, explains the organization's purpose and reason for existence. Mission statements are usually very broad and generally limited to no

EXHIBIT 3-1: THE PROCESS OF STRATEGIC MANAGEMENT

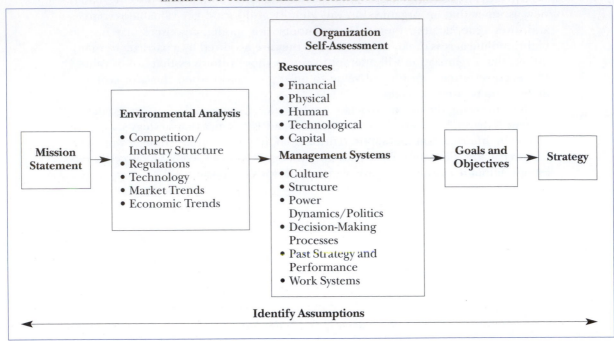

more than a couple of sentences. Although the statement appears to be simple, it is often very difficult to construct because it serves as the foundation for everything that the organization does. It requires those formulating it to have a clear and articulated understanding and vision of the organization and to be in consensus on what the organization is all about and why it exists in the first place.

Exhibit 3-2 presents the mission statement for Solectron. Established in 1977, Solectron is the world's largest electronics manufacturing services organization, offering supply-chain management systems for many of the world's leading electronics equipment manufacturers. Solectron has received more than 200 quality and service awards and was the first company to win the Malcolm Baldrige National Quality Award twice.[13]

Analysis of Environment

Upon establishing a mission statement, the next step is to analyze the external environment in which the organization operates consistent with the I/O model of strategic management. Decision makers need to analyze a variety of different components of the external organization, identify key "players" within those domains, and be very cognizant of both threats and opportunities within the environment.

EXHIBIT 3-2: SOLECTRON MISSION STATEMENT

"Our mission is to provide worldwide responsiveness to our customers by offering the highest quality, lowest total cost, customized, integrated, design, supply-chain and manufacturing solutions through long-term partnerships based on integrity and ethical business practices."

Among the critical components of the external environment are competition and industry structure, government regulations, technology, market trends, and economic trends, as indicated in Exhibit 3-1.[14]

In examining competition and industry structure, critical issues that need to be identified include who the chief competitors are, the means by which they compete, where "power" lies within the industry, barriers to entry, opportunities to acquire and merge with other organizations, critical success factors within the industry, and industry "maturity level." In addition, consideration must be paid to industries that produce complementary or substitute goods or services that may impact the demand for the organization's output.

In examining government regulation, critical issues that need to be identified include the scope of laws and regulations that may impact what the organization does. This involves everything from federal laws regulating the industry and the employment relationship to local zoning ordinances that may affect the size, scope, and location of operations. A significant number of strategic human resource management decisions that must be made have to be done within the context of federal, state, and local labor laws. Similarly, organizations need to establish beneficial relationships with agencies that enforce these laws and legislators who propose, pass, amend, and repeal such laws.

The technological sector of the environment involves looking at automation processes, new materials and techniques for producing goods and services, and improved products and special features. It also involves an assessment of how to obtain new technology and the decision as to whether the organization wants to pioneer new technology or allow others to do so and then attempt to copy it.

Analyzing market trends involves examining who existing customers are, their needs and wants, and how well satisfied they are. It also involves looking at potential customers who don't utilize the product or service and determining how existing products and services can be adopted or modified to address the needs of different target groups of consumers and developing strategies to increase the rate or level of usage by current customers. It also involves examining demographic, psychographic, and lifestyle issues among consumers, such as family status, age, interests, residence, education, and income level and determining shifts that are taking place in society relative to these areas.

Analyzing economic trends involves forecasting the condition and direction of the national and local economy. Although it is critical to remember that any kind of forecasting is not an exact science and that no one can accurately predict the future, organizations need to plan for what may happen in the economy that can have a significant impact on operations. Interest rates, levels of inflation and unemployment, international exchange rates, fiscal and monetary policy, and levels of GNP and economic growth clearly will impact what an organization will be able to accomplish; these need to be factored in to any assessment of future direction of the firm.

Organization Self-Assessment

Once an organization has scanned and assessed its external environment and identified any threats and opportunities, it then turns to the third stage of strategic management: assessing the internal environment of the organization. In this stage, the key outcome is for decision makers to identity the organization's primary strengths and weaknesses and find ways to capitalize on the strengths and improve or minimize the weaknesses, as espoused by the resource-based view of strategic management. This requires the organization to examine both its resources and its internal management systems, as illustrated in Exhibit 3-1.

RESOURCES

Financial resources can significantly affect an organization's competitive advantage. An organization that has the ability to generate internal funds and/or borrow significant sums is able to convert these funds into other assets. Virtually all components of an organization's business can be purchased, so the presence or absence of financial resources can have a significant impact on an organization's performance.

Physical resources include the actual equipment and machinery owned or leased, as well as the location of the business and its proximity to customers, labor, raw materials, and transportation. Physical location is clearly a more important resource in some industries than others. A large manufacturing facility has far different choices and considerations with its physical resources than does a small electronic-commerce business.

Human resources include not only the sum of technical knowledge of employees but also their personal traits, including commitment, loyalty, judgment, and motivation. An organization is only as strong or as weak as its employees, and the skills, backgrounds, and motivation these employees bring to their jobs will therefore be a key factor in the organization's overall performance. The organization also needs to consider the kinds of obligations it has to employees in the form of contracts or agreements to continue to employ them and the extent that it wishes to enter into such agreements in the future.

Technological resources include the processes by which the organization produces its goods and services. The technology used by an organization can be a major influence on its cost structures and measures of efficiency. A large number of organizations leverage this resource to their advantage by obtaining patents, trademarks, or copyrights. The extent to which an organization is able to safeguard its production processes can be a tremendous resource.

Capital resources include all other items of value including brand names, reputations with customers, relationships with key constituents in the environment, and goodwill. Many items that can be grouped here are intangibles that don't show up on an organization's financial statements. It has been argued that the more unobservable or intangible a resource is, the more sustainable an advantage it might supply.[15]

MANAGEMENT SYSTEMS

In assessing culture, an organization needs to understand the core values and philosophies that guide its day-to-day activities. Many aspects of culture are covert and not clearly articulated but rather assumptions that individuals in the organization make about the company. It is critical, as part of the strategic planning process, that elements of culture be identified and that an understanding be achieved of how these elements of culture influence behavior and impact overall performance.

There is no standard type of organization structure or way to draw up an organization chart. However, certain types of structural configurations may be more suited to certain types of conditions than others.[16] Organization structure has a significant impact on how work is carried out, how groups and departments interact with each other, and where accountability for performance lies. Certain types of structures are most conducive to certain strategic objectives as well. Essentially, an organization's structure can act as a catalyst for achieving certain strategic objectives or as an impediment to performance.

Assessing power dynamics and politics allows an organization to see who *really* controls what happens in an organization. Power is not necessarily related to hierarchical position; those in low-level positions can often obtain significant amounts of power and influence behaviors and activities of others in organizations. Politics is a process by which people utilize the power they have in order to influence outcomes in a manner that they desire. How power and politics are utilized in an organization can allow it to achieve its objectives or be self-serving obstacles to success.

Decision-making processes can be a competitive advantage to an organization or a weight that inhibits timely, effective action. In assessing decision making, one needs to look at whether decisions are made by individuals or groups; who gets involved in decision making; how information is collected, distributed, and made available to which individuals in the organization; how long it takes for decisions to be made; and the information criteria that are employed in reaching decisions. These assessments can allow the organization to see whether its decision-making processes promote or inhibit effective performance as defined by the organization's strategic objectives.

An examination of the organization's past strategy and performance is critical to understanding its internal environment. By looking at past strategic initiatives and measuring the organization's success in meeting them, an organization can attempt to determine how and why it was or was not successful in the past, reexamine the processes that facilitated or hindered its success, and take action that attempts to capitalize on its successes and remedy its shortcomings.

Finally, it is critical to examine the organization's work systems. Work systems involve the design of jobs and allocation of responsibilities to assist an organization in meeting its objectives. Considerations that need to be addressed include the "fit" between job requirements and employee skills and the extent to which changes in how work is done can be met by either providing current employees with further training or seeking applicants from outside the organization. The organization needs to ensure that is has designed work systems in an optimal manner to allow the organization to pursue its current and future objectives.

Establishing Goals and Objectives

Once the organization has established and articulated its mission, assessed its external environment, and identified internal resources and management systems that affect its performance, it is then ready to establish its goals and objectives for the next time period. Goals should be specific and measurable; in fact, at the same time they are established, decision makers should also identify *how* performance toward these goals will be measured and evaluated. In the planning process, measurement of goals is often overlooked. It serves little purpose to set goals and subsequently have no means to measure performance toward them.

Goals also need to be flexible. Because the whole process of setting goals involves dealing with the future and anticipating what might or might not happen, realistic goals should *not* be "carved in stone." What will actually happen in the external environment may likely be different from that which was assumed or anticipated when the goals were set. To maintain goals that were set under assumed conditions that have not materialized is unrealistic and impractical. Goals can be adjusted upward as well as downward in response to how events in the environment have unfolded. For this reason, some organizations, particularly those that operate in highly volatile environments, rely more on a strategic vision for the organization over the longer term. Visions are generally less detailed and formal than strategic plans but can still guide managers at all levels in their day-to-day decision making.

Setting Strategy

Once goals have been defined, an organization is then ready to determine its strategy. Strategy, very simply, is *how* the organization intends to achieve its goals. The means it will use, the courses of action it will take, and how it will generally operate and compete constitute the organization's strategy.

The strategic choices an organization makes then need to be incorporated into a general human resource strategy, which will be discussed in subsequent chapters. Ideally, this HR strategy will serve as a framework by which the organization can develop a consistent and aligned set of practices, policies, and programs that will allow employees to achieve the organization's objectives. Ideally, HR strategy will serve to ensure a "fit" between corporate strategy and individual HR programs and policies. It is important to remember that there is no one "model" way to manage human resources strategically because every organization is different. One organization shouldn't necessarily copy the management systems of another organization, even a successful organization that operates in the same industry. Every organization is unique, and any "best practices" that are considered or even adopted should be evaluated within the context of the specific organization in which they are being implemented.

First Tennessee National Corp.

Eyebrows were raised when First Tennessee National, a bank holding company and financial service organization, hired an executive who had a background in finance to head its HR function. HR was given the directive to not only maximize financial performance but also to demonstrate to shareholders the value-added benefits of HR programs and policies. This decision resulted in a strategic partnership between HR and finance that has greatly aided the profitability of First Tennessee. Studies were undertaken that aligned the organization's reward system with business strategy. Several years of data were mined that related HR activities to employee performance, retention, market share, profitability, customer value, and loyalty. Relationships between tenure, retention, and team performance were established. As a result, more visible career paths for high-potential and high-performing employees were established to aid in retention and, ultimately, profitability.[17]

CORPORATE STRATEGIES

Different types of organization strategies will require different types of HR programs. In essence, there are three different generic organization strategies,[18] and each would require a significantly different approach to managing people.

The first strategy is growth. Growth can allow an organization to reap the benefits of economies of scale, to enhance its position in the industry vis-à-vis its competitors, and to provide more opportunities for professional development and advancement to its employees. Growth can be pursued internally or externally. Growth can be achieved internally by further penetrating existing markets, developing new markets, or developing new products or services to sell in existing and/or new markets. Chief strategic HR issues associated with a growth strategy involve adequate planning to ensure that new employees are hired and trained in a timely manner to handle market demand, alerting current employees about promotion and development opportunities, and ensuring that quality and performance standards are maintained during periods of rapid growth.

External growth comes from acquiring other organizations. This is commonly done with competitors or with other organizations that might supply raw materials or be part of the organization's distribution chain (called *vertical integration*). There are two key strategic HR issues associated with external growth. The first involves merging dissimilar HR systems from different organizations. It is probable that two different systems existed for staffing, compensation, performance management, and employee relations, and the appropriate new system may or may not be one of the previous systems or even a hybrid of such. The process may involve starting from scratch and establishing an entirely new HR strategy for the "new" organization. The key factor to be considered here is whether the organization's overall strategy has changed as a result of the merger or acquisition and how this strategy changes.

The second strategic HR issue involves the fact that mergers and acquisitions usually result in the dismissal of employees. Critical decisions will need to be made concerning who will be retained and who will be let go, and a well-developed retention program should be developed that is cognizant of all legal obligations to employees that the organization might have.

The second organizational strategy involves stability or simply "maintaining the status quo." An organization pursuing this strategy may see very limited opportunities in its environment and decide to continue operations as is. The critical strategic HR issue for this type of organization would be the fact that an organization that is not growing will also be limited in the opportunities it is able to offer to its employees. There may be fewer opportunities for upward mobility, and employees may decide to leave and pursue opportunities with other employers. Hence, it is critical for the employer to identify key employees and develop a specific retention strategy to assist in keeping them.

The third type of overall strategy is a turnaround or retrenchment strategy. Here, the organization decides to downsize or streamline its operations in an attempt to fortify its basic competency. Often, a large organization will grow to the point where it becomes inefficient, particularly relative to smaller competitors, and finds itself unable to respond quickly to changes in the marketplace. Decision makers may see the environment as offering far more threats than opportunities and the organization's weaknesses as exceeding its strengths. Therefore, the organization tries to retool itself to capitalize on its existing strengths and remain solvent. In a retrenchment strategy, a key issue that needs to be addressed is cost-cutting; in many organizations, particularly service organizations, payroll is the chief expense. As with an acquisition strategy, the organization must be careful to adhere to all laws that regulate the employment relationship in selection of individuals to be terminated.

At the same time, the organization also needs to develop a strategy to manage the "survivors." This is, without question, one of the most neglected aspects of downsizing in organizations. It is often assumed by managers that those whose jobs are spared will be relieved that their employment is maintained and will consequently be grateful and return to their jobs motivated and productive. However, the opposite is often true. Many organizations announce the intention to lay off employees well in advance of the actual notification of individually affected employees. As a result, many of these "survivors" may have been working for several months in fear that their employment was in jeopardy. When their jobs are retained, they then find many friends and coworkers, with whom they may have worked alongside for many years, gone. They are often asked to assume additional job responsibilities of those who have departed, generally without any additional compensation. Further, they may feel that during any subsequent layoffs, they may not be as "fortunate" and lose their jobs. Boosting the morale of these employees is a significant HR challenge. Many are demoralized, depressed, significantly stressed, and less loyal to their employer. However, the organization now depends on these employees for high performance more than it ever did. Consequently, these individuals will directly affect whether the organization stays in business.

BUSINESS UNIT STRATEGIES

There is a significant and growing trend for larger organizations to break their operations into smaller, more manageable, more responsive units. Subdivisions are often established by product or service, customer group or geographic region. In addition to the general, corporate-level strategies explained earlier, many individual business units or product, service, or customer divisions develop a more specific strategy to fit the circumstances of their marketplace and competitive environment. Consequently, there are three different business unit strategies that require correspondingly different strategic approaches to HR.[19]

The first of these business unit strategies is cost leadership. An organization pursuing this strategy attempts to increase its efficiency, cut costs, and pass the savings on to the consumer. It assumes that the price elasticity of demand for its products is high or, in other words, that a small change in price will significantly affect customer demand. It also assumes that consumers are more price sensitive than brand loyal or, in other words, they see the product or service of each organization as being nondistinguishable. Suave has successfully utilized this strategy in the shampoo market. Knowing that a large segment of consumers are price sensitive in shampoo purchase decisions has allowed Suave to compete quite successfully in a very competitive industry.

This type of organization would center its HR strategy around short-term, rather than long-term, performance measures that focused on *results*. Because efficiency is the norm, job assignments would be more specialized, but employees might be cross-trained during slack or downtime periods. Cost-cutting measures might also result in developing incentives for employees to leave the organization, particularly higher salaried managerial employees.

The second business unit strategy is differentiation. An organization pursuing this strategy distinguishes its product or service from those of competitors or, at least, attempts to make consumers *perceive* that there are differences. This allows the organization to demand a premium price over the price charged by competitors and attempts to gain the loyalty of consumers toward a particular brand. Nike has successfully utilized this strategy to gain tremendous loyalty among its customers. Whether there are actual or perceived performance benefits for athletes or some status identification with the brand name, many consumers will not wear any other brand of athletic footwear.

With this type of strategy, creativity and innovation in product design or service delivery are important in developing such a distinction. Consequently, this type of strategy would involve the organization offering incentives and compensation for creativity. Measures for performance might be more long term in establishing and building brand names. Staffing may focus more on external hiring and recruiting individuals who bring a fresh, unique, outside perspective to the organization rather than being bound by existing ways of doing things.

The third business unit strategy is a focus strategy. An organization pursuing this strategy realizes that different segments of the market have different needs and attempts to satisfy one particular group. This might involve, for example, a restaurant that targets families, a clothing store that targets larger individuals, or a retail business that targets a particular ethnic group. Big 'N' Tall clothing stores for men and Dress Barn for women have successfully used this strategy to gain a loyal following among an often neglected group of consumers.

The key strategic HR issue here is ensuring that employees are very aware of what makes the particular market unique. Training and ensuring customer satisfaction are

EXHIBIT 3-3: DYER AND HOLDER'S TYPOLOGY OF STRATEGIES

	Logics		
Goals	**Investment**	**Inducement**	**Involvement**
Contribution	High initiative and creativity; high performance expectations; some flexibility	Some initiative and creativity; very high performance standards; modest flexibility	Very high initiative and creativity; very high performance expectations; high flexibility; self-managed
Composition	Comfortable head count (core and buffer); high skill mix; moderate staff	Lean head count (core and buffer); low skill mix; minimal staff	Comfortable head count; protected core; high skill mix; minimal staff
Competence	High	Adequate	Very high
Commitment	High; identification with company	High; instrumental	Very high; strong identification with work, team, and company
Practices			
Staffing	Careful selection; extensive career development; some flexibility; minimal layoffs	Careful selection; few career options; use of temps; minimal layoffs	Very careful selection; some career development; extreme flexibility; minimal (or no) layoffs
Development	Extensive; continuous learning	Minimal	Extensive; continuous learning
Rewards	Tall structure; competitive, fixed, job based, merit; many benefits	Flat structure; high, variable, piece rate; profit sharing; minimal benefits	Flat structure; high, partially variable, skill and competency based; gain sharing; flexible benefits
Work system	Broad jobs; employee initiative; some groups	Narrow jobs; employee paced; individualized	Enriched jobs; self-managed work teams
Supervision	Extensive, supportive	Minimal, directive	Minimal, facilitative
Employee relations	Much communication; high voice; high due process; high employee assistance	Some communication; some voice; egalitarian	Open and extensive communication; high voice; some due process; egalitarian, some employee assistance
Labor relations	Nonissue	Union avoidance or conflict	Union avoidance and/or cooperation
Government relations	Overcompliance	Compliance	Compliance

Source: Dyer and Holder (1988, pp. 1–21).

critical factors in this strategy. An organization often attempts to hire employees who are part of the target market and therefore are able to empathize with customers. A large woman would probably be more comfortable dealing with a salesperson in a clothing store who was also large than one who was slim and svelte.

Another framework developed for examining business unit strategy depicts strategies by "logics of control" and identifies three separate strategies: an investment logic, an inducement logic, and an involvement logic.[20] An investment logic is adopted by organizations concerned with adaptability to changing market conditions. Consistent with the I/O model, it bases strategic decisions on external considerations and utilizes very loose control of day-to-day operations. A minimum of formal rules and procedures facilitates adaptability and change in response to the organization's environment. Jobs and responsibilities are broadly defined, and compensation programs encourage and reward initiative and creativity.

An inducement logic is adopted by organizations concerned largely with cost containment and efficiency. Day-to-day management decisions are governed by tight control mechanisms in the form of budgets and special reports. Job responsibilities are narrowly defined to promote maximum efficiency in operations. Loyalty and commitment are rewarded to discourage excessive amounts of turnover.

An involvement logic is adopted by organizations that have a dual strategy of cost containment and innovation. This type of organization tends to adopt management practices that have some consistency with both the investment and inducement logics, as illustrated in Exhibit 3-3. Some systems are consistent with those of the investment logic while other are consistent with those of the inducement logic.

CONCLUSION

Many organizations have difficulty achieving their strategic objectives because employees don't really understand these are or how their jobs contribute to overall organizational effectiveness. Fewer than 50 percent of employees understand their organization's strategy and the steps that are being taken toward fulfilling the organization's mission. Further, only 35 percent see the connection between their job performance and their compensation. Effective strategic management requires not only that the organization's strategic objectives be communicated to employees but that there be a link between employee productivity—relative to these objectives—and the organization's reward system, as will be discussed in Chapter 10. Organizations that communicate their objectives to employees and tie in rewards with objectives-driven performance have much higher shareholder rates of return than organizations that do not.[21]

A critical lesson to be learned is that the development of an organization's strategy is a process unique to every individual organization. The factors identified in Exhibit 3-1 can vary dramatically from one organization to another. Even organizations in the same industry can have radically different strategies. ▼▼

The process of setting an organization's strategy should be the driving force in the establishment of all HR policies, programs, and practices. ▼▼▼ A strategic approach to

▶▶ Reading 3.2, "Distinctive Human Resources Are Firms' Core Competencies," illustrates a number of pairs of high-performing organizations that compete in the same industry, yet utilize vastly different strategies for managing their operations and their people. The success of each organization can be traced to the fact that its people management systems clearly support its mission and strategy.

▶▶▶ Reading 3.3, "Strategic Human Resources Management: Linking the People with the Strategic Needs of the Business," provides some examples and insights as to how this can be accomplished.

HR provides an organization with three critical benefits: (1) it facilitates the development of a high-quality workforce through its focus on the types of people and skills needed; (2) it facilitates cost-effective utilization of labor, particularly in service industries where labor is generally the greatest cost; and (3) it facilitates planning and assessment of environmental uncertainty and adaptation to the forces that impact the organization, as will be further discussed in Chapter 4.

CRITICAL THINKING

1. Compare and contrast the premises and assumptions of the industrial organization and resource-based models of strategic planning. What benefits does each model offer that aid in strategic planning?

2. Identify the HR challenges associated with each of the three major corporate strategies.

3. Identify the HR challenges associated with each of the three major business unit strategies.

4. Critique the model presented in Exhibit 3-1. What benefits can be gained from this process? What shortcomings exist within the model?

5. Examine your current organization's process of strategic management. How effective is this process relative to the organization's performance? What factors contribute to its effectiveness or ineffectiveness?

Reading 3.1

6. Trace the development of strategic human resource management from the resource-based view of the firm. How does the resource-based view of the firm facilitate and inhibit the actual practice of strategic human resource management?

Reading 3.2

7. Examine each of the pairs of organizations the authors discuss. Determine whether their strategies are based on I/O or RBV assumptions. What does this imply about strategic planning in general?

Reading 3.3

8. Examine the process by which Grand Union transformed its business. Do you feel that McDonald's could utilize such a process? Should McDonald's utilize such a process? Why or why not?

EXPERIENTIAL EXERCISES

1. Obtain a copy of a publicly held organization's most recent annual report. To what is its performance for the past year attributed? What strategy does it seem to be following and how integrated with this strategy do the operating units appear to be?

2. Apply the I/O and RBV models of planning to your college or university. What are the key factors in the environment that impact the school's performance? What are its key resources, and how can they best be deployed?

INTERNET EXERCISES

1. Select a particular industry (i.e., pharmaceuticals, shipping, auto, or manufacturing) and identify at least three major competitors in that industry. Visit their Web sites and identify key strategic issues within the industry as well as key strategic issues for the individual firms.

CHAPTER REFERENCES

1. For a discussion of this, see Kerr, S. "On the Folly of Rewarding A, While Hoping for B," *Academy of Management Journal*, 18, 1975, pp. 769–783.
2. Barney, J. B. "Firm Resources and Sustained Competitive Advantage," *Journal of Management*, 17, 1991, pp. 99–120.
3. Schendel, D. "Introduction to Competitive Organizational Behavior: Toward an Organizationally Based Theory of Competitive Advantage," *Strategic Management Journal*, 15 (2), Special Winter Issue, 1994.
4. Seth, A. and Thomas, H. "Theories of the Firm: Implications for Strategy Research," *Journal of Management Studies*, 31, 1994, pp. 165–191.
5. Hitt, M. A., Ireland, R. D. and Hoskisson, R. E. *Strategic Management: Competitiveness and Globalization*, 3d ed., Cincinnati: South-Western College Publishing, 1998, 19.
6. Cool, K. and Dierckz, I. "Commentary: Investments in Strategic Assets; Industry and Firm-Level Perspectives," in Shrivastava, P., Huff, A., and Dutton, J. (eds.), *Advances in Strategic Management* 10A, Greenwich, CT: JAI Press, 1994, pp. 35–44.
7. Barney, op. cit.; Hitt et al., op. cit., pp. 1–41.
8. Barney, op. cit., pp. 113–115.
9. Hitt et. al., op. cit., p. 21.
10. Barney, op. cit.
11. McGahan, A. M. and Porter, M. E. "How Much Does Industry Matter, Really?" *Strategic Management Journal*, 18, 1997, Special Summer Issue, pp. 15–30; Henderson, R. and Mitchell, W. "The Interactions of Organizational and Competitive Influences on Strategy and Performance," *Strategic Management Journal*, 18, Special Summer Issue, 1997, pp. 5–14.
12. Heuring, L. H. "Patients First," *HR Magazine*, July 2003, pp. 65–69.
13. Taken from http://www.solectron.com.
14. For an excellent discussion of the components of an organization's external environment, see Hitt, op. cit., Chapter 2, pp.42–81.
15. Godfrey, P. C. and Hill, C. W. L. "The Problem of Unobservables in Strategic Management Research," *Strategic Management Journal*, 16, 1995, pp. 519–533.
16. For a complete discussion of the different forms of organization structure and their appropriateness, see Daft, R. L. *Organization Theory*, 6th ed., Cincinnati: South-Western College Publishing, 1998, pp. 200–233.
17. Bates, S. "First Tennessee—Talking to the People," *HR Magazine*, 48, (9), September 2003, p. 48.
18. This typology was developed by Michael E. Porter. *Competitive Strategy*, New York: Free Press, 1980.
19. This typology was developed by William F. Glueck. *Business Policy: Strategy Formulation and Management Action*, New York: McGraw-Hill, 1976.
20. Dyer, L. and Holder, G. W. "A Strategic Perspective of Human Resources Management," in Dyer, L. and Holder, G. W. (eds.), *Human Resources Management: Evolving Roles and Responsibilities*, Washington, DC: American Society for Personnel Administration, 1988, pp. 1–45.
21. Bates, S. "Murky Corporate Goals Can Undermine Recovery," *HR Magazine*, November 2002, p. 14.

Human Resources and the Resource-Based View of the Firm

Patrick M. Wright, Benjamin B. Dunford, and Scott A. Snell, *Journal of Management*

1.   Introduction

The human resource function has consistently faced a battle in justifying its position in organizations (Drucker and Stewart). In times of plenty, firms easily justify expenditures on training, staffing, reward, and employee involvement systems, but when faced with financial difficulties, such HR systems fall prey to the earliest cutbacks.

The advent of the sub field of strategic human resource management (SHRM), devoted to exploring HR's role in supporting business strategy, provided one avenue for demonstrating its value to the firm. Walker's (1978) call for a link between strategic planning and human resource planning signified the conception of the field of SHRM, but its birth came in the early 1980s with Devanna, Fombrum and Tichy's (1984) article devoted to extensively exploring the link between business strategy and HR. Since then, SHRM's evolution has consistently followed (by a few years) developments within the field of strategic management. For example, Miles and Snow's (1978) organizational types were later expanded to include their associated HR systems (Miles & Snow, 1984), Porter's (1980) model of generic strategies was later used by SHRM researchers to delineate the specific HR strategies that one would expect to observe under each of them (Jackson & Schuler, 1987; Wright & Snell, 1991).

Though the field of SHRM was not directly born of the resource-based view (RBV), it has clearly been instrumental to its development. This was largely because of the RBV shifting emphasis in the strategy literature away from external factors (such as industry position) toward internal firm resources as sources of competitive advantage (Hoskisson, Hitt, Wan & Yiu, 1999). Growing acceptance of internal resources as sources of competitive advantage brought legitimacy to HR's assertion that people are strategically important to firm success. Thus, given both the need to concep-

tually justify the value of HR and the propensity for the SHRM field to borrow concepts and theories from the broader strategy literature, the integration of the RBV of the firm into the SHRM literature should surprise no one.

However, two developments not as easily predicted have emerged over the past 10 years. First, the popularity of the RBV within the SHRM litertture as a foundation for both theoretical and empirical examinations has probably far surpassed what anyone expected (McMahan, Virick & Wright, 1999). Second, the applications and implications of the RBV within the strategy literature have led to an increasing convergence between the fields of strategic management and SHRM (Snell, Shadur & Wright, 2001). Within the strategic literature, the RBV has helped to put "people" (or a firm's human resources) on the radar screen. Concepts such as knowledge (Argote; Grant and Liebeskind), dynamic capability (Eisenhardt and Teece), learning organizations (Fiol and Fisher), and leadership (Finkelstein; Norburn and Thomas) as sources of competitive advantage turn attention toward the intersection of strategy and HR issues.

The purpose of this paper is to examine how the RBV has been applied to the theoretical and empirical research base of SHRM, and to explore how it has provided an accessible bridge between the fields of strategy and HR. To accomplish this, we will first review the specific benchmark articles that have applied the RBV to theoretical development of SHRM. We will then discuss some of the empirical SHRM studies that have used the RBV as the basis for exploring the relationship between HR and firm performance. Finally, we will identify some of the major topic areas that illustrate the convergence of the fields of strategy and HR, and propose some future directions for how such a convergence can provide mutual benefits.

2. Applying the RBV to SHRM

While based in the work of Penrose (1959) and others, Wernerfelt's (1984) articulation of the resource-based view of the firm certainly signified the first coherent statement of the theory. This initial statement of the theory served as the foundation that was extended by others such as Rumelt and Barney, and Dierickx and Cool (1989). However, Barney's (1991) specification of the characteristics necessary for a sustainable competitive advantage seemed to be a seminal article in popularizing the theory within the strategy and other literatures. In this article he noted that resources which are rare, valuable, inimitable, and nonsubstitutable can provide sources of sustainable competitive advantages.

Although debates about the RBV continue to wage (e.g., whether the RBV is a theory, whether it is tautological, etc. Priem; Priem and Barney) even its critics have acknowledged the "breadth of its diffusion" in numerous strategic research programs (Priem & Butler, 2001a, p. 25–26). With its emphasis on internal firm resources as sources of competitive advantage, the popularity of the RBV in the SHRM literature has been no exception. Since Barney's (1991) article outlining the basic theoretical model and criteria for sources of sustainable competitive advantage, the RBV has become by far, the theory most often used within SHRM, both in the development of theory and the rationale for empirical research (McMahan, Virick & Wright, 1999).

3. RBV and SHRM Theory

As part of *Journal of Management*'s Yearly Review of Management issue, Wright and McMahan (1992) reviewed the theoretical perspectives that had been applied to SHRM. They presented the RBV as one perspective that provided a rationale for how a firm's human resources could provide a potential source of sustainable competitive advantage. This was based largely on what was, at the time a working paper, but later became the Wright, McMahan and McWilliams (1994) paper described later.

Almost simultaneously, Cappelli and Singh (1992), within the industrial relations literature, provided an examination of the implications of the RBV on SHRM. Specifically, they noted that most models of SHRM based on fit assume that (1) a certain business strategy demands a unique set of behaviors

and attitudes from employees and (2) certain human resource policies produce a unique set of responses from employees. They further argued that many within strategy have implicitly assumed that it is easier to rearrange complementary assets/resources given a choice of strategy than it is to rearrange strategy given a set of assets/resources, even though empirical research seems to imply the opposite. Thus, they proposed that the resource-based view might provide a theoretical rationale for why HR could have implications for strategy formulation as well as implementation.

Shortly thereafter, two articles came out arguing almost completely opposite implications of the potential for HR practices to constitute a source of sustainable competitive advantage. Wright et al. (1994), mentioned above, distinguished between the firm's human resources (i.e., the human capital pool) and HR practices (those HR tools used to manage the human capital pool). In applying the concepts of value, rareness, inimitability, and substitutability, they argued the HR practices could not form the basis for sustainable competitive advantage since any individual HR practice could be easily copied by competitors. Rather, they proposed that the human capital pool (a highly skilled and highly motivated workforce) had greater potential to constitute a source of sustainable competitive advantage. These authors noted that to constitute a source of competitive advantage, the human capital pool must have both high levels of skill and a willingness (i.e., motivation) to exhibit productive behavior. This skill/behavior distinction appears as a rather consistent theme within this literature.

In contrast, Lado and Wilson (1994) proposed that a firm's HR practices could provide a source of sustainable competitive advantage. Coming from the perspective of exploring the role of HR in influencing the competencies of the firm, they suggested that HR systems (as opposed to individual practices) can be unique, causally ambiguous and synergistic in how they enhance firm competencies, and thus could be inimitable. Thus, whereas Wright et al. (1994) argued for imitability of individual practices, Lado and Wilson noted that the system of HR practices, with all the complementarities and interdependencies among the set of practices, would be impossible to imitate. This point of view seems well accepted within the current SHRM paradigm (Snell, Youndt & Wright, 1996).

Boxall (1996) further built upon the RBV/SHRM paradigm, suggesting that human resource advantage (i.e., the superiority of one firm's HRM over another) consists of two parts. First, human capital advantage refers to the potential to capture a stock of exceptional human talent "latent with productive possibilities" (p. 67). Human process advantage can be understood as a "function of causally ambiguous, socially complex, historically evolved processes such as learning, cooperation, and innovation." (p. 67). Boxall (1998) then expanded upon this basic model presenting a more comprehensive model of strategic HRM. He argued that one major task of organizations is the management of mutuality (i.e., alignment of interests) to create a talented and committed workforce. It is the successful accomplishment of this task that results in a human capital advantage. A second task is to develop employees and teams in such a way as to create an organization capable of learning within and across industry cycles. Successful accomplishment of this task results in the organizational process advantage.

Most recently, Lepak and Snell (1999) presented an architectural approach to SHRM based at least partly in the RBV. They proposed that within organizations, considerable variance exists with regard to both the uniqueness and value of skills. Juxtaposing these two dimensions, they built a 2×2 matrix describing different combinations with their corresponding employment relationships and HR systems. The major implication of that model was that some employee groups are more instrumental to competitive advantage than others. As a consequence, they are likely to be managed differently. While the premise of an architectural perspective is rooted in extant research in HR (cf., Baron; Osterman and Tsui) and strategy (cf., Matusik & Hill, 1998). Lepak and Snell (1999) helped SHRM researchers recognize that real and valid variance exists in HR practices within the organization, and looking for one HR strategy may mask important differences in the types of human capital available to firms (cf. Truss & Gratton, 1994).

In essence, the conceptual development within the field of SHRM has leveraged the RBV to achieve some consensus on the areas within the human resource architecture in which sustainable competitive advantage might be achieved. Figure 1 depicts these components.

First, the human capital pool refers to the stock of employee skills that exist within a firm at any given point in time. Theorists focus on the need to develop a pool of human capital that has either higher levels of skills (general and/or firm specific), or achieving a better alignment between the skills represented in the firm and those required by its strategic intent. The actual stock of human capital can and does

FIGURE 1: A MODEL OF THE BASIC STRATEGIC HRM COMPONENTS

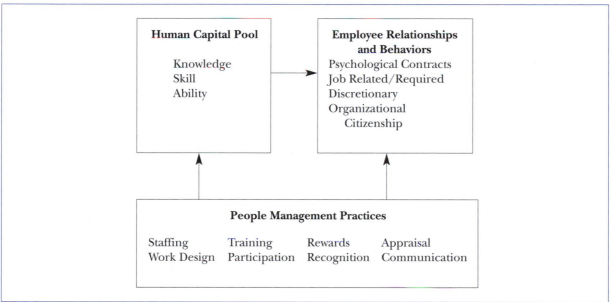

change over time, and must constantly be monitored for its match with the strategic needs of the firm.

Second, an increasing consensus is emerging among researchers that employee behavior is an important independent component of SHRM. Distinct from skills of the human capital pool, employee behavior recognizes individuals as cognitive and emotional beings who possess free will. This free will enables them to make decisions regarding the behaviors in which they will engage. This is an important, if subtle, distinction. A basic premise of human capital theory is that firms do not own it; individuals do. Firms may have access to valuable human capital, but either through the poor design of work or the mismanagement of people, may not adequately deploy it to achieve strategic impact. For example, MacDuffie (1995) focuses on the concept of discretionary behavior. Discretionary behavior recognizes that even within prescribed organizational roles, employees exhibit discretion that may have either positive or negative consequences to the firm. Thus, a machine operator who hears a "pinging" has discretion to simply run the machine until something breaks or to fix the problem immediately, and thus save significant downtime. Similar to March and Simon's (1958) concept of "the decision to contribute" SHRM's focus on discretionary behavior recognizes that competitive advantage can only be achieved if the members of the human capital pool individually and collectively choose to engage in behavior that benefits the firm.

Finally, while many authors describe HR practice or High Performance Work Systems, a broader conceptualization might simply be the people management system. By using the term *system*, we turn focus to the importance of understanding the multiple practices that impact employees (Wright & Boswell, in press) rather than single practices. By using the term *people*, rather than HR, we expand the relevant practices to those beyond the control of the HR function, such as communication (both upward and downward), work design, culture, leadership, and a host of others that impact employees and shape their competencies, cognitions, and attitudes. Effective systems for managing people evolve through unique historical paths and maintain interdependence among the components that competitors cannot easily imitate (Becker & Huselid, 1998). The important aspect of these systems is that they are the

means through which the firm continues to generate advantage over time as the actual employees flow in and out and the required behaviors change because of changing environmental and strategic contingencies. It is through the people management system that the firm influences the human capital pool and elicits the desired employee behavior. This dynamic process, while not depicted in the figure, will be taken up later in the paper.

The implications of our figure and this model are that while a firm might achieve a superior position in any one of the three, sustainable competitive advantage requires superior positions on all three.

This is because of three reasons. First, the value that skills and behaviors can generate requires that they be paired together (i.e., without skills, certain behaviors cannot be exhibited, and that the value of skills can only be realized through exhibited behavior). Second, it is difficult to conceive of a firm's human capital pool containing both the highest levels of skills and exhibiting optimal behaviors in the absence of an aligned people management system. Finally, the effects of the people management systems are subject to time compression diseconomies (Dierickx & Cool, 1989). While these systems might be immediately imitated, a significant time lag will occur before their impact is realized, thus making it costly or difficult for competitors to imitate the value generated by the human capital pool. We will later build upon this model to explore how this fits within the larger organization.

3.1. SUMMARY OF RBV-BASED CONCEPTUAL LITERATURE

In summary, the RBV has proven to be integral to the conceptual and theoretical development of the SHRM literature. Our brief review demonstrates how the RBV-based SHRM research has evolved in the last decade. This evolution began when HR researchers recognized that the RBV provided a compelling explanation for why HR practices lead to competitive advantage. Ensuing scholarly debate about the specific mechanics of this relationship advanced the SHRM literature to its current state. The net effect has been a deeper understanding of the interplay between HRM and competitive advantage. The model depicted in Fig. 1 demonstrates that sustained competitive advantage is not just a function of single or isolated components, but rather a combination of human capital elements such as the development of stocks of skills, strategically relevant behaviors, and supporting people management systems. Although there is yet much room for progress it is fair to say that the theoretical application of the RBV has been successful in stimulating a substantial amount of activity in the SHRM arena. Having summarized the conceptual development, we now turn to the empirical research.

4. RBV and Empirical SHRM Research

In addition to the many applications of the RBV to theoretical developments within SHRM, this perspective also has emerged as one of the more popular foundations for exploring empirical relationships within SHRM. In fact, one is hard pressed to find any SHRM empirical studies conducted over the past few years that do not at least pay lip service to the RBV. In the interest of brevity, we will cover a sample of such studies that illustrate the application of RBV concepts to empirical SHRM research. We chose these studies either because they specifically attempt to build on resource-based theory or because they tend to be most frequently cited within the SHRM literature and at least tangentially rely on resource-based logic.

In an early application, Huselid (1995) argued at a general level that HR practices could help create a source of competitive advantage, particularly if they are aligned with the firm's competitive strategy. His study revealed a relationship between HR practices (or High Performance Work Systems) and employee turnover, gross rate of return on assets, and Tobin's Q. That study received considerable attention because it demonstrated that HR practices could have a profound impact on both accounting and market-based measures of performance.

Koch and McGrath (1996) took a similar logic in their study of the relationship between HR planning, recruitment, and staffing practices and labor productivity. They argued that ". . . a highly productive workforce is likely to have attributes that make it a particularly valuable strategic asset" (p. 335). They suggested firms that develop effective routines for acquiring human assets develop a stock of talent that cannot be easily imitated. They found that these HR practices were related to labor productivity in a sample of business units, and that this relationship was stronger in capital intensive organizations.

Boxall and Steeneveld (1999) conducted a longitudinal case study of participants in the New Zealand engineering consultancy industry. They suggested that one of the firms in the industry had achieved a superior competitive position because of its human resource advantage in 1994, but that by 1997 two of the competitors had caught up in the competitive marketplace. They posited that this could mean that either the two competitors had been able to successfully imitate the former leaders' human resource advantage, or that the former leader has developed an advantage about which there is presently uncertainty, but which will be exploited in the future.

Diverging from the focus on HR practices, Wright, McMahan and Smart (1995) studied NCAA Men's basketball teams using an RBV framework. They focused on the skills of the team members and experience of the coach, and examined how a fit between skills and strategy impacted the team's performance. They found that the relationship between certain skills and team performance depended upon the strategy in which the team was engaged. In addition, their results indicated that teams whose coaches who were using a strategy different from their preferred strategy performed lower than teams where the coach was able to use his preferred strategy.

Recent empirical studies using the RBV build on Lepak and Snell's (1999) architectural framework discussed above. Lepak and Snell (in press) asked executives to describe the HR systems that existed for jobs that represented particular quadrants of their model. They found considerable support for the idea that the value and uniqueness of skills are associated with different types of HR systems within the same organization. These results were mostly consistent with the Lepak and Snell (1999) model, and supported the basic proposition that diverse HR strategies exist within firms. A follow up study (Lepak, Takeuchi & Snell, 2001) indicated that a combination of knowledge work and contract labor was associated with higher firm performance. This finding not only raises some interesting ideas about the development of valuable human resources, but also highlights the importance of combinations of various types used in conjunction with one another.

In another example of examining the human capital pool, Richard (2001) used resource-based logic to examine the impact of racial diversity on firm performance. He argued that diversity provides value through ensuring a variety of perspectives, that it is rare in that very few firms have achieved significant levels of diversity, and that the socially complex dynamics inherent in diversity lead to its inimitability. He found in a sample of banks that diversity was positively related to productivity, return on equity, and market performance for firms engaged in a growth strategy, but negatively related for firms downsizing.

In an effort to look beyond human capital pool alone, Youndt and Snell (2001) studied the differential effects of HR practices on human capital, social capital, and organizational capital. They found that intensive/extensive staffing, competitive pay, intensive/extensive training and promotion from within policies were most important for distinguishing high levels of human capital in organizations. In contrast, broad banding, compressed wages, team structures, socialization, mentoring, and group incentives distinguished those with high social capital (i.e., relationships that engender knowledge exchange) but had very little effect on human capital itself. Finally, organizational capital (i.e., knowledge embedded in the organization's systems and processes) was established most through lessons learned databases and HR policies that reinforced knowledge capture and access.

4.1. SUMMARY OF RBV-BASED EMPIRICAL RESEARCH: LIMITATIONS AND FUTURE DIRECTIONS

Recent debate about the usefulness of the RBV provides an interesting commentary about the current state of SHRM research (Barney and Priem). In response to claims that the RBV is tautological and does not generate testable hypotheses, Barney recognizes that most research applying the RBV has failed to test its fundamental concepts. Rather, he notes that much of the existing research has used the RBV to "establish the context of some empirical research—for example that the focus is on the performance implications of some internal attribute of a firm—and *are not really direct tests of the theory developed in the 1991 article.*" (Barney, 2001, p. 46, emphasis added).

Much of the existing SHRM research falls into this category. Although the empirical application of the RBV has taken a variety of forms, ranging in focus from High Performance Work Systems and stocks of talent, to the fit between employee skills and strategy it has employed a common underlying logic: Human resource activities are thought to lead to the development of a skilled workforce and one that engages in functional behavior for the firm, thus

forming a source of competitive advantage. This results in higher operating performance, which translates into increased profitability, and consequently results in higher stock prices (or market values) (Becker & Huselid, 1998). While this theoretical story is appealing, it is important to note that ultimately, most of the empirical studies assess only two variables: HR practices and performance.

While establishing such a relationship provides empirical evidence for the potential value of HR to firms, it fails to adequately test the RBV in two important ways. First, no attempt has yet been made to empirically assess the validity of the proposition that HR practices (or HPWS) are path dependent or causally ambiguous, nor whether they are actually difficult to imitate. While intuitively obvious and possibly supported by anecdotal data, the field lacks verifiable quantitative data to support these assertions. In fact, Boxall and Steeneveld's (1999) findings might suggest that HR systems are more easily imitated (or at least substitutable) than SHRM researchers previously believed. Certainly, efforts such as King and Zeithaml's (2001) study assessing causal ambiguity of competencies could be replicated with regard to SHRM issues. These authors asked managers to evaluate their firm's competencies and the generated measures of causal ambiguity based on these responses. While ambiguity was negatively related to firm performance in their study, they provide an example of how one might attempt to measure some of the variables within the RBV.

Second, few attempts have been made to demonstrate that the HR practices actually impact the skills or behaviors of the workforce, nor that these skills or behaviors are related to any performance measures. Arthur (1994) and Huselid (1995) did find a relationship between HR practices and turnover. Wright, McCormick, Sherman and McMahan (1999) found that appraisal and training practices were related to executives' assessment of the skills and that compensation practices were related to their assessments of workforce motivation. However, as yet no study has demonstrated anything close to a full causal model through which HR practices are purported to impact firm performance.

In short, a major step forward for the SHRM literature will be to move beyond simply the application of RBV logic to HR issues toward research that directly tests the RBV's core concepts. In fairness, this state of affairs does not differ from attempts to study competitive advantage within the strategy literature. As noted by Godfrey and Hill (1995), it is impossible to assess the degree of unobservability of an unobservable, and inimitable resources are often purported to be unobservable. Thus, strategy researchers are often left to using proxy variables that may not be valid for measuring the underlying constructs (Hoskisson, Hitt, Wan & Yiu, 1999).

However, given the single respondent, cross-sectional, survey designs inherent in much of this research, one cannot rule out alternative explanations for the findings of empirical relationships. For example, Gerhart, Wright, McMahan and Snell (2000) and Wright, Gardner, Moynihan, Park, Gerhart and Delery (in press) both found that single respondent measures of HR practices may contain significant amounts of measurement error. Gardner, Wright and Gerhart (2000) also found evidence of implicit performance theories suggesting that respondents to HR surveys might base their descriptions of the HR practices on their assessments of the organization's performance. This raises the possibility that research purporting to support the RBV through demonstrating a relationship between HR and performance may result from spurious relationships, or even reverse causation (Wright & Gardner, in press). The point is not to discount the significant research that has been conducted to date, but rather to highlight the importance of more rigorous and longitudinal studies of HR from a RBV perspective.

Taking a deeper understanding the resource-based view of the firm into empirical SHRM research entails focusing primarily on the competencies and capabilities of firms and the role that people management systems play in developing these. It requires recognizing that the inimitability of these competencies may stem from unobservability (e.g., causal ambiguity), complexity (e.g., social complexity), and/or time compression diseconomies (e.g., path dependence). This implies that rather than simply positing a relationship between HR practices and sustainable competitive advantage, one must realize that people management systems might impact this advantage in a variety of ways.

For instance, these systems might play a role in creating cultures or mindsets that enable the maintenance of unique competencies (e.g., the safety record of DuPont). Or, these systems may promote and maintain socially complex relationships characterized by trust, knowledge sharing, and teamwork (e.g., Southwest Airlines' unique culture). Finally, these systems might have resulted in the creation of a high quality human capital pool that cannot be easily imitated because of time compression diseconomies (e.g., Merck's R&D capability). Whichever the case, it certainly calls for a more complex view of the relationship between HR and performance than is usually demonstrated within the empirical literature.

In addition to a more complex view, such grounding would imply different strategies for studying HR and competitive advantage. For instance, recognizing time compression diseconomies implies more longitudinal or at least historical approaches to examining competitive advantage as opposed to the more popular cross-sectional studies. Focusing on causal ambiguity and social complexity might suggest more qualitative approaches than simply asking subjects to report via survey about the HR practices that exist. In sum, strategic HRM research more strongly anchored in the RBV of the firm would look significantly different than what currently exists. However, such research would shed light on both HR and strategy issues.

Extending this further, strategists who embrace the RBV point out that competitive advantage (vis core competence) comes from aligning skills, motives, and so forth with *organizational systems, structures, and processes* that achieve capabilities at the organizational level (Hamel; Peteraf and Teece). Too frequently, HR researchers have acted as if organizational performance derives solely from the (aggregated) actions of individuals. But the RVB suggests that strategic resources are more complex than that, and more interesting. Companies that are good at product development and innovation, for example, don't simply have the most creative people who continually generate new ideas. Product development capabilities are imbedded in the organizational systems and processes. People execute those systems, but they are not independent from them. So while core competencies are knowledge-based, they are not solely human. They are comprised of human capital, social capital (i.e., internal/external relationships and exchanges), and organizational capital (i.e., processes, technologies, databases) (Snell, Youndt & Wright, 1996).

That doesn't negate the importance of HR; it amplifies it and extends it. The RVB provides a broader foundation for exploring the impact of HR on strategic resources. In this context, HR is not limited to its direct effects on employee skills and behavior. Its effects are more encompassing in that they help weave those skills and behaviors within the broader fabric of organizational processes, systems and, ultimately, competencies.

Notwithstanding a great deal of room for development, it is clear from the preceding review that the conceptual and empirical application of the RBV has led to considerable advancement of the SHRM literature. In a broader sense, the RBV has impacted the field of HRM in two important ways. First, the RBV's influence has been instrumental in establishing a macro perspective in the field of HRM research (Snell et al., in press). This macro view has provided complimentary depth to a historically micro discipline rooted in psychology. Relatedly, a second major contribution of the RBV has been the theoretical and contextual grounding that it has provided to a field that has often been criticized for being atheoretical and excessively applied in nature (Snell et al., 2001).

5. The Convergence of RBV and SHRM: Potential Mutual Contributions

Thus far, we have discussed how the RBV has contributed to the field of SHRM. As noted before, however, that the RBV has also effectively put "people" on the strategy radar screen (Snell et al., in press). In the search for competitive advantage, strategy researchers increasingly acknowledge human capital (Hitt, Bierman, Shimizu & Kochar, 2001), intellectual capital (Edvinsson & Malone, 1997) and knowledge (Grant; Liebeskind and Matusik) as critical components. In so doing, the RBV has provided an excellent platform for highlighting the importance of people to competitive advantage, and thus, the inescapable fact that RBV strategy researchers must bump up against people and/or HR issues.

In fact, recent developments within the field of strategy seem to evidence a converging of that field and SHRM (Snell et al., in press). It seems that these areas present unique opportunities for interdisciplinary research streams that provide significant leaps forward in the knowledge base. We will discuss the concept of core competencies, the focus on dynamic capabilities, and knowledge-based views of the firm as potential bridges between the HR and strategy literatures. We choose these concepts because of both

their popularity within the strategy literature and their heavy reliance on HR related issues.

6. Core Competencies

Prahalad and Hamel (1990) certainly popularized the core competency concept within the strategy literature. They stated that core competencies are ". . . the collective learning in the organization, especially how to coordinate diverse production skills and integrate multiple streams of technologies" (p. 64), and that they involve "many levels of people and all functions" (p. 64). While the distinctions between core competencies and capabilities (Stalk, Evans & Schulman, 1992) seems blurred, one can hardly conceptualize a firm capability or competency absent the people who comprise them nor the systems that maintain them.

For example, competencies or capabilities refer to organizational processes, engaged in by people, resulting in superior products, and generally these must endure over time as employees flow in, through and out of the firm. Numerous researchers within the strategy field focus on firm competencies (e.g., King; Leonard and Leonard). These researchers universally recognize the inseparability of the competence and the skills of the employees who comprise the competence. In addition, some (e.g., Leonard-Barton, 1992) specifically also recognize the behavioral aspect of these employees (i.e., their need to engage in behaviors that execute the competency) and the supportive nature of people management systems to the development/maintenance of the competency. However, often these treatments begin quite specifically when examining the competency and its competitive potential within the marketplace. However, they then sometimes become more generic and ambiguous as they delve into the more specific people-related concepts such as knowledges, skills, abilities, behaviors, and HR practices.

This illustrates the potential synergy that might result from deeper integration of the strategy and strategic HRM literatures. To deeply understand the competency one must examine (in addition to the systems and processes that underlie them) the people who engage in the process, the skills they individually and collectively must possess, and the behavior they must engage in (individually and interactively) to implement the process. In addition, to understand how such a competency can be developed or maintained requires at least in part examining the people management systems that ensure that the competency remains as specific employees leave and new employees must be brought in to replace them. This again exemplifies the interaction of people and processes as they comprise competencies.

Focusing on the people-related elements of a core competency provides a linking pin between the strategy and HR literatures. Traditional HR researchers refer to a "competence" as being a work-related knowledge, skill, or ability (Nordhaug, 1993) held by an individual. This is not the same as the core competencies to which strategy researchers refer. Nordhaug and Gronhaug (1994) argue that firms possess individuals with different competences that they refer to as a portfolio of competences. They further propose that a core (or distinctive) competence exists when a firm is able to collaboratively blend the many competences in the portfolio, through a shared mindset, to better perform something than their competitors. For SHRM researchers, this implies a need to develop an understanding of firms, the activities in their value chains, and the relative superiority in value creation for each of these activities. For strategy researchers, it suggests a need to more deeply delve into the issues of the individuals and groups who comprise the competency, and the systems that develop and engage them to exhibit and maintain the competency. Lepak and Snell's (1999) model provides one tool for making this link between the firm's competency, the people that comprise it, and the systems that maintain it.

7. Dynamic Capabilities

The RBV has frequently focused on resources or competencies as a stable concept that can be identified at a point in time and will endure over time. The argument goes that when firms have bundles of resources that are valuable, rare, inimitable, and nonsubstitutable, they can implement value creating strategies not easily duplicated by competing firms (Barney; Conner; Peteraf; Wernerfelt and Wernerfelt).

However, recent attention has focused on the need for many organizations to constantly develop new capabilities or competencies in a dynamic environment (Teece, Pisano & Schuen, 1997). Such capabilities have been referred to as "dynamic capabilities" which have been defined as:

The firm's processes that use resources—specifically the processes to integrate, reconfigure, gain, and release resources—to match and even create market change. Dynamic capabilities thus are the organizational and strategic routines by which firms achieve new resource reconfigurations as markets emerge, collide, split, evolve, and die (Eisenhardt & Martin, 2000).

Such dynamic capabilities require that organizations establish processes that enable them to change their routines, services, products, and even markets over time. While in theory, one can easily posit how organizations must adapt to changing environmental contingencies, in reality changes of this magnitude are quite difficult to achieve, and the difficulty stems almost entirely from the human architecture of the firm. The firm may require different skill sets implying a release of some existing employees and acquisition of new employees. The change entails different organizational processes implying new networks and new behavioral repertoires of employees. The new skills and new behaviors theoretically must be driven by new administrative, (i.e., HR) systems (Wright & Snell, 1998).

This implies the centrality of HR issues to the understanding and development of dynamic capabilities. This centrality is well articulated by Teece et al. (1997) who note:

"Indeed if control over scarce resources is the source of economic profits, then it follows that such issues as skill acquisition, the management of knowledge and know how and learning become fundamental strategic issues. It is in this second dimension, encompassing skill acquisition, learning and accumulation of organizational and intangible or invisible assets that we believe lies the greatest potential for contributions to strategy" (pp. 514–515).

8. Knowledge-Based Theories of the Firm

Unarguably, significant attention in the strategy literature within the RBV paradigm has focused on knowledge. Efforts to understand how firms generate, leverage, transfer, integrate and protect knowledge has moved to the forefront of the field (Hansen; Hedlund; Nonaka; Svieby and Szulanski).

In fact, Grant (1996) argues for a knowledge-based theory of the firm, positing that firms exist because they better integrate and apply specialized knowledge than do markets. Liebeskind (1996) similarly believes in a knowledge-based theory of the firm, suggesting that firms exist because they can better protect knowledge from expropriation and imitation than can markets.

Interestingly, knowledge-centered strategy research inevitably confronts a number of HR issues. Knowledge management requires that firms define knowledge, identify existing knowledge bases, and provide mechanisms to promote the creation, protection and transfer of knowledge (Argote; Henderson and Liebeskind). While information systems provide a technological repository of knowledge, increasingly firms recognize that the key to successful knowledge management requires attending to the social and cultural systems of the organization (Conference Board, 2000).

Knowledge has long been a topic within the HR literature, whether the focus was on testing applicants for job-related knowledge (Hattrup & Schmitt, 1990), training employees to build their job-related knowledge (Gephart, Marsick, Van Buren & Spiro, 1996), developing participation and communication systems to transfer knowledge (Cooke, 1994), or providing incentives for individuals to apply their knowledge (Gerhart, Milkovich & Murray, 1992). The major distinctions between the strategy and HR literatures with regard to knowledge has to do with the focus of the knowledge and its level. While the HR literature has focused on job-related knowledge, the strategy literature has focused on more market-relevant knowledge, such as knowledge regarding customers, competitors, or knowledge relevant to the creation of new products (Grant and Liebeskind).

In addition, while HR literature tends to treat knowledge as an individual phenomenon, the strategy and organizational literatures view it more broadly as organizationally shared, accessible, and transferable (cf. Argyris; Brown and Snell). Knowledge can be viewed as something that characterizes individuals (i.e., human capital), but it can also be shared within groups or networks (i.e., social capital) or institutionalized within organization processes and databases (organizational capital).

These distinctions represent something of a departure for HR researchers. However, the processes of creation, transfer, and exploitation of knowledge provide common ground across the two fields, again highlighting their potential convergence within the RBV paradigm. Although theorists such as Argyris and Schon (1978) argue that all learning begins at the individual level, it is conditioned by the social context and routines within organizations (Nonaka & Takeuchi, 1995). Coleman (1988), for example, noted that social capital has an important influence on the creation of human capital. What seems clear is that these different "knowledge repositories" complement and influence one another in defining an organization's capabilities (Youndt & Snell, 2001).

But there are substantial differences between HR systems that support individual learning and those that support organizational learning. Leonard-Barton (1992), for example, noted that organizational learning and innovation were built on four inter-related processes and their related values: (1) owning/solving problems (egalitarianism), (2) integrating internal knowledge (shared knowledge), (3) continuous experimentation (positive risk), and (4) integrating external knowledge (openness to outside). Each of these processes and values works systemically with the others to inculcate organizational learning and innovation. Each process/value combination is in turn supported by different administrative (HR) systems that incorporate elements of staffing, job design, training, career management, rewards, and appraisal. Again, the concept of knowledge brings together the fields of strategy and HR. But a good deal more work needs to be done to integrate these research streams. Strategy theory and research provides the basis for understanding the value of knowledge to the firm and highlights the need to manage it. The HR field has lacked such a perspective, but has provided more theory and research regarding how knowledge is generated, retained, and transferred among individuals comprising the firm.

9.   Integrating Strategy and SHRM within the RBV

We have discussed the concepts of core competencies, dynamic capabilities, and knowledge as bridge constructs connecting the fields of strategy and SHRM. We proposed that both fields could benefit greatly from sharing respective areas of expertise. In fact, at the risk of oversimplification, the strategy literature has generated significant amounts of knowledge regarding who (i.e., employees/executives or groups of employees/executives) provides sources of competitive advantage and why. However, absent from that literature are specific techniques for attracting, developing, motivating, maintaining, or retaining these people. SHRM, on the other hand has generated knowledge regarding the attraction, development, motivation, maintenance, and retention of people. However, it has not been particularly successful yet at identifying who the focus of these systems should be on and why.

The strategy literature has also highlighted the importance of the stock and flow of knowledge for competitive advantage. However, it has not explored in great detail the role that individuals as well as their interactions with others contribute to this. Conversely SHRM has missed much of the organizational view of knowledge, but can provide significant guidance regarding the role that individuals play.

This state of affairs calls for greater integration between these two fields. Figure 2 illustrates this potential integration. Overall, the figure depicts people management systems at the left, core competencies at the right, intellectual capital and knowledge management as the bridge concepts between the two, and dynamic capability as a renewal component that ties all four concepts over time.

Note that the basic constructs laid out in Fig. 1 still appear in this expanded model, yet with a much more detailed set of variables. At the right-hand side of the model we place the people management systems construct. This placement does not imply that all competitive advantage begins with people management systems, but rather, that this represents the focus of the HR field. We suggest that these people management systems create value to the extent that they impact the stock, flow, and change of intellectual capital/knowledge that forms the basis of core competencies.

FIGURE 2: A MODEL FOR INTEGRATION STRATEGY AND STRATEGIC HRM

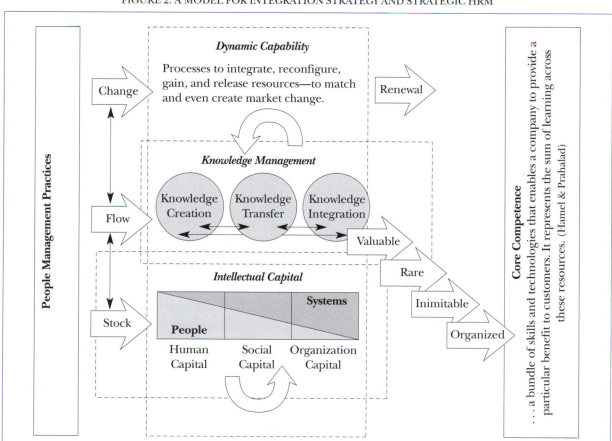

Rather than simply focusing on the concepts of "skills" and "behavior" we propose a more detailed analysis with regard to the stock and flow of knowledge. To this end we suggest that the "skill" concept might be expanded to consider the stock of intellectual capital in the firm, embedded in both people and systems. This stock of human capital consists of human (the knowledge skills, and abilities of people), social (the valuable relationships among people), and organizational (the processes and routines within the firm). It broadens the traditional HR focus beyond simply the people to explore the larger processes and systems that exist within the firm.

The "behavior" concept within the SHRM literature can similarly be reconceptualized as the flow of knowledge within the firm through its creation, transfer, and integration. This "knowledge management" behavior becomes increasingly important as information and knowledge play a greater role in firm competitive advantage. It is through the flow of knowledge that firms increase or maintain the stock of intellectual capital.

At the right-hand side of the model we place the core competence, one of the major foci of the strategy literature. We propose that this core competence arises from the combination of the firms stock of knowledge (human, social, and organizational capital embedded in both people and systems) and the flow of this knowledge though creation, transfer, and integration in a way that is valuable, rare, inimitable, and organized. This provides a framework for more specifically exploring the human component to core competencies, and provides a basis for exploring the linkage between people management systems and core competencies through the management of a firm's stock and flow of knowledge.

Finally, the dynamic capability construct illustrates the interdependent interplay between the workforce and the core competence as it changes over time. It represents the renewal process that organizations must undergo to remain competitive. Dynamic capability requires changing competencies on the part of both the organization and the people who comprise it. It is facilitated by people management systems that promote the change of both the stock and flow of knowledge within the firm that enable a firm to constantly renew its core competencies.

This model by no means serves as a well-developed theoretical framework, but rather simply seeks to point to the areas for collaboration between strategy and SHRM researchers. These two fields share common interests in issues and yet bring complementary skills, knowledge, and perspectives to these issues. The RBV highlights these common interests and provides a framework for developing collaborative effort.

10. Conclusion

The RBV has significantly and independently influenced the fields of strategy and SHRM. More importantly, however, it has provided a theoretical bridge between these two fields. By turning attention toward the internal resources, capabilities and competencies of the firm such as knowledge, learning, and dynamic capabilities (Hoskisson et al., 1999), it has brought strategy researchers to inescapably face a number of issues with regard to the management of people (Barney, 1996). We would guess that few strategy researchers are well versed in the existing research base regarding the effectiveness of various specific HR tools and techniques for managing people, and thus addressing these issues with necessary specificity.

This internal focus also has provided the traditionally atheoretical field of SHRM with a theoretical foundation from which it can begin exploring the strategic role that people and HR functions can play in organizations (Wright & McMahan, 1992). In addition to the lack of theory, this literature has also displayed little, or at least overly simplistic views of strategy, thus limiting its ability to contribute to the strategy literature (Chadwick & Cappelli, 1998). The RBV provides the framework from which HR researchers and practitioners can better understand the challenges of strategy, and thus be better able to play a positive role in the strategic management of firms.

We propose that both fields will benefit from greater levels of interaction in the future. This interaction should be deeper than simply reading each other's literature, but rather organizing conferences aimed at promoting face-to-face discussions of the common issues and challenges. In fact, we believe that future interdisciplinary research studies conducted jointly by strategy and SHRM researchers would exploit the unique knowledge and expertise of both fields, and synergistically contribute to the generation of new knowledge regarding the roles that people play in organizational competitive advantage (Jackson et al., 1989).

Source: Wright, Patrick M., Dunford, Benjamin B., and Snell, Scott A. *Journal of Management* 27, 2001, p. 701. Used by permission of Elsevier Science Ltd.

Selected Bibliography

L. Argote and P. Ingram, Knowledge transfer: A basis for competitive advantage in firms. *Organizational Behavior and Human Decision Processes* **82** 1 (2000), pp. 150–169.

C. Argyris and D. A. Schon, *Organizational learning: A theory of action perspective*, Addison-Wesley, Reading, MA (1978).

J. B. Arthur, Effects of human resource systems on manufacturing performance and turnover. *Academy of Management Journal* **37** 3 (1994), pp. 670–687.

J. N. Baron, A. Davis-Blake and W. T. Bielby, The structure of opportunity: How promotion ladders vary within and among organizations. *Administrative Science Quarterly* **31** (1986), pp. 248–273.

J. Barney, Firm resources and sustained competitive advantage. *Journal of Management* **17** 1 (1991), pp. 99–120.

J. Barney, The resource-based theory of the firm. *Organizational Science* **7** (1996), p. 469.

J. Barney, Is the resource-based view a useful perspective for strategic management research? Yes. *Academy of Management Review* **26** (2001), pp. 41–56.

B. E. Becker and M. A. Huselid, High performance work systems and firm performance: A synthesis of research and managerial applications. *Research in Personnel and Human Resources Management* **16** (1998), pp. 53–101.

J. S. Brown and P. Duguid, Organizational learning and communities-of-practice: Toward a unified view of working, learning, and innovation. *Organizational Science* **2** (1991), pp. 40–57.

P. F. Boxall, The Strategic HRM debate and the resource-based view of the firm. *Human Resource Management Journal* **6** 3 (1996), pp. 59–75.

P. F. Boxall, Human resource strategy and industry-based competition: A conceptual framework and agenda for theoretical development. In P. M. Wright, L. D. Dyer, J. W. Boudreau and G. T. Milkovich (Eds.), Research in personnel and human resources management (Suppl. 4, pp. 1–29). Madison, WI: IRRA (1998).

P. F. Boxall and M. Steeneveld, Human resource strategy and competitive advantage: A longitudinal study of engineering consultancies. *Journal of Management Studies* **36** 4 (1999), pp. 443–463.

P. Cappelli and H. Singh, Integrating strategic human resources and strategic management. In: D. Lewin, O. S. Mitchell and P. D. Sherer (Eds.), *Research frontiers in industrial relations and human resources*, IRRA, Madison, WI (1992), pp. 165–192.

C. Chadwick, & P. Cappelli, Alternatives to generic strategy typologies in strategic human resource management. In P. M. Wright, L. D. Dyer, J. W. Boudreau & G. T. Milkovich (Eds.), *Research in personnel and human resources management* (Suppl. 4, pp. 1–29). Greenwich, CT: JAI Press, Inc.(1998).

J. S. Coleman, Social capital in the creation of human capital. *American Journal of Sociology* **94** (1988), pp. s95–s120.

Conference Board. *Beyond knowledge management: New ways to work*. Research Report 1262–00RR (2000).

W. Cooke, Employee participation programs, group-based incentives, and Company performance: A union-nonunion comparison. *Industrial and Labor Relations Review* **47** (1994), pp. 594–609.

K. R. Conner and C. K. Prahalad, A resource-based theory of the firm: Knowledge versus opportunism. *Organization Science* **7** (1996), pp. 477–501.

M. A. Devanna, C. J. Fombrun, & N. M. Tichy, A Framework for Strategic Human Resource Management. *Strategic Human Resource Management* (Chapt. 3, pp. 33–51). New York: Wiley (1984).

I. Dierickx and K. Cool, Asset stock accumulation and sustainability of competitive advantage. *Management Science* **35** (1989), pp. 1504–1511.

P. Drucker *The practice of management*. Harper, New York (1954).

L. Edvinsson and M. Malone *Intellectual capital*. Harvard Business School Press, Cambridge, MA (1997).

K. M. Eisenhardt and J. A. Martin, Dynamic capabilities: What are they? *Strategic Management Journal* **21** (2000), pp. 1105–1121.

C. M. Fiol and M. A. Lyles, Organizational learning. *Academy of Management Review* **10** (1985), pp. 803–813.

S. Finkelstein and D. Hambrick, *Strategic leadership: Top executives and their effects on organizations*. West Pub. Co, Minneapolis/ St. Paul (1996).

S. R. Fisher and M. A. White, Downsizing in a learning organization: Are there hidden costs? *Academy of Management Review* **25** 1 (2000), pp. 244–251.

T. M. Gardner, P. M. Wright, & B. Gerhart, The HR-Firm performance relationship: Can it be in the mind of the beholder? Working Paper, Center for Advanced Human Resource Studies, Cornell University (2000).

B. Gephart, M. Marsick, V., Van Buren, M., & M. Spiro, Learning Organizations come alive. *Training and Development*, **50,** (1996), pp. 34–35.

B. Gerhart, G. Milkovich and B. Murray, Pay, performance and participation. In D. Lewin, O. Mitchell and P. Sherer (Eds.), *Research frontiers in industrial relations and human resources*, IRRA, Madison, WI (1992).

B. Gerhart, P. M. Wright, G. C. McMahan and S. A. Snell, Measurement error in research on human resources and firm performance: How much error is there and how does it influence effect size estimates? *Personnel Psychology* **53** (2000), pp. 803–834.

P. C. Godfrey and C. W. L. Hill, The problem of unobservables in strategic management research. *Strategic Management Journal* **16** (1995), pp. 519–533.

R. M. Grant, Toward a knowledge-based theory of the firm. *Strategic Management Journal* **17** Winter Special Issue (1996), pp. 108–122.

G. Hamel and C. K. Prahalad, Competing for the future. *Harvard Business Review* **72** 4 (1994), pp. 122–129.

M. T. Hansen, The search-transfer problem: The role of weak ties in sharing knowledge across organization sub units. *Administrative Science Quarterly* **44** March (1999), pp. 82–111.

G. Hedlund, A model of knowledge management and the N-form corporation. *Strategic Management Journal* **15** (1994), pp. 73–90.

K. Hattrup and N. Schmitt, Prediction of trades apprentices' performance on job sample criteria. *Personnel Psychology* **43** (1990), pp. 453–467.

R. Henderson and I. Cockburn, Measuring competence? Exploring firm effects in pharmaceutical research. *Strategic Management Research* **15** (1994), pp. 63–84.

M. A. Hitt, L. Bierman, K. Shimizu and R. Kochhar, Direct and moderating effects of human capital on the strategy and performance in professional service firms: A resource-based perspective. *Academy of Management Journal* **44** (2001), pp. 13–28.

R. E. Hoskisson, M. A. Hitt, W. P. Wan and D. Yiu, Theory and research in strategic management: Swings of a pendulum. *Strategic Management Journal* **25** 3 (1999), pp. 417–456.

M. A. Huselid, The impact of human resource management practices on turnover, productivity, and corporate financial performance. *Academy of Management Journal* **38** 3 (1995), pp. 635–672.

S. E. Jackson, R. S. Schuler and J. C. Rivero, Organizational characteristics as predictors of personnel practices. *Personnel Psychology* **42** (1989), pp. 727–786.

A. W. King and C. P. Zeithaml, Competencies and firm performance: Examining the causal ambiguity paradox. *Strategic Management Journal* **22** (2001), pp. 75–99.

M. J. Koch and R. G. McGrath, Improving labor productivity: Human resource management policies do matter. *Strategic Management Journal* **17** (1996), pp. 335–354.

A. A. Lado and M. C. Wilson, Human resource systems and sustained competitive advantage: A competency-based perspective. *Academy of Management Review* **19** 4 (1994), pp. 699–727.

D. Leonard-Barton, The factory as a learning laboratory. *Sloan Management Review* **34** 1 (1992), pp. 23–38.

D. Leonard-Barton, *Wellsprings of Knowledge*. Harvard Business School Press, Boston (1995).

D. P. Lepak and S. A. Snell, The human resource architecture: Toward a theory of human capital allocation and development. *Academy of Management Review* **24** (1999), pp. 31–48.

D. P. Lepak, & S. A. Snell, Examining the human resource architecture: The relationships among human capital, employment, and human resource configurations. *Journal of Management* (in press).

D. P. Lepak, R. Takeuchi, & S. A. Snell, An empirical examination of employment mode use and firm performance. Working paper, University of Maryland (2001).

J. P. Liebeskind, Knowledge, strategy, and the theory of the firm. *Strategic Management Journal* **17** Winter Special Issue (1996), pp. 93–107.

J. March and H. Simon, *Organizations*. Wiley, New York (1958).

J. P. MacDuffie, Human resource bundles and manufacturing performance: Organizational logic and flexible production systems in the world auto industry. *Industrial & Labor Relations Review* **48** 2 (1995), pp. 197–221.

S. F. Matusik and C. W. L. Hill, The utilization of contingent work, knowledge creation, and competitive advantage. *Academy of Management Review* **23** (1998), pp. 680–697.

G. C. McMahan, M. Virick, & P. M. Wright, Alternative theoretical perspective for strategic human resource management revisited: progress, problems, and prospects. In P. M. Wright, L. D. Dyer, J. W. Boudreau, & G. T. Milkovich (Eds.), *Research in personnel and human resources management* (Suppl. 4, pp. 99–122). Greenwich, CT: JAI Press, Inc. (1999).

R. E. Miles and C. C. Snow, *Organizational strategy, structure and process*. McGraw-Hill, New York (1978).

R. E. Miles, & C. C. Snow, Designing strategic human resources systems. *Organizational Dynamics*, Summer, (1984), pp. 36–52.

I. Nonaka, The knowledge creating company. *Harvard Business Review* **69** 6 (1991), pp. 96–104.

I. Nonaka and H. Takeuchi, *The knowledge-creating company: How Japanese companies create the dynamics of innovation*. Oxford Press, New York (1995).

D. Norburn and S. Birley, The top management team and corporate performance. *Strategic Management Journal* **9** (1988), pp. 225–237.

O. Nordhaug, *Human capital in organizations: Competence, training and learning*. Scandinavian University Press/Oxford University Press, Oslo/London (1993).

O. Nordhaug and K. Gronhaug, Competences as resources in firms. *The International Journal of Human Resource Management* **5** 1 (1994), pp. 89–106.

P. Osterman, Choice of employment systems in internal labor markets. *Industrial Relations* **26** 1 (1987), pp. 48–63.

M. A. Peteraf, The cornerstones of competitive advantage: A resource based view. *Strategic Management Journal* **14** (1993), pp. 179–191.

E. T. Penrose, *The theory of the growth of the firm*, Wiley, New York (1959).

M. E. Porter, *Competitive strategy*. New York: Free Press, pp. 34–46 (1980).

C. K. Prahalad, & G. Hamel, The core competence of the corporation. *Harvard Business Review*, May/June (1990), pp. 79–91.

R. L. Priem and J. E. Butler, Is the resource based "view" a useful perspective for strategic management research? *Academy of Management Review* **26** 1 (2001), pp. 22–40.

R. L. Priem and J. E. Butler, Tautology in the resource based view and the implications of externally determined resource value: Further comments. *Academy of Management Review* **26** 1 (2001), pp. 57–66.

O. C. Richard, Racial diversity, business strategy, and firm performance: A resource-based view. *Academy of Management Journal* **43** 2 (2001), pp. 164–177.

R. Rumelt, Toward a strategic theory of the firm. In R. Lamb (Ed.), *Competitive strategic management* Prentice-Hall, Englewood Cliffs, NJ (1984), pp. 556–570.

S. A. Snell, M. A. Shadur, & P. M. Wright, The era of our ways. In M. A. Hitt, R. E. Freeman, & J. S. Harrison (Eds.), *Handbook of strategic management* (pp. 627–629). Oxford: Blackwell Publishing (2001).

S. A. Snell, D. Stueber, & D. P. Lepak, Virtual HR departments: Getting out of the middle, In: Robert L. Heneman & David B. Greenberger, *Human resource management in virtual organizations*. Information Age Publishing (2001).

S. A. Snell, M. A. Youndt, & P. M. Wright, Establishing a framework for research in strategic human resource management: Merging resource theory and organizational learning. In G. Ferris (Ed.), *Research in personnel and human resources management* (Vol. 14, pp. 61–90), (1996).

G. Stalk, P. Evans and L. Schulman, Competing on capabilities: The new rules of corporate strategy. *Harvard Business Review* **70** (1992), pp. 57–69.

T. A. Stewart, Human resources bites back. *Fortune*, May, (1996). pp. 175.

K. E. Svieby *The new organizational wealth: Managing and measuring knowledge based assets*. Berrett-Koehler, San Francisco (1997).

G. Szulanski, Exploring internal stickiness: impediments to the transfer of best practice within the firm. *Strategic Management Journal* **17** Winter Special Issue (1996), pp. 27–43.

D. J. Teece, G. Pisano and A. Shuen, Dynamic capabilities and strategic management. *Strategic Management Journal* **18** 7 (1997), pp. 509–533.

A. B. Thomas, Does leadership make a difference in organizational performance? *Administrative Science Quarterly* **33** (1988), pp. 388–400.

C. Truss and L. Gratton, Strategic human resource management: A conceptual approach. *International Journal of Human Resource Management* **5** (1994), pp. 663–686.

A. S. Tsui, J. L. Pearce, L. W. Porter and A. M. Tripoli, Alternative approaches to the employee-organization relationship: Does investment in employees pay off? *Academy of Management Journal* **40** (1997), pp. 1089–1121.

J. Walker, Linking human resource planning and strategic planning. *Human Resource Planning* **1** (1978), pp. 1–18.

B. Wernerfelt, A resource-based view of the firm. *Strategic Management Journal* **5** (1984), pp. 171–180.

B. Wernerfelt, The resource based view of the firm: Ten years after. *Strategic Management Journal* **16** (1995), pp. 171–174.

P. M. Wright, & W. Boswell, Desegregating HRM: A Review and Synthesis of Micro and Macro Human Resource Management Research. *Journal of Management* (in press).

P. M. Wright, & T. M. Gardner, Theoretical and empirical challenges in studying the HR practice-firm performance relationship. In D. Holman, T. D. Wall, C. Clegg, P. Sparrow, & A. Howard (Eds.), *The new workplace: People technology, and organization.* New York: John Wiley and Sons (in press).

P. M. Wright, T. M. Gardner, L. M. Moynihan, H. Park, B. Gerhart, & J. Delery, Measurement error in research on human resources and firm performance. Additional data and suggestions for future research. *Personnel Psychology* (in press).

P. M. Wright, B. McCormick, W. S. Sherman and G. C. McMahan, The role of human resources practices in petro-chemical refinery performance. *The International Journal of Human Resource Management* **10** (1999), pp. 551–571.

P. M. Wright and G. C. McMahan, Theoretical perspectives for strategic human resource management. *Journal of Management* **18** 2 (1992), pp. 295–320.

P. M. Wright, G. C. McMahan and A. McWilliams, Human resources and sustained competitive advantage: A resource-based perspective. *International Journal of Human Resource Management* **5** 2 (1994), pp. 301–326.

P. M. Wright, D. L. Smart and G. C. McMahan, Matches between human resources and strategy among NCAA basketball teams. *Academy of Management Journal* **38** 4 (1995), pp. 1052–1074.

P. M. Wright and S. A. Snell, Toward an integrative view of strategic human resource management. *Human Resource Management Review* **1** 3 (1991), pp. 203–225. *Abstract*

P. M. Wright and S. A. Snell, Toward a unifying framework for exploring fit and flexibility in strategic human resource management. *Academy of Management Review* **23** 4 (1998), pp. 756–772.

M. A. Youndt, & S. A. Snell, Human resource management, intellectual capital, and organizational performance. Working Paper, Skidmore College (2001).

Distinctive Human Resources Are Firms' Core Competencies

Peter Cappelli and Anne Crocker-Hefter, *Organizational Dynamics*

Find a firm with a reputation for excellence in some function, copy its practices, and your company, too, will excel. Advice such as this, under the rubric of "best practices" or "benchmarking," has flooded the popular business literature. Each article implicitly extends the argument that superior management practices are readily identifiable and can be transferred across organizations.

The best practices advocates, however, must contend with a discomforting reality: *Many firms—some very successful—stubbornly refuse to adopt those practices.* Are we to assume, perhaps, that competition drives out firms that do not adopt the most efficient techniques—and that the intractable companies will ultimately fail? Hardly the case.

To understand what is happening, we need to look at a counterpoint to the best practices approach. When it comes to explaining how and why certain firms have carved out competitive advantages, attention increasingly focuses on unique, *differentiating* resources—the notion of "core competencies" being perhaps the best known of these resource arguments.

We believe that the notion of a single set of "best" practices may, indeed, be overstated. As we illustrate below, there are examples in virtually every industry of highly successful firms that have very distinct management practices. We argue that these distinctive human resource practices help to create unique competencies that differentiate products and services and, in turn, drive competitiveness. Indeed, product differentiation is one of the essential functions of strategic management, and distinctive human resource practices shape the core competencies that determine how firms compete.

The argument that there should be a "fit" between human resource practices and business strategies can be traced back to manpower planning and is certainly not new in management circles. What is new here is the argument that people management practices are the *drivers*—the genesis of efforts to create distinctive competencies and, in turn, business strategies.

We illustrate this point by examining pairs of successful organizations competing in the same industry. We chose the paired companies by asking analysts, consultants, and other industry experts to help us identify successful organizations in their industry that appeared to have very different employee management practices. We began our investigation with financial reports and other publicly available information on the organizations, including stories in the business press over the past five years. We also contacted each organization for information and in most cases visited them. The most revealing sources of information, however, tended to be competitors and former employees. The competitors in particular, typically the other member of an industry "pair," had a keen sense for what was truly distinctive in each organization. Former employees also have a clear sense about what actually happens inside organizations, as opposed to what the written practices say.

With the help of industry experts and competitors, we then identified the distinctive competencies and competitive advantages of each organization. There was remarkably little variance across respondents in what they believed these competencies to be. In most cases, competencies were clearly associated with particular employee groups—customer service, for example, or marketing.

The next step was to describe the employment practices associated with the relevant employee group. In cases where practices have recently changed, we describe the longstanding practices that were in place when the distinctive competencies were developed. In our final step, we compared the distinctive competencies for each organization with the employment practices for the relevant employee group to suggest how these competencies were created.

When Employees Are the "Product"

The link between people management practices and the way organizations compete is most direct in industries where employees, by themselves, create what the organization sells—where the "product" is a service provided directly by employees interacting with customers. Consider the following cases.

PROFESSIONAL SPORTS

Professional sports are obviously big businesses in their own right, and it's easy to see how "employee performance" matters in this arena. The rules governing each sport standardize the equipment, playing fields, and time limits for all competitors. Within those parameters, each club must deliver its services—an event that attracts an audience.

Sports are idiosyncratic in other ways as well. The fact that there is no "open" labor market and that teams tend to control hiring through drafts may make it easier to align organizations and employees than in other industries. Financial success and the success of the team in its sport are not always related, which may reduce somewhat the financial incentives to seek out the most effective strategies and employee matches on the field.

The San Francisco 49ers and Oakland Raiders have been among the most successful teams in American sports, yet they represent very distinct models of player management. The 49ers have succeeded by using a strategy of long-term player development—recruiting through college drafts rather than through trades, developing talent within the team, and then holding on to the best players by keeping them happy. Their salaries are among the most generous in the league, and more than in other clubs, the 49ers players have some influence on team decisions and feel that they are a part of the organization.

On the field, the club relies on experienced athletes who have worked with their coaches for years and who act as team leaders. (The coaches and management staff also have long tenure with the team.) They have a reputation for playing as a precise, well-disciplined unit. Long-tenure players also help create long-term relationships with fans, helping cement their loyalty to the club. If production language could be applied to sports, this is a "high commitment" organization that operates as a "quasi-autonomous team" on the field. The approach has apparently paid

off—the 49ers have won at least ten games a year every year since 1983.

The Raiders, in contrast, do not as a rule develop their own players, but instead use trades to scoop up talented players who fail or do not fit in elsewhere. The club has a very high player turnover and a repu-

How Do Management Practices Help Build Distinct Competencies?

Employee selection, i.e., the selection of employees with distinctive capabilities, provides the most obvious example of how management practices create distinct competencies. Moreover, a company's reputation for certain employment practices may attract employees and thus push the process along, aligning individual and organizational attributes. In practice, this is an imperfect mechanism. It requires that both employers and prospective employees have accurate information about each other and it assumes stable characteristics and mobility between organizations. But there is considerable evidence that this matching process between organizations and employee characteristics does occur.

In addition, each organization has its own training programs, rewards systems, and work organization, and these systems develop skills and behaviors that help an organization create distinctive competencies for attacking markets.

tation as a collection of individuals who often do not fit together well. As an organization, the Raiders are not known for treating players especially well, or for letting them have much influence on team decisions. The team, which has been called "an organizational anomaly," has an autocratic owner who is personally involved in coaching and personnel decisions. No employee participation here.

On the field, the Raiders are known for their individual performances and wide-open playing style, a style that makes good use of their pool of individual talent. The players are not known for their personal discipline either, having "swashbuckled through Bourbon Street" during Super Bowl week, for example, and recovered by game day.

The practices of these two clubs create reputations that contribute to some self-selection of players, reinforcing their systems; those comfortable working in disciplined systems go to the 49ers while players who bridle at the constraints such systems impose go to the Raiders. It makes sense for the 49ers to staff their team with inexperienced players from the college draft in order to better "stamp" them with their own system; players from other pro teams are more likely to come in with expectations and playing habits that might be incompatible with the 49ers' system. Similarly, the fact that the Raiders hire experienced players who bring disparate attitudes and reputations that are not easily blended helps create their more individualistic playing style.

To some extent, football teams compete for fans the same way that firms compete for customers, and having distinct styles of play may help build a national audience. A distinctive and unusual style may be useful on the field as well, in that it demands unusual responses from the other side that may be difficult to master.

RETAILING: SALES AS THE SERVICE

Sears and Nordstrom are both legends in the retailing industry.

Sears was the world's largest retailer for generations and has outlasted all of its historical competitors. During the 1980s, Nordstrom set service and growth standards for the industry. Although Sears stumbled in this period—as did most department stores—it has recently reorganized with improved performance.

Sears and Nordstrom are very different companies, with different employment practices, especially with reference to sales positions—the key job in retailing. Yet each company's practices make sense for its operations.

Sears has been and remains one of the pioneering firms in the science of employee selection. It relies on some of the most sophisticated selection tests in American industry. The company has refined these tests over time to achieve extremely high predictive power. Once hired, employees receive extensive training in company practices. Management also keeps track of employee attitudes and morale through frequent and rigorous employee surveys.

Two practices are especially noteworthy in the management of sales representatives. The first is intensive training in Sears products, operating systems, and sales techniques. The second is the pay program: a great many sales employees work on straight salary—not commissions—and the commissions that are paid at Sears are modest. (They have recently been cut to one percent of sales.)

Nordstrom operates with virtually none of the formal personnel practices advanced by Sears.

Indeed, its practices appear downright primitive in comparison. Nordstrom's hiring is decentralized and uses no formal selection tests. Managers look for applicants with experience in customer contact—not necessarily prior retailing experience (which is often seen as a drawback). The important qualities are a pleasant personality and motivation. The company has only one rule in its personnel handbook: "Use Your Best Judgment at All Times." Individual sales clerks run their areas almost as if they were private stores.

Nordstrom maintains a continuous stream of programs to motivate employees toward the goal of providing intensive service, but it offers very little of what could be thought of as training. The pay system is leaded toward commissions, which makes it possible for clerks to earn sizable incomes. Nordstrom sales personnel are also ranked within each department according to their monthly sales: the most successful are promoted (virtually all managers are promoted from within) and the least successful let go.

In Nordstrom's fashion-oriented retail business, the service that customers demand is not detailed knowledge of the products, but personal contact. The clerk's emotional energy is important—and hustle, running across the store to match an item, remembering an individual customer's tastes, etc. Impulse purchases are more important in fashion than in other segments of retailing, and the clerk's effort can be especially important in such sales.

The Nordstrom employment system fuels an intense level of personal motivation and customer contact. The commissions, internal competition, and motivation programs provide the drive, while autonomy and the absence of rules allow it to be exercised. Many new hires do not survive—Nordstrom's turnover ranks among the highest in the industry. But because the investment in each employee is relatively small, such turnover is not a real problem.

Sears is also in the retail business, of course, and service is part of what it sells. But it is service of a different kind, in part because housewares, rather than fashion, dominate its product line. Customers buying home appliances or hardware want information about the products and how they are used. Sears also sells financing and warranties, reasonably complicated services that require some background knowledge. As evidenced by its marketing ("The Name You Can Trust"), Sears trades, in part, on a reputation for steering the customer in the right direction.

With this strategy, training is important, and turnover is costly—hence the emphasis on selection. Salary pay systems, as opposed to commissions, create no incentives to push products irrespective of customer needs or to cut back on "non-selling time" associated with providing information. Personal relationships with customers also help build a reputation for honest and reliable service. Sears customer satisfaction data finds that the stores with the lowest employee turnover and the least temporary help have the highest satisfaction ratings. (Interestingly, Sears' problem with fraud in its automotive business a few years ago provides an exception that proves the rule—automotive managers operated on commissions and quotas that provided the incentives to encourage repairs that in many cases were apparently not needed.)

The restructuring of Sears during the past two years smashed its no-layoff policy, but left other principles of employment intact. In fact, the amount of training for sales representatives has increased and the limited commission-based pay reduced further.

PROFESSIONAL SERVICE FIRMS: INFORMATION AND ADVICE AS THE PRODUCT

Boston Consulting Group (BCG) and McKinsey & Company are among the world's leading strategic consulting firms. Both have world-wide operations, and their reputations for thoughtful leadership and quality service to management are comparable. Both firms hire from the best undergraduate and MBA programs and compete for the top students. Both have rigorous selection procedures and exceptional compensation. Yet the characteristics of the people the two firms hire, and the way each firm manages people, differ in important ways. Again, the practices relate to the companies' approaches to their markets.

BCG tends to attract candidates with very broad perspectives on business. Some have started their own businesses, and others leave BCG to found new companies. BCG also maintains something of a "revolving door" with academia, hiring business school professors as consultants and sometimes losing consultants to faculty positions in business schools. Once hired, consultants jump right into work, albeit closely supervised, and the formal training they receive is likely to be from outside courses.

BCG has an entrepreneurial environment—an expectation that each project team will come up with its own innovative approach. Each office is seen as having a slightly different culture. BCG pays less than many of its competitors, but offers more individualized incentive pay, reinforcing the entrepreneurial culture.

While BCG has some standard "products" such as time-based competition and capabilities-based strategies, these are not the source of its competency. Indeed, some products, such as the "Growth-Share" matrix, are well-publicized and basically given away. The value-added comes from the customized application to the client's situation. Many of BCG's projects do not even start with these products but rather with a "clean sheet of paper" approach. What clients buy, therefore, are original solutions and approaches to their problems. And these approaches begin with consultants whose varied backgrounds and entrepreneurial spirit help produce a unique product.

McKinsey, on the other hand, has historically taken virtually all of its new hires from on-campus recruiting and rarely hires from other employers. It tends to prefer candidates with technical backgrounds, such as engineering and computer science, who have depth in some functional business area. The new entrants vary less in terms of their management experience and come in as "blank slates" in terms of their consulting ideas. If McKinsey consultants leave, they are more likely to take senior line management positions in corporations than entrepreneurial positions.

McKinsey provides new consultants with extensive training in the company's method of project execution and management, even though this is highly tailored to each client's situation. McKinsey's size—3,000 consultants compared to 800 at BCG—may create scale economies in training new entrants that make it easier for the firm to provide such programs itself. The firm expects the career path to the highest position, senior partner, to take approximately 12 years (versus six to eight at BCG), which gives the consultants a long period to learn how to fit in.

The company is known for the "McKinsey way." McKinsey believes that it is important to provide its clients with consistent services; the client knows what to expect from the project teams whose products and techniques are regarded as proprietary and are not publicized. The firm's core competency, therefore, is in the consistent products and techniques that constitute the "McKinsey way." This standardization is especially notable given the far-flung nature of McKinsey's empire. Half of its senior partners are abroad, and 27 of the 33 offices it has opened since 1980 are outside the U.S.

BUSINESS SCHOOLS

A similar pattern of employment practices applies across business schools. And because these schools serve as supply channels for business, the pattern also influences the relationships with firms that recruit at those schools.

As an employer, the Harvard Business School represents the end of the spectrum associated with internal development of skills. Harvard is well-known for identifying bright young academics who, in many cases, come from fields largely unrelated to business. Harvard hires them as assistant professors and turns them into business experts. Harvard is also known for a faculty with unique skills and abilities: a deep and practical knowledge of business problems typically acquired through clinical methods, and the ability to teach "cases" using the Socratic method. Compared with other schools, Harvard is organized more by problem areas and teaching responsibilities than by traditional academic fields.

Several personnel practices support the development of these skills. Until recently, a system of post-doctoral fellowships specifically for Ph.D.s in non-business fields helped them learn about business. The best of these fellows were then hired as assistant professors. A second practice is a longer tenure clock than at many schools—nine years—which makes it easier for candidates to make the significant investment in Harvard-specific methods and for the institution to observe who is really fitting in. The tenure evaluation is more likely to stress factors specific to Harvard, such as course development, and to rely on evaluations from internal faculty. Finally, Harvard has been much more inclined than most schools to hire its own students as faculty, providing a more direct way of ensuring that the faculty "fit" into the organization.

The Wharton School exemplifies the other end of the continuum. It seeks faculty whose work is recognized as excellent in academic fields such as finance, accounting, and management. Like most business schools, Wharton hires its faculty from the network of Ph.D. programs and competitor schools with similar departments that make up the academic labor market. It is extremely rare that Wharton will hire one of its own Ph.D. students. Indeed, a majority of the tenured professors have been hired away from a faculty position elsewhere. The tenure decision is based largely on evaluations from faculty at other schools as a way of ensuring that successful candidates truly have skills recognized elsewhere. And a shorter tenure clock makes it easier to move faculty in and out, making use of the outside market.

What Wharton gets from its faculty, then, are skills oriented toward academic functional areas. Within the school, departments are organized according to academic fields. And the fact that it is the largest of the major business schools ensures that each department has considerable depth.

Given these different orientations, it is not surprising that the two schools produce different "products"—MBA students with different strengths. Harvard graduates are known for their general management orientation and superior discussion skills, while Wharton graduates have superior analytic skills associated with functional areas. It makes sense, therefore, that companies interested in general talent like McKinsey prefer Harvard's MBAs while those interested in specific skills, like the investment banks, prefer Wharton graduates. In 1992, for example, 26 percent of the Harvard MBA class went into consulting compared with 20 percent at Wharton, while 27 percent of the Wharton class went into commercial and investment banking compared with only 18 percent at Harvard.

FINANCIAL SERVICES

The property and casualty section of the insurance industry is based, perhaps more directly than other businesses, on knowledge and skills. The ability to identify and assess risk in unique situations, for example, is the central issue in the business, so it may not be a surprise that employees and the practices used to manage them are at the heart of competencies in this industry.

Yet we find a very wide range of people management practices and policies in the property and casualty business, a range that once again appears to result from different competitive strategies that are driven by different competencies. The two property and casualty firms exemplifying the most marked difference with respect to people management are Chubb and American International Group (A.I.G.).

Yet both are among the most profitable firms in the entire insurance business.

Chubb, often described by competitors as the "Cadillac" of its industry, is successful by being the best at what it does. Chubb does not create new markets or drive the ones that it is in through low prices. Instead, in the property business, it tries to find the very best risks that will provide a high return on its premiums. Chubb often goes after customers of other firms who it believes are good risks, identifies "gaps" or problems in their coverage, and offers them superior insurance protection. For both businesses and individuals, Chubb also looks for customers who are willing to pay a premium for superior service that is manifested by intensive customer contact. It has a reputation for being the "insurer of choice" for the very wealthy who are willing to pay a premium for superior service and customer contact.

In short, Chubb earns above-market profits by targeting those customers who will pay some premium for superior products and service and by identifying particularly good risks not spotted by competitors. These competencies—superior underwriting and service—are generated by Chubb's employee management practices.

Chubb makes a substantial investment in its employees, beginning with recruitment. Historically, it has recruited graduates, regardless of major, from the most prestigious undergraduate schools. These candidates, often from the liberal arts, come with the interpersonal and communication skills upon which insurance-specific skills can be built. The recruiters seek out applicants who "look like" Chubb's customers—i.e., who have personal contacts in the monied class and are comfortable with potential customers in that social stratum. New hires participate in several months of intensive training and testing before going to the branch into which they were hired. For the next 6 to 12 months, they work alongside established underwriters in an apprentice-like system.

With this substantial investment in skills, the company goes to great lengths to ensure that the new workers (and their skills) stay around long enough for the investment to be recouped. First, Chubb keeps its underwriters from the boredom of desk jobs, which often produces turnover elsewhere, by making them agents. The fact that underwriters go to the field to do the selling is a key factor in creating Chubb's competency. It eliminates communication problems that might otherwise exist between the sales and underwriting functions. The underwriter gets better information for assessing risks, and also provides customers with better service, including better information about their risks. The superior abilities of the underwriter/agents make it possible to combine these two roles.

Second, Chubb fills vacancies internally, moving people frequently and retraining them for new jobs. The pace of work eventually pushes some people out of the organization, but they rarely go to other insurance companies and more typically become independent agents, helping to expand the network for Chubb's business. And this turnover expands what would otherwise be very limited opportunities for career development in a reasonable stable organization.

American International Group (A.I.G.) achieves its high level of profitability in a different way, but one that also relies on its human resources. A.I.G. is a market maker. It identifies new areas of business, creates new products, and benefits from "first mover" advantages. It was the first insurer allowed into communist China and has recently entered the Russian market. A.I.G. thrives by finding markets where it has little competition, often high-risk operations that competitors avoid. Once companies that compete on price enter its markets, A.I.G. might well move on to another product.

The company's competencies, therefore, are in marketing—identifying new business areas—and in the ability to change quickly. It pursues change with a set of policies that are virtually the mirror opposite of Chubb's. Operating in a highly decentralized manner by creating literally hundreds of subsidiary companies, each targeted to a specific market, it creates new companies to attack new markets and staffs them by hiring experts with industry skills from other firms. It has been known to hire away entire operations from competitors, typically for much higher pay. For example, it hired the head and seven other members of Drexel Burnham Lambert's interest rate swap department in 1987 as part of its move into capital markets.

A.I.G. has little interest in developing commonalities across its companies. The executives in each company are managed through a series of financial targets—with generous rewards for meeting the targets—and are otherwise given considerable autonomy in running the businesses. When a market dries up or tough competition enters the picture, A.I.G.

may close shop in that arena. For example, the company's top executives forced out most of the original management team at A.I.G. Global Investors after determining that the profit potential in that market was no longer there. The fact that the company changes markets so quickly would make it difficult to recoup an investment in developing employees with market-specific skills itself, so it relies on the outside labor market instead.

The advantages of speed in attacking markets effectively make other ways of competing difficult. For example, hiring experienced employees away from competitors without offering any real job security means that A.I.G. is paying top dollar to get them, an expense that would make it difficult to compete as a low-cost provider. The reverse argument could be made about Chubb, that the investment in people required to develop the competencies needed to exploit existing markets would be too slow and expensive for attacking new markets as they emerge.

Beyond Direct Services

The link between employees and product market strategy is sometimes less direct when one moves away from services. But there are still relationships between the way employees are managed, the competencies employees help produce, and the way companies compete. Let's consider two examples, one from a service industry that relies heavily on technology, the other from food and beverage manufacturing.

THE SHIPPING BUSINESS

It is difficult to find two companies with people management systems that are more different than those at Federal Express and United Parcel Service. FedEx has no union, and its work force is managed using most of the "hot" concepts in contemporary human resource management. The company has pay-for-suggestions systems, quality-of-worklife programs, and a variety of other arrangements to "empower" employees and increase their involvement. The most important of these may be its "Survey-Feedback-Action" program that begins with climate surveys and reviews by subordinates and ends with each work group developing a detailed action plan to address the problems identified by the surveys and reviews.

Employees at FedEx play an important role in helping to design the work organization and the way technology is used, and employee hustle and motivation have helped make FedEx the dominant force in the overnight mail business. As evidence that initiatives paid off, FedEx claimed the honor of being the first service company to win the Malcolm Baldrige National Quality Award.

One of the goals at FedEx is that every employee should be empowered to do whatever is necessary to get a job done. Decentralized authority and the absence of detailed rules would lead to a chaotic pattern of disorganized decisions in the absence of a strong set of common norms and values. FedEx achieves those with an intensive orientation program and communication efforts that include daily information updates broadcast to each of its more than 200 locations. Empowering individual employees also requires that they have the information and skills to make good decisions. FedEx requires that employees pass interactive skills tests every six months. The tests are customized to each location and employee, and the results are tied to a pay-for-skill program.

UPS, on the other hand, has none of these people management practices. Employees have no direct say over work organization matters. Their jobs are designed in excruciating detail, using time-and-motion studies, by a staff of more than 3,000 industrial engineers. Drivers are told, for example, how to carry packages (under their left arm) and even how to fold money (face up). The company measures individual performance against company standards for each task, and assesses employee performance daily. There are no efforts at employee involvement other than collective bargaining over contract terms through the Teamsters' Union. The union at UPS does not appear to be the force maintaining this system of work organization. The initiative on work organization issues has been with management, which has shown little interest in moving toward work systems such as FedEx champions. Indeed, the view from the top of the company has been that virtually all of the company's problems could be addressed by improving the accountability of employees—setting standards for performance and communicating them to workers.

The material rewards for working at UPS are substantial and may, in the minds of employees, more than offset tight supervision and the low level of job enrichment. The company pays the highest wages and benefits in the industry, and it also offers employees gainsharing and stock ownership plans. UPS remains a privately held company owned by its employees. In contrast to FedEx, virtually all promotions (98 percent) are filled from within, offering entry-level drivers excellent long-term prospects for advancement. As a result of these material rewards, UPS employees are also highly motivated and loyal to the company. The productivity of UPS's drivers, the most important work group in the delivery business, is about three times higher (measured by deliveries and packages) than that at FedEx.

Why might it make sense for UPS to rely on highly engineered systems that are generally thought to contribute to poor morale and motivation, and then offset the negative effects with strong material rewards, especially when FedEx offers an alternative model with high levels of morale and motivation and lower material rewards? Differences in technology do not explain it. FedEx is known for its pioneering investments in information systems, but UPS has recently responded with its own wave of computerized operations. Yet the basic organization of work at UPS has not changed.

The employment systems in these two companies are driven by their business strategies. FedEx is much the smaller of the two companies, operating until recently with only one hub in Memphis, and focusing on the overnight package delivery service as its platform product. UPS, in contrast, has a much wider range of products. While its overnight delivery volume is only 60 percent of FedEx's, its total business is nine times as large (11.5 million deliveries per day versus 1.2 million at FedEx).

The scale and scope of UPS's business demand an extremely high level of coordination across its network of delivery hubs, coordination that may be achievable only through highly regimented and standardized job design. The procedures must be very similar, if not identical, across operations if the different delivery products are to move smoothly across a common network that links dozens of hubs.

The highly integrated system at UPS parallels the experience with assembly line production, where workers are closely coupled to each other by the line. The elimination of "buffers" or inventory stocks between work stations associated with just-in-time systems increases the coupling and dictates that the pace at which work flows be the same across all groups, substantially eliminating the scope for autonomy within groups and increasing the need for coordination across groups. The delivery business is like an extreme version of a just-in-time system in that there can be no buffers. A package arrives late from another hub, and it misses its scheduled delivery—clearly a worse outcome even than a temporary break in the flow of an assembly line. And the more points of interchange, the more the need for coordination. Changes in practices and procedures essentially have to be system-wide to be effective. Such coordination is incompatible with significant levels of autonomy of the kind associated with shop floor employee decision making. It is compatible with the system-wide process of collective bargaining, however.

In short, the scale and scope of UPS's business demand a level of coordination that is incompatible with individual employee involvement and a "high commitment" approach. UPS substitutes a system of unusually strong material rewards and performance measurement to provide alternative sources of motivation and commitment. Having historically one hub at FedEx meant that there were fewer coordination problems, allowing considerable scope for autonomy and participation in shaping work decisions at the work group level and more of a "high commitment" approach.

FOOD AND BEVERAGES

Few products appear to be more similar than soft drinks, yet "The Cola Wars" that marked the product market competition between Coke and Pepsi show how even organizations with highly similar products can be differentiated by their business strategies.

Coke is the most recognized trademark in the world. First marketed some 70 years before Pepsi, Coke has been a part of American history and culture. In World War I, for example, Coca-Cola set up bottling plants in Europe to supply the U.S. forces. With such enormous market recognition, Coke's business strategy centers on maintaining its position and building on its carefully groomed image. Compared with other companies its size, Coca-Cola owns and operates few ventures besides Coke (especially now that its brief fling with Columbia Pictures is over) and has relatively few bottling franchises with which to deal. Indeed, the largest franchisee, which controls 45 percent of the U.S. market, is owned by Coca-Cola itself.

Given its dominance, the Coke trademark is akin to a proprietary technology, and Coca-Cola's business strategy turns on subtle marketing decisions that build on the trademark's reputation. This is not to suggest that running Coke's business strategy is easy. Rather, the decisions are highly constrained within a framework of past practices and reputation. (One of the reasons that "New Coke" was such a debacle, it can be argued, was that it broke away from the framework represented by Coke's tradition.)

Managing Coca-Cola therefore requires a deep firm-specific understanding and a "feel" for the trademark that cannot be acquired outside the company—

History as Influence

What determines the investments in particular employment practices in the first place is a fascinating question. Often, the differences in practices seem to be associated with the period when the organization was formed. UPS for example, was founded in 1907 when the scientific management model for effective work organization was in full bloom. Federal Express, in contrast, was founded in 1971 when job enrichment and work reform programs were the innovations taught in every major business school. Similarly, companies like Sears (founded in 1886) grew up in the period where top-down, command-and-control systems of work organization dominated American industry. While Nordstrom began as a shoe store in 1901, it did not sell apparel until 1966 and became a major organization some time later, when more decentralized management structures became popular.

In the pairs discussed here, the older companies are the ones with employment practices that invest in their employees. Whether the different practices of the newer member of the pair resulted simply from growing up in a different period (i.e., Federal Express) or from a need to differentiate itself from the more established competitor (i.e., Pepsi), or both is an open question.

---

or even quickly inside it. What Coke does, then, is build an employment system that both creates those skills and hangs onto them. Coke typically hires college graduates—often liberal arts majors and rarely MBAs—with little or no corporate experience and provides them with intensive training. Jobs at Coke are very secure. Adequate performers can almost count on lifetime employment, and a system of promotion-from-within and seniority-based salary increases provides the carrot that keeps employees

from leaving. The internal company culture is often described as family-like. Decision making is very centralized and there is little autonomy and a low tolerance for individual self aggrandizement: No one wants an unsupervised, low-level decision backfiring on the trademark. To reinforce the centralized model, performance is evaluated at the company or division level.

Coca-Cola slowly steeps its new employees in the company culture—in this case, an understanding of the trademark's image. The people management system then ensures that only career Coke managers who have been thoroughly socialized into worrying about the company as a whole get to make decisions affecting the company.

Perhaps the main point in understanding Pepsi is simply that it is not Coke. Pepsi has prospered by seeking out the market niches where Coke is not dominant and then differentiating itself from Coke. From its early position as a price leader ("Twice as Much for a Nickel") to contemporary efforts at finding a "New Generation" of consumers, Pepsi cleans up around the wake left by the Coke trademark.

Pepsi has found new markets by becoming highly diversified. Its fast food operations—Taco Bell, Pizza Hut, Kentucky Fried Chicken—provide proprietary outlets for Pepsi soft drinks. Pepsi markets more aggressively to institutional buyers like hotels and restaurants than does Coke, which is focused on individual consumers. Pepsi also has many more bottling franchises that operate with some autonomy.

Given this strategy of operating in many different markets, Pepsi faces a much more diversified and complicated set of management challenges. It relies on innovative ideas to identify market niches, and it needs the ability to move fast. Its people management system makes this possible. Pepsi hires employees with experience and advanced degrees—high-performing people who bring ideas with them. In particular, Pepsi brings in more advanced technical skills. Once in the company, Pepsi fosters individual competition and a fast-track approach for those who are successful in that competition. The company operates in a much more decentralized fashion with each division given considerable autonomy, and performance is evaluated at the operating and individual levels. The recent restructuring has moved toward further decentralization and introduced the "Sharepower" stock option program designed to push entrepreneurial action down to individual employees.

Pepsi employees have relatively little job security, which is accentuated by the absence of a strong promotion-from-within policy. One Pepsi insider commented: "Whenever anybody is either over 40 or has been in the same Pepsi job for more than four or five years, they tend to be thought of as a little stodgy." In part because of higher turnover, Pepsi employees have significantly less loyalty to the company than do their counterparts at Coke. Indeed, the main issue that unites them, some say, is their desire to "beat Coke."

What Pepsi gets from this system is a continuous flow of new ideas (e.g., from experienced new hires), the ability to change quickly (e.g., hiring and firing), and the means for attacking many different markets in different ways (e.g., decentralized decision making with individual autonomy).

Conclusions

Our paired comparisons uncover clear patterns in the relationships between business strategies and employment practices. Organizations that move quickly to seize new opportunities compete through flexibility and do not develop employee competencies from within. It does not pay to do so. Instead, these organizations rely on the outside market to take in new competencies, individualism to sustain performance, and the outside market to get rid of old competencies. Organizations that compete through their dominance in an established market or niche, on the other hand, rely on organization-specific capabilities developed internally and group-wide coordination.

Exhibit 1 illustrates the relationship between the way in which human resource competencies are generated and the business strategies that flow from them. The "flexibility" dimension is associated with "prospectors"—companies that seek first-mover advantages in attacking new markets or quick responses to changing customer preferences. The "established markets" category is linked to classifications like "defenders," firms that maintain stable market niches. The most interesting part of the chart is the absence of cases in the off-diagonal quadrants. It is difficult to think of companies with a tradition of internal development that are known for their flexibility in response to markets or ones with reputations

EXHIBIT 1: HR COMPETENCIES AND BUSINESS STRATEGIES

Business Strategies	HR Competencies	
	"Outside" Development	"Inside" Selection
Flexibility	Raiders BCG A.I.G. Pepsi	—
Established Markets/ Niches	—	49ers McKinsey Chubb Coke

for outside hiring that have the kind of proprietary competencies associated with established products and market.

There may well be a natural equilibrium in the marketplace between the flexible and established market firms. Companies like Pepsi and A.I.G. exist in part because they have competitors like Coke and Chubb that do not (perhaps cannot) adapt quickly to new opportunities; similarly, companies like McKinsey succeed because their competitors cannot easily match the depth of competencies and long-term investments that they have established.

One factor that helps sustain this equilibrium is the difficulty in changing strategies. Historical investments in a particular approach create considerable inertia and reputations that, in turn, affect employee selection long after those investments have been exhausted. Going from an "inside" employment strategy to a market or "outside" approach, and in turn from the "established market" to the "flexibility" quadrant in business strategy, can probably be done more easily than the reverse (i.e., discarding the firm-specific assets and going to the market for new ones).

General Electric under Jack Welch may represent one of the more successful attempts to make such a change in HR competencies and in business strategy, and even there it has taken about a decade. It is very difficult, however, to find examples of mature firms that have gone from a market approach to an inside employment strategy. Start-up firms and those that are growing rapidly have no choice but to rely on a market approach to get staff, and some of these firms eventually switch to an inside strategy. But that is not the same as the transition from outside to inside for mature firms.

The fact that employment practices are so difficult to change and transfer helps explain the basic notion that core competencies should drive business strategy and not vice versa: It may be easier to find a new business strategy to go with one's existing practices and competencies than to develop new practices and competencies to go with a new strategy.

Companies that secure skills and competencies in the outside market, on the other hand, are pursuing a strategy that is not difficult to reproduce. And if these competencies are in fact available to everyone on the open market, how can they generate a unique competency and competitive advantage for any one firm? One answer is that a firm may be better at spotting talent on the open market or at managing that talent than are those competitors that are also trying to secure skills and competencies directly from the market. The Raiders' player management, for example, has been particularly good at incorporating and accommodating talented players who have trouble playing effectively under other systems. The fact that BCG is able to hire new consultants at salaries somewhat below those of its leading competitors suggests a competency in recruiting—an ability to identify underpriced talent and/or job characteristics that substitute for salary.

THE NEED FOR CHANGE

The increase in the need for flexibility and change, pressures that virtually all firms feel, may be exacting a toll on employers that develop their own competencies. Competitive pressures may be pushing more of them toward the "outside"/"flexibility" quadrant. UPS, for example, did not mount an overnight delivery business until 1982, despite 10 years of lessons from FedEx that customers would pay almost twice as much for it. It also delayed automating its operations until 1986. It was also slow to develop modern computer and information systems because it did not have the skills in-house to build them and no experience in getting such skills on the outside.

A portion of IBM's recent troubles has been attributed to its inability to respond to changing markets, due in part to a lack of new talent and ideas from the outside. Sears' high-quality but high-cost sales force became a disadvantage when it confronted competition from low-cost discounters that sold reliable brand-name products. Its delay in restructuring its operations despite a decade of decline has been attributed in part to inbred management. Companies like Coca-Cola and McKinsey have begun to take in more talent from the outside, and schools like Wharton that traditionally supplied functional skills have changed curricula to ensure that their graduates are broader and more flexible. The increased need for flexibility may erode the market niches mined by firms with high competencies and specific skills like Chubb. Perhaps these firms will find lower cost ways of creating the necessary competencies in the future, possibly assembling them from the outside market.

Whether firms with highly skilled, broadly trained employees can be more flexible in their product markets than firms that hire-and-fire to change their competencies is an important empirical question. The former may well be better at creating flexibility within their current product market (e.g., "quick response" or customized production) although the latter may achieve more flexibility in moving across product markets.

Public policy discussions about changing employment practices in the nation as a whole—increased levels of employer investment in skills or introducing "high performance" systems of work organization—must be thought through very carefully in light of the above arguments. Mandated changes in employment practices could well alter the competencies of organizations and their business strategies. Some might argue that changing business strategies is a desirable outcome. The constraints on dismissing employees in European countries, for example, encourage investments in existing employees and, it is argued, shift production toward the higher quality (and higher cost) markets that make use of higher skills. But they may also drive out of business firms that rely on first-mover advantages based on very high levels of internal flexibility. The fact that distinctive ways of competing appear to be driven by competencies and capabilities that are created by unique sets of employee management practices helps explain the long-standing puzzle noted earlier: Why is there so much variance in management practices? Even practices that appear to have been demonstrated to be "best" in some firms never seem to sweep over the business community as a whole.

None of this suggests, of course, that all practices are equally good. For practices that are not central to an organization's core competency, there may indeed be best practices that clearly cut across firms; for companies with similar business strategies, hence similar core competencies, it may also be possible to identify management practices that dominate others—"lean production" among auto assemblers, for example. But it should come as no surprise that variety in employment practices, as in other aspects of life, can be a source of distinctiveness and competitive advantage.

Source: Cappelli, Peter and Crocker-Hefter, Anne. "Distinctive Human Resources Are Firms' Core Competencies," *Organizational Dynamics*, Winter 1996, pp. 7–22. Reprinted with permission from Elsevier Science.

Selected Bibliography

Resource-based arguments in the strategy field suggest that the source of competitive advantage lies within the firm, not in how it positions itself with respect to the market. See Robert M. Grant, "The Resource-Based Theory of Competitive Advantage: Implications for Strategy Formation," *California Management Review*, Vol. 33, 1993. Among the most influential of the resource-based arguments has been C. K. Prahalad and G. Hamel, "The Core Competence of the Corporation," *Harvard Business Review*, May–June 1990, which suggests that the key resource of a firm lies on the procedural side. Several articles document differences in human resource practices among otherwise similar firms. One of the most interesting of these sees the differences as relating to business strategies: Jeffrey B. Arthur, "The Link Between Business Strategy and Industrial Relations Systems in American Steel Minimills," *Industrial and Labor Relations Review*, Vol. 45, 1992.

Among more behaviorally oriented research, many studies find that the process of selection may create distinctive organizational characteristics. See Ben Schneider, "The People Make the Place," *Personnel Psychology*, Vol. 40, 1987.

Evidence about the organizations described in this article often included published material. Interesting evidence explaining the link between employment strategies and business needs at Sears is reported in Dave Ulrich, Richard Halbrook, Dave Meder, Mark Stuchlik, and Steve Thorpe, "Employee and Customer Attachment: Synergies for Competitive Advantage," *Human Resource Planning*, Vol. 41, 1992. Complete references for the company material presented in this paper are available from the authors.

Strategic Human Resources Management: Linking the People with the Strategic Needs of the Business

Randall S. Schuler, *Organizational Dynamics*

There really shouldn't be any mystery about the word *strategic* in the phrase *strategic human resources management.*

According to Horace Parker, director of strategic education at the Forest Products Company, a 17,000-person division of Weyerhaeuser in Seattle, Washington, strategic human resources management is about "getting the strategy of the business implemented effectively." For Bill Reffett, senior vice president of personnel at the Grand Union, a 20,000-person supermarket operation of the East Coast, strategic human resources management means "getting everybody from the top of the human organization to the bottom doing things that make the business successful."

The viewpoints of the academics, although stated in slightly different terms, echo the same themes. A composite definition from this source might include the following: Strategic human resources management is largely about integration and adaptation. Its concern is to ensure that: (1) human resources (HR) management is fully integrated with the strategy and the strategic needs of the firm; (2) HR policies cohere both across policy areas and across hierarchies; and (3) HR practices are adjusted, accepted, and used by line managers and employees as part of their everyday work.

Together, these viewpoints suggest that strategic HR management has many different components, including policies, culture, values, and practices. The various statements also imply what strategic human resources management *does,* i.e., it links, it integrates, and it coheres across levels in organizations. Implicitly or explicitly, its purpose is to more effectively utilize human resources *vis-à-vis* the strategic needs of the organization.

While all of this helps us identify the general purview of the subject, it does not provide a framework for melding together the separate components as defined by the practitioners and academics. The purpose of this article is to provide a model for just such an integration, forming a basis for further research as well as more effective practice.

The 5-P Model

The 5-P Model of strategic human resources management, shown in Exhibit 1, melds various HR activities with strategic needs. Viewed this way, many activities within the five "P's" (HR Philosophy, Policies, Programs, Practices, and Processes) can be strategic. Thus, categorizing these activities as strategic or not depends upon whether they are *systematically linked to the strategic needs of the business,* not on whether they are done in the long term rather than short term or whether they focus on senior managers rather than nonmanagerial employees.

One benefit of the 5-P Model is that it shows the interrelatedness of activities that are often treated separately in the literature. This separate focus, perhaps necessary for research purposes, tends to understate the complexity of how HR activities influence individual and group behavior. Thus, by using the 5-P Model, we may gain greater understanding of this complex interaction. Another benefit of the 5-P Model is that it highlights just how significant the strategy-activity link can be, as the case histories included in this article illustrate.

Defining Strategic Needs

Typically, organizations define (or redefine) their strategic business needs during times of turbulence. As such, these needs reflect management's overall plan for survival, growth, adaptability, and profitability. Internal characteristics (e.g., culture, the nature of the business) as well as external characteristics (e.g., the state of the economy, critical success factors in the industry) may well influence the definition of needs. But the biggest factor affecting strategic HR management is not a particular characteristic so much as it is experience with this mode of planning.

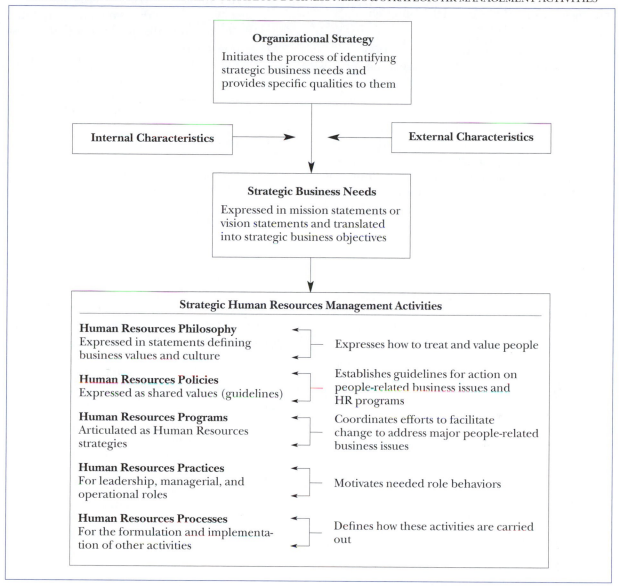

HR managers who have never before been asked to meld human resources activities with strategic needs will find that the process takes time, persistence, and a detailed understanding of the needs that have been defined. In fact, linkages between human resources activities and business needs tend to be the exception even during nonturbulent times. When such linkages do occur, they are usually driven by the organization's efforts to formulate and implement a particular strategy.

To trigger specific actions, the business needs are generally translated into more actionable statements,

which might be called *strategic business objectives*. For example, at Pepsi-Cola International, the strategic business objectives are:

- Committed bottling organization
- Uncompromising dedication to quality
- Development of talented people
- Focus on growth
- Quality business plans

For other organizations, these might be called *business vision statements*. By calling them strategic business objectives, Pepsi-Cola believes that the statement conveys a more specific action element, starting with an influence on HR philosophy.

HUMAN RESOURCES PHILOSOPHY

This is a statement of how the organization regards its human resources, what role the resources play in the overall success of the business, and how they are to be treated and managed. This statement is typically very general, thus allowing interpretation at more specific levels of action within an organization. A firm's HR philosophy can be found in its *statement of business values*. For example, one of the four value statements used at the Forest Products Company (FPC) describes the company's philosophy of what employees mean to the company and how they are to be managed:

- People are mature, responsible individuals who want to contribute.
- People hold themselves to high standards of integrity and business ethics; they are responsible stewards of the land and environment.
- Our work environment is based on mutual respect, personal satisfaction, and growth opportunities for everyone.
- People recognize that teamwork, cooperation, and a clean, safe, well-maintained work place are essential to fulfilling our customer commitments.
- Continuing education is an ongoing commitment that involves everyone.

Instead of using the terms *HR philosophy* or *HR values* to describe how human resources are regarded, treated, and managed, some organizations use the term *culture*. That is, "We will create a culture that recognizes the importance we place on people, and that builds trust and cooperation." The difference, however, may be more semantic than real. For comparison, here is a statement of the culture at Pepsi-Cola International (PCI):

LEADERSHIP IN PEOPLE

We will develop an excellent organization focused on building the business by:
- Empowering people to drive the business from the closest point to the market
- Developing the right skills to be the best in the business
- Building career opportunities
- Building teamwork:
  - With bottlers to ensure that we maintain strong partnerships

  - Among area, division and headquarters staff to ensure that we coordinate functional strengths to produce the best possible results
  - Across markets to ensure that we share the best practices throughout the enterprise
- Helping people succeed by building an environment with:
  - High integrity
  - Strong and consistent values
  - Continuous improvement

For both PCI and FPC, these descriptions of HR philosophy are part of a larger statement of *business (corporate) culture* or *business values*. These statements describe the importance to the firm of other, broader aspects of the organization: customers, operations, marketing, products, and general patterns of organization. These generally follow from a statement of the firm's vision or strategic business objectives, and vision and objectives follow from its strategy. For example, PCI's strategy is "Being No. 1 by Creating Value through Leadership and Excellence." This vision includes being:

- The fastest growing
- The most committed to customer service and attuned to customer needs
- The best operators
- The best selling and marketing company
- The best people-oriented company

And PCI's business values include:

LEADERSHIP IN OUR BRANDS

We will achieve brand superiority by:
- Delivering the best products in the marketplace:
  - The highest quality
  - The best tasting
  - The most consistent
  - Communicating these benefits in a high-impact, persuasive and consistent manner

LEADERSHIP IN MARKETING

We will build on our brand platforms by:
- Creating new brand, channel, and package segments that build the business:
  - Faster off the mark

- o Better ideas
- o Quicker to create and take advantage of opportunities

LEADERSHIP IN OPERATIONS

We will build excellence in our own and bottler operations by:

- Being the low-cost provider
- Establishing and maintaining a strong focus on customer services and sales management:
  - o These cornerstones will make us the best sales company
- Standardizing operating systems to:
  - o Enhance our ability to provide the highest level of customer service
  - o Develop an ability to measure and manage key parameters of the business in a consistent fashion
  - o Provide a common set of practices and disciplines for the organization

HUMAN RESOURCES POLICIES

All of these statements provide guidelines for action on people-related business issues and for the development of HR programs and practices based on the strategic needs. The term *HR Policy*, as used here does not mean *HR Policy Manual*. While a policy manual may contain statements of general guidelines, employees often perceive the manual as a "rule book" prescribing very specific actions permitted in very specific situations.

People-related business issues are those that affect the immediate and future success of the business and involve people. Flowing from the strategic business needs, they may include the need to hire skilled workers, the need to improve worker productivity, or the need to reduce health care costs. Other people-related business issues include the need to develop a top cadre of international managers, the need to have an adaptable and skilled workforce under changing environmental conditions, and the need to reduce excessive turnover of younger, talented individuals who are blocked by the limited number of traditional promotion opportunities.

One example, drawn from PCI, illustrates how an HR policy can link values with a particular people-related business need. The value, in this case, is stated in corporate literature as "high standards of personal performance," and the need was to develop communication skills that would foster such performance in a decentralized international environment.

HR Policy at PCI. Communication in an international environment is difficult even under the best of circumstances, as any diplomat knows. For PCI, the overlay of 150 potentially different national cultures makes it likely that some level of misunderstanding on almost any topic will occur on a regular basis.

In the early 1980s, it was clear to almost every manager in Pepsi-Cola International that expectations for individual performance standards varied from country to country. For example, in Eastern Europe it was acceptable for a manager to meet his quota and take the rest of the day off. In Germany, however, managers expected continuous improvement, a more demanding standard. Thus, the company needed a simple yet direct and culturally flexible tool to develop more consistency in managing performance. The answer turned out to be something called "instant feedback"—a device that any sophisticated human resources executive would have called too simple and unstructured to work globally. Stated simply, the principle of instant feedback says that if you have a problem or an idea about any aspect of the business, or about an individual's performance, then the organization demands that you raise the issue appropriately and discuss it maturely. A twenty-minute video tape was used to dramatize and explain how instant feedback could be applied in an international environment. Over time, instant feedback became the connecting link in a chain of feedback systems designed to improve and maintain high levels of personal performance.

Pepsi-Cola International is fundamentally a "feedback driven" organization. This feedback is now mirrored in every tool used to measure and improve performance, and the language of feedback has become part of the everyday vocabulary. It is heard when someone with an issue or problem says to another individual, "Let me give you some instant feedback." With travel schedules, frequent phone contact and constant time-zone pressures, instant feedback has become a shorthand for getting to the point and communicating clearly.

But perhaps the most fascinating aspect of the concept is that it has worked in every nation, although with some cultural modifications. Americans use it because it fits the fast-paced way we do business. In most Asian cultures, feedback may be tough and direct, but it should never be given in public. Also in Asian cultures, there may be a lot of head nodding during instant feedback, as if signifying agreement. In reality, the nods mean only that the message has been heard. Some Latins will argue very strongly if they do not agree with the feedback, and some nationalities (e.g., Indian) will insist on a great deal of specificity. Canadians will say that Americans are too direct and some Europeans will say that Americans are too demanding and critical.

Instant feedback works amid cultural diversity because the focus is always on how to improve business performance, not on cultural-specific behavior. Some would argue that this method is nothing more than effective communication. This is only partially correct. It is communication directed at solving performance problems, and while total cultural neutrality is not possible, instant feedback says, in effect, "It doesn't really matter *how* you do it, as long as you do it."

This instant feedback example also illustrates the impact of *organization structure* on strategic HR management. PCI refers to its globally dispersed organization structure as "mature decentralization" and considers this structure as a key to success in global markets. Essentially, mature decentralization means that as many decisions as possible be made in the field, as close to the consumer as possible.

Despite the emphasis on decentralization, PCI recognizes the need for operating units to be globally integrated and cooperative. The human resources challenge is to assure that a level of trust and open communication prevails so that needed resources, regardless of their source, can be brought to bear on a given problem. Common business objectives and human resources practices are certainly critical in this. But in the face of diversity, global cooperation is also accomplished by:

- Identifying values that support the objectives of the business, the organizational structure, and the needs of the individual employee, and
- Developing a set of shared understandings concerning individual performance that flow from the values that shape the human resources practices.

Thus, at PCI shared values (reflected in HR policies) result in part from the organization's structure that in turn results in part from the firm's strategic

directions. For PCI, policies serve to integrate the company's global operation by providing a basis for the development of HR practices and programs.

HR PROGRAMS

Shaped by HR policies, HR programs represent coordinated HR efforts specifically intended to initiate, disseminate, and sustain strategic organizational change efforts necessitated by the strategic business needs. These efforts may begin at the top of the organization and filter down, or they may begin elsewhere. They may even begin in two places at the same time. For example, Ford's early-1980s strategic decision to emphasize quality evolved at the top-management level and the plant level simultaneously, a serendipitous development.

HR programs can be initiated, disseminated, and sustained for many types of strategic organizational change efforts. These efforts, however, have several elements in common. First, they receive their impetus from the firm's strategic intentions and directions. Second, they involve human resources management issues, i.e., they represent major people-related business issues that require a major organizational change effort to address. They also share the reality of having *strategic goals* against which program effectiveness can be measured.

A number of generic questions help to identify the fundamental issues for these types of programs:

- What is the nature of the corporate culture? Is it supportive of the business?
- Will the organization be able to cope with future challenges in its current form?
- What kind of people and how many will be required?
- Are performance levels high enough to meet demands for increased profitability, innovation, higher productivity, better quality, and improved customer service?
- What is the level of commitment to the company?
- Are there any potential constraints such as skill shortages or HR problems?

Programs formulated in answer to such questions are typically associated with the term *HR strategies*. This makes sense because, after all, HR strategies are essentially plans and programs to address and solve fundamental strategic issues related to human resources management. For this reason alone, HR strategies and HR programs are used interchangeably in the framework here. Again, an example from the Forest Products Company illustrates this concept.

In the early 1980s, FPC became aware of a decline in large-volume, commodity lumber business and growth among small mills that tailor-made products to meet customers' demands. The small, nonunion, owner-operated, entrepreneurial mills were more market-oriented *and* operated at lower cost.

Deciding that going out of business was not an alternative, Charles Bingham, Forest Products' CEO, suggested that something needed to be done, preferably sooner than later. Together, the top dozen managers decided that a massive reorganization was called for, accompanied by a radical change in strategy. According to Bingham, the change in strategy went something like this:

> Approximately 80 percent of our sales dollars in 1982 represented products sold as commodities. By 1995 . . . we must reverse the proportions.

The result was a decision to dramatically decentralize. The three operating units, of which FPC was one, were given free reign on how to conduct their businesses. In addition, Bingham and his top team split operations into 200 profit centers, each center largely responsible for its own bottom line.

This restructuring proved to be only one step in the right direction. The top team soon realized that there would have to be a total transformation—the corporate culture, knowledge base, skill levels, style of leadership, and team orientation would all have to change. And this change would have to impact everything, from the way business was conducted at headquarters to how a salesperson dealt with customers. To meet this massive challenge, top management established a Leadership Institute. This institute, they felt, could become a powerful catalyst to accelerate the normal process of change.

The institute's first major objective was to develop and implement a four-week HR program for top executives, followed by a similar program for middle managers. A key element in both programs was attention to new HR practices, the fourth component of the Five-P Model.

HUMAN RESOURCES PRACTICES

One useful way to approach this component of HR strategy is from the framework of roles. Generally speaking, the roles that individuals assume in organizations fall into three categories: leadership, managerial, and operational. In each case, behaviors associated with a given role should support strategic needs.

Leadership Roles. These include establishing direction, aligning people, motivating and inspiring individuals, and causing dramatic and useful change. Within the FPC, *leadership roles* are defined and measured with statements like these:

- Live by the basic values of the Forest Products Company
- Demonstrate honesty and ethical behavior in business transactions
- Show a high degree of personal integrity in dealing with others
- Avoid wasting time or resources
- Strive for continuous improvement in all you do
- Demonstrate confidence in yourself as a leader

By the way, these statements are taken from a more extensive questionnaire used in the company's leadership program. Managers complete the questionnaire (i.e., rate themselves on each point) and ask their employees and customers to provide similar assessments.

Managerial Roles. Another part of the questionnaire contains statements on managerial roles. Basically, these are the traditional roles of planning, directing, delegating, organizing and coordinating. Here are some examples:

- Make sure that objectives are clearly understood
- Level with people on what is not negotiable
- Give appropriate orientation to people on new assignments
- Deal effectively with performance problems
- Give people the information they need to be successful
- Give developmental performance feedback in a timely manner
- Give people the freedom they need to do their jobs
- Give co-workers the opportunity to try out their new ideas

- Encourage appropriate collaboration on work assignments
- Encourage people to participate when appropriate

Again, managers use self-assessment and assessment from employees and peers to gauge how well they are playing the roles.

Operational Roles. These are the roles needed to deliver services or make products. In essence, they are "doing" roles, and as such their content is far more specific than for the other roles. In a service setting, a role statement might be "greets customers as they enter the sales area." In a manufacturing organization, a role might be "reads blueprints accurately" or "performs soldering operations consistent with quality standards."

Roles Can Move. Although these three roles are labeled leadership, managerial, and operational, this doesn't necessarily mean that only nonmanagers perform the operational roles or only managers perform the managerial and leadership roles. In the process of formulating and implementing new strategic objectives, organizations typically evaluate the "who does what" question. In some cases, this results in a shift of role responsibilities. For example, at the Nissan Motor Manufacturing Plant in the United Kingdom and the Honda Manufacturing Plant in Marysville, Ohio, an analysis of roles and responsibilities performed by first-level supervisors led to a more effective allocation of work. The main activities associated with first-line supervision are identified in Exhibit 2. Many of these activities, it turned out, could be distributed to nonmanagerial employees.

Matching Practices and Roles. Once the role behaviors, whether leadership, managerial, or operational, are identified, HR practices can be developed to cue and reinforce role performance. While many HR practices are used in organizations without regard to organizational strategy, some practices tie role behavior directly to strategic needs. Consider, for example, a company that has defined a need to improve quality. HR practices might provide cues for group participation in problem solving, training in statistical measures of quality control, and the like.

HR PROCESSES

This area deals with "how" all the other HR activities are identified, formulated, and implemented. Thus, it is a significant strategic human resources management activity. In the FPC situation, the process for establishing the Leadership Institute and the HR programs was accomplished through a great deal of interaction among the director of strategic education and the line managers. According to Horace Parker.

> The trump card in closing the deal [to establish the Leadership Institute and the HR programs] was to involve the executives at various levels of the organization in the planning stages.

This process of involvement at the FPC was not aimed solely at helping executives and HR people understand the organizational change strategy. It also provided opportunity for others to "buy into" the change process. Moreover, involvement is *in itself* consistent

EXHIBIT 2: MOST COMMON ROLES AND RESPONSIBILITIES OF SUPERVISORS

- Absence control
- Employee appraisal
- Bonus calculations
- Deployment of staff
- Discipline
- Drawing up shift rotations
- Employee welfare
- Handling grievances
- Health and safety
- Induction training
- Keeping personnel records
- Keeping production records
- Leading quality circles
- Planning/allocating work
- Quality control
- Recruitment
- Team briefing
- Team building
- Communicating

with the aims of the programs and the strategic business needs. That is, the executives' participation in change helps orient these individuals toward giving their employees more participation and involvement in devising tactics to meet strategic business needs. (Most quality improvement programs, for example, rely heavily on employee participation.) On the other hand, to the extent that suggestions, commitment, and executive willingness to change are not necessary, the need for a participatory HR process diminishes. These situations are increasingly rare, however, as employees at all levels continue to call for empowerment, ownership, and participation.

Thus, HR processes seem to vary along a continuum of extensive participation by all employees to no participation by any employees. Two continua could be used to differentiate between the formulation and implementation stages: e.g., high participation/involvement during formulation, but low involvement at implementation. But it appears that there is a need for consistency across these two process dimensions.

This need for consistency becomes evident across *all* the strategic human resources management activities. This need arises because all such activities influence individual behavior. If they are not consistent with each other, i.e., if they are not sending the same messages about what is expected and rewarded, the organization is likely to be an aggregation of people pulling in different directions. This is hardly a situation for the successful implementation of strategic business needs.

Recognizing this need for consistency, then, is an important component. This need, along with an awareness of the other aspects of strategic human resources management, translates into a greater need to be systematic. Strategic human resources management requires consistency and a systematic orientation. An example might illustrate how these two needs actually get played out.

Putting It All Together: The Case of Grand Union

The Grand Union is a large retail grocery operation with the majority of stores located in well-established neighborhoods. In the mid-1980s, a new phenomenon appeared in the traditional retail grocery business: the advent of the super store, the smallest of which was about twice the size of Grand Union's largest store.

The Grand Union had always defined itself as a grocery store—a traditional high-volume, low-margin, limited-selection, discount-driven, 40,000 square foot *grocery store*. Five years ago, the top management team decided that competing with the new 100,000 square foot stores (Wal-Mart's largest Hypermart is 260,000 square feet) was not a viable merchandising strategy. A directly competitive strategy would have called for moving stores from their current space-bound locations and uprooting relationships with customers, suppliers, and communities.

NEW STRATEGIC BUSINESS NEEDS

The top managers found themselves faced with the need to redefine what it meant for Grand Union to be a grocery store. Taking into account both competitive pressures and new customer habits and preferences, the team saw the need for a basic change in direction—from a commodity, undifferentiated business to a high-quality, customer-driven business.

From an individual store perspective, this meant eliminating many of the current items to make room for more national brands and merchandise with higher margins. A major objective was to sell the best quality products, which meant having a deli section (with the smells of barbecued chicken), an expanded fresh fruit section (more tropical fruits), a variety of small, ethnic food booths (for eating in or taking home), and a pastry shop.

The culture of the firm changed to emphasize listening to and serving customers. Store managers and top management started to provide the leadership John Kotter talks about, i.e., articulating and providing excitement, showing confidence in the firm's ability to successfully change in the new, more uncertain environment, and setting objectives that would relate to the new way of doing business.

LINKING HR WITH THE STRATEGIC BUSINESS NEEDS

Under the guidance of Senior Vice President of Human Resources Bill Reffett, the firm developed an HR philosophy that said the employee was a valuable, long-term source of competitive advantage, and that all efforts would be made to provide exciting jobs, promotion opportunities, and retraining as needed. The firm described this philosophy as developmental. It was apparent that role behaviors for all employees would need to change to match the needs of the new business.

While the physical size of the stores remained the same, employees were added to staff the new sections. It was important to keep these employees longer so that they could get to know the customer and the store. Consistent with the new business, the traditional command-and-control relationships across all levels were modified to accommodate a more self-directed, self-managed approach. Similarly, an individual orientation gave way to a team orientation.

Major effort was directed toward identifying new role behaviors for supervisors and other staff. This required the intense involvement of the employees, with guidance provided by the senior vice president of human resources. Together, they identified needed supervisory (first-level managerial) and staff role behaviors based upon what they saw as characterizing a customer-driven grocery store. Then they compared these with current role behavior.

This resulted in a critical redistribution of supervisory role behaviors. By recognizing the distinction between supervisors *as an employee group* and *supervisory activities* (responsibilities associated with the supervisory role) it became easier to define role activities in ways that would enhance the level of customer service.

The nonsupervisory employees also addressed the question. "What does this new business orientation mean for us at the store?" Because the focus was on the customer, they first asked, "How do we currently interact with customers?" This resulted in a before-and-after analysis of customer relationships. The "before" analysis produced the following list:

- We do not know customer desires
- We make limited use of customers
- We are space-driven, not customer-driven
- We have traditional departments, low margins, high turnover rates
- We feel no ownership of service
- We lack management skills

In contrast, the employees felt that the new direction would require management to initiate new practices:

- Holding focus groups with customers
- Being customer-driven
- Including service as part of the product
- Adding high-margin departments
- Having stores coordinate efforts; exchanging best practices
- Expanding management skills

In addition, these employees asked, "From the broader, store viewpoint, what are the characteristics that reflect a solutions-oriented, customer-driven service operation?" This question resulted in the list of characteristics for the store shown in Exhibit 3.

Based upon these characteristics, the staff analyzed the needed role behaviors, vis-à-vis the customer, and concluded that substantial changes were in order. The before-and-after role behaviors for the major job categories are listed in Exhibit 4.

In the final stage, the employees identified the HR practices that had to be formulated to match the business, based upon the role behaviors needed from the employees, especially those in direct contact with the customers. The analysis and formulation resulted in several HR practices that represented significant change (see Exhibit 5). While these changes in HR

EXHIBIT 3: ORGANIZATIONAL CHARACTERISTICS OF A CUSTOMER-DRIVEN SERVICE ORGANIZATION

- Just-in-time inventory
- Just-in-time working commitment
- Team-oriented
- Multi-skilled—technical, process, interpersonal
- Flexibility
- Trust, harmonious employee relations
- Communications
- Egalitarianism
- Distributed leadership
- Responsibility for customers
- Standard operating procedures
- Continuous improvement
- No-fault policies
- Job grade reduction
- Rewards for small improvements/suggestions
- Supplier and customer involvement
- Site visits, comparisons, benchmarks
- Customer knowledge

Employees	Behaviors Before the Change	Behaviors After the Change
Bag Packers	Ignore customers Lack of packing standards	Greet customers Respond to customers Ask for customers' preference
Cashiers	Ignore customers Lack of eye contact	Greet customers Respond to customers Assist customers Speak clearly Call customers by name
Shelf Stockers	Ignore customers Don't know store	Respond to customers Help customers with correct production/ location information Knowledgeable about product location
Department Workers	Ignore customers Limited knowledge	Respond to customers Know products Know store
Department Managers	Ignore customers Ignore workers	Respond to customers Reward employees for responding to customers
Store Managers	Ignore customers Stay in booth	Respond to customers Reward employees for service Appraise employees on customer service

practices were prompted by what the employees thought was necessary for the business, they were driven, in large part, by what employees thought would enable them to perform as needed by the customer.

Role of the Department

As the Grand Union example suggests, the HR department is in an ideal position to take charge of the 5-P's of strategic human resources management. In general it can:

- Assist in the formulation of the firm's strategic direction and needs
- Identify the HR philosophies or culture consistent with the business needs
- Develop and implement HR policies, programs, and practices consistent with the HR culture
- Ensure that the HR process is consistent with the other HR activities

If, as in the case of the Grand Union or the Forest Products Company, the organization must change in response to strategic needs, the HR department

can play a critical role as change agent. In this process, the HR department can establish an HR initiative, i.e., a specific HR program to serve as catalyst for change. The initiative can involve:

- Establishing a senior HR council and executive operating committee
- Mounting major activities to rally all employees to the change
- Developing a leadership program to ensure that the change clearly includes top management

In the development of the senior management program (and further programs that facilitate the change throughout the organization), the director of executive development or strategic education can often take the lead. This individual knows the top team perhaps better than any other HR person. This being the case, this person can then be in a position to orchestrate the entire change process—and thus the entire strategic human resources management function.

Within the HR department there can be further division of roles and responsibilities. This can be done by distinguishing between the corporate HR department and the business-unit or division HR

- **Human Resource Planning**
  Longer term focus
  Tie to the needs of the business

- **Staffing**
  More socialization
  More opportunities

- **Training and Development**
  More skill training
  Customer service training

- **Performance Appraisal**
  Customer service measures feedback

- **Compensation**
  Relate to performance appraisal
  Awards and celebration

departments. Taking a very proactive stance, the corporate HR department can:

- Assist senior managers in formulating change
- Become a model of change
- Develop and guide divisional HR
- Change organizational structure
- Serve as clearinghouse
- Serve as trainer for other HR personnel
- Do benchmark analysis
- Develop HRIS capability
- Audit competencies

HR activities at the divisional level can then reflect corporate activities. In situations where the corporate HR department abdicates to the divisions, or where the divisions simply seize the initiative, they can essentially perform the roles just ascribed to the corporate HR department. The Grand Union and FPC case studies offer a flavor of both of these situations.

The fact is that while there may be variations in *how* the roles are shared between corporate and divisional HR staffs, there should be little variation in *whether* these roles are performed. Indeed, in the extreme case, many of these roles could be performed by the line managers with or without the assistance of others.

Implications and Summary

The concept presented here proposes that the framework of strategic human resources management is made up of all activities affecting the behavior of individuals in their efforts to formulate and implement the strategic needs of the business. This rather broad concept carries several significant implications.

First, successful efforts at strategic HR management begin with the identification of strategic business needs. If these needs are important to the success of the business, and if strategic human resources management can be instrumental in meeting these needs, then these needs should be systematically analyzed for their impact on human resources management activities, including HR philosophy, HR policies, HR programs, HR practices, and HR processes.

Another implication is that, because all employees are affected by strategic human resources management, participatory processes may help cement the link between strategy and HR practices. At both Grand Union and FPC, employees helped to analyze and define the new roles they would play vis-à-vis the strategic business needs. HR management then developed practices to cue and reinforce role behaviors. While a participatory process may not always be necessary, there is mounting evidence that employees respond favorably to it when it is an option.

A third implication is that strategic human resources management depends upon a systematic and analytical mindset. At Grand Union, Forest Products, and Pepsi-Cola International, the executives formulated and implemented HR activities in a systematic and analytical manner, first identifying strategic needs and then designing HR activities with consistent cues and reinforcements. While the effectiveness of this approach has yet to be formally measured, indicators such as market share, profitability, and productivity suggest a fair amount of success. A fourth implication is that HR departments have a significant opportunity to impact their organizations' efforts to successfully launch strategic initiatives. This argues strongly for HR's participation in the formulation of strategy—if for no other reason than to get a head start on the systematic analysis of what the strategic needs of the business are vis-à-vis HR.

A final implication relates to the formal study of strategic human resources management. As practitioners do their work, HR academics have a significant opportunity to observe organizations in transition, a real-life laboratory for learning. This paper is evidence of the type of insight such observation can provide. Hopefully it will also stimulate further research, particularly in the areas of identifying employee role behaviors and linking HR practices to them, and in mapping the patterns of consistency within and across the strategic human resources management activities.

Source: Schuder, Randall S. "Strategic Human Resources Management: Linking the People With the Strategic Needs of the Business," *Organizational Dynamics*, Summer 1992, pp. 18–32. Reprinted with permission from Elsevier Science.

Selected Bibliography

Several individuals have written articles relevant to this topic and their ideas have been incorporated here. They include: F. K. Foulkes, *Strategic Human Resource Management* (Englewood Cliffs, NJ: Prentice-Hall, 1986); J. Butler, G. R. Ferris, and N. K. Napier, *Strategy and Human Resource Management* (Cincinnati: South-Western, 1990); and R. Cooke and M. Armstrong, "The Search for Strategic HRM," *Personnel Management*, December 1990, pp. 30–33.

For an insightful discussion of the impact of strategic intent and its implications for strategic human resource management, see G. Hamel and C. K. Prahalad, "Strategic Intent," *Harvard Business Review*, May–June 1989, pp. 63–76; and C. K. Prahalad and G. Hamel, "The Core Competence of the Corporation," *Harvard Business Review*, May–June 1990, pp. 79–91.

For how strategy and strategic directions determine various aspects of human resource management, see D. C. Hambrick and C. C. Snow, "Strategic Reward Systems" in C. C. Snow, ed., *Strategy, Organization Design and Human Resource Management* (Greenwich, CT: JAI Press, 1989); E. E. Lawler III, "The Strategic Design of Reward Systems," in R. S. Schuler and S. A. Youngblood, eds., *Readings in Personnel and Human Resource Management*, 2d ed. (St. Paul, MN: West Publishing, 1984); and J. J. Sherwood, "Creating Work Cultures with Competitive Advantage," *Organizational Dynamics*, Winter 1988, pp. 5–27.

Comments about Pepsi-Cola International are based upon numerous discussions with J. Fulkerson, vice president of HR for PCI. Some of these comments are expanded upon in J. Fulkerson and R. S. Schuler, "Managing Worldwide Diversity at Pepsi-Cola International," in S. E. Jackson, ed., *Working Through Diversity; Human Resources Initiatives* (New York: Guilford Publications, 1992). For further descriptions of international HR issues, see D. Lei and J. W. Slocum, Jr., "Global Strategic Alliances: Payoffs and Pitfalls," *Organizational Dynamics*, Winter 1991, pp. 44–62.

For further examples of people-related business issues, see R. S. Schuler and J. W. Walker, "Human Resources Strategy: Focusing on Issues and Actions," *Organizational Dynamics*, Summer 1990, pp. 5–19.

Descriptions of the HR activities at the Forest Products Company are from conversations with Horace Parker, director of strategic education, and Bill Maki, director of human resources, Weyerhaeuser Company, July 1990; and from J. F. Bolt, *Executive Development: A Strategy for Competitiveness* (New York: Harper & Row, 1989), pp. 139–158. Descriptions of leadership and managerial roles are also in J. Kotter, *A Force for Change: How Leadership Differs from Management* (New York: The Free Press, 1990). Comments on Nissan and Honda from interviews with Peter Wickens, director of personnel and information systems, Nissan UK, February 1991; and from interviews reported in R. S. Schuler and S. E. Jackson, "Linking Competitive Strategies and Human Resource Management Practices," *Academy of Management Executive*, August 1987, pp. 207–219.

The material describing the Grand Union is based on interviews with Bill Reffett, senior vice-president of human resources, during March 1989 and July 1991. The material here refers only to HR management-related changes; changes, of course, were also made in purchasing, merchandising, and operations. For more detail in using human resource management service organizations, see D. E. Bowen, R. B. Chase, and T. G. Cummings & Associates, *Service Management Effectiveness* (San Francisco, CA: Jossey-Bass, 1990); and S. W. Brown, E. Gummesson, B. Edvardsson, and B. Gustavsson, Service Quality (Lexington, MA: Lexington Books, 1991).

A final, but important note: As times change so do companies and individuals. The Forest Products Company was recently divided into two equal-sized groups, Wood Products and Timberland. Bill Reffett is now with Korn Ferry International.

CHAPTER

4

THE EVOLVING/STRATEGIC ROLE OF HUMAN RESOURCE MANAGEMENT

In 1998, *Fortune* cited General Electric (GE) as one of the most admired corporations in America. With revenues exceeding $100 billion annually, GE operates in more than 100 countries, employing more than 290,000 people, including 155,000 in the United States. A key component to GE's success is the belief that the HR function is a critical factor in driving its performance, worldwide. The importance of GE's people to the attainment of its corporate objectives is echoed at even the highest levels of the organization. GE CEO Jack Welch, in his annual letter to shareholders, refers to GE as "evolving to a company of 'A' products and 'A' services delivered by 'A' players."

Susan Peters, vice president of HR at GE Appliances, has noted that at GE, the human resources function is "truly a value-added business partner who is a fully participating member of the business decision-making team." At GE, HR executives are expected to have a keen understanding of the factors that are critical to the success of the business, including finance, marketing, and operations issues. Top management feels that, otherwise, it would not be possible to develop HR programs and policies that support business goals.

To support this need, newly hired HR professionals attend a comprehensive Human Resources Leadership Program (HRLP), designed to allow them to assume this critical role as a strategic partner. Those who enroll in the HRLP commit to an extensive period of training, conducted over a 2-year period. During this time, they develop skills through a combination of hands-on rotational assignments and training seminars. These assignments include working both in HR as well as in non-HR operating divisions to allow enrollees to develop an understanding of the numerous factors that impact the success of the individual business units. In addition to recruiting talent from top business schools across the country, GE also recruits internally from other functions within GE. These individuals receive specialized training in HR that augments the operating experience they have within GE. In both cases, GE ensures that its HR professionals have technical HR knowledge as well as a keen understanding of the business in which they work to allow them to meet expectations and fully contribute to their business as a true strategic partner.

Source: Stockman, J. "Building a Quality HR Organization at GE," *Human Resource Management*, Summer 1999, Vol. 38, No. 2, pp. 143–146.

The role of human resource management in organizations has been evolving dramatically in recent years. The days of human resources as the "personnel department"—performing recordkeeping, paper pushing, file maintenance, and other largely clerical functions—are over. Any organization that continues to utilize its HR function solely to perform these administrative duties doesn't understand the contributions that HR can make to an organization's performance. In the most financially successful organizations, HR is increasingly being seen as a critical strategic partner and assuming far-reaching and transformational roles and responsibilities.

Taking a strategic approach to human resource management involves abandoning the mindset and practices of "personnel management" and focusing more on strategic issues than operational issues. Strategic human resource management involves making the function of managing people the most important priority in the organization and integrating all human resource programs and policies within the framework of a company's strategy. Strategic human resource management realizes that people make or break an organization because all decisions made regarding finance, marketing, operations, or technology are made by an organization's people.

Strategic human resource management involves the *development of a consistent, aligned collection of practices, programs, and policies to facilitate the achievement of the organization's strategic objectives.* It considers the implications of corporate strategy for all HR systems within an organization by translating company objectives into specific people management systems. The specific approach and process utilized will vary from organization to organization, but the key concept is consistent; essentially all HR programs and policies are integrated within a larger framework facilitating, in general, the organization's mission and, specifically, its objectives.

Probably the single most important caveat of strategic human resource management is that there is no one best way to manage people in any given organization. Even within a given industry HR practices can vary extensively from one organization to another. This point was evident in Reading 3.2, "Distinctive Human Resources Are Firms' Core Competencies," from Chapter 3. In any organization, a critical prerequisite for success is people management systems that clearly support the organization's mission and strategy.

Establishing a strong HR strategy that is clearly linked to the organization's strategy is not enough. HR strategy needs to be communicated, practiced, and—perhaps most important—spelled out and written down. A recent study by global consulting firm Pricewaterhouse-Coopers found that those organizations with a written HR strategy tend to be more profitable than those without one.[1] It appears that writing down an organization's HR strategy facilitates the process of involvement and buy-in on the parts of both senior executives and other employees. The study found that organizations with a specific written HR strategy had revenues per employee that are 35 percent higher than organizations without a written strategy, and that those organizations with a written strategy 12 percent less employee absenteeism and lower turnover.[2] ▼

▶ Reading 4.1, "Strategic Human Resource Management: An Organisational Leadership Perspective," presents a theoretical perspective that forms a foundation for understanding how to develop appropriate HR systems. The authors center their thesis around the process by which knowledge development becomes the basis for organizational learning that, in turn, provides the basis for a competitive advantage.

Strategic HR can be contrasted to the more traditional administrative focus of HR through an examination of four different roles that HR can play in an organization. Ulrich developed a framework, presented in Exhibit 4-1, that proposes an entirely new role and agenda for HR that focuses less on traditional functional activities, such as compensation and staffing, and more on outcomes.[3] In this scenario, HR would be defined not by what it does, but rather by what it delivers. Ideally, HR should deliver results that enrich the organization's value to its customers, its investors, and its employees. This can be accomplished in four ways: (1) by HR becoming a partner with senior and line managers in strategy execution; (2) by HR becoming an expert in the way that work is organized and executed; (3) by HR becoming a champion for employees, working to increase employee contribution and commitment to the organization; and (4) by HR becoming an agent of continuous transformation that shapes processes and culture to improve an organization's capacity for change.

The first role involves becoming a partner in strategy execution. Here, HR is held responsible for the organizational architecture or structure. HR would then conduct an organizational audit to help managers identify those components that need to be changed to facilitate strategy execution. HR should then identify methods for renovating the parts of the organizational architecture that need it. Finally, HR would take stock of its own work and set clear priorities to ensure delivery of results. These activities require HR executives to acquire new skills and capabilities to allow HR to add value for the executive team with confidence.

For decades, HR professionals have fulfilled an administrative function within their organizations. In the administrative expert role, these individuals would shed their image of rule-making police while ensuring that the required routine work still gets done effectively and efficiently. This requires improving or "rethinking" a number of traditional HR functions, such as benefits and selection, which now can be automated

EXHIBIT 4-1: POSSIBLE ROLES ASSUMED BY THE HR FUNCTION

using technology, and therefore be more cost-efficient. Such streamlining of functions would help HR professionals become strategic partners in their organizations and enhance their credibility.

An organization cannot thrive unless its employees are committed to and fully engaged in the organization and their jobs. In the new role of employee champion, HR professionals are held accountable for ensuring that employees are fully engaged in and committed to the organization. This involves, in part, partnering with line management to enhance employee morale and training line managers to recognize—and avoid—the causes of low morale, such as unclear goals, unfocused priorities, and ambiguous performance management. It also involves acting as an advocate for employees, representing them and being their voice with senior management, particularly on decisions that impact them directly.

The pace of change experienced by organizations today can be dizzying. As a change agent, HR has to be able to build the organization's capacity to embrace and capitalize on new situations, ensuring that change initiatives are defined, developed, and delivered in a timely manner. HR also needs to help the organization plan for and overcome any resistance to change that might present itself. Particularly challenging are any efforts to alter the organization's culture.

HR Roles at Mercantile Bank

One organization that has effectively redesigned its HR function to assume all four roles is Mercantile Bank. Headquartered in St. Louis, Mercantile Bank is a multibank holding company, with $131 billion in assets and more than 10,000 employees. The bank strategically redesigned its HR function during the 1990s, when it went through more than 39 mergers and acquisitions. As part of this process, Mercantile's HR function moved beyond traditional recordkeeping and compliance to become more strategic in nature. This transformation happened through streamlining work processes, eliminating unnecessary activities, reevaluating technology, and outsourcing nonstrategic functions. Further, some retained HR functions remain centralized at headquarters; others are deployed to operating divisions. Consequently, Mercantile's HR function is able to assume the roles of strategic partner, change agent, administrative expert, and employee champion simultaneously.[4]

A number of other models have been developed relative to the portfolio of roles that HR can and/or should play in becoming a strategic partner in the knowledge-based economy. Lengnick-Hall and Lengnick-Hall found that, for HR to build strategic credibility, new roles needed to be assumed that expanded both the methods and processes traditionally, used in HR.[5] These roles include human capital steward, knowledge facilitator, relationship builder, and rapid deployment specialist, as illustrated in Exhibit 4-2.

EXHIBIT 4-2: HR ROLES IN A KNOWLEDGE-BASED ECONOMY

- Human capital steward
- Knowledge facilitator
- Relationship builder
- Rapid deployment specialist

The human capital steward role involves the creation of an environment and culture in which employees voluntarily want to contribute their skills, ideas, and energy. This is based on the premise that, unlike raw materials, plant, and equipment, human capital is not "owned" by the organization; it can move freely from organization to organization at the employee's whim. A competitive advantage can be maintained only when the best employees are recruited, duly motivated, and retained.

The knowledge facilitator role involves the procurement of the necessary employee knowledge and skill sets that allow information to be acquired, developed, and disseminated, providing a competitive advantage. This process can succeed only as part of a strategically designed employee development plan, whereby employees teach and learn from each other and knowledge sharing is valued and rewarded.

The relationship builder role involves the development of structure, work practices, and organizational culture that allow individuals to work together, across departments and functions. To ensure competitiveness, networks need to be developed that focus on the strategic objectives of the organization and how synergies and teamwork that lead to outstanding performance are valued and rewarded.

The rapid deployment specialist role involves the creation of an organization structure and HR systems that are fluid and adaptable to rapid change in response to external opportunities and threats. The global, knowledge-based economy changes quickly and frequently and success in such an environment mandates flexibility and a culture that embraces change.

In addition to these models, a study sponsored by the Society for Human Resource Management (SHRM) and Global Consulting Alliance found that HR's success as a true strategic business partner was dependent on five specific competencies being displayed by HR,[6] as illustrated in Exhibit 4-3. These competencies are radically different from those required in the past, when HR played a more administrative role. The first, strategic contribution, requires the development of strategy, connecting organizations to external constituents, and implementing systems that align employee performance with company strategy. The second, business knowledge, involves understanding the nuts and bolts of the organization's operations and leveraging this knowledge into results. The third, personal credibility, requires that measurable value be demonstrated in programs and policies implemented. The fourth, HR delivery, involves serving internal customers through effective and efficient programs related to staffing, performance management, and employee development. The fifth, HR technology, involves using technology to improve the organization's management of its people.

Whereas the SHRM study identifies a set of competencies that all HR executives will need, others conclude that HR roles may need to become more highly specialized. One set of roles identifies five competencies that easily might become areas of specialization.[6] The first role is "chief financial officer" for HR, an individual who is

EXHIBIT 4-3: SHRM CRITICAL HR COMPETENCIES

- Strategic contribution
- Business knowledge
- Personal credibility
- HR delivery
- HR technology

an expert at metrics, financial analysis, and can argue the cost-effectiveness of various HR programs. The second role is "internal consultant," an individual who trains and empowers line managers to assume much of the day-to-day responsibility for managing employees and understanding the legal aspects of the employment relationship. The third role is "talent manager," an individual who focuses on finding, developing, and retaining the optimal mix of employees to facilitate the organization's strategic objectives. The fourth role is "vendor manager," an individual who determines which functions can be better handled internally or externally and assumes the responsibility for sourcing and selecting vendors, as well as managing vendor relations. The fifth role is "self-service manager," an individual who oversees the technology applications of human resource management, including all aspects of e-HR.

So far our discussion has focused on roles that HR needs to assume and competencies that need to be demonstrated to ensure that HR be seen as a true strategic partner, as well as to facilitate high performance. This discussion has ignored the fact that different organizations engage in different types of employment in pursuing their strategies. To better understand these employment models, a system was developed by Lepak and Snell that identifies four different employment models and examines the types of HR systems required by each.[7]

Lepak and Snell first analyzed the characteristics of human capital using two dimensions. The first is its *strategic value*, or the extent of its potential to improve efficiency, effectiveness, exploit market opportunities, and/or neutralize potential threats. The authors found that as the strategic value of human capital increased, the greater the likelihood that the organization would employ it internally rather than externally. The second is its *uniqueness*, or the degree to which it is specialized and not widely available. The authors found that the more unique an organization's human capital, the greater potential source of competitive advantage it would provide. These two dimensions form the matrix, presented in Exhibit 4-4, which identifies the four types of employment modes.

EXHIBIT 4-4: LEPAK AND SNELL'S EMPLOYMENT MODELS

	Quadrant 4: Alliances / Partnerships Collaborative-Based HR Configuration	**Quadrant 1:** Knowledge-Based Employment Commitment-Based HR Configuration
	Quadrant 3: Contractual Work Arrangements Compliance-Based HR Configuration	**Quadrant 2:** Job-Based Employment Productivity-Based HR Configuration

Uniqueness: High / Low (vertical axis)

Strategic Value: Low / High (horizontal axis)

Quadrant 1 illustrates knowledge-based employment, human capital that is unique and has high strategic value to the organization. This type of employment requires *commitment-based* human resource management. Commitment-based HR involves heavy investment in training and development, employee autonomy and participation, employment security, and compensation systems that are long-term (i.e., stock options) and knowledge-based.

Quadrant 2 illustrates job-based employment, human capital that has limited uniqueness but is of high strategic value to the organization. This type of employment requires *productivity-based* human resource management. Less investment will be made in employees and the organization will seek to acquire individuals with the requisite skills rather than provide training in skills that are generic. Shorter time frames will be established for performance and rewards and jobs will be more standardized.

Quadrant 3 illustrates contractual employment, human capital that is not unique nor of strategic value to the organization. This type of employment requires *compliance-based* human resource management. Structure and direction would be provided for employees and systems established to ensure that employees comply with rules, regulations, and procedures. Workers would receive little discretion and any training, performance management, and compensation would be based on ensuring compliance with the set work structures.

Quadrant 4 illustrates alliance/partnership employment, human capital that is unique but of limited strategic value to the organization. This type of employment requires *collaborative-based* human resource management. Much of the work would be outsourced to an outside vendor based on the sharing of information and establishment of trust. The organization would select alliance partners who are committed to the relationship as well as the organization's success. Performance standards and incentives would be established that mutually benefit both partners. ▼▼

Strategic Human Resource Management at Southwest Airlines

Southwest Airlines (SWA) was one of the most successful airline companies in the 1990s. Throughout the decade, it was the only major domestic airline to turn a profit, and it consistently outperformed its competitors in customer service. A key factor in the success of SWA has been its unique corporate culture and the human resource management practices that have been developed as part of this culture. These practices are integrated with each other and directly developed under founding CEO Herb Kelliher and maintained as part of Southwest's competitive strategy of delivering both low costs and superior service. These human resources practices create shareholder value through employees via low turnover and high productivity, and allow employees to experience significant job satisfaction.

Southwest's success centers around a "value cycle": Southwest first creates value through its HR practices for employees; this value is then converted, in part, to customer value via the design of specific operating processes, then captured through the provision of low costs and superior service relative to competitors. This cycle of

---

▶▶ Reading 4.2, "Understanding HRM-Firm Performance Linkages: The Role of the 'Strength' of the HRM System," develops a model for understanding how strong HRM systems impact overall strategic performance. It proposes that the sum of a strong HRM system is a performance-inducing climate in which desirable employee behaviors are clearly understood and rewarded.

creating, converting, and capturing value is unique among not only airlines but labor-intensive organizations in general. Other airlines traditionally have competed by creating barriers to entry via the development of hub and spoke networks, and by sophisticated customer segmentation and information processing via computer reservation systems.

Southwest sees its competition not as other airlines but, rather, the automobile. Most of its flights are "short-haul" (less than 90 minutes) and involve quick turnaround of planes at the gate and the use of less congested airports. The company also restricts its growth relative to the rate at which it can hire and train new employees who fit with the company culture.

Southwest practices an alternative strategy called value analysis. Here, a value chain is created for the buyer, firm, and supplier. SWA does this by increasing its passengers' willingness to pay, decreasing the price passengers are charged, decreasing its own costs, and reducing employees' opportunity cost. SWA increases its passengers' willingness to pay by providing a higher level of service than its competitors, offering more frequent departures, and amusing its passengers, which makes the end of a long workday more entertaining. SWA also attempts to offer the lowest airline fare in a specific market. This allows SWA to differentiate itself from competitors that offer a relatively generic service.

Personnel is one of the most significant costs an airline incurs. At SWA, however, employees are more productive than at other major airlines. Most SWA employees are directly involved in moving passengers from departure to destination as gate agents, ramp agents, baggage handlers, flight attendants, or pilots. The result? An average airplane takes 45 minutes to turnaround: SWA averages only 17 minutes.

SWA can turn around its aircraft in 17 minutes for three reasons. First, it uses standardized aircraft—737s only. Second, no meals are provided on flights, enhancing efficiency and reducing costs. Finally, the airline has designed its work systems to allow cross-functional coordination by all its employees. From the moment a SWA flight touches down until the minute it clears the gate, every member of the flight and ground crews does everything necessary to get the next flight segment out on time.

Southwest has a culture that stresses "LUV" and "FUN." "LUV" refers to one of the company's core values, involving respect for individuality, and a genuine concern for others. "FUN" refers to the company's philosophy of employees enjoying themselves at work and creating an atmosphere that allows customers to have fun as well. FUN and LUV are critical elements of SWA's culture and are embedded in the hiring process, with prospective employees being asked to describe their most embarrassing moment. FUN and LUV are also critical components of SWA's compensation system. Actual salaries are at the industry average, but most employees consider SWA's work environment to be a form of nonmonetary compensation.

SWA uses a variety of HR practices to create its unique labor force. Starting with a rigorous selection process, employees are paid an average compensation, combined with significant nonmonetary awards. Employees treat one another well, and there is a focus on ongoing training and development. Employees' suggestions are also constantly solicited. The nurturing, ongoing development of the organizational culture is critical to Southwest's competitive advantage.[8]

Strategic HR differs radically from traditional HR in a number of ways, as illustrated in Exhibit 4-5. In a traditional approach to HR, the main responsibility for people management programs rests with staff specialists in the corporate HR division. A strategic approach places the responsibility for managing people with the individuals most in contact with them, their respective line managers. In essence,

EXHIBIT 4-5: TRADITIONAL HR VERSUS STRATEGIC HR

	Traditional HR	**Strategic HR**
Responsibility for HR	Staff specialists	Line managers
Focus	Employee relations	Partnerships with internal and external customers
Role of HR	Transactional, change follower, and respondent	Transformational, change leader, and initiator
Initiatives	Slow, reactive, fragmented	Fast, proactive, integrated
Time horizon	Short-term	Short, medium, long (as necessary)
Control	Bureaucratic—roles, policies, procedures	Organic—flexible, whatever is necessary to succeed
Job design	Tight division of labor, independence, specialization	Broad, flexible, cross-training, teams
Key investments	Capital, products	People, knowledge
Accountability	Cost center	Investment center

strategic HR would argue that any individual in an organization who has responsibility for people is an HR manager, regardless of the technical area in which he or she works.

Traditional HR focuses its activities on employee relations, ensuring that employees are motivated and productive and that the organization is in compliance with all necessary employment laws, as illustrated in the operational quadrants in Exhibit 4-1. A strategic approach shifts the focus to partnerships with internal and external constituent groups. Employees are only one constituency that needs to be considered. The focus on managing people is more systemic, with an understanding of the myriad factors that impact employees and the organization and how to manage multiple relationships to ensure satisfaction at all levels of the organization. Critical partners in the process include, but are not limited to, employees, customers, stockholders/owners, regulatory agencies, and public interest groups.

Traditional HR assumes a role of handling transactions as they arise. These may involve compliance with changing laws, rectifying problems between supervisors and subordinates, recruiting and screening applicants for current needs, and basically responding to events after they happen. Strategic HR is much more transformational and realizes that the success of any initiatives for growth, adaptation, or change within the organization are dependent upon the employees who utilize any changes in technology or produce any changes in the organization's product or service. HR therefore plays more of a transformational role in assisting the organization in identifying and meeting the larger challenges it faces in its external environment by ensuring that the internal mechanisms that facilitate change are in place.

Similarly, any initiatives for change coming from traditional HR are usually slow and fragmented, piecemeal, and not integrated with larger concerns. Strategic HR is more proactive and systemic in change initiatives. Rectifying a specific employee discipline problem or moving to a new sales commission system are examples of the former approach. Strategic HR is flexible enough to consider the various time frames (short, medium, and/or long-run) as necessary to facilitate the development of programs and policies that address the critical strategic challenges being faced by the organization. At the same time, these strategically conceived initiatives must be developed and implemented in concert with other HR systems.

As an example, the HR systems at Mercantile Bank were not developed independent of each other. As the HR function evolved with subsequent mergers and acquisitions, HR initiatives were developed in tandem with other HR programs and policies. For example, job analysis procedures developed competencies that formed the basis for recruiting, testing, performance feedback, and compensation programs. The performance feedback program was developed in tandem with a succession planning program and incentive programs for high performers. These types of integrated initiatives are one of the principle differences between traditional and strategic human resource management.

The traditional approach to HR manifests itself in bureaucratic control through rules, procedures, and policies that ensure fair treatment of employees and predictability in operations. Indeed, Exhibit 4-1 notes the role of HR as administrative expert in developing and enforcing rules and standards of behavior for employees. Strategic HR, on the other hand, realizes that such an approach limits an organization's ability to grow and respond to a rapidly changing environment. Strategic HR utilizes control that is much more "organic," or loose and free-flowing, with as few restrictions on employee actions and behaviors as possible. Flexibility in work processes and job responsibilities are common and will be discussed in Chapter 6. Rather than being bound by excessive rules and regulations, operations are controlled by whatever is necessary to succeed, and control systems are modified as needed to meet changing conditions.

Traditional HR grew out of principles of scientific management and job specialization to increase employee efficiency. A tight division of labor with independent tasks allowed employees to develop specific skills and maintain a focus on their specific job responsibilities. A strategic approach to HR allows very broad job design, emphasizing flexibility and a need to respond as change takes place in the external environment. Specialization is replaced by cross-training, and independent tasks are replaced by teams and groups, some of which are permanent, some of which are temporary, and many of which are managed autonomously by the workers themselves.

The traditional approach to HR sees an organization's key investments as its capital, products, brand name, technology, and investment strategy. Strategic HR sees the organization's key investment as its people and their knowledge and abilities. This approach realizes that competitive advantage is enjoyed by an organization that can attract and retain "knowledge workers" who can optimally utilize and manage the organization's capital resources. In the long run, people are an organization's only sustainable competitive advantage.[9]

Finally, accountability for HR activities in the traditional approach considers functions, including HR, as cost centers with an emphasis on monitoring expenditures and charging overhead to fiscal units. An investment approach considers returns as well as expenditures with attention paid toward the "value added" by HR activities.

BARRIERS TO STRATEGIC HR

Although the concept of strategic HR may make sense logically and intuitively, many organizations have a difficult time taking a strategic approach to HR. A number of reasons contribute to this. The first is that most organizations adopt a short-term mentality and focus on current performance. Performance evaluations and compensation throughout organizations tend to be based on current performance. This is not surprising given the emphasis by most shareholders and Wall Street on short-term organizational performance in terms of quarterly measures of profitability and return on investments. CEOs need to focus on short-term quarterly financial performance in order to retain their jobs. Several consecutive "down" quarters will often result in dismissal. This philosophy then trickles throughout the organization. Rewards are not provided for laying plans that may (or may not) provide significant gain three or five years in the future. Most owners and investors don't take a longer-term view of their investments; they expect to see quarterly progress in wealth-building. There are few, if any, clear incentives for managers to think long term in making their decisions. Consequently, although many organizations desire management decisions that will benefit the organization in the long run, rewards are based on short-term performance.[10]

A second barrier to strategic HR is the fact that many HR managers are unable to think strategically, given their segmented understanding of the entire business. Human resource management is a complex and ever-changing function, requiring a tremendous amount of technical knowledge. HR managers often have insufficient general management training to understand the entire organization and the issues and challenges being experienced in the finance, operations, and marketing sides of the company. Consequently, their ability to think strategically may be impaired, and their ability to influence colleagues in other functions may be limited. Unless senior HR managers can appreciate these functional issues and speak the language of these disciplines, they can not fully contribute to the organization in a strategic manner nor gain the support of managers in these areas.

A third barrier is that most senior managers lack appreciation for the value of HR and its ability to contribute to the organization from a strategic perspective. Many simply understand the traditional or operational function of HR and fail to realize the contributions HR can make as a strategic partner. Managers throughout the organization often see the HR function as providing unnecessary bureaucracy to their work and being more of an adversary than an ally. Their perception of HR is that it is inflexible and rules-oriented (You can't do this . . . you have to do that) and that it delays their ability to do their jobs (taking time to get job descriptions written and approved, postings, delays, procedures). Although a key function of HR is ensuring compliance with laws that regulate the employment relationship, many managers see the HR function as detracting from their ability to do their jobs because of the perceived added administrative work required by HR.

A fourth barrier is that few functional managers see *themselves* as HR managers as well and are concerned more with technical aspects of their areas of responsibility than the human aspects. Regardless of the function or technical specialty of a manager, any individual who has responsibility for people is an HR manager. Although a controller, chief financial officer, or information technology manager might not consider herself to be an HR manager, any individual responsible for the performance of other employees is, in fact, an HR manager. The role of HR as a strategic partner involves line managers assuming more responsibility for day-to-day operational issues, with HR providing internal support or assistance for employee relations rather than assuming full and sole responsibility for it.

A fifth barrier to strategic HR is the difficulty in quantifying many of the outcomes and benefits of HR programs. With competitive pressures making organizations more bottom-line oriented, programs that may not have any direct quantifiable benefit, such as team building, may be disregarded or shelved. Senior HR managers

EXHIBIT 4-6: BARRIERS TO STRATEGIC HR

- Short-term mentality/focus on current performance
- Inability of HR to think strategically
- Lack of appreciation of what HR can contribute
- Failure to understand general manager's role as an HR manager
- Difficulty in quantifying many HR outcomes
- Perception of human assets as higher-risk investments
- Incentives for change that might arise

consistently find resistance toward resources being allocated to programs that have less tangible, measurable benefits than those that do.

Another barrier to strategic HR is the fact that human assets aren't owned by organizations and, therefore, are perceived as a higher risk investment than capital assets. Particularly in highly competitive industries where key executives may be recruited from competitors, there is an incentive to invest less in employees than in technology and information, which are more proprietary. Organizations adopting this mindset fail to realize that it is the people who utilize the technology and information that provide an organization with stellar performance and a competitive advantage; investments in these individuals can be more critical than corresponding investments in technology and information. Although technology and information constantly need to be replaced due to depreciation in their value, an organization's human resources hold their value and can have this value enhanced by minimal investments in them.

Finally, strategic HR may be resisted because of the incentives for change that might arise. Taking a strategic approach to HR may mean making drastic changes in how work is organized; how employees are hired, trained, and developed; how performance is measured; how employees are compensated; standards of performance; and relations between employees and supervisors, and among employees themselves. Because people tend to be creatures of habit and enjoy maintaining the status quo—particularly older workers and those with less training and skills—organizations often find resistance to any change initiatives. Such significant changes can be very risky for those responsible for implementation if such efforts fail. An organization that "punishes" those responsible for unsuccessful change efforts instead of looking at such endeavors as learning experiences provides disincentives for change. Exhibit 4-6 summarizes these barriers to change.

Most of these barriers are rooted in the culture of an organization. As noted, the organization's history, values, and management practices can act as disincentives for any change initiative. The question remains concerning if and how an organization's HR systems can promote or encourage change initiatives. ▼▼▼

CONCLUSION

Recognizing that a strategic approach to human resource management needs to be undertaken within the context of a specific organization is paramount to successful implementation: What works for one organization won't necessarily work for another.

▶▶▶ Reading 4.3, "Culturally Compatible HR Strategies," illustrates how HR systems can be used as a lever to shape organizational culture toward desired strategic objectives.

This point is well illustrated by looking at how two large organizations revamped their HR functions. One did so by making HR more centralized, whereas the other did so by making HR more decentralized. Both efforts were successful because they were designed and implemented within the context of the organization's strategy.

Strategic Reorganization of the HR Function at General Motors

We might logically assume that larger and older organizations would be less prone to dramatic changes in their operating practices; however, one of the most venerable corporations in the United States has been among the most innovative in its HR practices. General Motors, like other domestic automakers, watched its market share shrink as Japanese, German, and Korean competitors captured the American consumer's dollar. When Rick Wagoner became CEO in the late 1990s, one of his primary objectives was to shake up the status quo at the organization through its HR practices. Wagoner had the head of HR join the senior management team and pushed HR into a more strategic role. At the time, the HR function at GM was totally "siloed," with a highly decentralized structure in which every GM facility administered HR in its own way. Each plant had its own HR staff, which operated with near total autonomy. Wagoner brought in Kathleen Barclay to head HR, which she revamped through a strategy she called the 3Ts: technology, talent, and transformation.

Technology was used to overhaul HR by creating an effective and accessible corporate intranet and transforming that site into a full-service HR portal. This system was described more fully in Chapter 2. The focus on talent resulted in the development of GM University, one of the largest corporate education and training programs in the world. The university has 15 separate colleges that develop training and curricula tailored to the professional needs of and challenges faced by the organization's employees. The transformation component has standardized operations, resulting in greater efficiency, improved communications and interaction, and tighter coordination of operations. The "siloed" nature of GM has been replaced by an organization that now operates as a true global entity.[11]

Strategic Reorganization of the HR Function at Wells Fargo Bank

San Francisco based Wells Fargo Bank has 185 branches, more than 3,000 employees, five separate division presidents, and does more than $20 billion in business annually. In such a large organization, HR had performed many of its traditional administrative roles. To become more competitive, Wells Fargo saw the need to move to a more strategic approach to human resource management. Line managers needed specific HR solutions to help them improve their operations and impact the bottom line, but HR was unable to deliver this under its existing administrative structure. That structure was highly centralized, with all HR consultants and staffing managers assigned to separate divisions but working out of headquarters. That was changed to create a new structure in which HR staff worked at the branch level to become more integrated with operations and support local management.

To facilitate this process, an outside trainer was brought in to work with the HR staff to refocus their responsibilities and skills. HR professionals were trained in facilitation *and consultation, technical issues, and strategizing and partnering, using a four-phase consultative methodology that ranged from the creation of work agreements, problem identification, data analysis and implementation, and follow-up. The transformation occurred over a year and has reduced turnover by 19 percent and pay problems by 99 percent. By centralizing some generic administrative duties, the organization was able to save close to $1 million annually. New hire time was reduced from 14 days to seven. The end result is that the reorganization has allowed managers to reach their strategic and business goals by moving HR closer to these managers and creating value-added processes.*[12]

Top management in most organizations doesn't realize the contribution that HR can make to overall organizational performance because they still perceive HR in more traditional ways. A contributing factor to this is that senior HR managers themselves may not understand how they can contribute to their organizations strategically. Without a holistic understanding of the organization, HR managers have limited ability to contribute to high-level strategic thinking. Until HR managers take the initiative to gain technical knowledge about their organizations, products and services, competition and markets and learn how to work politically with other senior managers, their organizations will not be able to fully integrate HR strategy with corporate strategy and will continue to operate at less-than-optimal levels of performance and efficiency.

The key to achieving this is for HR managers to realize that strategic HR can provide three critical outcomes: increased performance, enhanced customer and employee satisfaction, and enhanced shareholder value, as outlined in Exhibit 4-7. These outcomes can be accomplished through effective management of the staffing, retention, and turnover processes; selection of employees that fit with both the organizational strategy and culture; cost-effective utilization of employees through investment in *identified* human capital with the potential for high return; integrated

EXHIBIT 4-7: OUTCOMES OF STRATEGIC HR

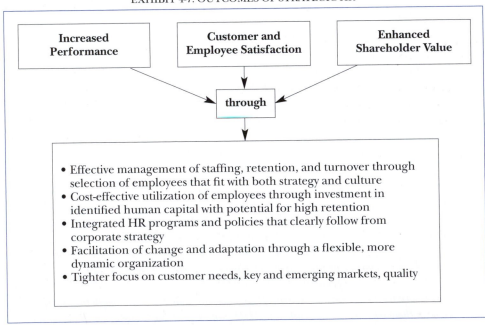

EXHIBIT 4-8: A MODEL OF STRATEGIC HUMAN RESOURCE MANAGEMENT

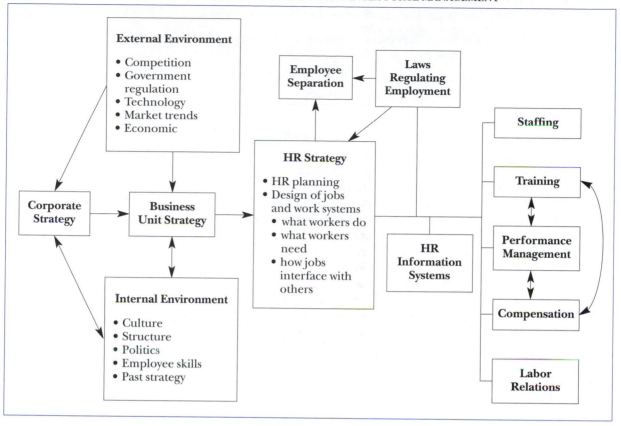

HR programs and policies that clearly follow from corporate strategy; facilitation of change and adaptation through a flexible, more dynamic organization; and tighter focus on customer needs, key and emerging markets, and quality.

A model that illustrates how this can be accomplished is presented in Exhibit 4-8. This model will provide the framework for the remainder of this book. At this point, we have discussed how corporate and business unit strategy are formed as well as organizational and external environment factors that need to be considered when developing strategy. The next two chapters, 5 and 6, will focus on the HR strategy component of the model, examining human resource planning and the design of jobs and work systems. The remaining chapters will focus on how each of the functional areas of HR can be derived from this strategy. Finally, Chapter 14 will conclude by examining strategic human resource management from an international perspective.

CRITICAL THINKING

1. Compare and contrast traditional and strategic HR. In what types of organizations might traditional HR still be appropriate?

2. What are the main barriers that prevent an organization from taking a more strategic approach to HR? Why do they exist, and how can they be overcome?

3. What is the role of HR in your current organization? What could it be? What should it be? Why does HR assume the role that it does?

4. Analyze the four HR roles presented by the Lengnick-Halls. How might the criticality of each of these roles be impacted by different strategies?

5. To be a true strategic partner, does HR need to take on a more generalized or specialized approach to its work? Why?

Reading 4.1

6. Explain the process by which knowledge development results in organizational learning and provides a basis for competitive advantage.

Reading 4.2

7. Explain the components of a "strong" HRM system. How does a strong HRM system result in the attainment of strategic objectives?

Reading 4.3

8. This reading implies that HR programs and policies can influence or change an organization's culture. Do you agree with this? Does an organization's culture need to grow/evolve naturally or can it be "shaped" or "manipulated"? To what extent does an organization's culture determine its strategy? To what extent does an organization's strategy determine its culture?

EXPERIENTIAL EXERCISES

1. Assume the position of a consultant hired to assess the approach toward human resource management taken by a client organization. What factors might you evaluate in determining whether an organization uses a traditional or strategic approach to managing its human resources? Develop specific questions that will need to be answered and determine which key decision makers in an organization should be asked these questions.

2. Select a local organization and investigate these factors by interviewing selected key decision makers.

INTERNET EXERCISES

1. Visit the Web site for the Society for Human Resource Management (http://www.shrm.org). SHRM is the largest professional association for HR practitioners in the world. Determine whether this organization encourages HR professionals to approach HR from a traditional or strategic standpoint. Print examples of pages that support your conclusion and be prepared to present them to the class.

CHAPTER REFERENCES

1. Bates, S. "Written HR Strategy Pays off," *HR Magazine*, April 2003, p. 12. Bates, S. "Facing the Future," *HR Magazine*, July 2002, pp. 26–32.
2. Ibid.
3. Ulrich, D. *Human Resource Champions: The Next Agenda for Adding Value and Delivering Results*, Boston: Harvard Business School Press, 1997.
4. Forbringer, L. R. and Oeth, C. "Human Resources at Mercantile Bankcorporation, Inc.: A Critical Analysis," *Human Resource Management*, 37, (2), pp. 177–189.
5. Lengnick-Hall, M. and Lengnick-Hall, C. *Human Resource Management in the Knowledge Economy*, Berrett Koehler, 2003.
6. Meisinger, S. "Adding Competencies, Adding Value," *HR Magazine*, July 2003, p. 8.
7. Lepak, D. P. and Snell, S. A. "Examining the Human Resource Architecture: The Relationships among Human Capital, Employment and Human Resource Configurations," *Journal of Management*, 28, (4), pp. 517–541.
8. Hallowell, R. "Southwest Airlines: A Case Study Linking Employee Needs Satisfaction and Organizational Capabilities to Competitive Advantage," *Human Resource Management*, 35, (4), pp. 513–534.
9. Pfeffer, J. *Competitive Advantage Through People: Problems and Prospects for Change*, Boston: Harvard Business School Press, 1994.
10. Kerr, S. "On the Folly of Rewarding A, While Hoping for B," *Academy of Management Journal* (18), 1975, pp. 769–783.
11. Leonard, B. "GM Drives HR to the Next Level," *HR Magazine*, March 2002, pp. 47–50.
12. Fox, A. "HR Makes Leap to Strategic Partner," *HR Magazine*, July 2003, p. 34.

Strategic Human Resource Management: An Organisational Learning Perspective

Jesus M. Rodriguez and Patricia Ordonez de Pablos, *International Journal of Human Resources Development and Management*

Abstract: This study is based on three perspectives from the strategic management literature—organisational learning, resource-based view of the firm, and organisational configurations, to develop a framework for hot topics in strategic human resource management. By merging the criteria for sustained competitive advantage with key organisational learning processes knowledge creation, transfer and institutionalisation, we analyse how strategic human resource management may facilitate the development and maintenance of a competitive advantage for the firm. By developing appropriate human resource systems firms can create and deploy their most strategic resource: organisational knowledge. In addition, the utility of the configurational approach for the analysis of human resources systems and their relationship with adaptation, renewal and organisational learning is considered.

1.   Introduction

Perhaps the organisational resources most difficult to control of all are people. Therefore, executives have traditionally based their competitive strategies on other factors, such as product and process technology, protected market niches, access to financial resources and economies of scale. However, in an entrepreneurial environment such as the present one, characterised by market globalisation, the intensification of competition and the high rate of technological change, tangible assets no longer provide sustainable competitive advantages. As firms are focusing on their intangible assets, intellectual capital can be viewed as the future basis of sustained competitive advantage. This is particularly true in industries based on knowledge, such as information and software services. Competitive advantage depends more and more on 'people-embodied *know-how.*'[1] Accordingly, it is human capital, rather than physical or financial capital, which distinguishes the leaders in the market. For these reasons, and given the fact that employee knowledge, skills and abilities constitute one of the most significant and renewable resources which a company can take advantage of, the strategic management of this capital now has greater importance than ever.[2]

The aim of this study, in keeping with Snell, Youndt and Wright,[3] is to provide a framework for the analysis of contemporary issues relating to strategic human resource management. This framework is based on a combination of three perspectives from the strategic management literature: the resource-based view of the firm, organisational learning and organisational configurations. In the first section, we emphasise the importance of organisational knowledge for the attainment of a sustainable competitive advantage. The different stages that knowledge management comprises are also presented. In the following section, organisational learning, understood as a process of knowledge creation, transfer and institutionalisation, is associated with the criteria for the attainment of a sustainable competitive advantage, and the implications of this framework on strategic human resource management are analysed. Finally, in the last section we consider the usefulness of the organisational configurations perspective for the study of the concept of fit in human resource management, and the relationship between human resource systems, organisational learning and competitive advantage.

2.   Knowledge Management and Entrepreneurial Competitiveness

2.1   ORGANISATIONAL KNOWLEDGE AND COMPETITIVE ADVANTAGE

The resource-based view of the firm[4–6] examines the manner in which organisational resources are applied and combined, the causes which determine the attainment of a sustainable competitive advantage, and the nature of rents generated by organisational resources.

On the basis of this theory, the firm is viewed as the accumulation of unique resources of a diverse nature.[7] In general terms, resources are defined as assets of different types that enable the firm to conceive and implement strategies leading the firm to improve its efficiency and effectiveness, and generating an increase in its competitiveness.[8-11]

In order for organisational resources to become a source of sustainable competitive advantage, certain characteristics must be present. On the one hand, Barney[4] argues that these resources must be rare, valuable, without substitutes and difficult to imitate. Moreover, Dierickx and Cool[12] suggest the following characteristics:

1. that they cannot be commercialised, as they are developed and accumulated within the company
2. that they display a strong intrinsic character as well as social complexity
3. that their origins lie in organisational skill and learning
4. that they should be strongly linked to the firm, with a high component of immobility
5. that their development is path dependent, that is, being conditioned on the level of learning, investment, stocks, and previous activities.

Organisational knowledge is one of the organisational resources that presents these characteristics.

2.2 TYPOLOGY OF ORGANISATIONAL KNOWLEDGE: TACIT VS. EXPLICIT KNOWLEDGE

Despite the fact that the literature includes numerous typologies for organisational knowledge—scientific and practical,[13] objective and based on experience,[14] procedural,[15] incorporated,[16] migratory and embedded[17] and codified[18]—the most frequently used is the one that distinguishes between tacit and explicit knowledge, proposed by Polanyi[19] and later utilised by other authors.

Tacit knowledge[20,21] is acquired through experience. It is a form of knowledge with which we are all intimately familiar. It appears as if it were acquired through 'osmosis' when we enter into a new organisation, or when we begin an activity that is different from what we are accustomed to. On the other hand, explicit or codified knowledge[19] is transmittable through formal, systematic language, and may adopt the form of computer programs, patents, diagrams, or similar.[22] Essentially, tacit knowledge should not be considered independently from explicit knowledge, as there is a tacit dimension to all forms of knowledge.[19] Table 1 shows the main differences between the two types of knowledge.

On the other hand, much of organisational knowledge is tacit.[24] That is, it is generated through the experience which the daily work consists of. Due to these experiences, employees who make up the organisation maintain a 'shared meaning network'. The creation of tacit knowledge is a continuous activity in organisations, and represents what Bateson[25] denominated 'analogical' quality as opposed to explicit knowledge, which is discretional or 'digital'.

2.3 KNOWLEDGE MANAGEMENT: STRATEGIC MANAGEMENT AND OPERATIVE MANAGEMENT

Managing knowledge is a key element in the achievement and sustainability of a competitive advantage. The knowledge management concept is defined as the necessary identification of knowledge categories for the support of the global firm strategy, the evaluation of the firm's present state of knowledge management, and the transformation of the current knowledge foundation into a new, powerful basis for knowledge, filling in any existing gaps.[26] In this vein, knowledge management should be developed not only within organisations, but also among organisations.[27] This last possibility is at least as attractive, if not more so, than the first. It implies sharing knowledge between partners, allies, intermediaries, suppliers and customers.

Another definition of knowledge management states that it is a collection of processes that enables

TABLE 1: TWO TYPES OF KNOWLEDGE

Tacit knowledge (subjective)	Explicit (objective)
Knowledge of experience (body)	Knowledge of rationality (mind)
Simultaneous knowledge (here and now)	Sequential knowledge (there and then)
Analog knowledge (practice)	Digital knowledge (theory)

Source: Nonaka and Takeuchi,[23] p. 61

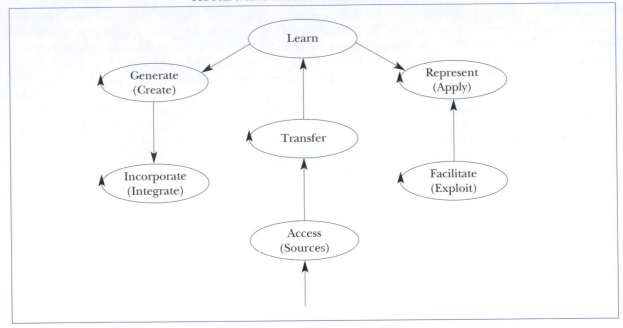

Source: Bueno[31]

knowledge to be utilised as a key factor in adding and generating value.[28] In this respect, Garvin[29] points out that it not only includes the processes of creation, acquisition and knowledge transfer, but is also a reflection of this new knowledge on organisational behaviour.

Moreover, it is possible to differentiate between strategic management and operational management of knowledge.[30] Operative management uses computer technology to organise and distribute information to and from employees. Strategic management is a process that relates the firm's knowledge to:

1. the design of organisational structures that promote knowledge
2. firm strategy
3. the development of knowledge professionals.

Any firm that undertakes initiatives in knowledge management tends to have a basic aim that is complemented with aspects of their other goals. These firms must evaluate the effectiveness of their objectives for knowledge management initiatives and their benefits, generally indirect, and establish a link between financial and knowledge results. This is a task which often shows difficulties.[32]

2.4 STAGES OF KNOWLEDGE MANAGEMENT

The aims pursued by organisational strategy for knowledge management are structured into four basic stages that constitute the knowledge management process (see Figure 2):

1. generating or capturing knowledge
2. structuring and providing value to gathered knowledge
3. transferring knowledge
4. establishing mechanisms for the use and reuse of this knowledge, both for individuals as well as for groups of individuals within the organisation.

The attainment of these objectives is accompanied by the use of knowledge management tools; that is, technology that broadens knowledge and allows for the generation, codification and transfer of this asset. This enhances the knowledge processes within the organisation. It is worth taking into account the observation made by Ruggles,[33] who points out that not all knowledge management tools are computerised. This author differentiates between three categories of knowledge management tools:

1. Those intended for knowledge generation, which is one of the keys for the firm's long-term viability, as well as its competitiveness. This category

FIGURE 2: KNOWLEDGE MANAGEMENT

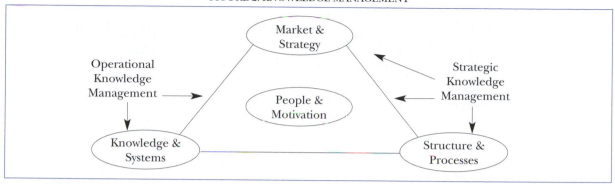

Source: Adapted from Tissen, Andriessen and Deprez,[30] pp. 26, 34

includes the creation of new ideas, the recognition of new models, the synthesis of separated disciplines and the development of new processes.

2. Those applied to knowledge codification, as this intangible asset is not useful in an isolated form. Its results must be made available to others, within and outside of the organisation. These tools allow the representation of knowledge to take place in a manner that may be accessible and transferable.

3. Those used for knowledge sharing, which face three important obstacles:
   - temporal distance, both historical (relating to organisational memory), as well as present (pertaining to the difficulty in coordinating two schedules to share sufficient common time to reach the desired interchange)
   - physical and spatial distance
   - social, which includes hierarchical, functional and cultural differences restricting common understanding.

Some companies, such as *Root Learning Inc.*, have developed tools such as the *Learning Map Process*, used by *Boeing*, *Pepsi-Cola* and *Allstate Insurance*, among others, which facilitate the social translation of knowledge. These tools enable the following objectives to be attained:

- translating corporate-level plans into clear ideas, or breaking them down into goals and activities that give an impulse to organisational success, and
- opening a dialogue regarding these learning maps during the months following their implementation.

3. Organisational Learning and Sustainable Competitive Advantage: Implications for Strategic Human Resource Management

In the context of strategic management, organisational learning can lead to the attainment of a sustainable competitive advantage if it facilitates the creation, transfer and institutionalisation of knowledge that is valuable, rare, inimitable and non-substitutable. By developing appropriate human resource systems firms can create and deploy their most strategic resource: organisational knowledge. In this respect, human capital plays a central role in the success or failure of organisations. Snell et al.[3] emphasise the complementary ground between the resource-based theory of sustained competitive advantage and the theory of organisational learning. These authors propose a framework which links the three processes of organisational learning[34] (knowledge creation, transfer and institutionalisation), with the criteria for sustained competitive advantage (value, rarity, inimitability and non-substitutability) to highlight several areas where strategic human resource management plays a role in building a firm's competitive advantage.

3.1 KNOWLEDGE CREATION

Organisational learning begins with the development of new ideas. However, knowledge creation is a process that depends on actions and requires experience, experimentation and reflection.[35,36] This idea is clearly reflected in the distinction between *single* and *double loop* learning.[37] Single loop learning consists of comparing the consequences of actions with desired outcomes, and modifying behaviour if deviations

TABLE 2: FRAMEWORK OF ORGANISATIONAL LEARNING AND SUSTAINED COMPETITIVE ADVANTAGE

	Creating Knowledge	Transferring Knowledge	Institutionalising Knowledge
Valuable	Create knowledge that enhances customer value by developing HR systems that embrace errors and encourage double loop learning	Enhance customer value by creating organisation-wide core competencies that reflect collective learning	Capitalise on learning curve effects to lower costs and enhance customer value
Rare	Attract exceptional employees and develop internal labour markets to create firm specific skills	Create organisation-wide core competencies which are distinctive and firm specific	Create first mover advantage and entry barriers by institutionalising learning curve effects
Inimitable	Utilise teams and other synergistic approaches that make the knowledge creation process socially complex and causally ambiguous	Utilise apprenticeships, mentoring cross-functional teams, and information sharing to promote the transfer of tacit knowledge and co-specialisation	Institutionalise knowledge in firm specific culture, transformations, and structures that are co-specialised and path dependent
Non-substitutable	Encourage demonstration projects, sabbaticals, and reflection time in an effort to nurture continually new ideas and recreate paradigms	Promote interplay between knowledge and transfer that leads to transformation and continuous renewal	Use memory/experience as a lever for further knowledge acquisition. Avoid organisational routines that lead to 'competency traps'

Source: Snell et al.,[3] p. 69

exist. This is an incremental process of action and reflection, focused on the continuous improvement of the existing system. Double loop learning, on the other hand, is a process that goes beyond the mere detection and correction of errors. It entails examining actions and outcomes, as well as the underlying assumptions on which they are based. In this vein, Levitt and March[38] posit that without purposeful analysis of the underlying assumptions and systems, organisations may become victims of 'competency traps' (i.e., inferior institutionalised procedures but which nevertheless lead to acceptable performance).

Organisational learning is inherently rare, inimitable and immobile, as it has a strong tacit dimension and is socially complex and path dependent.[12,5] Both single and double loop learning can contribute to the creation of value. However, single loop learning will lead to incremental improvements, whilst double loop learning tends to generate innovative or radical changes.

In keeping with this, double loop learning implies a very different human resource management approach. Traditional models of human resource management have placed great emphasis on the prevention, detection and correction of errors, taking the system as a given and attempting to maximise productivity within it.[39] However, knowledge creation requires systems that tolerate errors. Instead of focusing on the errors per se, mistakes should be considered to be one of the costs of human capital.[3] To ensure that these costs are more than offset by competitive advantages, researchers should focus on how human resource management systems can contribute to the development of organisational knowledge that is valuable, rare, inimitable and non-substitutable. First of all, the labour markets can be exploited in order to attract and select individuals with high cognitive abilities.[40,41] Likewise, research should focus on the contribution of internal labour markets to the development of firm specific assets,[42] and how cross-functional and interorganisational teams can be utilised for the creation of socially complex and causally ambiguous knowledge.

However, it must also be taken into account that although firm-specific human capital may not be transferred to other organisations, the knowledge itself can be appropriated by competitors under certain circumstances.[3] Tacit knowledge, that is, knowledge that is embedded in the minds and behavioural repertories of the organisational members as intuitive *know-how*, is not accessible to outside parties.[19] On the other hand, when knowledge is *explicit* and articulated, in such a way that it may be transmitted in standardised ways, it is easier to appropriate by competitors. For this reason, it is necessary to analyse the advantages derived from knowledge creation processes with a strong tacit component. This might include sabbaticals and demonstration projects that allow for experimentation,[43] job rotations,[35] or simply providing employees with some reflection time.[22]

3.2   KNOWLEDGE TRANSFER.

Although knowledge creation constitutes the foundation of organisational learning, the transfer of knowledge across individuals, groups, and organisations is vital for organisational adaptation.[22,35,44,45] Snell et al.[3] emphasise that transferring knowledge throughout the organisation is fundamental for building competitive capabilities. Moreover, when knowledge is transferred, co-specialised assets are created,[46] which tend to limit mobility and imitation by competitors. Furthermore, because this transfer is based on processes that are socially complex and causally ambiguous,[47] the paths tend to be difficult to replicate in a different context. In summary, knowledge transfer may constitute a source of sustainable competitive advantage for the firm.

In the context of strategic human resource management, greater attention should therefore be paid to how human resource systems can support and enhance knowledge transfer. For instance, the establishment of apprenticeship and mentoring opportunities and cross-functional teams may constitute processes of knowledge transfer with a strong tacit component, which is more difficult for competitors to imitate.[3]

A second aspect to consider is the analysis of how the knowledge transfer processes enhance the configuration of skills within the organisation. Competitive capability is something more than a simple aggregation of individual skills. Human resources programs that stimulate and reward information sharing, provide free access to information, and make use of job rotations may encourage inter- and intra-level

dialogue.[43,35] However, dysfunctional policies may discourage the exchange of information thereby obstructing efforts to facilitate knowledge transfer. For instance, competitive reward systems, based on individual performance, may impede cooperation and information exchange.

Finally, research should examine how human resource departments play a boundary spanning role between business units, in such a way that they become one of the main channels for knowledge distribution and transfer within and across organisational boundaries.[48]

3.3   KNOWLEDGE INSTITUTIONALISATION

Thus far, we have analysed the competitive advantages that may be derived from the creation and transfer of knowledge, but the capacity to institutionalise knowledge must also be taken into account. In accordance with numerous researchers, it may be stated that organisations, to a certain extent, have memory (i.e., historical information that is stored and can be brought to bear on current decisions). Walsh and Ungson[49] identified five distinct 'storage bins' in which this organisational memory can reside: individuals (assumptions, beliefs, and cause maps), culture (stories, myths, and symbols), transformations (work design, processes and routines), structure (organisational design) and ecology (physical structure and information systems).

Institutionalised knowledge can provide value to the organisation in various ways. For instance, learning curve effects act as entry and mobility barriers for competitors. As organisational learning entails costs (e.g., mistakes tolerated, time incurred), organisational memory provides a first mover advantage to those organisations that have suppressed old mistakes and capitalised on previous experiences. It must also be taken into account that, by its own nature, most institutionalised knowledge tends to be firm specific, socially complex and causally ambiguous. Specifically, for knowledge residing in culture, transformations and structures, organisational memory tends to take the form of co-specialised assets.[46] Furthermore, new knowledge usually builds upon the previous levels of learning, which are stored in myths, stories, structures, processes and organisational policies. This makes imitation on the part of competitors very difficult, as this knowledge loses much of its meaning and relevance when it is disconnected from its historical context. For these reasons, institutionalised knowledge may become a source of competitive advantage for the firm.

In the context of strategic human resource management, it would be worth studying how organisations develop complex and comprehensive memories through explicit forms such as information systems and organisational development programs,[48] as well as through mechanisms of a tacit nature, such as organisational cultures and social networks.[50]

In addition, researchers should develop ways of mapping a firm's knowledge base, and consider how different skill configurations lead to the attainment of competitive advantage. Snow and Hrebiniak[51] have initiated this type of analysis by examining the managerial competencies associated with particular strategies (e.g., defender, prospector, analyser). Although their study makes no explicit reference to the processes of knowledge institutionalisation, it does show the connection between the knowledge embodied in managers and the firm's strategic orientation.[3]

4. Fit of Human Resource Systems and Sustained Competitive Advantage

In this section, we refer to the manner in which human resource systems support organisational learning and a sustainable competitive advantage through people. Strategic human resource management should focus on how the integration and complementarity of organisational resources, practices and capabilities facilitate a sustained competitive advantage.

As set forth by Barney and Wright,[52] companies must organise themselves in such a way that they are able to capitalise on the potential value of people. Therefore, it is necessary to understand the manner in which human resource systems and practices should be configured for the development of a sustainable advantage. The literature on strategic human resource management has used the concepts of internal and external fit to refer to the integration and complementary nature of human resource practices. Internal fit refers to the degree to which the different components of the human resource system are logically connected and support each other mutually. External fit examines the integration between the human resource system and the firm's strategy.[53] It is often stated that organisational effectiveness is dependent on achieving internal and external fit.[54]

In this respect, Wright and McMahan[55] suggest that the configurational perspective may be appropriate for strategic human resource management.

According to the perspective of organisational configurations[56] certain organisational variables, including human resources, tend to be applied collectively, giving rise to coherent models or patterns. The configurational approach is consistent with the concepts of horizontal and vertical fit.[57–61] In the previous sections, different human resource practices—such as learning systems, job rotation and rewards that encourage information sharing—facilitating adaptation, renewal and organisational learning, have been considered. However, it is very unlikely that any of these practices, on their own, might lead to a sustainable competitive advantage. Though each one of them may generate organisational learning, they can be easily imitated by competitors and, therefore, are not sustainable as a source of competitive advantage. On the other hand, multi-functional systems of human resource practices may provide a sustained competitive advantage for the firm if they generate value and exhibit the characteristics of causal ambiguity and social complexity. That is, although each individual practice is easily identifiable, the entire system is more difficult to duplicate.

As mentioned previously, external fit is focused on the connection between the firm's strategy and its human resource systems. In the past, researchers had assumed that the achievement of external fit in one area impeded or limited the pursuit of other courses of strategic action. For example, Lengnick-Hall and Lengnick-Hall[62] argue that this fit may prove counterproductive from a competitive perspective, given that it may inhibit innovation and restrict the firm's repertory of skills.

Nevertheless, the concepts of fit and flexibility should not be considered opposite ends of a continum.[3] At a minimum, the two are independent dimensions that can be, and should be, managed in concert.[63] In this respect, Snell et al.[3] go a step further by pointing out that the fit among human resource practices, as well as fit of these practices with other organisational variables may be crucial for the development of organisational capabilities that enhance learning, adaptation and organisational renewal.

In Figure 3, the potential overlap is shown between different orientations of fit in strategic human resource management. On the one hand, fit can be considered exclusively as an integrative mechanism that links the different variables of the human resource infrastructure. Alternatively, fit may mean that human resource systems are aligned with a particular foundation of sustained competitive

FIGURE 3: ALTERNATIVE ORIENTATIONS OF FIT IN STRATEGIC HUMAN RESOURCE MANAGEMENT

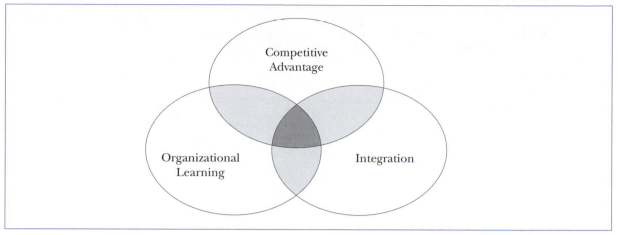

Source: Snell, Youndt and Wright,[3] p. 83

advantage. Or, fit can be interpreted as coherent efforts to facilitate organisational learning. Finally, Snell et al.[3] argue that fit implies managing all of these relationships simultaneously. This is what Miles and Snow[54] denominate the achievement of a *dynamic fit*: creating a self-renewing organisation with the ability to achieve competitive capability rapidly across a variety of situations and/or criteria.

5. Conclusions

In this study, we have related concepts from the resource-based view of the firm, knowledge management organisational learning and strategic human resource management. The aim is to develop a broader view of how firms 'compete through people'. Human resource practices exercise a strong influence on the processes of creation, transfer and institutionalisation of knowledge. In addition, fit among human resource practices, as well as among these practices and the foundations of a competitive advantage and organisational learning, is crucial for the development of organisational capabilities that enhance learning, adaptation and organisational renewal. In keeping with this, configurational research will be useful to gain a better understanding of the underlying human resource mechanisms that create a certain type of fit, of how those types of fit tend to be combined, how these combinations are related to organisational performance, and how they change over time.

Source: Rodriquez, J.M., and Ordonez de Pablos, P. "Strategic Human Resource Management," *International Journal of Human Resources Development and Management*, 2002, pp. 249–263.

Endnotes

1. Prahalad, C. K. (1983) 'Developing strategic capability: an agenda for management', *Human Resources Management*, Vol. 22, pp. 237–254.
2. Ulrich, D. (1991) 'Using human resources for competitive advantage', in R. Kilmann & Associates (Eds.) *Making Organizations Competitive*, Jossey-Bass, San Francisco, pp. 129–155.
3. Snell. S. A., Youndt, M. A. and Wright, P. M. (1996) 'Establishing a framework for research in strategic human resource management: merging resource theory and organizational learning', *Research in Personnel and Human Resource Management*, Vol. 14, pp. 61–90.
4. Barney, J. (1991) 'Firm resources and sustained competitive advantage', *Journal of Management*, Vol. 17, No. 1, pp. 99–120.
5. Peteraf, M. A. (1993) 'The cornerstones of competitive advantage: a resource-based view', *Strategic Management Journal*, Vol. 14, pp. 179–191.
6. Ventura, J. (1996) *Analisis dinamico de la estrategia empresarial: Un ensayo interdisciplinar, (Dynamic analysis of firm's strategy: An interdisciplinary essay)* (In Spanish), Servicio de Publicaciones, Universidad de Oviedo.
7. Wernerfelt, B. (1984) 'A resource based view of the firm', *Strategic Management Journal*, Vol. 5, pp. 171–180.
8. Amit, R. and Schoemaker, P. J. (1993) 'Strategic assets and organizational rent', *Strategic Management Journal*, Vol. 14, pp. 33–46.
9. Grant, R. (1991) 'A resource-based theory of competitive advantage: implications for strategy formulation', *California Management Journal*, Vol. 33, No. 3, pp. 114–135.

10. Grant, R. (1996) *Dirección estratégica: Conceptos, técnicas y aplicaciones*, Editorial Civitas, Madrid.

11. Schoemaker, P. and Amit, R. (1994) 'The two schools of thought in resource-based theory: definitions and implications for research', in P. Shrivastava, A. Huff and I. Dutton (Eds.) *Advances in Strategic Management: Resource-Based View of the Firm*, Vol. 10, pp. 3–33.

12. Dierickx, Y. and Cool, K. (1989) 'Asset stock accumulation and sustainability of competitive advantage', *Management Science*, Vol. 35, pp. 1504–1511.

13. Hayek, F. A. (1945) 'The use of knowledge in society,' *The American Economic Review*, Vol. 35, No. 4, pp. 519–530.

14. Penrose, E. T. (1959) *The Theory of the Growth of the Firm*, John Wiley & Sons, New York.

15. Winter, S. G. (1987) 'Knowledge and competence as strategic assets,' in D. Teece (Ed.) *The Competitive Challenge: Strategies for Industrial Innovation and Renewal*, Ballinger, Cambridge, Ma, pp. 159–184.

16. Zuboff, S. (1988) *In the Age of the Smart Machine: The Future of Work and Power*, New York: Basic Books.

17. Badaracco, J. (1991) *The Knowledge Link: Competitive Advantage through Strategic Alliances*, Harvard Business School Press, Boston, Massachusetts.

18. Blacker, F. (1993) 'Knowledge and the theory of organizations: organizations as activity systems and the reframing of management,' *Journal of Management Studies*, Vol. 30, pp. 863–884.

19. Polanyi, M. (1966) *The Tacit Dimension*. Routledge & Kegan Paul, London.

20. Spender, J-C. (1996) 'Organizational knowledge, learning and memory: three concepts in search of a theory,' *Journal of Organizational Change Management*, Vol. 9. pp. 63–79.

21. Spender, J-C. (1996) 'Making knowledge, collective practice and Penrose rents,' *International Business Review*, Vol. 3, p. 4.

22. Hedlund, G. (1994) 'A model of knowledge management and the N-form corporation,' *Strategic Management Journal*, Vol. 15, pp. 73–90.

23. Nonaka, I. and Takeuchi, H. (1995) *The Knowledge Creating Company: How Japanese Companies Create the Dynamics of Innovation*, Oxford University Press.

24. Cook, S. D. N. and Yanow, D. (1993) 'Culture and organizational learning,' *Journal of Management Inquiry*, Vol. 2, No. 4, pp. 373–390.

25. Bateson, G. (1973) *Steps to an Ecology of Mind*, Paladin, London.

26. Gopal, C. and Gagnon, J. (1995) 'Knowledge, information, learning and the IS manager,' *Computerworld (Leadership Series)*, Vol. 1, No. 5, pp. 1–7.

27. Earl, M. J. and Scott, I. A. (1999) 'Opinion, what is a chief knowledge officer?,' *Sloan Management Review*, Winter.

28. Tejedor, B. and Aguirre, A (1998) 'Proyecto Logos: Investigación relativa a la capacidad de aprender de la empresa espanola,' *Boletin de Estudios Económicos*, Vol. LIII. No. 164, Agosto, pp. 231–249.

29. Garvin, D. A. (1994) 'Building a learning organization,' *Business Credit*, Vol. 96, No. 1, January, pp. 19–28.

30. Tissen, R., Andriessen, D. and Deprez, F. L. (1998) *Value-Based Knowledge Management*, Addison-Wesley, Longman.

31. Bueno, E. (1998) 'El capital intangible como clave estratégica en la competencia actual,' *Boletin de Estudios Económicos*, Vol. LIII, Agosto, pp. 207–229.

32. Eccles, R. G. (1991) 'Performance measurement manifesto,' *Harvard Business Review*, January–February, pp. 131–137.

33. Ruggles, R. (1997) 'Knowledge tools: using technologies to manage knowledge better,' *Working Paper*.

34. Snell et al. [3] conceive organisational learning as a process of creation, transfer and institutionalisation of knowledge that leads to organisational adaptation.

35. Nonaka, I. (1991) 'The knowledge-creating company,' *Harvard Business Review*, November–December, pp. 96–104.

36. Senge, P. M. (1990) *The Fifth Discipline: The Art and Practice of the Learning Organization*, Doubleday Currency, New York.

37. Argyris, C. A. and Schön, D. (1978) *Organizational Learning: A Theory of Action Perspective*, Reading, MA: Addison-Wesley.

38. Levitt, D. and March, J. G. (1988) 'Organizational learning,' *Annual Review of Sociology*, Vol. 14, pp. 319–340.

39. Snell, S. A. (1992) 'A test of control theory in strategic human resource management: The mediating effect of administrative information', *Academy of Management Journal*, Vol. 35, pp. 292–327.

40. Snow, C. C. and Snell, S. A. (1993) 'Staffing as strategy,' in N. Schmitt, W. C. Borman and Associates, *Personnel Selection in Organizations*, Jossey-Bass, San Francisco, pp. 448–478.

41. Wright, P. M., McMahan, G. C. and McWilliams, A. (1994) 'Human resources and sustained competitive advantage: a resource-based perspective', *International Journal of Human Resource Management*, Vol. 5, No. 2, pp. 301–326.

42. Williamson, O. E. (1975) *Markets and Hierarchies: Analysis and Antitrust Implications*, Free Press, New York.

43. Garvin, D. A. (1993) 'Building a learning organization,' *Harvard Business Review*, July–August, pp. 78–91.

44. Nonaka[35] and Hedlund[22] have developed a useful framework for describing knowledge creation and transfer based on the distinction between tacit and explicit knowledge. Nonaka[35] proposes four approaches to knowledge transfer: socialisation (tacit to tacit), combination (explicit to explicit), articulation (tacit to explicit) and internalisation (explicit to tacit). Hedlund and Nonaka[45] have broadened this model, including knowledge transfer across different organisational levels: extension (from individuals to the groups or organisations), appropriation (from organisations to individuals), assimilation (from outside the organisation inward) and dissemination (from inside the organisation out).

45. Hedlund, G. and Nonaka, I. (1993) 'Models of knowledge management in the West and Japan,' in P. Lorange, B. G. Chakravarthy, J. Roos and H. Van de Ven (Eds.) *Implementing Strategic Processes, Change, Learning and Cooperation*, Basil Blackwell, London, pp. 11–144.

46. Teece, D. J. (1986) 'Firm boundaries, technological innovation, and strategic management,' in L. G. Thomas, III (Ed.) *The Economics of Strategic Planning*, Lexington, Lexington, MA, pp. 187–199.

47. Reed, R. and DeFillippi, R. J. (1990) 'Causal ambiguity, barriers to imitation, and sustainable competitive advantage,' *Academy of Management Review*, Vol. 15, No. 1, pp. 88–102.

48. Dixon, N. M. (1992) 'Organizational learning: a review of the literature with implications for HRD professionals,' *Human Resource Development Quarterly*, Vol. 3, No. 1, pp. 29–49.

49. Walsh, J. P. and Ungson, G. R. (1991) 'Organizational memory,' *Academy of Management Review*, Vol. 16, pp. 57–91.

50. Brass, D. J. (1995) 'A social network perspective on human resources management,' in M. Dunnette and L. Hough (Eds.) *Research in Personnel and Human Resources Management*, JAI Press, Greenwich, CT, Vol. 13, pp. 39–79.

51. Snow, C. C. and Hrebiniak, L. G. (1980) 'Strategy, distinctive competence, and organizational performance,' *Administrative Science Quarterly*, Vol. 25, pp. 317–336.

52. Barney, J. B. and Wright, P. M. (1998) 'On becoming a strategic partner: the role of human resources in gaining competitive advantage,' *Human Resource Management*, Vol. 37, No. 1, pp. 31–46.

53. Baird, L. and Meshoulam, I. (1988) 'Managing two fits of strategic human resource management,' *Academy of Management Review*, Vol. 13, No. 1, pp. 116–128.

54. Miles, R. E. and Snow, C. C. (1994) *Fit, Failure and the Hall of Fame*, Free Press, New York.

55. Wright, P. M. and McMahan, G. C. (1992) 'Theoretical perspectives for strategic human resource management,' *Journal of Management*, Vol. 18, No. 2, pp. 295–320.

56. Doty, D. H. and Glick, W. H. (1994) 'Typologies as a unique form of theory building: toward improved understanding and modeling,' *Academy of Management Review*, Vol. 19, No. 2, pp. 230–251.

57. As can be seen in Arthur,[58,59] Huselid[60] and MacDuffie.[61]

58. Arthur, J. B. (1992) 'The link between business strategy and industrial relations systems in American steel minimills,' *Industrial and Labor Relations Review*, Vol. 45, pp. 488–506.

59. Arthur, J. B. (1994) 'Effects of human resource systems on manufacturing performance and turnover,' *Academy of Management Journal*, Vol. 37, No. 3, pp. 670–687.

60. Huselid, M. A. (1995) 'The impact of human resource management practices on turnover, productivity, and corporate financial performance,' *Academy of Management Journal*, Vol. 38, No. 3, pp. 635–672.

61. MacDuffie, J. P. (1995) 'Human resource bundles and manufacturing performance: organizational logic and flexible production systems in the world auto industry,' *Industrial and Labor Relations Review*, Vol. 48, No. 2, pp. 197–221.

62. Lengnick-Hall, C. A. and Lengnick-Hall, M. L. (1988) 'Strategic human resources management: a review of the literature and a proposed typology,' *Academy of Management Review*, Vol. 13, No. 3, pp. 454–470.

63. Ulrich, D. and Lake, D. (1991) 'Organizational capability: creating competitive advantage,' *Academy of Management Executive*, Vol. 5, No. 1, pp. 77–92.

Understanding HRM–Firm Performance Linkages: The Role of the "Strength" of the HRM System

David E. Bowen and Cheri Ostroff, *Academy of Management Review*

In recent years scholars have devoted a great deal of attention to examining the linkage between HR practices and firm performance. Based on research evidence to date, it is becoming increasingly clear that the HR system is one important component that can help an organization become more effective and achieve a competitive advantage (Becker & Huselid, 1998). However, a larger question remains unanswered: *How* does HRM contribute to firm performance?

> More specifically, if there is indeed an impact of HRM systems on firm performance, how do these effects occur? What are the mechanisms through which these effects manifest themselves? . . . These questions call for theory refinement and the development of more comprehensive models of the HRM-firm performance relationship that include intermediate linkages and boundary conditions. . . . this type of research should be given a high priority by HRM scholars (Ferris, Hochwarter, Buckley, Harrell-Cook, & Frink, 1999: 394).

In research on the HRM–firm performance relationship scholars have often assumed two perspectives. One has been based on a systems approach. Research in this area has moved from a focus on *separate* HRM practices and *employee* performance to a more macro focus on the overall *set* of HRM practices and *firm* performance (e.g., Arthur, 1992; Huselid, 1995; Huselid & Becker, 1996; Huselid, Jackson, & Schuler, 1997). That is, the dominant trend in research on the HRM-firm performance linkage has been to take a systems view of HRM by considering the overall configuration or aggregation of HRM practices (Ferris, Arthur, Berkson, Kaplan, Harrell-Cook, & Frink, 1998), rather than by examining the effects of individual HRM practices on firm performance (e.g., Delaney & Huselid, 1996; Delery & Doty, 1996) or on individual performance.

A second approach has been the strategic perspective on HRM, which has taken on different meanings in the literature (Ferris et al., 1999). In one strategic-based approach, researchers have examined the particular "fit" between various HRM practices and the organization's competitive strategy (e.g., Miles & Snow, 1994; Wright & Snell, 1991). Embedded in this view is the notion that organizations must also horizontally align their various HRM practices toward their strategic goal and that practices must complement one another to achieve the firm's business strategy (Schuler & Jackson, 1987a,b; Wright & Snell, 1991; Wright, McMahan, & McWilliams, 1994). The guiding logic is that a firm's HRM practices must develop employees' skills, knowledge, and motivation such that employees behave in ways that are instrumental to the implementation of a particular strategy. Similarly, researchers have taken a contingency perspective, with the assumption that the effectiveness of the HR system depends on contextual features such as industry, firm size, or manufacturing policies (e.g., MacDuffie, 1995; Youndt, Snell, Dean, & Lepak, 1996).

A related approach within the strategic perspective on HRM pertains to how the overall set of HRM pertains to how the overall set of HRM practices is generally associated with firm performance and competitive advantage (Ferris et al., 1999). Central here is the resource-based perspective (Barney, 1991) such that, collectively, a firm's human resources are believed to have implications for firm performance and provide a unique source of competitive advantage that is difficult to replicate (Wright et al., 1994). The guiding proposition is that HRM practices are socially complex and intricately linked in ways that make them difficult for competitors to copy (Boxall, 1996). More fully, the complexities of the human resource value creation process make HRM a source of competitive advantage that is rare, inimitable, and nonsubstitutable (Barney, 1991; Ferris et al., 1991). The resource-based view has prompted recent work on how HRM practices contribute to firm performance by leveraging human capital, discretionary effort, and desired attitudes and behaviors (e.g., Becker & Gerhart, 1996; Lado & Wilson, 1994; Wright et al., 1994).

Taken together, these two perspectives on the HRM–firm performance relationship—the systems and strategic perspectives—help stage how HRM practices and their influence on employee attributes can lead to desired outcomes at the firm level, such as productivity, financial performance, and competitive advantage. Yet still left unanswered is the process through which this occurs. Although both perspectives take a macro approach, they assume implicit, multilevel relationships among HRM practices, individual employee attributes, and organizational performance (Huselid, 1995; Wright et al., 1994). The features of HRM that are necessary to facilitate these linkages have not been well addressed.

In what follows we develop a framework for understanding how HRM practices, as a system, can contribute to firm performance by motivating employees to adopt desired attitudes and behaviors that, in the collective, help achieve the organization's strategic goals. We first focus on climate as an important mediating variable in the HRM–firm performance relationship. The HRM system itself is discussed not so much in terms of content (e.g., the specific set of HRM practices necessary for achieving an organizational goal) but rather process (the features of an HRM system that send signals to employees that allow them to understand the desired and appropriate responses and form a collective sense of what is expected). We describe how a "strong climate" (Schneider, Salvaggio, & Subirats, 2002) can be viewed as a "strong situation" (Mischel, 1973, 1977), in which employees share a common interpretation of what is important and what behaviors are expected and rewarded. We then introduce the concept of "strength of the HRM system" and specify the metafeatures of the overall HRM system that would lead to strong climates, after which we examine the consequences of strong versus weak HRM systems, arguing that the emergence of the intended organizational climate from psychological climates is moderated by the strength of the HRM system. We close with directions for future research on this new strength of the HRM system construct and its antecedents and consequences. Our discussion is framed within the mesoparadigm that concerns the simultaneous study of organizational, group, and individual processes and specifies how levels are interrelated in the form of linking mechanisms (House, Rousseau, & Thomas-Hunt, 1995).

Climate as a Mediator of the HRM–Firm Performance Relationship

We begin our framework with the notion that different business strategies are linked to different sets of HRM practices, based on the contingency perspective of strategic human resource management (e.g., Schuler & Jackson, 1987b, 1995). For example, a strategy of innovation should foster adoption of HRM practices that share a focus on innovation; a strategy of customer service should be linked to a set of practices that center around service. We then build on the view that HRM systems influence employee attitudes and behavior, as well as organizational outcomes, through employee interpretations of the work climate (Ferris et al., 1998; Kopelman, Brief, & Guzzo, 1990).

Before developing climate as a mediator, it is important to note that other perspectives delineate different variables that can operate as a mediator in the HRM–firm performance relationship. For example, the technical subsystem perspective focuses on task requirements and task accomplishment (Katz & Kahn, 1978) and has historically dominated HRM research (Schuler & Jackson, 1995). The underlying assumption is that HRM practices lead to employee knowledge, skills, and abilities (KSAs) that, in turn, influence firm performance at the collective level (Schuler & Jackson, 1995).

Additionally, there are perspectives that focus on "higher-order" socially interactive constructs—what Ferris and his colleagues (1998) term *social context theory* views of the relationship between HRM and performance. By higher order, we mean social structures that cannot be reduced to an aggregation of the perceptions of the individuals currently composing the organization.

Although we focus on climate, two examples of higher-order social structures are organizational culture and the organization role structure. Culture, conceptualized as organizationally embedded assumptions and values, can function both as an antecedent to the HRM system and as a mediator of its linkage to firm performance (Denison, 1996). Organizational assumptions and values shape HRM practices, which, in turn, reinforce cultural norms and routines that can shape individual and firm performance. Role theorists conceptualize the organization as a system of formal roles, existing apart from any one current occupant, which serve to convey standardized information to employees about expected patterns of activity (Ashforth, 2001; Katz & Kahn, 1978). In this view the HRM system can be seen as part of the "maintenance subsystem" (Katz & Kahn, 1978) that defines roles, which, in turn, influence individual and firm performance.

Our focus on climate complements the technical and higher-order social structure perspectives on the HRM–firm performance relationship. We focus on climate because of our interest in multilevel relationships, since both psychological climates—as individual-level perceptions—and organizational climate—as a shared perception at the firm level—have been positioned as mediators of the relationship between HRM practices and performance (e.g., Kopelman et al., 1990; Ostroff & Bowen, 2000). Additionally, given our interest in strategic perspectives on HRM, climate is an appropriate construct for developing our framework, based on the recent emphasis on climates around strategic objectives that are purported to enhance effectiveness (e.g., Schneider, 2000).

Psychological climate is an experiential-based perception of what people "see" and report happening to them as they make sense of their environment (Schneider, 1990, 2000). This sensemaking is relative to the goals the organization pursues; how employees are to perform their daily activities; the management practices under which employees work; and the perceptions of the kinds of behaviors that management expects, supports, and rewards (Schneider, Brief, & Guzzo, 1996). Organizational climate is a *shared* perception of what the organization is like in terms of practices, policies, procedures, routines, and rewards—what is important and what behaviors are expected and rewarded (e.g., James & Jones, 1974; Jones & James, 1979; Schneider, 2000)—and is based on shared perceptions among employees within formal organizational units.

Climate researchers have acquired a strategic focus over the years, with the move from viewing climate perceptions as shared perceptions about global, generic issues to linking climate perceptions to a shared, specific, strategic content criterion of interest, such as a climate for innovation (Delbecq & Mills, 1985; Klein & Sorra, 1996) or service (Schneider, 1990). Individual-level psychological climates may emerge as a shared organizational climate, which, in turn, ultimately relates to organizational performance.

Climate is a critical mediating construct in exploring multilevel relationships between HRM and organizational performance. Because climate is widely defined as the perception of these formal and informal organizational policies, practices, and procedures (Reichers & Schneider, 1990), it follows that the HRM practices and HRM system will play a critical role in determining climate perceptions. In turn, empirical demonstrations have indicated that organizational climate is related to higher-level behaviors and organizational performance indicators, including customer satisfaction, customer service quality, financial performance, organizational effectiveness, and total quality management outcomes (e.g., Borucki & Burke, 1999; Johnson, 1998; Ostroff & Schmitt, 1980; Schneider & Bowen, 1985).

Although the above variables are well established in the literature, the mechanisms by which they interrelate are poorly understood. For example, as Boxall (1996) has observed, knowledge of HRM practices is widespread, but knowledge of *how* to refine and implement them within a particular context (e.g., a particular strategic focus) may not be. With respect to climate, Schneider (2000) has observed that there is little research or understanding of how organizational climate actually develops. Intuitive acceptance of an HRM-climate linkage far exceeds theory development of the mechanisms responsible.

Integrating HRM Content and Process

Two interrelated features of an HRM system can be distinguished; content and process. By content, we mean the individual practices and policies intended to achieve a particular objective (e.g., practices to promote innovation or autonomy). The content of the HRM system refers to the set of practices adopted and, ideally, should be largely driven by the strategic goals and values of the organization. That is, given some strategic goal such as service, efficiency, or quality, a set of HRM practices should be devised to help direct human resources in meeting this goal. To be effective in terms of content, the foci of the HRM practices must be designed around a particular strategic focus, such as service or innovation.

While a number of different models detailing the appropriate HRM practices for different strategies have been offered (e.g., Dyer & Holder, 1988; Miles &

Snow, 1994; Schuler & Jackson, 1987b), rhetoric about this contingency perspective outpaces data supporting it (cf. Huselid, 1995; MacDuffie, 1995; Schuler & Jackson, 1987a; Youndt et al., 1996). It is likely that there is not a single most appropriate set of practices for a particular strategic objective. Rather, different sets of practices may be equally effective (Delery & Doty, 1996), so long as they allow a particular type of climate around some strategic objective (e.g., climate for innovation or service) to develop Klein & Sorra, 1998).

We propose that HRM content *and* process must be integrated effectively in order for prescriptive models of strategic HRM actually to link to firm performance. By process, we refer to how the HRM system can be designed and administered effectively by defining metafeatures of an overall HRM system that can create strong situations in the form of shared meaning about the content that might ultimately lead to organizational performance.

Given a desired content of the HRM system, the HRM system may still not elicit appropriate collective behaviors and attitudes needed for effectiveness, because individuals may interpret the HRM practices idiosyncratically, leading to variability in psychological climate perceptions. HRM practices can be viewed as a symbolic or signaling function by sending mesages that employees use to make sense of and to define the psychological meaning of their work situation (e.g., Rousseau, 1995). *All* HRM practices communicate messages constantly and in unintended ways, and messages can be understood idiosyncratically, whereby two employees interpret the same practices differently (Guzzo & Noonan, 1994). Although much has been written about the substantive content of HRM—that is, the specific practices that can build task-relevant skills and motivations such as those for a climate for innovation (Delbecq & Mills, 1985), service (Schneider, 1990), change (Schneider et al., 1996), or safety (Zohar, 2000)—little attention has been given to the social constructions that employees make of their interactions with HRM across practices and time (Rousseau & Greller, 1984).

In what follows we focus on how HRM can send unambiguous messages to employees that result in a shared construction of the meaning of the situation. Thus, we concentrate on understanding what features of HRM process can lead employees to appropriately interpret and respond to the information conveyed in HRM practices. We develop the notion

that characteristics of a strong HRM system must be present in order for a shared, strong organizational climate to emerge (at the aggregate level) from psychological climates (at the individual level) and propose that the strength of the HRM system is a linking mechanism that builds shared, collective perceptions, attitudes, and behaviors among employees.

Climate as the Situation: The Concept of Situational Strength

Kurt Lewin's early work on climate is the foundation of discussions of situationism in social psychology (Ross & Nisbett, 1991). Lewin and his associates (Lewin, Lippit, & White, 1939) demonstrated that different leadership styles created different climates, which, in turn, led to different behavioral reactions and attitudes of members in the groups studied. As Ross and Nisbett summarize, "The main point of Lewin's situationism was that social context creates potent forces producing or constraining behavior" (1991: 9).

STRENGTH OF SITUATION

The situation, as developed in situationism, entails the psychological meaning of situations for the individual *and* the behavior potential of situations for the individual (Endler & Magnusson, 1976). The interest is not in the physical or actual situation per se but, rather, the situation individuals "see" based on their perceptions, cognitive maps, schemata, enactments, and even behavior in the situation (Drazin, Glynn, & Kazanjian, 1999).

In an attempt to explain when the characteristics of a situation would most likely lead to consistency in behaviors, Mischel developed the concept of the relative power of situations to control individual behavior:

Psychological "situations" and "treatments" are powerful to the degree that they lead all persons to construe the particular events the same way, induce *uniform* expectancies regarding the most appropriate response pattern, provide adequate incentives for the performance of that response pattern, and instill the skills necessary for its satisfactory construction and execution. Conversely, situations and treatments are weak to the degree that they are not uniformly encoded, do not generate uniform expectancies concerning the desired behavior, do not offer sufficient incentives for its performance, or fail to provide the learning conditions for successful construction of the behavior (Mischel, 1973: 276).

In sum, situational strength deals with the extent to which a situation induces conformity—a strong situation—or is interpreted as ambiguous—a weak situation (Mischel & Peake, 1982). The interest is in specifying situational contingencies that identify when individual differences will or will not control individual behavior (Mischel, 1997).

STRONG CLIMATES

Only when perceptions are shared across people does organizational climate become a meaningful construct (James, 1982). Recently, the notion of strong or weak climates has begun to emerge in the literature, with a focus on the *extent* to which employees interpret the situation similarly, thereby producing low variance in perceptions about the situation (Jackofsky & Slocum, 1988; Payne, 2000; Schneider et al., 2002). As such, an organizational climate can *act as* a strong situation when employees develop a shared interpretation of the organization's policies, practices, procedures, and goals and develop shared perceptions about what behaviors are expected and rewarded in the organization. Additionally, the work on strategic climate content—for example, for safety and innovation (e.g., Schneider, 1990)—assumes that the more HRM practices send strong signals about what strategic goals are most important and what employee behaviors are expected, supported, and rewarded relative to those goals, the more likely it is those goals will be achieved.

Strength of the HRM System

What are the features of an HRM system that allow for the creation of a strong situation? Although suggestions for appropriate process for separate practices have been offered (e.g., employee participation in the design and administration of performance appraisal), *metafeatures* of an HRM system overall have not been identified. Using social cognitive psychology and social influence theories, we propose a set of characteristics that allow HRM systems to create strong situations in which unambigious messages are communicated to employees about what is appropriate behavior. These characteristics refer to the *process* by which a consistent message about HRM *content* can be sent to employees.

HRM practices can be viewed as communications from the employer to employee (Guzzo & Noonan, 1994; Rousseau, 1995; Tsui, Pearce, Porter, & Tripoli, 1997). The literature on message-based persuasion (Chaiken, Wood, & Eagley, 1996) has its roots in McGuire's (1972) two-step process of "reception"—encoding of the message (exposure to the message, attention to the content, comprehension of the content)—and "yielding"—acceptance of the message (agreeing with the message and storing it in memory). For a message to have its desired effect, both reception and yielding are necessary. Yet making sense of the environment often entails numerous cycles of attending to information, interpreting information, acting on it, and receiving feedback to clarify one's sense of the situation, particularly when events are highly ambiguous or subject to change (Weick, 1995; Wicker, 1992).

Attribution theory has been useful in helping explain message-based persuasion and in helping identify key features that will allow for messages to be received and interpreted uniformly among employees (Fiske & Taylor, 1991). In the HRM context, employees are required to infer cause-effect attributions from these communications to determine what behaviors are important, expected, and rewarded. Causal inference can be understood not solely as the inner workings of the mind but also as a process by which people gather and elicit causal explanations from others and communicate their explanations to others (Fiske & Taylor, 1991).

In order to function effectively in a social context and make accurate attributions about a situation, an employee must have adequate and unambiguous information. Although attributional frameworks have been used to explain whether an individual attributes the cause of another person's behavior to internal or external factors, Kelley's (1967) attribution theory details the process for making attributions not only to other people but to situational factors as well. According to Kelley's (1967) covariation model, an individual can make confident attributions about cause-effect relationships in situations depending on the degree of distinctiveness (the event-effect is highly observable), consistency (the event-effect presents itself the same across modalities and time), and consensus (there is agreement among individuals' views of the event-effect relationship). Indeed, Mischel's (1973,

1977) explication of a strong situation implies that it is one in which there is distinctiveness, consistency, and consensus.

We propose that when the HRM system is perceived as high in distinctiveness, consistency, and consensus, it will create a strong situation. Using literature on message-based persuasion and social influence, we elucidate nine metafeatures of HRM systems that build distinctiveness, consistency, and consensus, thereby creating a strong influence situation in which employees share constructions of the situation. As such, the features help foster the emergence of a strong organizational climate, as opposed to iodosyncratic psychological climate perceptions. The strength of the HRM system can be conceptualized in terms of its effectiveness in conveying the types of information needed to create a strong situation.

DISTINCTIVENESS

Distinctiveness of the situation generally refers to features that allow it to stand out in the environment, thereby capturing attention and arousing interest. We elucidate four characteristics of HRM that can foster distinctiveness: visibility, understandability, legitimacy of authority, and relevance.

Visibility. Visibility of the HRM practices refers to the degree to which these practices are salient and readily observable. This is a basic prerequisite for interpretation involving whether an HRM practice and its component parts are disclosed to employees, affording them the opportunity for sensemaking. Visibility or salience has long been identified as an important characteristic in determining not only whether people attend to information but how they cognitively organize it (e.g., Tajfel, 1968) and make cause-effect attributions (Taylor & Fiske, 1978). For example, if performance criteria are not transparent or if pay administration outcomes are withheld, such as with pay secrecy, this certainly will not create Mischel's (1973) strong situation, in which everyone has shared constructions of the situation and uniform expectancies regarding the most appropriate response pattern and what incentives are available.

The creation of a strong organizational situation requires that situational characteristics be salient and visible throughout much of employees' daily work routines and activities. When the HRM system includes a wide spectrum of HRM practices—for example, selection, training, diversity programs, employee assistance programs, and so forth—that

affect a large number of employees, visibility is likely to be higher. Expanding the number and range of practices should enhance salience and visibility, because it increases complexity and allows for the set of practices to be more figural relative to other stimuli—both of which are principles of salience (Fiske & Taylor, 1991). Additionally, shared meanings cannot be developed unless most or all employees are subjected to and can perceive the same practices.

Understandability. Understandability of HRM content refers to a lack of ambiguity and ease of comprehension of HRM practice content. An organizational communication that cannot be understood can have no authority (Barnard, 1938). Features of the stimulus or situation evoke cognitive categories (e.g., schemas, scripts, cognitive maps), drawing attention to some features and away from others. Sometimes profound differences exist in category systems across people (Kelley, 1955). To the extent that the situational stimulus is ambiguous or unclear, multiple categorizations are likely (Feldman, 1981). That is, different people are likely to use different cognitive categories to attend to different aspects of the information, resulting in different attributions. For example, employees must be able to understand how the practice works. HRM practices such as benefit plans, gain-sharing plans, and succession plans are easily misunderstood or at least open to multiple interpretations.

Legitimacy of authority. Legitimate authority of the HRM system and its agents leads individuals to consider submitting to performance expectations as formally sanctioned behaviors. Influence by legitimate authority is essentially a perceptual process—that is, one sees the behavioral requirements of one's own role as subordinate to another that stands out as the legitimate authority (Kelman & Hamilton, 1989). It is the concept of authority whereby individuals are willing to submit to the necessities of cooperative systems (Barnard, 1938).

The HRM system is most likely to be perceived as an authority situation when the HRM function is perceived as a high-status, high-credibility function and activity. This is most likely when HRM has significant and visible top management support in the firm and can be achieved through investments in HR practices or the HRM function, or perhaps by placing the director of HRM in a high-level managerial position. This fits the observation about the requirements for the success of HRM systems generally; namely, success depends largely on top management support, including top managers' beliefs about the importance of people, investment in human resources, and involvement of HRM professionals in the strategic planning process (Ostroff, 1995). In such a way, the signal sent from top management is that HRM is "legitimate" or "credible."

This notion is related to message source in social cognition, since the characteristics of the message source are linked to attributions made and the outcomes of persuasion (Fiske & Taylor, 1991). Communicator credibility (Chaiken et al., 1996) is a critical component in attribution, persuasion, and influence attempts. However, the elaboration likelihood model of persuasion (Petty & Cacioppo, 1986) indicates that persuasion and influence are not simply functions of features of the communicator and credibility but, rather, joint functions of the communicator's credibility *and* the recipients' involvement in the outcomes (Hass, 1981). Relatedly, obedience to legitimate authority is a function of more than the individual's subordination to a position of "higher office"; it also involves an individual's interpretation of the *relevance* of influence attempts to them (Kelman & Hamilton, 1989).

Relevance. Relevance of the HRM system refers to whether the situation is defined in such a way that individuals see the situation as relevant to an important goal (Kelman & Hamilton, 1989). Relevance, coupled with legitimate authority, means that influence is based on both a perception of superordinate authority and what Kelman and Hamilton (1989) term *motivational significance*. For the latter, individuals must perceive the situation as relevant to their important goals, that the desired behaviors are clear and optimally suited for goal attainment, and that influencing agents have the personal power to affect the achievement of these goals (Kelman & Hamilton, 1989).

Here, consideration of both individual goals and organizational goals—in our case, the strategic goal desired in the form of HRM content—is important in that individual goals should be fostered to align with those of the organization. Alignment or congruence between individuals' and managers' goals has been shown to have important consequences for both individual attitudes and behaviors, as well as for effective organizational functioning (Vancouver & Schmitt, 1991). Thus, the situation must be defined in such a way that individuals are willing to work toward goals that not only allow them to meet their own needs but, in doing so, also allow the organization to achieve

its goals. For example, if the organization has a strategic goal of customer service and an employee values financial gain, then service-based bonuses will heighten relevance and allow both the individual and organization to achieve their goals. Relatedly, the relevant desired behaviors must be specified and obstacles to their performance removed.

Additionally, relevance is a function of the perceived power of the influencing agent(s) to help individuals achieve relevant goals (Kelman & Hamilton, 1989). Influence is based on the extent to which an agent (e.g., HRM staff member or line manager enacting HRM practices) is perceived as possessing *personal* capabilities and is willing to use them to aid goal achievement—separate from his or her influence based on position power and legitimate authority. Perceived power of the influencing agent(s) depends on two factors. One is whether the agent can affect some of the conditions necessary for the achievement of relevant goals through, for example, the application of unique expertise or the allocation of necessary resources. Characteristics of the agent that bear on this issue include his or her prestige, special knowledge or expertise, representativeness, control of resources, and ability to apply sanctions. A second is the perceived likelihood that the agent will actually use his or her relevant capabilities in ways that will affect the likelihood of goal achievement.

Taylor and Fiske (1991) explain the relationship between relevance and the credibility or legitimacy of the message source. If outcomes (rewards, punishments, goal attainment) depend on someone else's actions as well as the individual's actions, then this creates a condition of outcome dependency, which, in turn, affects perceptions and attributions. When people are more outcome dependent, particularly when the outcomes are relevant, they direct more active attention to the person or source of communication. At the same time, when outcomes are particularly relevant, credibility of the message source has less of an influence. Thus, it appears relevance alone can enhance distinctiveness; when relevance is not strongly established, legitimacy plays a greater role.

CONSISTENCY

The above features of visibility, understandability, legitimacy of authority, and relevance help draw attention to the message and communicator, thereby increasing the probability that the HRM message will be encoded and interpreted uniformly among employees. However, distinctiveness alone is not likely sufficient enough for people to view the situation uniformly and to respond to the message sent by the set of HRM practices. For employees to make accurate attributions about what behaviors are expected and rewarded, attributional principles of causation must be present. Fundamental principles for causal attribution include priority, whereby causes precede effects, and contiguity with the effect, whereby causes occur close in time to an effect (Kassin & Pryor, 1985).

Similarly, as alluded to above, the literature on authority and influence indicates that individuals who are to be influenced must perceive instrumentalities in the situation whereby behaviors lead to rewards. That is, the distinctiveness characteristics ensure that the HRM system is viewed, overall, as significant in defining the social context for employee behavior; a consistent pattern of instrumentalities across HRM practices, time, and employees that link specific events and effects further enhances the likelihood that desired specific behaviors will be displayed.

These notions are related to Kelley's (1967) concept of consistency. Consistency generally refers to establishing an effect over time and modalities whereby the effect occurs each time the entity is present, regardless of the form of the interactions. Thus, we focus on features that establish consistent relationships over time, people, and contexts: instrumentality, validity, and consistent HRM messages.

Instrumentality. Instrumentality refers to establishing an *unambiguous* perceived cause-effect relationship in reference to the HRM system's desired content-focused behaviors and associated employee consequences. It ensures that there are adequate incentives associated with performance of the desired behavioral pattern. Strong instrumentalities, combined with the earlier "relevance" of social influence, leverage influence within an expectancy theory of motivation perspective (e.g., Vroom, 1964).

Perception plays a central role in instrumentality because it emphasizes how employees anticipate likely consequences of behavior. Instrumentalities are shaped largely by reinforcement consistency and are established by consistency and repetition over time, particularly through application of reinforcement principles. Employees are more likely to perceive the instrumentality when behavior and outcomes are closely linked in time (evoking the contiguity causation attribution principle) and when

they are administered consistently over some time schedule (evoking the priority causation attribution principle). To the extent that HRM staff and line managers have the resources and power to link outcomes to behavior or performance on a timely and consistent schedule, they will be able to influence cause-effect attributions.

Validity. Validity of HRM practices is important because message recipients attempt to determine the validity of a message in making attributions (Fiske & Taylor, 1991). Thus, HRM practices must display consistency between what they purport to do and what they actually do in order for them to help create a strong situation. Selection tests, for example, must validly screen on desired employee abilities, thereby making a substantive contribution to human capital development. Recall that one aspect of a strong situation is that employees have the skills necessary to execute the behaviors expected of them. Barnard (1938) long ago observed that employees would view a communication as authoritative only if they were able mentally and physically to comply with it.

Validity also makes a symbolic contribution by signaling to employees what KSAs are valued in a setting and by adding more employees with specified skills to the workforce. Further, when a practice is implemented and advertised to have certain effects, and then does not do what it was intended to do, the message sent to employees is contradictory, and employees are left to develop their own idiosyncratic interpretations.

Consistent HRM messages. These convey compatibility and stability in the signals sent by the HRM practices. Considerable evidence indicates that individuals desire consistency in organizational life (e.g., Kelley, 1973; Lidz, 1973; Siehl, 1985). The lack of consistency in "double-bind" communication can lead to particularly intense cognitive dissonance (Siehl, 1985). Double-bind communication occurs when a person is faced with significant communication involving two separate messages (Bateson, Jackson, Haley, & Weakland, 1956). The messages are related to each other and deal with the same content area, but they are incongruent or contradictory. Consequences of inconsistency can be severe (Lidz, 1973).

Three types of consistency are required, each of which entails the need to avoid sending double-bind communications to employees and to allow for HRM content to be perceived consistently. One is between what senior managers say are the organization's goals and values and what employees actually conclude those goals and values are based on their perceptions of HRM practices. Inconsistency here is a difference between what has been termed *espoused* values and *inferred* values (Martin & Siehl, 1983). For example, managers may espouse a value of risk taking, but employees may infer that performance appraisal and reward system practices reinforce playing it safe.

A second requirement for avoiding double-bind communication is internal consistency among the HRM practices themselves. In recent years, much has been written on the importance of designing an HRM system with practices that complement one another and fit together as a whole in achieving the organization's goals (e.g., Becker & Gerhart, 1996; Delery & Doty, 1996; Schuler & Jackson, 1995; Wright & McMahan, 1992; Wright & Snell, 1991). Internal alignment among practices should result in performance advantages for firms, because the different sets of HRM practices will elicit, reward, and control the appropriate employee behaviors for achieving strategic objectives (Arthur, 1992; Ulrich & Lake, 1991; Wright et al., 1994). For example, if the ability to work in teams is a screening focus in selection, then internal consistency will be ensured if group, rather than individual, performance is the basis for rewards. Furthermore, if each employee encounter with an HRM practice (e.g., hiring decision, performance appraisal interview) is conceptualized as a separate situation, then, following Mischel (1968), the functional similarity of these situational stimuli will influence the generalizability of team-oriented behavior across on-the-job situations.

A third dimension of consistency is stability over time. HRM practices are situational stimuli, the meaning of which is acquired across time. Certainly, how one responds to a situation depends on one's prior history with the stimulus (e.g., Mischel, 1968). Behaviors and behavioral consequences remain stable when the evoking conditions remain stable. In organizations where practices have been in place a long time, there is stronger agreement among employees as to what is expected of them and what they expect of the organization in return (Rousseau & Wade-Benzoni, 1994).

CONSENSUS

Consensus results when there is agreement among employees—the intended targets of influence by the HRM system—in their view of the event-effect relationship. More accurate attributions about what behaviors and responses lead to what consequences are more likely to be made when there is consensus (Kelley, 1972). Several factors can help foster consensus among employees and can influence whether individuals perceive the same effect with respect to the entity or situation in question. Among these are agreement among message senders, which can foster consensus (Fiske & Taylor, 1991), and the fairness of the HRM system, which can also influence consensus inasmuch as fairness involves whether employees understand the distribution rules by which they do, or do not, receive what they feel they deserve for their contributions.

It is also important to point out that consistency and consensus are distinct but interrelated concepts. For example, when individuals throughout the organization experience consistency in HRM practices, consensus is more likely to be fostered. At the same time, when message senders cannot agree among themselves on the intended message, consistency is likely to be hampered.

Agreement among principal HRM decision makers. Agreement among these message senders helps promote consensus among employees. Within a strategic HRM perspective, the principal decision makers in the organization (e.g., top managers, HR executives) set the strategic goals and design the set of HRM practices for achieving those goals. When individuals view message senders as strongly agreeing among themselves on the message, they are more likely to form a consensus (Fiske & Taylor, 1991). This perception of agreement can be facilitated in several ways and is related to distinctiveness and consistency.

First, when multiple decision makers agree on the message, distinctiveness can be enhanced because a larger number of individuals can send similar communications (increasing visibility). As more employees "see" the practice and perceive that top decision makers agree on it, consensus can be facilitated. Further, integration and close interactions among HRM professionals, managers, and top managers foster the exchange of tacit knowledge for the formulation and implementation of an organizational strategy and HRM system that reflect the firm's strategic direction (Lado & Wilson, 1994). These integrations among decision makers can help promote relevance by clearly identifying important goals and means to goal attainment, as well as enhance legitimacy of authority of the HR managers and line managers enacting the HRM policies.

Second, to the extent that members of the top management team disagree among themselves about the goals of HRM and/or disagree with HRM professionals or managers, and to the extent that HRM managers and staff members disagree among themselves, it becomes difficult to send unambiguous and internally consistent messages to employees. Low consistency of HRM practices and lack of consensus are related in that disagreement among decision makers is likely to produce poor consistency in delivering practices; thus, different employees will experience different event-consequence relationships. Overall, then, agreement among top decision makers can help foster greater consensus among employees, since it allows for more visible, relevant, and consistent messages to be conveyed to employees.

Fairness. Fairness of the HRM system is a composite of employees' perceptions of whether HRM practices adhere to the principles of delivering three dimensions of justice: distributive, procedural, and interactional (e.g., Bowen, Gilliland, & Folger, 1999; Folger & Cropanzano, 1998). Research indicates that the perceived fairness of HRM affects how positively HRM activity is viewed and the capability of the HRM system to *influence* employee attitudes and behaviors. Researchers have argued that there is a positive relationship between perceptions of HRM fairness and what has been termed the *acceptability* criterion of HRM practices (Bretz, Milkovich, & Read, 1992; Waldman & Bowen, 1998), which refers to the extent to which employees contribute to and utilize HRM (e.g., complete 360 degree appraisals and use feedback from it to shape their behavior).

Agreement among employees' perceptions of event-effect relationships will be influenced by whether employees have similar perceptions of what distribution rules—principles of distributive justice—apply in what situations. Outcomes such as rewards can be distributed based on an "equality" rule, in which all receive the same outcome; an "equity" rule, in which subsets of employees receive different amounts based on relevant differences, such as in a merit pay system; or an "individual need" rule, such as flexible working hours for a single mother in unique circumstances (Bowen et al., 1999).

Management practices that lead to employee perceptions of procedural and interactional justice increase the transparency of these distribution rules (Bowen et al., 1999) and, by so doing, increase the likelihood that the HRM system will be characterized by consensus about event-effect relationships.

Procedural justice can be enhanced by giving employees a voice in determining the methods by which outcome decisions are made—for example, involving employees in designing behavior or outcome-based performance appraisals. Interactional justice involves managers' openly and respectfully explaining to employees the reasons behind decisions and the distribution of outcomes. It can include clarifying what distribution formula was used in making individual pay increase decisions in situations where not all employees received the same pay increase.

Consequences of the Strength of the HRM System

HRM practices influence employee perceptions of climate at the individual level. Further, the characteristics of strong HRM systems are more likely to promote shared perceptions and give rise to the emergence of a strong organizational climate about the HRM content. That is, we propose that *the strength of the HRM system will foster the emergence of organizational climate (collective perceptions) from psychological climates (individual-level perceptions).*

In a *strong* situation, variability among employees' perceptions of the meaning of the situation will be small and will reflect a common desired content. In turn, organizational climate will display a significant association with employee attitudes and behaviors. This occurs because a strong HRM system can foster similar viewpoints such that the situation leads everyone to "see" the situation similarly, induces uniform expectancies about responses, provides clear expectations about rewards and incentives for the desired responses and behaviors, and induces compliance and conformity through social influence. Therefore, we propose that a *strong HRM system process can enhance organizational performance owing to shared meanings in promotion of collective responses that are consistent with organizational strategic goals (assuming the appropriateness of those goals).* More specifically, an *HRM system high in distinctiveness, consistency, and consensus should enhance clarity of interpretation in the setting, thereby allowing for similar "cognitive maps" or "causal maps" to develop among people, as well as to create an "influence situation" whereby individuals yield to the message and understand the appropriate ways of behaving.*

Further, while interactions and communication among employees are likely to result in collective sensemaking (Jackofsky & Slocum, 1988), regardless of the strength of the HRM system, we argue that in cases where the strength of the HRM system is strong, the sensemaking process will be most likely to result in the *intended* organizational climate. If the HRM system is *weak*, HRM practices will send messages that are ambiguous and subject to individual interpretation. Given ambiguity, one of two things may happen: variability or unintended sensemaking.

First, with a weak system, variability of individual responses may be large (Mischel, 1973). Considerable variance across individuals' perceptions of psychological climates will exist, and shared perceptions in the form of organizational climate will not emerge. Individuals can construct their own version of reality (House et al., 1995) or their own version of what messages are being communicated by HRM practices and use this to guide their own behavior. Thus, in *weak situations (low distinctiveness, consistency, and consensus), constructs at the individual but not the organizational level are likely to show strong relationships; psychological climate perception will have a significant association with individual attitudes and behaviors.*

While a weak situation is produced by low distinctiveness, consistency, and consensus, we also argue that *the most ambiguous or weakest situation is produced when distinctiveness is high, coupled with low consistency and consensus.* Distinctiveness drives up attention. That is, HRM practices are salient or visible, and employees are aware of them. However, if the messages that employees are now attending to are inconsistent or conflicting, as different individuals are subjected to different experiences with the HRM practices, confusion, disillusionment, or other negative reactions will likely result. In such a case, not only will shared perceptions about the practices and climate particularly be unlikely to emerge, but many employees may have negative attitudes.

Alternatively, the ambiguity inherent in weak situations may cause employees to engage in collective sensemaking (House et al., 1995). When faced with an equivocal situation or attributional uncertainty, individuals may attempt to reduce this uncertainty by engaging in a social process of interacting and consulting with one another to develop their own shared interpretations (Drazin et al., 1999; Fiske & Taylor, 1991; Weick, 1995). The danger here is that the collective interpretation that employees draw from the ambiguous situation is not the one intended by the organization. That is, the "strong" climate that emerges does not match the intended climate content; hence, it may conflict with organizational goals and strategies and may ultimately lead to conflicts, poor productivity, or low effectiveness. This is particularly likely to occur when "distinctiveness" is low (although low consensus and consistency will also play a role). When practices are not made salient, visible, and understandable, ambiguity is high, and employees are more likely to refer to one another in an attempt to define the situation in their own way. Thus, we propose that *low distinctiveness of the HRM system contributes to a collective sensemaking process that may result in unintended organizational climates.* Further, *a weak HRM system process is unlikely to promote organizational effectiveness because it creates a weak situation in which either individual processes dominate or collective sensemaking results in shared interpretations that may be inconsistent with organizational strategic goals.*

It is important to note that this process of emergence of similar perceptions of climate does not occur in a vacuum. While the HRM system and the strength of this system form the fundamental basis of whether similar perceptions will be derived, scholars have argued that interactions among employees are also relevant (Jackofsky & Slocum, 1988). Morgeson and Hofmann (1999) provide rationales for the importance of these interactions in forming collective constructs. Within any collective, individuals are likely to meet one another and interact. Each interaction results in a discrete event, and subsequent interactions are termed *event cycles*. The structure of any collective group can be viewed as a series of ongoing events, activities, and event cycles among the individuals. These interdependencies and interactions among individuals over time can result in jointly produced responses, and it is this structure that forms the basis for the eventual emergence of collective constructs—one that can transcend individuals, individual behaviors, and individual perceptions.

This process is similar to the emergence of overlapping "causal maps" through cognitive processing (e.g., Weick, 1995; Wicker, 1992). Individuals develop causal maps, which are cognitive representations of the entities in the situation, certain qualities of those entities, and perceived linkages among them. Overlapping causal maps can be facilitated through social exchange and transactions among employees. In such a way, *employees* can *collectively* agree on the appropriate aspects of the environment to attend to, as well as how to interpret these aspects and how to respond to them appropriately. Thus, we propose that *a strong HRM system facilitates interactions, interdependencies, and event cycles such that fewer event cycles are needed to develop shared interpretations.*

Context and HRM System Strength

In the preceding discussion we implicitly assumed *an* organizational climate. Yet researchers and theorists recognize the multidimensional nature of climate such that multiple types of organizational climates can exist within a firm and at different levels of analysis in the organization (Schneider, 1990). That is, different functional areas, departments, or groups may develop different subclimates (e.g., Payne, 2000). Likewise, cluster analysis has been used to demonstrate different collective climates within an organization—climates that represent clusters of employees who perceive the organization similarly and span formal organizational units (e.g., Jackofsky & Slocum, 1988; Joyce & Slocum, 1984).

We acknowledge that the *content* of the climate can vary across groups within the organization. Further, different HRM practices around a different content might be applied to different groups of employees. We propose that *if the process of the HRM system is strong, a shared perception of the climate will emerge in organizational subunits, albeit with some differences in content or strategic focus across groups.* Indeed, for many firms this may be strategically desirable—for example, in diversified firms, firms with multiple locations, international firms, or firms pursuing multiple strategic objectives in different parts of the organization. It is also likely that, for some groups in the organization, a shared climate will emerge, whereas for others it will not, owing to differences in the HRM process across different groups.

Another concern is the possibility that a strong climate might be inflexible and resistant to change, thereby compromising organizational effectiveness. The literature on strong cultures offers a resolution of this issue. A culture whose content comprises values and beliefs that support flexibility can be strong, without limiting the organization's ability to adapt to its environment (e.g., Sathe & Davidson, 2000). Similarly, we propose that a strong climate that has elements of what has been termed a *climate for innovation* (e.g., Klein & Sorra, 1996), for example, can be simultaneously strong and adaptable. In other words, *the process of the HRM system can create a strong climate adaptable to change, if the content of the climate includes elements that focus on flexibility and innovation.* Although individual employees' behaviors may differ so as to be innovative or flexible, all employees should still share the idea that this type of adaptability is what is expected of them. Thus, perceptions of the climate will be the same with a strong system that encourages innovation or flexibility, but there may be variance and changes in actual behavior over time.

Future Research and Theory Development

Research is needed on the properties of the HRM *process*, as distinct from research on the properties of practices (e.g., reliability) and the content of HRM practices and systems (e.g., the specific practices that make up different systems). That is, research is needed to delineate how these processes influence the attributes of the work situation as perceived by employees.

Little is known about the important parameters underlying organizational situations (e.g., Bem & Funder, 1978; Chatman, 1989; Fredrickson, 1972). We have proposed a set of features, based on social influence and social cognition theories, that should help create a strong situation and shared meaning. It is critical that the viability of these metafeatures of the organization be tested as important elements that create strong situations. Frederiksen (1972) proposes a number of different means for attempting to classify and develop taxonomies of situations. In this case, it may be useful to attempt to group or cluster situations on the basis of their tendency to elicit similar behaviors. This would require a three-dimensional data matrix, with the dimensions representing person, behavior, and situational attributes (Frederiksen, 1972). With such a procedure, one could derive clusters of responses or behaviors that differentially correspond with the nine HRM process features.

In addition, research is needed to determine the most appropriate means for "combining" the metafeatures of the HRM system. As suggested earlier, it is likely that some features are more critical than others in creating a strong situation. For example, without consistent HRM messages, distinctiveness and consensus may lose impact. Alternatively, although we believe this is less likely, a compensatory model may be appropriate in that a high level of one feature will make up for a low level of another feature. Thus, one could compare and test the viability of an additive model (i.e., the sum across all features), a configural model (i.e., different profiles of features), and a multiplicative or contingency model (i.e., interactions among the features).

Further, it is important to determine the relative impact of and interrelationships between HRM system strength and other determinants of strong situations or climates. Factors such as leadership, social relationships, and structural design features can also affect the strength of the situation and can foster the development of a shared climate (Ashforth, 1985; Ostroff, Kinicki, & Tamkins, 2003). HRM features are likely to interact with these other factors to further foster a shared sense of the situation. For example, supervisors can serve as interpretive filters of HRM practices, and when they are visible in implementing practices or promote high-quality exchanges with employees, they can introduce a common interpretation among unit members (Kozlowski & Doherty, 1989; Naumann & Bennett, 2000).

Thus, a strong HRM system coupled with a visible supervisor may foster stronger relationships among HRM, climate, and performance than each would individually. Similarly, while our primary intent was to elucidate the characteristics of an HRM process that would allow for shared perceptions of climate to emerge, additional research is needed to determine the extent to which these HRM system characteristics can also impact other social structures such as culture, roles, communication patterns and networks, and social capital, all of which may enhance the relationship between HRM and performance.

RELATIONSHIPS BETWEEN CONTENT AND PROCESS

Research is needed to test interrelationships between HRM process strength and content. The configural approach examines how a pattern of numerous HRM practices is related to firm performance so that the total effect of HRM is greater than the sum of the individual practices themselves (Becker & Gerhart, 1996; Delery & Doty, 1996; Inchniowski, Shaw, & Prennushi, 1997). The focus of this approach is on the sets of mutually reinforcing practices that may be related to firm performance. The strength of the HRM system may be a factor influencing whether the configural approach to HRM–firm performance relationships is supported in empirical studies. The likelihood that individual HRM practices would function as a set, in a mutually reinforcing manner, may be a function of the internal consistency of those

practices and the effectiveness with which they are implemented together.

A similar case can be developed for assessing interactions between strength and content across climates *for* different strategic foci. For example, on the one hand, it may not be difficult to incorporate features of a strong HRM system for a climate focused on cost leadership or safety, given that the desired outcomes and behaviors associated with those criteria can be specified clearly. On the other hand, it may be more difficult to create a strong HRM system for a climate for service, given that the intangibility of service makes it difficult to specify service quality goals and the employee behaviors that will lead to them (Bowen & Schneider, 1988). This may either complicate the ability to create a strong HRM system or moderate the relationship between that strength and the uniformity of employees' perceptions in the form of organizational climates.

METHODOLOGICAL AND MEASUREMENT ISSUES

Two interrelated methodological issues are raised by our proposals. The first of these concerns appropriate measurement for the strength of the HRM system. The second concerns levels of analysis and aggregation issues in moving from individual-level perceptions of climate to collective constructs. A full discussion of these issues is beyond the scope of this article.

New measures will need to be developed to assess the strength of the HRM system. It is important to note that this construct is a situational context variable, and, as we have defined it, it represents a higher-level construct. In past research on HRM practices and systems, scholars have typically relied on reports from a higher-level manager or HR executive. In our case, HR directors and top managers could be asked to evaluate the dimensions of strength of the system. This procedure has the obvious advantage of obtaining a single, global measure for each dimension of strength of the system. However, this measurement technique focuses only on measures of the attributes from a single source that is at a higher level in the organization, while our primary theoretical focus lies in the impact these practices have on perceptions of employees. Because the concept of strength requires judgments and perceptions of employees, we suggest that a better alternative is to assess these characteristics of the HRM system from employees themselves. That is, the appropriate unit of measurement of assessing strength is the individual, since employee attributions and perceptions reside in the individual.

Future work should be directed at developing a valid measure of HRM strength. For example, to assess visibility, employees could be given a list of a variety of HRM practices and asked to indicate the extent to which each is utilized in the firm. A comparison between those practices that agents of the HRM function assert are in place and those that employees indicate are used would provide some assessment of how visible the practices are to employees.

Similarly, to assess consistency, employees could be asked to what extent they have actually participated in or experienced each of these practices (e.g., received a semiannual performance review). The percent of people indicating they experienced the practice would provide some indication of how consistently the practice is administered across employees in the organization. As an alternative, employees could be asked to indicate the extent to which they believe the practice applies to all employees.

Agreement might be assessed by asking top decision makers to delineate the strategic goals related to HRM and the intended message of the HRM practices (e.g., promote innovation and risk taking, promote loyalty and longevity, promote safety). High agreement among decision makers should be related to higher consensus among employees as to what practices are salient, visible, administered consistently, and so forth.

Such measures would be useful from multiple perspectives. First, the mean score on the dimension would provide an indication as to the level at which these characteristics are present. That is, a higher mean score on measures tapping distinctiveness, consistency, and consensus would be one indicator of strong HRM process. Second, researchers could assess the extent to which employees perceive characteristics in the same way—that is, they could assess the extent of agreement or variability in responses among employees. Higher agreement would support consensus and a strong system, whereas high variance in responses would indicate a weak system.

As to assessments of climate, agreement among employees about their perceptions must be demonstrated before aggregated measures of psychological climate perceptions can be used to represent a unit-level or organizational-level climate construct (James, 1982). Further, it is important to examine both the level (e.g., the level of rating on a dimension of climate) and the variability in responses. Level is an indicator of "content," whereas variability is an indicator of situational "strength." At the individual level of analysis, if one is interested in examining the relationship between perceptions of the climate and individual responses, the level of the individual's responses on the variables is most useful. However, when moving to higher levels of analysis, additional measurement issues emerge. Strong and well-designed HRM systems produce greater homogeneity of perceptions and responses within the organization, resulting in organizational climate. The strength of the climate is indicated by the degree of variability in responses, regardless of the level of the aggregate rating on the content of climate. An indication of whether the HRM system creates a strong situation is the extent of agreement on climate ratings (Payne, 2000).

Final Thoughts

In listing challenges that the HRM community faces in the future, Ulrich cites the need for HR practice to be guided by HR theory. He reminds HRM professionals that theory helps explain the manner in which outcomes emerge:

> To make HR practices more than isolated acts, managers and HR professionals must master the theory behind HR work; they need to be able to explain conceptually *how* and *why* HR practices lead to their outcomes . . . Regardless of the preferred theory, managers and HR professionals should abstract from it a higher level of reasoning for their day-to-day work and thus better explain why their work accomplishes its goals (1997: 238; emphasis added).

Recently, in the literature scholars have developed "why" HR practices lead to sustainable competitive advantage. Hopefully, this present effort at theory building on the strength of the HRM system can begin to help explain "how" HRM practices lead to outcomes the organization desires.

Selected Bibliography

Arthur, J. B. 1992. The link between business strategy and industrial relations systems in American steel minimills. *Industrial and Labor Relations Review*, 45: 488–506.

Ashforth, B. E. 1985. Climate formation: Issues and extensions. *Academy of Management Review*, 10: 837–947.

Ashforth, B. E. 2001. *Role transitions in organizational life*. Mahwah, NJ: Lawrence Erlbaum Associates.

Barnard, C. I. 1938. *The functions of the executive*. Cambridge, MA: Harvard University Press.

Barney, J. 1991. Firm resources and competitive advantage, *Journal of Management*, 17: 99–120.

Barteson, G., Jackson, D. D., Haley, J., & Weakland, J. H. 1886 Toward a theory of schizophrenia. *Behavioral Science*, 1: 251–264.

Becker, B., & Gerhart, B. 1996. The impact of human resource management on organizational performance: Progress and prospects. *Academy of Management Journal*, 39: 779–801.

Becker, B. E., & Huselid, M. A. 1998. High performance work systems and firm performance: A synthesis of research and managerial implications. *Research in Personnel and Human Resources Management*, 16: 53–101.

Bem, D. J., & Funder, D. C. 1978. Predicting more of the people more of the time—assessing personality of situations. *Psychological Review*, 85: 485–501.

Borucki, C. C., & Burke, M. J. 1999. An examination of service-related antecedents to retail store performance. *Journal of Organizational Behavior*, 20: 943–962.

Bowen, D. E., Gilliland, S. W., & Folger, R. 1999. HRM and service fairness: How being fair with employees spills over to customers. *Organizational Dynamics*, 27(3): 7–23.

Bowen, D. E., & Schneider, B. 1988. Services marketing and management: Implications for organizational behavior. *Research in Organizational Behavior*, 10: 43–80.

Boxall, P. 1996. The strategic HRM debate and the resource-based view of the firm. *Human Resource Management Journal*, 6: 59–75.

Bretz, R. D. Jr., Milkovich, G. T., & Read, W. 1992. The current state of performance appraisal research and practice: Concerns, directions, and implications, *Journal of Management*, 18: 321–352.

Chaiken, S., Wood, W., & Eagly, A. H. 1996. Principles of persuasion. In E. T. Higgins & A. W. Kruglanski (Eds.), *Social psychology: Handbook of basic principles*: 702–744. New York: Guilford Press.

Chatman, J. A. 1989. Improving interactional organizational research: A model of person-organization fit. *Academy of Management Review*, 14: 333–349.

Delaney, J. T., & Huselid, M. A. 1996. The impact of human resource management practices on perceptions of organizational performance. *Academy of Management Journal*, 39: 949–969.

Delbecq, A., & Mills, P. K. 1985. Managerial practices that enhance innovation. *Organizational Dynamics*, 14(1): 24–34.

Delery, J. E., & Doty, D. H. 1996. Modes of theorizing in strategic human resource management: Tests of universalistic, contingency, and configural performance predictions. *Academy of Management Journal*, 39: 802–835.

Denison, D. R. 1996. What is the difference between culture and organizational climate? A native's point of view on a decade of paradigm wars. *Academy of Management Review*, 21: 819–854.

Drazin, R., Glynn, M. A., & Kazanjian, R. K. 1999. Multilevel theorizing about creativity in organizations: A sensemaking perspective. *Academy of Management Review*, 24: 286–307.

Dyer, L., & Holder, G. W. 1988. A strategic perspective of human resource management. In L. Dyer (Ed.), *Human resource management: Evolving roles and responsibilities*: 1–45. Washington, DC: Bureau of National Affairs.

Endler, N. S., & Magnusson, D. 1976. Personality and person by situation interactions. In N. S. Endler & D. Magnusson (Eds.), *Interactional psychology and personality*: 1–25. New York: Hemisphere.

Feldman, J. M. 1981. Perception, cognition, and the organization. *Journal of Applied Psychology*: 66: 128–138.

Ferris, G. R., Arthur, M. M., Berkson, H. M., Kaplan, D. M., Harrell-Cook, G., & Frink, D. D. 1998. Toward a social context theory of the human resource management-organization effectiveness relationship. *Human Resource Management Review*, 8: 235–264.

Ferris, G. R., Hochwarter, W. A., Buckley, M. R., Harrell-Cook, G., & Frink, D. D. 1999. Human resource management: Some new directions. *Journal of Management*, 25: 385–415.

Fiske, S. T., & Taylor, S. E. 1991. *Social cognition*. New York: McGraw-Hill.

Folger, R., & Cropanzano, R. 1998. *Organizational justice and human resource management*. Newbury Park, CA: Sage.

Frederiksen, N. 1972. Toward a taxonomy of situations. *American Psychologist*, 26: 114–123.

Guzzo, R. A., & Noonan, K. A. 1994. Human resource practices as communications and the psychological contract. *Human Resource Management*, 33: 447–462.

Hass, R. G. 1981. Effects of source characteristics on cognitive responses and persuasion. In R. E. Petty, T. M. Ostrom, & T. C. Brock (Eds.), *Cognitive responses in persuasion*: 141–172. Hillsdale, NJ: Lawrence Erlbaum Associates.

House, R., Rousseau, D. M., & Thomas-Hunt, M. 1995. The meso-paradigm: A framework for the integration of micro and macro organizational behavior. *Research in Organizational Behavior*, 17: 41–114.

Huselid, M. A. 1995. The impact of human resource management practices on turnover, productivity, and corporate financial performance. *Academy of Management Journal*, 38: 635–672.

Huselid, M. A., & Becker, B. E. 1996. Methodological issues in cross-sectional and panel estimates of the human resource management-firm performance link. *Industrial Relations*, 35: 400–422.

Huselid, M. A., Jackson, S. E., & Schuler, R. S. 1997. Technical and strategic human resource management effectiveness as determinants of firm performance. *Academy of Management Journal*, 40: 171–188.

Ichniowski, C., Shorav, K., & Prennusht, G., 1997. The effect of human resources management practices on productivity: A study of steel finishing lines. *American Economic Review*, 87: 291–313.

Jackofsky, E. F., & Slocum, J. W., Jr. 1988. A longitudinal study of climates. *Journal of Organizational Behavior*, 9: 319–334.

James, L. R. 1982. Aggregation bias in estimates of perceptual agreement. *Journal of Applied Psychology*, 67: 219–229.

James, L. R., & Jones, A. P. 1974. Organizational climate: A review of theory and research. *Psychological Bulletin*, 81: 1096–1112.

Johnson, J. W. 1996. Linking employee perceptions of service climate to customer satisfaction. *Personnel Psychology*, 49: 831–852.

Jones, A. P., & James, L. R. 1979. Psychological climate: Dimensions and relationships of individual and aggregated work environment perceptions. *Organizational Behavior and Human Decision Processes*, 23: 201–250.

Joyce, W., & Slocum, J. 1984. Collective climate: Agreement as a basis for defining aggregate climates in organizations. *Academy of Management Journal*, 27: 721–742.

Kassin, S. M., & Pryor, J. B. 1985. The development of attribution processes. In J. Pryor & J. Day (Eds.), *The development of social cognition*: 3–34. New York: Springer-Verlag.

Katz, D., & Kahn, R. L. 1978. *The social psychology of organizing*. New York: Wiley.

Kelley, G. A. 1955. *A theory of personality: The psychology of personal constructs*. New York: Norton.

Kelley, H. H. 1967. Attribution theory in social psychology. In D. Levine (Ed.), *Nebraska symposium on motivation*: 192–240. Lincoln: University of Nebraska Press.

Kelley, H. H. 1972. Causal schemata and the attribution process. In E. E. Jones, D. E. Kanouse, H. H. Kelley, R. E. Nisbett, S. Valins, & B. Weiner (Eds.), *Attribution: Perceiving the causes of behavior*: 151–174. Morristown, NJ: General Learning Press.

Kelley, H. H. 1973. The processes of causal attribution. *American Psychologist*, 28: 107–128.

Kelman, H. C., & Hamilton, V. C. 1989. *Crimes of obedience: Toward a social psychology of authority and responsibility*. New Haven, CT: Yale University Press.

Klein, K. J., & Sorra, J. S. 1996. The challenge of innovation implementation. *Academy of Management Review*, 21: 1055–1080.

Kopelman, R. E., Brief, A. P., & Guzzo, R. A. 1990, In B. Schneider (Ed.), *Organizational climate and culture*: 282–318. San Francisco: Jossey-Bass.

Kozlowski, S. W. J., & Doherty, J. L. 1989. Integration of climate and leadership: Examination of a neglected issue. *Journal of Applied Psychology*, 74: 721–742.

Lado, A. A., & Wilson, M. C. 1994. Human resource systems and sustained competitive advantage: A competency-based perspective. *Academy of Management Review*, 19: 699–727.

Lewin, K., Lippit, R., & White, H. 1939. Patterns of aggressive behavior in experimentally created social climates. *Journal of Social Psychology*, 10: 271–299.

Lidz, T. 1973. *Origin and treatment of schizophrenic disorders*. New York: Basic Books.

MacDuffie, J. P. 1998. Human resource bundles and manufacturing performance: Organizational logic and flexible production systems in the world auto industry. *Industrial and Labor Relations Review*, 48: 199–221.

Martin, J., & Siehl, C. J. 1983. Organizational customer and counterculture: An uneasy symbiosis. *Organizational Dynamics*, 12(2): 52–64.

McGuire, W. J. 1972. Attitude change: The information processing paradigm. In C. G. McClintock (Ed.), *Experimental social psychology*: 108–141. New York: Holt, Rinehart & Winston.

Miles, R. E., & Snow, C. C. 1994. *Fit, failure and the hall of fame*. New York: Free Press.

Mischel, W. 1968. *Personality and assessment*. New York: Wiley.

Mischel, W. 1973. Toward a cognitive social learning conceptualization of personality. *Psychological Review*, 80: 252–283.

Mischel, W. 1977. The interaction of person and situation. In D. Magnusson & N. S. Endler (Eds.), *Personality at the crossroads: Current issues in interactional psychology*: 333–352. Hillsdale, NJ: Lawrence Erlbaum Associates.

Mischel, W. 1997. Personality dispositions revisited and revised: A view after three decades. In R. Hogan, J. Johnson, & S. Briggs (Eds.), *Handbook of personality psychology*: 113–132. New York: Academic Press.

Mischel, W., & Peake, P. K. 1982. Beyond déjà vu in the search for cross-situational consistency. *Psychological Review*, 89: 730–755.

Morgeson, F. P., & Hofmann, D. A. 1999. The structure and function of collective constructs: Implications for multilevel research and theory development. *Academy of Management Review*, 24: 249–265.

Naumann, S. E., & Bennett, N. 2000. A case for procedural justice climate: Development and test of a multilevel model. *Academy of Management Journal*, 43: 881–889.

Ostroff, C. 1995. SHRM/CCH survey. *Human Resources Management: Ideas and Trends in Personnel* (356): 1–12.

Ostroff, C., & Bowen, D. E. 2000. Moving HR to a higher level: Human resource practices and organizational effectiveness. In K. J. Klein & S. W. J. Kozlowski (Eds.), *Multilevel theory, research, and methods in organizations*: 211–266. San Francisco: Jossey-Bass.

Ostroff, C., Kinicki, A. J., & Tamkins, M. M. 2003. Organizational culture and climate. In W. C. Borman, D. R. Ilgen, & R. J. Klimoski (Eds.), *Comprehensive handbook of psychology, volume 12: Industrial and organizational psychology*: 565–594. New York: Wiley.

Ostroff, C., & Schmitt, N. 1993. Configurations of organizational effectiveness and efficiency. *Academy of Management Journal*, 36: 1345–1361.

Payne, R. L. 2000. Culture and climate: How close can they get? In N. M. Ashkanasy, C. P. M. Wilderom, & M. F. Peterson (Eds.), *Handbook of organizational culture and climate*: 163–176. Thousand Oaks, CA: Sage.

Petty, R. E., & Cacioppo, J. T. 1986. The elaboration likelihood model of persuasion. In L. Berkowitz (Ed.), *Advances in experimental social psychology*, vol. 19: 189-203. San Diego: Academic Press.

Reichers, A. E., & Schneider, B. 1990. Climate and culture: An evolution of constructs. In B. Schneider (Ed.), *Organizational climate and culture*: 5–39. San Francisco: Jossey-Bass.

Ross, L., & Nisbett, R. E. 1991. *The person and the situation: Perspectives of social psychology*. Philadelphia: Temple University Press.

Rousseau, D. M. 1995. *Psychological contracts in organizations*. Thousand Oaks, CA: Sage.

Rousseau, D. M., & Greller, M. M. 1994. Human resource practices: Administrative contract-makers. *Human Resource Management*, 33: 385–402.

Rousseau, D. M., & Wade-Benzoni, K. A. 1994. Linking strategy and human resource practices: How employee and customer contracts are created. *Human Resource Management*, 33: 463–490.

Sathe, V., & Davidson, E. J. 2000. Toward a new conceptualization of culture change. In N. M. Ashkanasy, C. P. M. Wilderom, & M. F. Peterson (Eds.), *Handbook of organizational culture and climate*: 279–296. Thousand Oaks, CA: Sage.

Schneider, B. 1990. The climate for service: An application of the climate construct. In B. Schneider (Ed.), *Organizational climate and culture*: 383–412. San Francisco: Jossey-Bass.

Schneider, B. 2000. The psychological life of organizations. In N. M. Ashkanasy, C. P. M. Wilderom, & M. F. Peterson (Eds.), *Handbook of organizational culture and climate*: xvii–xxii. Thousand Oaks, CA: Sage.

Schneider, B., & Bowen, D. E. 1985. Employee and customer perceptions of service in banks: Replication and extension. *Journal of Applied Psychology*, 70: 423–433.

Schneider, B., Brief, A. P., & Guzzo, R. A. 1996. Creating a climate and culture for sustainable organizational change. *Organizational Dynamics*, 24(4): 7–19.

Schneider, B., Salvaggio, A. N., & Subirats, M. 2002. Climate strength: A new direction for climate research. *Journal of Applied Psychology*, 87: 220–229.

Schuler, R. S., & Jackson, S. E. 1987a. Organizational strategy and organization level as determinants of human resource management practices. *Human Resource Planning*, 10: 125–141.

Schuler, R. S., & Jackson, S. E. 1987b. Linking competitive strategies and human resource management practices. *Academy of Management Executive*, 1(3): 207–219.

Schuler, R. S., & Jackson, S. E. 1995. Understanding human resource management in the context of organizations and their environment. *Annual Review of Psychology*, 46: 237–264.

Slom C. J., 1985. After the founder: An opportunity to manage culture. In P. Frost, L. Moore, M. Louis, C. Lundberg, & J. Martin (Eds.), *Organizational culture*: 125–140. Beverly Hills, CA: Sage.

Tajfel, H. 1968. Social and cultural factors in perception. In G. Lindzey & E. Aronson (Eds.), *Handbook of social psychology*: 315–394. Reading, MA: Addison-Wesley.

Taylor, S. E., & Fiske, S. T. 1978. Salience, attention, and attributions: Top of the head phenomena. In L. Berkowitz (Ed.), *Advances in experimental social psychology*: 249–287. New York: Academic Press.

Tsui, A. S., Pearce, J. L., Porter, L. W., & Tripoli, A. M. 1997. Alternative approaches to employee-organization relationship: Does investment in employees pay off? *Academy of Management Journal*, 40: 1089–1121.

Ulrich, D. 1997. *Human resource champions: The next agenda for adding value and delivering results*. Boston: Harvard Business School Press.

Ulrich, D., & Lake, D. 1991. Organizational capability: Creating competitive advantage. *Academy of Management Executive*, 5(1): 77–91.

Vancouver, J. B., & Schmitt, N. W. 1991. An exploratory examination of person-organization fit: Organizational goal congruence. *Personnel Psychology*, 44: 333–352.

Vroom, V. 1964. *Work and motivation*. New York: Wiley.

Waldman, D. A., & Bowen, D. E. 1998. The acceptability of 360-degree appraisals: A customer-supplier relationship perspective. *Human Resource Management*, 37: 117–130.

Weick, K. E. 1995. *Sensemaking in organizations*. Thousand Oaks, CA: Sage.

Wicker, A. W. 1992. Making sense of environments. In W. B. Walsh, K. H. Craik, & R. H. Price (Eds.), *Person-environment psychology*: 157–192. Hillsdale, NJ: Lawrence Erlbaum Associates.

Wright, P. M., & McMahan, G. C. 1992. Theoretical perspectives for strategic human resource management. *Journal of Management*, 18: 295–320.

Wright, P. M., McMahan, G. C., & McWilliams, A. 1994. Human resources and sustained competitive advantage: A resource-based perspective. *International Journal of Human Resource Management*, 5: 301–326.

Wright, P. M., & Snell, S. A. 1991. Toward an integrative view of strategic human resource management. *Human Resource Management Review*, 1: 203–225.

Youndt, M. A., Snell, S. A., Dean, J. W., Jr., & Lepak, D. P. 1996. Human resource management, manufacturing strategy, and firm performance. *Academy of Management Journal*, 39: 836–866.

Zohar, D. 2000. A group-level model of safety climate: Testing the effect of group climate on microaccidents in manufacturing jobs. *Journal of Applied Psychology*, 85: 587–596.

Culturally Compatible HR Strategies

Robert J. Greene, *HR Magazine*

Organizations must consider their internal and external realities when formulating human resource strategies. Successful HR strategies fit current realities and can be realigned when realities change. Culture—the shared basic assumptions and beliefs developed by an organization over time[1]—is one of the key components of any organization's internal realities. The following approach to defining and evaluating culture explores how human resource strategies and programs can be fashioned to support or change the desired culture. In other words, how to make human resource strategies "culturally compatible."

Defining and Evaluating an Organization's Culture

To define and evaluate an organization's culture, conduct a survey that asks key parties-at-interest to determine what they believe the existing culture is and what they believe it should be. Then compare the answers. The following topics should be included in the questionnaire:

- Performance: Is it defined as meeting organizational goals or as satisfying customers? Are results attributed to a few key individuals or to all employees? Is the focus on short-term results or long-term success?
- Information and resources: How are they managed and allocated? Who gets to know what? How much autonomy are employees given?
- Operational philosophy: Does the culture value balanced risk-taking or safety at all costs? Is management close control or leadership? Are managers taught to care only about their own units or are they concerned about overall results?
- Human resources: Are employees viewed as costs or assets?

The questions should be designed to draw out the values and philosophies of respondents and assess how appropriate those beliefs are for the organization at a given time. Each question should ask respondents 1) what the culture is, 2) what they believe it should be, 3) why a gap (if any) exists between what is and what should be, 4) the importance of closing the gap and consequences of failing to do so, and 5) what is required to close the gap and how this can best be done.

Selecting the right people or constituencies to provide input is critical to the success of the assessment. Be aware that if only those with vested interests in the existing culture determine who participates in the evaluation, the status quo will have the best chance of emerging as the "ideal." Key executives will almost certainly participate, since they have the broadest viewpoint and are the ones who must accept the need to change. But if the assessment is intended to identify subcultures and recognize variations between how constituencies view the organization's culture, the sample must be broader and representative, reaching both horizontally across functions or businesses and vertically through management levels.

Before beginning the cultural assessment, clarify and communicate the organization's vision or mission to ensure that it is widely understood. Scan the current environmental realities to confirm that the vision or mission is still viable. The communication process will strengthen the vision or mission, since publicly articulating a guiding philosophy strengthens belief in it.[2] Respondents evaluating the culture will then be able to base their input on the best available information. However, make sure respondents know that responses to the questionnaire should express their actual values, rather than values they believe to be "politically correct."

Interpreting the Results

The completed questionnaires provide a basis for a constructive dialogue on the key gaps between what the organization's culture is and what it should be.

At this point there is often a tendency to try to identify an "ideal" culture that can immediately be adopted. Other organizations cited as having effective cultures may be contacted, outsiders familiar with current trends or supposed "best practices" may be brought in, and so forth. While all of this "benchmarking" activity is an honest attempt to gather more information and may be productive, the real issue is how well an existing—or alternative—culture fits the organization's current internal and external realities. The search for an ideal, one-size-fits-all cultural profile is misguided.

Popular culture often assumes that the "correct" choice will be apparent on careful examination. But it is not clear that any one culture will be effective for all organizations, or even for a specific organization at a particular point in time. Respondents must understand that there are no "superior" answers on the questionnaire and that the critical goal is to arrive at an appropriate balance of viewpoints.

To illustrate this point, compare two very different organizations: a major utility, long recognized as relatively innovative and effective in serving its customers, and a large software firm, a leader in software packages and processing services supporting a high technology application. These examples show how the gaps between what is and what should be are identified and how this knowledge can be used to determine what is appropriate and effective for the organization, as well as what needs to change. The process of comparing the two organizations illustrates how one organization's "ideal" culture can differ from another organization's.

Formulating Strategies to Fit or Support the Culture

Human resource strategy is like a hologram: it consists of interrelated functional strategies that must be carefully integrated to form an effective whole. The functional components most often defined are selection and staffing, organizational and human resource development, and rewards. Another possible component of HR strategy encompasses how workplaces and employee roles are designed, although this functional strategy often does not fall completely within the purview of HR.

The utility and the software firms will almost certainly require different human resource strategies to meet their critical needs. Since their respective strategies must operate in very different cultures, it seems reasonable that they attract, retain and motivate different kinds of people and use different systems to do so.

The Utility

The culture of the utility is reasonably well-suited to a regulated monopoly. Maintaining consistent performance is viewed as more critical than continuous innovation, both because of the utility's primary mission and because mistakes can be extremely costly. As a result, policies and procedures that emphasize error avoidance are usually preferred, even when they result in some redundancy of resources or somewhat higher costs. Those values are reflected in the strategy of the organization.

If the utility were to compete directly with unregulated private sector organizations, its culture might not be as appropriate as it was when competition did not exist. The critical needs for effecting cultural change would be:

1. Increased sensitivity to satisfying customer needs.
2. Increased emphasis on doing what will benefit the entire organization, even though short-term interests of a unit may be in conflict.
3. More emphasis on cost management, without substantially increasing the risk of error or decreasing product quality or reliability.
4. Increased appreciation of employees' potential value and a stronger belief in investing in them when a high payback is likely.

HR strategy and fit to desired culture: staffing. The utility has operated with a relatively closed internal labor market, "growing its own" technical and managerial talent. Employees have typically been socialized to the organization's way of doing things and rewarded for following the "script."

Although this approach ensured employees were well-oriented to the vision, mission and objectives of the organization—and probably encouraged reliable execution of policy—it also may have created an internal-oriented, rather than a customer-focused, point of view. A new staffing strategy might be required to change it. One way of promoting a customer focus would be to hire people with experience in organizations where organizational survival depends on satisfying customers.

Mission: To provide high-quality services on demand, reliably, and at a reasonable cost.

Current Culture	Desired Culture	Gap
Performance de ned as organization meeting goals	Performance de ned as customer being satis ed	Signi cant; need to refocus on customer
Performance attributed to all employees/units	Same as Current	None
Performance thought of as both short- and long-term	Same as Current	None
Information communicated widely and completely	Same as Current	None
Focus is on unit/function performance	Focus should be on overall organizational performance	Signi cant; need to refocus on overall results
Increased ef ciency key to future performance	Same as Current	None
Operational philosophy = minimum risk approach	Operational philosophy = balance: risk vs. cost	Signi cant; need to change views about playing it safe
Human resources are costs, but some recognition that investment in HRD desirable	Human resources are investments; their "human capital" can contribute as much as nancial capital	Moderate; need to increase managerial appreciation for potential HRD paybacks
Employees have a right to annual increases, no matter the impact on rates	Pay increases must be earned with performance/cost effectiveness	Signi cant; need to replace time-based pay with merit pay

Overall Observations: The stable, highly internalized culture can be explained at least in part by the organization's history and the nature of its mission; stability and reliability have and continue to be critical to performance, even when dramatic innovations must be foregone to ensure reliability.

Development. All four of the critical needs are changes that can be met, at least partially, through revisions in the utility's current training and education programs. Management education should be used to sell managers on the idea that human resources are assets, since managers make the investment decisions and are typically responsible for assisting employees with their career progression.

Rewards. The utility has always used a time-based "step-rate" pay increase program. Because there has been little focus on merit or performance pay, there has been little in the rewards program that encouraged employees to do more than "follow the script." The "pay increases come first" attitude revealed in the cultural assessment needs to be broken down—probably by changing the base pay program.

Incentive programs could be instituted using customer satisfaction ratings to drive rewards. Performance criteria could also incorporate cost management effectiveness, while maintaining a balance between costs and results. To help managers think beyond their own unit's results and understand the downside of trying to get the most pay for their own people without regard to equity or costs, at least one incentive pay plan based on overall results should be instituted. Finally, management personnel could be evaluated and rewarded based on how well they develop their employees, which will be likely to increase their focus on this objective.

Design. Reorganizing the customer service process to provide a single contact or service point—probably a team—could help the utility focus on customer satisfaction. This approach would lend itself to investing in human resources by creating a multiskilled workforce with more autonomy to satisfy customers and handle complete transactions as a way of improving the service level.

The Software Firm

The culture of this organization is very different from the utility's but reasonably well-suited to its environmental and contextual realities. The organization's driving need at this time is to continuously develop and use the skills and creativity of employees. As a result, a flexible structure with defined roles that are temporary and change frequently will best allow the organization to succeed in a wide variety of future endeavors.

Although dramatic changes are not required, some critical needs are

1. More delegation by managers.
2. More recognition of support functions and their contributions.
3. Better creation and communication of long-range plans.
4. According equal weight to overall organizational performance and product or unit performance.

HR strategy and fit to desired culture: staffing. Traditionally, the firm has hired and promoted people with the best technical skills. Selection criteria for entry into management should probably be modified to ensure that successful candidates possess or can develop the particular management style and philosophy needed to improve organizational performance. Even if managers continue to be drawn from within the organization, training and management education may increase the effectiveness of those promoted.

Development. Management education could play a large role in improving this culture, with delegation, planning and communication of strategy being key topics. Because technically oriented professionals tend to focus on their own development and task accomplishments, their thought models must often be changed drastically if they are to manage effectively. Even in work team environments there is a big difference between the role of a team member and that of a team leader.

FIGURE 2: CULTURAL ASSESSMENT OF A LEADING SOFTWARE FIRM

Mission: To provide the most advanced technology that best serves customer needs and priorities, and to be evaluated by customers as a business partner who contributes significantly to customer success.

Current Culture	Desired Culture	Gap
Performance defined as customers being satisfied	Same as Current	None
Performance created by Sales, Design and Customer Service	Performance created by all employees/units	Moderate; support units need recognition
Performance thought of as principally short-run	Performance thought of as between short- and long-run	Moderate; more focus needed on long-run
Information managed fairly tightly	Information needs to be given to all who need it	Significant; managers need to increase trust placed in key people
Focus is on specific product/ business unit performance	Focus is on both unit and organizational performance	Moderate; more emphasis on overall results
Future performance requires continuous innovation	Same as Current	None
Operational philosophy = balance: risk vs. cost	Same as Current	None
Human resources are assets but must be well-managed to stay competitive	Same as Current	None
Shareholders have a right to a fair return before pay levels are increased	Same as Current	None

Overall Observations: The rapidly changing technological environment demands continuous innovation and improvement, and the current culture is reasonably well-suited to the demands of the organization.

Rewards. In this organization, the "spoils" have historically gone to direct sales people who participate in volume-based individual incentive programs, and to technical contributors responsible for creating breakthrough products or technologies. Incentive plans could be developed to increase recognition of the contribution support functions make to the firm's overall success. To encourage a broader perspective on the part of managers, some incentives could be based, at least in part, on organization-wide results. Long-term or project-based incentives also could be used to increase emphasis on long-range planning and sustained performance in all parts of the organization.

Design. Because of the nature of the work, this organization already operates in a project-focused manner. The workplace structure and defined employee roles fit the work to be done. The firm may want to consider incorporating staff support functions into the project teams, but will need to balance efficiency concerns against the benefits of supporting this aspect of its desired cultural change.

Organizations with Poorly Defined or Fragmented Cultures

Both the utility and the software firm seem to have a fairly good consensus among key managers about what the organization's culture is and what it should be. Many organizations that perform a cultural assessment will identify disagreement among key functions or businesses, all of whom are constituencies.[3] In fact, resolving differences is a prerequisite for improving the effectiveness of the culture organization-wide.

The utility had conflicting cultural expectations between the information systems function, the customer service function and the more mainstream functions related to production and delivery of primary services. For that organization, conducting cultural assessments within these functions and then determining key points of difference between senior management's desired culture and the culture desired by people in the functional businesses was beneficial.

Assessments will not necessarily light a clear path to reconciliation between functions. The result could be an agreement that cultural differences are acceptable or manageable, or perhaps, that the differences warrant an outsourcing of one or more "culturally incompatible" functions. One research organization created a new company to market a product it developed because the reward systems required for sales force effectiveness were culturally incompatible with the values and beliefs of the rest of the organization. In another organization the information systems function was outsourced because its culture supporting continuous, dramatic innovation did not fit the rather pedestrian needs of the rest of the organization.

Organizations with Dysfunctional Cultures

Neither the utility nor the software firm had a seriously misaligned or dysfunctional culture. In fact, many organizations would be happy with a similar degree of fit between their culture, their mission and their environmental or contextual realities.

In organizations with significant misalignments of culture—very large gaps between what the culture is and what people feel it should be—key constituencies must come to some consensus about:

- Which components of the culture are misaligned.
- What priorities should be assigned each of the gaps.
- What resources are needed and how they should be used.
- How the change effort should be managed and who does what.
- What role human resource strategy should play in signaling, making and reinforcing the necessary changes.

In many cases cultural misalignments are a byproduct of major organizational change initiatives, such as total quality management, employee involvement or reengineering. Each of these initiatives typically requires some cultural adjustment to be effective, even though they all seem to have similar goals, such as treating employees as critical assets, focusing on customer satisfaction and delegating authority broadly. Even when the optimal culture for supporting these initiatives has been identified and agreed to, the difficulties associated with making adjustments to the current culture must still be dealt with.

Each organization must decide whether it has the right people in the right places to make the changes, whether these people have been adequately trained, given the necessary resources and focused on the right objectives, and whether they believe they will be rewarded for their contributions. HR strategy must be consistent with the needs of the organization, and its component strategies must provide alignment with the organization's objectives.

Conclusion

Human resource strategies can be powerful tools for signaling cultural change and reinforcing those changes once they are made. Who is hired and retained, how people are paid, and what behaviors are deemed desirable all send strong messages about the desired culture. The potential of HR strategies and programs for shaping organizational culture cannot be overestimated. For HR strategy to realize its full potential, the organization must first determine what its culture is and what it should be. Then the organization can create a plan for aligning culture with its mission and environmental or contextual realities by managing the culture from what it is to what it should be.

Source: *HR Magazine* by Greene, Copyright © 1995 by the Society for Human Resource Management Reproduced with permission of the Society for Human Resource Management in the format Textbook via Copyright Clearance Center.

Endnotes

1. E. Skein. *Organizational Culture and Leadership* (San Francisco: Jossey-Bass, 1985).
2. J. Person & J. Sorensen. *Organizational Cultures In Theory & Practice* (Aldeshot, England: Avery, 1989).
3. J. Collins & J. Porras. *Built To Last* (New York: Harper Business, 1994).

CHAPTER

5

HUMAN RESOURCE PLANNING

For the past decade, Dell Computer has remained one of the world's fastest growing companies. Founded in 1984, the organization now has over 35,000 employees, does business in more than 170 countries, and has over $27 billion in annual revenues. One share of Dell stock purchased in its initial public offering in June 1988 at $8.50 was worth $4,812 as of April 2000. In 1998 alone, Dell's workforce increased by 56 percent over the previous year. Dell executives attribute much of this success to Dell's approach to managing human resources. Dell HR professionals have dual reporting relationships to both the vice president of a Dell business unit and the vice president of HR. They attend business unit management team meetings as internal consultants and are involved with developing the business unit's leadership team, measuring turnover and productivity, and developing a customized HR strategy for each particular business line. Clearly, such phenomenal growth and performance can only be achieved through a well-designed system for recruiting new hires.

A key to Dell's success has been its Organizational Human Resources Planning (OHRP) process. The OHRP process helps Dell to anticipate its demand for workers to facilitate its growth. The process involves mapping a set of key job openings that are used to forecast and source inside and outside talent in advance. Dell also requires its HR function to spot the competencies and skills its new employees will need by analyzing its existing highest performing employees and determining the keys to their success. Steve Price, vice president of HR at Dell, notes, "We look at people who have been given the biggest merit increases, the best appraisals, and so forth, and then we interview against these competencies."

Dell also utilizes flexible deployment of its HR staff to facilitate its OHRP process. Line managers in technical areas are utilized as "rotational recruiters," whereby they spend three- or four-month periods assisting HR with staffing, orientation, and training during peak periods. These individuals lend keen insights toward recruiting and training as they are the individuals who actually do and oversee the functional areas. Conversely, during slower recruiting periods such as the Christmas holidays, HR recruiting staff move over to sales and customer service to assist with peak customer demand experienced during that time. After the holidays, they return to their HR functions.

Source: Joinson, C. "Moving at the Speed of Dell," *HR Magazine*, Vol. 44, No. 4, April 1999. See also http://www.dell.com.

Once the corporate and business unit strategies have been established, then the human resource strategy can begin to be developed. The HR strategy involves taking the organization's strategic goals and objectives and translating them into a consistent, integrated, complementary set of programs and policies for managing employees.

This does not imply, however, that strategic HR is reactive in nature. Although it is derived from corporate and/or business unit strategies, HR strategy is developed in a proactive manner, with HR staff attempting to design and develop appropriate HR systems to meet the anticipated conditions under which the organization will be operating. The senior HR professional, as a vital member of the top management team, should also be heavily involved in corporate or business unit strategic planning so that the top management team is able to include human resource management concerns in its overall planning. HR needs to inform the top management team of the skills and capabilities of the organization's workforce and how they might impact strategic plans.

The first component of human resource management strategy is human resource planning. (The second component, the design of work systems, will be covered in Chapter 6.) All other functional HR activities, such as staffing, training, performance management, compensation, labor relations, and employee separation, are derived and should flow from the human resource planning process. When undertaking human resource planning, the organization considers the implications of its future plans on the nature and types of individuals it will need to employ and the necessary skills and training they'll require. The organization will also need to assess its current stock of employees as well as those available for employment externally. The key facet of human resource planning is that it is a *proactive* process. It attempts to plan and anticipate what might happen in the various domains of the organization's internal and external environments and to develop plans to address these events prior to their actually happening. Rather than react to changes in the industry, marketplace, economy, society, and technological world, human resource planning ensures that the organization will be able to adapt in tandem with these changes and maintain the fit between the organization and its environment. HR planning is particularly important during periods of organizational turbulence, such as during a merger or acquisition, when labor market conditions are tight, or when unemployment is low.

Because human resource planning involves making assumptions about the future, particularly the status of the economy, competition, technology, regulation, and internal operations and resources, it is critical that all human resource planning initiatives be flexible. If events and circumstances materialize differently from how they are anticipated, then the organization should not be bound by prior and existing plans. Changes to any planning initiatives should not be viewed as a weakness in the planning process. Rather, they should be a positive sign that the organization is carefully monitoring its external environment and responding appropriately to any changes taking place.

In order to facilitate this flexibility, it is critical that key decision makers in the organization *clarify and write down* all assumptions they make about the external environment and the organization when developing the human resource plan. If the organization has difficulty achieving its strategic objectives despite following a carefully wrought human resource plan, there is a very good chance that inaccurate assumptions were made about what might happen in the future or when expectations failed to materialize.

Clarifying and writing down these assumptions make subsequent intervention and corrective action much easier. Many interventions become complicated and time-consuming because when decision makers revisit the process, the strategy seems to flow logically from the process outlined in Chapter 3. However, as previously noted, much of the assessment of the external environment involves assumptions that various conditions of the economy, technology, marketplace, competition, and regulatory environment will remain the same or change. These assumptions are often held by key decision makers but not verbalized. As a result, corrective action may be stymied due to an inability to identify the key problem.

Human resource planning goes far beyond simple hiring and firing. It involves planning for the deployment of the organization's human capital in the most effective and efficient ways, in line with organization and/or business unit strategy. In addition to hiring and/or separation, human capital management may involve reassignment, training and development, outsourcing, and/or using temporary help or outside contractors. Modern organizations need as much flexibility as possible in how they utilize human talent in the pursuit of their strategic goals.

Human Resource Planning at Drexel Heritage Furnishings

Drexel Heritage Furnishings is a North Carolina–based, century-old manufacturer of premium quality furniture. To plan its workforce needs in such a competitive, volatile, and seasonally cyclical industry, the organization carefully monitors a variety of internal and external indicators. The vice president of HR carefully tracks incoming orders to monitor and project volume over the coming quarter. In addition, the Purchasing Managers Index, a monthly measure of nationwide business activity, is tracked. This index is a gauge of consumer sentiment about the economy and is based on new orders, prices, inventories, and backlogs. Additional indicators such as real estate activity—including construction activity, mortgage rates, relocations, and market prices—are monitored by HR as well, as these factors can be tied to demand for home furnishings. Finally, trends in employee compensation, including bonuses and stock options, are considered, as such "add-on" compensation may be used as discretionary income for the purchase of home furnishings.[1]

The need to carefully monitor human resource planning activities will become even more acute in the coming years. The U.S. Bureau of Labor Statistics estimates that during the current decade, the civilian labor force will increase by only 1 percent and that after that, the retirement of baby boomers will slow the growth to only two tenths of a percent until the year 2025.[2] Probably nowhere is this creating more challenges than with the federal workforce. Recent reports published by the U.S. Merit Systems Protection Board (MSPB) have determined that the federal government's recruiting processes greatly hamper its ability to hire needed employees. With an average age of approximately 50 years, between one half million and one million federal employees are expected to retire by 2010. Because little concerted effort is being made to replace such workers or to provide training for those who will remain after these retirements, the future looks grim. In addition, the process for hiring new employees has been found to be so cumbersome that many qualified workers are discouraged from applying for federal jobs.[3] However, one federal employer, the U.S. Postal Service, has developed a model for human capital management that is exemplary for government agencies.

Human Capital Management at the United States Postal Service

With more than 800,000 employees, the U.S. Postal Service (USPS) has the second-largest workforce in the country. The 230-year-old post service has an operating budget of $65 billion and has been under increased competitive pressure from organizations such as Federal Express, United Parcel Service, and Internet service providers, all of whom have eroded market share and offered alternatives to the traditional monopoly enjoyed by the USPS. Current projections are that 85 percent of its executives, 74 percent of its managers and supervisors, and 50 percent of its career workforce will be eligible to retire by 2010.

The postal service has developed a strategy to ensure that it attracts the right people and then deploys them effectively to where they are most needed. To ensure that the best employees are retained, performance management and leadership development programs have been created to motivate and reward them. At the center of its human capital management plan are four key strategies: (1) aggressive recruitment of future leaders; (2) building of an effective, motivated workforce in which individuals and teams are recognized through a performance-based pay system; (3) establishment and maintenance of a good work environment, based on cooperative working relationships between unionized employees and management; and (4) creation of a flexible workforce that can be readily adjusted as conditions change and new needs arise.

To facilitate these goals, back-office functions have been reorganized and consolidated into 85 separate "performance clusters." Each cluster has its own HR staff that applied reengineering principles and technology tools to repetitive transactional service work to create more self-service transactions for employees and managers. Performance management is being integrated into virtually every organizational initiative to ensure that rewards are commensurate with productivity. Succession planning and corresponding training and development initiatives have been established to ensure that vital skills are identified and transferred to up-and-coming employees. The Advanced Leadership Program has been developed as a premier program for high-potential future executives that trains them to understand the strategic challenges being faced by the organization and to develop the skills that allow participants to creatively address those challenges.[4]

OBJECTIVES OF HUMAN RESOURCE PLANNING

There are five major objectives of HR planning, as outlined in Exhibit 5-1. The first is to prevent overstaffing and understaffing. When an organization has too many employees, it experiences a loss of efficiency in operations due to excessive payroll costs and/or surplus production that can't be marketed and must be inventoried. Having too few employees results in lost sales revenue as the organization is unable

EXHIBIT 5-1: KEY OBJECTIVES OF HUMAN RESOURCE PLANNING

- Prevent overstaffing and understaffing
- Ensure the organization has the right employees with the right skills in the right places at the right times
- Ensure the organization is responsive to changes in its environment
- Provide direction and coherence to all HR activities and systems
- Unite the perspectives of line and staff managers

to satisfy existing demand of customers. Moreover, the inability to meet current demand for products or services due to understaffing can also result in the loss of future customers who turn to competitors. Human resource planning helps to ensure that operations are not only efficient but also timely in response to customer demand.

The second objective is to ensure that the organization has the right employees with the right skills in the right places at the right times. Organizations need to anticipate the kinds of employees they need in terms of skills, work habits, and personal characteristics and time their recruiting efforts so that the best employees have been hired, fully trained, and prepared to deliver peak performance exactly when the organization needs them. Specific techniques for accomplishing this will be discussed in Chapter 8. Nonetheless, the planning process needs to consider myriad factors including skill levels, individual employee "fit" with the organization, training, work systems, and projected demand and integrate these factors as a critical component of its HR strategy.

The third objective is to ensure that the organization is responsive to changes in its environment. The human resource planning process requires decision makers to consider a variety of scenarios relative to the numerous domains in the environment. For example, the economy might grow, remain stagnant, or shrink; the industry might remain the same or become either more or less competitive; government regulation may remain the same, be relaxed, or become more stringent; technology may or may not be further developed. Human resource planning forces the organization to speculate and assess the state of its eternal environment. Anticipating and planning for any possible changes, rather than passively reacting to such conditions, can allow the organization to stay one step ahead of its competitors.

The fourth objective is to provide direction and coherence to all human resource activities and systems. Human resource planning sets the direction for all other HR functions, such as staffing, training and development, performance measurement, and compensation. It will also ensure that the organization takes a more systemic view of its human resource management activities by understanding the interrelatedness of the HR programs and systems and how changes in one area may impact another area. A coherent human resource plan will ensure, for example, that the areas in which employees are being trained are being incorporated into their performance measurements and that these factors are additionally considered in compensation decisions.

The fifth objective is to unite the perspectives of line and staff managers. Although human resource planning is usually initiated and managed by the corporate HR staff, it requires the input and cooperation of all managers within an organization. No one better knows the needs of a particular unit or department than the individual manager responsible for that area. Communication between HR staff and line managers is essential for the success of any HR planning initiatives. Corporate

HR staff need to assist line managers in the planning process but simultaneously acknowledge the expertise of and responsibility assigned to individual line managers in considering their input to the planning process.

TYPES OF PLANNING

Planning is generally done on two different levels. *Aggregate planning* anticipates needs for groups of employees in specific, usually lower-level jobs (the number of customer service representatives needed, for example) and the general skills employees need to ensure sustained high performance. *Succession planning* focuses on key individual management positions that the organization needs to make sure remain filled and the types of individuals who might provide the best fit in these critical positions.

Aggregate Planning

The first step in aggregate planning is forecasting the demand for employees. In doing so the organization needs to consider its strategic plan and any kinds and rates of growth or retrenchment that may be planned. The single greatest indicator of the demand for employees is demand for the organization's product or service. It is imperative when forecasting the demand for employees to clarify and write down any assumptions that might affect utilization of employees (new technology that might be developed or acquired, competition for retention of existing employers, changes in the production of a product or provision of a service, new quality or customer service initiatives, or redesign of work systems).

Although there are several mathematical methods, such as multiple regression and linear programming, to assist in forecasting demand for employees, most organizations rely more on the judgments of experienced and knowledgeable managers in determining employee requirements. This may be done through unit forecasting (sometimes called *bottom-up planning*), top-down planning, or some combination of both.

In unit forecasting, each individual unit, department, or branch of the organization estimates its future needs for employees. For example, each branch of a bank might prepare its own forecast based on the goals and objectives each branch manager has for the particular office. These estimates are then presented to subsequent layers of management, who combine and sum the totals and present them to senior management for approval.

This technique has the potential for being the most responsive to the needs of the marketplace because it places responsibility for estimating employee needs at the "point of contact" in service provision or product production. However, unless there is some mechanism for control and accountability for allocating resources, such a technique can easily lead managers to overestimate their own unit needs. Without accountability and control measures for costs and productivity, this technique can become quite inefficient as lower-level managers attempt to hoard employees without regard as to whether these human assets might better be deployed in another division of the organization. Consequently, any system of unit forecasting needs to have an accompanying program of accountability for performance based, at least in part, on headcount. This underscores the need for having integrated HR systems and programs.

Top-down forecasting involves senior managers allocating a budgeted amount for employee payroll expenditures and then dividing the pool at subsequent levels down the hierarchy. Each manager receives a budget from her/his supervisor and then decides how to allocate these funds down to the next group of managers. This technique is similar to sales and profit plans in many organizations whereby each unit is assigned a budgeted amount and then required to make decisions on deploying those resources in the manner most consistent with business objectives. Although this technique may be efficient, as senior management allocates HR costs within a strict organization-wide budget, there is no guarantee that it will be responsive to the needs of the marketplace. Allocations are based solely on what the organization can afford, without regard to input concerning demand and marketplace dynamics.

Unit forecasting promotes responsiveness to customers and the marketplace; top-down forecasting promotes organizational efficiency in resource allocation. Consequently, an organization can choose a planning technique that is consistent with its overall strategy. An organization whose key strategic objectives involve cost minimization can opt for top-down forecasting. An organization more concerned with change and adaptability can opt for unit or bottom-up forecasting. However, if an organization has objectives of both responsiveness and efficiency, it is possible to use both forms of forecasting and have middle levels of management responsible for negotiating the differences between the two techniques.

In addition to the demand for actual headcount of employees, the organization also needs to consider the demand for specific skills that it will require of its employees as part of the HR planning process. Changes in workplace demographics are having a significant impact on the skills that job applicants bring to an organization. Technology is also having an impact on the skills required of employees. Assessment of the demand for employees needs to consider not only numbers but also the kinds of workers who will best fit with the organization relative to personal characteristics, work habits, and specific skills.

Once demand for employees has been forecasted, the organization then has to plan for an adequate supply of employees to meet this demand. This process involves estimating the actual number of employees and determining the skills that these employees must have, and whether their backgrounds, training, and career plans will provide a sufficient fit for the organization's future plans. This chapter focuses on the internal supply of labor. Chapter 8 will expand the discussion to consider external labor markets.

One way to assess the abilities, skills, and experiences of existing employees is by using a skills inventory. In the past, these inventories were usually compiled and processed manually, but now skills inventories are usually computerized databases that are part of the organization's overall human resource information system. Each employee provides information on his or her experience, education, abilities, job preferences, career aspirations, and other relevant personal information. This allows an organization to gain a collective sense of who their employees are and what capabilities they have. Skills inventories must be constantly updated to be of any value to an organization. Changing employee backgrounds and preferences mandate that the skills inventory be updated at least annually.

Estimates of the existing supply of human resources relative to quantity is not a static measure; rather, it is dynamic. In the majority of medium and large organizations, employees change positions and job levels constantly or leave the organization. Consequently, any attempt to assess the supply of employees needs to assess mobility within the organization, as well as turnover rates. This can be done through a mathematical technique known as *Markov analysis*, which describes the probability of

EXHIBIT 5-2: TRANSITION PROBABILITY MATRIX FOR A RESTAURANT

		One Year From Now			
		Servers	**Hosts**	**Buspersons**	**Exit**
Current Year	Servers	.80	.10	0	.10
	Hosts	.10	.70	0	.20
	Buspersons	.15	.05	.40	.40

Analysis of Matrix

Retention Levels

Servers	80%
Hosts	70%
Buspersons	40%

Forecasted Levels

Incumbents		**Servers**	**Hosts**	**Buspersons**	**Exit**
60	Servers	48	6		6
10	Hosts	1	7		2
20	Buspersons	3	1	8	8
	Totals	52	14	8	16

employees staying with the job in any job category, moving to another job, or leaving the organization over a given time period, usually one year. It uses a transition probability matrix that is established based on historical trends of mobility. Markov analysis can also be utilized to allow managers to identify problem departments within an organization or positions that appear to be less desirable as reflected in high rates of turnover or low rates of retention. A sample Markov analysis is illustrated in Exhibit 5-2.

The top portion of this exhibit presents a sample transition probability matrix. For the sake of simplicity, we will assume that there are three job classifications in the restaurant: servers, hosts, and buspersons. Horizontal readings show the movement anticipated during the coming year for each job classification based on historic trends. For example, 80 percent of the current staff of servers would be expected to remain employed in that capacity one year from now; 10 percent will become hosts; none will become buspersons, and 10 percent will leave the organization.

The bottom half of the exhibit first shows retention levels, followed by a forecast of the supply of employees expected in each position. To calculate these values, we take the number of incumbents and multiply them by the percentages from the transition probability matrix. Summing each of the columns that pertain to job classifications allows us to determine, given normal movement, expected supply levels of employees one year from now.

After reliable estimates have been made for both supply and demand of employees, programs can be implemented to address any anticipated surplus or shortage of employees in a particular job category. In planning for anticipated shortages, the organization first needs to consider whether the shortage is expected to be temporary or indefinite. This has implications for whether the organization should hire temporary or permanent employees or even consider subcontracting work to an outside vendor. If permanent employees are to be hired, the plan needs to be comprehensive and consider the types of employees that should be recruited, whether they should be recruited internally or externally, how long they will need for training to perform at acceptable

EXHIBIT 5-3: STRATEGIES FOR MANAGING EMPLOYEE SHORTAGES AND SURPLUSES

Strategies for Managing Shortages	Strategies for Managing Surpluses
• Recruit new permanent employees	• Hiring freezes
• Offer incentives to postpone retirement	• Do not replace those who leave
• Rehire retirees part-time	• Offer early retirement incentives
• Attempt to reduce turnover	• Reduce work hours
• Work current staff overtime	• Voluntary severance, leaves of absence
• Subcontract work out	• Across-the-board pay cuts
• Hire temporary employees	• Layoffs
• Redesign job processes so that fewer employees are needed	• Reduce outsourced work
	• Employee training
	• Switch to variable pay plan
	• Expand operations

Adapted from Fisher, Schoenfeldt, and Shaw. *Human Resource Management*, 4d, 1999.

levels, and how long the recruiting process has historically taken. Issues and strategies for addressing these concerns will be discussed in Chapter 8.

Another important consideration is whether the individuals will need the latest skills or whether the organization requires more hands-on practical experience. The former strategy would suggest recruiting younger employees directly out of formal schooling or training programs; the latter strategy would suggest recruiting from competitors or possibly having older workers postpone retirement or work on a contract or part-time consulting basis.

If a surplus of employees is anticipated, a critical strategic issue that must be addressed is whether this surplus is expected to be temporary or permanent. The most extreme action to reduce a surplus is to lay off employees. Layoffs should usually be conducted only as a last resort, given the effects they can have on the morale of remaining employees as well as the significant economic costs that often result from large-scale layoffs. Surpluses can also be addressed through early retirement programs, transfer and retraining of existing employees, and/or an across-the-board reduction in salaries or working hours. Exhibit 5-3 summarizes some strategies for managing employee shortages and surpluses. Shortages will be discussed in more depth and detail in Chapter 8 while surpluses will be discussed in Chapter 13.

Succession Planning

Succession planning involves identifying key management positions that the organization cannot afford to have vacant. These are usually senior management positions and/or positions that the organization has traditionally had a very difficult time filling. Succession planning serves two purposes. First, it facilitates transition when an employee leaves. It is not unusual to have a departing employee work alongside her or his successor for a given period prior to departure to facilitate the transition. Succession planning aids in this process. Second, succession planning identifies the development needs of high-potential employees and assists with their career planning. By identifying specific individuals who might be asked to assume high-level responsibilities, the organization can attempt to develop key skills in these individuals that might be needed in subsequent assignments.

Although succession planning programs are relatively easy to understand in concept, actual practice shows that, even though organizations realize how critical the processes is, they may fail to implement succession planning effectively. ▼

Succession Planning at K. Hovanian Enterprises

Red Bank, New Jersey–based K. Hovanian Enterprises is one of the nation's largest homebuilders. The $2.6 billion company recently was cited by Fortune *as the nation's fifteenth-fastest-growing company. As it has acquired seven other homebuilding companies within a three-year period, senior management saw the need to develop a succession planning committee to select and approve candidates who had high potential to move the organization ahead. In assessing candidates, data is collected in confidence on each candidate that consists of detailed feedback provided by 12 to 14 direct reports, colleagues, and senior managers. This data is used to assess leadership ability and potential. After a candidate is accepted by the committee, that person is notified and he or she creates a plan for personal development that reflects his or her experience and background. Employees are expected to devote 10 to 20 percent of their time to their personal development plan. The company has reported successful results, to date. One hundred percent of the employees who have completed the program have been promoted, whereas those hired from the outside have a promotion success rate of only 50 percent.*[5]

Traditional succession planning utilizes a relatively simple planning tool called a replacement chart. Replacement charts identify key positions, possible successors for each of these positions, whether each potential successor currently has the background to assume the job responsibilities, or the expected amount of time it will take for the potential successor to be ready. Replacement charts are easily derived from the organization chart and are often part of the human resource information system: They can narrow in on one key position and the subordinates reporting to the individual holding that position. A sample replacement chart is presented in Exhibit 5-4.

EXHIBIT 5-4: SAMPLE REPLACEMENT CHART

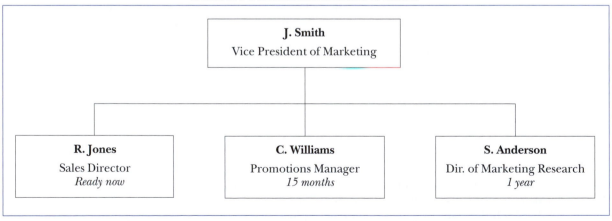

▶ Reading 5.1, "Heirs Unapparent," discusses some of the practical difficulties in succession planning, particularly in light of some of the demographic changes taking place in the workforce.

In this example, Smith is the vice president of marketing and has three direct reports: Jones, Williams, and Anderson. Beneath the three reports' job titles is the expected period of additional time each will need to be ready to assume the vice president responsibilities. The assessments of time are generally not objective. They are usually based on the opinions and recommendations of higher-ranking managers. In this example, Smith may have provided the time estimates for the three subordinates based on subjective personal assessments.

Some organizations, however, are much more systematic about their succession planning. Their replacement charts may contain specific skills, competencies, and experiences rather than subjective estimates of time-readiness. This may help to overcome problems associated with personal bias and ensure that the most qualified individuals are promoted. Moreover, it allows an organization to provide its high-potential employees with more specific feedback regarding developmental needs. Such an approach might ensure that women and minorities have equal access to high-level management positions.

Clearly, the more volatile competitive organizations of the 21st century may need to develop much larger pools of talent with very broad sets of skills. Consequently, many organizations are beginning to embrace the development of succession planning strategies that are based more on organization-needed competencies and flexibility than focusing on subjective assessment of "readiness." ▼▼

Succession planning not only helps to ensure that key management positions remain filled, but it also helps to identify critical training and development needs of both individual managers and the organization as a whole. Succession planning clearly involves taking an investment-oriented approach toward employees. Although the benefits of a well-developed succession planning program can be significant, such programs can also come at a significant cost to an organization. An employer should ensure that there is at least one individual able to assume every critical position if something prevents the incumbent from continuing in it; however, the more prepared an individual is for a promotion that he or she does not receive, the greater the possibility that he or she might seek such a position elsewhere. This is particularly true for succession planning programs built around defined management competencies. The end result of this process is the organization invests in an individual and a competitor receives the return on that investment. Succession planning initiatives aimed at key managers need to be coupled with a specific retention strategy designed for potential successors.

One key issue that organizations must address in their succession planning is the extent to which these efforts will be public and whether those targeted for grooming for higher-level assignments are to be informed of their "high-potential" status. These questions have been the subject of ongoing debate, as outlined in Exhibit 5-5. Telling employees that they have been identified as key potential players in the organization's future plans might reinforce these employees' decision to stay with the organization for a longer period of time in light of alternative career opportunities. At the same time, it may create expectations for these employees that advancement is guaranteed and/or imminent. In addition, it could create a kind of implied contract to workers that they are guaranteed continued employment, eroding the employment-at-will doctrine, which will be discussed in Chapter 7. Not telling employees has the benefit of the employer "not committing" to employees and allows some flexibility in changing the mix of employees as business needs and the skill sets and experiences required to run

▶▶ Such a system is outlined in Reading 5.2, "Designing Succession Systems for New Competitive Realities." Here, a complex system was designed to fit with the organization's strategic goals.

EXHIBIT 5-5: PROS AND CONS OF DISCLOSING SUCCESSION PLANNING

	Disadvantages	Advantages
Do Not Tell	High performers may leave the organization, unsure of their future	Allows flexibility as business needs change
Tell	Unrealistic expectations and implied contracts	Retention strategy

the business change. On the other hand, if individuals are not aware that they have been targeted as "high potential," they may be more receptive to opportunities with other employers or consider going out on their own. One recent survey found that 37.5 percent of employers tell employees that they have been targeted; another found that 64 percent did so.[6] There is clearly no consensus as to whether such information should be kept confidential among the senior management team and each organization should weigh the pros and cons presented in Exhibit 5-5 when deciding its strategy.

Succession Planning at Dole Food

California-based Dole Food Company, Inc., which produces and markets fruits, vegetables, and flowers, has more than 61,000 employees in more than 90 countries with annual revenues of more than $4.6 billion. As the company grew from its humble origins, a decentralized structure was kept in place that allowed each unit to remain flexible relative to local market conditions. However, as Dole has become a worldwide conglomerate, this structure has inhibited the effective management of human capital at the executive level. To facilitate the global deployment of human capital, Dole instituted a succession planning model that revolves around four strategic competencies: accountability, business acumen, multifunctionality (cross-training), and vision/originality. Conducted entirely online, the program allows top managers access via a password. Employees provide a resume and fill out personal data, including career interests and mobility restrictions, and assess themselves on the four competencies. The information is then made available to managers who can assess the data for promotability as well as identify those employees for whom a special retention strategy should be developed. The data is then used to create a career development plan for each employee and to keep executives informed about those internal candidates who might be best suited for an opening. The system also allows Dole to identify those areas where it has a "talent gap" so that development opportunities might be provided, candidates sourced externally, or both, until those competencies are fully contained in-house.[7]

Succession planning efforts for the top executive spots have taken on more importance in recent years. With increasing pressure from boards and shareholders for continual profitability, the job of CEO has become far less attractive, particularly as the economy slows. Approximately 20 percent of the CEOs of America's 200 largest corporations were replaced in a recent year and the average CEO tenure currently is less than three years.[8] Even more startling is the number of high-profile CEOs who have departed after 18 months or less on the job, either by resignation or ouster, including the CEOs of Procter & Gamble, Mattel, Gillette, and Maytag.[9] Although turnover at the CEO level can be beneficial for an organization, it also can be highly disruptive. Consequently, organizations need to pay special attention to planning at the CEO level.

CEO Succession Planning at General Electric

When legendary General Electric (GE) CEO Jack Welch announced his pending retirement, there was not as much concern among GE stakeholders as might be expected. In keeping with GE's reputation as one of the best organizations at grooming senior management, Welch had planned his succession for more than 6 years prior to his public announcement. Within one month of Jeffrey Immelt being named President and Chairman-elect of GE as Welch's successor, two other top GE executives were named CEOs of Minnesota Mining and Manufacturing (3M) and Home Depot, Inc., affirming that GE is known for its superb training of senior executives for the chief executive's role.

GE's plan is relatively simple. Managers and executives are rotated from job to job every two to three years, with each new assignment being carefully designed to build experience and skills, creating a knowledgeable and experienced team of managers who have been exposed to a range of the giant corporation's divisions. Each new assignment involves a specific set of goals and expectations that must be met to ensure further advancement. The model is relatively simple and easy to duplicate, yet it takes a tremendous amount of time, energy, and commitment to make it succeed. At GE, the model is firmly ingrained in the corporate culture and creates a highly competitive system of performance management in which only the best and brightest executive will ultimately succeed.[10]

CONCLUSION

Effective human resource planning is the first key component for developing a human resource strategy. Human resource planning involves translating corporate-wide strategic initiatives into a workable plan for identifying the people needed to achieve these objectives; simultaneously, planning serves as a blueprint for all specific HR programs and policies. It is critical for the success of smaller, rapidly growing companies to ensure that their growth is properly managed and focused. Human resource planning allows the HR function to contribute to an organization's effectiveness by laying a foundation for proactive management that is strategically focused. ▼▼▼

More specifically, human resource planning facilitates a number of key processes within an organization. First, it facilitates leadership continuity through succession

▶▶▶ Reading 5.3, "If HR Were Strategically Proactive: Present and Future Directions in HR's Contribution to Competitive Advantage," outlines how strategically proactive thinking is critical to an organization's competitive advantage. Human resource planning is the critical first step in this process.

planning. It ensures that there will be no, or at most minimal, disruption of day-to-day operations due to unplanned departures.

Second, it facilitates strategic planning by examining the future availability of employees and their skill sets. Although human resource planning follows from the strategic plan, the information collected in the human resource planning process contributes to the assessment of the internal organization environment done in subsequent strategic planning.

Third, it facilitates an understanding of shifts and trends in the labor market through an examination of job requirements and employee capabilities. By assessing demographics, skills, and knowledge of employees and applicants vis-à-vis job requirements, the organization can remain ahead of its competitors in understanding the changing labor force.

Fourth, it facilitates employee development by determining the skills that will be needed to achieve strategic objectives as well as to ensure future career success in the organization. Ideally, this can serve as a catalyst for investing in employees through targeted training and development programs.

Fifth, it facilitates budget planning and resource allocation by determining needs for employees in response to the organization's strategic plan. This is particularly important in labor-intensive service industries where a significant portion of the budget is assumed by direct and indirect payroll expenditures.

Sixth, it facilitates efficiency by estimating future employee surpluses and shortages. Costs of overstaffing and understaffing can be significant and are minimized by the human resource planning process, allowing organizations to maintain a more competitive cost structure.

Finally, it facilitates the organization's adaptation to its environment. By assessing the external factors that can affect the organization against existing employee skills and background, the organization is better able to maintain an appropriate fit with its environment by ensuring that it has the in-house talent to manage its relationship with its environment.

CRITICAL THINKING

1. What are the major objectives of human resource planning? Why are each of these objectives critical for an organization's success? What benefits are provided by each that can result in a competitive advantage?

2. Why are aggregate and succession planning of critical importance? How might failures in these areas impact an organization's ability to compete?

3. What role might human resource planning play in each of the following organizations?
   - A small, rapidly growing technology company
   - A medium-size nonprofit
   - A state government agency social services agency
   - A professional sports franchise
   - A company planning on acquiring or merging with a key competitor

4. Discuss the implication and pros and cons for managing surpluses and shortages using the various strategies presented in Exhibit 5-3.

5. Discuss the pros and cons of informing employees that they have been targeted as part of the organization's succession planning process. What particular business conditions and/or strategy might make telling or not telling the more advantageous option?

6. Identify the steps you might take in consulting with the federal government about human resource planning. What factors would you suggest senior managers examine and what obstacles to implementing change might exist?

7. Select three organizations in which a new CEO has assumed responsibility during the past year. Identify via news sources factors that may have led to the change at the top of the organization. What appears to be the reason for the succession and what was the general reaction to the succession?

Reading 5.1

8. What problems are demographic shifts and layoff practices causing for succession planning? What role do competencies play in the succession planning initiatives of leading organizations?

Reading 5.2

9. Identify the positions within your school for which you feel succession planning is critical, such as deans, program directors, or department chairs. What critical skills or competencies are needed to perform these jobs? Design a succession planning program that is consistent with the strategic objectives of your school, utilizing the four phases of the succession model presented in the reading.

Reading 5.3

10. Compare and contrast the strategically reactive and strategically proactive approaches to managing HR. How does HR add value by being more strategically proactive than reactive? Can/should HR be both strategically proactive and reactive?

EXPERIENTIAL EXERCISES

1. Explain how the dean of your school would employ techniques of human resource planning to decide how many faculty and staff to employ in the coming academic year and which specific employees to retain, reassign, or release. What critical pieces of information would the dean need in order to arrive at these decisions?

INTERNET EXERCISES

1. Visit the Web site for the Human Resource Planning Society, a professional organization of those who are involved with HR planning, at http://www.hrps.org. Identify the programs that they offer that might be of value to various organizations.

CHAPTER REFERENCES

1. Wells, S. J. "Keeping Watch: Tracking the Evidence," *HR Magazine*, April 2002, pp. 34–35.
2. Wells, S. J. "Catch a Wave," *HR Magazine*, April 2002, pp. 31–37.
3. Leonard, B. "Study Shows U.S. Government Needs to Restructure Recruiting, Training Tactics," *HR Magazine*, June 2003, p. 36.
4. Staisey, N., Treworgy, D. and Shiney, M. "Managing for the Future: Human Capital Strategies at the United States Postal Service," *The Business of Government*, Spring 2002, pp. 47–50.
5. Ibid.
6. Wells, S. J. "Who's Next?" *HR Magazine*, November 2003, pp. 45–50.
7. Roberts, B. "Matching Talent With Tasks," *HR Magazine*, November 2002, pp. 91–96.
8. Leonard, B. "Turnover at the Top," *HR Magazine*, May 2001, pp. 46–52.
9. Ibid.
10. Ibid.

Heirs Unapparent

Robert J. Grossman, *HR Magazine*

When U.S. Commerce Secretary Ron Brown's airplane crashed in Croatia in 1996, 16 corporate executives were among the casualties. Most of the organizations they left behind foundered—at least initially—reeling from the sudden void in leadership.

For HR, hand-wringing over the absence of succession plans is an old story. Sudden disasters can reveal glaring inattention to leadership development and succession planning in organizations of all sizes. Each time it's understandable, if not particularly wise, why executives at the top of their game put off asking, "What happens if I get hit by a bus?" until it is too late.

With every disaster, there's a flurry of activity—enthusiastically promoted by HR—as corporations pay more attention to building bench strength. Soon, the urgency fades as more pressing issues crowd the agenda.

But now, with the millennium around the corner, experts are looking more carefully at leadership needs for the 21st century. They're warning of a shrinkage in the pool of available managers, escalating costs in recruiting outside talent and a startling lack of attention to developing leaders from within.

The Leadership Gap—Real or Contrived?

Cassandras such as William Byham, CEO of Development Dimensions International (DDI), a global HR consulting firm headquartered in Bridgeville, Pa., compare the myopia toward the leadership gap to the computer industry's looming Year 2000 bug that has threatened to plunge the computer-dependent world into chaos at the dawn of the new century. The computer industry has known of the problem for a decade, but it remained under wraps until the eleventh hour.

Similarly, Byham says, the avoidance of succession planning is a costly time bomb that's been ticking steadily for a decade or more. The death of a top executive, like a stricken canary in a coal mine, is merely a portent of what lies ahead.

Byham, 62, contends the leadership gap is pervasive and will bedevil the corporate world for decades to come. "We surveyed 150 *Fortune 500* companies, and the results were sobering," he says. "The average company expects 33 percent turnover at the executive ranks in the next five years, and fully one-third said they're not confident that they will be able to find suitable replacements."

There's more. Three-quarters of corporate officers surveyed for a study by McKinsey and Co., an international management consulting firm based in New York, said their companies had insufficient talent or were chronically talent-short across the board. In a survey of 500 HR executives, RHR International Co.

Growing Leaders—Sun Microsystems

At Sun, as the company evolves rapidly from an entrepreneurial upstart into a $10 billion-plus kingpin, opportunities for fast-track executive growth have never been better. "Our senior executives are in the biggest job they've ever had," says Ken Alvares, vice president of human resources. "We have to get them to grow into these jobs."

One of 11 executives on Sun Microsystems' senior management team, Alvares takes direct interest in leadership development at the upper levels. Six hundred directors, the entry-level executive job, report to 110 vice presidents. "We watch the directors closely, but give more attention to the VPs," he says. "We look at each person's particular profile and tailor individual coaching to their needs." This personalized approach seems to be working.

In most cases, Alvares says, he has a pretty good idea who would fill a job if something happened to a given person. Still, he's uneasy. "When you look at our bench strength, I don't get the feeling that we've got ourselves covered," he says. "I worry about developing people to step up to the next level. In some cases, I have one guy who can fill 10 jobs. If I have to use him, then I'll have to do some scrambling."

---

of Wood Dale, Ill., a firm of management-coaching psychologists, discovered that half the respondents felt their companies were not doing effective succession planning and were unprepared to replace key executives.

Still, others are not so sure. The need to develop and recruit top-flight talent, now and in the future, has never been far from the minds of visionary organizations, counters Murray Dalziel, managing director of the Hay Group, North America, in Philadelphia. "To suggest that savvy executives have lost sight of it, or are not building a talent base for the future is to underestimate them," he says. "The good ones have always been thinking about it. It's an issue that's been on the minds and agendas of every good CEO and board for a very long time."

GE Lighting is a good example. "We have a very rigorous process established many years ago that has been refined over time," explains James K. Jones, GE Lighting's human resource manager for North America, in Cleveland. "Twice a year we focus on development and succession issues. First we examine our business needs, then we look at the implications for our people." Jones scoffs at predictions of a leadership crisis. "In the future, we'll be developing them differently, but there will be plenty of people."

But the problem may be how companies find these people, observes Steve Kirn, vice president of organizational learning and development at Sears in Chicago. Kirn recalls a recent meeting with HR executives from 30 blue chip companies including Johnson and Johnson and Procter and Gamble. "We were sitting around lamenting this lack of people in succession, and almost everyone said it's a huge problem for them. When I asked what they would do about it, they said, 'We'll have to go outside to solve it.' I said what that means is we have to hire from one another—which is to say we all have the people internally but are not recognizing it."

Still, Kirn concedes there's a widely shared perception at Sears that there's a talent drain. "We just asked our own people on our attitude survey if they felt that we have a ready and able supply of successors and they said no."

The Downside of Downsizing

Blame the inattention to succession planning on the corporate world's concentration on cost-cutting and downsizing. "People just didn't think about it much when they were reorganizing and slashing jobs,"

Growing Leaders—U.S. Postal Service

Steve Levy, the U.S. Postal Service's manager for corporate personnel management, focuses on filling and building bench strength for 800 senior management positions, readying talented executives to advance to these positions and—for a select few—to move up the ladder to the elite 45-person officer team.

With almost 800,000 employees to manage and motivate, Levy is looking for people-oriented executives. "We don't want directive, dictatorial-type leaders," he says. "We're looking more for responsiveness characteristics—people who know how to build a business and how to motivate and develop employees."

Levy's team directs a process that taps current and potential leaders and prepares them for advancement. He's building a strong bench with multiple backup candidates. "It's 4,000 people backing up 800 jobs. We're three to five people deep in key positions like information technology, engineering and government relations." Five back-ups for every key position means even with the Postal Service's awesome turnover rate, some people will not advance. But holding managers in place, Levy says, is not necessarily bad. "Leadership development helps people do their current jobs better as well as preparing them to move up."

How effective is the program? Since it began four years ago, it's accounted for 90 percent of the senior management and executive hiring. "That means the job hasn't gone begging for weeks or months on end," Levy says. "It's a seamless process, offering us total continuity."

Still, Levy realizes that developing leaders at the very top of the management pyramid is only the beginning. "We're in the process of pushing this process below the executive level," he says. "We realize that we have to reach down lower and younger if we are to remain competitive."

Byham says. But now, as they look to grow, the environment is not conducive to developing talent. "A lot of people are retiring and the back-ups you used to rely on are gone. There's no farm club there; we've taken out the ready talent pools. And the problem is exacerbated because with elimination of middle management and 'assistant to' jobs, the jumps between positions are higher."

UNUM Corp., the Maine-based insurance company, is a case in point. It is seeking to grow after slicing whole layers of management from the organizational chart during dicier times. Now, the wisdom of some of the downsizing moves is being questioned.

Growing Leaders—Ernst and Young's FT&A Division

Steve Sitek, director of performance development and training for Ernst and Young's 6,500-employee internal support division (Finance, Technology and Administration), reasons that it's fiscally sound to develop leaders internally.

"I've identified the very top leadership—about 100 people—and the costs of replacing them annually," he says. "If we have a turnover rate of 25 percent, the cost of replacing executives with an average salary of $140,000 is more than $1 million a year; and that's just for the direct costs of acquiring the new executive."

Sitek oversees a senior development program that helps executives gain feedback on how they measure up against 11 critical leadership characteristics. Internal studies have shown a direct correlation between executive performance and the 11 characteristics, which include being innovative, excited, persuasive and strategic.

In one-on-one encounters with superiors, managers discuss their assessments to identify characteristics that need strengthening and are charged with structuring their own development plans. "The underlying theme is that you're responsible and you take charge of your leadership potential," Sitek explains. "We give you the tools and resources." Managers are encouraged to work on the characteristics they need to grow incrementally over a multi-year period.

Sitek produces specific training geared to each characteristic. "I have a training program for each one," he says. "For example, the No. 1 development gap that we discovered was the characteristic of persuasiveness. I offer a one-day program on this characteristic." Sitek also uses case studies and literary works to develop leadership skills. Among the reading: *Twelve O'Clock High*, *The Hunt for Red October*, and *Twelve Angry Men*.

"A lot of companies are recognizing that middle management was a lot more important than we thought it was," observes Tammie Snow, UNUM's manager of training in Portland, Maine.

"Some of those positions are being reinvented and we're having to develop people for them," she says. "Today, there just aren't enough managers to meet the demand. Skills like good old critical thinking are hard to find. People who can take responsibility, who don't need hand-holding and who can make decisions quickly are at a premium."

Meanwhile, search firms' revenues have grown twice as fast as the Gross Domestic Product over the past five years. And the costs of recruiting outside have reached heights that will attract the eye of any CEO with an aversion to red ink. Recently, DDI asked 110 managers and executives to estimate first-year costs of filling an executive vacancy. "The average one-year estimated replacement cost is $750,000," Byham says. "That includes finding the new one, training and development costs and opportunity costs of getting the new hire up to speed."

Not surprisingly, executive loyalty is at an all-time low. "Holding on to people is a big problem," says Matt Paese, practice leader of executive development at DDI. "Seventy-five percent of executives are currently marketing themselves in some active way—sending out resumes, in contact with headhunters or the like," he estimates. Search experts estimate the average executive will change jobs from five to seven times during his or her career.

Voodoo Demographics?

Like it or not, it seems that most organizations will be required to go to the market to replenish their executive ranks. But fewer home-grown prospects will be available. The number of 35- to 45-year-olds in the United States, currently in the early stages of their careers, is projected to decline by 15 percent between 2000 and 2015, reducing the talent pool from which new leaders will emerge. The situation will come to a head as the number of 25- to 34-year-olds continues to decline over the next decade, as their perception of future opportunities dims with the preponderance of older executives occupying the top positions in most companies and as they're lured away with lucrative offers from other talent-hungry companies.

Business Week reports that, of the 500 companies in the Standard and Poor's Index, 17 percent have CEOs age 63 and older. While people at all levels have the option of working beyond usual retirement ages, the actual trend is to retire earlier. And the long bull market in stocks has opened the prospect of early retirement to thousands who until recently could only dream of it. For example, when AT&T offered an early retirement window to middle managers last June, 15,300 of the company's 62,000 middle managers opted out, 50 percent more than the buyout plan was designed to attract.

Don Clifton, chairman of the Gallup Organization in Lincoln, Neb., acknowledges the projected dip in people in the 35 to 45 age range but cautions that leadership need not come only from that age

Growing Leaders—Sonoco

Sonoco's succession plan—which targets 300 executives in its top management group—has been operational for four years. "Our goal is to meet present needs and prepare for the future at the same time," says Cindy Hartley, vice president of human resources. "Leadership development is individualized by tailoring the manager's work assignment, special assignments and teams he or she is asked to serve on."

Each of Sonoco's operating units worldwide goes through succession planning for each of its key people annually. "Our CEO and senior management team of seven, including me, spends three-and-a-half days in a succession planning review," Hartley says. "We meet with our division presidents and general managers to discuss our key people; we explore what we want to do to develop them and identify who we have tapped as potential successors. Later, when an opening occurs, we revisit the data that we discussed in the review from a global perspective."

About 20 percent of Sonoco's executive jobs turn over annually as a result of retirements, job changes within the company and departures. The general policy is to promote from within. "It's important that the majority of our people come from within. It's costly and risky to go outside," Hartley says. "When you interview somebody, you see their very good points; it's hard to understand how well they'll manage and operate in your business and culture. And it's a lengthy and costly process. They say it takes three months, but it's more like six and then you keep your fingers crossed."

---

group. "I think it will offer a good opportunity to bring young people along faster," he says. "I saw it work well in the military. It's amazing how quickly young people can advance when they're given the opportunity. We need to try to tap talent earlier—identify them, educate them and give them a mission they believe in."

The rush to push seasoned executives into early retirement should be rethought, Clifton adds. "Keep the good ones; let the others retire. Many older executives can be persuaded to stay on because they like the mission—it's the most important thing they can do. Some companies, like Caterpillar, already are doing this."

The Hay Group's Dalziel observes further that relying on U.S. demographics disregards an important aspect of globalization. "The U.S. numbers are largely irrelevant because you're talking about a global economy," he says. "One of the advantages is

that there will be a worldwide pool of executives to choose from."

But for Kenneth Alvares, 54, Sun Microsystems' vice president of human resources in Palo Alto, Calif., the focus on demographics misses the point. "When I look beyond 2000, the projected shrinking candidate pool doesn't bother me. My focus is on quality and finding leaders who will be effective down the road. I'd rather have one charismatic, dynamic leader than 10 mediocre leaders," says Alvares.

Modernizing Succession Planning

Old solutions to succession planning—computer programs that slot people on organizational charts or training programs that bump people up a pyramid-shaped hierarchy—won't work in an increasingly complex world. Succession planners are searching for new ways to develop executives who can cope with globalization and flourish in a new corporate climate buffeted by seismic changes over the past 10 years—downsizing, reengineering, decimated organizational levels, broadened spans of managerial controls.

"The expectations of what's required to succeed at the executive level have changed more rapidly than we have been able to prepare people for," says Kirn at Sears. "We were so focused on the operational levels of our business that we failed to think strategically. As we stripped out managerial layers to increase productivity, the people left behind are running like crazy to keep the business running. Now, we're finding that developing broad strategic thinking as opposed to operational thinking is paramount. We need people who can think strategically with a broader perspective on the marketplace and our changing customers."

But beware of simple, one-size-fits-all solutions. "When you think about how complex an executive's world is today, to think we could simplify it with common skill sets misses the point," Alvares warns. "HR comes in with these simplified solutions and it doesn't have any effect. The CEO says, 'why are we wasting time on these HR guys who don't understand the problem?' You can't say, here are the six skill sets we need, develop people and voila."

Steven Sitek, director of performance development and training at Ernst and Young's Finance, Technology and Administration division (FT&A) in Lyndhurst, N.J., has advice for HR managers when making the case for succession planning. "The problem in the past was that HR people thought that, if we knew an organization needed succession planning, the top executives would accept our word. I know that you need to have a business case, whether it be from a financial perspective, a retention perspective or a process improvement perspective. The business case needs to be in place to be able to show the benefits of leadership development to people. Otherwise people will think these programs are running in a vacuum. Don't waste anyone's time unless you have a strong case to do it."

Emerging Executive Profile— Balancing Competencies

As the millennium approaches, succession planners must find ways to prepare the next wave of leaders to operate effectively in different cultures and to make teams work well.

"As the post–World War II generation has moved into positions of responsibility, we've seen the positive results from teamwork that necessitates a very different kind of management," says Rick Maloney, director of organizational development at Sonoco, the global packaging company with 17,000 employees headquartered in Hartsville, S.C. "Ten years ago you rarely heard about management competencies; the focus was on business goals and

---

Growing Leaders—UNUM

At UNUM, the insurance company with 7,000 employees in Portland, Maine, growth and a merger with Provident Insurance in Texas is intensifying the search for executive talent. "We've created new leadership positions and don't have the people inside who can fill them," says Tammie Snow, head of training. "Like many insurance companies, we've also had to go outside because we realize that we have to get new blood in to implement new ideas."

For the past 10 years UNUM has been targeting 200 of its managers as "emerging leaders of the future" and putting the most promising ones through a management internship program. "We provide management assistantships to a select number of people, about 12 each year, who have reached the director level, the stepping-stone tier into a management level position," Snow says. "We identify the high potential people and for a year, or year-and-a-half, they shadow a key executive. They travel with the executives, attend meetings with them, literally do everything with them."

---

objectives. Now we're focusing on behaviors that are needed—teamwork, collaboration, coaching, and developing."

Proof there's a better way is the bottom-line performance of leaders who bring "emotional intelligence" and highly developed interpersonal skills to an organization. Leadership is becoming more focused on the psychological needs of human beings, says Gallup's Clifton, "We've done more than a million surveys and have found that the old dictator-type leadership style doesn't work nearly as well as a more caring one. Workers who believe their supervisors care for them perform better, and financial results bear this out."

Cindy Hartley, vice president of human resources at Sonoco, agrees. "Today's workforce requires a different kind of leader than 10 years ago, leaders who can inspire people and lead teams are essential. Because of these requirements, the bar has been raised in terms of what we expect."

General Electric, an acknowledged pacesetter in succession planning, has defined the characteristics it is seeking in leaders for the 21st century. "We have constructed what you might call a composite sketch of our leadership team for the next generation," explained Dennis D. Dammerman, GE's chief financial officer, in a recent speech at Cornell University in Ithaca, N.Y. "These individuals, in addition to possessing the obvious non-optional qualifications of absolute integrity, high intelligence, global and diverse business experience and the like, will have what we call the three 'E's'—high energy, the ability to energize others and something called 'edge'—the courage to remove from the organization those who can't or won't buy in."

Peter Neary, director of executive programs at the Center for Creative Leadership in Colorado Springs, Colo., helps managers acquire the skills that GE and other organizations prize. He directs Leadership at the Top, a week-long development seminar restricted to top-level executives. "Attention has to be balanced when developing executives. You have to push technical competence, but not at the expense of wisdom and sensitivity."

"There is an inverse ratio between their technical competence and their civility," he goes on. "The more technically competent they are, the more they need to learn about basic human relations. Recently, I was observing a program where instructors would throw out a case study. It was like throwing raw meat to the sharks. They would have a technical answer immediately, but any subtleties around human relations or motivations, they would miss completely."

Indeed, many companies are learning this lesson the hard way. "The balance has tipped too far toward technical skills, diluting the quality of management," says UNUM's Snow. "In the past, we got it backwards. People got promoted on their technical skills without regard to their leadership ability. The result: they're abysmal leaders. Now, to develop people as potential leaders, we have to build leadership development as well as technical training into their career paths."

Keeping Your Eye on the Ball

When succession planning and leadership development become hot topics in *Fortune 500* boardrooms, there will be no dearth of benchmarking opportunities from organizations that are doing it well, such as GE, Motorola and Allied Signal. Still many large companies don't get around to making the long-term time and financial commitments. "Succession planning is not in place because companies focus on how they're going to deliver the quarter and make new profits," explains Sun Microsystem's Alvares.

"The daily pressures are so demanding that when someone talks about the future, it's a very difficult conversation to have," says Alvares. "And when you ask top management to discuss who will replace them, it's a hard topic to address. It's an uncomfortable thought and, of course, nobody can possibly do the job better than you can."

At the U.S. Postal Service, now four years into formal succession planning, Steve Levy, manager for corporate personnel management, says succession is the most serious problem that organizations face. For HR leaders he advises: "If you're not developing an ongoing succession plan, you're doing a disservice to your organization. It's one of the most important things a senior executive can do. The company that's going to succeed needs a visionary who plans for succession."

But even the best intended executives can get sidetracked. "The biggest threat is that we get into an economic crisis that causes us to slip back from our thinking that succession planning is key," Sears' Kirn says. "But as our chairman says, 'It's hard to think strategically when your hair's on fire.' The goal is to make certain that our most senior executives continue to think that succession planning is critical and fail to slip back into a more operational focus. You have to focus on the strategic and operational. Managing at both levels simultaneously is the ultimate challenge."

Growing Leaders—Sears

Recently, Sears created its Corporate Leadership Team (CSLT, pronounced sea-salt) to develop bench strength from among its top 220 executives. "We weren't satisfied with the bench for our executives, so we began a process to move the bench, to develop successors for our top dozen executives," says Steve Kirn, vice president of organizational learning and development, who sits on Sears' top-level executive committee. "It's a huge priority at the top of our organization. . . . We really got serious about it about four years ago. The executive committee is spending days and days on it."

Sears analyzed each of the jobs that CSLT execs perform and targeted about 40 jobs that offer unique development opportunities. "We look at each position, identify the unique experiences and challenges that the job provides, then look at the people on the bench and match them with the appropriate position."

To prepare executives to think strategically, Sears builds strategic components into key operational jobs. "We also move them across lines to give them multi-line exposure and in and out of staff positions," Kirn says. "In addition, they study strategy at the in-house Sears University and attend external management development programs."

Meanwhile, Sears' culture is going through a subtle shift, and the CSLT executives are major change agents. "We traditionally had a lot of internal competition," Kirn notes. "Now we just can't compete with one another; our success depends on leveraging our abilities to win against the competition. So the team way of making decisions is critical."

Designing Succession Systems for New Competitive Realities

Edmund J. Metz, *Human Resource Planning*

Utility industry deregulation has forced utilities to seek new patterns of leadership and to transform their leadership planning, selection, and development systems. Future competitive success requires not only a different leadership success model but also a succession system that is feedback-rich, highly flexible, cloaked in less secrecy, and that accelerates the development of the next generation of leaders.

Change drives more change!

Change driven by competitive forces drives changes in an organization's internal processes and systems. The challenge faced by anyone who must redesign such processes and systems is to assure that the new design paradigms are appropriately supportive of the organization's revised strategy. Such redesigns must proactively anticipate and be responsive to new competitive realities that are emerging and that will characterize the competitive landscape in three to five years.

Many readers of this article who have worked in business organizations for a longer career period have experienced career advancement through the casual "tap on the shoulder." We often were promoted into a new and higher position by the "powers that be," who decided that such a move was in our best career interest. Sometimes, the move involved a relocation. We all knew that if we were so "tapped" and that if we refused the offer, it could result in an invisible career derailment for us. And that was the way it was done for many years. In the past, organizations controlled and dictated a person's career steps.

But competitive forces have been driving many organizations to change the way they identify and select leaders. The challenge of providing for leadership continuity in a climate of rapid and unpredictable change and discontinuity has become a catalyst for transforming succession systems by making them more flexible and responsive to such forces.

What Is Driving the Change?

Succession systems that provide leadership continuity are in place in many organizations. Traditionally, succession planning systems have been built upon a position-person matching model (often termed "replacement charting"), where they help to pinpoint voids in leadership continuity, and then identify candidate replacement slates. They have, however, been primarily focused on a few more highly placed individuals.

These succession systems were installed when organizations were more stable, competitive forces were much less global and turbulent, job security and career predictability were higher, individual development was more linear, and organizations were willing to invest more in the long-term development of people.

But traditional and long-used succession processes have become too time-consuming and inflexible to meet the leadership continuity needs of organizations facing such competitive forces as:

- continual corporate restructurings
- the increasing use of team-based work systems
- mergers, acquisitions, and divestitures
- rising diversity issues
- reengineering
- increasing global outsourcing
- newer computing technology
- more partnerships, joint ventures, and strategic alliances
- shifting demographics and workplace shortages of talent

- shifting career-ownership responsibility
- continual massive downsizing in middle management ranks

These change forces have proven that position-person succession planning models are too time-consuming to develop because with a sudden shift in any one or more external or internal forces, many succession plans become obsolete and useless. More importantly, the qualities sought in leaders may shift suddenly as a result of external forces, and traditional systems have been much less responsive in identifying and developing the leadership talent required for the new competitive realities.

New Succession Planning Paradigms

The U.S. business world has been undergoing numerous shifts in business paradigms over the past 10 years. Evolving patterns of managing the business and developing management philosophies have been reshaping internal business processes. Exhibit 1 summarizes a few of the many shifts in business and succession planning paradigms.

So what do these types of shifts imply about the design of succession systems? In designing a succession process for a business to meet these expectations as well as current and future demands, there are at least five key design shifts that are important.

EXHIBIT 1: SHIFTS IN PARADIGMS

BUSINESS

From	To
Organizational pyramids with multiple layers	Flatter organization structures
Desire for "seasoned" leaders	Want the "seasoning" developed sooner in careers
Stability	Flexibility with faster market responsiveness

SUCCESSION SYSTEMS

From	To
Groom a backup for each position	Develop pools of broadly qualified candidates; have position pools
Specialty disciplines in candidates	More broadly disciplined candidates
Business unit autonomy	More centralization and integration of systems and information
Siloed career growth	Cross-boundary fertilization to develop broader skills and perspectives
Largely human resources driven	Largely line driven
Subjective and informal criteria; personality/image oriented	Strategic competencies and models define success; 360 degree feedback
Technical competence a key factor	Cross-functional management capability; quick learner; manage change
Tolerate marginal performers	Fewer positions for development requires removing marginal blockers
Company directs and controls career	Individual sets career direction
Controlled and confidential process	Input from multiple sources; more open planning and development process
"Promises"	No "promises"
Focus on training and seminars as primary development vehicle	Sequential job assignments provide primary development experience supplemented by specific training
Take advantage of vacancies to promote candidates	Create assignments for development (e.g., exchanges, trades, special projects)
Promote from within when fully qualified	Promote when about 70% qualified; hire less experienced talent at entry level

Design Shift #1: Core Capabilities/Competencies

Start the design process by identifying the core capabilities of the business. This is a shift away from the "replacement charting" process of the past, in which each position had a slate of ready candidates identified regardless of what capabilities were needed for strategic success. Instead, strategic business competencies are identified, and from this a leadership competency model is defined that can be used to evaluate positions requiring core strategic competencies. Position pools might also be created (positions sharing a number of identical or similar core strategic competencies). Candidate pools can be formed to match single or multiple position pools.

Design Shift #2: Candidate Choice

Design the process so candidates can express an interest in pursuing leadership track positions. This opens the process to candidates beyond the immediate business unit pool and makes more opportunities possible for diversity candidates. Many organizations have increasingly encouraged employees to take more responsibility for their own individual career development. A process more aligned with the competitive realities of the 1990s is one that places more responsibility on the individual for choosing and putting more energy into pursuing a leadership career track. The new process must also accommodate the individual candidate as a team member, and not just an individual contributor.

Design Shift #3: Competency-Focused Development

Design the development process to make it focused on learning of competencies necessary for business success, provide a more feedback-rich environment through using 360 degree multi-rater development assessment systems, and build multiple on-the-job learner opportunities to develop more broad-based skills. The pace of change and competition requires that executives begin to think differently about where and how the organization's future leadership is developed. The design needs to accommodate the reality that people will change employers and possibly careers several times during their working lives. This requires changes in assumptions about what characterizes success. It also requires more structured and managed development tracks that can provide the broad-based exposure and skills in a shorter period of time.

Development processes should also include more feedback-rich developmental assessment utilizing 360 degree feedback tools and leadership competency models. While knowledge of the industry is no less important, there must be an increased recognition that other leadership competencies are just as critical for success.

Design Shift #4: More Communication Openness

Design the entire process to be more open and less exclusive and secretive. Move away from the silent "tap on the shoulder" process of the past. Provide more communication to everyone about how the process works, and build more open feedback systems into the environment, fostering and supporting personal and career development. A process shrouded in mystery and secrecy is one that does not help to retain talented candidates who have no idea where they stand. The new process needs to foster more open dialogue, help candidates understand the expectations of the new leadership competency model, and demystify the basis on which executive selections are made. Published leadership competency models help everyone to clearly understand the critical and desired behaviors leaders must demonstrate.

Design Shift #5: Continuous Review

Design the process to be more ongoing, more fluid, and more of a continuous review system rather than a ritualized annual "planning event." Strategy execution capability and candidate competency development progress are related, and it makes sense to review both at least quarterly, if not more frequently.

Design Issues to Be Addressed

Regardless of design, there are other important issues any system must address:

- The system must make sense for and be usable by different business units, each having some unique needs.
- The system must have a process to focus and guide the development of executives to meet strategic purposes.

- The system must align with other human resource processes that are also undergoing transition (e.g., selection, reward systems, performance management, etc.).
- The system must assure that a cadre or pool of potential leaders is being prepared for executive positions.
- The system must be owned by the senior management team.
- The system must deal with diversity issues and changing demographics.
- The system must add value and contribute to business success in some measurable way.

Moving from Concept to Reality— Succession Planning at ComEd

Commonwealth Edison (ComEd) is a $6.9 billion revenue electrical utility with 16,800 employees providing electricity to 3.4 million customers representing eight million people in northern Illinois.

ComEd is engaged in the production, purchase, transmission, distribution, and sale of electricity to both wholesale and retail customers.

With electric utility deregulation driving fundamental changes in the electric utility industry, it became very apparent to ComEd leaders that in order for the company to continue to excel and grow in a fiercely competitive environment, future company success would depend on new core capabilities to support a new vision for the utility: *to become a leading national energy services provider.*

The Commercial Division of ComEd is responsible for the transmission and distribution of electric power to commercial and residential customers in the northern Illinois service territory. Leaders in the Commercial Division recognized that new competitive realities required having leaders who were prepared to succeed in a competitive environment. They especially needed leaders who were customer-focused, able to achieve results, and capable of developing strong internal and external relationships. This required a better succession process—one that was appropriate for a fast-changing environment; one that could change and adjust quickly to unanticipated external shifts.

A cross-functional design team consisting of line and staff managers was charged with the responsibility of designing a succession process more attuned to meet these new competitive realities and one that would provide a much more objective measure of candidates for particular leadership positions.

The Commercial Division designed its new succession process around a four-phase model. Exhibit 2 provides an overview of this model.

The Commercial Succession Design Team used this model to design each aspect of its new succession system. This redesigned succession system had to achieve the following goals:

- Provide a minimum of two to three qualified candidates that are "ready now" for any position that may become open
- Assure that everyone that is accepted into a candidate pool has a written development plan on

EXHIBIT 2: SUCCESSION MODEL

ComEd Strategic Model
- Strategic Goals
- Competency Models
- Corporate Values
- Career Development Philosophy

PHASE 1 Business Unit Alignment Review
- Key Business & Leadership Issues (1–3 years)
- Agreement on Critical Competency Model Priorities

PHASE 2 Identification
- Critical Positions
  1. Position pools
  2. Unique positions
  3. Positions targeted for external selection
- Threshold Candidate Criteria
- Candidates
  1. Pools
  2. Unique candidates
  3. Diversity

PHASE 3 Development
- Development Assessment (360 degree developmental assessment)
- Individual Development Plans and Follow-Up Actions
- Development Reviews

PHASE 4 Selection
- Job-Specific Requirements
- Competency-Based Selection Matching
- Multi-Selector/Team Interview Process

file with their manager, and that their progress has been reviewed at least twice a year

- Through external recruitment or internal accelerated development and mentoring, increase the number of minority and female employees in the development pool by 50% for grades 11 and above
- Assure that all managers involved in candidate interview assessments have completed a specific and custom-designed three-day competency assessment/behavioral interviewing training workshop prior to being utilized for candidate selection interview purposes
- Assure that all candidates selected for the candidate pool complete a 360 degree feedback assessment for development and receive follow-up assistance from a Career Development Administrator or other qualified person regarding using their feedback for development purposes
- Allow for a follow-up succession planning focus meeting with managers annually to review the effectiveness of the succession planning process, and identify any potential improvements for further consideration and review
- Fill a position covered by the succession planning process with a qualified internal candidate from the candidate pool within 14 days

How the Process Works

The process starts with the Business Unit Alignment Review (Phase 1 of the model outlined in Exhibit 2). The senior leaders of the business unit review key business and leadership issues that are likely to influence the business in the next one to three years. The business unit has a Leadership Competency Model consisting of 22 strategic competencies. This is reviewed to see if the competency success requirements for any key positions are likely to be affected by these near-future issues and challenges. If any changes/shifts in competency priority are required, this information is then factored into the next three phases of the model. This keeps the process future-focused and flexible to respond to change.

If any manager or supervisor wishes to be considered for a future executive position, they are responsible for initiating a self-nomination (Phase 2— Identification). They provide their Process Head (immediate supervisor) with a list of eight names (five peers and three managers). The Process Head selects a peer and a manager from the list, who along with the candidate's supervisor fills out a detailed candidate assessment covering all the leadership competencies in the model. This assessment is scored, and a minimum score is needed on both the top three most important Commercial competencies as well as on the rest of the general competencies in order to be considered further. The higher a position is on the organizational hierarchy, the higher the average qualifying score a candidate must get to enter a candidate pool. Another candidate screen is his or her performance rating for the past three years, and those who are interested in entry supervisory positions must achieve a passing score on a validated supervisory effectiveness assessment test. If the candidate achieves or exceeds all the minimum threshold criteria, they are accepted into one of three succession pools, depending on their salary grade level.

Each candidate is individually informed regarding their admittance to a pool(s) but they do not know the names of other candidates in the pool(s). All candidates who apply to a candidate pool are given feedback regarding the results of their assessments. They end up knowing what their initial candidate competency profile looks like as well as which position pools they are in. Key positions are grouped into four position profile groups depending on the critical competencies that they share. Candidates know what they must do to stay in the pool, and they know what the objective criteria for selection will be when a position opens. There is very little secrecy in this system.

Once in the pool (Phase 3—Development), each candidate participates in a full 360 degree developmental assessment. Candidates use the results to put together a focused development plan with their manager. They must continue to maintain their performance as well as demonstrate developmental progress in order to stay in the succession pools. Each candidate is also free to consult confidentially with a highly experienced leadership mentor (the Director of Organizational Capability) regarding the best development options to meet their specific needs.

When a position opens (Phase 4—Selection), this position is posted internally to all candidates in the pool eligible for that position (each key leadership position is in one of four profile groups, which has a corresponding candidate pool). If candidates are interested in the open position, they submit an application for consideration. Applications are reviewed along with their competency profile data to determine which candidates most closely match the position success competencies. These candidates are then interviewed for the position. The interview is an in-depth assessment by a team of managers who decide whether or not to recommend the candidate for final consideration.

If there are no internal candidates, external candidates are recruited through professional recruitment, and they will also go through a thorough team interview assessment. If they pass these screens, they then go through an in-depth external assessment comprised of tests and competency simulations, and this information is factored into the final decision of whether or not to hire.

What Have Been the Benefits of This New Succession Process?

Overall, this new succession process is simplified, requiring less time to administer and manage. It uses candidate pools, thus making opportunities available to more candidates with diverse backgrounds. The evaluation and selection criteria are both more open and objective, and the use of competency models helps to target individual development and obtain best value for the training time and dollars. The entire process is more feedback-rich because of the multi-rater assessment methods. It supports a philosophy of career ownership by individuals and fosters continuous learning. Most importantly, the process is flexible in response to uncertainty in the increasingly unregulated competitive environment in which the utility industry finds itself. Lastly, the process was designed, is owned, and is managed by the line managers in the Commercial Division of ComEd.

Learning from This Process

The process used to develop the new succession system provided many valuable lessons in designing a system to meet the new competitive realities. Although no one could have predicted how the effort would turn out, each phase evolved using the four-phase model as the roadmap, and helped to enhance a new culture of involved ownership by the line organization.

Looking at the last year in retrospect, it became apparent that the new succession system also required additional supportive elements to make it

a success: helping managers develop more effective coaching skills; incorporation of the competencies into the performance management model; and building a leadership skills training system that helped individuals enhance high-performance success competencies.

Learning how to design and manage this system has provided some valuable lessons for ComEd's Commercial Division managers. First of all, no progress could have been made without their active involvement. The active involvement of line managers in working through the many design issues was always actively sought and never assumed. Although the design process moved a little more slowly at times, Al Wozniak, Human Resources and Management Development Director, believes it is essential to "include line management in the design process to gain their buy-in and support. It should not be identified as a human resource initiative." A similar sentiment is echoed by Greg Welch, Commercial Vice President—Technical Services and Supply Management, who says, "Resources must be dedicated to this type of task. Managers who are involved in creating a new system should be prepared to spend a lot of time at the process because design work takes longer than most managers expect. But the payoff comes when people are more responsible and involved, and candidates take more ownership for their own careers. This helps make the process more flexible."

The second lesson is that it helps to be able to have a vision or model first for the new system. This model helps keep managers focused and moving ahead, and less likely to be derailed by current crises and shifts in work priorities. The design was managed by an identified team of managers who also developed new competencies during the design process. The design effort was also aided by having an experienced facilitator who served as a sounding board for ideas and was a knowledge resource on succession systems and competency models.

Third, it is very important that the ultimate beneficiaries of this process, the candidates themselves, believe it is a process that demonstrates the value of integrity and that the process can be trusted much more than the "tap on the shoulder system." Said one candidate, "I now know, for the first time, what the specific competencies are for some positions I am interested in. More importantly, with the 360 degree feedback process, I have received more valuable and helpful feedback in the last month than I have received in the past few years." Candidates will be able to accelerate their development through a feedback-rich process that also very specifically and accurately targets critical competencies and related behaviors for development.

The last and probably most important lesson is that a competitively focused succession system must be linked directly to the corporation's vision and strategy. Developing a new leadership competency model reflecting the business's core strategic success competencies of the future was critical. As the effort progressed, the use and understanding of competencies as a strategic tool was enhanced greatly, and its importance for other human resource systems became more apparent to all in management. Commercial Division managers now realize that having strategic competencies as a foundation for their succession system is a critical tool for building an enhanced performance capability in potential leaders and in other members of the professional team at ComEd.

Source: Metz, Edmund J. "Designing Succession Systems for New Competitive Realities," *Human Resource Planning, 21*, (3), 1998, pp. 31–37. Reprinted with permission from Human Resource Planning, by the Human Resource Planning Society, 317 Madison Avenue, Suite 1509, New York, NY 10017, Phone: (212) 490–6387, Fax: (212) 682–6851.

If HR Were Really Strategically Proactive: Present and Future Directions in HR's Contribution to Competitive Advantage

Wayne Brockbank, *Human Resource Management*

Introduction

At the end of this special issue of *Human Resource Management* on HR best practices, it is appropriate to review the evolution of the HR field and to examine its future high value-added practices. Over the last few years, knowledge of the human side of business has dramatically increased. While HR practices substantially lag behind HR knowledge, practices in the HR field are evolving at an accelerated rate, and the lag between knowledge and practices appears to be shrinking. The field is learning better how to learn and more quickly apply what has been learned.

This article begins by arguing that HR's centrality to business success has never been so pronounced. It then provides a framework for examining the field's evolution in adding competitive advantage. It concludes with an examination of the progress of the field from being operationally reactive to adding greater value by being strategically proactive. The stages of evolution between these two extremes will be defined and examined in some detail.

While this article is not intended to be a quantitative analysis of the field's evolution, it is also not intended to be a theoretical essay. Rather, this article draws on the author's methodological observations with thoughtful HR professionals from 66 outstanding companies (see Appendix). Between 1990 and 1998, the author interviewed key HR professionals and, in most cases, senior line executives about the logic, strategic framing, and best practices of their HR organizations. This article is based on insights[1] gained from these companies.

Emergence of HR's Importance

Substantial empirical as well as anecdotal evidence supports the notion of HR's growing importance. In 1992, 2,961 executives, consultants, and academicians participated in a study on the future of HR (Towers Perrin, 1992). Twenty-five percent of the respondents stated that the first or second most important goal for HR was that it be more strongly linked to business strategy. Thirty-two percent stated that this goal would be adequately accomplished by the year 2000. Line executives alone projected a 10% increase in the importance of ensuring that HR be linked to business strategy, whereas HR respondents projected only a 5% increase.

In three rounds of data gathering in 1988, 1992, and 1997, more than 20,000 individuals participated in the Human Resource Competency study at the University of Michigan (Brockbank, Ulrich & James, 1997). In 1988, the HR departments of the highest performing firms had a strong and equal focus on both the strategic and operational aspects of HR. In 1992 and again in 1997, firm performance was found to be higher as HR departments focused more on the strategic aspects of HR and relatively less on operational agendas. High performing firms reduced the time and effort spent on operational HR activities so that they could focus on higher valued HR agendas. The alternative mechanisms for accomplishing the operations work done are discussed later in this article.

The seminal and ongoing work to date on the relationship between financial performance and HR practices has been conducted by Brian Becker and Mark Huselid (1998). In their study of 740 firms, they found that firms with greater intensity of HR practices had greater market value per employee. Specifically, they found that a standard deviation's increase in a firm's HR practices resulted in a $45,000 increase in market value per employee. If a firm with 10,000 employees were to make such an improvement, the firm's market value would increase approximately half a billion dollars.

In addition to direct and indirect empirical evidence concerning the emerging importance of HR, the field is rife with supporting anecdotal evidence such as the following:

1. The number of companies in which senior HR executives report to the CEO appears to be increasing.

2. CEOs in high performing firms are giving greater focus to HR issues (General Electric, Allied Signal, Hewlett Packard, Herman Miller, Sears, Disney, Intel, Texas Instruments, Ford).
3. Improvement in firm performance is increasingly attributed to HR's contributions (Sears, Ford, Baxter International, Harley Davidson, Quantum, Unilever, Arco).

Finally, the fact that the membership of the Society of Human Resource Management has reached 120,000 in 1999 and that the membership of the Human Resource Planning Society has increased 50% between 1992 and 1997 are further indirect evidence that HR professionals are finding a greater need for knowledge and professional development than ever before.

This increase in the importance of HR has not happened accidentally. Rather, these trends are a function of specific changes in the business environment. With the increased rate of transnational wealth, a firm's ability to compete in a global environment becomes increasingly contingent on having the right people, transnational learning systems, and optimal measures and incentives for measuring and rewarding individual and firm effectiveness. Pressures from competitors, shareholders, and customers require that people create new products, services, and processes ahead of the competition. In a world of hyper speed, people ultimately create changes in microchips, computers, disk drives, printers, and grocery products. As the workplace becomes increasingly diverse (Cox, 1993; Thomas, 1996), companies must leverage the full capabilities of all employees regardless of differences in demographics, different levels, departments, functions, regions, and disciplines. The explosion of service vocations and the reliance of these vocations on people has likewise propelled the human side of the business equation to the forefront. In 1998 the dollar volume of mergers and acquisitions in the United States was three times greater than ever before. Because people are required to conceptualize portfolio opportunities, identify merger and acquisition candidates, conduct due diligence and negotiations, and make new alliances work, the HR systems that provide and support people and influence their mindset and technological capabilities become increasingly important. This is especially true given that 65% of mergers and acquisitions fail to achieve their stated goals (Krallinger, 1997).

Competitive Advantage: From the Past to the Future

The human resource management field has responded to these conditions by conceptualizing and implementing higher value-added HR agendas. This section provides a general framework for analyzing current HR trends. It then extends the logic of the framework to assess the emerging generation of value-added HR agendas.

The distinction between the operational and strategic levels of HR has received considerable attention in the literature (Brockbank, Ulrich, & James, 1997; Ulrich, 1997a). Operational HR activities generally refer to the routine, day-to-day delivery of HR basics. The strategic level of HR activity is more complex and involves five criteria:

- Long term—Is the activity conceptualized to add long term as opposed to short term value?
- Comprehensive—Does it cover the entire organization or isolated components?
- Planned—Is it thought out ahead of time and is it well documented or does it occur on an ad hoc basis?
- Integrated—Does it provide a basis for integrating multifaceted activities that might otherwise be fragmented and disconnected?
- High value-added—Does it focus on issues that are critical for business success or does it focus on things that must be done but are not critical to financial and market success?

In the last three or four years, the field has begun to use the term "proactive" as a criterion for HR success. Two issues may cloud the use of this concept. First, "proactive" is one of those words that is often a "feel good" word rather than one that actually describes what people do. For example, it is easy to agree on the importance of being proactive, but being proactive in "strategic" ways leads to very different activities than being proactive in "operational" ways. Second, as "proactive" has become popular, "reactive" has become less popular. While there are times to be proactive, there are clearly times to be reactive. Being quickly reactive against strategic criteria can often create substantial competitive advantage.

Combining these two dimensions yields a framework around which the HR field may organize its thinking about the past, present, and future of HR.

Before examining each quadrant in detail, I will provide an overview of the model including a brief description of each quadrant and a sample of associated activities.

Operationally reactive HR focuses on implementing the basics; it addresses the question of, given the day-to-day demands of the business, how should HR react to ensure that the basics are addressed? Such activities include administering benefits, maintaining market-based salary grids, hiring entry level employees, and providing basic skill training.

Operationally proactive HR improves on the design and delivery of the HR basics; it addresses the question of how HR can improve the quantity and quality of the HR basics before problems occur. Such activities include reengineering HR processes, applying TQM principles to HR activities, and ensuring positive morale in the workforce.

Strategically reactive HR focuses on implementing the business strategy; that is, given a clearly formulated business strategy (e.g., growth, new product, innovation, cycle time reduction, new market entry), how can HR help support its successful implementation? Such activities include identifying and developing the technical knowledge, tactical skills, and business culture that are consistent with the demands of the business strategy. They may also include facilitating change management and organizing HR into service centers.

Strategically proactive HR focuses on creating future strategic alternatives. Such activities include creating a culture of innovation and creativity; identifying merger and acquisition possibilities; and creating internal capabilities that continually track and align with the marketplace for products, markets, and capital with their respective lead indicators.

This framework provides a basis not simply for describing alternative arenas for HR involvement; it also suggests a measuring stick against which to assess the progress of HR's value added at both the discipline and firm levels. This matrix from Table 1 may be reconfigured to create a linear scale for measuring HR as a competitive advantage.

Competitive advantage entails having the capability to provide *better* products, services, or financial returns than the competition does. HR should help its firm create value in the marketplaces for said capital, products, and services *before* its competitors do. As HR creates this kind of value in a timely manner, it contributes to its firm's competitive advantage. Thus, some categories of HR practices create greater competitive advantage than do others. This is indicated by the HR Competitive Advantage Index in Table 1. As discussed above, the strategic versus operational dimension suggests that HR creates competitive advantage when it creates, over the long run, greater value than its competitors' HR activities, optimizes the entire organization instead of subcomponents, and focuses the firm on issues that are critical for market success. The proactive versus reactive dimension suggests that value creating HR activities be done before that are done by the competition. It requires that a firm's HR function creates a temporal window within which the firm can dictate competitive rules and command monopoly position. The combination of these two dimensions into the HR Competitive Advantage Index enables HR to calibrate the extent to which an HR practice or set of practices creates strategic value before the competition. Thus, an HR department increases its potential to create competitive advantage as it moves from being operationally reactive to being strategically proactive.

Given the pressures on HR to add greater value before the competition and the emerging arsenal of HR practices, it follows that the above index may be superimposed onto a product life-cycle logic (see Figure 1).

HR Competitive Advantage

Placing the HR competitive advantage index into a life-cycle logic provides a useful logic for assessing the extent to which HR creates true competitive advantage (see Figure 2). Virtually all firms have HR departments or functions that provide operationally reactive HR practices and processes. Even the most

TABLE 1: DIMENSIONS OF COMPETITIVE ADVANTAGE FOR HR ACTIVITIES

	Reactive	Proactive
Strategic	Makes strategy happen	Creates strategic alternatives
Operational	Implements the basics	Improves the basics

FIGURE 1: HR COMPETITIVE ADVANTAGE INDEX

| Operationally Reactive | Operationally Proactive | Strategically Reactive | Strategically Proactive |

Low → High

Competitive Advantage

elementary business requires that people are paid, benefits are administered, people are hired, and basic skills are ensured.

Operationally proactive HR agendas were generally the state-of-the-art in the late 1980s and early 1990s. Reacting to the recognition of the unacceptable cost of hierarchical bureaucracy (Ashkenas, Ulrich, Jick & Kerr, 1995) and the recession of 1991–1992, many companies required reductions in the proportion of their staff functions. The mandate of "more with less" became the order of the day. Thus, a dominant agenda of conferences, seminars, and professional publications focused on the application of reengineering and Total Quality Management (TQM) to HR (Yeung & Brockbank, 1995). Service centers were born (Ulrich, 1995). Today one must look long and hard to find conferences and articles on these topics. Late adopters are

a relatively small proportion of the total population, and the demand for HR expertise in these arenas is shrinking.

The HR agenda of the late nineties—the state-of-the-art—is linking HR to the business strategy: Given the business strategy, what is HR's role in making the strategy happen? Again, articles, seminars, conferences, and university-based executive programs abound to help HR play a more powerful and effective role in strategy implementation. Major consulting firms have established specialty consulting in HR strategy, change management, culture change, and other related areas (e.g., Arthur Anderson, Deloitte and Touche, Bain, McKinsey, Mercer, Watson-Wyatt, etc.). In addition, many companies including Sears, Lucent, Coca Cola, Dow Corning, and General Motors have made aligning HR with business strategy a successful HR priority.

FIGURE 2: LIFECYCLE OF HR COMPETITIVE ADVANTAGE

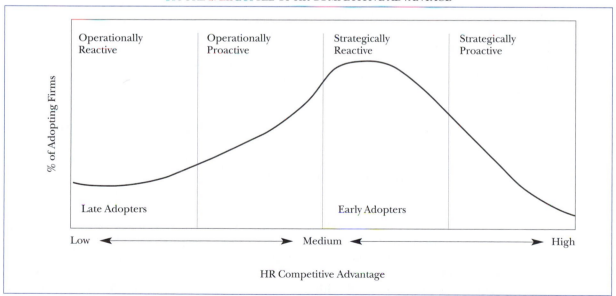

Relatively few early adopters are venturing into the realm of strategically proactive HR. Nevertheless, there are clear examples of HR departments moving into this arena. Strategically proactive HR agendas include identifying portfolio requirements, selecting merger and acquisition candidates, creating institutional change capacity, building organizational cultures of radical innovation, and identifying social trends that can be parlayed into products and services. These activities represent the logical extension of the HR field. Those HR departments with the capability to do so will lead the field in creating competitive advantage.

Application of the HR Competitive Advantage Index

The remainder of this article examines each of the four levels of HR's competitive advantage with major focus on HR's role in being strategically reactive and strategically proactive.

OPERATIONALLY REACTIVE HR

As Figure 1 suggests, relatively few firms are currently in the mode of adopting operationally reactive HR practices. The main reason is that virtually all firms already do the HR basics; that is, they pay employees, have benefits of some kind (even if nothing more than the processing of federal and state tax information), hire entry level employees, and ensure at least remedial competence through formal or on-the-job training. Even sole proprietors and partnerships ensure that these functions are carried out. The fact that the great majority of college level HR text books focus on this level of HR thinking evidences that this arena of HR involvement is a commodity (e.g., Cascio, 1995; Schuler, 1997). Without these activities a firm will fail, but with them, little competitive advantage is gained.

OPERATIONALLY PROACTIVE HR

Firms in the operationally reactive mode focus on improving the productivity of their HR departments and the quality of their HR practices. Much of the breakthrough work on improving quantitative and qualitative aspects of HR occurred in the late 1980s and early 1990s. Driven by global competition in the 1970s and 1980s, firms were required to improve productivity and efficiency. A major response was the emergence of reengineering that combined with

information technology to enable the automated processing of considerable volumes of transactional HR work (Yeung & Brockbank, 1995). During this time other practices took root that helped HR do more with less. These practices included outsourcing (e.g., benefit and payroll administration firms), work elimination (e.g., reducing steps in answering benefit inquiries), reallocation of activities to the line (e.g., having line managers handle grievances), and the creation of HR service centers (centralized transactional work processing centers). Firms such as Intel, Hewlett-Packard, Sears, Cisco Systems, Amoco, and Texas Instruments provided ground-breaking work in these arenas.

By applying the principles of TQM, the HR field sought to improve the accuracy of its HR work. Consistent with the requisites of TQM, during the 1990s the field made considerable progress in its ability to set clear standards of measurement for HR practices (Ulrich, 1997b; Yeung & Berman, 1997; Wintermantel & Mattimore, 1997). Alcoa and Motorola developed robust lists of measurements for productivity in HR functional areas including recruitment, benefits and salary administration, training and development, career management, diversity, health and safety, communications, and performance management. Employee attitude surveys that focused on the internal customers' perceptions of HR gained substantial popularity with virtually every HR-related consulting firm providing internal HR audits. HR mission statements abounded, which promised to "surprise and delight" internal customers and to provide "error-free HR work." Finally, to ensure that employee dissatisfaction would be addressed before major problems emerged, internal customers became more heavily involved in designing key elements of HR practices.

STRATEGICALLY REACTIVE HR

HR may be strategically reactive in business strategy implementation through two dominant avenues: (1) supporting the execution of tactics that drive the long-term strategies and (2) developing the cultural and technical capabilities necessary for long-term success. HR may also assist in the process of strategy implementation by providing change management support for tactical activities.

Tactical Support. The capacity of HR to be strategically reactive assumes the presence of a business strategy with its accompanying operational tactics. With the firm's strategic and tactical logic in place, HR's role becomes relatively obvious. How many people do we need? Where do we get them? What training do they require? How do we measure and reward desired behaviors and results?

Creating the Strategy-Focused Culture. The second channel through which HR practices may be linked to business strategy is through the establishment of a powerful and strategically focused culture[2] and in the continual availability of state-of-the-art technical knowledge and skills.[3] The process by which this linkage may be established can be divided into eight steps.

Step 1: Define the business unit for which the HR practices are being designed. Is the process used defining an HR strategy for a plant, business unit, division, sector, department, or for the company as a whole?

Step 2: Specify the key trends in the external business environment. What are the dominant trends that indicate key threats or opportunities? Trends among customers, competitors, informational technology, owners' expectations, regulatory requirements as well as product and process technologies must all be considered. Since it is difficult to define a company's culture around a large number of such trends, however, it is imperative that a clear and weighted prioritization be established among the frequently competing and contradictory requirements (Brockbank, 1995). The rationale for beginning with the environmental analysis instead of with the business strategy is threefold. *First,* the business strategy should be based on the environmental analysis. *Second,* it is useful practice for those who develop the business-based human resource strategy (including but not limited to the firm's key HR professionals) to examine marketplace realities in a clear and focused manner. *Third,* many business strategies are not HR-friendly; that is, they are not formulated to facilitate the mindset and technical requirements of individuals who make strategy happen.

Step 3: Identify and prioritize the firm's sources of competitive advantage. The key issue here is identifying how the company is choosing to compete. Is it choosing to compete on the basis of cost, quality, speed, innovation, service, relationships, convenience, branding, and/or distribution? Since a firm's culture should be defined in a way to be consistent with these foundational strategic assumptions, it is necessary to have a clear sense of priority among these alternatives.

In the automotive industry, for example, both cost and quality are important; however, if cost is assumed to be 90% and quality 10% of a firm's competitive focus, a different culture should dominate than if it is assumed that cost and quality should receive equal focus.

Step 4: Define the required culture (including specific behaviors) and technical knowledge and skill areas that the firm requires to create and support the sources of competitive advantage that were identified in Step 3. In the past few years, companies have moved beyond superficial culture definitions and are now specifying cultures and behaviors directly aligned with marketplace requirements. A sampling of such cultural definition includes restless creativity (Unilever), lean and unencumbered teamwork (Cathay Pacific Airways), and focused agility (Enron Corp.). While the meaning and passion behind these constructs may not be accessible to the outsider, to those who develop and apply them, they convey definitions of culture that serve as key supporting elements of business strategy. Complementing the cultural competencies are the required technical competencies. With the ever-decreasing life span of technical knowledge and skills, cultural competencies become increasingly important. Nevertheless, a substantive base of technical knowledge and skills is warranted in virtually every industry.

Step 5: Identify the cultural characteristics that the firm should reduce or eliminate if it is to optimize competitive advantage. Such undesirable cultural traits might include being internally focused, slow, complacent, arrogant, oblivious to competitive realities, or risk averse.

Step 6: Design the HR practices that will have greatest impact on creating the desired culture. This can be accomplished by evaluating the extent to which each HR practice is aligned with the desired culture. If an HR practice is not aligned with the desired outcome, then an evaluation must be made about the extent to which the practice would have impact on creating the desired culture if it were aligned. It is useful at this stage to distinguish between traditional and nontraditional HR practices. Traditional HR practices are generally under the direct influence of most HR departments. They include staffing, performance management, financial and nonfinancial incentives, and training and development. Nontraditional HR practices, on the other hand, are those not generally under HR's direct influence, but which have substantial influence on the mindset and technical capabilities of the firm. Such practices include organization design, reengineering, office or plant layout, job design, leadership communications, information systems design, and customer contact programs. It is HR's task to ensure that both traditional and nontraditional HR practices are mutually consistent in influencing the human side of the business equation.

Identifying action plans for enhancing the technical knowledge and skills is relatively easy. Two questions must be addressed. Do a lot of people require them or few? Are these technical capabilities best acquired through training, through recruitment or through borrowing (in the form of consultants and other external vendors)?

Step 7: With these decisions made, the firm should establish action plans for detailed design of the HR processes. Who will do what, by when, with whom, with what resources? What will be the mechanism of reporting to line management?

Step 8: The final step specifies the means by which effectiveness of the entire process is measured. Are the HR practices successfully creating the strategically targeted cultural and technical capabilities?

This framework has been widely used by many companies such as Texas Instruments, Alcoa, General Motors, Coca Cola, ITT, Dow Corning, and Unilever as the logic and process by which to link HR practices to preestablished business strategies.

Management of Change. The third set of activities by which HR is strategically reactive is found in change management programs. Organizational development and other change management activities assist in the implementation of general strategies and/or specific tactics. Multiple frameworks for change management may be found in the literature. One that has appropriately received considerable recognition (Ulrich, 1997a) specifies seven critical success factors for change:

- Ensuring support from key executives
- Creating a shared need for change among those who live with the change, including both employees and management
- Ensuring a clearly articulated vision of the end-state of change
- Eliciting the commitment of key stakeholders to the change vision and to the steps necessary to achieve desired outcomes
- Leveraging the management and HR systems that support and drive the change

- Defining insightful measurement by which the progress of change can be monitored
- Establishing learning loops through which change efforts may ensure ongoing improvements and progress

While each of these phases contains much of what has been documented over the years' experience with change management, the primary utility of this model is the structuring of the many details of change management into compact bundles of actions. When applied to the implementation of specific strategies and tactics, this model can assist HR professionals in reacting to strategic direction and tactical initiatives. It is also possible, however, for companies to use these steps not simply to implement change but to develop the capacity for change. This potentiality will be addressed in the next section.

STRATEGICALLY PROACTIVE HR
As discussed above, being strategically proactive prompts the question, "What is HR's role in creating strategic alternatives?" HR's position at the proactive strategy table can be earned in two ways: (1) by learning enough about the other functional areas (i.e., finance, marketing, production) to be able to contribute to business discussions in the terms and concepts of the other functional areas, and (2) by expanding and enriching the parameters of HR agendas through which strategic alternatives may be defined and created. To be a full partner at the strategy table, HR professionals must be capable of contributing at both levels. In the first, HR professionals create business alternatives through their ad hoc knowledge of other fields; in the second, they create business alternatives through the application of HR assumptions and logic.

As suggested in Figure 2, a relatively small number of HR departments are early participants in strategically proactive HR activities, so few reap the resultant competitive advantage. As an initial foray into the arena of strategically proactive HR, this article suggests three avenues through which HR can be strategically proactive: (1) creating the culture of creativity and innovation, (2) being involved in the full breadth of mergers and acquisition activities, and (3) creating internal capabilities based on future external environmental requirements.

HR can proactively add strategic value by enhancing the innovative capability of the firm. In so doing HR can improve the probability that the firm will bring to market new products and services before the competition, thereby reaping the pricing benefits of short-term monopoly market positions. The firm's innovative capability may be evidenced in providing new and improved products and services, reducing costs, improving quality, entering new businesses, and discovering new applications for existing products in either existing or potential markets. As HR plays a central role in these activities, it enhances the firm's ability to create market turbulence to which its competitors must respond rather than being in the position of responding to the rule-defining turbulence that its competitors may create.

Of course, no set of practices can guarantee that creativity will occur in a given situation. Innovation may not occur even where the conditions appear correct. Likewise, serendipitous innovation may occur where least expected. A reasonable expectation is that HR will enhance the firm's probability that innovative breakthroughs will occur.

Books and articles contain hundreds of anecdotes and stories about innovation in organizational settings (see, for example, Robinson & Stern, 1997; Isaksen, 1987; Drucker, 1985). Anecdotes and stories may inspire and reveal the possibilities, but they often fail to make explicit the levers that organizational leaders apply to increase the likelihood of innovation. Underlying nearly all discussions of creative breakthroughs in corporations is the conclusion that HR practices play a major role in the success of virtually every innovative organization.

To enhance the probability of innovation, two preconditions generally must exist. First, there must be a conscious decision by key decision makers that innovation is a desirable corporate focus or agenda. While this condition is reasonably obvious, it bears repeating since many management teams fail to make innovation a company focus even as they contemplate why their firms lack creative break-throughs (Robinson & Stern, 1997). Second, obstacles to creativity must be removed. Such barriers include overly bureaucratic infrastructures, too many layers of approval, and supervisors who are threatened by subordinate initiative. The reduction of such barriers is well reviewed by Ashkenas, Ulrich, Jick, and Kerr (1995).

With these preconditions in place, firms may then build the HR infrastructure that fosters and maintains the innovative ethos:

Communications. Is there an orchestrated communications initiative through which the priority of innovation is communicated? Do senior leaders discipline themselves to consistently communicate the innovation agenda and avoid the "crisis-of-the-week" communication pattern? Are role models of creativity publicly acknowledged through multiple media? Are upward communication channels available through which important breakthrough ideas are passed to potential senior level champions? Has management legitimated forums for the discussion of innovative ideas both in existing teams as well as in ad hoc groups? Are the time, space, and other resources available to support the effectiveness of such forums? Are channels established through which creative needs and innovative ideas can be communicated across business units and departments? Are information technology systems designed to provide easy access to information that might prompt innovative thinking? Is the physical setting designed to facilitate communication within and across teams and among organizational layers?

Staffing. Is the evidence of creativity explicitly applied as a criterion for hiring at all levels? When members are selected for major task forces, is a history of innovative contributions used as a selection criterion? Are individuals transferred across business units and functions to enhance the likelihood that the resultant diversity of ideas will spawn innovation? Are people promoted who have evidenced creative capabilities or who are committed to fostering and nurturing creativity in others? Are nonhierarchical promotions (i.e., fancier titles) applied to allow creative people to continue to be creative rather than moving them to managerial roles and responsibilities?

Training and Development. Are creativity skills included in corporate-wide training initiatives? Are customers included in action learning in order to directly access customers' needs and passions? Do training efforts include competitive benchmarking to create urgency around proactive innovation? Do cross-functional developmental efforts facilitate exposure to nontraditional sources of creative supply and demand? Do on-the-job developmental expectations and experiences explicitly focus on innovation? Are senior executives involved as trainers to role model and encourage openness to innovative ideas?

Measurement and Rewards. Does the firm have clear output as well as behavioral measures of creativity? Are there formal mechanisms to acknowledge and reward important creative contributions? Does the firm reward risk-taking without tolerating long-term failure? Does the reward system encourage the excitement of innovation without displacing it with extrinsic greed motives? Are rewards for innovation publicied to enhance the value of the reward to the innovator and to signal the importance of innovation as a corporate priority? Do the rewards for innovation recognize contributions of both individuals and teams? Are innovative breakthroughs quickly rewarded to enhance the motivating value of the reward?

HR can also exert strategically proactive influence in the arena of mergers and acquisitions. Defining the corporate portfolio is a fundamental mechanism by which firms strategically create their future. HR's role in merger and acquisition activities has emerged quickly over the past few years (Mirvis & Marks, 1992; Clemente & Greenspan, 1998).

As noted above, 65% of mergers and acquisitions fail to achieve the commitments that are stated to the financial community. The cause of these failures may occur at any phase in the acquisition process. The stages of mergers and acquisition include conceptualizing the firm's portfolio needs, identifying and selecting candidates, negotiating the deal, and integrating the two entities. HR can play an active role at each phase of the acquisition[4] process.

The merger and acquisition process begins with conceptualizing the firm's portfolio logic. A key element of this logic is the ability to understand the firm's core capabilities (Prahalad & Hammel, 1990) and the demand of the marketplace for these core capabilities. Three categories of core capabilities can be distinguished: what the firm knows (knowledge); what a firm does (skills); and how the firm thinks (culture). It may be assumed that the unique value added of the HR function is the creation and maintenance of the human element. HR has greater responsibility for conceptualizing and understanding the firm's core capabilities than any other function (with perhaps the exception of the CEO). The HR professional should then conceptualize existing portfolio deficiencies and opportunities and identify the core capabilities that might be acquired through a merger or acquisition. For example, a dominant logic in Microsoft's acquisition strategy is not just the acquisition of technological, market, or financial synergies but also the acquisition of fast and brash innovative cultures. An HR professional who is effective

in this area will not be limited to a domestic perspective. In Enron Corp., HR professionals have played a central role in identifying potential merger and acquisition candidates in South America.

When a potential buyer has conceptualized its portfolio needs, it then begins the process of identifying potential candidates and making a final selection. Finding a suitable candidate requires evaluating up to 100 firms in order to find one that meets the criteria of availability, fit, and price (Krallinger, 1997).

In the process of examining firms against these criteria, HR may contribute in two primary ways. First, the technical, market, financial, cultural, and managerial capabilities of the potential seller must be evaluated. HR professionals with the knowledge to conduct internal cultural, technical, and skill audits should now apply that knowledge to the merger or acquisition candidate. The audit logic will be similar, although gathering data from indirect sources requires considerably greater ingenuity. Since mergers and acquisitions tend to fail not because of financial, technological, or market reasons but because of people or cultural problems (e.g., Mirvis & Marks, 1992), HR's role in examining cultural incompatibilities is essential. Second, HR also contributes to the evaluation phase as it raises important issues during due diligence. What salary, benefits, and pension commitments does the buyer incur? What is the nature of union relations and existing contractual obligations? Should the buyer's reward system be superimposed onto the workforce of the seller? What are the strengths and weaknesses of exempt, nonexempt, and salaried workforces? Is there pending litigation between the selling firm and any of its employees? What will the staffing requirements of the combined entities be? What is the age, gender, and racial profile of the firm and what are their implications? How is the seller organized? What are potential pitfalls in merging structures? Third, HR should play an important role in determining the staffing requirements of the merger and acquisition team. The technical and interpersonal skills of the team members must be carefully selected, because it is for these reasons that deals often fall apart before they are consummated.

As the negotiation phase begins, HR again brings important value to the process. During this phase, HR has both a content role and a process role. In its content role, HR continues the in-depth probing of issues that it raised during due diligence, but now it is done opportunistically, with the potential partner seeking the highest possible selling price and with HR looking for potential problems that might influence the buying price. HR's process roles during negotiations include maintaining functional working relationships within its own company's team and with the members of the other company's negotiating team. Everything else being constant, it is better to begin the new relationship on a nonadversarial note. Thus, the creation of a merged whole that is greater than the sum of the parts begins during the negotiations. An HR professional can facilitate this goal by being aware of key subtleties during negotiations and by helping the senior executives of both sides maintain good working relationships while keeping them insulated from irksome details. HR's process role may also include knowing the negotiating style on the other side of the table and providing negotiation training as needed to her/his own team. Finally, since the ultimate selling price is often a function of the intervention of the seller's board of directors (Cotter, Shivdasani, & Zenner, 1997) the buyer's HR professionals should ensure their team is aware of the involvement level and historical opinions of the seller's board members.

It is at the integration phase that the majority of the 65% of merger and acquisition failures occur (Clemente & Greenspan, 1998). While this is the phase at which merger and acquisition value is suboptimized, it is also the phase at which HR's contributions can most easily rectify the most damaging problems. These problems include allowing cynicism-inducing politics instead of business logic to dominate the selection and placement of people and failing to integrate the merged cultures around critical, market-based criteria.

Two considerations are paramount in deciding which individuals get which positions: (1) ensuring that the "best" people are placed in the correct positions and (2) ensuring that the placement process is seen as fair and credible. The importance of the first consideration is obvious. Fairness and credibility of the placement process are critical to ensure that political considerations are minimized. If the placement is perceived to be tainted by politics instead of achievement and capability, cynicism sets in; capable people leave; the legitimacy of leadership is eroded; and the organization turns away from the customer and into itself.

The rules for deciding who gets what positions and for minimizing political influence are well known and straightforward but often ignored. Exact and explicit criteria about performance and capability should be specified for each relevant position in the merged or acquired unit. Considerable data should be gathered against these criteria from multiple sources including subordinates, peers, supervisors, customers, suppliers, board members, and the candidate. To the extent possible, objective (i.e., politically impartial) individuals should evaluate candidates against these criteria. Such individuals may include a team of peer executives representing both of the merging organizations, a team of internal staffing consultants such as exists at General Electric, or senior HR executives. This last step is the most difficult to do correctly because political criteria such as whom a senior line executive knows and "feels" most comfortable with have such a strong tendency to dominate placement logic. One *Fortune 200* top HR executive submitted his resignation three times during a major merger. Several senior line executives demanded that their favorite candidates be placed in specific positions without meeting the predetermined performance and capability criteria better than other candidates. In order to maintain the integrity of the placement process, the senior HR executive played his ultimate hand: he resigned from the process and the company rather than succumb to subtle and not-so-subtle political pressures and threats. Luckily, in each case, the line executives backed down, and the placement process continued with full integrity and credibility.

Equally important is deciding which culture should dominate. Three assumptions are necessary to ensure that the process for deciding which culture should dominate results in optimal outcomes. *First*, the most important element of organizational culture is shared mindset. *Second*, shared mindset is a key element of corporate success and, therefore, shared mindset should be defined by the requirements of the competitive marketplace. *Third*, it may be the case that the dominant firm in the merger or acquisition situation has the culture that is most aligned with the demands of the marketplace. It may also be the case, however, that the less dominant firm may have a culture that is best aligned with industry success criteria. It may also be the case that neither firm has the optimal culture and that the combined cultures must be defined and created anew. The key issue is to ensure that the components of the merged or acquired entities both have the cultures required for success, whether the cultures are similar or different.

With these assumptions in place, the process for merging the two cultures is fairly straightforward. The *first* step is for both entities to conduct a detailed analysis of the requirements for their respective marketplaces for capital, products, and services. This analysis should include viewing the marketplace from an "HR-friendly" perspective, that is, each component of the marketplace should be addressed, asking the question: "What should be known about this component of the business environment in order to determine what culture my organization should have?" The *second* step is to identify the sources of competitive advantage that a firm must have, the accompanying tactical actions that a firm must execute, and the relevant measures. The *third* step is to identify the cultural mindset that both firms must have in order to execute their respective strategies within their respective market requirements. *Fourth*, the merged partners may then compare their environmental assumptions, business strategies, and required cultures. By so doing they can assess which culture should dominate.

A third avenue through which HR may be strategically proactive is in linking the external market environment with key internal factors. HR's most fundamental and important corporate role focuses on optimizing the human side of the business equation. The problem is that most HR thinking addresses only 50% of the human side of business focusing on the internal "customer"—to the exclusion of external customers. Yet, HR's ultimate goal is to link the external human requirements with the internal human capabilities, thereby optimizing the utility of both. Several implications follow from this premise.

First, the HR goal is not to make employees happy or satisfied at work; rather, the HR goal should be to make those employees happy who are happy making the marketplace happy. This makes sense; yet, people in the HR field often fail to act in accord with this supposition. For example, HR professionals support company mission statements that boldly proclaim "People are our most important asset." Not only do HR professionals themselves not entirely believe such statements, neither do employees or even the executives who penned them in the first place. (This is the stuff of which Dilbert is made.) The problem with such mission statements is that in virtually every company there are people whose leaving would be in the best interest of the company. So, management rationalizes, "Well, what we meant to say is that *some* of our people are our most important assets." And thus the cynicism begins. In fact what we meant to say is: "People who are happy making customers happy are our most important asset. Other people we must either convert to being happy making customers happy or make them so unhappy that they leave the firm."

A *second* implication is that HR adds considerable value when it creates a customer-focused corporate culture. An important aspect of HR is to enhance each employee's understanding and valuing of marketplace realities. In so doing, HR not only helps facilitate the company's reactive responses to short-term market demands, but also helps to create the organization's capability to proactively track future market directions and create products and services that either lead future markets or that respond to current demands (Cespedes, 1995).

Initial research on the practices that have greatest influence on creating customer-focused value systems suggests that HR plays a central role in creating and executing these practices (Brockbank, Yeung, & Ulrich, 1989). These practices include the following: (1) providing a free flow of information directly from buying customers through the entire organization via customer focus groups, video tapes, audio tables, in-house visits, visits by employees to customer settings, and employee involvement in market research; (2) orchestrating comprehensive communication programs with the involvement of key institutional leaders who communicate the importance of the company being unified around winning the hearts, minds, and wallets of the marketplace; (3) ensuring that measurement, rewards, training, and promotions reinforce the importance of customer focus; and (4) designing organizational structures and physical settings that facilitate team work around customer requirements.

If HR is to play a more effective role in linking internal capabilities with external market realities, a third implication naturally follows: HR professionals must be highly knowledgeable about the marketplace for capital, products, and services. If HR is to lead in creating a customer-focused organization, HR itself must be relentlessly and intimately knowledgeable about external customers. The HR Competency Study at the University of Michigan has provided initial findings that knowledge of competitors, customers, marketing, and sales are critical aspects of an HR professional's knowledge base (Brockbank, Ulrich, & James, 1997). It has been furthermore suggested that a major contributor to the suboptimization in marketing activities is the lack of marketing's full integration with HR (Ballantyne, Christopher, & Payne, 1995; Clark, Peck, Payne, & Christopher, 1995).

In order to robustly link internal capability and external requirements, HR must not only be knowledgeable of specific customer issues but also of key aspects of the macro-societal environment including the following: basic social trends that are ultimately translated into market demands for specific products and services, changing values and meaning structures, major problems and challenges that are shared by large segments of the population, and structures of interpersonal relationships that influence buying processes (Cespedes, 1995). Within the context of these broadly defined social directions, marketing departments then work on niche analysis, short-term customer need identification, consumer communications, pricing tactics, field sales management, account management, competitive analysis, product positioning, channel management, branding, and product development. To facilitate internal and external linkages, HR should also be knowledgeable in these marketing areas, though these areas of HR contributions are secondary to the more fundamental social trend analysis.

These are agendas in which HR does not traditionally have substantial expertise or responsibility; however, if HR professionals are to become strategically proactive, this type of expertise will be increasingly required.

Summary

This article has argued that HR can add greater value by holding itself to the standards of being more strategic (as opposed to operational) and more proactive (as opposed to reactive). As HR moves from operationally reactive to strategically proactive, it moves from a position of adding relatively less to adding relatively more to a firm's competitive advantage. Specific HR agendas and activities may be associated with each of these levels of HR as competitive advantage. This article focuses primarily on the strategically reactive and strategically proactive HR roles. Among the strategically reactive arenas of HR involvement, three stand out: linking HR tactics to specific business strategies and associated tactics, creating the culture that is necessary to execute business strategies, and providing change management techniques and processes. Three agendas that help HR meet the criteria of strategically proactive include creating the corporate culture of innovation and creativity, contributing to each phase of the merger and acquisition processes, and leading the effort to link internal capabilities to external market requirements. These are not meant to be comprehensive lists of HR contributions in each of these areas of involvement, but they are mean to be important examples of the ways in which HR can add greater value in creating competitive advantage.

Source: Brockbank, Wayne. "If HR Were Strategically Proactive: Present and Future Directions in HR's Contribution to Competitive Advantage," *Human Resource Management*, 38, (4), 1999, pp. 337–352. Reprinted with permission of John Wiley & Sons, Inc.

Appendix: Corporate HR Information Sources

Abbott Laboratories	Champion Paper	Godrej Group (India)
Air Products and Chemicals	Citicorp	Harley Davidson
Alcoa	Coca Cola	Herman Miller
Allstate	Daewoo	Hewlett Packard
American Express	DataCard	IBM
Arco	Dow Chemical	ICI (UK)
AT&T	Dow Corning	ICICI (India)
Banco Rio (SA)	Edison Electric	Intel
Bank of Boston	Enron	ITT
Baxter International	Exxon	Johnson Controls
Boeing	Ford	Johnson and Johnson
British Oxygen	General Motors	Kodak
Cathay Pacific Airways	General Electric	Levi Strauss

Lucent Technologies	Quantum	Steelcase
L'Oreal	Raytheon	Techint (SA)
Marketing Displays International	Royal Bank of Canada	Texas Instruments
Merck	Sears	The Timken Company
Michcon	Sentara Healthcare System	Thomson Publishing
Motorola	Sheraton Inns	Unilever
Norwest	Singapore Air	University Hospitals of Cleveland
Perez Companc (SA)	Singapore Civil Service	Walt Disney Corporation
Polaroid	Smith Klein Beecham	Xerox

References

Ashkenas, R., Ulrich, D., Jick, T., & Kerr, S. (1995). *The boundaryless organization: Breaking the chains of corporate structure.* San Francisco: Jossey Bass.

Ballantyne, D., Christopher, M., & Payne, A. (1995). *Improving the quality of services marketing.* Journal of Marketing Management, II: 1, 7–24.

Becker, E. & Huselid, M. (1998). *High performance work systems and firm performance: A synthesis of research and managerial implications.* Research in Personnel and Human Resource Management, 16, 53–101.

Brockbank, W. (1995). *Conflict and contradiction in corporate values.* Paper presented to the Oxford Conference on Values in Business. Oxford University, Oxford, England.

Brockbank, W., Ulrich, D., & James, C. (1997). *Trends in human resource competencies.* Third Conference on Human Resource Competencies. University of Michigan School of Business, Ann Arbor, Michigan.

Brockbank, W., Yeung, A., & Ulrich, D. (1989). *Cultural unity: Institutional practices and individual outcomes.* Presentation at the Annual Meetings of the National Academy of Management. Washington, D.C., August.

Cascio, W. (1995). *Managing human resources productivity.* 5th ed. New York: McGraw-Hill.

Cespedes, F. (1995). *Concurrent marketing: Integrating product, sales, and service.* Boston: Harvard Business School Press.

Clark, M., Peck, H., Payne, A., & Christopher, M. (1995). *Relationship marketing: Toward a new paradigm.* In A. Payne (Ed.,), Advances in relationship marketing. London: Kagan Page.

Clemente, M. N., & Greenspan, D. S. (1998). Winning at mergers and acquisitions. New York: John Wiley & Sons, Inc.

Cotter, J. F., Shivdasani, A., & Zenner, M. (1997). *Do independent directors enhance target shareholder wealth during tender offers?* Journal of Financial Economics, 43:2, 153–193.

Cox, Jr., T. (1993). *Cultural diversity in organization.* San Francisco: Berret-Koehler.

Drucker, P. (1985). *Innovation and entrepreneurship: Practice and principles.* New York: HarperCollins.

Isaksen, S. G. (1987). *Frontiers of creativity research.* Buffalo, NY: Bearly Press.

Krallinger, J. (1997). *Mergers and acquisitions: Managing the transaction.* New York: McGraw-Hill.

Mirvis, P. H., & Marks, M. L. (1992). *Managing the merger.* Paramus, NJ: Prentice Hall.

Prahalad, C. K. & Hamel, G. (1990). *The core competency of the corporation.* Harvard Business Review, 68:3, 79–91.

Robinson, A., &Stern, S. (1997). *Corporate creativity.* San Francisco: Berrett-Koehler.

Schuler, R. (1997). *Managing human resources.* 6th Edition. Cincinnati: South-Western Publishing Company.

Thomas Jr., R. R. (1996). *Redefining diversity.* New York: AMACOM.

Towers Perrin. (1992). *Priorities for competitive advantage.* New York: IBM and Towers Perrin.

Ulrich, D. (1995). *Shared services: From vogue to value.* Human Resource Planning, 18:3, 12–24.

Ulrich, D. (1997a). *Human resource champions.* Harvard Business School Press.

Ulrich, D. (1997b). *Measuring human resources: An overview of practice and a prescription for results.* Human Resource Management, 36:3, 229–301.

Wintermantel, R., & Mattimore, K. (1997). *In the changing world of human resources: Matching measures to mission.* Human Resource Management, 36:3, 337–356.

Yeung, A., & Berman, B. (1997). *Adding value through human resources: Reorienting human resources measurement.* Human Resource Management, 36:3, 321–335.

Yeung, A., & Brockbank, W. (1995). *Re-engineering HR through information technology.* Human Resource Planning, 18:2, 25–37.

Endnotes

1. Many insights about the "state-of-the-art" stem from my association with four esteemed colleagues: Dave Ulrich (University of Michigan); Steve Kerr (General Electric); Warren Wilhelm (Global Consulting Alliance); and Dick Beatty (University of Michigan). I thank them readily and gladly.

2. Nearly all of the companies listed in the Appendix focus on establishing the strategically focused culture as a key element of their HR strategy. Culture is discussed under multiple rubrics including shared mindset, shared values, organization capability, human organization, and organizational competitiveness. The underlying similarity of these concepts is

that they all focus on (1) improving the organization as a whole rather than individuals or teams and (2) defining and creating the desired corporate culture rather than merely enhancing short-term knowledge and skills.

3. In an informal survey conducted during the senior line and HR executive programs at the University of Michigan, approximately 550 executives indicated that culture and shared mindset were more important to address as dominant business challenges than were technical knowledge skills. The ratio of their relative importance was 3:1.

4. This section is written from the buyer's perspective. The mirror image of much of this logic is relevant for the seller.

CHAPTER

6

DESIGN AND REDESIGN
OF WORK SYSTEMS

Quantum is the highest volume global supplier of hard disk drives for personal computers, a leading supplier of high-capacity hard drives, and the worldwide revenue leader among all classes of tape drives. In 1994, Quantum had less than $2 billion in annual revenue and approximately 2,500 employees, and was based primarily at corporate headquarters in Milpitas, California. By 1999, revenues exceeded $5 billion, and the employee headcount exceeded 7,500 worldwide, two thirds of which were outside of Milpitas.

In order to facilitate this phenomenal growth, Quantum needed to take a bold move in redesigning its HR function. When all functions were under competitive pressure to reduce both costs and headcounts while simultaneously adding value to the company's operations, HR moved from a function that took care of employees to one that provided systems for managers to use.

Quantum transformed its HR function from one of functional specialists to one of internal consultants who work directly with line managers. To assist with this process, initial and ongoing training is provided to these internal consultants to allow them to assist their operating units with growth and to properly manage the associated changes that accompany growth. Largely accomplished through in-house training and workshops facilitated by outside consultants, HR is now called upon to respond to changes in the external environment that impact the organization's people and to design organizational systems for managing change and increasing competitiveness.

Source: Baill, B. "The Changing Requirements of the HR Professional—Implications for the Development of HR Professionals," *Human Resource Management*, Summer 1999, Vol. 38, No. 2, pp. 171–176; http://www.quantum.com.

The second component in the development of human resource management strategy, in addition to human resource planning, is the design of work systems. The organization must consider the implications of its future plans on how tasks and responsibilities should be assigned to individuals and groups within the organization and decide how to redesign existing work systems. A model for the design of work systems is presented in Exhibit 6-1.

DESIGN OF WORK SYSTEMS

In Exhibit 6-1, three primary considerations are presented that decision makers need to consider in designing jobs: what workers do, what workers need, and how jobs interface with other jobs within the organization.

What Workers Do

One of the more challenging tasks in organizations is allocating specific tasks and job responsibilities to employees. Those who assign responsibilities need to ensure that employees are not overwhelmed by their jobs yet, at the same time, ensure that employees have sufficient work to keep them both productive and motivated. In addition, job titles and content serve as an important basis of comparison for employees within the organization relative to status, power, and appropriateness of compensation.

There are various strategies for the design of individual jobs. Those responsible for designing jobs and work systems need to fully assess the skills, knowledge, and abilities required by the organization both currently and in the future and consider both existing and possible future technologies. As noted in Chapter 5, a critical component of human resource planning is anticipating changes in the organization's environment. Work systems need to be constantly assessed and evaluated to ensure that the organization has assigned workers tasks and responsibilities that assist in achieving organizational objectives.

EXHIBIT 6-1: A MODEL FOR THE DESIGN OF WORK SYSTEMS

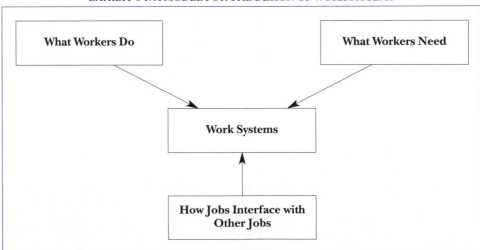

Early approaches to work system design focused on individual employees' jobs. In the late 19th and early 20th centuries, industrial engineering prescribed work systems with jobs that had very narrow task assignments, thus giving rise to the term *job specialization*. These systems attempted to promote efficiency in industrial operations by allowing workers to specialize in particular tasks and gain high levels of competence in their work. Jobs had a limited number of tasks assigned that required little thought, but precise execution. Not surprisingly, although these efforts toward simplified, specialized jobs provided efficiency, they also resulted in creating jobs that were boring and monotonous for employees. Because employees were not encouraged to go beyond a basic robotic function in most of their work, they were consequently unable to contribute to the organization in any meaningful way. This does not mean, however, that job specialization is inappropriate or never works. In fact, United Parcel Service, as discussed in Chapter 1, uses techniques of job specialization extensively. Job specialization can be a viable strategy for the design of work systems in organizations that require high levels of efficiency and cost minimization in order to compete effectively. It can also be appropriate for organizations that employ workers who do not seek to grow and be challenged in their careers.

Initial efforts to relieve this boredom and design more stimulating work for employees focused on providing them with tasks outside of the scope of their previously narrowly defined jobs. *Job enlargement* provides some variety by increasing the number of tasks, activities, or jobs to help alleviate the boredom of highly specialized work. A variation of job enlargement is *job rotation*, where workers are rotated across different specialized positions within the organization. Both techniques of designing jobs rest with providing employees with more variety in the tasks they perform. However, although these approaches add variety to tasks, they don't necessarily involve giving employees more responsibility. This does not mean that efforts to allow or require workers to perform additional tasks are necessarily useless. Employees who assume responsibility for additional tasks can have their understanding of organizational production processes enhanced and have a greater appreciation of how their specialized job contributes to the overall organization. Several studies have documented the success of both job enlargement and job rotation. Shortly after World War II, IBM instituted a job enlargement program and found a significant increase in product quality and a reduction in down or idle time.[1] Pharmaceutical company Eli Lilly utilized a popular job rotation program that allowed employees to qualify for salary increases and promotions while enhancing career development opportunities.[2]

Job rotation has become increasingly popular in recent years as a key tool by which employees are developed through exposure to different roles and functions within an organization. This is particularly true for HR professionals. In order for HR to be a true strategic partner, HR executives must understand fully not only the functional aspects of human resource management but also the nature of the organization's business. One of the best ways to obtain this understanding is to work within the organization in an operating division outside of the HR function. Ironically, for many years HR has developed programs that rotate employees across functions such as marketing, finance, operations, and accounting, providing those in rotation with a better grasp of the entire organization and an appreciation for how individual functions contribute to overall strategy. HR executives, however, are usually not part of such programs because the traditional "administrative" role that HR played. In order to participate in an organization's success at the highest levels, HR executives need to avail themselves of opportunities to "learn the business" by actually participating in and learning about the entire organization and its various units. Until they do so, they cannot contribute to the organization as a true strategic partner.

Job Rotation at General Electric

General Electric (GE) has always been a leader in employee development among large organizations. For many years, entry-level HR managers have been placed in a two-year job rotation program on joining the organization. New hires spend three 8-month rotations within the HR function. Although they might end up in different business units or divisions, these rotations were still within the HR domain and confined to areas such as labor relations, compensation, staffing, and benefits. The goal of this program was to develop strong HR generalists who could eventually become senior HR executives within GE. In the mid-1990s, GE added cross-functional rotations to the mix whereby individuals would leave HR for at least one rotation, working in areas such as audit, marketing, finance, or operations. This rotation program can continue throughout the employee's career as new skills, competencies, experiences, and knowledge bases are sought. HR executives in GE now have far greater credibility among their non-HR peers given this experience and are also better able to understand the business and develop HR solutions to key business challenges faced by divisions.[3]

Job enrichment initiatives involve going beyond merely adding tasks to employees' jobs. Job enrichment involves increasing the amount of responsibility employees have. Work is designed so that employees have significant responsibility for their own work. In many cases, the employee becomes more accountable for his or her own performance because responsibility for quality and productivity that previously were assigned to the employee's supervisor are redirected to the employee. This process of reassigning what were formerly supervisory responsibilities to employees is commonly referred to as *vertical loading*.

To assist organizations in designing enriched jobs, a model was developed that illustrated the relationships between redesigned jobs and ultimate performance and behavioral outcomes.[4] The Job Characteristics Model is presented in Exhibit 6-2. The model suggests that five core job characteristics can impact certain employee psychological states that will impact certain work-related outcomes. These five core job characteristics are skill variety, the extent to which the work allows an employee to use a variety of acquired skills; task identity, the extent to which the work allows an employee to complete a "whole" or "identifiable" piece of work; task significance, the extent to which the employee perceives that his or her work is important and meaningful to those in the organization or those outside of the organization; autonomy, the extent to which the employee is able to work and determine work procedures at her or his own discretion, free of supervision; and feedback, the extent to which the work allows the employee to gain a sense of how well job responsibilities are being met. The model argues that work systems can be designed to enhance motivation, performance, and satisfaction and reduce absenteeism and turnover.

Frequently, the job characteristics model can be utilized to allow workers to assemble an entire product or provide a wider range of services to customers. For example, at Motorola's Communications Division, individual employees assemble, test, and package paging devices whereas previously these tasks were performed on an assembly line with 100 workers performing 100 different steps.[5] Similarly, the job responsibilities of a group of employees may be enriched by allowing the work group the autonomy to complete an entire range of tasks in a manner determined by the group.

EXHIBIT 6-2: THE JOB CHARACTERISTICS MODEL

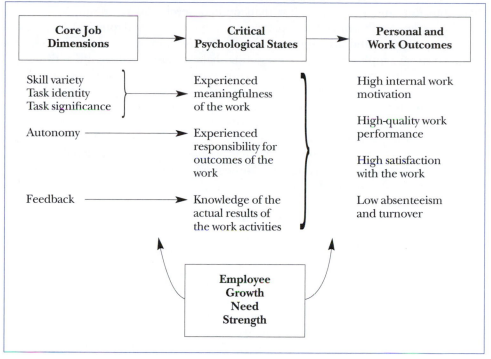

Source: J. R. Hackman and G. R. Oldham, "The Relationship Among Core Job Dimensions, the Critical Psychological States, and On-the-Job Outcomes," *The Job Diagnostic Survey: An Instrument for the Diagnosis of Jobs and the Evaluation of Job Redesign Projects*, 1974.

What Workers Need

The design of work systems also needs to consider what workers need and want in order to carry out their job responsibilities. Certainly, all employees do not work for the same reasons, nor do they expect the same things from their employers. However, employers must consider a number of important universal considerations in designing work systems to ensure that workers are motivated, productive, and happy.

The first of these considerations is the changing demographics and lifestyles of the labor market. As noted in Chapter 2, there are some significant differences in the composition of the 21st century workforce. No longer are the majority of employees married white males who are considered the breadwinners of their families. In fact, white males now make up less than 50 percent of the U.S. workforce. Organizations need to realize that employees no longer have generic needs. Employees expect their employers to understand their needs and respect them as individuals. Worker needs will vary among and between those of different age groups, genders, races, religions, physical abilities, sexual orientations, and marital and family status. In order to perform at peak levels, employees need to remain free from bias or prejudice in hiring, treatment, performance management, compensation, and advancement decisions and programs. This diversity of worker needs creates a significant challenge for allocating work in organizations.

Organizations also need to be more aware of employee needs for work/life balance. All employees, but particularly younger employees, are far less loyal to their employers than they were a generation ago. Employers who design work systems that do not allow employees to have the balance they desire in their life activities will find workers who not only are less committed to the organization but who may also suffer from burnout and perform at less than optimal levels. An increasing number of employers are establishing stress management programs and physical health and wellness programs and are contracting with outside employee assistance programs to ensure that employees retain an essential balance among their life activities. In response to the particularly stressful work environments in which many high-technology executives find themselves, the Growth and Leadership Center of Mountain View, California, was established to work with executives from nearby Silicon Valley. Leading employers such as Sun Microsystems, Intel, and Netscape sent employees at risk for burnout to the center for weekly coaching sessions.[6] A typical 10-week program costs $12,000 per employee. Such excessive costs can be avoided through the development of work systems that are strategically designed to allow the organization's employees to retain the right balance in their life activities and can be a key catalyst to high performance.

A third consideration in determining what employees want is ensuring that employees have some form of representation, or "voice." More highly skilled and trained workers do not expect to be micromanaged. They expect to use their training and experience to make a contribution to the organization, and they expect the organization to listen to their concerns. Systems for employee input are not only motivational to employees but they also allow the organization to fully utilize its existing human capabilities by encouraging employees to get involved in work-related issues that impact them. Work systems need to be designed so that employees have sufficient voice to allow them to contribute their perspectives and expertise.

In unionized organizations employee voice is formalized and centralized. However, less than 20 percent of the U.S. workforce is unionized. Unions also restrict the individual employee's right to have an independent voice, apart from the majority. In the absence of and even with a formal union, employers need to design their work systems to ensure that employees are able to communicate their needs and concerns in a constructive manner within an atmosphere of mutual respect. Both employees and the organizations win when this is accomplished.

One final consideration that needs to be incorporated in work system design under worker needs is workplace safety. The United States has established numerous guidelines for employers, administered by the Occupational Safety and Health Administration (OSHA), which oversees the Occupational Safety and Health Act. The act largely addresses employer liability for on-the-job injuries and occupationally acquired diseases. In addition to the traditional concerns of hazardous products or waste and unsafe physical conditions, increasing attention is being paid to safety issues regarding technology. Ergonomics is a relatively new science that explores the relationship between injuries and physical office working conditions. The National Institute for Occupational Safety and Health reported that in 1997 musculoskeletal disorders related to the neck, shoulders, elbow, hand, wrist, and back generated more than $13 billion in worker's compensation claims.[7] Consequently, OSHA has been developing national standards relating to ergonomics.

The near-constant use of computers with video display monitors has ignited debate concerning radiation hazard and the potential long-term effects of sustained gazing at video display monitors on an individual's vision. Because many employees also spend significant amounts of time at their desks or workstations, concern is also being addressed toward the ergonomics of work sites. Work systems and jobs need to be designed to be consistent with employees' physical capabilities and allow them to perform their jobs without any undue risks.

How Jobs Interface with Other Jobs

The final component of designing jobs is an understanding of how individual jobs may have interdependencies with other jobs as well as how individual jobs can or should interface with others. There are three traditional types of task interdependence: pooled, sequential, and reciprocal.[8] Pooled interdependence is where individual employees can work independently of each other in performing their tasks but utilize some coordination of their activities. Bank loan officers utilize this kind of work system. Each loan officer works independently of peers, yet the work of each officer is coordinated within the rules and procedures outlined by the bank for lending. In addition, experienced loan officers may often assist newer officers with specific tasks or questions they might have.

Sequential interdependence refers to work that flows from one individual to another, where one individual depends on the timely completion of quality work from another coworker. Mass-production assembly line workers utilize this kind of work system. Here, the output of one employee becomes the input for the next employee. Timely completion of work to be "passed on" is essential to avoid any slack or downtime, which creates inefficiencies and may strain relations between coworkers.

Reciprocal interdependence occurs when the workflow is not linear (as in sequential interdependence) but random. Employees can process work so that its flow is not necessarily predictable and often spontaneous to suit an immediate situation. Teammates on a basketball or hockey team utilize reciprocal interdependence as would the different departments within a hospital. Employees in a reciprocal interdependence need to be flexible and are often configured as a team, with joint and shared responsibility.

When the work of one employee interfaces with another, concern must be paid to designing the work system to allow as efficient a flow as possible. Higher levels of interdependence require higher levels of coordination and attention. In designing work systems, organizations need to consider the implications that the levels of interdependence have for management practices that facilitate control of processes and communication among the interdependent tasks. For example, higher levels of interdependence might require more frequent meetings between employees, regular status reports, and more careful monitoring of performance and processes by management.

The design of organizational work systems is not an easy task. Allocation of tasks and responsibilities must be balanced with worker needs. Consideration must also be paid to the need for interdependencies among workers. Because changes in technology and changes in workforce composition continue to present ongoing challenges, the design of work systems is not a static activity.

REDESIGN OF WORK SYSTEMS

The redesign of work systems represents one of the most radical yet common changes taking place in organizations from an HR perspective. Traditional work systems that stressed individualized jobs that were specialized and hierarchical have inhibited organizations and hindered performance. Current and future work systems are becoming much more broadly defined and stress designing jobs not solely around technical measures for efficiency but around strategic choices made by management. The greater the volatility in an organization's environment, the greater the need for more flexible, adaptive work systems. In fact, a new model for organizational effectiveness requires organizations to be agile or infinitely adaptable.[9] Although redesign efforts may initially be a very time-consuming process, well-designed flexible work systems can provide an organization with the ongoing ability to respond quickly to a changing environment.

Although key decision makers can and do approach work redesign from a more macro, holistic perspective, individual employees' main concerns usually involve their individual jobs. This is not to say that employees are not concerned about larger, systemic types of organizational change; individuals, understandably, have the greatest concern about changes that directly impact their careers and livelihoods. Many of the most significant change initiatives being undertaken in contemporary organizations involve job design, notably, what workers do, what workers are given and need in terms of resources, how jobs interface with each other, and skills requirements. Changes in these areas may be referred to in a number of ways, particularly reengineering, but the bottom line is that employees' jobs are changing faster than they ever have before, particularly in light of how information processing technology is impacting the nature of work.

The trend toward reengineering has resulted in numerous changes in the fundamental ways in which work is carried out. Unnecessary activities that add no value are eliminated; tasks are outsourced; work is consolidated; and divisions are restructured in the interest of increased efficiency and enhanced performance. These efforts often result in the establishment of cross-functional teams that have a very high potential for conflict as areas of responsibility are redefined and positions are eliminated. At the same time, these changes can have a negative impact on employee motivation and morale, as workers may feel some threat to their job security. Therefore, management needs to consider and plan for those possible effects prior to implementation, when redesign initiatives are being initially considered.

The increased use of teams and project groups in organizations has provided a number of challenges as well. Because U.S. culture is so highly individualistic, there is some discomfort as to the role that teams and group decision making should play vis-à-vis individual initiative. Employees who have been brought up in such an individualistic culture need training to be effective team members. In some instances, teams function more effectively than individuals, but in others, they don't. Although teams are becoming more prevalent, organizations still struggle with how to effectively manage them. ▼

STRATEGIC WORK REDESIGN IN ACTION

Outsourcing and Offshoring

Developing an organization's strategy involves, in part, an assessment of the organization's strengths and weaknesses, as discussed in Chapter 3. This process increasingly forces senior management to consider how best to leverage these strengths and minimize weaknesses. Frequently, the result is the decision to outsource some of the work being done by in-house employees.

▶ Reading 6.1, "Restructuring Teams for the Re-Engineered Organization," illustrates how an organization can strategically redesign its work systems for competitive advantage. A critical factor in the success of these programs is the process by which the change to these work teams was managed. As a result, one of the key responsibilities of strategic human resource management is guiding the change processes caused by job and work redesign.

Outsourcing involves the contracting out of some of the organization's noncore work activities to outside specialists who can do the job more effectively, often for less than it costs the organization to do such work in-house. Once an organization identifies its core competencies—the things that it does better than its competitors—anything remaining may be expendable. A simple cost-benefit analysis can allow managers to determine the efficacy of outsourcing a particular function. Within HR, payroll and benefits are two areas that are frequently outsourced. Technological support is often outsourced because of the high costs involved with keeping an organization's technology support systems from becoming obsolete. Training and capital investment in this area often provide limited return because of the rate of change in the application of information technology in organizations. Such work often is better handled by outsourced specialists, usually at a lower cost to the organization. ▼▼

Outsourcing by Federal and State Governments

The popularity of outsourcing is not limited to for-profit organizations. In late 2002, President Bush announced plans to put out for bid up to 850,000 federal jobs, close to half of the non-postal civilian positions within the federal government. One successful outsourcing bid involved the merging of 22 separate payroll systems into only two systems, at a projected savings of more than $1 billion over the coming decade. The State of Florida has been a leader in outsourcing, taking its entire HR function for 189,000 state employees and elected officials, and outsourcing it under a seven-year, $280 million contract. This action is anticipated to save the state an average of $24 million annually, in addition to the $65 to 90 million it avoided having to spend to update its antiquated software system. The contractor operates "employee care service centers" in Jacksonville and Tallahassee to handle administrative work, and remaining HR employees with the state now focus on strategic issues such as collective bargaining and specialized training and staffing.[10]

One recent study showed that more than 75 percent of organizations outsource at least one HR function.[11] A particular benefit for HR in outsourcing is that the assignment of transactional and administrative work, such as payroll and benefits administration, can free up HR staff to focus on more strategic issues. In considering whether to outsource any function, either within or outside of HR, decision makers need to consider not only costs but also whether the contractor can deliver a higher level of performance; where control and responsibility will lie, particularly in areas where compliance with laws is necessary; and how outsourcing might affect employees whose jobs might be lost, as well as the morale of remaining employees.

The importance of the compliance aspect of outsourcing cannot be overemphasized. In October 2003, Wal-Mart made headlines not for increasing its sales, profits, and market share but for the raids by federal agents at 60 of its stores that rounded up 250 illegal workers. The employees were cleaners, employed by a contractor to whom Wal-Mart outsourced this area of its retail operations. Two weeks later, a number of these workers turned around and sued both Wal-Mart and the cleaning contractor, alleging that they did not receive overtime pay to which

▶▶ Reading 6.2, "Human Resource Management Outsourcing: The Make or Buy Decision," illustrates how this practice can be carried out within the HR function.

they were entitled and that taxes and workers' compensation premiums were not being withheld from their wages. Employers who outsource may be considered "joint employers" if they exert a certain level of control over these employees. An organization can give contractors complete latitude in their hiring and compensation practices, but the organization may still face legal liability if a court finds that the organization exerts control over the work performed by the subcontractor's staff.

Decisions to outsource some or all of the work being done in an organization usually are driven by projected cost savings. Employers in our information and services-based economy frequently have labor as their chief expense. While many domestic outsourcing contractors can provide cost savings relative to labor, they are often limited by laws that mandate minimum wages and/or by the forces of supply and demand relative to the market value of certain skills and competencies. As a result, many organizations are taking outsourcing one step further, using a practice known as "offshoring." Offshoring involves the exporting of tasks and jobs to countries where labor costs are significantly less than comparable costs in the United States. Offshoring was once considered a threat only to manufacturing and assembly jobs that required relatively low levels of skill and education. Many domestic workers in these jobs were unionized, with correspondingly high wages, particularly relative to those that could be earned in less-developed countries. Because these jobs required basic manual skills that were easily taught, organizations began to enjoy significant cost savings when they exported such jobs to Mexico and underdeveloped areas in Central America and Asia. More recently, many white-collar, professional jobs have been the target of offshoring and decisions by organizations to engage in such practice have been controversial.

Chief among the jobs that are offshored are those in the information technology sector, computer programming, back-office accounting, and customer service call centers.[12] India remains the largest market for offshoring, accounting for as much as 90 percent of the industry.[13] The workforce there is largely fluent in English and highly educated with approximately 2 million university graduates annually, many with science and engineering backgrounds.[14] Most important to organizations, however, is the fact that wages for these workers—at approximately 10 percent of those that would be paid for the same work done in the United States—are considered good by local standards.[15] Oracle Corporation recently offshored more than 2,000 software development jobs to India. China, Russia, and Ireland are also popular locations for the offshoring of white-collar jobs.

Offshoring has presented an unprecedented challenge to organizations via the means of managing virtual global teams. The projected cost savings that can be realized by offshoring some work can be lost if employees from different regions of the world fail to work together effectively. A nonstop, 24-hour work environment creates a dispersed global team with sequential and reciprocal interdependence. Managers responsible for such dispersed teams need to exercise tight organizational and operational control to ensure coordination and communication.

Offshoring is certainly a controversial practice, as was seen in January 2004, when an IBM company memo was leaked to the *Wall Street Journal*. Meant for internal consideration, the memo reported that IBM could save $168 million annually by offshoring programming jobs to China, where the going wage rate was 20 percent of that in the United States.[16] Offshoring has been criticized for a number of reasons, but its proponents argue not only its merit but its necessity if domestic organizations are to continue to be successful and build the U.S. economy. These pros and cons are illustrated in Exhibit 6-3.

EXHIBIT 6-3: ADVANTAGES AND DISADVANTAGES OF OFFSHORING

Advantages	Disadvantages
• Cost savings • Extend work day to 24 hours (continuous)	• Loss of domestic jobs • Transfer of technical knowledge • Demoralizing • Public image/loyalty concerns

The chief advantage of—and often motivating factor behind—the decision to offshore is the savings that can be realized through reduced labor costs. It has been argued that this can make the U.S. economy more efficient and competitive and is necessary to allow domestic organizations to compete with their foreign counterparts who already enjoy such reduced labor costs. In addition, offshoring can extend the work day around the clock. This can be particularly beneficial for functions such as software development, allowing production time to be reduced considerably as the work is transferred across time zones. Call center operations can also claim enhanced 24-hour customer service through offshoring. The biggest criticism of offshoring involves the fact that offshored jobs usually result in job loss for domestic workers, hampering our domestic economy. In addition, offshoring often involves the transfer of technical knowledge overseas, developing the workforces of other countries rather than benefitting domestic employees. Job losses through offshoring can also be detrimental to the morale and loyalty of employees who remain, fearing that their jobs might next be exported. Finally, because offshoring can be viewed as unpatriotic, organizations who offshore have to be concerned about their public image and take steps to maintain the loyalty of their customers, the public, and government agencies and officials who have decried the practice of offshoring.

MERGERS AND ACQUISITIONS

Throughout the 1990s and into the 20th century, merger and acquisition activity in the United States has grown at a frenetic pace. An increasing number of domestic organizations are merging and/or being acquired by both domestic and international partners. While most merger activity is fairly well-planned relative to financial, product line and operational decisions, the human element of mergers and acquisitions is often ignored. In a study of merger activity in the banking industry, the International Labour Organization found that neglecting human resource activities in merger and acquisitions results in a much higher risk of failure.[17] It found that mergers are pursued for a variety of reasons, including economies of scale in operations, consolidation in saturated markets, and improving competitive position through a larger asset base. Employees, however, often first gain knowledge of pending merger and acquisition activity through the news media rather than from their employers. This lack of communication erodes trust and loyalty, resulting in increased job insecurity and workplace stress. The ILO report states that a full two thirds of mergers fail to achieve their objectives, largely because of the inability to merge cultural and other human factors into the combined enterprise or a blatant failure to even consider such issues.

The Human Side of Creating AOL Time Warner

The $162 billion merger of America Online (AOL) with Time Warner was the largest in corporate history. Whereas much has been written about the strategic and financial aspects of the merger, little insight has been shared as to the role that HR played in the merger to ensure its success. HR focused on five critical areas in attempting to merge the organizations as seamlessly as possible. First, HR restructured itself. Some operating units didn't need a full-time HR presence, so HR managers divided their time among units as necessary. Routine administrative work was outsourced to allow HR to focus on strategic and human resource planning. Second, the foreign HR staff was flown to corporate headquarters to collaboratively work on global strategy. Foreign operations were centralized in London, Paris, and Hong Kong to speed up both production and communication. Third, talent profiles were developed for 300 key executives to assist with the most efficacious deployment of talent worldwide. Fourth, recruiting practices were redesigned to facilitate an expedited review process as well as the sharing of applicant information across the different business units. Finally, an Internet tutorial, AOL Time Warner 101, was developed that explained the reasons for the merger as well as the benefits that it could provide to employees. As one of the most closely watched business transactions ever undertaken, the AOL Time Warner merger has been facilitated by the involvement of HR as a true strategic partner from the initial stages of merger planning onward.[18]

Successful merger and acquisition activity has been described as progressing through four distinct stages.[19] The first is the pre-deal, or selection of the target organization. The second is due diligence, during which time the parties meet and disclose all information relevant to the merger or, in the case of a hostile takeover, the acquiring company gathers its information on its own. The third is integration planning, or pre-merger activity just prior to the formal launch. The fourth is the actual implementation. HR plays a critical role in each of these stages, as identified in Exhibit 6-4.

EXHIBIT 6-4: HR'S ROLE IN MERGERS/ACQUISITIONS

HR Roles	Stage of Merger/Acquisition			
	Pre-deal	**Due Diligence**	**Integration Planning**	**Implementation**
	• Identifying people-related issues	• Estimating employee-related costs	• Developing communication strategies	• Managing employee communications
	• Assessing individual's fit with new needs	• Estimating employee-related savings	• Designing talent retention programs	• Aligning rewards with organizational needs
	• Assessing "cultural fit" between organizations	• Assessing cultural issues as potential challenges	• Planning for overcoming resistance	• Monitoring the new culture and employee dynamics
	• Educating top management on HR aspects of transaction			

Source: Adapted from Schmidt, J. A. "The correct spelling of M&A Begins with HR," *HR magazine*, June 2001, pp. 102–108.

Teams at Dow Chemical

Michigan-based Dow Chemical has been a leader in the use of employee teams since it began the practice in Europe in 1994. The large, bureaucratic organization felt that it was not using the skills and talent of its employees as well as it might, which led to a restructuring of plant operations. Work processes, from budgeting to actual production, were examined and a three-tiered system was developed for rating the degree of autonomy each team displayed. With the goal of removing day-to-day control and responsibility from a supervisor and giving it to a team—allowing individuals to contribute more fully to the organization—Dow developed audit systems that assessed teams and their independence. Rewards were developed commensurate with team performance and autonomy. The teams have saved Dow more than $1 billion in their first 10 years of operation. The process also has allowed Dow staff engineers to spend more time on improving plant processes rather than its operations.[20]

UNDERSTANDING CHANGE

The pressure to change can be a constant force in many organizations. Small organizations try to grow to gain the economic and market advantages that come with larger size. At the same time, larger organizations try to become smaller—either by streamlining operations or dividing into smaller subsidiaries—to increase efficiency and responsiveness to marketplace changes. Multinational organizations try to change to adapt to different economic, political, social, and market conditions faced in various locations around the world.

Despite the need for and pressure to change, any change initiatives in organizations are often met with resistance. There are several reasons for such resistance. One is the real or perceived costs of change. Change involves disrupting the status quo and entering areas of uncertainty. It also generally involves commitment of resources (financial, time, capital, human) that could be deployed otherwise. Particularly when there is a mentality of "If it ain't broke, don't fix it," the opportunity cost of the resources being committed to an uncertain change initiative may be questioned. If employees fail to see any real need to change the design of work systems, they are less likely to support changes in their job or work environment, particularly if they enjoy things as they are.

Resistance to change can also be found when those involved with and impacted by the change efforts fail to perceive any benefits for themselves. Rank-and-file employees, in particular, may have no incentive to do things differently, be retrained, or have their jobs restructured if they see no personal benefit. Employees may adopt the attitude that the organization is trying to get them to do more without compensating them for their efforts. This can be particularly problematic in union settings where union representatives often reject any initiatives that may alter the collective bargaining agreement in spite of benefits they may provide.

A third barrier to change involves risk and the uncertainty inherent in doing something differently. There is no assurance that the change initiatives will result in higher performance, greater efficiency, better working conditions, or improved morale. Older workers with greater tenure in an organization are more likely to be creatures of habit and find the risk to greatly outweigh any return they or the organization might receive. Employees who question the utilization of and need for new technology or distrust team-based responsibility may be particularly resistant to work redesign.

Finally, poor coordination and communication often undermine change initiatives. Managers are well aware that change initiatives are often met with some resistance and, therefore, they may refrain from informing workers about new projects and programs that are being considered or developed. Unfortunately, the organization's grapevine invariably gets a sense that something may be happening and often produces exaggerated and/or more threatening rumors than what is actually being planned. Although senior managers may wish to develop change initiatives in a vacuum, that vacuum always has leaks. Misinformation unrefuted by managers can result in the departure of employees who may sense a threat to their jobs.

MANAGING CHANGE

The management challenge then becomes how to overcome resistance to change. First, organizations need to plan to promote and implement change so that it provides benefits to the users—those who will be most affected by the change. This might be in the form of incentives to learn, an understanding of how it will make a job easier or more enjoyable, enhanced marketability of skills, an upgrading of a position, or some form of "gain sharing" of the results for employees. Work redesign strategies need to consider the employee perspective as to how the changes will improve work and organizational life for them.

Second, those responsible for change initiatives need to promote and invite participation. Employees will generally be much more committed to any course of action they have been consulted on and agreed to than one that is forced upon them. In addition, the organization stands to benefit from the most fundamental rule of managing people in organizations: No one knows a job better than the person doing it. An employee who "lives" with a job day in and day out can provide far keener insights as to how to improve the job, working conditions, or efficiency than virtually anyone else. Consider how many senior managers in organizations know what it's like to work in a mailroom day after day, week after week, year after year; how many have ever worked swing shifts, cleaning the offices after everyone has left; how many have ever worked at a fast-paced reception desk/switchboard all day long. An individual does not need an advanced degree in management to be able to make significant recommendations and contributions relative to work design based on their own *real* experiences in living with a job.

Finally, change is facilitated by open, two-way communication. In addition to seeking input from those affected by change, managers also need to keep all employees informed of what is being considered and planned. This is particularly true when nothing has yet been decided. A lack of any information at all can cause employees to suspect that something significant may be in the works. Again, the informal rumor mill will often manufacture scenarios that are far more threatening than anything that might be under consideration. Employees who are apprehensive and have dubious perceptions of what management might be planning will be more stressed and less productive. Seeking employee input is not only motivating and beneficial for the organization in soliciting relevant expertise, but communicating with employees also fosters an atmosphere of trust and allows the organization to determine where resistance might lie prior to implementation of change rather than after.

CONCLUSION

The changing nature of work requires organizations to strategically manage change processes as part of work design and redesign. Redesigning work to create more flexible, responsive organizations is probably the biggest unmet need in modern organizations and a key, ongoing strategic issue for organizations of all sizes, in all industries and in all locations.

Restructuring an organization is a risky undertaking and provides no guarantee of success. One 18-year study of *Standard and Poor's 500* companies found no correlation between an organization's decision to downsize and its profitability.[21] To optimize performance, organizations need to determine the factors that distinguish successful reorganizations and restructurings from those that are less successful. Cascio has identified the practices that correlate with successful restructuring as

- Skills training and continuous learning
- Increased employee participation in the design and implementation of work processes
- Flattened organizational structures
- Labor–management partnerships
- Compensation linked to organizational performance[22]

Clearly, HR plays a critical role in the success of any restructuring efforts. In partnering with senior executives on strategic objectives and how the organization's human capital might best be deployed toward those objectives, HR can facilitate the effective implementation of change that accompanies restructuring decisions and increase the probability that such efforts will be successful.

A strategic approach to human resource management involves HR acting as a change agent to drive, facilitate, and strategize change in organizations. Although some areas and functions, notably marketing, may respond to and/or drive change external to the organization, no other area drives change within the organization as the human resources function does. ▾▾

CRITICAL THINKING

1. Obtain the job description for your current or most recent job (prepare one yourself if one does not exist). Redo this description using the job characteristics framework presented in Exhibit 6-2. Design a job that would be more interesting, challenging, and enjoyable for you.

2. What are the critical factors to consider in the design of work systems? What particular role does technology play in the design of work systems?

3. Compare and contrast job enlargement, rotation, and enrichment. How are they similar to and different from each other?

▸▸ The HR function itself does more than just drive, facilitate, and manage change. Strategic human resource management involves managing change within HR, as well. The move from traditional HR functions and activities may involve restructuring and/or reconceptualizing HR. An increasing amount of HR activities are also being outsourced, as noted in Reading 6.2, "Human Resource Management Outsourcing: The Make or Buy Decision." In managing change, HR must be willing to practice what it preaches if it is to fulfill its strategic role and allow an organization to establish and maintain competitive advantage. A self-examination of how HR accomplishes its responsibilities allows the HR function to lead by example.

4. What barriers to change exist in most organizations, and how can they be overcome?

5. Describe a successful and unsuccessful attempt at job redesign that you have experienced or observed. What factors contributed to the success or failure of the change initiative? How could the unsuccessful attempt have been managed better?

6. Debate how offshoring might impact the U.S. economy. Do you feel that it will cause domestic organizations to become more competitive in the global marketplace through increased efficiency and reduced costs, or will it simply result in higher unemployment and an erosion of the consumer segment of our economy?

Reading 6.1

7. Explain the four different types of teams. Propose an organizational setting where each type of team would be most appropriate.

Reading 6.2

8. Why might work redesign result in outsourcing of some functions? What factors, both pro and con, might impact the decision to outsource a function?

Reading 6.3

9. Could the model presented in this reading be applied to an organization that is not experiencing a downsizing or restructuring? If so, how? Which components of the model might need modification? ▼▼▼

EXPERIENTIAL EXERCISES

1. Apply the job characteristics model in Exhibit 6-2 to the following positions:
   - an order taker at McDonald's
   - an usher in a movie theater
   - a receptionist
   - a manager of an auto rental company
   - a computer programmer
   - an insurance salesperson

INTERNET EXERCISES

1. Visit the Web site for Kaiser Permanente health maintenance organization (HMO) at http://www.kaiserpermanente.org. If you are a member, go to Kaiser Permanente Online. This site allows the organization to extend member services to the Web by allowing community members to interact with one another and

▶▶▶ Reading 6.3, "Work Redesign and Performance Management in Times of Downsizing," takes this process one step further by highlighting the importance of managing retained employees whose work duties and responsibilities may have been reconfigured during a downsizing or restructuring. The authors illustrate the importance of an effective performance management system during times of downsizing or restructuring to ensure that efforts have the highest chance of success.

with physicians in moderated sessions. Members can also research their own health-care needs as well as arrange appointments. The goal of this site is to improve outcomes and lower operating costs by fostering preventive care. This form of "redesigning" the work of health care enables Kaiser to get feedback that can be used to improve the delivery of services.

CHAPTER REFERENCES

1. Walker, C. R. "The Problem of the Repetitive Job," *Harvard Business Review*, 28, 1950, pp. 54–58.
2. Campion, M. A., Cheraskin, L. and Stevens, M. J. "Career-Related Antecedents and Outcomes of Job Rotation," *Academy of Management Journal*, 37, 1994, pp. 1518–1542.
3. Grossman, R. J. "Putting HR in Rotation," *HR Magazine*, March 2003, pp. 51–57.
4. Hackman, J. R. and Oldham, G. R. "The Job Diagnostic Survey: An Instrument for the Diagnosis of Jobs and the Evaluation of Job Redesign Projects," *Technical Report No. 4*, New Haven, CT: Department of Administrative Sciences, Yale University, 1974.
5. Gomez-Meija, L. R., Balkin, D. B. and Cardy, R. L. *Managing Human Resources*, 3 ed., Upper Saddle River, NJ: Prentice Hall, 2001.
6. "Tough Love for Techie Souls," *Business Week*, November 29, 1999, p. 164.
7. Gomez-Meija, L. R., Balkin, D. B. and Cardy, R. L. *Managing Human Resources*, 3 ed., Upper Saddle River, NJ: Prentice Hall, 2001.
8. Thompson, J. D. *Organizations in Action*, New York: McGraw-Hill, 1967.
9. Shafer, R. A. "Only the Agile Will Survive," *HR Magazine*, July 2000, pp. 50–51.
10. Overman, S. "Federal, State Governments Fishing for Business Process Outsourcing Bounties," *HR Magazine*, September 2003, p. 32.
11. Pomeroy, A. "Telecom Leaders Share HR Outsourcing Tips," www.shrm.org/hrnews_published/articles/CMS_003846.asp
12. "Job You Like May Be Going Overseas Soon," *Baltimore Sun*, December 30, 2002, p. 14D.
13. Babcock, P. "America's Newest Export: White-Collar Jobs," *HR Magazine*, April 2004, pp. 50–57.
14. Schramm, J. "Offshoring," *Workplaces Visions*, Society for Human Resource Management, 2004, No. 2.
15. "Job You Like May Be Going Overseas Soon," *Baltimore Sun*, December 30, 2002, p. 14D.
16. Babcock, P. "America's Newest Export: White-Collar Jobs," *HR Magazine*, April 2004, pp. 50–57.
17. "Financial Sector Workforce Hit by Mergers and Acquisitions," "'Human Factor' is Key Element in Success Rates for Merged Companies," International Labour Organization, www.ilo.org/public/english/burea/inf/pr/2001/06.htm
18. Adams, M. "Making a Merger," *HR Magazine*, March 2002, pp. 52–57.
19. Schmidt, J. A. "The Correct Spelling of M&A Begins with HR," *HR Magazine*, June 2001, pp. 102–108.
20. Bates, S. "Accounting for People," *HR Magazine*, October 2002, pp. 31–37.
21. Cascio, W. *Responsible Restructuring*. San Francisco: Berrett-Koehler, 2002.
22. Ibid.

Restructuring Teams for the Re-Engineered Organization

Afsaneh Nahavandi and Eileen Aranda, *Academy of Management Executive*

Since the mid-eighties, searching for ways out of their quality and performance crises, U.S. corporations have turned to a team concept. This turning to teams is appropriate for several reasons. First, organizations are now so complex that it is virtually impossible for an individual to have all the information necessary to make a good decision. Second, improvement efforts are often focused on process flow, and cross-functional teams can provide both needed information and "buy-in" to process improvements. Third, managers believe that if they put people into ongoing work teams, they will be better motivated and more productive. Fourth, recent models for "learning" organizations further suggest that teams are natural ways to gain and share the new information vital to organization growth and flexibility.[1] Finally, organizations even see teams as a way of assuring quality "in process" by making teams responsible for internal quality control.

Two major factors fostered U.S. corporations' implementation of teams. First, managers looked at global competitors and attributed their success partially to team-oriented management styles. Japan and Sweden, in particular, stand out as "teaming" exemplars.

Second, managers discovered the very large body of research which indicates that groups can be highly creative and effective.[2] The quality of work life research, for example, suggests that people in ongoing teams that are given wide latitude in self-management, and are made responsible for large tasks, are better motivated and produce higher quality work.

The early uses of teams were focused on quality circles (QC) which addressed specific organizational issues, and on project teams. While these QC teams were worthy efforts at developing teams in the organizations, the teams needed for the restructuring and re-engineering processes of the 1990s are quite different.

As a matter of fact, teams are now the central piece of many corporate restructuring and re-engineering efforts. For example, Motorola for many years now has successfully used teams in decision making and production. In another case, the much publicized Johnsonville Sausage Company[4] has made teams the successful cornerstone of its strategic planning.

Uneven Success

Despite the many success stories on the use of teams for organizations both in Japan and the U.S., success has been uneven.[5] Recently, there has been much frustration on the part of managers and employees, and a growing concern on the part of many observers, that teams might not be the panacea everyone hoped for. Complaints about teams being poorly trained and poorly supported abound. Teams are rarely well integrated into the organization's hierarchy.[6] For example, the results of a new survey of 4,500 teams across fifty organizations point to inappropriate compensation and reward systems, competitive departments, and the inability of employees to change as problems typically faced by teams.[7] Furthermore, teams continue to be a rare occurrence at the top executive levels of many organizations,[8] thereby sending a mixed message to middle-level managers and employees about their importance.

As a result, many employees feel that teams are a waste of time. The time spent on developing trust and agreement does not translate easily into high creativity and performance. Individual stars often feel that contributions in a team environment dilute their personal success. In addition, few teams have learned to deal constructively with "freeloaders." During a recent training session with a high-tech and team-intensive Fortune 50 company, one of the authors earned cheers and applause when she voiced reservations about the success of teams. Employees and managers expressed anger and exasperation at the teams' inability to make good decisions and at upper management's lack of support for them.

Overall, teams have not done consistently for the U.S. what they did and are continuing to do for Japan. Dramatic improvements rarely emerge with increased use of teams. There is little evidence that employees are more creative or more motivated when they work in teams. While quality improvements are evident in many organizations, the role of teams in these improvements remains unclear. Along with some success stories, we have many examples of teams that did not work.[9] The failures indicate the need to actively continue our attempts to discover better team processes.

Surprisingly, although we do not seem to know how to implement teams well, we continue to believe in them. We continue to use them in our organizations. As a matter of fact, in light of the considerable reduction in force in many corporations, the reliance on teams has increased. For example, the recent practice of re-engineering builds on a cornerstone of flexible and efficient cross-functional teams.[10] Given the potential benefits of teams and their persistent growth, we propose that managers can build climates for effective teaming.

Considering Culture When Creating Teams

The successful use of teams in the U.S. depends primarily on building structures that capitalize on cultural values. The first step then should be to understand how U.S. values differ from Japanese culture, particularly around issues that relate to teams (see Table 1 for a summary). Although much has been written about the differences between the two national cultures, the analysis is rarely applied specifically to understanding the effectiveness of teams.

U.S. and Japanese Culture

Individualism vs. collectivism. In the U.S., individual ingenuity and creativity are at the core of performance. Accordingly, the key to motivation lies within the individual employee.[11] Our organizational reward systems are a clear indication of such orientation. In spite of many teams in organizations, we steadfastly continue to reward individual performance. In Japan, on the other hand, the emphasis is on group harmony and unity, often at the expense of individual needs. The success of the organization is more important than the achievement of the individual. Work and responsibility are defined and described in collective rather than individual terms, and the source of progress and good is considered to be the team. The collectivism of the Japanese culture supports the use of teams and collective decision making. In contrast, the individualistic American culture often works against team harmony and cohesion.

Conflict and conformity. In Japan, direct conflict is often avoided, and equity is more important than reward. The harmony of the group is a primary and essential element of Japanese society. Conformity is expected and open conflict highly frowned upon. The U.S. culture, in contrast, through its focus on individual rights and independence, is more tolerant of conflict; competition is encouraged, as is non-conformity.[12] Once more, the Japanese culture supports the use of teams and the building of harmony, whereas the U.S. culture does not fit well with

TABLE 1: CULTURAL DIFFERENCES BETWEEN THE U.S. AND JAPAN
THAT INFLUENCE THE SUCCESS OF TEAMS

United States	Japan
• Core of performance is the individual	• Core of performance is the group
• Preservation of individual rights is key	• Preservation of harmony is key
• Conflict and competition are allowed	• Conflict is dangerous to group harmony
• Striving for egalitarian membership	• Status within groups is important
• Focus on present and quick results	• Focus on past and future
• Need for dynamic actions	• Need for slow progress
• Heterogeneous cultural values	• Homogeneous cultural values

the traditional definition of team effectiveness which assumes lack of conflict and acceptance of norms.

Power and hierarchy. Another factor which influences team processes is the acceptance of power and hierarchy. Whereas the Japanese respect their managers, U.S. employees are generally distrustful of management.[13] In Japanese teams, status is important and relationships are often formal. U.S. teams, on the other hand, strive for egalitarian positions and are generally informal. Where hierarchy is respected, it is much easier to subordinate the individual for the good of the collective. Where the "self-made person" is considered to be the ideal, acceptance of hierarchy within a team becomes harder.

Time orientation. Yet another cultural factor that affects our teaming efforts is the time orientation. The U.S. culture tends to be present-oriented, and focuses on fast results. The focus on the present creates a highly dynamic environment where part of the definition of success is the speed with which it occurs. On the other hand, the Japanese culture is more strongly embedded in the past and future. Its focus on the present is often colored by history and a long-term view of events. As a result, there is no compulsion to jump into action and to gain quick results. In such an environment, slow incremental change is tolerated and even valued. This tolerance for the passage of time favors the use of teams.

Cultural and demographic homogeneity. The final cultural element which affects the implementation of teams is the differential level of cultural and demographic homogeneity of the two cultures. Where Japan is culturally homogeneous, the U.S. has tremendous diversity. Reaching agreement is considerably simpler in homogeneous groups whose members share central cultural values. Where there is culturally heterogeneous membership, agreement becomes more difficult. The U.S. cultural diversity, therefore, presents a challenge to team process and cohesion. Such challenge is likely to increase as the U.S. organizations come to reflect even more the social and cultural diversity of the overall population.

Overall, Japan's cultural values of collectivism and conformity paired with high power-distance allow for relatively easy use of teams in organizations.[14] The current Japanese management techniques fit well with the Japanese cultural values, and the culture reinforces and supports the implementation of group-oriented techniques. Harmony and cohesion easily follow.

The U.S. import of Japanese techniques has ignored the role and dynamics of collectivism and individualism in the success of teams. As a result, our efforts to use teams rest on inaccurate cultural assumptions. We teach our teams that they need to first and foremost become cohesive. We try to get team members to leave behind their deeply ingrained cultural values and become more collectivist, cooperative, and patient with process and slow change. Under such conditions, it is not surprising that many of our teaming efforts have been less than successful. The application of Japanese style teams in the U.S. is culturally incompatible. Given the mainstream U.S. cultural values, it is unreasonable to expect Japanese style team-based decision making to succeed.

The Three Keys to Successful Teams in the U.S.

Our challenge is to create team processes that capitalize on U.S. cultural values. Teams in U.S. corporations need to feel competent and confident in the knowledge that their decisions are valued. Individuals need to contribute and have their contributions recognized and valued. Teams require a dynamic and independent quality that fits U.S. cultural values. We propose three key changes essential to having those teams work well as the core of U.S. restructuring efforts. They are: 1) value and endorse dissent; 2) encourage fluidity in team structure; and 3) enable and encourage teams to make decisions (see Figure 1 for a summary). These recommendations require management and employees to move outside of the current mind-set of "appropriate team behavior" and to learn to capitalize on U.S. cultural values and diversity. Once implemented, these changes can lead to higher levels of performance than is possible when teams rely on culturally incompatible assumptions.

VALUE AND ENDORSE DISSENT

The U.S. mainstream culture is based on individualism, conflict, competition, quick results and success, and fast-paced actions. Our teams are not likely to ever achieve the Eastern-style harmony that is at the core of Japanese decision making. This difficulty with harmony will increase as our organizations increasingly reflect the U.S. demographic and cultural diversity. People who hold diverse cultural values do not

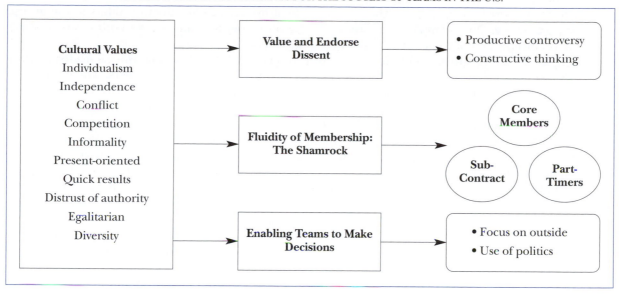

reach harmony easily. In fact, attempts at forced harmony may eliminate the benefits of diversity. Members' disagreement and differences should form the basis for team creativity.

Because of the way teams are structured and trained in many U.S. organizations, members are usually taught to seek internal agreement. However, recent information on effectiveness in organizations has indicated the need to foster tension.[15] Complacency is identified as one of the greatest dangers to continued success of an organization. Without active dissent, it is easy for managers and employees to consider "our" way as the "right" way, or to focus on incremental improvement rather than innovation. Since many in the organization have a vested interest in maintaining the status quo, few will argue. Controversy is therefore discouraged. Such thinking can be the pathway to failure. The decline of many of our major corporations such as GM and IBM can be partially attributed to their inability to tolerate deviation from what was considered to be the "right" product or strategy. To value and endorse dissent, organizations and teams must learn the techniques of productive controversy and constructive thinking.[16]

Productive controversy involves learning how to "fight" over the issues. Team members must learn to draw out and to value different points of view. Overall, the use of productive controversy fits well with values of individualism and independence.

A recent example at the Phoenix Fire Department provides a case in point. The department, like many others around the country, had a long history of union conflicts. Ten years ago, it began a process of Results by Objectives (RBO) which created teams of union and management people charged to address specific organizational issues. The teams received training on how to bring up controversial issues, explore alternatives, and reach consensus while focusing on the outcome. The RBO process has been continued over the years and has been expanded to areas beyond union-management relationships. The city's fire department has, as a result, one of the best working relationships with its union in the country, and has become a model for other fire departments.

Similar to the fire department example, teams need to adopt a view that sees differences as enriching a discussion rather than impeding it. To engage in productive controversy, teams must establish processes and ground rules that focus on issues rather than people, preserve all ideas regardless of the position of the proposer, and put off decisions until all issues and ideas are explored.

Closely related to productive controversy is the process of constructive thinking. Team members often do not know how to be creative. It is not enough to be cloistered together and assigned a task; team members have to learn to think better.[17] Organizations should teach teams and team members how to attack problems and create innovative ideas. Several organizations have moved on the path to constructive thinking. One example is the Creativity Center developed by DuPont where teams and individual employees are taught to think in innovative ways. Participants are trained in the skills of lateral thinking and are encouraged to challenge assumptions and practices in their organizations.[18]

Encouraging tension and teaching individual team members to be innovative draw upon existing U.S. values of individualism and competitiveness and capitalize on U.S. cultural diversity. U.S. teams are likely to find these behaviors easier to learn and to apply than achieving harmony and conforming to group decisions.

FLUIDITY OF MEMBERSHIP

The second key to successful U.S. teams is increased fluidity of membership. We have tried to make work teams harmonious and stable social units, when harmony and stability are inconsistent with U.S. cultural values. Although respect and good interpersonal skills are essential to productive team processes, it is not clear that stability of team membership is in the best interests of either teams or organizations. In fact, we have long been aware of the detrimental effects of too much stability and cohesion.[19] Recent advice for redesigning organizations into fluid shamrock structures can be applied to team development and membership.[20] Such advice is also in line with the movement toward a contingency workforce which has allowed many employers to maintain flexibility in uncertain and changing times.

A shamrock team structure would have three components. The first one would be a stable core of three to five members who stay with the team until the task is done. These members have the technical, problem-solving, and interpersonal skills necessary to address issues and to generate and consider new ideas. They also provide continuity and some measure of stability to the team.

The second component would be resource people with specialized skills and expertise who enter and exit the team as needed. They belong to the team for varying periods of time (sometimes quite long) and play many different roles. They bring new ideas and differing perspectives to problems, thereby preventing complacency and lack of creativity. Because they enter and exit frequently, resource people offer the team a vehicle to learn new skills and to renew itself. Their continued interaction with the core members also makes them insiders, rather than outsiders to the group. Resource people can include both customers and suppliers.

The third leaf of the shamrock is made up of the temporary or part-time members. These members are called upon at special times; for example, when the team needs to gather information from customers or to advocate a particular point of view. Both part-time members and resource people play a key political role for the team. They can be the team's advocates and idea champions in the organization by disseminating information and sending up trial balloons. They form the core of the team's coalition.

The use of a shamrock team structure challenges the common wisdom that teams need stability in order to be productive. The dynamic structure of a team shamrock allows organizations to deal with highly diverse and complex issues. It is also compatible with the U.S. cultural values of conflict, focus on the present, and quick and constant actions. The continual movement of members in and out of teams, together with the presence of the core members, prevents the development of too much cohesion and complacency, allows for the dynamic renewal of teams and their members, and leads to better use of our diverse population.

ENABLING TEAMS TO MAKE DECISIONS

The final key to building effective teams is to empower them with decision-making authority. One of the major complaints about teams is that they are not trusted with major decisions and their tasks are often not clearly tied to strategic plans and initiatives.[21] As a result, they are prevented from addressing fundamental issues in the organization. Additionally, teams are usually required to seek "permission" before they can implement any of their recommendations, thereby minimizing the timeliness, ownership, and the potentially innovative and unorthodox nature of their recommendations. In order to gain permission to implement their ideas, teams are forced to suggest easily acceptable and non-controversial solutions to problems.

Truly effective teams empower themselves. Recent work by Peter Block further emphasizes the need to allow teams autonomy to define their goals and their area of impact.[22]

Effective teams are anchored in organizational realities. Therefore, the focus of the team effort should include external factors. Acceptance of the team's idea becomes as much a goal as the idea itself. The team is forced to look outside itself for ideas and feedback. As mentioned earlier, the fluid shamrock can provide a strong external link for the team. Another key tool for the team is the use of organizational politics. The team needs to understand other people's needs and perspectives and define an optimal solution. Cooperation, coalition building, and cooptation provide the means for team success and empowerment.

A large public sector organization recently struggled with the implementation of new work processes in its accounting department. The need for change was well recognized and accepted by most of the forty employees of the department. The manager therefore appointed a ten-member cross-functional team to study the existing work process and propose alternatives. As the team started its deliberations, the members found the large size to be an impediment to speed. In spite of the initial plans to rotate membership, the team leader recommended a limit of four members. Throughout a six-month period, very little feedback was provided about the team's deliberations. Finally the team presented a single creative and innovative proposal for changing the existing processes to the department. The proposal involved the learning of many new skills and change in a number of schedules and internal and external relationships. Department members complained; external customers panicked. The team members and the department manager were left frustrated and angry at the department's lack of willingness to change and lack of confidence in the team. The team had not taken any steps to anchor its proposal in organizational realities. Coalitions had not been built. The team failed to empower itself.

A Model for Understanding Types of Teams

Figure 2 presents four types of teams, three of which are extensively used in today's organizations. The teams vary on the two dimensions of fluidity of team membership, and task complexity. The oldest and simplest type of team, Type I, has stable membership and performs relatively simple tasks. The Quality Circles of the 1970s and 1980s are an example of such teams. Their goal was basic and simple problem solving. They were focused on internal issues and were often made up of workers reporting to managers or other workers. Many such teams exist in organizations to deal with basic

FIGURE 2: TEAM DEVELOPMENT MODEL

HIGH

TASK COMPLEXITY

TYPE II		**TYPE IV**	
GOAL:	Problem solving and selling of ideas	GOAL:	Creative problem solving and implementation
FOCUS:	External	FOCUS:	Strategic
BLOCKS:	Lack of empowerment	BLOCKS:	Preparedness
LEVELS:	Management teams	LEVELS:	All levels
EXAMPLES:	Top management teams	EXAMPLES:	Shamrock teams
TYPE I		**TYPE III**	
GOAL:	Simple problem solving	GOAL:	Integration in structure and setting ground rules
FOCUS:	Internal	FOCUS:	Internal
BLOCKS:	Lack of training	BLOCKS:	Organization structure
LEVELS:	First level work teams	LEVELS:	First and middle levels
EXAMPLES:	Quality circles	EXAMPLES:	Cross-functional teams

LOW

LOW   TEAM MEMBERSHIP FLUIDITY   HIGH

work problems. Type II teams have generally stable membership. However, they deal with complex tasks and problems. They often need to consider many stakeholders in their deliberations and recommendations. They, therefore, not only have to solve problems, but also "sell" and implement their ideas. As a result, their focus is often outside the team and their major obstacle is the lack of empowerment to implement their ideas. As opposed to the membership of Type I teams, these teams often include or are exclusively made up of middle and top-level managers.

Type III teams have a fluid membership although they do not typically deal with highly complex problems. Cross-functional teams used in some organizations are examples. In addition to problem solving, one of their major goals is to create and set the ground rules that would support the interaction of people with diverse functional backgrounds. The focus of such teams is often internal, and a major obstacle they face is the organizational structures within which they operate.

The fourth type of teams are the shamrocks we are proposing. These teams can function in highly complex organizations and deal with broad organizational issues. Their membership is fluid and flexible. In addition to problem solving, politics, and integration within existing structures, the goal of such teams is primarily constructive thinking. Their focus is both internal and external and they operate at all levels of the organization.

Although the proposed model does not follow a linear path, there appears to be some consistency in the manner in which many organizations develop teams. Many of our organizations have started with Type I teams through QCs and task forces. They have typically moved to more complex structure and they now include several Type II or Type III (or in some cases both simultaneously) teams depending on their strategic needs. Given the current highly complex business environment, the radical changes in the structures of our organizations, the fluidity of organizational membership, and the redefinitions of organizational boundaries to include customers and in some cases competitors, many organizations need to move towards the shamrock teams we are proposing. Such teams need to understand and capitalize on diversity, include many outsiders—both outsiders to the team and to the organization—in their deliberations and implementation, and face complex problems in a highly creative manner.

For organizations to implement the proposed team structures, it is important to start the changes in the structure in small doses. For example, the use of the shamrock team structure does not require a wholesale organizational change. Many organizations already rely on part-time employees and subcontractors in a variety of functions. Shamrock teams can start with few members. Here once again, the organization that does not have existing teams may be at an advantage in that it will not have to dismantle existing teams; fluidity can be built in from the beginning. One of the keys to the success of newly structured teams is, as it has always been, providing them with training. The major difference here is that training should be focused on productive controversy, constructive thinking, and creativity. Team members should be taught how to disagree with one another productively, not how to reach consensus and agreement above all else. It is also important that training be provided to team members in a "cafeteria-style" fashion, so that they can pick and choose the type and quantity that they need when they need them. The use of the shamrock teams may also reduce the need for training since both the subcontractors and part-timers can bring expertise to the group without the group members having to master new skills for every new project and task.

In addition to the above training, team members also have to acquire a number of "political" behavior such as building of coalitions with outside members and managing their image with internal customers. Such behaviors are often developed through experience, and observation of positive role models rather than through formal training sessions. Managers can be extremely effective in helping team members to acquire such skills. Furthermore, managers have a particular responsibility to make productive use of the newly created teams. Their tasks should be at the center, rather than on the fringes, of the organizational strategic efforts.

Implementation of the restructured teams requires some of the same tools that have been used in more traditional teams. However, the content of the training has to be drastically changed and directed by the team. Furthermore, the productive use of teams has to become, more than ever, the center of the organization's efforts.

Conclusion

The use of teams in the U.S. makes sense for several reasons. The complexity of our organizations, the virtual inability for any one individual to acquire all the necessary skills and knowledge to make good decisions, the rapid pace of technological change, and improvement efforts focused on process flow, all make teams the ideal mechanism to provide both the information and the "buy-in" needed for process improvements. Additionally, the continuing customer demands for responsiveness and product/service innovation make the potential benefits of the collective thinking of teams a competitive advantage. However, our present-, individual-, competitive-oriented cultural values, together with unsupportive and hierarchical organizational structure that expect but do not encourage creativity, have set the stage for the current, culturally incompatible implementation of teams. Instead of constructing teams based on U.S. cultural values and creating structures that can support them, we have borrowed from other cultures and partially implemented research findings. The hierarchy in which most teams currently operate, together with management's lack of faith in them, neutralize a team's most valuable outcome, its creativity and its chance to bring change to the organization.

For teams to be effective in U.S. corporations, they need to capitalize on the U.S. cultural values of individualism, competitiveness and conflict, and focus on rapid results. These can be achieved through the creation of teams that build on dissent through the use of productive controversy and constructive thinking; have fluid rather than stable membership; and, are enabled, not only through management support, but through their own focus on championing their ideas to their external constituents. Given the key role of teams in U.S. restructuring efforts, it is essential that the teams be created to fit the culture and the goals of the organization.

We see an additional advantage for organizations redesigning their teams. As the U.S. becomes more culturally diverse, teams will have to regularly adjust to the evolving culture. The skills proposed here will allow teams to accept the constant challenges of change and to dynamically and systematically consider new approaches to teamwork. Thus we can move beyond the simple-minded teams of the 80s.

Source: *Academy of Management Executive: The Thinking Manager's Source* by Nahavandi. Copyright © 1994 with permission of Academy of Management in the format Textbook via Copyright Clearance Center.

Endnotes

1. P. Senge, *The Fifth Discipline: The Art and Practice of the Learning Organization* (New York, NY: Doubleday, 1990).
2. For an excellent recent review of social science research about teams see S. Worchel, W. Wood, and J. A. Simpson (Eds.), *Group Process and Productivity* (Sage Publications, 1992).
3. Quality of work life research on success of teams.
4. R. Stayer, "How I Learned to Let my Workers Lead," *Harvard Business Review*, 1990.
5. For research about quality circles see E. E. Lawler, III, and S. A. Mohrman, "Quality Circles: After the Honeymoon," *Organizational Dynamics*, Spring 1987, 42–54; and G. E. Ledford, Jr., E. E. Lawler, III, and S. A. Mohrman, "The Quality Circle and its Variations," in J. R. Campbell and Associates (Eds.), *Productivity in Organizations* (San Francisco, CA: Jossey-Bass, 1988), 255–294.
6. For some examples see D. D. O'Connor, "Trouble in the American Workplace: The Team Player Concept Strikes Out," *ARMA Record Management Quarterly*, 24(2), 1990, 12–15; and J. F. Vogt and B. D. Hunt, "What Really Goes Wrong with Participative Work Groups?" *Training and Development Journal*, 42(5), 1991, 96–100.
7. For results of the survey see "The Downfall of Teams," *Training and Development Journal*, February 1993, 9–10; and "Why Teams Don't Work," *Sales and Marketing Management*, April 1993, 12.
8. M. Hequet, "Teams at the Top," *Training*, April 1994, 7–9.
9. See example in J. R. Hackman, *Groups that Work (and those that Don't): Creating Conditions for Effective Teamwork* (San Francisco, CA: Jossey-Bass, 1990).
10. M. Hammer, and J. Champy, *Reengineering the Corporation: A Manifesto for Business Revolution* (New York, NY: Harper Business, 1993).
11. For research on cultural differences, see G. Hofstede, *Culture's Consequences* (Sage Publications, 1980); N. Adler, *International Dimensions of Organization Behavior*, 2nd edition (Boston, MA: PWS-Kent Publishing Company, 1991); and V. Terpstra and K. David, *The Cultural Environment of International Business*, 2nd edition (South-Western Publishing Company, 1985).
12. For a brief example see H. Aaron, "Something's Wrong with American Business," *Business Marketing*, 77(1), 1992, 38–39.
13. D. L. Kanter and P. H. Mirvis, *The Cynical Americans: Living and Working in an Age of Discontent and Disillusion* (San Francisco, CA: Jossey-Bass, 1989).

14. P. R. Harris and R. T. Moral, *Managing Cultural Differences* (3rd ed.) (Gulf Publishing Company, 1991).

15. R. T. Pascale, *Managing on the Edge* (New York, NY: Touchstone, Simon & Schuster, 1990).

16. The idea of valuing and endorsing dissent was proposed by Pascale, *op. cit.*

17. E. DeBono proposes a number of ways for teams to improve their thinking in his book, *Serious Creativity: Using the Power of Lateral Thinking to Create New Ideas* (New York, NY: Harper Business, 1992).

18. E. DeBono, *op. cit.*

19. See the work of I. I. Janis, *Victims of Groupthink* (Boston, MA: Houghton Mifflin, 1972).

20. See C. Handy, *Age of Unreason* (Cambridge, MA: Harvard Business School Press, 1990) for details of the shamrock structure.

21. Pascale, *op. cit.*

22. P. Block, *Stewardship: Choosing Service over Self-Interest* (Berrett-Koehler Publishers, 1993).

Human Resource Management Outsourcing: The Make or Buy Decision

Charles R. Greer, Stuart A. Youngblood, and David A. Gray, *Academy of Management Executive*

Just-in time human resource (HR) management, sell and lease-back human resource programs, and do-it-yourself HR—all of these phrases characterize how companies manage outsourced HR functions. This article reports results of interviews conducted with senior HR executives and professionals in 25 organizations to identify outsourcing rationales and consequences. Companies were found to use HR outsourcing for both operational and strategic reasons. Based on these findings, we present guidelines for selecting vendors, managing the outsourcing transition, managing vendor relations, and monitoring vendor performance. HR outsourcing is not a fad, and it can enhance the HR value chain as well as support the development of HR as a business partner and strategic contributor to the organization's goals.

The Trend Toward Outsourcing

Does outsourcing of human resource activities spell doom for the HR department? Is this phenomenon a short-term response to the corporate downsizing of the 1990s? Are senior HR executives supporting or resisting outsourcing pressures from their executive teams? The answers to these questions and other regarding the role of HR outsourcing depend in large part on how senior HR executives view the roles of the HR function. To address these questions, we interviewed 26 executives and professionals, including senior HR executives from 25 different organizations with experience in outsourcing.[1] Many of the larger companies are industry leaders, and seven are ranked in the top half of their specific industries in *Fortune*'s list of American's most admired companies.[2]

HR executives view the process of outsourcing differently from purchasing, procurement, and subcontracting. In their view, outsourcing occurs when a company contracts with a vendor to perform an activity previously performed by the company. In contrast, procurement generally means that the company has not performed the activity before. Outsourcing also has a temporal dimension in that some executives view outsourcing as permanent, whereas subcontracting is temporary. Thus, a subcontracted activity is expected to return to the company at some point, whereas outsourcing is not. We refer to outsourcing as the performance, by outside parties on a recurring basis, of HR tasks that would otherwise be performed in-house.

The market for providers of outsourced services of all types is growing rapidly. In 1996, American firms spent over $100 billion in outsourced business activities. Globally, outsourcing usage grew by 35 percent for the 12 months ending in June 1997 and the total market for outsourced services is expected to increase to $200 billion by the year 2000. A 1996 Hewitt Associates survey of large employers found that 93 percent of respondents outsourced some of their HR functions. Similarly, an American Management Association survey found that 77 percent of firms surveyed in 1996 outsourced some of their HR activities, up from 60 percent in 1994. The 1997 Survey of Human Resource trends of 1,700 organizations reported that 53 percent planned to outsource more in the future.[3] HR departments are facing the classic make-or-buy decisions that other functional areas confront when considering the outsourcing of services or products.

From our review of the outsourcing literature and interviews with HR professionals, we identified five competitive forces that are driving more companies to outsource some or all of their HR activities: downsizing, rapid growth or decline, globalization, increased competition, and restructuring. Over the past decade, these forces have significantly altered the strategy and structure of many firms. During this time, firms have attempted to refocus their businesses, lower their costs while increasing service, and improve capabilities to respond to future business challenges.

For the HR executive, the imperatives are similar. By refocusing the HR function, executives hope to achieve a closer alignment of HR practices with business strategy. HR managers, in turn, have been admonished to partner with line managers to deliver more value-added services at a lower cost. In addition, HR executives feel more pressure to improve their service response time for internal and external customers. In the words of professor and consultant Dave Ulrich, the world of HR has evolved to producing "deliverables," as well as "doables."[4] Consequently, HR tasks, functions, and entire departments are being reexamined to see which HR activities are needed, and who can best provide them.

One of the five forces, downsizing, has dominated HR thinking for the past decade, although there are some signs that the trend is diminishing. In the early 1990s, as many as 3,100 layoffs per day were announced, with over 650,000 jobs lost each year.[5] The inevitable restructuring of entire industries has recast HR departments as formulators and implementors of downsizing and as targets of downsizing themselves. HR outsourcing decisions are frequently a response to an overwhelming demand for reduced costs for HR services.

Many firms have also undergone changes related to restructuring, mergers, and acquisitions. Retrenched firms, or those in decline, face incredible pressures to reduce costs, while high-growth firms face similar pressures to monitor costs. HR outsourcing presents the option of cost reduction and the choice to hold or release control of selected HR activities. The choice depends on whether an activity is deemed a core competency within the HR department.

The global imperative for outsourcing accelerates as firms evolve from sellers of products and services abroad to setting up operations in foreign countries and staffing those operations with host country or third party nationals. Several HR executives in our study described needs related to moving a global workforce across geographical boundaries. Harmonizing pay and benefit packages as well as complying with local laws demands specialized expertise. Larger vendors that focus on compensation and benefits offer these specialized services and deliver expertise built on experience and concentration in particular regions of the world.

Increased competition, both domestic and international, emphasizes the value-added role of products and services. Firms that subscribe to the balanced scorecard approach to measuring effectiveness look not only at financial measures of firm success, but also at customer and employee measures of service quality.[6] General Electric's CEO Jack Welch captures best the balanced scorecard approach to measuring business effectiveness. He pays attention to only three measures of firm effectiveness—cash flow, customer satisfaction, and employee satisfaction.[7] If HR departments are to be responsible to both internal and external customers, they must look for ways to improve the quality and responsiveness of their services. Proponents argue that outsourcing offers HR an option to satisfy competing demands for improved service and responsiveness at a reasonable cost.

Strategically, outsourcing provides HR departments with a tool for producing competitive advantage for the firm. Outsourcing for the sake of outsourcing or to imitate competitors offers no basis for sustainable competitive advantage. Operationally, many firms are pursuing low-hanging fruit by choosing, for example, to outsource benefits administration with a vendor that provides the latest in automated technology. Because all firms have access to these vendors, no firm achieves any discernible advantage over the others.

To the extent that outsourcing decisions are a part of a larger plan to restructure the HR department, refocus activities, and/or redeploy HR resources, competitive advantage is attainable. Firms that redeploy HR generalists to serve key divisions or business units of the organization can transform HR into a service role. Such a transformation serves as a source of competitive advantage for the firm. These new, service-quality cultures are not easy to build and sustain, particularly among established, traditional, or entrenched HR departments. Strategically, HR outsourcing decisions can potentially be part of a larger pattern of responses designed to deliver hard-to-imitate, hard-to-substitute, value-added services that enhance the value and quality of the firm's products and services.[8]

Operational Rationales for Outsourcing

STAGE OF EVOLUTION OF THE HR FUNCTION

HR outsourcing is sometimes driven by the evolution of the HR function within the organization. We found very extensive outsourcing in some young or small companies where the HR function was relatively undeveloped or was being restructured. These activities were essentially confined to administering compensation and benefits, record keeping, and applicant screening. Extensive outsourcing was used to quickly fill voids in critical HR capabilities by purchasing services from outside the organization. In such circumstances, outsourcing has the critical advantage of providing HR capabilities while not adding to HR headcount. One executive mentioned that HR outsourcing allowed the company to do more without additional staff or with fewer staff. Although some companies with highly developed HR functions have outsourced the entire HR function, none of our interviewees described such extreme outsourcing.[9]

We found extensive HR outsourcing among some very large companies, a relationship consistent with findings in a recent survey of workplace trends.[10] However, in other very large companies, we found only limited outsourcing, such as the almost universal outsourcing of 401(k) retirement plans and some recruitment activities. Some interviewees explained that existing scale effects in their large companies eliminated any potential savings from outsourcing, and that shared services companies within their corporate families sometimes provided similar services. Thus, the relationship between the evolutionary stage of HR development and outsourcing rationales or extent of outsourcing is complex.

NEED FOR SPECIALIZED EXPERTISE

As one highly respected senior HR executive stated: "You outsource when someone else can perform the activity better than you." Another said that companies should ask, "What is it we will never be experts at or shouldn't spend time doing?" These attitudes are consistent with the results of a recent survey that identified vendor expertise, along with time savings, as the most frequently cited rationales for outsourcing HR activities.[11] The demand for specialized expertise is not surprising, given the growing complexity of HR tasks and the decline in staff HR specialists resulting from organizational downsizing. HR specialists, many in their 40s or 50s with relatively high salaries, become tempting targets for cost cutting, and many have been downsized or offered options for early retirement.[12] Companies that have undergone repeated downsizings have dismantled staffing functions and lost requisite expertise. As companies require more specialized HR expertise, their best alternative is to hire external HR vendors to perform activities that were formerly performed in-house. Some executives argued that in tight markets for HR services, such as for specialty searches or recruiting, they cannot permanently employ the best specialists. Specialists such as executive search experts can earn more by operating their own search firms.

Agents and consultants can also provide special knowledge of regulatory compliance criteria and regulators gained from experience and personal friendships formed during prior employment with governmental agencies.[13] A consultant who has worked for the Office of Federal Contract Compliance can guide a company through a difficult compliance problem based on knowledge of the regulatory criteria that federal agents apply. Outside vendors can be more objective than internal staff members in conducting training program evaluations. Furthermore, when the HR function lacks credibility with the company's senior management, evaluations or research performed by outside vendors perceived to have expertise and objectivity are given more credibility.

HR INFORMATION TECHNOLOGY

Innovations in HR information technology also influence outsourcing practices. Many outside vendors are installing integrated or enterprise software, such as PeopleSoft or SAP, with human resource information system (HRIS) components. Most HR executives cited recent or planned conversions to new, fully integrated information systems that would simplify the transaction components of HR services. These systems enable HR executives to make informed business decisions on both operational and strategic issues. HR information can also be downloaded for processing by outside vendors. HRIS implementation is one of the driving forces for restructuring jobs, processes, and entire departments, including the HR department. Although outsourcing to gain technological capabilities is an operational necessity, upgrading the HRIS has an important strategic implication. As one HR executive stated: "We had to rethink all of our processes when we began working with the HRIS consultant to begin our conversion to a new information platform." From a different perspective, outsourcing provides another means for obtaining the benefits of technology, particularly in organizational cultures that emphasize cost control. According to one interviewee: "Outsourcing provides access to technology without [the requirement of] purchasing it."

TIME PRESSURES

HR outsourcing enables executives to cope with time-sensitive issues and competing demands. One HR executive outsourced recruiting when the company had 50 openings and he did not have time to hire or train a recruiter. The training function provides another example of how time pressures often do not allow internal development of trainers or program design. Vendors can supply generic programs, such as diversity training, that can be customized and delivered quickly.[14]

COST SAVINGS

The expectation that outsourcing will cut costs is consistent with the strategic management view of competitive resource allocation. This perspective holds that all activities unrelated to strategic core competencies should be outsourced since economies of scale allow specialized vendors to provide services at lower costs. One interviewee observed that the fees charged by vendors decreased because of increasing economies of scale. Another senior HR executive commented: "We gain credibility with senior management when we demonstrate that we can manage budget and headcount."

In contrast to the conventional wisdom about cost savings, a recent study of information technology found that efficient vendor management practices drive costs down more than economies of scale.[15] As noted earlier, several HR executives from large companies reported that, because of the magnitude of their internal HR operations, specialized vendors were unable to achieve greater economies of scale and cost savings. One interviewee observed that outsourcing produces no cost savings when only two or three vendors dominate a specialized market. As noted, cost savings are often an important rationale for outsourcing, but another interviewee warned: "Don't let cost be the absolute driver!"

VENDOR EFFICIENCIES AND SERVICE

For some activities, the decision to outsource is straightforward. For example, many large mutual fund or financial services companies can administer 401(k) retirement plans competently and at very low cost. Decisions are similarly straightforward for benefits administration such as relocation services, unemployment compensation, Consolidated Omnibus Budget Reconciliation Act (COBRA), and medical claims processing. For specialized vendors, these activities are their core business and constitute their strategic focus. As a result, they produce high service and customer satisfaction.[16] One HR executive suggested that exceptional service is another reason his company outsourced services: "We are willing to pay more for a vendor service because we are buying specialized expertise and exceptional service."

On the other hand, several executives claimed that better service could not be obtained with most outsourced services. They argued that the pursuit of cost savings often resulted in the loss of service quality. For example, one interviewee reported unsatisfactory experience in two attempts to outsource unemployment claims because "the vendors had an exploit-the-employees philosophy."

FIRMS' HR CAPACITY

According to our interviewees, HR activities are occasionally outsourced because of such extraordinary circumstances as an activity level that is too overwhelming for in-house personnel to perform. Extreme demands for services take place during natural disasters or strikes. Planning for an anticipated pilots' strike in 1997, American Airlines made arrangements with an outside vendor to handle COBRA processing for some 80,000 employees.[17] Outsourcing is also used when companies are operating at full capacity and do not have additional staff to handle increased activity. Because such levels of business will eventually decline, companies may prefer to outsource some activities rather than hire more staff. This approach is similar to using overtime to handle peak workloads, instead of hiring new permanent employees. One interviewee summarized this point by stating that "we use outsourcing to handle peak demand, and staff only for the baseline."

BENEFITS OF AN AGENT IN NEGOTIATIONS

Outsourcing gives firms the benefits of using agents in negotiations. Several HR executives championed the use of third parties or agents for executive-level searches. Use of a search firm to find qualified candidates and to conduct salary and benefit negotiations reduces an HR executive's involvement in the negotiation phase. This can be advantageous since, as one executive said, "Negotiations [by search firms] don't leave [the company's] fingerprints when it's the search firm that is the bad guy. You don't want your new boss leaving bruises on you."

REDUCTION OF LIABILITY OR RISK

Outsourcing an HR activity can reduce liability and risk, which is critical for smaller companies that do not have the resources to employ staff specialists who are fully informed on the legal requirements of HR programs. For example, substantial expertise is required to insure that a retirement program conforms to the Employee Retirement Income Security Act (ERISA). As a result, smaller companies sometimes outsource the administration of their entire retirement programs. Employee assistance programs (EAPs) and drug testing are also frequently outsourced regardless of company size, thus reducing legal liability associated with divulgence of confidential information.

Strategic Rationales for Outsourcing

STRATEGIC FOCUS

HR departments often lack a clear strategic focus because they are preoccupied with operational activities. Outsourcing nonstrategic activities permits HR departments to move away from routine administration toward a more strategic role.[18] As one HR executive said: "I like doing the value-added strategic aspects of my job, not the administrative, paper-pushing pieces." But outsourcing is only one component of the strategic transformation process. One senior vice president for HR advised: "It is difficult to change your role to strategic by dumping activities via outsourcing. It is easier if you are already in the strategic role." Numerous executives wanted to shift more of the HR responsibilities to the line managers and to transform the HR staff to an internal consultant role. By considering the old HR function as a candidate for outsourcing, the

executives explicitly redefined the roles of their HR staffs. Another HR executive stated that HR departments are more likely to stick to their knitting when they perform only those activities related to the implementation of their companies' strategies, rather than less essential functions.

DECENTRALIZED STRUCTURE

HR outsourcing is associated with decentralized or matrix structures and extensive internal networking. One of the highest levels of HR outsourcing we found was in a significantly matrixed telecommunications organization. The company, which relies heavily on internal networking and deemphasizes departmental barriers, has a very informal culture with a heavy emphasis on flexibility. Its decentralized structure, lean staffing, and informal, fast-paced culture is consistent with its outsourcing arrangements. The firm's HR executive explained that, except for benefits and compensation outsourcing, she does not sign contracts with HR outsourcing vendors. Instead, she relies on trust in established relationships. Her company also uses vendors that operate internationally to supply the same service to its operations throughout the world.

Decentralization of the HR function through redeployment of some of its assets to operating units is another strategic rationale for outsourcing. By outsourcing specialized services, the HR function can redeploy HR expertise from the corporate level to provide HR services at the operational level. Such generalists help operating managers access HR services, including those provided by vendor specialists. One senior HR executive emphasized using HR generalists who know the business to manage outsourcing relationships because they enhance the perception and reality of HR as a true business partner. Another HR executive stated: "HR generalists view their role differently when they sit in the decision maker's chair instead of the chair next to it." For these generalists, knowing where to get a problem solved is more important than having specialized HR knowledge.

REDUCTION OF BUREAUCRACY AND CULTURE CHANGE

An important rationale for outsourcing is to develop less bureaucratic HR departments, which are often criticized for the constraints they impose on operational flexibility.[19] As one interviewee stated, successful outsourcing vendors emphasize customer service that permits the HR executive to deal with only the most extreme cases. Outsourcing also replaces bureaucracy with market forces. As one senior vice president stated, outsourcing allows his firm to "harness the power of the bidding process." Because of their size and focus, outsourcing firms are often more nimble and agile, and can deliver services more quickly than in-house HR staff.

INTERNAL POLITICS

Downsizing has frequently required HR departments to share the pain of widespread organizational restructuring by reducing their staffs. One HR executive stated that outsourcing and staff reductions made his department "look less bloated and more like a real business partner." Under such circumstances, maintaining specialized in-house expertise is nearly impossible. One interviewee claimed that his medium-sized company obtained better HR staff utilization and flexibility by employing only HR generalists rather than specialists. For specialized HR services, he relied on vendors. Some of the largest companies made similar arguments for HR generalists.

Staff reduction is often an important consideration for companies in the evolutionary phase when senior management is skeptical about the value of a more comprehensive HR function.[20] In addition, economy of scale effects from in-house HR activities are virtually impossible for smaller companies to achieve.

One interviewee argued that an unspoken rationale for outsourcing is that it enables an executive to cover up unsatisfactory performance. Sometimes an HR executive can reduce personal risk, at least in the short run, by outsourcing a troublesome activity. If problems persist, blame can be attributed to the vendor, who can be replaced.

MANAGEMENT AND ORGANIZATIONAL DEVELOPMENT

One HR executive wryly suggested that "outsourcing is the antidote to inward thinking." Another said that outsourcing stimulated his thought processes and kept him in contact with consultants who had current and specialized information that could accelerate his progress on the learning curve. Outsourcing provides a big picture perspective, as one HR executive exclaimed, because "sometimes I can't

see the forest for the trees." Another senior HR executive compared HR outsourcing with genetics, arguing that the use of vendors improves the HR gene pool and produces new capabilities and out-of-the-box thinking. A senior executive responsible for executive compensation alternates outsourcing and insourcing approaches to enhance organizational learning. After a year in which he outsources the activity to learn the latest techniques, he insources it the next year for cost savings, and then outsources again the next year to learn more. When HR activities are outsourced, however, fewer career development opportunities exist for the HR staff. When only a limited number of activities are performed in-house, broad or general HR experience is more difficult to obtain.

Outsourcing Outcomes

From these interviews we learned that most good reasons for outsourcing translated into advantages when outsourcing remained in effect for extended periods. Several HR executives mentioned that lower HR costs were achieved, along with higher service quality, and that these activities enhanced HR focus on areas directly contributing to firm success. Some by-products or unintended benefits were realignment or redeployment of internal HR expertise, development of negotiation and broker skills, and enhanced credibility of the HR function. Another benefit was risk and uncertainty absorption by the HR vendor, especially where rapid changes in technology or regulatory issues occurred. One interviewee suggested that the use of HR outsourcing is a way to "syndicate the risk" when the organization cannot stay current on all the new developments in the HR field. One measure of satisfaction with outsourcing was reflected in the comments of a senior HR executive who views any area of HR as an outsourcing opportunity, and who feared that "my replacement will tell me that my job is too easy!"

However, not all outsourcing experiences were positive, and one interviewee stated: "Outsourcing is not the silver bullet." Some HR executives found that outsourcing does not always produce significant cost savings, and in one case, costs actually increased. When HR vendor service quality is unsatisfactory, vendor switching costs and long-term vendor contracts block immediate improvements. One interviewee cautioned that when the primary motivation for outsourcing is cost reduction instead of superior service at a reasonable cost, "senior management often gets what it pays for." Outsourcing can disrupt the firm's culture if the vendor becomes a noticeable third party instead of a seamless extension of the HR function. The HR department's loss of skills or competencies can produce excessive reliance or dependence on the vendor. Many interviewees cautioned against outsourcing activities that could remove or distance the HR function from employees. Another interviewee observed that when HR vendor relations go sour, in many instances the people working for the vendor lack critical expertise and a customer-service focus, or fail to take the interests of their client into account when delivering their services.

On balance, virtually all the HR executives we interviewed expressed satisfaction with their outsourcing arrangements because the benefits outweighed the costs and produced a more robust HR function. Based on their evaluative comments, we have developed the following guidelines for successful HR outsourcing.

Guidelines for HR Outsourcing

Table 1 provides a summary of guidelines using categories that follow a chronology similar to the outsourcing phases identified by Professor Scott Lever.[21]

MAKING THE OUTSOURCING DECISION

Except for such core competencies as employee relations or performance appraisal, most HR activities should be subject to outsourcing. Immunity from outsourcing should result only when the company's competitive position will be compromised by a loss of specialized expertise. Insufficient focus on retaining HR activities that support core competencies can have unintended consequences. One such consequence is HR anorexia, which occurs when key HR activities are hollowed out of the old HR department, resulting in lost capability and diminished customer service quality. According to one highly regarded HR executive, outsourcing is a truth serum for what is going on in HR, and it has a potential role in providing competitive advantage. As a result of the downsizing-induced malaise affecting some companies, some HR executives are making the mistake of outsourcing key activities. Several HR executives identified core areas that should not be outsourced.

The interviewees were unanimous in their advice not to outsource core competencies such as labor relations, employee relations, or performance management functions. Effectiveness in these functions requires consistency, trust, an understanding of long-term effects in relationships and control of confidential information. Thus they should not be outsourced. One interviewee told us that his company keeps the people-to-people activities in-house because management wants "someone from the company who can do something about the problem, and we can't outsource the mechanism [employee relations] that communicates to employees that we care about them." In addition, although fewer interviewees agreed, many executives would not outsource compensation or training design. Because HR departments run the risk of losing their identities with extreme levels of outsourcing, a mixture of outsourcing and in-house activities seems optimal in many circumstances.

The need to preserve confidentiality and an appropriate amount of control are important considerations, particularly for activities involving sensitive information. For example, in executive searches some companies outsource only the research needed to identify names of potential candidates. After the vendor supplies the names, the company performs the remainder of the recruitment activity. Although many companies outsource wage and salary surveys or job evaluations, they often retain in-house wage and salary adjustments, performance-based pay incentives, or other sensitive aspects of compensation. Similarly, a defense contractor may choose not to outsource some selection activities because staffing specialists require security clearances. Nonetheless, the pressure to produce cost savings appears to override important sensitivity considerations. Even such sensitive functions as EAPs are outsourced primarily because of cost pressures, or to reduce risk and legal liability.

When making decisions to outsource HR activities, executives need to recognize that performance is typically the most important consideration. One interviewee noted the importance of the service quality his staff provides and the direct impact on his own job security: "If I don't support the organization, I'll get in trouble quickly. This may be more important than headcount or budget." The president of an HR service firm mentioned that when an executive comes to him seeking cost savings, he tells the executive that his is not the right firm for

Making the Outsourcing Decision

- Don't allow sacred cows. Except for core competencies, all other HR activities should be considered as candidates for outsourcing.
- Determine whether the desire to outsource an activity is driven by its low contribution to core competencies, influences from the external environment, or poor management of the activity.
- Recognize that performance is more important than low HR department headcounts or lower costs.
- Beware of vendors that supply off-the-shelf solutions that do not fit the company's needs.
- Avoid excessive reliance on vendors.
- Decide how much control is needed for various HR activities and whether control can be retained with outsourcing.
- Identify critical personal benefits of outsourcing.

Selecting and Negotiating with Outsourcing Vendors

- Assign a high weighting to vendors' knowledge of the industry.
- Perform reference checks of potential vendors.
- Understand the costs involved in switching vendors for outsourced services.

Managing the Outsourcing Transition

- Expect the internal HR team to resist outsourcing and develop ways of managing this resistance.
- Anticipate conflict and develop a plan for resolving it in a manner that supports the relationship with the vendor.
- Anticipate changes to HR culture and careers.

Managing Vendor Relationships

- Develop long-term relationships with outsourcing vendors where such continuity is critical.
- Develop staff members to become effective managers of vendor relationships.
- Maintain stability of the in-house staff who oversee vendor relationships and understand the performance expectations originally negotiated.
- Require competitive bidding for each outsourced service at regular intervals.

Monitoring and Evaluating Vendor Performance

- Establish expectations, measures, and reporting relationships up front for both outsourcing parties.
- Insist on high quality performance by HR vendors.
- Insist on accurate and frequent status reporting by HR vendors and immediate notification when problems arise.
- Establish performance targets for vendors with the assistance of outside consultants when necessary.
- Enhance vendor performance through performance standards.
- Consider internal customer surveys to evaluate vendor performance.

the job. Problems can result from a shortsighted emphasis on cost savings, which may not be realized if employees lost confidence in vendor services or when vendors supply off-the-shelf solutions that do not fit the company's needs.

Quality is particularly important when services are provided for highly skilled or educated employees who are in great demand. A pharmaceutical company that went to great lengths to attract and retain a highly educated workforce rejected most outsourcing alternatives and any potential associated savings. Executives felt that retention of world-class talent required pampering through personalized service and error-free administration of its generous benefit package. They also felt that outsourcing would be inconsistent with their red-carpet treatment of employees and the company's culture. Furthermore, HR executives might lose direct feedback on the quality of benefit services. In a few small to medium-sized companies, we found only limited outsourcing, while some customer-intensive HR activities in the benefits areas were retained to preserve cultures focusing on employee welfare.

HR executives must also exercise caution to avoid becoming overly dependent on vendors for essential personnel services that cannot be performed competently by other vendors. Competitors could pirate services, for example, placing a company at a disadvantage. Reliance on a single vendor means that learning accrues to the vendor—not to the client organization. Thus, organizational learning cannot be captured or adapted into other capabilities.

SELECTING AND NEGOTIATING WITH OUTSOURCING VENDORS

Decision makers selecting vendors should, in the words of one HR executive, "treat the selection as you would when conducting due diligence during a planned acquisition." The executive also noted that selection criteria should include a high criterion weighting for vendors' knowledge of the industry because HR practices differ across industries. Thus, reference checks are important. Even when a large outsourcing firm has a good overall reputation, there is no guarantee that its specialty areas are of uniformly high quality. HR executives must also understand the costs involved in switching vendors for outsourced services.[22] For some activities, high switching costs can lead to weak power bases in subsequent negotiations with vendors. Furthermore, firms frequently enter into bad contracts with vendors and then find terminating the agreements extremely difficult.[23]

MANAGING THE OUTSOURCING TRANSITION

Since HR outsourcing entails change, executives must be prepared to manage resistance mounted by the internal HR team, especially specialists in functions retained within the company who may perceive only limited opportunities for upward mobility. Executives also need to be aware of the impact of outsourcing on the staff's sense of job security, loyalty, and organizational commitment. Loss of job security and loyalty can lead to decreased productivity and other dysfunctional actions, and can have severe consequences for the organization.

Companies contemplating an outsourcing relationship should anticipate conflict with the vendor and develop a plan for resolving it.[24] One interviewee who provides legal services to corporate clients said problems often arise because of lack of vendor competency and the failure of the vendor to represent fully the interests of the client. Another HR executive warned that hasty outsourcing arrangements usually produce unsatisfactory results. Thus, it is important to set clear expectations at the outset to create safeguards that permit termination of the contract for noncompliance. Clarifying expectations at the outset can produce a healthy alliance in which each party is motivated to work through problems. Terminating vendor contracts is not easy because replacement vendors are often unavailable on short notice. Bringing the service back in-house is also not always feasible in the short run.[25] Problems sometimes arise even when the service performed by the vendor is good. For example, when the vendor's employees perform excellent services in-house, the host company may have an incentive to buy out the vendor's operations. Specifying the conditions for such a buy-out before the service is initiated can eliminate related problems.

MANAGING VENDOR RELATIONSHIPS

HR executives should be prepared to develop long-term relationships with outsourcing vendors where continuity is critical, as with actuarial firms and search firms. In the case of executive search firms, one interviewee stated that a long-term relationship is conducive to the vendor's learning the company's culture to achieve better employee-organization fit. Also, if competitive intelligence has been obtained ethically as a byproduct of the in-house search process, alternative intelligence sources must be established when search activities are outsourced. To the extent that long-term relationships exist and conflicts of interest are avoided for the contracting search firm, there may be a willingness to allow some capturing of intelligence. Moreover, some vendors supply competitive intelligence as part of their normal services. On the other hand, some companies require vendors to sign nondisclosure agreements that prevent them from revealing such information.

Even long-term vendors must understand that work is awarded on the basis of performance, not relationships. One interviewee made the comparison of HR vendors to at-will employees as a reminder that no vendors should ever believe that they have a non-expiring contract. Executives should choose vendors that deliver the right service at the right price. While firms sometimes need special long-term relationships, these are not required for all activities. HR executives should require competitive bidding for each outsourced service at regular time intervals, such as every three years.

In addition, outsourcing requires companies to develop managers of vendor relationships. While talent for managing outsourcing relationships may exist even one or two levels below vice president, it is not always present. When it is not, executives should assign capable staff members to teach negotiating skills to experienced sales or engineering managers who perform these activities on a regular basis. Several HR executives noted that they learned how to outsource by "jumping into the hip pockets" of line managers with experience in outsourcing some of their own activities.

MONITORING AND EVALUATING PERFORMANCE

HR executives should communicate performance expectations and establish measurement criteria from the outset. Vendor and customer expectations must be identified and articulated, along with the performance measures and reporting routines. Executives should insist on honest and frequent reporting by HR vendors and on immediate notification when problems arise. Common measures of vendor performance include cost-per-hire and turnover rates. Vendor performance is enhanced by performance standards, and outside consultants can help establish performance targets for vendors. For example, an actuary can provide advice on performance targets for health care coverage. Similarly, a consulting firm can help identify the top money managers needed to handle investments for company-administered pension funds. Vendor performance is also enhanced by the use of performance standards in which savings, for example, from reduced workers' compensation claims, are shared with the vendor. Similarly, the performance of HMOs can be enhanced by sliding scale standards that share risk and cost savings with the HMO. One company's experience in competing for a Baldrige National Quality Program award taught it how to better select and partner with vendors, including HR vendors.

Because outsourcing is often motivated by a need for better service, HR executives should insist on high quality performance by HR vendors. Unlike employees, vendors do not have to be paid until contracted levels of service quality are provided. Staff members charged with monitoring the quality of vendor performance have the option of using internal customer surveys.[26]

Evolving Issues and Conclusions

HR outsourcing is a byproduct of the restructuring of HR departments underway in organizations in virtually every industry, regardless of size. Some HR departments are restructuring because of growth, mergers, acquistions, or top executive turnover, others to deliver better service at a reasonable cost to multiple stakeholders. Executives are asking how they can provide valued services to both internal and external customers in light of scarce organizational resources. The old HR staffing rule of one HR staff member for every 100 employees is not as meaningful today as a measure of HR efficiency or effectiveness as in the past.

HR outsourcing is consistent with the business partner role that internal service staffs are attempting to assume. HR is a service that is coproduced with line managers and employees. HR executives are being asked to help provide business solutions for employee and customer problems. HR executives are being challenged to develop core competencies to help formulate and deliver these business solutions. HR departments are being challenged to change their bureaucratic culture and to be customer-oriented and deliver exceptional service. Outsourcing can be used in conjunction with an internal HR focus on core competencies to produce these solution, especially when that means partnering with an HR vendor.

Information technologies are fueling the growth of new organizational forms, such as networks and highly decentralized organizations. The outsourcing business has tapped into these technologies and is serving a growing demand for technology-related services such as HRIS. Outsourcing provides support for the new HR role and structure of redesigned organizations. Restructured HR departments will continue to increase their use of outside service providers.[27] In restructured HR departments, HR generalists will be challenged to develop consultant and brokering skills that identify client needs and negotiate and manage vendor relations to meet business needs. HR professionals must discover a set of core competencies to be retained and services to be provided by outsourcing vendors.

The dynamics of outsourcing are complex and paradoxical. The relationship between HR department evolution and outsourcing is anything but linear. Some HR departments are more evolved than others and employ strategic rationales for outsourcing. Less-evolved departments resist change and embrace outsourcing in a reactive mode and for short-term considerations. Small and large organizations alike have adopted outsourcing. Some firms seek outsourcing to replace whole jobs, functions, or departments. Others unbundle HR services and retain some functions in-house while brokering others to vendors. Some firms outsource HR services with no motivation to bring them back in-house. Other firms in-source previously outsourced services because learning is accuring to the vendor, or because of dissatisfaction with the service or recognition that the HR activity is a core competency.

The choice to outsource some or all of the HR domain is becoming increasingly likely for most firms. Macroeconomic and environmental forces have compelled organizations to restructure and reexamine all management processes, including HR management. Little empirical research exists to guide informed decision making.[28] Our purpose here has been to identify the critical issues confronting executives who must choose which HR outsourcing path to follow.

Endnotes

1. We obtained data from intensive interviews of 26 senior HR executives and professionals from 25 organizations. To obtain a broad sampling of companies with a variety of approaches to outsourcing practices, we purposely selected large and small companies from a variety of industries. With one exception, interviews were conducted between February 1997 and March 1998. All three researchers were present for more than 60 percent of the interviews. Fewer than 25 percent of the interviews were conducted by only one of the researchers. Our sample organizations ranged in size from *Fortune* 500 to smaller employers having fewer than 200 employees. In addition, we included a few small HR service providers with a small number of employees. Industries represented in the sample were airlines, electronics-semiconductors, engineering-construction, entertainment, food services, HR services, legal services, manufacturing, petroleum, pharmaceuticals, publishing, railroads, search firms, specialty retailers, telecommunications, and utilities. We interviewed one executive vice president, three senior vice presidents of HR, 11 vice presidents of HR, four directors of HR, one director of learning services, two HR managers, three presidents, managing directors, or owners of their own personnel services firms, and one employment attorney. Nineteen of the interviewees were men and seven were women.

2. Our interviews followed a semistructured format developed from the authors' reviews of practitioner and academic literature. Each executive interview took approximately one hour. We revised the format as we conducted the interviews when comprehensive responses on the initial issues were obtained and as new issues emerged. Our interview and analytical procedures are similar to the "template" approach described by B. F. Crabtree and W. L. Miller (eds.). 1992. *Doing qualitative research.* Newbury Park, CA: Sage Publications. This approach is comparable to content analysis in that the text is analyzed with the application of content categories or themes. Template analysis varies from content analysis in that a qualitative interpretation of themes is employed, rather than a statistical analysis. Our analytical approach placed substantial emphasis on determining the range of practices and identifying outliers because of our interest in unique practices.

3. Carney, W. 1997. Outsourcing HR and benefits: Navigating the right course. *Benefits and Compensation International,* 26 (7): 15–23; Directors and boards, 1997. *Business Process Engineering,* 21(3): 37–43; Weinfurter, D. J. 1997. Project outsourcing offers a career alternative. *HR News,* 16(12), 14; Jones, M. 1996. Four trends to reckon with. *HR Focus,* 73(7): 22–23; *HR Focus,* 1997. Outsourcing of HR continues, 74(3): 2; *HRMagazine,* 1997. HR today and tomorrow: 1997 survey of human resource trends, 42(8): 33–41.

4. Ulrich, D. 1997. Judge me more by my future than my past. *Human Resource Management,* 36(1): 5–8.

5. Byrne, J. A. 1994. The pain of downsizing. *Business Week,* May 9:61.

6. Kaplan, R. S. & Norton, D. P. 1996. *The balanced scorecard: translating strategy into action.* Boston: Harvard Business School Press; Beatty, R. W. & Schneier, C. E. 1997. New HR roles impact organizational performance: From partners to players. *Human Resource Management,* 36(1): 29–37.

7. Tichy, N. M. & Sherman, S. 1993. *Control your own destiny or someone else will.* New York: Currency Doubleday, p. 246.

8. Pfeffer, J. 1997. Pitfalls on the road to measurement: The dangerous liaison of human resources with the ideas of accounting and finance. *Human Resource Management,* 36(3), 357–365; Pfeffer, J. 1994. *Competitive advantage through people: Unleashing the power of the work force.* Boston: Harvard Business School Press; Huselid, M. A. 1995. The impact of human resource management practices on turnover, productivity, and corporate financial performance. *Academy of Management Journal,* 38: 635–672; Arthur, J. B. 1994. Effects of human resource systems on manufacturing performance and turnover. *Academy of Management Journal,* 37: 670–687.

9. Seely, R. S. 1993. HR redesigns for optimizing effectiveness. *HRMagazine*, 35(11): 44–46; Laabs, J. J. 1993. Why HR is turning to outsourcing. *Personnel Journal*, 72(9), 92–101.

10. *Training*, 1997. 1997 industry report: Workplace trends. October: 61–65.

11. Harkins, P. J., Brown, S. M., & Snllivan, R. 1995. Shining new light on a growing trend. *HRMagazine*, 40(12): 75–79.

12. Hoffman, E. B. 1976. *Unionization of professional societies.* New York: Conference Board; Raelin, J. A. 1987. Job security for professionals. *Personnel*, 64(7): 40–47.

13. Rubin, J. A. & Sander, F. E. A. 1988. When should we use agents? Direct versus representative negotiation. *Negotiation Journal*, October: 395–401.

14. Kaeter, M. 1995. An outsourcing primer. *Training and Development Journal*, 49(11): 20–25.

15. Lacity, M. C., Willcocks, L. P., & Feeny, D. F. 1996. The value of selective IT sourcing. *Sloan Management Review*, 37: 13–25.

16. Marinaccio, L. 1994. Outsourcing: A strategic tool for managing human resources. *Employee Benefits Journal*, March, 19: 39–42.

17. Allison, J., vice president of human resources, American Airlines. Address to the Human Resource Round Table, Texas Christian University, Fort Worth, TX, April 15, 1997.

18. Marinaccio, L., op cit.

19. Cantoni, C. J. 1995. A waste of human resources. *Wall Street Journal*, May 15: A18.

20. Stewart, T. A. 1996. Taking on the last bureaucracy. *Fortune*, January 15: 105; Stewart, T. A. 1996. Human resources bites back. *Fortune*, May 13: 175–176; Ellig, B. 1996. SHRM rebuts *Fortune* article. *HR News*, 15(2): 5.

21. Lever, S. 1997. An analysis of managerial motivations behind outsourcing practices in human resources. *Human Resources Planning*, 20(2): 37–47.

22. Mullin, R. 1996. Managing the outsourced enterprise. *Journal of Business Strategy*, 17(4): 28–38.

23. Cascio, W. F. 1993. Downsizing: What do we know? What have we learned? *The Academy of Management Executive*, 7(1): 95–104; Cook, D. S. & Ferris, G. R. 1986. Strategic human resource management and firm effectiveness in industries experiencing decline. *Human Resource Management*, 25(3): 441–457; Laabs, J. J. 1993. Successful outsourcing depends on critical factors. *Personnel Journal*, 72(10): 55.

24. Lacity, M. C., Willcocks, L. P., & Feeny, D. F. op cit.

25. Kaeter, M. op cit.

26. Lacity, M. C., Willcocks, I. P., & Feeny, D. F. op cit.

27. Miles, R. E. & Snow, C. C. 1992. *Fit, failure, and the hall of fame: How companies succeed or fail.* New York: Free Press; Miles, R. E. & Snow, C. C. 1995. The new network firm: A spherical structure based on a human investment philosophy. *Organizational Dynamics*, 23: 5–18.

28. Lever, S. op cit.

Work Redesign and Performance Management in Times of Downsizing

A. S. Evangelista and Lisa A. Burke, *Business Horizons*

The decade of the 1990s yielded a false sense of security among management and employees that the economy was boundless. However, the topic in many copy rooms, cubicles, and break areas today is downsizing, or the inevitability of more corporate bloodletting. Executives are rallying back to the lines to reengage, where they sense little time for streamlining, reevaluating, or reallocating business processes, tasks, and activities. The reality of the present corporate situation is that many downsizing firms face the immediate challenge of keeping operations going with a minimum number of staff, at least for a short term until the outlook becomes more stable. With layoffs occurring across many industries—the tech sector, retailing, entertainment, manufacturing, and air travel, to name a few—the situation presents an opportunity to address associated issues of downsizing for sensible recovery.

Although management literature has focused on certain aspects of downsizing, such as communication strategies, employee cynicism, stress, potential litigation, morale, retention, and survivor support, one area remains essentially untouched: the effect of reductions in force on employee workloads and the troubling ripple effect on the integrity of performance management systems. Even though the topics of downsizing and performance management each boasts an established practitioner literature base, research at the intersection of these topics remains scant.

Thus, it is our purpose here to help organizations and managers who are operating "in extremis"—doing as much or more but with fewer people—reconfigure work duties and establish a fair performance management process for surviving employees. The framework proposed here is targeted for solution-hungry managers caught in the throes of downsizing organizations who need a solid recipe for work redesign.

Productivity in Downsizing

A recent article in *HR Focus* that summarized data gathered by the Families and Work Institute ("Focus resources now . . ." 2001) reported that corporate downsizings often mean extended hours and a heavier workload for surviving employees. The effects of the resulting stress vary from making more errors to feeling bitter toward coworkers to simply leaving the job altogether. Assuming that companies keep their best employees and managers during downsizing, organizations should theoretically be in a position to perform better. But case studies have shown that productivity often declines. In *The People Side*, by Richard Koonce (1991), Dr. Jackie Greaner refers to the productivity paradox as a source of regression:

> Let's say a corporation decides, for financial reasons, to undertake a downsizing or restructuring to improve its bottom-line profitability and productivity. If it doesn't deal with the "people factors" associated with change—that is, effectively manage the human resources issues that are part of any corporate reorganization—its productivity and profitability will suffer anyway. This is the so-called "productivity paradox." It's quite common in organizations going through transition today.

Such an observation highlights the inadequate attention paid to the "people aspects" of previous organizational restructurings. Clearly, one goal of these types of corporate change must be to provide indubitable improvement in productivity and profitability so that surviving employees remain viable stakeholders in corporate progress. But as Slavin (1994) suggests, "If you eliminate people, the ones who remain will make choices about how to react. The best often leave the company—the brain drain. The rest either work longer or harder, or they just don't do certain tasks."

Many more authors also point out that in corporate downsizings the survivors end up working longer and are heavily taxed with a bigger workload. As a result, morale often goes into the proverbial dumpster. Place the performance management process against this backdrop and it is easy to discern potential problems.

DOWNSIZING AND PERFORMANCE MANAGEMENT DILEMMAS

Consider the following: Caroline has escaped a recent volley of layoffs at her manufacturing firm. The company's dreary situation will likely continue into the foreseeable future and she is concerned about her job security. She has been a superior performer who takes pride in being able to complete all assigned duties well and on time. When the latest cuts trimmed several people from her department and management divided up the work among those who were left, Caroline took over much of the workload of one of the terminated employees. The stress of the current work environment is taking a toll on her and her peers and is beginning to affect her work. Caroline knows that her annual performance appraisal is around the corner and that she has not performed up to her usual potential, although she has tried. There is just too much to do and too little time to get it all done; some tasks never get touched and others are only half-heartedly completed. This once exemplary employee now actually feels she is average, and she is distressed about it. She fears not only that she will be appraised unfairly because she has been asked to do so much more and has done all that she could, but that others might actually get away with task avoidance, something she does not feel comfortable doing.

Michael, Caroline's supervisor, is also under a great deal of stress. Not only is he responsible for his own performance but that of the Quality Assurance Department as well. The department has consistently produced above average performance. But lately Michael has noticed that several of his key employees—employees that he urged be saved from the corporate chopping block—are performing marginally. Several work assignments that absolutely must be done are either late or inadequate. Even employees he relies on the most, such as Caroline, are turning in weaker performances. He also senses they are on the verge of a morale slump as a result of the burgeoning workloads. Performance appraisals

are due in six months and Michael prides himself on being fair and accurate. Given that the departmental workload has increased, however, he feels there will be several challenges to confront.

This scenario illustrates some of the complexities surrounding the fallout from corporate downsizing, especially concerning employee workloads and performance management. Before the company cut heads, Caroline was working at or near her effective capacity—she had the time, opportunity, ability, and energy to be a superior performer. She completed all of her duties and did so in an outstanding manner; plus, she enjoyed her work. Michael regards Caroline as one of his best employees. But left with additional duties to distribute among his remaining employees after the layoffs, he effectively gave her the work of at least two people. He sees her performance faltering, sees her turning in relatively lackluster work and even failing to complete a couple of tasks.

Michael realizes he must now get his group focused appropriately (and quickly) on their new work reality if he is to maintain the unit's performance. He also wants to deliver fair and accurate performance appraisals in the post-downsizing environment. Stepping back, he realizes he needs to first review departmental tasks in this environment to maximize his unit's productivity; then he will be in a better position to evaluate employee performance fairly. Our framework can help him do just that.

Work Redesign

In downsizing situations, it is vital for managers to assess business unit obligations and internal tasks to effectively and fairly manage and balance workloads among remaining employees. Typical problems they may face during employee reductions are: (1) the failure or inability to identify and categorize duties and assignments, (2) the failure to identify when they have over-tasked an employee, and (3) the failure to see when a business unit's demands exceed its capacity.

When a firm enters the downsizing mode, the top managers need to redefine their goals for the restructured company in order to meet the demands of their business environment. According to Slavin, this process also involves examining and identifying the more essential operational tasks. Maintaining that certain tasks are more strategically important than others is consistent with Wright,

McMahan, McCormick, and Sherman (1998), who demonstrated that a focus on the most strategically important tasks in a performance management system will enhance company performance. As such, we propose a process for this important task categorization duty, as shown in **Figure 1**.

FIGURE 1: WORK REDESIGN PROCESS

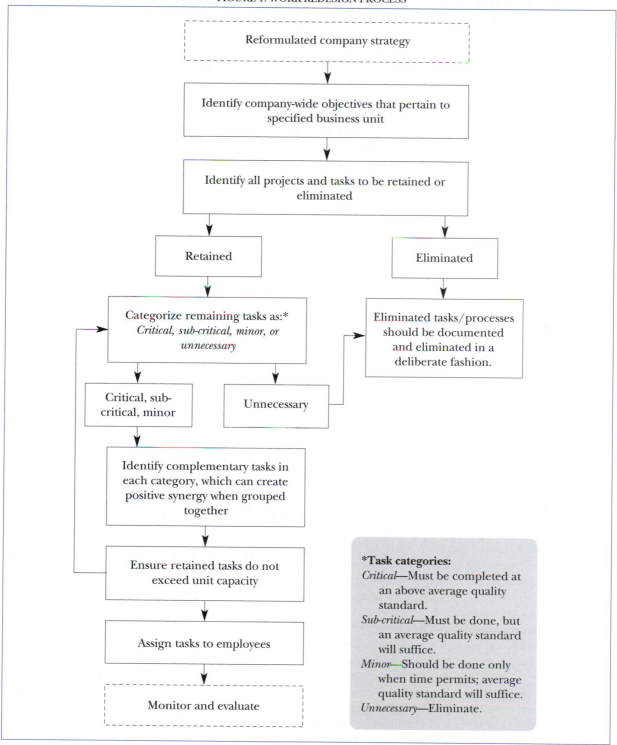

To proceed in this new corporate direction, managers need to identify and categorize all projects and tasks to determine which activities are to be retained and which are to be eliminated. *Critical tasks* are those that enable a company to accomplish its primary organizational objectives; they are essential to maintaining the firm's strategic intent, and must be performed to completion at the highest quality standard. One example from Michael's department is the task of quality control, a vital function that is performed on incoming parts to the department and that requires certain sample inspections to ensure that those parts meet or exceed standards. There is no wiggle room in this function—failure to identify problems could lead to catastrophic results.

A *sub-critical task* is one that needs to be performed, but an average standard of quality will suffice. An example might be a job that is perceived as critical in the near future once the company restabilizes, thus requiring that it be maintained to ensure proficiency when reinstated. All sub-critical duties contribute to the achievement of organizational goals but are just as effective when a bare-bones approach to completion is taken. One example in Michael's department that fits this category is a specific quality monthly report. Prior to the downsizing the report was a work of art. The responsible team member had the opportunity to produce a visually stimulating presentation reporting certain quality assurance data. The data could have been presented just as accurately in a straightforward, "no-frills" report and still would have met the needs of the recipients while taking less than half the time. Another sub-critical example could be maintenance on a piece of test equipment that is not used at current production levels but is likely to become critical when production rebounds.

A *minor task* is one that adds value to the firm but will not hinder operations or organizational goals if left undone. An example would be maintaining workplace tidiness. And an *unnecessary task* is one that can be discarded because it most likely drains needed resources away from the critical or sub-critical tasks—for example, quality inspections of products that have been temporarily ceased until demand picks up again. Denoting such tasks is particularly relevant in a restructured firm, as business goals may have changed. Taking the time to document discarded tasks and the lessons learned may prevent future mistakes and yield valuable information if the company decides to resurrect similar projects.

In most cases, an employee does not need to stop performing critical or sub-critical tasks to advance workplace aesthetics. Because the opportunity to do each task will vary daily, regardless of category, time management skills will be ever-important. Some tasks complement each other and may be more effective when assigned together. This may seem intuitive, but synergy can lead to greater efficiency and productivity. Examples are tasks that require close coordination with another department or specific areas within another department. If Michael's unit has a critical task and some sub-critical and minor ones that all require coordination with the marketing department, then these tasks should be assigned together.

After formulating the work redesign process outlined in Figure 1, we modified our model in response to an interview with Steven Finch, a supervisor at Philips Broadband Networks of Manlius, New York. Mr. Finch said that when his company began to downsize, he knew his department would need to do a task assessment in order to pare down the workload into "necessary" and "unnecessary" components. He requested that each member of his department brainstorm and produce a task list, including all steps necessary to accomplish assigned duties. Then he compared their lists with departmental functions, as conceived in the company's new focus. If certain functions were no longer necessary, he removed them and their corresponding tasks. Finally, he allocated the downsized employees' duties to remaining members to ensure that necessary functions were completed. This approach to task categorization is consistent with Figure 1 and provides some semblance of face validity verification.

Reconceptualizing Performance Management

As Figure 1 shows, then, redesigning work around critical, sub-critical, and minor tasks while eliminating unnecessary ones forms the foundation for performance appraisal content. Using this framework, managers can assess the completion of each type of task, as well as the specified level of quality for each. The output from the work categorization process must be shared with all employees so they have a list of the critical, sub-critical, and minor tasks they are accountable for. These same tasks are then used to drive the performance management process. Employee communication and understanding will be vital to the success of this effort because the manager will formally evaluate the three types of duties as performed by that group of employees.

The manager must evaluate the level of work that was assigned to employees and then assess whether they are performing those duties at the appropriate levels. Because each task has been categorized, the manager can ensure that critical tasks are all being performed to the highest standards, sub-critical tasks to adequate levels for functional requirements to be met, and minor tasks only when possible or as needed. Each employee is then in a much better position to receive a fair and accurate performance appraisal, further removed from problems that occur due to ineffective task assignment after downsizing.

Figure 2 outlines a proposed method for effectively and fairly dealing with employee overload in

FIGURE 2: PERFORMANCE MANAGEMENT IN TASK OVERLOAD SITUATIONS

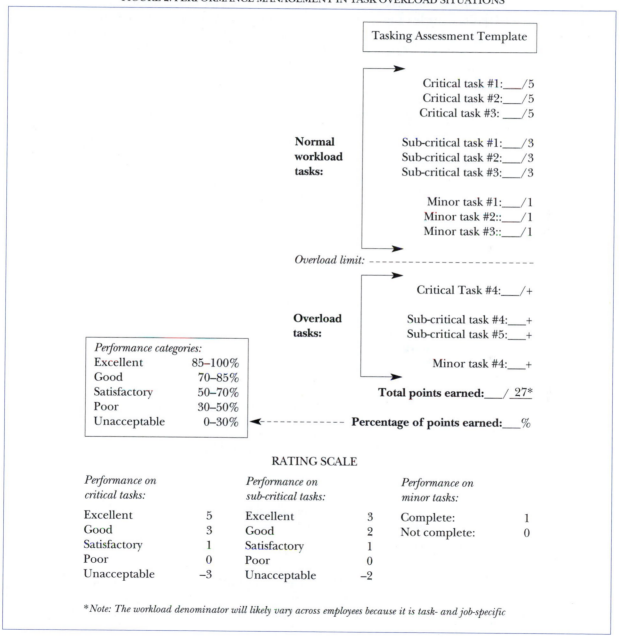

Tasking Assessment Template

Critical task #1:___/5
Critical task #2:___/5
Critical task #3: ___/5

Normal workload tasks:

Sub-critical task #1:___/3
Sub-critical task #2:___/3
Sub-critical task #3:___/3

Minor task #1:___/1
Minor task #2::___/1
Minor task #3::___/1

Overload limit: -

Critical Task #4:___/+

Overload tasks:

Sub-critical task #4:___+
Sub-critical task #5:___+

Minor task #4:___+

Total points earned:___/ 27*

Performance categories:

Excellent	85–100%
Good	70–85%
Satisfactory	50–70%
Poor	30–50%
Unacceptable	0–30%

Percentage of points earned:___%

RATING SCALE

Performance on critical tasks:		*Performance on sub-critical tasks:*		*Performance on minor tasks:*	
Excellent	5	Excellent	3	Complete:	1
Good	3	Good	2	Not complete:	0
Satisfactory	1	Satisfactory	1		
Poor	0	Poor	0		
Unacceptable	–3	Unacceptable	–2		

*Note: The workload denominator will likely vary across employees because it is task- and job-specific

the performance management process. A generic example of translating reengineered workloads for performance management purposes is illustrated, with the goal of assigning each newly sorted task a proper weight. It is essentially a weighted evaluation system, in which managers translate each member's workload into numerical values so that they can evaluate each task and obtain an overall percentage for each employee. More specifically, the manager creates a task assessment, including both normal workload and overload tasks. Various tasks of all types exist, both above and below the "overload limit line," each with a different rating scale because of varying importance. For example, while critical tasks are rated on a scale of 5 (excellent) to –3 (unacceptable), sub-critical tasks are on a 3 to –2 scale, and minor tasks are either complete (1) or incomplete (0). These varying endpoints communicate to employees the relative importance across the task types in the thrust of their daily efforts.

The "total points earned" ratio comprises a numerator (the employee's total earned points across all tasks) and a denominator (the manager's determination of a fair workload). Note that this workload denominator, being task- and job-specific, will likely vary across employees and organizations. Regardless, an employee's total earned points divided by his workload denominator gives a percentage of points earned and places his performance in a category of excellent, good, satisfactory, poor, or unacceptable. Of course, firms can tailor these ratings and categories for their particular needs.

Our suggested process requires managers to acknowledge when employees are overloaded, while subordinates must acknowledge that the manager values the completion of various tasks differently. Examining employee overload based on the *importance* of tasks, and then explaining to the employees what *level* of performance is expected on the various tasks and how the appraisal process will work, allows a

FIGURE 3: EXAMPLE OF PERFORMANCE MANAGEMENT IN TASK OVERLOAD SITUATION

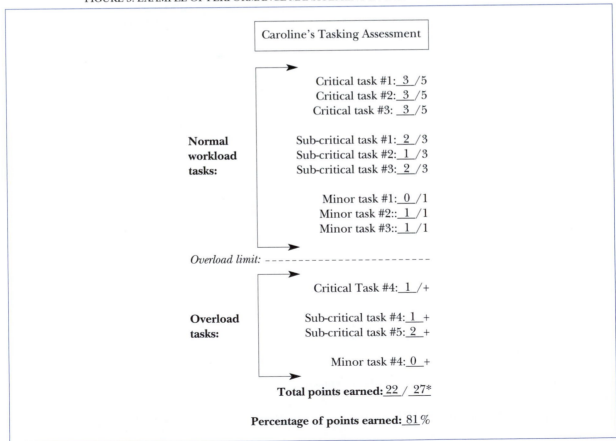

Caroline's Tasking Assessment

Critical task #1: 3 /5
Critical task #2: 3 /5
Critical task #3: 3 /5

Normal workload tasks:

Sub-critical task #1: 2 /3
Sub-critical task #2: 1 /3
Sub-critical task #3: 2 /3

Minor task #1: 0 /1
Minor task #2:: 1 /1
Minor task #3:: 1 /1

Overload limit: -

Overload tasks:

Critical Task #4: 1 /+

Sub-critical task #4: 1 +
Sub-critical task #5: 2 +

Minor task #4: 0 +

Total points earned: 22 / 27*

Percentage of points earned: 81 %

manager to more fairly administer periodic formal evaluations. For example, it may be tempting to give a high performance rating when an employee is overloaded; however, based on our approach, the rating would depend on the employee's performance and not simply on emotional appeal. In addition, downsizing firms can more closely tie any merit bonuses to deserving performances in order to keep a "pay for performance" mentality foremost in employees' minds and ensure corporate dollars are wisely distributed.

To illustrate our point, we apply our task assessment framework to Caroline's situation. As shown in **Figure 3**, Caroline has made a concerted attempt over the last four or five months to complete work assigned in Michael's task categorization system. Even though she is only producing mostly "good" results, she is performing consistently across assigned tasks, both old and new. Adding up her task scores, we see that she has produced a value of 22, resulting in an 81 percent of points earned and a good rating. As such, her performance appraisal reflects her results across the various tasks.

Caroline's normal workload was broken down by task type to encourage appropriate focus—all complete with clear performance standards. Michael assigned what he determined to be a fair workload in the employees' restructured work reality and a fair division of departmental work responsibilities. But performance appraisal results are based on the types of tasks that were assigned and, more important, on the level at which those tasks were performed. Caroline is not an average performer, as she has lately felt; instead, she has exhibited quite good performance over the last several months. Michael gives her clear direction on which tasks are valued the most, and with continued coaching and experience, Caroline will likely make it to the excellent category soon. Ultimately, Michael is confident that his department's task load has been fairly and accurately distributed and that employees will become more comfortable and proficient with the new system over time.

Perhaps organizations other than downsized firms could benefit from considering our outlined approach as well. When a firm becomes mature and duties become routine, this method could be useful in revitalizing it—to do some housecleaning by identifying critical, sub-critical, and minor tasks and eliminating unnecessary ones. Nevertheless, it is crucial in a downsized environment for managers and supervisors to reexamine workloads, prioritize duties, and communicate how the task hierarchy will be reflected during the performance appraisal process. The effort must be made to ensure that employees who are retained are being used effectively, treated fairly, and rewarded appropriately for their contribution to the organization.

Source: Reprinted with permission from *Business Horizons* March/April 2003. Copyright © 2003 by the Trustees at Indiana University, Kelley School of Business.

References and Selected Bibliography

Appelbaum, Steven H. 1991. How to slim successfully and ethically: Two case studies of "downsizing." *Leadership & Organization Development Journal* 12: 11–17.

Beam, Henry H. 1997. Survivors: How to keep your best people on board after downsizing. *Academy of Management Executive* 11: 92–94.

Feldman, Daniel C., and Carrie R. Leana. 1994. Better practices in managing layoffs. *Human Resource Management* 33 (Summer): 239–261.

Finch, Steven. 2001. Supervisor, Philips Broadband Networks, Manlius, New York, phone interview (17 November).

Focus resources now on retained employees. 2001. *HR Focus* 78/10: 11–16.

Gutknecht, John E., and J. Bernard Keys, 1993. Mergers, acquisitions and takeovers: Maintaining morale of survivors and protecting employees. *Academy of Management Executive* 7/3: 26–37.

Koonce, Richard. 1991. The "people side" of organizational change. *Credit Magazine* 17/6: 22–25.

The negative effects of overwork and related stress. 2001. *HR Focus* 78/11 (November): 9+.

Siriginidi, Subba Rao. 2000. Enterprise resource planning in reengineering business. *Business Process Management Journal* 6: 376.

Slavin, Roy H. 1994. Re-engineering: A productivity paradox. *Quality* 33/6 (June): 18.

Wright, Patrick M., Gary C. McMahan, B. McCormick, and W. S. Sherman. 1998. Strategy, core competence, and HR involvement as determinants of HR effectiveness and refinery performance. *Human Resource Management* 37/1 (Spring): 17–29.

CHAPTER

7

EMPLOYMENT LAW

On June 1, 2000, the United States Equal Employment Opportunity Commission (EEOC) announced that a subsidiary of W.R. Grace & Co. and a company that subsequently operated one of its facilities had agreed to pay $1 million to the victims of widespread sexual harassment at one of its food processing plants in Laurel, Maryland. The class-action lawsuit had been filed by the EEOC on behalf of 22 Hispanic females, all recent immigrants from Central America who spoke limited English, who had been routinely subjected to unwanted groping and explicit requests for sexual favors from male managers and coworkers over a period of several years.

The harassment directed at the workers took many forms. One woman was locked in a freezer by her supervisor upon turning down his request for a sexual favor. Two other women, who were pregnant at the time, were asked to perform sexual favors and subsequently demoted and fired following their refusal to comply with the requests. Many of the other women had their job duties reassigned to especially menial or difficult tasks when refusing requests for sexual favors from plant management.

EEOC Chairwoman Ida L. Castro noted that the EEOC would "remain vigilant to ensure that no worker endures this type of discrimination in order to earn a paycheck and support their family."

Source: EEOC Press Release, "EEOC Obtains $1 Million for Low-Wage Workers Who Were Sexually Harassed at Food Processing Plant," June 1, 2000, available at http://www.eeoc.gov.

The increasing scope, complexity, and ambiguity of federal laws that regulate the employment relationship have contributed to making employment law more of a critical strategic issue for employers than it has been in the past. Organizations that knowingly or unknowingly violate these laws can be saddled with significant litigation costs, negative press and public relations, and lowered employee morale, even if the organization is eventually cleared of the allegations. When employers are found to have violated laws, the consequences can be even more severe.

Employment law can have a significant impact on an organization's cost structure. The establishment and maintenance of internal mechanisms, such as training and reporting systems, to ensure compliance with laws can be time-consuming and costly. Violations of the law can result in significant monetary penalties and damage an organization's name and reputation.

Several federal laws protect individuals from unfair treatment in the workplace. Congressional intent in passing these laws is to ensure that all Americans receive equal access to and treatment in employment. In other words, all Americans should enjoy equal opportunity in employment. From an organizational perspective, there are two reasons why it makes sense to be an equal opportunity employer. First, federal laws provide for a variety of penalties for organizations that violate such laws. Second, it is in an organization's best interest to hire the most qualified applicant for any job or to promote the most qualified individual, regardless of factors that do not impact the individual's ability to perform the job in question.

A critical component of the strategic management of human resources involves attracting, developing, and retaining the highest quality workforce. Decisions regarding staffing, compensation, and other HR programs and policies are mitigated by laws regulating employment, as noted in Chapter 4. Employment law has a significant impact on an organization's ability to implement strategic human resource management for two reasons. First, any strategic HR initiatives must be tempered and structured within the context of applicable laws that regulate the employment relationship. Second, there is a significant cost to organizations for noncompliance with these laws. Pretrial costs to defend an allegation of illegal employment discrimination can exceed $1 million. These costs are incurred regardless of whether the complaints are judged to be valid. Additional costs include the impact of litigation and publicity on the organization's reputation with customers and prospective employees as well as on the morale and productivity of current employees.

SCOPE OF LAWS

Laws passed by Congress at the federal level are binding on each of the 50 United States as well as the U.S. territories. Individual states can pass their own additional, supplemental laws as long as these laws do not violate or contradict federal laws. These state laws are then binding on all cities, towns, and municipalities in that state. Individual municipalities can also pass their own laws that extend state laws, as long as the municipal laws do not contradict or violate state and, consequently, federal laws. For example, there is currently no federal law that prohibits discrimination in employment on the basis of sexual orientation. Although such a bill has been proposed in Congress, it has not received sufficient support to be passed into law at this writing. However, ten individual states have decided to offer this protection at the state level. California is one such state. One municipality within California, San Francisco, has decided to extend this protection under the law even further and prohibit discrimination based on gender orientation, or that directed at transgendered individuals. In this example, each lower level of government has exercised the freedom to extend or supplement the laws that have been passed by higher legislative bodies.

An organization that operates in multiple states or even within multiple municipalities within a single state may find that it needs to comply with different legal requirements in different locations. This would require the employer to have separate HR programs and policies at different locations or one blanket policy that covers all locations and considers state and local laws in all locations in which it operates.

The process of selecting applicants for positions requires employers to discriminate in their selection decisions. The process of discrimination, in and of itself, is not an illegal action. To discriminate simply means "to make or note a distinction." Employers do this all the time; they discriminate, for example, regarding the number of years' prior experience and levels of education applicants have. Discrimination becomes illegal, however, when it is directed at groups that Congress has decided to protect under federal law. Groups that enjoy protection against illegal job discrimination are referred to as "protected classes."

FEDERAL ANTIDISCRIMINATION LAWS

The first law passed by Congress that impacted the employment relationship was the Civil Rights Act of 1866. This law literally gave all citizens the right to enter into contracts as "white citizens." Although this terminology may sound racist, it is important to interpret this language within its historical context. The year 1865 marked the end of the Civil War and the abolition of slavery. Congress' intent in passing this law was to ensure that the former slaves enjoyed freedom in their lives and were able to obtain gainful employment on an equal basis with Caucasians. Congress, however, was a bit naive in assuming that just because it passed a law, employers would comply. No remedies for unjust treatment were provided in this law when it was passed. Not surprisingly, racial discrimination did not end upon passage of the law; however, those discriminated against had no recourse. Consequently, Congress passed the Civil Rights Act of 1871, which gave individuals the right to sue if they felt that they had been deprived of their rights under the Civil Rights Act of 1866.

Equal Pay Act

Nearly a century passed before Congress ratified another law aimed at protecting workers from discrimination in employment. In 1963, Congress passed the Equal Pay Act, which prohibits wage discrimination based on sex or gender for jobs that require equal skill, effort, and responsibility and are performed under similar working conditions. In short, it states that women cannot be paid less than men for doing the same jobs. However, more than 35 years have passed since the passage of this act, and women still make, on average, somewhere around 70 to 75 cents on the dollar of what men make.

One reason for this discrepancy is that Congress provided four exceptions, or exclusions, to the law. If satisfied, these conditions allow an employer to legally pay women less than men. The first exception is a bona fide seniority system. When compensation is based on seniority and men have held jobs longer than women, pay differentials are legitimate. Throughout American labor history, Congress and the courts have readily embraced the idea of seniority as a legitimate criterion in making employment-related decisions because it is an objective standard. The term "bona fide" in describing a seniority system refers to the fact that the seniority system must not be self-serving as a means of facilitating wage discrimination. It must be an existing, legitimate, and enforced system of managing various aspects of employee relations.

The second exclusion to the Equal Pay Act is differences in quality of performance. If the employer can show that men perform at higher levels than women, then the pay differential is justified. This, however, can be problematic as most assessments of performance are highly subjective in nature. Organizations need to ensure that any merit-based pay system does not intentionally or inadvertently discriminate against women. This will be discussed in greater detail in the chapter on performance management systems.

The third exception to the law is pay plans that are based on quantity of output. Traditionally called "piece-rate" systems in manufacturing organizations, compensation is based on how much an individual produces. This is somewhat analogous to commission-based sales in today's organizations or wages based on the number of transactions completed or customers serviced.

The final exception is for "factors other than sex." Although this term is often treated with cynicism, Congress realized when passing the law that it could not anticipate every possible contingency that might arise in establishing a basis of equity in pay. Therefore, it allowed this exclusion to give employers some latitude if they had some other means of compensation that resulted in gender-based pay differentials that did not take gender into account. This is one of many laws that Congress has passed that has included a provision allowing somewhat of an open option for employers to articulate a legitimate, nondiscriminatory means for treating employees as it does.

Civil Rights Act of 1964

The following year, Congress passed the Civil Rights Act of 1964, which is often regarded as being the single most important piece of social legislation of the 20th century. The act is broken into a number of different sections, called *titles*; Title VII pertains to employment. As a result, when referring to this particular act, most employers, policy makers, and members of the legal and judiciary communities simply refer to it as "Title VII."

Title VII prohibits discrimination in employment based on race, color, religion, sex, and national origin. Conditions of employment included under Title VII include hiring, firing, promotion, transfer, compensation, and admission to training programs. Title VII applies to all private employers with 15 or more employees as well as state and local governments, colleges and universities, and employment agencies and labor unions.

The law also established the Equal Employment Opportunity Commission (EEOC), which was charged with overseeing Title VII. Prior to the passage of this law, employees who felt that they had been discriminated against had no means by which to pursue their complaints outside of hiring a private attorney. Because many employees could not afford the kind of costly legal counsel that their employers could, the playing field was hardly level. Consequently, Congress saw a need to establish a federal agency to enforce federal labor laws and receive employee complaints. In addition to Title VII, the EEOC is also charged with oversight of the Equal Pay Act of 1963 and all other federal labor laws subsequently discussed in this chapter.

Racial Discrimination at Coca-Cola

In late 2000, Coca-Cola made the largest settlement in history related to a race discrimination case. The organization agreed to pay $192.5 million to a group of African-American employees and former employees and also agreed to institute significant changes in its employment practices relative to the ways it manages and promotes minority employees. The lawsuit began when four employees came forward with their allegations; the case escalated into a highly publicized event as 45 current and former employees traveled from Coke's Atlanta headquarters to Washington, D.C. on a "bus ride for justice." Reverend Jesse Jackson joined the fray by calling for a consumer boycott of the company and its products.

In addition to paying the monetary settlement, Coke created a panel of outside monitors to perform independent audits of the organization's performance on diversity issues as well as to mandate changes in HR practices. The panel's recommendations are binding on the organization, unless Coke can prove in court that they are financially impossible to implement. In addition to the panel, Coke's board of directors also agreed to establish a Public Issues and Diversity Review Committee to oversee corporate equal employment opportunity programs and devise a strategy for tying executive compensation to successful EEO efforts.[1]

Age Discrimination in Employment Act of 1967

The Age Discrimination in Employment Act of 1967 prohibits employment discrimination against employees who are age 40 or older and prohibits the setting of mandatory retirement ages (although mandatory retirement ages are allowed in some occupations that deal with public safety). This act was amended in 1990 by the Older Workers Protection Act, which prohibits employers from discriminating based on age when providing benefits to employees or from asking older workers to sign waivers of any future age discrimination claims when being laid off. The EEOC has oversight of this law, which applies to all employers covered under Title VII in addition to the federal government.

Rehabilitation Act of 1973

The Rehabilitation Act of 1973 prohibits discrimination by organizations with federal contracts against applicants or employees who are handicapped. It should be noted that, by requiring compliance only by federal contractors, the majority of private employers are not covered under this act. The act has a three-pronged definition of what constitutes an individual with a handicap: (1) an individual with a physical or mental impairment that substantially limits one or more major life activities; (2) an individual with a history or record of such impairment; (3) an individual regarded as having such an impairment. The act requires individuals with these conditions to be "otherwise qualified" to perform job responsibilities (in spite of their handicap) in order to receive protection against discrimination and also requires employers to provide "reasonable accommodation" to such qualified individuals with handicaps.

The Supreme Court has ruled that "reasonableness" of an accommodation would be determined on a case-by-case basis relative to the specific facts of the case, including the cost of the accommodation, the resources of the employer, the nature of the job, workplace safety issues, and any relevant collective bargaining provisions.

Pregnancy Discrimination Act of 1978

The Pregnancy Discrimination Act of 1978 prohibits employers from discriminating against pregnant employees by requiring employers to allow pregnant employees to take leave for pregnancy and childbearing, as it would for any other medical disability. In short, the law requires the employer's existing policy on disability leave to be extended to include pregnancy. This act does not require the employer to reinstate the employee in the same job upon return from leave and does not allow the employer to determine the dates of leave. It further prohibits employers from refusing to hire or promote because of pregnancy or from providing health insurance plans that do not cover pregnancy.

Americans with Disabilities Act of 1990

The Americans with Disabilities Act (ADA) of 1990 greatly extends the protection first offered under the Rehabilitation Act. The act covers all public and private employers with 15 or more employees and utilizes much of the same language as the Rehabilitation Act. The ADA's definition of disability is adapted from the Rehabilitation Act, and the ADA retains the Rehabilitation Act provisions for being "otherwise qualified" and providing "reasonable accommodation."

The extension of the coverage of the Rehabilitation Act under the ADA to so many additional Americans with disabilities has resulted in a flood of litigation. The courts have found many of the provisions of the ADA to be quite ambiguous and open to interpretation. For example, there is some concern as to whether certain medical conditions really are impairments and whether they limit any major life activity. This is particularly problematic when a condition can be controlled by medication or some prosthetic device. Courts have issued ambiguous rulings in this regard related to a number of medical conditions including diabetes, epilepsy, asthma, HIV, hypertension, and lymphoma. They have also disagreed as to whether any major life activities other than earning a living are relevant to consider in employment discrimination cases.

The courts have ruled that "otherwise qualified" and "reasonable accommodation" need to be determined on a case-by-case basis. Some courts have been sympathetic to those with disabilities by granting great latitude to employees or applicants stating a claim; others have been very strict in their interpretations of the provisions of the ADA in ruling for employers. Similarly, some courts have granted wide latitude as to what constitutes a disability. In certain instances, aspects of physical appearance including weight and poor dental health have been considered disabilities under the third prong of the definition in the statute. Although the ADA has provided the more than 43 million Americans with disabilities wide protection against discrimination in employment and in other areas of their lives, the statute as it stands is very vague, flexible, and open to the interpretation and whim of the courts. ▼

▶ Reading 7.1, "Responding to the Supreme Court: Employment Practices and the ADA," explains how the Supreme Court has interpreted some of these ambiguous ADA issues and concepts.

Employees with Disabilities at IBM

Since 1995, Armonk, New York–based IBM has sponsored an employee disabilities task force. One of eight diversity task forces within IBM, this group was asked first to address four issues. The first is what IBM could do to make employees with disabilities feel welcome and valued. The second was what IBM could do to maximize disabled employees' productivity. The third was what IBM could do to maximize business opportunities with consumers with disabilities. The fourth was an inquiry as to what community organizations employees would like to see IBM participate in. The task force was designed with a dual purpose: to assist in the recruiting and retention of employees with disabilities and to capitalize on new market opportunities. As part of its initiatives, IBM has created a partnership with the American Association for the Advancement of Science, which recruits and screens undergraduate students with disabilities in math- and science-related disciplines for positions at IBM. It has also allowed IBM to develop a number of products that make workplace and home technology more accessible to individuals with disabilities.[2]

The Supreme Court has issued several landmark rulings on the Americans with Disabilities Act that have clarified some areas of ambiguity. In *Toyota v. Williams*, the Court unanimously held that an employee's carpal tunnel syndrome, which prevented her from doing her job without accommodation, did not provide her with protection under the ADA. While she was unable to perform some of the manual tasks required by her job, the Court did not find that she was "substantially limited" in any "major life activity." In a split decision, the Court held in *Barnett v. US Airways* that an employer that utilizes a bona fide seniority system is not required to provide a disabled employee with a job when the action involves displacing an employee with greater seniority. Finally, in what probably has been the Court's most controversial ADA ruling, it found in *Sutton v. United Airlines* that disabilities needed to be considered in their "mitigated" states when deciding whether an applicant or employee has ADA protection. Because medication and assistive devices can be used by many individuals with disabilities, the Court found that the finding of whether an individual had an ADA-protected disability needed to consider the use of any such medication or device and whether such use still resulted in the substantial limitation of a major life activity.

In response to this latter condition, California passed a law that expressly went beyond the ADA requirement. While the law applies only to California employers, it still has a significant effect on tens of thousands of employees and employers. This law, A.B. 2222, went into effect in 2001 and has five less restrictive requirements than those set forth in the ADA. First, in response to the *Sutton* decision, the law requires that disabilities be evaluated without consideration of mitigating measures, such as medications, assistive devices, or accommodations. Second, the law removes the "substantially" component of the ADA and requires simply that an individual be "limited" in a major life activity. Third, the determination of whether an activity is limited under the ADA requires that its performance be "unusually difficult," whereas under the California statute, the requirement is that it be "difficult" only. Fourth, in response to the Supreme Court's decision in *Toyota*, the California statute protects individuals whose impairment excludes them from a specific job rather than the ADA requirement of preclusion from a class or broad range of jobs. Finally, whereas the ADA does not delineate "major life activities," the definition of major life activities under A.B. 2222 is to be "broadly construed and shall include physical, mental and social activities and working."

In addition to these less stringent requirements than those found under the ADA, A.B. 2222 provides no limits to damages that an individual can receive, in contrast to the ADA's cap of $300,000. The net effect of the California statute is that the burden of proof in disability-related cases largely is shifted from the employee to the employer. Because California law is often the harbinger of laws that are adopted elsewhere, the potential ramifications of A.B. 2222 could be significant relative to the employment rights of individuals with disabilities in the United States.[3]

Civil Rights Act of 1991

Congress extended the rights of individuals protected under Title VII when it passed the Civil Rights Act (CRA) of 1991. This law has four specific provisions that amend the coverage of Title VII: (1) It extends the protection of Title VII to federal government employees; (2) It allows litigants to sue for compensatory and punitive damages, in addition to back pay, benefits, and attorney's costs; (3) It requires a heavier "burden of proof" on the part of employers in rebutting claims of unlawful discrimination; (4) It provides for "extraterritorial enforcement" of federal labor laws, protecting U.S. employees on overseas assignments unless compliance would violate laws of the foreign country where the employee is on assignment. The additional protection and benefits offered to employees under the CRA of 1991 has resulted in a dramatic increase in Title VII filing with the EEOC.

Family and Medical Leave Act of 1992

The Family and Medical Leave Act (FMLA) of 1992 requires employers to provide up to 12 weeks unpaid leave for the birth, adoption, or serious illness of a child, family member, or the employee during any 12-month period. It only covers organizations with 50 or more employees. In order to receive protection, an employee has to have been employed a minimum of 25 hours per week for one year, or 1,250 hours in total. Employees whose salaries are among the highest 10 percent of the employer's workforce do not receive FMLA protection.

The employer is required to continue the employee's group health insurance during the leave, and the employee must be allowed to return to the same job or an equivalent position upon returning to work. The employer may require that the employee utilize any accrued vacation or sick time as part of the leave. It is important to remember that this law sets a minimum federal standard for compliance. Any organization is obviously free to provide more generous options, such as longer leave, paid leave, or other accommodations such as working at home when the leave time period has been completed.

Interestingly enough, when President Clinton signed the Family and Medical Leave Act into law, its passage was hailed as a major victory for families and parents. It had taken a number of years and several congressional revisions of the act before it was finally passed. Although an earlier version had been passed by Congress, it had been vetoed by President George H. W. Bush. However, despite its family-friendly provisions, the FMLA provides far less extensive coverage than comparable laws of other industrialized countries. European countries, for example, tend to be far more generous in both the length of the leave that they provide as well as the compensation and benefits offered to employees. Sweden offers up to one full year parental leave for either parent, with the first 38 weeks at 90 percent salary with guaranteed job security. Italy provides mothers with up to

40 weeks, with 100 percent salary for the first 22 weeks with guaranteed job security. Finland provides either parent 35 weeks of leave at 100 percent salary with guaranteed job security. It is worth noting, however, that citizens of these countries are taxed at a significantly higher rate than those in the United States. However, these European countries share a philosophy that children are a "national resource" to be properly nurtured and developed and that the future of the nation is dependent on proper childrearing. The United States, on the other hand, considers children to be the "personal property" of parents, with responsibility for childrearing lying with the parents rather than the state, unless the state can find abusive treatment of the child.

ENFORCEMENT OF FEDERAL LAWS UNDER THE EEOC

As previously mentioned, Title VII created the EEOC to oversee and enforce federal labor laws. Any individuals who feel that their rights under Title VII have been violated may file a complaint with the EEOC in an attempt to remedy the situation. The procedures that are followed in an EEOC investigation are outlined in Exhibit 7-1.

The first requirement is that the charge be filed within 180 days of the alleged discriminatory act. The charge can be filed with the federal EEOC office or a state or local agency responsible for overseeing claims of employment discrimination. If charges are initially filed with a state or local agency and the complainant is dissatisfied with the outcome, the individual may refile the charge with the EEOC within 30 days of the initial decision.

The EEOC will then investigate the complaint to determine if there is reasonable cause to believe that discrimination has occurred. If no cause is found, the complaint will be dismissed, although the complainant still retains the right to hire a private attorney. If cause is found, the EEOC will notify the employer of the charge and attempt to mediate the dispute with the employer on behalf of the complainant. The EEOC will first meet with the complainant to determine what would constitute a satisfactory settlement and then attempt to have the employer sign a conciliation agreement. If the employer refuses, the EEOC may file suit on behalf of the complainant or issue the complainant a "right to sue" letter.

In proving illegal discrimination, the burden of proof first falls with the employee or applicant to establish a prima facie case. *Prima facie* means "on the surface" or "at first look," and prima facie status is established by showing either disparate treatment or disparate impact. It should be noted that disparate treatment/impact is sometimes referred to as *adverse treatment/impact*.

Disparate or adverse treatment happens when an employee is treated differently from others based on some dimension of protected-class status, such as age, race, sex, religion, national origin, or disability. Disparate or adverse impact is a bit more subtle. Here the same standards and treatment are applied to all workers, but the outcomes or consequences of this treatment are different for different groups. For example, a requirement that all employees be a certain height might result in adverse impact for an applicant who uses a wheelchair. Similarly, an employment test in which individuals from one ethnic or religious background consistently score higher than individuals from other backgrounds would establish adverse impact. Disparate impact is usually illustrated statistically using the four-fifths rule. Under this, if the selection rate for a protected group is less than 80 percent of the selection rate

EXHIBIT 7-1: EEOC COMPLAINT PROCESS

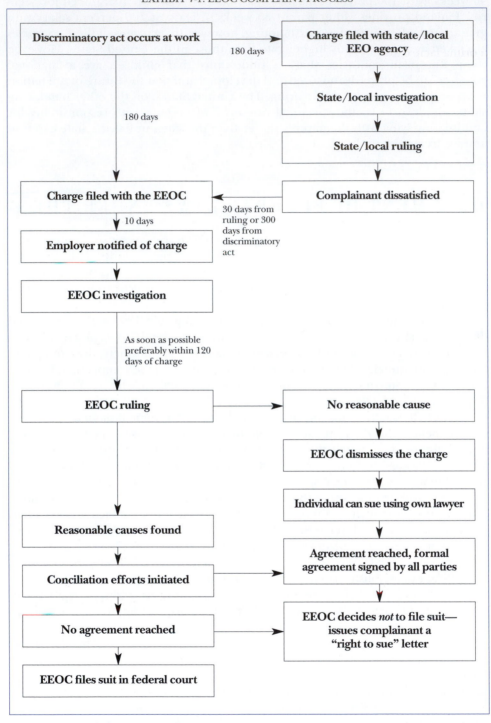

for a majority group, then adverse impact is established. For example, if an employment test resulted in 20 out of 100 males being qualified, then at least 16 out of 100 (16 being four-fifths of 20) females should be assessed similarly to refute the fact that the test results in disparate impact.

Once the complainant has established disparate treatment or impact, the burden of proof then shifts to the employer to provide a legally justifiable, nondiscriminatory reason for the action. There are essentially four ways in which an employer can rebut a prima facie case.

The first is through showing job-relatedness. To do this, the employer illustrates that the criteria utilized to select applicants is essential for performance of the job. Proving job-relatedness is not easy; employers usually have to perform validation studies of tests or other criteria used to screen applicants or provide performance data of past employees to support their contentions.

The second means is by claiming a bona fide occupational qualification (BFOQ) defense. This defense requires the employer to explain why it is essential for the employee to be a member of a certain group. This defense has been utilized most frequently in gender and religious discrimination cases. It would be legitimate, for example, to deny a woman a job as a men's locker room attendant. Customer preferences for a certain "type" of individual do not support the BFOQ defense. When an airline refused to hire male flight attendants, claiming that being female was a BFOQ due to "customer preferences," they were found in violation of Title VII.

The third defense is a bona fide seniority system. As previously discussed, courts support the use of seniority in employment decisions due to the objectivity of seniority. As long as the system is bona fide, meaning it was not set up to discriminate or perpetuate discrimination, seniority systems are a justifiable defense. When the city of Memphis used seniority as the criterion to lay off firefighters, African-American firefighters who had been hired under an affirmative action program were disproportionately affected. Because the department had traditionally used seniority in making other personnel decisions, the criterion was upheld, even though it had significant adverse impact on a protected class.

The final defense is "business necessity." This defense requires the employer to show that the criteria used are essential to the safe and efficient operation of the enterprise. However, the courts have rejected business necessity claims that were based on profitability or other economic concerns of the business owners. Instead, this condition applies more to factors related to the safety of employees and customers. For example, a postal worker who was of short stature sued the U.S. Postal Service when it refused to provide him with a reasonable accommodation in the form of a stepstool so that he could reach mail slots that were outside of the reach of his arms. The postal service successfully argued that having an employee constantly climbing up and down a stepstool would be unsafe for the employee and coworkers around him.

Although the EEOC has broad oversight of federal antidiscrimination laws, it does not serve as a judiciary authority and has limited power over employers. It is empowered by Congress to perform only a conciliatory role between employers and those who file discrimination charges and relies on the federal court system to enforce charges it brings against employers. ▼▼

Under a new chair, the EEOC recently has taken a very aggressive stance in attempting to reduce the backlog of cases on its docket. Over 95,000 private sector charges were filed in 2002 and the average time to process these complaints declined to 171 days, despite the increased caseload.[4] To assist with the resolution of claims, the EEOC Web site now has a special page that assists employers with investigations.

▶▶ Currently, the EEOC has a backlog of tens of thousands of cases because it is being called upon to play a different role than that envisioned by Congress when it passed Title VII. This backlog is severely undermining Congress' intentions to have discrimination-free workplaces. Reading 7.2, "The Dual Loyalty Dilemma for HR Managers Under Title VII Compliance," explains how judicial interpretations have served to limit the protection offered under Title VII.

- Prevent discrimination through education and partnerships with other like-minded organizations.
- Efficiently track and resolve charges of discrimination, evaluate data and report trends to employers.
- Develop efficient working relationships between attorneys and investigators for more strategic enforcement and litigation.
- Expand the mediation program and increase use of external mediators.
- Become a model workplace and an example for the private sector to follow.

Much of the EEOC's success can be attributed to its strategic plan, which provided much-needed direction to agency activities and initiatives. The plan is presented in Exhibit 7-2.

Perhaps the EEOC initiative that has had the most impact on resolving discrimination charges against employers has been its voluntary mediation program. While the program has been in existence since the early 1990s, it really had not had a tremendous impact until the new chair decided to emphasize its use. Mediation involves the employee and employer attempting to resolve their differences outside of a courtroom through the assistance of an EEOC mediator. The process is designed to be fair, impartial, and unbiased and has met with resounding success. Ninety-six percent of employers and 91 percent of employees who engaged in EEOC-assisted mediation reported that they would do so again. However, when offered mediation services by the EEOC, only 30 percent of employers agreed to mediation, as opposed to 83 percent of employees.[5] Despite the fact that the EEOC uses what it calls "facilitative mediation," many employers initially view EEOC-assisted mediation with some skepticism because the EEOC was established to ensure compliance with federal laws as well as to assist employees with their claims. Employers also may reject mediation when they are certain that the claims against them eventually will be judged unfounded after an investigation. Also, by refusing mediation, employers may force the employee to go to court, becoming involved in an often lengthy, expensive resolution process that the employee may not be able to afford either financially or emotionally. To an extent, when an employer refuses mediation, it "dares" the employee to continue the process. This dare, however, is not without risk: Litigation is time-consuming and expensive for the employer as well as the employee. It also can be disruptive to the employer's workplace during the investigatory process and may result in hard feelings toward the employer among other employees, who may sympathize with the charging employee. Essentially, the decision by an employer to accept or reject EEOC-assisted mediation may come down to a simple cost-benefit analysis. However, even through many of those costs and benefits can be estimated, their certainty of incurrence is unknown.

EXECUTIVE ORDERS

In addition to federal laws that regulate the employment relationship, certain employers are required to comply with executive orders. Executive orders are issued by the President and apply to all federal agencies and organizations with federal contracts.

Executive Orders 11246 and 11375, taken together, prohibit those organizations from discriminating against the same protected classes that Title VII does. Compliance with executive orders is overseen by the Office of Federal Contracts Compliance Programs (OFCCP), an agency of the U.S. Department of Labor, which performs similar investigatory functions as the EEOC. However, unlike the EEOC, the OFCCP actively monitors compliance with laws and executive orders instead of waiting for employees or job applicants to file complaints. The OFCCP also has enforcement power, unlike the EEOC, allowing it to levy fines and punishments, including revocation of the federal government contracts.

AFFIRMATIVE ACTION

Executive orders also require organizations with 100 or more employees *and* $50,000 or more in federal contracts to develop, implement, and maintain a program of affirmative action. The concept of affirmative action addresses the fact that there has been significant past discrimination in employment and other aspects of life in the United States and attempts to remedy these injustices. Affirmative action requires organizations to make special efforts to ensure that their workforce is representative of the society where the business operates. Affirmative action rests on the assumption that we still have not progressed to the point, as a society, where we can treat all individuals equally and that the only way to rectify past injustices is to provide individuals from protected classes special consideration and treatment in employment opportunities.

Although the doctrine of equal employment opportunity (EEO) requires that organizations provide a discrimination-free workplace, it does not imply that organizations should attempt to go back and correct past injustices. EEO rests on the assumption that any initiatives to show preference to any member of a protected class would be, in and of themselves, illegal and just turn the tables by unfairly discriminating against the majority. Therefore, the only way to ensure a discrimination-free society and workplace is to wipe the slate clean. History cannot be rewritten, and past injustices cannot be corrected by discriminatory treatment in the present. In short, EEO argues that "two wrongs do not make things right."

Affirmative action plans, however, are usually meant to be temporary measures that require organizations to take corrective action to address "underutilization" of certain protected classes. Preferential treatment, in this regard, is a means of allowing the organization to ensure that its workplace is well represented by various protected classes. Nonetheless, critics of affirmative action have called for dismantling affirmative action programs due to the problems of reverse discrimination that they create. Proponents of affirmative action argue that such programs are necessary because our society is not yet blind to personal characteristics that have nothing to do with the ability to perform a given job. ▼▼▼

Affirmative action plans are filed with the Department of Labor and monitored by the OFCCP. They consist of four separate sections. The first section is a utilization analysis in which the employer identifies its employees by gender, race, ethnicity, religion, physical ability, and any other protected class. This is merely a counting and summation and is often performed for various levels of employment in the organizational hierarchy, rather than being aggregated, to ensure that representation of

▶▶▶ Reading 7.3, "In Defense of Preference," illustrates that affirmative action is problematic in both concept and practice but argues that society without affirmative action is worse off than with it.

protected classes is not limited to low-level positions. The second portion is an availability analysis that examines the availability for employment of all protected classes in the immediate recruiting vicinity. The third portion is an identification of problem areas in which the employer notes over- and underutilization of certain groups in the employee mix. The final section is a narrative statement of a corrective action in which the organization details plans with timetables to rectify the discrepancies between utilization and availability.

Those who support and those who oppose affirmative action do agree on one thing: Our society has unfairly and unlawfully discriminated against a variety of protected classes for a long period of time. Where they disagree is the means of correcting such injustices. Those who argue that EEO laws are sufficient without affirmative action feel that affirmative action does nothing more than perpetuate the discrimination that federal law tries to prohibit by merely shifting the target of unfair treatment from the minorities to the majorities. This group argues that our society *can* treat all individuals equally. Proponents of affirmative action argue that discrimination is still rampant in our society, and the only way to remedy this is to force organizations to employ and promote individuals from all protected classes through government regulation because the organizations, themselves, are not capable of doing this on their own. Even proponents of affirmative action realize that it can be problematic: Individuals in protected classes often argue that they are never really sure whether they receive jobs or promotions because of their protected-class status or their own individual abilities, qualifications, and accomplishments.

Affirmative action does not require organizations to hire individuals who are not qualified to hold positions for which they apply. If the organization has a clear job description and qualifications that it can prove are specifically job-related—and can show that it has made a sincere effort to recruit individuals from underutilized populations—it may continue to show discrepancies between utilization and availability.

SEXUAL HARASSMENT

In 1986, the Supreme Court ruled in *Meritor Savings Bank v. Vinson* that sexual harassment constituted a form of sex discrimination under Title VII. To date, the majority of sexual harassment cases have involved situations where a man sexually harasses a woman who holds a lower or equal position. In 1998, the high court further ruled in *Oncale v. Sundowner Offshore Services, Inc.*, that same-sex harassment was also actionable under Title VII. Every year, organizations pay workers millions of dollars in claims involving allegations of sexual harassment. In addition to the direct monetary costs of sexual harassment, there can also be significant costs in terms of negative public relations and damaged employee morale. Managing sexual harassment becomes even more complicated in light of the fact that sexual attraction and even interoffice romances between consenting adults do happen in the workplace. As a result, sexual harassment compliance remains one of the more challenging aspects of legal compliance for employers.

What Sexual Harassment Is

Courts have identified several key concepts that influence whether behavior constitutes sexual harassment. The first is that the advances are of an "unwelcome" nature. It is imperative in sexual harassment cases that the individual who is the target of the harassment make clear that the behavior is considered offensive and inappropriate. Two individuals may be privy to the same behavior; although one may find the behavior offensive, the other may find it perfectly acceptable. Sexual harassment, being subjective in nature, places the initial burden on the complainant to communicate the "unwelcomeness" to the alleged harasser.

The second key concept is the nature of the harassment. The courts have identified two kinds of harassment: quid pro quo and hostile environment. Quid pro quo, which translated from the Latin means "this for that," happens when certain benefits are promised to an individual in return for sexual favors, or threats of punishment are made if sexual favors are withheld. Hostile environment constitutes the majority of sexual harassment claims and is much more subtle than quid pro quo. Hostile environment happens when the employee is subjected to an offensive working environment. However, the subjective nature of what constitutes an offensive or hostile working environment can make it difficult for employers to identify whether sexual harassment is taking place.

In an attempt to alleviate the uncertainty of defining a working environment as "offensive," the courts have utilized the standard of "reasonable woman." Realizing that in some cases employee claims of harassment may be unwarranted, the courts have attempted to apply a neutral standard to determine whether the working environment is indeed offensive. This involves an assessment of how a reasonable woman (or reasonable person, if the complainant were male) would be expected to react to such working conditions.

Another key consideration in sexual harassment claims concerns whether a pattern of behavior was displayed. Isolated incidents of alleged harassment usually carry less weight with the courts than continued harassment of an individual or ongoing harassment of a number of individuals perpetrated by a single individual. The courts will also attempt to determine whether the organization took any action if and when it was made aware of earlier allegations of harassment in determining ultimate liability for the conduct and the full extent of such liability.

A final concern is that many incidents of harassment involve the words of one employee against those of another and can be difficult to prove. Allegations need to be provable and verifiable. Such evidence is often provided through witnesses and/or written or printed documentation that supports the allegations of harassment.

Cleaning Up Sexual Harassment at Dial

Sexual harassment can be very costly to an organization. In 2003, Dial Corporation agreed to pay $10 million in settlement of a federal lawsuit brought when women at its Aurora, Illinois, plant argued that the employer had ignored their sexual harassment complaints. The suit charged that 90 current and former female employees had been groped, shown pornography, and called names on the job. This settlement was eclipsed by one involving Mitsubishi Motors in 1998. Facing allegations that women working on an assembly line were groped and insulted and their complaints then met with indifference, Mitsubishi settled this case, which involved 486 plaintiffs, for $34 million.[6]

Problems in Managing Sexual Harassment

In managing sexual harassment, organizations have to deal with four specific problems. The first is that many workers and managers are not aware of what sexual harassment is and what constitutes harassment. Several key management challenges need to be addressed in remedying this: Employees have different perceptions and standards of what is offensive; sexual harassment can be difficult to identify; and the intention of the harassing party is irrelevant relative to how the receiving party interpreted the behavior or action.

These challenges can be dealt with effectively through training that centers on *discussion rather than merely knowledge or skills.* Awareness of and attitudes toward sexual behavior at work need to be addressed among both men and women. Perceptions need to be shared and clarified, and employees, particularly managers, need to be aware of different ways of understanding or framing action and behaviors that may be sexual in nature.

The second problem is that although an organization may have a policy that prohibits sexual harassment, many employees may be unaware of the policy or know that there is a policy but not know what it says. A challenge that management faces in addressing this problem is that although every allegation of sexual harassment is unique, any established policy needs consistency in application but flexibility in enforcement to suit the specific circumstances and their severity. This issue can be dealt with through training that focuses on procedures, policies, and processes. Employees need to understand exactly the organization's position on sexual harassment and how it will be enforced. This type of training is probably most effective when conducted in conjunction with training that deals with attitudes and awareness.

The third problem in managing sexual harassment is that employees often fear reporting any incidents of sexual harassment. For the average employee, reporting sexual harassment means challenging the power base of the organization and often confronting a direct supervisor. Employees need to know that their claims will be taken seriously. Although Title VII expressly prohibits retaliation against any employee who files a claim under the law, it is not difficult for a supervisor or an organization to "dance around the law" and make an employee's life miserable without running afoul of the law. Employees often feel that challenging the organization is a losing proposition in which the individual employee is pitted against a large, powerful, resource-abundant organization. This also has significant implications for those who investigate any such charges within the organization. This individual or these individuals need to be objective. If employees distrust the process or investigator, they are more likely to allow acts of harassment to continue. To encourage reporting of sexually offensive behavior, it is important to create a climate of trust within the organization. Employees need to be assured of some confidentiality and provided with some support in continuing in their jobs during the course of the investigation into the allegations. Investigations also need to be conducted by an impartial, preferably neutral, outside source to prevent bias.

The fourth problem is determining how best to investigate allegations of sexual harassment. The challenges to doing this effectively involve the fact that there are two sides to every story, and often there are neither witnesses nor evidence to support the claims levied by one or both parties. To facilitate the investigation, those looking into claims of sexual harassment should seek out all others who may have knowledge about the effects of the harassment, particularly on the complainant, or of other incidents that might support or disclaim the allegations of harassment. Complaints should also be investigated immediately. This might help in curtailing any ongoing harassment or offensive behavior, and it is also generally looked upon favorably by the courts. In investigating claims of sexual harassment, if the charges cannot be proven, it can be useful to notify the accused party in writing that, if the

EXHIBIT 7-3: PROBLEMS AND CHALLENGES IN MANAGING SEXUAL HARASSMENT

Problems	Challenges	Strategies

• Workers/managers still not sure what it is	• Perceptions
	• Difcult to identify
	• Intention irrelevant, interpretation important
		• Training
		  • Centering on discussion among men and women
		  • Not skills: awareness and attitudes

• Workers unaware of policy or know there's a policy but not what it says	• Need consistency in application (to ensure fair and legal treatment of employees) but exibility in enforcement (to suit specic circumstances)	• Training • Centering on policy, processes, etc.
• Fear of reporting	• Retaliation • Biases of investigators	• Create climate of trust • Investigation by impartial, outside source • Condentiality • Support those ling allegations
• How to investigate	• Two sides to every story • Often no outside witnesses	• Seek out others for any knowledge about effects, other incidents • Investigate immediately while issue is still "fresh"; also looks good with courts • If no resolution, notify accused in writing that if conduct did occur it would constitute sexual harassment

conduct did occur, it would constitute sexual harassment and be in violation of company policy. A notification using neutral language serves notice to the employee without accusing the employee of wrongdoing and setting up a potential defamation claim. Exhibit 7-3 summarizes how to overcome some of the problems inherent in addressing sexual harassment in organizations.

Strategy for Managing Sexual Harassment

Exhibit 7-4 presents some general guidelines organizations can use to strategically manage sexual harassment in the workplace and minimize both legal liability and other adverse consequences of sexual harassment. First, the organization should investigate *all* allegations of harassment. Lack of knowledge or ignorance concerning the harassment would not be an acceptable defense in court. Second, a thorough and prompt investigation of all charges should be conducted. Determining potential liability is critical, as is dealing with the charges and curtailing any harassment in a timely manner. Third, the investigator that is appointed needs to be unbiased and objective. This is critical in avoiding company politics and preventing conflicts of interest. An improperly or poorly conducted investigation will not only be a waste of time and resources but may further damage employee trust and morale. Fourth, steps should be taken to ensure that no retaliation takes place against the complainant. As stated, such action is prohibited under

- Investigate *all* allegations (lack of knowledge, ignorance not a defense)
- Conduct a thorough and prompt investigation (determining actual liability often easier at this point)
- Ensure that investigator is unbiased, objective (avoid company politics, conflicts of interest)
- Ensure that no retaliation takes place (could result in additional Title VII liability)
- Treat accused employee fairly (hear his or her side, avoid wrongful discharge)
- Have both parties sign written statements (prevents "facts" in stories from changing)
- Take prompt action and equate consequences with behavior (goal is to ensure that behavior never happens again)
- Have clear, defined process for investigation (apply consistently, document everything)

Title VII, regardless of whether the allegations of harassment are ultimately proven. Even if no harassment has taken place, a Title VII violation may be found in how the complainant was subsequently treated. Unfounded claims do not remove the retaliation protection offered by Title VII. Fifth, the accused employee must be treated fairly. There are two sides to every story, and the accused's story should be heard in a nonjudgmental manner. Many unfairly accused employees have turned around and successfully sued their employers for wrongful discharge. Sixth, both parties should sign written statements that outline facts and completely disclose all pertinent information and clarify where they stand. This assists the investigator and prevents the parties from subsequently changing their stories. Seventh, in cases where harassment is found, employers need to take prompt action to rectify the situation and equate the consequences with the behavior. Any and all appropriate measures should be taken to ensure that the behavior never happens again. Finally, the organization needs to develop a clear, well-defined investigative process. This process should be applied consistently across cases and involve extensive written documentation of every step of the investigation. Information collected should be held in confidence due to its sensitive nature.

Complications Abroad

The increasing rate at which U.S. organizations set up operations abroad has some significant implications for how sexual harassment is handled. Although the Civil Rights Act of 1991 provides for extraterritorial enforcement of U.S. labor laws, many cultures do not acknowledge sexual harassment as a workplace or societal problem. Ethical dilemmas arise concerning how such behavior should be tolerated when it is not considered inappropriate in another culture.

In managing sexual harassment in the workplace, employers *always* have a chance to rectify wrongdoings if they have a policy in place. Although courts place a responsibility on complainants to inform harassers that advances or behaviors are "unwelcome," this does not relieve the employer of the burden of establishing, communicating, and implementing a clear policy on sexual harassment. Sexual harassment can and will happen in virtually any workplace. Clear measures can be taken to strategically manage this form of unlawful discrimination, ensuring that all employees have a workplace more conducive to high performance.

CONCLUSION

Although employment law is a key strategic area for HR, it remains the single area in which managers throughout organizations are most uninformed and ill-prepared to manage. The laws regulating employment relationships are numerous, complex, and ambiguous. Although no manager can be expected to be a legal expert, the move toward decentralized operations and the establishment of autonomous subsidiaries and work groups requires line managers to increasingly have full responsibility for HR issues. However, of all the traditional HR functions, employment law is probably the most difficult to manage effectively. Not only are there myriad laws and technical details as to how the laws have been interpreted by the courts, but there is also ambiguity in most of the newer laws (and many of the older laws, as well) that requires informed strategic decision making by managers at all levels in an organization.

One strategy that employers are using to prevent having to pay large settlements in discrimination cases is obtaining employment practices liability insurance (EPLI). EPLI has becoming increasingly popular as large settlements are offered and judgments rendered against employers. In 2003, the median judgment in employment discrimination cases ranged from $125,000 for sex discrimination to $266,852 for age-related discrimination.[7] EPLI assumes some of the risk incurred by an employer's illegal or questionable employment practices. With employment law becoming an increasingly complicated dimension of the employment relationship, it is more likely that managers and supervisors unversed in the changing aspects of the law may commit violations. Premiums for EPLI are dependent on the size of the employer and the frequency of past serious claims. Much like various kinds of consumer insurance, EPLI assesses an employer based on risk. Insurers who offer EPLI look favorably on employers who provide ongoing training for managers and supervisors and have strong policies against sexual harassment—and all kinds of discrimination—as well as procedures that call for a quick, thorough, and impartial investigation of complaints.

CRITICAL THINKING

1. What is a protected class, and what laws exist that safeguard the rights of each protected class?

2. Explain the process under which an EEOC complaint is processed. To what extent is it more advantageous for an employee to file an EEOC complaint at the local or federal level?

3. How can an employer lawfully respond to an allegation of employment discrimination?

4. Why does illegal discrimination persist nearly 40 years after the passage of Title VII?

5. What constitutes sexual harassment? What rights and responsibilities does an alleged recipient of sexual harassment have?

6. To what extent do cultural norms influence how other societies and cultures deal with the issue of sexual harassment in the workplace?

7. What are the pros and cons of mediation for an employer? What factors might influence whether an employer agrees to the mediation of an employee charge? What can be done to make mediation more attractive to employers?

Reading 7.1

8. What questions were left unanswered in the Supreme Court decisions in *Toyota* and *Sutton*? How might other courts interpret these questions and, until these questions are decided, what advice would you give to an employer?

Reading 7.2

9. The reading outlines a problem with Title VII, which has backlogged the court system with cases. What are the pros and cons of providing the HR manager with antiretaliation protection under Title VII? How can the problem addressed in this article be rectified?

Reading 7.3

10. Why is affirmative action such a controversial issue? Is society better served with or without affirmative action? In small groups, take a position either in favor of or against affirmative action and debate the issue within your group.

EXPERIENTIAL EXERCISES

1. In small groups, investigate any laws that prohibit employment discrimination in the European Union, Australia, Japan, or China. Note similarities and differences from American laws. What values or assumptions do the laws of these countries make about the employment relationship?

2. You are an HR manager for a medium-size financial services institution. You overhear an employee, Pat, tell a coworker, Chris, that a third employee, Jamie, told Pat about being the recipient of harassing behavior from Chris. How would you handle this situation? Role-play this with several classmates and have the remainder of the class critique the approach used.

3. Evaluate California law A.B. 2222. Does it go too far in protecting the rights of employees with disabilities? Break into two groups, with one arguing the need for the provision of the law and the other arguing against the law.

INTERNET EXERCISES

1. Visit the Equal Employment Opportunity Commission Web site at http://www.eeoc.gov. Identify current trends in complaints being filed with the EEOC and the processes by which claims are being resolved. Review the EEOC press releases posted on the site. What appear to be the agency's current priorities, and how appropriate do you feel these priorities are for the U.S. society?

CHAPTER REFERENCES

1. Schafer, S. "Coke to Pay $193 Million in Bias Suit," *Washington Post*, November 17, 2000, p. A1.
2. Wells, S. "Is the ADA Working?" *HR Magazine*, April 2001, pp. 38–46.
3. Minehan, M. "California Law Expands ADA Protections," *HR News*, 20, (3), 2001, p.1.
4. From the EEOC Web site, www.eeoc.gov/press/2-6-03.html.
5. Barrier, M. "The Mediation Disconnect," *HR Magazine*, May 2003, pp. 54–58.
6. "Dial to Pay $10 Million to Settle Sexual Harassment Case," *Baltimore Sun*, April 30, 2003, p. 9C.
7. Greene, K. "Odds on Age-Bias Suits," *South Florida Sun-Sentinel*, August 31, 2003, p. 6H.

Responding to the Supreme Court: Employment Practices and the ADA

Michael T. Zugelder and Paul J. Champagne, *Business Horizons*

On January 8, 2002, the United States Supreme Court decided in favor of Toyota Motor Manufacturing of Kentucky in a case brought by Ella Williams, a female assembly-line worker who had developed carpal tunnel syndrome in her wrists and bilateral tendinitis in her neck, shoulders, and arms as a result of gripping pneumatic tools to perform her job at the plant. Because she could no longer perform certain job functions, the company, as an accommodation, assigned her to two of the simpler jobs at the plant. However, after several years, management began to require other tasks that she was unable to do because of her medical problems. She requested that her job be modified to include only the simpler activities that did not exacerbate the carpal tunnel problem. Toyota management refused this request, and the employee was ultimately forced to resign. She brought suit under the Americans with Disabilities Act, alleging that Toyota had failed to provide her reasonable accommodation as required by statute.

The District Court granted Toyota summary judgment, holding that Williams's impairment did not qualify as a disability under the Act because it did not substantially limit any "major life activity." The Sixth Circuit reversed this ruling, finding sufficient evidence of an impairment that substantially limited the major life activity of "working" because she could not perform the repetitive motions and do the lifting necessary for assembly-line jobs.

In its reversal, the Supreme Court concluded that the Sixth Circuit had not applied the proper standard in making its determination because it analyzed only a "limited class of manual tasks" and failed to ask whether the employee's medical impairments restricted or prevented her from performing tasks that are "central to daily life," such as household chores, bathing, and brushing one's teeth. The Court also suggested that "working" may no longer be an appropriate "major life activity" under the ADA.

The *Toyota* case is another recent decision of the high court restricting the reach of the ADA. Yet while these decisions clearly side with employers, they also leave open many questions and probably create new ones with respect to the rights and responsibilities of employers and employees under the ADA.

Here we address the changing environment of the workplace as affected by the ADA. Following a brief discussion of the Act, we examine the recent Supreme Court decisions that clearly appear to restrict its coverage, draw management implications, and offer suggestions for employers in light of these decisions.

History and Framework of the ADA

Congress enacted the Americans with Disabilities Act with the clear intent of eliminating discrimination against disabled but otherwise qualified persons. Title 1 of the ADA is aimed at employment discrimination, prohibiting firms from evaluating employees based on a disorder rather than on their qualifications, skills, and abilities.

An individual who wishes to bring an employment discrimination claim under the ADA must demonstrate that several conditions are present. First, he must have a disability within the meaning of the ADA. Second, he must be qualified for the job with or without reasonable accommodation. Third, he must have been discriminated against in an employment situation because of the alleged disability. A person is disabled under the Act who (1) has a physical or mental impairment that substantially limits one or more of life's major activities, or (2) has a record of the impairment, or (3) is regarded as having such an impairment. The first part of this definition is supposed to cover actual disabilities, while the second and especially the third address stereotypes, stigmas, and social perceptions that cause people to be treated as if they were disabled.

At first glance, the law and its application may seem to be relatively clear; indeed, the descriptions of a physical or mental impairment within the language of the ADA are fairly straightforward. The problem, however, is that beyond the broadly constructed statutory language, the ADA lacks clear definition, thus leaving the question of what is or is not a covered condition open to interpretation on a case-by-case basis. For small to medium-size firms that lack in-house legal staff and human resource specialists, this may be especially difficult.

In an effort to address this problem, Congress empowered the EEOC to issue regulations in order to clarify ambiguities for courts and plaintiffs. In response, the Commission constructed interpretive guidelines in the appendix to the Code of Federal Regulations. However, because those guidelines are not congressionally mandated, they are binding on courts only to the extent that the courts unequivocally adopt the Commission's interpretations of the statute. In fact, the courts have often disagreed with the Commission. As a result, opinions have differed over time, and the question of what level of impairment constitutes a true ADA disability has been an active area of debate.

At the center of this debate is the following question: Is an individual who suffers from a condition that substantially limits a major life activity disabled, and must this determination be made without regard to mitigating measures? Until recently, the EEOC's guidelines said yes. Where an impairment was controlled by the mitigating measure, the plaintiff could expect protection even if he did not experience, or had never experienced, any limitations from the condition. Thus, people suffering from mild diabetes, treated hypertension, vision impairments requiring normal glasses and/or contacts, periodic but manageable depression, and so on could still be disabled and thus expect accommodation in the form of preferential treatment and certain working conditions.

Although the majority of the federal circuit courts have deferred to the EEOC's view concerning mitigation, others have taken the opposite view. The split opinion led to the US Supreme Court hearing and deciding three companion cases in 1999 that directly addressed the role of mitigation under the ADA.

A Mitigation Trilogy

In the first of the three 1999 cases, *Sutton v. United Airlines, Inc.*, the Court held that two applicants for commercial pilot jobs, who had very poor visual acuity without eyeglasses but perfect vision with corrective lenses, were not disabled under the ADA because disability must be determined taking into account the corrective mitigation measures they used. The twin sisters, Karen Sutton and Kimberly Hinton, applied for the positions but suffered myopia. Without eyeglasses or contact lenses, neither could see sufficiently to do many things, including driving a car, watching television, or flying an airplane; with corrective lenses, each had 20/20 vision and functioned normally. United, however, had a minimum vision standard for the position and required uncorrected visual acuity of 20/100. Because neither sister met the standard, they were both rejected for the position.

The sisters brought suit, claiming they were refused the position because of their disability or, in the alternative, because United regarded them as disabled.

The trial court dismissed the sisters' complaint, saying they were not disabled under the ADA because their impairment was fully correctable. Nor were they "regarded as" disabled by United. Merely being unable to satisfy the physical requirements of the job of commercial airline pilot did not constitute a perceived ADA disability. The Tenth Circuit affirmed the decision, as did the US Supreme Court, which addressed for the first time whether a court should consider the effect of measures that mitigated an individual's impairment. The Court held that such measures must be considered, and based its decision on several grounds. First, the ADA uses the present tense "substantially limits," requiring that a person be "presently"—not potentially or hypothetically—disabled in order to qualify. A corrected impairment, therefore, does not substantially limit a major life activity. Second, the statute requires an "individualized" inquiry into the effects of the impairment on the person's life. If people were viewed in their unmitigated states, courts and employers would have to speculate on their condition, looking to generalized information rather than actual effect. Third and finally, the Act's findings that some 43 million Americans have disabilities are inconsistent with the definition that includes people in their uncorrected states, because the latter definition would give as many as 160 million people ADA coverage.

The Court in *Sutton* also said that an employer does not "regard" an individual as disabled merely because the individual cannot meet the physical standards defined by a particular job. In their words, "The ADA allows employers to prefer some physical attributes over others and to establish physical criteria."

In *Murphy v. United Parcel Service, Inc.*, the Court ruled that a mechanic who used medication to control high blood pressure was not disabled under the Act. Vaughn Murphy's condition was controlled by medication, enabling him to function normally. However, once UPS became aware of his medical problem, it terminated his employment because his blood pressure exceeded Department of Transportation requirements. Murphy sued, alleging UPS violated the ADA by firing him based on his disability of hypertension or, in the alternative, because it regarded him as disabled. Affirming the rulings of the trial and appellate courts, the Supreme Court held that Murphy's hypertension did not substantially limit a major life activity because it was controlled with medication. Even though DOT regulations precluded him from mechanic jobs that required driving, his impairment did not exclude him from a wide range of other mechanic jobs, so he was not disabled in a major life activity of "working." Further, as in *Sutton*, the Court rejected Mr. Murphy's "regarded as" claim because UPS did not consider him unable to perform a class of jobs, just one specific job—a mechanic job requiring driving. In addition, the Court stressed that employers have the right and obligation to abide by federal safety standards, and Murphy's condition made him unqualified under those standards.

In *Albertson's, Inc. v. Kirkingburg*, the Court ruled that a truck driver who had vision in only one eye was not disabled because his disorder did not substantially limit the major life activity of seeing. Hallie Kirkingburg applied for a truck-driving job with Albertson's Grocery Store. Although the store hired him, it later discovered that he had not met DOT vision requirements for drivers of commercial vehicles. When the company learned of his monocular vision, Kirkingburg obtained a waiver under an experimental DOT program, but Albertson's fired him anyway, prompting his suit. The trial court granted summary judgment in favor of Albertson's, reasoning that the plaintiff's failure to pass a vision test made him unqualified for the essential functions of the truck driver job. The Ninth Circuit found that the plaintiff's brain had developed an ability to cope with his visual impairment.

Expanding on *Sutton*, the Court ruled that mitigation measures can include those undertaken by the body's own system in response to the impairment, and must be considered just like medication and eyeglasses in determining the question of ADA disability. Because Kirkingburg was able to see through the adjustments made by his body, such mitigation negated his principal disability claim. Further, the Court again ruled that the employer was entitled to rely on minimum safety standards, and the failure of the employee to meet such standards made him unqualified for the job, but did not make him disabled or "regarded as" disabled by the employer.

In addition to this mitigation trilogy, *Toyota v. Williams* (2002), discussed previously, has introduced further restrictions to the ADA's practical application to any workplace disability by holding that the phrase "a major life activity" means only those basic activities "of central importance to most people's daily lives," rather than any work-related tasks.

These Supreme Court decisions all balance in favor of the employer's hiring prerogative and would appear to add further support for employers when ADA claims reach federal court. But the time and expense associated with EEOC investigations and subsequent litigations still remain a problem. In addition, the recent decisions have their limitations and leave a number of important questions unanswered, as we will discuss.

Management Implications: Limitation to Cases and Open Questions Remaining

The four decisions cited above note specific limitations to mitigation, and have raised a series of questions regarding the responsibilities and rights of employers and employees. Unfortunately, many of these questions have not been answered clearly. For example: What if the mitigation is only partially corrective? Can an employer lawfully inquire about mitigation in order to determine whether an applicant or current employee is subject to accommodation and preferential treatment? Does the employee have an obligation to take medication or agree to use other mitigative aids if this would completely or generally control the impairment? And would failure to use available mitigating measures disqualify an employee from ADA protection? How are cases involving a "record" or "perceived as" having a disability affected by the decisions? Can a company reject or terminate a fully mitigated applicant or current employee just because it is uncomfortable with certain corrected disorders, or because a refusal to hire or termination might lower health insurance costs?

WHEN MITIGATION IS NOT TOTAL

In *Sutton*, the plaintiffs' vision was corrected to 20/20; in *Murphy*, high blood pressure was controlled by medication to within normal limits; and in *Albertson's*, the driver's monocular eyesight still did not disqualify him from a broad range of other job opportunities. Although these people were not ADA-disabled, the Court in *Sutton* clearly stated that the mitigation is only one factor and people who use mitigating measures may still be substantially limited in a major life activity and thus covered by the ADA. The Court also noted that even people who use mitigating measures may, in spite of or because of them, still be disabled under the Act.

As noted above, most lower courts are ruling in favor of employers when considering conditions/impairments that are fully controlled by medication or other forms of treatment. Individuals with an array of physical impairments—asthma, correctable hearing loss, epilepsy, sleep apnea, even diabetes, heart disease, blood cancer, and depression—have been found not to be disabled under the Act. But still other cases have sided with the employee, leaving the basic question unanswered. Thus, in *Carruth v. Continental Gen. Tire* (2001), an Illinois federal district court upheld a jury award of $175,000 in damages, along with $250,000 in punitive damages, to a diabetic who suffered from blood sugar flareups, even though the condition was largely controlled by corrective measures. In another decision, *Rowles v. Automated Production Systems, Inc.* (1999), the Court found the claimant's epilepsy presented a triable legal issue, denying the employer summary judgment based upon *Sutton*. Similarly, in *Bazert v. State Dept. of Public Safety and Correction* (2000), the Court found an ADA violation for the correction system's refusal to reassign an officer suffering from asthma.

To make matters even more complex, the EEOC's recently amended guidelines now take mitigative measures into account. Still, the new instructions to its field offices stress in detail that the Commission shall investigate and will pursue claims of disability discrimination where allegedly illegal treatment has occurred in the workplace based on a partially mitigated mental or physical condition or, in the case of a completely mitigated condition, as a result of a record of that condition or stereotypes about it. In particular, the Commission directs investigators to determine how well the mitigating measure controls the symptoms or limitation identified. For instance, a person who has a prosthetic hand, arm, or leg may continue to experience substantial limitations in performing certain manual tasks and thus be able to claim protection under the law. Another question would be whether the mitigating measure tends to become less effective under certain conditions, such as stress, weather conditions, illness, or other factors. Does the medication work long-term or does it tend to be effective only for a short period of time, such as someone with bipolar disorder whose medication wears off, or someone with Parkinson's Disease whose condition worsens over time, making the mitigation measure ineffective? The Commission will also investigate whether the individual has negative side effects from medication, using as an example a person with attention deficit disorder whose medication causes substantial inability to sleep. Further, the EEOC notes that impairments such as diabetes and the need for prosthetic limb devices may well continue to be disabilities, despite all efforts to mitigate. In short, the matter of mitigation is far from settled, and employers will still have to deal with employees and job applicants on a case-by-case basis.

CONTINUED PROHIBITION OF INQUIRY AND TESTING

The three 1999 Supreme Court decisions we discussed involved people who had already undertaken steps to control impairments that they admitted were totally mitigated as far as major life activities are concerned, though not sufficiently controlled for an employer's particular job requirements. Because fully mitigated people could not support a disability claim in those cases, employers might reasonably assume that such individuals are no longer protected from pre-hiring inquiries about disabilities. For instance, one question employers might want to ask in an interview or on an application would be: "Please describe any medical or mental impairment that you are able to control with medicine or other device." But although such a question might now seem permissible, the EEOC's latest guidance reinforces its position that the ADA's prohibition against pre-job offer disability inquiries and examinations remains intact. Thus, it is the Commission's position that if employers test for or ask about disabilities or mitigations of any applicant prior to the conditional job offer, they violate the Act. Only after the job offer is made can any medical examinations or inquiries be had, and even then they must be applied to all employees in the same class of jobs. Further, unless business necessity can be demonstrated, medical monitoring and testing for employees on the job continue to be very limited.

The EEOC's view was driven home in its August 31, 2000, announcement of a huge $6.8 million consent decree against retail giant Wal-Mart Stores, arising from a storewide Wal-Mart pre-employment questionnaire that sought disability-related information used to screen applicants from 1994 to 1998 before conditional job offers were made. Although the settlement occurred prior to *Sutton*, its announcement telegraphs to employers that prohibition against pre-employment inquiry and testing shall continue to be vigorously enforced.

DOES A DUTY TO MITIGATE EXIST? DOES REFUSAL DISQUALIFY?

Although employers have an obligation to offer reasonable accommodation once a physical or mental disability has been identified, no clear parallel can be drawn from the ADA or EEOC guidelines or case law decisions obligating the employee to take medication or employ some other mitigative device. But the issue has been squarely addressed in *Capizzi v. County of Placer* (2001). A carpet installer for the county, suffering from tendinitis, was fired and sued for wrongful dismissal and a failure to reasonably accommodate. The employer argued in summary judgment that the woman was a "disqualified" employee for her refusal to undertake cortisone shots or surgery to correct the tendinitis. The Court here refused to require the plaintiff to undertake those mitigations, holding that the ADA does not mandate employees to do so. The Court also stated that *Sutton* provided no basis on which to conclude otherwise.

A contrary view, however, was suggested in *Rose v. Home Depot USA, Inc.* (2002). Mr. Rose, suffering

from vasomotor rhinitis and a variety of other impairments, refused to obtain a physician's diagnosis for proper treatment. The Court found that the employee's refusal made him unqualified, reasoning that the opportunity to obtain a medical diagnosis for proper treatment was akin to refusing a reasonable accommodation by the employer. Moreover, in *Roberts v. County of Fairfax* (1996), the Court held that an employee with asthma who refused treatment was "unqualified" and therefore without ADA protection. Because the case law and the EEOC's guidelines on point are in conflict, the issue of whether an employee who could mitigate must do so or face disqualification is a long way from being settled. If this is true, fitness-for-duty tests used to determine whether a person is still otherwise qualified may be of dubious purpose.

CASES INVOLVING A "RECORD" OR "PERCEIVED AS" HAVING A DISABILITY

The Court's mitigation trilogy expressly warns employers about these types of discrimination cases. When the employer has relied on an old medical history or has made adverse employment decisions based on stereotypes concerning individual impairments, there may be ADA discrimination, even if an impairment is fully mitigated. In fact, this type of claim may become even more frequent.

When the employer, acting on the belief that the individual with a disability who mitigates it cannot perform the job simply because of the status of the disability, a claim is definitely stated for discrimination. For example, when a firm erroneously believes someone with a moderate hearing loss cannot be a secretary because a hearing aid will not, under any circumstances, allow him to hear telephones or clients needing assistance, the plaintiff's case would be strong. Same for an individual with epilepsy who does not actually have a substantially limiting impairment but is disqualified by an employer who has a generalized fear of seizures.

DISCRIMINATING AGAINST FULLY MITIGATED INDIVIDUALS

The Supreme Court decisions favoring the employer's hiring prerogative may lead employers to press that prerogative in other ways. For example, the cases suggest that a company is now allowed to reject an applicant or terminate a current employee whenever it is uncomfortable with a corrected disability. An applicant with, say, a controlled condition of bipolar disorder could lawfully be rejected just because the employer is uncomfortable with people whose behavior is chemically influenced. Further, a company might be moved to use the cases as a way to minimize health insurance costs by not hiring people with controlled impairments that require extensive medication and other medical treatments. While such employer actions may seem permissible, none of them have been addressed or expressly authorized by the decisions and could likewise lead to "regarded as" litigation.

DEBATABLE ISSUES

In many ways, the recent Supreme Court decisions make disability questions in employment more complex rather than less so. As the federal law now stands, impairments that are fully mitigated and therefore not substantially limiting no longer seem to qualify under the ADA. Still, if the condition is only partially mitigated or becomes a concern only under specific circumstances, then the protection of the law may apply. Moreover, the EEOC continues to aggressively pursue complaints and appears intent on enforcing the law as it sees it. This includes continuing prohibitions on tests and other prejob offer inquiries, as well as the employer's basic duties to disabled employees or job applicants. All of this leaves employers squarely in the middle of an ongoing debate between the federal courts and the EEOC. Conceding that mitigation must now be considered, the Commission apparently intends to enforce the balance of its earlier guidelines. So although the courts have not been terribly sympathetic to plaintiffs, there are still EEOC investigations and lawsuits that must be defended.

Beyond this, the fact is that the mitigation decisions are factually narrow. All three involved safety rules in regulated industries. The claimants had routine medical conditions that were already mitigated. The conditions were physical and not mental, and there were no substantial limitations in terms of major life activities. The claimants may not have qualified for a particular job, but they could certainly do many other things. *Sutton* held that rejected applicants for hiring or promotion no longer suffer "regarded as" discrimination simply because their impairments disqualify them from a particular job. Still, employers must be able to show that the job qualifications are based on essential job functions and that the adverse employment decision is not based on a "record" of prior treatment or mitigation, or on stereotypes and unwarranted bias that

the impaired but impairment-controlled individual cannot perform the job.

In addition, employers must continue to monitor hiring and other employment decisions so that they do not fall victim to litigation stemming from other civil rights statutes. A good example would be the well-known disparate impact test as established by *Griggs v. Duke Power* (1971). This test essentially means that an employer may establish job requirements, but if they result in substantially fewer members of a protected class being qualified, the standard itself must be consistent with business necessity and the specific requirements of the job. The *Sutton* language appears to deny the disparate impact test to plaintiffs claiming discrimination under the ADA. Again, however, this is not entirely clear.

The ADA is not the only law prohibiting disability discrimination. There is also the matter of state-by-state cases. The ADA does not preempt state disability discrimination laws from providing more generous remedies or broader definitions of disability, and many do not exclude mitigated impairments. In *Dahili v. Police Dept. of Boston* (2001), a police officer with a hearing impairment corrected to normal limits by hearing aids had no claim under the ADA but a valid one under the Massachusetts state disability law, which does not consider mitigation. Likewise, in *Shaw v. Greenwich Anesthesiology Associates, P.C.* (2001), under Connecticut law, an anesthesiologist was awarded $785,000 in back pay and compensatory damages from her practice for its refusal to accommodate her arthritis with leave time—even though she would not be disabled under the ADA because her condition was largely mitigated and, at worst, only affected a narrow range of work.

Disability-related cases in California have also become more complicated. As of January 1, 2001, the state provided sweeping new protections to people with disabilities. Although California law had previously followed the ADA, a condition or impairment under the new legislation can be considered a disability if it merely "limits" (not "substantially limits") a major life activity. The law also lowers the standard for determining when a major life activity is limited. The statute characterizes "limited" as an impairment that makes a life activity "difficult" but not impossible or extremely difficult to achieve. In addition, the California legislature rejected the Supreme Court decisions and wrote the law to say that employers have to evaluate someone's impairment without considering mitigating measures. Therefore, even if a condition can be controlled through treatment or medication, the person qualifies as disabled.

Employers must be alert to state law in their jurisdiction. The ADA does not prohibit state law from exceeding ADA protections, and most state disability statutes do not consider mitigation in assessing protection. Moreover, before employers place undue lasting reliance on the Supreme Court's ADA decisions, they should be aware that even those decisions can be reversed by an act of Congress. On several occasions in the past, Congress has amended civil rights legislation to specifically reverse decisions of the high court when it was found that the court's decisions defeated legislative intent. A legislative response could therefore ultimately reverse these ADA decisions.

The recent Supreme Court decisions narrowing the coverage of the Americans with Disabilities Act hold that mitigating measures must be considered in determining whether one has a disability within the Act's meaning. Though the mitigation trilogy and subsequent *Toyota* decision balance in favor of employers' prerogatives with respect to disabled individuals in the workplace, those decisions do have limitations and leave many questions unanswered. In light of the EEOC's aggressive posture toward enforcement of the ADA, employers must give due consideration before they conclude that any individual applicant or employee falls outside the ADA's protections. As always, professional legal advice in this regard is recommended.

Source: Reprinted with permission from *Business Horizons*, Jan–Feb 2003, pp. 30–36. Copyright © 2003 by the Trustees at Indiana University.

References and Selected Bibliography

Albertson's v. Kirkingburg, 527 U.S. 555 (1999).

Americans with Disabilities Act of 1990, 42 U.S.C. 12101 (2001).

Bazert v. State Dept. of Public Safety and Correction. 768 So.2d 279 (La.App. 1 Cir. 2000).

Burke, Debra, and Malcolm Abel. 2001. Ameliorating medication and the ADA protection: Use it or lose it or refuse it and lose it? *American Business Law Journal* 38/4 (Summer): 785–817.

California Law Expands ADA Protection. 2001. *HR News* 20/3 (March): 1,4.

Capizzi v. County of Placer, 135 F.Supp.2d 1105 (E.D.Cal. 2001).

Carruth v. Continental Gen. Tire, 12 A.D. Cases 1244, 2001 W.I. 1775992 (S.D.Ill. 2001).

Coleman, Charles J. 2001. The Sutton trilogy: Changing the landscape of the ADA. *Journal of Individual Employment Rights* 9/1: 55–69.

Dahill v. Police Dept. of Boston, 434 Mass. 233, 748 N.E.2d 956 (Mass. 2001).

Equal Employment Opportunity Commission. 2001. Comprehensive EEOC. *Wal-Mart Settlement Resolves Disability Lawsuit* Washington: EEOC.

Equal Employment Opportunity Commission. 2000. *EEOC enforcement guidance on disability-related inquiries and medical examiniations of employees under the Americans With Disabilities Act* (ADA). Washington: EEOC.

Griggs v. Duke Power, 401 U.S. 424 (1971).

Harrington, Christine M. 2000. The Americans With Disabilities Act: The new definition of disability post-Sutton v. United Airlines, Inc. *Marquette Law Review* 84: 251–271.

Murphy v. United Parcel Service, Inc., 527 U.S. 516 (1999), *aff'g* 946 F.Supp. 872 (D.Kan 1996).

Roberts v. County of Fairfax, 937 F.Supp. 541 (E.D.Va. 1996).

Rose v. Home Depot USA, Inc., 186 F.Supp. 2d 595, 2002 W.L. 334107 (D.Md. 2002).

Rowles v. Automated Production Systems, Inc., 92 F.Supp.2d 424, 10 A.D. Cases 1542 (M.D.Pa. 1999).

Shaw v. Greenwich Anesthesiology Associates, P.C., No. 3:99CV1076 (D.Conn. 2001).

Sutton v. United Airlines, Inc., 527 U.S. 471 (1999).

Thompson, Ian D. 2000. Medicating the ADA—*Sutton v. United Airlines, Inc.*: Considering mitigating measures to define disabilities. *Pepperdine Law Review* 28: 257–288.

Toyota Motor Mfg., Kentucky, Inc. v. Ella Williams, 534 U.S. 184 (2002).

The Dual Loyalty Dilemma for HR Managers Under Title VII Compliance

Jeffrey A. Mello, *SAM Advanced Management Journal*

Introduction

When Congress passed Title VII of the Civil Rights Act of 1964 (42 U.S.C. Sect. 2000e, *et. seq.*), it sought to eradicate employment discrimination based on race, color, national origin, sex, and religion. Under the Act the Equal Employment Opportunity Commission (EEOC) was created with an envisioned role of conciliating allegations of discrimination as opposed to functioning as a watchdog agency. Congress intended the main responsibility for compliance with Title VII to rest with employers, who were expected to establish their own internal voluntary Title VII compliance mechanisms.

To ensure that any employee allegations of unlawful discrimination were not met with any kind of employer retaliation, the Act expressly prohibits employers from engaging in any such behavior. A problem has arisen, however, because judicial interpretations of this retaliation provision have excluded managerial personnel, particularly human resource and equal employment opportunity (HR/EEO) managers, from its protection. By excluding these managers from protection, the courts have favored management prerogatives to terminate employees perceived to be disloyal to the employer over the rights provided to employees under Title VII. Consequently, the protection Congress intended to afford employees under Title VII has been severely undermined. This article discusses the purpose of Title VII, its anti-retaliation provision, the dual and conflicting roles of the HR manager relative to Title VII, and the need for a judicial interpretation of role of the HR/EEO manager that is more consistent with Congressional intent.

The Purpose of Title VII

When Congress enacted Title VII, it sought to create a largely self-regulating system by which employers would voluntarily abandon the discriminatory practices prohibited in the Act and do so with minimal outside intervention by government agencies. Congress sought to promote voluntary compliance due to its serious concerns that any governmental oversight and control efforts to eradicate employment discrimination would prohibitively interfere with individual business prerogatives. In fact, when Congress established the EEOC, it envisioned an agency that would respond to complaints rather than initiate them and would perform a mediation or conciliation function as opposed to an adjudication role (42 U.S.C. Sect. 2000e – 5(f) and (g)). This very point was noted by the Supreme Court in *Alexander v. Gardner-Denver Co.* (415 U.S. 36, 44, 94 S. Ct. 1011, 1017, 39 L.Ed. 147 (1974)), which also noted that the EEOC was not empowered by Congress with any direct authority to enforce Title VII. Such powers rested with the federal court system.

It has become apparent to even the Commissioner of the EEOC that Congress's intended voluntary compliance scheme is not working; EEOC Vice-Chairman Paul Igalaski recently commented that "our process is broken and needs substantial reform" (Lawyers Committee for Civil Rights Under Law, 1995). Each year, the volume of discrimination litigation continues to soar. In fiscal year 1994, the EEOC received 91,189 charges of discrimination compared to 63,898 in 1991, a 42.7% increase in three years (EEOC Annual Report; Fiscal Year 1994). As a result, there has been increased and unwelcome government intervention through judicial scrutiny of business affairs that Congress intended to remain as prerogatives of individual businesses through its voluntary compliance plan. Even though Congress designed Title VII to keep employment discrimination allegations out of court, dockets continue to be flooded with such cases.

At first glance the cause of this is not readily apparent. The means of enforcing Title VII are relatively sound, and the role of the EEOC is quite clear. The EEOC receives employee complaints for the purpose of conciliation as a prerequisite for obtaining relief through the courts. The EEOC conducts a preliminary investigation, and complaints without merit are dismissed, with the complainant presumably discouraged from litigating. EEOC investigations that find charges with merit provide an incentive for employers to rectify behavior and practices because the EEOC has the power to file suit on behalf of the aggrieved employee or employees. Hence, there is a strong incentive for employers, if they do unlawfully discriminate, to resolve matters in-house quickly and quietly.

Ideally the process outlined in Title VII should dispose of most claims without litigation. The voluntary compliance mechanism would allow an organization to keep its "dirty laundry" from the public domain and, in cases where the EEOC found discriminatory behavior on the part of employers and attempted conciliation, there was a clear incentive for organizations to cooperate, given the cost and time involved with litigation, not to mention having a mark on their records with the federal government and EEOC.

In 1991, Congress passed an amendment to Title VII which greatly altered employee/employer Title VII dynamics. In the years that had passed since the original passage of Title VII, a number of EEOC complaints had made their way to the courts, and it became painfully apparent that Title VII's remedies for aggrieved plaintiffs were far inferior to those found in other federal anti-discrimination laws. For example, the Age Discrimination In Employment Act of 1967 (29 U.S.C. Sect. 626(b)) allows punitive double liquidated damages and jury trials. In contrast, Title VII prior to the 1991 amendment, provided neither compensation or punitive damages nor jury trials.

As a result, Congress enacted the Civil Rights Act of 1991 (42 U.S.C. Sect. 1981 A(2)), which added compensatory and punitive damages as well as the opportunity for jury trials as remedies for Title VII violations. These new remedies gave grievants an additional incentive to file complaints and to litigate. The combination of these new remedies with the passage of the Americans With Disabilities Act of 1990 (42 U.S.C. Sect. 12101, *et. seq.*) caused EEOC litigation to skyrocket. Since 1992, the EEOC has averaged more than 85,000 charges per year (Shapiro, 1998). As employment discrimination complaints have overwhelmed the EEOC and litigation has swamped the courts, the EEOC has responded by instituting mandatory mediation programs as well as limiting EEOC investigations to selected cases (Bureau of National Affairs, 1996). In fact, the EEOC has attempted to slash its pending caseload by offering mediation-based alternative dispute resolution for nearly half the charges it finds valid (EEOC Annual Report: Fiscal Year 1997).

Unfortunately, the effect of such selective enforcement of laws does not prevent the type of employment discrimination Congress sought to eradicate when it passed Title VII. Certainly, employers who become aware that the EEOC selectively enforces Title VII, due to the hemorrhaging burdens on the agency, may be more likely to discriminate, given the lesser likelihood of incurring Title VII enforcement and penalties. The commission had more than 100,000 backlogged cases by 1995, which caused Vice Chairman Igasaki to state that "the enormous build-up of pending cases has resulted in a serious loss of public confidence and faith in the EEOC's ability to effectively carry out its responsibilities" (Lawyers Committee for Civil Rights Under Law, 1995).

While the source of this problem may largely rest with the fact that the EEOC has strayed from its role as originally envisioned by Congress, there is an additional issue contributing to the problem that relates to the failure of voluntary compliance mechanisms. Judicial interpretations of Title VII have essentially debilitated the key persons, human resource managers responsible for EEOC, who would be overseeing internal compliance systems from effectively performing this role. As a result, the system that attempts to resolve claims of discrimination under Title VII has been brought to the virtual standstill.

The Nature of the Role of the HR Manager

In many organizations the role of the HR manager is often somewhat ambiguous. Ideally, when chasms exist between employees and management, the role of the human resources function is to bridge these chasms and resolve conflict between employees and management in creating and maintaining a motivating work environment conducive to high performance. Whether the HR manager is principally more a representative of management to handle employee problems or an advocate of employee concerns to management is not always clear, and the dual expectations often placed on the HR manager can create an ambiguous and conflicting dual loyalty.

This has been especially true as the role of HR has evolved in modern organizations. While HR was once largely an administrative function, its role has changed to one that is centrally involved in top management arenas such as strategic planning and legal compliance. In managing workplace dynamics such as conflict resolution and change processes such as restructuring, HR is often called upon to bridge the needs of the organization and the rights and interests of workers, particularly in collective bargaining environments. The HR manager is expected to establish an atmosphere of trust and confidentiality with employees to facilitate in-house resolution of grievances.

In many instances, advocating for employees or employee groups does not conflict with the responsibility of loyalty to the employer, and the HR manager avoids any duality of responsibility. In many organizations, the HR manager is relied upon to be the voice of the employees in bringing up and resolving employee concerns. However, in certain instances, the role of employee advocacy can directly conflict with the employer's interests and goals for the organization and, therefore, creates a tension for the HR manager between loyalty to employer and responsibility to employees. In this regard, the HR manager's primary role is far less apparent.

The management literature is conspicuously silent concerning any examination or study of this potential conflict of interest. Even the Code of Ethics of the nation's largest professional HR organization, the Society of Human Resource Management, states that the HR manager is supposed "to make the fair and equitable treatment of all employees a primary concern" while simultaneously stating expectations "to maintain loyalty to the employer, even while upholding all laws and regulations relating to the employer's activities."

Because HR generally has principal responsibility for compliance with EEOC legislation, HR is usually the place where employees initially file complaints of behaviors that violate their Title VII rights. Ideally, HR tries to resolve any such complaints in-house. This process is not only in line with what Congress intended but is also clearly in the employer's best interest (in maintaining employee morale, minimizing the time and cost of possible litigation, and avoiding any public disclosure of claims) as well as the best interest of the employee (in securing a more timely resolution and avoiding the stressful EEOC investigation and possible litigation). Clearly, the appropriate posture for HR is not to simply advocate or, at worst, defend management's position nor to do anything to placate a disgruntled employee, but to ensure that the issues are resolved fairly in-house. This may involve attempting to persuade management that the employee's point of view is more valid than that of management from a practical, ethical, or most important, legal perspective.

The HR manager will only succeed to the extent that employees perceive that he or she is their advocate against allegedly unlawful management practices. If HR lacks credibility, employees are far more likely to seek redress outside of the organization. The role of the HR manager in developing and managing an internal grievance policy requires a delicate balancing act between the interest of employees and those of the employer. Given this tension, an HR manager in an organization in which senior management supports full compliance with Title VII will find it rarely necessary to advocate employee positions that may be at odds with those of management. Management's support of Title VII should prevent such adversarial dilemmas. However, in an organization where commitment to Title VII and EEO are absent or, at worst, where management knowingly or unknowingly continues to illegally discriminate against employees, the HR function may find itself in a precarious position.

The HR manager clearly needs to be able to promote a law-abiding workplace in which employee trust can be maintained without fear of reprisal by the employer in cases where HR must challenge management. This is in the best interest of the employer and is clearly consistent with Congressional intent. Even though this posture would strengthen the system that Congress sought to establish under Title VII, Congress itself has made this end unobtainable due to judicial interpretations of a provision in Title VII that pertains to anti-retaliation protection.

Anti-Retaliation Under Title VII

Title VII's anti-retaliation provision has been described as the broadest found in any federal law where rank-and-file employees are concerned (Walterscheid, 1988). A specific portion of Section

704(a) of the Civil Rights Act of 1964 prohibits employers from discriminating against any employee who has opposed any practice made unlawful by the Act, filed any charge under the Act, or testified, asserted or participated in any manner in an investigation, proceeding or hearing under the Act. It states, "It shall be an unlawful employment practice for an employer to discriminate . . . against any employee or applicant for employment . . . because [the employee or applicant] has opposed any practice made an unlawful employment practice by this title, or because [the employee or applicant] has made a charge, testified, assisted or participated in any manner in an investigation, proceeding or hearing under this title" (42 U.S.C. Sect. 2000e-3(a)). Even employees who participate in a process in which the employer's conduct is deemed lawful would receive protection under 704(a) as long as the opposition was done in good faith and based on an objectively reasonable belief that unlawful discrimination had in fact occurred (Bales, 1994). Acts of retaliation by employers are extensive. The EEOC reports that 22.5% of the complaints it receives pertain to employer retaliation (Shapiro, 1998).

While the language and framework that prohibit retaliation may seem cut and dried, a series of retaliation cases have revolved around the argument by the employer that when the employee was "punished," the action was not taken on account of his or her oppositional position or conduct but rather because the employee had been disruptive or disloyal to the employer in the course of opposing the allegedly discriminatory employment practice or had caused the employer excessive harm that infringed on the employer's right to run his business. The first federal appellate court to address this issue was the First Circuit Court of Appeals in *Hochstadt v. Worcester Foundation for Experimental Biology* (545 F.2d 222 (1st Cir. 1976)). In this case, a research scientist claimed illegal sex discrimination based on a perceived pay disparity and filed charges with the Massachusetts Commission Against Discrimination, the EEOC, the Department of Labor and the Department of Health, Education, and Welfare. In preparing her claim, Hochstadt conducted her legal business on company time and solicited information from coworkers, who, in turn, complained that she disrupted their work. Hochstadt alleged that her termination was in retaliation for her sex discrimination claim, while the employer said she was terminated for her performance and disruptive behavior.

As the court weighed the respective interests of the parties, it sought to determine whether the plaintiff's oppositional conduct was "excessive" in terms of its injury to the employer's interests. In attempting to find the appropriate balance between the rights of the employer (to "run his business") versus the rights of the employee (to "express her grievance and promote her own welfare"), the court reasoned that Section 704(a) did not afford employees unlimited license to complain at any and all times and places and that oppositional conduct should not be deliberately calculated to inflict needless economic hardship on the employer. It ruled that Hochstadt's poor work performance and disruptive behavior resulted in the discharge, and that while her complaint had some merit, her actions were so excessive as to be outside of the protection of section 704(a).

The Hochstadt case became a precedent for other courts who followed by denying anti-retaliation protection to employees who engaged in a variety of behaviors including disclosing confidential records, making loud threats of calling the "labor board" in the presence of others, participating in a disruptive, noise demonstration during working hours, making militant demands for paid time to prepare EEO complaints, and engaging in loud and insubordinate conduct in public working areas. The Ninth Circuit later questioned the logic behind the Hochstadt court's reasoning in *EEOC v. Crown Zellerbach Corporation* (720 F.2d 1008 (9th Cir. 1983)) when it ruled that under the Hochstadt decision every oppositional action by employees can be deemed disloyal or disruptive and, hence, virtually every opposition claim could easily be defeated by employers.

While the *Hochstadt* precedent has made it relatively easy for employers to defeat the retaliation charges levied by nonmanagerial employees, cases in which the plaintiffs were management-level employers have been even easier to defeat. In *Hicks v. ABT Associated, Inc.* (572 F.2d 960 (3d Cir. 1978)) and *Silas v. City Demonstration Agency* (588 F.2d 297 (9th Cir. 1978)), the courts found that anti-retaliation was not available when the employees' directly conflicted with their job duties. One court ruled, in *Notovny v. Great American Federal Savings & Loan Association* (539 F.Supp. 437 (W. D. Pa. 1982)), that the higher an employee is on the management ladder, the more circumspect that employee should be in expressing opposition to employment practices of which he disapproves. This argument essentially eradicates any protection managerial employees could expect to receive for any perceived opposition, given the fact that managers are essentially "agents" of their employers.

This raises the questions as to how the HR manager with EEO responsibility can be assertive concerning compliance with and violations of Title VII's express terms and policies when he or she is totally deprived of any protection from retaliation. The first court to address this problems was the Court of Appeals for the District of Columbia in *Pendleton v. Rumsfield* (628 F.2d 102 (9 D.C. Cir. 1980)). In this case, two individuals who were employed as EEO counselors attended an employee demonstration protesting employer policies relating to EEO and were fired for doing so and sued under the 704(a) anti-retaliation provision. The sharply divided court in this case noted the dual responsibilities of the counselors, particularly in light of the fact that the employer had provided the counselors with a very ambiguous job description. The majority of the court held that the counselors constantly needed to reaffirm their "undivided loyalty" to management in a way that did not tolerate oppositional conduct such as attending the protest. The dissent recognized that the counselors attending the protest were acting as true intermediaries in attempting to gain the confidence of employees and information necessary to settle the disputes.

This decision was followed by a redefining of the role of the HR/EEO manager in very narrow, one-dimensional terms, in which managers engaged in any conduct perceived by management as oppositional may be viewed as "ineffective" if management decide it can no longer place absolute trust in such employees. In *Smith v. Singer* (650 F.2d 214 (9th Cir. 1981)), an EEO counselor himself contacted and filed a charge with the EEOC on behalf of an employee after attempts to reconcile the complaint with management were futile. In upholding the counselor's dismissal based on disloyalty, the court ruled that "to grant protection to a manager engaged in oppositional conduct would force the company to keep in its ranks an adversary who would be forever immune from dismissal" and that once a manager becomes an adversary, he or she is "wholly disabled" from "representing the company before any agencies as well as working with executives in the voluntary development of nondiscriminatory hiring programs." This court took the express position that adversarial views within the management ranks threaten rather than foster voluntary compliance. It reasoned that an interpretation of Section 704(a) to protect oppositional conduct by HR/EEO managers "would render wholly unworkable the program of voluntary compliance which [the manager] was employed to conduct."

Similarly, in *Jones v. Flagship* (793 F.2d 714 (5th Cir. 1986), cert. denied, 479 U.S. 1065 (1987)), the Fifth Circuit ruled and the Supreme Court affirmed that an EEO counselor's need to maintain the trust and confidence of management superseded any rights or goals that might be advanced by affording the manager anti-retaliation protection under Section 704(a). The court reasoned that in providing aid and comfort to an employee, Jones had undermined her role in "acting as the representative of the company before administrative agencies in cases filed against the company" and "critically harmed [the employer's] posture in the defense of discrimination suits brought against the company." Likewise in *Herrera v. Mobile Oil, Inc.* (53 Fair Empl. Prac. Cas. (BNA) 1406 (W. D. Tex. 1990)), the court found that when Herrera, an employee relations advisor, counseled and advised a disgruntled employee to file an EEOC charge, such action placed Herrera in a "squarely adversarial position" with his employer, leaving the employer "no option but to terminate him."

Lack of confidence was also upheld as a legitimate reason to usurp any protection an EEO manager might expect against retaliation in the Sixth Circuit case of *Holden v. Owen-Illinois* (793 F.2d 745 (6th Cir. 1986), cert. denied 479 U.S. 1008 (1986)). In this case the dismissal of a plaintiff who had been hired to design and implement an affirmative action program and subsequently developed a stronger program than her employer desired was upheld. The Eleventh Circuit also failed to provide Section 704(a) protection to an EEO officer in *Hamm v. Members of Board of Regents of State of Florida* (708 F.2d 647 (11th Cir. 1983)). When the officer released reports to newspapers and files to employees, the court found that such a breach of duty was outside of the protection of Section 704(a). The court also found that the plaintiff's duties required obedience to management prerogatives, as opposed to discretionary conduct.

Need for a New Interpretation

A call has been made for all opposition activity by rank-and-file employees to be afforded unconditional 704(a) protection to prevent judicial abandonment of employees' anti-retaliation rights and to ensure that Title VII's protection is not totally undermined (Bales, 1994). However, this argument for reform has also provided for retaining the lack of 704(a) protection to managerial employees involved with EEO enforcement due to the precarious nature of their roles.

Management staff, particularly HR managers, have been clearly distinguished from rank-and-file employees by the courts, who have denied protection against employer retaliation. Because HR managers are an increasingly integral part of their organization's management teams, they obviously should be expected to comply with and enforce their employer's policy decisions. No employer should be forced to tolerate disruption, disloyalty, or insubordination from key players of its management team.

However, a critical problem remains in that the courts have placed the HR manager's responsibility to employers on a direct collision course with the intentions of Congress in eradicating many types of discrimination in employment. An HR manager who values his or her job and career may be forced to make a difficult choice when these two responsibilities collide. In fact, when this paper was presented at the 1998 International Society for the Advancement of Management Conference in Washington, DC, one individual in the audience described how she had been faced with this very dilemma as a senior HR manager with EEO responsibility. When asked how she handled it, she replied, "I was in a no-win situation and did the only thing I could do—I resigned," to audible gasps in the room. She further noted that resignations of senior HR officials for that reason were common and accepted within her professional network.

In the public sector, the issue becomes even more complex. First Amendment rights can be raised in connection with the government's action as an employer seeking to discharge or discipline an HR manager or any other employee. Employees' rights to be free from government restriction on speech involving matters of public concern would also need to be balanced (along with Title VII protection against retaliation) with the government employer's right to set management policy. The public employee's ultimate loyalty should be to the public, which places further strain on efforts to promote loyalty and strict obedience to agency leadership (Rosenbloom, 1998).

Summary

Clearly there is a need to reexamine the roles, rights, and responsibilities of the HR manager relative to Title VII. If the HR manager is expected to be the catalyst to promoting voluntary compliance, her or she needs to be able to be more of an intermediary and not just a "management employee whose job is to make claims go away." The dual roles of HR in attending to the needs and upholding the legal rights of employees while simultaneously looking out for the interests and needs of management involves a precarious balancing act. This is particularly true when the issues involve Title VII compliance.

As it stands, Title VII's anti-retaliation provision effectively prohibits the HR manager from any employee advocacy whatsoever, assuming that the HR manager values and wishes to retain his/her job. As a result, the burden is essentially imposed on individual employees to challenge management and file their own claims, further burdening the EEOC and court system. If the HR manager had a reasonably good faith belief that management practices or behavior were in violation of Title VII, anti-retaliation protection should not be denied, as it is not denied to rank-and-file employees. Without 704(a) anti-retaliation protection, the HR manager has little choice than to advocate management's point of view and totally abandon the employee advocacy role intended by Congress to be played by someone internal to the organization. Absent this protection, the EEOC is forced to assume this advocacy role, unleashing the floodgates of litigation on an agency and court system that are already overburdened and unable to respond to complaints in a timely manner, if at all. The end result is that employers are afforded the opportunity to ignore Title VII, at least in the short run, and frustrated employees, feeling that the system is unresponsive to their needs, are forced to live with and accept the various forms of discrimination in employment that Congress sought to eradicate under the Title VII. Moreover, the human resources function will be able to gain the trust and confidence of employees, deepening any chasms that might exist between employee groups and management.

As long as any opposition whatsoever by managerial employees, particularly HR/EEO managers, continues to be seen by the courts as disloyal and indefensible and outside of Section 704(a) protection, the interests and goals of Title VII will be undermined. Absent an act of Congress to amend Title VII and provide anti-retaliation protection for HR managers, HR/EEO managers must be afforded some alternative interpretation of their job duties and responsibilities by the courts that will allow the internal compliance function to operate effectively. Until HR/EEO managers can persuade the courts to adopt a different rule of law, the internal compliance ideal of Congress will remain just that, an ideal, and the provisions of law of Title VII will continue to be undermined and circumvented in the workplace.

Source: *SAM Advanced Management Journal* by Mello. Copyright © 2000 by Society for Advancement of Management. Reprinted with permission of Society for Advancement of Management in the format Textbook via Copyright Clearance Center.

References

Bales, R. (1994). A New Standard for Title VII Opposition Cases: Fitting the Personnel Manager Double Standard Into A Cognizable Framework. 35 *South Texas Law Review*, 95.

Bureau of National Affairs. National Enforcement Plan of the Equal Employment Opportunity Commission in *Employment Discrimination Report*, 6, 18 February, 1996.

Equal Employment Commission. *EEOC Annual Report: Fiscal Year 1994*.

Equal Employment Commission. *EEOC Annual Report: Fiscal Year 1997*.

Lawyers Committee for Civil Rights Under Law, *Civil Rights Act and EEO News*, 19, May, 1995.

Rosenbloom, D. (1998). *Public Administration*. New York: McGraw-Hill.

Shapiro, L. (1998). EEOC Backlog Reduced: Race Bias Charges Most Common. *California Employer Advisor*, 7, (10), 8.

Waltersceid, E. C. (1988). A Question of Retaliation: Opposition Conduct As Protected Expression Under Title VII of the Civil Rights Act of 1964. *Boston College Law Review*, 29.

In Defense of Preference

Nathan Glazer, *The New Republic*

Affirmative action is bad. Banning it is worse.

The battle over affirmative action today is a contest between a clear principle on the one hand and a clear reality on the other. The principle is that ability, qualifications, and merit, independent of race, national origin, or sex should prevail when one applies for a job or promotion, or for entry into selective institutions of higher education, or when one bids for contracts. The reality is that strict adherence to this principle would result in few African Americans getting jobs, admissions, and contracts. What makes the debate so confused is that the facts that make a compelling case for affirmative action are often obscured by the defenders of affirmative action themselves. They have resisted acknowledging how serious that gaps are between African Americans and others, how deep the preferences reach, how systematic they have become. Considerably more than a mild bent in the direction of diversity now exists, but it exists because painful facts make it necessary if blacks are to participate in more than token numbers in some key institutions of our society. The opponents of affirmative action can also be faulted: they have not fully confronted the consequences that must follow from the implementation of the principle that measured ability, qualification, merit, applied without regard to color, should be our only guide.

I argued for that principle in a 1975 book titled, provocatively, *Affirmative Discrimination*. It seemed obvious that that was what all of us, black and white, were aiming to achieve through the revolutionary civil rights legislation of the 1960s. That book dealt with affirmative action in employment, and with two other kinds of governmentally or judicially imposed "affirmative action," the equalization of the racial proportions in public schools and the integration of residential neighborhoods. I continued to argue and write regularly against governmentally required affirmative action, that is, racial preference, for the next two decades or more; it was against the spirit of the Constitution, the clear language of the civil rights acts, and the interests of all of us in the United States in achieving an integrated and just society.

It is not the unpopularity of this position in the world in which I live, liberal academia, that has led me to change my mind but, rather, developments that were unforeseen and unexpected in the wake of the successful civil rights movement. What was unforeseen and unexpected was that the gap between the educational performance of blacks and whites would persist and, in some respects, deepen despite the civil rights revolution and hugely expanded social and educational programs, that inner-city schools would continue to decline, and that the black family would unravel to a remarkable degree, contributing to social conditions for large numbers of black children far worse than those in the 1960s. In the presence of those conditions, an insistence on color-blindness means the effective exclusion today of African Americans from positions of influence, wealth, and power. It is not a prospect that any of us can contemplate with equanimity. We have to rethink affirmative action.

In a sense, it is a surprise that a fierce national debate over affirmative action has not only persisted but intensified during the Clinton years. After twelve years under two Republican presidents, Ronald Reagan and George Bush, who said they opposed affirmative action but did nothing to scale it back, the programs seemed secure. After all, affirmative action rests primarily on a presidential executive order dating back to the presidencies of Lyndon Johnson and Richard Nixon which requires "affirmative action" in employment practices from federal contractors—who include almost every large employer, university, and hospital. The legal basis for most of affirmative action could thus have been swept away, as so many noted at the time, with a "stroke of the pen" by the president. Yet two presidents who claimed to oppose affirmative action never wielded the pen.

Despite the popular majority that grumbles against affirmative action, there was (and is) no major elite constituency strongly opposed to it: neither business nor organized labor, religious leaders nor university presidents, local officials nor serious presidential candidates are to be found in opposition. Big business used to fear that affirmative action would undermine the principle of employment and promotion on the basis of qualifications. It has since become a supporter. Along with mayors and other local officials (and of course the civil rights movement), it played a key role in stopping the Reagan administration from moving against affirmative action. Most city administrations have also made their peace with affirmative action.

Two developments outside the arena of presidential politics galvanized both opponents and defenders of affirmative action. The Supreme Court changed glacially after successive Republican appointments—each of which, however, had been vetted by a Democratic Senate—and a number of circuit courts began to chip away at the edifice of affirmative action. But playing the largest role was the politically unsophisticated effort of two California professors to place on the California ballot a proposition that would insert in the California Constitution the simple and clear words, taken from the Civil Rights Act of 1964, which ban discrimination on the basis of race, national origin, or sex. The decision to launch a state constitutional proposition, Proposition 209, suddenly gave opponents the political instrument they needed to tap the majority sentiment that has always existed against preferences.

While supporters of affirmative action do not have public opinion on their side, they do have the still-powerful civil rights movement, the major elites in education, religion, philanthropy, government, and the mass media. And their position is bolstered by a key fact: how far behind African Americans are when judged by the tests and measures that have become the common coin of American meritocracy.

The reality of this enormous gap is clearest where the tests in use are the most objective, the most reliable, and the best validated, as in the case of the various tests used for admission to selective institutions of higher education, for entry into elite occupations such as law and medicine, or for civil service jobs. These tests have been developed over many years specifically for the purpose of eliminating biases in admissions and appointments. As defenders of affirmative action often point out, paper-and-pencil tests of information, reading comprehension, vocabulary, reasoning, and the like are not perfect indicators of individual ability. But they are the best measures we have for success in college and professional schools, which, after all, require just the skills the tests measure. And the test can clearly differentiate the literate teacher from the illiterate one or the policeman who can make out a coherent arrest report from one who cannot.

To concentrate on the most hotly contested area of affirmative action—admission to selective institutions of higher education—and on the group in the center of the storm—African Americans: If the Scholastic Assessment Test were used for selection in a color-blind fashion, African Americans, who today make up about six percent of the student bodies in selective colleges and universities, would drop to less than two percent, according to a 1994 study by the editor of the *Journal of Blacks in Higher Education.*

Why is this so? According to studies summarized in Stephan and Abigail Thernstrom's book, *America in Black and White,* the average combined SAT score for entering freshmen in the nation's top 25 institutions is about 1300. White applicants generally need to score a minimum of 600 on the verbal portion of the test—a score obtained by eight percent of the test-takers in 1995—and at least 650 on the mathematics section—a score obtained by seven percent of the test-takers in 1995. In contrast, only 1.7 percent of black students scored over 600 on the verbal section in 1995, and only two percent scored over 650 on the math. This represents considerable progress over the last 15 years, but black students still lag distressingly far behind their white counterparts.

There is no way of getting around this reality. Perhaps the tests are irrelevant to success in college? That cannot be sustained. They have been improved and revised over decades and predict achievement in college better than any alternative. Some of the revisions have been carried out in a near-desperate effort to exclude items which would discriminate against blacks. Some institutions have decided they will not use the tests, not because they are invalid per se, but because they pose a barrier to the increased admission of black students. Nor would emphasizing other admissions criteria, such as high school grades, make a radical difference. In any case, there is considerable value to a uniform national standard, given the enormous difference among high schools.

Do qualifications at the time of admission matter? Isn't the important thing what the institutions manage to do with those they admit? If they graduate, are they not qualified? Yes, but many do not graduate. Two or three times as many African American students as white students drop out before graduation. And the tests for admission to graduate schools show the same radical disparities between blacks and others. Are there not also preferences for athletes, children of alumni, students gifted in some particular respect? Yes, but except for athletes, the disparities in academic aptitude that result from such preferences are not nearly as substantial as those which must be elided in order

to reach target figures for black students. Can we not substitute for the tests other factors—such as the poverty and other hardships students have overcome to reach the point of applying to college? This might keep up the number of African Americans, but not by much, if the studies are to be believed. A good number of white and Asian applicants would also benefit from such "class-based" affirmative action.

(I have focused on the effect of affirmative action—and its possible abolition—on African Americans. But, of course, there are other beneficiaries. Through bureaucratic mindlessness, Asian Americans and Hispanics were also given affirmative action. But Asian Americans scarcely need it. Major groups—not all—of Hispanic Americans trial behind whites but mostly for reasons we understand: problems with the English language and the effect on immigrant children of the poor educational and economic status of their parents. We expect these to improve in time as they always have with immigrants to the

---

Testing Texas

The University of Texas Law School is ground zero of the post–affirmative action world. In a 1996 case, *Hopwood v. Texas*, the Fifth Circuit Court of Appeals struck down the law school's affirmative action policy. To ensure that each entering class of 500 or so included about 75 black and Hispanic students, the law school had been operating, in effect, a "dual" admissions system under which minority and nonminority students were being admitted by separate criteria—a method that the Supreme Court had struck down in the 1978 *Bakke* case. This fall, at the beginning of the first semester since *Hopwood*, 26 Mexican-American students, and four blacks, enrolled in Texas's first-year class—only a few more than the law school had had during the late '60s. Back then, the lack of minority representation hadn't been a big issue at the law school. Now, it is seen as a political and marketing disaster. Qualified minority students, whom schools fight over like star quarterbacks, are proving reluctant to apply to Texas. And so are the kind of progressively minded, out-of-state white students who help make the law school a national, rather than local, institution. "There have been times at recruitment events when majority and minority students approach the table together and say 'What does the entering class look like?'" Shelli Soto, the law school's assistant dean of admissions, told me.

Since *Hopwood* the law school has labored mightily to thread the eye of a legal needle—to admit large numbers of minority students without applying explicitly racial or ethnic criteria. The law school's application now includes an optional "Statement on Economic, Social or Personal Disadvantage"—an effort to tease more minority applicants out of the pool. "'Qualified' really means a combination of your accomplishments and your experiences," Soto explains. But this effort to side-step such statistical criteria as LSAT results doesn't really work. Black students do not have more extracurricular activities than whites and do not have better grade-point averages relative to their LSAT scores. And, because so few black students from truly disadvantaged backgrounds do well enough academically to qualify even under affirmative action criteria, "class-based" affirmative action doesn't help either. It seems the only way to admit large numbers of blacks is to admit them *because* they are black.

When I posed this problem to William Cunningham, the chancellor of the U.T. system, he said that the University of Texas Medical School had already adjusted its admissions criteria. "They want to look at people's motivation," the chancellor said, "the human traits that have to do with their wanting to be doctors." Was this being done in the hope that it would have a "race-positive effect"? I asked. Cunningham paused for a long, careful moment. "I don't want to say 'race-positive,'" he said. It wasn't clear what he *could* say without violating

continues on next page

United States. And, when it comes to women, there is simply no issue today when it comes to qualifying in equal numbers for selective institutions of higher and professional education.)

How, then, should we respond to this undeniable reality? The opponents of affirmative action say, "Let standards prevail whatever the result." So what if black students are reduced to two percent of our selective and elite student bodies? Those who gain entry will know that they are properly qualified for entry, that they have been selected without discrimination, and their classmates will know it too. The result will actually be improved race relations and a continuance of the improvements we have seen in black performance in recent decades. Fifteen years from now, perhaps three or four percent of students in the top schools will be black. Until then, blacks can go to less competitive institutions of higher education, perhaps gaining greater advantage from their education in so doing. And,

meanwhile, let us improve elementary and high school education—as we have been trying to do for the last 15 years.

Yet we cannot be quite so cavalier about the impact on public opinion—black and white—of a radical reduction in the number of black students at the Harvards, the Berkeleys, and the Amhersts. These institutions have become, for better or worse, the gateways to prominence, privilege, wealth, and power in American society. To admit blacks under affirmative action no doubt undermines the American meritocracy, but to exclude blacks from them by abolishing affirmative action would undermine the legitimacy of American democracy.

My argument is rooted in history. African Americans—and the struggle for their full and fair inclusion in U.S. society—have been a part of American history from the beginning. Our Constitution took special—but grossly unfair—account of their status, our greatest war was fought over their status, and our

---

Hopwood. "We want to have a diverse student body," he said, "and we want to look at broader criteria than we have in the past to insure that we have a diverse student body." I told Cunningham that some law school faculty members were concerned about diluting admissions standards. The chancellor said very carefully, "I do think this is a time for us to be thoughtful and flexible." Was it possible to be "flexible" without either violating the terms of *Hopwood* or lowering standards? "It is," Cunningham signed, "a difficult problem."

U.T.'s administrators are also looking over their shoulders at the Texas state legislature. A quarter of a century ago, it was virtually all white; now it has significant, and growing, black and Hispanic representation. As Russell Weintraub, a professor of contracts at the law school who was uneasy about affirmative action, says: "If the majority of people in this state are going to be Mexican-American and African American, and they are going to assume many of the leadership roles in the state, then it's going to be big trouble if the law school doesn't admit many minority students—it's going to be a bomb ready to explode."

Indeed, a few small bombs have detonated already. Soon after the *Hopwood* decision the state legislature passed a law that would require the University of Texas undergraduate college to accept the top ten percent of graduates from every high school in the state. This law, which would increase minority enrollment by automatically admitting the best students from heavily minority high schools, effectively

reinstated a rule the college had abandoned three years ago in order to strengthen its standards.

The legislature then passed another law that requires public universities to apply the minimum grade-point average demanded of entering students to everyone—including athletes admitted on scholarship. The law, whose interpretation is now a matter of debate, would destroy the Texas Longhorn football team. Its sponsor, Ron Wilson, is a black State Assemblyman from Houston who attended both U.T. and U.T. Law. Wilson freely admits that the bill was designed to punish the university, which he saw as complicit in the Hopwood ruling. "If you're just a regular African American student with a two-point-five grade-point average, you can't get into the University of Texas," he told me. "But, if you can play the court jester out there on the football field and earn the university a million dollars, you can get it. As far as I'm concerned, that's hypocrisy. My bill says you can't have it both ways."

Wilson's real goal, of course, is not to exclude the athletes but to force the university to take everyone else. One solution, Wilson said, was "open admission." I asked if that wouldn't lead to a lowering of standards. Wilson said: "I don't look at academic standards as the Bible for academic excellence. There hasn't been enough input into those standards from African Americans and Hispanics to make them relevant to their community." And he added one more threat: if the university couldn't counteract the effect of *Hopwood,* he said,

continues on next page

most important constitutional amendments were adopted because of the need to right past wrongs done to them. And, amid the civil rights revolution of the 1960s, affirmative action was instituted to compensate for the damage done to black achievement and life chances by almost 400 years of slavery, followed by state-sanctioned discrimination and massive prejudice.

Yet, today, a vast gulf of difference persists between the educational and occupational status of blacks and whites, a gulf that encompasses statistical measures of wealth, residential segregation, and social relationships with other Americans. Thirty years ago, with the passage of the great civil rights laws, one could have reasonably expected—as I did—that all would be set right by now. But today, even after taking account of substantial progress and change, it is borne upon us how continuous, rooted, and substantial the differences between African Americans and other Americans remain.

"We're going to move the money to follow the students to historically black colleges, if necessary."

The revenge of the legislature implies that the costs of doing away with affirmative action may turn out to be higher than the costs of keeping it. One of the most intriguing documents of the post-affirmative action era is an amicus brief which three professors at U.T. Law submitted to the Supreme Court in an affirmative action case last year. The three made the usual case in favor of affirmative action—but added a more novel, purely pragmatic argument: "A large public institution that serves the whole state cannot maintain its legitimacy if it is perceived to exclude minority students." The authors described the two bills that had passed the Texas legislature and noted that the University of California system is considering waiving its SAT requirement. If *Hopwood* becomes law for the country as a whole, the authors declared apocalyptically, "there will eventually be no great public universities—not for the nation and not for the white plaintiffs either."

In other words, affirmative action represents not a threat to academic standards but the surest means of preserving them. This argument sounds so perverse that it's hard to take seriously, but it's not without foundation. Douglas Laycock, one of the authors of the brief, said: "We're in the middle of a full-blown attack on every means we have to measure merit and on the very idea of merit, and it's mostly driven by the issue of race." What Laycock was suggesting is that, in a straightforward battle between the old meritocratic principle on which conservatives make their stand on the new ideals of diversity and inclusion, meritocracy is likely to lose. And, several weeks later, *The New York Times* inadvertently confirmed his point in a front-page story headlined, "COLLEGES LOOK FOR ANSWERS TO RACIAL GAPS IN TESTING." Donald M. Stewart, president of the College Board, lamented the "social cost" of relying on standardized tests on which minority students fare poorly. "America can't stand that," Stewart said.

Should we regret the political and marketplace dynamics that essentially force institutions like the University of Texas Law School to practice affirmative action? The original rationale for affirmative action was that it helped disadvantaged students overcome the effects of discrimination, both current and historical. No one questions that U.T. Law is guilty of past discrimination. The school was off-limits to black students as a matter of state law until a celebrated 1950 Supreme court decisions, *Sweatt v. Painter.* But most of the black students who attend the law school now come from other states, and they are scarcely more likely than the white students to come from a disadvantaged background.

What about "diversity"? The diversity argument has rapidly eclipsed the past-discrimination argument, because it is so much rosier and more consensual. It's hard to dispute the notion that institutions benefit from "diverse" points of view. But is that a large enough good to justify disadvantaging whites? And there's something arbitrary about the math. Randall Kennedy, a professor at Harvard Law School and another uneasy supporter of affirmative action, says: "I have my problems with the idea that we've got to have diversity because in the year 2000 the census says this and this about a jurisdiction. Does that mean that, if you're in Maine, you don't have to have more than one black student?"

The simple and painful truth is that affirmative action rests on a bedrock of failure. The reason why the University of Texas Law School needed affirmative action in the first place is that, according to a university deposition in *Hopwood,* only 88 black students in the entire country had a combination of grades and law boards in 1992 that reached the mean of admitted white students; only one of those black students came from Texas. One lesson of post-*Hopwood* Texas is that eliminating affirmative action would virtually wipe out the black presence in top schools. For conservatives, that's just the way the meritocratic cookie crumbles, but for most Americans, justly proud of the extent

continues on next page

to which our leading institutions have been integrated over the last quarter century, that's likely to be an unacceptable outcome.

Affirmative action is, at bottom, a dodge. It allows us to put off the far harder work: ending the isolation of young black people and closing the academic gap that separates black students—even middle-class black students—from whites. When we commit ourselves to that, we can do without affirmative action, but not before.

James Traub

The judgment of the elites who support affirmative action—the college presidents and trustees, the religious leaders, the corporate executives—and the judgment even of many of those who oppose it but hesitate to act against it—the Republican leaders in Congress, for example—is that the banning of preference would be bad for the country. I agree. Not that everyone's motives are entirely admirable; many conservative congressmen, for example, are simply afraid of being portrayed as racists even if their opposition to affirmative action is based on a sincere desire to support meritocratic principle. The college presidents who support affirmative action, under the fashionable mantra of diversity, also undoubtedly fear the student demonstrations that would occur if they were to speak out against preferences.

But there are also good-faith motives in this stand, and there is something behind the argument for diversity. What kind of institutions of higher education would we have if blacks suddenly dropped from six or seven percent of enrollment to one or two percent? The presence of blacks, in classes in social studies and the humanities, immediately introduces another tone, another range of questions (often to the discomfort of black students who do not want this representation burden placed upon them). The tone may be one of embarrassment and hesitation and self-censorship among whites (students and faculty). But must we not all learn how to face these questions together with our fellow citizens? We should not be able to escape from this embarrassment by the reduction of black students to minuscule numbers.

The weakness in the "diversity" defense is that college presidents are not much worried about the diversity that white working-class kids, or students of Italian or Slavic background, have to offer. Still there is a reputable reason for that apparent discrepancy. It is that the varied ethnic and racial groups in the United States do not, to the same extent as African Americans, pose a test of the fairness of American institutions. These other groups have not been subjected to the same degree of persecution or exclusion. Their status is not, as the social status of African Americans is, the most enduring reproach to the egalitarian ideals of American society. And these other groups have made progress historically, and make progress today, at a rate that incorporates them into American society quickly compared to blacks.

This is the principal flaw in the critique of affirmative action. The critics are defending a vitally important principle, indeed, the one that should be the governing principle of institutions of higher education: academic competence as the sole test for distinguishing among applicants and students. This principle, which was fought for so energetically during the 1940s and 1950s through laws banning discrimination in admission on the basis of race, national origin, or religion, should not be put aside lightly. But, at present, it would mean the near exclusion from our best educational institutions of a group that makes up twelve percent of the population. In time, I am convinced, this preference will not be needed. Our laws and customs and our primary and secondary educational systems will fully incorporate black Americans into American society, as other disadvantaged groups have been incorporated. The positive trends of recent decades will continue. But we are still, though less than in the past, "two nations," and one of the nations cannot be excluded so throughly from institutions that confer access to the positions of greatest prestige and power.

On what basis can we justify violating the principle that measured criteria of merit should govern admission to selective institutions of higher education today? It is of some significance to begin with that we in the United States have always been looser in this respect than more examination-bound systems of higher education in, say, Western Europe: we have always left room for a large degree of freedom for institutions of higher education, public as well as private, to admit students based on nonacademic criteria. But I believe the main reasons we have to continue racial preferences for blacks are, first, because this country has a special obligation to blacks that has not been fully discharged, and second, because strict application of the principle of qualification would send a message of despair to many blacks, a message that the nation is indifferent to their difficulties and problems.

Many, including leading black advocates of eliminating preferences, say no: the message would be, "Work harder and you can do it." Well, now that affirmative action is becoming a thing of the past in the public colleges and universities of California and Texas, we will have a chance to find out. Yet I wonder whether the message of affirmative action to black students today really ever has been, "Don't work hard; it doesn't matter for you because you're black; you will make it into college anyway." Colleges are indeed looking for black students, but they are also looking for some minimal degree of academic effort and accomplishment, and it is a rare ambitious African American student seeking college entry who relaxes because he believes his grades won't matter *at all.*

One of the chief arguments against racial preference in college and professional school admissions is that more blacks will drop out, the quality of blacks who complete the courses of instruction will be inferior, and they will make poorer lawyers, doctors, or businessmen. Dropping out is common in American higher education and does not necessarily mean that one's attendance was a total loss. Still, the average lower degree of academic performance has, and will continue to have, effects even for the successful: fewer graduating black doctors will go into research; more will go into practice and administration. More blacks in business corporations will be in personnel. Fewer graduating black lawyers will go into corporate law firms; more will work for government.

And more will become judges, because of another and less disputed form of affirmative action, politics. Few protest at the high number of black magistrates in cities with large black populations—we do not appoint judges by examination. Nor do we find it odd or objectionable that Democratic presidents will appoint more black lawyers as judges, or that even a Republican president will be sure to appoint one black Supreme Court justice. What is at work here is the principle of participation. It is a more legitimate principle in politics and government than it is for admission to selective institutions of higher education. But these are also gateways to power, and the principle of participation cannot be flatly ruled out for them.

Whatever the case one may make in general for affirmative action, many difficult issues remain: What kind, to what extent, how long, imposed by whom, by what decision-making process? It is important to bear in mind that affirmative action in higher education admissions is, for the most part, a policy that has been chosen (albeit sometimes under political pressure) by the institutions themselves. There are racial goals and targets for employment and promotion for all government contractors, including colleges and universities, set by government fiat, but targets on student admissions are not imposed by government, except for a few traditionally black or white institutions in the South.

Let us preserve this institutional autonomy. Just as I would resist governmentally imposed requirements that these institutions meet quotas of black admissions, so would I also oppose a judicial or legislative *ban* on the use of race in making decisions on admission. Ballot measures like Proposition 209 are more understandable given the abuses so common in systems of racial preference. But it is revealing that so many other states appear to have had second thoughts and that the California vote is therefore not likely to be repeated. (A recent report in *The Chronicle of Higher Education* was headlined "LEGISLATURES SHOW LITTLE ENTHUSIASM FOR MEASURES TO END RACIAL PREFERENCES"; in this respect, the states are not unlike Congress.)

We should retain the freedom of institutions of higher and professional education to make these determinations for themselves. As we know, they would almost all make room for a larger percentage of black students than would otherwise qualify. This is what these institutions do today. They defend what they do with the argument that diversity is a good thing. I think what they really mean is that a large segment of the American population, significant not only demographically but historically and politically and morally, cannot be so thoroughly excluded. I agree with them.

I have discussed affirmative action only in the context of academic admissions policy. Other areas raise other questions, other problems. And, even in this one area of college and university admissions, affirmative action is not a simple and clear and uncomplicated solution. It can be implemented wisely or foolishly, and it is often done foolishly, as when college presidents make promises to protesting students that they cannot fulfill, or when institutions reach too far below their minimal standards with deleterious results for the academic success of the students they admit, for their grading practices, and for the legitimacy of the degrees they offer. No matter how affirmative action in admissions is dealt with, other issues remain or will emerge. More black students, for example, mean demands for more black faculty and administrators and for more black-oriented courses. Preference is no final answer (just as the elimination of preference is no final answer). It is rather what is necessary to respond to the reality that, for some years to come, yes, we are still two nations, and both nations must participate in the society to some reasonable degree.

Fortunately, those two nations, by and large, want to become more united. The United States is not Canada or Bosnia, Lebanon or Malaysia. But, for the foreseeable future, the strict use of certain generally reasonable tests as a benchmark criterion for admissions would mean the de facto exclusion of one of the two nations from a key institutional system of the society, higher education. Higher education's governing principle is qualification—merit. Should it make room for another and quite different principle, equal participation? The latter should never become dominant. Racial proportional representation would be a disaster. But basically the answer is yes—the principle of equal participation can and should be given some role. This decision has costs. But the alternative is too grim to contemplate.

Source: *New Republic* by Glazer. Copyright © 1998 by New Republic. Reproduced with permission of New Republic in the format Textbook via Copyright Clearance Center.

PART 2

IMPLEMENTATION OF STRATEGIC HUMAN RESOURCE MANAGEMENT

CHAPTER

8

STAFFING

Kroger Co. is currently the nation's largest supermarket chain with over 1,400 supermarkets, 200,000 employees, 500 convenience stores, 40 manufacturing plants, and $27 billion in annual sales. Faced with a constant need to hire new employees and with problems concerning the quality of new hires, Kroger set out to improve its selection processes. Kroger's goal was to enhance the effectiveness of its ability to hire and retain outstanding customer service employees. Its traditional structured interview approach was very time-consuming. Numerous interviewers needed to be trained and certified, and each interview took an average of 45 minutes of management time. At the same time, Kroger faced pressures to develop a system that was efficient and cost-effective. The answer was a computer-based, self-administered employee selection system.

Kroger began by conducting a survey of its customers to gather information regarding customer perceptions of customer service. This information was then converted to scales that measured the knowledge, skills, and competencies that impact outstanding customer service. The end result, an employability index, was able to evaluate an applicant's thought process, management of job-related stress, self-control, and general job-related attitudes. The index was determined entirely by an online, interactive interview with applicants; a recommendation was then offered as to whether the individual should be offered a job. This innovative approach is designed to improve both effectiveness and efficiency by matching selection criteria with carefully chosen strategic objectives. Although the program has not been formally evaluated, Kroger has already determined the three criteria by which it will assess the program: customer service measures, turnover rate, and employee safety.

Source: Murphy, T. E. and Zandvakili, S. "Data- and Metrics-Driven Approach to Human Resource Practices: Using Customers, Employees and Financial Metrics," *Human Resource Management*, Vol. 39, No. 1, pp. 93–105.

Staffing, the process of recruiting applicants and selecting prospective employees, remains a key strategic area for human resource management. Given that an organization's performance is a direct result of the individuals it employs, the specific strategies used and decisions made in the staffing process will directly impact an organization's success or lack thereof.

Decisions made as part of the staffing process can have a significant impact on an organization's bottom line. One study found that 45 percent of companies calculated the cost of turnover at more than $10,000 per person, while 10 percent calculated it at more than $40,000 per person.[1] Turnover costs tend to rise as the level of the job and its complexity increase. In technology companies, the costs of turnover can be staggering. Agilent Technologies of Palo Alto, California, estimates an average turnover costs of $200,000 per departing employee and $250,000 per software engineer.[2]

The activities performed as part of recruiting and selection offer an organization numerous choices for finding and screening new employees. These options can have a significant impact on an organization's efficiency because some are much more extensive, costly, and time-consuming than others. Organizations have great latitude to select from a variety of staffing techniques, each of which offers various degrees of sophistication and selectivity; however, such benefits come at a price.

In addition to the time and financial costs involved with staffing, many changes are taking place concerning how work is performed. Trends such as broader job scope and responsibilities, the move toward leaner staffing and operating with fewer full-time permanent employees, smaller autonomous units, pay for company-wide performance, and flatter organization structures affect the types of individuals and skills that organizations seek and influence how organizations find and screen applicants. The staffing process must be more strategically focused: Newer challenges and considerations must be directly incorporated into an organization's staffing strategy.

Staffing takes on even greater importance in the service sector, which continues to create the largest number of jobs in our economy. However, a service-based economy requires different skills and has higher turnover costs than those associated with manufacturing. In addition, payroll typically assumes a higher percentage of overall costs in service organizations. Companies in this traditionally high-turnover sector need strategic staffing initiatives that allow them to attract and retain productive employees, thereby minimizing operating expenses.

Probably most important is ensuring that employees fit with the culture of the organization. Technical skills alone do not guarantee high performance, particularly as organizations move toward process- and project-oriented work teams. ▼

RECRUITING

Temporary Versus Permanent Employees

When an organization needs to increase its headcount, the first strategic choice is whether to hire temporary or permanent employees. To do this, the organization must forecast accurately how long it expects the employee shortage to last. Temporary

▶ Reading 8.1, "Hiring for the Organization, Not the Job," presents a model that outlines issues surrounding person-organization fit and illustrates an investment approach to staffing.

employees obtained from an agency usually cost more per hour to employ than permanent worker; however, unlike permanent employees, temporary employees are not paid when there's no work for them to do, particularly if they are hired on a project basis. Temporary employees are not provided benefits so, unlike permanent employees, they cannot file claims for unemployment compensation when their employment ends. Temporary employees also provide flexibility for employers because payroll can be quickly and easily contracted during downturns without having to result to layoffs.

In addition to hiring temporary employees from an agency, an organization can subcontract work to an outside vendor; this is usually done on a project basis. Larger organizations can also move permanent employees from department to department as needs dictate. This promotes efficiency through lower costs and flexible utilization of employees. These in-house "temporary" employees have more permanent status, including benefits; are generally more committed to the organization; and know the inside workings of the organization. They can be extremely useful when regular employees take extended vacation or sick leaves. In-house temporary employees provide the organization with more flexibility and efficiency than it would garner from outside temps; also, employees have more variety in their work assignments.

Internal Versus External Recruiting

If an organization decides to hire permanent employees, the first critical question it needs to address is whether to recruit internally or externally. Recruiting from the current employee pool can benefit the organization in a number of ways. First, the organization already has performance data on employees. Ample opportunity has been afforded to observe the applicant's work habits, skills and capabilities, ability to get along with others, and fit with the organization.

Second, promotion from within motivates employees. Employees feel that the organization is trying to provide them with promotional and developmental opportunities in reward for their performance and loyalty. Third, training and socialization time are reduced. Current employees know the organization, its procedures, politics, and customers and have already established relationships with coworkers. Consequently, they need far less formal or informal socialization time than those hired from the outside. Finally, internal recruiting is often much faster and far less expensive than going outside of the organization for applicants.

Although internal recruiting has advantages, this approach also has some disadvantages. First, internal recruiting can become very political and competitive, particularly when coworkers apply for the same position. Dysfunctional conflict may result, and collegiality and interpersonal relationships can be strained. Second, those employees not selected for the position can suffer from diminished morale and performance, particularly when they feel equally or better qualified than the candidate selected.

Third, the organization can become inbred through excessive internal recruitment. Continuing to promote from within can encourage maintaining the status quo. An organization that needs to improve organizational processes should usually recruit from the outside. Finally, excessive internal recruitment can cause inefficiency by creating multiple vacancies. For instance, if a senior-level manager leaves the organization and is replaced by a direct subordinate, that subordinate's job will then need to be filled. As this promotion chain continues down the hierarchy, an initial vacancy could spur promotions for a large number of people. Nearly all employees require a certain period of time to learn a new job. Even when an employee has worked in the organization for several years, a new position requires adjusting to new responsibilities and redefining interpersonal relationships with coworkers. Internal recruiting can exacerbate this effect by creating a large number of employees having new positions. Until these employees gain the level of competence that their predecessors had and sufficiently redefine their working relationships, inefficiency will result.

Internal recruiting has its advantages and disadvantages. It is probably best utilized when the organization pursues a strategy related to stability, faces few major threats from its external environment, and is concerned with maintaining the status quo relative to its operating systems. When time and/or money are limited, internal recruiting can be beneficial, as well.

External recruiting also has advantages and disadvantages. Not surprisingly, the advantages of external recruiting are consistent with the disadvantages of internal recruiting. External recruiting facilitates change and tends to be more useful for organizations with volatile external environments. External recruiting can allow an organization to expand its knowledge base beyond that of its existing employees and bring in new ideas and viewpoints; external recruits are not bound by existing ways of thinking or doing things. They can bring a fresh approach to problems that have plagued the organization. At the senior level, candidates are often recruited for their history of bringing about high-level change in other organizations.

External recruiting, however, can be expensive and time-consuming. Employees from outside the organization will often need a longer socialization period to know the organization, its products or services, coworkers, and customers. External recruits are also unknown entities in that the organization has no experience working with them. Although an applicant may have outstanding skills, training, or experience and may have had past success in another organization, those factors do not guarantee similar success with a new organization or an ability to fit with a new organization's culture. Finally, external recruiting can have detrimental effects on the morale of those employees who have applied for the job internally, but have not been selected. Exhibit 8-1 summarizes the strategic issues surrounding internal versus external recruiting.

EXHIBIT 8-1: ADVANTAGES AND DISADVANTAGES OF INTERNAL AND EXTERNAL RECRUITING

	Advantages	Disadvantages	When Useful
Internal	Have performance data available Motivational Less training/socialization time Faster Less Expensive	Possible politics "Loser" effects Inbreeding Promotion chains	Stability strategy Stable external environment Limited time and money
	Advantages	**Disadvantages**	**When Useful**
External	Fresh ideas and viewpoints Expand knowledge base	Unknown entities Detrimental to internal applicants Training and socialization time Time-consuming Can be expensive	Need for change Volatile external environment

When recruiting employees from outside of the organization, employers have a variety of applicant sources from which to choose. Proper sourcing can save not only time and money but also can reduce the time it takes to have new employees actually on the job. A recent survey of recruiters found that the top five recruitment goals were (1) generating high-quality employment applications, (2) generating the best possible return on investment, (3) stimulating a desire to work for the organization, (4) filling specific positions, and (5) generating diversity.[3]

When and How Extensively to Recruit

Regardless of whether recruiting is done internally or externally, effective planning and strategizing are essential to the success of the process. An organization needs to know that it has the right employees with the right skills in the right places at the right time. This involves determining (1) how large an applicant pool is needed and (2) when recruiting efforts should begin. Both of these questions can be answered by reviewing data from past recruiting efforts. A recruiting pyramid can be constructed using yield ratios that show, traditionally, how many employees pass from one stage of the recruiting process to the next. This can help the organization determine how large an applicant pool to seek. An example of a recruiting pyramid is presented in Exhibit 8-2. In this case, the organization could use historic yield ratios to determine how extensively to recruit. For example, if the organization is seeking 20 new employees, it should obtain 240 resumes.

An organization must determine when to begin its recruiting efforts to ensure that trained employees will be ready when the organization needs them. Timelines of past recruiting efforts can help the organization determine when to time its recruiting efforts. Here, an organization works backward from the time employees will be needed to determine when to begin recruiting. An example of a recruiting timeline is presented in Exhibit 8-3. In this case, the organization should begin recruiting 14 weeks before the intended start date.

EXHIBIT 8-2: RECRUITING PYRAMID

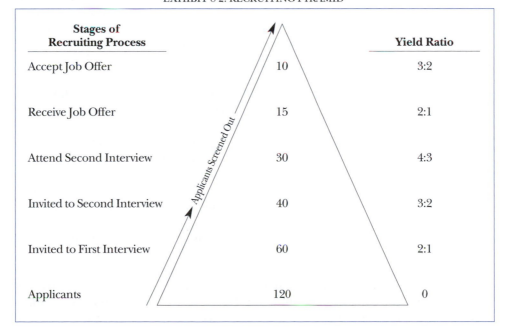

Stages of Recruiting Process		Yield Ratio
Accept Job Offer	10	3:2
Receive Job Offer	15	2:1
Attend Second Interview	30	4:3
Invited to Second Interview	40	3:2
Invited to First Interview	60	2:1
Applicants	120	0

EXHIBIT 8-3: RECRUITING TIMELINE

Stages of Recruiting Process	Normal Time Taken to Complete
Candidate begins work	2 weeks
Acceptance of offer by candidate	1 week
Making of offer to candidate	1 week
Second interview cycle	1 week
Arranging second interviews	2 weeks
First interview cycle	1 week
Arranging first interviews	2 weeks
Screening resumes	2 weeks
Recruiting for position	3 weeks

One caveat must be issued concerning the use of recruiting pyramids and time-lines. Because they are based on past recruiting data, they may need to be adjusted if labor market conditions have changed dramatically. Higher or lower unemployment, changes in the competitiveness of the industry, and/or the attractiveness of the employer vis-à-vis competitors might make the staffing process easier or more difficult than it had been in the past. Managers should assess how any changed conditions might impact the size of the applicant pool, the ratios, and the timeline.

Methods of Recruiting

Small organizations often do their recruiting very informally. Job openings or new positions may be communicated by word of mouth or by allowing the direct supervisor to find someone of his or her own choosing. Most larger organizations do their internal recruiting through some means of formal job posting. This process involves posting the available position where all employees have access, such as a physical or online bulletin board. Employees then decide whether they want to apply for any position.

When such a system is used and several people apply for the job, the detrimental effects of nonselection on employee morale can be minimized by providing non-selected employees with specific, objective feedback concerning the screening process. These employees should also be counseled regarding how they might enhance their skills and experience if they plan to apply for future job openings. However, no guarantee or promise of appointment or promotion should be made.

If the organization maintains employee information in a computerized database, the skills inventory component of the human resource information system can be used to assist in internal recruiting. The employee database can be searched for employees having skills, experiences, and personal qualities that are required for a job. This can save the organization a great deal of time in identifying strong internal candidates for a job. These candidates can then be contacted to determine their interest in a position.

External recruiting may also be done informally through contact with friends and acquaintances of existing employees; this process is usually limited to small organizations. However, informal recruiting tends to be the norm at the executive level. A recent survey found that 64 percent of executives found their jobs through peer networking.[4] In the year 2000, the number of CEOs who had been hired from outside of the organization had doubled from 1990 levels.[5]

A primary source of recruiting for larger organizations is targeted advertising in selected media. In writing and designing a help-wanted ad, it is important to be accurate and specific and provide sufficient information about the position and organization to encourage applicants to apply. Interestingly, studies have shown that fewer than 20 percent of those who read help-wanted ads are actively looking for employment. Competitors, current employees, investors, stockbrokers and analysts, recruiters, and regulators also read such ads to gain information about organizations. Consequently, employers who use recruitment advertising need to take these audiences into account without losing sight of the need to attract strong applicants.

Recruiting on the Internet is one of the fastest-growing recruitment methods. A 1998 survey found that 70 percent of HR professionals were already using the Internet for recruiting.[6] Most found using the Internet more cost-effective than news-paper advertising.[7] Internet recruiting can be extremely effective in generating applicants due to its low cost, speed, and ability to target applicants with technical skills. A recent survey of undergraduate and graduate students found that 75 percent used the Internet for job searches.[8] Information on the organization is readily avail-able, which allows applicants to assess their interests and needs with the employer's offerings. However, poorly designed or user-unfriendly Web sites can damage an organization's reputation and its ability to attract applicants. The same survey found that 25 percent of job candidates rejected a potential employer on account of its Web site.[9]

Because Internet recruiting is worldwide, it gives an employer global expo-sure to potential applicants, which can be critical if particular language skills or cul-tural backgrounds are needed. Technology-based employers have found the Internet to be a fertile recruiting ground for applicants who are technologically savvy. For example, Cisco Systems receives more than 80 percent of its resumes electronically.[10]

Interestingly, the strategies used by recruiters often do not fit the job search strategies being used by applicants. Networking, or the use of personal and profes-sional contacts to obtain employment, is the strategy of choice for the majority of job seekers 78 percent use this approach.[11] Sixty-seven percent of recruiters, how-ever, find that the Internet is their top source for attracting new employees.[12] This is not to say that job seekers do not use the Internet, as they have been shown to utilize more search tactics than recruiters,[13] but rather, implies that HR professionals need to think carefully about their recruiting sources and think strategically about how best to achieve the recruitment goals they have set.

Internet recruiting has become increasingly popular with employers and can cut the search process time by as much as 75 percent.[14] Sophisticated technology allows employers to quickly process large numbers of applications through the use of spiders, programs that search resumes for specific characteristics or words. Many employers attempt to attract applicants by developing Web sites that provide information about the organization that can allow applicants to determine if there might be an optimal "fit" between their career goals and the goals of the organization, guide candidates through the application process and even allow prospective applicants to take a virtual tour of the organization. While Internet recruiting can speed up the employment process, it is also fraught with some potential challenges that must be weighed by an organization considering Internet recruiting.[15]

The first of these challenges is ensuring security. Online recruiting means that the employer will be receiving electronic inquiries from unknown sources. Many of these communications will include attached files, making viruses a security concern; another consideration is ensuring that those visiting the Web site do not obtain access to unauthorized areas of the site. A second challenge is that overreliance on Internet recruiting can result in disparate impact against certain protected classes of applicants. Studies have shown that members of certain ethnic minority groups, women, and older individuals either may not have access to, or be less likely to use, the Internet.[16] Individuals with disabilities may have conditions that limit or prevent their ability to easily access the Internet as well. Consequently, employers may unintentionally screen out large groups of potential applicants who are members of protected classes in the interest of the efficiency afforded by Internet recruiting. Finally, Internet recruiting can complicate reporting of data related to compliance with federal and state laws. A difficult question arises whether an individual who sends an unsolicited resume via the Internet needs to be "counted" and considered an "applicant" for the purpose of federal reporting. The EEOC and OFCCP have continuously wrestled with the definition of "job applicant" for reporting purposes; combining this with the greatly increased number of job applicants that result from Internet recruiting creates a challenging situation for employers.

E-cruiting at Air Products and Chemicals, Inc.

One organization that has developed a satisfactory strategy for reporting its Internet recruiting activities to federal agencies is Air Products and Chemicals, Inc. (APC). Based in Allentown, Pennsylvania, APC supplies gases and chemicals to various industries as well as to the federal government. With 16,000 employees worldwide, including 9,000 in the United States, APC falls under the purview of the Office of Federal Contracts Compliance Programs as a government contractor. As APC began to use the Internet for recruiting with greater frequency, a conflict arose relative to its reporting with the OFCCP. The OFCCP considered resumes submitted electronically as an expression of interest in employment and APC's reading of that resume constituted acceptance of it, making the submitting party an "applicant" for reporting purposes. Because the organization could not control who submitted unsolicited resumes, it found itself at a disadvantage relative to its affirmative action goals. APC eventually solved the dilemma. Each unsolicited resume received an automatic e-mail reply, instructing the individual to apply for a specific open position listed on the company Web site. Only when a position was chosen would the individual be considered an "applicant." In addition, applicants were required to submit information identifying their race and gender. This system met with the OFCCP's enthusiastic approval and has allowed APC to reap the benefits of Internet recruiting while satisfying the OFCCP's reporting requirements for federal contractors.[17]

An organization's existing employees often can be a very valuable source for recruiting new employees. Consumer products manufacturer Johnson & Johnson relies extensively on its employee referral program to recruit new hires. J&J offers up to $1,500 for each employee recruit, paid in full two weeks after the new employee's start date.[18] Hartford-based Lincoln Financial's referral program results in 55 percent of all external hires and saves the organization more than 97 percent of the costs it would incur using an executive search firm.[19] One innovative approach to staffing has existing employees recruit themselves, as illustrated below.

Staffing at St. Peter's Health Care

St. Peter's Health Care is an Albany, New York–based hospital that, like many health care institutions, suffered from a severe shortage of qualified nurses. Nurses hired from outside agencies to assume unstaffed shifts not only commanded a premium price but also were unfamiliar with operations and procedures at St. Peter's. To alleviate this problem, St. Peter's launched an online bidding system by which any nurse could bid for an open shift. Nurses must be existing employees or approved to work for the hospital and bid on shifts for a certain pay rate per hour. Nurse managers have the authority to accept or reject any bid, and applicants whose bids have been rejected are free to rebid at a lower pay rate. Because the hospital cannot mandate overtime for workers, this system allows maximum flexibility for both St. Peter's and nurse-employees. In 2002, St. Peter's filled 43,400 available hours under the bidding system at an average pay rate of $37 per hour. Two thirds of those hours were filled by existing employees. Outside agency nurses would have cost the hospital $54 per hour. In addition to the cost savings, turnover among nurses has decreased from 11 percent to under 5 percent annually and both patient and employee satisfaction have increased.[20]

Organizations can also address their staffing needs by turning to other organizations and outsourcing all or part of their staffing. Employment agencies, more commonly called *staffing agencies* or *staffing services*, can locate and prescreen applicants for an employer. Because locating and prescreening applicants are often the most time-consuming, expensive, and laborious processes for managers, many organizations are quite willing to use staffing agencies to perform these functions. In addition, the risk of running afoul of the law and having initial screening influenced by the biases of current employees is minimized, because the staffing service is often able to bring a more objective perspective to the process.

In addition to traditional staffing agencies, there are several other kinds of organizations that may help an employer with external recruiting. The first of these are state job service agencies. State job service agencies are public funded by the federal government but are operated by individual states. All citizens who file unemployment compensation claims are required to register with the state job service agency and remain actively looking for work as a condition of receiving ongoing unemployment compensation. Employers can call and list positions with their state job service agency for no fee and, at the same time, assist those who have lost their jobs.

Another source of prospective employees is the Private Industry Council (PIC), a local agency that administers federal funds to assist individuals who are hard to employ in finding jobs. These individuals are generally those who depend on public welfare assistance but have either limited or no marketable job skills or lack the means to obtain appropriate training. Employers who are willing to train individuals for entry-level jobs can obtain assistance in locating such applicants from the local PIC. If the organization provides training and then subsequently hires the individual referred from the PIC for a permanent position, then the employer can seek partial reimbursement for the wages paid during the training period from the PIC. The Private Industry Council receives federal money for such reimbursement under the Job Training Partnership Act.

Executive search firms are a specialized type of staffing agency that assist organizations in filling skilled technical and senior- and executive-level management positions.

Executive search firms usually charge significant fees for their services; these fees are paid by the employer. Searches are usually conducted for a contracted period of time and for a set fee, which is paid regardless of whether the search is successful. Estimates are that fewer than 50 percent of searches are successful during the contracted time period.[21]

Despite their relatively low rates of success, the services of executive search firms continue to be in demand because search firms provide employers with several benefits. First, search firms are usually better and faster than the organization's in-house recruiters in locating talent. The majority of search firms focus on specific industries, and they have extensive networks and numerous contacts. Consequently, they can locate and attract candidates who are not actively looking for new jobs. Although most employers would not directly call someone who works for a competitor to recruit that individual, an executive search firm can and does. The executive search firm can also keep the organization's identity confidential during the recruiting and prescreening process. Some organizations have hired executive search firms to contact their own employees in efforts to determine whether the employees might have any interest in leaving the organization. Although this kind of behavior may be unethical, it shows that executive search firms can offer an organization a means of secretly recruiting candidates. Finally, executive search firms will often, upon request, provide their client organizations with a written and signed "anti-raiding" agreement, whereby the search firm promises not to contact or recruit any of the organization's employees for a given time period in searches being conducted for other client organizations.

Outsourced Recruiting at Kellogg

Michigan-based cereal manufacturer Kellogg recently revamped its recruiting function for all of its nonhourly employees. With more than 14,000 employees worldwide, coordination of the recruiting function had become cumbersome, prompting Kellogg to outsource its entire exempt recruiting operation. Because the industry is highly cyclical, Kellogg did not want to have to continuously hire and lay off recruiting staff and sought a system that was more flexible and better aligned with its business needs and strategy. When Kellogg needed to hire 200 new salespeople in a short time, the vendor was able to fill the positions much more quickly and efficiently than Kellogg would have been using its own staff and an outside search firm. The vendor's performance is overseen by a project manager at Kellogg and evaluated according to a variety of metrics including cost, timeliness, quality of applicants, service to managers, and diversity. During the first year of implementation, the outsourced recruiting program saved Kellogg more than $1.3 million and reduced average cost per hire by more than 35 percent.[22]

Many organizations use college and university on-campus recruiting as a means of attracting a relatively large number of qualified applicants. Campus recruiting can generate a large applicant pool in a short time period at a minimal cost and, therefore, create efficiency in the recruiting process. However, this can also create inefficiencies, due to having to screen an excessively large number of applicants. Campus recruiting can often result in motivated, highly skilled, energetic applicants, but these applicants are usually available only at certain times of the year; they may also have very limited prior work experience. Success in the classroom does not necessarily translate to success in the workplace. Campus recruiting involves higher risk, given the practical inexperience of most applicants; however, there is a potential for higher return, given the intelligence, level of training, energy, and ambition that many applicants possess.

To alleviate some of the difficulties associated with campus recruiting, an increasing number of employers are offering co-op and/or internship programs. Such programs allow both the employer and student a trial period with no obligation. Employers have an advantage in recruiting interns for permanent positions; students gain marketable experience for their resumes.

College Recruiting via Internships at Microsoft

Redmond, WA–based Microsoft is one of the most sought-after employers in the world. The software giant receives upwards of 50,000 resumes a month and is clearly an "employer of choice" for many applicants. One way to heighten one's chances of obtaining employment with Microsoft is through interning at the organization. While the internship program itself is highly competitive, it provides Microsoft and interns with an opportunity to try each other out for a limited time period. Microsoft provides paid internships to approximately 800 college students each summer. After a rigorous screening process, fewer than 10 percent of applicants eventually end up with Microsoft for the summer. Those who do receive "competitive salaries," company-subsidized housing, training, and full benefits. Microsoft, with employee turnover at less than 6 percent hires as many as 45 percent of its interns for permanent positions. Microsoft expects that after the 12-week internship concludes, each intern will be ready for permanent full-time employment.[23]

SELECTION

Once a sufficient pool of applicants has been recruited, critical decisions need to be made regarding applicant screening. Selection decisions can and do have significant economic and strategic consequences for organizations, and these decisions need to be made with great care. Before the application of any selection tools or criteria, the organization needs to determine that the methods being employed are both reliable and valid.

Reliability refers to the consistency of the measurement being taken. Ideally, the application of any screening criteria should elicit the same results in repeat trials. For example, if an applicant is asked to take a pre-employment test, the test should have consistent results each time it is administered to an applicant. Similarly, when different interviewers evaluate an applicant's ability to make spontaneous decisions, they should assess the applicant's skill level similarly. Consequently, in planning a screening process, the organization needs to ensure that there is reliability on two levels: across time and across evaluators.

Because many factors can impact assessment, 100 percent reliability is rarely, if ever, achieved. An individual might score poorly on a test on a given day due to preoccupation with personal matters. Interrater reliability, which is the correlation among different judges who interview an applicant, is often low because these evaluators may bring different perceptions and biases to the process. However, low interrater reliability is not always bad. A supervisor might evaluate an applicant by using different criteria from those a subordinate might use. Such differences in perception are important in getting a holistic assessment of a potential employee.

Low reliability is often the result of one of two types of errors in assessment. The first of these is deficiency error. Much as the name implies, deficiency error occurs when one important criterion for assessment is not included in the measure. For example, if the test for an applicant for an editor's position did not attempt to measure the applicant's writing ability, deficiency error would be present.

The second type of error is contamination error. Contamination error is caused by unwanted influences that affect the assessment. If an interviewer is under intense time pressure to complete other tasks and rushes the interview process so that it is impossible to gather sufficient information on a candidate, contamination error would result. Similarly, if a test measures knowledge, skills, or abilities that are not essential for the job and the evaluation of these noncritical factors impacts the ratings for the more important dimension, contamination error would result.

Reliability is a prerequisite for validity. A test cannot be valid without first being reliable. Validity refers to whether what is being assessed relates or corresponds to actual performance on the job. It examines whether the skills, abilities, and knowledge being measured make a difference in performance. Validity is critical not only to ensure proper selection, but it also becomes the chief measure by which employers defend discrimination allegations in court. Although no laws specifically require employers to assess the validity of their screening devices, illustrating that specific criteria are valid selection measures and are, therefore, job related is the major way for employers to respond to such claims.

There are two types of validity that support selection criteria. The first is content validity. Content validity illustrates that the measure or criterion is representative of the actual job content and/or the desired knowledge that the employee should have to perform the job. Content validity is determined through the process of job analysis, which was discussed in Chapter 6. For example, in order to receive a real estate license and work as a licensed salesperson or broker, an individual must pass an exam that tests knowledge of job-related concepts, activities, and processes. Content validity, in and of itself, does not guarantee successful performance on the job, much as completing a prerequisite course in a degree program does not guarantee successful completion of a later course.

The second validity measure is empirical or criterion-related validity. This measure demonstrates the relationship between certain screening criteria and job performance. If individuals who obtain higher scores or evaluations on these screening criteria also turn out to be high performers on the job, then this type of validity is established.

It is important to realize that reliability alone is not sufficient for determining the appropriate screening criteria. These criteria must be valid as well. Validity not only ensures the best possible strategic fit between applicant and job, but it also ensures that the organization will have a readily accepted means of defending discrimination charges at hand. Criteria cannot be valid that are not already reliable. Conversely, criteria can be reliable without being valid. It is critical for decision makers to understand this difference and develop their screening criteria accordingly.

Interviewing

The first set of critical decisions in the selection process involves the interviewing process. Employers first need to determine who should be involved in interviewing applicants. A number of different constituents can provide input.

Prospective immediate supervisors, peers, and/or subordinates might be asked to participate in interviewing candidates. Coworker input can be critical in organizations that emphasize teams and project groups. The input of customers might also be sought, particularly for employers in service industries. Those involved in selecting appropriate interviewers must consider the different perspectives that different individuals or groups offer and the relevance of these perspectives for selecting the best applicant. Interviewers should be chosen from diverse racial, ethnic, age, and gender backgrounds. Another decision must be made as to whether interviews will be conducted in an individual or group format. Group interviews can save time for both the organization and applicant, but they often involve creating a less personal atmosphere for applicants. Group interviews may make it more difficult for interviewers to get a sense of the applicant's interpersonal style.

Interviewing applicants involves making subjective assessments of each applicant's qualifications for a job. However, interviewers commonly make interpretation errors that should be avoided in an effective interviewing process. Among these are similarity error, in which the interviewer has a positive disposition toward an applicant considered to be similar to the interviewer, in some way; contrast error, in which the candidates are compared to each other during the interview process instead of the absolute standards and requirements of the job; first impression error, in which the interviewer immediately makes a positive or negative assessment of the candidate and uses the remaining interview time to seek information to support that contention; halo error, in which a single characteristic, positive or negative, outweighs all other dimensions; and biases that are based on the interviewee's race, gender, religion, age, ethnicity, sexual orientation, or physical condition rather than factors that relate to job performance.

Group interviewing allows different interviewers to compare and contrast their interpretations of the same interview information. Consequently, this often helps overcome many of the errors that individual interviewers might make.

One interviewing technique that has become increasingly popular in recent years is behavioral interviewing, which involves determining whether an applicant's anticipated behavior in a variety of situations and scenarios posed in interview questions would be appropriate for the employer. Behavioral interviewing can be used with experienced applicants as well as with those who have little or no professional work experience because it asks about situations the candidate might likely find herself or himself facing on the job. Behavioral interviewing with candidates who have professional experience can also involve candidates presenting real-life situations in which they were involved and how they handled them.

To use behavioral interviewing, the first step is to determine the most important behavioral characteristics required for a given job or to work in a certain unit. These can be identified by examining the key traits displayed by high-performing incumbents. Behavioral interviewing assumes that candidates have already been screened for technical skills, and focuses more on the human interaction traits and people skills an applicant would bring to a job. Questions might be what an applicant did in a certain past situation or might do in a given situation, as well as things he or she most enjoyed, least enjoyed, and would opt to change about a given situation. Behavioral interviewing is used extensively by Dell Computer, AT&T, and Clean Harbors Environmental Services.[24] Dell collects data from 300 of its executives to determine the qualities most needed for success within the organization. AT&T has developed a series of behavioral questions that address the core competencies of organization, interpersonal communication style, decision making, and problem analysis. Clean Harbors, which specializes in cleanups of hazardous materials in the environment, looks for problem-solving ability, openness to new ideas, and enthusiasm.[25]

Regardless of who conducts the interviews and whether they are administered in a group or individual format, a decision needs to be made as to whether the actual format or process of the interviews should be structured or unstructured. Structured interviews follow a set protocol: All interviewees are asked the same questions and are given the same opportunity to respond. There is standardization in that it becomes easier to compare applicant responses to identical questions, and legal liability can be minimized because all applicants are treated the same. However, structured interviewing provides limited opportunity to adapt the interview process to any unique circumstances surrounding any applicant.

An unstructured interview is totally spontaneous and one in which questions are not planned in advance. The topics of discussion can vary dramatically from one candidate to another. Such a process allows interviewers to gain a greater sense of the applicant as an individual, but it often makes comparison among different candidates difficult. A semistructured interview would fall somewhere between these two extremes. With a semistructured interview, the interviewer asks each candidate a set of standard questions. However, the interviewer can determine exactly which questions each candidate is asked and can be flexible and probe for specifics when answers are provided. Although structured interviews provide the greatest consistency, unstructured interviews provide the greatest flexibility. The organization must determine which is more important strategically. For example, in interviewing for jobs that require a great degree of creativity, the interviewer may wish to use a less-structured approach to determine how the applicant handles an unstructured situation. If it is critical to compare candidates closely across several criteria, a more structured approach might be more advantageous.

Regardless of interview structure, the selection process is aided when the interviewer asks specific, pointed questions. Asking candidates to describe behaviors they have engaged in or actions they have taken in specific situations is far more meaningful for assessment purposes than closed-ended "yes or no" questions. This strategy of behavioral interviewing has become increasingly popular in organizations. Candidates can and should be presented with scenarios they might expect to encounter in the job for which they are interviewing and be asked how they would handle the situation. This can assist the organization in determining the fit between the applicant and organizational culture and processes. Interviewing by itself generally has relatively low reliability and validity. Consequently, it is critical to employ other criteria in the screening process to increase the likelihood of selection of the best applicants.

Testing

Another critical decision in the selection process involves applicant testing and the kinds of tests to use. The needs of the organization and job structure (specific responsibilities, interpersonal relationships with others, and so forth) will determine whether any or all of the following should be assessed: technical skills, interpersonal skills, personality traits, problem-solving abilities, or any other job-related performance indicators. The key variable that should influence testing is job requirements. Any testing that is not specifically job-related could be legally challenged, particularly if adverse impact can be shown.

The timing of testing can vary from organization to organization. Traditionally, testing has been conducted after the interviewing and screening process due to the expense of testing and time required to score and evaluate test results. However, some organizations are now testing earlier in the selection process because costs involved with interviewing often exceed the costs of testing. Clearly, it makes sense for an employer to use more cost-effective screening techniques earlier in the selection process.

Perhaps the most useful types of tests are work sample and trainability tests. Work sample tests simply involve giving the applicant a representative sample of work that would be part of the job and asking the individual to complete it. These tests are useful when the employer needs employees who will be able to perform job responsibilities from the first day of employment. Trainability tests measure an applicant's aptitude and ability to understand critical components of the job that the company may be willing to teach once the employee is hired. They are useful when the employer needs some familiarity with the nature of the work but seeks to train the new employee in the organization's way of doing things.

Both work sample and trainability tests can provide candidates with realistic job previews. Traditionally, organizations emphasized only the positive aspects of jobs during the recruiting process. This approach kept the applicant pool large and allowed the organization to reject the applicant, instead of vice versa. However, by hiding negative aspects of jobs, employers often hired individuals who became disillusioned once employed and left the organization shortly after hire. This results in a waste of both time and money and a loss of efficiency. The idea behind realistic job previews is to make applicants aware of both positive and negative aspects of the job. If the applicant is hired, the new employee has realistic expectations and is less likely to become dissatisfied with the job and quit. Realistic job previews also increase the likelihood of a candidate's self-selecting out of a position; however, this is in both the applicant's and employee's best interests. The predictive power of work sample and trainability tests for an appropriate fit between an applicant and job/organization has been found to be quite high.

Applicants might also be asked to provide samples of their previous work. A means of assessing the validity of collected information (such as samples of work and past work projects) needs to be determined, as well. Such work may be falsified. Its integrity can be verified by asking candidates detailed questions about its content or the process by which it was completed.

Other types of testing need to be administered very carefully. Personality testing often centers around what have been called the "Big Five" personality dimensions.[26] Those traits considered most relevant to performance in any kind of work environment. As illustrated in Exhibit 8-4 they are sociability, agreeableness, conscientiousness, emotional stability, and intellectual openness. Personality testing can be useful to anticipate how employees might behave, particularly on an interpersonal level, but personality tests can be problematic on two levels. First, personality testing has been successfully challenged in many courts due to the impact of certain questions on members of protected classes. Second, few, if any, jobs require one specific type of personality to ensure success. No employer has ever been able to argue successfully in court that a specific personality type or dimension was necessary for effective job performance.

Under the Americans with Disabilities Act, physical testing can be done only after a job offer has been made unless an employer can show that there are specific, critical physical requirements for job performance. The use of honesty testing has been declining since Congress passed the Employee Polygraph Protection Act in 1988. This act, which prohibits such tests, is problematic and generally unreliable. Research has shown that employee theft is usually influenced more by factors external to the individual (pay inequity, working conditions, or abusive treatment from superiors) than internal factors such as inherent dishonesty. Drug testing has been challenged

EXHIBIT 8-4: THE BIG FIVE PERSONALITY DIMENSIONS

Personality Dimension	Characteristics of a Person Scoring Positively on the Dimension
1) Sociability	Gregarious, energetic, talkative, assertive
2) Agreeableness	Trusting, considerate, cooperative, tactful
3) Conscientiousness	Dependable, responsible, achievement-oriented, persistent
4) Emotional stability	Stable, secure, unworried, confident
5) Intellectual openness	Intellectual, imaginative, curious, original

in the courts under the legal doctrine of invasion of privacy; however, no federal right-to-privacy statutes prohibit testing of either on- or off-the-job drug use by employees. Drug testing is, however, coming under increased scrutiny by the courts and rulings favoring employers versus employees/applicants have been inconsistent. If any drug testing is conducted, those who sanction and administer the tests need to ensure that they do not unduly target members of protected classes.

Call-Center Staffing at Capital One

Capital One is one of the largest suppliers of consumer MasterCard and VISA credit cards in the world, with more than 44 million cardholders and more than 20,000 employees. More than 75 percent of its employees are call-center customer service associates and 3,000 new call-center employees are hired annually. The tremendous growth of the organization required that it develop a strategy for staffing its call centers that would recruit and retain the best individuals, reduce turnover and associated costs, and increase sales volume. After a three-year planning period, Capital One rolled out its company information-based strategy (IBS) in 2001. A major component of IBS is the proprietary database software that allows Capital One to achieve its staffing goals. Applicants for call-center associate jobs can either call a toll-free telephone number and proceed through a battery of screening questions or answer the same questions online. These questions relate to the job characteristics deemed to be most critical to success as a call-center associate at Capital One. Those who receive acceptable scores are invited to a regional assessment center where they undergo an average of five hours of a additional computer-based tests and assessments spread over a two-day period. The IBS uses multiple technologies, including real-time automated decision making, simulations, and online videos. The IBS has decreased time-to-hire by 52 percent, increasing the rate at which Capital One can hire by 71 percent. Moreover, the system has resulted in a 12 percent increase in the number of calls handled per hour, a 36 percent increase in the rate of closing sales, an 18 percent decrease in unproductive downtime, and a 75 percent decrease in involuntary attrition during the first six months on the job.[27]

References

Reference-checking is usually part of the selection process; however, most prospective employers do little more than waste valuable time during this process. Generally, employers contact individuals whose names have been provided by the applicant, despite the fact that common sense dictates that an applicant would not submit a reference who would provide a negative recommendation. However, few employers bother to investigate the applicant's background any further. Employers can and should call individuals other than those named by the applicant. When contacting references the applicant has provided, requests can be made for additional contacts within or outside of the organization. Once an individual has worked within a given industry in a given geographical location for a few years, he or she becomes well networked within the local industry. These contacts can and should be used for checking references. There are often far fewer degrees of separation between an applicant and an employer than the employer might imagine.

Much like testing, reference-checking was often done after the interviewing process and usually as the final step in the selection decision. More recently, however, many organizations have begun checking references prior to interviewing to allow them to eliminate candidates and gather information to be used later in the interviewing process.

One potential limitation with reference-checking is that many past employers will not provide any information at all; they may do nothing more than verify the dates of employment, position held, and/or salary level. Increasing liability for libel, slander, and defamation of past employees has caused more organizations to adopt a policy of not commenting on past employees' employment history. This can be overcome at times through a well-established professional network, whereby individuals will confidentially tell those in other organizations whom they know and trust about a problem former employee.

Reference-checking has become more critical for organizations because courts have been holding employers responsible for an employee's acts if the employer did not conduct a reasonable investigation into the employee's background. The doctrine of negligent hiring requires employers to balance an applicant's right to privacy with the responsibility for providing a safe workplace for employees and customers. At the very least, the employer should verify all dates of employment and education and investigate any time gaps on an applicant's resume.

In attempting to balance the need to avoid defamation suits brought by former employees with the need to avoid possible negligent referral charges for failure to warn another employer about a past employee's suspected potential to cause harm, employers are faced with a Catch-22: giving either too much or too little information can expose them to a lawsuit. As a public policy issue, many states have adopted laws that provide qualified immunity to an employer who provides reference information in good faith. Employers who knowingly provide false or misleading information are not immune from liability. To date, 35 states have enacted such legislation, which has been supported by the Society for Human Resource Management.[28]

INTERNATIONAL ASSIGNMENTS

One final challenge that organizations face in staffing is selecting among current employees for overseas assignments. Traditionally, such assignments have been made based on past proven successes within the organization and the employee's work-related technical skills. Although technical ability is certainly a valid selection criterion, the main reason employees fail on international assignments has less to do with technical skills than with interpersonal and acculturation abilities. Lack of adaptation of not just the employee but the employee's family has caused problems for numerous organizations in their international operations as well as with relations with foreign officials, customers, and business partners. ▼▼

Organizations are now realizing that assessing the technical backgrounds of such employees is merely an initial screening criterion. To ensure the success of overseas assignments, employers are increasingly testing employees' adaptability, open-mindedness, ability to tolerate uncertainty and ambiguity, and independence. Similarly, many are also interviewing and screening family members who would be accompanying the employee on the assignment. In certain cases, the employee is able to adapt, but problems with family member adaptation either require the employee to return home before the end of the assignment or have a negative impact on the employee's performance. Screening employees as part of staffing international operations has consequently become much more elaborate and strategic to ensure the success of the assignment. This will be discussed in greater depth in Chapter 14. ▼▼▼

DIVERSITY

When developing an integrated, strategic approach to staffing, initiatives, programs, and policies must remain in compliance with federal, state, and local labor laws that prohibit discrimination. To ensure compliance with these laws and to assist with staffing, many organizations have developed formal diversity management programs. Successful diversity initiatives have been developed not in a piecemeal manner but in conjunction with the organization's strategic objectives.

CONCLUSION

An organization can only be successful and reach its strategic objectives by employing individuals who have the capacity and desire to contribute to its mission. The staffing function, therefore, plays an important role in facilitating an organization's success. When unemployment is low, organizations face even greater challenges in staffing as the forces of supply and demand drive wages up and provide greater career opportunities with other organizations.

An effective staffing strategy requires in-depth planning for the recruiting process to ensure efficiency and generation of a qualified applicant pool. How selection will proceed relative to process and the kinds of applicant information needed must also be determined. The strategic decisions organizations need to make relative to staffing are summarized in Exhibit 8-5. Staffing is the key or core component that forms the backbone of an integrated, strategic system of human resource management by ensuring that there is an optimal fit between employees and the strate-

▶▶ Reading 8.2, "Causes and Consequences of Declining Early Departures from Foreign Assignments," examines the challenges associated with selecting individuals for international assignments.

▶▶▶ Reading 8.3, "Designing and Implementing Global Staffing Systems: Part I—Leaders in Global Staffing," provides examples of six leading organizations who have successfully implemented strategic global staffing systems.

EXHIBIT 8-5: STRATEGIC ISSUES IN STAFFING

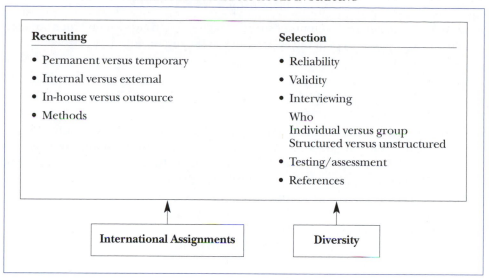

gic needs of the organization. If an organization's staffing is deficient, the effectiveness of its HR programs and policies will be impaired. As one HR professional commented, "Good training will not fix bad selection."

CRITICAL THINKING

1. How does an organization's investment in staffing benefit the organization after an applicant becomes an employee?

2. What problems can result from cutting corners to save time or money in the staffing process?

3. What are the major strategic choices an organization faces concerning staffing? What are the advantages and disadvantages of each alternative?

4. Devise a staffing strategy for the following organizations:
   • A church-based soup kitchen staffed with volunteers
   • A professional baseball team
   • A small, Internet start-up
   • A publisher of a large, daily newspaper in a major city
   • A police department
   • A 400-room luxury hotel

Reading 8.1

5. Is it more important for an employer to establish a person-job fit or a person-organization fit? Why? Can you think of situations where one would be preferable to the other?

Reading 8.2

6. What can an employer do to make international assignments more attractive to its employees?

Reading 8.3

7. What are the key components of successful global staffing systems? Identify similarities and differences in the approaches of the organizations described.

EXPERIENTIAL EXERCISES

1. Visit a major employer's Web site (such as those provided here or any others). Apply for a specific job with the same company both via online means and through submitting a resume by surface mail. Compare and contrast the processes. As an applicant, which did you find preferable, and why?

Cisco Systems	http://www.cisco.com
GE Energy	http://www.gepowercareers.com
Advanced Micro Devices	http://www.amd.com
Booz • Allen & Hamilton	http://www.bah.com
Bank of America	http://www.bankof america.com
Compaq Computer	http://www.compaq.com
Eastman Kodak	http://www.kodak.com
Specialized Bicycles	http://www.specialized.com

2. In small groups, discuss your experiences and determine the pros and cons of online recruiting from the *employer's* perspective.

3. Develop a behavioral interviewing protocol for your current or most recent job.

INTERNET EXERCISES

1. Visit the Web sites for the following employment services:

   http://www.monster.com
   http://www.hotjobs.com
   http://www.careerbuilder.com

   Compare and contrast the features and attractiveness of each site.

CHAPTER REFERENCES

1. Joinson, C. "Capturing Turnover Costs," *HR Magazine*, July 2000, pp. 107–119.
2. Ibid. p. 118.
3. McConnell, B. "Recruiting How-tos As Important As Who-tos, SHRM Survey Reveals," *HR News*, December 2002, pp. 2, 5.
4. Miraz, P. "Networking: An Executive Recruiter's Best Friend," *HR Magazine*, September 2000, p. 22.
5. Miraz, P. "Where Are All the Home-Grown CEOs?" *HR Magazine*, September 2000, p. 22.
6. Leonard, B. "Online and Overwhelmed," *HR Magazine*, August 2000, pp. 37–39.
7. Ibid.
8. Leonard, B. "Job Candidates Judge Employers by Their Web Sites," *HR Magazine*, July 2000, pp. 30–31.
9. Ibid.
10. Martinez, M. N. "Get Job Seekers to Come to You," *HR Magazine*, August 2000, pp. 45–52.
11. "Networking Rules, Say Job Seekers and Employers," *HR News*, 20, (5), May 2001, p. 2.
12. Leonard, B. "Job-Hunting Professionals Rank Networking over Internet," *HR Magazine*, May 2002, pp. 25–26.

13. "Networking Rules, Say Job Seekers and Employers," *HR News*, 20, (5), May 2001, p. 2.
14. McConnell, B. "Recruiting How-tos As Important As Who-tos, SHRM Survey Reveals," *HR News*, December 2002, pp. 2, 5.
15. Grensing-Pophal, L. "The Perils of Internet Recruiting," www.shrm.org.hrresources.whitepapers_published/CMS_000408.asp
16. Ibid.
17. Roberts, B. "System Addresses 'Applicant' Dilemma," *HR Magazine*, September 2002, pp. 111–119.
18. Martinez, M. N. "The Headhunter Within," *HR Magazine*, August 2001, pp. 48–55.
19. Ibid.
20. Robinson, K. "Online Bidding Fills Nursing Jobs," *HR Magazine*, December 2003, p. 44.
21. Fisher, C. D., Schoenfeldt, L. F. and Shaw, J. B. *Human Resource Management*, 4th ed. Boston: Houghton Mifflin Co., 1999, p. 274.
22. Martinez, M. N. "Recruiting Here and There," *HR Magazine*, September 2002, pp. 95–100.
23. Hirsh, S. "Software King Builds Young Careers, Too," *Baltimore Sun*, March 9, 2003, p. 1D.
24. Poe, A. C. "Graduate Work," *HR Magazine*, October 2003, pp. 95–100.
25. Ibid.
26. Goldberg, L. R. "An Alternative 'Description of Personality': The Big-Five Structure," *Journal of Personality and Social Psychology*, 59, (6), December 1990, pp. 1216–1229.
27. Romeo, J. "Answering the Call," *HR Magazine*, October 2003, pp. 81–84.
28. "SHRM Board Oks Investment Advice, Safety, Reference Positions," *HR News*, May 2002, p. 11.

Hiring for the Organization, Not the Job

David E. Bowen, Gerald E. Ledford, Jr., Barry R. Nathan, *Academy of Management Executive*

Conventional selection practices are geared toward hiring employees whose knowledge, skills, and abilities (KSAs) provide the greatest fit with clearly defined requirements of specific jobs. Traditional selection techniques rarely consider characteristics of the organization in which the jobs reside. Traditional techniques also ignore characteristics of the person that are irrelevant to immediate job requirements. In common management parlance, the organization hires new "hands" or new "heads"—that is, parts of people.

A new model of selection is emerging, however, that is geared toward hiring a "whole" person who will fit well into the specific organization's culture. It reflects a fundamental reorientation of the selection process toward hiring "people," not just KSAs, for "organizations," not just jobs. This leads to hiring practices that seem peculiar, and needlessly extravagant, from a traditional human resource standpoint. Consider the hiring practices of three different organizations.

- AFG Industries builds two new float glass plants. The plants use practices such as work teams, extensive training, and skill-based pay that create a high level of employee involvement. The hiring process for factory workers includes screening formal resumes (not job applications), personality testing, pre-employment training that simulates some plant jobs, interviews with panels of managers and/or employees, and a medical exam.
- Sun Microsystems is the fastest-growing U.S. company in the past five years, with annual growth averaging more than 100 percent.[1] Filling open jobs is critical to Sun's effectiveness, phenomenal growth, and profitability. Yet, the hiring process is extremely time-consuming and labor-intensive. Potential hires at all levels are brought into the organization from four to seven times for interviews with up to twenty interviewers. The process is full of ambiguity, lacks formal rules, and

demands that all employees engage in problem solving to get themselves hired.
- Toyota (USA) screens 50,000 applicants for 3,000 factory jobs in the initial staffing of its plant in Georgetown, Kentucky.[2] Each employee hired invests at least eighteen hours in a selection process that includes a general knowledge exam, a test of attitudes toward work, an interpersonal skills assessment center, a manufacturing exercise designed to provide a realistic job preview of assembly work, an extensive personal interview, and a physical exam.

As we shall see, these organizations adopt unusual hiring practices to find employees who fit the organization and to encourage those who do not fit to seek employment elsewhere. Although potential hires with skills that meet the demands of specific jobs are not ignored, these companies maintain that the person-job fit needs to be supported and enriched by person-organization fit. These companies are willing to invest substantial resources in rigorously assessing this fit. Why and how organizations approach hiring in this way are explored in this article.

HOW IMPORTANT ARE HIRING DECISIONS, REALLY? THE PERSON-SITUATION CONTROVERSY REVISITED

Is individual behavior, such as job performance, a function of the person (attributes of an employee), the situation (characteristics of the work setting), or the interaction of the person and situation? This question is age-old. Proponents of employee selection as a key to human resource effectiveness answer that individual behavior is largely a function of the person. Selection techniques attempt to capitalize on enduring differences between individuals by choosing those individuals who are best suited to the job. Conversely, advocates of socialization and training practices that attempt to mold employees after they are hired assume that the situation is the principal determinant of individual behavior.[3]

The majority of researchers and managers subscribe to some form of the interactionist perspective. They assume that both the person and the situation matter, and that the combination of the two determines individual performance and other behavior.

We argue that both researchers and managers have overemphasized the situation and have paid only lip service to the individual in recent years. In research on organizational behavior, people variables (for example, needs) usually are treated as secondary to situational variables (for example, job designs) and researchers generally are skeptical about the ability of personality variables to predict job performance.[4] Managerial interest in individual testing appears to have dropped sharply after several 1970 court decisions held that unvalidated and discriminatory selection procedures were illegal.

An overemphasis on the importance of the situation fits the managerial ideology dominant among American corporations. A basic assumption of bureaucratic organizations is that individuals cannot be trusted to manage their own behavior. Thus, management designs the organization to control employee behavior as tightly as possible, through the managerial hierarchy, impersonal rules and procedures, close supervision, and extensive socialization and training. This curtails the expression of individual differences in behavior. As a result, the organization is designed to be what researchers have called a "strong situation," one in which the intensity of the situation suppresses variation in behavior that is attributable to the person.[5] Thus, managers create a self-fulfilling prophesy. The belief that the situation is the most important predictor of behavior leads to the organizational design which suppresses individual differences. This self-fulfilling pattern is further reinforced by basing hiring decisions on a single, brief interview, which has proved to be unreliable and of poor validity.[6] It is not surprising, then, that managers often conclude that the selection system is not a key success factor.

Yet, some organizations are designed as "weak situations," allowing a range of employee responses to work requirements.[7] These organizations have less control over individuals and the effects of person variables are greater. In such organizations, it is more important than in traditional organizations to do a good job of hiring the right people.

Consider the three organizations we described at the beginning of this article. They are more different than similar. They include high-tech and moderately low-tech, manufacturing-driven and engineering-driven, white collar and blue collar, and U.S.-owned and Japanese-owned firms. Yet these organizations share a set of management assumptions about organizational success. Each is attempting to build a distinctive culture that is intentionally "fragile," meaning that management relies heavily on self-motivated, committed people for system effectiveness.[8] While all three organizations have management hierarchy, organizational policies, and other tools of external control, all rely to an unusual degree on employees to make the system work effectively. And they use sophisticated selection systems to hire the whole person whose skills and personality fit the type of organization, not just a job.

The New Selection Model: Hiring for Person-Organization Fit

Exhibit 1 presents the new selection model for hiring for person-organization fit. As we shall see, it differs from the traditional selection model in several important ways.[9] Our model represents a synthesis of the steps taken by the organizations mentioned in our opening case examples as well as by other progressive firms. Although any one firm may not fully implement every step, all of these steps together offer the best guarantee of person-organization fit.

We will describe the steps in the model and then present a case description of a firm where hiring practices are a close match to the ideal. First, however, we clarify the meaning of "person-organization fit."

PERSON-ORGANIZATION FIT

The model in Exhibit 1 places the selection process in the context of a rich interaction between the person and the organization, both of which are more broadly defined and assessed than in the traditional selection model.

Person-organization fit requires that two types of fit be achieved in the hiring process: (1) between the KSAs of the individual and the task demands or critical requirements for the job; and (2) between the overall personality of the individual (e.g., needs, interests, and values) and the climate or culture of the organization.

The traditional selection model focuses almost exclusively on the first type of fit (KSAs—job) while tending to ignore, or assessing far less rigorously, the second type (personality—climate/culture).[10] The narrow focus of the traditional selection model

1. Assess the Overall Work Environment

- Job Analysis
- Organizational Analysis

2. Infer the Type of Person Required

- Technical Knowledge, Skills and Abilities
- Social Skills
- Personal Needs, Values, and Interests
- Personality Traits

3. Design "Rites of Passage" for Organization Entry That Allow Both the Organization and the Applicant to Assess Their Fit

- Tests of Cognitive, Motor, and Interpersonal Abilities
- Interviews by Potential Co-Workers and Others
- Personality Tests
- Realistic Job Previews, Including Work Samples

4. Reinforce Person-Organization Fit at Work

- Reinforce Skills and Knowledge Through Task Design and Training
- Reinforce Personal Orientation Through Organization Design

reflects several factors. One is that managers tend to think of individual job performance as the key outcome of the hiring process and they believe that job performance is a function of the fit between KSAs and task demands. Additionally, the traditional selection model is more concerned with finding new employees than with retaining them. There is less attention to whether the whole person finds the organization's culture satisfying enough to stay. Organizations have also been constrained by the unavailability of proven selection technologies for producing the fit between personality and climate/culture. This situation can be improved, we believe, by following the steps for hiring that are described next.

STEP ONE: ASSESS THE WORK ENVIRONMENT

The job analysis of the traditional model of selection is also conducted in the new model. It remains instrumental in achieving the fit between individual KSAs and task demands. Alternative job analysis techniques include the position analysis questionnaire, task inventories, and critical incident techniques.[11]

The purpose of an organizational analysis is to define and assess the work environment in terms of the characteristics of the organization, rather than just in terms of the characteristics of a specific job. It identifies the behaviors and responsibilities that lead to organizational effectiveness, and implies the personal characteristics most likely to be associated with such behaviors and responsibilities. Organizational analysis also is important because job analysis data may quickly become outdated as rapidly changing products and technologies reshape employees' jobs. The organization's overall philosophy and values are likely to be more stable and consequently, the more important long-term focus for fit.

Techniques for organizational analysis are not well-established, largely because there is little research that systematically associates the characteristics of organizations and individual behavior patterns. Managers need to identify the important dimensions of the organization and their implications for the kinds of employees who would best fit those situations. Although organizational analysis techniques are not nearly as well-developed as job analysis techniques, a variety of methods are available. For example, the training field offers guidelines for conducting an organizational analysis as one component of a training needs analysis. Organization characteristics assessed include short- and long-term goals, staffing needs, properties of the environment (for example, stability), and employee perceptions of organization climate. Organizational culture audits have emerged in the last decade that offer both qualitative and quantitative methods for describing an organization's norms and values.[12] Quite promising is a sophisticated Q-sort methodology that assesses the content, integrity, and crystallization of organizational values and matches them with an assessment of individual values.[13] Finally, there is a long-standing approach to diagnosing the characteristics of an organization's four subsystems (individuals, tasks, organizational arrangements, informal organization) that can yield organizational analysis data.[14]

Organization analysis does not replace job analysis. Rather it ensures that important components of the work context as well as its content are identified and evaluated for their importance to job success. While many job analyses include evaluations of the work context, the person-organization fit model explicitly recognizes that successful employees have knowledge, skills, abilities, and other personal characteristics that match both the content and the context of the job.

STEP TWO: INFER THE TYPE OF PERSON REQUIRED

In step two, managers deal with applicants in terms of who they are, not just what they can do. It is still necessary to infer from the job analysis the KSAs that employees need to be technically competent. However, step two also requires inferring, from the organizational analysis, the needs, values and interests—that is, the personality—an employee must possess to be an effective member of the organization. For example, if the organizational analysis reveals that teamwork is a key norm or value in the setting, then selection tools must be used to find people who are team players. Furthermore, social and interpersonal skills will be necessary, in addition to the cognitive and motor abilities that are the dominant skills-focus of the traditional selection model.

The move by some organizations toward hiring the total person coincides with a renewed interest by researchers in personality as a predictor of job attitudes and behaviors. These researchers believe that studies in which personality measures fail to predict job performance often have been plagued by problems such as focusing on personality aspects of questionable relevance to the job, poor research methods, and so on.[15] These problems have given personality a bad name and fostered the impression that the situation matters much more than the person in influencing job attitudes and performance. In contrast, more recent research has yielded such interesting findings that individual personality attributes can predict job satisfaction later—more than fifty years and even for different jobs. The research implies that job satisfaction may be associated with a stable, enduring personality attribute rather than a function of the situation.[16] This indicates that the types of people hired is very important.

Organizations also must pay attention to technical skills needed by the organization. Often applicants with the most appropriate personalities and social skills are not those with the right technical skills. If the organization faces the need to upgrade technical skills quickly, it may be forced to make tradeoffs. Organizations in this situation often place greater weight on personality and social skills, on the grounds that it is easier to train technical skills than change personalities or develop social skills. This can lead to increased short-term training costs and temporary overstaffing. However, if the work technology is complex and training times are long, management may be forced to hire some employees who better fit the organization's technical requirements than its cultural requirements. Douglas Bray, noted pioneer of the AT&T Management Progress Study, considers this tradeoff and suggests that selection decisions about needs, values, and interests may be more critical than those for skills.[17] For example, a desire to learn new jobs is an attribute that cannot be taught easily to employees, as job skills can. You either hire people who have this attribute, or do without.

STEP THREE: DESIGN "RITES OF PASSAGE" THAT ALLOW THE ORGANIZATION AND THE INDIVIDUAL TO ASSESS FIT

The battery of screens used in the new approach to hiring may seem designed to discourage individuals from taking the job.[18] Yet, these screens have several purposes. First, the use of multiple screening methods, raters, and criteria has long been recommended by researchers as the best approach to hiring.[19] Yet most organizations still hire employees using a single interview with a single interviewer. More sophisticated techniques, if used, typically are reserved for executives and sometimes sales people. Second, multiple screenings not only allow the organization to select employees, but also provides applicants with sufficient realistic information about the work environment so that they can make an informed choice about whether they even want the job. Third, the people who join the organization feel special. They have survived the elaborate rites of passage necessary to join the organization. They experience the sense of accomplishment associated with completing boot camp when entering military service.

A recent *Fortune* article described these fresh approaches as "The New Art of Hiring Smart."[20] One ingredient has been increased use of job simulation exercises for assembly workers. These simulations, or work sample tests, help both the person and the organization assess fit. The applicant receives a realistic job preview of the work. The organization has an opportunity to assess applicants' technical skills and, when group interaction is required in an exercise, their interpersonal skills as well. Intelligence tests also seem to be on the rebound.

Personality tests are another way to assess mutual fit. It appears that "personality tests are back."[21] For example, the Meyers-Briggs Type Indicator is used by companies such as Allied Signal, Apple, AT&T, Citicorp, Exxon, G.E., Honeywell, and 3M. These tests are used primarily in management development programs. However, personality tests are used increasingly as selection tests, particularly for assembly worker positions.

There is renewed interest in personality tests even though past efforts to validate them have been largely unsuccessful.[22] However, there is a growing belief that personality tests can be validated under the proper conditions.[23] These include:

1. Using personality measures that are tailored to the work setting. Major personality tests were not developed for work settings, so their poor track record in validation studies is not surprising.
2. Using personality measures to predict global criteria. That is, multi-faceted measures of job attitudes and behaviors, rather than one specific criterion such as quarterly sales.
3. Using measures of personality dimensions that are logically or theoretically associated with the work in the organization. This contrasts with screening for personality attributes that are not job related but hold some particular interest to managers.

Sun Microsystems offers a good example of the use of rites of passage to allow mutual assessment of fit. This fast-growing Silicon Valley firm, like many high-technology companies, is constantly changing in response to rapidly developing markets, evolving technologies, and the pace of internal growth. Employees who prefer clear job descriptions, stability, a leisurely pace, and predictability would be unhappy at Sun. The hiring process is such a challenge, and so full of ambiguity, that unsuitable applicants tend to give up before the process is completed. Those hired have survived multiple interviews with many different possible co-workers. A joke at Sun is, "after seven sets of interviews, we put applicants on the payroll whether they've been hired or not." The hiring process thus introduces prospective employees to the culture of the organization.

Whereas personality tests provide organizations with information about applicants, realistic job previews (RJPs) provide applicants with information about organizations. Examples of RJPs are the Toyota USA job simulations/work sample tests that show applicants the repetitive nature of manufacturing work and the requirements for teamwork. Applicants can then make informed choices about whether they would be satisfied there. "Turned-off" applicants may drop out of the hiring process. Those hired are more likely to join the organization with a sense of commitment and realistic expectations. Fundamentally, an RJP helps individuals decide if they want to join an organization, based on their own assessment of their personality and how it might fit with a particular type of organization.[24]

STEP FOUR: REINFORCE PERSON-ORGANIZATION FIT AT WORK

Selection is clearly the first and, arguably, the most important step in implementing a fragile system philosophy. However, the hiring process must be integrated with, and supported by, the firm's other human resource management practices. Japanese-owned plants in the U.S. and high involvement organizations illustrate this point.

Japanese automobile manufacturers operating in the United States provide examples of how to accomplish this. The Japanese "Auto Alley" in the U.S. provided more than 6,000 assembly jobs in 1989. Key operations include Nissan in Smyrna, Tennessee; Toyota in Georgetown, Kentucky; Honda in Marysville, Ohio; Mazda in Flat Rock, Michigan; and Diamond-Star Motors Corporation in Normal, Illinois.[25] The

Japanese have attempted to create a certain type of organization, characterized by now-familiar values of teamwork, consensual decision-making, peer control, egalitarianism, and non-specialized career paths. Broad job classifications encourage employee flexibility, rather than identification with specific jobs. Extensive on-the-job training and job rotation further increase flexibility. Group activities encourage employees to contribute ideas for organizational improvement and promote teamwork. Employment stability helps the organization realize a return on its training and other investments in human resources, and increases employee loyalty to the organization. Thus, a selection system in such organizations typically screens for interest in work variety, social needs and skills, and organization commitment.

High involvement organizations (HIOs) are another class of organization that uses multiple systems to support hiring for person-organization fit. HIOs are a relatively new organizational form; there are perhaps a few hundred examples now existing in the U.S.[26] HIOs have two key characteristics.[27] First, the organization is designed to create very high levels of employee involvement. Power, information, skills, and rewards for performance are pushed down to the lowest levels of the organization. Self-managed teams or other structures enable employees to share decision-making power. Extensive training in technical, social, and business skills provides team members with the skills needed for effective self-management. Information systems communicate the performance data that teams need to manage themselves. Reward systems such as skill-based pay and gainsharing motivate needed behaviors, such as learning and problem solving. For obvious reasons, hiring practices in HIOs typically attempt to select employees who prefer working in groups and who have high needs for personal growth and development. Thus, the hiring process is one design element of many that must fit with the overall design.

The following case description of the hiring process in a new HIO illustrates all four steps of the new selection model.

HIRING FOR PERSON-ORGANIZATION FIT: THE CASE OF A START-UP HIGH INVOLVEMENT ORGANIZATION

The research reported here was conducted as part of an action research project at a new float glass plant in the western United States.[28] The plant is a classic new HIO. Research on the selection system described here is part of a larger, on-going action research effort. Management was interested in developing selection procedures and tools for hiring employees with the necessary job skills, needs, and aspirations to fit the organization design. Researchers helped design the hiring process, conducted extensive research on the initial hiring process at the plant, and explored the validity of personality measures as possible future selection tools. The overall effort essentially followed the four steps previously discussed for hiring for person-organization fit.

STEP ONE: ASSESS THE WORK ENVIRONMENT

Since the plant was a start-up operation, there were no existing jobs to analyze in this initial step. There were individual jobs with comparable content at other organizational sites, but management was committed to designing the new plant as the first high involvement organization in the company. Thus, analyzing the work environment of the existing plants would have been of limited use in designing a hiring process to match the new HIO. Instead, top management and two of the researcher/consultants (the second author and Tom Cummings of the University of Southern California) conducted an organizational analysis to assess key desired organizational characteristics, norms, and values. This analysis followed standard sociotechnical systems procedures, and specifically considered requirements for the level of employee growth and social needs. This led to the development of the management philosophy and practices that would define the new organization. A customized version of the HIO concept, tailored to the needs of the organization, emerged from this work.

Glass-making lent itself to an HIO design for several reasons. First, there was a great deal of task interdependence which required worker cooperation and teamwork. Second, technical uncertainty was high. Workers were responsible for making immediate decisions about the glass-making process from the procurement to furnace melting of raw materials and various stages of cooling, inspecting, cutting, packing, and storing. The plant's profitability is directly related to production efficiency and glass quality. Quality is directly dependent on workers' ability to maintain a continual, steady flow of glass, by constantly monitoring and regulating the temperature and speed of flow of the product through the system. Deviations from desired parameters must be corrected as soon as possible after detection. Internal control by employees is more responsive to system fluctuations than external control through supervision, rules, and procedures.

The work environment led management to adopt a work design that encouraged high levels of employee teamwork and decision making. Employees were organized into self-regulating work teams at each sequential stage of production. Management saw this job design as most appropriate for the relatively high task interdependence and task uncertainty of the plant technology. Management expected that as team members developed technical and social skills, they would make joint decisions about work methods and assignments and solve production problems on the line.

STEP TWO: INFER THE TYPE OF PERSON REQUIRED

Since work in the high involvement glass plant required understanding and becoming involved in the entire production process, selecting on the basis of technical skills was not enough. Basic KSAs, such as motor and arithmetic skills, while necessary, would not be sufficient for organizational success. Workers also had to feel a sense of commitment to working in this type of organization. Furthermore, the jobs were to be dynamic. Over time, employees were expected to learn different skills within their team and in other teams, and to take on an increasing share of decision making. Top management expected that the number of supervisors and layers of management would be reduced as the teams matured. A fit between applicant characteristics and the work requirements of a high involvement organization as a whole was required.

In addition to the necessary technical skills, two personality characteristics were especially important to the organization. One was growth need strength. The HIO design placed many demands on employees for continuous learning, decision-making, and assuming responsibility for organizational structuring, functioning, and performance. For example, employees were required to train each other, give feedback to fellow team members on their performance and help design organizational changes. Applicants who desired little challenge or learning opportunity and those who prefer narrowly defined jobs would have been misfits with this organization. Conversely, those who valued or had strong needs

for personal growth, accomplishment, and personal development would be more committed to working in the new plant.

A second relevant personality characteristic was social needs. This was obvious because self-regulating teams demand cooperation and teamwork. In addition, management planned to make heavy use of special problem-solving groups, committees, and task forces. Those who saw working with others as a burden would have been misfits in such a setting, while people with high social needs were expected to prefer group forms of work and group activities.

STEP THREE: DESIGN "RITES OF PASSAGE" THAT ALLOW THE ORGANIZATION AND THE INDIVIDUAL TO ASSESS FIT

The hiring process consisted of several stages that involved multiple methods, raters, and criteria. A state agency conducted an initial screen of approximately 1000 candidates responding to local advertisements about job openings at the plant, which was then under construction. At this stage applicants received scores for their education and experience, such as a high school degree or GED, manufacturing or related experience, and ability to understand process instrumentation and complete a time card. In addition, tests using potential predictors based on personality and other survey questions also were administered at this time. Personality characteristics were assessed using the Personality Research Form— Form E, or PRF, a highly regarded personality assessment instrument.[29] The PRF measure of affiliation needs is very similar to social needs as described previously. Three PRF measures were relevant to growth needs: achievement, endurance, and dominance. (The dominance items measure desire to influence others or social achievement, not oppressiveness.) These two personality dimensions, affiliation and growth needs, were logically associated with the nature of work in an HIO and the PRF measures were moderately tailored to better fit the work setting. Of the 540 applicants who passed the initial screening and were invited to a pre-employment assessment and training program (described below), approximately 500 candidates responded.

Performance was assessed in four half-day sessions of a pre-employment assessment and training program, designed to capture characteristics of work in a high involvement float glass factory. The company used this program both as a selection tool and as a realistic job preview. As an RJP, the program showed how a high involvement organization is designed to operate, technical and social requirements, what it would be like to handle glass (for example, lacerations are common and special protective clothing is used to minimize the likelihood of injury), and various tasks employees would be expected to perform.

The program was divided into two approximately equal segments. One part involved work simulations consisting of handling and packing glass and operating hand tools and equipment required for glass making. Participants were given instructions about work methods, rules, and safety procedures, and engaged in glass making and packing tasks as a team. The second part of the training program involved classroom learning and experiential exercises aimed at group decision making. Almost half of the classroom time was used to present information about glass making and the design features of the high involvement plant, including self-regulating groups, participative leadership, egalitarian human-resource practices, skill-based pay, and gainsharing. Participants were given a realistic portrayal of what it would be like to work in a team-based, high involvement structure, including the kinds of work behaviors that would be expected. They also were tested on basic math and measurement skills needed to perform glass making and packaging tasks, as well as given homework covering basic processes and terminology used in making glass as well as the nature of one's work and responsibility in a high involvement organization.

For more than half of the classroom time, participants engaged in exercises designed to simulate the kind of group interaction and decision-making occurring in self-regulating groups. One exercise, for example, involved reaching a group consensus about the ranking of items needed to survive in the rugged outdoors. Another exercise involved role playing a group decision about which department should receive a new piece of equipment. These exercises were followed by extensive debriefing about members' behaviors and interactions and how the learning applies to the work of teams in the plant.

The scoring procedure evaluated applicants from a holistic perspective, that is how well each applicant fit in a high involvement setting rather than how he or she performed on individual job-related tasks. Applicants were evaluated by managers and supervisors who had received training on how to avoid common rater errors. Classroom activities, group exercises, and work simulations were scored. Applicants were evaluated on the quality and thoroughness of homework assignments and were required to attain minimum passing scores on arithmetic and tape measure reading tests. Group exercises were scored on the degree applicants exhibited participating, negotiating, gatekeeping, and probing behaviors. Finally, work simulations were scored on four factors: absence and tardiness over the four days; safety behavior; responsibility, meaning following instructions and not exhibiting disruptive or distracting behavior; and general behavior, meaning exhibiting team skills, paying attention to instructors, and not breaking plant rules or abusing equipment. Thus, the work simulations were not scored on task performance per se. Instead, they were scored on behaviors relevant to the overall success of the organization. The focus on behaviors ensured that the selection process could be defended legally, if necessary, on the basis of content validity.

Those who passed this program were invited to a final selection interview with a panel of managers. This structured interview consisted of questions

---

The pre-employment assessment and training program met two important goals. First, it was consistent with technical and professional standards for employment selection. As in assessment centers, job behaviors were sampled systematically across different situations. Multiple and diverse activities and assessment methods afforded evaluators an opportunity to assess how well applicants would fit into an HIO generally, rather than just on how well applicants could perform specific tasks. The use of global criteria satisfied another condition for successfully validating a personality test as selection tools. Second, the program gave applicants a realistic job preview of what working in a high involvement glass plant would be like. The task activities provided applicants with a preview of the physical and potentially dangerous nature of the work. (One of the authors was present when a piece of tempered glass was mishandled and literally exploded in an applicant's hands.) The classroom activities prepared applicants for the organization's emphasis on working together and taking responsibility for action.

---

regarding manufacturing experience, education, understanding the high involvement and autonomous work group design, past experience and interest in group activities, and other performance skills and creative experiences. Finally, applicants were required to pass a physical examination including a drug screen. Ultimately, 250 applicants of the original 1000 applicants successfully completed these phases and the physical examination.

We subsequently validated the PRF personality test. Specifically, scores on the PRF were significantly correlated with performance in the pre-employment training program and with applicants' anticipated satisfaction with work in the organization.[30] This means that it would be appropriate and legal for the company to use measures of social and growth needs from this test in future hiring decisions. Since the analysis was completed long after most employees had been hired at the site, however, the company did not use the test in hiring decisions.

STEP FOUR: REINFORCE PERSON-ORGANIZATION FIT AT WORK

The objectives of the hiring process were reinforced by various organization design features that emphasized high involvement and team functioning. For example, extensive training was provided, both in technical skills and in social skills such as group decision making. A skill-based pay system gave employees increases in base pay for learning new jobs within their team. This in turn reinforced employees' interest in receiving training, which enabled them to earn pay increases. The plant adopted a gainsharing plan from the beginning that provided generous plant-wide monetary bonuses when plant performance met specific objectives. This reinforced the need for teamwork, since no individual could win a bonus at the expense of another. The gainsharing plan also provided incentives for exemplary performance and for developing improvements in the production process that could result in greater payouts. Extensive business information was routinely shared with employees, in part to make the gainsharing plan work more effectively. Employees were also involved as needed in task forces of various kinds to solve business, personnel, and other problems. In short, there was extensive reinforcement for the behaviors and characteristics that management sought during the hiring process.

The results of the hiring process have been positive. A survey of employees after startup indicated that employee quality of work life, according to various measures of satisfaction, organization commitment, and so on, was very high—a likely indication of person-organization fit. After an initial period of high turnover, turnover has dropped below national norms. On most key performance measures, the plant is one of the most effective in the company. Its main rival is another new high involvement plant that opened shortly after startup of the plant described here; it was developed on the same HIO model and used a similar hiring process. On the whole, it appears that the plant has been a very effective organization and that hiring for the organization, not just the job, has contributed to that effectiveness.

Benefits and Problems from Hiring for Person-Organization Fit

Clearly, the new approach to hiring for person-organization fit requires more resources than the traditional selection model. Is it worth the cost? Consider the potential benefits (see Exhibit 2).

(1) Employee Attitudes. Researchers have long proposed that a fit between individual needs and organizational climates and cultures would result in greater job satisfaction and organization commitment.[31] There is ample data documenting that the realistic job previews typically used in the new selection model are associated with higher on-the-job satisfaction.[32] Greater team spirit also is likely when new employees have shared the experience of moving successfully through the demanding rites of passage that lead to organizational entry.

Surveys of applicants in our case example indicated that these favorable attitudes were associated with the hiring process. For example, the majority of applicants felt the pre-employment training program accurately measured how well they could do the job and get along with others, and was a help in subsequent performance on the job and interacting with co-workers. Applicants also felt it provided a realistic preview of working at the plant. An overwhelming seventy-seven percent reported that after going through pre-employment training, the work seemed more satisfying than when they first applied for the job. Only two percent thought it would be less satisfying.

EXHIBIT 2: POTENTIAL BENEFITS AND PROBLEMS WITH HIRING FOR PERSON-ORGANIZATION FIT

Potential Benefits

1. More favorable employee attitudes (such as greater job satisfaction, organization commitment, and team spirit)

2. More desirable individual behaviors (such as better job performance and lower absenteeism and turnover)

3. Reinforcement of organizational design (such as support for work design and desired organizational culture)

Potential Problems

1. Greater investment of resources in the hiring process

2. Relatively undeveloped and unproven supporting selection technology

3. Individual stress

4. May be difficult to use the full model where payoffs are greatest

5. Lack of organizational adaptation

(2) Employee Behaviors. Studies indicate that high involvement organizations, which typically use the new selection model, have low rates of absenteeism, turnover, and grievances.[33] The data are even clearer that using realistic job previews in Step 3 is associated with lower turnover.[34] We also have presented a strong case that person-organization fit will result in employees displaying more of what have been labelled "organizational citizenship behaviors." These are behaviors that employees perform above and beyond explicit job requirements. The thinking here is that fitted employees see themselves as really belonging to the organization and willing to invest their own resources in its on-going maintenance.[35]

(3) Reinforcement of Organization Design. The effectiveness of Japanese transplants that hire according to this model is common knowledge. HIOs often are very high performers. For example, a study of a large sample of high-involvement organizations found that HIOs outperformed their industry on return on sales by an average of 532 percent and outperformed their industry on return on investment by an average of 388 percent.[36] Researchers often argue that the power of such an organization derives from the mutual reinforcement of its parts, including the selection process. The hiring process in HIOs helps select employees who are interested in challenging, responsible, varied jobs and pay systems that reward needed behaviors and performance.

POTENTIAL PROBLEMS

Hiring for person-organization fit may also have its disadvantages (see Exhibit 2).

(1) Greater Investment in Hiring. This model requires a much greater investment of resources in the hiring process. For example, Mazda in Flat Rock, Michigan, spends about $13,000 per employee to staff its plant.[37] It appears that organizations hiring within this model are spending the same time and money on hiring an assembly worker as they do in conducting an executive search.

The costs of making revisions in the hiring process also are different in the new model. A traditional hiring process needs to be revised whenever the requirements of the job change significantly. A hiring process for person-organization fit needs to be changed whenever the business, technological, or cultural requirements of the organization change significantly. This means that changes in hiring practices for person-organization fit are likely to be less frequent but much greater in scope than changes in traditional hiring processes. A change in hiring practices for person-organization fit may well involve a change in how every new employee is hired.

(2) Undeveloped Selection Technology. The supporting selection technology is still relatively undeveloped and unproven. One problem is the still-thin track record of successfully validating personality tests against job performance. However, the present authors' study in which measures of

growth needs and social needs predicted candidates' performance in a pre-employment simulation of high-involvement work demonstrates that personality measures, carefully chosen and developed, can be validated. Yet until personality tests acquire a deeper inventory of successful validation studies, organizations will doubt their usefulness.

In the context of person-organization fit, techniques for assessing people are more developed than those for assessing work environments. Even on the people side, though, the field is not nearly as sophisticated in measuring work-related personality facets as it is in assessing KSAs. Moreover, there is a great need for techniques of organizational analysis that are as sophisticated as those for job analysis (e.g., the PAQ). Overall, the challenge in organizational analysis is to: (a) identify relevant underlying dimensions of settings and how they can be measured, (b) determine the major impact on individual attitudes and behaviors, and organizational effectiveness, and (c) determine how such impacts differ depending upon individuals' personality.[38]

Managers may be concerned about the legality of these developing tools. More broadly, managers may be concerned about whether selecting for organization fit is legal. This concern is groundless, in our view. The legal standards for person-organization fit are not different than those for person-job fit. In general, selection procedures that do not result in adverse impact on protected minorities and women are not illegal. If the selection system does result in adverse impact, then evidence of job-relatedness must be presented. Job-relatedness is based on the content, construct, and criterion-related validity of the selection procedures. The procedures we have described establish job-relatedness.

In fact, there may be less adverse impact as a result of hiring for organization fit than in traditional hiring systems. Traditional systems rely mostly on tests of abilities to predict job performance. Intellectual ability tests typically result in adverse impact against minorities, and physical ability tests often result in adverse impact against women. Organization fit, in contrast, is based largely on values, needs, and motives that may be more evenly distributed in the population.

(3) Employee Stress. Individuals fitted to "fragile systems" may find their organizational lives to be more stressful. The firms in the Japanese Auto Alley, high-involvement organizations, firms in the Silicon Valley, and so on, which rely on carefully selected people for system effectiveness are also laying substantial claims to those people's lives. This higher level of involvement at work may be associated with experiencing more stress on the job. These workers have reported that they now take work problems home with them and feel the strains more typically associated with managerial roles.[39]

(4) Difficult to Use the Full Model Where the Benefits Are Greatest. A new hiring model may offer the greatest potential benefits to new organizations, such as new plants and startup companies. This is because hiring the right kinds of employees can help establish the desired culture of the organization from the very beginning. In existing organizations that are attempting to change their culture, there may be a long period in which the proportion of employees with unwanted attributes drops through attrition, while the proportion of employees with desired attributes gradually increases due to an improved hiring process.

Most of the hiring model we have described can be used in new organizations. However, one component of the model, specifically formal selection testing, often cannot be used appropriately or legally early in the life of the organization because the tests have not yet been validated. By the time the validation studies have been conducted, most of the workforce will have been hired. In some circumstances, it may be possible to avoid this problem by validating the tests before hiring in the new organization. For example, many companies that develop one high involvement organization (or other unusual culture) go on to develop others. It may be possible to validate the tests in an existing location if the culture of the existing organization and that desired of the new location are similar. AFG Industries, for example, could use the PRF test to hire employees in other plants that are designed as high-involvement organizations.

Another way to avoid this problem is taken by Development Dimensions International, a consulting firm that designed the hiring system for Toyota's Kentucky plant as well as other hiring systems aimed at person-organization fit.[40] DDI identifies the desired characteristics of new hires through a diagnosis conducted with senior managers of the organization. Potential hires explicitly are told about the desired characteristics during the orientation process. Then, the new hires complete a Job Fit

Inventory, which includes items relevant to the desired qualities of employees in the organization. The instrument intentionally is very "transparent" and fakeable. Thus, it does not serve the same purposes as personality tests. Rather, it is used to screen out the bottom five to fifteen percent of applicants—those who admit they lack the attributes that they are told explicitly that the company is seeking.

(5) Lack of Organizational Adaptation. A problem could arise in hiring for the organization if it led to a workforce in which everyone had the same personality profile. The organization might become stagnant because everyone would share the same values, strengths, weaknesses, and blindspots. (Obviously, the issue is the same whether employees all tend to have the same point of view because of the selection system or because of training and socialization.) There has been considerable debate about whether a powerful organizational culture, whatever its source, leads to success or leads to dry rot and lack of innovativeness. There is some evidence, for example, indicating that organizations with little internal variability in employee perspectives perform better in the short run but worse in the long run, presumably as a result of inferior adaption.[41]

However, we expect that significant internal variability will co-exist with person-organization fit. Even the best selection system is still imperfect; we do not succeed in hiring only the "right types." More fundamentally, the hiring process still results in variability on the desired characteristics. Even though all those hired may meet minimum standards, some will be higher than others on the desired characteristics. Finally, employees are not clones of one another just because they are similar on some personality dimensions. We would expect considerable variation on demographic, cultural, and personality dimensions that were not the basis for selection.

The Future of Hiring for Person-Organization Fit

What does the future hold for this more sophisticated and elaborate approach to employee selection? Will it be adopted by an increasingly large share of corporations?

We believe that hiring for the organization, not the job, will become the only effective selection model for the typical business environment. The defining attributes of this business environment—such as shortened product life cycles, increasingly sophisticated technologies, growing globalization of markets, shifting customer demands—make for very transitory requirements in specific employee jobs. Organizational success in this environment requires hiring employees who fit the overall organization, not those who fit a fixed set of task demands. Employee personalities must fit the management philosophy and values that help define the organization's uniqueness and its fitness for the future.

We also believe that senior managers must become more "person-oriented" in their own implicit resolution of the person-situation controversy if hiring for person-organization fit is to become a more common approach to selection. Again, generally speaking, managers tend to believe that tightly controlled situations are more effective in shaping employee performance than less-structured situations that allow the expression of individual differences. Managers who believe this are more inclined to spend resources on creating strong situations via job descriptions, close supervision, and so on than on sophisticated selection procedures.

Finally, we offer an important caveat to "person-oriented" managers who are committed to hiring for person-organization fit. They must manage a paradox. They must build strong organizational cultures yet, at the same time, design work situations that are weak enough to allow the unique qualities of individual employees to impact work performance. The key ingredient in balancing this paradox is to create a strong organizational culture with values that empower employees to apply their individual potentials to the conduct of their work. In this way, fragile systems release the employee energy necessary to compete in today's business environment.

Source: *Academy of Management Executive: The Thinking Manager's Source* by Bowen. Copyright © 1991 by the Society for Advancement of Management. Reprinted with permission of the Society for Advancement of Management in the format Textbook via Copyright Clearance Center.

Endnotes

1. See William E. Sheeline, "Avoiding Growth's Perils," *Fortune*, August 13, 1990, 55.

2. "Japan's Gung-Ho U.S. Car Plants," *Fortune*, January 30, 1989, 78–85.

3. For a review of the person-situation controversy, see Larry James and Terrence Mitchell (Eds) of several articles in a special forum, "Situational versus Dispositional Factors: Competing Explanations of Behavior," *Academy of Management Review*, 1989, *14*. In particular, see Jennifer Chatman, "Improving Interactional Organizational Research" in that issue for implications of the controversy for selection and training.

4. See, for example, Terrence Mitchell, "Organizational Behavior" in M. R. Rosenzweig and L. W. Porter (Eds), *Annual Review of Psychology, Vol 30* (Palo Alto, CA: Annual Reviews, 1979); Howard Weiss and Seymour Adler, "Personality and Organizational Behavior," in Barry Staw and Larry Cummings (Eds), *Research in Organizational Behavior, Vol 6* (Greenwich, CT: JAI Press, 1984).

5. See, for example, Chatman, op. cit.; Weiss and Adler, op. cit.

6. A number of research reviews have documented the low validity of the employment interview. For example, see R. D. Arvey and J. E. Campion, "The Employment Interview: A Summary and Review of Recent Research," *Personnel Psychology*, 1982, *35*, 281–322. For an overview of higher validity coefficients reported for appropriately designed, or structured, interviews, see Neal Schmitt and I. Robertson, "Personnel Selection," in M. R. Rosenzweig and L. W. Porter (Eds), *Annual Review of Psychology, Vol 41* (Palo Alto, CA: Annual Reviews Inc., 1990).

7. See, for example, Chatman, op. cit.; Weiss and Adler, op. cit.

8. John P. MacDuffie, "The Japanese Auto Transplants: Challenges to Conventional Wisdom," *ILR Report*, Fall, 1988, *26* (1), 12–18; Huaro Shimada and John Paul MacDuffie, "Industrial Relations and' Humanware,' Japanese Investments in Auto Manufacturing in the United States," Working Paper, Sloan School of Management, MIT, 1987.

9. For an overview of the steps in the classic selection model, see Benjamin Schneider and Neal Schmitt, *Staffing Organizations*, Second Edition (USA: Scott Foresman and Company, 1986). The goal of the traditional selection model is to produce a fit between the critical requirements of a particular job and the job-relevant KSAs of job applicants. This approach consists of three steps. First, a job analysis is conducted to determine the critical requirements of a particular job. Second, on the basis of the job analysis the analyst infers the knowledge, skills, and abilities that are needed for the job. Finally, selection tests are chosen or developed that are intended to indicate the degree to which job applicants possess the KSAs needed on the job. The tests are administered to all applicants. The tests are validated by collecting data on criteria measures, such as job performance, and then examining the correlation between applicant test scores and criteria measures. A statistically significant and reasonably high correlation indicates that the test is capable of discriminating appropriately between employees who do well and those who do poorly on the criteria measures.

10. See John P. Wanous, *Organizational Entry: Recruitment Selection, and Socialization of Newcomers* (Reading, MA: Addison-Wesley Publishing Company, 1980) for a more complete discussion of these two types of fit and how both the organization and individual approach them.

11. For more detail on job analysis techniques, see Schneider and Schmitt, op. cit.

12. Caren Siehl and Joanne Martin, "Measuring Organizational Culture: Mixing Qualitative and Quantitative Methods," in M. O. Jones et al. (Eds), *Inside Organizations* (Beverly Hills: Sage, 1988).

13. Chatman, op. cit.

14. Michael Tushman and David Nadler, "A Diagnostic Model of Organizational Behavior."

15. As examples of this thinking, see Barry M. Staw, Nancy E. Bell, and John A. Clausen, "The Dispositional Approach to Job Attitudes: A Lifetime Longitudinal Test," *Administrative Science Quarterly*, 1986, *31*, 56–77; Weiss and Adler, op. cit.

16. Staw et al., op. cit.

17. "Doug Bray: You've Got to Pick Your Winners," *Training*, February, 1988, 79–81.

18. Richard Pascale, "Fitting New Employees into the Company Culture," *Fortune*, May 28, 1984, 28–42.

19. For an overview of this issue, see Schneider and Schmitt, op. cit.

20. Brian Dumaine, "The New Art of Hiring Smart," *Fortune*, August 17, 1987, 78–81.

21. Wilton Woods, "Personality Tests Are Back," *Fortune*, March 30, 1987, 74–82.

22. For a review of the track record of validation studies of personality tests as selection tools, versus other measures, see R. M. Guion and R. F. Gottier, "Validity of Personality Measures in Personnel Selection," *Personnel Psychology*, 1965, *18*, 49–65; R. M. Guion, "Changing Views for Personnel Selection Research," *Personnel Psychology*, 1987, *40*, 199–213; Schmitt and Robertson, op. cit.; N. Schmitt, R. Gooding, R. Noe, and M. Kirsch, "Meta-Analysis of Validity Studies Published Between 1964 and 1982 and the Investigation of Study Characteristics," *Personnel Psychology*, 1984, *37*, 407–422.

23. Schneider and Schmitt, op. cit., 353.

24. See Wanous, op. cit.

25. "Japan's Gung-Ho U.S. Car Plants," op. cit.

26. Richard E. Walton, "From Control to Commitment in the Workplace," *Harvard Business Review*, March–April 1985, 76–84.

27. Edward E. Lawler III, *High-Involvement Management* (San Francisco: Jossey-Bass, 1986); S. Mohrman, G. Ledford, Jr., E. E. Lawler III, and A. M. Mohrman, "Quality of Work-Life and Employment Involvement," in C. L. Cooper and I. Robertson (Eds), *International Review of Industrial and Organizational Psychology* (New York: John Wiley & Sons, 1986).

28. The case description is an illustrative overview of the steps and some techniques associated with hiring for the organization, not the job. Readers may contact the authors if they are interested in more details about the hiring process, such as assessment methods, validation strategies, scoring of simulation, and so on.

29. D. N. Jackson, *Personality Research Form Manual*, 3rd ed., (Port Huron, MI: Research Psychologists Press, 1984). For a review of the PRF, see J. S. Wiggins, *Personality and Prediction: Principles of Personality and Assessment* (Reading, MA: Addison-Wesley, 1973).

30. The significant correlation between scores in the composite growth needs scale and performance in the pre-employment training program was a 0.22 (and it was 0.27 after correction for unreliability in the criterion). This compares favorably to the average validity of 0.15 found in a recent review of research using personality measures (N. Schmitt, R. Z. Gooding, R. A. Noe, and M. Kirsch, "Meta-Analysis of Validity Studies Published between 1964 and 1982 and the investigation of study characteristics," *Personnel Psychology*, 1984, *37*, 407–422). In addition, scores on the social needs measure were significantly correlated (.16) with anticipated satisfaction.

31. See Wanous, op. cit., for a discussion of this proposition.

32. For a review of the research findings, see S. C. Premack and J. P. Wanous, "A Meta-Analysis of Realistic Job Preview Experiments," *Journal of Applied Psychology*, 1985, *70*, 706–719.

33. R. A. Guzzo, R. D. Jette, and R. A. Katzell, "The Effects of Psychologically Based Intervention Programs on Worker Productivity: A Meta-Analysis," *Personnel Psychology*, 1985, *38*, 275–291; G. E. Ledford, Jr., T. G. Cummings, and R. W. Wright, "The Structure and Effectiveness of High Involvement Organiza-

tions," Working Paper, Center for Effective Organizations, University of Southern California, 1991.

34. Premack and Wanous, op. cit.

35. See Chatman, op. cit.

36. Ledford et al.

37. William J. Hampton, "How Does Japan Inc. Pick Its American Workers?" *Business Week*, October 3, 1988, 84–88.

38. For a discussion of these issues, see J. L. Holland, "Some Speculation About the Investigation of Person-Environment Transactions," *Journal of Vocational Behavior*, 1987, *31*, 337–340; R. H. Moos, "Person-Environment Congruence in Work, School and Health-Care Settings," *Journal of Vocational Behavior*, 1987, *31*, 231–247; and J. B. Rounds, R. V. Dawis, and L. H. Lofquist, "Measurement of Person-Environment Fit and Prediction of Satisfaction in the Theory of Work Adjustment," *Journal of Vocational Behavior*, 1987, *31*, 297–318.

39. E. E. Lawler III, "Achieving Competitiveness by Creating New Organizational Cultures and Structures," in D. B. Fishman and C. Cherniss (Eds), *The Human Side of Corporate Competitiveness* (Newbury Park: Sage Publications), 69–101.

40. *Assessment Strategies for Selection* (Pittsburgh, PA: Development Dimensions International, 1990).

41. D. R. Denison, *Corporate Culture and Organizational Effectiveness* (New York: Wiley, 1990)

Causes and Consequences of Declining Early Departures from Foreign Assignments

Gary S. Insch and John D. Daniels, *Business Horizons*

Although expatriate managers are expensive compared to their local and domestic counterparts, US companies employ more than a quarter of a million executives abroad. The reasons are varied: to use their specific competencies; to transfer technologies to other locations; to train transferees by broadening and deepening their understanding of global operations; to employ them as instruments of corporate control. A Windham study (1999) indicated that two-thirds of companies expect their expatriate employment to grow in the future.

Many researchers maintain that a high proportion of expatriates depart their foreign assignments prematurely, with estimates ranging anywhere from 10 to 50 percent. Nevertheless, a few have questioned whether premature departures are this extensive. Daniels and Insch (1998) theorized how evolving conditions should be lowering premature departure rates; however, international human resource scholars still disagree about the relative importance of factors influencing premature departure and how these factors are evolving.

Even if premature departure rates are lower than is customarily estimated, there is a near consensus that costs are still high. Benesh (2000) estimates the price tag for each early departure to be upwards of $1 million. Companies incur measurable expenses (even for well-performing expats) that include time and effort to find replacements, additional international relocation expenses if successors are other expats, and decreased productivity until replacements are contracted, trained, and fully effective in their new jobs.

Companies also incur significant costs that are difficult to estimate, such as when foreign subsidiary personnel discredit headquarters' ability to appoint well-performing expats who complete their assignments. Such mistrust may hinder a subsidiary's acceptance of future expats and its commitment to implement HQ directives. When managers depart foreign assignments early because of poor performance, the discredit may be even greater. Moreover, there are the costs of earning inadequate returns from corporate investments in these managers. First, the managers may join other companies (particularly competitors), taking with them the human capital investment that their present employers have contributed. Second, they may be demotivated by their overseas experience and perform inadequately in new assignments. Third, their superiors may see them as poor performers and give them assignments that do not challenge their abilities. Finally, other managers may be hesitant to accept expatriate posts if they have observed their colleagues' early returns and subsequent career problems.

Given the disagreement about the extent and causes of premature departure rates and the agreement that costs are high regardless, there is clearly a need to explore this area further. So we set out to study companies appearing on 1998 S&P, *Fortune*, and Dun & Bradstreet lists as having international operations. We gathered data primarily from four-page questionnaires sent out to the heads of human resources and international operations in 74 large US corporations with expatriate employees. The 74 participating companies number almost 3.6 million employees (48,000 average per company) and roughly 12,500 expatriates (170 average per company). The questionnaire included semantic differentiation statements and short answer questions. Our purposes were to estimate current premature departure rates for expats in US companies, discuss what constitutes high versus low rates, rank the reasons for early departures, determine the dynamics of factors affecting them, and suggest evolving HR issues and practices as changes occur in these rates.

Extent of Premature Departure

Foreign assignments are almost always for a multi-year duration, and their length may be open-ended or of a fixed term. In fact, there are examples of foreign assignments having exceeded 20 years. Thus, a premature departure of an open-ended foreign assignment after many years in the location may have very different implications than one that occurs shortly after arrival for a fixed-term assignment. However, other studies and estimates have not made this distinction; they have simply estimated premature departures over the length of the assignments. Thus, an annualized early departure rate is more descriptive of the situation.

In light of the lack of annualized turnover estimates, we asked each company how many expats it currently employs and how many had left their foreign assignments early during the previous year. This allowed us to closely approximate a recent annual premature departure rate of 3.2 percent. Of the 71 companies that answered this question, 39 reported that no expat had returned early during the previous year, whereas another 19 reported premature departure rates of 5 percent or less (cumulative sample total 81 percent). Six companies rated between 5 and 10 percent, five between 10 and 20 percent, and two at 20 percent or higher.

Our findings seem consistent with a Windham (1994) survey that estimated an 8 percent early departure rate, mainly US multinational enterprises, during the duration of an assignment. Although that survey did not consider the length of expected assignments, an average assignment of slightly less than three years—a seemingly reasonable average length—would equate with our finding of 3.2 percent per year. Very few writers in the international human resource area estimate rates this low.

ARE PREMATURE DEPARTURE RATES TOO HIGH?

Even though our findings show low rates of premature departures in comparison with almost all other estimates, we must subjectively decide whether

3.2 percent per year is high. One point of reference could be what happens domestically. Unfortunately, we do not have comparable domestic data, but we do have some estimates of annual executive turnovers. For instance, a 1997 *Toronto Star* survey of 1,343 HR professionals found that an annual executive turnover rate of around 10 percent is normal. But a turnover rate does not capture premature departures from posts that entail reassignments within the same company; nor do all premature departures from foreign assignments result in turnovers because many early returnees take new posts within their companies. Thus, we must conclude that our 3.2 percent is very low compared to domestic rates.

Nevertheless, regardless of whether the rate for foreign assignments is higher or lower than for domestic assignments, a key issue is whether companies perceive that early expatriate departure is a problem for them. We asked respondents to rate the statement. "The noncompletion of expatriate assignments is a major problem" on a five-point scale. Table 1 shows the results and indicates that a majority of respondents did not consider it to be a major problem for them. In fact, fewer than 3 percent strongly agreed it was. Surprisingly, none of the 13 respondents who gave a score of four or five to the statement had a premature departure rate above 8 percent.

Reasons for Premature Departure

Up to this point, researchers have focused mainly on poor job performance and poor adjustment by both expat and family as reasons for leaving foreign assignments early. In turn, they have tied poor performance to poor adjustment. The director of

TABLE 1: ACCEPTANCE AND COMPLETION OF EXPATRIATE ASSIGNMENTS

	No. of firms	Strongly disagree	Disagree	Don't know	Agree	Strongly agree
The non-acceptance of expatriate assignments is a major problem.[a]	73	31.5	30.1	28.8	8.2	1.4
The non-completion of expatriate assignments is a major problem.[b]	71	40.8	26.8	14.1	15.5	2.8

[a] χ^2 29, 123, p = .000   [b] χ^2 29, 493, p = .000

development for Danone articulated the belief in this connection when she said, "Failures in foreign postings are always tied to a problem of cultural adaptation" (Woodruff 2000). Moreover, some researchers have tied expatriates' satisfaction with their assignments to their perceptions of what the assignments will do to their careers and to whether they view their compensation packages as sufficient.

Although fewer than half of our companies had experienced any premature departures during the previous year, those that did indicated why, as shown in Table 2. The number one answer for almost half the respondents was poor job performance. Interestingly, the second most common was that the expats had received better offers from other companies. Apparently, expats were leaving either because they were doing too bad a job or too good a job. Adjustment issues continue to contribute to early departure but at a lower rate than historically reported. Although corporate staff cited "Not performing job effectively" as the most frequent reason for early departure, their citations may reflect what they are able to discern most easily. In other words, some other items in Table 2 may be less discernible, although they may underlie and cause poor performance.

Contrary to earlier findings, none of our respondents cited inadequate compensation as a cause for early departure. Similarly, fewer than 8 percent of respondents mentioned children's education issues, spousal career concerns, and fears that the foreign assignment would slow career advancement. Only about 10 percent of the companies indicated that health/safety concerns or deprived living standards were contributors.

Dynamics Reducing Premature Departures

Although previous researchers have used slightly different terminologies, they have consistently classified adjustment factors affecting early departure from foreign assignments into similar categories: individual and family, work/organizational, and environmental. We used these same categories to test our theory that changing conditions are keeping more expats in their assignments longer.

INDIVIDUAL AND FAMILY FACTORS
The most frequently cited cause for early departure has remained fairly constant and includes individual and family issues and adjustment problems. Here we will examine three individual factors: homesickness, the ability to turn down unwanted foreign assignments, and the size of the pool of qualified managers who want such assignments.

Homesickness. The inability to adjust to a foreign culture may well boil down to "homesickness" or the longing for the familiar, contact with support systems, and news from the home country. "Familiar" things include the availability of their accustomed purchases of products and services.

TABLE 2: REASONS FOR EXPATRIATE EARLY DEPARTURE

Reason	Percent in agreement
Not performing job effectively	48.4
Received other, more rewarding offers from other companies	43.7
Expatriate or family not adjusting to culture	36.6
Expatriate or family missing contact with family and friends at home	31.0
Received other, more rewarding offers from our company	17.2
Unable to adjust to deprived living standards in country of assignment	10.3
Concerned with problems of safety and/or health care in foreign location	10.3
Believed children's education was suffering	7.1
Feared that assignment would slow career advancement	7.1
Spouse wanted career	6.1
Compensation package was inadequate	0.0

Globalization—the deepening relationships and broadening interdependence among people from different countries—has improved the ability of expats to obtain familiar home country products and services almost anywhere in the world. Advances in and decreased costs of international communications and transportation (compared to incomes) enable expats to keep in closer contact with support systems in their home countries. For example, Windham (1999) reports that 86 percent of expat families used e-mail in 1998, and the number of firms providing allowances for personal long-distance phone calls, e-mail, and home faxes has also grown. Moreover, expat managers now have better links with their home bases and colleagues through online corporate newsletters and shared corporate databases. They can more easily gain access to newspapers and view satellite newscasts in their own language, especially if that language happens to be English. Hence, with expats and their families being able to stay in touch more and more with family, friends, and developments at home, their general feelings of alienation and loneliness should be greatly lessened. So we expected that the reduction in premature departure rates would be due in part to the reduction in expatriate, spousal, and family homesickness. Table 3 shows that respondents overwhelmingly agreed with our expectation both in terms of the increased availability of familiar goods and services and the improved ability to keep in close contact with people back home.

Refusal of foreign assignments. Employees' refusals to accept either a domestic or foreign transfer have become more commonplace, largely because of the higher instances of dual careers. A Pricewaterhouse-Coopers survey of 270 companies (Flynn 2000) found that 80 percent had experienced turndowns due to spouses' careers. With more dual-career families refusing transfers, those that are accepting foreign assignments may have spouses who are either focused on home and family maintenance or more willing to suspend their own career opportunities in order to support the expat. This may reduce tension in the home and lead to an easier adjustment to the foreign assignment because what the spouse cares about most is being with family. Consequently, we expected the lower early departure rates to be due in part to the rise in dual-career families, which is simultaneously raising the number of job turndowns while also increasing the portion of "stay at home" or "willing to forgo career" spouses accompanying managers in their foreign assignments.

Table 4 supports our expectations and reasoning. Over the past decade, more employees have been turning down foreign assignments because of spouses' careers. The table also includes information on employees who accepted foreign assignments. Slightly fewer than half of the respondents indicated that expats' spouses had to forgo careers because of the assignments, whereas only about 9 percent agreed that premature departures occurred because of spouses wanting careers. Thus, we conclude that in the face of spousal career conflicts, managers are prone to turn down foreign assignments rather than get into situations where the conflicts will mean they have to leave early.

TABLE 3: H1: LESS HOMESICKNESS

	No. of firms	Strongly disagree	Disagree	Don't know	Agree	Strongly agree
Over the past decade, the availability of goods and services similar to those in the home country has improved.[a]	71	0.0	2.8	33.8	54.9	8.5
Over the past decade, the ability of expatriates and their families to keep in close contact with people in their home country has improved.[b]	72	0.0	1.4	25.0	50.0	23.6

[a]χ79.493, p = .000   [b]χ60.639, p = .000

TABLE 4: H2: FEWER SPOUSAL CAREER CONFLICTS

	No. of firms	Strongly disagree	Disagree	Don't know	Agree	Strongly agree
Over the past decade, fewer employees have been turning down foreign assignments due to spouses' careers.[a]	69	24.6	43.5	20.3	8.7	2.9
Expatriate turndown was due to spousal career (other than compensation).[b]	47	12.8	2.1	21.3	51.1	12.8
Premature departure was because spouses wanted career.[c]	34	47.1	23.5	20.6	8.8	0.0
Expatriates' spouses generally have careers that they forgo when going on foreign assignment.[d]	72	1.4	15.3	33.3	36.1	13.9

[a] χ 94.261, p = .000   [c] χ 21.588, p = .000
[b] χ 32.681, p = .000   [d] χ 30.361, p = .000

Pool of candidates for expat positions. Although nonacceptance of transfers may be on the rise because of dual careers, more of the remainder of managers may be eager to work abroad. There are two reasons for this. First, more companies are publicizing future career enhancement advantages from foreign assignments. As GE's former chairman said, "The Jack Welch of the future cannot look like me; I spent my entire career in the United States" (Melymuka 2001). Tung's 1996 study supports the link between a growing perception of enhanced upward mobility from foreign postings and the improved pool of candidates for those postings. In addition, globalization issues are being included more and more in senior management evaluations.

Second, Carpenter, Sanders, and Gregersen (2001) have found evidence that CEOs with international assignment experience have recently been able to negotiate higher compensation for themselves. This contrasts sharply with earlier perceptions of foreign assignments. In the early 1980s, according to *Sales & Marketing Management* ("Executives . . ." 1982), 41 of 100 executives surveyed following their return to the United States said they would avoid another foreign assignment because they felt forgotten and less well compensated upon their return than those who did not take such assignments.

Indeed, according to Table 5, almost two-thirds of the respondents agreed with the statement that over the past decade more employees have come to believe more strongly that foreign assignments will help their careers. Almost 90 percent also agreed that a foreign assignment should help an expat's career. More than half disagreed that turndowns were caused by concerns about career advancement. Finally, two-thirds disagreed that premature departures from a foreign assignment were related to fears that the assignment would slow their career advancement.

WORK/ORGANIZATIONAL FACTORS

An upward trend in the number of expatriate managers led Hunt (1996) to conclude that the availability of international opportunities is also on the rise. This means employees may no longer need to jump at the first foreign assignment offered but may instead be able to pick and choose. Thus, the greater availability of international job opportunities may allow managers and their families to more easily choose where they want to go and where they expect to feel comfortable.

Moreover, although there is limited information on the historical locations for foreign assignments, anecdotal evidence indicates that major shifts have occurred since the 1970s. The big infrastructure projects that necessitated the deployment of thousands of expat managers and technical personnel and their families to remote areas in oil-producing developing countries are less prevalent. These were often in areas climatically harsh and

TABLE 5 : H3: OVERSEAS ASSIGNMENT ENHANCES CAREER

	No. of firms	Strongly disagree	Disagree	Don't know	Agree	Strongly agree
Over the past decade, more employees have come to believe more strongly that foreign assignments will help their careers.[a]	72	0.0	6.9	30.6	47.2	15.3
The expat's career with our company should be enhanced by taking this assignment.[b]	73	1.4	1.4	9.6	52.1	35.6
Assignment turndown is due to the fear that the assignment would slow career advancement.[c]	46	30.4	23.9	26.1	17.4	2.2
Premature departure is due to the fear that the assignment would slow career advancement.[d]	33	45.5	21.2	27.3	6.1	0.0

[a] χ52.028, p = .000   [c] χ11.174, p = .025
[b] χ75.699, p = .000   [d] χ21.394, p = .000

culturally difficult for Westerners, who have comprised the bulk of expat managers and technical personnel. Recent years have seen evidence of a shift toward greater needs for expatriates in more economically advanced countries, where adjustment may be easier. Indeed, Windham (1999) reported that the four most common international locations for expats are the UK, the US, Hong Kong, and Japan. Thus, we expected the lower early departure rates to be due in part to greater international employment opportunities, which in turn has resulted in expats and their families having a greater opportunity to go to potentially compatible locations.

Table 6 on the next page shows the responses to two statements included in our survey. Contrary to our expectations, respondents overwhelmingly rejected the notion that expats have considerable discretion in foreign assignment location. Nor did they accept that foreign assignments had shifted to more locations with fewer hardships. Thus, our results do not support the hypothesis that decreases in premature departures are influenced by the ability of managers to work in more compatible foreign locations than in the past.

ENVIRONMENTAL FACTORS

Environmental factors—mainly, standard of living and cost of living—significantly affect job and location turnover. We examined three such factors

here: comparative living standards, availability of education for children, and existence of acceptable health services and safety.

Comparative living standards. Historically, to ensure the maintenance of an acceptable standard of living, expatriate compensation packages have generally been much larger than those for comparable home- or host-country nationals. Latta (1999), however, reports that such packages are becoming less extravagant, especially in terms of foreign service and hardship premiums, because the differences in living standards have generally narrowed among many countries, particularly between those countries from which the majority of expat managers emanate and those where they are assigned. The overall reduction in benefits is occurring even though multinationals need more expatriate managers and must offer new benefits such as job assistance for spouses. Table 7 shows that respondents were mixed in agreeing with this reasoning. However, most respondents did not believe that turndowns or early departures were related to concerns about living conditions. Thus, comparative living standards seem to be at best a weak explanation for fewer premature departures.

Available education for children. Solomon's (1996) Shell Oil survey showed that potential expatriate managers' concerns about the quality of their

TABLE 6: H4: GREATER CHANCE TO GO TO COMPATIBLE LOCATIONS

	No. of firms	Strongly disagree	Disagree	Don't know	Agree	Strongly agree
Employees have considerable discretion as to the location of the assignment (e.g., choosing between Country A vs. Country B).[a]	73	43.8	39.7	13.7	2.7	0.0
Over the past decade, foreign assignments have shifted more to locations with fewer hardships for expatriates.[b]	71	15.5	25.4	28.2	31.0	0.0

[a] χ 61.863, p = .000   [b] χ 22.592, p = .000

children's education, including separation from family while attending boarding schools, was the second main impediment to their international mobility. Although companies have traditionally provided education allowances, these have not always prevented the children from being separated from their parents. However, private schools catering to expatriates have proliferated. And improvements in international transportation and communications have lessened the hardship of having parents in one country and children in another. Thus, we expected that lower early departure rates were due in part to fewer family concerns about education. Overall, Table 8 shows support for these expectations, though not as much as we had predicted. Respondents strongly agreed that the educational needs of expat children have improved and that these concerns are not a cause for leaving an assignment prematurely. However, opinions about the turndown situation regarding children's education were not so clear-cut.

Acceptable health services and levels of safety. Birdseye and Hill (1995) found that the quality of host country medical facilities was an important factor in premature departure. Nevertheless, we believed that improvements in the quality and availability of medical facilities and care along with the emergence of international medical services and medical evacuation companies to handle expats' needs have lessened the importance of that factor. Table 9 supports our belief.

TABLE 7: H5: LESS TURNOVER DUE TO NARROWING DIFFERENCES IN STANDARDS OF LIVING

	No. of firms	Strongly disagree	Disagree	Don't know	Agree	Strongly agree
Over the past decade, the difference between the standard of living for US expatriates and that for managers in the United States at a comparable level has been narrowing.[a]	72	2.8	9.7	45.8	38.9	2.8
Assignment turndown is due to concern about deprivation of current living standards in country of assignment.[b]	46	19.6	37.0	21.7	17.4	4.3
Premature departure is due to the inability to adjust to deprived living standards in the country of assignment.[c]	34	38.2	20.6	26.5	11.8	2.9

[a] χ 62.028, p = .000   [b] χ 12.478, p = .014   [c] χ 12.471, p = .014

TABLE 8: H6: FEWER FAMILY CONCERNS ABOUT CHILDREN'S EDUCATION

	No. of firms	Strongly disagree	Disagree	Don't know	Agree	Strongly agree
Over the past decade, the ability to deal with children's educational needs has improved.[a]	69	1.4	10.1	36.2	47.8	4.3
Assignment turndown is due to concern over children's education.[b]	47	17.0	21.3	25.5	31.9	4.3
Premature departure is due to concern over children's education.[c]	33	48.5	18.2	18.2	15.2	0.0

[a] χ^2 59.478, p = .000   [b] χ^2 10.128, p = .038   [c] χ^2 20.485, p = .000

Evolving HR Issues

Factors affecting the premature departure of expatriate managers fall into two categories: those that companies can control (predeparture training about host country's environment, upward mobility for returning expats) and those they cannot (spouses' desires for careers, quality of infrastructure and social services). Overall, controllable and uncontrollable factors are becoming more favorable to the completion of foreign assignments. However, some are two-edged swords. On one hand, they help solve early departure problems; on the other hand, they contribute to different international human resource problems.

One of the trends is the increased ability of managers to turn down foreign assignments. If companies exclude managers who do not want foreign assignments from their candidate pools, they are left with managers who may be more dedicated and more likely to avoid many of the pitfalls of family adjustment abroad. This possibility harbingers fewer early departures and improved performance. But will companies be left with a large enough pool of qualified managers for foreign assignments? So far, they have been. Our respondents indicated that turndowns are not a major problem for them. Only 10 percent or so of the respondents agreed with the statement that "The non-acceptance of expatriate assignments is a major problem," whereas about 62 percent disagreed. Apparently, the smaller expatriate manager pools because of turndowns has been more than offset by the higher number of managers who want foreign assignments to enhance their careers.

TABLE 9: H7: LESS TURNOVER DUE TO IMPROVED HEALTH CARE ACCESS

	No. of firms	Strongly disagree	Disagree	Don't know	Agree	Strongly agree
Over the past decade, the risk of inadequate health care for expatriates has increased in so-called hardship areas. (R)[a]	69	5.8	24.6	46.4	21.7	1.4
Assignment turndown is due to concern about safety and/or health care in foreign location.[b]	47	21.3	25.5	31.9	19.1	2.1
Premature departure is due to problems of safety and/or health care in foreign location.[c]	34	38.2	20.6	26.5	11.8	2.9

[a] χ^2 43.681, p = .000   [b] χ^2 11.617, p = .000   [c] χ^2 9.235, p = .055

There are some worrisome signs, however, that the pools may shrink too far. Turndowns are caused largely by the trend toward more dual-career families, a trend that does not seem to be abating, while companies are needing more expats than ever before. Companies are already responding by including job assistance for spouses or added packages to entice dual-career families to accept foreign assignments. They may have to move further with spousal assistance, perhaps by shifting expat compensation packages away from hardship and standard of living allowances. If the candidate pools shrink too far, companies may encounter two types of problems, which would require adjustments in their international HR practices. First, it may be harder to infuse managerial and technical skills into their foreign operations. Second, it may be harder to give managers the international experience necessary to develop the global mindset that makes them more effective as they move into higher-level positions, and that enables the firm to develop synergies among diverse operating locations. Let's examine these points.

Anecdotal evidence holds that many companies are beginning to respond to turndowns by transferring managers abroad without their families and for shorter periods of time, perhaps less than a year. Others are not transferring them per se, but are sending them on consecutive business trips without their families for a duration of several years while bringing them back home as often as every weekend. Such business trips may offer more managers the opportunity to visit their companies' foreign facilities, customers, suppliers, and partners. This is a logical outcome of increased production rationalization, network organizations, and transnational strategies. However, these alternatives are often more expensive than traditional transfers. In the long run, working without family support and enduring frequent long flights through multiple time zones may be more stressful than regular foreign assignments, especially with heightened anxiety about hijacking and added travel time as airlines and airports deal with security. Moreover, there is a dearth of information about managers' turnover from foreign projects (as opposed to turnover from the company) as they find they cannot cope with the stress of travel and work on a multicultural team.

At the other extreme, there is also anecdotal evidence of longer, rather than shorter, stints abroad. For example, because many managers and their families thrive on foreign assignments, companies are moving some of them from one to another. However, this approach seems to revert back to earlier periods when many companies employed managers—many of whom were children of diplomats and expats—whose entire career might be abroad. Most firms abandoned this approach because their managers lost contact with headquarters' viewpoints and new home-country technologies.

Another approach for dealing with shrinking management pools for foreign assignments is to better tap underused groups. One possibility is to use more women, who, says Maitland (2000), account for 49 percent of middle managers in the United States but only 13 percent of US managers sent abroad. A further option is to use first- or second-generation immigrants, such as those from the growing Asian and Latin American populations in the United States. However, this does not solve the dual-career problem, unless the transferees happen to be single. Still another option is to use more third-country nationals who have limited opportunities in their own countries. For example, Tenorio (2001) reports that Nestlé assigned only 15 expats to the Philippines while using 45 Filipinos as third-country nationals. However, nationals from emerging economies more likely lack the headquarters experience necessary either for infusing the latest technology abroad or for serving as effective control instruments for global operations. Moreover, tapping underused groups begs the question of how to get more international exposure for domestically focused managers at headquarters.

Although most executives now perceive that foreign assignments will help their careers, only time will tell whether those perceptions are correct. If not, then the pool of candidates for expat positions will likely suffer. In this respect, we found an interesting anomaly in our study. Our respondents indicated that the second most cited cause of early departure from a foreign assignment was a better offer from another company. On one hand, this highlights the potential career value of an overseas assignment. On the other hand, it means that companies stand to lose the investment they have made in these managers.

The loss of managers with international experience to other companies is an area that warrants further research, particularly in light of recent reports that a high proportion of managers leave their firms within a short time after being repatriated. Why? One possibility is that many foreign assignments are not really career enhancing; rather, companies simply send people abroad to solve skill shortages with no expectation that they will gain new skills abroad to make them more upwardly mobile when they return. A manager should know this in advance because disgruntled repatriates have historically been an impediment to finding future expats. Another possibility is that companies are simply underusing the skills of returning expats as a source of country and cultural knowledge. Still another possibility is that some people so like foreign assignments (and the perks that go with them) that they take new foreign positions with other companies rather than transfer to domestic operations. Finally, people might be leaving to join some of the fast-growing start-up companies, sometimes called "born global" firms, which begin with a global orientation and provide opportunities for former expats to use the skills they have gained abroad.

A final factor apparently reducing the incidence of early expat departures is the improved standard of living in many countries. This may not only alleviate initial culture shock and adjustment, but may also lead to lower expat costs in the future. In fact, if premature departures are declining because of conditions external to companies, then perhaps companies can cut costs by trimming down or eliminating certain expensive personnel practices designed to entice managers to accept and complete foreign assignments. These include expensive selection processes, predeparture training, and complex compensation packages. However, companies need to ascertain how these expensive practices interplay with the changing environment.

The research reported here confirms that premature departure rates among expatriates are low, in part because of the international environment. Improved global telecommunications and transportation help ease family homesickness. There is greater availability of educational opportunities for children and improved medical care. And economic improvements make fewer places hardships. However, this study focused primarily on the environmental changes influencing early departure. It does not discount the potential impact of improved corporate policies (selection, training) that may also

have contributed to the decline in early departures. Nevertheless, although the fact of such a decline is not particularly surprising, the findings may be valuable for firms expanding abroad because improved environmental conditions indicate greater odds of expatriate success.

Rather than explaining why premature departure from foreign assignments takes place, our study emphasizes why it does not. Hence, an interesting extension of this research is the examination of why people take and complete foreign assignments. Moreover, continued research on factors that companies can control, such as repatriation planning and pre-departure training, should also be fruitful because performance from these programs has not been adequately addressed. If these factors are indeed responsible for lowering premature departures, then programs addressing these issues should continue to be developed and promoted to the extent that they are cost-efficient. To complete this picture, the effectiveness of company programs and actions are the next logical step for evaluation.

For example, there is probably a need to refocus research away from premature departure, which is often considered a surrogate for success, and focus instead on performance. A 1997 Employee Relocation Council study based on 162 companies with nearly 26,000 expatriates reported that 10 percent of foreign assignments were unsuccessful. But what are "unsuccessful assignments" and "expatriate failure"? The 1994 Windham study defines them as "failing to meet the assignment's objectives." We need to know more about companies' criteria for "unsuccessful" and "failure." Perhaps the problem lies as much with headquarters' failure to define objectives clearly or to expect results too soon.

Expatriate performance measurement has always been a difficult task because many prematurely returning managers know they are not generally meeting the corporate objectives and leave before more formal review processes are completed. Others may not be successfully achieving their goals, but they stay and endure the assignments to their own and their companies' detriments. Such managers may be creating far greater costs for their employers than the managers who are relocated and replaced. Companies need firsthand information from line managers on expatriate performance, and HR managers may require a more comprehensive evaluation system to track how many and how well expats are meeting their assigned objectives. Both theory and practice would benefit from exploring expatriate failure.

We do not mean to imply here that premature departure is no longer a problem or that companies should no longer strive to keep such departures in check. Despite the environmental changes that are easing homesickness, spouse and family adjustment continue to be challenges. For such families, alternative assignment structures may be helpful. Some families may be more comfortable in less "foreign" or more economically advanced countries, such as allowing a family to live in Singapore or Hong Kong while the expat "commutes" to Cambodia or relatively isolated areas in mainland China.

As early departure rates fall among managers abroad, discovering the reasons for the decline has widespread implications for the management of expats, including the expansion or reduction of compensation packages, predeparture training, and repatriation planning. It also has implications for other international HR practices because conditions that improve early departure rates may simultaneously worsen other HR areas. Thus, examining external factors influencing these rates may help companies predict and plan their international HR practices.

Source: Reprinted with permission from *Business Horizons*, November 2002, pp. 39–48. Copyright © 2002 by the Trustees at Indiana University, Kelley School of Business.

References and Selected Bibliography

Benesh, Peter, 2000. As more Americans work abroad, risks, rewards for both sides rise. *Investor's Business Daily*, 10.

Birdseye, Meg G., and John S. Hill. 1995. Individual, organization/work and environmental influences on expatriate turnover tendencies: An empirical study *Journal of International Business Studies* 26/4: 787–813.

Black, J. Stewart, 1988. Work role transitions: A study of American expatriate managers in Japan. *Journal of International Business Studies* 19/2: 277–294.

Black, J. Stewart, and Hal B. Gregersen, 1999. The right way to manage expats. *Harvard Business Review* 77/2 (March–April): 52–62.

———. 1991(a). When Yankee comes home: Factors related to expatriate and spouse repatriation adjustment. *Journal of International Business Studies* 22/4: 671–694.

———. 1991(b). The other half of the picture. Antecedents of spouse cross-cultural adjustment. *Journal of International Business Studies* 22/3: 461–477.

Caligiuri, Paula M. 1997. Assessing expatriate success: Beyond just being there. In *New approaches to employee management*, ed. D.M. Saunders, 117–140. Greenwich, CT: JAI Press.

Carpenter, Mason A., W. Gerald Sanders, and Hal B. Gregersen, 2001. Bundling human capital with organizational context: The impact of international assignment experience on multinational firm performance and CEO pay. *Academy of Management Journal* 44/3: 493–511.

Daniels, John D., and Gary S. Insch. 1998. Why are early departure rates from foreign assignments lower than historically reported? *Multinational Business Review* 6/1 (Spring): 13–23.

Employee Relocation Council, 1997. Results from ERC's International Survey, *Monitor* 2/1: 1–5.

Executives are less than thrilled about overseas assignments. 1982. *Sales & Marketing Management* (17 May): 85.

Expatriate job satisfaction said to hinge on benefits, 1996. *National Underwriter* (11 March): 13.

Flynn, J. 2000. Multinationals help expatriate couples deal with the strain of living abroad. *Wall Street Journal* (8 August): A19.

Forster, N. 1997. The persistent myth of high expatriate failure rates: A reappraisal. *International Journal of Human Resource Management* 8: 414–433.

Frankenstein, John, 1985. The quality of life: Americans in Beijing complain, but admit conditions are improving. *China Business Review* 12/6: 22–26.

Gupta, Anil K., and Vijay Govindarajan. 2002. Cultivating a global mindset. *Academy of Management Executive* 16/1: 116–126.

Guzzo, Richard A. 1996. The expatriate employee. In *Trends in organizational behavior*, ed. D.M. Rousseau, 123–127. Chichester, UK: Wiley.

Harveston, Paula D., Ben L. Kedia, and Peter S. Davis. 2000. Internationalization of born global and gradual globalizing firms: The impact of the manager. *Advances in Competitiveness Research* 8/1: 92–97.

Harvey, Michael G. 1997. Dual-career expatriates: Expectations, adjustment and satisfaction with international relocation. *Journal of International Business Studies* 28/3: 637–658.

Harzing, Anne-Wil K. 1995. The persistent myth of high expatriate failure rates. *International Journal of Human Resource Management* 6 (May): 457–475.

Hunt, Neil A. 1996. Employees overseas: SOS. *Risk Management* (October): 45.

Kraimer, Maria L. Sandy J. Wayne, and Renata A. Jaworski. 2001. Sources of support and expatriate performance. *Personnel Psychology* 54/1 (Spring): 71–99.

Latta, Geoffrey W. 1999. Expatriate policy and practice: A ten-year comparison of trends. *Global Compensation* 3/4: 35–39.

Lublin, J.S. 2001. Managers and managing: Benefits from overseas jobs. *Wall Street Journal* (6 July): 24.

MacErlean, Neasa. 2001. Work: How to cope with a short assignment. *The Observer* 1: 16.

Maitland, Alison. 2000. America's gender gap travels abroad. *Financial Times* (20 October): 16.

McEvoy, Glenn M., and Barbara Parker. 1995. Expatriate adjustment: Causes and consequences. In *Expatriate management: New ideas for international business*, ed. J. Selmer, 97–114. Westport. CT: Quorum Books.

Melymuka, Kathleen, 2001. Global woman. *Computerworld* 35/32: 34–35.

Misa, Kenneth F., and Joseph M. Fabricatore. 1979. Return on investment of overseas personnel. *Financial Executive* 47/4: 42–46.

Naumann, Earl. 1993. Organizational predictors of expatriate job satisfaction. *Journal of International Business Studies* 24/1: 61–80.

Osland, Joyce S. 1995. *The adventure of working abroad.* San Francisco: Jossey-Bass.

Richter, David. 1996. On and off the beaten path. *China Business Review* 23/4: 26–31.

Solomon, Charlene M. 1995. Global compensation: Learn the ABCs. *Personnel Journal* 74/7: 70–76.

———. 1996. Expats say: Help make us mobile. *Personnel Journal* 75/7: 47–52.

Tenorio, Arnold S. 2001. Executives still hopeful on RP. *Businessworld* (17 August): 1.

Timberlake, Cotten. 2001. Experts advise on the pitfalls of jobs abroad. *Wall Street Journal* (25 June): np.

Tung, Rosalie L. 1987. Expatriate assignments: Enhancing success and minimizing failure. *Academy of Management Executive* 1/2: 117–26.

———. 1996. Acculturation of expatriates. Paper presented at the annual meeting of the Academy of Management, Cincinnati.

Turnover trend rising for managers. 1997. *Toronto Star,* Business section: D2.

Voigt, Keith. 2001. Timing the time abroad: Overseas work assignments are getting shorter. *Wall Street Journal* (2 March): W3.

Windham International and National Foreign Trade Council. 1994. Global relocation trends 1994 survey report. Windham International: 1–30.

Windham International, IIHR, and National Foreign Trade Council. 1999. 1998 Global relocation trends survey report. Windham International.

Woodruff, D. 2000. Conjuring up a crisis—firms put candidates through a battery of tests before shipping them overseas. *Asian Wall Street Journal* (17 November): P3.

Designing and Implementing Global Staffing Systems: Part I—Leaders in Global Staffing

Darin Wiechmann, Ann Marie Ryan, and Monica Hemingway, *Human Resource Management*

Introduction

As more and more organizations extend their reach globally, HR managers are faced with questions regarding to what extent HR tools and systems should be applied on a global basis. While it may be challenging for an organization to align all of its quality assurance or manufacturing processes globally, it is conceivable to do so. However, many in HR remain skeptical about the ability and the appropriateness of applying HR systems on a global basis. There is a general sentiment that "one size fits all" will not work. This is particularly true in the staffing area, where differences across countries in educational systems, credentialing, available labor pools, works councils and unions, and equal employment-related legislation make the concept of a global staffing system seem to be an unobtainable goal. Yet, there are a few leading organizations that have taken on this challenge.

With funding provided by the Society of Human Resource Management (SHRM) Foundation, we were able to take an in-depth look at six organizations that are, to at least some degree, attempting to institute globally standardized staffing tools and systems. In this article, we describe the kinds of things these organizations have been successfully able to implement on a global basis, the challenges they have faced, and how they have created successful global HR practices. In a companion paper in this same issue (Ryan, Wiechmann & Hemingway, 2003), we describe the best practices for global selection system design that can be inferred from the activities of these six organizations.

We began our project by identifying organizations that were viewed by others as implementing truly global staffing practices. We limited our examination to U.S.-based multinationals, because of research that has shown that country of headquarters can make a substantial difference in multinational operations. Of interest, many leading U.S. multinationals do not have a global staffing strategy—while U.S.-based staffing functions may be viewed as the best in

their class by peer organizations, there is little that the organization is doing that is of a truly global nature. We then conducted interviews with key informants on staffing at six organizations: Agilent Technologies, Dow Chemical Company, IBM, Motorola, Proctor and Gamble (P&G), and Shell Oil. These informants were in high-level positions related to or overseeing staffing activities (e.g., European staffing and workforce programs manager, global design director for workforce planning, program manager for Asia-Pacific staffing, director of global selection and assessment operations). The informants have an average of over five years in a global context and spend approximately 40% of their staffing time on global issues.

Below we describe each organization, components of their staffing systems that they have implemented on a global or near global basis, obstacles and cross-cultural differences that they have faced, success stories of overcoming these hurdles, and views on technology as a help or a hindrance in globalization. In Ryan et al. (2003), we describe the best practices in global selection system design that these organizations emulate.

Agilent Technologies

Agilent Technologies is a technology organization with 2001 annual sales of US$8.4 billion and 40,000 employees, located in more than 40 countries. Agilent has a diversified set of operations that exist within three primary businesses: (1) test and measurement, (2) semiconductor products, and (3) chemical analysis.

GLOBAL TOOLS AND PRACTICES

Agilent has a global policy of posting jobs to internal candidates while posting the jobs to external candidates. To reduce costs associated with development and retention, Agilent also has a practice that if both internal and external candidates are equally qualified, the hiring manager should select the internal candidate.

Agilent uses a face-to-face interview for all of its candidates worldwide. Although successful in its rollout, Agilent still faces the difficulty of standardizing the way in which interviewers use and interpret the interview results. Agilent attempts to standardize tool use by using educational programs that train HR personnel on the tools being used, why they are used, and how to interpret and use the test results. In addition, an internal website provides interviewers with various tool formats, general tips on interviewing, and the legal issues regarding interviews for the country in which they are located.

Last year, Agilent implemented a global talent acquisition system based on the Recruitsoft system. At the beginning of its development, Agilent created a global team that clearly defined its goal to create a product that represented Agilent employees worldwide. Hiring managers use the system to create their job requisition, select a recruiting/ selection template related to the global job classification, and select questions that every candidate will be asked as part of their prescreening tool. Through Agilent's website, candidates complete a profile, submit a resume, and fill out other application forms. Candidates are then part of a global database on which HR personnel can search based on skill sets and even send e-mail messages when positions become available. Agilent has found that the system allows them to more quickly identify candidates who will suit the needs of locations worldwide.

OBSTACLES

In designing their global talent acquisition tool, Agilent's regional managers found that legal issues may be obstacles. They noted the need for clear definitions of what the operating principles are, what the business rules are, and what the legal requirements within each region are. Specifically, Agilent found that managers in some countries require that prescreening questions of any type be approved by local agencies before they are used.

A common obstacle to all business ventures relevant to global staffing is the role that economic factors play in the success of rolling out a global system. Global rollouts present unique issues with timing because dealing with multiple labor markets and economic conditions around the globe is much more challenging than planning around one labor market or one economy.

Agilent has also found that differences in the value given to material goods, individualistic goals, and the role of work in peoples' lives can have significant influences on reactions to HR practices. For example, Agilent has found that cultures that see work as a means to living seem to be less likely to use stock options in recruiting as opposed to more work-oriented cultures. Agilent also found that taxation rules also impact reactions to recruiting practices such as offering stock options, as some countries immediately tax stock options. Thus, negative reactions to practices or tools may be due to true cultural differences in how these are viewed or differences in financial and economic systems or government regulations.

Agilent has also faced the obstacle of overcoming the perception that because its headquarters is in the United States, everything proposed by corporate HR is U.S.-centric. In order to successfully create and implement a global HR system, Agilent has found that creating a truly global team is important to helping all HR personnel see HR systems as globally representative.

SUCCESS NEGOTIATING CULTURAL DIFFERENCES

Agilent has found that one of the keys to overcoming cultural differences is to keep the candidates' and hiring managers' perspectives in mind at all times. The result of this approach is that the global HR team is able to anticipate cultural reactions by both applicants and HR personnel to new or uncommon practices in their location. Agilent has used focus groups of hiring managers to examine new staffing processes and tools, so they can provide input into the process and determine any change that should be made in the process or the tool.

Agilent's regional managers have also found that the values of the organization can help to overcome differences between cultures. The fact that trust is one of Agilent's fundamental values helps the global team to build on that level of trust already present in its team members and keep the best interests of the organization in mind throughout the process. Agilent's strong corporate culture has helped to overcome many of the cultural differences that might have hindered development of global staffing systems.

Another component of overcoming cultural barriers is to recognize fundamental values that people have, regardless of where they are. For example, most people value participation, so explicitly recognizing this as a shared value helps create an understanding of what the process of creating a global staffing system will be.

Modification to incorporate cultural considerations also ensures success. Agilent uses a global employee referral program that rewards employee referrals but does so with cultural differences in mind. As it is offensive in some cultures to be rewarded for recommending acquaintances, Agilent modified their program so that employees in some countries are not required to receive a bonus, or the bonus can be shared between people engaging and referring a hire.

TECHNOLOGY AS A HELP OR HINDRANCE

Agilent's experience with technology is that issues of generation and age may be just as important as those of culture. A gap in Internet use exists between those under and over 25 years of age; thus, reactions to new tools/practices may be more a function of generational differences that may be addressed with more exposure to new technologies.

Although technology is an enabler for global HR systems, Agilent also recognizes that because many of the technologies come out of the United States, the new products and tools can be more technologically advanced than systems in many countries are able to handle. Thus, technology can be an enabler as long as issues of connection quality, stability, speed, and cost are considered through a worldwide lens.

Dow Chemical Company

Dow Chemical Company is a science and technology organization with 2001 annual sales of US$28 billion and 50,000 employees, located in 38 countries. Dow provides innovative chemical, plastic, and agricultural products and services to many essential consumer markets in 170 countries. Dow is organized around a global business model where all strategic decisions are taken from a global perspective and it is commonplace for leaders to have direct reports in multiple locations and countries. This drives the necessity for HR systems that are globally consistent, yet are implemented locally.

GLOBAL TOOLS AND PRACTICES

Several of Dow's staffing system components are global. First, their processes for strategic HR planning and the roll-up of annual hiring plans are consistent globally. Second, their external hiring process and the business rules driving this process were developed by a global team and implemented globally. Third, both their value proposition, which is used in recruiting and states what kind of work one can expect at Dow and the values of the organization, and the generic expectations of what the competencies needed for success in Dow are used on a global basis. This enables Dow to send a consistent message to anyone recruited for working at the organization, regardless of where they live and helps to ensure corporate culture continuity.

Fourth, Dow uses Recruitsoft as a tool for taking applications online. Since instituting Recruitsoft, Dow has had tremendous increases in both the quantity and quality of applicants in regions initially resistant to the idea of online applications.

Dow also has interview guides, based on a competency model, that are used with all job families and provides training for all interviewers. Selection tests for administrative jobs are used in four of the five global regions Dow operates in, with the last expected to implement the tools over the next year. Dow has just completed a global job analysis for technical jobs and plans to roll out a selection system for global use for technical hires in the near future.

Internally, Dow has a Job Announcement System (JAS), also based on their global competency model, which enables employees globally, in all job families and all but the top management levels, to view and self-nominate for open jobs. This is an important component in Dow's journey to top-quartile employee satisfaction and below industry norm attrition. JAS has helped shape Dow's culture to an employee-centric model which, in turn, has created a greater global talent pool from which Dow can fill needed positions. Dow also has standardized processes for identification and development of future leaders at all levels and global succession planning for higher levels within the organization.

Dow has a global testing policy for its administrative and technical jobs that covers re-testing issues, requirements for various positions, selection qualifications, etc. Dow also mandates that all test administrators receive a standardized training program before they can test any applicants.

Dow also uses a global separation process for all employees that states policies for making termination decisions and how to carry out the process. Although the process is largely standardized, Dow allows for accommodations due to works councils, unions, or labor laws.

OBSTACLES

Dow has found that a variety of obstacles exist when creating global staffing systems. The fact that countries differ widely in regard to educational systems makes it difficult for Dow to create a standard set of requirements for its global applicants in terms of years of education, type of degree, and amount of job-related experience.

Dow also finds that there are often many misperceptions of the differences between cultures that create resistance to global staffing systems. Through follow-up examinations (e.g., job analysis, needs analysis, quality comparison) of potential differences between locations, Dow finds that the differences are often quite minimal. Dow also finds that the basic competencies, knowledge, skills, abilities, and job requirements are largely similar across the globe. This is helped significantly by consistent technology and work processes being deployed globally for all Dow functions.

Given the number of countries in which Dow is located, another obstacle has been providing training and materials to every site, regardless of size. Dow's experience looking for global selection tools has also lead them to struggle to find appropriate, off-the-shelf tools. To have a truly global tool, Dow must search for those products that are appropriate across cultures, are interpreted the same, have translated versions, have similar norms across countries, are available in all locations, and so forth.

Dow has found that although candidates around the globe are concerned with a tool's face validity, candidates outside of the U.S. are often more sensitive to face-validity issues than their U.S. counterparts. Finally, Dow also finds that understanding of test validation largely does not exist across its global locations.

SUCCESS NEGOTIATING CULTURAL DIFFERENCES

Dow has found that staffing managers in many global locations do not have backgrounds in testing practices that are common to U.S. staffing personnel. Dow has found that in order to successfully implement new practices or tools, they must be able to provide data to locations that is meaningful to local values and business needs. To gain local acceptance, Dow conducts extensive focus groups and interviews with local personnel. Dow also uses results from stakeholder surveys to understand the views of all personnel to be affected by a new staffing system.

Dow gains acceptance for new practices or tools by including as many people as possible in the development process. This makes everyone feel part of the process as well as provides Dow with information on important cultural differences that may necessitate making changes in the selection tool/process. For example. Dow incorporated an English fluency test for its Asian locations that wanted a required level of proficiency for reading manuals and operating disciplines. Before rolling out the Recruitsoft system for its professional managerial population, Dow found that hiring managers were resistant to its use and thought that applicants would be turned off from applying to Dow. After bringing the system online, Dow found the number and quality of applicants significantly increased; thus, the success of the system convinced hiring managers worldwide of the use of the system.

TECHNOLOGY AS A HELP OR HINDRANCE

Dow has created a global technology infrastructure, which means that Dow uses a single type of workstation, laptop, and the like across the globe. This singular approach to information technology (IT) has helped reduce the number of cross-country technology differences that had previously impeded the work of global team members.

Over the years, Dow has found that online server-based technology may not be cost effective in instances with low-volume hiring. Dow also finds that technology may often make the process of creating global staffing tools more difficult as the number of nuances added to the mix increases greatly. In addition, access issues have led Dow to provide multiple options for applicants to complete initial selection materials.

Despite these problems, technology allows Dow to provide a seamless application process to candidates that also provides managers with immediate access to a list of candidates meeting the minimum job requirements. Through the Recruitsoft technology, Dow is able to e-mail candidates throughout the process to update them on their standing. The system automatically provides turndown letters as well as information letting candidates know that someone will be contacting them regarding their application.

IBM

IBM is an electronics organization with 2001 annual sales of US$85 billion and 320,000 employees, located in 67 countries. IBM is involved in creating, developing, and manufacturing advanced information technologies such as computer systems, software, networking systems, storage devices, and microelectronics. IBM's worldwide network of solutions and service professionals helps customers translate these technologies into business value for their organizations.

GLOBAL TOOLS AND PRACTICES

IBM has implemented a variety of global tools and practices. IBM uses an Information Processing Aptitude Test (IPAT) to select entry-level technical applicants (i.e., software, hardware, and application programmers) in 11 languages in 22 countries. In developing the current version of the IPAT, a team of global representatives was formed to identify specific aspects of the English-language version that may cause difficulties across cultures. To finalize the product, an internal translation team was used to create the tests. IBM also used a global team to create a training manual and test results sheet to aid in the testing and subsequent interpretation of the testing results for the IPAT.

In 2001, IBM rolled out a toolkit that was developed with the participation of 18 countries. From the beginning, management and HR representatives from all countries were involved in the toolkit's development. The toolkit consists of a resume screening, phone interview, face-to-face assessment consisting of a Behavior Based Structured Interview (BBSI) and two simulation exercises that hiring managers can use, and a job match which attempts to assess the fit of the candidate to IBM. Although the general framework of the toolkit was standardized globally, IBM remained flexible in allowing for regional differences in what and how the pieces are used in the hiring process. To aid in the initial rollout, IBM's corporate HR aided in the training and implementation in each country via a two-day conference, and

appropriate modifications were made based on specific country needs.

IBM also uses an online training tool for the BBSI to teach employees about behavioral interviewing. After its initial rollout, the toolkit has been successfully implemented in a number of other countries worldwide.

OBSTACLES

IBM finds resistance to new policies or practices may not always be based on culture; it may also be based on tenure or experience. Prior to becoming a global organization, many regions across IBM had autonomy over their policies, programs, and processes. When IBM moved to a global HR system, those regions with more autonomy tended to resist changes more, while regions new to IBM or those traditionally having less autonomy were more likely to accept new HR policies, programs, and processes.

One of the obstacles IBM has faced in creating global staffing tools is the different role that HR plays across cultures. For example, in countries with a strong union pressence, HR tends to control much more of the employment functions than in other cultures. Countries also differ in the level of development for selection tools and processes. Managers in countries with a longer history of test use and development are often more reluctant to give up what they are currently using.

IBM has also experienced obstacles relating to cultural differences. In implementing a phone interview. IBM found that resistance may be due to cultural differences in how people interact with each other or to the practice not being a common one within that country.

IBM has also found that limited resources are an obstacle for countries looking to implement tools or practices requiring validation. Because of resource issues, managers in countries differ in the value they attach to research and benchmarking. In addition, resources often drive what becomes a global priority versus a regional priority. For example, different regions may have different hiring needs, which may not be addressed globally if those needs do not affect every region. As regions may be at different stages in their HR functions, IBM perceives challenges in gaining agreement as to the focus of its global HR systems.

With regard to specific tool use, IBM has found obstacles in the use of reference checks. Although managers in many countries still use this method, privacy laws and legal rulings have eliminated or reduced the role of this method in a number of locations.

Although cultural differences are present, IBM has found that cultures are changing over time. For example, managers in cultures that were once more passive in response to new tools or practices are becoming more vocal in stating the problems they see with the new materials and how to address those problems.

SUCCESS NEGOTIATING CULTURAL DIFFERENCES

As noted above, IBM attempts to use business necessity as a means to convince managers in different countries as to why they should adopt new policies or practices. As with any venture, a successful strategy is to always sell the bottom line to the hiring managers. No matter where they are located, managers want to know what the value of new tools are and how they will impact their business. As the value of tools/practices may differ across countries (e.g., due to differences in selection ratios, nature of applicant pools), the key is to identify what each location values and align both the tool and the sales pitch with those values.

To allow for cultural differences, IBM allows each country to adjust the tools within their toolkit and when they are used in the process. For example, for sales positions, IBM mandated that the face-to-face tools are used but allowed flexibility in the rest of the process.

A successful method for overcoming obstacles has been to gain the support of key players within the region of interest. If the initial sales pitch does not work, the global team may have to go up the ladder to gain support within that country.

One of the most widely used methods for accommodating cultural differences is to adapt the way a test looks and is used. IBM's main concern is to make sure that the content of the tool or test is consistent across the globe, but changes may be made in the test's formatting, how it is implemented, and where it fits in the process.

A final practice used to negotiate cultural differences is to get continuous feedback from each country regarding the development of the tool or practice. Feedback can be from speaking to the hiring manager, running focus groups, or surveying employees from each country. To gauge the success of a global rollout, IBM looks at a variety of factors such as the number of add-on countries using the tool or process, the number of countries asking about the new tool or process, and the number and nature of questions from those adopting the tool or process.

TECHNOLOGY AS A HELP OR HINDRANCE

IBM has found that advances in technology are helping to create centralized databases where content revisions can occur; thus, global HR personnel have continuous access to the latest versions of products and tools. Technology allows the global HR team to interact better. IBM's databases also contain global norms that allow IBM to compare staffing results across all of its locations.

Technology issues also affect how a product or tool is implemented globally. The testing volume and distance between locations differ greatly among countries, so creating computerized testing centers may not be as practical for high-volume countries and countries with distanced locations. Using unproctored environments allows IBM to overcome the disadvantages of testing remote applicants and/or high numbers of applicants.

Another problem with technology is the bandwidth differences around the globe. Bandwidth issues led IBM to create CD-ROM versions of a web-based training tool for those countries with low bandwidth. Despite these problems, IBM has found that countries are quickly catching up with each other in technology, so these problems may not persist for long.

Motorola

Motorola is a communications and electronics organization with 2001 sales of US $30 billion and 111,000 employees, located in 37 countries. Motorola's products and services include such things as wireless telephone and messaging, interactive digital video systems, embedded semiconductors, and integrated electronic systems for automotive, Telematics, industrial, telecommunications, computing, and portable energy-systems markets.

GLOBAL TOOLS AND PRACTICES

Motorola uses a standardized, structured interview process in most of its locations, but allows locations and functions to adapt the details to their needs. To support the interview process, Motorola has developed a globally used training program for those implementing the interviews.

Motorola also uses standardized test batteries to select for manufacturing operators and technicians in most locations worldwide. For their manufacturing operator battery, Motorola implemented and validated the test in over 20 countries in a five-year period. During the validation phase, Motorola also provided a standardized test administrator training program. In addition, Motorola also conducted phone training or follow-up on-site training for those locations that needed help when they were ready to roll out the test battery. The success of the test battery allowed Motorola to gauge the skill levels of its global locations against each other.

On a global basis, Motorola gives applicants a preparation book that familiarizes applicants to the types of questions they should expect. The preparation booklet also gives U.S. applicants information about Americans with Disability Act regulations and what should be done if they need accommodation during testing.

OBSTACLES

Motorola found that cultures differ in the extent to which formalized testing sessions are commonplace, thus making the introduction of testing a challenge in certain locations. In developing their manufacturing operator test, Motorola found that translation issues can be quite challenging. Using translation, back translation, and local validation gives Motorola the types of information to ensure that the same meanings are conveyed across cultures and languages.

Motorola has also found that data protection laws are challenging their ability to create global databases. In order for Motorola to keep data tied to identifying information (i.e., IDs and names), they must clearly identify where the information is to be stored, how it is stored, and so forth in order to get approval from local agencies. Because of compliance issues, Motorola often uses internal standards that are more rigorous than local agencies require in order to avoid potential obstacles on a global basis.

Motorola finds that local resistance often comes more from the staffing and HR employees who perceive more work from the new tools or practices rather than from the hiring manager who often just wants to find the best people possible.

Motorola finds that managers in some cultures like to make sure they are collecting as much information as possible, so that often they are collecting redundant information from the applicants. Some managers also prefer to take a more clinical approach to selection, which often involves asking personal questions that are not appropriate in other cultures. Although personal questions are not illegal to ask. Motorola tries to guide local HR personnel on the basis of a corporate ethical standard to avoid such questions.

SUCCESS NEGOTIATING CULTURAL DIFFERENCES

One of the most useful ways Motorola has found to convince managers in different countries and cultures to implement new tools or practices is to show added value to their business. Motorola assesses value by conducting return on investment (ROI) studies and conducting local validations. Motorola also sells the value to local HR personnel by sharing success stories and telling them about the costs and benefits associated with the tools or practices.

Familiarity with practices varies across countries. Testing tools such as opscan sheets are not common in all countries. Thus, Motorola had to include a brief training session on what opscan sheets were and how to complete them during testing.

In order to successfully overcome resistance to new practices or tools, Motorola has found it is vital to get backing from key personnel within each location. Although resistance may be uncomfortable for all those involved, Motorola suggests that unless open discussions about the cultural issues at hand take place, there is little chance that an agreement will be reached between the global team members. For those countries reluctant to give up commonly used selection tools that are not established as valid, Motorola lets managers continue to use the locally endorsed tools but adjusts their weight in the selection decision to minimal.

Technology as a Help or Hindrance

Motorola finds that the use of computerized testing is not appropriate for all testing programs. For example, countries that have group testing sessions are not able to afford the hardware necessary to test large groups of applicants. In those instances, local HR personnel use the low-tech opscan sheets that work more effectively for their situation. Motorola does find that technology can be useful for exercises such as assessment centers or business simulations so that the applicant does not have to travel in order to participate in the selection process.

Proctor and Gamble

Proctor and Gamble (P&G) is a manufacturing organization with 2001 annual sales of US$39 billion and 106,000 employees, located in more than 80 countries. P&G develops, distributes, and markets a number of consumer products in the fabric and home care, baby care, feminine care, family care, beauty care, health care, and food and beverage areas.

GLOBAL TOOLS AND PRACTICES

P&G has implemented a global candidate management system which uses a common set of assessment factors and common assessment tools, such as a scorable application with an embedded biodata instrument, a problem solving test, an English proficiency test, and a structured interview. The structured interview is supported by standardized interview guides to train all interviewers. The success of the system has allowed P&G to calibrate scores and interviews around the world. P&G uses this global database as an internal benchmark of how well they are doing in different parts of the world.

P&G also has cognitive-based tests, translated into many languages, which are used to select entry-level managers, professionals, and plant technicians. P&G has specialized tests for plant technicians (English only), electrical and instrumental positions, and accountants. Recently, P&G has begun to implement a global trainer training program for test administrators and interviewers.

Currently, P&G recruits based on a global core set of values and provides similar materials to all candidates. Regional websites give tailored information to local candidates. P&G also uses a web-based job posting system that has been developed in North America and Asia and has the potential to be completely global.

To support its management selection system, P&G is using a global steering team to create a standardized set of recruiting policies and practices.

OBSTACLES

Variations across regions can occur due to local practices, local labor pools, or lack of trust in validated assessment tools. Generalizing across cultures, P&G tends to find that applicants generally prefer biodata instruments to cognitive tests.

P&G has found that not all countries have local employees with significant (i.e., five or more years) staffing experience as opposed to experience in other HR functions. In addition, local units differ greatly in their ability to acquire and use information technology, especially tools that are web-based. P&G finds that less developed locations tend to be more receptive to input and guidance from experienced global team members. Those countries with more HR experience tend to be more resistant to change, technology, or policy support.

P&G finds that local candidates also have trust issues based on their lack of experience with new selection tools or practices. Finally, P&G has found that relationship-oriented cultures are often suspect of any type of assessment tool or technology that is put between the hiring manager and the candidate.

SUCCESS NEGOTIATING CULTURAL DIFFERENCES

To successfully account for cultural differences, P&G conducts a number of steps to insure legitimate variations are incorporated into the assessment tool. For cognitive-based tests. P&G conducts item analyses, reviews of content by local employees, translation checks by local psychologists, and predictive validation studies. While developing their biodata instrument, P&G found that they needed to include culturally sensitive questions to reflect what is valued in the different cultures. For example, P&G assesses leadership skills, so they looked for the patterns of behavior that reflect leadership in each country. P&G used these differences to create questions and score them to reflect what leadership means in each country. P&G also found that their biodata items had to be carefully reviewed and modified due to wide variations in educational practices and systems across countries. Although educational variations did exist among countries, P&G found that their predictor of scientific innovation within their biodata measure had significant cross-cultural validity in the United States, Europe, and Asia.

P&G also conducts research studies to assess cultural reactions to assessment tools and their effectiveness. For example, P&G conducted a study in the United Kingdom to assess whether an application including biodata was less likely to be returned than an application without the biodata. As P&G found no differences, they implemented the tool without negative reactions due to cultural differences.

To help negotiate cultural differences, P&G trains HR personnel working in recruiting and assessment in ways that can help them create acceptance of the tests by applicants and hiring managers.

P&G also allow candidates the option of taking their problem-solving test in their local language or in English. If they take it in English, candidates are given additional time to take the test. Finally, for countries where multiple-choice testing is not a common aspect of their selection processes, P&G has practice tests that simulate what taking the test will involve.

TECHNOLOGY AS A HELP OR HINDRANCE

P&G has found that their move to a global staffing strategy was driven by the capabilities provided by the Internet. P&G sees the progress of globalization, the Internet, and new technologies as creating vast new opportunities to create global HR systems.

P&G feels that changes in candidates' demographics and skills as well as their mobility are creating more intra-regional staffing issues that they must address. Companies that do not address these changes will lose out on the global talent pool being created. In some ways, P&G feels that they have little choice in becoming more global.

P&G sees technology as helping to redefine the role of HR in attracting and selecting global candidates. Technology is allowing hiring managers and applicants to directly interact without the influence of HR personnel. Thus, P&G is in the process of trying to understand where HR fits into global systems and how it can remain a value-added component of the process to both hiring managers and applicants.

Shell Oil

Shell Oil is the U.S.-based affiliate of the Royal Dutch/Shell Group of Companies. Shell is involved in exploring, developing, producing, purchasing, transporting, and marketing crude oil and natural gas. Shell also purchases, manufactures, transports, and markets oil and chemical products and provides technical and business services. Shell had 2001 annual sales of US$29 billion and nearly 20,000 employees. The Shell representatives that we interviewed are part of Shell People Services, which handles all of the hiring for professional level employees within the Royal Dutch/Shell Group of Companies. Shell People Services handles the professional hiring for over 100 countries.

GLOBAL TOOLS AND PRACTICES

Shell follows the philosophy of thinking globally, but acting locally. Shell People Services provides only English-based tools and practices as English is the global language of all professional employees within Shell. Shell uses a global assessment center and has standard training for all assessors who administer the assessment center. To ensure success of the assessment center, Shell allows for local accommodation due to compliance and cultural differences.

Shell also uses a global system to select for administrative, clerical, and technician positions. Shell uses globally standardized structured interview protocols for every job group (i.e., engineering, business, science, and technology) for which they hire.

Shell has put a great deal of effort in creating a strong recruiting function. To aid in recruiting globally, Shell uses SAP, which provides a common database and a common workflow process. Shell provides all potential candidates with global information about Shell as a global organization. Shell uses the website as a global posting board for opportunities across the globe. Shell also provides some general information to potential candidates around the world such as the job description, whether global travel may be required, the initial location of the position, and, more generally, how the position fits within Shell. In addition to the global information, Shell has materials that are more relevant to the opportunities available within that location.

OBSTACLES

Shell finds that it often faces a lack of understanding among managers of different countries concerning the influence of legal issues upon each other's HR practices or policies. Shell has found that managers in nonlitigious countries often do not fully appreciate the rigor needed to insure local compliance or the legal issues behind other team members' concerns. Shell's experiences suggest the failure to understand the legal concerns of all team members may impede the team's ability to adequately address everyone's concerns. Shell has found that, over time, countries are implementing laws that may look different, but have similar intent. For most HR practices, Shell finds that work councils, unions, government regulations, and so forth present similar issues and concerns across countries. Thus, the changing legal environment may help to create a shared understanding of the issues in global staffing.

In creating global staffing systems, Shell also faces issues of how to assess competencies on a global basis. Shell's goal is to understand what each competency means across cultures and devise assessment methods that will allow them to capture those culture-specific behaviors. As Shell penetrates more markets over time, HR finds itself trying to keep up with these differences. In addition, Shell also tries to insure that candidates from different cultures are not assessed differently because of the cultural differences between those conducting the assessments or interviews. For example, Shell would want to ensure that an assessor from an outgoing culture does not rate a candidate who is from a reserved culture as inadequate.

Shell suggests that an "us versus them" mentality may exist between global HR partners unless a team mentality is created among regions. Shell suggests that a global practice leader can provide the structure needed to create an effective global HR system. The global practice leader can also provide some of the authority needed to attach consequences for creating a global system; thus, the leader pushes the team to design and implement practices that are truly globally integrative.

Shell's emphasis has been to hire locals within each of their operating units, but this practice has come under pressure due to the increasing number of global HR candidates. Shell has found it difficult to remain loyal to the local hiring practice, but, at the same time, utilize the talent that they are able to attract worldwide.

SUCCESS NEGOTIATING CULTURAL DIFFERENCES

Shell has found that one factor in overcoming cultural differences is to build personal relationships with global team members. By creating relationships with key players in policy creation and implementation, Shell has found that perceptions of an "us versus them" situation are less likely to come between global team members. In addition, Shell has found that their successes have been due to making the intent of new initiatives clear to all countries involved. Each culture and location has their own interests that they think are the most important, so Shell tries to make global partners realize this fact and identify the many options available for creating a global system. To support this process, Shell representatives suggest having a strong integrating force such as a global practice leader or center for global practices.

In creating a new selection process for college graduates, Shell found that U.S. locations were an obstacle for creating a global system. Managers thought that U.S. employees would react negatively to an assessment center, so they were somewhat hesitant to fully accept that the process would work for U.S. candidates. To determine if this process would hurt Shell in the United States, a group of candidates went through the assessment center and then participated in a focus group to understand how they viewed the process. To management's surprise, U.S. candidates saw the process as useful for showing Shell their capabilities and that it was cutting edge compared to other organizations.

In addition to internal testing, Shell also uses market testing to ensure that cultural differences do not impact the success of new practices or tools. Finally, Shell has found that working with external firms with experience in different countries has helped to create tools and practices that will be successful within that culture.

TECHNOLOGY AS A HELP OR HINDRANCE

Shell has found that technology has allowed them to effectively coordinate their global HR functions. Technologies such as LiveLink allow Shell to share best practices, previously learned information, and newly learned information on a routine basis.

Despite the potential benefits of technology for global staffing systems, Shell has found that technology may also be a hindrance to creating global systems. Whenever technologies created in the United States are exported, they must pass export compliance regulations; thus, the technology needs to be modified to support the legal compliance issues within each country. The result of these issues is that Shell has ended up with multiple recruiting systems instead of a globally standardized recruiting system. Shell finds that they put considerable energy into making sure technology for staffing systems complies with all of the differences around the globe.

Because of these problems, Shell does not automatically push for a global platform; instead, they determine its usefulness and then use regional systems when problems are encountered. Although technology currently may be a limiting factor, Shell still believes that it will and should help them to create a globally standardized recruiting system.

TABLE I: FREQUENTLY MENTIONED OBSTACLES AND BENEFITS TO A GLOBAL STAFFING SYSTEM

Obstacles to a Global Staffing System	*Benefits of Global Staffing Systems*
• Legal requirements across countries/regions • Educational systems across countries/regions • Economic conditions across countries/regions • Ability to acquire and use technology • Labor market variations • Value differences across cultures • Availability of off-the-shelf translated tools • Level of HR experience varies across regions • Role of HR in hiring varies across regions • Familiarity with a tool or practice varies • Misperceptions that something is a cultural difference • Limited local resources for implementation • Beliefs about whether a global system is U.S.-centric or imposed	• Global database of qualified talent • Quick identification of candidates to meet needs of a specific location • Provision of a consistent message about the company to candidates worldwide • Quality of all hires is ensured • Better understanding of country/regional needs by all HR • Global succession planning is enabled • Global HR personnel have access to the latest versions of products/tools • Shared vision of HR globally • Comparisons of staffing results across locations • Global database as an internal benchmark of achievement in different parts of the world

Conclusions

Our interviews with six leaders in developing and implementing global staffing systems have indicated the ability to be successful in adopting global strategies, policies, and tools in this area of HR functioning. Our analysis also indicates that this is not an easy process, and these global leaders have indicated the importance of flexibility, of developing a global team, and of gathering data to assess cultural concerns. Table I provides a summary of the obstacles and benefits in designing global staffing systems mentioned by our respondents.

While the multinationals in our study are U.S.-based, presenting perhaps a U.S. view of staffing, a number of our interviewees were directors or managers of various global regions and added a similar but unique perspective. In particular, regional staffing managers emphasized the importance of global input in system planning and development as key to avoiding perceptions of a "U.S.-centric" imposed staffing system. A truly global staffing practice is not one that is simply exported from the United States to other countries, but one that is developed by a global team.

Source: Wiechmann, D., Ryan, A.M., and Hemingway, M. "Designing and Implementing Global Staffing Systems: Part 1—Leaders in Global Staffing." *Human Resource Management* 2003 pp. 71–83. Copyright © 2003 John Wiley & Sons. This material is used by permission of John Wiley & Sons, Inc.

Reference

Ryan, A.M., Wiechmann, D., & Hemingway, M. (2003). Designing and implementing global staffing systems: Part II—Best practices. *Human Resource Management*, 42, 85–94.

CHAPTER

9

TRAINING AND DEVELOPMENT

Corning was one of the first major U.S. employers to realize the value of taking a strategic approach to human resource management, particularly in investing in employees relative to training. Like many other American manufacturers, by the late 1980s Corning had begun to suffer in the marketplace due to increased competition from abroad. Foreign competitors had been able to develop the same technology that had been the basis for Corning's competitive advantage, and the lower labor costs of these organizations had allowed them to compete successfully against Corning. Corning was faced with the prospect of moving its production overseas unless it could develop a whole new approach to its business.

In 1989, Corning reopened a plant in Blacksburg, West Virginia, and reinvented the way in which it did business. One hundred fifty production workers were hired from a pool of 8,000 applicants and given extensive training. In fact, training time for employees accounted for 25 percent of total working time during the plant's first

year of operation. The training involved workers' taking on responsibilities previously reserved for management and the development of a broad range of skills that were to be utilized in a team-centered environment. Workers were required to master three different skill modules within two years in order to keep their jobs, which allowed the plant to retool itself with minimal downtime. The "new" plant had only four job classifications as opposed to the previous 47 classifications. This training provided efficiencies in both flexibility of employees, decreased supervision costs, and increased productivity. The end result was that during the first eight months of operations, the plant turned more than $2 million in profit as opposed to the expected $2.3 million start-up loss. Clearly, the strategized training provided to employees was a wise investment of organizational resources.

Source: Hoerr, J. "Sharpening Minds for a Competitive Edge," *Business Week*, December 17, 1990, pp. 72–78.

If an organization considers its employees to be human assets, training and development represents an ongoing investment in these assets and one of the most significant investments an organization can make. Training involves employees acquiring knowledge and learning skills that they will be able to use immediately; employee development involves learning that will aid the organization and employee later in the employee's career. Many organizations use the term *learning* rather than *training* to emphasize the point that the activities engaged in as part of this developmental process are broad-based and involve much more than straightforward acquisition of manual or technical skills.

Learning implies ongoing development and continuously adding to employees' skills and knowledge to meet the challenges the organization faces from its external environment. A focus on learning, as opposed to training, emphasizes results rather than process, making such an approach more palatable to senior executives. Any kind of employee learning that is not reinforced by the organization's reward system has little chance of impacting employee behavior and performance.

Employee training and development is increasingly becoming a major strategic issue for organizations for several reasons. First, rapid changes in technology continue to cause increasing rates of skill obsolescence. In order to remain competitive, organizations need to continue training their employees to use the best and latest technologies available. Managing in such a turbulent environment has created the need for continuous learning among managers.[1] Second, the redesign of work into jobs having broader responsibilities (that are often part of self-managed teams) requires employees to assume more responsibility, take initiative, and further develop interpersonal skills to ensure their performance and success. Employees need to acquire a broader skill base and be provided with development opportunities to assist with teamwork, collaboration, and conflict management. Third, mergers and acquisitions have greatly increased. These activities require integrating employees of one organization into another having a vastly different culture. When financial and performance results of merger and acquisition activity fall short of plans, the reason usually rests with people management systems rather than operational or financial management systems. Fourth, employees are moving from one employer to another with far more frequency than they did in the past. With less loyalty to a particular employer and more to the employees' own careers, more time must be spent on integrating new hires into the workplace. Finally, the globalization of business operations requires managers to acquire knowledge and skills related to language and cultural differences.

These strategic challenges for training exist alongside standard types of training that are done for new organizational hires (orientation and socialization) and for those employees assuming new job responsibilities. In organizations that emphasize both promotion from within and the career development of existing employees, continual training and development opportunities are critical. Employees must be updated in industry best practices and changing technology. For an employer who hires a significant number of skilled workers from outside the organization, new employees need to understand rules, policies, and procedures and be socialized into company operations and employee networks.

New employee orientation can be a daunting challenge for employers. New hires are often inundated with forms, procedures, and people but lack a strong sense of the business and operations in which they have begun to work. While new-hire orientation programs can attempt to assist new employees in their transition into the workplace, if the programs were not developed in tandem with any strategic objectives or in concert with other HR programs and/or critical operational areas of the organization, they often don't have a significant impact on the new hire's ability to fully understand the entire organization and their place in it. Exemplary new employee orientation/training programs have been developed at Black and Decker and MicroStrategy.

New Employee Training at Black and Decker

Towson, Maryland–based tool manufacturer Black and Decker (B&D) has developed a new employee training program that literally puts employees to work. College grads who gain entry-level professional employment in sales with B&D traditionally received their training via a three-ring binder that provided information about B&D products. New employees would study and learn the material to assist them with their selling. Establishing credibility was not part of the training equation and many trainees never even touched the products they were selling, let alone used them. Black and Decker has recently revamped its sales training for new hires to combine classroom training, online courses, and, most important, a training floor where new hires engage in hands-on learning about construction and tool use. This program, a component of Black and Decker University, enrolls 100 to 200 new sales and marketing employees annually. B&D University has a staff of 15 employees and an annual budget of $3 million. As part of their training, sales and marketing trainees take an online course that explains the four basic applications of tools: cutting, removing, fastening, and making holes. They then go to work in a product training area where they must use the tools to build things such as roofs, moldings, and stairs. Such experience allows them to go to retailers and fully explain product features and benefits. As a result of its program, Black & Decker has drastically reduced turnover, sent out more credible sales staff, enhanced the Black & Decker name, and reported higher employee satisfaction and loyalty.[2]

Boot Camp at MicroStrategy

MicroStrategy is a Vienna, Virginia–based organization that provides data mining services and has long held a spot on Fortune's *best employers' list. With a strong corporate culture, based on the convictions and beliefs of its founder, Michael Saylor, MicroStrategy has developed a new-hire orientation program that attempts to infuse elements of its culture into employees from the first day of work. The program, known as "boot camp," goes beyond mere orientation and is a written requirement in every employment contract for MicroStrategy employees, who work in 18 states and 35 countries. It is an intensive immersion into MicroStrategy culture to which Saylor wants each employee exposed and committed. There are three different variations of boot camp, each targeted to a different group of employees. The first is a three-day general boot camp that concludes with a 20- to 25-question exam that covers information such as MicroStrategy's products and company structure. The second is a two-week sales boot camp that culminates in a mock marketing presentation. The third is a five-week technical boot camp that features continuous testing. Despite its intensity, employee feedback on boot camp has been very positive and the only complaint heard is that it is too short.[3]*

Another approach to new-employee training is rotation. Discussed in Chapter 6, rotational programs can have an added benefit for new employees, particularly those who have limited full-time professional work experience. Rotations allow new hires to sample different kinds of work within the organization and determine an optimal fit between their needs and interests and those of the organization. Rotation programs can be expensive in the short run but they represent a longer-term investment in employees that can provide significant benefits to an organization. Employers benefit in that rotation programs allow more flexibility in work assignments. Employees who have been cross-trained not only better understand how their individual jobs contribute to the whole but also can be reassigned as business and organization conditions change. Rotational programs also have the benefit of minimizing the chance that specialized knowledge will be vested in only one individual in the organization, causing disruptions when such an individual resigns, retires, or otherwise leaves the organization. In addition to helping develop a knowledgeable and flexible workforce, rotation programs can enhance retention because the versatility they offer allows employees to pursue more opportunities within the organization.[4]

Organizations that wish to remain competitive must consider the types of employees they should hire and the skills and knowledge these employees will need to ensure optimal performance over time. Ironically, however, training budgets and programs are usually one of the first expenses organizations cut in response to economic downturns. Many key decision makers consider these to be luxury expenditures for prosperous times instead of the necessary investments in the organization's future that they are.

Training and development activities are equally important to both employees and employers. One recent survey found that 96 percent of job applicants reported that the opportunity to learn new skills was very important when evaluating a prospective employer.[5] Employers also see a bottom-line benefit from strategically designed training activities. One study found that employers who were in the top quartile of their peers relative to the average training expenditure per employee experienced 24 percent higher-gross profit margins, 218 percent higher income generation per employee, and a 26 percent higher price-to-book value of company stock price relative to those employers in the bottom quartile.[6] Investment in training and development, however, remains a Catch-22 for employers. While additional training can improve bottom-line operating results, that same training can make employees much more attractive targets of competitors' recruiting efforts. This is particularly true for technical employees, a majority of whom view training primarily as an opportunity to obtain another job.[7]

BENEFITS OF TRAINING AND DEVELOPMENT

Training involves some kind of change for employees: changes in how they do their jobs, how they relate to others, the conditions under which they perform, or changes in their job responsibilities. Although some employees may find any kind of change threatening, change that results from employee training and development has nothing short of win-win outcomes for both employees and employers. Strategically targeted training in critical skills and knowledge bases adds to employee marketability and employability security that is critical in the current environment of rapidly developing technology and changing jobs and work processes. Organizations continue to seek out and employ knowledge workers rather than workers with narrowly defined technical skills.

Organizations can benefit from training, beyond bottom line and general efficiency and profitability measures, when they create more flexible workers who can assume varied responsibilities and have a more holistic understanding of what the organization does and the role they play in the organization's success. Providing employees with broader knowledge and skills and emphasizing and supporting ongoing employee development also help organizations reduce layers of management and make employees more accountable for results. Everyone (employees, employers, and customers) benefits from effective training and development programs. The key strategic issue then becomes how to make training effective.

In order for organizations to provide effective employee training and development, key decision makers must consider employees from the investment perspective described earlier in this book. Training and development quite frequently involve short-term costs (for design and delivery of the learning activities) and long-term benefits. Particularly with issues of employee development, there may be no return on investment for the immediate time period. Organizations that are bound by short-term financial performance indicators are less likely to value training and less likely to create and support a culture that fosters employee development.

Organizations that take a strategic approach to human resources can find that employee training can be much more efficacious as part of an integrated approach to HR. For example, training and development are greatly assisted by having appropriate and well-thought-out staffing strategies. Judicious recruitment and selection of new employees will not only allow more targeted training that addresses specific needs but also minimize the need to conduct any extensive or remedial training among new employees.

PLANNING AND STRATEGIZING TRAINING

There are two keys to developing successful training programs in organizations. The first is planning and strategizing the training. This involves four distinct steps: needs assessment, the establishment of objectives and measures, delivery of the training, and evaluation. A model for planning and strategizing training is presented and explained in Exhibit 9-1.

Needs Assessment

The first step, needs assessment, involves determining why specific training activities are required and placing the training within an appropriate organizational context. Needs assessment involves three levels of analysis: organizational, task, and individual. At the organizational level, the training is considered within the context of the organization's culture, politics, structure, and strategy. This analysis considers how the training will assist the organization or unit in meeting its objectives and how the

EXHIBIT 9-1: STRATEGIZING TRAINING

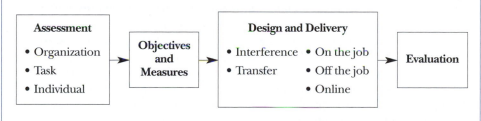

EXHIBIT 9-2: LEVELS OF NEEDS ASSESSMENT

Organizational Level

- How does the training relate to organizational objectives?
- How does the training impact day-to-day workplace dynamics?
- What are the costs and expected benefits of the training?

Task Level

- What responsibilities are assigned to the job?
- What skills or knowledge are needed for successful performance?
- Should the learning setting be the actual job setting?
- What are the implications of mistakes?
- How can the job provide the employee with direct feedback?
- How similar to or different from the training needs of other jobs are the needs of this job?

Individual Level

- What knowledge, skills, and abilities do trainees already have?
- What are the trainees' learning styles?
- What special needs do the trainees have?

training may affect day-to-day workplace dynamics between and among different units. It also considers the cost of training relative to the benefits that may be expected and considers the opportunity costs of foregoing the training.

Task-level assessment involves looking at specific duties and responsibilities assigned to different jobs and the types of skills and knowledge needed to perform each task. This level also considers whether the learning can or should take place on or away from the job, the implications of mistakes, and how the job can be designed to provide the employee with direct feedback on his or her performance. This level also involves determining whether the training needs of certain jobs are similar to or different from the training needs of other jobs in the organization.

The individual level of assessment considers the people to be trained. It requires an analysis of their existing levels of knowledge and skills as well as factors relating to their preferred learning styles, personality, interpersonal styles in interacting with others, and any special needs individual employees might have, such as any physical or mental condition that might need to be addressed in the design and delivery of the training. The three levels of needs analysis are summarized in Exhibit 9-2.

Objectives

After training needs have been assessed, objectives for the training activities must be developed. These objectives should follow directly from the assessed needs and be described in specific, measurable terms. Measures should be stated in terms of both desired employee behaviors as well as the results that are expected to follow such behavior. A common problem at this stage is that an organization's objectives may be so vague that success in achieving them cannot be accurately measured or evaluated. On the other hand, an organization may have no plan for measuring these objectives. Training programs that cannot be evaluated are of little value to the organization in the long run.

One important source of information in setting objectives can be the data contained in the organization's performance management system, which will be discussed in detail in Chapter 10. Specific training objectives can be derived from the performance deficiencies noted in the performance feedback process. Both individual and group training can be developed around these measures. ▼

Using Training to Facilitate a Merger at Hewlett-Packard

When computer giants Hewlett-Packard (HP) and Compaq completed their controversial merger in 2002, HP faced the daunting task of integrating the two organizations. Training via e-learning played a major role in ensuring that the merger went smoothly. The existing portal, Learn@HP, was used as a single gateway for employees in nearly 60 countries. The portal was redesigned to help define the new company identity and structure and to communicate HP's new vision to employees. This helped to speed up the merger and saved the organization an estimated $50 million. Learn@HP's success in facilitating the merger has led to its continued growth and development as a critical management tool. From 2003 to 2004, e-learning increased from 25 to 40 percent of the total time employees spent in training. A new agreement with Microsoft required the retraining of 3,000 HP/Compaq employees. E-learning not only reduced the training time for certification from eight to three weeks, it also saved the organization an estimated $10 million.[8]

Design and Delivery

After objectives and measures have been set, the next step is the design and delivery of the training itself. Two critical issues must be considered in the design of the training prior to its delivery. The first is interference. Interference occurs when prior training, learning, or established habits act as a block or obstacle in the learning process. Anyone who learned to drive an automobile having an automatic transmission and later attempted to drive a manual or standard transmission probably experienced interference in their learning. The more experience someone has in behaving in a certain way, the more difficult it may be to modify the response they display. When individuals are stressed, they tend to revert to conditioned behavior.

The second critical issue that must be addressed in design is transfer. Transfer refers to whether the trainee or learner can actually perform the new skills or use the new knowledge on the job. In other words, transfer is the extent to which the trainee or learner is able to "transfer" the learning to the actual job setting. Many training programs that are conducted away from the work site have been criticized for their lack of transfer because the conditions under which employees have been trained are vastly different from those in which they actually work. Obviously, it is inefficient to conduct training and receive no benefit from it in terms of employee job performance; those responsible for training need to ensure that it provides maximum transfer.

▶ Reading 9.1, "The Imperative of Developing Global Leaders," provides recommendations for the development of global leaders in government that could serve as a blueprint for a comprehensive training program.

The delivery of the training should anticipate any interference that might be present, and a strategy should be planned to overcome it and ensure transfer. Interference is not caused only by conditioned or learned behavior. The attitudes of supervisors or peers may produce interference as well. Coworkers who publically express negative concerns about the training may cause learners to be predisposed against the training. When trainers examine the potential sources of interference, they need to look beyond the backgrounds, skills, and habits of the trainees themselves to the broader organizational context, which includes culture, politics, and organization structure. Training and development will not be effective unless it is conducted within a larger supportive organizational environment. Having the CEO or other senior executives attend training sessions communicates strong organizational support for training.

Transfer can be facilitated by delivering the training in an environment that simulates the actual job conditions as much as possible. In some cases, it may be feasible to provide direct, on-the-job training where the employee is trained under the exact working conditions in which he or she will be expected to perform. However, in other cases, on-the-job training may not be feasible, and the delivery of the training should then replicate exact working conditions as much as possible. Airline pilots do not learn to fly by going up in an airplane and being told what to do. Their training involves extensive exposure to simulated flight conditions on the ground, which tests their learning and ability to react to a variety of situations, including crisis situations.

On-the-job training may help to maximize transfer, but it is obviously not feasible for all jobs. In addition, off-the-job training allows learners to focus on their learning by minimizing interruptions or distractions that might take place in the actual work environment. An increasing amount of training is being conducted away from the workplace. This sort of training utilizes techniques that attempt to simulate what happens on the job. Instructional techniques that facilitate such simulation involve the use of case studies, role-plays, and interactive and experiential methods of learning. Individuals being trained are asked to assume a role and the responsibilities that they might have on the job and then perform accordingly.

An increasing amount of organizational training is being conducted online. Many organizations have entire training libraries consisting of skills-related training and information/knowledge-based learning that have been packaged into computer-based instruction modules or programs. Colleges and universities are offering an increasing number of courses and even entire degree programs online as well.

Computer-Based Training at QUALCOMM

San Diego–based QUALCOMM is unquestionably one of the leaders in computer-based training for its employees. The 6,000-plus employee organization, which invented the multiple access technology used in digital wireless communication worldwide, offers more than 250 custom-designed courses online. These courses include offerings in both technical and professional/management development areas and were initially designed for delivery to fit different learning schedules and different learning styles. Online courses are offered 24 hours a day, seven days a week, but certain courses are still available in a traditional classroom delivery setting for those who prefer this type of learning environment.

Probably most critical is the fact that the training is strategically focused. All instruction is developed in concert with QUALCOMM's culture and business needs. Learning specialists are assigned to track the needs of various business units by attending staff meetings, meeting regularly with senior management, and conducting group needs assessments. They are then charged with identifying training needs and then working with vendors and management to define the course and create appropriate and unique content geared to the needs of the business unit and QUALCOMM.

Training at QUALCOMM is tightly integrated with the organization's competency management initiative, MySource. MySource is an intranet-based employee development tool that allows employees to access their employment records and view their skills and accomplishments. Individuals can map out career options and then enroll in the appropriate learning modules to facilitate promotion and skill development.

In moving to computer-based training, QUALCOMM has saved millions of dollars from the cost of ineffective centralized training. More important, its system successfully unleashes the full potential of its employees through training and skill development, career planning, and competency management.[9]

Online computer-based instruction provides a number of benefits. It is self-paced, allowing different individuals to learn and absorb material at their own level of comfort and understanding. It is adaptive to different needs and can be customized for different employees. It is also easy to deliver: All an employee has to do is turn on a computer at a workstation or at home. There is no need to leave one's desk or coordinate schedules with trainers or trainees, nor a need to have trainers and trainees in the same physical space. Computer-based training is also usually less expensive to administer when different units in the organization are geographically dispersed. Finally, training can be conducted whenever it is convenient for the employee. An employee who has finished assigned work early no longer needs to look busy or find a way to kill time. The training can be undertaken without any advance scheduling.

The popularity of online training cannot be underestimated. A recent survey of 100 companies with an average of 15,000 employees each found that 42 percent currently used online learning applications. More important, however, 92 percent of the respondents planned to introduce or accelerate the volume of online training within 12 months.[10]

Despite its popularity, there are some drawbacks to computer-based instruction. First, learners must be self-motivated and take both initiative and responsibility for their learning. Second, the cost of producing online, interactive materials can be quite high. The content of the learning can become outdated quickly and require revision and possible redesign of the entire online learning environment. Finally, the lack of both interaction with others and two-way communication may work against the needs and preferred learning styles of many employees, particularly adult learners. Consequently, computer-based training can either be advantageous for an employer or a waste of time, resources, and money. Clearly, it needs to be considered within the larger context of the training objectives and the assessed organizational, task, and individual considerations discussed previously.

E-Learning at EMC Corporation

EMC is a Hopkinton, Massachusettes–based supplier of software, networks, and services for data and information storage. Dramatic improvements in technology related to data storage and retrieval have made product life cycles at EMC increasingly short. This has prompted a need for continuous new product development and, consequently, training. The use of traditional classrooms to meet these accelerated training needs would have involved great expense as it required the building or leasing of physical space as well as the cost of moving employees out of the field to the training site. As EMC expanded globally there was also a need to deliver more standardized training to prevent inconsistencies that were taking place in different locations relative to content and approach. In response to these challenges, EMC installed a single learning management system that moved training from a traditional instructor-led process to an integrated e-learning process. This move has allowed new employees to complete product training in five months, rather than the nine months previously required, and sales staff are now able to meet quotas in four months rather than nine to twelve months. Perhaps the biggest benefit has been realized with new product launches. Updated courses are available to coincide with a new product's release, resulting in increased customers' willingness to become early adapters. Customers also are now more prone to buy multiple products, knowing that online support is readily available for them. While EMC initially developed its e-learning program with an eye on costs, the longer-term investments in this area are also yielding significant productivity and revenue gains.[11]

Evaluation

After the training has been delivered, it needs to be evaluated. This evaluation should be an integral part of the overall training program. The organization needs to receive feedback on the training and decide whether the training should be continued in its current form, modified, or eliminated altogether. The ultimate evaluation criteria should also be assessed prior to training delivery to provide a comparison basis for post-training assessment. Evaluation techniques that are not developed when objectives are set will usually have little value to the organization. The decision of how to evaluate training should be made at the same time the training objectives are set.

A highly regarded model has been developed for training evaluation that suggests that evaluation can take place on four levels and that these levels form a hierarchy, meaning that lower levels are prerequisites for higher levels.[12] In other words, if one of the lower-level measures is not affected, then those measures that follow it will automatically not be affected as well. These levels are reaction, learning, behavior, and results and are illustrated in Exhibit 9-3.

Reaction measures whether the employees liked the training, the trainer, and the facilities; it is usually measured by a questionnaire. If employees have less-than-favorable reactions to the program, it is unlikely that other employees will have an interest in the training or that employees attending the training received anything of value from it. A favorable reaction, in and of itself, does not ensure that the training was effective.

Learning measures whether the employees know more than they did prior to undertaking the training. Knowledge-based training can be measured by tests; skills-based training can be measured through demonstrations or simulations. If employees did not learn anything, then obviously we can expect no change in their behavior on the job. For any change to occur as a result of training, the trainees must have learned something.

Behavior measures what employees do on the job after the training. This measure allows organizations to assess not only whether transfer has taken place but also whether the employees are able to do anything differently (skills-based training) or think or solve problems in different ways (knowledge-based training). Behavioral impact is usually measured through performance appraisal, which is done by those who are able to witness and observe the employee. If there is no change in behavior, we cannot expect employees' performance to have been enhanced.

EXHIBIT 9-3: FOUR LEVELS OF TRAINING EVALUATION

Level	Questions Being Asked	Measures
Results	Is the organization or unit better because of the training?	Accidents Quality Productivity Turnover Morale Costs Profits
Behavior	Are trainees behaving differently on the job after training? Are they using the skills and knowledge they learned in training?	Performance appraisal by superior, peer, client, subordinate
Learning	To what extent do trainees have greater knowledge or skill after the training program than they did before?	Written Tests Performance Tests Graded Simulations
Reaction	Did the trainees like the program, the trainers, the facilities? Do they think the course was useful? What improvements can they suggest?	Questionnaires

Source: Kirkpatrick, Donald. "Four Steps to Measuring Training Effectiveness," in *The Personnel Administrator*, Volume 28, #11, November 1983, p. 19. Reprinted with permission.

Evaluation of results looks at the overall outcomes of the training and the impact that the training has had on productivity, efficiency, quality, customer service, or any other means the organization uses to measure contributions and performance of employees. This can be assessed by budget and cost reports, sales figures, production, customer surveys, or any other means that correspond to the organization's performance measures. However, results of training programs are often not immediate. Training programs may be ongoing or involve employees' developing a level of proficiency, which takes time to achieve and master. Although results-based measures of training are usually the most meaningful and economically significant for an organization, undue reliance on them may cause key decision makers to abandon training programs that do not produce immediate short-term results. Consequently, the evaluation of training should consider all four levels in conjunction with the organization's overall strategic objectives.

INTEGRATING TRAINING WITH PERFORMANCE MANAGEMENT SYSTEMS AND COMPENSATION

The second key factor in strategizing training programs is to ensure that desired results of training are reinforced when employees achieve or accomplish them. In larger organizations, it is not uncommon to see an entire department devoted solely to employee training and development. This unit may be separate and autonomous from other human resource functions such as performance measurement (appraisal) and

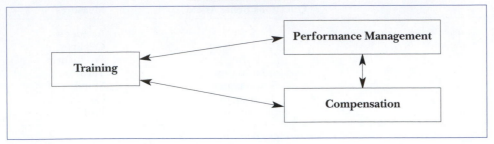

compensation and benefits administration. When employees expend the effort to learn new skills and knowledge and are expected to implement such learning in their jobs, there should be some incentive to do so and some acknowledgment and reinforcement of that performance once it is achieved. However, when training, performance measurement, and compensation are administered separately and not integrated within a larger, integrative HR strategy, there is less chance of that appropriate and necessary reinforcement.

When employees are asked to learn critical new skills and/or absorb important new knowledge and apply this in their jobs, the means by which their performance is assessed must reflect these changes. The more critical the skills and knowledge are to the organization's strategy, the greater the emphasis that should be placed on assessing them in the organization's performance management system. Similarly, compensation should reflect the results of training. If employees have learned new skills and knowledge and successfully implemented this learning to enhance the performance of the organization, they should be compensated accordingly in a way that is significant to them. A training program that is not linked to the organization's performance management and compensation systems, as indicated in Exhibit 9-4, has far less chance of success than one that does. Training should be conceptualized, designed, and delivered within a larger strategic context and receive an organization-wide commitment to ensure its success.

Strategizing Training and Performance Management at Anheuser-Busch

The past decade has seen a tremendous boom in the use of online training programs. One of the most comprehensive was developed by St. Louis–based beer brewer Anheuser-Busch. Anheuser-Busch has developed its Wholesaler Integrated Learning (WIL) program for its 13 company-owned branch operations, 12 breweries, and 700 independent distributors. The WIL took more than a year to develop, starting with data collection related to employee skills, knowledge, and attributes that was used to create a competency database, which in turn was used to create unique job descriptions based on almost 400 different competencies. The WIL allows employees to access the company Web site from virtually anywhere to take advantage of e-learning opportunities and measure proficiencies deemed critical for a given job description. Immediate feedback is offered and a gap analysis prepared that shows employee skill levels relative to those needed for a position, along with specific suggestions which might include classroom training, online training, reference materials, apprenticeships, coaching, and on-the-job training, for bridging any gap. WIL is far from being a simple testing and assessment program, though;

the program also ties a comprehensive performance management system into its training components. WIL analyzes employee performance relative to individual jobs and increases manager accountability by tracking when managers evaluate their employees, whether the manager has produced a development plan for each employee, and how the employee acts on that plan throughout the year.[13]

CONCLUSION

▼▼ Training and development of employees is a key strategic issue for organizations: It is the means by which organizations determine the extent to which their human assets are viable investments. Because much of the return on investment in training and development may be difficult to quantify, particularly in the short run, organizations should take a holistic view of training and development, particularly with regard to the kinds of employees and the skills and knowledge bases necessary to achieve strategic objectives. Changes in how work is performed and the organizational contexts in which work is conducted mandate that organizations conduct specific, targeted, strategic training and development initiatives as a prerequisite for continued success. ▼▼▼

CRITICAL THINKING

1. Why is training such a critical strategic issue for organizations?

2. What is transfer, and how can it best be facilitated?

3. What are the advantages and disadvantages of on-the-job, off-the-job, and online training? For what types of training is each approach most appropriate?

4. How is training likely to change in the future?

5. Using Exhibit 9-1, develop a training module to teach your classmates about your company and job responsibilities.

Reading 9.1

6. What are the competencies needed for global leaders in government? What similarities and differences exist from those needed in private industry? To what can these similarities and differences be attributed?

Reading 9.2

7. What key factors influence the success of the training programs noted in Reading 9.2?

▶▶ There is no model or ideal program for employee training and development. Effective training programs should be appropriate for the particular organization. Reading 9.2, "Designing Management Training and Development for Competitive Advantage: Lessons from the Best," illustrates several successful strategically focused training and development programs. All of these programs are conceptualized, designed, delivered, and evaluated with a strategic focus.

▶▶▶ Reading 9.3, "The Strategic Training of Employees Model: Balancing Organizational Constraints and Training Content," presents a model for the strategic conceptualization of training that is linked to the organization's objectives.

Reading 9.3

8. Explain the key concepts of the STEM model of training. Apply this model to the delivery of the course in which you are currently enrolled.

EXPERIENTIAL EXERCISES

1. In small groups, develop a tool to evaluate the learning/training taking place in the course in which you are enrolled. Be sure to consider the needs of the organization, task, and individuals; specific objectives; and design and delivery issues.

INTERNET EXERCISES

1. Visit the Web site for Virtual Learn, Inc. (http://www.virtuallearn.com). This site offers thousands of products from nearly 100 well-known vendors and publishers. Select a subject module and evaluate the opportunities for training with the following media:
   * Web
   * Book
   * Live
   * Video
   * Audio
   * CD-ROM

   What modes of delivery appear to be most popular for various subject areas? To what do you attribute this?

CHAPTER REFERENCES

1. Alutto, J. A. "Just-in-time Management Education for the 21st Century," *HR Magazine*, July 2000, p. 57.
2. Henry, K. "Local Grad School Teaches Power Tools," *Baltimore Sun*, October 13, 2002, pp. 1C, 8C.
3. Garvey, C. "The Whirlwind of a New Job," *HR Magazine*, June 2001, pp. 111–118.
4. Frase-Blunt, M. "Ready, Set, Rotate," *HR Magazine*, October 2001, pp. 46–53.
5. Leonard, B. "Training Can Be a Valuable Job Perk," *HR Magazine*, February 2001, p. 37.
6. Wells, S. "Stepping Carefully," *HR Magazine*, January 2001, 461. pp. 44–49.
7. Leonard, B. "Training Can Be a Valuable Job Perk," *HR Magazine*, February 2001, p. 37.
8. Overman, S. "Dow, Hewlett-Packard Put E-Learning to Work to Save Time and Money," *HR Magazine*, February 2004, p. 32.
9. Greengard, S. "Keyboarding Courses at Work or Home," *Workforce*, March 2000, pp. 88–92.
10. Anonymous. "Growing Number of Employers Jump on E-Learning Bandwagon," *HR Magazine*, September 2000, p. 34.
11. Silberman, R. "E-Learning Is Strategic Corporate Move, Not Just Cost-Saver," *HR News*, May 2002, p. 15.
12. Kirkpatrick, D. L. "Four Steps to Measuring Training Effectiveness," in Kirkpatrick, D. L. *Evaluating Training Programs: The Four Levels*. San Francisco: Berrett-Koehler, 1994, pp. 19–25.
13. Tyler, K. "Take E-Learning to the Next Step," *HR Magazine*, February 2002, pp. 56–61.

The Imperative of Developing Global Leaders

Dana Brower, Terry Newell, and Peter Ronayne, *The Business of Government*

Introduction

Throughout U.S. history, the domestic and foreign policy arenas have been viewed as mostly separate and distinct spheres of action. Government executives who worked in domestic agencies felt they needed to know little about other countries and seldom interacted with them, if at all. In recent years, this view has begun to change. The combined and accelerating forces of globalization and technology have forged an interconnected world in which change—and the need to anticipate and respond to it—is both faster and more complex and where the international and the domestic are inextricably linked. The United States' economic, military, and cultural power and influence make it a global actor by default, and therefore federal organizations and the people who lead them find themselves increasingly thrust into the global context.

As countless observers have noted and as individual experience tells us, with each passing day the public policy agenda is increasingly both international and domestic, or "intermestic." Indeed, "global" is the word of the new century, filling newspapers, journals, and books on current events. The new century brings with it accelerated globalization, complete with a proliferation of international agreements, institutions, and mechanisms for consultation and partnership. The events of September 11th, 2001, further these developments and remind us of the United States' role in and connection to the world.

With these thoughts in mind, the U.S. Office of Personnel Management (OPM) Federal Executive Institute (FEI), a residential executive education center for senior career government leaders, hosted a colloquium in November 2001. The colloquium, attended by over 40 leaders from the United States and other nations' governments, the private sector, academe, and the nonprofit sector, focused on the evolving global leadership role of government executives and the competencies needed to succeed in international work. This article reports on the colloquium and the implications of its findings for developing global leaders.

Whether due to the importance of building bilateral relationships or international coalitions, the heightened priority of improving homeland defense, or the simple realization that the domestic and international arenas are intricately connected, colloquium participants concluded that it is imperative that government executives lead in a global context. "So many of the issues that we deal with now, such as organized crime, are transnational in nature. We need to continually build coalitions and dialogue with leaders of all countries to address these matters in a global manner," said Jean M. Christensen, district director for the Immigration and Naturalization Service's Asia District, a colloquium participant. "We must develop leaders to work globally who fully understand the issues, possess diplomatic skills and cultural sensitivity, and can speak on behalf of the U.S. government in a multinational environment."

Like their private-sector counterparts, a considerable and growing number of federal agencies are involved in international work in this networked world. The Social Security Administration, for example, has bilateral agreements with 18 nations. The Environmental Protection Agency works with foreign counterparts to implement the Montreal Protocol, designed to protect the ozone layer from chlorofluorocarbons. The promise of agricultural biotechnology depends in large part on the U.S. Department of Agriculture and its work to ensure that biotech products can access markets abroad. The U.S. Customs Service works to combat money laundering, a transnational threat estimated at a minimum of $600 million annually. The U.S. Geological Survey faces international challenges ranging from protecting diverse biological resources to identifying the world's remaining energy resources.

The imperative of global leadership is felt particularly at the National Aeronautics and Space

Administration (NASA), which has more than 3,000 international agreements with over 130 countries. NASA's approach to leadership development includes emphasis on several international competencies (Figure 1). "Global competencies are critical in today's ever changing world, from an understanding of the political, social, and economic environment to cross-cultural relationships and international partnerships and alliances," explains Jan Moore, program manager for NASA's Leadership and Management Development. "At NASA," explains Moore, "international cooperation and an understanding of working in a global environment are critical to organizational success. Understanding and cooperation create access to unique capabilities and expertise, provide access to locations outside the United States, and open new avenues for discovery."

A 2001 State Department working paper observed, "Currently, there are approximately 42 different U.S. federal agencies in more than 160 countries performing a variety of functions that serve the national interest and help assure national security. These functions have significant impact on our domestic economy as well as on U.S. world relations. U.S. government personnel, regardless of agency, performing these core functions at home and abroad face significant challenges as they struggle to keep pace with world events and represent the U.S. from an informed position." Similarly, in a report on the future of human capital in the federal workforce, the General Accounting Office emphasized that "government organizations must undergo a cultural transformation allowing them to work better with other governmental organizations, non-governmental organizations, and the private

FIGURE 1: NASA LEADERSHIP MODEL

sector, *both domestically and internationally* [emphasis added], to achieve results."

Mirroring federal agency trends, a significant number of federal executives are involved in international work. Overall, the federal government has more than 50,000 employees stationed overseas. It is important to keep in mind, however, that global leadership does not require travel abroad. Many federal executives act and lead in a global context from the confines of their offices in the United States.

Recent surveys by the FEI help illustrate the extensive international roles filled by today's executives. Although only about 3 percent of the career federal executives (GS-15s and Senior Executive Service) who attend FEI are actually stationed abroad, a much higher percentage is involved in international work. For example, 37 percent report collaborating with other agencies or organizations on international projects, 37 percent report traveling abroad for work, and 20 percent report managing programs that provide goods or services to other nations. (See Table 1.)

"Going Global" Requires Globally Competent Leaders

Although executives' roles overseas are expanding, their preparation for success in international work may not be keeping pace. The State Department's Overseas Presence Advisory Panel (OPAP), established in the wake of the 1998 terrorist bombings of U.S. embassies in Nairobi and Dar es Salaam, looked at the readiness of State Department personnel to succeed internationally. The OPAP report cited human resource issues in overseas posts as a major concern, stating that "there was universal agreement that more training was needed in languages, leadership and management, and new issues." The report also estimated that "up to one-half of Department personnel who took assignments abroad last year did so without appropriate training. In addition, the training available was truncated or ignored." Finally, the OPAP report recommended "that the Department and other agencies mandate that all employees undergo security training and area studies before going overseas."

If the State Department recognizes a need to augment its training programs for employees assigned overseas, it seems logical that other domestic agencies might also have work to do in training their employees for international work. A series of leadership development surveys conducted by FEI in 2001–2002 bear this out. The surveys found that 57 percent of executives reported that their responsibilities included some type of international work. Yet among those executives involved in international work, almost 60 percent received no formal preparation for their assignments. Over two-thirds (68 percent) of federal executives surveyed reported that they spoke no language other than English, and executives rated their own proficiency for international work below the midpoint of a five-point scale on six of eight key topics. (See Figure 2.)

The President's Management Agenda (PMA) calls for establishing a "right-sized" U.S. overseas presence, which includes better coordination among federal agencies to ensure that the right number of people with the right talents are deployed internationally. President Bush's call for better strategic management of human capital also supports the notion that all personnel involved in international work should be recruited, selected, trained, and managed effectively. Without sufficient attention to developing the global leadership competence of U.S. government executives, it will be difficult to achieve these

TABLE 1: TYPES OF INTERNATIONAL WORK REPORTED BY FEDERAL EXECUTIVES

- Collaborating with other agencies/organizations on international projects (37%)
- Travel abroad (37%)
- Managing programs that provide goods/services to other nations (20%)
- International negotiations (16%)
- International policy development (14%)
- Managing programs that receive/inspect people, goods, and services from other nations (10%)
- Supervising government workers/contractors abroad (8%)
- Living abroad (3%)

Source: 2001–2002 Survey by Federal Executive Institute

FIGURE 2: EXECUTIVES' PERCEIVED PROFICIENCY IN WORKING INTERNATIONALLY
Where 1 = poor and 5 = excellent

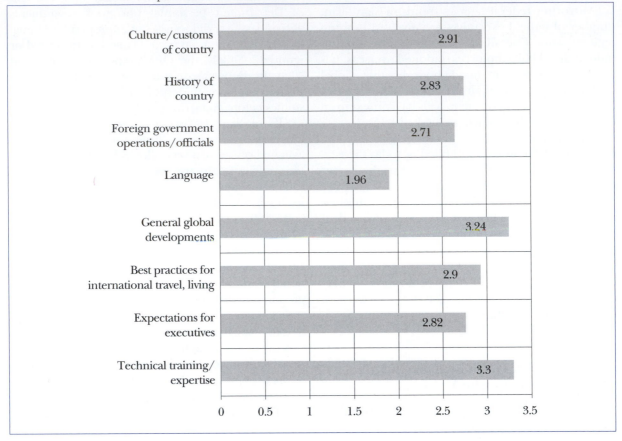

PMA goals and effectively serve the interests of the United States in an age of globalization. Patricia McGinnis, president and CEO of the Council for Excellence in Government, underscores this point: "The Council believes that career federal executives must be able to lead for results in all aspects of their work. Today, an increasing number of career public servants outside the federal government's traditional foreign affairs community have responsibilities with an international dimension. Improving their ability as leaders in a global context has therefore become a very important goal."

The World of Global Competencies

Although no concrete consensus or definitive work exists on exactly what skills and attitudes federal executives need to succeed as global leaders, experts echo common themes and elements. Lists of critical global competencies invariably include emphasis on

the need for effective intercultural communication skills and broader knowledge of world affairs and trends, combined with the ability to represent U.S. interests effectively.

The Centre for Intercultural Learning of the Canadian Foreign Service Institute recently conducted a major research project on intercultural effectiveness. Their Year 2000 report identified nine critical competencies, including understanding the concept of culture, intercultural communication, and an attitude of modesty and respect. All nine competencies are outlined in Table 2.

In his research on global leadership effectiveness in the private sector, Dr. Robert Rosen of Healthy Companies International found four broad areas of competence critical to global leadership success. In his book *Global Literacies*, he labels these as personal literacy (understanding and valuing yourself), social literacy (engaging and challenging others), business literacy (focusing and mobilizing

In 1995, the Centre for Intercultural Learning at the Canadian Foreign Service Institute began a project to more fully understand executive effectiveness in a global context. According to the Centre's findings, globally effective executives possess the following nine competencies:

1. Adaptation skills—the ability to cope personally, professionally, and in one's family context with the conditions and challenges of living and working in another culture.

2. An Attitude of Modesty and Respect—demonstrating modesty about one's own culture's answers to problems, a respect for the ways of the local culture, a willingness to learn from and consult with locals before coming to conclusions.

3. An Understanding of the Concept of Culture—and the pervasive influence it will have on life and work abroad.

4. Knowledge of the Host Country and Culture—and trying constantly to expand that knowledge.

5. Relationship-Building Skills—both social/personal and professional.

6. Self-Knowledge—one's own background, motivations, strengths, and weaknesses.

7. Intercultural Communication—the ability to convey thoughts and expectations in ways that are understandable and culturally sensitive, without fear of participating in the local culture and language, and that empathize with how locals see the world.

8. Organizational Skills—improving organizational structures, processes, and morale in ways that balance one's own and the host culture's values.

9. Personal and Professional Commitment—to the intercultural assignment and the life experience in another culture.

your organization), and cultural literacy (valuing and leveraging cultural differences).

Explains Rosen: "To thrive, all companies must adopt a global-centric approach to business. They must develop a multi-cultural perspective, an international knowledge base, and a global imagination—in other words, a cultural literacy." While Rosen's work focused on the private sector, he finds the lessons equally applicable, indeed perhaps even more essential, for the public sector. "The public sector faces the same trends—namely the new context of interconnectedness and globalization—that are influencing the private sector. These trends are likewise transforming the roles of federal, state, and local government in a global society." And, adds Rosen, "America's role as the sole superpower requires that government executives be prepared for global responsibility."

The frameworks offered by Rosen and the Canadian Foreign Service Institute have much in common, including the strong emphasis on learning other languages—not only to be able to communicate but also to appreciate another's culture. Those gathered at FEI's global leadership colloquium validated and stressed these frameworks. Given the unique role of U.S. government executives in representing not only their agencies and their missions but also the United States and its Constitution, additional global leadership competencies were identified:

- Understanding the history of U.S. foreign relations, its constitutional history, and how both are understood and examined by the rest of the world.
- Understanding U.S. business, global economics, and key U.S. government domestic and international goals and policies and how they interact with each other—sometimes in consistent and reinforcing ways and sometimes in ways that make the nation's international agenda more challenging to implement
- Understanding the evolving structure of international relationships, including regional and international organizations and alliances and how these influence U.S. policies and agencies
- Strong negotiation skills
- Security consciousness

These competencies are critical for government executive leadership in international work *whether or not* an executive actually travels or works overseas. It is a potentially costly myth that a government executive sitting in an office in the United States can succeed internationally by relying solely on technical competence.

A Food and Drug Administration Experience

Of course, models and lists of competencies only go so far in communicating what executives must know and be able to do in their international work. The presentation by one of the colloquium participants, Naomi Kawin, put the competencies in context. As the associate director for International Agreements of the Office of International Programs of the Food and Drug Administration (FDA), Kawin's job involves no less than helping ensure the safety of foods and medical products coming to the United States from abroad. Although she travels overseas only occasionally in her work, she interacts extensively with other nations. To succeed, she and her FDA colleagues must wear at least three hats: regulator, diplomat, and leader. Reflecting on her work, Kawin offered a set of competencies for federal executives drawn from her experience.

Kawin's comments and suggestions bear a striking resemblance to the global literacies identified by Rosen and the critical skills identified by the Canadian government. The benefit and importance of global leadership competencies have strong domestic connections as well. Many of the skills essential for leadership in a global context, especially those related to understanding and working with people from other cultures, are increasingly important to government executive effectiveness *within* U.S. society. U.S. Census Bureau data and projections demonstrate that our society is already very culturally diverse and will become more so. California, for example, no longer has an ethnic group that constitutes more than half of the population. Successful domestic programs thus demand leadership from executives knowledgeable about and comfortable working across the cultures that define not only the world but also U.S. society in the 21st century.

Lessons from the Food and Drug Administration

International work takes several forms in the FDA. Inspectors travel to other countries to examine industry and government practices, Scientists work on international issues, including the development of international standards. And FDA staff work on negotiating international agreements and other collaborative international ventures.

Whether or not they travel overseas, all these staff need an awareness of cultural differences including how another's culture can affect regulation and product safety. In light of the September 11th attacks, personal security awareness is critical. Another set of skills—"International Survival 101"—includes protocol, diplomatic sensibilities, how to work with American embassies and interpreters, and being cognizant of ethical issues. In terms of effective leadership in a global context, federal executives across government need to possess a fuller understanding of international organizations, trade agreements and regional blocs, prominent global trends, and the influence of all of these on the United States. Also needed is openness both to collaboration and to new ways of doing business, supported in turn by knowledge of negotiation skills—even for seemingly non-negotiating contexts.

Developing Global Leaders

Although we may know what competencies government leaders need for effective global leadership, we do not excel at providing them. A few agencies, including the State Department and OPM, have programs to address some of the essential skills and attitudes.

Agencies are clearly at various stages in implementing development programs focused on global leadership. At OPM's FEI, the four-week long *Leadership for a Democratic Society* experience includes a central "global perspectives" theme as part of FEI's ongoing work to prepare senior civil servants for leadership in a global context. The sessions and courses on this curriculum theme provide an opportunity for executives to examine critical global developments and their implications for U.S. society and government. In addition, FEI works to foster global perspectives by periodically hosting international executives as participants in the program.

The State Department has long stood at the forefront of international and multi-cultural development in the federal sector. The Foreign Service Institute (FSI) is the U.S. government's primary training institution for officers and support personnel of the U.S. foreign affairs community, preparing U.S. diplomats and other professionals to advance U.S. foreign affairs interests overseas and in Washington, D.C. At the National Foreign Affairs Training Center, the FSI provides more than 400 courses, including some 60 foreign languages, to more than 30,000 enrollees a year from the State Department and to more than 40 other government agencies and the military service branches.

More recently, the State Department has placed renewed focus on leadership issues and competency development with the establishment of FSI's School of Leadership and Management. Inaugurated in June 2000, the School of Leadership and Management offers a competency-based curriculum with classes that emphasize valuing diversity, creativity, flexibility, ethical behavior, strategic thinking, transparency, and effective communication. The School's first dean, Ambassador Aurelia E. Brazeal, stressed the importance of its mission: "Clearly, the challenges to American global leadership are unprecedented. FSI's School of Leadership and Management is committed to bringing innovative, world-class leadership development programs to professionals in our foreign affairs community. Our curriculum is designed to foster leadership qualities that are, in my view, essential to effectiveness in our rapidly changing world." These and similar programs play an important role in fostering global leadership competencies in the federal executive corps. However, the U.S. government has no comprehensive approach or system in place to deliberately and carefully develop public-sector leaders for success in their critical "intermestic" work. An unwavering federal commitment to *this type* of global leadership training needed by government executives will be a requisite first step in developing such a system of executive development.

Participants in the November colloquium called for just this type of comprehensive, systemic approach in which training would play a key role but by no means the only role in developing government leaders to succeed in their international assignments.

The colloquium identified seven specific recommendations aimed toward building this comprehensive development system for our nation's global leaders.

Recommendation 1: Build the business case for global leadership competence. Without a shared understanding of how and where effective global leadership matters to government agencies, it will be hard to enlist support for developing global leaders. The consensus at the colloquium was that there is a need but that need has not been well documented in business terms.

Recommendation 2: Build support for developing global leaders in government among government agencies and in the broader society. Although a documented business case may serve the needs of policy makers, more broad-based support is needed within agencies and from the public. Public events, speeches, and other means are needed to demonstrate that effective global leadership is as important in building a healthy food supply as it is in building foreign policy.

Recommendation 3: Develop a model of global leadership competence. The colloquium participants urged that specific competencies be identified and communicated to illustrate what effective global leaders do. What skills, knowledge, and attitudes do they need to be competent internationally? The colloquium concluded that the competencies government executives need, for example, can be thought of as falling into three broad groups:

- **Broad-based leadership knowledge**—for example, U.S. and foreign government operations, U.S. foreign and domestic policies, and global economics
- **Generic leadership skills**—for example, self-knowledge, communication, cultural sensitivity, security consciousness, and negotiation skills
- **Agency-, sector-, or country-specific knowledge and skills**—for example, international trading blocs, intellectual property protection, international labor agreements, global environmental issues, and Chinese history and politics

The third group is important for executives working in specific areas or countries. The first and second skill areas can reasonably be delivered to a more diverse government audience.

Recommendation 4: Integrate global competencies into leadership selection and development programs. Identifying needed competencies is necessary but not sufficient for leadership development. The colloquium urged that these competencies be integrated into OPM's Executive Core Qualifications and that they be used to help select, develop, and appraise leaders with significant international responsibilities.

Recommendation 5: Strengthen interagency and public/private partnerships to provide for global leadership development. Global leadership in government depends on a collaborative partnership among the public, private, and nonprofit sectors. So too should the *development* of global leaders in government. There was consensus at the colloquium that the three sectors working collaboratively could produce more innovative and effective models of developing leaders for the "intermestic" world than just relying on government to do it alone.

Recommendation 6: Create certification programs for developing global leaders in government. Such programs would draw attention to this important area and ensure the sufficient depth and breadth of coverage needed to go beyond "awareness" to skill mastery.

Recommendation 7: Develop a center of excellence—a place or consortium that could gather, offer, and spread the best programs, tools, and resources for developing global leaders in government. The colloquium recognized that many innovative training and development resources already exist within and outside the United States, while others need to be created. But it is nearly impossible for a busy government worker to find and access what is available, much less what needs to be created. Until such resources become easy to access, global leadership development remains a promise, not a program.

The development of public-sector leaders prepared for success in a dynamic global context is a long-term journey that members of the federal community must travel together. U.S. leadership on the world stage requires individual leaders prepared for the international context in which they operate. Overall, a commitment to a globally savvy leadership corps represents a farsighted vision of leadership development: one that provides government executives with a greater perspective with which to lead organizations and design public policy in the global context of the 21st century.

Source: Brower, D., Newell, T., and Ronayne, P. "The Imperative of Global Leaders." *The Business of Government* 2002 pp. 18–24.

Designing Management Training and Development for Competitive Advantage: Lessons from the Best

Judy D. Olian, Cathy C. Durham, Amy L. Kristof, Kenneth G. Brown,
Richard M. Pierce, Linda Kunder, *Human Resource Planning*

Increasingly, exemplary organizations are recognizing that a workforce with superior skills is a primary vehicle for sustainable competitive advantage. Although selection is one traditional means to accomplish this advantage, strategically focused training and development offers a more flexible and long-term advantage. A few outstanding organizations use training and development to sustain competitive advantage through continuous learning. In this benchmarking study, we identified "best-in-class" organizational leaders in management-level training and development. We reviewed training system materials and interviewed training and development executives from these organizations to understand and describe how the elements of their training and development systems are linked to, and advance, the leadership's strategic agenda.

"In the 21st century, the education and skills of the workforce will end up being the dominant competitive weapon."

[Lester Thurow, *Head to Head*, 1992].

Organizations can buy skills through hiring, or they can develop skills through training and development (T&D) activities. This paper focuses on strategically aligned training and development systems that advance and sustain the organization's competitive position in its market. Traditionally, T&D systems were relegated to narrowly defined support roles, where individuals were trained around current job-based deficiencies or predicted knowledge and skill needs. A few exemplary organizations, however, view a workforce with superior skills as a primary source of sustainable competitive advantage. In these organizations, T&D becomes the critical means for creating readiness and flexibility for change across all organizational levels, and there are strong linkages between all facets of the T&D system and the strategic leadership and planning processes of the business. Readiness and flexibility are achieved largely through supervisory, management, and executive training, as these individuals set the boundaries for modification and continuous improvement of existing organizational practices.

Investment in T&D is highly variable across U.S. employers. In 1995, U.S. organizations allocated approximately $52.2 billion for informal employee T&D (Industry Report, 1995). It has been estimated that over half the money invested in training annually (approximately $27 billion) is spent by just 15,000 organizations, or merely 0.5% of all U.S. employers. Among those, only about 100 to 200 spend more than 1.5% of their payroll on T&D (Stone, 1991). These disproportionate expenditures are made because of the presumed market returns on the investment in employee development and learning.

Despite these presumed benefits, few prescriptions are available to executives on how best to create systems that are aligned with, and actually advance, the organization's strategic agenda. Although much has been written about the design of T&D systems from an instructional perspective, little has been offered on how to include the T&D function in the leadership agenda or the strategy implementation process. Yet, organizations that have "best-in-class" T&D systems offer certain insights. This study was designed to understand and describe how these best-in-class organizations design and utilize supervisory and management T&D to achieve and sustain competitive advantage.

Method

Benchmarking is frequently used to identify the practices of organizations recognized as leaders and innovators in a particular area (Xerox, 1992; Weatherly, 1992). Once these best-in-class practices have been identified, other organizations can use them as a comparison point for assessing their own progress. Thus the goal of this paper is to collect benchmark information and derive an integrated model of how the best T&D organizations structure, implement, and conduct management-level T&D.

The benchmark organizations in T&D were selected if included in at least one of the following five sources: Malcolm Baldrige National Quality Award winners (1988–1992), *FORTUNE Magazine* "Top 20 Managed Companies" (1990–1993), American Society for Training and Development "Corporate Award" winners (1985–1992), *Training Magazine* "Readers' Survey Award" winners (1992), or identified by subject matter experts. A total of 62 organizations were thus identified and contacted.

Forty-two percent of the organizations (26 of the 62) served as the final benchmark sample by submitting written information describing their organization-wide T&D practices and by participating in a structured 45 to 90 minute telephone interview. Responses to the structured interview questions were summarized and tabulated into means and frequencies, where appropriate. Fifty percent of participants interviewed were the heads of their units and all were specialists, key consultants, managers, or executives in their organization's T&D operation. A complete list of participating organizations is available from the authors. T&D practices from the benchmark organizations were supplemented with materials mailed by the participating organizations and culled from the literature. Throughout this paper, all references to company policy and practices were derived from these interviews and sources, except where otherwise noted.

A "best-practices model" was developed from commonalities in the information we collected. This article summarizes interview results around elements of the model. We focus primarily on the T&D elements that (1) provide non-technical training to managers and executives, and (2) create a context for linkages between the leadership's strategic business agenda and a change in, or renewal of, workforce skills. We de-emphasize parts of the model that have been addressed adequately elsewhere (e.g., content and delivery methods [Goldstein 1993]).

Overview: The T&D Framework

The major elements of the T&D framework adopted in this paper are portrayed in Exhibit 1. These elements were derived from analysis of the critical success factors in organizations we studied, expert knowledge, and a review of the T&D literature.

As shown in Exhibit 1, the framework's major elements are organized around a Plan, Do, Check, Act cycle, sometimes known as a Shewhart or Deming cycle. This model provides both a conceptual and a practical means to distinguish between the different components and stages of training and development.

Benchmark organizations engage in a significant amount of strategically oriented "planning," often involving the organization's leadership, prior to the introduction of T&D activities. They then implement the T&D ("do") and critically evaluate ("check") the success of T&D activities against their strategically driven objectives. The "act" phase reflects the

EXHIBIT 1: TRAINING AND DEVELOPMENT FRAMEWORK: BEST PRACTICES ELEMENTS

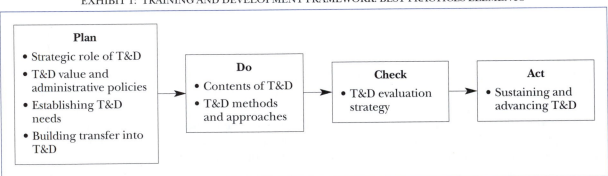

sustained effort and renewed commitment that preserve T&D activities as a continuously improving process and an integral element of the organization's execution of its strategy. The practices comprising the present model represent an idealized system—one that combines system elements across the exemplary organizations studied here, rather than reflecting any single organization's T&D system.

T&D Framework, Phase I: Plan

T&D planning is the first step in creating systematic linkage between the business strategy and the T&D system. It establishes T&D as a strategic priority involving the creating of policies and values that support T&D programs, assessment of strategically relevant T&D needs, and development of plans for the transfer of T&D into job performance. Benchmark company practices in each area of planning are discussed below.

HOW DO EXEMPLARY COMPANIES TIE T&D TO THEIR STRATEGIC BUSINESS PLANS?

In benchmarking organizations, the T&D system advances the organization's mission and is exploited as a source of strategic advantage. In these organizations, there is an intimate and structured linkage between the organization's strategic mission and the goals of the T&D program. T&D goals and processes are reviewed and updated annually around the changing strategic needs of the business units or organizational components. T&D executives are integrated into the strategic planning process to assure that strategic goals are formulated using accurate information about the availability of the necessary talent to realize the goals (Casner-Lotto, 1988).

Apple uses both human and information support systems to fold business executives into the T&D mission and goal formulation process. At Apple's corporate T&D headquarters—Apple University— regular forums with executives are conducted to exchange information about the strategic direction of the firm and its business units. In addition, professionals from Apple University are permanently assigned to business units and serve as a continuous information funnel between these units and the university. Apple also uses its worldwide information network as an electronic campus to collect information about changing business requirements, and to facilitate immediate responsiveness in T&D offerings.

In another corporation, Motorola, the CEO is one of four "outside" members of the Advisory Board of Directors to Motorola University (Wiggenhorn, 1990). This assures tight coupling between the CEO's agenda and its implementation through T&D.

Procter & Gamble's (P&G) executives demonstrate the significance they attach to internal development through their personal involvement. The interview conducted for this study indicated that members of the executive committee teach at P&G College whenever they are physically nearby. For example, over the course of 1992, the CEO had taught at P&G College nine times.

In benchmark organizations, deliberation over and approval of the organization's T&D objectives are among the Board of Directors' management oversight priorities. This is true of the Corning Glass Corporation, where the question "What do we need to do with people to meet the development needs of the company?" has been addressed by the Board of Directors annually since 1979.

WHAT POLICIES AND VALUES DO EXEMPLARY COMPANIES USE TO SUPPORT T&D SYSTEMS?

Many factors define whether a T&D system is strategically aligned and a critical contributor to the organization's competitive advantage. Some of those factors are structural, such as the previously discussed linkages between the organization's planning process and the T&D operation. Two additional factors discussed below are policies, formal means of communicating T&D expectations, and value statements, more informal and decentralized means of pushing managers to develop attitudes toward T&D that are aligned with the business strategy.

Policy statements provide clear and consistent communication regarding expected attitudes and behaviors that support learning. According to Chairman James Houghton of Corning Glass, mandatory policies helped his company move T&D success to a new level:

"We talked about the importance of training for years, but until we instituted comprehensive and mandatory programs, our efforts never matched our intentions" (cited in Carnevale, 1990).

Fifty-eight percent of the organizations we interviewed have some form of explicit T&D policies. Some T&D policies have straightforward objectives of achieving consistent employee access to, and participation in, T&D. Most of these "rules" address budget allocation for T&D, required levels or hours of T&D participation, or required T&D before or after promotions.

Although not always articulated as a policy, these benchmark companies allot, on average, over three percent of their payroll to employee T&D. Andersen Consulting reports an investment as high as seven percent of payroll. Professional and nonprofessional (e.g., technical) employees receive, on average, a four percent allocation, compared to three percent for managers, supervisors, and executives. U.S. national averages are far lower, estimated at no more than 1.4% of payroll among private employers (Carnevale, 1990). About 90% of U.S. private employers make almost no investment in T&D, compared to T&D investments of three percent to four percent of payroll in the average German or Japanese company (Bernstein, Brandt, Carlson & Padley, 1992). Nevertheless, establishing policies and rules regarding T&D expenditures may be associated with increased T&D support in the U.S.

Other rules-oriented policies refer to the annual number of hours each employee is obliged to spend in T&D. In these best-in-class organizations, executives spend an average of almost 45 hours in annual training, and supervisors and managers almost 51 hours. Some companies, such as ARCO and 3M, specify a minimum of 40 hours of training per year, regardless of organizational level. AT&T Universal Card requires 80 hours of annual training per employee, and at Andersen Consulting, Zytec, and the Saturn division of General Motors, the figure is 100 hours.

Finally, many organizations establish T&D policies as part of structured career paths, a prerequisite for consideration for promotion, or a requirement once the promotion is obtained. P&G requires employees to go back to school each time they receive a new promotion. Other organizations specify that eligibility for promotion is contingent upon successful completion of certain mandatory programs or developmental assignments.

Benchmark organizations also strive to mold the attitudes and behaviors of their supervisors and managers through values-oriented T&D statements. These values are most effective if reinforced by relevant organizational outcomes. For instance, some of these organizations assert that "every manager is held accountable for the development of his/her employees." If managers' own rewards and promotions are made contingent upon their success as developers of talent, the value is likely transformed into practice. For example, Coca-Cola's mission statement, Vision 2000, includes four components, one of which emphasizes the responsibility of managers to develop their subordinates.

> [Coca-Cola] has a Competency/Success model which targets commitment to development at two levels: Self and Others. This is measured in managers' performance reviews. Managers are given feedback on their developmental success, and compensated for how well they do it.

In other organizations, statements and policies laud the value of self-driven T&D—that it is the individual employee's responsibility to seek out and capitalize on T&D opportunities. When managers and supervisors internalize these attitudes, a vibrant and supportive learning environment is created, in which employees feel encouraged to constantly expand their knowledge base. For example, Digital Equipment proclaims that employees own their own careers and employees are responsible for structuring their career development and seeking out T&D opportunities (Fossum, 1991).

HOW DO EXEMPLARY COMPANIES LINK BUSINESS STRATEGY WITH T&D NEEDS ASSESSMENT?

In addition to structures, policies, and values, T&D practices also account for an effective T&D system. The first of these practices relevant to planning is the process for establishing T&D needs. Needs are influenced by factors both internal and external to the organization. The interviews were designed to assess the relative reliance on environmental, organizational, job, and person information. Which of the following questions (rated on a 7-point scale: 1 = minimal reliance and 7 = heavy reliance) is most likely to drive needs assessment in participating organizations? (1) "What is changing in the external environment that demands employee T&D?" (2) "What types of T&D support the organization's mission or strategy?" (3) "What jobs/tasks need improvement through T&D?" elicited job information, and (4) "Which individuals need T&D?"

In these benchmark organizations, the establishment of T&D needs is driven most often by the organization's mission and strategy, with an average rating of 6.27. Individual performance factors, environmental trends, and job-based information appear to be less influential in establishing T&D needs, at 5.31, 5.08 and 5.04 respectively.

Although some information is derived from employee needs surveys, T&D needs assessment appears weighted toward information collected from top management. Several organizations, including Apple, Corning, and Motorola, conduct annual conferences with the organization's most senior executives to elicit their views of the skills that will be needed to achieve strategic short-term and long-term goals.

Even though environmentally focused needs assessment is not the foremost driver of T&D, benchmark organizations engage in significant environmental scanning to remain informed about, and responsive to, changing external trends and requirements. For example, Xerox benchmarks other exemplary companies and collects information from their partners and suppliers to best understand the economic, cultural, and technological trends affecting their business. Similarly, Northern Telecom uses customer focus groups to learn about product and service requirements and to garner suggestions regarding employee development needs. In these companies, however, environmental demands drive adjustments to the business strategy, with T&D changes implemented as a result of decisions to modify the business strategy.

HOW DO EXEMPLARY ORGANIZATIONS BUILD TRANSFER INTO T&D?

As companies assess employees' developmental needs and begin making plans to deliver T&D, an important consideration is T&D transfer. Transfer refers to the degree of continuity between learning in the T&D context, and behaviors and results in the job environment. There are three basic approaches to maximizing transfer: overlap between T&D and job contexts, integration between T&D and other elements of the human resource management system, and integration of management into the T&D process.

The first critical requirement for transfer is an overlap between learning in training, and requirements on the job. The overlap assures that the knowledge, abstract concepts, attitudes, or behaviors acquired through T&D match the strategic business needs.

The best and easiest way to select a proper [T&D] technique is to ask whether it will have the participants doing the things we want them to be able to do when they get back to the job. . . . Computerized management games are great—provided the decisions people are asked to make while running the imaginary company are the same kinds of decisions they will make in the real one. Otherwise, the supervisors have a lot of fun running the fictitious company, then go back . . . [and continue] to make the same mistakes they always did (Broadwell, 1993).

The relevance of T&D content is enhanced when there is an obvious connection between T&D objectives and the strategic mission and goals of the organization; such relevancy enhances transfer. Indeed, in the interviewed companies, the linkage of T&D to the business strategy was the most prominent transfer strategy (rated 5.81 on a 7-point scale), followed by transfer maximized through similarity between T&D content and the job environment (5.31).

The simplest way to maximize overlap between the job and training environments is through on-the-job training. Even though most T&D occurs away from the job (65% in our sample), there is a noticeable trend toward incorporating learning into the job itself. Taking people off the job to learn is simply becoming too costly. On-the-job T&D reduces downtime, eliminates travel costs, maximizes content relevance, and increases the likelihood that the learning will become embedded into routine processes and interactions among colleagues. Moreover, management is an observer to, if not a participant in, the learning process and is able to facilitate and reinforce the continuation of the desired behaviors. General Mills indicated that only about 10% of its training occurs away from the job. The interviewee noted that, "[General Mills has] a very large focus on on-the-job training. . . . We feel that most of the training comes from experiential learning."

A second transfer strategy is making T&D part of an overarching human resource framework that systematically hires, promotes, develops, and rewards people using a core set of competencies and behaviors. Such continuity across HR systems helps translate T&D learning into behaviors and results on the job. Texas Instruments, for example, uses a single integrated HR system in which critical competencies are derived from job analyses. These critical competencies drive all HR subsystems and serve as the common underlying competency framework for selection, promotion, and reward decisions, and for establishing T&D requirements for a given job.

In a random survey of U.S. T&D directors, 21.5% reported that supervisory trainees are held accountable for improved performance following training, as part of their performance appraisals (Taylor, 1992). Transfer is greatly encouraged when promotion decisions are predicated on evidence of T&D transfer, for example, that the trainee's performance appraisal documents that he or she is successfully applying newly acquired skills. Pay-for-knowledge systems are also a way to translate T&D into results on the job.

Another strategy that integrates T&D with other HR functions is structured career pathing, mentioned previously as a T&D policy option. Individuals receive T&D at critical junctures in their careers, and it is reinforced through their career progression. Northern Telecom has an executive career path that is interspersed with four T&D phases: MLF (Manager Leader Forum) I, for employees about to become managers or very new managers; MLF II, for first- and second-level managers; MLF III, for Director level and up; and Global Leadership Forum, for only the most senior executives, by invitation from the CEO. Continued promotion at Northern Telecom requires active participation in these milestone training activities.

The third transfer mechanism recognizes that it is not enough that co-workers and supervisors are passive observers of the trainee's improvement following T&D. To ensure transfer, they must be involved in proactively supporting knowledge-based and behavioral improvements from T&D. Involving management in all aspects of T&D is critical in obtaining this level of support.

As an example, in the quality management area, Xerox implements T&D sequentially across the organization, from the top down. With the exception of the chief executive and the most junior person in the organization, everyone receives the T&D twice, once as trainee and once as trainer to his/her direct reports or peers. In Xerox's vernacular, this is called "LUTI"—Learn, Use, Train, and Inspect. The result is that every manager at Xerox knows how to support the new behaviors, and no manager is surprised by behavioral changes in the workplace that come as a result of training.

Target, an operator of retail stores with over 90,000 employees, uses line managers as the primary deliverers of T&D. In its interview, Target reported that 2,000 workshops were delivered in 1991, of which only 150 were conducted by corporate training staff. The remaining training sessions were conducted by line managers, many of whom clamored to be trainers. Training is not a dead-end career choice for these managers—many current executives at Target were former trainers.

An alternative way of familiarizing trainees' managers with training content is practiced by BellSouth and Coca-Cola. These organizations provide managers with written or video reports summarizing the content of employees' T&D and suggesting strategies to reinforce learning. Managers also are held accountable for the returns on dollars invested in employee T&D, around behaviors and results directly tied to T&D objectives.

Finally, management is involved through the active planning of T&D with employees. Noel and Dennehy (1991) suggest a "partnership" between learners and their supervisors, who meet together before and after T&D to go over expectations and results. The process can be made explicit through pre-T&D "contracts" between employees and their managers. Expected T&D results are specified, including how they will be monitored and facilitated, and a trainee re-entry plan is designed to create continuity between learning in the T&D environment and behaviors and results on the job.

T&D Framework, Phase 2: Do

The Do phase involves selecting specific training program content and choosing how to deliver it. Because there is a wealth of useful information in the T&D literature about content and delivery methods, we discuss these parts of the T&D framework only briefly.

HOW DO EXEMPLARY ORGANIZATIONS DETERMINE THE CONTENT OF T&D?

Benchmark organizations derive the content of T&D from their strategic objectives, culture and values, and their present and predicted competency and skill needs. That is, decisions about T&D content logically follow the earlier phases of the framework. Unfortunately, T&D is fraught with fads, and in no area is this more evident than in choices about T&D content and methods. Often, organizations are swept into supporting T&D programs because they are "in," without examining whether the purposes served by these programs fit their own profile of objectives and needs.

The most commonly addressed T&D area is leadership training. Many organizations provide leadership training through short courses. For example, in an attempt to boost the probability of success when employees receive promotions into management, Federal Express developed a series of critical hurdles for entry into its Leadership Institute. Hurdles for prospective managers include attending a class designed to provide a realistic preview of managerial responsibility, receiving leadership coaching, obtaining a recommendation from one's next-level manager, receiving anonymous peer evaluations, and making a presentation to a panel of senior managers (Galagan, 1991)—and that's what it takes just to enter the program.

A few organizations have developed leadership programs that become integrated capstone events in a structured career path. An example is Coca-Cola's 10-week management development program for persons in line to become general managers. The program includes traditional leadership training, as well as internally designed simulations that are "mirror images of business in Coca-Cola," and an action learning program in which four member teams are given cross-functional and cross-cultural project assignments and sent to locations outside their native countries.

GE also employs an action learning approach in its four-week training program for mid- to senior-level executives. Teams of executives are given actual business problems identified by the company's top officials, such as Chief Executive Jack Welch. After a month, teams make presentations to Welch and other senior managers. With the help of consultants and business school professors, the student executives go around the world learning to function effectively in teams, finding the information they need, and making decisions with little time and information (O'Reilly, 1993).

HOW DO EXEMPLARY ORGANIZATIONS CHOOSE THE BEST T&D METHOD?

Just as T&D content areas are varied, so too are methods for T&D delivery. Choice of T&D delivery methods depends on the organizational culture and values, T&D objectives and content, the profiles of trainees and trainers, financial and technological resource availability, time, location, and political

constraints. One study suggests that organizations are relying quite heavily on in-house T&D services. Sixty-nine percent of T&D is designed and delivered in-house, compared to 31% purchased from outside vendors (Carnevale, 1990). However, a more recent survey suggests that in contrast to training for sales, customer service, and production workers (which is more likely delivered in-house), many managerial and executive training programs are purchased from outside suppliers (Industry Report, 1995). Thus, there seems to be a range of alternatives for delivery, with the most popular option being a combination of in-house and outside suppliers (Industry Report, 1995).

Several developments are occurring with regard to T&D methods of delivery: a shift toward on-the-job training, increased efficiency, exploitation of technology to aid learning, increased emphasis on teams, and a focus on mentoring. First is the shift to on-the-job training mentioned previously. Although the most common T&D methods continue to be classroom-based, many best-in-class companies are increasing the proportion of on-the-job T&D experiences. A problem with this approach is that on-the-job training is often unplanned and unsystematic. Increasingly, however, organizations are realizing that systematically planned on-the-job training can be more efficient and cost-effective than off-the-job training. General Mills' enthusiasm for on-the-job training was described earlier, and Hewlett-Packard has almost 80% of T&D delivered through the job.

Beyond the transfer and efficiency advantages of on-the-job delivery, T&D incorporated into the job provides an opportunity to accomplish organizational business during the training. Similar to the GE program mentioned earlier, ARCO utilizes an action learning approach:

> . . . where training is part of the real life [business] situation. During training, managers will address and come up with solutions to real-world ARCO problems and issues. . . . [Action learning] ties all training to reality, to the actual daily business of the people who are in the courses.

A second development with regard to T&D methods of delivery involves attempts to increase the efficiency and cost-effectiveness of off-the-job T&D. For example, management at Andersen Consulting has determined that half of the firm's training costs ($270 million in 1989) are in trainees' time. If they can find a way to reduce that time investment, they stand to reap substantial benefits (Graham, 1990). Similarly, between 1991 and 1994, Motorola University's goal has been to achieve a 50% per year reduction in the cycle time for design, delivery, and administration of new T&D products and services (Moskal, 1990).

One way T&D program times are shortened is through mechanisms that make the learning curve steeper (e.g., simulations). Another way is to shift the burden for learning to employees. Company supported off-hour learning is becoming increasingly popular.

> [At Boeing] we offer an extensive program of Off Hours Training and self-paced instruction to all employees. This is training that is free to employees, but they do it on their own time (mostly on week-nights). . . . It is basically a supplement to the training presented during work hours, geared toward employees who are eager to learn and get ahead. Currently, about one-third of our employees are taking advantage of this Off Hours Training.

Another example of a strategy to increase T&D cost-effectiveness is drawing on customers as "suppliers" of T&D. In many instances, customers are quite willing to partner with their suppliers in delivering T&D as a means of elevating the quality of the goods or services supplied and reducing their costs. GE, for example, opens its doors to customers and suppliers to participate in its unique "Work Out" training programs (Stewart, 1991).

A third development in T&D delivery methods is the increased exploitation of technology-aided learning—especially information and telecommunications technologies. For example, at IBM during the 1980s, technology was used to deliver no more than five percent of the company's T&D. By 1990 that figure stood at 30%, and by the end of the decade it is expected to rise to 60% of all T&D delivered (Geber, 1990).

Apple's "electronic campus" draws on the computer manufacturer's globally networked information system to facilitate T&D information exchange. In a sense, Apple's electronic campus is an example of broadly defined team-based learning, facilitated through a far-flung information network. Other companies are using distance learning methods (e.g., satellite communications or teleconferencing) to deliver T&D programs to managerial and non-managerial trainees in their local environments.

Federal Express relies on an interactive video network to deliver training to 45,000 employees and delivers college courses and degree programs via personal computers. They even have a leadership series broadcast on an internal television network, FXTV (Galagan, 1991). Federal Express also developed a series of interactive videodisks related to customer service processes for managers and service providers. Comparing the effectiveness of T&D delivered in the classroom to videodisk technology revealed that, although both groups of trainees scored the same on learning outcomes, the conventional T&D took 7.5 hours, versus 2.6 hours for the videodisks (Wilson, 1991).

A fourth development in the delivery of T&D is an increased emphasis on teams. This emphasis takes a variety of forms, including training intact work teams to maximize relevance to job conditions, delegating decision making authority to the team to determine perceptions of its T&D requirements, including the team in T&D design and, most importantly, using the team or selected team members as deliverers of the T&D content. The Colgate-Palmolive plant in Cambridge, OH, allots 40 hours annually to interaction training for the entire team, most of it on the job.

Finally, mentoring is becoming an increasingly important vehicle for the development of management and executive succession capabilities, especially with regard to historically disadvantaged groups. For example, at Corning:

> Every minority (Black, female or other) employee has a mentor/coach within the company. Any non-minority who wants a mentor can also have one. Corning also has Quality Improvement Teams (QITs) for Blacks and women, to provide [developmental] feedback and input to the employees. The QITs are made up of members of that minority in managerial positions within Corning.

T&D Framework, Phase 3: Check

One of the most seriously lacking activities in T&D is evaluation. However, evaluation has improved considerably over the last few years, possibly due to the ease of collecting and analyzing data with desktop computers (Industry Report, 1995). These exemplary companies make a serious effort to ascertain whether or not their programs are having the intended effects.

HOW CAN ORGANIZATIONS EVALUATE THE VALUE ADDED BY THEIR T&D INVESTMENTS?

Few organizations evaluate their T&D expenditures against returns on those investments. Carnevale and Schulz (1990) reported that although two of three T&D professionals felt increased pressure to show that their efforts affect the bottom line, fewer than 20% of their organizations conducted return on T&D investment studies. Kirkpatrick's (1976) survey of 100 companies indicated that while over 75% of the firms measured participant reactions, fewer than 50% measured knowledge changes or skills learned, and still fewer measured changes in behaviors (20%) or results (15%). More recently, an Industry Group study (1995) reported that 43% of the firms in their survey measured business results attributable to training and 60% evaluated behavior on the job relevant to training. Even with this improvement, the classic problem of causality continues to hamper this assessment—can the returns (or the failures) be attributed to the T&D investments? Commenting on Corning's Blacksburg plant:

> . . . Corning has learned to view extensive training as an investment rather than a cost. The payoff is improved product quality, productivity, and profits. Corning's return on equity jumped from 9.3% in 1984, when it began emphasizing employee training, to 15.9% in 1989. "In my gut, I can tell you a large part of our profit increase has come about because of our embarking on this way of life," says Chairman James R. Houghton (Hoerr, 1990).

Organizations interviewed for this study focused primarily on two activities for assessing T&D effectiveness—gauging on-site participant reactions to T&D and measuring learning by means of behavioral exercises during T&D. The missing pieces of evaluation continue to be assessments of post-training behaviors and control groups, both of which provide less ambiguous information about the effectiveness of training efforts.

There are a few noteworthy exceptions to these statements. Xerox uses multiple methods, including observations of trainees once they return to their regular positions, interviews with trainees' managers,

and examination of trainees' post-T&D performance appraisals, to ascertain whether T&D has impacted job behaviors (Carnevale & Schulz, 1990). American Express provides another example with its Leadership Development Program. The organization implemented T&D according to a "rolling" cycle, where the first group completed T&D at the time the second group was beginning, the third group beginning at the time the second group completed, and so on. Pre-post measures and control group (i.e., trained compared to not-yet-trained group) comparisons were made for reactions, learning, and behavior measures. Managers' evaluations and trainees' self-ratings of performance were collected two weeks prior to the program and three months after its completion (Tannenbaum & Woods, 1992).

Andersen Consulting evaluated results of a tax law training program against quantity of work and revenue data. The study demonstrated that Andersen's tax consultants who had taken the course had more billable hours than their counterparts who had not been trained (Galagan, 1993). Motorola University utilizes the six sigma quality framework followed throughout the corporation. Any form of negative feedback is counted as a "defect," with the goal of having less than four defects per million T&D sub-processes delivered.

A number of organizations also publish cost savings to training expenditure ratios. Motorola claims that in some of its T&D operations, the ratio of T&D savings to costs is 33:1 (Fierman, 1991). The figure is 27:1 in three Baldrige award-winning companies (Ford, 1993). Precisely how these ratios are computed is unclear; however, the ratios are supposed to reflect post-training performance returns against the direct and indirect costs of training.

Some organizations also incorporate 360 degree appraisal (for example, evaluations by the employee's superior, direct reports, peers, customers, and self-ratings) into their T&D evaluation portfolio. For example, Johnson & Johnson uses a post-training selfreport form to evaluate participants' on-the-job changes. Subordinates of managerial and supervisory trainees are surveyed annually about their perceptions of changes in their manager's performance (Carnevale & Schulz, 1990).

A small number of organizations are moving toward a profit-centered approach to the T&D function, where T&D services are "sold" to internal customers. This forces responsiveness to the needs of internal customers and demonstration of value added if in-house units will continue purchasing T&D services. Although this profit-centered orientation to T&D is not evaluation in the classic sense, it constitutes a "market-driven" approach to assessing perceptions of return on T&D investments. It also forces continuous improvement because of discipline introduced through competition with outside vendors. T&D at Bristol-Myers Squibb operates this way:

> [We] use what's called a "charge-back" program where the individual departments make a financial commitment to training. Training budgets for individual programs are usually zero-based, and are funded through the individual units that decide to put their employees through those programs. . . . If an employee decides to go to that training, his/her department pays for the training just as if they were paying an outside vendor. . . . We are competing with outside vendors for the 'business' of the local departments.

Clearly, the evaluation phase of T&D is an area in which even the best organizations practice only a minimum level of on-site assessments. One reason for this is that T&D in exemplary organizations is part of the organization's mission and values and is not subject to the rules of cost-benefit evaluation. T&D represents a belief in the value of continuous learning, that over time a highly skilled and informed workforce will be more focused on the organization's strategic goals and values, and more capable, productive, and creative in ways that might not be immediately measurable. In the words of the Federal Express Chairman:

> You could never justify the cost of our FXTV network or our interactive video training system. But if you ask me, those would be among the top 10 highest payoff projects we've ever done at Federal Express. Maybe even in the top three. [I believe that] it is important for the company's leadership to support those things, such as quality and learning, that cut across the organization and don't have a clear ROI (Smith, cited in Galagan, 1991).

A call for systematic T&D evaluation, however, need not be construed as a challenge to the unquestionable value of human resource development. Instead, systematic T&D evaluation provides insights into the relative returns of one form of T&D versus another,

measured against the organization's strategic priorities and specific customer requirements. It enables data-driven choices among, for example, longer university-delivered management programs, company-designed action learning modules, or team-based learning approaches.

T&D Framework, Phase 4: Act

Act involves sustaining effort on T&D activities. Training can be a one-shot deal, but it will then fail to support continuous learning. Thus, after every cycle of planning, implementing, and evaluating a program, the organization must be ready and willing to make modifications to the program based on evaluation information and to start the whole process again.

HOW DO BENCHMARK ORGANIZATIONS SUSTAIN AND ENHANCE THE ROLE OF T&D?

T&D budget preservation during financially difficult times is integral to demonstrating leadership's commitment. One recent study found that training budgets tend to take a bigger "hit" than some other organizational functions when the going gets rough (Lee, 1992). That is not the case, however, in benchmark organizations. Ninety-two percent of interviewees indicated that T&D is central to the organization's goals—so important that only 15% expressed a willingness to cut T&D during tough times.

Because they are critical to the organization's strategic mission, investments in T&D by best-in-class organizations are supported by a central T&D budget or are required as a line item in the budgets of divisions. Budget priorities within the T&D function are tied directly to the strategic mission. Moreover, there is a visible presence of T&D at the central organizational level. Often, this takes the form of an organizational "university" or campus (62% of organizations interviewed had a central T&D campus). This type of visible investment in T&D sends a message about the organization's continuing commitment to T&D.

An effective T&D process cannot be a one-time event. It requires a sustained and deepening investment in the factors mentioned earlier, to the point that T&D is a cornerstone of the organization's value system, part of the routine behaviors of all of its employees from the most senior on down, and preserved during financial downturns. The T&D

system does not achieve this status solely due to the vision and loyal support of the organization's leaders. It does so by providing a compelling case for itself as a critical ally in realizing the organization's mission and goals.

The only legitimate reason to put in place an executive development program is that it is integral to the business strategy. Any other reason will result, at best, in a series of interesting training programs tangentially related to the business or, at worst, in a variety of expensive activities conveying irrelevant or contradictory messages. The only way to sustain the necessary commitment of time, passion, and resources to executive development is through a bedrock belief that leadership is a critical source of competitive advantage and that leadership can be developed through systematic attention to development (McCall, 1992).

The framework presented in this paper includes structural features, policies, and practices that together add up to a climate of continuous learning. No single factor is responsible for a strategically aligned T&D system that supports continuous learning. An effective T&D system is a result of the confluence of elements of the T&D framework, and the extent to which they are embedded in the organization's structures, policies, and practices.

Executives today confront unprecedented uncertainty, given the magnitude and rate of technology and market transformations. No organization can have the foresight to predict the precise talents it will need 10, or even five years from now. How can organizations respond to and overcome the risks associated with market uncertainty? By developing an internal discipline that creates readiness for several alternative strategic directions. Tight linkages between organizational planning and T&D systems create leadership and skill readiness. As demonstrated in these benchmark organizations, T&D can be a powerful strategic lever.

Source: Olian, J. et. al. "Designing Management Training and Development for Competitive Advantage: Lessons from the Best," *Human Resource Planning*, 21, (1), 1998, pp. 20–31. Reprinted with permission from Human Resource Planning, by The *Human Resource Planning* Society, 317 Madison Avenue, Suite 1509, New York, NY 10017, Phone: (212) 490–6387, Fax: (212) 682–6851.

References

Baird, L., Briscoe, J., Tuden, L., and Roansky, L. M. H. "World Class Executive Development," *Human Resource Planning*, Vol. 17, No. 1 (1995): 1–15.

Bernstein, A., Brandt, R., Carlson, B., and Padley, K. "Teaching Business How to Train," *Business Week*, October 23 (1992): 82–90.

Broadwell, M. M. "How to Train Experienced Supervisors," *Training*, Vol. 30, No. 5 (1993): 64.

Carnevale, A. P. "America and the New Economy: A Special Report from the ASTD," *Training & Development*, Vol. 44 (1990): 31–49.

Carnevale, A. P. and Schulz, E. R. "Economic Accountability for Training: Demands and Responses," *Training & Development*, Vol. 44, No. 7 (1990): S2–S4.

Carnevale, A. P. and Schulz, E. R. "Evaluation Practices," *Training & Development*, Vol. 44, No. 7 (1990): S23–S29.

Casner-Lotto, J. *Successful Training Strategies: Twenty-six Innovative Corporate Models*. San Francisco: Jossey-Bass, 1988.

Fierman, J. "Shaking the Blue-Collar Blues," *Fortune*, April 22 (1991): 209–218.

Ford, D. J. "Benchmarking HRD," *Training & Development*, Vol. 47, No. 6 (1993): 36–41.

Fossum, J. A. "Issues in the Design and Delivery of Corporate Training Programs," *Labor Law Journal*, Vol. 42 (1991): 575–580.

Galagan, P. A. "Training Delivers Results to Federal Express," *Training & Development*, Vol. 45, No. 12 (1991): 27–33.

Galagan, P. A. "Training Keeps the Cutting Edge Sharp for the Andersen Companies," *Training & Development*, Vol. 47, No. 1 (1993): 30–35.

Geber, B. "Goodbye Classrooms (Redux)," *Training*, Vol. 27, No. 1 (1990): 27–35.

Goldstein, I. L. *Training in Organizations: Needs Assessment, Development and Evaluation (3rd ed.)*. Monterey, CA: Brooks/Cole, 1993.

Graham, E. "High-Tech Training: Companies Turn to Technology to Try to Bring Their Employees Up to Speed," *The Wall Street Journal*, February 9 (1990): R16–18.

Hoerr, J. "With Job Training, A Little Dab Won't Do Ya," *Business Week*, September 24 (1990): 95.

Hoerr, J. "Sharpening Minds for a Competitive Edge," *Business Week*, December 17 (1990): 72–78.

Industry Report, 1995, *Training*, October (1995): 37–74.

Kirkpatrick, D. L. "Evaluation of Training," in R. L. Craig (Ed.), *Training & Development Handbook (2nd ed.)*. New York: McGraw-Hill, 1976.

Lee, C. "The Budget Blahs," *Training*, Vol. 29, No. 10 (1992): 31–38.

McCall, M. W. "Executive Development as a Business Strategy," *The Journal of Business Strategy*, January/February (1992): 25–31.

Moskal, B. S. "Just a Degree of Confidence," *Industry Week*, February 19 (1990): 65–66.

Noel, J. L. and Dennehy, R. F. "The Learner's Manager: The Bridge from Classroom to Workplace," *The Journal of European Industrial Training*, Vol. 15, No. 6 (1991): 17–18.

O'Reilly, B. "How Execs Learn Now," *Fortune*, April 5 (1993): 52–58.

Stewart, T. A. "GE Keeps Those Ideas Coming," *Fortune*, August 12 (1991): 41–49.

Stone, N. "Does Business Have Any Business in Education?" *Harvard Business Review*, Vol. 69, No. 2 (1991): 46–62.

Tannenbaum, S. I. and Woods, S. B. "Determining a Strategy for Evaluation Training: Operating within Organizational Constraints," *Human Resource Planning*, Vol. 15, No. 2 (1992): 63–81.

Taylor, P. "Training Directors' Perceptions about the Successful Implementation of Supervisory Training," *Human Resource Development Quarterly*, Vol. 3, No. 3 (1992): 243–259.

Thurow, L. *Head to Head*. New York: William Morrow, 1992.

Vicere, A. A. and Graham, K. R. "Crafting Competitiveness: Toward a New Paradigm for Executive Development," *Human Resource Planning*, Vol. 13, No. 4 (1990): 281–295.

Weatherly, J. D. "Dare to Compare for Better Productivity," *HR Magazine*, September (1992): 42–46.

Wiggenhorn, W. "Motorola U: When Training Becomes an Education," *Harvard Business Review*, Vol. 68, No. 4 (1990): 71–83.

Wilson, B. "Federal Express Delivers Pay for Knowledge," *Training*, Vol. 28, No. 6 (1991): 39–42.

The Strategic Training of Employees Model: Balancing Organizational Constraints and Training Content

Dan Wentland, *S.A.M. Advanced Management Journal*

Introduction

In the early 1980s U.S. Steel (now USX) underwent massive downsizing and invested more than $1 billion to upgrade and computerize its production processes. Worker skills needed to be upgraded, for the new technology to pay off. But as part of its restructuring, the company had eliminated an apprenticeship program that provided in-depth training in a number of crafts. Now the company needed a training program that would cut across craft lines. USX found that an investment in physical resources often requires an investment in human resources (Gomez-Mejia, Balkin and Cardy, 1995).

The extent to which organizations will support employee training and development certainly varies, and that variability leads to an interesting question— why do some organizations value training more than others? Of course, organizational constraints can limit the amount of training regardless of how much the company values it.

This article develops the Strategic Training of Employees Model (STEM). STEM advances the literature by giving human resource practitioners a comprehensive framework that balances the need for training against the organizational constraints, STEM assumes that an organization consists of three components people, a goal or goals, and structure (Robbin, 1998). Of the three, the people factor is the most important because without them the other two cannot exist. People form the structure of an organization and set the goals or standards. Any product value an organization brings to the marketplace is fundamentally dependent upon the abilities of the employees at all levels. As the USX example illustrated it is the decisions and capabilities of management and nonmanagerial personnel that ultimately determine organizational results.

Historical Perspective

When establishing a training program it is important to determine the content. However, because of organizational constraints, usable content tends to be less than the potential content. Constraints can include restrictions on time, personnel and spending; lack of training facilities, materials or equipment; and the attitude of senior management. The relationship between potential and usable training content can be expressed in the following equation (Finch, 1989, p. 161):

The Training Content Decision-Making Equation
$$UC = PC - C$$
Where: UC = usable content,
PC = potential content, C = constraints

Therefore, any training program must balance the need to provide the proper level of training against organizational constraints. A tilt one way or the other could be detrimental. Too much training is a waste of resources, but too little could damage an organization's competitive position. Any training model that does not reflect this delicate balance will be useless for human resources practitioners. A training model that captures the reality of organizational constraints is needed because, despite spending more than $50 billion per year on training, the effectiveness of American companies' training is questionable compared with many other countries (Hicks, 2000; Idhammar, 1997). Much of the training in the U.S. is the "follow Joe" type. This means new employees are teamed with experienced employees and are expected to learn on the job. However, this method does not always ensure that all the necessary information is passed along to the new employee. For instance, let us suppose that Joe, an experienced worker, is responsible for teaching Mike, who is new. First of all, Joe might only possess a certain percentage of the knowledge he should have. In addition, Joe might not teach Mike everything he knows, keeping some skills to himself because of pride or job security. However, even if Joe teaches Mike everything he knows, Mike might not be able to remember all of it (Idhammar, 1997).

To improve the effectiveness of the training function, a systematic process is needed that provides a framework for evaluating training goals and techniques subject to organizational constraints.

Literature Review

As background, this paper will briefly review research relating to the development of human capital and pertaining to the learning process, with an emphasis on adult learning and the implications for organizational training.

ECONOMIC LITERATURE AND HUMAN CAPITAL

In his seminal article, Gary Becker (1962) laid the foundation for the study of human capital acquisition when he distinguished between "general human capital" and "specific human capital." General human capital has multiple uses and is portable, while specific human capital is useful in a narrow line of work and has limited portability (Loewenstein and Spletzer, 1999; Bassi, 1994). Accordingly, any "completely general training" is an investment in human capital that increases an employee's overall productivity and could be transferred to any employment situation, while "completely specific training" only increases worker productivity for the employer who provided it. Becker concluded that within a perfectly competitive market any general human capital formulation would be financed by the individual while any specific human capital acquisition would be shared by individuals and firms (Bassi, 1994).

Following the publication of Becker's work, most of the research regarding workplace analysis examined physical capital issues; recently, however, several researchers (Elbaum, 1990; Parson, 1990; Lynch, 1991, 1992; Bishop and Kang, 1996; and Loewenstein and Spletzer, 1997, 1998a, 1999) have begun investigating topics relating to human capital development. In sum, this line of research serves as a valuable reminder of the tug of war between employee training and the associated costs. Most organizations (with the exception of academic institutions) do not exist for the sole purpose of educating their employees, so a managerial decision must be made regarding the level of training that will be provided. This dilemma once again focuses attention on the concepts of potential and usable content

as outlined by Finch (1989) in the "Training Content Decision-Making Equation."

LEARNING THEORIES AND TRAINING IMPLICATIONS

Learning is defined as a relatively permanent change in human capabilities that is not a result of growth processes. These capabilities are related to specific learning outcomes (verbal information, intellectual skills, motor skills, attitudes and cognitive strategies). Several learning theories can provide a foundation for understanding how a trainee is motivated to learn.

1. Reinforcement theory emphasizes that people are motivated to perform or avoid certain behaviors because of past outcomes that have resulted from those behaviors. From a training perspective, reinforcement theory suggests that the trainer needs to identify what outcomes the learner perceives as being positive (or negative). Trainers then need to link these outcomes to learners' acquiring knowledge, skills, or new behaviors (Noe, 1999; Robbins, 1998).

2. Social learning theory suggests that learners first watch others who act as models. In a training scenario, a group of trainees can be presented with models of effective behaviors, such as serving customers or performing managerial analyses, as well as the relationship between these behaviors and favorable consequences, such as praise, promotions, or customer satisfaction. Trainees then rehearse the behaviors and consequences, building cognitive maps that intensify the links and set the stage for future behaviors. The learning impact occurs when the subject tries the behavior and experiences a positive result (Gordon, 1996).

3. Goal-setting theory implies that establishing and committing to specific and challenging goals can influence an individual's behavior. From a training perspective, goal-setting could be utilized to identify the specific outcomes that should be achieved from the training (Hellriegel, Slocum and Woodman, 1995).

4. Need theories (Maslow's Hierarchy of Needs, Alderfer's ERG Theory, Herzberg's Dual Structure Theory and David McClelland's Need Theory) assume that need deficiencies cause behavior. Need theories suggest that to motivate

learning, trainers should identify trainees' needs and communicate how training program content relates to fulfilling those needs (Noe, 1999; Moorhead and Griffin, 1995).

5. Expectancy theory implies that an individual's behavior is a function of three factors (expectancy, instrumentality, and valence). The expectancy factor refers to an individual's belief that effort will lead to a particular performance level, that the performance level is associated with a particular outcome (instrumentality factor), and that the outcome is valued by the individual (valence factor). From a training perspective, expectancy theory suggests that learning is most likely to occur when employees believe they can learn the content of the program (expectancy), when learning is linked to outcome such as better job performance, a salary increase, or peer recognition (instrumentality), and when employees value the outcomes (Noe, 1999).

ADULT LEARNING THEORY (ANDRAGOGY) AND IMPLICATIONS FOR WORKPLACE TRAINING

Traditionally, pedagogy dominated the literature in education. More recently, educational psychologists recognized the need to focus on adult learning and developed the theory of adult learning, andragogy. Malcolm Knowles (1990) is most frequently associated with adult learning theory. Some implications regarding adult learning theory for workplace training are summarized below (Noe, 1999):

• Employees learn best when they understand the objective of the training program. The training objective should have three components: an explanation of what the employee is expected to do (performance); a statement of the quality or level of performance that is acceptable (criterion); and, finally, a declaration of the conditions under which the trainee is expected to perform the desired outcome (conditions).

• Employees tend to learn better when the training is linked to their current job experiences, because this enhances the meaningfulness of the training. By providing trainees with opportunities to choose their practice strategy as well as other characteristics of the learning situation the training experience can be further enhanced.

• Employees learn best when they have the opportunity to practice. In addition, the trainer should identify what the trainees will be doing when practicing the objectives (performance), the criteria for attaining the objective, and the conditions under which the practice sessions will be conducted.

• Employees need feedback, and, to be effective, the feedback should focus on specific behaviors and be provided as soon as possible after the trainee's behavior.

• Employees learn by observing and imitating the actions of a model. To be effective, the model's desired behaviors or skills need to be clearly specified and the model should have characteristics (such as age or position) similar to the target audience. After observing the model, trainees should have the opportunity to reproduce the skills and behaviors shown.

• Employees need the training program to be properly coordinated and arranged. Good coordination ensures that trainees are not distracted by events (such as an uncomfortable room or poorly organized materials) that could interfere with learning.

The linking of adult learning theory with the strategic objectives of the organization is referred to as high-leverage training. High-leverage training helps to establish a corporate culture that encourages continuous learning. Continuous learning requires employees to understand the entire work system, including the relationships among their jobs, work units, and the overall company. Employees are expected to acquire new skills and knowledge, apply them on the job, and share them with other employees (Noe, 1999).

The Foundations of the Strategic Training of Employees Model (STEM)

The concept of high-leverage training is embedded in the framework of STEM. The model is built on the realization that organizations have limited resources (capital, financial, human) and those resources must be allocated in an efficient manner. STEM directly links employee training and career development with the strategic objectives set by management so that the focus of any workplace training will be centered on organizational goals. This fundamental bond defines the content direction for the entire training development process. Specifically, the usable content can be defined by modifying Finch's earlier equation.

The Strategic Training Decision-Making Equation
USC = PC − NSC − C
Where USC = Usable Strategic Content, PC = Potential Content, NSC = NonStrategic Content, C = Constraints

Usable strategic training content can alternatively be identified as employee training plus career development associated with obtaining strategic organizational goals.

USC = SET + SCD
Where USC = Usable Strategic Content, SET = Strategic Employee Training, SCD = Strategic Career Development

Therefore, the strategic decision-making equation can be rewritten as

SET + SCD = PC − NSC − C
Where SET = Strategic Employee Training, SCD = Strategic Career Development, PC = Potential Content, NSC = NonStrategic Content, C = Constraints

STEM directs the flow of the training process by focusing on the organization's strategic objectives and then designing specific training and career development activities to obtain those goals. By effectively and efficiently allocating training content (as well as dollars), an organization should be able to improve the value of the products that it brings to the marketplace.

To make sure that training content and dollars are properly allocated, the training function is analyzed at two levels.

The first is the macro-organizational training level while the second is the micro-organizational training level. At the macro level, the focus is on identifying the strategic objective of the organization or business unit as well as task analysis. At the micro level, specific training content is developed to support the outcomes of the macro-level analysis. Following macro- and micro-level analysis, training programs are implemented. After implementation, the next step is to obtain feedback and evaluate the quality of the training.

Macro-Organizational Training Level Analysis

The macro-organizational training level begins by incorporating the business strategy (or strategies) formulated by senior management. Business strategies have been classified into four general categories: (1) concentration, (2) internal growth, (3) external growth, and (4) disinvestment (Noe, 1999). A concentration strategy focuses on increasing market share, reducing costs, or creating and maintaining a market niche for products and services. An internal growth strategy focuses on new markets and product development, innovation, and joint ventures. An external growth strategy (acquisitions) emphasizes acquiring vendors and suppliers or buying businesses that allow the organization to expand into new markets. A disinvestment strategy stresses liquidation and divestiture of businesses. These business strategies are not necessarily mutually exclusive, and once management has determined the organization's course of action the training function should concentrate on developing employee capabilities that will help achieve these objectives.

FIGURE 1: MACRO-ORGANIZATIONAL TRAINING LEVEL ANALYSIS (FOUR BUSINESS STRATEGIES AND TASK ANALYSIS)

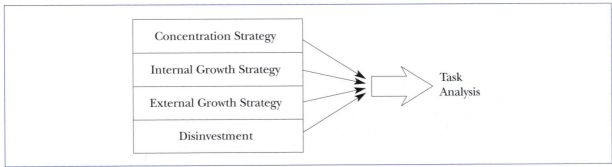

Given the business strategy, a task analysis should then be conducted to evaluate what jobs, tasks, and abilities are necessary to accomplish that strategy. A task analysis generally has four steps. The first is deciding which jobs to analyze. Second, a preliminary list of the tasks needed to perform a job is drawn up. Third, this list should be validated or confirmed. Finally, the knowledge, skills, and abilities required to perform the job are identified.

Micro-Organizational Training Level Analysis

After the task analysis, the focus of the training function is shifted toward developing specific training programs based on the task analysis. At this micro-organizational level, the training process includes identifying who needs to be trained (targeting) and the appropriate training content. The task analysis would have resulted in a list of specific jobs and the tasks and skills required to perform those jobs. Based on that information, the training function next targets specific employees for training and designs content to assist them in performing their jobs for the ultimate purpose of achieving management's objectives. When determining specific training content, a four P's approach can be utilized.

The Four P's of Micro-Organizational Training Level Analysis

Four key variables (place, product, promotion, and price) provide a framework for guiding training content decisions. Micro-organizational analysis using these four variables is a useful managerial and planning tool.

PLACE

"Place" analysis refers to location decisions such as on-the-job (OJT) or off-the-job training as well as equipment and other facilities criteria. OJT means trainee works in the actual work setting usually under the supervision of an experienced worker, supervisor, or trainer. Examples of OJT programs include job rotation, apprenticeships, and internships. An alternative is off-the-job training, such as formal courses or simulations and role playing in a classroom setting. In selecting a site, numerous factors should be evaluated: noise level, colors, room structure, lighting, wall and floor coverings, type of chairs, glare, ceiling height, electrical outlets, and acoustics. The seating arrangement should also be considered, such as fan-type, classroomtype, conference-type, or horseshoe.

Equipment decisions focus on any multimedia learning tools that may be required including audio-visual, computer-based, and possibly intelligent tutoring or expert systems equipment. In sum, a proper training location is comfortable, accessible, quiet, private, free from interruptions, and has sufficient space and equipment to ensure that a quality-training environment is created (Noe, 1999).

PRODUCT

Product analysis focuses on issues such as the purpose of the training. How should the training be presented? What organizational constraints limit the amount of training?

Two factors need to be considered regarding the training's purpose. The first is deciding whether the training is for its own sake or career development. Training typically provides employees with specific skills or helps to correct deficiencies in their performance, while development is an effort to provide employees with abilities the organization will need in the future (Gomez-Mejia, Balkin and Cardy, 1995). The second factor is to have a clear understanding of the type of skills the training is attempting to develop. Skill development could include improving basic literacy, technological know-how, interpersonal communication, or problemsolving abilities (Robbins, 1995). When a training program is being designed, the purpose behind it must be reflected in the content. For example, if the purpose is career development then several training activities are applicable, such as mentoring, coaching, job rotation, and tuition assistance (Gomez-Mejia, Balkin and Cardy, 1995).

Along with content decisions, the method of presentation should be determined. Training methodologies utilized by various companies include classroom training, videos, role-play, case studies, computer-based training, games, and adventure learning (Noe, 1999).

Besides determining methodologies, an overriding issue regarding training content is the "organizational reality" illustrated by the strategic decision-making equation. Any training program will be subject to organizational constraints that will affect the length and breadth of the content. By tying training activities into the strategic management process, some organizational constraints might be eased because the training function becomes an integral part of efforts to obtain management goals.

One final product consideration involves deciding whether training should be provided by an outside source. If a particular training activity can be provided by an outside vendor at a lower cost while ensuring quality, then it should be subcontracted.

PROMOTION

The main objective of the promotion element should be to build a relationship of trust between the training area and other departments so that the training function will be supported and viewed as a valuable asset to the organization. The level of management support for training can range from low, which means managers generally accept training and allow employees to attend training sessions, to high, where managers actually participate in the process (Noe, 1999).

The most effective method of promoting the training function is for the HR department to become more strategic and improve its overall image (HR Focus Survey, 2001). Other promotional avenues include the company newsletter (to report training events) and having training administrators and the trainers visit managers throughout the organization to promote the benefits of training. Finally, the best form of promotion is positive word-of-mouth communication among employees, which is only generated by providing a quality training experience.

PRICE

Price analysis focuses on budgetary considerations, and budgetary analysis begins with identifying the costs associated with a training activity. The seven traditional cost sources include: program development or purchase, instructional materials, equipment and hardware, facilities, travel and lodging, salary of trainer and support staff, and loss of productivity while trainees attend the program plus the cost of any temporary employees who replace the trainees while they are at training (Noe, 1999). Using these cost sources, an aggregate annual training budget can be determined by identifying each of these costs for a specific training activity and then multiplying the total cost of each by the number of training sessions forecasted for the year.

Once determined, the costs must be weighed against the benefits received from the training. To identify the benefits, it may help to review the

FIGURE 2: MICRO-ORGANIZATIONAL TRAINING LEVEL ANALYSIS (TARGETING AND THE FOUR P'S)

Target Market—Who will be receiving the training (executive, upper middle management, lower middle management, supervisory, non-management)?	
Place (location factors) • On-the-job • Off-the-job • Equipment required	**Product** (content of training program) • Purpose of training • Content and constraint factors • Presentation options

Promotion (communicating information about training programs)
 	
 • Strategic planning involvement
 • Company newsletter
 • Personal communication
 • Word-of-mouth
	Price (cost considerations)
	
	 • Budget allocation
	   • Employees
	   • Facility
	   • Material
	   • Equipment
	   • Travel

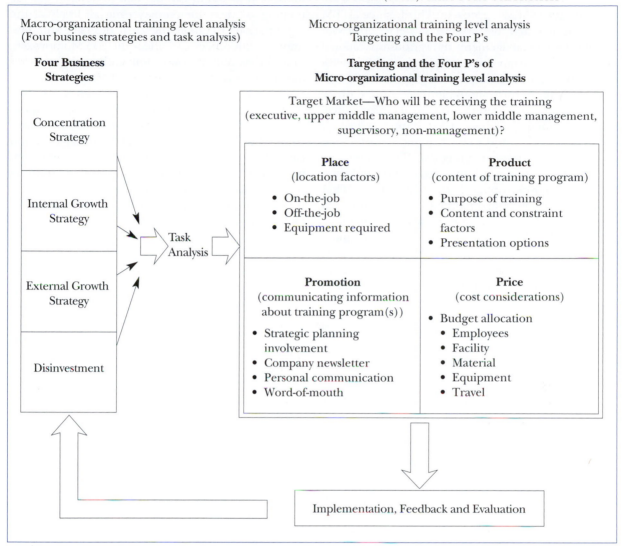

technical, academic, or practitioner literature that summarizes the benefits of a specific training program. Additionally, pilot training programs or observing on-the-job performance of employees after training can also help with the cost/benefit analysis (Noe, 1999).

Implementation, Feedback, and Evaluation

If the benefits of a training program exceed its costs, the program should be implemented. Following implementation, feedback will be needed, and an ongoing evaluation process should ensure that the quality does not diminish.

Suggestions for Future Research and the Conclusion

A range of future research possibilities can be developed from this initial presentation of STEM. First, the tug-of-war relationship between recognizing the importance of training and actually providing it requires additional exploration. This focuses on the difference between potential strategic content and usable strategic content and why management talks a good game about the need for training but, in many cases, will not support a thorough training process (remember the USX example). Second, a specific training activity based on the Four P's could be designed, and employee performance before and after receiving training can be compared to assess the value of the STEM approach. Third, since STEM links training activities to the strategic objectives established by management, the various operational goals that flow from the strategic planning process should be achieved in a more effective and efficient manner. This, in turn, should improve overall financial performance. To test this, financial performance, such as earnings per share, sales volume, return on equity, stock price, and so forth, could be compared before and after implementing the STEM approach.

Other research possibilities could include 1) surveying employee opinion regarding the STEM approach; 2) developing additional criteria for each of the Four P's; 3) using case studies to evaluate the impact of the STEM approach on specific organizations or industries; 4) studying the effect of the STEM approach on employee motivation at all levels within the organization; 5) further refining the model in terms of how STEM can be used to develop specific training activities for employees at all levels of the organization; 6) analyzing how diversity and pre-training differences can affect the STEM approach; 7) and researching how online and other computer technologies can influence the STEM approach.

In conclusion, employee capabilities and the strategic objectives are bound together in a relationship that ultimately determines an organization's competitiveness. By utilizing STEM, an organization can achieve its strategic objectives in a cost-efficient manner while also providing a quality training process that nourishes employee skills and abilities that enable an organization to flourish in today's global economy.

References

Abernathy, D. J. (1999, April). In gear. Training and Development, 53 (4), 61–63.

Atkinson, A. A. (1991, April). Training and control. CMA Magazine, 65 (3), 15.

Bassi, L. J. (1994, Winter). Workplace education for hourly worker. Journal of Policy Analysis and Management, 13, (1), 55–75.

Callahan, M. R. (1995, December). Training on a shoestring. Training and Development, 49 (12).

Cohen, S. (1996, December). Online organizational training. Training and Development, 50, (12), 62.

Finch, C. R., & Crunkilton, J. R. (1989). Curriculum development in vocational and technical education: Planning, content, and implementation (3rd ed.). Allyn & Bacon.

Gefen, D., & Straub, D. W. (1997, December). Gender differences in the perception and use of e-mail: An extension to the technology acceptance. MIS Quarterly, 21 (4), 389–401.

Gomez-Mejia, L. R., Balkin, D. B., & Cardy, R. L. (1995). Managing Human Resources. Prentice Hall.

Gordon, J. R. (1996). Organizational behavior (5th ed.). Prentice Hall.

Hellnegel, D., Slocum, J. W., Jr., & Woodman, R. W. (1995). Organizational behavior (7th ed.). West Publishing Company.

Hicks, S. (2000, May). Successful global training. Personnel Management: International Business Enterrises, 54 (5), 95.

Hill, C. W. L., & Jones, G. R. (1998), Strategic management: An integrated approach (4th ed.). Houghton Mifflin.

HR focus survey. (2001, January). HR Focus, 78 (1), Special Report on Strategic Planning.

Hubbard, A. (1999, February). Too much money. Mortgage Banking, 59 (5), 97.

Idhammar, C. (1997, November). Retaining valuable skills. Pulp and Paper, 71(11), 35.

Jentsch-Smith, K. A., Jentsch, F. G., Payne, S. C., & Salas, E. (1996). Can pre-training experiences explain individual differences in learning? Journal of Applied Psychology, 81, 110–116.

Knowles, M. (1990). The adult learner (4th ed.). Gulf Publishing.

LaLonde, R. J. (1995, Spring). The promise of public sector sponsored training program. Journal of Economic Perspectives, 9 (2).

Lapidus, T. (2000, July). High impact training: Getting results and respect (book review). Training and Development, 54 (7), 62–64.

Loewenstein, M. A., & Spletzer, J. R. (1999, Fall). General and Specific training: Evidence and implications. Journal of Human Resources, 34 (4), 710–734.

McCarthy, J. E., & Perreault, W. D. (1994). Essential of marketing (6th ed.). Irwin.

Miller, J. S., & Cardy, R. L. (2000, Summer). Technology and managing people: Keeping the 'human' in human resources. Journal of Labor Research, 21 (3), 447–462.

Moorhead, G., & Griffin, R. W. (1995). Organizational behavior: Managing people and organizations (4th ed.). Houghton Mifflin.

Noe, R. A. (1999) Employee training & development. Irwin McGraw-Hill.

Payne, S. (2000, November 13). Corporate training trend: Building leadership. Grand Rapids Business Journal, 18 (46), p. B2–4.

Robbins, S. P. (1998). Organizational behavior (8th ed.). Prentice Hall.

Survey says. (2001, January). Training and Development, 55 (1), 17.

Wentland, D. (1999, May). A guide for expatriate training ERIC Clearinghouse for Adult, Career, and Vocational Educational-Center on Education and Training For Employment, The Ohio State University, May 1999.

Zemke, R., & Armstrong, J. (1996, August). Evaluating multimedia. Training, 48–52.

CHAPTER

10

PERFORMANCE MANAGEMENT AND FEEDBACK

Farmington, Connecticut–based Otis Elevator is the world's largest manufacturer, installer, and servicer of elevators, escalators, moving walkways, and other vertical and horizontal passenger transportation systems. Otis products are offered in more than 200 countries worldwide, and the company employs more than 63,000 people. Among its many installations are the human transport systems of the Eiffel Tower, Sydney Opera House, Vatican, CN Tower (Toronto), and Hong Kong Convention Center.

For years, the company had an ineffective performance management system that was excessively time-consuming and inspired little confidence among employees or managers. In revamping its performance management, Otis moved toward a system that provided performance feedback based on critical strategic competencies related to the company's new focus on project teams. For this realignment into project teams to be successful, managers were required to demonstrate specific competencies in both team leadership and project management, as well as remain accountable for the financial and operating results of projects.

Realizing that critical feedback in these areas could not come exclusively from immediate supervisors, Otis had a custom-designed 360-degree feedback system developed that provided managers with feedback from those most directly affected by their performance: their subordinates, peers, and customers. The system provides ratings on several critical core competencies and is administered entirely online via the company intranet. The online system is easy to use, employs encryption technology to secure all data, and allows a performance review to be completed in 20 minutes. The system allows Otis to provide performance feedback in tandem with the organization's strategic objectives; is far more efficient than the previous paper-driven system; and perhaps, most important, has restored employee faith in the company's performance feedback system.

Source: Huet-Cox, G. D., Neilsen, T. M. and Sundstrom, E. "Get the Most from 360-Degree Feedback: Put It on the Internet," *HR Magazine*, May 1999, pp. 92–103; http://www.otis.com.

An organization's long-term success in meeting its strategic objectives rests with its ability to manage employee performance and ensure that performance measures are consistent with the organization's needs. Consequently, performance management—also called *performance evaluation, performance appraisal,* or *performance measurement*—is becoming more of a strategic issue for organizations than in the past. The term *performance feedback* will be used frequently in this chapter to stress that the performance management system needs to be understood and accepted by the organization's employees and must provide them with meaningful information if it is to be effective. Effective performance management systems require employees and supervisors to work together to set performance expectations, review results, assess organizational and individual needs, and plan for the future. On the other hand, the terms *performance appraisal* and *performance evaluation* imply a one-sided judgmental approach to performance management, where employees have little involvement in the process.

Performance management systems need not be formal in order to be effective. The most important concern in designing a performance management system is its fit with the organization's strategic objectives and the most important concern in providing performance-related feedback is its fit with the organization's culture. SAS, an international, 8,000-employee software company headquartered in Cary, North Carolina, decided to do away with formal performance feedback entirely. Instead, SAS opted for a system that provides continuous dialogue on performance-related matters. Executives report that the system works well because it is built on the values of open communication, trust, and self-motivation of employees to do their best. Moreover, any performance-related issues are dealt with in a timely manner because the lack of formality in the process allows feedback to be provided on an ongoing basis.[1]

The trends toward more streamlined organizations and hierarchies with fewer employees having broader job assignments have resulted in performance feedback taking on a more critical role than it has assumed in the past. Organizations today cannot afford to have weak links or unproductive employees. More than ever, organizations need broader measures of employee performance to ensure that (1) performance deficiencies are addressed in a timely manner through employee development programs that meet the changing needs of the organization and its markets, (2) employee behaviors are being channeled in the appropriate direction toward performance of specific objectives that are consistent with the work unit and organization's strategy, and (3) employees are provided with appropriate and specific feedback to assist with their career development.

An effective performance management process can be conceptualized as one that connects three time periods, as illustrated in Exhibit 10-1. It utilizes data about past performance to set goals, plans, and objectives for the present that should result

EXHIBIT 10-1: PERFORMANCE MANAGEMENT TIMELINE

Past	**Present**	**Future**
Data related to past performance, →	allows work plans, goals, and development opportunities to be set, →	resulting in the achievement of strategic objectives.

in high levels of performance in the future. However, a number of critical strategic issues must be addressed to establish an effective performance management system, as will be discussed below.

USE OF THE SYSTEM

An organization faces five strategic decisions in establishing its performance management system, as illustrated in Exhibit 10-2. The first is a determination of the purpose of the system and how it will be used. A performance management system can serve multiple purposes and it is important for the organization to strategize why the system is being used before further design decisions can be made. The organization also needs to ensure that, if the system is developed to serve several purposes, these

EXHIBIT 10-2: STRATEGIC CHOICES IN PERFORMANCE MANAGEMENT SYSTEMS

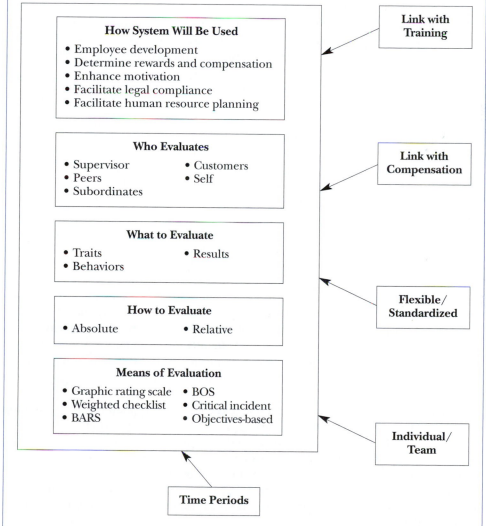

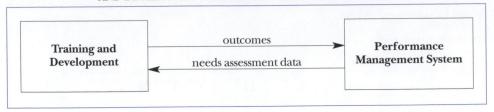

purposes not be at odds with each other and that any purpose not undermine data collection for the other(s).

One purpose of performance management systems is to facilitate employee development. By assessing deficiencies in performance levels and skills, an organization can determine specific training and development needs. In fact, the performance feedback process can be designed to provide information to fuel the organization's training and development programs. Assessing individual and team strengths and weaknesses can allow employee and team development plans to be established. A reciprocal relationship exists between the two as the desired outcomes of training and development initiatives must be incorporated into the performance management system, as discussed in Chapter 9. At the same time, the performance management system provides data that impacts the needs assessment of training and development, as displayed in Exhibit 10-3.

A second purpose of performance management systems is to determine appropriate rewards and compensation. Salary, promotion, retention, and bonus decisions are frequently based on data collected as part of performance measurement. Therefore, employees must understand and accept the performance feedback system as a prerequisite for accepting decisions made relative to rewards and compensation. Any perceived unfairness of the performance feedback system on the part of employees will result in a perceived unfairness of the compensation system.

A third purpose of managing performance is to enhance employee motivation. A formal process that allows for employee acknowledgment and praise can reinforce the behaviors and outcomes that are beneficial to the unit or organization. Employees can be told specifically what the organization's expectations for them are, and employees can inform their employers of the types of job assignments and responsibilities they desire.

A fourth purpose of performance management systems is to facilitate legal compliance. Claims of unfair dismissal and/or Title VII violations are best supported when the organization has documentation of performance deficiencies. Such information is often admitted into court to prove nondiscriminatory means of taking remedial action against employees and for termination of employment. Data showing unacceptable performance, particularly over a period of time, is a strong defense against such charges of unlawful bias.

Finally, performance management systems facilitate the human resource planning process. Performance data can alert the organization to deficiencies in the overall level and focus of employee skills and can be used in critically planning for future staffing needs relative to the skills and abilities of current employees. Because performance feedback can perform multiple functions in any organization, the organization must determine how it will be used prior to developing the system. This will keep the system focused, rather than random, and allow the organization to determine the specifications of its design.

The second strategic decision that must be made relative to the development of the performance management system concerns who provides performance data. Traditionally, performance evaluation was performed by the employee's immediate supervisor, who communicated to the employee the supervisory assessment of performance. This system offered very little opportunity for input or feedback from the employee. This approach, by itself, can be problematic for a number of reasons. Immediate supervisors often do not have the appropriate information to provide informed feedback and do not observe the employee's day-to-day work enough to assess performance accurately. It is also common in today's organizations for supervisors not to be current on the technical dimensions of a subordinate's work, which may be best evaluated by peers, customers, or other external constituencies. Technical line managers often have no training in or appreciation for the process and can see it as nothing more than an administrative burden. Finally, performance assessment is an inherently subjective process that is prone to a variety of perceptual errors by supervisors.

These errors include the halo effect, in which the rater allows one positive or negative trait, outcome, or consideration to influence other measures (for example, if an employee is often late for work, that fact may impact ratings having nothing to do with tardiness); stereotyping or personal bias, in which the rater makes performance judgments based on characteristics of the employee rather than on employee performance (for example, a bias that older workers are more resistant to change, less mentally agile, and less capable than younger workers of working longer hours); contrast error, in which the employee's assessment is based on those being given to other employees; recency error, in which the evaluation is biased toward events and behaviors that happened immediately prior to the time the evaluation is completed, with little or no consideration given to events occurring earlier in the evaluation period; central tendency error, in which the evaluator avoids the higher and lower ends of performance assessment ratings in favor of placing all employees at or near the middle of the scales; and leniency or strictness error, in which employees are generally all rated well above the standards (making the supervisor look effective and/or attempting to appease employees) or well below the standards (making the supervisor look demanding). Personal biases and organizational politics may have a significant impact on the ratings employees receive from their supervisors.

There may also be a number of reasons why supervisors might intentionally inflate or deflate employee ratings. For example, an empathetic supervisor might inflate the rating given to an employee having difficulties with personal matters. Conversely, a supervisor who sees a subordinate as a threat to the supervisor's job might intentionally deflate performance ratings. The performance management process can be inherently political in many organizations. In most instances, when supervisors conduct performance evaluations, they personally have job and career issues at stake in the ratings they give to their employees.

In addition to these errors, supervisors and subordinates may agree on levels of performance but disagree on the causes for such performance. Research has shown that supervisors are much more likely to place the responsibility for poor performance with the employee, whereas the employee is likely to cite organizational factors outside of his or her control for performance deficiencies.[2] Employees are much more likely to attribute their own job success to their own behaviors rather than to external factors such as easy job assignments or assistance from others.

For these reasons, organizations have been moving away from traditional means of performance feedback where only one assessment of an employee's performance is conducted and completed by the immediate supervisor. In addition to supervisory input, performance feedback can also be sought from peers, subordinates, customers, and/or the employee. Feedback from peers can be useful for developmental purposes, but peer feedback systems must be administered with care. They can be very political and self-serving in organizations where employees compete with each other either formally or informally. When a peer has personal gain or loss at stake in the assessment of a colleague, he or she can hardly be expected to exercise objectivity. Competitive organizational cultures could cause a peer evaluation system to raise havoc throughout the organization by escalating conflict. This could have detrimental effects on morale and teamwork. Peer feedback systems can only be effective when political considerations and consequences are minimized (meaning that peers have nothing at stake in their assessments of colleagues) and employees have a sense of trust in the organization and its performance measurement system.

Performance feedback from subordinates can provide insights into the interpersonal and managerial styles of employees and can assist the organization in addressing employee developmental needs, particularly for high-potential employees. Subordinate evaluations are also excellent measures of an individual's leadership capabilities. However, subordinate evaluations can suffer from the same political problems as peer evaluations. They can also be used by either the supervisor or subordinates to retaliate against each other. However, in assessing an employee's ability to manage others, valuable performance data pertaining to behavior and skills can be uniquely provided from subordinates.

Because our economy is becoming increasingly service-oriented and because many organizations emphasize customer service as a key competitive and strategic issue, customers are increasingly being sought for feedback on employee performance. In most instances, customers can provide the feedback that is most free from bias: They usually have little or nothing at stake in their assessment of employees. Feedback from customers can be critical for facilitating employee development and determining appropriate rewards because it is most clearly related to the organization's bottom line.

Self-evaluations allow employees to provide their own assessments and measures of their own performance. Although it should be obvious that self-evaluation can be self-serving, allowing employees to evaluate their own performance has at least two important benefits for organizations. First, it can be motivating because it allows the employee to participate in a critical decision that impacts his or her employment and career. Second, the employee can provide insights, examples, and a more holistic assessment of performance than that provided by supervisors or peers, who generally spend a limited time observing and interacting with each employee. Individual employees are far more likely to remember significant examples of effective performance than their supervisors, and they can often provide specific examples of behaviors and outcomes rather than the generalities often cited by supervisors. Individual employees may also be able to provide performance information of which others may be unaware.

Performance management systems that solicit the input and advice of others besides the immediate supervisor are referred to as multirater systems or 360-degree feedback systems. These systems can be beneficial because the organization and employee gain multiple perspectives and insights into the employee's performance. Each of these sources of performance feedback can balance each other relative to any inherent organizational politics that may be at play in the process. However, there is a cost to such systems: They can be very time-consuming and laborious to administer. Data from numerous sources needs to be analyzed, synthesized, and, occasionally, reconciled. There is inherently a cost-benefit aspect to any type of multirater performance feedback system. The more performance data collected, the greater the overall facilitation of the assessment and development of the employee. At the same time, larger volumes of data are costly to collect and process. At some point, the collection of additional data will undoubtedly provide diminishing returns. ▼

The popularity and use of 360-degree feedback programs has increased dramatically in recent years: More than 65 percent of organizations now use some form of multirater feedback, despite the fact that 360-degree feedback programs have been associated with a 10.6 percent decline in shareholder value.[3] The reason appears to be that many organizations have jumped on the 360-degree bandwagon without careful planning and strategizing about why and how the program is being used within the organization. Unless each rater has a consistent view of effective performance relative to the organization's strategy, disagreements can cause unexpected conflicts and problems, and result in communication breakdowns that require time to resolve. Despite their popularity, 360-degree feedback programs can create severe problems if not designed, implemented, and managed carefully. The organization's strategy and culture must support such a system. Otherwise, the organization runs the risk of performance problems that inevitably will impact bottom-line profitability and value.

Despite the advantages of multirater systems, collecting additional performance data results in a greater economic cost (relative to opportunity cost of the time of those involved in the process) and a more complex process in attempting to process and analyze the data to provide meaningful feedback to employees. If not designed and implemented carefully, 360-degree feedback systems can result in the collection and processing of excessive amounts of information that provide no benefit to either the organization or the employee. Such data overload can cause the most relevant, critical performance data to be lost or obscured in the process.

WHAT TO EVALUATE

The next strategic question that needs to be addressed involves determining what is to be evaluated. Essentially, employee evaluations can be based on their traits, their behaviors, or the results or outcomes they achieve. Traits-based measures focus on the general abilities and characteristics of the employee. They might include dimensions like loyalty to the organization, industriousness, and gregariousness. Although assessment of traits can often allow the organization to determine how the employee fits with the organization's culture, such measures ignore what the employee actually *does*. Traits-based measures, therefore, are of limited use or value; the subjective nature of such nonperformance-related criteria would probably not hold up well in court in a discrimination complaint.

Behavior-based measures focus on what an employee does by examining specific behaviors of the employee. Factors assessed here might include the employee's ability to get along with others, punctuality, willingness to take initiative, and ability to meet deadlines. Behavioral measures are very useful for feedback purposes because they specify exactly what the employee is doing correctly and what the employee should do differently. This is critical; work-related behaviors are generally within the control of

▶ Reading 10.1, "Has 360-Degree Feedback Gone Amok?" addresses why organizations have embraced the idea of 360-degree feedback and provides strategies for getting the maximum benefit from 360-degree systems.

most employees. However, it is possible for employees to engage in appropriate behaviors but not achieve results for the organization. Although employees may do the right things, their performance may not make a difference for the organization in terms of performance that relates to strategic objectives.

The third basis for performance feedback is to assess outcomes or results. Results-based measures focus on specific accomplishments or direct outcomes of an employee's work. These might include measures of number of units sold, divisional profitability, cost reduction, efficiency, or quality. Unlike traits and behaviors, results-based measures are often criteria than can be measured objectively. More important, results are generally more meaningful to the organization due to their more direct correlation with performance relating to the divisional or organizational strategy.

Although results may be a more significant measure of performance than traits or behaviors, there are some limitations to the utilization of results-based feedback measures. First, it may be difficult to obtain results for certain job responsibilities. Any tasks that involve dealing with the future (i.e., forecasting and planning relative to competition or assessing other dimensions of the external environment) will not show immediate results nor will the quality or accuracy of the work be assessable until sometime in the future. Second, results are sometimes beyond an individual employee's control. Budget cuts and resource availability may be at the discretion of others, but they may impact the employee's ability to generate specific performance objectives. Third, results, taken by themselves, focus on the ends or outcomes while ignoring the means or processes by which the results were obtained. An employee might achieve targeted goals but do so in an unproductive way by incurring excessive costs, alienating coworkers, or damaging customer relations. Finally, results are limiting in that they fail to tap some critical areas of performance for modern organizations such as teamwork, initiative, and openness to change. The need for organizations to remain flexible and responsive to change in their environments requires them to have internal processes to facilitate internal change. Results-based measures would ignore these processes.

As can be seen, all three types of performance measures have some limitations. However, the strengths of one approach can offset the limitations of the others. Nothing prevents an organization from utilizing any combination of traits, behaviors, and results-based measures in attempting to develop a performance feedback system that is in sync with the organization's strategic objectives. In short, the decision of what to evaluate is contingent upon what the organization seeks to achieve. ▼▼

Strategic Performance Management at Continental Airlines

When Gordon Bethune became CEO of Continental Airlines in the mid-1990s, he faced a daunting challenge. Years of cost-cutting measures had resulted in a consumer image of the airline as unreliable and unpredictable, employees were deeply unhappy and distrustful of management, late and canceled flights were costing Continental $6 million each month, and Continental was dead-last in the Department of Transportation's monthly performance rankings. Bethune decided to implement one overriding measure of performance in this complex work environment and industry to help turn the struggling airline

---

▶▶ Reading 10.2, "Aligning Service Strategy Through Super-Measure Management," examines how service organizations can link performance management to a customer-focused strategy via the use of one principal measure of performance.

around. He proposed that if Continental were to attain a top-three on-time ranking in the Department of Transportation's monthly rankings, half the cost savings incurred would be split with every nonmanagement employee. No other performance measures were to be considered. This risky strategy paid off well. By the second month of the offer, Continental had moved from last to first in the rankings and each employee enjoyed a $65 bonus. However, as on-time performance improved, the number of lost customer baggage increased. As a result, the program was modified to include baggage handling, with Continental immediately moving into the top three in the rankings for this measure. By 2000, Continental was consistently ranked number one in on-time arrivals among all U.S. airlines and named number one in customer satisfaction in industry surveys. In that year, bonuses of $785 were paid to employees. Continental's program was a resounding success because of the importance of the performance measure to the organization (and industry) and the means by which it was communicated, implemented, and rewarded.[4]

In addition to traits, behaviors, and outcomes, one area that employers are beginning to measure is the job performance competencies the employee displays. Competencies often can be closely tied to an organization's strategic objectives and therefore provide a more critical measure of performance—as well as more valuable feedback for employees in their careers. A competency-based performance management program can take a tremendous amount of time to establish, must be communicated clearly to employees, and also tied in with the organization's reward structure. Core competencies should be limited in number to those most central to the organization's success, and corresponding opportunities should be established by which employees can obtain and build on these competencies. Exhibit 10-4 presents a sample competency model for managers that cuts across organization size and industry.

EXHIBIT 10-4: MULTILEVEL CORPORATE COMPETENCY MODEL

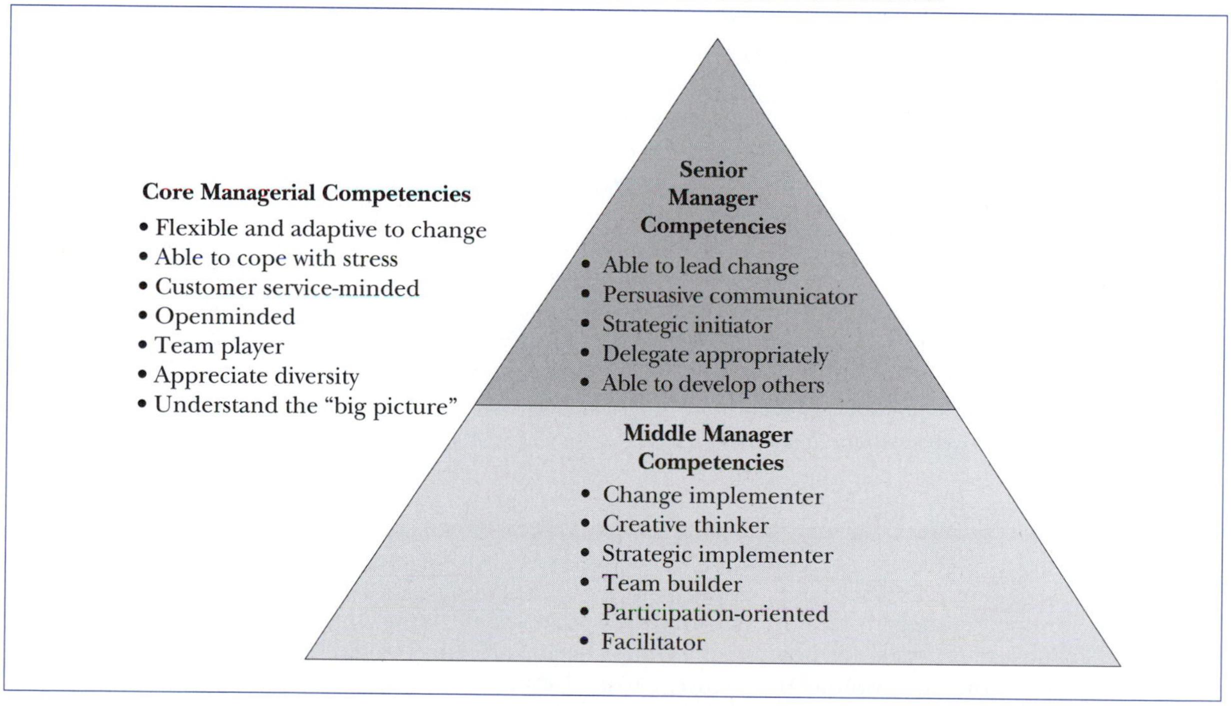

Core Managerial Competencies
• Flexible and adaptive to change
• Able to cope with stress
• Customer service-minded
• Openminded
• Team player
• Appreciate diversity
• Understand the "big picture"

Senior Manager Competencies
• Able to lead change
• Persuasive communicator
• Strategic initiator
• Delegate appropriately
• Able to develop others

Middle Manager Competencies
• Change implementer
• Creative thinker
• Strategic implementer
• Team builder
• Participation-oriented
• Facilitator

Source: Adapted from Elmer Burack, Wayne Hockwarter and Nicholas Mathys, "The New Management Development Paradigm," *Human Resource Planning*, Vol. 80(1), 1997, pp. 14–21.

EXHIBIT 10-5: CAPITAL ONE COMPETENCIES

Success Factors	Competencies
Builds relationships	1 Communicates clearly and openly
	2 Treats others with respect
	3 Collaborates with others
Applies integrative thinking	4 Analyzes information
	5 Generates and pursues ideas
	6 Develops and shapes strategies
	7 Identifies and solves problems
	8 Applies integrated decision-making
Drives toward results	9 Focuses on strategic priorities
	10 Organizes and manages multiple tasks
	11 Directs and coordinates work
	12 Gets the job done
Leads in a learning environment	13 Recruits talent
	14 Motivates and develops
	15 Builds and leads teams
	16 Influences others
	17 Promotes the culture
Takes personal ownership	18 Takes responsibility
	19 Learns continuously
	20 Embraces change
	21 Initiates opportunities for improvement
	22 Shows integrity
	23 Maintains perspective

Competency-Based Performance and Development at Capital One

Capital One is one of the world's fastest-growing consumer credit companies. In 2002, Capital One developed a competency-based performance management system, known as the Success Profile, which is designed to support the organization's strategy and long-term growth objectives. The Success Profile is designed to provide specific measurable performance feedback as well as to allow employees to plan their own professional development activities. The Success Profile contains 23 competencies that are seen as critical to the mission and objectives of Capital One. These competencies are grouped together into five access Factors, as illustrated in Exhibit 10-5. Each competency is measured on a behavioral-based rating scale containing up to four stages. Employees receive detailed performance feedback and work with their managers to develop a personal development plan for the future.

HOW TO EVALUATE

The next strategic decision that must be addressed in designing the performance management system is how to assess employees. Performance feedback can be performed on an absolute or relative basis. Absolute measures evaluate employees strictly according to the performance requirements or standards of the job; relative measures evaluate employees in comparison to coworkers. Relative measures may further involve slotting employees into categories, such as the top 10 percent of the employees in the work unit receiving an overall outstanding evaluation, similar to what is known in education as grading on a curve.

Relative assessment of employees can be useful in allowing the organization to identify overall top performers, much as high schools provide class rank to their students to facilitate college and university assessments for admission. However, if performance is not normally distributed, skewed results can provide misleading data: If all employees are outstanding performers, some will still be ranked poorly. Conversely, if all employees are deficient in performance, some will still be ranked as outstanding. For example, in a classroom setting, assume that there are 30 students in a class and that on a midterm exam all 30 students score 90 or above. If performance was ranked on a relative basis, a student who scored 90 would be ranked 30th out of 30, despite the fact that the student did "A" work in absolute means. Similarly, if on the final exam the highest grade was a 55, that student would be ranked 1st out of 30, despite the fact that, on an absolute basis, the student failed the exam. Relative measures can easily facilitate distorted perceptions of performance when all employees are superior or deficient. Although they are useful in identifying the best employees, they should not be used without some supplementary absolute assessment and ratings that are specifically related to strategic objectives.

One popular, although controversial, means of relative assessment is forced ranking. Forced ranking, or forced distribution, involves placing employees into clusters or groupings based on a distribution schema. Forced ranking is premised on social science theory that finds that human phenomena tend to distribute normally, along a bell-shaped curve, when measured using sufficiently large samples.[5] Forced rankings ideally can help build a high-performance organization by ensuring that managers clearly distinguish among employee performance levels.

Forced ranking systems were pioneered by General Electric, under former CEO Jack Welch. At GE, employees are sorted into three groups: the top 20 percent on whom rewards, promotions and stock options are showered; a "high performing" middle 70 percent with promising futures; and a bottom 10 percent whose employment is terminated, either voluntarily or involuntarily.[6] Other large employers who use forced ranking systems include Cisco Systems, Hewlett-Packard, Microsoft, Sun Microsystems, and Pepsico.[7]

Those who favor forced ranking argue that it is the best way to identify both the highest-performing employees, who should receive generous incentives, and bottom performers, who should be helped up or out. It also provides data-driven bases for compensation decisions and forces managers to make and justify sometimes tough decisions and won't allow them to avoid giving employees needed feedback. Critics, however, argue that forced ranking can be arbitrary, unfair, and expose an organization to lawsuits.[8] Ford Motor Company abandoned its practice of forced rankings in 2001 when it settled two class-action lawsuits for $10.5 million.[9] To avoid some of the inherent subjectivity that might come with the final rankings, some employers outsource the final distributions to outside consultants who are able to analyze trends and correct biases in final ratings.[10]

While forced rankings may be controversial they tend to be more effective in organizations with a high-pressure, results-driven culture.[11] Forced rankings are certainly not appropriate for every organization, but in concept, forced rankings are consistent with a strategic approach toward human resource management because they emphasize differentiating employees by performance level and investing more resources in those human assets that have displayed the highest returns.

MEASURES OF EVALUATION

Another strategic decision that needs to be made in the design of the performance management system is the means of evaluation. There are a variety of tools or formats to use in measuring performance. These include graphic rating scales, weighted checklists, behaviorally anchored rating scales, behavioral observation scales, critical incident measures, and objectives-based measures.

Graphic rating scales are one of the most widely used assessment and feedback devices. Relatively easy to design, use, and update as job requirements change, they involve a scale that gives the evaluator the performance measures for traits, behaviors, or results. Some examples of graphic rating scales are illustrated in Exhibit 10-6.

Weighted checklists provide the evaluator with specific criteria on which performance is to be assessed and ask the evaluator to check those criteria that apply to the employee. The different dimensions are weighted based on their importance to the organization; weights are unknown to the evaluator as the checklist is being completed. A sample weighted checklist is presented in Exhibit 10-7.

A behaviorally anchored rating scale (BARS) is a more specific type of graphic rating scale. The evaluator is given specific descriptions of behaviors along a numerically rated scale and is asked to select the behavior that most corresponds to the

EXHIBIT 10-6: EXAMPLES OF GRAPHIC RATING SCALES

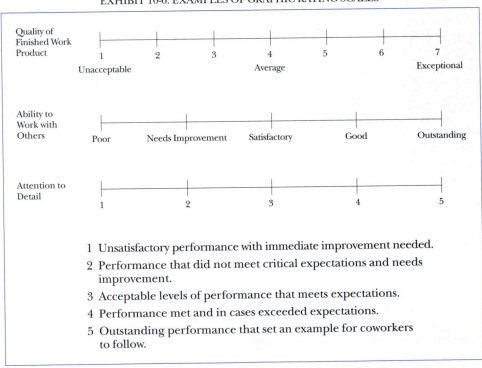

1 Unsatisfactory performance with immediate improvement needed.

2 Performance that did not meet critical expectations and needs improvement.

3 Acceptable levels of performance that meets expectations.

4 Performance met and in cases exceeded expectations.

5 Outstanding performance that set an example for coworkers to follow.

EXHIBIT 10-7: EXAMPLE OF WEIGHTED CHECKLIST

Instructions: Check all of those qualities that are accurate assessments of the employee's performance.

		Weight
_____	Is able to address routine day-to-day problems effectively.	4.2
_____	Maintains cordial and productive relationships with coworkers.	3.7
_____	Displays the ability to delegate effectively and develop subordinates.	4.1
_____	Works well without direct supervision.	5.1
_____	Is able to meet deadlines and follow through on commitments.	4.8
_____	Engages in appropriate activity to further individual career development.	2.9
_____	Adheres to rules, procedures, and standard operating protocols.	3.4

Note: The weights are not included on the actual rating form that the evaluator completes. Higher values indicate more critical requirements for the job.

employee's performance for the time period being evaluated. BARS can be difficult and time-consuming to develop, but it can help to overcome some of the subjectivity and biases that may result when evaluators are given no set descriptions for performance measures. A sample BARS is presented in Exhibit 10-8.

A potential problem with BARS may be that an employee's behavior is inconsistent. Sometimes, the employee might merit a 6 on a scale of 1 to 7; at other times, performance would be closer to 2. A behavioral observation scale (BOS) addresses the problem of inconsistent employee performance by measuring frequencies along the scale. Instead of providing examples of different behaviors as would be presented in a BARS, the BOS determines which behavior of a BARS is optimal and asks for an assessment of the frequency with which the employee displays it. A sample BOS is presented in Exhibit 10-9.

Critical incident measures do not generally utilize a scale. The evaluator provides specific examples of the employee's critical behaviors or results, either outstanding or problematic, during the performance period. The evaluator must maintain a log or diary for each employee and make periodic notation of noteworthy behaviors or results that were particularly effective or ineffective. This process can be very time-consuming, but it allows the feedback to cite specific examples of performance measures instead of general impressions. Feedback that is specific and directed is not only more meaningful to the employee, but it can also be targeted to specific objectives of the work unit or organization. The critical incident technique can be utilized by itself or incorporated into a rating scale where space is provided for open-ended comments by the evaluator.

A final way to assess performance is to base feedback on predetermined, negotiated work objectives. Traditionally called *management by objectives (MBO)*, this process involves having the employee meet with his or her immediate supervisor prior to the time period for which performance is to be assessed. The two parties jointly agree on the employee's work objectives for the forthcoming time period. The process of

EXHIBIT 10-8: EXAMPLE OF BEHAVIORALLY ANCHORED RATING SCALE

Position: _____

Job Dimension: _____

Plans work and organizes time carefully in order to maximize resources and meet commitments.

9

8 — Even though this associate has a report due on another project, he or she would be well prepared for the assigned discussion on your project.

This associate would keep a calendar or schedule on which deadlines and activities are carefully noted, and which would be consulted before making new commitments.

7

As program chief, this associate would manage arrangements for enlisting resources for a special project reasonably well, but would probably omit one or two details that would have to be handled by improvisation.

6

Plans and organizes time and effort primarily for large segments of a task. Usually meets commitments, but may overlook what are considered secondary details.

5 — This associate would meet a deadline in handing in a report, but the report might be below usual standard if other deadlines occur on the same day the report is due.

4 — This associate's evaluations are likely not to reflect abilities because of overcommitments in other activities.

3 — This associate would plan more by enthusiasm than by timetable and frequently have to work late the night before an assignment is due, although it would be completed on time.

2 — This associate would often be late for meetings, although others in similar circumstances do not seem to find it difficult to be on time.

Appears to do little planning. May perform effectively, despite what seems to be a disorganized approach, although deadlines may be missed.

1 — This associate never makes a deadline, even with sufficient notice.

Source: Anthony, W. P. et al. *Human Resource Management*, 3 ed. Dryden, 1999, p. 389.

EXHIBIT 10-9: EXAMPLE OF BEHAVIORAL OBSERVATION SCALE

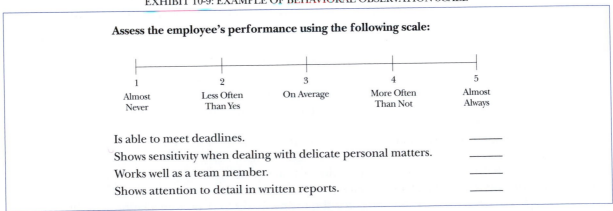

Assess the employee's performance using the following scale:

1	2	3	4	5
Almost Never	Less Often Than Yes	On Average	More Often Than Not	Almost Always

Is able to meet deadlines. _____

Shows sensitivity when dealing with delicate personal matters. _____

Works well as a team member. _____

Shows attention to detail in written reports. _____

negotiation is important here. Ideally, this process involves setting objectives that are simultaneously consistent with the organization's strategy and satisfy job requirements and also provide challenging work assignments that are consistent with the employee's developmental needs and career aspirations.

Objectives-based performance management systems are based on goal-setting theory, which was pioneered by Edwin Locke.[12] Goal-setting theory assumes that motivation is enhanced when individuals work toward a specific, targeted goal or goals and also receive feedback as to their progress toward reaching their goals.[13] Even though objectives are determined for a set time period, commonly six months or one year, this does not mean that performance feedback should be withheld until the end of the time period. Informal, regular feedback is more effective; particularly when it is provided immediately following some outcome or behavior, it has a far stronger and more constant impact on motivation than feedback that is only provided annually in a more formal manner.

Objectives-based performance measurement systems often result in enhanced employee motivation because employees are allowed to provide input in determining their job responsibilities and in discussing critical organizational goals to which they can contribute.[14] Employee commitment is usually enhanced as well; employees can be expected to be far more committed to reaching performance objectives that they have agreed to and negotiated for themselves rather than having objectives determined for them by the organization.[15] When an employee participates in this process, the employee's trust and dependability are placed on the line. Nonperformance cannot be as readily dismissed through claims that the supervisor does not understand the job or the pressures inherently involved with it or that the objectives set were therefore unrealistic.

Three common oversights can inhibit the effectiveness of any objectives-based feedback system. These oversights are (1) setting objectives that are too vague; (2) setting objectives that are unrealistically difficult; and (3) not clarifying how performance will be measured, particularly when the objective itself is not quantifiable and requires some subjectivity in evaluation. Any objectives set as part of such a process must be specific, measurable, and within the employee's control if the feedback system is to be beneficial to the organization and to the employee. Objectives also need to be challenging, but obtainable. Unrealistic goals may hamper motivation; supervisors need to have faith in their employees' abilities yet realize where to draw the line. When the objectives are set, the parties must also reach agreement as to how the performance criteria will be measured and assessed. This is particularly important when there are no objective measures available for assessing performance.

The objectives selected must also be valid. Much as selection measures need to be valid, objective performance measures must be valid, as well. Occasionally, inappropriate objective measures may be selected. These measures may be easily quantifiable and accurately measurable, but not directly related to performance. For example, a teacher could be evaluated on the test scores of students. Although this is an objective measure, it might encourage the teacher to teach students to maximize test scores rather than learn. A salesperson could similarly be evaluated on sales volume, which is easily measurable, but not get evaluated on expenses incurred, customer service, returns, or professional demeanor. Most employees will focus on the behavior or outcome that is evaluated and rewarded at the expense of other elements of the job.[16]

These various means of measuring performance are not mutually exclusive. Nothing prevents an organization from using some combination of methods. However, it should be remembered that, much like the decision of who should provide performance feedback, more is not necessarily better. Organizations need to ensure that the methods employed in measuring performance are not cumbersome, contradictory, or excessively laborious. The methods of providing performance data must be consistent with the uses of the system and the organization's strategic objectives.

OTHER CONSIDERATIONS

In addition to the five strategic design decisions previously outlined, several other critical factors must be considered when developing an effective performance management system. First, the organization needs to ensure the link between the performance management system and the training and development and compensation systems. This link was explained in Chapter 9, but it bears reiteration here. Training and development goals and objectives must be reflected in performance feedback systems. Subsequently, the criteria by which performance is evaluated must be incorporated into the compensation or reward system. If either of these two links is not established and maintained, the performance management system will be of limited value. The performance management system lies within the much larger framework of human resource management systems and must be conceptualized and designed with this strategic perspective in mind.

Traditional performance evaluation systems stress the most recent, immediate time period and evaluate individual employee performance. However, many organizations have strategic initiatives that involve long-range planning and growth, requiring the use of criteria that cannot be measured based on performance during the immediate past time period. In addition, many organizations are moving toward more flexible job assignments and responsibilities. Organizations having self-managed work teams place more responsibility for performance on the group rather than at the individual level. Traditional means of performance evaluation may need to be significantly recast in the light of changes taking place in contemporary organizations. There are few, if any, models of evaluation systems that can assess work responsibilities associated longer-range objectives or team-based evaluation.

A final consideration is the degree of standardization or flexibility of the performance management system. Standardization is important to prevent job bias or allegations of discriminatory treatment. Flexibility in the system is important because jobs have different levels of responsibility and accountability and require different types and mixes of skills (technical, interpersonal, or administrative). Organizations need to strike a balance between having some consistency (standardization) and some variance (flexibility) in their performance feedback systems. The single most important criterion in addressing this issue is the nature of the job responsibilities assigned to the employee. Specific job-related criteria are not only most meaningful for feedback and developmental purposes but are also most defendable under the law. This does not imply that each individual job should have a unique means and method for measuring performance. That is clearly impractical and unrealistic. It does mean, however, that there is no one appropriate way to develop a performance management system in any organization; the system must be tailored to the objectives of the organization.

Why Performance Management Systems Often Fail

Despite the importance of performance management systems, many managers and executives are not committed to providing performance feedback. The process is often

EXHIBIT 10-10: REASONS MANAGERS RESIST OR IGNORE PERFORMANCE MANAGEMENT

- Process is too complicated
- No impact on job performance
- Possible legal challenges
- Lack of control over process
- No connection with rewards
- Complexity and length of forms

Source: Adapted from Grensing-Pophal, L. "Motivate Managers to Review Performance," *HR Magazine*, March 2001, pp. 45–48.

seen as time-consuming and cumbersome and can make managers uncomfortable. This dissatisfaction is also seen in the HR suite. One survey of HR directors and executives found that 90 percent felt that their performance management system needed reform.[17] Exhibit 10-10 outlines some of the reasons managers may resist—or totally ignore—performance management processes.

First, many managers are disheartened by the complexity of the process. Performance data may be subject to multiple levels of review and/or require the collection of large amounts of data that must be analyzed and condensed. A system that requires the collection of data from multiple individuals may further require that contradictory and/or inconsistent feedback be reconciled. Second, unless the performance management process involves some planning by which managers and subordinates use the performance data to set clear goals for future performance, there may be little, if any, impact on subsequent job performance. An ideal performance management system connects data about recent past performance to future plans that incorporate the employee's career goals and the strategic goals of the organization and/or unit. Third, when salary, promotion, and retention decisions are made based on performance management data, claims of unlawful discrimination may be made by employees who did not feel appropriately rewarded. The inherently subjective nature of performance management data fuels this possibility and, as a result, may cause organizations to limit the performance feedback given and/or how such feedback is used. Fourth, many managers feel that they have little control over the process by which they manage their subordinates' performance. When standards related to expectations of the end results are set by senior management, managers may feel that the process is less than legitimate. Fifth, employees and managers alike lament the fact that many performance management systems are totally divorced from the organization's reward system. If there are no consequences, results, or outcomes from the performance management process, it most likely will be shortchanged and not taken seriously by those at all levels in the organization. Finally, the forms and paperwork that often accompany the performance management system can be lengthy and complex. A process that takes managers away from their day-to-day responsibilities for an unduly long time may result in them looking for shortcuts that compromise the efficacy and integrity of the overall process. ▼▼▼

►►► Reading 10.3, "Strategic Performance Appraisal in Team-Based Organizations: One Size Does Not Fit All," examines the relationship between different types of teams and the appropriate performance measures for each.

- Involve managers in the design of the system
- Hold managers accountable for the performance and development of their subordinates
- Set clear expectations for performance
- Set specific objectives for the system
- Tie performance measures to rewards
- Gain commitment from senior management

Addressing the Shortcomings of Performance Management Systems

The challenge then becomes how to get buy-in from managers to improve the performance management system. Exhibit 10-11 highlights some strategies for addressing some of the managerial reluctance or resistance to commit fully to performance management. First, managers should be involved in the design of the system. Because they are its true users, their input as "consumers" should be sought to facilitate the design of a system that works both for them and the organization. Second, managers should be held accountable for the performance of their subordinates as well as for the development of their direct reports. By tying managers' performance in meeting organization and divisional goals to their effective use of the performance management system, managers are more likely to take the system seriously. Third, clear expectations should be set for individual performance at all levels of performance review to facilitate a timely review of recent performance data and allow more specific feedback to be provided to employees. Fourth, the organization should identify the specific purpose and goals of its performance management system. Clarification of the relationship of the system to the organization's strategy makes the system more salient and relevant to organizational participants and further legitimizes the entire process. Fifth, performance measures should be clearly linked to rewards, solidifying the legitimacy of the system. Finally, absolute commitment to the performance management system needs to be gained from top management. One recent survey found that at the executive level, 42 percent of executives do not even review the performance management system at all.[18] When senior managers publicly support and personally use the performance management system, a strong message is sent regarding its importance to all employees.

CONCLUSION

Performance management systems can significantly impact organizational performance and processes. However, there is no one optimal way to develop and design an effective performance management system. Organizations face a number of strategic choices as to how they measure performance and provide employees feedback on the process.

Although effective performance management systems need to be developed within the context of specific organizational contingencies, five critical guidelines should be followed in any performance management system: (1) Any feedback provided to employees should be specific rather than general; (2) Feedback should only be provided from credible, trustworthy sources that have ample opportunity and background to make an assessment of performance; (3) Feedback should be provided as soon as possible after events, behaviors, or outcomes take place to be of maximum benefit; (4) Performance measures should be based on clear, measurable goals; and (5) The process should involve a dialogue between the employee and the manager that addresses the most recent period and also plans for the future.

CRITICAL THINKING

1. Identify the major strategic issues an employer faces in designing a performance management system.

2. What are the major purposes of a performance management system? To what extent can all of the purposes be realized simultaneously?

3. What are the advantages and disadvantages of 360-degree feedback systems? How should an organization decide whose feedback to seek?

4. Describe the strengths and weaknesses of traits, behavior, and outcomes-based measurements. For what kinds of positions is each appropriate?

5. Do performance management systems usually measure the right things? How can performance management systems encourage performance that is more consistent with long-range rather than short-term issues?

6. Devise an appropriate performance management system for your current position.

7. Debate the pros and cons of forced rankings. What kinds of organizations would most benefit from forced ranking systems?

Reading 10.1

8. What recommendation can be provided to an organization considering the implementation of a 360-degree feedback system? What limitations exist to the success of these programs?

Reading 10.2

9. What is a Super-Measure? Chose five organizations in different industries and determine how a Super-Measure might be implemented in each of these organizations.

Reading 10.3

10. Explain the different kinds of teams and the appropriate performance measures for each.

EXPERIENTIAL EXERCISES

1. Individually or in small groups, select one occupation and design a performance management system for this position.
   - University professor
   - Convenience store clerk

- Attorney
- Marriage counselor
- Software engineer
- Clergy member

2. Develop a competency-based performance management system for a student in the degree program in which you are enrolled. How would you go about determining and measuring important competencies? What benefits might such a system provide?

3. In an organization of your choosing, briefly interview three managers who work in different divisions/departments/units and are at different levels of managerial responsibility. How does each feel about performance management in the organization?

INTERNET EXERCISES

1. This chapter begins with a description of a 360-degree performance management system that is administered on an intranet. What are the pros and cons of an intranet-based performance management system compared to a paper-based system? Investigate the costs of moving a traditional, paper-based performance management system to an online system in economic terms, technical terms, and human terms.

CHAPTER REFERENCES

1. Johnson, C. "Making Sure Employees Measure Up," *HR Magazine*, March 2001, pp. 36–41.
2. Carson, K. P., Cardy, R. L. and Dobbins, G. H. "Performance Appraisal as Effective Management or Deadly Management Disease: Two Empirical Investigations," *Group and Organization Studies*, 16, 1991, pp. 143–159.
3. Pfau, B. and Kay, I. "Does 360-degree Feedback Negatively Affect Company Performance" *HR Magazine*, June 2002, pp. 55–59.
4. Morgan, I. and Rao, J. "Aligning Service Strategy through Super-Measure Management," *Academy of Management Executive*, 16, (4), 2002, pp. 121–135.
5. Guralnik, O. and Wardi, L. "Forced Distribution: A Controversy," www.shrm.org/hrresources/whitepapers_published/CMS_005247.asp
6. Grote, D. "Are Most Layoffs Carried Out Fairly? Yes," www.optimizemagazine.com/issue/002/squareoff_yes.htm
7. Ibid.
8. Guralnik, O. and Wardi, L. "Forced Distribution: A Controversy," www.shrm.org/hrresources/whitepapers_published/CMS_005247.asp
9. Bates, S. "Forced Ranking," *HR Magazine*, July 2003, pp. 63–68.
10. Guralink, O. and Wardi, L. "Forced Distribution: A Controversy," www.shrm.org/hrresources/whitepapers_published/CMS_005247.asp
11. Bates, S. "Forced Ranking," *HR Magazine*, July 2003, pp. 63–68.
12. Locke, E. "Toward a Theory of Task Moves and Incentives," *Organizational Behavior and Human Performance*, 3, 1968, pp. 157–189.
13. Pinder, C. *Work Motivation*. Glenview, IL: Scott, Foresman, 1984.
14. Ibid.
15. Ibid.
16. Kerr. S. "On the Folly of Rewarding A, While Hoping for B," *Academy of Management Journal*, 18, 1975, pp. 766–783.
17. Grensing-Pophal, L. "Motivate Managers to Review Performance," *HR Magazine*, May 2001, pp. 45–48.
18. "Performance Management Gaps Need Filled, Survey Says" *HR News*, November 2000, pp. 14, 21.

Has 360-Degree Feedback Gone Amok?

David A. Waldman, Leanne E. Atwater, David Antonioni, *Academy of Management Executive*

Three hundred sixty degree feedback programs have been implemented in a growing number of American firms in recent years. A variety of individual and organizational improvement goals have been attributed to these feedback processes. Despite the attention given to 360 feedback, there has been much more discussion about how to implement such programs than about why organizations have rushed to join the bandwagon or even what they expect to accomplish. Are companies doing 360 degree feedback simply because their competitors are? What evidence exists to suggest that 360 degree feedback prompts changes in managers' behavior? This article explores the outcomes that organizations can realistically expect and provides recommendations for implementing innovations such as 360 feedback to best ensure improvements will be realized and the process will be a success.

Three hundred and sixty degree feedback programs can involve feedback for a targeted employee or manager from four sources: (1) downward from the target's supervisor, (2) upward from subordinates, (3) laterally from peers or coworkers, and (4) inwardly from the target himself. Studies show that about 12 percent of American organizations are using full 360 degree programs, 25 percent are using upward appraisals, and 18 percent are using peer appraisals.[1] Furthermore, it appears that the trend is growing.[2] The most obvious reasons for this growth include the desire on the part of organizations to enhance management development, employee involvement, communication, and culture change.

The rise of 360 degree feedback can be traced to the human relations movement of the 1950s and 1960s, when organizations attempted to improve organizational processes and communication through various forms of what came to be known as organizational development. One popular form of organizational development was survey/feedback.

Survey/feedback involves a general employee survey of such factors as jobs, benefits, pay, and organizational communication. Traditional survey/feedback was geared toward overall organizational processes, while 360 degree feedback programs are targeted toward supplying information to specific individuals, e.g., supervisors and managers, about their work behaviors. Traditional survey/feedback was an upward feedback process. While 360 degree programs have relied heavily on upward feedback, at least some attempts have been made to gather peer, supervisor, and/or customer feedback.

Reasons for Adopting 360 Degree Feedback

A key purpose driving the present use of 360 degree feedback is the desire to further management or leadership development. Providing feedback to managers about how they are viewed by direct subordinates, peers, and customers/clients should prompt behavior change. Many managers have not received as much honest feedback as is necessary for an accurate self-perception. When anonymous feedback solicited from others is compared with the manager's self-evaluations, the manager may form a more realistic picture of his or her strengths and weaknesses. This may prompt behavior change if the weaknesses identified were previously unknown to the manager, especially when such change is encouraged and supported by the organization.

Other potential benefits of 360 degree initiatives are targeted ultimately toward organizational change and improvement. These initiatives reflect resource dependence theory, which views organizational change as a rational response to environmental pressures for change or strategic adaptation.[3]

By increasing managerial self-awareness through formalized 360 degree or upward feedback, an organization's culture will become more participatory and will be able to react more quickly to the needs of internal and external customers. This should ultimately lead to increasing levels of trust and communication between managers and their constituents, fewer grievances, and greater customer satisfaction.

In addition to the logical, performance-based reasons for pursuing a 360 degree feedback program, at least three other reasons account for its proliferation.

IMITATION

Institutional theory suggests that organizations make attempts to imitate their competition or other firms in an organizational network.[4] This suggests that the choice to adopt 360 degree feedback reflects a response to environmental pressures. Such conformity gives a firm a sense of external legitimacy.

As an example, we worked closely with a large telecommunications firm to implement an upward feedback program. From the beginning, we sought to determine the precise reasons why the firm wanted to pursue this program. A consistent reason simply seemed to be a desire to keep up with the competition. Managers asked us to provide lists of other companies using upward feedback, almost as if that alone were reason to adopt it. Performance-based thinking was not absent, but a form of "satisficing" might have been at play whereby improved performance was expected simply by imitating others.

A similar phenomenon of imitation occurred years ago regarding quality circles and has occurred more recently with TQM. TQM can be implemented in a number of different ways. These include the use of various scientific and statistically oriented approaches to solving quality problems, and an increase in activities directed toward understanding customers' perceptions and desires pertaining to quality. In an attempt to achieve external legitimacy, later adopters have often not been overly concerned about the specifics of TQM implementation and how or whether such specifics are actually linked with performance outcomes.

The recent implementation of teams in organizations provides another relevant example. Organizations have created teams to mimic the competition. Managers reason that if the competition is using teams and they are doing well, they should use them or fall behind. Little thought has gone into determining what improvements can be expected, or how

technical and managerial systems would require change to support teams.

Institutional theory and imitation become more and more relevant as organizations face uncertain situations. Indeed, this may still be the case for 360 feedback since little research evidence exists regarding the precise methods and contexts in which it can positively affect organizational outcomes. In such situations, attempts to copy the actions of reputable others seem reasonable, and late adopters may not seriously question the potential effectiveness of 360 feedback. That is, they see no need to systematically demonstrate performance improvements before engaging in a widespread rollout.

A case can be made that given the increasing uncertainty, rapid change, and increasing competition facing organizations, managers feel that spending additional time and money testing the usefulness of such innovations prior to full implementation is not cost effective. It may be smarter in the long run to adopt the innovation and simply drop it later if it is unsuccessful. In short, we acknowledge the logic of attempting to imitate what other firms are doing with regard to 360 feedback initiatives. But imitating without clearly understanding what other firms have accomplished, or the likely outcomes for one's own firm, may be a questionable strategy.

360 DEGREE FEEDBACK AS PART OF PERFORMANCE APPRAISAL

A second alternative reason for the proliferation of 360 degree feedback is the desire to expand formal appraisal processes by making such feedback evaluative, thereby linking it directly with a manager's or employee's performance appraisal. Our most recent experiences suggest that there are pressures to make 360 feedback evaluative because companies want to get their money's worth.

In theory, the use of 360 feedback for evaluative purposes seems logical. An individual held directly accountable for ratings received will be more motivated to take action to make improvements based on the feedback. Unfortunately, problems exist that may negate the possible benefits of 360 degree feedback if it is made evaluative. Employees may rebel and try to sabotage the program. For example, in the case of upward feedback, implicit or even explicit deals may be struck with subordinates to give high ratings in exchange for high ratings. Such maneuvering is less likely when the feedback is being provided strictly for developmental purposes.

Research has demonstrated that when ratings become evaluative rather than purely developmental, some raters (up to 35 percent) change their ratings.[5] UPS tested the potential of using 360 ratings for evaluation. The company asked employees after they had provided upward ratings whether they would have altered the ratings if they knew they would be used as part of their managers' formal performance evaluations. Their findings suggested that some individuals would raise, and some would even lower, ratings if they were to be used for evaluation. Changes in ratings were made primarily in order to affect outcomes, i.e., keep the manager from trouble, or in some cases to get the manager in trouble. Three hundred sixty degree ratings are typically collected anonymously. Ratings that are not anonymous may differ from those that are. Ratings become less genuine if the rater believes he or she will be identified. Not surprisingly, some raters indicate that they would raise their ratings if they were going to be identified to their managers. Anonymous ratings also have potential drawbacks. If anonymous 360 ratings were used as part of the documentation for a personnel action involving a manager—e.g., demotion, dismissal, or unattained promotion or pay raise—that manager could potentially make a legal case against the firm. Since the ratings are anonymous, they cannot be traced to specific individuals, and hence their validity could come into question in a court action. In contrast, traditional performance appraisal ratings are typically signed by the rater, i.e., one' supervisor, making them more verifiable.

A rating should be used for appraisal purposes only when the raters are committed to the goals of the organization, rather than merely to their own personal goals. This is often not the case, as the rater is primarily concerned with his or her own short-term needs. For example, a subordinate may only provide high upward feedback ratings to a manager who maintains the status quo, even though the individual and the organization could use a high degree of challenge.

This suggests another caution regarding ratings: be careful what you measure. If a manager's 360 ratings depend on creating a positive or even relaxed climate, these factors may actually detract from work directly geared toward bottom line results. For example, customers may call the manager away from the office frequently, or necessitate many hours on the phone, thus making the manager less available to employees. If this customer-oriented behavior is not part of the criteria measured and availability to subordinates is part of the criteria, customer-oriented behavior will diminish over time and be replaced by more frequent interactions with employees. Yes, relationships with employees may improve, but at what cost?

Some companies have abandoned the use of 360 feedback for appraisal purposes. For example, half of the companies surveyed in 1997 that had implemented 360 degree feedback for appraisal had removed it because of the negative attitudes from employees and the inflated ratings.[6]

Not all experts agree that using 360 degree feedback for evaluation is a problem. If traditional appraisal depends on the opinion of a supervisor who is not always in the best position to judge, and is never anonymous, wouldn't 360 appraisal be an improvement even if not always totally honest? Ratings from multiple sources also usually produce more reliable data. Data from a variety of organizations indicated that ratees were more satisfied with multi-rater appraisal than single-rater appraisal.[7] Obviously, some ratees believe that 360 appraisal is an improvement over traditional appraisal, while other do not. This belief likely stems from such factors as levels of trust in the organization, and the type of traditional appraisal used.

We would suggest caution in adopting 360 appraisal. Use 360 feedback strictly for development at first. Let managers and others become comfortable with the process. Once employees see that negative repercussions are unlikely and managers see that the information truly is helpful, they will be less apprehensive about using 360 ratings for evaluation.

A pertinent example of using upward feedback involves student evaluations of teaching. Beginning mainly in the 1970s, student evaluations have provided a form of customer-based feedback (some might argue upward feedback) to faculty members at universities. In line with institutional theory, such evaluations have now become so commonplace in universities as to represent an institutional norm. Student evaluations were originally designed to be mainly developmental in nature, providing faculty with information that could be used to improve teaching. Over time, university administrations have increasingly used this feedback for evaluative purposes, e.g., for promotion and tenure decisions.

Has this feedback process resulted in improved student-faculty relationships, trust, and communication? Has it had any effect on student learning outcomes and the satisfaction of the ultimate customers—employers and society? Student feedback, especially when used for evaluation, can certainly modify a teacher's style without having an impact on student learning. It is also possible that universities have not had clear goals nor good outcome measures for the student feedback process. Instead, student evaluations represent an easy way to evaluate teaching, and in some cases, to provide information for students selecting professors. One university recently experienced pressure from other local universities to publish student ratings of faculty. The university decided to publish its student ratings, with the intent of giving students more information on which to base course selections. The criteria students would consider important were unknown. The decision to publish student ratings was based on customer demand, and mimicked the actions of other universities.

USING 360 DEGREE FEEDBACK FOR POLITICAL PURPOSES

A third reason that companies engage in 360 feedback is politics.[8] There is often competition among individuals and groups over ideas and the individuals or groups pushing those ideas. Individuals or groups try to impress higher level management with their innovative ideas and plans. A manager with authority to make an implementation decision may attempt to appropriate credit. In an organization that we helped to implement upward feedback, we communicated initially with a training director. Once his boss bought into the plan, the boss assumed ownership and credit. Indeed, the training director eventually left the organization.[9]

Similarly, a company as a whole may adopt 360 degree feedback to manage an impression. Organizations may embrace 360 feedback to convey an impression of openness and participation to clients or recruits when, in fact, this is not part of the organizations' culture. While the innovations themselves may not be very successful, the political gains from impression management may be valuable.

Where Are the Data?

A problem related to the absence of purpose in implementing 360 feedback is the absence of data, as well as the resulting dearth of knowledge on how or even whether 360 feedback really works. In recent telephone interviews with individuals who had spear-headed the implementation of 360 degree feedback in a number of *Fortune* 500 companies, the availability of effectiveness data was discouraging. The only data available were employee and manager perceptions of the process, random anecdotes, or, on rare occasions, changes in employee ratings of managers before and after upward feedback. Recent research in a retail store setting has shown that subordinate and peer ratings of managers increased after managers received 360 feedback, but managers' ratings from their supervisors and customers did not change. In addition, this research revealed that store sales volume was unaffected by the 360 feedback intervention.[10]

There are some data suggesting productivity improvements among university faculty and improved customer satisfaction ratings following the implementation of 360 feedback. However, the research generating these data did not include a control group, so it is difficult to conclude that the 360 process was solely responsible for the improvements.[11]

We expect that in the future, few organizations will be able to afford to engage in costly training or development activities purely altruistically, or on the basis of speculative success. Rather, decision-makers and participants will need to be convinced that the development effort can be expected to have a positive impact on the bottom line.

Evaluating 360 Degree Feedback Efforts

The above arguments suggest that little is known about the effects of 360 degree feedback programs in organizations. The following recommendations are offered in the hope of realizing more systematic knowledge regarding ways to ensure the effectiveness of 360 degree feedback programs. These recommendations should apply equally well to other organizational innovations, such as TQM and teams.

MAKE CONSULTANTS/INTERNAL CHAMPIONS ACCOUNTABLE FOR RESULTS AND CUSTOMIZATION

How often are the people who are pushing an organizational innovation told that they must go into the process with specific goals, realistic timetables, and a plan for measuring results? We would argue that this is a rare event. Instead, consultants may jump on the 360 bandwagon, put together enticing packages, and subsequently feel reluctant to charge companies for evaluation. They may also fear demands from managers to explain the need for evaluation.

The result is a rush to implementation without a clear understanding of needs or expected results. Consultants, both internal and external, may simply implement the programs or activities of other organizations without systematic testing. One common example is the use of off-the-shelf 360 surveys. Although leadership may be a common factor of importance in, say, a mining organization, a police agency, and a high-tech think tank, a one-size-fits-all approach to survey items is not likely to be effective. The items will need to be customized.[13]

Conflicts of interest can result when program evaluation is left in the hands of people who have either marketed or championed a process. Care must be taken to make sure that the evaluation process is objective, and that the data are verifiable.

ENGAGE IN A PILOT TEST INITIATIVE

Firms should learn to crawl before they walk. Managers tend to want immediate action, while a pilot study may last a year or longer. However, the benefits of a pilot study can be immense. In organizations with traditional hierarchies, the inversion of the organizational pyramid that accompanies 360 degree feedback can be threatening and problematic. Pilot studies can identify the threat and problems.

A pilot test we ran in a few departments before full-scale implementation of upward feedback in a large telecommunications firm identified problems with our original survey items that could be modified. We discovered both employee and management resistance and fear, which we were able to counteract with general information sessions for all employees in the targeted departments. We identified concerns with confidentiality and anonymity that stemmed from an earlier survey intervention by another company where breaches of confidentiality were suspected. We were able to present our strategies for ensuring anonymity and confidentiality to ease these concerns. Because these problems were corrected, we were able to implement a relatively smooth roll-out across the division. In addition, we were able to follow up the pilot group before implementation and obtain some initial effectiveness data. Our ability to demonstrate at least some success on a small scale helped convince reluctant managers that the roll-out could be beneficial to the company.

CREATE FOCUS GROUPS TO IDENTIFY EFFECTIVENESS CRITERIA MEASURES

The list of possible effectiveness criteria measures for an intervention such as a 360 degree feedback program can be quite extensive. Measures should focus on activity levels as well as results. Possibilities include:

1. ratee and rater reactions to the program, i.e., the extent to which they believe the process is valuable;
2. response rates—obviously a program cannot succeed if potential raters do not respond when surveyed;
3. grievance rates;
4. customer satisfaction;
5. employee satisfaction;
6. absenteeism/turnover;
7. recruiting success, e.g., strong qualifications of applicants and new hires;
8. work behaviors, e.g., leadership, communication, employee development efforts;
9. work performance, e.g., individual work output or contributions to work unit output; and
10. positive image with clients, customers, competitors, and suppliers.

One way to identify criteria is to form focus groups. The groups could be asked what they think would improve if those being rated got better at the dimensions on which they were being rated. The groups should be pressed for specifics and then guided to systematically monitor progress on the identified criteria before and after the innovation was fully implemented.

EVALUATE USING A PRE-POST CONTROL GROUP DESIGN

Evaluation of the process is crucial to ensure that it is aiding in the accomplishment of the organization's goals, and working as intended. At least in the early stages, the organization should adopt a pre-post control group design to assess the impact of the process. Behaviors and outcomes should be measured prior to feedback, as well as after feedback, and some individuals should be selected to take part while others are not.

This recommendation may cut against the grain of typical managerial thinking. Many managers assume that if something is worth doing, it is worth doing for everybody right now. Managers also do not like their people being used as guinea pigs. We urge a reconsideration of this line of thought. In fact, this evaluation design could be implemented simply by beginning the process in stages in various parts of the organization.

Clearly, more experimental field studies on 360 degree feedback are needed. Research partnerships between the academic institutions and business organizations should be established. Research is needed on whether improvements in managerial or leadership behaviors cause improvements in performance and on whether the improvements have an effect on employee satisfaction, absenteeism, and turnover. With proper control for other factors that could affect the results, it is possible to determine what needs to be done to improve the 360 degree feedback process and, ultimately, whether the process is worth the time, money, and effort.

BE CAREFUL WHAT YOU MEASURE AND HOW IT'S USED

What gets measured (and rewarded) drives behavior. Even when 360 degree feedback ratings are used strictly for developmental purposes, individuals will tend to modify behaviors in ways to receive more positive ratings. Therefore, it is extremely important that 360 degree surveys reflect those behaviors that the organization values most highly. Care should also be taken to ensure that behaviors measured are closely tied to the accomplishment of the organization's goals.[14]

Student evaluations of teaching should encourage better teaching styles and classroom relationships. Communication between instructors and students should also improve. However, it can be argued that the process may also encourage behaviors and outcomes that are not always beneficial. Instructors may avoid challenging students for fear of upsetting them and obtaining lower student evaluations at the end of the semester. Assignments and readings may be made easier, and faculty may be hesitant to disagree with students' comments or concerns for fear of appearing disagreeable. Moreover, sensing that students dislike ambiguity, instructors may "teach the test" (i.e., virtually announce what will be on exams through the use of study guides) and provide a lockstep method of accomplishing assignments and research projects. The growing phenomenon of grade inflation should not be surprising. However, the ultimate customers, society

and future employers, need and seek students who have been challenged and can adequately deal with ambiguity in solving problems. Future employers and graduate schools want to be able to look at grade point averages that have meaning. Although this example of upward feedback can provide valuable information for its recipients, we need to realize that people generally modify their behavior toward what gets measured and rewarded. Such behavior may not always lead to the realization of long-term goals and outcomes.

TRAIN RATERS[15]

Almost all 360 degree instruments rely on rating scales. Research has clearly established that raters commit different types of rating errors, such as rating too leniently or too harshly.[16] Some raters play it safe by consistently using the central rating point. Other errors include halo effects (generalizing from doing well in one area to perceptions of doing well in other areas) and recency effects (weighting heavily behavior observed most recently). Raters need training in how to complete forms and how to avoid rating errors. Training should also cover the objectives of the surveys and the overall process. UPS, for example, explains the appraisal feedback process, and discusses how data will be used.

A few medium-sized organizations in the midwest have indicated to us that they are providing raters with a frame of reference training and teaching raters how to keep a log of observed behavior that correspond with survey items. Frame of reference training covers the roles, responsibilities, and accountabilities of the ratee. Survey items are linked to roles and responsibilities in an attempt to help raters create a common frame of reference when they rate a ratee. To improve observations, raters are given surveys to keep throughout the year and are instructed to record their observations of incidents that they would use to help them determine their final ratings. Raters are encouraged to take their record of work incidents and supplement their ratings with written feedback. According to the HRM Directors in these organizations, raters thus far are willing to take risks to provide raters with specific written comments. Furthermore, the amount of written feedback has remained about the same over the last three years. Finally, ratees have indicated that the written feedback is more valuable to them than numerical ratings.

A Typical Case of 360 Degree Feedback Implementation

A CEO from a large size manufacturing company attended an executive development conference and heard about 360 degree feedback programs. He liked the idea. At the conference he heard all about the benefits of 360 degree feedback. He persuaded his senior management that the company should use 360 degree feedback because it would be a lot better than their current annual performance appraisal. He stated, "360 feedback comes directly from people who are in the best positions to evaluate the performance of the people they work with. Supervisors will have more information to support their appraisals of others and, therefore, more leverage to do something about some people's performance. We'll use the 360 feedback to help determine peoples' merit raises. That way, we'll make sure that people make improvements based on the feedback they received." The CEO asked the human resource management (HRM) department in the company to recruit a consulting firm that specialized in 360 degree feedback. HRM found a firm and then used a small focus group to help customize the firm's 99-item 360 degree survey.

After the first round of 360 degree feedback, almost everyone in the organization, including the CEO, was at least a little frustrated or disappointed with the outcomes of the process. People complained about how many surveys they had to fill out and how long the process took. Supervisors felt that many of the 360 ratings were inflated. In short, the data were not worth much. The company was faced with a decision about whether to continue or discontinue the 360 feedback program. What should the organization do? What should it have done at the beginning of the process?

Management decided to start over and took the next year to engage in several activities. A 360 feedback project team was formed, comprising representative employees from different areas and levels of the organization. The team's mission was to design, implement, and evaluate a 360 feedback process that would be acceptable to organizational members and would produce results. The following outcomes were defined: (1) improve communication by reducing the undiscussables between raters and ratees; (2) increase alignment of expectations between raters and ratees; and (3) improve ratees' work behaviors and performance.

The team, facilitated by the consultants, conceptualized how the 360 process should work in order to produce results. The team developed its own 360 feedback survey items based on values the organization deemed important and included a written feedback section on the survey. Pilot tests of survey items were conducted before producing the survey that would be used in a roll-out. In addition, the team explored the use of putting the survey on the computer network. Anonymity was still maintained, and this process eliminated the need to have someone outside the organization type the written comments. Raters, ratees, and coaches were trained about different aspects of the 360 process.

A decision was made that 360 surveys should be administered throughout the year. This procedure addressed the issue of overburdening people within one particular month. The team wanted the 360 process to provide individuals with information they could use to set specific improvement goals. Individuals were expected to review their 360 results with their respective coaches, who helped prepare those individuals for a discussion of appropriate 360 results with their respective raters. Thus, managers were expected to share the results of their upward appraisals with people reporting directly to them, and to share the results of their peer feedback with their peers. This took place during regularly scheduled meetings. The HRM area provided facilitation, if needed, when managers shared results with their raters.

Based on input from focus groups, the team also decided that the purpose of the 360 feedback process was to be primarily developmental, but with accountability. That is, individuals needed to use the feedback to set developmental goals. As part of this process, they had to meet with their respective supervisors and share the data. They were subsequently responsible for attaining their developmental goals. Consequences for failing to meet development goals ranged from being put on notice if no improvements occurred in the work behaviors targeted for improvement, to potential demotion if no changes occurred after three years. 360 feedback information would be used in annual performance appraisals only in cases of obvious need for corrective action and/or demotion.

In conjunction with the consultant, a three-year research program was designed to assess the 360 process. A number of research questions were formulated, and a research proposal was submitted to senior management. One question was whether those individuals who were trained to seek additional, follow-up feedback from respondents actually obtain more feedback and positive outcomes, as opposed to those who did not receive such training. Several meetings took place with management about the rationale for the research questions and the reasons for experimental field studies.

Finally, a 360 feedback steering committee was formed consisting of one member from the board of directors, one manager each at senior, middle, and first-line levels, and three employees. The committee is similar to the steering committees that help provide structure and guidance to TQM initiatives.

Conclusions

Unfortunately, in many organizations, 360 degree feedback or other innovations may be viewed increasingly as just another management fad. Employees and managers have seen a number of change initiatives begin abruptly with much fanfare, only to end abruptly, and often for little apparent reason.

It is obvious that organizations, like individuals, cannot erase their pasts. However, at the same, it is possible to keep new initiatives like 360 feedback from running amok, and to realize degrees of success. The case reviewed here can provide some lessons to avoid faddism and the potential cynicism it engenders. Specifically, this case demonstrates the need to systematically determine how 360 feedback (or other interventions) will be used and what outcomes can be expected. It also shows how the process needs to be tailored to the needs of the organization and subsequently scrutinized in terms of undergoing careful evaluation. The process was primarily developmental in nature, but with increasing accountability for ratees over the long-run implementation. With careful planning and implementation, the benefits of 360 feedback can be clearly realized, rather than merely taken on faith.

Source: *Academy of Management Executive: The Thinking Manager's Source* by Waldman. Copyright © 1998 by the Society for Advancement of Management. Reprinted with permission of the Society for Advancement of Management in the format Textbook via Copyright Clearance Center.

Endnotes

1. See Antonioni, D. 1996. Designing an effective 360 degree appraisal feedback process. *Organizational Dynamics*, 25(2): 24–38.

2. As examples, see *Training and Development*. 1995. First-rate multirater feedback. August: 42–43. Also see *APA Monitor*. 1995. Subordinate feedback may foster better management. July: 30–31. Also see *Fortune*. 1994. 360 feedback can change your life. October: 93–100.

3. For a more complete description of resource dependence theory, see Ulrich, D., & Barney, J. 1984. Perspectives in organizations: Resource dependence, efficiency and population. *Academy of Management Review*, 9: 471–481. Also see Oliver, C. 1991. Strategic responses to institutional processes. *Academy of Management Review*, 16: 145–179.

4. For a more complete description of institutional theory, see Tolbert, P. S. 1985. Institutional environments and resource dependence: Sources of administrative structure in institutions for higher education. *Administrative Science Quarterly*, 30: 1–13.

5. See London, M., & Smither, J. 1995. Can multi-source feedback change perceptions of goal accomplishment, self-evaluations and performance related outcomes? Theory-based applications and directions for research. *Personnel Psychology*, 48: 803–839.

6. The results presented here were part of a survey of companies that belonged to a 360 degree feedback consortium. Results were presented by Timmreck, C., & Bracken, D. 1996. *Multisource assessment: Reinforcing the preferred "means" to the end*. Paper presented at the meeting of the Society for Industrial and Organizational Psychology, San Diego.

7. See Mark Edwards' and Ann Ewens' accounts of productivity improvement and improved customer satisfaction ratings follow a 360 feedback intervention in their 1996 book, *360 degree feedback*, AMACOM, New York.

8. For an interesting look at how the exercise of politics and other forms of power affect organizations, see Pfeffer, J. 1992. *Managing with power*. Boston: Harvard Business School Press.

9. Similar examples can be found in Jackall, R. 1988. *Moral mazes: The world of corporate managers*. New York: Oxford University Press.

10. See Bernardin, J., Hagan, C., & Kane, J. 1995. The effects of a 360 degree appraisal system on managerial performance: No matter how cynical I get, I can't keep up. In Tornow, W. (Chair), *Upward feedback: The ups and downs of it*. Symposium conducted at the Tenth Annual Conference of the Society for Industrial and Organizational Psychology, Orlando, FL.

11. See note 7 above.

12. The issue of activity-centered programs versus results-driven programs is discussed in more depth in the following article:

Shaffer, R. H., & Thomson, H. A. 1992. Successful change programs begin with results. *Harvard Business Review*, 70(Jan.–Feb.): 80–89.

13. We wish to thank an anonymous reviewer for pointing out the need for customizing innovations such as 360 feedback.

14. See Kerr, S. 1995. An Academy classic: On the folly of rewarding A while hoping for B. *Academy of Management Executive*, 9: 1, 7–16.

15. This recommendation is specific to 360 degree feedback interventions or those that include survey or rating instruments.

16. See Landy, F. J., & Farr, J. L. 1980. Performance rating. *Psychological Bulletin*, 87: 82–107.

For an in-depth consideration of the antecedents and consequences of organizational cynicism, see Reichers, A. E., Wanous, J. P., & Austin, J. T. Understanding and managing cynicism about organizational change. 1997. *Academy of Management Executive*, 11(1): 48–59.

Aligning Service Strategy through Super-Measure Management

Ivor Morgan and Jay Rao, *Academy of Management Executive*

An Example of Super-Measure Management (SMM)

When Gordon Bethune took over as CEO in late 1994, Continental Airlines, the fifth-largest U.S. airline with nearly 50,000 employees,[1] had lost on average $960 million per year for the previous four years, and its stock sold for $5 per share. Years of cost cutting had left Continental with a customer image of unreliability and unpredictability. Its employees were deeply unhappy, thought everyone was taking advantage of everyone else, and had little trust in their management or pride in the company. The results were aircraft that were dirty and late, and baggage that was lost.

Bethune and his executives estimated that the late and cancelled flights were costing Continental $6 million a month, mainly to put stranded passengers on rival airlines, to house them in hotels, or to feed them. Though most customer satisfaction studies had showed that on-time performance was very important to travelers,[2] in January 1994 only 61 percent of Continental's flights were on time. The airline was last in the Department of Transportation's monthly on-time performance rankings.

To stop the employee squabbling and the company's decline, Bethune declared that if Continental were to rank among the top three airlines in the Department of Transportation's monthly on-time performance rankings, he would split half of the $6 million (or $65 per person) each month with every non-management employee—this included gate agents, flight attendants, baggage handlers, and reservation agents. By March 1995, the second month of his $65 offer, Continental had moved from last to first in the on-time rankings.[3] Bethune paid up six times in 1995.

Instead of arguing over whose job it was to carry wheelchairs to the gate, ramp workers and gate agents began working together—and helping passengers. Realizing that missing parts would delay flights, the stockroom employees began paying closer attention to inventory-level accuracy. If a catering truck pulled up with fewer than the ordered meals, instead of delaying the flight, flight attendants would offer gifts to passengers in lieu of a meal to ensure that the flight left on time.

When the program first started, aircraft on-time arrivals improved, but the number of lost bags went up. So the program was restated as "the whole system has to be on time," not just parts of the system. Lost bags and dirty aisles were therefore not acceptable. Soon, Continental started to figure in the top three rankings for baggage handling as well. The use of an SM had jump-started Continental on a revitalization path.

The on-time incentive program got so much press that other airlines began to copy it. So Continental had to adjust its incentive. Even when Continental was only fifth-best in a month, if 80 percent of the flights were on time, that could be considered good work and worth a reward. In 1995, Continental netted $215 million. By 1998, this figure had steadily increased to $385 million, and in mid-year the stock price hit an all-time high of $65. In 1997 Continental paid out $21 million ($490 per employee) in on-time bonuses, and in 1998 it paid out $23 million. In 2000, Continental was ranked #1 in on-time arrivals among all U.S. airlines, named #1 in customer satisfaction by J.D. Power, and paid on-time bonuses (worth $785 per employee) in 11 out of 12 months.

Though on-time arrival is an old measure, what set the Continental measure apart was the singleness of purpose tied to the airline's strategy, the breadth of the measure's interpretation, and the way it was implemented and communicated. Even after other airlines attempted to stress the on-time measure, Continental was able to stay ahead of the pack. Its leadership maintained this position using sensitive adjustments to the measure and its rewards.

In the airline industry, most late arrivals are due to air traffic control problems or the weather. So selecting on-time arrival as the SM to turn the heads of employees and the direction of an airline is counterintuitive, perhaps more so because this measure is almost always part of an airline's measurement set.

While Continental's on-time performance was ranked against that of other airlines, the real impact at Continental was in both perceived and actual improvements for their passengers. Continental Airlines had been at the bottom of most rankings and had a poor self-image. Getting to the top of any ranking was a stunning achievement. Once at the top of one ranking, they quickly climbed to the top of another. And being the best at anything is a strong motivating factor. Moving from a negative to a positive state opened up Continental's management and employees to the realization that they could compete with the best.

What Is a Super-Measure?

A "Super-Measure" (SM) is a single measure that has great relevance up, down, and across the organization and to its customer base. An SM is one that can be used to align the behaviors and actions of the various parts of a firm with the firm's value proposition or customers' needs. An SM is one on which all eyes within the firm are firmly fixed and which can be used to propel the firm in a unified fashion in its chosen direction.

This article defines the characteristics of Super-Measures, presents their benefits and potential applications in service enterprises, and reviews some of the difficulties encountered with their use. The focus is on why they work, why they sometimes don't work, and on what managers need to do to select and implement them.

Why Every Manager Should Know About SMM

The onset of the 21st century has not diminished the challenges facing business enterprises. They are like ships navigating in uncharted seas, with major obstacles lurking below tranquil waters, and storms sometimes come unexpectedly with great ferocity. Consequently, all connected to an enterprise—from front-line workers through to presidents, shareholders, customers and suppliers—must align themselves continuously to the firm's strategy and execute it. The problem for managers lies not simply in setting the direction but in getting the firm to follow it.

There is often a gap between intended strategy and its execution.

In their seminal article, Floyd and Wooldridge[4] argued that the successful execution of an intended strategy is the result of middle- and operating-level managers acting on a common set of strategic priorities achieved through a shared level of understanding and commitment. They termed this "strategic consensus." Further, they suggested that a firm's rewards, systems, and structures embodying the intended strategy are likely to be more powerful than any words. And these elements are key to building commitment by aligning the execution of the firm's strategy with the interests of the people within the firm.

The challenging process of aligning strategy and its implementation has long been supported by the use of performance measures. The most pervasive and traditional of these have been developed by financial and management accountants, with specific systems for meeting statutory requirements and others for supporting managerial decision-making. Unfortunately many of these accounting systems slowly lost their managerial relevance as the 20th century progressed, in part because their logic was based on labor-intensive processes.[5]

Along with these developments came a growing need for line managers to look to the future rather than to the past. Using profitability and some other financial measures was, for some, like steering a sailing ship by looking backwards at the ship's wake: the view gave little information about how the ship had reached its position or what lay ahead. So profitability and many other financial measures came too late and gave little information about the future.

With historical measures alone proving to be misleading or inadequate, managers tried to "do the right things" in the hope that so doing would lead to the right financial result. The problem was to define the right things—and then to get the organization to do them. Developments in measurement systems have led to considerable changes in the way we look at data and the data items thought to be relevant. "Time to market" data for new products are now commonly published, for example, and such numbers would have been difficult to find even a decade ago.

Complicating the picture, as gathering, analyzing and distributing data became easier, was a boom in performance-measurement tools. Two concepts—Economic Value Added and the Balanced Scorecard—have received special attention from practitioners, consultants and academics.[6]

The Balanced Scorecard[7] in particular introduced a much broader set of metrics—external, internal, financial, and learning and growth—to support the firm's strategy. Though most Balanced Scorecard measures are of a non-financial nature, financial figures invariably form part of the set. Many scorecards have 10 measures or more, and some many more than 20. A firm's total of measures is usually much more than this because new measures are added as the scorecards are cascaded down through the organization, the thinking being to make measurements relevant both to the firm's strategy and to those using them.[8]

The 1992 Kaplan and Norton Balanced Scorecard article[9] contrasts flying a modern jet aircraft with its many instruments and controls to managing a complex firm. Indeed where the relationship between an action and its result is well known, it is possible for humans to handle a large number of measures simultaneously. But success for a firm is not an easy matter of cause and effect. Some actions of considerable importance in terms of cost may be very hard to demonstrate when it comes to their effect. The investment in information technology is but one example. Investing in image advertising is another. And outcomes such as changes in market share may be more a matter of competitive behavior than results of actions by a firm's management. This is a far cry from the operation of a jet aircraft where every meter and control has specific meaning to the pilot.

Aligning a firm's forces according to a large number of measures is a difficult proposition, particularly since the measures may be in part financial, in part physical, and sometimes with outcomes that are difficult to measure. Given the dynamic nature of our focus, we asked: what is the number of measures that can be handled by humans? Our discussions with executives confirm that people often find it hard to relate to more than a handful of measures. Simons and Davila[10] suggest a maximum of seven. However, in a very dynamic environment, even this number could provide several potentially different directions for a company. And the number could be greater if the measures themselves were not clearly understood. While senior management may use a Balanced Scorecard for benchmarking externally and internally, an SM is used to "fire up" the organization.[11]

Since all the firm's employees need to understand the firm's strategic direction—and measures associated with it should connect employees' actions to the short- and long-term success of the firm—the simplest system to articulate, communicate, and monitor would be a system using very few measures, ideally a single SM.

An SM is therefore a measure that transcends other measures by unifying the actions of disparate organizational functions and levels. In the language of Floyd and Wooldridge,[12] the aim is to produce a clear alignment of the firm's strategic direction with the actions of the firm.

Who Uses Super-Measure Management and When?

We were looking for firms that used very few measures—ideally single ones—and had disseminated these measures throughout the enterprise. We expected to find great clarity of direction in these firms, a unified team approach, and real punch behind the measures. Though our search for SMs led us to a number of firms and situations, the clearest examples came from firms within the service sector, or service divisions of manufacturing enterprises.

Service encounters—the interaction between the customer and the service delivery system—often require various elements of the supply system to have a direct customer interface. Furthermore, these supply elements may themselves be working together simultaneously to produce the service. Hence the service, unlike the production of tangible goods, often cannot be decoupled from the customer. And service characteristics call for clear definitions of process and careful management of customers' expectations and perceptions. Overall, these characteristics lend themselves particularly well to measures that span the firm horizontally.

Although our focus here is on service enterprises, we omitted companies using service guarantees—Lands' End, Federal Express, Virgin Atlantic, "Bugs" Burger Bugs Killers[13]—from our search. A service guarantee is a publicized contract between a firm and its market that sets specific performance standards, system failure recovery processes, and penalties. The customer evaluates the firm's performance against this guarantee. For a service guarantee to be effective, it is important that there be a visible cost to the firm to recover from a service failure, the thinking being that these failure costs will encourage alignment of the firm's internal behaviors with its external market demands.

The most powerful service guarantees are those that guarantee satisfaction—with no exclusions. Thus though a firm may manage a customer's prior service perceptions, the determination of satisfaction rests ultimately with the customer, leaving the nature of the recovery cost and process to the firm. The force of such a system lies in creating a close link between the firm and its customers, a motivation for better alignment and a strict monitoring system of failure.

A service guarantee could form an SM if properly implemented, well timed, well communicated, and appropriate to a firm's strategic alignment requirements. It would then serve as an aid to continuous improvement. Limited guarantees—those with an abundance of small print—are unlikely to meet SM criteria due to their restricted scope externally and internally.

A firm normally offers a full guarantee only when it is a high performer but has not had the performance recognized. The guarantee works to maintain and improve this performance. But poor performers are not advised to offer guarantees as they would damage the firms' competitive position and be costly financially. Yet this is the time when alignment and strategic direction are most needed, as seen in the case of Continental.

The following cases demonstrate some important aspects of SMM: EMC, Fairfield Inn (Marriott), Nordstrom, AT&T Universal Card Services, and US West.

EMC

EMC, headquartered in Hopkinton, MA, manufactures mainframe and midrange storage products for computer systems. When Mike Ruettgers took over as CEO in 1989, EMC had about 2 percent of the market, faced a quality crisis—with disk drives from its principal supplier crashing—and was on the verge of bankruptcy. Ruettgers instituted a 100 percent inspection and test policy—for incoming and outgoing product—in an industry that then had a norm of testing only 10 percent of its final products.

Until the early 1990s, IBM was synonymous with great service and the undisputed leader in market share and technology. Then, as IBM started to face competition from technical advances by its competitors, its service support faltered. That created an opening, and EMC, having fixed its product-quality problems, channeled its entire service organization to go after IBM. Within 5 years, EMC had captured 41 percent of the mainframe storage market, and IBM was down to 35 percent from its earlier 80 percent.

One of the key differentiating factors in EMC's quest to topple the then king-of-the-hill was its approach to customer service and its focus on one SM—customer satisfaction. The firm had determined that the keys to customer satisfaction were the availability of the customer's system and the availability of support personnel. Hence, bonuses (nearly 20 percent of salary) were tied directly to the customer-satisfaction measure. Consequently EMC's customer service vice presidents (VPs) were more hands-on than their counterparts in other firms.

A priority escalation process aided EMC's undivided attention to customer service. When problems escalated beyond the first level of service support, the VPs of Customer Service, Field Services, Tech Support, and Engineering were all notified, and one of them would stay on top of the problem to see it through to its resolution. The VPs' beepers were on all the time. If a problem was not resolved within 24 hours, the CEO was notified.

In 1999 EMC became the world's first company to earn the prestigious Support Center Practices (SCP) certification in both North America and Europe. In 2001, FastCompany named EMC "Best of the Best" for customer service.

Nordstrom

Nordstrom is an upscale department store known for its unparalleled focus on customer service. Nordstrom viewed its floor staff as "individual entrepreneurs" and encouraged them to nurture long-term personal relationships with shoppers. Sales staff earned sales-based bonuses as long as they exceeded minimum sales-per-hour quotas. But the staff with the highest sales per hour in turn received the most profitable work hours. Thus success led to further opportunity for success.

To obtain high sales-per-hour performances, it was necessary for Nordstrom employees—known as Nordies—to cultivate their customer bases by maintaining client records of sizes and style preferences, jotting down thank-you notes, and often going to superhuman lengths to make a sale. These "heroic" efforts were widely publicized within and without the firm.

Nordies used their detailed customer knowledge to connect themselves to the store buying process to ensure product availability. And this availability allowed them to call their clients when suitable merchandise arrived, thus enhancing the bond between the seller and buyer. The resultant match of customer size, taste, and desires ensured a speedy sales process, further enhancing the productivity of the salesperson.

The success of many service systems requires a careful matching of employees with the culture and the strategy of the firm. In the case of Nordstrom, newcomers not well acquainted with the norms of Nordstrom strategy and culture might never rise above the minimum sales per hour and then leave the firm in a dissatisfied state. It was therefore incumbent upon Nordstrom management to set clear expectations of job requirements and widely publicize them. In this way, newcomers would self-select themselves into Nordstrom with an understanding of the major emphasis on customer interaction and support systems.

Several hundred successful Nordies were permanently transferred from existing Nordstrom stores to provide a cultural base for new stores as they opened. And the status and image of these high performers inspired a stream of other outstanding salespeople to join the firm to fuel company growth.

Many retailing firms pay their salespeople a bonus that is tied to sales volumes. However, few use this bonus to motivate their staff to manage the buying process, the store inventories, and their client lists as well. Such an approach has major strategic implications for a retailing firm. One consequence is the decentralization of much of the purchasing, with the hope that a higher service level to a regular customer will offset the disadvantages of a loss of scale.

Fairfield Inn

In 1987, Marriott launched Fairfield Inn into the economy limited-service motel industry, a sector saturated with excess rooms and with low 55 percent occupancy rates. Marriott wanted to gain market share quickly by creating an enhanced service focus—a focus somewhat foreign to this segment of the industry. Marriott's careful hotel designs matched the needs of this segment but resulted in construction costs that were higher than those of the competition. Furthermore, ideal sites were scarce. Consequently, Marriott was faced with higher break-even costs than its competitors and a requirement for much higher occupancy levels than the industry average.

In the hotel business, once the site has been selected and the unit constructed, much of the success is a direct result of the people employed. There are also network effects on booking and issues of brand. Marriott chose to focus on service as a key differentiator. They implemented this focus with the support of very selective hiring—an approach used by Southwest Airlines, for example, and many other service enterprises as an aid for aligning their culture—and a new customer feedback mechanism for evaluating staff and unit performance.

Each Fairfield Inn operated an SM system that allowed guests to rate three aspects of service: cleanliness, friendliness, and efficiency. The three individual scores were then aggregated to give an overall guest score. This score (the SM in this case) affected bonuses for everyone at the property from the guestroom attendant to the Inn manager. These scores were publicized across the firm to allow for easy comparison between all Fairfield Inns. Thus there was considerable motivation for all unit members and area managers to investigate opportunities and effect improvements.

Fairfield Inn won awards for the best hotel in its segment only two years after opening. It has continued to win awards over the last decade. This SM system lasted seven years and served to establish the service culture of Fairfield in the minds of both customers and employees. Today, its implementation is left to the discretion of the unit managers.

Why Did They Adopt Super-Measure Management?

Our examples demonstrate that SMs do provide a powerful thrust to a firm's direction. EMC and Continental adopted their measures in order to provide a very sharp focus to their businesses. In Continental's lowly position, the question on CEO Bethune's mind may have been "Where do we start?" and at EMC, when CEO Ruettgers took over with a quality crisis on hand, a similar question must have come to mind. Leadership clarity would hardly have been enhanced by a multitude of measures. These crises[14] may have provided the pressure for resolving conflicts between factions to arrive at consensus. And a crisis demands acute attention to direction. Having achieved "Best in Industry" status, these firms still use the SM for continuous improvements and to achieve a better alignment with their strategies.

Fairfield Inn entered a market late that had excess capacity. Its market-share-grabbing strategy was through superior unit design, construction, and customer service. The customer service SM was used to aid the alignment of the firm with this strategy.

Nordstrom—a small regional shoe retailer until the 1960s—tasted initial success through great service with the aid of its SM. And the firm kept to its measure to achieve rapid growth, maintain its "Nordie" culture, and decentralize its management.

If the examples so far describe success, the following two cases give a flavor of some of the difficulties in choosing, implementing, and maintaining an SM.

AT&T Universal Card Services: Problems with a Measure

When AT&T launched its card,[15] it was the first mover in a new world of no-fee credit cards. Top management chose customer service as its primary differentiator and used a composite SM—an amalgam of many measures—thought to be in line with this differentiator. However, as competition increased and margins fell, the SM required adjustment to maintain its relevance and to spur employees on to greater things.

On many counts the firm was successful—as was the measure—receiving the Baldrige Award in 1992. But its service strategy ran into difficulties as an increasing number of competitors used clearer market segmentation, gave rewards to cardholders, and added other services. Rewards tied to AT&T's SM became increasingly difficult to obtain, and there were serious questions about the relevance of the customer service strategy.

AT&T management however kept raising the hurdle in an attempt to keep pace with the changes but ultimately lost employee commitment as their market share eroded. The leadership was unable to convince employees that even greater efforts on their part would win out in the market. Both the strategy selected and managing the measure proved to be problematic.

US West: Additional Problems

In 1998, after years of downsizing, Denver-based telecommunications giant US West was fined thousands of dollars by the Public Utilities Commission for poor customer service. The firm responded with a bonus scheme for its 7,100 field technicians, potentially adding over 20 percent to their salaries. The declared aim was to create a high customer service level.[16]

The program tied field technician performance to the sales dollars they generated in a given month. Base targets were set, such as number of repair calls completed during a specific period, and values were assigned to every task a technician performed. The technician's monthly bonus pay was then determined from the points—an SM—accumulated from extra sales generated, service quality, and the number of complaints.[17]

In late 1998, union members held a two-week strike protesting that the plan was geared towards revenue generation and not service to customers. A post-strike plan, implemented in July 1999, focused on the time it took technicians to finish a job in the field. This program, made voluntary for existing employees, was mandatory for new employees. A union spokesperson subsequently declared their disagreement again, not with the service intent of management but with the means of its implementation.

The US West measure provided little incentive for employees other than the technicians to support the service effort. Customer service in the telephone business is far more complex than finishing a job quickly and requires many support personnel to ensure correct failure diagnosis, quick response, and parts availability. Furthermore, the components of the US West measure were not clearly aligned with the firm's declared strategic direction. These components could cause a technician to trade off customer service against productivity in order to gain a bonus. The measure failed on strategic alignment, its lack of impact across the organization, and low commitment and resistance by the employees.

In June 2000, US West was acquired by Qwest Communications, and the firm ranked last nationwide in customer-satisfaction among residential phone service providers in a 2002 J.D. Power & Associates study.

Selecting and Implementing the SM

From the cases described here, we can define some general characteristics of successful measures and the conditions that make it easier to adopt the SM approach.

SM FOLLOWS STRATEGY

A clear strategy is the normal starting point. Not only are SMs industry specific; they are company specific. They tie directly to a firm's market and strategy for competing in that market.

SIMPLE AND COMMON

SMs are not unusual in character. Most of the measures we have cited are in common use and consequently may be overlooked. What sets them apart is the reliance on this measure rather than on a basket of measures, and on the way the measure is implemented. An on-time arrival measure has always been in common use in the airline industry, but Continental raised its importance to a strategic level. Similarly the sales per hour of Nordstrom and the customer satisfaction of Fairfield Inn are far from unique but were chosen to differentiate the strategy of their firms from their competitors at critical points in time.

An SM need not be comprehensive or balanced. The Continental case demonstrates the power of selecting an important dimension and managing it well.

HORIZONTAL AND VERTICAL RELEVANCE

What does on-time arrival for an aircraft have in common with retail sales per hour or with a hotel's customer satisfaction index? Closer examination shows that the measures are particularly relevant from executives to employees, and across functional departments, and are linked to the market. Hence, our prescription is for the measure to be relevant across all functional areas and sufficient to focus the firm's strategy.

Reliance on one measure may be very uncomfortable, and that is why many firms have adopted a multi-measure approach. Even reducing the number of key measures down to ten requires considerable discussion and concession among disparate parts of the firm. Reaching the SM state generally results in a measure that may not seem obvious. A single measure to which most can relate has the potential for unleashing a great deal of aligned energy.

REWARDS

In all cases rewards—both monetary and behavioral—were tied to the SM. Further, the employees of the successful firms clearly believed that improvement in the SM would result in improved performance of their firms. Indeed the successful cases cited here have received industry awards beyond those mentioned here. Only Nordstrom, in our sample, used personal rather than group rewards.

LEADERSHIP, COMMUNICATION, EDUCATION, AND COMMITMENT

Choosing the strategy and developing the SM and its reward system is the first phase of SM management that falls to a firm's leadership. Implementation requires leaders to follow with careful communication and education to create the commitment necessary to use the SM to align the organization with the chosen strategy.

Though an SM may be easily understood, its connection to the overall strategy of the firm or the connection of any one person to the SM may be far from simple. It may not be obvious to personnel in airline food preparation or baggage handling how their efforts can affect an airline's on-time performance. And it may not be clear to "back-room" service personnel in a hotel such as cleaners that their performance can significantly affect a guest's satisfaction. The eyes of the firm are on the SM. Though the improvement in the SM may benefit everybody, all employees must understand how they can affect the SM in order to release its full power. And they must understand the connection between the SM and strategy. Creating these connections requires a system for educating company members and communications links between members to identify opportunities from which they can benefit.

The clarity of the SM and the connections to individual effort and company strategy, a careful administration of the reward system, and a sense that the firm's leadership is in full support of the strategy are important for developing a strong commitment by a firm's members to the SM implementation. In the case of Continental, the reward was given even if the target rank had not been achieved, provided that performance was satisfactory.

Modifying the SM and its reward requires a sensitive finger on the pulse of the organization, and this extends to the removal of blocks that stand in the way of change or communication.

THROW OUT THE MANUAL

A firm with rigid procedural controls may find it difficult to implement an SM since success requires freedom to act. Should inappropriate procedures be in place, a first step for successful SM implementation would be to relax these procedures and open up the organization to allow employee flexibility to support the SM and the firm's strategy SMM would have limited impact in a firm governed by inflexible policies or a rigid organization.

Implementation requires leadership skills to create a conviction that the firm's strategy makes sense and that the SM will aid in its achievement. A dynamic reward system, whether behavioral or monetary, is an essential aid in gaining commitment and in achieving consensus, resulting in an alignment of effort. Implicit in requiring this freedom to act is the assumption that when employees experience ownership, involvement, and responsibility for the firm's future, they gain a sense of achievement and personal growth.

Managing the SM

Managing the measure incorporates two key dimensions: modifying the SM's definition and changing its scope of application. Why do measures require management? The short answer is that the world is always changing. Measures may indeed have a half-life in managerial terms and lose their effectiveness over time.

ADAPTABILITY AND SCOPE
The Continental case shows the adaptability of an SM and the considerable flexibility in the way rewards were managed along with it. From an early definition of on-time arrival referring only to aircraft, the scope of the measure was broadened to include baggage. In doing so, the number of departments affected grew considerably. And ultimately, on-time arrival was broadened even further to that of a satisfied passenger on time. Thus both the meaning of "on-time" and the scope of its application changed dynamically. The starting $65 bonuses were adjusted constantly to accommodate competitors' moves. By 1999, every time Continental got first place in the DOT monthly on-time arrival rankings, every employee (not just non-management) received $100.[18]

EVOLUTION AND SCOPE
EMC also shows a very evolutionary approach to the definition of measure. Only after achieving the highest system availability (product quality) in the industry could EMC redefine—and broaden—its key measure to that of customer satisfaction. Indeed it would be unthinkable for a firm that did not have an outstanding quality process to contemplate a service priority escalation system like that practiced by EMC. Correcting the quality was a necessary precursor to adopting the customer-satisfaction measure. And the scope of the customer-satisfaction measure forced the involvement of all functions from new product development through to after-sales service, thereby ensuring not only high-performing existing products but the incorporation of customers' ideas and challenges into new product and service designs.

LIFE SPAN
That measures have limited lives is a given in our dynamic world. The SM for Nordstrom, for example, implemented in the mid-1960s and unchanged to this day, may present a danger. The SM suited the firm's focus on a relatively affluent market that valued service highly—and a vigorous expansion resulted. But the decentralized nature of buying linked to its excellent market information impacted the firm's ability to gain the scale economies that are open to competitors. With cost a larger factor and service less an issue, a firm more narrowly targeted in terms of style could pick off parts of the Nordstrom market, and this attack may already be underway. Under these circumstances, the firm's strategy could require substantial adjustment—as could the measure.

The AT&T measure was very effective as the firm ramped up its initial volumes. Only when the nature of competition changed did the SM fail. And Fairfield chose to move its SM to an optional use once its mission of aiding the establishment of a service culture had been accomplished. At EMC and Continental, the SMs have survived and have become instruments for continuous improvement and alignment.

ADVANTAGES AND DISADVANTAGES OF SM
We have summarized the steps for creating, implementing, and managing an SM in Table 1. Though there is logic to the sequence of the seven steps, many of these actions may at times progress simultaneously. In particular, the actions under "Implementing the SM" and "Managing the SM," once started, require continuous efforts.

SM ADVANTAGES
A single Super-Measure is easier to communicate than multiple measures, and the greater opportunity to clarify its meaning should lead to fewer misunderstandings than under a multiple-measure approach.

Creating the SM

	Action	Criteria	Comments
Stage 1	Select a strategic direction	Spur growth Get out of crisis Late market entry Attain leadership position Create a service culture Continuous improvement	Clear and concise No need to pick something performed (unless the goal is continuous improvement)
Stage 2	Create an SM	Cross-functional Executive to employment Tie to market	Look for simple common measures
Stage 3	Develop a reward system	Tie to SM	Likely to be group reward, both both monetary and behavioral

Implementing the SM

	Action	Criteria	Comments
Stage 4	Communicate and educate	Tie SM to strategy Tie every individual to SM	Encourage communication between work groups Create ideas for improvement and implementation
Stage 5	Demonstrate top management support	Leadership visibility and action	Ensure flexible organization, remove communication and action blockages

Managing the SM

	Action	Criteria	Comments
Stage 6	Modify the SM	Scope	Expanding the scope pulls more people into the SM system increasing its power
		Adaptability and evolution	Maintain alignment
Stage 7	Manage SM life span	Strategy revision	Requires careful monitoring of the environment and of the internal culture of firm
		Adjust measure and rewards	Ensure continued alignment with strategy

Explaining even seven measures—their meanings, interactions, and relative importance—presents a major task. The close tie between the rewards and the SM should propel the firm rapidly down its chosen path.

The SM also allows managers to select any major dimension that they believe could lead to competitive advantage. As Continental demonstrated, a firm does not have to select something they perform well. And the measure selected does not have to be unusual.

Overall, the SM approach can produce outstanding vertical alignment within the firm, excellent horizontal alignment from the firm's suppliers, across its functional areas to its customer base, and a clear attention to the present and the future.

SM Disadvantages

A Super-Measure would appear to be unsuitable at the highest levels of an organization that has multiple markets, a portfolio of diversified services, or a multi-divisional form, though individual divisions could manage with SMs of their own. And because SMs do not have to be comprehensive, they may miss their target. This was demonstrated in the AT&T case.

A particular challenge for leadership may be the need for firms to have the flexibility to communicate easily across levels and departments, and take actions accordingly. A rigid organization is unlikely to be able to align the forces necessary for the impact we look for here. We recognize the difficulties associated with changing such an organization and culture. This challenge may deter some leaders from SM use.

Final Words

Most of the firms we have cited had a compelling need to differentiate themselves from their competitors. The success stories of Continental and Fairfield Inn are not lessened by the relatively short-term use of their SMs. The Continental SM had to be adjusted often, and the Fairfield Inn measure eventually became optional.

The cases of EMC and Nordstrom show SMs of considerable life span. The progress of Nordstrom has already raised some questions, but the deep-seated nature of the sales-per-hour approach at Nordstrom makes for a complex change. The very nature of the "Nordie" is embodied in the rewards that flow from this system.

An SM and its tie to the firm's leadership and strategy are complex relationships. When the on-time arrival measure of Continental Airlines is examined in detail, one can see its possibilities. Schedules can be changed to include slack time. Passengers may have their expectations managed. Baggage handlers, re-fueling crews, ground staff, and cabin crews may all have a role to improve the turnaround time of an aircraft. And unions may be brought into the changes too. That such complex effects may occur in one airline does not guarantee the same effects in others. And indeed the success of Continental has led others to try the same thing but with less success.

Overall it may be possible to keep modifying and replacing SMs to create a longer-term management system. The cases we have reviewed have not carried this logic beyond the modification phase. A dynamic environment requires considerably work to ensure the strategic alignment of any measurement system. The difficulty in constructing effective SMs may make changes difficult, though benefits from the ease of communication, monitoring, and understanding should offset this difficulty considerably. In short, like many other ideas, the SM approach needs to be managed.

Source: *Academy of Management Executive: The Thinking Manager's Source* by Morgan. Copyright © 2002 by the Society for Advancement of Management. Reprinted with permission of the Society for Advancement of Management in the format Textbook via Copyright Clearance Center.

Endnotes

1. O'Reilly, B. The mechanic who fixed Continental. *Fortune*, 23 April 1999, 176–186.
2. Welch, N. From worst to first. *Fortune*, 25 May 1998, 185–190.
3. McCartney, S. Continental is back on course: Morale, passengers return. *The Wall Street Journal Interactive Edition*, 15 May 1996.
4. Floyd, S., & Wooldridge, B. 1992. Managing strategic consensus: The foundation of effective implementation. *The Academy of Management Executive*, 6(4): 27–39.
5. Miller, J., & Vollmann, T. 1985. The hidden factory. *Harvard Business Review*, 83(5): 142–150.
6. Ampuero, et al., tabulate the number of articles devoted to these two tools that have appeared in prestigious business journals in the last decade. Please see Ampuero, M., Goranson, J., & Scott, J. 2002. Solving the measurement puzzle. *Perspectives on Business Innovation Journal*, 2. Center for Business Innovation. Cap Gemini Ernst & Young.
7. Kaplan, R., & Norton, D. 1992. The balanced scorecard—Measures that drive performance. *Harvard Business Review*, 70(1): 71–79.
8. Kaplan, R., & Norton, D. 1996. Using the balanced scorecard as a strategic management system. *Harvard Business Review*, 74(1): 75–85.
9. Kaplan & Norton. 1992. op. cit.
10. Simons, R., & Davila, A. 1998. How high is your return on management? *Harvard Business Review*, 78(1): 71–80.
11. We thank an anonymous referee for this suggestion.
12. Floyd, S., & Wooldridge, B. 1992. Managing strategic consensus: The foundation of effective implementation. *The Academy of Management Executive*, 6(4): 27–39.
13. Hart, C. 1988. The power of unconditional service guarantees. *Harvard Business Review*, 66(4): 54–62.
14. The crisis-management literature views crises as low-probability, high-impact events rather than a gradual erosion of a firm's performance over time. Hence, the literature's

prescriptions to manage a turnaround in crises due to gradual erosion are also limited. See, for example, Pearson, C., & Clair, J. 1998. Reframing crisis management. *Academy of Management Review*, 23(1): 59–76; and Pearson. C., & Mitroff, I. 1993. From crisis prone to crisis prepared: A framework for crisis management, *The Academy of Management Executive*, 7(1): 48–59. On the other hand, the services management literature, specifically case studies of SAS and British Airways (like our example of Continental Airlines), help to understand the process of turnarounds. Management literature is quite limited when dealing with performance measures for the effective turnaround of ailing firms.

15. A measure of delight: The pursuit of quality at AT&T Universal Card Services (A). 1993. Harvard Business School case #9–694–047.
16. Gonzales, L. 1998. US West seeks to link pay to customer service goals. *The Colorado Springs Gazette*, 21 May 1998.
17. Diddlebock, B. 1998. Pay-for-performance program separates US West, striking employees. *The Denver Post*, 29 May 1998.
18. Puffer, S. 1999. Continental Airlines' CEO Gordon Bethune on teams and new product development. *The Academy of Management Executive*, 13(3): 28–35.

Strategic Performance Appraisal in Team-Based Organizations: One Size Does Not Fit All

Susanne G. Scott and Walter O. Einstein, *Academy of Management Executive*

In the early 1990s, a prominent high-tech firm in the northeastern United States enthusiastically rolled out a new performance-management system to improve the performance of its professional work teams. The program was comprehensive, with details contained in two large, beautifully written, leather-bound volumes prepared by external consultants following nearly a year of work. Top management introduced the program with much public fanfare and pledges to implement it.

Three years after the launch, the second author happened to run into a colleague who was doing research at the firm on the human resource system and productivity:

Q: How's the performance management system working?

A: What performance management system?

The program introduced with such hope had come and gone within the space of a year, leaving in its wake frustration, anger, and cynicism.

This may be an extreme example. But it is no secret that many performance-appraisal systems fail to deliver their anticipated benefits in team-structured organizations. Working with teams in our consulting practice has convinced us that one-size-fits-all performance-appraisal systems are largely to blame. A generic system applied across an organization ignores important differences among teams. For example, intact, colocated work and service teams still attend to the core work in many organizations, while virtual teams, geographically or organizationally dispersed, are used for more complex tasks.[1] This trend has accelerated with the move from a manufacturing to a knowledge-based economy. In the same organizations, we often see rapid-response teams of loosely networked professionals who manage strategic initiatives in the face of technology change, continued globalization, and hyper-competition.[2]

These are all teams, yet each presents a different challenge to performance management and its

bedrock—employee performance appraisal. Employee performance appraisal influences motivation and development, provides documentary support for rewards and recognition, and links the activities of individuals to organizational effectiveness. But the movement to team-based structures in the 1990s raised new questions and revived old controversies regarding the efficacy of traditional appraisal systems.

For example, who should be appraised in team-structured organizations—individuals or teams? Should the focus of appraisal be on attaining specified outcomes, or on nurturing appropriate behaviors to achieve those outcomes, or on acquiring competencies and skills? Should the focus be the same or different for individual and team appraisal? And who should provide the data on performance—a manager who is not really part of a team? Other team members? Customers?

Designing effective performance-appraisal systems requires careful consideration of a number of team contingencies. In this article, we discuss three—team membership configuration, team task complexity, and the nature of the interdependencies among a team and external groups—that, when taken together, define three prototypical team types. We then specify the appropriate performance appraisal target, type, and data source for each type. To ground our discussion, we begin with a brief review of what is meant by employee motivation and performance, and specify how three different types of performance appraisal—outcome, behavior, and competency-based—affect these processes.

Employee Motivation and Performance

Performance appraisal influences employee motivation by identifying and specifying mutually agreed on outcomes (outcome-based performance appraisal); directing attention to specific tasks, objectives, and assignments and specifying the behaviors that are needed to accomplish them (behavior-based performance appraisal); recognizing skill acquisition and identifying skill deficits for further training and development (competency-based performance appraisal); providing feedback on progress toward outcome attainment and actual task performance (outcome and behavior-based performance appraisal); and establishing the process and providing the rationale for distributing rewards (outcome-based, behavior-based, and competency-based performance appraisal).[3]

Outcome-based performance appraisal is used most successfully when it is part of a comprehensive goal-setting program that includes clearly defined, specific, challenging goals.[4] Appraisal of behavior has possibly been the most used form over the last 30 or so years, and it involves identifying and rating observable behaviors relevant to individual work roles. Finally, competency-based appraisal consists of assessing an individual's skills or knowledge relative to that required to perform a specific job.[5]

Work Roles and Performance-Appraisal Criteria

Performance appraisal, whether outcome-, behavior- or competency-based, traditionally focuses on the formal requirements of specific jobs. With the introduction of team structures, employee-involvement programs, and total quality management, employee roles in the workplace have expanded, and now include activities that go beyond task performance. The following work roles have been identified as important in today's workscapes:[6]

- Job role: Concerned with quality, quantity, and customer service provided.
- Context role: Being a good organizational citizen, continuous improvement of organizational processes, personal self-development in career, and continuous learning.
- Teamwork role: Collaborating in problem solving and conflict resolution, communicating openly, goal setting and performance appraisal of the team, as well as planning and task coordination among members.

Employee job-role performance contributes most directly through the organization's core technical processes, while performance in context and teamwork roles contributes to the broader organizational,

social, and psychological setting in which job-role performance occurs.[7] Generic performance appraisal systems that specify work-role definitions, behavioral descriptors, and competencies are available in the commercial market, or organizations can develop their own. In either case, it is important to involve employees and supervisors early in the process to assure their acceptance of the system.[8] Mutual development by employees and supervisors of work roles, and the outcomes, behaviors, and competencies necessary for their enactment, serves four purposes:

- influencing employees and supervisors to think deeply about which of the roles are most supportive of department goals and of the organizational mission;
- providing specific direction on the behaviors and competencies needed to adequately perform in each role;
- communicating to supervisors which roles an employee is most interested in; this information can be considered for future job assignments;
- resulting in a concrete agreement between employees and supervisors on where time and energy will be focused.

Sources of Performance Data

Much has been written about the use of 360-degree (multirater) feedback as an effective tool for performance appraisal.[9] At its most basic, a multirater feedback system gathers ratings of an employee's work-role behaviors from those in the best position to observe it, including subordinates, customers, and peers, as well as supervisors. Since its inception in the early 1990s, 360-degree performance appraisal has been criticized as often as lauded. A number of recent articles have summarized concerns with the validity of the measurement instruments, the process through which they are administered, and how the feedback is eventually used by organizations.[10] Yet many scholars and managers agree that multisource feedback is fundamentally a good idea that deserves further development.

We will not review the technical discussions related to the validity of 360-degree feedback instruments, which have been thoroughly covered elsewhere,[11] other than to note that such discussions are important with any performance instrument.

Experts do agree that 360-degree performance appraisal should:[12]

- be used more for employee development than for making personnel decisions;
- be part of a formal goal-setting system;
- be administered on a regular basis rather than only once;
- provide aggregated, anonymous feedback to recipients;
- assure that raters evaluate employee behaviors only in work roles for which they have adequate knowledge and first-hand experience;
- provide orientation and training to performance raters;
- provide training and guidance on effectively interpreting and constructively using feedback to recipients.

Performance Appraisal Target: Team Member or Team?

Despite admonitions by many management scholars and consultants to abandon individual performance appraisal for team appraisal,[13] U.S. corporations have been slow to do so. Their reticence may be justified, as team effectiveness is founded on individual behavior and performance, and individuals vary in the amount of effort and capability they bring to the workplace. Social loafing is likely to result when individual effort is not recognized and assessed. This conscious or unconscious tendency to shirk responsibilities by withholding effort toward group goals while sharing in rewards occurs more often when group members believe that their individual contribution (or lack thereof) cannot or will not be identified or assessed. People do show fewer signs of social loafing in small teams than in large groups, but they are still more likely to loaf when rewards (including recognition) are tied to team effort rather than individual effort.[14] This tendency is markedly stronger in individualistic western cultures than it is in more collectivist societies such as Israel and Japan.[15]

If a team must support a free rider without recourse, other team members often withdraw effort.[16] Social loafing spreads among team members like flu, poisoning the work climate. Individual performance appraisal helps discourage social loafing by providing each team member with feedback on the acceptability of his or her individual behavior, and on the need to further develop skills and competencies. High-ability team members are likely to be reassured that equity will be restored, and that all members will have the necessary skills and abilities to contribute.

Individual-level performance appraisal helps reduce social loafing, but it ignores the interaction and synergy that characterize excellent team performance. Team performance assessment gives a team the information it needs to identify team problems and to develop team capabilities. It heightens team pride and ownership, increasing commitment and identification of members with the team. Many team performance measurement systems, such as that at Xerox, are developed jointly by teams, managers, and customers as part of total quality management efforts.[17] Joint accountability helps assure that the criteria and standards for performance are aligned with organizational and team strategies. Such measurement systems are largely outcome-based with some behavioral measures, but there is little reason that they could not also include team competencies. Teams are typically trained to prepare and interpret their own performance data as part of continuous improvement efforts.

Team Types and Performance Appraisal

In this section, we examine the fit of performance appraisal target, type, and data source with different types of teams. We begin by identifying three types of teams—work teams, project teams, and network teams—based on two important dimensions—membership configuration and task complexity. (See Figure 1.)

Membership configuration refers to the expected tenure of a team, the stability of its membership, and the allocation of members' work time, and it varies along a continuum from static to dynamic.[18] Static teams are characterized by full-time team members, membership that remains constant throughout the life of the team, member expectations of a future, and a common level of activation or involvement of members throughout the life of the team. At the other extreme, dynamic teams are characterized by shorter tenure tied to task completion, members who come and go depending on task demands, and members who also work on other teams or nonteam tasks simultaneously.

The second team dimension, task complexity, recognizes that organizational teams engage in a wide variety of work that varies from the routine to the nonroutine.[19] Routine tasks are well scripted and

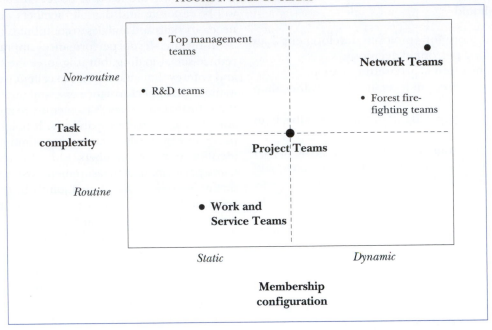

defined, and people encounter relatively few exceptions to the rule in completing them. Cycle time (the time needed to finish one complete unit of work) on routine tasks is specified in advance and is of relatively short duration. Outcomes are easily assessed soon after task completion against specific, quantifiable criteria. In contrast, nonroutine tasks tend to be emergent—the desired outcome and the means to accomplish it are impossible to define in advance. At the extreme, everything encountered in performing a nonroutine task is an exception to the rule. Nonroutine tasks require applying multiple knowledge bases or skill sets learned through education in specific disciplines or through extensive training. Cycle time is longer on nonroutine tasks and indeterminate; at the extreme, cycle time can be decades, such as in developing a new drug.

The dimensions of membership configuration can vary independently. For instance, an airline flight crew is stable, with dedicated members, but of short duration. The dimensions of task type can also vary, but we find common patterns among them that define three types of teams used in organizations.

WORK OR SERVICE TEAMS

At one extreme of membership configuration and task complexity, we find intact work teams engaged on routine manufacturing or service tasks. Those in production at Saab, Saturn, and Xerox are good examples that have been discussed often in the business media. These teams have been in existence for a long time, their membership has changed little or not at all since formation, and team members anticipate membership stability in the future. Members have similar skill sets and are cross-trained to perform many of the tasks necessary for the team to reach its goals. The team's tasks are standardized, cycle time is generally short, and multiple task cycles occur in each performance appraisal period. The team's output tends to be easily and objectively evaluated, there is minimal disagreement among stakeholders about the criteria for success, and feedback on performance is often provided by the task itself.

The work team is a well-developed social system. Members have interpersonal knowledge of each other's likes, dislikes, and personalities such that task interaction is more predictable. The quality of interpersonal relationships is important to all members. Trust reflects knowledge gained over time through experience with each other, but trust is also a matter of confidence that the needs, preferences, and goals of all team members are similar. This is enhanced by the team's regularly engaging in team building and training as an intact unit.

As shown in Table 1, individual and team performance appraisals are recommended for work and service teams. Conditions operating in these teams—an atmosphere of trust, expectations of a future together, shared knowledge of members' differences and similarities, and shared interest in the continuous improvement of the team members and the team—create an optimal environment for conducting performance appraisal at both the individual and team levels.

These same conditions make peer ratings a useful supplement to managers' evaluations of individual team members' behaviors and competencies assuming other conditions of use are met. For instance, the feedback report is used only for developmental purposes, and individual raters' anonymity is assured. Team members are in a good position to assess and certify each other's competencies related to job and nonjob roles, as they have personal knowledge of and experience with them. They also are in an excellent position to assess each other's job behaviors because they observe them daily. Since the team works together over multiple appraisal cycles, useful feedback can be given on improvements that have

TABLE 1: PERFORMANCE APPRAISAL METHODS FOR DIFFERENT TYPES OF TEAMS

Team type	Who is being rated	Who provides rating	What is rated?			How is the rating used?		
			Outcome	Behavior	Competency	Development	Evaluation	Self-regulation
Work or service team	Team member	Manager	✔	✔	✔	✔	✔	
		Other team members		✔	✔	✔		
		Customers		✔		✔		
		Self	✔	✔	✔	✔		✔
	Entire team	Manager	✔	✔	✔	✔	✔	
		Other teams		✔		✔		
		Customers	✔	✔		✔		
		Self	✔	✔	✔	✔		✔
Project team	Team member	Manager	✔		✔	✔	✔	
		Project leaders		✔	✔	✔		
		Other team members		✔	✔	✔		
		Customers		✔				
		Self	✔	✔	✔	✔		✔
	Entire team	Customers	✔	✔			✔	
		Self	✔	✔	✔	✔		✔
Network team	Team member	Manager		✔	✔	✔	✔	
		Team leaders		✔	✔	✔		
		Coworkers		✔	✔	✔		
		Other team members		✔	✔	✔		
		Customers		✔	✔	✔		
		Self	✔	✔	✔	✔		✔
	Entire team	Customers	✔				✔	

occurred in individual behaviors and competencies since the previous appraisal. The feedback report also provides a foundation for individual goal setting, and for a constructive dialogue among members on how to improve team functioning.

Outcome-based performance appraisal is recommended for the team but not for individual team members, as the tight interdependence among team tasks makes it difficult to accurately determine who did what toward achieving team goals. (If this is not the case, we question whether a team actually exists.) Individual outcome-based appraisal shifts the team's focus from teamwork to individual work and promotes a view of teamwork as no more than the sum of the individual parts. It encourages finger pointing and assigning blame by the team rather than problem solving, and it undermines concepts of mutual accountability.

Yet individual team member task proficiency is essential to team effectiveness,[20] and feedback to team members on their own task accomplishment helps them regulate their own performance.[21] Thus work and service team members are typically responsible for monitoring and documenting their own performance on individual tasks. This information is then used by the team as a whole to identify training and development needs and plan skill-building exercises for each member.

At the team level, measurement systems often reflect various types of outcome measures (e.g., productivity, sales volume, and customer complaints), and these act as a signaling device to the team for problem solving and corrective action. Teams are held accountable for monitoring and documenting their own performance against standard goals and against team goals, and they are also held accountable for results. When outcomes do not meet standard or team goals, teams are responsible for exploring potential sources of performance variability and for minimizing and eventually eliminating those over which they have control. Sources of variability outside the team's control are also identified and documented for management action. It is difficult to conceive of a situation where teams have 100 percent control over outcomes, and it is important that this be acknowledged. The weaker the effort-performance linkage (the more factors outside the team's control affect performance), the more important it is that behavioral measures be used to supplement outcome-based measures. Behavioral measures can include jointly attending team-training sessions during the performance cycle and arranging equal opportunities for all team members to master task proficiencies through job rotation.

Three hundred and sixty-degree feedback is sometimes collected on teams as a unit, and most of the same principles apply as those identified for individual multirater feedback. This type of feedback from internal and external customers can be especially useful when work teams are delivering a service and objective measures are difficult to identify. But care must be taken that raters actually assess the team as a unit rather than just the one or two members of the team with whom they interact.

PROJECT TEAMS

Project teams are distinguished from work teams by expectations of a limited future. Members are assembled for a specific purpose and they expect to disband once their task is complete. Well-known examples of successful project teams include the team that developed the first of IBM's PCs and the team that developed the original Taurus/Sable at Ford. Projects can range from relatively short to longer term, but members know they are on loan and will return to their functional areas on completion of the project.

Project teams engage in work that is outside the core production or service work of the organization and inherently less routine than that of work or service teams. Members typically come from different functional areas and have differentiated skills and knowledge bases; they lack expertise or deep understanding of each other's specialties. The difficulty and the tempo of team tasks vary across the life of the project and members' involvement waxes and wanes with project need. Project teams must learn and adapt to task realities.

As a result of their particular task demands and membership configuration, project teams tend to be focused more on tasks than on team members.[22] Project teams have high goal interdependence among members—they are dependent on each other to meet project goals—but the degree of task interdependence among members varies considerably. Training and development of members does not occur as an intact unit, and members are left to apply and integrate individual training with their team experience. Team members' competencies include functional expertise, political skills, creative problem solving, and critical decision making skills, but there is less emphasis on team self-management skills.[23] Paradoxically, team self-management is often less appropriate in these teams of highly educated specialists than it is for work and service teams. Members are functional specialists rather than team specialists, and the priority on meeting project deadlines makes it difficult to engage in team training. In general, the less variable membership dynamics are, and the more routine the task, the more possible and desirable it becomes to move leadership and routine management functions into the team and to make members jointly responsible for team goal attainment. As team-membership dynamics become more fluid and team tasks become more specialized, there are greater needs for coordination and integration of the work across time, space, and members, and strong centralized leadership becomes more critical to goal accomplishment.

The determinant existence and shorter duration of project teams limits the usefulness of team outcome-based assessment because the project cycle does not coincide with the typical appraisal cycle. End-of-project outcome measures do not benefit the team's development as the team has likely dissolved by then. Instead, metrics are developed that relate to the various stages of a project so that teams can self-correct before things go too far off course. These include the continuous tracking of time, cost, and return-on-investment, as Hewlett-Packard does in its product development teams.[24] Interim metrics are carefully designed with the input of project team members to eliminate or account for extraneous sources of variability that the team does not control.

Team members are expected to understand team metrics, work together to track them, revise them as needed, and use them to set downstream project goals. Multisource performance appraisal is particularly useful for rating performance of project team members on these behaviors and competencies. Because project team members are assigned and reassigned to different projects and often serve simultaneously on multiple teams, no one functional manager, team leader, or set of peers observes behavior over the many different work situations in which they perform. Under these circumstances, it makes sense to collect ratings from each of the team leaders and team members of the various projects an employee participates in during a performance cycle.

Project leader and peer ratings are good sources of behavioral ratings related to a team member's context and teamwork roles. But peers lack knowledge of other members' functional disciplines or understanding of their technical specialities, and they generally cannot assess the goodness or value of individual team members' inputs. As shown in Table 1, functional managers, who are responsible for technical mentoring, and who typically retain administrative responsibility for employees,[25] are in a better position to provide behavioral ratings of job roles and to assess competencies pertaining to specific functional expertise. Functional managers and employees use the feedback report from peers and project leaders to identify developmental needs and schedule training. Thus people who are assigned to project teams as part of their job roles are rated on both their individual performance and their contribution in their team role. Training focuses on the development of behaviors and competencies that are transferable from one team assignment to the next.

NETWORK TEAMS

Network teams are virtual in that their potential membership is not constrained by time or space; they include geographically dispersed members who collaborate through a combination of telecommunications and information technologies.[26] Their membership is not limited by organizational boundaries, and frequently includes contingent workers, customers, vendors, and consultants, as well as organizational employees. It is difficult to draw boundaries around a network team, as potential membership includes all who are committed to the goal.

Network teams also differ from project teams because their work is extremely nonroutine. Most network teams engage in one task cycle, the nature of which is unlikely to be repeated. For example, Fleet Focus, a team composed of dispersed specialists, was assembled by Fleet Financial Group of Providence, RI, to reorganize and reengineer Fleet's structure and processes during its acquisition of Shawmut Bank's portfolio in 1994. A similar network team functioned during Fleet's merger with BankBoston in 1999.

Membership configuration in these teams is dynamic, shifting in response to changing task needs, which are themselves emerging in response to rapidly changing environmental and technological conditions and from unique interactions among customers, suppliers, and team members. The timing and intensity of members' participation and the nature of the interaction and level of exchange among members is not scripted, but is dependent on task needs. Network teams are rapid-response units charged with strategically responding to market challenges and exploiting market potentials. Thus their primary competency is the ability to rapidly select and assemble the most appropriate member configuration for the task at hand, even when that task cannot be clearly specified. Team performance is a matter of strategic responsiveness.

The performance emphasis for team members shifts from what they did yesterday or last year to what they are willing and capable of doing tomorrow, where tomorrow is still largely undefined. Network teams, more than any other, rely on a cadre of potential members who are continuously engaged in self-directed learning to improve skills, knowledge, and competencies. Team members must be able to continuously reframe and rethink how things are done. Further, because membership configuration and task requirements are emergent and dynamic, collaborative, intensive communication is especially important to coordinating effort and achieving team effectiveness. Distant members must rely on electronic technologies to maintain coordinated action and commitment to goals. These include audio and video teleconferencing, chat groups, e-mail, bulletin board software, group decision-support systems, and project-management calendars.

Network teams are transitory structures that engage in unique tasks as they arise. Their performance cycle is at odds with annual performance-appraisal systems, and performance of the team as a whole is often not assessed in any formal way. However, there is evidence that this type of improvisational action is becoming increasingly important to organizations operating in highly turbulent industries, and it is important that their employees be prepared to participate in network teams as needed.[27] Thus appraisal is focused on developing individual capacity to initiate, participate, and lead improvisational action, rather than on assessment of past outcomes.

Competency-based appraisal systems are optimal for assessing the potential of all employees to participate in network teams. Knowledge, behaviors, and skills, including individual adaptive ability, are appraised and used for evaluation and developmental purposes. Behavior-based appraisal can also be used to assess the extent to which employees participated in learning activities during performance cycles. These can be self-paced programs, in-house training, or courses at educational institutions. To avoid simply rewarding attendance in training programs, employees are assessed on the extent to which they apply learning to current activities, set developmental goals, and seek out feedback from others as an input into the self-regulatory process.[28] Finally, behavior-based appraisal is used to assess the extent to which members engage in collaborative communication and teamwork behaviors when participating in network teams. Multirater behavioral assessment is essential in networked organizations, because team members are working in multiple performance settings during any given performance cycle.

External Interdependence: A Final Contingency

Our analysis would be incomplete without considering the interdependencies among a team and other teams, individuals, and groups within an organization. At its simplest level, interdependence exists when a team is dependent on the contributions of nonmembers to complete tasks and goals. High interdependence exists when teams are dependent on multiple outsiders for information, resources, and support, and, when the need for the exchange emerges with the task, such exchanges are not well understood and procedures for them are not formalized. Low interdependence implies that teams are dependent on only a few outsiders, and procedures can be set up to manage the exchange of resources and information.

As the complexity of interdependence increases, teams face escalating needs to manage extensive interaction with others inside the organization. Care must be taken to assure that performance-measurement systems focused at the team level do not encourage teams to optimize their own performance at the expense of other teams and the system as a whole. Motorola's experience with team incentive systems is instructive in this regard. The firm found that the outcome of focusing on team productivity in its production facility was anything but teamwork. While some teams did perform better, the cost of open competition, griping, and conflict among teams caused suboptimization in the plant as a whole.[29] Team-focused outcome measures are important tools for team-development purposes, but the more the team is interdependent with others, the greater the need is to balance outcome measures with behavioral measures related to citizenship and teamwork with other teams.

Putting It All Together

One-size-fits-all prescriptions for performance appraisal methods are still all too common, despite strong differences among the types of teams commonly found in organizations. Further, the three types of teams we discussed here do not cover all the possible permutations of team membership dynamics, task complexity, and internal and external interdependencies. Project teams or work teams certainly vary greatly in work organizations. Such teams are prototypical; real teams must be evaluated on many dimensions to determine the most useful and appropriate performance-appraisal target, type, and data source.

As teams move from the stable, routine, and self-contained end of the continuum to the dynamic, emergent, and interdependent end, performance-appraisal systems must move from a focus on the outcomes, behaviors, and competencies of teams to those of individuals. At one extreme—the intact work or service team—the focus is on developing better teams. At the other extreme—network teams—the focus is on developing better team members. These members include those who can and will accurately and quickly assess the task and interpersonal idiosyncrasies of their interaction partners at any given moment and adapt their behavioral repertoire to fit the unique needs presented by both.

Effective performance appraisal is a matter of fit between characteristics of the team and the target of assessment, as well as the rating type, source, and purpose. Performance-appraisal systems that result from careful consideration of these contingencies have the greatest probability of being effective—that is, of eliciting employee behavior that contributes to an organization's goals. Allstate Insurance, Xerox, Hewlett-Packard, and many other organizations have demonstrated that a strategic approach to performance-appraisal design dramatically increases the likelihood that team structures will contribute to greater organizational effectiveness.[3]

Source: *Academy of Management Executive: The Thinking Manager's Source* by Scott. Copyright © 2001 by the Society for Advancement of Management. Reprinted with permission of the Society for Advancement of Management in the format Textbook via Copyright Clearance Center.

Endnotes

1. Townsend, A. M., DeMarie, S. M., & Henrickson, A. R. 1998. Virtual teams: Technology and the workplace of the future. *The Academy of Management Executive*, 12(3): 17–29.
2. Ibid.
3. Steers, R. M., Porter, L. W., & Bigley, G. A. 1996. *Motivation and leadership at work*. 6th ed. New York: McGraw-Hill; Einstein, W. O. 1995. The challenge of leadership: The key to a successful reward strategy or be a pathfinder instead of a firefighter. *The Journal of Applied Management and Entrepreneurship*, 2: 10–26; Cardy, R. L., & Dobbins, G. H. 1994. *Performance appraisal: Alternative perspectives*. Cincinnati: South-Western College Publishing; and Murphy, K. R., & Cleveland, J. N. 1995. *Understanding performance appraisal*. Thousand Oaks, CA: Sage.
4. Locke, E. A., & Latham, G. P. 1984. *A theory of goal-setting and task performance*. Englewood Cliffs, NJ: Prentice Hall; Pritchard, R. D., Roth, P. L., Jones, S. D., Galgay, P. J., & Watson, M. D. 1988. Designing a goal-based system to enhance performance: A practical guide. *Organizational Dynamics*, 16: 69–78.
5. Reilly, R. R., & McGourty, 1999. Performance appraisal in team settings. In T. A. Smither, (Ed.), *Performance appraisal: State of the art in practice*: 244–277. Newark, NJ: John Wiley & Sons.
6. Borman, W. C., & Motowidlo, S. J. 1993. Explaining the criterion domain to include elements of contextual performance. In N. Schmitt, W. C. Borman, & Associates, (Eds.), *Personnel selection in organizations*: 71–98. San Francisco: Jossey-Bass; and Campbell, J. P., Gasser, M. B., & Oswald, F. L. 1996. The substantive nature of job performance variability. In K. R. Murphy, (Ed.), *Individual differences and behavior in organizations*: 258–299. San Francisco: Jossey-Bass; Welbourne, T. M., Johnson, D. E., & Erez, A. 1998. The role-based performance scale: Validity analysis of a theory-based measure. *Academy of Management Journal*, 41: 540–555.
7. Borman & Motowidlo, op. cit.
8. Hedge, J. W., & Teachout, M. S. 2000. Exploring the concept of acceptability as a criterion for evaluating performance measures. *Group & Organization Management*, 25: 22–44.
9. Antonioni, D. 1996. Designing an effective performance appraisal feedback process. *Organizational Dynamics*, 25(2): 24–38; Borman, W. C. 1998. 360-degree performance ratings: An analysis of assumptions and a research agenda for evaluating their validity. *Human Resources Management Review*, 7: 299–315; DeNisi, A. S., & Kluger, A. N. 2000. Feedback effectiveness: Can 360-degree appraisals be improved? *The Academy of Management Executive*, 14(1): 129–139; Ghorpade, J. 2000. Managing five paradoxes of 360-degree feedback. *The Academy of Management Executive*, 14(1): 140–150; and

Waldman, D. A., Atwater, L. E., & Antonioni, D. 1998. Has 360-degree feedback gone amok? *The Academy of Management Executive*, 12(2): 86–94.

10. DeNisi & Kluger, op. cit.; Ghorpade, op. cit.

11. Dalessio, A. T. 1999. Using multisource feedback for employee development and personnel decisions. In T. A. Smither, (Ed.), *Performance appraisal: State of the art in practice*: 244–277. Newark, NJ: John Wiley & Sons; Tornow, W. W. 1993. Perceptions of reality: Is multi-perspective measurement a means or an end? *Human Resource Management*, 32: 221–229.

12. DeNisi & Kluger, op. cit.; Tornow, op. cit.: Ghorpade, op. cit.

13. This idea seems to have originated with W. E. Deming in his 1986 book, *Out of crisis*, Cambridge, MA: Center for Advanced Engineering Study, Massachusetts Institute of Technology. It continues to be advanced by adherents of total quality management such as Ghorpade, J., Chen, M. M., & Caggiano, J. 1995. Creating quality-driven performance appraisal systems. *The Academy of Management Executive*, 9(1): 32–39. See also Gomez-Mejia, L. R., & Balkin, D. B. 1992. *Compensation, organizational strategy, and firm performance*, Cincinnati: South-Western College Publishing.

14. Kidwell, R. E., & Bennett, N. 1993. Employee propensity to withhold effort: A conceptual model to intersect three avenues of research. *Academy of Management Review*, 18: 429–456; Heneman, R. L., & von Hippel, C. 1995. Balancing individual and group rewards: Rewarding individual contributions to the team. *Compensation and Benefits Review*, 27: 745–759.

15. Wagner, J. A. 1994. Studies of individualism-collectivism: Effects on cooperation in groups. *Academy of Management Journal*, 38: 152–172; Kirkman, B. L., & Shapiro, D. L. 1997. The impact of cultural values on employee resistance to teams: Toward a model of globalized self-managing work team effectiveness. *Academy of Management Review*, 22: 730–763.

16. Milkovich, G. T., & Widnor, A. K. 1991. *Pay for performance: Evaluating performance appraisal and merit pay*. Washington, DC: National Academy Press; Sheppard, J. A. 1993. Productivity loss in small groups: A motivation analysis. *Psychological Bulletin*, 113: 67–81.

17. Jones, S., & Moffett, R. G. 1999. Measurement and feedback systems for teams. In E. Sundstrom & Associates, (Eds.), *Supporting work team effectiveness: Best management practices for fostering high performance*: 157–187. San Francisco: Jossey-Bass.

18. Expanded theoretical analyses of membership dynamics in teams are provided in Arrow, H., & McGrath, J. E. 1993. Membership matters: How member change and continuity affect small group structure, process, and performance. *Small Group Research*, 24: 334–361; and Arrow, H., & McGrath, J. E. 1995. Membership dynamics in groups at work: A theoretical framework. In L. L. Cummings, & B. M. Staw, (Eds.), *Research in organizational behavior*, 17: 373–411. Greenwich, CT: JAI Press.

19. Mohrman, S., Cohen, S., & Mohrman, A. 1995. *Designing team-based organizations: New forms for knowledge work*. San Francisco: Jossey-Bass.

20. Salas, E., Dickinson, T. L., Converse, S. A., & Tannenbaum, S. I. 1992. Toward an understanding of team performance and training. In R. W. Swezey, & E. Salas, (Eds.), *Teams: Their training and performance*: 3–29. Norwood, NJ: Ablex Publishing, and Glickman, A. S., Zimmer, S., Montero, R. C., Guerette, P. J., Campbell, W. J., Morgan, B. B., & Salas, E. 1987. The evolution of teamwork skills; An empirical assessment with implications for training. Technical Report TR 87-016. Orlando, FL: Naval Training Center.

21. Kozlowski, S. W. J., Gully, S. M., Nason, E. R., & Smith, E. M. 1999. Developing adaptive teams: 241–292. In D. R. Ilgen, & E. D. Pulakos, (Eds.), *The changing nature of performance*: 240–292. San Francisco: Jossey-Bass.

22. Arrow & McGrath, 1995, op. cit.

23. Mohrman et al., op. cit.

24. House, C. H., & Price, R. L. 1991. The return map: Tracking product teams. *Harvard Business Review*, 1: 92–100.

25. Mohrman et al., op. cit.

26. Townsend et al., op. cit.

27. Crossan, M., & Sorrenti, M. 1997. Making sense of improvisation; and Hatch, M. J. 1997. Jazzing up the theory of organizational improvisation, both in J. P. Walsh & A. S. Huff, (Eds.), *Advances in strategic management*, 14: 181–191. Greenwich, CT: JAI Press.

28. London, M., & Mone, E. M. 1999. Continuous learning. In Ilgen & Pulakos, (Eds.), op. cit.: 119–153.

29. Lawler, E. E., 1999. Creating effective pay systems for teams. In Sundstrom & Associates, (Eds.), op. cit.: 188–193.

30. Jones & Moffett, op. cit.

CHAPTER

11

COMPENSATION

Founded in 1990, San Francisco–based Jamba Juice has expanded to 300 stores that employ more than 4,000 workers in 15 states. Jamba is a leading retailer of blended-to-order fruit smoothies, fresh-squeezed juices, and healthful soups and breads. Since its inception, one of Jamba's chief challenges has been finding and retaining qualified managers. In a high-growth company that has intense competition within the industry, Jamba is additionally challenged by its location in the San Francisco Bay area, which provides many other career opportunities to the younger employees Jamba recruits. A large number of these employers are technology based and offer more generous financial incentives than the typical food retailer.

In order to expand, Jamba must attract and retain these younger workers. To assist them in this objective, Jamba has developed an innovative compensation policy, which allows it to compete not only within the growing juice industry but also with the technology-based employers who attract the same young employees. Jamba's "J.U.I.C.E. Plan" allows general managers to receive a percentage of the store's cash flow, predicated on the financial performance of their business. To keep good managers on board, Jamba provides

opportunities for general managers to share in store profits over a three-year period. When general managers increase year-to-year sales in their operation, money accrues in a retention account, which is payable only in three-year cycles. Much like stock options that vest over three or five years in technology companies, Jamba's retention account not only provides short-term performance incentives, but it also provides incentives to stay with Jamba. On top of this, Jamba also provides all employees at the managerial level with traditional stock options, as well. When assistant managers are promoted, their general manager also receives a cash bonus of $1,000 for their development efforts.

In a fiercely competitive industry characterized by high turnover, Jamba was able to reduce turnover among managers during the first year of operating its J.U.I.C.E. Plan. Jamba has also received inquiries from Australia and Europe from prospective employees, managers, and franchisees. Ironically, the company's strategically designed compensation program has also provided the unintended benefit of fueling its growth.

Source: Sunoo, B. P. "Blending a Successful Workforce," *Workforce*, March 2000, pp. 44–48.

Compensation, a key strategic area for organizations, impacts an employer's ability to attract applicants, retain employees, and ensure optimal levels of performance from employees in meeting the organization's strategic objectives. Compensation is also a key economic issue: Compensation programs continue to assume an increasingly larger share of an organization's operating expenses. This is particularly true in service industries, which are highly labor-intensive. A critical balancing act must occur to ensure that compensation attracts, motivates, and retains employees; at the same time, compensation should allow the organization to maintain a cost structure that enables it to compete effectively and efficiently in its markets.

An organization's compensation system usually consists of three separate components, as illustrated in Exhibit 11-1. The first and largest component is the base compensation or salary system. The second is the incentive system, where employees

EXHIBIT 11-1: COMPENSATION SYSTEM

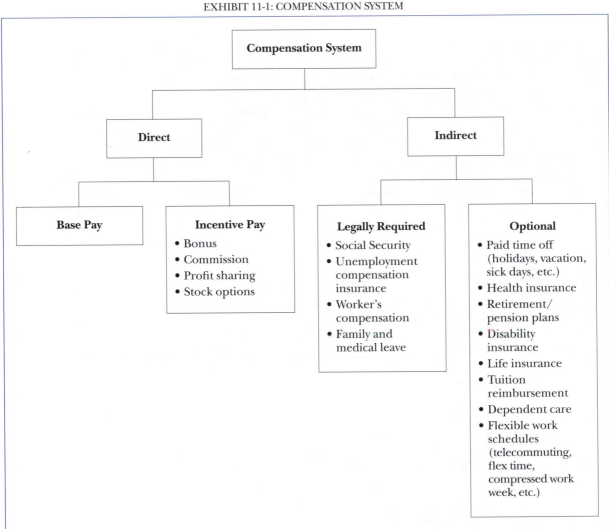

receive additional compensation based on individual, divisional, and/or organization-wide performance. Third is the indirect compensation system, where employees are provided with certain benefits, some of which are legally required and others are provided at the discretion of the employer. This chapter focuses on the strategic and policy issues associated with compensation, as opposed to presenting details concerning many of the components of indirect compensation.

EQUITY

In designing the overall compensation system, an organization needs to be concerned with the perceived equity or fairness of the system for employees. All employees should feel that they are being compensated fairly relative to their coworkers and to individuals who hold comparable jobs in other organizations. The equity theory of motivation holds that workers assess their perceived inputs to their work and their outcomes to those of others as depicted in Exhibit 11-2.[1]

When individuals perceive that they are being treated inequitably relative to their peers, they usually try to establish equity by increasing their outcomes or decreasing their inputs. Increasing outcomes might involve asking for additional compensation or pilfering from the organization. In the latter case, the individual might use the inequity to justify the theft. Decreasing inputs might involve not working as hard, taking longer breaks, coming in late, leaving early, or resigning.

The design of an equitable compensation system must incorporate three types of equity: internal, external, and individual. These perceptions of equity directly impact motivation, commitment, and performance on the job, as illustrated in Exhibit 11-3. It is important to remember that employee assessments of equity are, in fact, perceptions. They may be based, in part, on incomplete or inaccurate information. Few employees really know the extent of their coworkers' inputs unless they are together throughout the workday. The confidentiality of many compensation programs can also make it difficult for employees to obtain accurate information on coworker compensation. Nonetheless, these perceptions impact motivation, commitment, and performance and must be effectively managed. Although compensation is not the only work-related outcome employees receive, it often is the basis by which employees conclude that they are being treated appropriately.

The Internet can provide a wealth of information to employees about comparable salary data. A recent Google search turned up more than 28,000 hits for the search "salary comparison" sites. The most popular of these sites, www.salary.com, averages more than 26 million hits annually and hosts 1.7 million different visitors monthly. The *Wall Street Journal* even offers its own site, www.careerjournal.com.[2] Much of the salary information found by employees may be inaccurate, dated, or based on samples

EXHIBIT 11-2: EQUITY THEORY

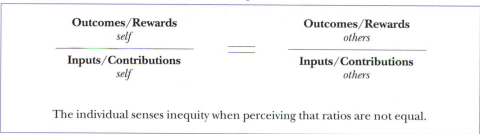

The individual senses inequity when perceiving that ratios are not equal.

EXHIBIT 11-3: EQUITY AND WORK-RELATED OUTCOMES

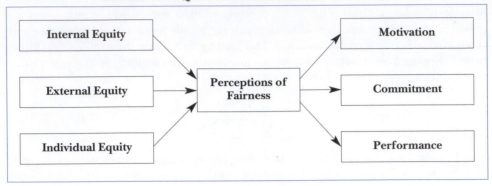

that are irrelevant to the individual employee's job. Employers, however, add to the confusion by failing to communicate compensation policy with employees. Although 60 percent of workers in one recent survey reported that their pay compares unfavorably to pay levels elsewhere, only 43 percent of that same group reported that their employers do a good job of explaining how pay is determined.[3] Hence, with the abundance of salary information available to employees, it is more important than ever that employers develop an equitable compensation system and explain it to employees.

Internal Equity

Internal equity involves the perceived fairness of pay differentials among different jobs within an organization. Employees should feel that the pay differentials between jobs are fair, given the corresponding differences in job responsibilities. In attempting to establish internal equity, employers can evaluate jobs by using four techniques. These are job ranking, job classification, point systems, and factor comparison.

Job ranking is a relatively simple, nonquantitative means of determining equity in compensation in smaller, less complex organizations. Senior management makes judgments as to which jobs are most challenging and ensures that the more challenging jobs receive higher compensation. This method, which is somewhat random and nonscientific, is more concerned with the hierarchical position of jobs rather than with the differential amounts of compensation. Because it is random, job ranking is used infrequently and usually only in small, informal organizations.

Job classification systems group jobs requiring similar effort, ability, training, and responsibility into predetermined grades or classes and compensates each job within a grade similarly. This method is more scientific than job ranking, but it has been criticized for lack of flexibility. Organizations must force each job into a specific category, and subjectivity is involved in classifying jobs, given the nonquantitative nature of the process.[4] However, job classification systems are easy to understand and explain and can be widely administered in large organizations. The federal government, for example, has an elaborate system of 18 job classes, each of which is distinguished by 10 levels of job difficulty or challenge; this impacts the compensation of more than 3 million federal employees. Exhibit 11-4 provides a sample of several of these job grades.

Point systems involve making a quantitative assessment of job content and are more scientific than job ranking or classification. Point systems are easy to understand and explain and, although difficult to design, are easy to implement once they are operational. The organization first creates a list of compensable factors—things that the organization is willing to pay its employees for, such as education, experience,

Grade Level	Grade Description	Jobs Included in Grade
GS 1	Includes those classes of positions the duties of which are to perform, under immediate supervision, with little or no latitude for the exercise of independent judgment: • The simplest routine work in office, business, or fiscal operations; or • elementary work of a subordinate technical character in a professional, scientific, or technical field.	Typist, Messenger
GS 2	Includes those classes of positions the duties of which are: • to perform, under immediate supervision, with limited latitude for the exercise of independent judgment, routine work in office, business, or fiscal operations, or comparable subordinate technical work of limited scope in a professional, scientific, or technical field, requiring some training or experience; or • to perform other work of equal importance, difficulty, and responsibility, and requiring comparable qualifications.	Engineering aide
GS 5	Includes those classes of positions the duties of which are: • to perform, under general supervision, difficult and responsible work in office, business, or fiscal administration, or comparable subordinate technical work in a professional, scientific, or technical field, requiring in either case— • considerable training and supervisory or other experience; • broad working knowledge of a special subject matter or of office, laboratory, engineering, scientific, or other procedure and practice; and • the exercise of independent judgment in a limited field; • to perform other work of equal importance, difficulty, and responsibility, and requiring comparable qualifications.	Chemist, Accountant, Engineer (civil), Statistical clerk

Source: From *The Management of Compensation* by Alan, N. Nash and Stephen J. Carroll. Copyright © 1976 by Wadsworth, Inc.

specific skills, working conditions, and responsibility. Each of these compensable factors is then assigned a factor scale, which describes progressive levels of mastery or accomplishment of each factor. Points are assigned to each level of each scale, and compensation is determined by the overall number of points that correspond to the job. A sample point system is presented in Exhibit 11-5. Note that some compensable factors receive higher points than others. For example, level one in technical skills receives 30 points; level one in working conditions receives only 5 points. Employers can determine the relative worth of each compensable factor by assessing its criticality for the organization's strategic objectives. The more a compensable factor relates to goals and objectives, the higher the values that should be present in the factor scales.

A special type of point system is often used for administrative and managerial positions. Developed by the consulting group Hay Associates, this system is known as the *Hay Plan* and is used by most of the *Fortune 500* companies, as well as over 5,000 organizations in more than 30 countries. The Hay Plan utilizes three factors, called *universal factors*, which are common to all managerial and administrative jobs: know-how, problem-solving, and accountability. Know-how pertains to the technical knowledge required to do the job. Problem-solving assesses the amount of independent thinking and decision making required in the job. Accountability considers the

EXHIBIT 11-5: SAMPLE POINT SYSTEM

| Factors | Level | | | | |
	1	2	3	4	5
Education	15	30	45	60	75
Experience	20	40	60	80	100
Technical Skills	30	60	90	120	150
Working Conditions	5	10	15	20	25
Responsibility	25	50	75	100	125

The compensable factor "technical skills" might have its five levels defined as follows:

Knowledge

This factor measures the knowledge or equivalent training required to perform the job duties.

1st Degree

Use of reading and writing, adding and subtracting of whole numbers; following of instructions; use of fixed gauges, direct reading of instruments, and similar devices; where interpretation is not required.

2nd Degree

Use of addition, subtraction, multiplication, and division of numbers including decimals and fractions; simple use of formulas, charts, tables, drawings, specifications, schedules, wiring diagrams; use of adjustable measuring instruments; checking of reports, forms, records, and comparable data; where interpretation is required.

3rd Degree

Use of mathematics with the use of complicated drawings, specifications, charts, tables; various types of precision measuring instruments. Equivalent to one to three years' applied trades training in a particular or specialized occupation.

4th Degree

Use of advanced trades mathematics, together with the use of complicated drawings, specifications, charts, tables, handbook formulas; all varieties of precision measuring instruments. Equivalent to complete accredited apprenticeship in a recognized trade, craft, or occupation; or equivalent to a two-year technical college education.

5th Degree

Use of higher mathematics involved in the application of engineering principles and the performance of related practical operations, together with a comprehensive knowledge of the theories and practices of mechanical, electrical, chemical, civil, or like engineering field. Equivalent to complete four years of technical college or university education.

Source: Adapted from *Compensation*, 3/e by George T. Milkovich and Jerry M. Newman. Copyright © 1990 by Richard D. Irwin.

direct responsibility for people, resources and results. A brief summary of the Hay Plan is presented in Exhibit 11-6.

Factor comparison is somewhat similar in concept to the point system. However, instead of assessing jobs independently of each other relative to compensable factors, factor comparison utilizes five standard factors in evaluating all jobs: responsibility, skills required, mental effort, physical effort, and working conditions. Jobs are evaluated relative to each other on each of these five dimensions to determine appropriate compensation. For example, an employer would try to determine whether the job of a paralegal required more or less responsibility, skill, mental effort, physical effort, or unusual working conditions relative to the job of an accounting clerk to determine appropriate compensation for each job. Factor comparison can be

EXHIBIT 11-6: HAY COMPENSABLE FACTORS

Know-How

Know-how is the sum total of every kind of skill, however acquired, necessary for acceptable job performance. This sum total, which comprises the necessary overall "fund of knowledge" an employee needs, has three dimensions:
- Knowledge of practical procedures, specialized techniques, and learned disciplines.
- • The ability to integrate and harmonize the diversified functions involved in managerial situations (operating, supporting, and administrative). This know-how may be exercised consultatively as well as executively and involves in some combination the areas of organizing, planning, executing, controlling, and evaluating.
- • • Active, practicing skills in the area of human relationships.

Problem Solving

Problem solving is the original "self-starting" thinking required by the job for analyzing, evaluating, creating, reasoning, and arriving at conclusions. To the extent that thinking is circumscribed by standards, covered by precedents, or referred to others, problem solving is diminished and the emphasis correspondingly is on know-how.

Problem solving has two dimensions:
- The environment in which the thinking takes place.
- • The challenge presented by the thinking to be done.

Accountability

Accountability is the answerability for an action and for the consequences thereof. It is the measured effect of the job on end results. It has three dimensions:
- Freedom to act—the degree of personal or procedural control and guidance.
- • Job impact on end results.
- • • Magnitude—indicated by the general dollar size of the areas(s) most clearly or primarily affected by the job (on an annual basis).

Source: Courtesy of the Hay Group, Boston, MA.

difficult to administer in organizations where job content and responsibilities change frequently. It has also been criticized for its assumption that the five factors are universal to and equally important in all jobs. Factor comparison is best utilized in organizations where there is limited change and job responsibilities and content remain somewhat stable.

The consequences of having a compensation system that employees perceive to be inequitable can be severe. Employers have a choice of four systems for developing an internally equitable compensation system based on whether they wish to consider complete or specified job factors as well as whether they wish to compare jobs to each other or to some standard. Exhibit 11-7 compares the four techniques, noting the relative strengths and weaknesses of each technique. Regardless of the method chosen, employees must understand and accept the system to ensure optimal motivation, commitment, and performance.

External Equity

External equity involves employee perception of the fairness of their compensation relative to those outside the organization. Obviously, employees would not be thrilled to discover that those who do similar work in other organizations receive greater

EXHIBIT 11-7: COMPARISON OF JOB EVALUATION METHODS

	Unit of Analysis	
	Whole Job	**Select Factors of Job**
Basis of Comparison	**Job Ranking**	**Factor Comparisons**
Job vs. Job	• Identify jobs based on "worth" to organization relative to other jobs	• Define compensable factors and evaluate jobs on these factors relative to other jobs
	▲ Simple, inexpensive, easy to understand	▲ Ease of employee comprehension
	▼ Random, subjective, not useful in large organizations	▼ Cumbersome and requires constant updating; universal importance of factors in all jobs questionable
	Job Classification	**Point Method**
Job vs. Standard	• Prepare job grades/classifications and assign jobs to appropriate class	• Define compensable factors and levels of accomplishment and determine levels for each job
	▲ Apply to large number of varied jobs: easy to understand: flexible	▲ Simple to understand and administer; easy for employees to aspire to high levels
	▼ Detailed and time-consuming to develop; lack of flexibility	▼ Extremely time-consuming to develop; lack of universal applicability of compensable factors

compensation. Employers need to be aware of salary structures of competitors and understand that this can impact motivation, commitment, and productivity.

Assessing external equity is relatively a straightforward process. Organizations should first collect wage and salary information to determine market wage rates. This information, which can be collected in-house or through sources external to the organization, is usually readily available relative to the industry and geographic area through professional associations, HR consulting firms, or through the organization's own primary research. When making assessments of external equity, it is important to consider not only salaries but also other forms of compensation, such as bonus and incentive plans and benefits packages. Information pertaining to these additional forms of compensation may be more difficult to obtain, but it must be incorporated into the analysis, especially for higher-level managerial and executive positions that may have a significant portion of the overall compensation based on incentive pay.

After an investigation of the market has been completed, the organization then determines its own pay strategy relative to the market. The three strategies an employer can choose are a lead, lag, or market policy. A lead policy involves paying higher wages than competitors to ensure that the organization becomes the employer of choice. In other words, this strategy assumes that pay is a critical factor in an applicant's decision in choosing an employer and attempts to attract and help retain the highest-quality employees. In short, the employer desires to be the first-choice employer; that is, the organization wants first selection from available talent. However, any organization that offers higher compensation than its competitors needs to ensure that it has a means of remaining competitive relative to its cost structure and market prices. This requires the organization to have operational efficiencies that its competitors lack, a higher rate of employee productivity than its competitors, and/or a product or service for which consumers are willing to pay a premium price.

With a lag policy, the organization compensates employees below the rates of competitors. An organization employing this strategy attempts to compensate employees through some other means, such as opportunity for advancement, incentive plans, good location, good working conditions, or employment security. The organization believes that work-related outcomes are multifaceted and, more important, that employees consider more than just salary in weighing their employment options. An organization employing a lag policy needs strong insights into the personal and lifestyle choices of the employees it recruits to allow it to tailor compensation options for these individuals that will allow them to accept a lower base salary than that offered by the competition.

With a market policy, the organization sets its salary levels equal to those of competitors. An employer following this strategy attempts to neutralize pay as a factor in applicant decisions, assuming that it can compete in the labor market in attracting employees by other means such as those listed in the discussion of lag policy. It should come as no surprise that the majority of employers set their salary levels at or very near market levels. Such a strategy assumes that employees are less likely to leave if their salaries would remain the same with a new employer.

Individual Equity

Individual equity considers employee perceptions of pay differentials among individuals who hold identical jobs in the same organization. Determining individual salary levels and pay differentials among employees in identical jobs can be done in a number of ways. The most basic is basing pay on seniority. Seniority-based systems determine compensation according to the length of time on the job or length of time with the employer. Although this rewards a stable and experienced workforce, it has no direct relationship to performance on the job. Seniority systems are very common in union settings. They are also usually looked upon favorably by the court system, because they are objective in nature. However, they provide little incentive to be more productive, and they encourage workers who may be mediocre or substandard performers to remain with the organization.

Merit pay systems compensate individuals for their proven performance on the job. Ideally, they provide an incentive for employees to work harder and accomplish more. Merit pay is generally permanently added to an employee's base pay. However, in practice, merit pay can be quite problematic. Because merit-based pay systems are anchored by the organization's performance feedback system, they can extend the subjectivity that is inherent in the feedback system. If an employee believes that the performance feedback process is biased or unfair, a compensation system that is based on this process can further add to the employee's perceptions of unfairness. Any merit-based pay plan must ensure that the performance feedback upon which it is built is understood and accepted by employees.

An increasing number of organizations are using incentive pay to compensate their employees. Incentive plans allow the employee to receive a portion of his or her compensation in direct relation to financial performance of the individual, unit, or entire organization. Incentive pay is provided for a given time period and is not added to the base salary. Consequently, it must be re-earned in subsequent time periods and can have a greater motivational impact than merit pay.

The philosophy behind this compensation system is to reward higher levels of performance by returning financial rewards to the employees who have been responsible for creating them. Incentive pay programs also allow organizations to adjust their compensation expenses based on organizational performance. These plans can take a variety of forms, such as commission sales plans, profit-sharing plans, gainsharing plans (in which cost savings are partially distributed to those responsible for them) and stock ownership, distribution, or option plans. Incentive plans also differ from merit pay plans in that the former are based on objective, measurable financial performance; the latter are based on subjective, generally nonfinancial performance-related criteria. A well-designed incentive pay plan can be the deciding factor in an applicant's decision to accept or reject a job offer when base compensation is set at market level and nondistinguishable from that of competitors.[5]

Performance-based pay that is variably tied into an employee's, work unit's, or organization's results is popular with both employers and employees. Until recently offered to senior executives only, performance-based pay is now extended to many other employees, as organizations realize how variable compensation programs can impact individual employees' behavior and performance. Approximately two thirds of U.S. companies offer some form of variable performance-based pay and about 10 percent of all compensation paid in the United States is variable.[6] More important, one survey found that employers who provide variable performance-based pay to their top employees are 68 percent more likely than those who don't to report outstanding bottom-line financial performance.[7]

Incentive pay is popular with employers, in part, because it is self-funded. Because it is tied into specific financial performance of a division or the entire organization and is not paid unless specific measurable financial metrics are achieved, it can and should appeal to even the most fiscally conservative organizations. The flexibility of variable compensation programs allows them to be tailored to organization-wide, divisional, team, or individual performance—or some combination thereof—depending on the interdependence present in jobs as well as organizational strategy. Perhaps their greatest value is that variable compensation programs, if well-communicated and implemented, allow employees to fully understand the organization's goals and objectives, as well as how their individual jobs impact organizational performance. As discussed in Chapter 10, Continental Airlines used a performance-based variable compensation program to turn around poor performance. The result? Continental won more awards for customer satisfaction than any other U.S. airline and was named one of "100 Best Companies to Work for in America" by *Fortune* for four consecutive years.[8]

Team-Based Incentive Pay at Children's Hospital Boston

The accounts receivable department at Children's Hospital Boston was suffering from low morale and inefficiencies after an unsuccessful change to a new billing system. With an average of more than 100 days from billing to payment, the organization was facing serious cash flow concerns in its fiscal operations. To alleviate this, management developed a team-based incentive plan that would allow employees to see the relationship between quarterly cash flow and the number of days a bill spent uncollected in accounts receivable. Employee-centered, the program allowed team members to set three possible goal levels—threshold, target, and optimal—with corresponding rewards of $500, $1,000, and $1,500 for the attainment of each. Meetings were set up with employees to explain the program and obtain employee input and support. Employees suddenly began to feel important, empowered, and energized: Weekly progress reports allow employees to self-monitor their progress. During the first year the average number of days *a bill spent in accounts receivable was reduced from more than 100 days to 76 and during the second year the average was reduced to the mid-60s, and the satisfaction with the program has reduced employee turnover in the department.*[9]

While performance-based rewards can be tremendous motivators and allow employees to see a stronger connection between their performance and organizational performance, they are clearly not for every organization. Cultural barriers, both institutional and national, can act as impediments to the successful implementation of a performance-based pay plan. Japanese conglomerate Fujitsu was the first Japanese organization to implement such a compensation plan. Hailed as a breakthrough and revolutionary when first introduced, the program ignited a trend in Japanese organizations to abandon archaic pay systems based almost entirely on seniority in favor of performance-based plans. After eight years, however, Fujitsu abandoned the program, calling it "flawed" and a poor fit with Japanese culture that respects and rewards loyalty and seniority. In addition, to maintain a positive self-image, employees fought to keep the performance standards under the plan as low as possible for fear of falling short and being embarrassed. Innovation was stifled as employees resisted change, fearing that results might not accompany the change.[10]

Skill-based pay systems have been increasing in popularity in recent years due to the ease of measurement of many specific skills and because skills relating to the organization's strategy can be readily identified. Skill-based pay involves basing the employee's compensation on the acquisition and mastery of skills used on the job. Skill-based pay programs not only give employees incentives to learn new skills or upgrade existing ones, but they also promote flexibility for the organization. They can easily be linked with training programs and the strategic needs of the organization. During the strategic planning process, the organization must determine which kinds of employee skills are most critical to its objectives and future success. Then, the organization must either hire employees with these skills or with the capacity to learn these skills.

Despite their popularity, skill-based pay systems are not without problems. Employers should remember that the acquisition of skills and improved performance are two different things. Skill-based pay systems often are based on the acquisition of skills, without regard to whether the employee has successfully transferred the training to the work setting or achieved any results from the skill-based training. In a rapidly changing work environment, skill obsolescence may result in a pay system that compensates employees for previously learned skills that have become outdated and are no longer of value to the employer. Most employees would find it unfair for the organization to reduce compensation because it no longer values certain employee skills, particularly if the organization has not provided opportunities for employees to upgrade their skills. Employers need to implement skill-based pay plans very carefully and with a clear sense of what the future might hold for how work is performed.

Team-based pay plans are also becoming more prevalent in many organizations. With more work and responsibility being centered around self-managed teams, such compensation plans provide incentives to cooperate and be more flexible in working with others in achieving group and organizational objectives. Administering team-based pay systems can be less time-consuming than administering individual reward systems. However, team-based pay plans may impact group dynamics and can adversely impact and intensify conflict within a unit, particularly if team members feel that certain teammates are not doing their share of the work and living up to their responsibility to the team. Such free-riders can greatly damage morale and enthusiasm for the plan, as well.[11] Consequently, team-based pay plans may require the oversight and attention of supervisors, particularly in their early stages of implementation.[12]

Team-based pay plans present a key strategic issue for organizations in determining the percentage of overall employee compensation that should be based on team rather than individual performance. ▼

Team-based pay systems need a decentralized decision-making system that gives the team some autonomy and responsibility in order to be successful; they also need to be tied into specific measures of accountability and results. To the extent that they foster unhealthy competition and conflict among different teams within an organization, they can have adverse effects on overall performance. Although team-based pay plans may make sense given the changing nature of work and the emphasis on project teams and groups, their potential impact on both individual teams and intrateam relations and performance needs to be assessed before the plan is implemented. Despite the changing nature of job design, technology, and work relationships, certain organizations may find that their culture does not support the team-based pay concept. Team-based pay plans must be implemented within the context of an organizational culture that values sharing and collaboration, cooperation, and open communication.

While many employers realize the critical role that effective teams play in the success of their organization, few have been able to implement compensation systems that encourage and reward team effort. The few that have done so find that three criteria influence the success of such a plan. First, there has to be a high level of communication with employees regarding the details of the plan. Second, employees should have a voice and provide input into the design and implementation of the plan. Third, team members need to feel that the system is fair and equitable.[13]

Team-Based Pay at Phelps Dodge

Phoenix-based Phelps Dodge has a copper-mining operation that employs more than 4,200 individuals at six North American locations. When the employees decided to decertify their existing labor union, management saw a golden opportunity to create a more incentive-based compensation system. The new plan involves a base salary with bonuses awarded for meeting team-based goals set for a specific location or mine. Goals are set by team members and the compensation is constantly being evaluated through the feedback provided by employees.[14]

LEGAL ISSUES IN COMPENSATION

Those designing compensation systems must also bear in mind that compensation is a condition of employment covered under Title VII of the Civil Rights Act of 1964. The design of any compensation system that intentionally or unintentionally discriminates against any protected class can subject the organization to legal action. The Equal Pay Act of 1963 also partially regulates compensation and must be considered when designing and administering compensation programs. These laws were discussed in Chapter 7.

▶ Decisions need to be made as to whether all team members should receive the same compensation or whether they should be rewarded individually. It must also be determined whether to reward behavior or results. With teams, process can be as important as outputs, so behavioral measures could be critical performance criteria. Reading 11.1, "Compensating Teams," addresses some of the strategic issues surrounding team-based pay.

Critics of the Equal Pay Act have noted that it has been of limited value because men and women often are not employed in the same jobs, and the act only requires equal pay for equal work. To combat this limitation, the concept of comparable worth has been advanced. Comparable worth argues that the standards of equal pay for equal work should be replaced with the doctrine of equal pay for equal value. Because many occupations, although becoming more gender-integrated, are still somewhat gender-segregated, women and men generally do not hold the same jobs or do the same work in our economy, so the Equal Pay Act does nothing to relieve the lower wages that women receive relative to men. For example, in a warehouse, men might be working on the loading dock, and women might be working in the office. Men will invariably be paid more, but the Equal Pay Act cannot address this because the jobs being performed by men and women are not the same. Comparable worth would argue that the work being done in the office (bookkeeping, clerical, and switchboard) has as much value as and is as important to the organization as that being done on the loading dock and should be compensated similarly.

Comparable worth of two different jobs, however, remains very difficult to prove because of the lack of objective, measurable data that would support an assessment of job value. Gender stereotyping of certain jobs creates an additional obstacle in this regard. For example, the majority of schoolteachers (particularly in elementary schools), secretaries, nurses, and flight attendants are female. Although the courts have been sympathetic to arguments for comparable worth, they have been extremely reluctant to take action, because the doctrine falls outside of existing federal law. In addition, the value of a particular job is very difficult to determine objectively and prove in a legal arena. Comparable worth may be our society's best hope for narrowing the gender gap in wages, in which women consistently have been found to earn 70 to 75 cents on the dollar of what men earn.[15] This is particularly true given that the Equal Pay Act does have exclusions that allow gender-based pay differentials to exist. Comparable worth, however, will most likely remain an unenforceable ideal until laws are passed that specifically address it. Equal pay for equal work is still the standard; the courts have refused to manufacture standards and policy that have not been legislated.

One additional law that impacts compensation is the Fair Labor Standards Act of 1938 (FLSA), which regulates the federal minimum wage, overtime policies, and the use of child labor. It exempts from minimum wage and overtime requirements certain groups of employees (managers, administrators, outside salespeople, and professionals) who exercise independent judgment in carrying out their job duties. However, there has been significant controversy concerning whether certain types of sales positions, temporary employees, and independent contractors are legally considered employees and/or covered under the FLSA. As nontraditional employment relationships continue to develop, this act will require the courts to increase scrutiny of the legal status of such nontraditional employees. In the interim, companies that employ these workers will have to exercise caution when designing compensation programs to ensure that they follow the law.

The FLSA has caused numerous problems for employers in recent years. Because it was written and passed long before our economy became based on services, knowledge, and information technology, Congress was unable to anticipate many of the changes that would take place relative to the nature of jobs, work, and organizational life. Problems have arisen because of the ambiguity of the law regarding specifically who is covered under the act and therefore is eligible for overtime pay. In response, there have been a number of high-profile class action lawsuits that have resulted in major payouts by employers. In 2002, RadioShack settled a class action lawsuit for

$30 million that was filed by managers who claimed that they were classified improperly under the act in an attempt to avoid paying them overtime.[16] Similar settlements were offered in the same year by Starbucks ($18 million), Rite Aid ($25 million), and Pacific Bell (two separate cases settled for $35 million and $27 million).[17] While the U.S. Department of Labor offers employers a comprehensive FLSA compliance assistance program, much confusion still exists and lawsuits continue to be filed. Congress has been debating amending the FLSA for several years, given the complicated political nature of reform in this area, but reform and relief have yet to be seen.

EXECUTIVE COMPENSATION

One important and controversial area of compensation concerns the pay received by executives. There is no real average or standard for executive compensation, largely because of differences between industries, as well as between organizations within a given industry. The demand for talented CEOs and other chief officers who can generate results for shareholders often results in significant compensation packages. Typically, a senior executive receives no more than 20 percent of annual compensation in the form of salary, with the remainder usually divided between annual (30 percent) and long-term (50 percent) incentives.[18] ▼▼

Executive compensation has been criticized for its excessiveness as well as for the fact that it often is unrelated to actual performance. In 1980 the average CEO made 42 times the average hourly worker's pay; by the year 2000, average CEO pay had grown to 531 times the average hourly worker's pay.[19] Recent corporate accounting scandals in which executives reaped millions of dollars in compensation while their organizations were going bankrupt has drawn even more attention to executive compensation. The lesson learned from the Enron scandal is that heavy reliance on stock options as part of executive compensation can create a culture obsessed with improving stock performance at the expense of all other concerns. Nonetheless, stock options remain a key component of executive compensation packages.

Stock options provide employees with the opportunity to purchase shares at some future date, at a price that is determined at the time the options are awarded. They are designed to focus employee attention on creating shareholder value and, in doing so, employees are also able to reap the benefits of the organization's financial performance. However, stock options can prompt executives to engage in creative accounting practices in which revenues and profitability are artificially inflated, driving up the value of the stock and the options. In addition, stock options are deductible on corporate income taxes despite the fact that they do not have to be reported as expenses in the organization's financial reports.[20]

Several large organizations, including Coca-Cola and Bank One Corp., however, have voluntarily decided to expense stock options offered to employees. Designed to ease concerns in the investment community in light of the recent accounting scandals, this move will make earnings appear lower. Ideally, this may reduce the use of stock options, particularly among rank-and-file employees, as stock options and cash will cost the organization an identical amount. With stock options requiring more time and recordkeeping for the organization and oversight by employees, both employers and employees might find simple equivalent cash compensation more

▶▶ Reading 11.2, "Executive Compensation: Examining an Old Issue from New Perspectives," examines some of the controversies surrounding executive compensation.

efficient than stock options. Regardless of the decisions that individual organizations make regarding the future of stock options, those organizations that continue to offer stock options to executives as well as other employees will now find their compensation practices more carefully scrutinized by those outside of the organization.

A number of employers have been moving away from stock options and instead compensating employees, particularly executives, with stock grants.[21] Stock grants require that the organization meet specific financial goals, such as a given return on capital or return on assets, as a condition of their issuance. From 2002 to 2003, the percentage of CEO long-term compensation that consisted of stock options decreased from 76 percent to 62 percent.[22]

CONCLUSION

Organizations face a number of key strategic issues in setting their compensation policies and programs. These include compensation relative to the market, the balance between fixed and variable compensation, utilization of individual versus team-based pay, the appropriate mix of financial and nonfinancial compensation, and developing an overall cost-effective program that results in high performance. ▼▼▼

In addition to these strategic issues, the fast pace of change in our society and the corresponding need for organizations to respond in order to remain competitive create challenges for all HR programs, but particularly for compensation. Probably more now than at any time in the past, organizations need to reevaluate their compensation programs within the context of their corporate strategy and specific HR strategy to ensure that they are consistent with the necessary performance measures required by the organization. Overly rigid compensation systems inhibit the flexibility needed by most contemporary organization's competitive strategies, so it is no surprise to see such flexibility being incorporated into compensation systems.

At the same time, organizations wishing to be more innovative may need to alter their compensation systems to promote more intrapreneurial behavior that encourages employees to act as risk-taking entrepreneurs. Similarly, smaller entrepreneurial organizations will usually need different compensation systems than their larger counterparts. Organizations taking a strategic approach to compensation realize the need for creativity to meet strategic objectives. Also, within a given organization, different compensation programs may be needed for different divisions, departments, or groups of employees. Compensation systems must grow and evolve in the same manner as the organization to ensure that what is actually being rewarded is consistent with the organization's strategic objectives. This link between strategy and compensation is essential for ensuring optimal performance.

CRITICAL THINKING

1. Does money motivate employees? Why or why not?

2. Why should compensation systems be equitable? How can an organization design an equitable compensation system?

▶▶▶ Reading 11.3, "Pay Strategy: New Thinking for the New Millennium," discusses some of the challenges organizations face in developing compensation systems that reflect the realities they confront.

3. Compare and contrast the four job evaluation methods. Give an example of an organization in which each of the four methods might provide an optimal strategic fit.

4. Discuss the pros and cons of employee pay being fixed versus variable and dependent on performance. How might such decisions impact recruiting, motivation, and retention?

5. Analyze your current job responsibilities. Determine whether the method by which you are compensated is appropriate.

6. Is performance-based pay effective? Why or why not? How can performance-based pay systems be better designed to ensure optimal results?

Reading 11.1

7. What are the critical factors in designing a team-based compensation system?

Reading 11.2

8. Is executive compensation excessive? Why or why not? What factors should influence executive compensation?

Reading 11.3

9. Critique the three strategies discussed for managing compensation systems of the future. What potential limitations or problems do you see with these strategies?

EXPERIENTIAL EXERCISES

1. Briefly interview an employee in his or her 20s, 30s, 40s, 50s, 60s, and 70s. Determine what motivates workers from different generations and design compensation plans for each generation that would result in high performance.

INTERNET EXERCISES

1. Visit the Web site http://www.salary.com. Click on "salary trends" and prepare a brief report on the latest developments in compensation practice.

2. At the same Web site, click on "salary wizard." Select a job category and determine the median compensation figures for this position in eight different United States locations. Should an organization that operates in these different locations pay different salaries for identical work? Is cost of living a sufficient explanation for an employee who senses inequity?

CHAPTER REFERENCES

1. Adams, J. S. "Toward an Understanding of Inequity," *Journal of Abnormal and Social Psychology*, October 1963, pp. 422–436.
2. Wellner, A. S. "Salaries in Site," *HR Magazine*, May 2001, pp. 89–96.

3. Shea, T. F. "Send Employees a Message—About Their Pay," *HR Magazine*, December 2002, p. 29.

4. Fisher, C. D., Schoenfeldt, L. F. and Shaw, J. B. *Human Resource Management*, 4th ed. Boston: Houghton Mifflin Co., 1999, p. 560.

5. Williams, V. L. and Grimaldi, S. E. "A Quick Breakdown of Strategic Pay," *Workforce*, 78, (12), December 1999, pp. 72–75.

6. Bates, S. "Pay for Performance," *HR Magazine*, January 2003, pp. 31–38.

7. Ibid.

8. Minton-Eversole, T. "Bethune Flies High with Continental," *HR News*, August 2002, pp. 1, 7.

9. Cadrain, D. "Put Success in Sight," *HR Magazine*, May 2003, pp. 85–92.

10. Tanikawa, M. "Fujitsu Decides to Backtrack on Performance-Based Pay," *New York Times*, March 21, 2001, p. W1.

11. Heneman, F. and Von Hippel, C. Interview appearing in The *Wall Street Journal*, November 28, 1995, p. A1.

12. Albanese, R. and VanFleet, D. D. "Rational Behavior in Groups; The Free-Riding Tendency," *Academy of Management Review*, 10, 1985, pp. 244–255.

13. McClurg, L. N. "Team Rewards: How Far Have We Come?" *Human Resource Management*, 40, (1), pp. 73–86.

14. Garvey, C. "Steer Teams with the Right Pay," *HR Magazine*, May 2002, pp. 71–78.

15. U.S. Bureau of the Census. *Current Population Reports*, No. P60–197, Washington, DC: U.S. Government Printing Office, 1997.

16. "RadioShack Agrees to Pay $30 Million to Settle Suit," *Baltimore Sun*, July 17, 2002.

17. Clark, M. M. "FLSA: Will Ya Still Need Me When I'm 64?" *HR News*, October 2002, p. 3.

18. Overman, S. "Executive Compensation to Undergo Intense Scrutiny," *HR News*, May 2002, p. 1.

19. Patel, D. "The Evolution of Compensation," *Work Visions*, No. 3, 2002.

20. Bates, S. "More Firms Take High Road by Expensing Stock Options," *HR Magazine*, August 2002, p. 10.

21. Gerena-Morales, R. "Balancing Pay and Performance," *South Florida Sun-Sentinel*, May 23, 2003, p. 1E.

22. Ibid.

Compensating Teams

Perry Pascarella, *Across the Board*

You want your team to be more than simply a bunch of individuals. So how do you achieve that end?

Watching the advent of quality circles in the early '80s and the mushrooming of quality teams in the late '80s and '90s has been thrilling to anyone who favors worker participation. Today, companies no longer need to prove that teams can generate great gains in productivity and quality even as employees earn psychic rewards from team involvement. They widely employ special-project, cross-functional, ad-hoc teams to find ways to cut costs, develop new products, re-align production processes, and engage in all sorts of problem-spotting and -solving activities.

But always lurking in the background are those nasty questions about whether and how to share the financial gains with workers: Should teams be compensated? In this day of pay-for-performance, the answer seems obvious. But do you pay them as individuals or as a group? The solution hinges on the answer to another question: Which way will make teams perform better?

And then there are the thorny issues of how and when. With money or "recognition" of deeds well done? If it's cash—how much is enough? As to the when, after the team's work is done—assuming you know when that is. But isn't it important for team members to know what their possible bonus is beforehand, so that it motivates them?

Nasty questions, indeed.

Although the types of work performed and the types of behavior required in teams do not fit within the bounds of traditional compensation systems, some managers continue to use old thinking to rec-ognize good performance. As David Goodall, corpo-rate director of compensation at Motorola Inc., puts it: "Organizations of the '90s are trying to manage with compensation tools of the '50s and '60s."

So what do you do? Establish your company's incentives and recognition practices with one over-arching principle in mind: Tailor what you do to the individual. Keep in mind:

1. Motivation comes from within the individual, not from the group.
2. The development of skills and behaviors is an individual undertaking.
3. Fairness in dealing with teams does not mean equal pay for all.
4. Expressing oneself within the context of coop-eration is replacing wild notions of individualis-tic behavior.
5. Team compensation is not a payoff but a means of nurturing behavior that benefits the group.

At most companies, people are not assigned full time to teams. Team activity is piggy-backed atop staff members' regular duties. As teams proliferate in a company, however, a person may spend a major portion of his time on these projects. "The more the project looks like your regular work," says Jerry McAdams, national practice leader for reward and recognition systems for Watson Wyatt Worldwide, St. Louis, "the harder it gets to operate a reward mechanism. If that's the case, I argue strongly for a much more extensive and pervasive recognition sys-tem so that managers have the right, after the fact, to recognize a team for having done good work."

Teams, for most companies, are still an intrusion on the standard operating procedure. William M. Mercer Inc. canvassed 2,500 corporations for its 1996/97 Compensation Planning Survey and found that the number of companies with "small-group incentives" (the type you would use with a project team) grew from 16 percent in 1995 to 19 percent in 1996. Meanwhile, 21 percent are considering such programs. That still leaves a huge number of com-panies without a team-based compensation plan. Unless your company uses the team approach from top to bottom in virtually all it does, people will hold teams under the magnifying glass to see how they are being rewarded and recognized vis-à-vis the mainstream compensation structure.

Adding on Incentives

Burying incentives and recognition for team membership in the company's basic compensation package can dampen the intended motivating effect on individuals, so look for ways to *add on* incentives and recognition for team participation. If you don't, says McAdams, you'll be carrying "a whole bunch of baggage that have always made compensation plans not as effective as they could be—lack of education, lack of communication, lack of management accountability for how well they develop people and how well they reward them. At the end of the line, we get our bonus check and don't know why we got it."

Companies are particularly likely to add incentives to support team activity when a person is assigned full time to a project. At TRW Inc.'s Cleveland-based automotive group, "We have something going on called Project ELITE [Earnings Leadership in Tomorrow's Environment]," says director of compensation Harvey Minkoff, "where a number of people there are temporarily assigned to the effort, and it's expected they'll return to their units or to a full-time permanent position sometime in the future. We have established specific goals for that project, and each individual, in turn, has established specific goals. A significant portion of their pay is tied to the accomplishment of their goals and the accomplishment of their organization's goals." This could range from 10 percent for lower-paid workers to 25 percent for those at higher levels. (Why do lower-paid workers get less? The thinking is that they should be exposed to less risk in their total compensation packages than should higher-paid workers. The lower the bonus, the higher the "guaranteed" portion of their total compensation.)

Teams abound at TRW, but not all are compensated in this fashion. "In any given year, any one of us can expect to perform on some kind of team in addition to doing our normal duties and responsibilities," says Minkoff, "but we don't have a separate salary structure or a special base pay plan."

Reward Behavior, Not Results

Traditional thinking may lead you to link the performance of your players to their results. In cost reduction, for instance, that's possible because the cuts are relatively easy to quantify. But in other areas measurement can be a nightmare. In his book *The Reward Plan Advantage* (Jossey-Bass), McAdams writes, "If it is not something that is easily measured, then you tend to measure on activities. Did you meet a milestone? Did you get it done? But it's harder to do that. That just may be a candidate for after-the-fact recognition rather than project-team incentives."

Motorola's Goodall offers a telling argument against trying to link rewards and results. "It's unfair to reward cross-functional teams solely on the basis of results, because they are often put into positions to move organizations forward by taking risks. Sometimes the risks they take might not be successful. The worst thing to do would be to rap their knuckles."

This has led Goodall to reward behaviors and activities rather than results. "Where people are working on cross-functional teams, management should look at the elements of team play when it is distributing rewards," he says. "It should ask, for example: 'does the person display participative behavior? Is the person an empowering individual? Does the person listen in a team environment?' A team may be unsuccessful because of the lack of team playing by certain individuals. That should be spotted in a one-on-one appraisal process and be reflected in the level of rewards given to the individual in base pay, or in promotion, or ability to maintain employment within the company."

Team performance can be judged as an employee goes through the normal evaluation process. Robert P. McNutt of Du Pont human resources says his company uses a 360-degree review process in which a person is evaluated by peers, subordinates, and supervisors. "As you go through that, you're going to get some of the input on a person's performance on a project," he allows.

Jay Schuster, partner at Schuster-Zingheim and Associates Inc. and co-author of an ongoing study of team pay sponsored by the American Management Association, also favors the 360-degree review process. But he feels that you can't just implement such a system overnight: "For our study, we looked at organizations that are team-based, like Honeywell and Selectron. We found that when pay is based on individual performance, it erodes team cohesiveness and makes it less likely that the team as a collaborative element will meet its goals. American culture is individualized: Gary Cooper in *High Noon* gets the job done by himself. As a result, pay systems have been individualized. But now, team organizations are becoming more prevalent, so the first thing to do is base all team members' pay on team performance only. Most teams are not ready to base pay on multisource performance management early in their formation. When the team becomes mature enough, the members will let you know they're ready to have pay based on individual performance. The best way to do that is 360-degree performance management.

If team members' pay levels vary from one another, so should their compensation for team participation. TRW's Minkoff says, "Many companies have a very structured compensation approach, and bringing a bunch of people together from all around the country with significant inequities in their pay is an issue for them. We tend to not overreact to that. We say to employees, 'We're paying you for what we

---

Tricky but Not Impossible
Making everybody happy—at a price.

Corporate life would be so much easier if every worker were an island. Just give each individual a job description and an appropriate pay package, right? Compensation specialists will tell you it's not that easy, and the growing use of teams makes motivating people through pay even tougher. What will make your stars shine yet keep the supporting players involved in the project?

Edward E. Lawler III has given some thought to this problem over the years. A founding director of the Center for Effective Organizations at the University of Southern California and author of *From the Ground Up: Six Principles for Building the New Logic Corporation* (Jossey-Bass), Lawler agrees that compensating teams is tricky, but feels there are proven methods for handling the problem. On a recent trip to New York, he talked with *Across the Board*'s managing editor, Geoffrey Loftus.

Let's cut to the chase: Do you motivate a team by a collective reward, or do you try to motivate individual by individual?
Well, the question I always ask is: What kind of team is this? Is it—to take a sports analogy—a soccer team where we constantly play off of each other? Or is it a golf team, where we add up the individual scores at the end of the day?

If it's a highly interactive team, you're probably better off rewarding the team as a whole. You might want to recognize a "most valuable player" with an extra award. Or use a group process—which is tricky—where group members decide on different rewards for different members.

Something similar to the way sports teams have the players divide shares of playoff bonus money.
Exactly. The evidence would say that's the best. But the worst thing is for management to come in and say, OK, it's a great win for the team, but in my judgment Joe contributed less than Sue, and so forth.

At the other extreme, let's take a group of salesmen who have a territory but basically have individual accounts within that territory. If you say there's going to be a bonus plan for the territory as a whole, you cause the team members to lose line of sight for their compensation system. There's a less direct connection between what each team member does and what he's rewarded for.

Going back to the highly interactive team, how do you rate the contribution of the individuals who form the team? Or would the peer-assessment process handle that for you?
In many team environments, the only well-informed judges about each other's performance are other team members. Usually no one else sees the individuals' performance. Others see the performance of the team as a whole in the end product, but they don't see the contributions of individuals that led to that end product. So you almost have to go to some form of peer-rating system.

Peer rating also usually handles the problems of poor performers on the team. The argument goes that if you have a system that individualizes the reward, you're happy to have the team slowpokes just tag along because they'll get their just desserts in the end—nothing. The more valuable contributors will get theirs. That's what typically happens when the members of the team do some sort of peer rating. You might have the project manager look the team over and say, this person did or didn't contribute, but ideally, the team divides the money.

In terms of compensation, is there a distinction between a permanent team and an ad-hoc or project team?
Very definitely. The easiest teams to deal with are permanent teams. You just build team compensation into the normal job description or role description. You can study the skills that are needed and put a compensation plan in place.

Regardless of the type of team, do you pay for results or activities? Do you pay teams that take risks and fail for their efforts?
There are really three ways you can reward teams. You can reward individuals for what they contribute to the team. That's probably the most common thing that goes on in the United States right now. Next is to reward the team as a whole for a performance.

continues on next page

---

expect you to do, and your value.' There may be big differences between team members, but we seem able to better tolerate those inequities than I find with some of my buddies in other companies."

If you're in a team-oriented company, you can handle rewards in still another way—a broader gain-sharing that puts dollars into everyone's pocket and gives appropriate recognition to the individual. James A. Tompkins, president of Tompkins Associates Inc., a Raleigh, N.C., consultancy, explains: "If I say 'I'm giving each one of these people a thousand bucks,'

people complain, 'Mary? She never did a day's work in her life. I don't believe this stupid company. They think they're going to save money on this; watch this, I'll fix them.' But if we are all sharing in the company's gains, then when Mary stands up, I'll be sitting there thinking, 'The work Mary and that team did brings me an extra 45 cents a hour in my paycheck.' Am I going to clap? You're darn right I am. I'm going to be so motivated that, next month, I want to be recognized as the guy who gives them 30 cents more in their paycheck."

But the third—and I predict that more and more firms are going to end up saying it—is: "We can't do this." When people are on five or six teams, trying to track what each team member did or didn't do is almost impossible—unless you want to build an incredible database that tells you that Joe spent 25 percent of his time on this team, 15 percent on that, two of his teams folded during the year, three more started up. At the end of the year you say, 'How do we reward Joe?' It's an administrative nightmare.

A lot of organizations, like the Motorolas and the HPs that have that kind of team structure, will say, "We've got to pay people for the success of the business that they're in. We're going to give them stock and individual pay based on measures of their competencies, capabilities, and skills."

Earlier you used the phrase "line of sight" when talking about team compensation. How does that tie in with managing a team's performance?
Teams perform best when the head of the team has reward power over members for the time they work together. If the primary reward power rests back at the home base, people don't make the effort and commitment to the team that they need to make. They're always looking back at their functional boss and saying, "Gosh, if I give in on this point, what will my boss in marketing say?" So that's a very relevant issue, and it needs to be clear to the team members that the project manager has that reward power from the beginning of the team activity.

What about nonmonetary rewards? Things like dinners, trophies, tickets to concerts or ballgames? Do you think those things motivate team members as well as—or better than—cold, hard cash?
I've found that, by and large, people who manage rewards for teams are much more favorable toward nonfinancial rewards than are team members. It turns out they cost less than financial rewards. But you've got to be careful when somebody tells you what somebody else wants.

That said, human beings differ a lot in what they value. Some people would rather have a dinner honoring their team, be congratulated by the CEO, who says, "This is the greatest team we've ever had." There are people who would rather have that event than a $5,000 bonus. No question about it. How many there are is an interesting question.

Particularly, the whole history of the quality-circle movement was built on nonfinancial recognition. My experience with a lot of those programs was that they got along pretty well with nonfinancial rewards for a while. People got a kick out of the T-shirts, hats, and newsletters with their pictures in them, and saving the company $100,000. Then they got to the point of saying, "I've saved the company $2 million, I think it's time I participated in the financial savings."

Which brings us back to motivating the individual team member—answering the question, "What's in it for me?"
One issue you've got to look at in this whole area is national culture. In the United States we have an individualistic national culture. If you ask people on teams what they think is fair—being rewarded as a team, or being rewarded as individuals—they typically say, "Both. Why should I give up one?" Other places in the world, particularly in Asia, people are much more comfortable saying, "We're all in this together, we ought to all sink or swim together."

Team-based organizations work best if you get a collective sense of responsibility. You want your people saying, "I'm responsible for what I do, but I'm also responsible for what you do. And I need to encourage you; I need to criticize you if you're not doing anything." That seems to be hard to do in the United States.

So the question sometimes of paying teams is, do you go with the national culture? Or do you go with what would be indicated by the structural nature of the team that you're trying to create? That's the challenge for Corporate America in the coming years.

Doing It Right

Money isn't everything, even when you're rewarding teams, and managers and consultants agree that the various other ways of saying "thank you" constitute the best incentive over the long run. You can select from the many forms of nonmonetary recognition—plaques, trophies, small gifts, vacation trips, and dinners with company officers. But, above all, give with sincerity. That is why, perhaps, some managers find it easier to pay someone in money. They can't muster up a genuine sense of closeness to the recipient in expressing appreciation for performance.

When they do try to give recognition, they may fall into the same traps again and again. If they give an outing to a ballgame as an award, for example, they may be overlooking the fact that not everyone likes ballgames. And they may fail to ensure that someone from management acts as a personal host—another important ingredient. A little investigation into an individual's tastes and backgrounds will help you select the most meaningful forms of recognition.

The where and when of granting recognition is all-important, too. "If you give the right recognition but do it two months late, you shoot yourself in the foot," Tompkins explains. "We have to give people recognition in a way that they feel is timely and to make sure we don't do it only in public—the guy is going to view us as grandstanding. We first have to give the recognition in private, *then* in public."

Recalling his experiences as Pet Inc. VP of manufacturing, Bernie Nagle, now a principal consultant with Price Waterhouse, says: "What worked best was recognition and celebration. Recognize the team. Let the team members speak to management or the whole plant and tell how they organized, how they implemented their idea, what results they had.

"Over the long haul, recognition is the best form of compensation. It pays dividends over time. But we take for granted what people do. We have to realize that people value each other and their relationships. People want to know they're valued by the company. We've got to celebrate a team's success. Create an event. Shut down the plant. But be sure you're sincere."

McNutt adds, "I think we're just beginning in business to really understand the hidden power of recognition. To have the boss or somebody in leadership, on a Friday afternoon, tell Mary, 'You did one heck of a job this week on that task' tends to make Mary's weekend." Recognition of team members

and other individuals "has been very under-utilized in American industry, but it's changing and it's changing quickly."

The Money Pit

Sometimes after-the-fact recognition may involve money—not enough to change a person's living standards but, rather, a gift of appreciation. Both DuPont and TRW employ spot monetary awards for significant achievements, but team members are not the only ones eligible for them. On a team or not, people are recognized for their individual performance.

But hundreds of managers can tell you from experience that expressing recognition in monetary terms invites complaints. Goodall cites the case of an international team made up of a half-dozen people representing different businesses from different regions. When they successfully completed their project, the organization decided it would give each individual a $1,000 after-tax bonus. Three of the six members felt the money was unnecessary. "We've already had the satisfaction of being on the team, having the recognition of being able to report back to the senior staff." They said another key reward had been the opportunity to travel to different regions of the world as they were doing their work.

These people were further disturbed by the fact that, irrespective of the level they were in the organization, each received the same dollar amount. "We want to be rewarded for the effort we put in as individuals," they said. Motorola has learned that treating members as a block of interchangeable parts is not good. "We've got to focus on the individual and how the individual is performing within that team," says Goodall. "People don't want to be rewarded for team results; they know some pull more weight than others."

Management needs to be careful about anything that may be viewed as "buying," warns Tompkins. "If I'm stuck on the side of the road and you stop and help me change a flat tire, and I give you $10, you are insulted. But if I send your wife a bouquet of flowers, you are complimented."

On the other hand, some people assume that anything done in the workplace is a tradeoff for money. Nagle reminds us of an often-heard complaint from persons who receive an award: "We saved the company millions and they gave me only a thousand." When you encounter this kind of thinking, be especially careful to divorce good performance from dollars and find other ways to say "thank you."

Management often overlooks the powerful intrinsic rewards that come from team participation and being part of the corporate decision-making process. Recognize that team participation takes people to new heights—a step up psychologist Abraham Maslow's hierarchy of needs toward fulfillment in nonmonetary terms. As much as people may want or need money, receipt of dollars after doing a good job can sometimes strike a sour note. Industrial psychologist Frederick Herzberg pointed out nearly four decades ago that people make comparisons about who got what, and dollars can become dissatisfiers.

"What would motivate you if you were part of a team?" Motorola asked individuals at all levels as it went around the world, interviewing teams. They all came up with the same answer, says Goodall. "The reward we get is the fact that we're on the team, and, if the team is successful, that gives us a sense of recognition and satisfaction."

Who Gets What?

A good way to avoid alienating recipients who feel team participation was uneven is to let the team decide who gets what from the awards basket. DuPont's McNutt says, "You can involve the team, after the task is completed, in recognizing the most significant contributor. We've done that. We may not set the dollar amounts, but we want the team to think in terms of the varying levels of contributors."

Consultant McAdams also believes teams should be given a role in distributing recognition awards. He tells of a company that had a serious problem with a product that had to conform to certain standards to be sold in Europe. "The documentation was a nightmare to translate. They pulled people together to work an intensive schedule for six months. They said, up front, 'If we meet this deadline, you will receive X amount of money.' That's a project-team incentive. They made equal distribution to everybody. The problem they had was, although there were 10 people in the core team, they drew on another 50 or 60 for part-time help. They should have given the team the right to recognize the people who helped them." That, however, could have raised endless questions. For example: Since the team was getting money, should the recognition passed on to others be monetary? If so, where would the money come from? In the case McAdams cites, only the core team received any money, so those questions did not have to be answered. But the unofficial team players were given the ultimate brush-off for their extra work: nothing.

True commitment to the team process starts with allowing the team to determine how it will accomplish its objectives and to suggest, if not to determine, how recognition will be distributed to members and other contributors. Which only stands to reason: After all, if you really support the team process, you give teams autonomy. That may put you in the position of not knowing for sure who did what. Even more difficult, it may leave you doing something many managers hate: keeping your hands off.

Source: Pascarella, P. "Compensating Teams," *Across the Board*, February 1997, pp. 16–22. Reprinted with permission.

Executive Compensation: Examining an Old Issue from New Perspectives

Parbudyal Singh and Naresh C. Agarwal, *Compensation and Benefits Review*

Executive compensation has attracted renewed attention as corporations such as ENRON and Worldcom tumbled, attributable in part to questionable practices, including excessive executive pay. In other instances, and even for well-respected companies such as Disney, Microsoft and General Electric, many think that executive pay is too high. (See Exhibit 1 for a sample of the top-paid CEOs in the United States in 2001.) Even Alan Greenspan recently lambasted corporate greed and CEO pay as excessive.

Many of us in the academic world are trying to make sense of executive compensation. Some researchers have investigated the traditional determinants of executive compensation (for example, firm size and performance), now documented in a voluminous body of literature.[1] However, as one leading author concluded, "it is amazing how little we know about executive pay in spite of the massive volume of empirical work available on this topic."[2] As such, there is still need for additional insights and new perspectives from which the determinants of executive compensation should be analyzed.

This article briefly reviews the main aspects of previous research and discusses one relatively new perspective—the role of firm strategy—an area that has not received much attention but holds reasonable promise in helping to explain the levels and structure of CEO pay. Furthermore, the vast majority of previous research on executive compensation focuses on the situation in the United States. Thus, we use data drawn from Canadian firms, many with U.S. operations, and discuss the implications of the results for a wider audience.

EXHIBIT 1: SAMPLE OF TOP CEO PAY, 2001
(IN U.S. DOLLARS)

Name of CEO, Company	Total Compensation, Including Option Values
Lawrence Ellison, Oracle	$706 million
John Chambers, CISCO Systems	$226 million
Edward Whitcare, SBC Communications	$141 million
Geoffrey Bible, Phillip Morris	$132 million
Louis Gerstner, Jr., IBM	$127 million
Richard Fuld, Lehman Bros Holdings	$127 million
William Esrey, Sprint	$114 million
L. Dennis Koslowski, Tyco International	$113 million
Douglas Daft, Coca-Cola	$101 million
Richard Bron, Electronic Data Systems	$81 million

Source: *USA Today*, March 25, 2002.

Size and Performance

One of the consistent findings in the literature is that size matters. CEOs in larger firms generally earn more money for their services. Two possible explanations have been provided for this finding: size maximization and human capital theories. The *size maximization hypothesis* posits that executives deliberately increase the size of their firms because larger firms are deemed to be more prestigious and more financially rewarding. Researchers using *human capital theory* argue that increasing firm size requires higher levels of human capital, such as education and experience, for organizational success. Increasing organizational size is associated with greater responsibility and tasks requiring better management skills and education. Size may also be a proxy for job complexity and levels of management.

Firm performance may also matter. Many argue that CEO pay should reflect the bottom-line performance of the firm, with executives in more successful firms earning more for their services. However, the evidence on the firm performance/executive compensation relationship is mixed, at best. Although some studies have reported a positive relationship between the two variables, others have found that the relationship is not significant, and yet others have reported a negative relationship.[3] The mixed empirical evidence on the relationship between executive compensation and firm performance, especially the negative results, has fuelled considerable criticism from various stakeholders (employees, shareholders, the general public, the press).

Such pressures, in part, have led to calls for more vigilance by the Securities and Employment Commission in the United States and the enactment of similar legislation in other jurisdictions (such as the amendments to the Ontario Securities Act, 1993) requiring public companies to disclose relevant information on executive compensation. As the recent spate of corporate problems reveals, there are questions as to whether these regulations are working or if there is a need for tougher sanctions for unethical and fraudulent behavior. We will return to this issue later.

Role of Firm Strategy

Recently, a number of researchers, some influenced by their work in organizations, have begun to search for new explanations for seemingly illogical executive pay. One such new perspective is the role of firm strategy, which may be explained from a *contingency theory* perspective. In essence, the argument is that an organization's functional strategies, such as compensation, are driven by the overall strategy. That is, compensation and other strategies must support the overall strategic direction of the firm for optimal results to be achieved. For example, a firm adopting an entrepreneurial and high-risk strategy in the semiconductor industry will want to use an aggressive pay strategy, including options, to attract, retain and motivate its workforce. From a contingency theory perspective, it is implied that executive compensation strategies are more likely to be effective if they are contingent on the overall strategy followed by the organization, other things being equal. That is, executive compensation is dependent on organizational strategy.

A number of empirical studies have examined how organizational strategy acts as a determinant of executive compensation. In these studies, various proxies were used to represent firm strategy: the extent and types of diversification activities,

organizational and product life cycles and industry type. Recently, a few researchers have used a more systematic approach in classifying firms into strategic groups. This involves using a system developed by Raymond Miles and Charles Snow, whereby statistical and self-classification techniques are used to determine the categories.[4] We adopted this system in our study, which is described below.

FRAMEWORK USED

Our study[5] uses the Miles and Snow framework in classifying firms into strategic archetypes. One of the major premises of the Miles and Snow typology is that there are identifiable strategic orientations within an industry. Using this framework, a firm can be classified as a prospector, a defender, an analyzer or a reactor. These strategic orientations reflect a firm's adaptation to the challenges/problems in the organization's entrepreneurial, engineering and administrative domains.

The key dimension underlying the categories is the rate at which an organization changes its products, markets or geographic areas of operation. Prospectors usually pioneer product and market/geographic development and tend to explore opportunities the most intensive. They compete primarily by stimulating and meeting new opportunities. Defenders are at the other end of the spectrum. They engage in little or no new product or market/geographic development and often control relatively secure niches within their industries. Such organizations compete primarily on the basis of price, quality or service. Analyzers are an intermediate type. They make fewer and slower market or product changes than do prospectors and are less committed to stability and efficiency than are defenders. Finally, reactors do not seem to follow a conscious strategy and are viewed as a dysfunctional organizational type.

In this study, we predicted that CEOs in prospector firms would be paid the highest, especially in stock options, given the risks and innovativeness required to work successfully in their domains. Similarly, we expected CEOs in defender firms to earn high fixed salaries but relatively smaller proportion of incentives and stocks.

METHOD

We obtained data from 102 Canadian metal-mining firms, many with holdings and business units in the United States. Metal-mining firms were selected because we wanted to control for industry. Furthermore, using a single industry takes cognizance of the fact that similar firm strategies may be classified differently across industries; for example, a prospector firm in the auto parts industry may be considered a defender firm in the high-tech industry. Relevant data for these firms were drawn from several reliable sources, including the Ontario Securities Commission, and cluster analyses were used to classify the firms into Miles and Snow's strategic archetypes. This classification was tested for reliability with a follow-up questionnaire to the CEOs in the study asking them to self-classify their firms. The CEOs were given short descriptions of the strategic types and asked to fit their organizations accordingly. Data on other variables were collected from various sources, including company documents. Five-year data were collected for firm performance and size.

We focused on three main aspects of executive compensation: fixed, short-term incentives and long-term incentives. Total compensation would, of course, be a combination of these components. Using various statistical techniques, we then assessed the relationship between CEO pay and firm strategy, as well as other variables such as firm size, performance, CEO tenure and education. Regression analyses were used to assess the unique effects of firm strategy on executive compensation.

THE RESULTS

Exhibit 2 shows the descriptive statistics of the relevant variables in the full sample and subsamples for prospector and defender firms. There were 68 prospector-type firms and 30 defender-type firms; 4 firms could not be classified. Many of the compensation variables vary considerably across strategic archetypes. Although CEOs in defender firms earned more than their counterparts in prospector firms, including all the components of the total compensation package, it is important to note that the proportion of long-term incentives/stock-based pay to total compensation is higher in prospector firms (approximately 47%) when compared to defender firms (24%). Prospector firms are also smaller, having lower earnings per share (EPS) on average (an accounting performance measure) but higher returns on stock investments to shareholders (a market-based performance measure). CEOs in prospector firms have also been in their current positions longer than their counterparts in defender firms (although not at a statistically significant level).

Despite our expectations, CEOs in prospector firms did not earn more in total compensation, including all its components. In fact, their counterparts in defender firms earned significantly more than they did, except for long-term incentives; however, the difference in this latter compensation component is not statistically significant.

EXHIBIT 2: DESCRIPTIVE STATISTICS

Variable	Total Sample		Prospectors (P)		Defenders (D)		Statistical Differences between P and D
	Mean	Standard Deviation	Mean	Standard Deviation	Mean	Standard Deviation	F Ratio
Fixed compensation	138.97	127.35	100.23	69.90	243.45	167.90	33.26**
Short-term incentives	36.37	134.10	9.70	37.68	101.51	230.33	9.57*
Long-term incentives	98.62	290.76	98.99	258.32	111.19	373.65	0.03
Total compensation	274.00	400.60	208.92	282.50	456.16	567.20	7.73*
Size (log assets)	9.84	1.86	9.40	1.24	10.96	2.56	16.52**
EPS	0.06	0.61	0.01	0.52	0.17	0.78	1.37
Market return	1.32	3.49	1.58	3.73	0.88	3.13	0.73
Tenure	6.43	3.81	7.09	2.91	5.83	4.53	0.61

Note: All monetary figures are in thousands of Canadian dollars (except log assets); U.S. dollars, when reported in the data, were converted using the appropriate rates for the various years.
$*p < .01.$ $**p < .001.$

The correlation and regression results confirm that firm strategy adds incrementally to the other predictors of executive compensation used in this study. For short-term compensation, EPS is positively correlated with fixed annual compensation (.23) and short-term incentives (.45) at significant levels. However, for long-term incentives, EPS loses its significance; instead, market return is positively correlated at a statistically significant level (.33). It is important to note that the market for metals, especially gold, experienced some decline in the study period; otherwise, this relationship might have been even stronger. In the regression analysis, EPS is a significant predictor of short-term incentives (.25, $p < .01$) and adds incrementally to adjusted R^2. For long-term incentives/exercised options, market return is significant (.36, $p < .01$).

For the control variables, firm size is positively related to all the components of executive compensation in the correlations and is a significant predictor in the regression analyses. On the other hand, a CEO's tenure in his or her current position showed no significant relationships with any of the compensation variables.

As can be recalled, we predicted that firm strategy would be a significant predictor of CEO compensation, controlling for other important variables. That is, it would add explanatory power to the predictor variables of firm size and firm performance. Our results reveal that although the direction of the effect is not in line with the proposition (more compensation for prospector firms), the size is significant for fixed compensation. That is, CEOs in defender firms earn significantly more in short-term compensation than their counterparts in prospector firms when all relevant variables are in the equation.

This effect does not apply for long-term incentives, which in turn affect total compensation, because the direction changes for these structural aspects of compensation. That is, for long-term incentives, the direction of the relationship is in line with that proposed in the hypothesis. In other words, CEOs in prospector firms earn more than their counterparts in stock-based compensation; however, the effect is not statistically significant.

DISCUSSION OF RESULTS

As outlined above, with the exception of long-term incentives, CEOs in prospector firms received significantly lower compensation, controlling for firm size

and other variables. Why is it that despite the inherent risks and innovative behaviors CEOs in prospector firms employ, their pay was less than their counterparts in defender firms? These findings can be explained using theory and research on firm life cycles and an examination of the structure of compensation packages across the strategic types.

Firm life cycle theory and research suggests that firms at the entrepreneurial and growth stages of their cycles tend to be relatively small and prospector-like, with research and exploration emphasized. Such firms usually have limited financial resources, and their ability to pay is consequently limited. Thus, they tend to emphasize performance-based and variable long-term incentive rewards, such as stock-based compensation. A post hoc analysis of the data revealed that prospector firms in the sample are significantly younger (measured as years since establishment) than defender firms are (18 years vs. 27 years, respectively; F ratio = 3.17; p value = .07).

The findings in this study suggest that prospector firms are emphasizing long-term incentives (stock-based pay) over salaries. This has allowed them to invest proportionately more in research, exploration and development, as well as marketing and advertising. Defender firms are more mature and stable, and risk is consequently reduced. Thus, as firms become more defender-like, they are more likely to emphasize fixed pay (salary and benefits) and provide proportionately less in variable long-term incentives. In fact, as Exhibit 2 shows, the stock-based component of the compensation package accounted for 47% of the total compensation package of CEOs in prospector firms, compared to 23% for defenders. Furthermore, among the 98 firms analyzed in this study, 10 reported no annual cash compensation for their CEOs; that is, chief executives in these firms had their compensation based totally on the firm's market performance (stock-based pay), thus putting their entire compensation package at risk. Of these firms, 90% (9 out of the 10) were prospector firms.

The bottom line of the foregoing discussion is that compensation for CEOs in prospector firms may be lower than that of their counterparts in defender firms because prospector firms are in the entrepreneurial stage of their life cycles and are thus placing emphasis on stock-based pay, some of which (namely, future options) could not have been calculated in this study.

With respect to the relationship between firm performance and executive compensation, the results suggest that although EPS (the accounting measure) is a significant predictor of short-term compensation, it loses its significance for long-term/stock-based compensation. In fact, the results show that share price growth and return on stocks are better predictors of such compensation. That is, accounting measures are better predictors of short-term compensation, and market measures better predict variable long-term incentives/stock options.

Thus, this research supports the view that although performance measures may not be demonstrating a significant impact on executive compensation in the literature, it is evident that an analysis of the impact of different performance measures does yield insights on the design of total compensation packages. Furthermore, in this study, unlike others, we used multiyear averages of past financial performance to assess the relationship between CEO pay and firm performance. It is interesting to note that although the three-year average performance variables displayed significant effects, similar one-year variables did not; this suggests that executive compensation may be based more on cumulative performance rather than just performance in the preceding year. This issue is not generally addressed in the popular press.

IMPACT OF FIRM SIZE AND PERFORMANCE ON EXECUTIVE COMPENSATION

As in U.S.-based research, firm size—and to a lesser extent, firm performance—affects executive compensation the most in this study. There are a few reasons why CEO compensation in Canada may be reflecting these dynamics evident in the United States. First, recent disclosure rules may be having a pull effect as Canadian CEOs compare their relatively low compensation with their U.S counterparts, some of whom work in U.S.-based subsidiaries of Canadian firms. That is, CEO compensation in Canada may be playing catch-up with, and be reflective of, CEO pay in the United States. Second, with the dismantling of trade barriers, Canadian CEOs are increasingly taking up worldwide positions, where they are probably making constant compensation comparisons with their counterparts.

One key limitation of this study is that because of a lack of relevant data required for calculating the value of future options, using, for example, the Black-Scholes option pricing formula, options were calculated as those exercised and not the value of future options. Although there is controversy on the method of calculations and the impact of future options, it would have been useful to incorporate it into the analysis because it appears as if prospector firms place a great deal of emphasis on this factor. In this study, the total compensation of prospector CEOs may have been underestimated because of a lack of incorporation of such stock grants; thus, both in-the-pocket (situation where the executives hold vested options whose prices are less than the market price; thus, options can be profitably exercised) and future compensation were ignored. Future studies should address this issue because data reliability emanating from firms, with guidance by the Securities Commissions, can only get better.

It should also be noted that we focused on just a few key variables in this study; there may be other forces and processes at work. For instance, other researchers focus on the role of CEO power and the issue of "interlocking" membership in boards of directors. An argument can be made that CEOs "pay themselves" through their direct and indirect control of compensation decisions. However, the research evidence is mixed on this issue.

Lessons for Management

A number of practical implications flow from the present study. First, the study shows a significant relationship between organizational strategy and executive compensation. This relationship stands to reason. Because executives play a key role in successful implementation of organizational strategy, it is critical that their compensation packages be designed in a way so as to motivate them toward that goal. This would require each organization to very carefully review its strategy and the resulting requirements and develop an executive compensation approach that is consistent with those requirements. No single compensation approach can suffice across organizations as their business strategies may vary from each other depending on their respective internal and external contexts.

Second, the present study confirms that firm size continues to be a major determinant of executive compensation, as CEOs of large firms make more money than those of small firms. Executive jobs in large firms, relative to those in small firms, are more complex, carry more responsibility and require higher levels of human capital, and therefore they should be paid more. But these job content and job requirement factors may not explain the entire story.

Many experts and practitioners in the field have begun pointing fingers at the process by which executive compensation is determined in large firms.

In these firms, the board of directors normally appoints a compensation committee, which in turn hires a consulting firm to do a market survey of comparators and uses the resulting data as a basis for making its decision. The CEOs can exercise a great influence over this process because board members and consultants get appointed usually on their recommendations. Shareholders in public companies, especially institutional investors (e.g., pension funds), are increasingly getting concerned about the executive compensation setting process and are demanding active participation in it. Public companies should attempt to make this process more objective and transparent and should consider having executive compensation discussed and voted on at their annual meetings to give shareholders a feeling of having a say in this matter.

Finally, the present study has implications with respect to the relationship between firm performance and executive compensation. The results of the study show that EPS is a significant predictor of short-term executive compensation earned as annual bonuses, and share price growth and return on stocks, market measures of firm performance, are better predictors of long-term executive compensation earned through the exercise of stock options. Although it is heartening to see a relationship between firm performance and executive compensation, major concerns have arisen in recent times with respect to stock options as a component of executive compensation.

Stock options were used in the past decade as a primary means to tie executive compensation to business results. The primary goal of corporations is to maximize the wealth of its shareholders, that is, stock price maximization. It makes logical sense, then, to link executive compensation to stock price appreciation. However, recent examples of Enron, WorldCom and several other corporations show that stock options as presently structured have become a flawed incentive for at least three reasons. First, they tend to encourage executives to take actions that boost short-term performance but may be disastrous for firms in the long run. Second, they may lead unscrupulous executives to engage in unethical behavior such as manipulating financial statements of their firms to make the short-term performance of the firm look artificially good. This practice recently led the SEC to require CEOs of the 1,000 largest American corporations to provide sworn statements vouching for the accuracy of financial statements. Third, stock price appreciation is an imperfect measure of management performance of executives as stock prices can be affected by a whole host of factors that are beyond the control of executives. Thus, stock options can work like a lottery, which produces windfall gains for executives during bullish market conditions and unnecessarily penalizes them in bearish market conditions.

In response to these emerging issues with the use of stock options in executive compensation, experts in the field have begun recommending a number of corrective measures. These include expensing the stock options in company financial statements, requiring executives to hold the majority of their shares until they have held their job for a predefined time period or until they leave the firm, not allowing options to be fully vested and exercised until they have been held for a certain minimum period of time, making greater use of restricted stock options and measuring firm performance relative to other firms in the industry to drive stock-based rewards. Some companies have already taken initiatives in this regard. Others need to follow their example.

Endnotes

1. See Gomez-Mejia, L. (1994). Executive compensation: A reassessment and future agenda. *Research in Personnel and Human Resource Management, 12*, 161–222; Gomez-Mejia, L., & Wiseman, R. (1997). Reframing executive compensation: An assessment and outlook. *Journal of Management, 23*, 291–374.

2. Gomez-Mejia (1994, p. 201).

3. For comprehensive reviews of the literature, see Gomez-Mejia (1994); Gomez-Mejia & Wiseman (1997).

4. Miles, R., and Snow, C. (1978). *Organizational strategy, structure, and process.* New York: McGraw-Hill.

5. A version of the results of this study was published by the Canadian Journal of Administrative Sciences (Vol. 19, 2002).

Pay Strategy: New Thinking for the New Millennium

Edward E. Lawler III, *Compensation and Benefits Review*

It is time for new thinking, new practices and more strategic direction in the pay systems of organizations. The simple fact is that organizations, the business environment and individuals are changing at a rate that is must faster than the rate of change with respect to the way organizations design and manage pay systems. There are a number of reasons for this. Pay practices are clearly hard to change. Pay system change is complex, in part because many individuals and organizations are comfortable with their existing pay practices and find it difficult to leave them behind. But this is not a sufficient reason to accept a slow rate of change and misaligned pay systems. It is simply too important to have a pay system that supports an organization's business strategy and contributes to organizational effectiveness.

All too often a misaligned pay strategy not only fails to add value, it produces high costs in the compensation area as well as inappropriate and misdirected behavior. Thus, organizations that fail to adapt their pay systems to today's business challenges operate with a significant handicap and at a tremendous disadvantage.

It is beyond the scope of this article to go into detail with respect to the major societal and business changes that have implications for pay system change. But it is worth highlighting some of the key ones in order to underline the amount of change that has occurred.

More and more products and services are competing globally and this has lead to much greater competition. Organizations increasingly need to operate globally—moving products and people across national boundaries in seamless ways. In order to be successful, organizations increasingly have to get their products to market more quickly and improve their customer service. The Internet is creating new sales channels and changing the way information is distributed and managed within organizations.

In order to be competitive, organizations increasingly have to operate with lateral processes that are supported by advanced information technology systems. Increasingly, work in a number of areas requires advanced knowledge and skills.

Organizations can no longer afford extensive hierarchies with command and control management structures. More and more individuals do not have stable work activities that can be described as jobs. Instead, they have roles and general areas of responsibility that they flexibly perform. Individuals no longer have a traditional loyalty contract with organizations. Instead, they have a temporary relationship in which they try to maximize their rewards while adding to their skills and capabilities. Because individuals don't see companies being loyal to them, they are not loyal to their employers and are increasingly willing to change jobs when better opportunities present themselves.

Key technical and management skills frequently have more demand than supply and as a result, certain individuals become "hot talent" and enjoy considerable leverage in negotiating for their working conditions. The work forces of many organizations are becoming more diverse and as a result, there are large, individual differences in what their employees want from work and how they want to be treated by reward systems. Individuals increasingly work in teams and are collectively responsible for producing products and services.

There is no reason to believe that business will return to the way work was done when most of the current pay practices used by organizations were developed and fine-tuned. If anything, with the increased development of e-business and the Internet, the rate of change is likely to accelerate. The explosive growth of the Internet, for example, is likely to lead to greater globalization. Employee mobility and work force diversity will continue to increase. We are likely to see more cases of "hot talent," and the growth of businesses in which knowledge development is the key to organizational success.

The challenge, and it is a significant one, is to develop pay systems that the way organizations, individuals and society are changing and to change pay systems at the speed of business. No single pay system or set of pay practices is likely to provide the answer to how organizations should alter their pay systems. I do believe, however, that there are three major strategic positions that organizations should take with respect to pay systems that will allow them to develop pay practices that will be effective in the future. These three strategic approaches are described below.

Pay the Person

Historically, the pay systems of most large organizations have been based on jobs and job evaluation technology. This approach made sense in a world in which individuals had stable duties and the market value of individuals was largely determined by the way in which their jobs were designed and managed. In a world in which individuals do not have traditional jobs and are often able to add considerable value because of their high levels of knowledge and skill, it is very dangerous and misleading to pay them according to job worth rather than their individual worth. It ignores the difference-making value that is added by people with high levels of knowledge and performance. It also fails to encourage individuals to develop the right skills and knowledge.

Increasingly, human capital is the key capital for an organization. Human capital must earn a fair return or like any other capital it will search for a higher rate of return and it will frequently find it. Thus, organizations must be sure that their people are paid according to their market value. Pricing the job that they are doing at the moment is simply not a good enough way to value individuals. They must be valued for the knowledge, skills and competencies that they have. This evaluation must take into account not just the internal labor market within their organization, but the external labor market as well. Indeed, it must primarily take into account the external labor market. Placing too much focus on the internal labor market runs the great risk of either underpaying highly valued individuals or overpaying individuals who do not have the knowledge and skills that the most valuable employees have.

Developing an approach that pays individuals according to their market value requires a pay system which measures the knowledge, skills and competencies of individuals and prices them in the external market. At this time, the technology to do this is admittedly still under development and in a rudimentary form, but organizations still can begin to pay individuals according to their market value. They often can get a good idea of the market value of their key individuals simply by monitoring the actual hiring transactions that go on in the labor market. This, of course, is a far different approach from the traditional one of looking at salary survey data in order to gain information about what individuals doing particular jobs are paid.

Perhaps the greatest challenge in paying individuals for their skills, knowledge and competencies is developing good measures of them. Too often organizations that have tried to measure them have chosen to measure the degree to which individuals possess very generic competencies, such as leadership ability and communication ability. They have not written specific knowledge and skill descriptions for the roles that individuals need to perform and then developed measures of whether individuals have these specific skills and knowledge. As a result, they have not developed systems that are particularly good at rewarding individuals for developing the kinds of technical and business knowledge that individuals need in order to perform effectively.

I believe that in the future we will increasingly see organizations develop detailed, intranet-based descriptions of the kind of knowledge and skills individuals need to be effective in their roles. They will also have skill and knowledge profiles of their employees available on the intranet. These person descriptions will be supported by measures of skill and knowledge mastery and used as a basis for the market pricing of individuals, the assignment of work and the development of individuals.

By tying increases in pay to the development of the skills and knowledge that is called for in person descriptions, organizations will be able to accomplish two very important objectives. First, they will have a positive effect in motivating individuals to learn the skills and knowledge they need to perform in their current role, and second, they will raise the pay of individuals as they become more valuable in the external labor market. These two outcomes are clearly key to developing pay systems that create learning organizations and organizations that develop and retain valuable human capital.

Rewarding Excellence

There are a number of reasons why an intense focus on paying for performance is appropriate. It is an important way to attract and retain top performers and it is a potentially powerful motivator that can be a partial substitute for a traditional loyalty employment relationship.

The research literature on pay has for decades shown that although pay can be an effective motivator, often it is not. A few theorists have argued that, in fact, pay cannot be a motivator, but the research evidence does not support this view. Instead, it argues that pay motivates behavior when there is a clear relationship between a significant amount of pay and behavior, but it goes on to argue that often because of poor plan designs, pay winds up motivating dysfunctional behavior as well as functional behavior. It also has conclusively established that the traditional approach to pay for performance—merit pay—is generally a failure. It is a failure for numerous reasons, including the fact that it is often based on poor measures and it usually delivers such small changes in compensation that it has no motivational impact. Further, it fails to pay good performers highly enough to retain them in a hot job market.

Perhaps the most important thing that we have learned from the research on pay for performance is that there is no silver bullet. No single plan fits all organizations nor is pay for performance an accomplishable objective in all organizations. Nevertheless, pay for performance needs to be an important part of most organizations' reward systems. The type of pay for performance that is utilized needs to very much reflect the strategy, structure, business processes and management style of the organization.

The pay for performance approach of an organization needs to effectively translate its business strategy into measures that can be used for reward system purposes and it needs to fit the characteristics of the organization's structure with respect to coordination and integration. It is unlikely that any one pay for performance plan or approach will be able to accomplish all the objectives that the reward system needs to accomplish. Thus, an effective pay for performance system for an organization is likely to have multiple pay for performance plans.

Individual pay for performance systems accomplish different objectives than do team and organization-wide pay for performance systems. Bonus systems have different impacts than do stock-based plans. Thus, organizations need to carefully design a combination of pay for performance plans that covers all the objectives they need to accomplish with their plans.

The point has already been made that merit pay increases are poor motivators. Part of the problem with them is that they create an annuity payment which employees receive as long as they are employed regardless of their future performance. This ties up a considerable amount of an organization's payroll in an inflexible base pay commitment. One of the major effects of this is that few salary dollars are left to reward present performance. Thus, one key recommendation is that in the future, organizations should rely on variable pay plans in order to reward performance.

Every organization needs to carefully consider the use of stock. Stock ownership and stock options are powerful ways to reward performance. They can be given to individuals based on performance and, of course, their value changes as an organization's performance changes. They do suffer from one major weakness, however. The line of sight from an individual's behavior to the value of stock is often poor, thus for many members of an organization they may not have a powerful, motivational impact. Nonetheless, when organizations are trying to integrate everyone toward a common set of goals and a mission, broad-based stock plans can be quite useful because they give everyone a common fate. Stock option plans also can be a powerful way to retain individuals if they require individuals to remain with an organization in order to exercise them.

One of the most difficult decisions in pay system design concerns whether to reward individuals, groups, business units or the organization as a whole. Plans that reward individuals clearly accomplish different objectives than plans that reward the organization as a whole. The former are a much more powerful motivator of individual behavior. Plans that reward the organization as a whole are good at integrating individuals and encouraging them to understand the business and develop effective lateral relationships, but poor at directly motivating individuals. Team bonus plans can be extremely powerful in motivating team performance and cause individuals to work together to accomplish the team's goals and objectives. On the other hand, they do little to encourage teams to work together.

Given the different impacts of individual, team, and business-based pay for performance plans, they may all have a place in a single organization's approach to paying for performance. For example, individuals may be paid based on their individual performance, their team's performance, as well as on their businesses' performance. This makes good sense in situations where individual performance can be measured; individuals are part of a team whose performance is well measured and the organization is practicing employee involvement in a way that encourages individuals to understand the business and participate in decisions affecting the entire organization. Under this set of conditions, it makes sense for an organization to have three different types of pay for performance plans.

If individual performance is not measurable because highly interdependent teams are used and the major focus should be on team performance, a system that rewards team performance and organizational performance may be most appropriate. Finally, in situations where individual performance is all that counts and the organization does not practice employee involvement, an individual pay for performance system that is highly leveraged with variable pay may be all that is appropriate.

Given the trends in organization design toward lateral organizations, employee involvement roles, rather than jobs, and the lack of loyalty, it is possible to make some general statements about what pay for performance approaches are likely to become more popular. Clearly broad-based stock plans are likely to become much more popular. They fit the idea of employee involvement and they support the development of lateral thinking in organizations. They also do not require the kind of individual performance metrics that are difficult to collect in a role-based organization. Team-based pay for performance plans are also likely to become much more popular. The increasing use of teams and the difficulty in measuring individual performance makes this particularly likely. Team-based cash bonus plans have the potential to develop a good line of sight and can be a direct motivator of individual performance.

The use of profit sharing plans and plans which pay bonuses based on business unit and operating unit performance is also likely to increase significantly. Particularly in small business units and in operating units such as plants, they have the potential to create a reasonably strong line of sight, and research on gainsharing and goalsharing suggests that they therefore can be quite effective motivators. With education and employee involvement, a reasonable line of sight can often be developed so that individuals see how their performance impacts performance measures and therefore the bonus that they receive.

Particularly if the bonus offered is of a significant size it can be an effective motivator of performance.

The loser is individual pay for performance. Not just merit pay, which has already been dismissed, but variable individual pay. It simply does not fit as well in lateral team-based organizations as does team and organization-based pay for performance.

When the practice of paying individuals for their skills and knowledge is combined with a system which rewards performance, organizations can use pay systems as an effective substitute for loyalty. The pay system can encourage people to develop the skills the organization needs to have and it can motivate them to stay with the organization. It can also motivate them to perform well. Thus, it can do much more than the loyalty system, because seniority-based loyalty systems are primarily effective at encouraging individuals to stay with an organization. Because loyalty systems do not reward skill development or performance effectiveness, they do not motivate individuals to improve their skills or perform effectively. Thus they fail to do a good job at developing the human capital or an organization and retaining the most valuable employees.

Individualizing the Pay System

Traditionally the pay programs of organizations have adopted a one-size-fits-all approach to rewards. Individuals are given little choice with respect to how they are rewarded and what rewards they receive. The differences that exist within organizations are usually the result of the type of work individuals do rather than their needs and desires. This approach generally fits a homogeneous work force but does not fit a diverse work force. With a diverse work force it runs a tremendous risk of giving individuals rewards that they do not value while failing to reward them with things that they value highly. This can obviously have negative consequences for both the attraction and retention of individuals as well as for motivation.

The obvious alternative to a one-size-fits-all reward system is one that gives individuals a significant amount of choice. In the United States, some organizations have taken one step in this direction with the installation of cafeteria or flexible benefit plans, but in most cases it is a small step. Individuals are given little choice and as a result, these plans are not very effective. With a diverse work force it may make sense to give individuals a considerable amount of choice in the reward packages that they are offered. This can include individuals being given options with respect to working simply for cash, having extensive benefit packages, and even choosing the type of pay for performance system that they are covered by. The advantages of greater flexibility include tailoring rewards to employee preferences and thus, greater effectiveness in attracting and retaining a diverse work force. The potential negative of this approach is that it may create too diverse a work force for a company that wants to establish a strong unified culture.

Because the reward system is a powerful tool for attracting and retaining individuals, a one-size-fits-all reward system tends to lead to a homogenous internal population of employees. This can be a real negative if it leads to not enough individuals wanting to work for an organization and/or a homogenous culture that lacks adaptability and flexibility, as well as the ability to understand diverse markets. On the other hand, it can be a positive if the organization has a very specialized niche and the kind of performance capabilities that it needs are best developed by having an internally homogenous work force.

Organizations need to think through the consequences of having a diverse versus a homogenous work force and then pick the reward profile that fits the degree and type of diversity they desire. Given that many organizations are moving towards a more diverse work force and becoming more global, it is likely that organizations will increasingly choose to have flexibility and individualization in their reward system. This simply makes sense with respect to optimizing the impact of the dollars organizations spend, particularly organizations which are dealing with diverse markets and multiple national cultures.

Creating the Strategic Reward System

What should the pay systems of organizations look like in the future? Based on how organizations are changing and the impact of reward systems, I have suggested that three strategic thrusts are appropriate:

- Person-based pay should be used to reward individuals for their skills, knowledge and competencies relative to their external market value.
- Multiple pay for performance approaches should be used, with variable pay and stock as rewards.
- Reward systems should be individualized to fit the characteristics of individuals that an organization wishes to attract and retain. In most cases, this can best be done by allowing individuals a choice in the rewards that they receive.

Although these strategic thrusts are widely applicable, they clearly do not fit all situations and they are only the first step in developing an actual reward system for an organization. The next step is to develop actual pay practices that follow them and fit with the management style, structure, and strategy of the organization. This step involves developing a good understanding of the business strategy, the appropriate measures of organizational effectiveness, and of course, an understanding of the kinds of relationships and communication patterns that are needed in order for an organization's structure to be effective. In short, the three approaches are the basic building blocks upon which an effective pay system can be built for tomorrow's organizations.

Source: *Compensation and Benefits Review* by Lawler. Copyright © 2000 by Sage Publications. Reprinted with permission of Sage Publications Inc. (J) in the format Textbook via Copyright Clearance Center.

CHAPTER

12

LABOR RELATIONS

In July 1994, United Airlines, the world's largest airline, announced an employee stock ownership plan (ESOP) that would allow its unionized employees to acquire 55 percent of the company's stock in exchange for reductions in pay and benefits. The plan was immediately hailed as a breakthrough in labor relations in the airline industry and applauded among investors, customers, employees, and management. Among the union members, United pilots were the biggest beneficiaries of the plan, receiving 25 percent of company stock despite the fact that they constituted only 10 percent of the workforce. However, the pilots had made the greatest financial concessions.

The initial results of the ESOP were overwhelmingly successful. Teams were set up to analyze every aspect of company operations, from fuel utilization to free-pass policies for employee family members. The teams developed numerous cost-saving and morale-boosting measures that significantly impacted profitability. In the following three years, the price of United stock nearly quadrupled in response to its enhanced financial performance.

The positive results, however, were short-lived. Flight attendants, who were not included in the ESOP, became irritated at not being able to share in the company's success. As the employees with the greatest amount of public contact, their dissatisfaction and damaged morale affected customer service. In addition, the plan was only scheduled to operate for five years and nine months. Therefore, in 2000, employees stopped receiving United stock, and pay levels returned to pre-ESOP levels. Consequently, employees no longer had as significant a personal stake in the company's ongoing financial performance. New employees were also not able to participate in the plan. Perhaps the biggest problem with the plan for employees is that they are not allowed to cash in their stock until they retired from the airline.

United management, seeing the ESOP as an unqualified success, reports that it allowed the company to reduce its cost structure and strengthen its competitive position. However, since United stock hit its peak in 1997, its value has declined by close to 50 percent. Labor unrest with the pilots, who refused to fly overtime during contract negotiations, severely curtailed operations during the summer of 2000. United lost millions of dollars in revenue and the business of many loyal customers. Customer complaints about in-flight service have skyrocketed. What initially appeared to be a strategic win-win approach to labor relations on the part of United has evolved into a longer term problem with no remedy in sight.

Source: Pender, K. "Employee Ownership Doesn't Solve Labor Woes at United Airlines," *San Francisco Chronicle*, August 15, 2000, pp. C1, 5.

Labor relations is a key strategic issue for organizations because the nature of the relationship between the employer and employees can have a significant impact on morale, motivation, and productivity. Workers who feel that the terms and conditions of their employment are less than advantageous will not be as committed to perform and to remain with an employer. Consequently, how organizations manage the day-to-day aspects of the employment relationship can be a key variable affecting their ability to achieve strategic objectives.

Workers who have unionized create special challenges for human resource management. When workers form unions, the employment relationship becomes more formal through a union contract and is subject to special provisions of the National Labor Relations Act. This act allows unions to be formed and exist as employee organizations that have the legal right to bargain with management over various terms and conditions of employment. Unions provide membership solely for employees; managers are prohibited by law from joining employee unions or from forming their own unions.

Organized labor in the United States has had a cyclical history, generally consisting of short periods of sharp growth in union membership and activity followed by extended periods of decline.[1] In the early part of the 20th century, employee-centered management practices were eroding interest in unionization. The Great Depression then ignited strong interest in unions with the resultant creation by John Lewis of the Congress of Industrial Organizations (CIO). At that time, both the CIO and the American Federation of Labor (AFL) were able to unionize large segments of the workforce. These organizing efforts were largely focused on second-generation immigrants, particularly Catholics, Italians, and Jews, as unions attempted to provide these individuals with the full benefits of working in the WASP-dominated economy.

Unions continued to enjoy increased membership until World War II. Interest in unions declined postwar until the mid-1960s, when unions began to reach out to African-Americans during the drive for civil rights and subsequently enjoyed a renewed popularity. Also at that time Cesar Chavez founded the National Farm Workers Association, drawing attention to the plight of Latino and Filipino farm workers who had been forced to endure deplorable working conditions and substandard wages. Chavez's efforts led to a grape boycott that was observed by more than 17 million Americans and more generally, resulted in widespread awareness and distrust of exploitation of workers by employers. These successes also led to a flurry of union organization among public sector employees that continued until the early 1980s. When President Reagan successfully dismantled the air traffic controllers' union in 1981, a turning point was reached for the strengthening of the antiunion movement, both politically and organizationally.

Union membership in the United States has been steadily declining for a number of years. In 1970, approximately 30 percent of the private workforce was unionized, in addition to a majority of public sector employees. By 1999, the United States Department of Labor reported that only 13.9 percent of the workforce was unionized. Government employees were four times more likely to be union members than were private sector employees (37.3 percent versus 9.4 percent). These numbers represented declines in overall union membership as well as in both the public and private sector union density.[2]

The decline in union membership can be attributed to a number of factors. First, many workers have become disenfranchised from their unions. Allegations of union corruption and misuse of funds, combined with the fact that workers some-times feel that the costs of union membership outweigh the benefits, have eroded union membership. Second, many organizations have moved their manufacturing and assembly operations outside the United States. Unions have traditionally had their strongest bases of support among these blue-collar workers, and the move-ment of those jobs overseas has hurt unions. Third, changes in the nature of work and technology have eliminated many of the traditional manual labor jobs in which union members were employed. Finally, many unions have refused to be flexible enough to allow organizations to grow and adapt in relation to the changes taking place in their industries, markets, and the technological, economic, and sociocul-tural environments. The traditional model of American labor unions, which guard employee rights by attempting to maintain the status quo, no longer benefits employers or employees. Unions of the future will have to be based on a different model and have different relationships with the organizations whose workers they represent, if they continue to exist.

Although overall union membership is declining, it is important to understand organized labor relations for at least three reasons. First, in many industries, union-ization is the norm. Many public sector workplaces are unionized. In the private sector, industries such as transportation, construction, hospitality, publishing, edu-cation, and health care are usually highly unionized. In fact, the transportation industry has the highest level of private sector union membership, at 25.5 percent.[3] Managers and business owners in these industries have no choice but to be well-versed on the laws that regulate the relationship with union employees. Second, competitors may be unionized, and settlements in those organizations may impact HR practices, programs, and policies needed to remain competitive in recruiting and retaining productive employees. Arguably, the most important reason for employers to have a sense of the labor relations landscape is that the NLR Act pro-vides all employees, rather than just those who have unionized, with specific rights. Consequently, many employers who operate in nonunion environments may be unfamiliar with some of the terms and conditions of employment outlined in the act. Section 7 of the act grants all employees, including those who are not members of unions, the right to engage in activities that support their "mutual aid or protec-tion." There are six notable provisions under this section that employers must know to avoid violations of the act.[4]

First is the right of employees to discuss employment terms. In order for employ-ees to consider whether they wish to organize, they must be able to discuss the terms and conditions of employment, including compensation, harassment, and discrimi-nation. This right, however, does not extend to the disclosure of confidential infor-mation, such as salaries, to which an employee might have access as part of her or his job. Second, employees reserve the right to complain to third parties, such as cus-tomers, clients, and the media, about their treatment by the employer. Again, how-ever, the employer retains the right to prohibit disclosure of any confidential or proprietary information. Third, employees have the right to engage in a work stop-page or collective walkout to protest working conditions without fear of retaliation. Any employee who is disciplined or discharged for engaging in such behavior has a valid claim against the employer under the National Labor Relations Act. Fourth, employees have the right to honor picket lines without fear of retaliation. This is considered protected activity regardless of whether the employee is a member of the picketing union or merely sympathetic to the cause and plight of the workers on the picket line. Fifth, employees have the conditional right to solicit and distribute union literature. Such behavior can be restricted but not fully prohibited, as will be discussed below. Finally, employers cannot unilaterally ban employees access to the work site while off-duty. Restrictions may be imposed that limit access to the interior of the facility if applied consistently to all employees for all purposes, but employees still retain the right to be present on company property, such as the employee parking lot, after working hours to engage in behaviors protected under the act.

Just because an organization is not unionized today does not mean that it may not be in the future. Managers in such organizations need to know why workers form or join unions, how the law requires the employer to behave during any union-organizing campaign and after a union has been voted in, how the collective-bargaining process is conducted, and how impasses may be settled.

The word *union* means that workers have agreed to work together in dealing with and negotiating the terms and conditions of their employment with management. The Latin root *uni* means *one*; in the sense of a union, it means that a plurality of workers have united to speak with "one voice."

Organized labor presents a number of key strategic challenges for management. First, when workers unionize, the power based within the organization is redistributed. Employers can find that their ability to manage workers at their discretion to achieve the organization's strategic objectives has been severely curtailed. Second, the process of unionization involves bringing in outside players: union representatives, who then become an additional constituency whose support must be gained for any new or ongoing management initiatives. Finally, a unionized work setting can greatly impact the organization's cost structure, particularly payroll expenses and work processes that may contribute to or retard efficiency in operations.

WHY EMPLOYEES UNIONIZE

Employees usually form or join unions because of the perceived benefits that unionization might provide them. These benefits can be economic, social, and/or political. Economic benefits can result from a union's ability to negotiate higher wages, better or expanded benefits, greater job or employment security, and improved working hours and conditions. Social benefits can be derived from the affiliation and sense of community that workers share when they are unionized. Their personal issues and needs relating to their jobs and lifestyles can often be integrated within the union agenda, with corresponding support gained from coworkers. Unions often sponsor social events for their members and their families as well. Is it not surprising that many unions have the word *brotherhood* in their name; this attempts to signify the family or community atmosphere the union tries to create for its members.

Political benefits can be gained through the sense of power in numbers. In negotiating with management over terms and conditions of employment, individual employees are relatively powerless. They often need the organization (to earn a living) far more than the organization needs them (individual workers can be easily replaced). When workers unionize and speak with one voice, they leverage their individual power against management and equalize the balance of power within the organization. Management may be able to do without individual employees, but they cannot do without their entire workforce. Unions can allow workers far greater say and involvement in negotiating and setting critical terms and conditions of employment and in ensuring fair treatment from the organization. Unions can often provide additional political benefits in a literal sense in that the power and strength of their united membership can be used to support and influence political races and legislation passed at the local, state, and federal levels.

No benefits come without some cost, and union membership is no exception. Union members pay at least two significant costs for their benefits. First are the economic costs of the fees or dues that unions charge their members to support the initiatives the union undertakes on behalf of its employees. Second are the political costs employees assume when they relinquish their individual freedom to deal with their employer and be represented by the union. Individual employees may not agree with the terms and conditions negotiated for them or the tactics and strategies the union uses in negotiating. Although individual employees do vote on the decision to strike, an employee who does not wish or cannot afford to go out on strike is basically stuck in accepting the majority position and then assumes any risk associated in deviating from the union majority.

THE NATIONAL LABOR RELATIONS ACT

In 1935, Congress passed the National Labor Relations Act (NLRA), also called the *Wagner Act*, which gave employees the right to unionize and to regulate union/management relations. This act has been amended several times, most notably in 1947, with amendments known as the *Taft-Hartley Act*, and in 1959, with amendments knows as the *Landrum-Griffith Act*.

The NLRA created the National Labor Relations Board (NLRB) to oversee the provisions of the act. Among other duties, the NLRB is responsible for overseeing union elections, certifying a particular union as the official bargaining representative of a group of employees, and hearing allegations of violations of the act from employers, unions, and employee groups. ▼

As a first step in establishing a union, a group of employees petitions the NLRB, often through the assistance of a union representative, to conduct an election. As a prerequisite for an election, the NLRB requires at least 30 percent of the employees to have signed authorization cards, which indicate an expressed interest in having union representation from a specific union. Most petitions to the NLRB involve the presentation of authorization cards from a far greater number of employees than 30 percent. These authorization cards are not a vote for the union; they are merely the means for establishing the level of employee interest to conduct an election. Some employees who are not in favor of union representation often sign authorization cards under peer pressure or to facilitate the election process. Union-organizing campaigns often create very stressful working conditions, and some employees who are against unionization may sign authorization cards to ensure that the election be held as soon as possible.

Once the NLRB has received the authorization cards and determined that there is sufficient interest to conduct an election, it will attempt to determine the appropriate bargaining unit. A bargaining unit is a group of employees who have similar wages, skill levels, working conditions, and/or levels of professionalism. The NLRB will determine whether the organization should have one bargaining unit that covers all employees or separate bargaining units for different groups of employees, given the differences in their jobs.

▶ Reading 12.1, "The Bush NLRB: Can Balance Be Restored?," examines recent history and functions of the NLRB as well as how politics influence its composition and behavior.

For example, airlines have separate bargaining units for flight attendants, pilots, and ramp workers, given the differences in job responsibilities, training, hours, and working conditions. Newspapers have separate unions for writers, printers, and presspeople, due to similar differences. A restaurant, on the other hand, might have one bargaining unit that includes waitstaff, cooks, hosts, bartenders, and bus staff. When a unionized organization has more than one bargaining unit, each bargaining unit negotiates a contract with management separately; however, the individual units are often impacted by what the other units negotiate, and each unit often lends support to the others during periods of labor unrest.

When the NLRB conducts an election, the option that receives the majority of the votes (50 percent plus one) wins the election. There may, however, be more than two options (union or no union) on the ballot. Given that the NLRB requires authorization cards from only 30 percent of employees, it is mathematically possible for more than one union to be part of an election. This has been the case when there has been public knowledge of dissatisfied employees, and more than one union attempted to organize workers simultaneously. If there were three options on the ballot (no union, Union A, Union B) and none of the options received more than 50 percent of the initial vote, then the option receiving the least support would be dropped, and a second ballot would be issued. Eventually, one option will have the support of more than 50 percent of the employees in the prospective bargaining unit.

BEHAVIOR DURING ORGANIZING CAMPAIGNS

Union-organizing campaigns often present difficult working conditions for employees, who are often continuously subjected to opposing information from management, union representatives, and pro-union coworkers in support of their respective positions. In passing the NLRA, Congress determined that it should regulate the behavior of management and union representatives in union-organizing campaigns to ensure that one does not have an unfair advantage over the other in communicating positions to employees.

The NLRA outlines specific provisions pertaining to employer conduct during union-organizing campaigns in its discussion of unfair labor practices. Section 8(c) of the act provides that "the expression of views, arguments or opinions, or the dissemination thereof, whether in written, printed, graphic or visual form shall not constitute or be evidence of an unfair labor practice . . . if such expression contains no threat of reprisal or force or promise of benefit." Therefore, employers have free rein to communicate their position concerning unionization to employees during working hours, which is only appropriate because the employers are paying employees for that time. However, employers are forbidden from making any threat or promise pending the outcome of the election. The reason for this directive is that allowing employers to do so would give employers an unfair advantage in the election. The union does not have the power to make any such promises, so to ensure a level playing field, the NLRB prohibits employers from doing so as well. Employers need to treat employees more favorably *before* the NLRB has stepped in and established employee interest in conducting an election.

The act also allows pro-union employees the full right to approach their coworkers at work and express their support of the union, as long as such contact takes place during nonworking periods in nonworking areas (such as the employee cafeteria during lunch breaks, the parking lot after leaving work, or in a restroom during a scheduled break). This is consistent with the constitutional guarantee of freedom of speech. Employers can prohibit employees who support the union from communicating this support to coworkers at any other time.

A more difficult question concerns the extent to which employers can prevent employee solicitation by union representatives at the worksite. The United States Supreme Court has issued several rulings in this area that continue to redefine the relative positions of unions and management. Generally, an employer can restrict nonemployee access to employees if two conditions have been met: (1) The non-employee, in this case, a union organizer, must have some reasonable means to access and communicate with employees outside the workplace, such as electronic or print media, and (2) The employer must have a general ban on all nonemployee solicitation. The latter condition is not limited to union solicitation; it might also include charitable appeals, blood drives, or employer-sponsored outings for which employees have to pay. If these two conditions are met, then the employer can restrict union organizers' access to employees.

Historically, this issue of access to employees has involved somewhat of a "chess game" between employers and union organizers. Subsequent to the Supreme Court rulings described above that restrict union organizer access to employees, unions have turned to a strategy called "salting" the workplace. Salting involves a paid union organizer applying for employment with an employer whose employees are the target of an organizing drive. The Supreme Court has held that under the NLRA an employer cannot discriminate against a person solely on the basis of his or her status as a salt and intention to organize the workplace. Employers have since countered salting efforts through the use of restricted hiring criteria that has the effect of eliminating salts from employment consideration. The portrayal of union organizing efforts and management responses as a chess game relates to the fact that each side is attempting to develop a response to counter the other side's most recent "move" or court victory. ▼▼

Employees who are dissatisfied with their union representative may elect to decertify the union. The process for decertification happens in exactly the same manner as certification, utilizing authorization cards and requiring a 50+ percent majority employee vote. The NLRA does, however, require employees to wait at least one year from certification until a decertification election can be held. This is to ensure that the union has had appropriate time to work on behalf of the employees and to ensure that employees do not drain the time and resources of the NLRB by continually calling for certification and decertification elections. Similarly, if a union loses an organizing campaign, the NLRA prohibits another organizing campaign and election for at least one year.

COLLECTIVE BARGAINING

When a union is elected to represent employees, the union representative and employer are jointly responsible for negotiating a collective-bargaining agreement that covers various terms and conditions of employment. There are no set requirements as to the term or content of any collective-bargaining agreement, but the NLRA classifies bargaining items as mandatory, permissive, or prohibited. Mandatory items

▶▶ Reading 12.2, "A Direct Defense: Using an Employment Practices Compliance Approach to Avoid Employee Lawsuits," examines the process by which employers minimize the likelihood of an employee lawsuit.

must be negotiated in good faith if one party chooses to introduce them to the negotiations. They consist of many of the economic terms of employment, such as wages, hours, benefits, working conditions, job-posting procedures, or job security provisions. Mandatory items also include management rights clauses and union security clauses. The two parties are not required to come to an agreement on these items, but they are legally required to discuss them and bargain in good faith if requested by the other party. Mandatory simply means that one party cannot refuse to discuss one of these items if the other party requests to do so.

Permissive items can be discussed if both parties agree to do so. Neither party can legally force the other party to negotiate over a permissive item, nor can either party pursue a permissive item to the point of impasse. Permissive items include things such as changes in benefits for retired employees, supervisory compensation and discipline, and union input in pricing of company products and services. Prohibited items are things neither party can negotiate because these items are illegal. They include featherbedding (requiring the employer to pay for work not done or not requested), discrimination in hiring, or any other violation of the law or illegal union security clauses. A listing of some of the items that fall under each classification is presented in Exhibit 12-1.

Unions often attempt to negotiate security clauses into the collective-bargaining agreement. These clauses are a mandatory bargaining item and an attempt to ensure that the union enjoys some security in its representation of employees and that the cost of the union's efforts on behalf of employees is covered. The two types of union security clauses are union shop agreements and agency shop agreements. Union shop agreements require all newly hired employees who are not union members to join the union within a specified time period after beginning employment. Agency shop agreements do not require employees to join the union but require all nonunion members who are part of the bargaining unit to pay the union a representation fee, usually equivalent to the amount of dues paid by union members. The rationale for collecting such fees is that although individual employees can maintain the freedom of being nonunion, as bargaining unit members they reap the advantages of what the union negotiates. Therefore, it is only fair that they should share equally in the cost of obtaining what the union is able to achieve for the bargaining unit. Although union security clauses are a mandatory bargaining item, the NLRA allows individual states to pass right-to-work laws that prohibit union and agency shop arrangements. To date, nearly half of the 50 states have passed such laws.

EXHIBIT 12-1: TYPES OF BARGAINING ITEMS

Mandatory	Permissive	Illegal
Base wages	Union representation on board of directors	Closed-shop agreements
Incentive pay	Benefits for retirees	Featherbedding
Benefits	Wage concessions	Discrimination in hiring
Overtime	Employee ownership	
Paid time off	Union input into company pricing policy	
Layoff procedures		
Promotion criteria		
Union security clauses		
Management rights clauses		
Grievance procedures		
Safety and health issues		

A third type of union security agreement that was originally allowed under the NLRA has since been outlawed. Closed-shop agreements required the employer to hire only applicants who were already union members. Congress found such arrangements to be detrimental to labor, because individuals without income were forced to pay union dues without the benefit of any employment. There was no guarantee that an applicant who belonged to a union subsequently would be hired, so closed-shop agreements eventually were outlawed.

FAILURE TO REACH AGREEMENT

When the union and the employer are unable to agree on the terms of the collective-bargaining agreement, workers have the right, under the NLRA, to strike. Whether employers are obligated to rehire striking employees at the conclusion of the strike depends on the kind of strike.

An economic strike is one in which the parties have negotiated in good faith but have been unable to settle on a contract or collective-bargaining agreement. The organization has the right to continue to operate during such a strike and often does so by utilizing management employees, hiring temporary workers, and/or hiring permanent replacements. The discretion of how to proceed rests with the organization. Economic strikers cannot be terminated simply for engaging in collective strike activity. At the conclusion of the strike, they must be reinstated if two conditions are met: (1) Their individual jobs still exist and (2) Permanent replacements have not been hired. Economic strikers run the risk that the employer may eliminate their jobs or hire replacements; both activities are protected under the NLRA.

An unfair labor practice strike is one in which employees strike in response to some action of management that the NLRA identifies as an unfair labor practice. These behaviors are outlined within the statute, and workers who go out on such a strike have a guaranteed legal right to reinstatement by the employer even if the employer has hired permanent replacements in the interim.

A wildcat strike is one in which workers decide not to honor the terms of the collective-bargaining agreement and walk out in violation of their obligation to the employer under the agreement. Because wildcat strikers have breached their contractual obligations to the employer, they have no right to reinstatement in their jobs. Wildcat strikes can be caused by perceived unfair treatment of an employee by management, or a worksite may be perceived as hazardous or dangerous, such as those found in the mining and construction industries. In certain industries, management will attempt to resolve the issue if the claims are deemed to have merit in lieu of fighting the union in court. In addition, federal workers are prohibited by law from striking for any reason, including an economic strike. Any strike by federal employees is not protected under the NLRA, and striking employees have no legal rights to return to their jobs. Such was the case in the early 1980s when the Professional Air Traffic Controllers (PATCO) union struck, and President Reagan immediately fired and replaced the striking workers.

The incidence of labor strikes in the United States is decreasing as both employees and employers realize that everyone loses during a strike. The company gets hurt financially and in the public domain; workers get hurt financially and emotionally; customers may be hurt operationally and financially, particularly if there are no substitute providers. Organizations can prevent strike activity in two principal ways: through the use of a formal grievance procedure or through the alternate dispute resolution (ADR) processes of mediation or arbitration.

Grievance procedures are a permissive bargaining item under the National Labor Relations Act, as indicated in Exhibit 12-1. Grievance procedures outline how conflicts or disagreements between workers and management over the terms of the collective-bargaining agreement will be handled. Grievance procedures are often the catalyst to resolving problems before the conflict escalates to a strike. They are also useful in helping union leaders and management identify weaknesses or oversights in the collective-bargaining agreement that can be addressed during the negotiations over subsequent collective-bargaining agreements. Grievance procedures are also useful as a means of communicating to management firsthand work-related sources of employee dissatisfaction that can hamper morale and productivity.

An increasing number of collective-bargaining agreements are calling for mediation or arbitration of labor disputes as a means of avoiding strikes. Mediation involves an outside third party who has no binding decision-making authority assisting both sides in reaching a settlement. This individual assists the two sides in finding some middle ground on which they can agree and facilitating dialogue and concessions. Arbitration works in a similar manner: It involves an outside, unbiased third party who listens to the arguments presented by both sides. However, the arbitrator renders a ruling or decision that binds both parties. Both sides agree to abide by the decision of the arbitrator prior to entering the arbitration hearing. Mediation is frequently used in public sector organizations where strike activity is outlawed at the federal level and often greatly restricted at the state and local levels. Arbitration is used quite frequently in professional sports in resolving salary disputes between union players and the owners of their teams.

UNIONS TODAY

One way in which unions are attempting to maintain their viability in light of declining membership is to recruit in organizations and industries with which they have no previous affiliation. With the demise of their traditional manufacturing base, many domestic unions have expanded their missions as efforts to recruit new members have become a top priority. Such recruiting efforts are seen as so central to the ongoing livelihood of unions that the AFL-CIO now earmarks one third of its operating budget for organizing, compared to just 5 percent ten years ago.[5] Consider the diversity now present in some of the leading labor unions: the United Steelworkers of America, established in 1936 to represent steelworkers, now includes employees from Good Humor/Breyers, the Baltimore Zoo, and Louisville Slugger; the United Auto Workers, established in 1935 to represent auto workers, now includes employees from Miller Beer, Planter's nuts, Kohler bathroom fixtures, Yamaha musical instruments, and Folger's Coffee; the International Brotherhood of Teamsters, established in 1903 to represent drivers in the freight-moving industry, now includes flight attendants, public defenders, and nursing home employees. There is no consensus regarding the value of such diversification by unions. Some argue that it provides more power to unions and their members by strengthening their numbers and preventing their dependance on one particular industry. On the other hand, critics argue that this prevents unions from being very influential in setting wages and policy in a particular industry, given the need to spread time and resources across multiple industries. However, given the demise of traditional manufacturing jobs from which unions originated and relied on for their support and power, unions have little choice but to reach out to new industries. The critical issue is whether this diversification is really strategic for the union or merely opportunistic.

Another new development in how unions operate is their reliance on technology. Unions have been using the Internet effectively to recruit new members, particularly those in technology-based industries, and to gain support from others in their organizing efforts. The South Bay Central Labor Council, based in California's Silicon Valley, consists of 110 affiliated unions that represent more than 100,000 employees in the area. The Council is using the Internet to communicate with and, it is hoped, organize contingent workers.[6] Similarly, the Service Employees International Union undertook a campaign to organize janitorial workers in the Silicon Valley. The union successfully used the Internet to publicize its case against Apple Computer, Oracle, and Hewlett-Packard worldwide via electronic bulletin boards that informed engineers and programmers about the wages and working conditions of those who cleaned their offices at night.[7] Finally, the Oakland-based Local 2850 of the Hotel Employees & Restaurant Employees International Union used the Internet in a campaign against software giant PeopleSoft. In attempting to organize workers from a hotel used extensively by PeopleSoft and its corporate partners and unable to gain the support of PeopleSoft, the union launched an Internet campaign that caused PeopleSoft's stock value to decline by more than $63 million, according to the company's own estimates.[8]

The NLRB has also considered the role of technology as it relates to worker rights under the NLRA. Given its charge to ensure that employees are able to communicate freely with each other about wages and all other conditions and terms of employment, the NLRB has endorsed e-mail communication between employees as a means of safeguarding those rights. Only when an employee's behavior is disruptive does NLRA protection cease. As a result, employer policies that ban all non-business and/or personal use of e-mail may interfere with the right to self-organize and therefore constitute a violation of the NLRA. A key issue here is the extent to which employees normally use the employer's computer system for their regular work and communication with coworkers. Employees who normally use a computer system in carrying out their regular job responsibilities will be considered differently from employees who generally do not use computers or e-mail to carry out their regular job responsibilities. In addition, the more e-mail normally is used in the workplace, the less restrictive a policy an employer can implement that regulates communication that might be considered protected concerted activity under the NLRA.[9]

CONCLUSION

Unions have a long and deep history in the United States and enjoy strong support under federal law. However, union membership is declining in America; unions in this country probably will not survive if they continue to display traditional adversarial relationships with employers. Traditional approaches to negotiation usually involved the union trying to gain concessions from management and winning the negotiation. To be successful in the future, unions must develop partnerships with employers and seek win-win outcomes to collective bargaining that strengthen both the union's position and employees' rights and enhance the performance of the organization. Rigid posturing by unions in attempting to maintain the status quo works against the many initiatives and innovations organizations develop at they attempt to respond to changes in their environments and remain more competitive. ▼▼▼

Given the changing nature of organizations and work, unions clearly need to reinvent themselves. Unions need to consider that the jobs of today and those of the future are quite different from the jobs of the past. Increasing global competition, changing technology, the heightened pace of merger and acquisition activity, the move toward smaller businesses and autonomous divisions, and the increasing diversity in the workforce represent broad changes for unions in the United States. The jobs being created in our economy are more service- than manufacturing-oriented; are much more complex, multifaceted, and broadly designed; involve teams, cooperation, and working with others; and involve more self or peer supervision than supervision by management. Countries such as Japan and Germany have extensive unionization and produce some of the highest quality, most technologically advanced products. Their unions facilitate worker involvement, development, and participation programs; also, the unions partner with employers in creating beneficial change rather than inhibiting change and attempting to ensure workers' rights by maintaining the status quo.

As unions decline in number and stature, workers become less powerful. Without union representation, employee interests can only be advanced through increased government regulation of the employment relationship or through innovative and responsive HR programs that organizations initiate themselves. Increased legislation may ensure worker rights, but it can also inhibit organizational flexibility and change. Innovative HR programs can provide workers with benefits, but usually the organization retains power and control over the workers, who maintain their individual status in dealing with separate issues with the employer. Legislation preserves rights and empowers workers to a limited extent, but it inhibits change. Organization-designed initiatives can promote change but still leave individual workers at a disadvantage when dealing with employers on issues of equity.

Very few unionized companies have developed effective worker participation programs because unions are interested in keeping workers insulated from management issues. Ironically, however, successful employee participation programs in nonunionized organizations have actually increased workers' power and voice in dealing with management. Union leaders need to create a new model of worker representation if they plan to survive in the 21st century. This can only be done if union leaders rethink their roles and adopt collective-bargaining strategies that allow both the employees and employers to benefit. Union leaders need not only political and negotiating skills but management skills as well in understanding the whole organization: strategic issues facing the employer and the organization's environment. Instead of seeing themselves as adversaries to management, they should envision themselves as facilitators and consultants. Although employers clearly need to consider labor relations from a strategic perspective, union representatives must do so even more if they are to keep their unions viable for tomorrow's organizations.

▶▶▶ Reading 12.3, "Embracing the Future: Union Strategies for the 21st Century," explains in more depth the issues and challenges facing unions and provides an example of labor-management cooperation that facilitated both employee productivity and satisfaction and organizational performance.

CRITICAL THINKING

1. With unionization on the downturn, why should an organization be concerned about labor relations?

2. What benefits are received and what costs are incurred when workers unionize?

3. Describe the process by which workers unionize.

4. What are the possible outcomes of failure to reach consensus on a collective-bargaining agreement?

5. Contrast the style of labor unions in the United States to that found in other countries.

6. Does union diversification make unions stronger or weaker? How would you feel as an auto worker to see the UAW representing employees outside of the auto industry?

Reading 12.1

7. Examine recent major decisions of the National Labor Relations Board. In what direction does it appear to be leaning relative to the rights of employees and employers under the NLRA?

Reading 12.2

8. Explain how an employment practices compliance system functions. How might one be applied to labor relations under the NLRA?

Reading 12.3

9. How can unions best serve the interests of American labor in the 21st century?

EXPERIENTIAL EXERCISES

1. Locate a local unionized organization. Interview both a manager and a union employee to determine the level of satisfaction each has with the employment relationship. What types of union activity/inactivity contribute to these positions?

2. Investigate one large union, such as the United Auto Workers, United Steel-workers, or Teamsters, in depth and examine its member base and recent activity on behalf of its members. Does it appear that diversification has made this union more or less effective?

INTERNET EXERCISES

1. Visit the Web sites for the AFL-CIO (http://www.aflcio.org) and Teamsters (http://www.teamsters.com). What programs does each union offer its members?

What are the main issues each union appears to be pursuing? Do these programs and issues appear to be well-matched to the needs of the U.S. labor force?

2. Visit the Web site for the National Labor Relations Board (http://www.nlrb.gov). Of what value is this Web site for employers? Of what value is this Web site for union leaders?

CHAPTER REFERENCES

1. Caudron, S., et al., "The Labor Movement to War" *Workforce*, January 2001, pp. 27–33.
2. United States Bureau of Labor Statistics, Labor Force Statistics from the *Current Population Survey, Union Members*, http://stats.bls.gov.
3. Ibid.
4. Segal, J. A. "Labor Pains for Union-Free Employers," *HR Magazine*, March 2004, pp. 113–118.
5. Hirsh, S. "Unions Reach Everywhere for Members," *Baltimore Sun*, January 25, 2004, p. ID.
6. Newman, N. "Union and Community Mobilization in the Information Age," *Perspectives on Work*, 6, (2), pp. 9–11.
7. Ibid.
8. Ibid.
9. Lyncheski, J. E. and Heller, L. D. "Cyber Speech Cops," *HR Magazine*, January 2001, pp. 145–150.

The Bush NLRB: Can Balance Be Restored?

Heather L. MacDougall, *Employee Relations Law Journal*

The National Labor Relations Board started 2002 with just two members on the five-member board, leaving it unable to issue decisions or take other official action. However, two recess appointments made by President George W. Bush on January 23, 2002 gave the NLRB a Republican majority for the first time since November 1993. While the recess appointments bring the Board up to four members, all four will leave office by December 2002 unless they are reappointed by the President or confirmed for regular terms. Hopefully, confirmation of a full complement of NLRB members will occur this year. In any event, with a Republican-majority in place, the Bush NLRB can begin to address correcting the pro-union tilt that characterized the NLRB throughout the Clinton years. After years of imbalance at the NLRB throughout the Clinton Administration, it is hopeful that the Bush NLRB will restore confidence in the NLRB's decision-making ability. This article provides a summary of the issues that the Bush NLRB may address.

The year 2001 was a harrowing odyssey for employers that, at the beginning of the year, had hoped that a change in administration would bring a correction of the pro-union tilt that had characterized the National Labor Relations Board (NLRB) throughout the Clinton years. However, a Democratic majority continued to churn out controversial decisions well beyond the inauguration of President George W. Bush. With Republican Chairman Peter Hurtgen gaining a long-awaited Republican majority in 2002,[1] employers can hope for a new balance. While the NLRB's agenda will by necessity be shaped by the cases brought before it, a preview of the kinds of changes that can be expected is provided by a review of the controversial decisions issued by the Democratic-majority NLRB of the Clinton era. One may speculate that many of these cases would likely have gone the other way under a Republican-majority NLRB. In addition, the Bush NLRB will address important issues that have arisen as a result of significant changes that have occurred

in the workplace. Many of these issues have not previously been decided by the NLRB but will have a profound impact on today's workplace. Ultimately, upon later review of all of the issues decided by the Bush NLRB, one can hope that some balance was restored that was lost during the Clinton era—an obviously difficult period of time for a management representative.

Possible Review of Clinton NLRB Decisions that Ignored Established Law or Set New Standards

Some of the more controversial rulings of the Clinton NLRB dealt with: (1) employee free choice; (2) temporary employees; (3) Weingarten rights; (4) withdrawal of recognition; (5) secondary activity; (6) discrimination; (7) employee involvement; and (8) union organizers' access to property. A summary of the cases decided by the Clinton NLRB on each of these issues and a discussion of the prospects for review by the Bush NLRB follows.

EMPLOYEE FREE CHOICE

In recent years, the NLRB has increasingly confronted the issue of whether a group of employees is entitled to a secret ballot election on whether to be represented by a union. This question not only arises in cases involving card check recognition but also where a union seeks to add ("accrete") a group of unrepresented employees to an existing bargaining unit already represented and where a group of employees seeks to rid itself of union representation through a decertification election. During the Clinton NLRB, the Board issued several decisions either reversing existing Board precedent or establishing new standards that impact employee free choice under the National Labor Relations Act (NLRA). These decisions favored the interests of the bargaining representative or a preference for collective bargaining agreements over the expression of employee free choice. It is hopeful that the

Bush NLRB will conclude that employees' exercise of their Section 7 right to select a union representative of their own choice or to have no union represent them at all is of paramount importance. The Bush NLRB may revisit several Clinton NLRB decisions that involve employee free choice.

In St. Elizabeth Manor, Inc., 329 NLRB No. 36 (1999), an employer initially recognized a union in a successorship context but filed a petition three months later challenging the union's majority status. Following existing NLRB precedent established in Sound Contractors, 162 NLRB 364 (1966), the regional director found no bar to the processing of the petition and directed an election. In a 3–2 decision, the Board reversed and held that the union was entitled to a "reasonable period of time to negotiate a contract."[2] In adopting the "successor bar rule," the Board majority analogized the case to the situation where there is voluntary recognition and where the union is given a reasonable time to negotiate before any challenge to its majority status can be mounted. The Board majority reasoned that there is a need to protect the bargaining relationship and the previously expressed majority choice against the "stresses of the organizational transition" that might have affected employee support for the union.[3]

However, the holding in St. Elizabeth frustrates important rights under the Act. Successorship should not be equated with voluntary recognition. When voluntary recognition has been extended, the rationale for barring challenges to the union's majority status has been that time should be given to allow the collective bargaining process to work as newly recognized unions need time to establish themselves among their new membership. With a successor, however, the employees already have experience with the collective bargaining process and the union has established a "track record familiar to the unit employees."[4] Thus, the desire to challenge the union's status in this setting should not be ignored. The Bush NLRB has already decided to revisit the holding of St. Elizabeth. The Bush NLRB has already granted requests for review in four cases to consider the issue of whether to overrule or modify St. Elizabeth Manor.[5]

The Clinton NLRB disfavored the right of employees to exercise their Section 7 right to select a union representative of their own choice or to have no union represent them at all in New Otani Hotel & Garden, 331 NLRB No. 159 (2000). In New Otani Hotel, the NLRB held that a union's request that the employer sign a neutrality/card check agreement does not constitute a present demand for recognition. The requested agreement would require the employer to refrain from campaigning against the union during an organizing campaign and to recognize the union as the employees' bargaining representative upon proof that a majority of workers have signed authorization cards. The NLRB found that the union's four-year picketing and boycotting campaign to pressure the employer into signing the agreement did not constitute a present demand for recognition as the majority representative of the employer's employees as the Board has construed Section 9(c)(1)(B) of the Act as requiring before an employer's petition will be processed.[6]

Taking the New Otani Hotel holding a step further, in Rapera, Inc., 333 NLRB No. 150 (2001), an employer sought an election by the NLRB, claiming that the union, which had put pressure on the employer to sign a neutrality/card check agreement, had evidenced a present demand for recognition through picketing, demonstrations, and letters to third parties that the employer sign the neutrality/card check agreement. Contemporaneously, the union had asserted in a court-filed affidavit that it had in fact achieved majority support through signed authorization cards. Upon finding that no such demand had been made through this conduct by the union, the employer's petition was dismissed by the regional director. An equally divided Board resulted in the dismissal being affirmed.[7] Chairman Truesdale and Member Hurtgen, who would have reinstated the employer's petition, noted that it was the combination of the union's actions and its sworn statement to the court, and not merely its picketing activities, that established the present demand for recognition. It is hopeful that the NLRB will revisit the holdings of New Otani Hotel and Rapera. The NLRB should view the totality of the circumstances to determine whether a union is seeking recognition.

The Clinton NLRB sacrificed employees' Section 7 rights in favor of the stability of continuing collective bargaining relationships even where it was clear that the employees at issue no longer wanted union representation. In MGM Grand Hotel, 329 NLRB No. 50 (1999), after three years of picketing and demonstrations, the hotel employer voluntarily recognized the union pursuant to a card check as the exclusive bargaining representative of its employees. The parties commenced bargaining. After 12 days of bargaining over five months, employees filed a decertification petition that was dismissed. After an additional 30 meetings over five more months, employees again filed a decertification petition that was dismissed. After another dozen or more meetings and only nine days short of the anniversary of the voluntary recognition, the employees filed a third petition that was also dismissed. In a 3–2 decision, the NLRB majority affirmed the three dismissals concluding that a "reasonable time to bargain" had not elapsed. In support of their decision, the Board majority weighed in favor of promoting voluntary recognition and nurturing collective bargaining relationships at the expense of repeated attempts at employee free choice. Clearly, in the name of "industrial stability," the majority "sacrificed employees' Section 7 rights to engage in selforganization or to refrain therefrom."[8]

These rights were again sacrificed in Wyndham Palmas Del Mar Resort and Villas, 334 NLRB No. 70 (2001), in which the NLRB ruled that the employees of the hotel could not vote to decertify their union because their petition was tainted by the employer's illegal action. The employer had withdrawn recognition from the union on the basis of an anti-union petition signed by employees during a 60-day notice-posting period as required as part of an informal settlement agreement resolving several unfair labor practice charges. The majority analyzed the case under Master Slack, 271 NLRB 78 (1984), which is used by the NLRB where proven unfair labor practices are followed by employee disaffection from the union. The Master Slack analysis determines whether the unfair labor practices caused the disaffection. However, in Wyndham Palmas Del Mar Resort, there were no proven unfair labor practices. As noted by Chairman Hurtgen in his dissent, the informal settlement agreement had a nonadmissions clause; thus, Master Slack has no relevance.[9] Furthermore, there was no evidence that the employer had any responsibility for the decertification effort. Clearly, the majority's opinion will act to decrease the likelihood that employers will voluntarily enter into agreements that settle unfair labor practice charges. Moreover, it interferes with employees' Section 7 right to decide whether they desire union representation.

Employees' Section 7 rights compromise the core of the Act and in balancing these rights against the need for stability in collective bargaining relationships, the NLRB must show special sensitivity toward employees' rights. To allow a union to represent employees while ignoring the desires of these very employees strikes at the core of the Act. It is hopeful that the Bush NLRB will restore the proper balance in this fundamental area of labor law.

TEMPORARY EMPLOYEES

One of the most controversial areas under the Clinton NLRB was the issue of whether to include temporary agency employees in the same bargaining unit as regular employees. In M.B. Sturgis, Inc./Jeff Boat Division of American Commercial Marine Services, 331 NLRB No. 173 (2000), the Board ruled, 3–1, that workers provided by a temporary employment agency may be included in the same collective bargaining unit as a client's regular employees without the mutual consent of the agency and its client. The Clinton NLRB's long-awaited decision threatens to wreak havoc in the use of temporary workers supplied by staffing agencies. In the words of Member Brame's dissent, the decision "throws a settled area into turmoil."[10]

Since the 2000 ruling in M.B. Sturgis, there have been several other cases by the Clinton NLRB applying the new rule, including Interstate Warehousing of Ohio, LLC, 333 NLRB No. 83 (2001), and Tree of Life d/bla Gourmet Award Foods, Northeast, 336 NLRB No. 77 (2001). Chairman Hurtgen, who has agreed with the Board's departure from Lee Hospital, 300 NLRB 947 (1990) and Greenhoot, Inc.,[11] has argued for a narrower reading of the application of M.B. Sturgis. For example, in Interstate Warehousing of Ohio, while the Democratic-majority combined temporary agency employees with regular employees in the same bargaining unit, Chairman Hurtgen dissented, finding that the employees did not share the necessary community of interest where the supplier set the economic conditions of the temporary employees and the user employer set the economic conditions of the regular employees. As Hurtgen noted, under these circumstances, it is not appropriate to combine the two groups of employees as bargaining will be frustrated by significant fractures within the bargaining unit.[12]

Chairman Hurtgen objected strenuously again when the Board took the M.B. Sturgis ruling even further in Gourmet Award Foods, by ruling that an employer commits an unfair labor practice by not applying the labor contract provisions governing its regular employees to the temporary agency employees working on-site. While in M.B. Sturgis the NLRB found that the employer and the supplier would have to jointly bargain with the union over temporary employees that are included in the same bargaining unit with regular employees, in Gourmet Award Foods, the Clinton NLRB eliminated the bargaining process altogether.

In Gourmet Award Foods, the Clinton NLRB ruled that the terms of the regular employees' contract automatically apply, to the extent that those terms regulate temporary employees' working conditions under the employer's control, where the temporary employees perform the same work as the regular employees and work side by side at the same facility, under the same supervision, and under common working conditions.[13]

In his dissent, Chairman Hurtgen noted that the case should properly be considered under an accretion analysis. Moreover, applying the accretion analysis to the facts of the case—that is, accretion will be appropriate only where the employees sought to be added to an existing bargaining unit have little or no separate identity and share an "overwhelming community of interest with the preexisting unit to which they are accreted"—the higher standard of accretion was not met where there were strong differences noted between the interests of the employee groups, including that the basic economic terms and conditions of employment are not only different but also set by different employers.[14]

The Clinton NLRB failed to recognize the realities of the collective bargaining process with regard to including temporary employees in the same unit as jointly employed regular employees. Where two groups of employees have different economic terms, and those terms are set by different employers, it is difficult to say that the two groups share a community of interests—let alone an overwhelming community of interests—that protects against the prospect that bargaining will be frustrated. In deciding cases in this area, hopefully, the Bush NLRB will not offend "appropriate unit" principles; thus, protect employees' Section 7 rights, not undermine them. With several cases already pending before the Bush NLRB, it will have an early opportunity to correct the turmoil created by M.B. Sturgis.[15]

REPRESENTATION RIGHTS FOR NONUNION EMPLOYEES (WEINGARTEN RIGHTS)

Another one of the Clinton NLRB's most controversial rulings was the extension of the "Weingarten" right to nonunion employees. The NLRB ruled, 3–2, in Epilepsy Foundation of Northeast Ohio, 331 NLRB No. 92 (2000), that employers must grant requests by nonunion employees to be accompanied by a co-employee of their choice at any investigatory meeting that the employee "reasonably believes" may result in disciplinary action. Prior to this ruling, this so-called Weingarten right, named after a 1975 Supreme Court decision, NLRB v. Weingarten, Inc., 420 U.S. 251 (1975), applied only in unionized workplaces.

The decision came as a shock to those who had assumed that the law in this area was well settled given that, in the 25 years since Weingarten, there was only a brief, three-year period during which the NLRB applied the Weingarten right to unionized workforces. Moreover, nothing had changed in either the legal landscape or in the workplace that compelled a change in the rules. In abruptly reversing precedent and applying Weingarten to nonunionized workforces, the NLRB majority ignored complaints by the two dissenting Republican members that the Supreme Court clearly did not contemplate applying Weingarten beyond union settings, where employers that deal directly with employees do so at their peril anyway. The D.C. Circuit enforced the NLRB's order in Epilepsy Foundation of Northeast Ohio v. NLRB, 268 F.3d 1095 (D.C. Cir. 2001), noting that it was the "province of the Board, not the courts, to determine whether or not the 'need' [for a Weingarten-type rule] exists" in a nonunion setting.[16]

It is likely that the Bush NLRB will revisit the ruling in Epilepsy Foundation of Northeast Ohio. Clearly, the Clinton NLRB ignored the realities of the nonunion workplace, particularly the fact that the relationship between nonunion employers and their individual employees differs greatly from the unionized conditions that underlay the Supreme Court's holding in Weingarten. The imposition of the Weingarten right upon nonunion employers conducting investigatory interviews creates irreconcilable conflicts with numerous other employer obligations and with settled nonunion employment practices. In particular, nonunion coworker representatives, unlike union shop stewards, have no obligation to safeguard the interests of the entire bargaining unit and may, in fact, be hostile to and impede an employer's investigation. In addition, the extension of the Weingarten right to nonunion employees chills employers' effective enforcement and efforts to curb workplace misconduct such as sexual harassment, employee theft, fraud, and workplace violence.

Hopefully, the Board will rethink the province of extending the Weingarten right to nonunion employees. At the least, the Board should provide additional guidance to employers, both union and nonunion, on the application of the right, including troubling issues such as what constitutes an investigatory interview triggering the Weingarten right.

WITHDRAWAL OF RECOGNITION

In Levitz Furniture Co. of the Pacific, Inc., 333 NLRB No. 105 (2001), the NLRB overruled established principles of law set forth in Celanese Corp., 95 NLRB 664 (1951), that an employer could withdraw recognition from an incumbent union if the employer has a good-faith uncertainty as to the union's majority status. Following Levitz Furniture, an employer can withdraw recognition only if the employer can prove that an incumbent union has, in fact, lost majority support.

In Levitz Furniture, the new rule was not applied retroactively; thus, the complaint was dismissed. Because Hurtgen agreed with the dismissal of the complaint, and thus concurred with the result, his opinion is written as a concurrence. However, he disagreed with much of the majority opinion. Hurtgen asserted that Celanese offered "stability in the law and due regard for Section 7 rights," while the new standard "is imprudent and unfair."[17]

Again, this time in Levitz Furniture, the Clinton NLRB failed to give due regard for Section 7 rights and the fundamental right to choose whether to engage in collective bargaining or not. The result of the new rule of Levitz may be to impose a union on employees when they may no longer wish to be represented and should be reconsidered by the Bush NLRB.

SECONDARY ACTIVITY

The protection of neutral employers against becoming embroiled in other employers' labor disputes was substantially weakened in United Food and Commercial Workers, Local No. 1996 (Visiting Nurse Health System, Inc.), 336 NLRB No. 35 (2001). In Visiting Nurse Health System, the NLRB ruled that companies that do business with an employer that chooses to contest a Board certification of a union are excluded from the secondary boycott protections of the Act. The primary employer in Visiting Nurse Health System—a company providing home health services to indigents—had refused to recognize the union after an NLRB election in order to challenge the election in the federal courts. The NLRB held that the union acted lawfully in picketing the United Way of Metropolitan Atlanta to try to shut off its support to the company.

As noted in Chairman Hurtgen's dissent, there is no support in the text of Section 8(b)(4), its legislative history, or the basic policies of the Act for the result reached in Visiting Nurse Health System.[18] Clearly the Act affords employers the right, through a "test-of-certification" proceeding, to obtain judicial review of a certification of representative issued by the Board. Yet, the majority found in Visiting Nurse Health System that the employer might lawfully be subjected to secondary boycotts. The result is patently unfair and will pressure employers into foregoing their right of judicial review of a certification of representative. Employers that do exercise their right to seek judicial review of a certification of representative will be subject to economic harm with no recourse even if they ultimately prevail before a reviewing court. It is clear that the Act did not intend such a result and obvious that it is for these reasons that the Board had never before recognized the exception created by Visiting Nurse Health System. For these reasons, the Bush NLRB should reverse Visiting Nurse Health System.

DISCRIMINATION

In another major ruling, the Clinton NLRB expanded an important 1967 Supreme Court doctrine. A bedrock principle of NLRB discrimination law has been that the employer must be shown to have intended to discriminate or acted based on "union animus." In NLRB v. Great Dane Trailers, 388 U.S. 26 (1967), the Supreme Court held that some conduct was so "inherently destructive" of union rights that intent to discriminate could be inferred. Previously, this foreclosure of a major employer defense had only been applied where intent to discriminate is shown on the face of the policy (for example, granting a higher level of seniority to employees who refused to strike). However, in Aztech Electric Co., 335 NLRB No. 25 (2001), the Clinton NLRB expanded this doctrine to hold that a policy that impacts adversely on union members is discriminatory, even without any showing of discriminatory intent or union animus.

In Aztech Electric, the Board found that the employer had no discriminatory intent or union animus, either in adopting or applying its policy, but the Board borrowed from the so-called disparate impact theory under Title VII and expanded the "inherently destructive" analysis to include policies that are facially neutral, but have an adverse impact. Then, going beyond Title VII law, which allows a defense of substantial business justification, the Board held that it could balance the employer's business need for the policy against the impact on union members and still decide that the policy was illegal."

In this "salting" case, the Board ruled illegal the employer's policy of not hiring any applicant whose recent wage history differed by 30 percent from its starting wages, even though the employer contended, and the Board agreed, that the policy was motivated by non-discriminatory, legitimate business needs. The Board found that this policy effectively excluded from eligibility for hire virtually all applicants who had recently worked for unionized construction employers and, on that basis alone, could not be allowed to stand.

Chairman Hurtgen objected strenuously, but futilely, to this policy shift. The Bush NLRB should reverse the Aztech Electric ruling and conclude that such policies, which have not been shown to be unlawfully motivated or discriminatorily applied, do not violate the Act—particularly where the employer has a legitimate business justification for its policy.

EMPLOYEE INVOLVEMENT

The Clinton NLRB issued many rulings following Electromation, Inc., 309 NLRB 990 (1992), enforced, 35 F.3d 1148 (7th Cir. 1994), affirming the illegality of employee involvement structures: Polaroid Corp., 329 NLRB No. 47 (1999); Naomi Knitting Plant, 328 NLRB 1279 (1998); EFCO Corp., 321 NLRB 372 (1998); Vic Koenig Chevrolet, 321 NLRB 1255 (1996); Aero Detroit, Inc., 321 NLRB 1101 (1996); Simmons Industries, 321 NLRB 228 (1996); Vons Grocery, 320 NLRB 53 (1995); Stoody Co., 320 NLRB 18 (1995); Dillon Stores, 319 NLRB 1245 (1995); Webcor Packaging, 319 NLRB 1203 (1995);

Keeler Brass, 317 NLRB 1110 (1995); and E.I. du Pont de Nemours & Co. 311 NLRB 893 (1993).

While most of the Clinton NLRB decisions regarding employee involvement demonstrate its lack of balanced decision-making, one recent decision gives employers hope the NLRB will recognize the merit of increasing the intellectual role of rank-and-file employees in the operation of a company. While there remain questions as to precise scope of the ruling, in Crown Cork & Seal, 334 NLRB No. 92 (2001), the NLRB effectively excluded from the definition of "labor organization" employee involvement groups that simply perform a management function that would otherwise be performed by management.

With this decision, the NLRB appears to finally have recognized that the role played by legitimate employee involvement structures is substantially different from that of sham unions and that these new structures can be allowed without threatening the right of employees to organize labor unions. There are questions as to how much interaction will be allowed between employee involvement structures and other layers of management, but it is hopeful that following Crown Cork & Seal, the Bush NLRB will find employee involvement structures lawful under more varying factual circumstances.

UNION ORGANIZERS' ACCESS TO PROPERTY

The Clinton NLRB sought to assist union organizers by extending property access rights to them in a number of cases. Where the issue was one of balancing union organizers' Section 7 rights and employers' property rights, the Clinton Board struck the balance in favor of Section 7 rights. Hopefully, the Bush NLRB will be more balanced in its approach.

For example, in First Healthcare Corp d/bla Hillhaven Highland House, 336 NLRB No. 62 (2001), the Clinton NLRB found illegal an employer's rule prohibiting employees of one of its facilities from accessing nonwork outside areas at any other of its facilities for the purpose of union organizing. Although the employees have a Section 7 right to assist employees elsewhere in their organizational drive, it does not follow from the governing precedent established in cases such as Hudgens v. NLRB, 424 U.S. 507 (1976), that they have a Section 7 right to come onto the property of the employer at a facility where they do not work. Here, the employees' interests must give way to the employer's property right.

In addition, the Clinton NLRB demonstrated an overly narrow understanding of how hospitals provide treatment and care to their patients. In Beth Israel Hospital v. NLRB, 437 U.S. 483 (1978), the Supreme Court upheld the Board's presumption that a hospital may lawfully prohibit solicitation and distribution in immediate patient care areas and in areas where it can show that such a ban is necessary to avoid disrupting care or disturbing patients. In cases such as Brockton Hospital, 333 NLRB No. 165 (2001), the Clinton NLRB was reluctant to find such a ban by hospitals was necessary.

The Bush NLRB should revise the Board's principles to allow prohibitions of solicitation and distribution in areas where patients, their families, and visitors spend a substantial amount of time. The Board should take into account that a modern hospital houses a complex array of facilities and techniques for patient care and therapy that defy simple classification. Patients are cared for in a variety of settings, such as recovery rooms, intensive-care units, patients' rooms, sitting rooms, and even corridors. The atmosphere in these areas may be critical to patients' well-being and should be favored over the exercise of employees' Section 7 rights.

The Clinton NLRB continued to find violations of the Act when employers removed union literature from company bulletin boards even where the employer maintained a written rule specifying that the company bulletin boards were to be used only for company business and enforced that rule against all outside organizations. In Fleming Companies, Inc., 336 NLRB No. 15 (2001), the Clinton NLRB, rather than focusing on this consistent application, noted minor exceptions, such as individual "thank you" notes and wedding announcements. The Bush NLRB should recognize that there is no Section 7 right to post literature on company bulletin boards. There is only a Section 7 right to be free from discriminatory treatment. Thus, the relevant inquiry is whether the employer's posting policy treats, evenhandedly, like postings. If it does, there is no warrant for a special exception for union literature.

Too often, the Clinton NLRB failed to start from the proposition that employers may control activities that occur in the workplace, both as a matter of property rights (the employer owns the building) and of contract (employees agree to abide by the employer's rules as a condition of employment). As the Supreme Court has stated, the Act "does not command that labor organizations . . . are entitled to use a medium [of communications in the workplace] simply because the employer is using it." Hopefully, the Bush NLRB will afford employers' property rights the protection they deserve.

Possible New Issues To Confront NLRB due to Changes in the Workplace

The Bush NLRB is likely to address important issues that have never been decided by the Board, the determination of which will have far-reaching consequences in the workplace. These issues may include: (1) new forms of union solicitation; (2) card check/neutrality agreements; and (3) corporate campaigns. A brief summary of these issues that might come before the Bush NLRB follows.

UNION SOLICITATION

Over the term of the Clinton NLRB, significant changes occurred in the workplace brought about by technological innovation. The NLRB has not yet decided many of the issues that have evolved as a result of these technological innovations. Significant attention has already been given the issue of solicitation and access by the Office of the General Counsel's Division of Advice.[22] For example, the Division of Advice has taken the position that the use of e-mail is akin to verbal solicitation between employees.[23] Employers, however, are more likely to view the use of e-mail as having little difference from the use of telephones and other employer-provided equipment that the Board has consistently held may be limited by the employer to business usage only as long as there is no discrimination against union activity.

However, is the use of e-mail a solicitation or should it be considered the distribution of material? Do these concepts even make sense in the context of today's workplace? Clearly, this is an issue for debate among the Board members that decide the case to first address it. There are many other issues that the Board will need to confront here, such as what restrictions an employer can place on the use of its e-mail systems. The resolution of these issues will have significant impact upon the productivity and efficiency of America's workplaces and deserves thoughtful and reasoned decision-making.

CARD CHECK/NEUTRALITY AGREEMENTS

Feeling a sense of desperation to organize workers, unions have increasingly turned to an organizing tactic called "card check recognition" that takes the decision to unionize away from workers by avoiding an NLRB-conducted secret ballot election and puts it in the hands of those workers' employers. Reversing the NLRB and agreeing with an amicus curiae brief filed by LPA and other employer groups, the D.C. Circuit ruled in Pall Corp. v. NLRB, 275 F.3d 116 (D.C. Cir. 2002), that a union cannot attempt to force an employer to bargain over a demand for a card check recognition agreement at one of the employer's other facilities. While the case is somewhat fact-specific, the Clinton Board's ruling in Pall Corp. was generally viewed as a potential precursor to a broader ruling that employer neutrality and card check recognition are generally mandatory subjects of bargaining. The court's ruling sets the stage for a more definitive ruling by the Bush NLRB.

CORPORATE CAMPAIGNS

Along with the increased use of seeking card check and neutrality agreements, unions that are unable to achieve their recognitional objectives are seeking to tarnish the image, and undermine the reputation, of the targeted company through constant and unyielding pressure and to cause so much disruption that the employer is forced to surrender to the union's demands. Again, unions are choosing warfare that is outside the confines of the representation procedures of the Act. Instead, unions use corporate campaigns—a coordinated attack using a variety of economic, legal, political, and psychological weapons against a company that has opposed unionization, refused to agree to the union's bargaining demands, or in some other way refused to yield on some issue of great importance to the labor organization waging the campaign.

The NLRB has yet to recognize corporate campaigns as a union tactic.[24] It is hopeful that the Bush NLRB will at least take this initial step. Furthermore, the NLRB should determine that non-employee union conduct, which does not deserve the same special protection as conduct by rank-and-file employees

engaged in workplace conduct, is unprotected activity under Section 7 of the Act or that the conduct of a union's corporate campaign is carried out by "indefensible" means as proscribed by NLRB v. International Brotherhood of Electrical Workers, Local 1229 (Jefferson Standard Broadcasting), 346 U.S. 464 (1953) (holding that certain attacks on an employer that are lawful may nevertheless lose protection by Section 7 of the Act).

Conclusion

This article has provided an overview of just a few of the issues that may come before the Bush NLRB. There are many others, including recurring issues that each new NLRB must address such as: the scope of the statutory coverage of the Act, what is protected speech under Section 8(c) of the Act, what constitutes protected activity, what is the ability of an employer to make changes prior to reaching agreement on a first collective bargaining agreement, what constitutes a collective bargaining impasse, when does an employer have a duty to bargain over operational changes, and what limitations are placed on an employer's duty to provide requested information.

However, in analyzing all of the issues it faces, the Bush NLRB should seek adequate comment from those affected by its rulings, such as using oral arguments more frequently and inviting participation by amid curiae in cases where this would be beneficial. Above all else, the NLRB must engage in reasoned decision-making, casting aside long-established precedent only where it is able to provide satisfactory reasons why it is taking such action. After years of imbalance at the NLRB throughout the Clinton Administration, it is hopeful that the Bush NLRB will restore confidence in the NLRB's decision-making ability.

Source:

Endnotes

1. President Bush made two recess appointments to the NLRB on Jan. 23, 2002: Michael Bartlett, director of labor law policy for the U.S. Chamber of Commerce, and William Cowen, a McLean, Virginia, management attorney with Institutional Labor Advisors, LLC. They join Chairman Peter Hurtgen,

also serving under a recess appointment, to constitute a Republican majority of three. The fourth member of the NLRB is Wilma Liebman, appointed by President Clinton.
2. 329 NLRB No. 36, slip op. at 1 (1999).
3. Id., slip op. at 5.
4. Id., slip op. at 9 (Hurtgen and Brame, Members, dissenting).

5. The cases that will be considered are: International Sec. Servs., Inc. (29-RC-9730); MV Transp. (33-RD-788); and Aramark School Servs., Inc. (7-RC-22114). The NLRB also granted review in Rubrpumpen, Inc. (17-RM-820), but the employer withdrew its request for review.

6. See, e.g., Windee's Metal Indus., 309 NLRB 1074, 1074 (1992).

7. Members Liebman and Walsh agreed with the regional director's dismissal. Chairman Truesdale and Member Hurtgen found that the union's conduct constituted a present demand for recognition.

8. 329 NLRB No. 50, slip op. at 6 (1999) (Brame, Member, dissenting).

9. 334 NLRB No. 70, slip op. at 8 (2001) (Hurtgen, Chairman, dissenting).

10. 331 NLRB No. 173, slip op. at 21 (2000) (Brame, Member, dissenting).

11. 205 NLRB 250 (1973). Although Hurtgen did not join in the decision of M.B. Sturgis, he later concurred with the ruling. See J. E. Higgins Lumber Co., 332 NLRB No. 109 (2000) (Hurtgen, Member, concurring).

12. 333 NLRB No. 83, slip op. at 2–3 (2001).

13. 333 NLRB No. 77, slip op. at 3 (2001).

14. Id., slip op. at 6.

15. These cases are: Microflect Co. (36-RC-6056); Massey Metals Co. (27-RC-8142); and Laneco Constr. Sys. (15-RC-8311).

16. 268 F.3d at 1100 (citing Weingarten, 420 U.S. at 266).

17. 333 NLRB No. 105, slip op. at 14 (2002).

18. 336 NLRB No. 35, slip op. at 10 (2001).

19. 335 NLRB No. 25, slip op. at 4 (2001).

20. See, e.g., Guardian Indus. Corp. v. NLRB, 49 F.3d 317 (7th Cir. 1995).

21. NLRB v. Steelworkers Union, 357 U.S. 357, 364 (1958).

22. See, e.g., Pratt & Whitney, Cases 12-CA-18446, et al., Advice Memorandum dated Feb. 23, 1998; TU Elec., Case 16-CA-19810, Advice Memorandum dated Oct. 18, 1999; Bureau of National Affairs, Case 5-CA-28860, Advice Memorandum dated Oct. 3, 2000.

23. See, e.g., Bureau of National Affairs, Case 5-CA-28860, Advice Memorandum dated Oct. 3, 2000.

24. For an overview of the tactics engaged in by unions employing a corporate campaign and the Clinton NLRB's refusal to find such tactics unprotected, see generally BE&K Constr. Co., 329 NLRB 717 (1999), enforced, 246 F.3d 619 (6th Cir. 2001), cert. granted in part, U.S. 122 S. Ct. 803, 151 L. Ed. 689 (2002) (petition for writ of certiorari granted limited to the following question: Did the Court of Appeals err in holding that under Bill Johnson's Restaurants, Inc. v. NLRB, 461 U.S. 731 (1983), the NLRB may impose liability on an employer for filing a losing retaliatory lawsuit, even if the employer could show the suit was not objectively baseless under Professional Real Estate Investors, Inc. v. Columbia Pictures Industries, Inc., 508 U.S. 49 (1993)?).

A Direct Defense: Using an Employment Practices Compliance Approach to Avoid Employee Lawsuits

Ken Thrasher, *Employee Relations Law Journal*

Few areas of the law have undergone such upheaval in the recent past as employee relations law. Organizations are confronted with sorting through the complexities of state and federal laws to ensure compliance while implementing policies and procedures to reduce liability risk.

The state of U.S. business is already on shaky ground and the number and complexity of new employment regulations adds confusion and frustration, taking focus away from profitability and productivity. Regulations are changing at such a rapid pace that corporations find it nearly impossible to keep up (Exhibit 1).

The Better Regulation Task Force published a report "Employment Legislation: Striking a Balance," which recommends that more consideration should

EXHIBIT 1: EMPLOYMENT REGULATION TRENDS

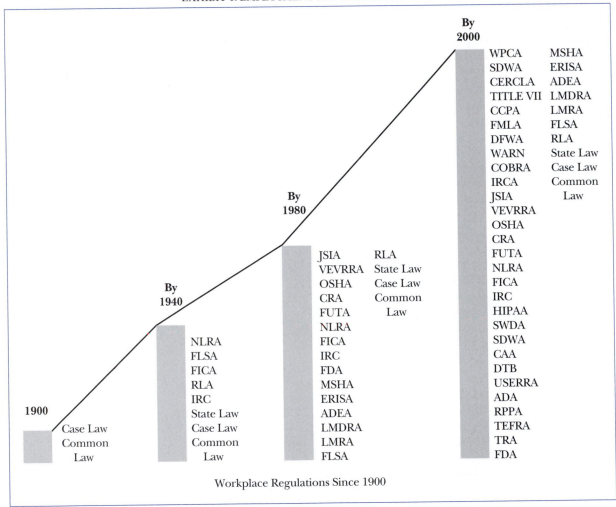

Workplace Regulations Since 1900

Source: NAPEO

be given to regulation alternatives to meet employment policy objectives. The report advises that greater thought must be given to how regulatory pressures on business can be reduced without lessening minimum standards for employees.[1] Employment legislation is particularly tough on small and mid-sized businesses. The red tape and ever changing rules make it next to impossible for companies to meet the demands of regulatory legislation, with already limited labor resources available to manage the workload of administration and tracking alone.

The State of Employment Litigation

Current statistics paint a troubling picture of the frequency and severity of employee lawsuits. Disgruntled workers typically allege discrimination based on sex, disability, age, race or religion; wrongful termination; invasion of privacy; and wrongful demotion or failure to promote. Employment liability claims have risen 400 percent in the past two decades, to the point that an average of 6.5 claims per 1,000 employees are brought annually. In fact,

according to a survey conducted by the Society for Human Resource Management (SHRM), more than 60 percent of all U.S. companies are sued by employees or former employees annually.

According to the 2001 Jury Verdict Research Report, 67 percent of plaintiffs win in trial and 90 percent of the claims brought against employers are settled for an average of $390,000. The remaining 10 percent of claims receive trial awards that average more than $500,000. In addition, the Equal Employment Opportunity Commission reports that 91 percent of all discrimination claims are successfully resolved through consent decrees, settlements, and favorable court orders—all unfavorable to most employers (Exhibit 2).

Moreover, when an employee brings a claim, a company suffers from more than the obvious financial and resource costs. Corporate reputation helps organizations attract and retain the best and brightest recruits. A lawsuit alleging that a company is not living up to its responsibilities for providing a fair workplace environment can damage that company's reputation and their ability to hire top talent. It can

EXHIBIT 2: PLAINTIFF RECOVERY & EPL AWARDS TRENDS

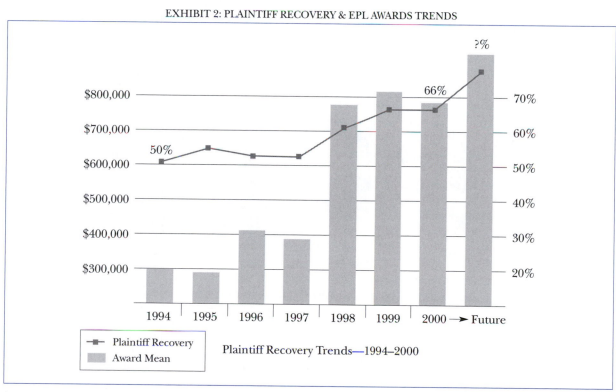

Plaintiff Recovery Trends—1994–2000

Source: Jury Verdict Research Reports 2001

also devastate employee morale. Once morale slips, the effect can snowball, further increasing a firm's vulnerability to lawsuits and regulatory violations.

At the federal level, in the 2002 fiscal year alone, the Department of Labor (DOL) collected a record $143 million in back wages for Fair Labor Standards Act (FLSA) violations. One of the reasons is that the DOL is getting more aggressive in making sure that employers comply with the FLSA. According to U.S. Labor Secretary Elaine L. Chao, "strong enforcement and compliance assistance programs are working to restore wages and protect the rights of workers." In more than a few federal rulings, employers have been required to find ways to engage in interactive efforts with employees to solve potential disputes and set a course for workplace environment where exposure risks are reduced, rather than adhering rigidly to arbitrary employment rules.

At the state level, another long list of hotbed issues have led to increased regulation as well as opportunities for litigation, including the following topics:[2]

- Employment discrimination
- Family and Medical Leave Act
- Privacy issues
- Civil rights issues
- Individual employment rights
- Wages and hours

In particular, litigation in the wage and hour and discrimination arenas inherently tends to result in lawsuits with large financial damages. For example, Starbucks agreed to pay up to $18 million to settle overtime claims alleging that California managers and assistants were not paid accurately. A commercial printer in Pennsylvania paid out more than $610,000 to settle a race discrimination lawsuit, while a major soft drink company disbursed more than $4.2 million to settle multiple discrimination claims. With the potential to reap large dollar damages like these, plaintiffs' lawyers are more likely to spend time and energy on pursuing these types of lawsuits.[3]

Employment Practices Liability Insurance Woes

In the last 10 years, as employers have struggled with escalating claims and expanding settlement and jury awards, insurance costs have also skyrocketed (Exhibit 3). The insurance industry has experienced a monumental shift over the past three years. September 11, the increasing cost of natural disasters, as well as corporate scandals, changed the market from one of low rates and high competition to one of high rates and consolidation. As costs have increased, adequate coverage is more difficult to come by, giving businesses fewer options

EXHIBIT 3: INSURANCE AND LITIGATION TRENDS

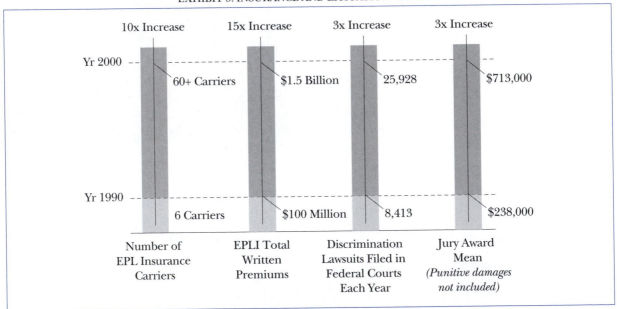

Source: The Batterley Report: EPLI Market Survey 2001; EEOC; U.S. Department of Justice; Jury Verdict Research Report 2001

for transferring their risk. This hard market situation—coupled with the increase in the frequency and severity of employment-related claims and low investment returns in a down economy—means insurers are losing money and corporations are being forced to assume the greater majority of risk exposure. Even companies with clean records are seeing premium increases of 20 to 50 percent. Employers are then faced with painful choices: either pay the increased policy rates or roll the dice, buy less coverage, and assume the risk directly. Avoiding the risk altogether has emerged as the only cost-effective option.[4]

MANAGING THE PAIN: REDUCING RISKS AND GAINING CONTROL

Reducing risk exposure and securing better, more reasonably priced insurance coverage can be accomplished with implementation of an employment practices compliance system (EPCS). While some companies have adopted such programs as a corrective action, many are taking a proactive approach to improve their workplaces before they are scrutinized under new regulations, such as the Sarbanes-Oxley Act, or are exposed to numerous lawsuits.

Companies that demonstrate a strong commitment to corporate values and good business practices to benefit their shareholders and employees can improve corporate culture, not only reducing the frequency of lawsuits but the severity of jury awards. Moreover, implementing an employment practices compliance framework and processes in the work environment can go a long way toward establishing indisputable transparency and accountability for renewed investor confidence.

The unfortunate reality is that traditional risk management tools and services—800 numbers, reference manuals, training seminars, and audits—while important elements to managing employment practice-related risks, are simply not enough to avoid exposure to risk that can result in costly litigation. They are typically employed as individual tools that are disconnected and passive, and have no meaningful connection across the enterprise. Effective risk management should be a pervasive responsibility throughout the organization, not just relegated to overburdened HR staff or general counsel. The greatest downfall of these disconnected tools is their failure to provide any consistent feedback or measurement mechanisms about the level of enterprise-wide compliance.

To address the problems that plague business today at a fundamental level, it is critical for organizations to be able to consistently monitor, quantity, and measure the effectiveness of their company's compliance program. More importantly, they not only need a way to determine if weaknesses exist, but to pinpoint exactly where they exist to take preventive action before an incident occurs. The statistics of increasing litigation and rising insurance rates alone provide evidence that these proactive processes are not taking place often enough in American businesses and organizations today.

Getting to the Heart of Compliance

The lingering question then, is how can employers adequately address employment practices liability risks? Forward-thinking companies have begun to implement EPCS to address their risk problems. As a way to integrate the information and tracking needs of training, human resources, risk management, and legal departments, an EPCS is an interactive, online tool that gives management an effective method of achieving nearly 100 percent workforce compliance.

An EPCS demonstrates a "standard of care" in terms of educating employees about company policies and procedures, such as workplace discrimination, corporate guidelines, sexual harassment, hiring and firing regulations, and so on. Through education, training, and real-time monitoring, a comprehensive compliance process can also act as a risk-management system. It reduces the likelihood that a claim will be made because the company can demonstrate that it has applied fair and consistent practices among all employees, while creating substantiated documentation that is an essential defense against a lawsuit.

Moreover, as a risk reducer, an EPCS can be an antidote to the hardening insurance market. Insurance carriers have already begun to offer better rates and more comprehensive coverage to companies using an EPCS because they see the potential for a positive impact on losses. According to Rick Betterley's October/December 2002 edition of The Betterley Report, "The frequency of claims bothers underwriters more than the ultimate cost of those claims." It stands to reason then that when corporations can reduce the actual number of claims as well as potential for future claims, they become a more desirable client for the insurer. To that end, an EPCS enables companies to provide comprehensive risk data to insurers, who in turn can then perform accurate qualitative analyses of the insured's actual risk levels. The result is enhanced ability to predict risk exposure, thereby enabling insurers to set reasonable policy rates and offer packages that better correspond with the actual needs of the employment practices liability insurance market and their clients.

Reaping the Rewards of Good Faith Efforts

Implementation of an EPCS has already been acknowledged as favorable for corporations in litigation. Recent court decisions have illustrated the corporate imperative for ensuring that employees at all levels in a corporation have been educated about employment laws, regulations, and policies. For example, in Kolstad v. American Dental Association, the U.S. Supreme Court established a defense to an employee's claim for punitive damages in discrimination suits. In the 1999 appeal of this case, the Supreme Court said, "an employer can't always be liable for the acts of its managers."[5] In the case, the justices set aside a lower court decision that said punitive awards were warranted in only the most egregious instances of sexual discrimination. Carole Kolstad's claim was she had been passed over for a key lobbying job for the ADA because she was a woman. In the lower court, a jury agreed she had been a victim of bias and awarded her back pay. But the judge in the case refused to let jurors consider punitive damages, which could have ranged from $50,000 to $300,000.

In 1991, Congress amended Title VII of the Civil Rights Act to allow awards for punitive damages in cases where employers act with "malice or reckless indifference." Kolstad, in her appeal, asked the high court to clarify what that meant.

Writing for the court, Justice Sandra Day O'Connor said the terms "malice" and "reckless" ultimately focus on the actor's state of mind. She added,

> While egregious misconduct is evidence of the requisite mental state . . . (the law) does not limit plaintiffs to this form of evidence, and the section does not require a showing of egregious or outrageous discrimination independent of the employer's state of mind.

The issue of punitive damages in Kolstad's case eventually wound up before the U.S. Court of Appeals for the District of Columbia. In a 6–5 vote, the appellate court said the alleged discrimination against Kolstad wasn't "egregious" enough to merit punitive damages. Only the worst cases of sex discrimination merit such awards, the majority concluded. But Kolstad's attorney, Eric Schnapper, said the appellate court adopted a tougher standard than Congress intended. Kolstad's appeal was backed by the Justice Department. Schnapper said the law envisions a two-pronged test for allowing punitive damages: The plaintiff must prove intentional bias on the part of the company, and must then show the company knew, or should have known, that the discrimination was illegal.

In their ruling, the justices said not all cases of intentional discrimination merit punitive damages, such as when an employer is unaware of relevant federal laws. The court also concluded that an employer is not necessarily liable for discrimination by its managers as long as it is trying to follow the law.

Upon granting certiorari. Justices O'Connor held that: (1) punitive damages could be imposed in Title VII action without showing of egregious or outrageous discrimination, independent of employer's state of mind; (2) the employer must at least discriminate in the face of perceived risk that its actions will violate federal law to be liable for punitive damages in Title VII action; and (3) the employer may not be vicariously liable for discriminatory employment decisions of managerial agents, for purposes of imposing punitive damages, when those decisions are contrary to employer's good-faith efforts to comply with Title VII.[6] Essentially, it is improper for courts to assess large settlements or awards against an employer that undertakes good-faith efforts to comply with employment discrimination laws.

An EPCS can be the company's best and most essential defense against monetary claim damages. Properly implemented, an EPCS will provide a near perfect level of protection against employment lawsuits and demonstrate "good faith efforts" (Exhibit 4). The strategy is two-fold: prevention by raising workforce compliance and understanding levels to near the 100 percent mark, and substantiation through systematic, centralized documentation of compliance activities to unequivocally refute legal challenges and prevent frivolous lawsuits.

While the steps to take in employment practices compliance may make common sense on paper, in

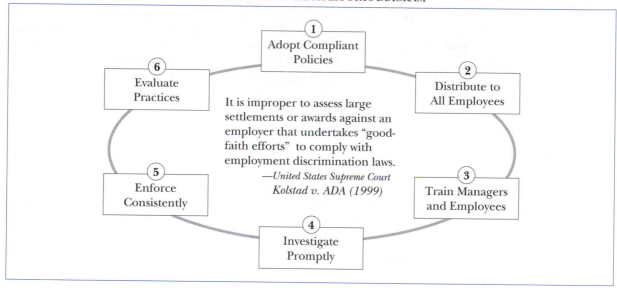

It is improper to assess large settlements or awards against an employer that undertakes "good-faith efforts" to comply with employment discrimination laws.
—*United States Supreme Court Kolstad v. ADA (1999)*

practice it can be difficult to effectively manage and implement this process. For example, as the number of employees rises, so does the complexity of system management. Add multiple national and international locations, new and changing regulations, employee turnover, promotions, and mergers and acquisitions, and it quickly becomes apparent how overwhelming undertaking good faith efforts can be for almost any company.

According to Gartner Group's May 2002 industry study on compliance,[7]

> The bottom line is that compliance is a significant work effort for all enterprises and ad hoc or departmental approaches will provide neither the needed efficiency nor effectiveness desired. Compliance should be viewed as an enterprise-wide process; it should be managed and supported by well-designed processes and appropriate technology.

Enterprise Compliance Management: Process vs. Document

Indeed, to fully understand and maximize enterprise-wide compliance management through an EPCS, it is imperative that risk management and compliance be viewed as processes, not simply documents or documentation. The focus on simply obtaining signatures, while important, misses the point. To truly adopt

practices that serve as counter-measures to litigation and risk reduction, the process needs to be ongoing, becoming an interactive aspect of the corporate culture. Being fully compliant requires going beyond collecting signatures into a pervasive process that engages the entire workforce and spreads accountability and responsibility throughout.

While many companies make huge efforts to implement effective employment practices compliance systems, they often miss the mark and run short of reducing risk exposure. Why? Because they have not seen compliance as an evolving process. Compliance does not have a start or finishing point. It is the result of proactive implementation of sound processes that result in measurable, actionable information. Most current workplace compliance programs are still based on the old rules, often resulting in a disjointed group of independent efforts. This paper-based process no longer produces the level of documentation demanded by courts.

Consider, according to the Gartner Group study,[8] the information associated with compliance tends to be viewed as an unconnected series of discrete activities motivated by specific regulatory requests. It is expected that these activities will be driven by HR personnel. For example, when a new piece of regulatory legislation is passed, the HR department scrambles to find clear information about the change, translate it into policy, then communicate the policy to their employees, and hopefully still find the resources to provide managers with some guidelines for implementing and enforcing the new policies. Once the policy document has been distributed, there is no systematic way to gather data regarding whether employees understand the new policies, which employees might require additional training, or how vulnerable the organization might be to potential claims from employees who state that they were neither made aware of nor understood the new policies.

Currently, there are several informational resources on the Internet that help managers gain up-to-date legal information and templates for translating changes in the law to language suitable for policies. While they may be effective at identifying changes in the law, these models fail to provide a means for trying information together in a coherent way that brings meaning to employees across the enterprise. A recent SHRM legal report states that the only way to ensure healthy best practices (thereby mitigating the threat of lawsuits) is to subscribe to a regular regimen of employment law and practices training for managers and employees.[9]

Traditional risk management programs have also failed to combine the four core elements of an effective compliance program—orientation, training, documentation, and reporting—into one intelligent system, flexible enough to handle almost any area of risk exposure while also complying with virtually any regulatory requirement. The key to achieving total corporate compliance, however, is the inherent combination of these four elements, which is the ability to monitor each employee's compliance activity to produce measurable, actionable information about an organization's compliance program.

To achieve total corporate compliance, organizations must move away from the "document-centric" model that places HR administrators or general counsel in a "compliance watchdog" role, and instead adopt compliance as a comprehensive system that involves all stakeholders within the corporation. "To be effective, compliance programs must be smoothly integrated into day-to-day operations," said Larry Butler, former vice president of human resources for PeopleSoft. "If such programs are perceived as 'compliance-specific,' people will respond in a negative way, as most view compliance as a painful process."

The Gartner Group recommends organizations adopt an EPCS where compliance-related content is available in an online environment, taking advantage of integrated technologies to manage an electronic workflow process. To be effective, the system must orient employees to changing policies or corporate procedures, train and assess comprehension of those policies, document all interactions systematically to reduce the level of exposure to claims, and report on exceptions to enable appropriate, preventative action to be taken.

To that end, an EPCS can create a benchmark for current levels of risk exposure. A fully implemented EPCS is dynamic, changing as an organization changes to accommodate the needs of its employees, current market conditions and regulatory requirements.

An EPCS can serve as the first line of defense against frivolous lawsuits. When such a system is in place, organizations gain peace of mind knowing that areas of greatest concern—harassment and discrimination—are being addressed throughout the organization. And, because the company can demonstrate that it has applied fair and consistent practices among all employees, an EPCS reflects the "good faith efforts" that, as we have discussed, have been shown to reduce the severity of claims awards.

While corporate governance has not been our focus in this discussion, it merits mention, given the new landscape for shareholder claims in light of corporate wrongdoing. The inherent process created by an EPCS is a natural demonstration of ethical operations, demonstrating accountability and transparency. In so doing, it fosters an environment of mutual trust between the company and its stakeholders—both internally and externally. It moves corporate standards and practices above board and promotes flexibility to meet evolving state and federal regulations, as well as stakeholder demands. An EPCS becomes a platform of proof if any questions should arise about corporate conduct, policies, and procedures.

A New Compliance Notion at Work

Qsent, a technology company focusing on applications for real-time contact information located in Portland, Oregon, recently adopted new EPCS technology. For Frank Garbayo, the company's senior vice president of human resources, the system promises relief from the masses of paper that have traditionally accompanied the compliance process.

"Our compliance philosophy is straightforward," explained Garbayo. "We want to do the right thing by our employees, and by doing the right thing, we'll be in compliance. The employee practices compliance system provides a framework for controlling the compliance-related paper that's a natural by-product of the compliance process."

Using Qsent as an example, the system works like this: attorneys at the EPCS provider monitor Oregon state and federal employment law for changes that impact companies like Qsent. When a change is mandated, Qsent's HR department is alerted of the change by the EPCS. They are then provided with a package of integrated information that includes an explanation of the change in law in layman's terms; how it affects the company, suggested new policy, supervisory guidelines, FAQs, relevant forms, and training assessments.

Once Qsent managers review and approve the policy language, all employees are notified of the new policy via e-mail, and provided with training assessment materials to measure employee comprehension. Employees acknowledge their understanding of the new policy via a secure, third party website. In addition to the general policy notification, supervisors receive guidelines for implementing the policy, so they know how to help employees understand what the new policy really means to them as individuals. The system also provides an automated tracking process that enables Garbayo and his staff to efficiently follow-up with employees who have not acknowledged the policy change.

Perhaps most significantly, Qsent can capture all system interactions, including training scores, in a central electronic repository through each step of the compliance process. From this repository, they can easily assess how well each employee understands the new policy and which employees may benefit from further training by running quick reports of real-time information. Flexible reporting capabilities pinpoint potential areas of weakness so they can be addressed prior to an incident or provide the means to defend against frivolous lawsuits should an incident occur.

For Kimberly Sullenger, director of finance and administration at Pixion, a Pleasanton, California–based provider of hosted and installed Web-conferencing products, using a Web-based compliance system has lowered legal bills and reduced administrative redundancies. "If a compliance-related issue came up in the past, I'd reach for the phone to call our attorneys," Sullenger noted. "Now, I can become better informed before calling them by reviewing the law in relation to our policies and guidelines through the Web site our provider built for us. In the past, I've also used Lawroom.com

to keep up to date on developments in the law. Since we've adopted a comprehensive EPCS that is customized for out industry, I can go to one place to stay current with regulations and then immediately distribute information and track compliance activities."

Realizing the Benefits

Concerns about compliance practices have taken on greater significance as the workplace becomes ever more litigious, the insurance market hardens, and as shareholders demand accountability and transparency from companies. "Most employers have compliance concerns looming large in the back of their minds. They come to us asking for guidance about how to put themselves in a better position to ward off potential damages," said Patrice D. Altenhofen, an attorney and director of human resource development services for Cascade Employers Association of Salem, Oregon.

In our efforts to address those concerns and provide businesses with practical support, we've come to believe in the power of employment practices compliance systems. From an exposure standpoint alone it gives workforce managers a cost-effective means to provide employees with regulatory and policy information that in the end will protect companies from lawsuits.

This discussion has shown the incredible value an EPCS can provide for managing employment practices–related claims. In the end, the entire workplace is improved; expansion of interdepartmental collaboration, the potential for reductions in insurance costs, increased worker morale and productivity, consistency in corporate governance and regulatory compliance, and reinvigorated shareholder confidence.

Most importantly, because every employee truly understands company policies and procedures and associated documentation is clear, an EPCS enables organizations to reduce the frequency and severity of employee claims, while minimizing unpredictability of risk exposure to obtain quality insurance coverage and reasonable rates. At a time when risk transference is no longer a viable option, companies must focus on avoiding risk. An EPCS is the most effective tool an organization can employ to accomplish this formidable task.

Source:

Endnotes

1. Armstrong, Geoff, Director. July 2002.
2. HR Focus, May 2002.
3. AHI's Employment Law Resource Center, available at www.ahipubs.com.
4. Id.
5. Ritter, Scott, "High Court Makes Punitive Damages Easier In Sex-Bias Suits," The Wall Street Journal, June 22, 1999.
6. 527 U.S. 526 (1999).
7. Harris, K. and Logan, D. "Compliance is Not a Document, It's a Process," Gartner Group 2002.
8. Id.
9. Turner, W. Kirk and Thrutchley, Christopher S. "Employment Law and Practices Training: No Longer The Exception—It's the Rule," SHRM Legal Report, July/August 2002.

Embracing the Future: Union Strategies for the 21st Century

Peter Lazes and Jane Savage, *The Journal for Quality and Participation*

"If we hadn't engaged with management in a restructuring process on the shopfloor in the way that we did, we would not have had the [necessary] information, nor developed a relationship with management in order to save the plant."

Mike Cavanaugh
International Representative, UNITE!

Since the 1960s, we have seen union membership continue to decline in the United States. U.S. companies continue to aggressively practice strategies that result in replacing workers with technology or, taking advantage of lower-cost labor markets, moving jobs offshore. Labor laws, long outdated, make it difficult for unions to organize. And in recent years, worker attitudes and interests have changed significantly. While many seek a living wage, others are no longer content with merely decent wages and working conditions—if in fact they do have such conditions. As the Boeing strike illustrated in 1999, today's workers want a greater voice in workplace decision making.

Such trends fundamentally challenge traditional unionism. Workers still turn to unions when they are treated unfairly, but they rarely recognize the union's role in giving them a voice for greater workplace control and employment security.

Hathaway Shirt Company: Expanding the Union's Tool Kit

In 1994, the Union for Needletrades, Industrial, and Technical Employees (UNITE!) established an unusual project with Hathaway Shirt Company at its plant in Waterville, Maine. The Waterville plant was the company's only domestic factory, employing more than 400 employees. Hathaway owned two additional plants, one in Canada and the other in Honduras. This project, initiated by the union, was established to find ways to keep the well-known shirt company profitable and to maintain employment for the current union-represented workforce. The project was particularly important to UNITE!, as during the previous decade most domestic unionized men's shirt companies had either closed their doors or moved production entirely offshore, thus causing significant job losses within the industry.

After several months of meetings between corporate management and the union, an agreement was negotiated that established specific shopfloor activities to increase profitability and maintain and/or increase current employment levels in the Waterville plant. The specific objectives of the agreement were to engage workers and managers in a process to redesign the shopfloor; improve the flow of work in the plant; retrain workers; upgrade cutting and stitching equipment; develop better systems for cutting shirts; and work with suppliers to improve the quality of raw material.

All proposals and changes were developed by worker/management design teams. These groups received assistance from the company, external consultants, the union's engineering department, and the union's regional international representative. Within six months, the teams made significant improvements in quality and throughput time. The morale of both labor and management improved as well.

A review of the initial work and the plant's financial performance, however, found that shopfloor activities alone were not sufficient to keep the company solvent or to meet either of the two primary strategic alliance goals: profitability and job stability/growth. The company needed to make major strategic changes. The quality of shirt design, product placement, and marketing of the Hathaway Shirt brand, for example, were identified as significant problems. In addition, retailers were requesting better coordination and communication coupled with a faster order response time. The company needed a low inventory/quick response capability. While these "beyond the shopfloor" changes were not anticipated during the earlier stage of the joint labor-management work, they would be critical to regaining the company's profitability.

Furthermore, research conducted at Harvard University's Center for Textile and Apparel Research confirmed that changes in manufacturing strategies, such as better control of inventory between the plant and the retailer, and maintaining a broader product mix, would be necessary to remain competitive.

Following this review, the company and union reached a second agreement. They immediately focused to improve communications between the plant and retailers, improve response time on orders, make changes in the design of the shirt, and continue the redesign of the shopfloor that was already in progress. Both parties viewed these activities as crucial to the plant's viability and future jobs.

Working with management in these new areas expanded UNITE!'s role and led the union into uncharted territory. The initiation of the shopfloor projects had been difficult enough for the local executive board and members, as they lacked both experience and confidence. With coaching and education, the local executive board and stewards gradually developed the capacity to understand and participate in shopfloor projects. By the time the need for a more strategic focus emerged, the union was prepared and more confident about assuming leadership. Meanwhile, from the inception of the joint work, the president of UNITE! continued to meet regularly with the president of the Hathaway Shirt Company to discuss the project as well as business conditions and obstacles to its progress. When appropriate, the president of Hathaway was approached to open doors to specific departments, making sure that design teams would gain access to the technical and financial resources they needed.

"We cut the cost of production work in half. It was not a question of 'Can it be turned around?' We just did it."

Neena Quirton
Chief Steward, Local 486

After two years of hard work, Hathaway's parent company, Warnaco, decided to sell the Hathaway Shirt division. This decision created a crisis for the plant, because the sale of the division foreshadowed the plant's closing. UNITE! became proactive and assertive, and secured the services of a union-friendly buy-out firm. At the same time, UNITE! organized a national political and media campaign to save the Hathaway Shirt brand and the Waterville manufacturing facility.

After several months spent approaching potential buyers and venture capital funds, a buy-out package was completed. Three prominent businessmen in Maine, including the ex-governor, finally bought the company and took control of operating responsibilities for the Waterville plant. This buy-out plan included provisions to honor the union contract, to continue investing in restructuring activities on the shopfloor, and to work strategically with retailers. As a result of these initiatives and its new ownership, the company is profitable for the first time in over a decade. The number of unionized employees now working at the Waterville plant has increased; the company reversed its outsourcing practice as a result of expanding its sewing department. In addition, the local union is more active in the plant and in the Waterville community.

"Hathaway meant everything to Waterville. There isn't a family who hasn't had a Hathaway employee."

Ruth Joseph
Mayor of Waterville, Maine

A New Union Approach

In our changing economy, negotiating pay, benefits, and basic working rights is not enough to sustain or grow a union and many recognize this.

Unions are experimenting with the following strategies to ensure their place in the 21st century (see figure on next page).

1) **Education and retraining.**
   Creating greater education opportunities for workers has long been an important priority for many unions. With the continuous advances in technology today, it has become even more urgent that employees gain new skills and keep abreast of progress in their field.

   Many unions recognize that promoting and maintaining a knowledge-based workforce is a

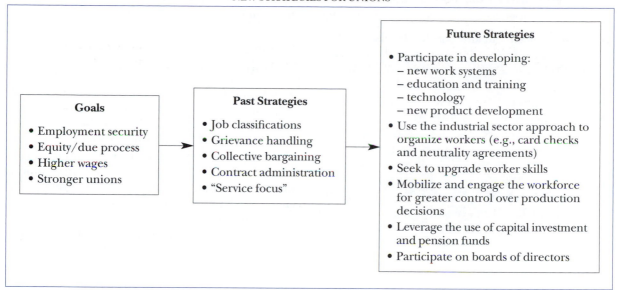

critical strategy for economic development and employment security. Most recently, in New York City, the Health and Human Service Union (1199/SEIU) has applied political pressure to obtain both state and federal funds for the re-training of health care workers, as their industry shifts from acute care to ambulatory and community care settings.

Currently the AFL-CIO's Working for America Institute is focused exclusively on:

- increasing worker-centered employment and training
- establishing ways to give workers more of a strategic voice in labor market decisions as a result of sector- and regionally focused activities; and fostering the development of joint activities with unions, community allies, and business groups to develop better and sustainable jobs in our fast-changing global economy.

In various countries abroad, including Norway and Ireland, unions are developing national agreements that provide for lifelong learning for all workers, not just those at risk.

2) Research and development.

Some unions are working with companies to improve and develop new products and services, an area generally left to the sole discretion of management. In addition to UNITE! at the Hathaway Shirt Company, the UAW/Saturn Cor-

poration and SEIU/KaiserPermanente Health Care System have adopted this strategy. In these situations, union involvement in research and business or product development has positively influenced services and marketing strategies. In all three of these cases, market share and sales volumes increased as a result of the union's involvement.

A similar strategy is currently emerging in New York City and Los Angeles, where hospital workers are involved in projects such as consolidating and redesigning laboratories and developing approaches to transition facilities from acute care to ambulatory care.

3) A voice in strategic management decision making and ownership.

Many unions are becoming more familiar with technology, market needs, and production methods within the industries they organize. This will allow them to actively participate in decisions that affect industry competitiveness where employees are organized. As UNITE! did at Hathaway, unions can counter the outsourcing trend by leveraging the knowledge and skills of the workforce to obtain a voice in both shopfloor and strategic decisions. This strategy could also include placing union representatives on plant management teams as well as on the board of directors of firms. The potential for employee stock ownership might also become an important strategy to increase the union's voice in plant and company decisions.

4) Capital investment and pension funds.

There is a growing interest in finding ways to creatively use employee pension-fund monies to achieve union interests. Such funds have helped finance new building and construction projects, which in turn are required to use unionized workers. A similar strategy leverages bonds and uses other financial tools to help fund the modernization of unionized companies, enabling them to restructure to keep up with the changing marketplace. Admittedly, significant Taft-Hartley issues can arise with such work. There is a growing understanding among many unions and the AFL-CIO, however, that pension funds could be better used to support companies in ways that support the growth of unions, rather than leaving such funds solely to serve the needs of other corporate stockholders.

5) Industrial sector approach.

This approach has been less developed in the United States but is more common in Australia, Ireland, and Norway. In these countries, projects are being organized around sectors such as food processing, nursing homes, and shipbuilding. Multiple unions have come together with employers to help coordinate training, education, marketing, technology, and the sharing of consulting resources to redesign companies.

In industrial-sector projects, unions have gained a broader understanding of significant changes that are taking place within an industry. These trends are less apparent when work is focused solely within a plant or even a company. As a result, unions can focus action on core strategic problems, rather than merely react to the symptoms arising at individual companies or plants.

One of the primary advantages to this strategy is that the union, by demonstrating its value added to management, can position itself to organize new workers in that industry using card checks, neutrality agreements, etc.

Pursuing this strategy, however, requires that unions build their own industry expertise. Although unions such as UNITE! and the UAW have had long-standing arrangements to obtain technical assistance and research from technical specialists and universities, these activities will need to be expanded and coordinated more aggressively within industrial sectors.

Initiating Nontraditional Strategies

Getting union staff, leaders, and members to support nontraditional strategies is tough work and not to be underestimated. Although these strategies can be positioned to save jobs (and this surely is an important outcome of much nontraditional work with management), it is important that unions embrace a broader approach or vision if they are to rebuild their positive influence and power in both workplaces and society.

Education is key—particularly education that builds awareness of economic and other "external" challenges. Whether it is the effects of managed care on hospital workers or the way the old Big Three auto companies demand cost reductions from their suppliers each year, union members need to be aware of—and ready to act upon—the external factors that affect their work environment.

In addition to understanding the big picture, unions need to have the specific knowledge necessary to contribute substantively to the topic at hand. Alternatively, they should have access to researchers or technical specialists who can provide such knowledge, whether the issue is how to streamline the manufacture of seat belts or how to provide better health care in an outpatient setting.

For these strategies to meet union-oriented ends, unions will need to develop an effective process for communicating with their members and involving them in changes. Union members—not just their representatives—must have a role in decisions that affect the workplace. Also, union representatives must prepare in advance for meetings with management by meeting with members and taking other steps to ensure that they are accurately representing the long-term concerns of the workers who might be affected by specific changes.

Finally, unions need a clear agenda for change, and "union building" from and with their members. While many unions have begun to experiment with the nontraditional union strategies outlined, they often neglect to identify an independent union agenda. Clarifying the needs and concerns of members and of the union as an organization is a critical step in the union-building process (see sidebar next page).

Unions should ask themselves the following questions as they consider new approaches to the challenges they face.

1) What do we need and expect to gain from initiatives with management?

2) How can shopfloor and strategic efforts be directly linked to the interests of the union and its members?

3) Will we be able to gain more influence and a greater role in decision making as a result of direct project work with management?

4) How can our membership grow at the facility and in the industrial sector as a result of participation?

5) Will more members have opportunities for training? Enhanced job responsibilities? Advancement?

6) Will involvement in such initiatives enable us to attract and organize new members or influence employers to make it less cumbersome for employees to become union members, such as allowing for card checks and neutrality for organizing new members?

7) Will workers view a particular strategy as providing them with greater opportunities for skill training, advancement, and employment security?

The challenges in a global and increasingly knowledge- and automated technology-based economy often do not yield to traditional union actions. Strategies such as collective bargaining and facility-based strikes or walk outs can be too slow or narrowly focused to achieve complex objectives. For example, collective bargaining alone, with implementation left to management, does not ensure that workers displaced by a cost-saving technology are retrained and employed in value-added work. To turn the tide from outsourcing and de-skilling toward a higher road, a strong, reoriented labor movement with a broader vision is needed.

Unions have much at stake as they move into the 21st century. To remain vital and relevant, unions will need to develop multi-level activities and make use of new skills. Linking the success of productivity projects to worker involvement as a way to obtain good wages, benefits, and working conditions will also help to organize the unorganized and increase the strength of the unions as an advocate for workers in society. By preparing for change and developing a flexible approach to today's swiftly moving marketplace, unions will be able to successfully confront the challenges that lie ahead.

Source: *Journal for Quality and Participation* by Lazes and Savage. Copyright © 2000 by the Association for Quality and Participation. Reprinted with permission of the Association for Quality and Participation in the format Textbook via Copyright Clearance Center.

CHAPTER

13

EMPLOYEE SEPARATION

Information technology (IT) is one of the most difficult areas for organizations to staff. The short supply of trained, experienced workers coupled with increasingly strong demand has presented almost limitless career opportunities for IT professionals. Most large organizations experience annual turnover in the 20 percent range. Kraft Foods, however, has developed a retention program that has resulted in the reduction of the turnover rate of its nearly 1,000 full-time IT professionals to a staggering 5 percent.

The program involved Kraft's chief information officer (CIO) partnering with HR to help HR understand the unique challenges being faced by IT. Kraft's retention program involves more than just the standard attractive stock options; it involves a holistic and integrated set of HR programs. Many of Kraft's IT professionals have come directly from its college internship program. Interns are given early responsibility for learning different technologies and are held accountable for rigorous performance outcomes early on. Seventy percent of IT interns who are offered permanent jobs accept.

Once hired on a permanent basis, employees are expected to engage in an objectives-based management system. Managers are specially trained to provide ongoing feedback and conduct developmental performance feedback sessions. Employees are allowed to pursue one of two career tracks within IT: technical or managerial. To assist

with development, an intranet site provides learning tutorials, links to job postings, formal training courses, and both division and functional area Web sites that discuss competencies required in these areas. Consequently, employees are allowed to develop a plan for career development within Kraft. IT employees are further encouraged to devote ten working days per year exclusively to career development pursuits. In addition to in-house development opportunities, a tuition reimbursement plan is offered for outside programs of study.

Employees also become part of the IT Leadership Program, where junior employees are paired with an executive mentor. The one-year program involves about 30 days of joint work activities and provides additional exposure to leadership and technology issues.

Probably most important, IT employees at Kraft note the top reason they stay is the sense of family they find at work. Ideas are solicited and accepted from every level in the organization, and inclusion is a strong company value. Kraft also understands the needs of its younger workers who populate the IT division. It offers flexible hours, telecommuting and part-time work options, a casual dress code, and a new campus that includes a company store and an on-site health club.

Source: Melymuka, K. "Kraft's 5% Solution," *Computerworld*, 32, (44): Nov. 2, 1998, pp. 69–71.

Organizations can expect continuing pressure to change and adapt. Societal changes affecting lifestyles, technology, and the economy create threats and opportunities for nearly all organizations. The organization of yesterday that was able to serve the same customers in the same markets, use the same production technology, and operate in a relatively stable domestic economic landscape no longer exists. Profitable markets invite entry of new competitors; technological changes in production impact efficiency; lifestyle changes alter preferences for certain types of products and services; and economic decisions must be made within a global context.

Contemporary organizations that wish to remain competitive need to be flexible and responsive to their environments. These organizations must develop ways to deal with increasing skill obsolescence among their employees and the labor market in general; they must also consider alternative forms of organization structure due to downsizing operations, selling off subsidiaries, and merger and acquisition options. From an HR perspective, this often involves employee training and development. In an increasing number of scenarios, however, the organization must strategically analyze its workforce and objectives and make decisions to sever relationships with employees. Similarly, employees today spend less time with individual employers than workers did in the past and make a greater number of career changes during their working years. Personal lifestyle decisions, opportunities with other organizations, and entrepreneurial motivations are causing many employees to leave their organizations.

The pressure to remain competitive and efficient, coupled with the fact that employees are less committed to individual employers than in the past, makes the process of employee separation a key strategic issue for organizations. An effective HR strategy involves managing the process by which employees leave the organization, regardless of whether such departure is by the employer's or employee's choice. Organizations can manage this separation process to ensure that transitions are smooth for both employers and employees, that operations are not disrupted, and that important professional relationships are not damaged. The three major ways that employees leave the organization are through reductions in force (initiated by the employer), turnover (initiated by either the employer or employee), or retirement. Organizations should have strategies for managing each form of separation.

REDUCTIONS IN FORCE

Reductions in force or employee layoffs are attempts by employers to reconfigure their workforces. Reductions in force are becoming increasingly common in nearly all industries and are often caused by organizational restructuring following merger or acquisition activity. A reduction in force is sometimes used to make an organization more competitive by reducing costs.

Organizations reduce the size of their workforces for three main reasons: inefficiency, lack of adaptability in the marketplace, and a weakened competitive position within the industry. In all regards, efficiency is a major driving force: In many organizations, labor or payroll is one of the largest expenses. This is particularly true in service organizations, which are making up an increasingly significant portion of our economy and gross national product (GNP). Efficiency is sought by attempting to reduce labor costs and accomplishing more work with fewer individuals by redesigning work processes. Interestingly, an organization's stock price often sky-rockets when layoffs are announced. Such decisions create expectations among investors of improved short-term financial performance.

One federal law regulates employer actions taken as part of reductions in force. The Worker Adjustment Retraining and Notification Act (WARN) went into effect in 1989 and requires employers with 100 or more employees to provide affected employees with a minimum of 60 days' written notice of any facility closings or large-scale layoffs of 50 or more employees. WARN does not apply to federal, state, or local government agencies. Employers found to be in violation of the law can be required to provide back pay, expenses, and benefits to all workers dismissed without appropriate notice in addition to fines.

Employers who conduct layoffs often provide affected employees with 60 days' notice and immediately relieve them of their job duties. The employees remain on the payroll for two months but are able to use the two-month period to adjust, seek new employment, and transition out of the organization. This not only assists the employee in his or her transition and job search, but it also helps to ensure that laid-off employees will be less likely to file for unemployment compensation insurance. State unemployment compensation insurance programs are funded by employers, with the percentage rate determined by the use of the funds by the employers' former employees. An employer who lays off a large number of employees who file for and collect unemployment compensation will have to reimburse the compensation insurance program proportionately.

To facilitate the transition (and ensure that their unemployment insurance payments remain lower), many organizations implement outplacement programs for laid-off employees. Outplacement services, which may be conducted in-house or contracted to an external vendor, assist not only with helping laid-off employees land on their feet but also serve as a public relations tool: These services help to retain the support and goodwill of remaining employees by making them feel that the organization will look out for them if future reductions are necessary. In addition to helping maintain the morale and motivation of remaining employees, outplacement programs reduce the risk of litigation by disgruntled former employees.

Realizing that in certain circumstances it might be unrealistic, impossible, or unfair to require employers to provide such written notification, Congress allowed several exceptions to WARN. These exceptions are for (1) a "faltering company" that is actively seeking capital to retain its scope of operations and reasonably believes that giving employees warning will jeopardize the financing, (2) an "unforeseeable circumstance," such as a strike at a supplier's business, (3) a natural disaster, such as a fire, flood, earthquake, or hurricane, and (4) any operation set up as a "temporary facility," where employees who were hired were informed that the facility and employment were nonpermanent.

Layoffs can sometimes be avoided through proper planning. The main benefit of strategic human resource planning is to ensure that supply and demand of employees are equated while avoiding the costs associated with severe overstaffing and understaffing. Effective human resource planning in most instances can reduce or eliminate the need for any kind of large-scale reductions in force or layoffs. Regardless of the size of the surplus, employers must identify the real reason for the excess number to determine an appropriate response. This strategic perspective determines whether the surplus is expected to be temporary or permanent in order to assist in developing a plan of action with a corresponding time frame. For example, longer-range surpluses can often be managed without the need for layoffs by utilizing hiring freezes, not replacing departing employees, offering early retirement incentives, and through cross-training of certain employees to allow them to develop skills that the organization anticipates needing. Short-run surpluses can be managed through loaning or subcontracting employees, offering voluntary leaves, implementing across-the-board salary reductions, or redeploying workers to other functions, sites, or units.

Two more policy-oriented solutions to remedy overstaffing might involve (1) tying a greater portion of compensation to division or organization performance and/or (2) regularly staffing the organization at less than 100 percent and making up the difference with temporary employees or offering overtime. The former strategy creates a flexible or variable pay plan to control costs because payroll expenses are directly related to the organization's profitability. Therefore, overstaffing is somewhat less of a concern. The latter strategy creates a flexible or variable workforce that can be expanded or contracted to meet business needs and conditions. These strategies are summarized in Exhibit 13-1.

As part of any layoff plan, the organization also needs to develop an appropriate strategy for managing the survivors. A key management challenge that is often overlooked is ensuring that the retained employees can adjust to the changes. It should not be assumed that these individuals will automatically be relieved (and thrilled) to have retained their jobs during the layoff and will still be motivated and productive. These individuals may feel less secure about the jobs they have retained; be asked to perform more work than previously without a corresponding increase in pay; have lost long-term friends and coworkers; and may have damaged morale and fear that they are vulnerable to future layoffs. Consequently, they may be less loyal to the employer and have strong incentives to leave the organization. The organization needs a separate strategy in addition to its layoff strategy to ensure that these retained employees remain committed, loyal, high performers. Retention of these employees and their level of productivity will probably determine whether the organization will survive. Ironically, downsizing organizations often ignore this critical fact and assume that retained workers will be happy to still have their positions and work harder than ever. Reality has shown that nothing could be farther from the truth.

Layoffs at Kodak

A critical component of the successful outcome of any layoff is the manner in which the survivors are managed. Rochester, New York–based Kodak actually had its surviving employees defend the organization's decision to lay off colleagues to the media during recent job cuts. When Kodak decided it needed to lay off 3,500 employees worldwide, it immediately considered how this decision would impact not only the employees being cut but those who were staying. One key to the positive response to the layoffs was the man-

EXHIBIT 13-1: STRATEGIES FOR MANAGING EMPLOYEE SURPLUSES AND AVOIDING LAYOFFS

Long Run	Short Run	Policy
• Hiring freezes • Attrition • Offer early retirement incentives • Cross-training of employees	• Loaning or subcontracting labor • Voluntary leaves • Across-the-board salary reductions • Redeploying employees	• Greater percentage of compensation tied to performance • Staff at less than 100%

ner in which communications were handled. To help minimize uncertainty and anxiety, complete and honest information was provided to employees as soon as it was available. Employees were informed that details had not been worked out yet, but that the downsizing was not temporary and would affect only certain, specified parts of the organization. A range of services was provided to those employees being let go, including a termination allowance of two weeks' pay for each year of employment; retained medical, dental, and life insurance for four months; outplacement counseling; and a retraining allowance of up to $5,000 for schooling. By strategically planning and implementing the layoffs, Kodak was able to enjoy, the continued support of its remaining employees and customers.[1]

TURNOVER

Employees who leave the organization at the organization's request (involuntary turnover) as well as those who leave on their own initiative (voluntary turnover) can cause disruptions in operations, work team dynamics, and unit performance. Both types of turnover create costs for the organization. In some cases, these costs may be short term but have longer-term benefits; in other cases, the costs may be significant and longer lasting. Costs of turnover include the direct economic costs of staffing and training new hires as well as the indirect costs of the downtime needed for the new employee to gain proficiency in his or her job and to become fully socialized and integrated into the organization. In addition, those responsible for training the new employee are pulled away from their regular job responsibilities. If an organization has made significant investment in training and developing its employees, that investment is lost when employees leave. Excessive turnover can also impact the morale of employees and the organization's reputation as being a good place to work, which makes retention and recruitment more challenging and time-consuming.

The economic costs of turnover can be staggering. In Chapter 8, it was noted that one technology company calculated turnover costs to average $200,000 per employee.[2] Merck and Company, the pharmaceutical giant, has estimated that its turnover costs are between 150 percent and 250 percent of the employee's annual salary.[3] Sears, Roebuck estimated that turnover among its retail sales staff amounted to $110 million annually, which constituted 17 percent of its operating income.[4] Sears also found a strong negative correlation between employee turnover and customer satisfaction. Merck and Sears are not alone; most large employers suffer from excessive turnover costs. A recent survey found that at companies with more than 1,000 employees, annual voluntary resignations averaged 21 percent.[5] For employers with more than 5,000 employees, the rate climbed to 26 percent.

Turnover can, however, be beneficial. It can allow the organization to hire new employees with more current training who are not locked into existing ways of doing things. Fresh ideas from outsiders can be critical to organizations that have become stagnant and are in need of innovation. Turnover can also lower the average tenure of employees and translate into lower payroll expenses. Turnover also affords opportunities to promote talented, high performers. Finally, when poor performers or disruptive employees leave the organization, morale can improve among coworkers.

It may be assumed that voluntary turnover generally provides more costs than benefits and that involuntary turnover is beneficial for the organization from a cost perspective. Both of these assumptions are often false. First, voluntary turnover may allow the organization to find an even better performer than the employee who left, possibly at a lower salary. Second, involuntary turnover often results in much higher costs than training or counseling an employee with performance deficiencies.

Both voluntary and involuntary turnover can be managed strategically to allow the organization to maximize the benefits of turnover and minimize the costs incurred with the process. Exhibit 13-2 presents a Performance-Replaceability Strategy Matrix that was developed by Martin and Bartol as a tool to allow organizations to manage turnover strategically.[6] The model on which this matrix is based argues that turnover in organizations, while unavoidable, can be strategically managed to allow organizations to minimize the disadvantages of turnover and maximize its advantages.

Martin and Bartol have classified turnover as being functional (beneficial) or dysfunctional (problematic) for an organization. Whether turnover is functional or dysfunctional depends on two factors: the individual employee's performance level and the difficulty the organization would have replacing the individual. In Exhibit 13-2, replaceability is depicted on the X axis and performance level on the Y axis. Each of the six cells is then classified as resulting in functional or dysfunctional turnover, and appropriate strategies for managing employees who fit into each of the cells are provided. Clearly, the more dysfunctional the turnover, the greater the attention that will be required by management to retain the employee. Retention strategies for such employees might involve additional career development opportunities, incentive compensation that rewards high performance, or innovative benefits that are tailored to the needs of the employee. Regardless of the performance level, backups should be developed by the organization for any employees who would be difficult to replace. Ideally, the strategy for managing turnover involves keeping high performers rewarded through innovative compensation and recognition and reward programs while engaging in human resource

EXHIBIT 13-2: THE PERFORMANCE-REPLACEABILITY STRATEGY MATRIX

		REPLACEABILITY	
		Difficult	Easy
PERFORMANCE	High	High performers—difficult to replace Highly Dysfunctional Turnover Retain/invest in employee: develop backups	High performers—easy to replace Dysfunctional Turnover Retain/invest in employee
	Average	Average performers—difficult to replace Dysfunctional Turnover Retain/provide performance incentives: develop backup	Average performers—easy to replace Dysfunctional Turnover if Replacement Costs Are High Retain/provide performance incentives
	Low	Poor performers—difficult to replace Short-Term Dysfunctional/Long-Term Functional Turnover Improve performance or terminate: develop backup	Poor performers—easy to replace Functional Turnover Improve performance or terminate

Adapted from Martin, David C. and Bartol, Kathryn M. "Managing Turnover Strategically," *Personal Administrator*, Volume 30, #11, November 1985, p. 63.

planning to ensure that as few employees as possible occupy positions that will make them difficult to replace. ▼

Exhibit 13-3 presents the eventual outcomes of a successfully managed employee turnover and retention program. All employees whose turnover would be disruptive would be reclassified as easy to replace once appropriate backups had been trained. At the same time, performance incentives and counseling should be provided to low performers to encourage and motivate them to become average performers. Similar incentives should be provided to average performers to encourage and motivate them to become high performers. If these lower performers do not improve in time, they should be terminated.

In cases of involuntary turnover or termination, employers need to have a strategy and standard policy that if followed would allow the employer to defend a charge of wrongful termination. In recent years, courts have been increasingly open to hearing complaints that an employer violated the public policy exception to employment at will, discussed in Chapter 7. Although there may be no legal responsibility to continue to employ individuals, many courts have found that employers have an ethical responsibility to discharge employees only for just cause. Consequently, employers who discharge their employees should have strong evidence of just cause that has been documented and communicated to the employee over time. Otherwise, the employer could incur significant costs in defending itself against the charges or face negative publicity and dissension among the ranks of its employees. The Martin and Bartol model argues that the organization's goal should not necessarily be to reduce all turnover but to reduce dysfunctional turnover by developing appropriate human resource programs and policies.

EXHIBIT 13-3: STRATEGIC MANAGEMENT OF TURNOVER AND RETENTION

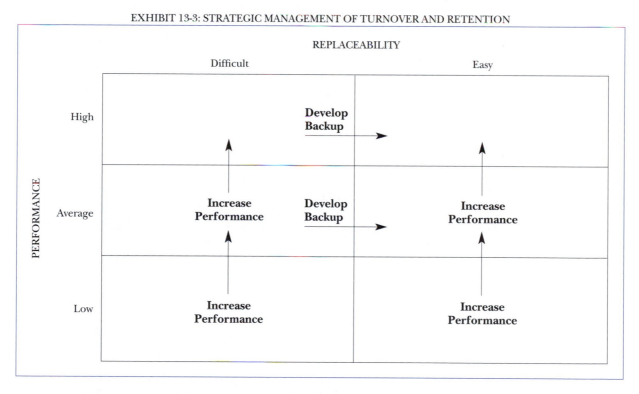

▶ Reading 13.1, "Holding On to High Performers: A Strategic Approach to Retention," describes some strategies used by organizations to ensure the retention of high-performing employees.

Managing Retention at Sprint PCS

In the early 2000s, Sprint PCS, a provider of consumer cellular telephone services, suffered from excessively high turnover, which exceeded 100 percent annually. Employees were leaving faster than new hires could be brought on board. Unfortunately, many of the organization's highest-performing employees were among those departing. Sixty-eight percent of employees reported in exit surveys that the organization could have done something to retain them. To address this, Sprint developed a strategy to address retention that focused not on pay and programs but on developing managers to become "retention agents." Through survey data Sprint learned that employees were leaving not because of issues related to compensation or benefits but because their managers were not seen as individuals who knew and understood them and therefore were deemed to be untrustworthy. Ten retention competencies were designed for managers: trust builder, esteem builder, communicator, climate builder, flexibility expert, talent developer and coach, high-performance builder, retention expert, retention monitor, and talent finder. Assessments were then done in five pilot customer contact centers to rate each manager on each of these competencies via 360-degree surveys. Each manager then received a plan that identified at least four competencies to be developed through e-learning modules. A survey was taken of over 7,000 PCS employees with their respones compiled into a database; that information illustrates three categories of factors that impact employee retention: organization-wide conditions, job conditions, and leader behaviors. Managers use this database to share specific "best practices" relative to retention with each other and to create a learning community around employee retention. The result is that every pilot site reported lower attrition and resultant cost savings, projected in the millions of dollars, than the control sites. The program is about to be rolled out to remaining customer service sites.[7]

Retention of top employees continues to be a vexing problem for a large number of employers. One study of HR professionals found that 75 percent of those surveyed reported that retention of high performers was the top HR problem they confronted.[8] A critical strategic issue for employers is the development of policies and programs that help retain high performers and/or those employees who are difficult to replace.

Strategic Retention at United Airlines

United Airlines recently developed a "key employee retention program" that focuses on 600 workers identified as critical to the organization's efforts to emerge from bankruptcy. These individuals, who were employed in the organization's information services division, received a cash payment equal to 20 percent of their base pay. Because these individuals were deemed to have highly marketable skills, be highly expensive to replace, and be critical to United's survival objectives, United justified the payments even as other employees were being laid off. Turnover rates among these technical workers had risen to 11 percent while the company's overall turnover rate stood at 7 percent. The plan, while popular with technical employees, was criticized by United's Association of Flight Attendants, which argued that the retention bonuses would come at the expense of other workers.[9]

When attempting to retain talented employees and top performers, employers face competition not only from other organizations but also from the very employees they are attempting to retain. Particularly in service and information-related industries, start-up costs for new businesses are often relatively low, creating opportunities for employees to start their own organizations. The access to information, such as client lists and marketing and strategic plans, that many employees have in the course of doing their jobs can provide strong support for such endeavors. In addition, these employees also may have built strong relationships with customers that transcend loyalty to the organization on the part of both parties. The number of lawsuits that involve employee start-up companies has increased greatly in recent years and many employers now require employees to sign "noncompete" agreements. However, such noncompete agreements frequently are not seen as legally valid and binding. For example, the courts in California, a state with some of the highest start-up activity, do not recognize any noncompete agreements.

When an employee decides to engage in an entrepreneurial endeavor, an employer essentially has two ways in which it can respond: it can treat the new business as an adversarial competitor or it can attempt to enter into a partnership with the new enterprise.[10] Many large organizations, including Xerox, General Motors, Sun Microsystems, and Microsoft, have been involved in the funding of new start-up organizations created by their employees. This funding, however, comes in exchange for some involvement with and control of the new enterprise.

Retaining Talent at Intel

One of the employers that not only supports but actively embraces start-up operations by employees is Intel. The Oregon-based computer chip manufacturer has an internal program called the New Business Initiative (NBI) that not only funds start-ups but actively solicits proposals for new businesses from Intel employees. The NBI has its own staff to examine proposals and determine whether NBI will provide funding. If approved, the employee works with the NBI to develop the project, becoming an entrepreneur while still remaining on the Intel payroll. Successful new enterprises may operate as independent organizations; others may be integrated into Intel's operations. The program is consistent with Intel's innovation strategy and entrepreneurial culture and has also served very successfully as both a retention and a training and development tool. Employees who decide to abandon their projects return to their jobs at Intel with new job skills and a stronger commitment to the organization. Employees are allowed to chase their dreams as technical entrepreneurs without the financial risk of investing in the business and having to leave their full-time employment. The program has also helped the company to retain many of the employees who have come on board as part of one of the many mergers or acquisitions completed by Intel.[11]

While the decision to lay off employees should usually be done as a "last resort," it is inevitable that sometimes an employer has no other choice. However, many layoff decisions by senior management are misguided and create additional problems for the organization. While the investment community may react to a layoff announcement with initial enthusiasm, the long-term performance results are often disappointing. One study found that employers that laid off more than 3 percent of their workforces saw little or no gain in their stock price over a three-year period whereas those that laid off 15 percent or more of their workforces performed significantly below average over the same time period.[12] Layoffs tend to have better results when done strategically as part of a merger or repositioning, rather than as a means to cut costs or impact stock price in the short-term. In 2001, Sears Roebuck & Company eliminated 2,400 jobs and closed 89 stores as part of a strategic restructuring. In the same year, Praxair, Inc., a $5 billion producer of specialty gases, eliminated 900 jobs as part of a plan to change its product mix. In both cases the value of the company stock rose 30 percent in three months.[13] The lesson here is that layoffs alone will not turn around a company whose strategy is ineffective. However, when layoffs are conducted as part of a strategic restructuring that involves fundamental changes in the direction of an organization, they have a higher probability of success. ▼▼

Strategic Downsizing at Charles Schwab

San Francisco–based discount brokerage Charles Schwab was hit hard in the early 2000s by the downturn in the stock market. However, given the cyclical nature of the economy, it was likely that many workers who were no longer needed might be needed again in the undeterminable future. In March 2001, when the company laid off 3,400 employees, each received a transition package that consisted of 500 to 1,000 stock options, cash payments to cover COBRA costs for benefits continuation, a stipend of up to $20,000 to cover tuition for schooling, and a full range of outplacement services. More important, however, was the $7,500 bonus to be provided to any employee who was rehired within 18 months of separation. This program greatly assisted in the quick rehiring of knowledgeable, trained employees when business improved, saved the organization a tremendous amount of money, and secured the goodwill of customers and remaining employees. Perhaps more important, when across-the-board pay cuts of 5 percent for rank-and-file employees were announced, it was also announced that any manager at the vice-presidential level or higher would be receiving a 25 percent pay cut. Schwab was cited as a model responsible employer within the business community and continued to be one of the most sought-after employers in the country.[14]

RETIREMENT

Employees also leave the organization through retirement. Except for certain occupations dealing with public safety (such as airline pilots), the Age Discrimination in Employment Act of 1967 prohibits an employer from setting a mandatory retirement age. Because medical advances are allowing individuals to live longer and stay healthier longer, older workers are maintaining a strong and increased presence in the workforce. Ironically, however, many older workers tend to be set in their ways and resistant to change, particularly to technological change. Employers have a distinct challenge in finding ways to keep older workers motivated and productive and ensuring that they do not violate the legal rights of these employees.

When older workers retire, the organization can hire new employees to replace older workers who may have less physical or mental energy or skills that have become dated or obsolete. These new employees may cost less than the older workers relative to salaries and health insurance premiums. Because many older workers are higher in the organizational hierarchy, promotion opportunities may be made available when they retire.

▶▶ Reading 13.2, "Strategies for Responsible Restructuring," explains many of the common problems that result from layoffs and examines how organizations can restructure themselves both strategically and responsibly.

However, significant costs are often associated with retirement. Retirees who have worked for the organization for many years usually have a wealth of knowledge about the industry and the marketplace. They also have extensive historical knowledge about the organization and experience with organizational processes, politics, and culture. Although fresh ideas from outsiders can be critical to an organization, knowledge and experience can be equally important, and decision makers need to ensure that the organization capitalizes on both to assist in meeting its objectives. The challenge again becomes how to maximize the benefits of retirement while simultaneously minimizing the costs.

Older workers will become more prominent in the workplace. Employers can usually not set mandatory retirement ages, force employees to retire, or treat older workers in a discriminatory manner in any employment decision. Particularly when conducting layoffs, employers must ensure that there is no adverse treatment of older employees, which would violate the Age Discrimination in Employment Act. Indeed, many large-scale reductions in force have been accompanied by lawsuits that allege discrimination based on age. This issue may be exacerbated in the very near future as the baby boom generation moves through middle age.

Older workers are becoming a reality for employers. A recent study by the American Association of Retired Persons found that 80 percent of the baby boom generation intends to continue to work during retirement.[15] This statistic helps to counteract existing fears concerning the mass retirement of baby boomers predicted to start later this decade. In fact, the number of Americans age 65 and older in the labor force recently grew by 7 percent, to a total of 4.5 million individuals.[16] In addition to the many seniors who wish to keep working, there are a number who *have* to keep working: Lack of adequate health insurance in postemployment years is keeping some seniors in the workforce.[17] Consequently, employers may face not the anticipated worker shortage but rather an older workforce.

Many older individuals seek to cut back on their working hours in what is known as a "phased retirement" stage of their careers. However, phased retirement can impact an employee's ability to collect retirement pensions, so it is critical that such programs be structured to benefit both the employee and the organization.[18] As part of overall human resource planning, employers need to determine how to deploy human assets for maximum organizational benefit. Assisting with retirement planning has become a critical strategic human resource function of which phased retirement programs may be a vital component.

Employers can develop programs to give older employees incentives to retire or to take early retirement as long as employees are not coerced into doing so. When older employees retire, the organization can replace them with younger workers, but the organization can lose a great wealth of knowledge and expertise. To remedy this, many employers rehire retirees on a part-time or consulting basis. This allows the organization to retain the benefits these older workers bring to the company and gives these individuals the opportunity to gradually transition into a shorter work week or semi-retirement. Retirees can enjoy more leisure time and work at a less hectic pace but also continue to make meaningful contributions to their employers, maintain their careers, and stay alert and challenged. ▼▼▼ Strategic management of the retirement process results in everyone winning: Retirees gain the best of both worlds; the organization retains their knowledge and experience

▶▶▶ Reading 13.3, "Retirement of Older Workers: Issues and Policies," shows how the establishment of flexible retirement policies can benefit organizations. Although focused on Canadian society, this reading presents concepts that are applicable in any industrialized society.

base; existing employees are afforded opportunities to be promoted; and new employees may be hired and learn from the experiences and knowledge bases of seasoned veterans.

CONCLUSION

Organizations have only recently begun to pay attention to the HR function of employee separation. The increased pace of merger and acquisition activity as well as downsizings have made HR programs and policies that address employee separation a key strategic issue in ensuring the new organizations's success.

For many years, managing turnover has been ignored, taken for granted, or assumed to be a simple process of automatically terminating poor performers and trying to fill the gaps when employees involuntarily left the organization. It was more of a coping process than any kind of active strategic management. Organizations today, however, are realizing that the effective strategic management of turnover can be a critical factor affecting overall performance.

Retirement is no longer a process of filing paperwork as employees reach mandatory retirement age. Effective management of employee retirement can provide organizations with an important competitive advantage: the means of retaining knowledge, expertise, experience, loyalty, and positive role models while simultaneously allowing an infusion of new ideas and energy. The development of creative, mutually beneficial programs and policies related to retirement will become even more critical as our population ages and baby boomers approach traditional retirement age.[19]

The reality of employee separation is that the organization relinquishes key assets. Every employee represents an investment by the organization in terms of direct and indirect expenditures relative to staffing, training, compensation, and benefits. Strategically managing employee separation entails determining the value of human assets from an investment perspective and considering the costs of discarding these assets. How this process is managed may be one of the most important investment decisions an organization makes.

CRITICAL THINKING

1. Why is it important to manage the process of employee separation?

2. What short-run, long-run, and policy options are available to employers in lieu of layoffs?

3. Under what conditions might layoffs be advantageous to an employer?

4. What costs are associated with turnover? What benefits can be derived from turnover?

5. Explain the Martin and Bartol matrix for managing turnover. How does this relate to taking an investment approach to human resources?

6. Because workers live and stay healthy longer, the workforce is aging. How might this impact an organization's competitive position?

7. Discuss the ways an organization might attempt to retain its most valued employees.

Reading 13.1

8. How can selection, training, and compensation programs be designed strategically to help an organization manage its retention and turnover?

Reading 13.2

9. Explain the link between strategic human resource management and responsible restructuring. How can restructuring be undertaken for maximum benefit?

Reading 13.3

10. What challenges does an aging workforce present to organizations? How can these challenges be managed to provide enhanced performance within organizations?

EXPERIENTIAL EXERCISES

1. Calculate the turnover costs for a university professor who voluntarily resigns, retires, or is dismissed. Be sure to consider both economic and noneconomic costs in your analysis. How difficult is it to gain an accurate accounting of these costs? How might you recommend to the university president that these costs be managed?

INTERNET EXERCISES

1. Visit the Web sites http://www.greenthumb.org, http://www.maturityworks.org, and http://www.50andoverboard.com. What unique characteristics and needs do older workers have? What special contributions can older workers make to an organization? How might organizations best strategically employ older workers?

CHAPTER REFERENCES

1. Juezens, J. "Motivating Survivors," *HR Magazine*, July 2001, pp. 92–99.
2. Joinson, C. "Capturing Turnover Costs," *HR Magazine*, July 2000, pp. 107–119.
3. Bacarro, J. P. "The Hidden Cost of Employee Turnover." Grant Thornton Benefits and HR Advisor, Grant Thornton, 1992.
4. Schlesinger, L. A. and Heskett, J. A. "The Service-Driven Service Company," *Harvard Business Review*, 69, September–October, 1991, pp. 71–81.
5. Barrette, D. L. "Survey Highlights Retention Concerns," *HR News*, 19, (10), October 2000. Alexandria, VA: Society for Human Resource Management, pp. 11, 16.
6. Martin, David C. and Bartol, Kathryn M. "Managing Turnover Strategically," *Personnel Administrator*, November 1985.
7. Taylor, C. R. "Focus on Talent," *Training & Development*, December 2002, pp. 26–31.
8. Ibid.
9. Cole, A. "Attendants Fight United Retention Plan," CBS.MarketWatch.com, July 7, 2003.
10. Leonard, B. "Inside Job," *HR Magazine*, October 2001, pp. 64–68.
11. Ibid.
12. Jossi, F. "Take the Road Less Traveled," *HR Magazine*, July 2001, pp. 46–51.
13. Cascio, W. F. "Corporate Restructuring and the No-Layoff Policy," *Perspectives On Work*, 7, (1), pp. 4–6.
14. Jossi, F. "Take the Road Less Traveled," *HR Magazine*, July 2001, pp. 46–51.

15. Carpenter, D. "Looking Forward to a Long Goodbye," *South Florida Sun-Sentinel*, September 18, 2002, p. 10D.
16. Ibid.
17. Grensing-Pophal, L. "Departure Plans," *HR Magazine*, July 2003, pp. 83–86.
18. Hirschman, C. "Exit Strategy," *HR Magazine*, December 2001, pp. 52–57.
19. Leonard, S. "The Aging Workforce; As Baby Boomers Retire, Employers Will Face New Challenges," *Workplace Visions*, No. 1 – 2000. Alexandria, VA: Society for Human Resource Management.

Holding On to High Performers: A Strategic Approach to Retention

Eileen M. Garger, *Compensation and Benefits Management*

As HR professionals everywhere can now attest, sustained economic prosperity also has its downside. Faced with the tightest labor market in nearly 40 years, many of them are finding it difficult to maintain minimum staffing requirements or are struggling to achieve the manpower targets they set to support continued growth. In many cases, resolving these staffing problems must involve more than just new ideas for recruitment. Also required is a systematic and focused review of what is being done to retain employees, especially those who are identified as high performers. It is becoming increasingly clear that, in today's dynamic business environment, companies that want to remain competitive must adopt a more strategic approach to retention.

Two major trends point to the growing importance of retention as an HR issue. One is the ongoing rise in turnover rates in virtually every economic sector and region that, if left unaddressed, can have a significant impact on bottom-line results and organizational success. The other is the ever-climbing cost of turnover, especially when it involves high performers.

A report released last year by the Bureau of National Affairs showed that turnover rates (which exclude layoffs) have soared to their highest levels of the decade, increasing for companies in both the service and manufacturing sectors. Employers in all parts of the country now face higher levels of turnover and, as a result, higher replacement costs.[1]

Though the direct costs associated with losing an employee are well documented—ranging anywhere from one to three times the employee's salary— these calculations often fail to factor in the hidden costs of turnover. These include lost productivity and missed revenues, as well as intangible repercussions such as reduced morale and diminished company reputation.

If the lost employees are high performers, turnover costs could rise dramatically. According to the Saratoga Institute, which specializes in quantitative HR measurement systems, the average company loses about $1 million with every 10 professional employees who leave.[2] Since these employees typically comprise the core managerial and technical talent within a company and are the leaders of mission-critical activities, their departure can have significant business consequences.

Uncommon Initiatives

Responding to what many experts now consider a retention crisis, some companies are implementing aggressive programs to manage turnover and hold on to those employees who contribute most to their business success. Microsoft, for example, has set up a special department within its corporate HR function that focuses exclusively on keeping annual attrition low, and Ernst & Young has founded an Office for Retention.

In our consulting work with HR professionals at two major technology companies, Drake Beam Morin has helped to implement similar initiatives. In one, we conducted more than 1,000 exit interviews to identify the key drivers of retention in the organization and then used the results to develop a formal retention strategy. For the other company, which had just completed two major buyouts, we performed a retention analysis to determine what had to be done to hold on to high performers in the acquired organizations.

Although such approaches can be highly effective, they are not yet common. In a recent study of more than 600 U.S. companies, only a third reported that they have developed strategies for retaining employees.[3] Another eye-opening statistic: According to McKinsey & Co., only 40 percent of HR executives in major corporations track the departure of high performers or document their reasons for leaving.[4]

Why are so few companies taking action to manage retention better? One reason may be the pervasive belief that high turnover is inevitable today, given the tight labor market and the "new employment contract," which tacitly endorses more frequent job changes. Some managers believe that, just as high rates of turnover seem almost endemic to certain industries (like health care) or certain professions (like sales), relatively little can be done to improve retention in a business environment characterized by rapid growth and rock-bottom unemployment.

But this viewpoint ignores the fact that, even when a certain amount of "churn" is normal—or even healthy—for an organization, losing high performers is always costly, not matter what the economic climate.

A Three-Part Strategy

Another reason why companies often fail to address the retention challenge is that they lack effective strategies for managing turnover or, when they do apply specific retention techniques (such as stock options), achieve only limited results because their approach is incomplete or misdirected. Based on our work with leading U.S. and international corporations, we have found that the best way to manage turnover and retain high performers is to implement a well-planned and coordinated retention strategy, which sometimes requires fundamental changes in how a company selects, develops, and rewards its employees.

This strategy should incorporate the elements that research and our experience show have a positive impact on retention and help in preserving the loyalty of high performers. These elements fall into three categories:

- Selection and Orientation
- Training and Career Management
- Motivation and Compensation

Selection and Orientation

An effective retention strategy begins at the earliest stages of the recruitment and selection process. Identifying and attracting good candidates for hire helps companies to select the "right" people—those who not only possess the skills that are needed but also demonstrate the attitudes, personality traits, and behaviors that ensure organizational "fit" and promote commitment.

This is critical to retention because most turnover is due, in fact, to poor chemistry or bad fit. A recent study showed that nearly 80 percent of turnover is the result of mistakes made during the hiring phase.[5] And our experience with outplacement over the past 30 years confirms that, in the vast majority of cases not involving layoffs, the primary basis for job loss is not because the departing employees failed to meet the requirements of their job but because they never really fit the culture of their organization. For this reason, many companies are now adopting the strategy of "hire for attitude, train for skill." They have come to realize that, in many instances, it is easier to develop the skills and capabilities that an employee needs than to attempt to change the employee's personality or mind-set.

Since compatibility is the key to long-term employment relationships, cultural issues need to be addressed throughout the selection process, beginning with recruitment. To determine cultural fit, companies must look beyond the information provided in job descriptions when assessing potential candidates and making hiring decisions. While job descriptions may help in establishing the basic requirements for a job, they do not provide the guidance needed to determine whether a candidate demonstrates the personal characteristics and attitudes that will ensure a good match.

One Fortune 500 company we worked with gained significant retention benefits by integrating cultural issues into its selection practices. While going through a period of explosive business growth, this company experienced such high levels of turnover in its call centers that personnel costs were skyrocketing and the quality of its customer service deteriorated. After conducting a retention analysis, the company decided to install prescreening selection software that could identify job candidates who not only have good communication skills, but also perform well in a fast-paced, high-stress work environment. In a matter of months, the turnover rate in this company's call centers dropped by 10 points.

Once a culture-based selection process is in place, a carefully designed orientation program can also help lay the groundwork for commitment by promoting the feelings of affiliation that characterize organizational fit. Though the structure of such programs may vary greatly among companies, the primary objective for each of them should never be to inundate new hires with company information. They should be designed, rather, to promote feelings of membership right from the start by celebrating the arrival of new employees and showing them how they fit into the organization's "big picture."

SELECTION AND ORIENTATION GUIDELINES

Introduce recruitment practices that focus on cultural fit. The best way to gain an accurate picture of what a candidate needs to succeed at a job in a particular culture is to conduct a strategic job analysis. This involves gathering data to establish the skills and competencies required for the job, analyzing the cultural context in which the job will be performed, and spending time with employees who excelled at the job in the past or with high performers who hold similar jobs.

A strategic job analysis helps to define the critical "success factors" for the job, that is, the specific behaviors and attitudes that are needed to perform the job successfully within its culture. These success factors can be used to create a profile of the ideal candidate for recruitment—one who is likely not only to do well at the job but also to stay on with the organization.

Conduct behavioral-based selection interviewing. When the selection process begins, the success factors identified for a job can provide the basis for an interviewing strategy that will assess the candidate's organizational fit. A good way to uncover evidence of these success factors is to incorporate behavioral-based questions that are designed to elicit stories from candidates about their work history and how they behaved in previous job situations. Examples: "Can you tell me about a time when you were under great pressure and had to resolve a difficult customer problem?" or "Can you give me examples of how you demonstrated creativity in your last two jobs?"

Behavioral-based interviewing encourages candidates to paint a picture of their qualifications and provides the information needed to determine whether their work styles and preferences match the cultural requirements of the job: how decisions are made, how problems are solved, how communication takes place, and how responsibilities are shared.

Integrate for success through effective orientation. A new employee's earliest impressions can have a significant impact on retention, but all too often these first impressions are negative because of weak orientation programs. When new hires are forced to spend their first day filling out complicated forms or viewing company videos, they may begin to regret their decisions to join the company and may experience feelings comparable to "buyer's remorse."

Dr. John Sullivan, head of the Human Resource Management Program at San Francisco State University, has written extensively on this subject. He claims that most companies need to reconstruct their orientation programs so that they make more favorable first impressions and "close the sale" on new hires.[6] Some of his suggestions:

- Involve the families of new employees in orientation programs.
- Ask senior managers to participate in orientations to show new hires that they are important to the organization.
- Assign a departmental mentor to assist new hires during their first month.
- Give line managers control of the orientation process, to integrate new hires into their work "family" as quickly as possible.

Training and Career Management

Today, the connection between development and retention is stronger than ever. Many employees now look to the companies they work for to provide them with growth and learning opportunities, and high performers often perceive development as a benefit they are entitled to. In addition, more employees are taking charge of their careers and recognize the need to continually upgrade their skills. Aware of the faster pace of change in the business world, they want to improve their "employability" and feel confident that they will be well-prepared wherever they go.

In light of these changing attitudes, some companies have dedicated themselves to creating a learning environment that energizes employees and wins their commitment by providing growth opportunities. Intel, for example, now spends more than $150 million a year—about 6 percent of its payroll budget—to maintain an inhouse university, and all senior managers are required to spend time teaching there each quarter. JCPenney has introduced "career pathing," a career-management tool that uses grids to compare jobs by level and skill requirements and helps employees to identify growth opportunities within the corporation.

Not all companies have embraced the concept of the learning organization, however. As turnover rates rise, many have been tempted to cut back on development expenditures and hesitate to allocate funds to train workers who are likely to leave. While these companies may be missing opportunities to build employee commitment through development, others actually undermine commitment by paying lip service to the concept of continuous learning without investing in programs that provide real opportunities for growth.

Though the concerns of these companies are understandable, their fears are generally unfounded because training and development tend to have a positive impact on retention. Ironically, when companies provide opportunities for their employees to become more marketable by acquiring new skills, job satisfaction increases and those employees are more likely to stay.

One company that realized this principle was a bank we worked with that was about to merge with another financial institution and expected to lose some of its best people during the change. To prevent this from happening, the bank offered career-transition workshops to help employees rework their resumes and prepare to interview for jobs within the new organization. Though some employees attended the workshops and then left the bank, a significant number stayed on and a mass exodus of key people was averted.

As this example shows, when employees see a positive and personal return from the training they receive, their organization usually benefits in the form of increased commitment. The challenge for companies today is to provide development opportunities that serve a dual purpose and meet the needs of both the organization and its employees. Companies that can achieve this alignment between the values, interests, and career aspirations of employees and the organization's business goals are the ones most likely to see improvement in both employee satisfaction and retention.

TRAINING AND CAREER MANAGEMENT GUIDELINES

Adopt an interactive approach to training and development. The traditional, paternalistic approach to career management no longer applies. Since companies cannot realistically offer the prospect of lifetime employment, they are not in a position to make life-altering career decisions for employees. The responsibility for mapping out careers now lies primarily with employees, and they want more say in deciding which development opportunities they will pursue.

In this climate, the most effective development programs are those that operate as interactive processes, in which managers and their direct reports work together closely to identify skill gaps that must be filled, satisfy the professional interests of employees, and develop the competencies that will be needed to ensure both individual and business success.

Establish development as a line responsibility. For employee development to become an organizational priority, it must be driven from the top and integrated throughout the company's culture. This means that executives and senior staff should consistently promote the benefits of development, and line managers at every level must work proactively to set developmental goals with employees, provide information on the resources available to meet those goals, and offer assistance to facilitate the development process.

When managers are held responsible for these activities—and their performance is evaluated on this basis—it ensures that employees develop the right competencies and sends a strong message to high performers that the company wants them to stay and is committed to their success.

Case Study: Guiding Careers to Retain Employees

Recognizing the link between development and retention, a major health care provider we work with has opened a career center dedicated solely to the redeployment and retention of key human assets. Whenever cutbacks are planned, the center works with employees whom the company wants to keep to improve their skills and help their transition to other parts of the organization. The center also provides ongoing career guidance to any employees who seek assistance in clarifying professional goals or accessing either internal or community-based development programs.

Working closely with the corporate HR department, the center's manager meets each week with supervisors at various levels and with their teams to talk about career planning and discuss training needs. A new initiative is under way to ensure that these efforts are focused strategically on high performers. The goal is to establish criteria that team leaders can use to identify their most valuable employees and provide them with the skills and competencies they will need to survive any future reorganizations.

Offer a variety of development opportunities at every level. Companies that use development effectively as a retention tool recognize that people learn in different ways, so they offer a variety of learning programs and growth opportunities. These may include mentorship programs, job rotations, and task force assignments, as well as classroom-based instruction, self-paced computer-based training, and even coaching at executive levels.

Some forward-thinking companies even provide assistance to employees in understanding how to best leverage their talents. One of our clients, for example, maintains a small staff of inhouse counselors who work with employees to assess their careers and skill levels and determine what re-skilling they may need to remain professionally competitive within the organization.

Motivation and Compensation

Though they represent some of the most traditional retention tools, the methods that companies typically use to motivate and compensate employees do not always produce good results and may be largely ineffective in retaining high performers. All too often, when companies design their reward systems, they end up relying on the approaches that are most familiar and widely practiced, such as financial incentives.

While financial incentives can sometimes work to improve performance, their value as a retention tool has diminished in recent years. The reason: In today's marketplace, there are just too many companies willing to match the financial offerings of their competitors in order to recruit top talent. Even when competing for high-level executives—where the battles often involve retention bonuses, stock options, and hefty salaries—companies are finding it increasingly difficult to come up with financial packages that cannot be readily duplicated.

There is also mounting evidence to suggest that, while companies should certainly strive to remain competitive in the pay and benefits they offer, it may not be wise to focus primarily on money when designing a retention strategy. With high performers in particular, nonfinancial incentives—especially those that promote feelings of achievement, ownership, and involvement—may be far more critical to retention.

This was confirmed by a recent survey in which 3,400 employees in a national representative sample were asked why they decided to leave their last job and take their current one. The desire to make more money was not among the reasons most frequently cited, the study found. These employees left, they said, because they wanted more open communications, a better balance between work and family life, and more meaningful work.[7] When one of our clients conducted employee interviews to identify the key drivers of retention in its workforce, it also came to the conclusion that nonfinancial rewards are more important than money.

How can companies determine what these rewards should be? Internal surveys and interviews can help in assessing whether reward systems are in sync with what employees want and provide guidance in designing compensation programs that reflect what matters most to employees. There is also a growing number of research studies that companies can look to for ideas on what kinds of rewards are most likely to help them achieve their retention goals.

The 1998 America @ Work Study, for example, found that having managers who recognize the need to balance work and family life is now the number one contributor of employee commitment.[8] The most recent National Study of the Changing Workforce found that job quality and organizational support are more important to retention than earnings or benefits.[9] These studies indicate that, when companies utilize rewards for the purpose of retention, they should think about what they can do to help employees balance work and family responsibilities, find job assignments that are both challenging and enjoyable, and feel better about their work.

MOTIVATION AND COMPENSATION GUIDELINES
Incorporate nonfinancial rewards into compensation programs. Companies should remember that commitment is an emotional bond that is based largely in intangibles, like feelings of being valued and appreciated. That is why offering nonfinancial rewards—giving employees more control over their work schedule, for example or providing exposure to decision makers—can add quality to the work life of employees and strengthen their feelings of affiliation.

In some companies, these practices are considered so important that managers are evaluated on how well they apply them. At Allstate Insurance, all new managers receive three days of training in fostering a supportive work environment and are expected to implement what they learn. At DuPont, managers are evaluated in part on the efforts they make to support the work/life goals of their direct reports.

Enlist high performers in solving business problems. High performers look for increased responsibility and challenges, tend to participate more than other employees, and offer more suggestions for improvement. Enlisting them as key problem solvers can help strengthen their feelings of engagement and enhance their self-image as stakeholders.

One company that used this approach well is a major provider of bedding and mattresses. When customers complained that delivery people were tracking mud into their homes, the company's CEO pulled together a group of high performers to brainstorm solutions. They came up with the idea of offering a white-glove service, complete with red carpet and shoe coverings for handlers. By soliciting ideas in this way, the company provided recognition to its high performers and also gained a new and distinctive marketing tool.

Recognize employee efforts more informally, more personally, and more frequently. Informal, spontaneous, and sincere forms of recognition—like a personal note—are often more meaningful to employees than service awards or write-ups in the company newsletter. These forms of recognition are especially valued by high performers, who take their work seriously and need to feel that they are making a contribution.

When rewards are customized to each employee, their impact on motivation and retention can increase significantly. Dr. Thad Green, a former management professor and recognized expert on motivation, has developed a system managers can use to get to know their employees and understand their needs, which he says can vary greatly among individuals. The system calls for frequent and facilitated discussions between managers and their direct reports, and includes surveys that are designed to identify the specific motivators that work best with each employee.[10]

Final Recommendations

Even when companies address all the factors discussed in this article as critical to retention, they should design strategies that reflect their particular situation: the composition of their workforce, the key drivers of retention in their organization, and the specific retention goals they set for themselves. Of course, they will have to take into consideration the time and costs involved in implementing these strategies and weight their investments in retention against other business priorities.

They should also evaluate the effectiveness of their efforts as systematically as possible. This should involve measuring the results they achieve, revisiting their underlying assumptions, and modifying their approach based on what they learn. As with any business strategy, success requires focus and buy-in from all levels, as well as mechanisms to ensure that the strategy is on the right track.

One of the most practical ways that companies can do this is to conduct exit interviews on a regular basis. Learning why employees leave—and tracking the reasons for their departure—often reveals patterns that can help companies determine where to focus their retention efforts in the future. To capture the most valuable data, companies should make sure that these interviews are conducted by people whom the departing employees feel they can trust or by an impartial third party. Also effective: Interview a sample of high performers who have been away from the company for at least six months. With time and distance, former employees are usually more honest in their feedback and, when vested in another position, tend to be less guarded in their responses.

Case Study: Motivating Employees to Improve Retention

In our work with a global manufacturing company that is going through a major reorganization, we were asked to design a strategy that would motivate key employees to stay on during the transition and relocate to new work sites. Though the company expects to lose some employees, the overriding concern is to hold on to the high performers who are critical to the business.

The strategy we came up with combines stay-on bonuses with nonfinancial motivators that we believe are critical to the retention effort. Among them: communicating more often to keep employees informed of the changes taking place, creating a vision of the new organization to show employees they have a future with the company, and providing positive images of the lifestyles employees could lead if they moved to the new locations. The strategy also includes workshops to facilitate employees' learning why and how decisions related to change are made and to help them develop personal action plans to make it through the transition.

Finally, companies should keep in mind that adopting a strategic approach to retention can produce benefits that go beyond meeting the immediate need to reduce turnover. Even when companies hire only talented people, give them plenty of opportunities to develop, and reward them appropriately, there is still likely to be some turnover. The upside is that the "alumni" of these companies may provide new business or referrals, or may even return after gaining valuable experience elsewhere.

Source: Garger, E. M. "Holding On to High Performers: A Strategic Approach to Retention." *Compensation and Benefits Management, 15*, (4), Autumn 1999, pp. 10–17. Reprinted with permission.

Selected Bibliography

Adams, Marc. "The Stream of Labor Slows to a Trickle." *HR Magazine*, Oct. 1998.

Laabs, Jennifer. "The New Loyalty: Grasp It. Earn It. Keep It." *Workforce*, Nov. 1998.

LaMotta, Toni. *Recognition, the Quality Way.* New York: Quality Resources, 1995.

Levesque, Joseph D. *Complete Manual for Recruiting, Hiring & Retaining Quality Employees.* Englewood Cliffs, NJ: Prentice Hall, 1996.

Lynn, Jacquelyn. "Hard to Hold: Conquer the Tight Labor Market by Retaining Valuable Workers." *Entrepreneur*, Oct. 1997.

Mendonsa, Robert. "Keeping Who You Want to Keep: Retaining the Best People." *Supervision*, Jan. 1998.

Ramsey, Robert. "How to Keep Key Workers." *Supervision*, Oct. 1998.

Scheig, Richard. "Employee Turnover and Its Hidden Costs." *U.S. Distribution Journal*, Jan./ Feb. 1997.

Sullivan, John. "Retention Is Like a Box of Chocolates." *Electronic Recruiting Exchange*, http://ourworld.compuserve.com/homepages/gately/ppl5js05.htm.

Endnotes

1. Bureau of National Affairs press release, issued Mar. 27, 1998.
2. Jac Fitz-enz, "It's Costly to Lose Good Employees." *Workforce* (Aug. 1997): 50.
3. Roger Herman, "You've Got to Change to Retain." *HR Focus* (Sept. 1998): S3.
4. Shelly Branch, "You Hired, 'Em, But Can You Keep 's Em." *Fortune* (Nov. 9, 1998): 248.
5. Carolyn Hirschman, "Playing the High Stakes Hiring Game." *HR Magazine* (Mar. 1998): 80.
6. John Sullivan, "How to Ruin a Great Recruiting Effort With the 'Orientation From Hell,'" available from Electronic Recruiting Exchange, www.erexchange.com/daily/default.asp?date = 1/15/99; Internet.
7. Cited by Catherine D. Fyock in "Retention Tactics That Work," a for-members-only white paper issued by the Society for Human Resource Management (Mar. 1998): 2.
8. *America @ Work: A Focus on Benefit and Compensation* (Chicago: Aon Consulting, 1998).
9. James Bond, Ellen Galinsky, and Jennifer Swanbert, *The 1997 National Study of the Changing Workforce* (New York: Families and Work Institute, 1998).
10. A description of Dr. Green's system and case studies of its implementation within AT&T are included in *Change of Heart, Change of Mind: Motivation, Beliefs, and Organizational Transformation* (Westport, CT: Quorum Books, 1999).

Strategies for Responsible Restructuring

Wayne F. Cascio, *Academy of Management Executive*

Employment Downsizing: The Juggernaut Continues

The job churning in the labor market that characterized the 1990s has not let up. If anything, its pace has accelerated. However, the free-agent mentality of the late 1990s that motivated some people to leave one employer so that they could make 5 percent more at another, a strategy that benefited men more than women,[1] is over. Layoffs are back—and with a vengeance. Thus, in 2001, companies in the United States announced layoffs of almost two million workers, with firms such as American Express, Lucent, Hewlett-Packard, and Dell conducting multiple rounds in the same year. Corporations announced 999,000 job cuts between September 11, 2001 and February 1, 2002 alone![2] Indeed, the 443,134 job cuts announced in the first quarter of 2002 exceeded those announced in the first quarter of 2001 by nine percent.[3] Medium- and large-sized companies announced most layoffs, and they involved *all* levels of employees, top to bottom. A study by Bain & Company's Worldwide Strategy Practice reported that in 2000, for example, 22 percent of the CEOs of the largest publicly traded companies either lost their jobs or retired, as opposed to just 13 percent in 1999.[4] Morgan Stanley estimates that about 80 percent of the U.S. layoffs involved white-collar, well-educated employees. According to Morgan Stanley's chief economist, that's because 75 percent of the 12.3 million new jobs created between 1994 and 2000 were white-collar jobs. What the companies created, they are now taking away.

Are there gender differences in the likelihood of layoffs and in their consequences? A longitudinal data set of more than 4,000 large Australian firms covering the period 1990–1998 found that men were more likely than women to experience employment downsizing, but that women's re-employment rates after downsizing were lower than men's.[5]

Evidence indicates that such career disruptions have particularly negative consequences on the future earnings of women.[6]

The Economic Logic That Drives Downsizing

What makes downsizing such a compelling strategy to firms worldwide? The economic rationale is straightforward. It begins with the premise that there really are only two ways to make money in business: either you cut costs or you increase revenues. Which is more predictable, future costs or future revenues? Anyone who makes monthly mortgage payments knows that future costs are far more predictable than future revenues. Payroll expenses represent fixed costs, so by cutting payroll, other things remaining equal, one should reduce overall expenses. Reduced expenses translate into increased earnings, and earnings drive stock prices. Higher stock prices make investors and analysts happy. The key phrase is "other things remaining equal." As we shall see, other things often do not remain equal, and therefore the anticipated benefits of employment downsizing do not always materialize.

What Does Research on the Economic Consequences of Employment Downsizing Tell Us?

In a series of studies that included data from 1982–1994, 1995–2000, and 1982–2000, my colleagues and I examined financial and employment data from companies in the Standard & Poor's 500. The S&P 500 is one of the most widely used benchmarks of the performance of U.S. equities. It represents leading companies in leading industries and consists of 500 stocks chosen for their market size, liquidity, and industry-group representation. Our purpose was to examine the relationships between changes in employment and financial performance. We assigned companies to one of seven mutually exclusive categories based upon their level of change in employment and their level of change in plant and equipment (assets). We then observed the firms' financial performance (profitability and total return on common stock) from one year before to two years after the employment-change events. We examined results for firms in each category on an independent as well as on an industry-adjusted basis.[7]

In our most recent study, we observed a total of 6,418 occurrences of changes in employment for S&P 500 companies over the 18-year period from 1982 through 2000. As in our earlier studies, we found no significant, consistent evidence that employment downsizing led to improved financial performance, as measured by return on assets or industry-adjusted return on assets. Downsizing strategies, either employment downsizing or asset downsizing, did not yield long-term payoffs that were significantly larger than those generated by Stable Employers—those companies in which the complement of employees did not fluctuate by more than ±5 percent.

This conclusion differs from that in our earlier analysis of the data from 1982 to 1994.[8] In that study we concluded that some types of downsizing, e.g., Asset Downsizing, do yield higher ROAs than either Stable Employers or their industries. However, when the data from 1995–2000 are added to the original 1982–1994 data, a different picture emerges. That picture suggests clearly that, at least during the time period of our study, it was not possible for firms to "save" or "shrink" their way to prosperity. Rather, it was only by growing their businesses (Asset Upsizing) that firms outperformed Stable Employers as well as their own industries in terms of profitability and total returns on common stock. With respect to such returns, Asset Upsizers generated returns that were 41 percent higher than those of Employment Downsizers and 43 percent higher than those of Stable Employers, by the end of Year 2.

This is not to say that firms should not downsize. In fact, many firms have downsized and restructured successfully to improve their productivity. They have done so by using layoffs as part of a broader business plan. As examples, consider Sears Roebuck & Company and Praxair, Inc. In January 2001 Sears cut 2,400 jobs as part of a restructuring that included closing 89 stores and several smaller businesses. Shares rose 30 percent in six months. Praxair, Inc., a $5 billion supplier of specialty gases and coatings, cut 900 jobs in September 2001 in response to the economic slowdown. At the same time, however, it also announced initiatives designed to pull it out of the slump, including two new plants for products where demand was on the rise. The result? The value of its shares rose 30 percent in three months.

In the aggregate, the productivity and competitiveness of many firms have increased in recent years. However, the lesson from our analysis is that firms cannot simply *assume* that layoffs are a quick fix that will necessarily lead to productivity improvements and increased financial performance. The fact is that layoffs alone will not fix a business strategy that is fundamentally flawed. Thus when Palm, Inc. trimmed 250 jobs in an effort to cut costs after a delayed product launch slowed demand, shares lost nearly half their value in one day and never recovered. In response, Palm's chief financial officer, Judy Bruner, noted, "There were a lot of questions about the viability of the business."[9]

In short, employment downsizing may not necessarily generate the benefits sought by management. Managers must be very cautious in implementing a strategy that can impose such traumatic costs on employees, both on those who leave as well as on those who stay.[10] Management needs to be sure about the sources of future savings and carefully weigh those against *all* of the costs, including the increased costs associated with subsequent employment expansions when economic conditions improve.

What's Different About Current Layoffs in the United States

In some important ways, the cuts that firms in the United States are making now differ from those they made in the 1990s.

PREEMPTIVE LAYOFFS BY LARGE FIRMS
Today's job cuts are not solely about large, sick companies trying to save themselves, as was often the case in the early 1990s (e.g., IBM, Sears). They are also about healthy companies hoping to reduce costs and boost earnings by reducing head count (e.g., Goldman Sachs and AOL). They are about

trying to preempt tough times instead of simply reacting to them. These layoffs are radical, preventive first aid.[11] On the other hand, small companies, especially small manufacturers, tend to resist layoffs because they are trying to protect the substantial investment they made in finding and training workers.[12]

TAILORING THE COMPLEMENT OF SKILLS

At the same time that firms are firing some people, they are hiring others, presumably people with the skills to execute new strategies. According to the American Management Association's annual survey of its member companies, which employ one-quarter of the American workforce, 36 percent of firms that eliminated jobs in the previous 12 months said they had also created new positions. That's up from 31 percent in 1996.[13] As companies lose workers in one department, they are adding people with different skills in another, continually tailoring their workforces to fit the available work and adjusting quickly to swings in demand for products and services. What makes this flexibility possible is the rise in temporary and contract workers.[14] On a typical day, they allow companies to meet 12 percent of their staffing needs. On peak days that figure may reach 20 percent.[15]

SYMPATHY TOWARD AN EMPLOYER'S REASONS FOR LAYOFFS, AND A REFUSAL TO PERSONALIZE THE EXPERIENCE

From the perspective of employees, layoffs have a new character. More managers are briefing employees regularly about the economic status of their companies. This information raises awareness and actually prepares employees for what might happen to them. To many, the layoffs seem justified because of the slowdown in economic growth, the plunge in corporate profits, and the dive in stock prices. While being laid off even once used to be traumatic, some employees can now expect to go through that experience twice or even three times before they reach 50.[16]

OUTPLACEMENT CENTERS AS HIRING HALLS

Outplacement centers have become America's new hiring halls—gathering places for those between assignments. As the managing principal of the New York office of outplacement firm Right Associates put it, "These people are not ashamed, but they do feel dislocated, and there is anger. They were on track, and now they are trying to get back on track." Right has redesigned its offices to accommodate

the new matter-of-factness about downsizing. Instead of enclosed offices and cubicles, where the downsized of the 1990s kept to themselves as they pursued jobs, there are many more glass walls and open gathering places where the downsized of the 21st century get to know each other. They socialize, and they even re-create office buzz. Said the managing principal, "It took us awhile to recognize that this had become important."

LAYOFFS IN OTHER COUNTRIES

The phenomenon of layoffs is not limited to the United States. Asia and Europe have been hard hit as well. Japan's chip and electronics conglomerates have shed tens of thousands of jobs in the past year as the worldwide information-technology slump and fierce competition from foreign rivals have battered their bottom lines. High-profile firms such as Hitachi, Fujitsu, NEC, Toshiba, Matsushita Electric Industrial, and Sony have cut deeply, as has Mazda in automobile production.[17] In Hong Kong, fully 43 percent of firms in a recent survey expect to lay off workers in 2002, and in mainland China, more than 25.5 million people were laid off from state-owned firms between 1998 and 2001. Another 20 million are expected to be laid off from traditional state-owned firms by 2006.[18]

The incidence of layoffs varies among countries in Western Europe. Labor laws in countries such as Italy, France, Germany, and Spain make it difficult and expensive for companies to dismiss workers. In Germany, for example, all "redundancies" must by law be negotiated in detail by a workers' council, which is a compulsory part of any big German company and often has a say in which workers can be fired. Moreover, setting the terms of severance is tricky, because the law is vague and German courts often award compensation if workers claim that they received inadequate settlements. In France, layoffs are rare. As an example, consider that now-bankrupt appliance maker Moulinex, once considered an icon of French industry, repeatedly tried to restructure in 2001 but was blocked by the French Socialist government because its cost-cutting plans included layoffs. At present, even if companies offer generous severance settlements to French workers, as both Michelin and Marks & Spencer did in 2001, the very announcement of layoffs triggers a political firestorm.[19]

Multinational companies are dealing with this problem in several different ways. One strategy is to turn to other locations within the 15-nation European Union where labor laws are more flexible. Thus Britain has attracted car assembly plants from Nissan Motor Company and PSA Peugeot Citroen, while Ireland hosts EU-wide operations for such technology companies as Microsoft and Intel. A second strategy, practiced by multinationals such as General Motors and Ford, is to move production to Eastern Europe, Turkey, and other lower-cost areas.[20]

U.S.-style layoffs are more common among some European multinationals. Thus London-based EMI Recorded Music, facing a declining global market and growing threat from Internet piracy, recently announced cuts affecting 18 percent of its workforce. Stockholm-based LM Ericsson, the world's largest manufacturer of equipment for cell-phone networks, with operations in 140 countries, had 107,000 employees in April 2001. By January 2002 it was down to 85,000, and in April 2002 it announced an additional 17,000 job cuts.[21] Such massive corporate and personal disruption once again raises important questions about the long-term benefits of strategies that emphasize reductions in the workforce. To put that issue into perspective, let us consider a key driver of business success in the new millennium: business concept innovation.

Business Concept Innovation

As Gary Hamel notes in his book *Leading the Revolution* (2000), the age of incremental progress is over. Its mantra—faster, better, cheaper—is true of fewer and fewer companies. Today change has changed. No longer is it additive. No longer does it move in a straight line. In many industries it is now discontinuous, abrupt, and distinctly non-linear, as radically different ideas and commercial developments render established products and services obsolete.[22] Perhaps the most far-reaching change of all is the Internet, which has rendered geography meaningless.

In the age of incremental progress, companies practiced rigorous planning, continuous improvement, statistical process control, six sigma quality-enhancement programs, reengineering, and enterprise resource planning.[23] If companies missed something that was changing in the environment—for example in TVs, stereos, and other consumer electronics, as in the 1970s and 1980s—there was plenty of time to catch up.

Today, if a company misses a critical new development—for example in digital phones, Internet auctions, or corporate extranets (networks that connect firms to their suppliers or customers, that is, the entire value chain)—it may never catch up. As an example of the latter, consider enterprise resource planning (ERP). Firms employed armies of consultants to help them use ERP to integrate internal operations like purchasing, manufacturing, and accounting. Such activities are important and useful, but now many companies use the Web to link up with suppliers and customers. Many ERP consultants (and their firms) are not players in this area, and the Web is the wave of the future.

Industrial-age management is a liability in a post-industrial world. Never before has there been such an incredible need for visionary leadership and the capacity to manage change effectively. Today the challenge is to think differently—to move beyond scientific management and kaizen (continuous improvement). As Hamel points out, the focus today is not on the slow accretion of scientific knowledge but on leaps of human imagination. In a non-linear world, only non-linear ideas will create new wealth and lead to radical improvements in human welfare.

The starting point today is not a product or a service. It's the entire business concept. Here are just a few examples:

- Internet telephony (the use of Internet facilities, where voice transmission is one form of communication) versus dedicated voice networks (e.g., telephones, allowing only voice transmission)
- Buying insurance over the Internet versus going to a physical agency
- Searching for a job at Monster.com versus help-wanted ads in a local newspaper
- Downloading music via MP3 files versus purchasing CDs at a music store
- Instant buyer co-operatives (Mercata.com) versus shopping at a mall

The list goes on and on. Now let's consider what business concept innovation is not.

What Business Concept Innovation Is Not

Some popular strategies today are spin-offs of non-core businesses, stock buy-backs, tracking stocks, and efficiency programs. All of these release wealth but they do not create wealth.[24] This is financial engineering, not business concept innovation. Strategies like these do not create new customers, markets, or revenue streams. Their only purpose is to wring a bit more wealth out of yesterday's strategies. Sure, money talks, but it doesn't think. Machines work efficiently, but they don't invent. Thinking and inventing are done by the only true, long-term source of innovation and renewal that organizations possess: smart, well-trained people.

How do you increase the probability that radical, new, wealth-creating ideas will emerge in your organization? Certainly not by indiscriminate downsizing of your workforce or by trying to imitate the best practices of other companies. Rather, a key task for leaders is to create an environment in which the creativity and imagination of employees at *all* levels can flourish. In many cases doing so requires a radical shift in the mindset of managers at all levels. That new mindset is called *responsible restructuring*.

Responsible Restructuring—What Is It?

In 1995 I wrote a publication for the U.S. Department of Labor entitled *Guide to Responsible Restructuring*.[25] As I investigated the approaches that various companies, large and small, public and private, adopted in their efforts to restructure, what became obvious to me was that companies differed in terms of how they viewed their employees. Indeed, they almost seemed to separate themselves logically into two groups. One group of firms, by far the larger of the two, saw employees as *costs to be cut*. The other, much smaller group of firms, saw employees as *assets to be developed*. Therein lay a major difference in the approaches they took to restructure their organizations.

- *Employees as costs to be cut*—these are the downsizers. They constantly ask themselves: What is the minimum number of employees that we need to run this company? What is the irreducible core number of employees that the business requires?
- *Employees as assets to be developed*—these are the responsible restructurers. They constantly ask themselves: How can we change the way we do business, so that we can use the people we currently have more effectively?

The downsizers see employees as commodities—like paper clips or light bulbs, interchangeable and substitutable one for another. This is a "plug-in" mentality: plug them in when you need them; pull the plug when you no longer need them. In contrast, responsible restructurers see employees as sources of innovation and renewal. They see in employees the potential to grow their businesses.

DOWNSIZING'S HIDDEN RISK TO LEARNING ORGANIZATIONS

Learning organizations, from high-technology firms to the financial services industry, depend heavily on their employees—their stock of human capital—to innovate and grow. Learning organizations are collections of networks in which interrelationships among individuals, that is, social networks, generate learning and knowledge. This knowledge base constitutes a firm's "memory." Because a single individual has multiple relationships in such an organization, indiscriminate, non-selective downsizing has the potential to inflict considerable damage on the learning and memory capacity of organizations.[26] That damage is far greater than might be implied by a simple tally of individuals.

When one considers the multiple relationships generated by one individual, it is clear that restructuring which involves significant reductions in employees can inflict damage and create the loss of significant "chunks" of organizational memory. Such a loss damages ongoing processes and operations, forfeits current contacts, and may lead to foregone business opportunities. Which kinds of organizations are at greatest risk? Those that operate in rapidly evolving industries, such as biotechnology, pharmaceuticals, and software, where survival depends on a firm's ability to innovate constantly.

TEN MISTAKES TO AVOID WHEN RESTRUCTURING

Downsizing a learning organization is not the only mistake that some companies make. Here are ten others to ponder and learn from.[27]

1. *Failure to be clear about long- and short-term goals.* Always ask: What do our customers expect from us, and how will restructuring affect our ability to meet those expectations?[28]
2. *Use of downsizing as a first resort, rather than as a last resort.* In some cases, firms downsize because they see competitors doing it. This is a "cloning" response, in which executives in different firms follow one another's actions under conditions of uncertainty,[29] but it fails to consider alternative approaches to reducing costs. Such alternative

include delaying new-hire start dates, reducing perks, revoking job offers, freezing salaries and promotions, and asking employees to take unpaid vacations.[30]

3. *Use of non-selective downsizing.* Across-the-board job cuts miss the mark. So also do cuts based on criteria such as last-in-first-out (because then firms lose all their bright young people), removing everyone below a certain level in the hierarchy (because top-heavy firms become even top heavier), or weeding out all middle managers (because firms lose a wealth of experience and connections).[31] Are all departments and all employees equally valuable to the firm? Probably not. With respect to employees, think about performance and replaceability.[32] Employees who are top performers and who are difficult to replace are most valuable. They are the "stars" that firms will depend on to innovate, to create new markets and new customers. Do everything you can to retain them.

4. *Failure to change the ways work is done.* Some firms mistakenly believe that they can keep making products or delivering services the same way as before downsizing. They fail even to consider changing from an old way to a new way of working. The same amount of work is simply loaded on the backs of fewer workers. Such a "pure-employment downsizing" approach does not lead to long-term improvements either in profitability or in total returns on common stock.[33]

5. *Failure to involve workers in the restructuring process.* It is a truism that employees are more likely to support what they helped to create. Yet many restructuring efforts fail to involve employees in any decisions either about the process or the desired outcome. As a result, employees feel powerless and helpless, and there is massive uncertainty in the organization. Conversely, when employees were asked to rate various factors that affect attracting, motivating, and retaining superior employees, one of the most important factors was "opportunities to participate in decisions."[34]

6. *Failure to communicate openly and honestly.* Failure to provide regular, ongoing updates not only contributes to the atmosphere of uncertainty; it also does nothing to dispel rumors. Open, honest communication is crucial if employees are to trust what management says, and trust is crucial to successful restructuring.[35] People trust leaders who make themselves known and make their positions clear.[36]

7. *Inept handling of those who lose their jobs.* Failure to treat departing employees with dignity and respect (e.g., having security guards escort them off company property), failure to provide training to supervisors in how to handle emotional factors, and failure to provide assistance to departing employees (financial, counseling, redeployment, training, outplacement) is another crucial mistake.[37]

8. *Failure to manage survivors effectively.* Employee morale is often the first casualty of downsizing, as survivors become narrow-minded, selfabsorbed, and risk averse.[38] Many firms underestimate the emotional damage that survivors suffer by watching others lose their jobs. In fact, a great deal of research shows that survivors often suffer from heightened levels of stress, burnout, uncertainty about their own roles in the new organization, and an overall sense of betrayal.[39] In unionized environments, downsizing may be related to increased grievances, higher absenteeism rates, workplace conflict, and poorer supervisor–union member relations.[40] In fact, survivors are looking for signals such as the following. Were departing employees treated fairly, and with dignity and respect? Why should I stay? What new opportunities will be available to me if I choose to do so? Is there a new business strategy to help us do a better job of competing in the marketplace?

9. *Ignoring the effects on other stakeholders.* In addition to survivors and victims, it is important to think through the potential consequences of restructuring on customers, suppliers, shareholders, and the local community. A comprehensive program addresses and manages consequences for each of these groups.

10. *Failure to evaluate results and learn from mistakes.* Restructuring is not a one-time event for most firms. I have found in my research that unless firms are brutally honest about the processes and outcomes of their restructuring efforts, they are doomed to repeat the same mistakes over and over again. Don't be afraid to ask employees and managers at all levels. "What did you like most and like least about our restructuring effort?" Don't be afraid to ask customers if the firm is now meeting their needs more effectively, and for suggestions on how it might do so.

Three Downsizing Strategies for Responsible Restructuring

Now that we have seen what so many firms do wrong, let's examine three responsible restructuring strategies that some firms are doing right. These examples are by no means exhaustive, but they do represent the strategies of firms in several different industries (financial services, management consulting, high technology, telecommunications, manufacturing) and countries (the United States and Singapore).

CHARLES SCHWAB & COMPANY: USE DOWNSIZING AS A LAST RESORT; AT THE SAME TIME REINVENT YOUR BUSINESS

At the end of the second quarter of 2001, Schwab's commission revenues were off 57 percent from their peak 15 months earlier. Overall revenue was down 38 percent, losses totaled $19 million, and the stock had dropped 75 percent from its high. Something had to give. How did the company respond? It took five steps *before* finally cutting staff.[41]

- When Schwab first saw business begin to deteriorate the year before it put projects on hold and cut back on such expenses as catered staff lunches, travel, and entertainment. Management went out of its way to explain to employees the short-term nature of these cuts.[42]
- As it became clear that more savings were needed, top executives all took pay cuts: 50 percent each for the company's two CEOs, 20 percent for executive vice presidents, 10 percent for senior vice presidents, and 5 percent for vice presidents.
- It encouraged employees to take unused vacation and to take unpaid leaves of up to 20 days.
- Management designated certain Fridays as voluntary days off without pay for employees who didn't have clients to deal with.
- Only after the outlook darkened again, at the end of the first quarter of 2001, did the firm announce layoffs: 2,000 out of a workforce of 25,000. Even then the severance package included a $7,500 "hire-back" bonus for any employee rehired within 18 months. It also included between 500 and 1,000 stock options, cash payments to offset the increased costs of healthcare insurance for laid-off employees, and a full range of outplacement services.[43] Further, everyone being laid off, nearly 5,000 people

by the end of September 2001, was eligible for a $20,000 tuition voucher paid for by the founder himself. That could cost him as much as $10 million.

Over the past decade or so, Schwab & Company has had a lengthy record of product innovation. Perhaps its greatest innovation was one of the gutsiest moves of the 1990s: offering online trading in a bigger and better way than anyone else, even though it meant cutting commission rates by more than half. The result? In early 2000 Schwab could boast of having generated a better 10-year return for investors than Microsoft!

Today, however, the company is reinventing its business model. Sure, it is cutting costs by making its website easier to use, thus cutting down on expensive phone traffic, and it is raising fees for customers who don't trade very often and are unprofitable for the firm. But its biggest bet—where it thinks the bulk of its future revenue will come from—will be a radical new approach to winning and keeping business. The firm that was founded on the principle that it would never tell customers what stocks to buy is about to do just that—but with an ingenious twist.

The plan is to have computers analyze customers' portfolios, compare them with a computer-generated list of Schwab-recommended stocks for that investor's risk profile, and then convey that message to the client. When the objective analysis is supplemented with research reports from partner Goldman Sachs, plus occasional access to a salaried investment specialist, the company feels that these steps will fill in the final gap in what will be a complete set of services for virtually every investor.[44]

Schwab is practicing responsible restructuring. How? At the same time that it is demonstrating by its actions that it sees its employees as assets to be developed, it is developing business concept innovations that will allow it to generate new customers and new streams of revenue in order to grow its business.

CISCO SYSTEMS, ACCENTURE, MOTOROLA: "PARK" THE BEST; RESPECT THE REST

A second downsizing strategy is to retain top employees, while generating good will, even loyalty, among those departing. The United States has just sailed through five years of labor shortfalls on a scale not seen in more than three decades. What's more, the unemployment rate, while still rising, remains at historically low levels. Indeed, the unemployment rate for white-collar workers remains at just 2.2 percent.[45]

Many employers are cautious about laying off too many workers, only to find themselves scrambling to refill the positions when demand picks up. To avoid that scenario, some are developing ingenious plans to "park" their most highly skilled employees until the economy recovers, and to promote good will, even loyalty, among those they have to let go.

Cisco Systems, which is shrinking its staff to 30,500 from 38,000 and paying six months' salary to those who sign severance agreements, is also trying a 21st-century version of the old industrial furlough. In a pilot program, it is paying 70 employees one-third of their salaries while lending them to non-profit organizations for a year. In effect Cisco is warehousing them until they might be needed.[46]

Accenture, a large management consulting firm, did cut 600 support staff last June. But to retain skilled employees, it developed the idea of partially paid sabbaticals. The firm pays 20 percent of each employee's salary for six to twelve months, plus benefits, and it lets the employee keep a work phone number, laptop, and email. About 1,000 employees took the offer. Said Accenture's managing partner for internal operations. "This is a way to cut costs that gives us the ability to hang onto people we spent so much time recruiting and training."[47]

Motorola has been hard hit by the global slowdown in telecommunications. As a result it is eliminating 30,000 jobs of the 147,000 that existed in January 2001, but at the same time it does not want to waste the results of its assiduous recruiting during the late 1990s. Every laid-off employee in the United States is getting a minimum of eight weeks' pay as severance, a benefit that until the late 1990s was not so broadly available to lower-ranking employees.

Motorola has also become more active in sponsoring job fairs and outplacement clinics where those leaving the company can receive help in writing resumes, honing interviewing skills, and making contacts.[48] Why is Motorola going to such lengths to generate goodwill among departing employees? It views these initiatives as subtle tools for future recruiting, once the economy revives and hiring resumes.

PHILIPS ELECTRONICS SINGAPORE: OFFER TRAINING, COUNSELING, AND JOB-FINDING ASSISTANCE TO DISPLACED WORKERS

A third downsizing strategy for responsible restructuring is to help displaced workers find new jobs.

Philips has operations in more than 60 countries in the areas of lighting, consumer electronics, domestic appliances, components, semiconductors, medical systems, business electronics, and information technology services. It began manufacturing operations in Singapore in 1969.[49]

Since the 1980s, manufacturing companies operating in Singapore have been following the global trend of relocating low-end production to lower-cost countries in the region. More recently, the trend has been to relocate to China and newly emerging economies with large supplies of low-cost labor and growing markets. In 1999 Philips Singapore took advantage of this opportunity to relocate part of its consumer electronics and domestic appliances business to China, Eastern Europe, and Mexico, thus lowering its operating costs while remaining based in Singapore. This restructuring exercise resulted in about 750 excess production operators, technicians, and related support staff.

In an effort to maintain a lean and flexible workforce in its low-end production in anticipation of an eventual relocation out of Singapore, Philips adopted the following human resource management strategies:

- Managers were required to assess long-term workforce projections carefully before recruiting new employees.
- Vacancies had to be filled from within the organization unless present staff could not meet the requirements.
- Philips recruited contract workers rather than full-time workers to meet increased demand and to provide flexibility when demand fluctuates.

When it became clear that the relocation would result in 750 excess employees, management informed the union, a branch of the Union of Workers in Electronics and Electrical Industries (UWEEI), of the situation. They worked together to ensure that the retrenched workers were given as much support and help as possible in finding alternative work.

Philips puts a high priority on employee self-development, with the belief that people are its most valuable resources. It has earned a reputation for being an enlightened and caring employer, having won several prestigious awards from the National Trade Union Congress (NTUC) and from the government. Its demonstrated commitment to its employees, as stated in its philosophy of management, is that employees should be respected, challenged, encouraged, and given equal opportunities.

KEY INITIATIVES AT PHILIPS

Skills upgrading and training for employability. Together with the UWEEI and the NTUC, Philips encouraged all of the affected workers to take advantage of a program that had been initiated by the NTUC: the Skills Redevelopment Program. That program provides attractive training grants to companies. Its objective is to help workers, especially those who are older and lower skilled, to become more employable through skills upgrading. Philips encouraged the 750 affected workers to enroll in the Certificate of Competence in Electronic Maintenance program under the Skills Redevelopment Program.

Counselling and employment assistance. On the day that the retrenchments were announced in December 1999, the company made sure that all affected workers were registered with the NTUC Employment Assistance Program, and company and union representatives were available to answer questions. Later, a job fair was organized by the Ministry of Manpower and union representatives to assist affected workers in their job search.

Job matching. The first priority was to help workers secure alternative employment, by trying to match them with vacancies in job data banks kept by the NTUC Employment Assistance Program and the government-sponsored Employment Services Department. In an initial effort in December 1999, more than 30 retrenched workers were identified as having the necessary qualifications to pursue further training for a higher skills job such as wafer fabrication. The union approached ST Microelectronics, which had vacancies in this area, and got its agreement to interview interested workers. The union encouraged other workers who were qualified or interested to undergo training in order to qualify for higher-paying employment opportunities.

Financial assistance. To minimize financial hardship, retrenchment benefits were paid according to the collective bargaining agreement: one month's pay for every year of service for those with three or more years of service, and one week's pay for every year for those with fewer than three years' service. In addition, workers received one month's pay in lieu of notice of retrenchment, and those retrenched in December still received the one-month annual wage supplement normally paid at the end of the year.

Outcomes

Many of the laid-off workers had worked for Philips for more than 20 years, and this had been their first job. They understood the company's need to reduce operating costs and to remain competitive. At the same time, they appreciated the support provided both by the management and by the union in helping them to adjust to the sad reality. Such support also boosted the morale and confidence of those who continued to work in the plants.

Restructuring Responsibly: What To Do

At this point you are probably wondering how to proceed. We have highlighted some things not to do and have provided examples of how to use downsizing as part of a strategy for responsible restructuring. We believe it can all be put together by following these suggestions.

1. *Carefully consider the rationale behind restructuring.* Invest in analysis and consider the impact on those who stay, those who leave, and the ability of the organization to serve its customers.[50] Do you have a long-term strategic plan that identifies the future mission and vision of the organization, as well as its core competencies? Does the plan consider factors such as changes in the firm's external environment and industry, the business cycle, the stage of internationalization of the firm, market segments, and life cycles of products in the various segments? Does the plan consider how processes can be redesigned while retaining the high performers who will be crucial to the firm's future success? Is there a plan to sell off unprofitable assets? Is employment downsizing part of a plan or is it *the* plan? All of these factors could impact the need for and extent of restructuring.

2. *Consider the virtues of stability.* In many cases, companies can maintain their special efficiencies only if they can give their workers a unique set of skills and a feeling that they belong together. Teams work best if the team members get to know and trust each other and if each team member masters a broad enough range of skills to be able to fill in for absent colleagues. Moreover, profit sharing as a reward system makes sense only if the employees are around when profits are disbursed.

Sometimes the virtues of stability outweigh the potential benefits of change.[51]

3. *Before making any final decisions about restructuring, managers should make their concerns known to employees and seek their input.* Sometimes workers have insightful ideas that may make layoffs unnecessary. However, even if layoffs are necessary, seeking employee input will foster a sense of participation, belonging, and personal control. Make special efforts to secure the input of "star" employees or opinion leaders, for they can help communicate the rationale and strategy of restructuring to their fellow employees and can also help to promote trust in the restructuring effort.[52]

4. *Don't use downsizing as a "quick fix" to achieve short-term goals in the face of long-term problems.* Consider other alternatives first, and ensure that management at all levels shares the pain and participates in any sacrifices employees are asked to bear. Make downsizing truly a last resort, not a first resort.

5. *If layoffs are necessary, be sure that employees perceive the process of selecting excess positions as fair, and make decisions in a consistent manner.*[53] Make special efforts to retain the best and the brightest, and provide maximum advance notice to terminated employees.

6. *Communicate regularly and in a variety of ways in order to keep everyone abreast of new developments and information.* Use newsletters, emails, videos, and employee meetings for this purpose. Sharing confidential financial and competitive information with employees establishes a climate of trust and honesty. High-level managers should be visible, active participants in this process. Be sure that lower-level managers are trained to address the concerns of victims as well as survivors.[54]

7. *Give survivors a reason to stay, and prospective new hires a reason to join.* As one set of authors noted, "People need to believe in the organization to make it work, but they need to see that it works to believe in it."[55] Recognize that surviving employ-ees ultimately are the people you will depend on to provide the innovation, superior service to customers, and healthy corporate culture that will attract and retain top talent. Do everything you can to ensure their commitment and their trust.

8. *Train employees and their managers in the new ways of operating.* Restructuring means change, and employees at all levels need help in coping with changes in areas such as reporting relationships, new organizational arrangements, and reengineered business processes. Evidence indicates clearly that firms whose training budgets increase following a restructuring are more likely to realize improved productivity, profits, and quality.[56]

9. *Examine all HR systems carefully in light of the change of strategy or environment facing the firm.*[57] Training employees in the new ways of operating is important, but so also are other HR systems. These include workforce planning based on changes in business strategy, markets, customers, and expected economic conditions; recruitment and selection, based on the need to change both the number and skills mix of new hires; performance appraisal, based on changes in the work to be done; compensation, based on changes in skill requirements or responsibilities; and labor relations, based on the need to involve employees and their unions in the restructuring process.

Above all, if you do choose to restructure, do it responsibly, and use it as an opportunity to focus even more sharply on those areas of the business where your firm enjoys its greatest competitive strengths. By restructuring responsibly through the use of effective downsizing strategies, your organization will be better able to achieve the 3C's of organizational success: Care of customers, Constant innovation, and Committed people.[58]

Endnotes

1. Brett, J. M., & Stroh, L. K. 1997. Jumping ship: Who benefits from an external labor market career strategy? *Journal of Applied Psychology*, 82(3): 331–341.

2. Shadow of recession. 9 February 2002. *http://www.cbsmarketwatch.com.*

3. Planned job cuts continue fall. 3 April 2002. *http://www.cbsmarketwatch.com.*

4. Morris, B. White-collar blues. *Fortune.* 23 July 2001, 98–110.

5. Dawkins, P., & Littler, C. R. (Eds.). July 2001. *Downsizing: Is it working for Australia?* http://www.ceda.com.au.

6. See, for example, Blau, F. D., & Ferber, M. A. 1987. *The economics of women, men, and work.* Englewood Cliffs. NJ: Prentice-Hall; Schneer, J. A., & Reitman, F. 1997. The interrupted managerial career path: A longitudinal study of MBAs. *Journal of Vocational Behavior,* 51(3): 411–434; and Schneer, J. A., & Reitman, F. 1995. The impact of gender as managerial careers unfold. *Journal of Vocational Behavior,* 47(3): 290–315.

7. Cascio, W. F., & Young, C. E. 2001. Financial consequences of employment-change decisions in major U.S. corporations: 1982–2000. In K. P. De Meuse & M. L. Marks (Eds.). *Resizing the organization.* In press, San Francisco: Jossey-Bass. See also Cascio, W. F., Young, C. E., & Morris, J. R. 1997. Financial consequences of employment-change decisions in major U.S. corporations. *Academy of Management Journal,* 40(5): 1175–1189; and Morris, J. R., Cascio, W. F., & Young, C. E. 1999. Have employment downsizings been successful? *Organizational Dynamics,* 27(3): 78–87.

8. Cascio, et al., op. cit.

9. Bruner, J., quoted in Lavelle, L. Swing that ax with care. *Business Week,* 11 February 2003, 78.

10. Cascio, W. F. 1993. Downsizing: What do we know? What have we learned? *The Academy of Management Executive,* 7(1): 95–104. See also Cascio. W. F. Strategies for responsible restructuring. Keynote address presented at the National Manpower Summit, Singapore. 18 October 2001.

11. Morris, op. cit.

12. Ansberry, C. Private resources: By resisting layoffs, small manufacturers help protect economy. *Wall Street Journal,* 6 July 2001, A1, A2.

13. American Management Association. 2000. *2000 American Management Association survey: Staffing and structure.* New York: Author.

14. Eig, J. Shrinking week: Do part-time workers hold the key to when the recession breaks? *Wall Street Journal,* 3 January 2002, A1, A2.

15. Uchitelle, L. Pink slip? Now, it's all in a day's work. *New York Times,* 5 August 2001. http://www.NYTimes.com.

16. Ibid.

17. Hitachi decides another 4,000 workers in Japan must go. *South China Morning Post,* 31 January 2002, 1; Kunii, I. Under the knife. *BusinessWeek,* 10 September 2001, 62; and Larimer, T. Worst-case scenario. *Time,* 26 March 2001, 54–56. See also Shirouzu, N. Leaner and meaner: Driven by necessity—and by Ford-Mazda downsizes, U.S.-style. *Wall Street Journal,* 5 January 2000, A1, A10. See also Sony's shake up. *BusinessWeek.* 22 March 1999, 52, 53.

18. 43pc of firms plan to cut staff, says poll. *South China Morning Post,* 26 February 2002, 1; and China warns of 20 million urban jobless. *South China Morning Post,* 30 April 2002, 1.

19. Winestock, G. A. reticent European right balks on labor *Wall Street Journal,* 21 June 2002, A6, A7; and Matlack, C. The high cost of France's aversion to layoffs. *BusinessWeek,* 5 November 2001, 56.

20. Winestock, op. cit.

21. Larsen, K. EMI plans job cuts, large cost savings. *Asian Wall Street Journal,* 21 March 2002, M6: Pritchard, S. Deregulation and debt serve to hasten inevitable. *South China Morning Post,* 26 March 2002, 2; and Gamel, K. Ericsson to cut 17,000 jobs. 22 April 2002. http://www.cbsmarketwatch.com.

22. Hamel, G. 2000. *Leading the revolution.* Boston: Harvard Business School Press.

23. Statistical process control (SPC) is a quality-control technique that is based on statistical theory. Its objective is to study the variation in the output of production processes. Six sigma is a standard in SPC where almost all variability in product or service output has been eliminated. In a six-sigma system, one expects only 3.4 defects per million units of output. Enterprise resource planning is a computer-based software system that integrates all departments and functions into a single information database.

24. Norris, F. Financial magic looked good, but left companies weak. *New York Times,* 28 September 2001. http://www.NYTimes.com.

25. U.S. Department of Labor. 1995. *Guide to responsible restructuring.* Washington, DC: U.S. Government Printing Office.

26. Fisher, S. R., & White, M. A. 2000. Downsizing in a learning organization: Are there hidden costs? *Academy of Management Review,* 25(1): 244–251.

27. The sources of these recommendations, unless otherwise noted, are my own research, as described in *Guide to responsible restructuring,* op. cit., as well as the following: Cravotta, R., & Kleiner, B. H. 2001. New developments concerning reductions in force. *Management Research News,* 24(3/4): 90–93. See also Moravec, M. The right way to rightsize. *Industry Week,* 5 September 1994, 46.

28. For more on this topic, see Seiders, K., & Berry, L. L. 1998. Service fairness: What it is and why it matters. *The Academy of Management Executive,* 12(2): 8–20.

29. McKinley, W., Zhao, J., & Rust, K. G. 2000. A sociocognitive interpretation of organizational downsizing. *Academy of Management Review,* 25(1): 227–243.

30. Lavelle, L. Thinking beyond the one-size-fits-all pay cut. *BusinessWeek,* 3 December 2001, 45.

31. Ibid. See also The year downsizing grew up. *The Economist,* 21 December 1996, 97–99.

32. Martin, D. C., & Bartol, K. M. 1985, Managing turnover strategically. *Personnel Administrator,* 30(11): 63–73. See also Cascio, W. F. 2000. *Costing human resources: The financial impact of behavior in organizations.* 4th ed. Cincinnati, OH: South-Western College Publishing.

33. Cascio & Young, op. cit.

34. Mirvis, P. H. 1997. Human resource management: Leaders, laggards, and followers. *The Academy of Management Executive,* 11(2): 43–56.

35. Mishra, K. E., Spreitzer, G. M., & Mishra, A. K. 1998. Preserving employee morale during downsizing. *Sloan Management Review,* 39(2): 83–95. See also Gray, R. Internal communication: Its critical role during business reorganizations. Presentation to the Australian Human Resources Institute, Sydney, 1 November 2001.

36. Darling, J., & Nurmi, R. 1995. Downsizing the multinational firm: Key variables for excellence. *Leadership & Organization Development Journal,* 16(5): 22–28.

37. As one example of this, see Barrionuevo, A. Jobless in a flash, Enron's ex-employees are stunned, bitter, ashamed. *Wall Street Journal,* 11 December 2001, B1, B12.

38. Cascio, W. F. Downsizing: What do we know?, op. cit.

39. Appelbaum, S. H., Everard, A., & Hung, L. T. S. 1999. Strategic downsizing: Critical success factors. *Management Decision*, 37(7): 535–552.

40. Wagar, T. H. 2001. Consequences of work force reduction: Some employer and union evidence. *Journal of Labor Research*, 22(4): 851–862.

41. Vogelstein, F. Can Schwab get its mojo back? *Fortune*, 17 September 2001, 93–98. See also Bernstein, A. America's future: The human factor. *BusinessWeek*, 27 August 2001, 118–122.

42. Boyle, M. How to cut perks without killing morale. *Fortune*, 19 February 2001, 241, 242, 244.

43. Jossi, F. Laying off well. *HRMagazine*, July 2001, 48.

44. Schwab versus Wall Street. *BusinessWeek*, 3 June 2002, 64–70.

45. Bernstein, op. cit.

46. Uchitelle, op. cit.

47. Bernstein, op. cit.

48. Uchitelle, op. cit.

49. Source: Singapore Ministry of Manpower. February 2001. *Managing excess manpower, case study series.* Singapore: Author.

50. *Guide to responsible restructuring*, op. cit.

51. Cascio & Young, op. cit. See also Conlin, M. Where layoffs are a last resort. 8 October 2001. *http://www.businessweek.com.*

52. See Roth, D. How to cut pay, lay off 8,000 people, and still have workers who love you. *Fortune*, 4 February 2002, 62–68.

53. Colquitt, J. A., Conlon, D. E., Wesson, M. J., Porter, C. O. L. H., & Ng, K. Y. 2001. Justice at the millennium: A meta-analytic review of 25 years of organizational justice research. *Journal of Applied Psychology*, 86(3): 425–445.

54. Feldman, M., & Spratt, M. 1999. *Five frogs on a log: A CEO's field guide to accelerating the transition in mergers, acquisitions, and gut-wrenching change.* New York: Harper.

55. De Vries, M., & Balazs, K. 1997. The downside of downsizing. *Human Relations*, 50(1): 11–50.

56. Appelbaum, S. H., Lavigne-Schmidt, S., Peytchev, M., & Shapiro, B. 1999. Downsizing: Measuring the costs of failure. *Journal of Management Development*. 18(5): 436–463.

57. Becker, B. E., Huselid, M. A., & Ulrich, D. 2001. *The HR scorecard: Linking people, strategy, and performance.* Boston: Harvard Business School Press. See also Delery, J. E., & Doty, D. H. 1996. Modes of theorizing in strategic human resource management: Tests of universalistic, contingency, and configurational performance predictions. *Academy of Management Journal*, 39(4): 802–835.

58. Darling & Nurmi, op. cit.

Retirement of Older Workers: Issues and Policies

Naresh C. Agarwal, Michael G. DeGroote, *Human Resource Planning*

Retirement of Older Workers: Issues and Policies

Today's organizations are faced with an aging workforce. Such a workforce represents both an opportunity and a challenge to organizations. It presents an opportunity because organizations can draw upon this growing resource to achieve their goals and strategies. An aging workforce poses a challenge because its effective utilization requires development of appropriate human resource policies. Included among these are retirement policies that are the primary focus of this paper.

The present paper consists of two parts. The first part examines key substantive issues that organizations should consider in developing retirement policies for older workers. These issues are discussed with particular reference to two basic policy options: mandatory and flexible retirement. The discussion of issues draws upon established theoretical and empirical literature from a variety of fields. While the context of discussion on some of the issues is Canada, the trends noted and the arguments made are generalizable to most industrialized countries. The second part of the paper derives policy implications with respect to retirement and effective utilization of older workers.

Substantive Issues and Arguments

INDIVIDUAL RIGHTS, NEEDS, AND PREFERENCES

Most Western societies have become increasingly committed to democratic principles of equality and freedom. At the workplace, these principles imply that employment decisions affecting individuals ought to be made without any regard to their personal and demographic characteristics. Instead, such decisions should be based on work-related criteria such as bona fide occupational requirements and performance. Accordingly, it can be argued that mandatory retirement, by singling out age rather than individual productivity or competence, is contrary to the principles of equality that our society has embraced.

Mandatory retirement can cause great economic and emotional hardship to many older workers. Before introducing legislation in 1978 prohibiting forced retirement at age 65 in the United States, public hearings were held by the House of Representatives on this subject. About the same time, in Canada, the Special Senate Committee on Retirement Age Policies also deliberated on this issue. According to the evidence presented before these bodies, mandatory retirement can cause severe economic hardship on older workers having financial obligations. This is particularly true for women, who have become very integral and critical participants in the labour market. Over the period 1976 to 1995, their labour force participation rate has increased from 45.2% to 57.4%; their relative share in labour force has gone up from 37.5% to 45.1%; and they have contributed 61.6% of the total labour force growth in Canada.[1] Due to the role they play in household and family activities, many women workers tend to have discontinuous and fewer years of service. Thus they may not qualify for full pension benefits if forced to retire at age 65.

Also, sudden shock of compulsory retirement and the resulting loss of productive work and earning power may often lead to impaired health and mental well-being. Studies have shown that voluntary retirees are more likely to be better satisfied than forced retirees (Roadburg, 1985). Flexible retirement policies enable older workers to make retirement decisions that are most consistent with their economic and non-economic needs. This may explain why a large majority of Canadians in a recent national survey indicated a strong preference for flexible retirement (Lowe, 1991). These preferences are also reflected in the widening of the age range within which people have begun retiring in recent years. For example, in the 1960s and 1970s, most people retired at or around age 65. But, retirement now occurs across an age span of 15 years or more, from the early fifties to the mid-sixties (Schellenberg, 1996).

DEMOGRAPHIC & LABOUR MARKET TRENDS

A strong case for flexible retirement policies can be made based on the emerging demographic and labour market trends in the Canadian economy. Similar trends are also noticeable in the United States (Kinsella & Gist, 1995) and many other industrialized countries (OECD, 1995). The key demographic and labour market trends are as follows:[2]

- The Canadian population is getting older. The median age of population increased from 26.2 years in 1971 to 33.9 years in 1993 and is expected to increase to 39.5 years by the year 2011. The aging index (i.e., the ratio of the number of persons aged 65 or over to those age 15 or under) increased from 27.4 in 1971 to 57.0 in 1993 and is expected to increase to 81.6 by the year 2011. Also, the proportion of population aged 55 years and older has increased from 20.2% in 1951 to 25.4% in 1991 and is expected to increase to 35.1% by the year 2011.

- People are living longer. For example, the life expectancy increased from 61.3 years to 74.6 years for men, and 70.8 years to 80.9 years for women over the 1951–91 period. It is expected to increase to 77 years and 84 years respectively for the two groups by the year 2011.

- The Canadian labour force is growing at a slower rate. The labour force grew by 24.6% over the decade of 1976–85. However, the rate of growth declined by more than half to 11.6% over the next decade 1986–95.

- The age distribution of the Canadian labour force is changing in favour of the older groups. The total number of youth (aged 15–24 years) in the labour force declined by 15.3% over 1976–95. Their proportion in the labour force fell from 28.3% in 1976 to 16.4% in 1995. In contrast, the number of those aged 25 and over increased by 70.1% and their proportion in the labour force rose from 71.7% in 1976 to 83.6% in 1995.

- The labour market activity is declining among older workers. For example, the labour force participation rate of those in the 55–64 years of age category fell from 53.5% in 1976 to 47.4% in 1995. The decline in the rate was even sharper for men in this age bracket, from 76.3% to 58.9% over the same period.

- The average retirement age is declining. Only 51% of those retiring between 1976 and 1980 were under age 65. This figure rose to 71% over the 1991–95 time period. As a consequence, the median age of retirement fell from 64.9 years in 1976–80 to 62.3 years in 1991–95 (Gower, 1997).

It is clear from the above data that the labour force in Canada is growing at a slower pace and getting older. Also, despite the fact that people are living longer, older people as a group are participating less actively in the labour market. Anticipating these demographic trends, the Federal Task Force on Labour Market Development in the 1980s examined, among other things, the resulting implications for labour market imbalances and mandatory retirement policies. The Task Force specifically concluded the following:

"There emerges a pattern of an increasing pool of older persons fully capable of continuing their attachment to the labour force at a time when serious industrial adjustment can be expected to require the skills they have developed.

These findings suggest that the management of labour shortages in some highly skilled trades in the next decade will require employment strategies that either slow down the withdrawal of older workers from areas of highest productivity and growth in the economy or prevent the total loss of such vital skills and expertise in the post-retirement period. Removal of mandatory retirement legislation and adoption of policies to encourage flexible work arrangements can facilitate employment for older workers" (Employment and Immigration Canada, 1981).

The same conclusions have been drawn for the 1990s in a recent survey study of respondents from over 400 public and private sector organizations in Canada (Towers Perrin and Hudson Institute Canada, 1991). The study found that even in the midst of widespread downsizing and layoffs, close to 60% of the respondents reported current difficulties in recruiting technical/technical support, supervisory/managerial, and professional employees. And a greater proportion of respondents expected these difficulties to continue or become worse in the coming years. The study observed that in view of these recruiting difficulties, "companies may be missing an opportunity to tap into an already existing and capable resource: their own aging employees." Similar conclusions concerning the current and expected shortages of skilled workforce are reported in more recent studies of local labour markets as well.[3]

It is difficult to predict whether or not retirement age will continue to decline. The statistics of the mid-1990s were undoubtedly affected by early retirement incentives offered by employers. As these incentives become less popular, retirement age may level out or even increase in future (Gower, 1997). Another emerging practice in industry is the increasing use of contingency employment contracts. These contracts generally provide lower job/income security, pension, and other benefits. As a result, many workers in future are likely to face more constrained retirement decisions (Chaykowski, 1995). There is also a mounting concern about the affordability of various retiree benefits plans. Faced with escalating health care costs of older workers, many employers in the United States have reduced health care benefits offered to retirees (Crown, 1996). In Canada, these reductions could occur through cuts to basic benefits available through the Canadian health system and extended/supplemental benefits available through employer health care plans. In addition, Canada's pension (social security in the United States) and other old age income supplements may become less generous due to concerns about the future solvency of these social plans. It is, therefore, conceivable that many older workers in future may stay longer in the labour force.

AGE-PERFORMANCE RELATIONSHIP

Age-performance related issues are among the strongest rationalizations offered in favour of mandatory retirement. These rationalizations take essentially two interrelated forms. First, it is argued that mandatory retirement enables older workers to "retire with dignity," for example, with a perception that they retired because of a personnel policy applicable to all employees. If mandatory retirement is eliminated, there may be a social stigma to retirement because it may be perceived as an indication of competence or performance problems.[4] Second, it is argued that mandatory retirement minimizes the need to monitor and assess job performance of older employees. It is claimed that workers nearing mandatory retirement age are generally permitted to continue their employment without careful review even if their job performance deteriorates below the acceptable level. If mandatory retirement is eliminated, employers will be obligated to use more careful and demanding performance appraisal systems for older employees, and this might put undue emotional pressures on the workers.

The above arguments appear to rest on two common assumptions: (a) after a certain age, job performance and age are negatively related, and (b) this negative relationship is generalizable across all older workers. The age-performance relationship has been a subject of so many empirical studies that literature review articles have periodically appeared attempting to summarize, interpret, and integrate the findings of these studies. Examples of such literature review articles include: Sonnenfeld (1977); Rhodes (1983); Waldman and Avolio (1986); McEvoy and Cascio (1989); and Forteza and Prieto (1994). Reviewing case studies and anecdotal evidence from a variety of sources and organizational settings, Sonnenfeld (1977) concluded that "the higher variation of manual labour performance within age groups, compared with the variation between ages groups, suggests that individual differences are much more important than age group differences. The need to evaluate potential on an individual basis, and not by age group has been convincingly established in these studies." The same finding appeared to generally hold for workers in other occupational categories as well.

The above conclusions have been largely confirmed in subsequent and more systematic reviews of published studies. In a qualitative review of 25 studies, Rhodes (1983) found roughly equal support for each of four possible age-performance relations: positive, negative, curvilinear ("inverted U"), and nonsignificant. Waldman and Avolio (1986) employed a quantitative technique, meta-analysis, with a view to provide a more precise interpretation of findings in the age-performance literature. Subjecting 13 published studies (with 37 samples) to this analysis, they found that the studies using objective performance found a small positive relationship between age and performance, whereas those using subjective measures (i.e., supervisory ratings) found a slight negative relationship. Overall, the study concluded that chronological age accounted for only a small percentage of the variance in performance and that it fell short in explaining the wide range of individual differences in job performance for people at various ages. In a subsequent meta-analysis review of a much larger group of 65 published empirical studies with 96 independent samples, McEvoy and Cascio (1989) reached essentially a similar conclusion that age and performance appeared to be generally unrelated. Finally, the same conclusion has been confirmed in a recent review of cross-cultural studies of the age-performance relationship (Forteza & Prieto, 1994).

A possible explanation for why empirical studies have failed to find a consistent, generalizable relationship between age and performance may lie in the moderating effects of various job and organizational-level factors (Avolio, Waldman & McDaniel, 1990). For example, some jobs may involve relatively low levels of complexity, autonomy, and variety, and high levels of potential physical and psychological stress. In such occupations, what might appear as declining performance with increasing age may be the result of accumulated boredom and burnout. The reverse might be true in occupations that involve an opposite profile of the above job contextual factors. Similarly, perceptions concerning organizational reward systems built over time can also influence performance (Cosier & Dalton, 1983). Older employees are likely to remain more motivated if they have experienced equitable rather than inequitable reward systems. In part, this experience may be dependent upon how employee performance is measured. It appears that the use of subjective measures tends to produce a negative relationship between age and performance; the reverse is true when objective measures of performance are used. A recent field study of a large U.S. corporation shows that a more consistent, positive relationship between age and performance results when both types of performance measures are used simultaneously (Liden, Stilwell & Ferris, 1996). It may be that when objective performance data are available, subjective performance ratings are less likely to be biased against older workers.

COMPENSATION SEQUENCING SCHEMES

Mandatory retirement is often justified on the grounds that it facilitates the existence of compensation sequencing schemes, which offer many economic advantages. Under such schemes, employees are underpaid (i.e., less than their productivity) in the first half of their employment contract and overpaid in the second half such that the expected present value of the employee's productivity equals the expected present value of compensation. It is argued that compensation sequencing schemes cannot exist without a pre-set mandatory retirement date. In the absence of such a date, employees can decide to postpone retirement. Thus, their compensation could exceed productivity for an indefinite period of time, thereby causing economic losses to employers and inequity feelings among younger employees.

Supporters of compensation sequencing schemes argue that these schemes prevent employees from "shirking" on the job (Lazer, 1979). The threat of being fired and thereby losing substantial deferred earnings at the end of their career keeps employees honest and working hard. In addition, it is suggested that compensation sequencing schemes reduce the need to constantly monitor and evaluate employee performance which would be required if employees were being paid exactly according to their current productivity. Periodic assessment of performance is less costly to employers and psychologically less threatening to older employees.

The above arguments in favour of mandatory retirement as a means to preserve the existence of compensation sequencing schemes do not appear to be particularly strong for three reasons. First, there are other, perhaps simpler and equally effective, ways than compensation sequencing schemes to prevent older employees from shirking on the job. For example, the threat of certain, immediate dismissal would be an extremely powerful incentive not to shirk on the job, considering the psychological damage to the employee's ego, the tarnishing of his/her employment record and the probably loss of income during the period of unemployment while searching for a new job (Reid, 1988). In addition, periodic bonuses based on acceptable past performance are an alternative and a positive way to motivate employees to maintain performance over time.

Second, a pre-set mandatory retirement age is deemed necessary for the existence of compensation sequencing schemes because, without such a date, compensation could exceed productivity for an indefinite period of time. This assumes that under an open-ended, flexible retirement system, older employees will choose to continue working past the traditional retirement age of 65. The available evidence from jurisdictions that have abolished mandatory retirement and companies that allow their employees to continue working past age 65 does not support this assumption. It indicates that only a small number of employees opt to continue working beyond age 65, and those who do tend to retire within a year or two thereafter (Dunlop, 1980; Labour Canada, 1985; and Gibb-Clark, 1990). Therefore, absence of a pre-set mandatory retirement age is not likely to jeopardize the operation of compensation sequencing schemes.

Finally, compensation sequencing schemes presuppose a long-term career with the same employer. Only then can underpayment in the first half of an employee's career be compensated through overpayment in the second half of that employee's career. However, the assumption of a lifelong career with the same employer is not a very realistic one. For example, the average tenure of paid workers in Canada was only 6.9 years in 1977 and 7.9 years in 1995 (Belkhodja, 1992; Statistics Canada, 1996). The slight increase in the average tenure observed over this period can be largely explained by the declining proportion of the youth (aged 18–24 years) in the labour force. The average tenure may become even lower under the emerging employment systems, which make much greater use of part-time, temporary, and contract workers. For example, the percentage of part-time workers in the labour force increased from 10.6% in 1975 to 18.6% in 1995 (Statistics Canada, 1996). Similarly, eight percent of employees, or about 799,000, identified themselves as being in temporary or contract positions in 1989. The figure increased to nine percent, or about 970,000, in 1994 (Krahn, 1995). Thus, compensation sequencing schemes will become even less applicable in future.

AGE AND TRAINING PERFORMANCE

Another potential argument in favour of mandatory retirement relates to the perceived lack of trainability of older workers. Given the accelerating pace of technological and other changes at the workplace, ability of workers to learn new skills and competencies has become a particularly important concern for employers. The cognitive ability literature indicates that the information processing system tends to become less efficient with age, and that such decrements in efficiency begin to appear past the twenties (Charness, 1995). This implies that older workers will be slower in acquiring new skills. A recent meta-analytic study investigated the relationship between age and job-related training outcomes (Kubeck, Delp, Haslett & McDaniel, 1996). The study found that, relative to younger workers, older workers showed less mastery of training material, completed the final training task more slowly, and took longer to complete the training program.

The adult education and training literature, however, points to a different conclusion. It indicates that individuals can maintain intellectual and learning abilities well into the seventies and beyond (Schaie, 1985; Sterns, 1986; Willis, 1985). While this literature recognizes that, relative to younger workers, older workers may require more time to learn, it indicates that these workers tend to do better if self-paced, non-competitive, and experiential training methods are used with them (Sterns & Doverspike, 1989). Once the new skills are learnt, older workers tend to perform them as well as their younger counterparts. These workers also exhibit lower absenteeism, turnover, and work injury/accident rates than younger workers (Barth, McNaught & Rizzi, 1996; Charness, 1995). It is thus possible that cost savings gained through these attributes of older workers may well offset any additional costs associated with longer training time needed for these workers.

ORGANIZATIONAL PLANNING AND RENEWAL

Two additional issues concerning mandatory versus flexible retirement policies need to be briefly reviewed here. The first issue relates to the degree of uncertainty faced under the two policies and the resulting implications for organizational planning efforts. It is sometimes argued that mandatory retirement provides a fixed termination date on the basis of which planning for recruitment, succession, and training can be undertaken. Without such a fixed date of retirement, the number of upcoming retirees will become indeterminate, rendering such planning more difficult. These concerns, however, seem to be overstated. For example, even under mandatory retirement policies, retirement is not an entirely certain or predictable flow. As discussed earlier in this paper, a large number of workers in Canada choose to retire prior to reaching the specified mandatory age of retirement. Also, uncertainty is inherent in the normal running of most organizations. In the area of human resources specifically, turnover, absenteeism, disability, and death are all uncertain, probabilistic flows with which organizations have to deal. General approaches, processes, and techniques that are used by organizations to forecast these flows can be adapted to forecast retirements under flexible retirement policies. As experience with such policies accumulates, more accurate prediction models can be developed to estimate the likely retirements in a given time period.

Finally, some may argue that mandatory retirement policies are needed to ensure organizational renewal through infusion of new blood and to protect job and promotional opportunities for the younger people. While these are very important goals, the critical question is the extent to which mandatory retirement can actually be a means to achieve them. The number of people retiring at the mandated age in most organizations is likely to be too small to contribute in any meaningful way to organizational renewal or employment opportunities for the youth. Also, as noted earlier, the evidence emerging from jurisdictions that removed mandatory retirement a few years ago indicates that the number of people opting for delayed retirement is rather small, and even those who do so tend to remain working only for one to three additional years. So, the adverse impact of removing mandatory retirement on organizational renewal and employment opportunities for the youth is likely to be largely transitional (Krashinsky, 1988).

CURRENT LEGAL SITUATION

In the United States, the Age Discrimination in Employment Act (ADEA) prohibits age discrimination in hiring, firing, and compensation of persons aged over 40. Initially, the coverage of ADEA was up to age 65. It was extended to age 70 in 1978. The upper limit of age 70 was removed altogether in 1986, virtually eliminating mandatory retirement in the United States. In contrast, the legal situation in Canada is less clear-cut. The Canadian Charter of Rights and Freedoms (Section 15) guarantees that: "Every individual is equal before and under the law and has the right to the equal protection and equal benefit of the law without discrimination and, in particular, without discrimination based on race, national or ethnic origin, colour, religion, sex, age or mental or physical disability." These rights and freedoms are "subject only to such reasonable limits prescribed by law as can be demonstrably justified in a free and democratic society" (Section 1). Thus, under the Charter, age is a protected category without any upper age limit. Consequently, in those sectors to which the Charter applies, mandatory retirement is illegal unless it can be justified as a reasonable limit.

In sectors not covered by the Charter, the human rights legislation is the appropriate law in respect to mandatory retirement. In all jurisdictions in Canada, such legislation prohibits age discrimination in employment, unless age can be demonstrated as a bona fide occupational requirement (BFOR).

Protection against age discrimination exists without any upper limit on age years in these nine jurisdictions: federal, Alberta, Manitoba, New Brunswick, Nova Scotia, Northwest Territories, Prince Edward Island, Quebec, and the Yukon Territory. Thus, in all these jurisdictions mandatory retirement is illegal under their respective human rights statutes. In contrast, protection against age discrimination in employment exists only up to age 65 in the remaining four jurisdictions: British Columbia, Newfoundland, Ontario and Saskatchewan. As such, mandatory retirement at age 65 or beyond is not illegal under the human rights statutes in these four jurisdictions.

Since 1990, the Supreme Court of Canada has dealt with four cases involving the issue of mandatory retirement and equality rights of older workers.[5] In all these cases, the Court ruled that mandatory retirement did violate the equality rights of older workers, but that this violation was justified as being reasonable in the specific circumstances of the employers in question. Interestingly, the employers involved in these four cases were universities and a public hospital. These organizations are heavily dependent on government funding and have experienced major funding cuts in recent years. Considering the specific circumstances of these organizations, the Supreme Court accepted the employers' argument that mandatory retirement was essential to permit flexibility in resource allocation, promote employee/organizational renewal, and protect job opportunities for the young workers. The Supreme Court is yet to rule on a similar argument made by a private sector employer.

A number of recent court cases have also dealt with mandatory retirement as a bona fide occupational requirement. The Supreme Court accepted mandatory retirement as a BFOR for firefighters on the grounds that a) firefighting was a strenuous occupation; b) the risk of failure by a firefighter endangered the firefighter, his/her colleagues, and the public; c) ability to perform the tasks of a firefighter decreased with age; and d) there was no reliable test to accurately determine how an individual firefighter would cope in an emergency situation.[6] A similar ruling was issued in a case involving police officers.[7] However, mandatory retirement was not accepted as a BFOR for army officers.[8] Based on the evidence before it, the Federal Court Trial Division rejected the employer's claim that mandatory retirement was needed to achieve the goals of organizational renewal, safety, and medical fitness. It found that a 10% turnover in personnel was necessary to achieve the organizational renewal objective, but the turnover attributable to mandatory retirement policies was only one percent, and further, that of this only a small fraction would choose to stay on if mandatory retirement policies were abolished. In relation to the medical fitness and safety goals, the Court ruled that age was a poor predictor of these conditions, and that more direct fitness tests and standards must be used as predictors instead.

Thus, it is clear from the court rulings that a BFOR defense for mandatory retirement policies can be established only if the employer is able to demonstrate that a) it is impossible or highly impractical to measure individual employee fitness or readiness for the job, and b) there is a clear basis in fact to believe that nearly all employees above a certain age cannot safely perform their job duties. Essentially the same rulings have been issued by the U.S. Supreme Court as well.[9] It is interesting to note that a BFOR defence for mandatory retirement policies is yet to be made in relation to the so-called knowledge occupations, in which physical/medical fitness is not a major job performance criterion. Nor is such a defence, even if made, likely to succeed given the standards for its acceptability laid down by the courts and the available evidence that job performance capacity of many knowledge workers, such as higher-level executives, continues to grow into their sixties or seventies (Brown & Jaques, 1971; Jaques, 1968).

Policy Implications and Conclusion

Conceptually, organizations have a choice among a variety of retirement policies. They can maintain the customary mandatory retirement age of 65, extend it beyond age 65, or replace mandatory retirement policies with flexible ones. These policy alternatives can also be supplemented with early and delayed retirement incentives. The choice among these policy options should depend on the specific economics and non-economic contexts of each organization. The analysis and discussion in this paper provides several policy implications and guidelines in this regard.

First, organizations must ensure that their retirement policies meet the requirements of the governing legislation. Clearly, organizations face no legal impediment to developing and implementing flexible retirement policies. The same, however, cannot be said about mandatory retirement policies. In this regard, the legislative requirements vary across jurisdictions. The existing human rights legislation in a majority of jurisdictions provides protections against age discrimination without any upper age limit, thereby rendering mandatory retirement policies illegal. In the remaining jurisdictions, mandatory retirement at age 65 or beyond is legally permissible as a justified violation of the equality rights only under certain circumstances. Through its recent rulings, the Supreme Court of Canada has specified what those circumstances are. Additionally, according to the existing legislation, mandatory retirement at any age is permissible in all jurisdictions if it can be justified as a bona fide occupational requirement. Here again, the court rulings provide information on what justification would be legally acceptable. Thus, in developing retirement policies, it is critical for the employers to be knowledgeable about the applicable legislation and its requirements and how these have been interpreted and applied by the courts.

Second, even in the midst of high unemployment, many studies and surveys point to the existence of current and impending skill shortages and imbalances. Organizations need to undertake human resource planning to determine their own specific situation in this regard. They should assess their future human resource requirements across occupations and identify areas of expected shortages and surpluses. If an array of imbalances is found, flexible retirement policies may be more appropriate. "Making more selective use of early retirement incentives, as well as implementing delayed retirement incentives . . . may help many companies see through the skills and labour shortage crunch in the years ahead" (Towers Perrin and Hudson Institute Canada, 1991). Delayed retirement may not appear to make much sense in today's environment of downsizing and restructuring. But, if a possibility of future human resource and skill shortages exists in an organization, it is advisable for that organization not to reject such initiatives out of hand. A major advantage in retaining older employees is that their accumulated work experience can be a real asset, particularly in jobs requiring high levels of complexity (Avolio, Waldman & McDaniel, 1990). Also, "the present euphoria over the benefits of early retirement has tended to mask some of the problems this trend has created in the past. These problems can only become worse in the future. Early retirement can result in the unnecessary loss of skilled, loyal, and experienced workers" (Ford & Fottler, 1985). Thus, employers need to take a longer-run perspective in implementing retirement policies.

Third, most organizations are increasingly faced with an aging workforce. They should carefully examine their existing human resource policies (including retirement) that discriminate against older workers not only for ethical and legal reasons but also for their own economic benefit. Age-neutral human resource policies are needed to ensure full and effective utilization of the expanding pool of older workers. Many studies point to the existence of various age stereotypes which may inhibit the development of such policies. According to these stereotypes, older workers have poorer health, lower productivity, rigid and less creative behaviour, inability to learn new skills, and higher accident rates (Rosen & Jerdee, 1977; Burack, 1988; Forteza & Prieto, 1994). There is, however, very little empirical evidence supporting these stereotypes. Human resource decisions based on such inaccurate beliefs can be economically costly to the organization because the available pool of employees considered for these decisions would be perceived to be smaller than it actually is. It is important for organizations to ensure that their human resource policies rely on objective, work-related criteria and that these policies are applied uniformly across all employees based on their respective productivity-related attributes. Chronological age of employees should not figure as a relevant consideration in this process. The presence of such human resource policies can enable the organization to handle performance or competence problems of older (indeed all) employees in a legally defensible manner and take action, if necessary, to "force them to retire" for cause. These policies can also assist the organization in making a more effective use of early and late retirement incentives based on actual as opposed to assumed performance contributions of older workers.

Fourth, supply-side policy measures are also needed to ensure effective utilization of older workers. The key issue here is the availability and willingness of these persons to work. Mandatory retirement policies do not guarantee that employees will continue working until they reach the mandatory age of retirement. Employees can, and

many do, leave the labour force prior to reaching that age. The labour force participation statistics reviewed in this paper clearly indicate that an increasing number of older workers are doing exactly that—taking early retirement. Many older people would prefer working under more flexible work arrangements than presently exist (Kraut, 1988). Such arrangements are likely to be better suited to meet the needs and preferences of older workers and, therefore, can influence their willingness and availability to work. For example, many older workers may prefer more developmental, mentoring, and advisory job responsibilities to exclusively operational/production responsibilties. Similarly, older workers may prefer some type of a reduced work option (e.g., part-timing, job sharing, or phased-in/gradual retirement) due to personal health reasons, desire for more leisure time, or need for time to provide care to family members and relatives. The last reason is particularly applicable to women, who continue to be the primary caregivers for their families. In a rigid employment system, older workers are forced to choose between continuing to work under the existing standard arrangements or to quit the job entirely by retiring early. Clearly, neither of these choices is optimal from the employee's perspective as his/her needs and preferences may remain unsatisfied. From the employer's perspective as well, neither situation may be satisfactory. For example, the forced standard employment situation may cause the employee to exhibit a higher absenteeism rate, while the forced early retirement situation may imply loss of a potential source of qualified and experienced talent. Thus, by developing more flexible work arrangements, including flexible retirement options, organizations can satisfy better the needs and preferences of their older employees, and also make a more effective use of this growing workforce.

Finally, individualized human resource planning should be implemented for older employees. It can serve as a useful tool for effectively utilizing these employees and managing their remaining careers with the organization. Such planning would require pertinent data to be regularly collected from employees upon reaching a certain age (e.g., 55 years). This database should cover such areas as retirement intentions, training needs, and job design and hours of work preferences. Individual employees must be active and responsible participants in this planning process. They must gain understanding of their personal needs, preferences, and competencies. They must also be willing to take advantage of relevant developmental opportunities offered them to remain current and competitive.

In conclusion, the demographic trends in most industrialized countries imply that older workers constitute an important component of labour supply in the economy. Effective use of this resource depends upon the ability and willingness of employers to develop human resource policies that manage older workers in a non-discriminatory manner and also accommodate their needs and preferences. In this regard, flexible retirement policies deserve serious consideration. Such policies are consistent with the existing human rights legislation and the generally accepted equity principles in our society. They are also suited to both employee as well as employer interests. Flexible retirement policies enable older employees to choose retirement dates that are most appropriate to their economic and non-economic circumstances. Similarly, these policies can assist employers in maintaining appropriate levels of older workforce to meet the expected skill and labour imbalances in the organization. Flexible human resource management policies are becoming more common among organizations. Flexible retirement policies can form part of this emerging trend and enable organizations to meet the challenges of a diverse labour force, and highly competitive and dynamic market environments.

Source: Agarwal, N. and DeGroote, M. "Retirement of Older Workers: Issues and Policies" *Human Resource Planning, 21*, (1). Reprinted with permission from *Human Resource Planning*, 1998, pp. 42–52, by The Human Resource Planning Society, 317 Madison Avenue, Suite 1509, New York, NY 10017, Phone: (212) 490–6387, Fax: (212) 682–6851.

Endnotes

1. These data are computed from the following Statistics Canada publications: Labour Force Annual Averages 1995, Cat. No. 71–220-XPB, February 1996; and Historical Labour Force Statistics 1995, Cat. No. 71–201, February 1996.
2. The data reported here are taken or adapted from these Statistics Canada publications: Population Ageing and Elderly, Cat. No. 91–533 E, March 1993; Population Projections for Canada, 1989–2011, Cat. No. 91–520, March 1990; Population Projections for Canada, Provinces & Territories, 1993–2016, Cat. No. 91–520, Occasional, 1994; and the two publications cited in the preceding footnote.
3. See "Skilled Labour Crunch" in the *Hamilton Spectator*, May 30, 1996, p. B10; and "Jobs Are Going Begging," in the *Hamilton Spectator*, June 13, 1996, p. C16.
4. For a more detailed discussion on this point, see the Report of the Ontario Task Force on Mandatory Retirement entitled Fairness and Flexibility in Retiring from Work, December 1987, pp. 156–157.
5. For a full discussion of these cases, see: McKinney v. University of Guelph, *Canadian Human Rights Reporter*, Vol. 13, Decision 29, March 1991, D/171-D 316; Harrison v. University of British Columbia, *Canadian Human Rights Reporter*, Vol. 13, Decision 30, April 1991, D/317-D/337; Stoffman v. Vancouver General Hospital, *Canadian Human Rights Reporter*, Vol. 13, Decision 31, April 1991, D/337-D/394; and University of Alberta v. Alberta (Human Rights Commission), *Canadian Human Rights Reporter*, Vol. 17, Decision 8, February 1993, D/87-D/89.
6. For a full discussion of these cases, see: Saskatchewan (Human Rights Commission) v. Saskatoon (City), *Canadian Human Rights Reporter*, Vol. 11, Decision 22, March 1990, D/204-D/217; and Saskatchewan (Human Rights Commission) v. Moose Jaw (City), *Canadian Human Rights Reporter*, Vol. 11, Decision 23, March 1990, D/217-D/222.
7. For a full discussion of this case, see Large v. Stratford (City) Police Department, Canadian Human Rights Reporter, Vol. 24, Decision 1, January 15, 1996, D/1-D/21.
8. For a full discussion of this case, see Martin et al. v. Department of National Defense and Canadian Armed Forces and Canadian Human Rights Commission, *Canadian Human Rights Reporter*, Vol. 21, Decision 27, February 8, 1995, D/373-D/400.
9. For example see Western Air Lines v. Criswell, 472 U.S. 450 (1985).

References

Avolio, B. J., D. A. Waldman, and M. A. McDaniel. "Age and Work Performance in Nonmanagerial Jobs: The Effects of Experience and Occupational Type," *Academy of Management Journal*, Vol. 33, No. 2 (1990): 407–422.

Barth, M. C., W. McNaught, and P. Rizzi. "The Costs and Benefits of Older Workers." In W. H. Crown (ed.), *Handbook on Employment and the Elderly*. Westport, CT: Greenwood Press, 1996.

Belkhodja, A. "Staying Put: Job Tenure Among Paid Workers," *Perspectives on Labour and Income*, Vol. 4, No. 4 (1992): 20–26.

Brown, Wilfred and Elliot Jaques. *Glacier Project Papers*. London, U.K.: Heinemann, 1971.

Burack, E. H. *Creative Human Resource Planning and Applications*. Englewood Cliffs, NJ: Prentice-Hall, 1988.

Charness, N. "The Aging Worker and Performance." In A. Joshi and E. Berger (eds.), *Aging Workforce, Income Security, and Retirement: Policy and Practical Implications*. Hamilton, Ontario: McMaster University, Gerontological Studies, 1995.

Chaykowski, R. "Workforce Transition and the Older Worker." In A. Joshi and E. Berger (eds.), *Aging Workforce, Income Security, and Retirement: Policy and Practical Implications*. Hamilton, Ontario: McMaster University, Gerontological Studies, 1995.

Cosier, R. A. and Dalton, D. R. "Equity Theory and Time: A Reformulation," *Academy of Management Review*, Vol. 8, No. 2 (1983): 311–319.

Crown, W. H. "The Political Context of Older Workers Employment Policy." In W. H. Crown (ed.), *Handbook on Employment and the Elderly*. Westport, CT: Greenwood Press, 1996.

Dunlop, D. P. *Mandatory Retirement Policy: A Human Rights Dilemma*. Ottawa, Ontario: The Conference Board of Canada, 1980.

Labour Market Development in the 1980s. Ottawa, Ontario: Employment and Immigration Canada, 1981.

Ford, R. C. and Fottler, M. D. "Flexible Retirement: Slowing Early Retirement of Productive Older Employees," *Human Resource Planning*, Vol. 8, No. 3 (1985): 147–156.

Forteza, J. A. and Prieto, J. M. "Aging and Work Behavior." In H. C. Triandis, M. D. Dunnette and L. M. Hough (eds.), *Handbook of Industrial and Organizational Psychology*, Palo Alto, CA: Consulting Psychologists Press Inc., Second Edition, Vol. 4, 1994.

Gibb-Clark, Margot. "Managers Applaud Decision," *Globe & Mail*, December 7 (1990): B3.

Gower, D. "Measuring the Age of Retirement," *Perspectives on Labor and Income*, Statistics Canada, Vol. 9, No. 2 (1997): 11–17.

Jaques, Elliot. *Progression Handbook*. London, U.K.: Heinemann, 1968.

Kinsella, K. and Gist, Y. J. *Older Workers, Retirement, and Pensions*. Washington, D.C.: U.S. Department of Commerce, 1995.

Krahn, H. "Non-Standard Work on the Rise," *Perspectives on Labour and Income*, Statistics Canada, Vol. 7, No. 4 (1995): 35–42.

Krashinsky, M. "The Case for Eliminating Mandatory Retirement: Why Economics and Human Rights Need Not Conflict," *Canadian Public Policy/Analyse de Politiques*, Vol. XIV, No. 1 (1988): 40–51.

Kraut, A. L. "Retirees: A New Resource for Flexible Industries," *Human Resource Planning*, Vol. 11, No. 4 (1988): 317–319.

Kubeck, J. E., Delp, N. D., Haslett, T. K., and McDaniel, M. A. "Does Job-Related Training Performance Decline with Age?" *Psychology and Aging*, Vol. II, No. 1 (1996): 92–107.

Labour Canada. *An Industrial Relations Perspective on Mandatory Retirement*. Ottawa, Ontario, 1985.

Lazear, E. P. "Why Is There Mandatory Retirement?" *Journal of Political Economy*, Vol. 87, No. 6 (1979) 1261–1284.

Linden, R. C., Stilwell, D., and Ferris, G. R. "The Effects of Supervisor and Subordinate Age on Objective Performance and Subjective Performance Ratings," *Human Relations*, Vol. 49, No. 3 (1996): 327–347.

Lowe, G. S. "Retirement Attitudes, Plans and Behaviour," *Perspectives on Labour and Income*, Vol. 3, No. 3 (1991): 8–17.

McEvoy, G. M. and Cascio, W. R. "Cumulative Evidence on the Relationship Between Employee Age and Job Performance," *Journal of Applied Psychology*, Vol. 74, No. 1 (1989): 11–17.

OECD. *The Labour Market and Older Workers*. Paris, France: Organization for Economic Co-Operation and Development, 1995.

Reid, F. "Economic Aspects of Mandatory Retirement: The Canadian Experience," *Industrial Relations/Relations Industrielles*, Vol. 43, No. 1 (1988): 101–114.

Rhodes, S. R. "Age-Related Differences in Work Attitudes and Behaviour: A Review and Conceptual Analysis," *Psychological Bulletin*, Vol. 93, No. 2 (1983): 328–367.

Roadburg, A. *Aging: Retirement, Leisure and Work in Canada*. Toronto, Ontario: Methuen Publications, 1985.

Rosen, B. and Jerdee, T. H. "Too Old or Not Too Old," *Harvard Business Review*, Vol. 55, No. 6 (1977): 97–106.

Shaie, K. "Intellectual Development in Adulthood." In J. Birren and K. Schaie (eds.), *Handbook of the Psychology of Aging*. New York: Van Nostrand Reinhold, Third Edition, 1990.

Schellenberg, G. "The Road to Retirement." In A. Joshi and E. Berger (eds.), *Aging Workforce, Income Security, and Retirement: Policy and Practical Implications*. Hamilton, Ontario: McMaster University, Gerontological Studies, 1995.

Sonnenfeld, J. "Dealing with the Aging Workforce," *Harvard Business Review*, Vol. 78, No. 6 (1978): 81–92.

Statistics Canada. *Worker Turnover in the Canadian Economy*. Cat. No. 71–539 (1992).

Statistics Canada. *Labour Force Annual Averages 1995*. Cat. No. 71–220-XPB (1996).

Sterns, H. and Doverspike, D. "Aging and the Training and Learning Process." In I. Goldstein (ed.), *Training and Development in Organizations*. San Francisco, CA: Jossey-Bass, 1989.

Towers Perrin and Hudson Institute Canada. *Workforce 2000*. Ottawa, Ontario: 1991.

Waldman, D. A. and Avolio, B. J. "A Meta-Analysis of Age Differences in Job Performance," *Journal of Applied Psychology*, Vol. 71, No. 1 (1986): 33–38.

Willis, S. "Towards an Educational Psychology of the Adult Learner." In J. Birren and K. Schaie (eds.), *Handbook of the Psychology of Aging*. New York: Van Nostrand Reinhold, Second Edition, 1985.

CHAPTER

14

GLOBAL HUMAN RESOURCE MANAGEMENT

In 1998, athletic shoe global industry leader Nike was hit by a wave of negative publicity regarding the conditions in many of its overseas factories. Growing reports of strikes, unsafe working conditions, poor wages, worker abuse, and the use of child labor aroused a fury within the United States. Although Nike's market share remained constant, its stock price sagged with each new report of labor abuse in Asia.

Reebok, one of Nike's main competitors and a company with a history of strong support for human rights, acted quickly to ensure that there were no similar problems at overseas sites owned by Reebok or those in which subcontractors produced goods for Reebok. Reebok contracted with a respected nonprofit social research group in Jakarta, Indonesia, for thorough inspections of two of its shoe factories that employed more than 10,000 workers. The researchers interviewed and surveyed workers, performed health and safety tests, and discussed operations with managers. These audits marked the first time that a U.S. company allowed truly independent outsiders with expertise in labor issues to inspect their factories and make their findings public.

The report found a range of problems including poor ventilation, the presence of harmful chemicals, inadequate toilet facilities, and sex bias. Reebok took immediate action but found some cultural challenges in addressing the problems. These problems were largely due to the difficulty of introducing industrialized-world work and culture environments. Workers did not report sexual harassment largely because they did not understand the concept of it. There was also a thriving local market for empty hazardous chemical containers. Reebok's vice president for human rights was relentless in his attempt to force Western values on the reluctant Indonesians. Workers and managers were trained in gender awareness and harassment; requirements were set for the safe disposal of chemical containers; and workers were educated as to the reasons and personal benefits for the protective clothing they were required to wear. Reebok's two Indonesian contractors were forced to spend more than $250,000 to address these issues or lose Reebok's business.

Reebok led the way in ensuring that oppressive sweatshop operations were curtailed. Within days, both Liz Claiborne and Mattel followed suit in having outside independent agencies review their operations and those of their subcontractors. Though these initiatives clearly show good business sense, particularly in light of what happened to Nike, they also show a sensitivity to basic human rights and the ethical treatment of their global labor force.

Source: Anonymous. "Business; Best Foot Forward at Reebok," *The Economist*, October 23, 1999, p. 74; Bernstein, A. "Sweatshops: No More Excuses," *Business Week*. November 9, 1999, pp. 104–106; Gilley, B. "Sweating It Out," *Far Eastern Economic Review*, December 10, 1998, pp. 66–67.

The strategic business decisions being made by modern organizations increasingly involve some plan to conduct business that was previously conducted domestically in the global arena. In some cases this may involve a minimal physical presence in another country; in others, it may involve setting up operations that will eventually exceed the size of domestic operations. We no longer live in a domestic economy, as evidenced by diminished trade barriers and regional economic alliances, such as the North American Free Trade Agreement (NAFTA) and the European Union (EU), and the acceleration of global financial markets and information networks. Tremendous opportunities exist to market goods and services abroad, particularly in less-developed countries; to participate in joint ventures with foreign organizations; and to outsource operations to other countries as a means of lowering costs. When one considers that less than 10 percent of the world population resides in the United States and that many domestic consumer markets are saturated, it should not be surprising that an increasing number of organizations are developing strategies to expand internationally.

These strategic opportunities are resulting in employers' sending an increasing number of employees abroad to start up, manage, and develop their global operations. While a greater percentage of the U.S. workforce is being moved abroad, an increasing number of U.S. domestic workers are natives of other countries. These trends are not just limited to larger organizations as they once were; small and medium-size employers are taking advantage of international opportunities and their workforces are becoming more culturally diverse.

An organization might focus on expanding globally for a number of reasons. Foreign countries may present enhanced market opportunities. In addition, expanding the scope and volume of operations to support global initiatives could result in economies of scale in production as well as in the administrative side of the organization. Competitive pressure may require an organization to enter foreign markets to keep pace with industry leaders. Finally, acquisition activity may result in the ownership of a foreign-based organization or subsidiary.

Regardless of the reasons a company may have for expanding operations globally, human resource management is critical to the success of any global endeavor. If one adopts the perspective that human resource strategy must be derived from corporate strategy and that people do determine an organization's success or failure, then the human resource function needs to be a key strategic partner in any global undertakings. Ironically, human resources is often neglected in the planning and establishment of global operations. ▼

Strategic Global HR at McDonald's

When fast-food king McDonald's initially expanded outside of the United States, it followed a very ethnocentric approach to going global. U.S. expatriates were sent abroad to develop the new sites and maintain as much consistency as possible with domestic operations. Locals were "McDonaldized"—taught the specific operations and

▶ Reading 14.1, "Managing the Global Workforce: Challenges and Strategies," addresses some of the major strategic issues that human resources faces from a global perspective and tells how some leading organizations are meeting these challenges.

business plans developed back in the United States. This approach has evolved over the years to one that is now very polycentric. When opening locations outside of the United States, expatriates are rarely used and HR professionals at McDonald's partner closely with locals to develop an operation that fits with local culture, customs, and lifestyles. A four-phase approach is used in which HR has a specific and critical role to play at each step. The first phase, development preparation, usually begins 18 to 24 months prior to the actual opening. During this phase, HR researches issues such as compensation and benefits, considers recruiting strategies, and secures a labor attorney or consultant. The second phase, resources selection, takes place 8 to 12 months prior to opening. HR takes the information gathered in phase one and begins to develop specific HR programs and plans and determines staffing needs and compensation levels. The third phase, resource development and strategy implementation, takes place 3 to 8 months prior to opening. HR puts together employee handbooks, considers the effects of local labor laws on operations, and begins to implement its staffing plan by hiring employees. The final phase, pre-opening preparation, begins 90 days prior to opening. Here HR conducts training and lays the groundwork for the performance review system. McDonald's strategy for its global operations includes HR as a key strategic partner, facilitating the implementation of the human and cultural dimension of the operation for maximum success.[1]

HOW GLOBAL HRM DIFFERS FROM DOMESTIC HRM

Despite the fact that the core principles of strategic human resource management also apply to global human resource management, global human resources presents some unique contingencies. First, managing people in global settings requires human resources to address a broader range of functional areas. These areas include clarifying taxation issues; coordinating foreign currencies, exchange rates, and compensation plans; and working directly with the families of employees who may be accepting overseas assignments. Second, it requires more involvement in the employee's personal life. The employee is usually assisted with acquiring housing in the host country; selling or leasing domestic accommodations; locating recreational and cultural opportunities for the employee and family; arranging and paying for school for the employee's children; and locating and securing domestic help for the employee. Third, the organization must often set up different human resource management systems for different geographic locations. Fourth, the organization is often forced to deal with more complex external constituencies, including foreign governments and political and religious groups. Finally, global assignments often involve a heightened exposure to risks. These risks include the health and safety of the employee and family; legal issues in the host country; possible terrorism; and the human and financial consequences of mistakes, which may greatly exceed the costs of those made domestically.

The threat of terrorism has added to many of the anxieties employees face when considering and undertaking a global assignment. A recent survey found that expatriates need and want more support from headquarters than they are receiving regarding health and safety concerns; only 20 percent responded that their employers were keeping them sufficiently informed about health and safety issues.[2] Dissatisfied expatriates can be expensive for an organization: the average cost of a three-year assignment abroad is $1.3 million.[3] In addition, concerns about the employee's and/or family safety can diminish productivity and cause stress. Consequently, employers need to communicate with—and provide the needed support for—expatriates about their safety to ensure that the assignment is a success.

The decision to expand globally first involves determining the appropriate strategy for involvement in the host country. For example, the organization may decide to simply export its goods to a foreign country; this might require very limited presence on the part of domestic employees. The organization might also decide to subcontract or license certain goods and services to a foreign partner. On a slightly more involved scale, a joint venture might be undertaken abroad with a foreign partner. Finally, the organization could decide to establish a significant presence abroad by setting up operations in the form of a foreign branch office or subsidiary.

ASSESSING CULTURE

Several factors will influence the level of involvement an organization might choose in its foreign operations. Economic, market, social, and political conditions will certainly play a significant role in any decision to go abroad. A larger issue might be the culture of the host country and how it compares to the national culture of the organization's home. National cultures differ on a variety of dimensions, and many global undertakings fail because of a lack of understanding or appreciation of cultural differences.

One of the most popular models of cultural differences among countries was developed by Hofstede, who explained cultural differences along four dimensions.[4] The first dimension is the extent to which a society emphasizes individualism or collectivism. Individualistic societies value the development of and focus on the individual; collectivistic societies value togetherness, harmony, belongingness, and loyalty to others. The second dimension is power distance. This dimension looks at the extent to which a society is hierarchical, with an unequal distribution of power among its members, as opposed to one where there are few distinctions and power is more evenly distributed among individuals. The third dimension is uncertainty avoidance, which refers to the extent to which the society feels comfortable with ambiguity and values and encourages risk-taking. The fourth dimension is the extent to which the society displays "masculine" or "feminine" tendencies. A masculine society is one that is more aggressive, assertive, and focused on achievements; the feminine society is one that emphasizes interpersonal relationships and sensitivity toward the welfare and well-being of others. Although many are uncomfortable with the sexist connotations of *masculine* and *feminine* and the stereotypes they encourage, this dimension does significantly explain many differences in cultural behavior in societies. Some researchers who have applied Hofstede's work have substituted *quantity of life* for *masculinity* and *quality of life* for *femininity*. Exhibit 14-1 illustrates how a number of countries fit Hofstede's model of culture.

Another well-known model that explains differences in culture was developed by Hall, who characterized culture by the patterns with which we communicate.[5] His work focused on the more subtle means by which we express and display our culture. These means might not be evident to someone from outside the culture, but they are well understood and accepted by insiders. Hall's model describes culture in terms of five silent "languages": time, space, material goods, friendships, and agreement.

The language of time considers how we use time to communicate and how we use it to manage our daily lives. For example, how much do individuals in the

EXHIBIT 14-1: EXAMPLES OF HOFSTEDE'S CULTURAL DIMENSIONS

Country	Individualism—Collectivism	Power Distance	Uncertainty Avoidance	Quantity of Life*
Australia	Individual	Small	Moderate	Strong
Canada	Individual	Small	Low	Moderate
England	Individual	Small	Moderate	Strong
France	Individual	Large	High	Weak
Greece	Collective	Large	High	Moderate
Italy	Individual	Moderate	High	Strong
Japan	Collective	Moderate	High	Strong
Mexico	Collective	Large	High	Strong
Singapore	Collective	Large	Low	Moderate
Sweden	Individual	Small	Low	Weak
United States	Individual	Small	Low	Strong
Venezuela	Collective	Large	High	Strong

* A weak quantity-of-life score is equivalent to a high quality-of-life score.

Source: G. Hofstede, "Motivation, Leadership, and Organization: Do American Theories Apply Abroad?" *Organizational Dynamics*, Summer 1980, pp. 42–63.

culture rely on schedules, appointments, and deadlines? Is it considered appropriate to keep someone waiting for a meeting? Do meetings usually have a timed agenda? Are meetings and appointments scheduled with an ending time or are they open-ended?

The language of space considers how we communicate through space and distance. For example, what is considered the appropriate physical distance between two people engaged in a conversation? Friendship, formality, and even intimacy are often communicated by distance. How are spaces in organizations arranged to communicate rank, power, and status? Does an organization have private offices and/or designated parking spaces? Are some offices larger than others?

The language of material goods can be similarly used to signify power, success, and status. In some cultures, these indicators are of critical importance in establishing one's personal and professional identity. In an organizational setting, this language might be communicated through generous perks such as a company car and might be further evidenced by executive salaries that are many times those of lower-level workers. Organizations that establish and maintain pay compression plans are attempting to silence this kind of language.

The language of friendships considers how we form interpersonal relationships. For example, are friendships formed and dissolved quickly, or are they built on a foundation over a long period of time? Is there a mutual sense of ongoing obligation in interpersonal relationships, or are they more transient and maintained only as long as both parties see some benefit? Some cultures communicate status via material goods; other cultures communicate status through one's network of friends and the support this network provides.

The language of agreement considers how consensus is reached among people. For example, are formal, written contracts signed under an oath of law the norm in business negotiations, or is a simple handshake sufficient guarantee? Is it acceptable to debate someone with whom you do not agree and, if so, is it acceptable to debate in front of others?

A key issue that impacts an organization's success in the global arena is an awareness of cultural differences and the development of both a business strategy and corresponding HR strategy that is consistent with the culture of the host country. Although it is beyond the scope of this chapter to detail how cultural differences might impact people management systems, a culture in which negotiations are based on trust and friendship that is built over time might pose some difficulty for an American, who might be used to getting down to business and negotiating without developing any kind of interpersonal connection. Also, the candor and outspokenness for which Americans are known could conflict with the styles of those from other cultures. In short, when cultures come together in organizational settings, special consideration must be paid to managing processes such as power dynamics and relationships, norms of participation and decision making, and performance management and compensation systems to prevent misunderstandings.

Much as societies have cultures, organizations also have their own cultures. As a result, decision makers need to examine the interface between the culture of the organization and the culture of the host country in determining whether an appropriate fit exists and, subsequently, in developing an optimal business strategy and appropriate human resource management strategies. For example, if the organization strongly values diversity, what will be done when a host country's culture fails to support these values? In many cultures, it is acceptable to discriminate on the basis of gender, race, ethnicity, age, disability, and sexual orientation. Does the organization extend its ban on smoking to all overseas locations? Will it prohibit facial hair on employees or prohibit employees from enjoying a glass of wine with their lunches? What will happen in a culture in which bribes are an accepted and expected means of conducting business?

In going abroad, an organization needs to decide what human resource policies will be implemented in the host country and needs to make these decisions prior to arrival. These decisions will force top managers to confront a number of ethical decisions and may test the strength of the organization's culture. Conflict issues will need to be resolved relative to incompatible local and corporate cultures. Decision makers need to understand which values the organization holds so deeply that it will not compromise, even in the face of significant financial consequences. Although these ethical decisions can present difficult choices, they can help to strengthen the organization's mission, strategy, and employment practices.

National culture can have a significant effect on an organization's ability to utilize strategic HR. A culture that is oriented toward tradition, for example, might not understand the logic of, or resist, any kind of planning. Certain cultures have stringent rules regarding staffing and may require the organization to employ individuals assigned to it by a centralized labor bureau. Individuals in some very strict hierarchical cultures would probably not respond well to upward performance feedback programs. In some cultures, it is considered inappropriate for a worker to report to a manager who is younger than the subordinate. The inappropriateness of using direct eye contact in conversation in some cultures might bias the results of the employment interview process. Where a culture fits on the individualism/collectivism continuum would influence how it defines acceptable performance and appropriate compensation. Consequently, in managing across cultures, it is critical to have a strong sense of cultural self-awareness yet remain aware that oversensitivity to cultural issues can be as detrimental as undersensitivity. ▼▼

▶▶ Reading 14.2, "Four Seasons Goes to Paris," presents a case study of how an organization with a very strong culture approached entry into a highly competitive foreign market that has a distinct and intense national culture, and the role that strategic HR played in this process.

STRATEGIC HR ISSUES IN GLOBAL ASSIGNMENTS

An organization can use several different approaches in managing the process of sending workers abroad. An administrative approach involves merely assisting employees with paperwork and minor logistics—for example, hiring movers, ensuring that taxes are paid, and obtaining a work visa for the employee and travel visas for family members. A tactical approach involves managing the risk or failure factor—for example, handling the administrative paperwork while also providing limited, usually one-day, training for the employee. This approach does only what needs to be done to prevent failure. A strategic approach to global assignments, however, involves much more support and coordination. In addition to those items cited previously, strategically managing such a process would involve adding extensive selection systems; ongoing, integrated training; a specific performance management system; destination services; and a strategized repatriation program at the end of the assignment. ▼▼▼

A model that outlines the strategic human resource issues in global assignments is presented in Exhibit 14-2. The first step in the strategic management of global assignments is the establishment of a specific purpose for the assignment. There may be numerous reasons for the assignment, including business or market development; the set-up, transfer, or integration of information technology; management of an autonomous subsidiary; coordination or integration of foreign with domestic operations; a temporary assignment to a vacant position; or the development of local management talent.

After the purpose of the assignment has been identified, the process of selecting an appropriate employee for the assignment can commence. Much as there is an organizational purpose for the assignment, there should also be an individual purpose for the assignment, as indicated in Exhibit 14-3. An employee could be chosen for and accept an international assignment to prepare that employee for a top management position, develop further technical or interpersonal skills, or allow an employee to follow a dual-career spouse/partner.

Both the organizational and individual purposes for the assignment must be identified and matched. The assignment needs to be conceptualized as a win/win proposition. There should be clear articulated gain for both the organization and the employee as a prerequisite to success on the assignment.

After an appropriate individual has been identified, it is important to assess the adaptability to the host culture of both the employee and any family members who will be accompanying the employee on the assignment. The single greatest reason for failure on an overseas assignment has to do with adaptability skills, rather than technical skills, and usually is a consequence of the adaptability of the employee's family to the host culture. Individuals and their families should be screened to determine their ability to be comfortable in the host culture. This might include sending the employee and family members to the host country for several weeks to test their adaptability. Among the areas that an organization will need to assess are the technical abilities of the employee; the adaptability, willingness, and motivation to live overseas; tolerance of ambiguity; communication skills; patience and openness to differences in others; and willingness to interact of both the employee and accompanying family members.

▶▶ Reading 14.3, "Adapting to a Boundaryless World: A Developmental Expatriate Model," illustrates the stressors experienced by employees who are sent abroad and how organizations can manage expatriate assignments for maximum chance of success.

EXHIBIT 14-2: STRATEGIC HR ISSUES IN GLOBAL ASSIGNMENTS

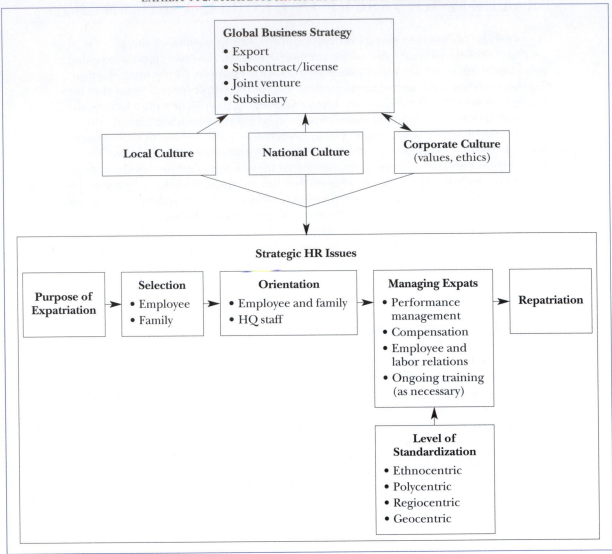

EXHIBIT 14-3: PURPOSES OF EXPATRIATION

Organizational	Individual
• Business or market development	• Skill development
• Set-up, transfer, or integration of information technology	• Preparation for top management
• Manage autonomous subsidiary	• Follow dual-career partner/spouse
• Coordinate or integrate foreign operation with domestic	
• Fill vacant position temporarily	
• Develop local management talent	

Expatriate Selection at Kellogg Co.

Given the high cost of most global assignments, it is critical for organizations to get some return on their investment in sending employees abroad. Battle Creek, Michigan–based breakfast cereal manufacturer Kellogg saw its turnover rate among expatriates reach 40 percent. Kellogg viewed the retention problem as being rooted in poor selection of candidates for global assignments. To remedy this problem, Kellogg first implemented a selection strategy for its global assignments, including a pilot program that identified the best candidates based on assessments from managers. HR and senior management partnered to narrow the list down to sixteen individuals who then were given assessment tests that examined work styles and habits, values, interests, and lifestyles. Employee spouses were also given the assessment. Key personality traits critical to assignment abroad, such as flexibility, willingness to learn, openness, sense of humor, adaptability, ability to handle ambiguity, and interest in others, were measured. The information was then analyzed and the results given to employees and their spouses to explain potential risks and areas of concern that needed to be addressed prior to any assignment. This new process has had a 100 percent success rate for Kellogg in its expatriate assignments.[6]

Once an employee has been selected for the overseas assignment, the organization then needs to provide the appropriate training for the employee and family members. The initial training should begin at least 6 to 9 months prior to the start of the assignment. Longer training periods will reflect the need to learn language skills necessary in the host country. Prior to departure, the employee and family, if possible, should be allowed a trial period living overseas (if this was not done as part of the selection process). Although this may involve significant costs, it should be viewed as an investment; the costs incurred for such a trip will be much less than the monetary, political, and reputation-damaging costs of a failed overseas assignment.

Also prior to departure, the employee and family should receive cross-cultural training in the norms and values of the host country, workplace and business practices, language training (as necessary), health and safety issues, and realistic expectations of what day-to-day life in the country will be like. This training should not be considered completed when the employee and family depart for the host country. A critical mistake made by many organizations is the lack of follow-up once employees have gone abroad to provide additional support to ensure that there have been no unexpected surprises or consequences.

While the employee and family are being trained, simultaneous training should be conducted for headquarters staff who will be supervising and/or interacting with the employee who is abroad. Clashes between local culture and headquarters are common on overseas assignments, and headquarters personnel should be provided with some sensitivity training. Sensitivity training will (1) help headquarters staff understand how and why local decisions are being made and (2) allow them to give the expatriate employee the necessary support and empathy while keeping the expatriate informed as to what has been happening at headquarters.

After employees have been relocated to the host country, the day-to-day issues in managing expatriates are not dramatically different from those involved in managing domestic employees. The same principles and practices of general human resource management apply with a few additional concerns. First, it is critical to assess ongoing training needs of the expatriate employee and family after they have arrived at the host country. Particularly if this is the first time an employee of the organization has been assigned to a particular country, it is likely that some unanticipated events that require additional support and training could materialize. Second, performance management will be more of a challenge; the expatriate's functional boss is usually located domestically, and others in the organization may not be aware of how economic, social, and political conditions and everyday living situations impact the expatriate's performance. Third, many aspects of employee and labor relations will be localized. The expatriate may have to manage a local workforce under far more challenging conditions than those presented domestically. The expatriate may also have to manage the dynamics of being a foreign manager of local employees. Finally, compensation for the expatriate will be different. It is costly to send an employee overseas, usually amounting to as much at three times the employee's annual domestic salary. Income tax payments for the employee may be complicated and costly. Benefits such as armed security guards or private schooling for the employee's children may be necessary. Although compensation for expatriates is often outsourced, organizations need to be very careful in this regard; compensation is a key strategic issue not only from a cost perspective but in impacting the employee family's ability to live in the host country, as well. Outsourcing compensation to a third party who does not fully understand the organization's overall strategy or have a holistic appreciation of all of the organization's human resource systems could result in disaster.

There are three traditional approaches to determining expatriate compensation. The first, and most common, is the balance sheet method. With this approach, salary is based on home country pay, and additional expenses associated with relocation and the assignment itself are added to arrive at an overall reimbursement and compensation level. These expenses might include the cost of housing in the host country, furniture, household help, a car and driver, or spousal/partner assistance. This approach ensures that the expatriate gains a sense of equity and fairness in the compensation package; however, the local employees, particularly if they are poor, may sense some inequity. This system can be complex to administer, but it is still widely used, particularly for short-term or temporary assignments.

The higher-of-home-or-host approach takes into account the employee's salary at home and adjusts it upward, as necessary, to account for a higher cost of living in the host country. This approach is usually accompanied by standard perquisites for executives in the host country and is used most commonly for intermediate term assignments of indefinite duration.

When the employee is assigned to a host country on a permanent basis, the localization approach is usually used. Here, the employee's salary is converted to the host country equivalent. Depending on the country, salary structures, and the cost of living, this approach can initially result in a salary decrease for the employee.

In establishing general human resource policy for the day-to-day management of all employees abroad, locals as well as expatriates, the organization also needs to make a strategic decision as to the level of standardization it desires across locations. Heenan and Perlmutter identified four different approaches an organization can take in setting and enforcing policy: ethnocentric, polycentric, regiocentric, and geocentric, as illustrated in Exhibit 14-4.[7]

An ethnocentric approach involves exporting the organization's home country practices and policies to foreign locations. This strategy is often used by organizations whose competitive strategy is focused on creating an image. An ethnocentric approach can be beneficial in allowing standardization, integration, and efficiency. However, if it is forced onto another culture that does not subscribe to the values on which the practices are based, there can be severe problems. Some turnover can and should be expected and even encouraged when using this approach. It can also help to make expatriate assignments more attractive to the organization's domestic employees.

EXHIBIT 14-4: FOUR APPROACHES TO IHRM

Aspect of the Enterprise	Orientation			
	Ethnocentric	**Polycentric**	**Regiocentric**	**Geocentric**
Standard Setting, Evaluation, and Control	By home country headquarters	By local subsidiary management	Coordination across countries in the region	Global as well as local standards and control
Communication and Coordination	From HQ to local subsidiary	Little among subsidiaries, little between subsidiary and HQ	Little between subsidiary and HQ, medium to high among subsidiaries in region	Totally connected network of subsidiaries and subsidiaries with headquarters
Staffing	Home country managers	Host country managers	Managers may come from nations within region	Best people where they can be best used

Source: D. A. Heenan and Howard V. Perlmutter, *Multinational Organizational Development* (pp. 18–19), © 1979 by Addison-Wesley Publishing Company.

A polycentric approach involves allowing each location to develop its own practices and policies that are consistent with the local culture and workforce characteristics. Management practices are localized to suit the existing needs of the marketplace, and adaptability to customer tastes is a key strategic initiative facilitated by this approach. Although this approach can be costly, it is also extremely responsive to local market and labor conditions and can help to reduce employee turnover in an acquisition, particularly if there are anti–foreign ownership attitudes among locals.

A regiocentric approach involves developing standardized practices and policies by geographic region; therefore, there is some consistency and efficiency within operations. At the same time, there is some variation among regions to support the local markets. This approach commonly involves establishing autonomously managed regional subsidiaries within a geographic region.

A geocentric approach involves developing one set of global practices and policies that are applied at all locations. This approach differs from the ethnocentric approach in that although the ethnocentric approach exports its one set of management systems based on home country culture to all locations, the geocentric approach considers the global workforce in all of its areas of operations as well as the numerous local cultures in which it operates and attempts to develop practices and policies that transcend cultural differences. This approach can be very difficult to implement, given different host government policies and regulations and the need to address them simultaneously. Compensation plans and standards of living can be difficult to unify in an equitable way across different cultures.

REPATRIATION

The final issue in managing international assignments is repatriation of returning employees. This function is probably one of the most neglected areas in global human resource management. Ironically, it is the one that has the greatest impact on the return on investment made in employees sent abroad.

Very few companies deal successfully with the issue of repatriation. Retention rates of repatriates during the first year of return are often as low as 50 percent in many companies. Organizations need to establish a strategy that allows them to take the valuable experience abroad and (1) integrate it with what is happening at home and (2) allow coworkers to learn of the repatriate's experience to enhance their own performance. As a prerequisite, repatriates need to be considered from an investment perspective. In many cases, the organization has invested a sizable amount of time and money in the global assignment of the employee, during which time the employee has further developed both personally and professionally. If the organization fails to develop career management programs that allow those returning from abroad to share their knowledge and insights—rather than leave the organization and share that knowledge with competitors—then the investment has a negative return. An employee who has worked in another country may be of great value to a competitor who would like to start up overseas operations.

Many repatriates return from overseas assignments and either have no job assignment waiting for them or receive a job that is considered a demotion. Expatriates often have high-ranking autonomous positions overseas and are forced to assume positions that strip them of this autonomy upon their return. It is not surprising that some expatriates choose to move to another expatriate assignment with the same employer or with a different employer rather than return to headquarters.

Any strategy for repatriation has to address the purpose of the expatriation. The process of repatriation can be greatly facilitated if a clear purpose for the assignment was established ahead of time based on the needs of both employer and employee.

A specific repatriation process needs to address several critical career and personal issues, as outlined in Exhibit 14-5. The first career issue is resolving career anxiety by helping the employee returning from abroad find an appropriate place that is connected with a career path for the future. The second career issue is the organization's reaction to the return. Is the repatriate made to feel welcome? Is any value placed on the global experience? Are new skills that have been developed being put to use? The third career issue is the loss of autonomy. In planning repatriation programs, some consideration must be given to the level of autonomy the repatriate enjoyed overseas and the correspondingly appropriate types of responsibilities, work assignments, and supervision for the return assignment. The fourth career issue is adaptation. During the expatriation period, there were probably some significant changes taking place at the home office. The repatriate needs to be provided with assistance in adapting to those changes to facilitate maximum performance in the new assignment.

On a personal level, three major issues need to be addressed in repatriation. The first is logistics. Personal savings will need to be transferred, currency converted, personal belongings inventoried and shipped, automobiles and homes possibly purchased and sold, school transfers arranged, and possibly spousal employment assistance arranged. The more logistical details with which the employee has to contend, the more he or she will be distracted from work. The second personal issue is readjustment and integration into the community for the employee. The third personal issue is

EXHIBIT 14-5: ISSUES TO BE ADDRESSED IN A REPATRIATION PROCESS

Career	Personal
• Career anxiety—current place, future	• Logistics
• Organization's reaction	• Personal readjustment
• Loss of autonomy	• Family readjustment
• Adaptation to change	

readjustment and integration into the community for the employee's family. Although it may seem logical that the return home should be a welcome and easy process, experience has shown that it often is not. Much as the workplace has changed, the community in which the employee family lives or is moving to may have changed dramatically during the time abroad. Support for such transition for the employee and family can greatly facilitate the repatriation process.

Repatriation at Colgate-Palmolive

One of the biggest problems with the traditional high attrition rate among repatriates is the loss of experience, skills, and knowledge that accompany the employee's departure. To address this, Colgate-Palmolive has established a global succession database. Used primarily for succession planning purposes, the database, available to the organization's management team worldwide, also contains information on experiences and skills related to work abroad in various cultures. Because Colgate-Palmolive operates over a widely dispersed global area, detailed information about local markets is critical to ongoing success. Seventy-five percent of the company's $9.5 billion annual sales comes from outside of North America. At any time, approximately 300 expatriate global managers are on assignment. Seventy-five percent of these managers have had two or more global assignments and 40 percent of these managers have had four or more. Because foreign assignments are seen as critical to an individual's career success within Colgate-Palmolive and the necessary track to senior management, global assignments are in demand. By collecting information related to success in a particular location, Colgate-Palmolive not only is able to provide assistance to managers going on a new assignment but also ensures that its investment in skills, knowledge, and experiences stays with the organization, given the longer "shelf life" of cultural information over market data.[8]

THE EUROPEAN UNION

Employers who choose to do business in the European Union (EU) do not have the option of taking an ethnocentric approach to HR in their operations there. The European Union has a large number of umbrella employment laws, the details of which vary from country to country, that provide workers with far more protection than their counterparts in the United States. The common intent of these laws is an employment relationship that is not adversarial or confrontational but one that protects the rights of workers via more collectivist social policy.

Unlike the United States, the EU does not follow the employment-at-will policy. Terminating an employee can be a very difficult and expensive undertaking and the laws regulating the ability to terminate, the notification period, and required severance vary from country to country. In the Netherlands, court approval may be needed to terminate an employee; even termination for cause requires very rigid and specific documentation. Germany requires three months' notification before terminations can take effect; Sweden requires up to six months' notice. In Belgium, where terminations are very difficult, employers may be required to pay up to four years' salary to an employee as severance.[9] Spain requires nine weeks of severance pay for each year of service.[10]

Other areas of the employment relationship are regulated in various EU countries as well. Most require a minimum of four weeks paid vacation but France requires 5 weeks, with an additional week for employees between 18 and 21 years of age.

Maternity leave in France is a minimum of 16 weeks, 10 of which must be taken after the child is born, and can extend up to 26 weeks for a third pregnancy. For any pending layoffs, Germany requires a "social plan," which outlines the specific selection criteria used and performance and education levels of workers. German employers must also report employee ages and number of dependants as older workers and those with more dependants enjoy a greater level of job security than others.[11]

One major way in which the employment relationship in the EU differs from that of the United States is the level of worker involvement seen in European organizations. U.S. employers generally have a unilateral right to make decisions that affect employees, but European employers are required to communicate and negotiate many of these decisions with employees as part of the EU's Directive on Information and Consultation. Works councils, composed of employee-elected worker representatives, are required to meet monthly with senior management to discuss all employment policy issues. Works councils operate at individual work sites and in Germany, France, and the Netherlands must approve many of the decisions that employers hope to implement. Employers who do not consult with their works council are subject to fines and possible recision of the decisions implemented. Germany requires works councils in organizations with five or more employees. France requires them in organizations with 50 or more employees. Larger employers, with at least 1,000 employees and at least 150 in each of two member countries, must also form an EU-wide works council. Decisions that affect workers in more than one country must be presented to these groups, which are employer-funded. U.S. employers operating in the EU are faced with a dramatically different mandate relative to how they manage their employees than what they are used to domestically. Works councils formalize the employment relationship far more than is seen with a typical collective-bargaining agreement.

CONCLUSION

Although the principles and processes of strategic human resource management are universal and apply to all organizational settings and cultures, an organization whose strategy involves multinational operations faces some additional challenges in ensuring the success of global assignments. The model for strategically managing global human resources presented in this chapter is independent of the larger model for the book for this very reason; it addresses a different set of issues and challenges that present themselves in the global arena. However, the underlying theme of strategic human resource management in looking at human assets as investments remains quite apparent when looking at global human resource management. Employees on global assignments represent valuable assets who need to be managed more systematically and strategically than they traditionally have been to ensure greater probability of success in global markets.

CRITICAL THINKING

1. How does global human resource management differ from domestic human resource management?

2. Explain the organizational and individual purposes for expatriation. Why do these need to be incorporated as part of a strategic approach to managing global assignments?

3. Describe the four levels of standardization of global human resource practices. For what strategic objectives might each level of standardization be best suited?

4. Explain how each of Hofstede's cultural dimensions might result in specific kinds of human resource programs and practices.

5. How can employers be more successful with retention of repatriates?

Reading 14.1

6. Explain the major challenges organizations face in managing a global workforce. Explain how each of the four strategies presented in the reading addresses these challenges.

Reading 14.2

7. What factors most influenced the success of Four Seasons' entry into the Paris market?

Reading 14.3

8. What stressors are present in the various stages of expatriation? How can expatriate employees and organizations manage the stressors inherent in these stages to ensure the success of the global assignment?

EXPERIENTIAL EXERCISES

1. Examine the four dimensions of culture presented in Hofstede's framework. What strategies would you recommend in dealing with a different culture that is polar on each of the dimensions? For example, what advice would you give to someone from a culture that stresses individualism when dealing with someone from a collectivist culture?

2. What challenges does doing business in the European Union present to an employer? In small groups, have each member investigate the HR environment in a different EU country and then compare and contrast your findings, making recommendations to U.S. organizations considering doing business there.

INTERNET EXERCISES

1. You have been asked to design a Web site that would assist expatriates in getting ready for their overseas assignments. What kinds of information would you include on the site? Locate appropriate Internet sites that provide either useful information about culture in general or guidance in how culture affects business relationships with citizens from a particular country.

CHAPTER REFERENCES

1. Overman, S. "HR Is Partner in 'McDonaldizing' Employees in New Countries," *HR News*, May 2002, p. 7.
2. Britt, J. "Expatriates Want More Support from Home," *HR Magazine*, July 2002, pp. 21–22.

3. Ibid.
4. Hofstede, G. *Culture's Consequences: International Differences in Work-Related Values*, Beverly Hills: Sage, 1984.
5. Hall, Edward T. "The Silent Languages in Overseas Business," *Harvard Business Review*, 1960.
6. Poe, A. "Selection Savvy," *HR Magazine*, April 2002, pp. 77–83.
7. Heenan, D. A. and Perlmutter, Howard V. *Multinational Organizational Development*, Reading, MA: Addison-Wesley, Inc., 1979.
8. Connor, R. "Plug the Expat Knowledge Drain," *HR Magazine*, October 2002, pp. 101–107.
9. Hirschman, C. "When Operating Abroad, Companies Must Adopt European-Style HR," *HR News*, 30, (3), pp. 1, 6.
10. Falcone, P. "Learning from Our Overseas Counterparts," *HR Magazine*, February 2004, pp. 113–116.
11. Ibid.

Managing the Global Workforce: Challenges and Strategies

Karen Roberts, Ellen Ernst Kossek, Cynthia Ozeki, *Academy of Management Executive*

The line went dead. Steve Prestwick slowly hung up the telephone, wondering what he could possibly say to the executive committee monitoring the Singapore R&D center project. Shortly after being assigned to help staff the facility, he had attended a committee meeting that left him excited about tapping into the potential of the company's large global work force. "Get the best people from everywhere," said one executive. "Don't just rely on information from headquarters. Try to find out what the people in Europe or Japan might know," chimed in another. And from the CEO, "Let's use this as an opportunity to develop a global mindset in some of our more promising people." The vision sounded great, and Steve's role seemed simple: put together a team with all the experts needed to get the new facility up and running smoothly in its first two years.

Right away Steve began having trouble finding out who had the right skills, and even where the choices seemed obvious, he wasn't getting anywhere. The engineer who refused the assignment over the telephone was the best the company had in her field. She told him that spending two years in Singapore wouldn't really help her career. Plus, it would be hard on her children and impossible for her husband, a veterinarian with a growing practice. Not only did he need a top engineering manager, but Steve also had to find a highly competent corps of technical researchers who knew about the company and its approach to R&D. He also needed technicians who could set up the facility. He thought he would bring in people from the U.S. to select and set up equipment, then lead a research team of local engineers that the U.S. engineers would train in company practices and technologies. To his chagrin, most of the U.S. technical people he had talked to weren't interested in such an assignment. A European perspective might be useful, but he didn't even have records on possible candidates from the other overseas offices. Steve was on his own, and he had less than a week to come up with a plan.

What Can Steve Do?

Although Steve is fictional, he is facing a composite of real problems for global HR managers. The need to develop a global perspective on human resource management has been part of the managerial landscape for well over a decade, but there is no consensus about what tools to use. Adler and Bartholomew noted that organizational "strategy (the what) . . . is internationalizing faster than implementation (the how) and much faster than the managers and executives themselves (the who)."[1] Steve has been given an assignment that reflects his organization's commitment to manage globally but little guidance about how to meet his goals.

The challenges, strategic approaches, and diagnostic framework we present are based on interviews with senior managers in large corporations with reputations for excellence in international operations. We chose the firms in this study using three criteria. First, we wanted firms experienced in operating internationally that could comment on the evolution of transnational HR management. Second, we wanted variation across industries to assure that we were not uncovering information idiosyncratic to certain types of industries. Third, we selected firms whose recruitment policies indicated a commitment to the strategic use of HRM in global management.

We sent the most senior international HR professional in each firm a letter describing our study and requesting an interview. We asked that they identify any other HR professionals in their organization whom we might also interview. Based on this process, we interviewed 24 professionals at eight firms.[2] The letter listed four questions that we wanted to cover during the interview:

1. What are the key global pressures affecting human resource management practices in your firm currently and for the projected future?
2. What is the level and substance of knowledge about human resource issues that human resource professionals should possess?

3. What are examples of leading edge international human resource practices in your organization?
4. To what extent is international knowledge needed by entry level professionals in human resource management at your organization?

The questions were deliberately broad, reflecting our exploratory approach. Each interview lasted 1½ to 2 hours. During the interviews, we asked for any additional materials the HR managers thought would be valuable to our study. Once we had begun to analyze our interview information, we used follow-up phone calls both to those we interviewed as well as to other professional contacts to supplement or clarify the data from the interviews.

The information from these interviews was distilled into a two-dimensional framework. One dimension was the set of challenges these executives saw confronting global managers. The second was a set of four prototypical strategies to address these challenges.

The Challenges

In the course of each interview, we asked these executives to describe their vision of the ideal global internal labor market. Three broad features emerged from their responses:

(1) Deployment: easily getting the right skills to where they are needed in the organization regardless of geographical location;
(2) Knowledge and innovation dissemination: spreading state of the art knowledge and practices throughout the organization regardless of where they originate; and,
(3) Identifying and developing talent on a global basis: identifying who has the ability to function effectively in a global organization and developing those abilities.

Although skill deployment, information dissemination, and talent identification have long been basic HR challenges, in the global environment, these issues are overlaid with the complexities of distance, language, and cultural differences. Part of the challenge to global management is to reinterpret successful past practices in terms of these complexities.

DEPLOYMENT
All the organizations had a history of operating internationally, but had relied on a headquarters-subsidiary structure and the traditional expatriate model of human resource staffing where U.S. nationals held most positions of authority. This arrangement was adequate in yesterday's international organization because leadership, decision-making authority, and organizational power flowed from the parent site to the foreign subsidiaries. Today, however, new technologies, new markets, innovation, and new talent no longer solely emanate from headquarters but are found cross-nationally, making the expatriate model obsolete.[3] Further, the cost of deploying an expatriate has become excessive. One Merck and Co., Inc., executive estimated that it was three times more expensive to have an expatriate than a local national in any given job.

All of the organizations were developing alternative ways to get the right people to where the work is on an as-needed basis. The key innovation is that organizations are making distinctions between when it is necessary to physically move a person to a particular location and when the person's skills can be delivered through other means. Permanent transfers are no longer seen as the only method for delivering certain services to parts of the organization, giving way to short-term assignments and virtual deployment. Getting managers to stop relying on physical transfers and to think globally about resources is not easy.

Managers will use company-wide job postings when there is a formal job opening, but will not think outside their units, let alone countries, when it comes to finding the expertise to solve a specific problem, such as poor market response to a new consumer product or dysfunctional work relationships that are due to cross-cultural ignorance.

KNOWLEDGE DISSEMINATION/ INNOVATION TRANSFER
The HR executives cited two global information flow blockages: disseminating knowledge from one location to another and spreading innovation. Under earlier expatriate structures, information flowed from the center out. Current global organizations need structures where all units concurrently receive and provide information. Valuable market and production technology information are being produced outside the parent location. One example of the perils of not using local expertise in collecting market information is Marks & Spencer, Britain's largest retailer. The company failed routinely overseas until

it found its niche by selling M&S branded clothes in Hong Kong, a former British colony.[4]

The executives at both Dow Chemical Co. and Merck saw this challenge as being one of cross-functional communication, where the greatest opportunities for growth and innovation are at hand-off points between functions. These executives saw hand-off opportunities as easily lost in a global environment, primarily because of the difficulties of establishing cross-cultural trust. As one manager noted:

> As long as diversity is not valued, trust of people from different backgrounds is not developed. There is a tendency to duplicate functions so one does not have to rely on people one does not trust. As a result, rather than having a single global enterprise, many international companies are operating more like a collection of lots of smaller companies.

All of the executives we interviewed noted that language compounded the trust problem. Although English was the business language in all of these organizations, halting speech, misused words, strange grammar, and mispronounced words can subtly undermine the perception that the speaker is competent.

TALENT IDENTIFICATION AND DEVELOPMENT

One executive at General Motors Corp. began his interview with us by noting that:

> . . . the key global issue [for GM] is how to transform the organization internally to become globally competitive. Even for employees who may never go overseas, it is necessary to constantly sensitize everyone to the fact that they are in a global business.

All the executives reiterated this theme in one way or another. But, eventually, each interview came to the reality that not everyone in the organization is going to thrive and prevail in a global environment. Therefore, one of the larger challenges of managing the global labor force is identifying who is most likely to grasp the complexities of the transnational operations and function well in that sort of environment. As one Merck executive described it:

> In the 1940s, transactions were the basis for determining the types of skills managers needed. The [new] challenge to [global

human resource management] is to learn to talk in terms of "stories." Organizations need people who understand the business and who are able to see where the business is going globally and the cultures that need to be bridged, people able to manage conflict and change.

One aspect of this challenge is that the scope of the transnational organization is so large that just collecting information about employees is difficult. Also, all of the executives we interviewed acknowledged that there were cultural biases in the selection process that probably caused talented people to be overlooked. One Amoco Corp. executive gave the example of their operations in Norway. Norwegian work-family values differ from those in the U.S., and it is common for men who are senior in their organizations to leave work at 3 p.m. to pick up their children after school. While U.S. norms are beginning to tilt somewhat more toward family in the work-family balance, leaving early still signals a lack of commitment to the job in most U.S. workplaces.[5] The Amoco executive noted that it was very difficult for U.S. managers to trust that their Norwegian employees would get the job done in a crisis and thus had trouble seeing them as potential global managers. Duplicative staffing was sometimes the result.

A final component of this challenge was motivating employees to want to spend time overseas. Most of the executives considered overseas experience a *sine qua non* for promotion to top jobs in their organizations. But, for a variety of reasons, many talented employees do not want to move overseas. One executive noted that, "talent marries other talent," and that spousal careers are increasingly an obstacle to overseas assignments.[6] Another point, made by both Merck and Amoco, was that the expected growth in their industries was in locations that were not viewed as desirable by employees from developed countries. An Amoco executive noted that in some West African countries where Amoco had operations, 30 to 35 percent of the population was thought to be HIV positive, dramatically undermining the appeal of those countries to potential expatriates.

Four Strategies for Managing the Global Workforce

The managers we interviewed described how their organizations had moved away from the traditional expatriate assignments and the new arrangements they were using to meet the three challenges above. Tables 1 through 4 summarize the key points of each of the strategies.

ASPATIAL CAREERS

Aspatial careerists have borderless careers, typically working in multiple countries over the course of their work lives. The chief difference between the aspatial career and the expatriate assignment is that these careers exist in an environment where authority and expertise are no longer thought to reside exclusively at the parent company. Aspatial careerists can come from any part of the globe.

Aspatial careers can take several forms. An employee may live and work overseas with frequent moves; others may have a geographically stationary home base but are required to travel and to have the ability to think about the organization in ways that are spatially neutral. If they relocate, their families go with them.

The aspatial careers model does not overcome the high costs associated with the traditional expatriate model. As a result, only a small percent of most organizations' employees follow aspatial career paths. GM estimates that there are only about 900 of its employees [who] pursue aspatial careers. Merck has approximately 250 employees on this path out of a workforce of 37,000.[7]

Aspatial careerists are usually managers, not technicians. Over the course of their several moves, they accumulate rich contextual knowledge, also known as tacit or implicit knowledge. Successful aspatial careerists develop an in-depth understanding of global organizations because they have managed across cultures and know how culture affects work.

They have also developed extensive global networks that help them identify and draw on expertise throughout their organizations. These managers' global insights tend to filter through the organization rather than be distributed by means of explicit training or the introduction of new technology. One exception is when companies use aspatial careers to develop technical personnel below the top management level. A plant manager at Dow described cross-national rotation of engineers as part of a strategy for cross-training and to assure comparability of engineering skill level across Dow plants in all countries.

Through long rotations with in-depth experience, aspatial careerists acquire globally applicable skills. One company had a manager who had begun his career as a health care expert in France. He then spent four years in London, three in Tokyo, and three in Switzerland, at each point deepening his health care expertise and expanding his network. He had become a repository of cross-cultural health care information as well as a someone who

TABLE 1: ASPATIAL CAREERS

Who	What
Globally oriented, highly mobile people, with proven ability and company loyalty	Corps of experts with borderless careers on long-term overseas assignment

How		
Deployment	**Knowledge Dissemination**	**Talent ID & Development**
Geographically relocate employees with high level skills and rich cross-cultural perspectives	Employees with in-depth global experiences & networks in leadership positions across sites	Rotation as development

Implementation Points

- Encourage company over country culture
- Assign within culturally homogenous regions
- Use pan-region selection meetings
- Evolve selection criteria that are shared across countries
- Provide cross-cultural training for families
- Recognize family life-cycle realities

TABLE 2: AWARENESS-BUILDING ASSIGNMENTS

Who		What
High potential employees early in their careers		3 to 12 month assignments

How		
Deployment	**Knowledge Dissemination**	**Talent ID & Development**
Technically competent, high potential employees	Cross-cultural immersion to produce global perspective	• Screening for ability to function out of own culture • Develop globally aware future performers

Implementation Points

- Use to bridge geofunctional disconnects
- Rotate employees with demonstrable competence
- Manage the adjustment cycle
- Use to develop local nationals

knew the players across these different sites. His gradually accumulated information made him an insightful manager and valuable to the company.

The talent identification potential of aspatial careers is not yet fully realized. Several companies noted that they are beginning to explicitly view their aspatial careerists as a recruiting pool for the highest level of corporate management. The underlying logic is that those who have rotated across different countries have the global perspective needed at the top of the organization. However, none of the companies we interviewed had fully committed to reliance on aspatial career experience as an indicator of top management potential. Rather, several admitted that their companies still had difficulties with recognizing the value-added of overseas experience when reintegrating those who have been overseas into home country operations.

AWARENESS-BUILDING ASSIGNMENTS

The primary purpose of awareness-building assignments is to develop cross-country sensitivity in high-potential employees in a short time. These assignments last anywhere from 3 months to one year. Families are not expected to relocate, so that depending on assignment length, regular home visits might be part of this strategy. Usually this assignment is made early in one's career and typically an employee will only have one such assignment.[8]

At the end of an awareness-building assignment, a high potential employee is expected to have a broadened cultural perspective and an appreciation of the diversity in the organization. One of the Dow executives summarized the purpose of these assignments:

> Overseas assignments are no longer used just to get the "overseas stamp" . . . We may transfer them to acquire knowledge available only overseas, or perhaps as a way to export a leading-edge practice to an overseas location. Often, though, an overseas assignment is not specifically a technical transfer—we are going more for [developing an employee with an] 'open mind'.

GM also incorporates a training component in the form of short-term cross-function transfers and/or cross-plant training. This can be a mechanism for innovation dissemination. GM has found that rotated employees must demonstrate technical competence to be accepted at the overseas site. As one GM executive described it:

> If the need is to cultivate openness and develop cross-cultural awareness, it has to be done early in one's career. However, the reality is that those who go overseas first have to demonstrate technical competence to be accepted in a different location, and this is more necessary than cultural awareness.

Several firms use these assignments to aculturate local nationals who after the rotation will spend

TABLE 3: SWAT TEAMS

Who	What
Technical specialists	Short-term, project-length assignments

How		
Deployment	**Knowledge Dissemination**	**Talent ID & Development**
Specialized skills on an as-needed basis	Transfer of technical processes & systems	Specialized skills honed through varied & frequent applications

Implementation Points

- Best SWAT team member has single contributor mindset
- Use to spread acultural innovation
- Good at smaller locations or at start-up
- Recognize clear limitation

most of their careers in their home countries. These assignments serve as screens for global awareness potential. Awareness-building assignments are not long enough to develop in-depth cultural knowledge. However, an employee who can shed provincialism and learn that value can be added from any location in the company is one who is likely to function effectively in the global organization.

SWAT TEAMS

SWAT teams are highly mobile teams of experts, deployed on a short-term basis, to troubleshoot, solve a very specific problem, or complete a clearly defined project. (The name derives from the special weapons and tactics units used by many police departments.) SWAT teams play a role like that of the technical troubleshooter, an individual sent to a foreign location to analyze and solve a particular operational problem.[9]

SWAT teams comprise nomadic experts who are identified internationally and deployed as internal consultants on an as-needed basis. As a Dow executive described the objective of this approach, the company does not "expect to move people across areas but does want to leverage resources across our different businesses." At GM, the SWAT team takes the form of an expert network, internal consultants deployed throughout the organization. The actual amount of time spent overseas varies with the purpose or project but in general is under three months.

The primary strength of this approach is that it permits the organization to cultivate highly specialized knowledge and expertise on a limited basis, and to apply that expertise wherever it is needed within the organization. One difference between SWAT teams and awareness-building assignments is that there is no explicit developmental component to the SWAT team model other than to complete whatever project is defined. Development of cross-cultural awareness on the part of SWAT team members may be a by-product of the job but it is not its intention.

Once a SWAT team has been assembled, it can be redeployed each time a situation requiring its skillset emerges. Frequent opportunities to apply their skills in different settings can add significantly to the existing skill accumulation of team members, providing the developmental component to the SWAT team strategy.

VIRTUAL SOLUTIONS

Virtual solutions are a collection of practices that exploit the rapidly evolving electronic communication technologies. These include use of all forms of the Internet and intranets, videoconferencing, electronic expert systems, and electronic databases coupled with user-friendly front-end systems. The chief advantages to this strategy are the low cost of communication and the uncoupling of real time from virtual time. Awareness-building and virtual solutions are the strategies with which most of the firms we interviewed had had the least experience, but also were the approaches they saw as having the most potential for managing and developing the global workforce.

Internet and intranets, including E-mail, are the most democratic form of overseas deployment, allowing communication among employees regardless of organizational level. Videoconferencing has a similar

TABLE 4: VIRTUAL SOLUTIONS

Who	What
Non-rotating employees who need overseas connections	Electronic communications

How		
Deployment	**Knowledge Dissemination**	**Talent ID & Development**
Videoconferencing & E-mail allow virtual deployment	Web pages, bulletin boards, intranets, distance learning & interactive training disperse information across locations	GHRIS, electronic job posting, video & virtual interviews ID and screen for assignments

Implementation Points

- Encourage virtual friendships
- Couple with cross-culture awareness training
- GHRIS works best with standardized information
- GHRIS trade-off between standardized information & universal access
- Global job posting for clearly defined jobs
- Don't expect instant results

advantage; however, videoconferencing facilities are a scarce resource compared with E-mail in most organizations. Both Dow and Merck managers said that their videoconferencing rooms were in constant use.

Virtual international teams design software at IBM Corp. Communication through intranets allows for 24-hour product development. One team includes software developers from the U.S., several former Soviet Union states, and India. The work is usually initiated in the U.S. At the end of the day, the U.S. team transmits its files via the intranet to the Soviet team, which works on the project until the end of the work day. The Soviet team then sends its work on to the Indian team whose work day ends at the start of business for the U.S. team, which picks up the files and continues the production cycle.

A more sophisticated virtual deployment tool is the use of virtual reality. NASA uses virtual reality to train international teams of astronauts.[10] These teams need to perform complex tasks requiring lengthy training. Actually convening these teams of astronauts from different countries at a single geographical location for months at a time is prohibitively expensive and disrupts family life. A virtual simulation of a repair of the Hubble telescope was constructed for training purposes and allowed team members to simulate the repair as though in the same room. One Russian and one U.S. member virtually shook hands at the end of the repair exercise.

However, this simulation took months to develop. While virtual reality is almost as good as being there, it is also almost as expensive.

All the companies have web pages on the Internet with company background and product information, as well as public information about new developments. E-mail is in common use and electronic bulletin boards to solve technical problems were becoming more common. At the time of our interviews, comparable intranet systems with proprietary information were in development. This sort of communication is one mechanism to break down some of the barriers to information flow erected by technical chauvinism. Reiterating the theme of cross-cultural distrust, one GM executive noted that "technically skilled people in one country feel their training and skills are superior [to those of employees from other countries] and they have little to learn from their international counterparts." He noted this was a substantial problem in motivating technical employees to rotate overseas and that use of E-mail and electronic bulletin boards is expected to ameliorate this problem as technical solutions are offered cross-nationally and recognized as valid.

One solution not yet widely implemented is distance learning. Ford Motor Co. uses this commonly to continuously update the skills of its engineers, videotaping classes that employees can play individually or as a group. The students can then hold discussion groups and interact with the instructor who holds electronic office hours at predetermined time. Another version is a highly interactive broadcast class where students can interact with the instructor across networks that permit student questions and discussion, even pop quizzes. However, distance learning is still in its infancy and was not cited as a commonly used tool.

All the firms had Global Human Resource Information Systems (GHRIS), which allowed for global job posting. The companies stressed that talent identification below the highest level on a global basis was key to the success of the company. Amoco Corp., Dow, and Merck used their GHRIS to store career data about their employees useful for selection and, on a more limited basis, for job posting. Amoco has implemented a worldwide job posting system that allows all employees to use electronic systems to learn about and apply for jobs.[11]

Diagnosing the Challenges

We developed a diagnostic framework for evaluating each of the challenges and deciding among the four strategies.

DIAGNOSING THE DEPLOYMENT CHALLENGE

The challenge of global deployment is getting the needed skills from one part of the organization to another inexpensively. Not all of the tools associated with each of the strategic solutions were equally effective in all situations. There are two components to deciding among the deployment strategies: contact time required and extent to which the skills can be applied out of cultural context.

If the need is for on-going on-site leadership, in-depth cultural understanding, and/or skills that can only be successfully applied if culturally embedded, use aspatial careers. To provide short-term training or skills application that requires cultural sensitivity, use awareness-building assignments. SWAT teams offer on-site technical skills, knowledge of production process, operations, and/or systems that need to be implemented, with little cultural content. Virtual solutions provide frequent, brief iterative interactions, with only a little cultural component to the interaction, or a wide sweep of the organization to search for or communicate technical details or information.

DIAGNOSING THE KNOWLEDGE AND INNOVATION DISSEMINATION CHALLENGE

The information organizations need to stay competitive ranges from highly technical to informally communicated background information. The effectiveness of each of the four strategies depends on the type of knowledge or innovation being disseminated. Choosing among the four strategies depends on the technical complexity of the information that is to be shared and the extent to which it must be culturally embedded. If the knowledge or innovations to be disseminated can be successfully shared only when communicated in a cultural context, use aspatial careers. Awareness-building assignments succeed when the knowledge is primarily cultural awareness and cross-cultural sensitivity training. If the knowledge is defined technology or practices with minimal cultural content, use SWAT teams. If the knowledge requires on-going and frequent information exchanges among dispersed employees, use virtual solution.

DIAGNOSING TALENT IDENTIFICATION AND DEVELOPMENT CHALLENGES

Development of a global mindset is essential to operating globally. Executives are looking for a similar set of characteristics among their global managers.[12] Merck looks for people who have a broad perspective and can intelligently apply practical leadership skills to guide change in the organization. Baxter International looks for "patience, flexibility, communication skills, intellectual curiosity about the rest of the world." GM looks for a skillset that includes, "communication skills, the ability to value diversity, and the ability to be objective."

Cultural training notwithstanding, a manager from Merck noted the difficulty of finding people with this skillset:

> Merck uses two-thirds selection and one-third development . . . [We rely more on selection than development in our selection criteria because] it is difficult to impart needed skills, and people don't get that much out of classroom training—they are more likely to remember what they had for dinner than what went on in the training session . . . We are looking for people with curiosity and a mix of skills.

This suggests that organizations should select well, then develop. Companies that need to identify and develop leaders with in-depth cultural knowledge and proven cross-cultural abilities and are willing to spend time and money to have those people, should use aspatial careers. To identify and develop high potential performers with an understanding that they are functioning in a global organization and an appreciation of cultural diversity, companies should use awareness-building assignments. SWAT teams provide mobile and technically competent specialists whose skills tend to be needed on a short-term basis. Virtual solutions identify employees using shared selection criteria to fill vacancies with well-understood job requirements.

Implementing the Strategies

Following are examples of how companies implemented each of the strategies, including some of the obstacles they have encountered.

IMPLEMENTING THE ASPATIAL CAREER STRATEGY

All the companies encourage the development of a culture of company over country. Baxter has deployed leadership throughout the organization regardless of national origin: the VP for the European region is of U.S. origin located in Germany; the VP for the Diagnostics division is an Italian located in Switzerland; the VP of Cardiovascular is Irish and located in France; the Hospital group is lead by French person in Belgium. This is not just a happy accident but the result of an explicit strategy on Baxter's part to develop a company-over-country identity, where the managers focus on the competitive strategies of the entire company, not only for the region in which they reside. Baxter has eliminated country-based organization and reorganized by product group or business function. Also, the position of country general manager has been eliminated to encourage a business-over-country orientation.

These geographically fluid careers are more successful if rotations occur within culturally homogeneous regions. Both Baxter and GM have divided their global operations into regions, and Baxter is deliberate about rotating employees within rather than across regions as much as possible. This policy is consistent with results from a study of Singaporean managers showing that the cultural similarity between origin and destination locations positively affected employee and spouse willingness to relocate.[13]

GM also uses a regional basis for determining benefit plans, distinguishing between intracontinental (policies reflecting continent-wide norms) and intercontinental policies (policies applied at GM sites world-wide). This distinction simplifies within-region rotations.

Schlumberger uses a "borderlands career track" version of aspatial careers in which rotating employees move often across adjoining borders. The cultural homogeneity of border areas allows the company to move people quickly with minimal adjustment.[14]

One identification mechanism used by several companies is the pan-regional meeting. This meeting takes place regularly, three to four times a year, where higher- (but not just the highest-) level managers and sometimes technical people within a geographical region meet to exchange information and network. The meetings last several days to a week and are used to showcase potential aspatial careerists. HR people are included and charged with identifying potential talent for global reassignment. Dow holds four annual meetings, one in each region, where managers are asked to recommend, review, and present the top 1.5 percent of the employees in terms of high management potential. Because it is important for managers to present very talented people, these annual meetings are high pressure events. These meetings are used also to identify candidates for awareness-building assignments.

An informal outcome from Dow's meetings is the evolution of a shared understanding of what is meant by global competencies. This evolves out of formal identification and presentation of high potential talent at the pan-regional meetings. Each meeting serves as an iteration in the development of global selection criteria. This evolving understanding of the managerial traits required by the global organization is used to identify candidates for both aspatial careers and awareness-building assignments.

A key component to motivating talented employees to go overseas, even for a short time, is their belief that the organization values overseas experience. This will be especially true for aspatial careerists, but also true to a lesser extent for awareness-building assignments and SWAT team employees. Most organizations send a mixed message to employees about the value of overseas experience.[15]

There is often a sharp decline in authority, responsibility, and autonomy for the employee returning to the parent company. Most aspatial careerists are at or near the top of the overseas organization and in many cases behave like CEOs. Their jobs at the parent site are of necessity of lower status. The more hierarchical an organization, the more difficult this problem will be. Structuring jobs of returning aspatial employees to allow sufficient autonomy and identifying explicit ways to fully utilize their overseas expertise is important. GM does this by using returned overseas employees in the first round selection process for aspatial careers and awareness-building assignment candidates.

The firms varied in how they valued overseas experience. At one firm it was impossible to receive more than 1000 Hay points (from the Hay Group's method of evaluating jobs based on technical skills, problem-solving, and accountability) without an international experience, so employees were willing to relocate to avoid that career ceiling. At another extreme, one executive candidly described his organization as having a top management that stressed overseas experience; below top management, however, was a headquarter-centered culture, where overseas experience was viewed as inferior.

GM sets up home-based mentor relationships between each overseas employee and what they call a repatriation facilitator. This provides a support system for the overseas employee but also helps home-based employees value what the overseas employee can contribute upon return. GM also uses home leave where rotated employees present their overseas projects and show how they will contribute to home operations. GM has found that repatriated employees are more successful when brought back into a unit where the manager has had some overseas experience.

Recognizing family needs is key to successful aspatial career development. According to numerous studies, family circumstances are the leading cause of overseas assignment failures.[16] Spousal careers and child care are important family considerations and cited in one survey as the top family reasons to refuse an overseas assignment.[17] Cultural awareness training for family members was just beginning at several of the companies we studied and held promise for smoothing family transitions. GM uses relocation facilitators and assigns mentor families to aspatial career families early in their assignments. Job seeking assistance and/or partial remuneration for loss of job income for spouses were provided by most of the companies we studied, but these were considered feasible only if the family was staying overseas at least two years.

It is also important to recognize that all aspatial careerists may not stay aspatial forever. Although some individuals will spend their entire careers outside of their native countries, most eventually return to the parent site. One driver of this decision is family life-cycle change, which pushes an employee to move the family back home. For example, executives wanting their children to go to U.S. high schools so they can get into U.S. colleges was a factor noted by GM.

IMPLEMENTING THE AWARENESS-BUILDING ASSIGNMENT STRATEGY

The missed opportunities at hand-off points described earlier by a Merck executive are often the result of geofunctional disconnects. These are points where functional and geographical boundaries are coterminous, compounding cross-functional cooperation problems. Awareness-building assignments can effectively bridge these gaps when they are used to collect consumer market information. Amoco uses awareness-building assignments to develop product preference sensitivity in employees who design products used or sold overseas. Two examples of the need to develop intimate knowledge of local markets are Procter & Gamble's faulty start selling all-temperature detergents to Japanese housewives who wash clothes only in cold water and GM's attempt to sell two-door trucks to Chinese with a strong preference for four-door vehicles.[18] Baxter learned this lesson after medical equipment intended for Japan was designed and sized using U.S. patients as the standard. The firm now has a cross-cultural training program, often in the form of awareness-building assignments, for engineers who design products for global markets.

Awareness-building assignments blur the traditional distinction between learning and contributing jobs. Most of the executives we interviewed noted that these assignments should be used judiciously. The awareness-building benefit will be lost if the rotated employee is perceived as having nothing to offer the overseas site. The challenge is to select people early enough in their careers that the assignments serve as screens for future potential but not so early that they have few skills to offer.

Merck gives awareness-building assignments to more mature employees, believing that generating a global mindset is more a selection than a developmental issue, and that mature workers can develop a global awareness if the predisposition is there. Both Merck and Baxter note, however, that language ability limits the candidate pool. At Merck, this has meant that more overseas employees are rotated for awareness-building assignments in the U.S. than the other way around.

Awareness-building assignments must avoid the negative effects of what is termed the "intercultural adjustment cycle."[19] A Dow executive described a cycle on long-term overseas assignments. During the first three months, employees are euphoric about the new country, soak up the culture, and enjoy the superficial differences between the overseas post and the home country. Because most rotated employees are top performers in their home country, however, by the third month they become discouraged by the drop in their productivity and by their lack of linguistic or cultural fluency. During the next three to six months, relocated employees and their families begin to miss their home countries and find fault with the overseas sites. At about nine months, the employees regain the confidence they had before being sent overseas and function as competent members of the overseas society.

Most aspatial careerists will pass through the cycle to regain their sense of competence, but an awareness-building assignment may not last through the entire adjustment cycle. An assignment that ends during the euphoric period will leave the employee with a superficial understanding of the overseas location. An assignment ending during the trough of the cycle may leave the employee soured about overseas experiences and negative about the global scope of the organization. Rather than trying to avoid the adjustment cycle, organizations should use training to prepare employees for it. The virtue of the adjustment cycle is that its low point prompts individuals to reconceptualize their mental frames and begin to develop in-depth understanding of the new cultures.

Since a solution to the problem of motivating aspatials to go to unattractive locations is to develop indigenous talent, Amoco, Baxter, and Merck give awareness-building assignments to local nationals. Rotations to headquarters familiarize them with the company mission and culture, while rotations to various world-wide production locations familiarize them with operations. Local nationals must be given challenging assignments in the U.S. or the rotation may be demotivating.

IMPLEMENTING THE SWAT TEAM STRATEGY

Two factors seemed to help optimize the staffing of SWAT teams. First, despite the likelihood that work will be done on a team basis, individual contributor-type employees with a technical orientation are the best candidates. Second, because technical challenges are what motivates them, mechanisms such as outside training are needed to keep SWAT team members on the leading edge.

SWAT teams are best used to export clearly defined technologies or practices. While some training may have to take place at the overseas site to allow those employees to become users, knowledge or innovations conveyed by a SWAT team do not usually have a developmental or cross-cultural component. The SWAT team approach is most easily applied in a manufacturing setting where production processes are less dependent on cultural idiosyncracies. For example, GM uses what they refer to as internal consulting teams to collect information about best manufacturing processes and to disseminate them to other plants world-wide.

In some cases, SWAT assignments are used at sites that are too small to have a sustained need for certain skills, especially in developing countries. In Pakistan, for example, where the human resource/industrial relations function is a part-time job, a traveling unit of negotiators travels from site to site at contract negotiation time, completes the negotiations, secures a contract, and leaves. Both GM and Merck use teams of internal experts and external consultants to do global benefit planning. These teams immerse themselves in local government regulations and set up the benefit plan for each site.

SWAT team assignments can be useful in setting up new operations where start-up skills are needed for a brief period. Amoco uses SWAT teams when it is deciding whether or not to permanently locate in a country. Because location usually depends on finding oil and securing drilling rights, Amoco may be in a country for a relatively long time before withdrawing.[20] Using SWAT teams during start-ups also requires more cultural-awareness training than the conventional SWAT team assignment.

SWAT teams have their very clear limitations, tending to draw on the manufacturing model to conceptualize deployment and information dissemination challenges, and applying that model to nonproduction situations. The pure SWAT team approach will be effective only when interpersonal relationships and cultural understanding are of minimal importance to the transfer of knowledge or innovation. The development of interpersonal relationships and cultural awareness is time consuming and the benefits are often intangible, but in many cases these are necessary prerequisites for information exchange and effective working relationships. If these are needed, the SWAT team strategy will fail.

IMPLEMENTING THE VIRTUAL SOLUTIONS STRATEGY

The virtual solutions model allows cross-national relationships to form below the level of top management. Virtual communications that are not necessarily task-oriented but that foster interpersonal exchanges enable task information to flow more smoothly. In addition, opportunities for innovation can occur at electronic hand-off points if information about production methods, problems, and solutions is shared informally.

In most cases, electronic communication is not yet a perfect substitute for direct contact. Small misunderstandings can become full-blown E-mail wars because of the absence of such communication cues as tone of voice and facial expression.

Cultural differences and differing abilities in the language of the exchange increase the likelihood of misunderstanding. Thus, virtual deployment is best used in conjunction with some other form of cultural awareness building. Recognizing this, one Dow executive encourages modest expectations for E-mail initially—to develop in employees "a different mentality, to get them to agree that there are more than one way to skin a cat."[21]

Both Dow and Baxter use employee questionnaires designed by international teams to collect information about operations, practices, and values across the firm to build cross-cultural data bases. These data bases can be retrieved by employees throughout the organization and can supplement other cultural training for virtual solution users. The Baxter survey is customized to fit local conditions and uses local terminology appropriate to each culture. The Dow instrument measures climate as well as management practices.

All of the companies had a Human Resource Information System (HRIS) in place, but varied in the degree to which it could be characterized as a global system. Merck has developed templates that vary with the employee's level in the organization. Employees lower in the organization are less likely to be relocated globally and thus fewer data are required about them for the GHRIS. Approximately one hundred pieces of data are entered into the GHRIS for lower level employees, compared with approximately four hundred entries for higher level employees.

Storing benefit information continues to be a GHRIS challenge. Dow has developed regional benefit models and determined that approximately 80 percent of the data needed for any given employee is standard across nations. The remaining nonstandard 20 percent is country-specific. However, some of this nonstandard information can be collapsed into a smaller number of models, each with its own data template. One example, cited by Dow, is that while there is no world-wide set of educational certifications, most countries' educational systems can be classified into one of a few models. Decisions about which information can be standardized globally and which need to reflect local custom were made after a series of global stakeholder meetings.

One Dow executive commented that to be truly valuable, a GHRIS must be a dynamic tool, evolving over time. He also said that this is easy to say, but something of a headache to implement. One significant gap between the ideal and the reality of a GHRIS is the ability to combine universal access with standardized information. Amoco uses a kiosk system to allow employees to enter information about themselves but has found that not all employees have the ability to do this. Dow has faced the same challenge and has decided to sacrifice universal access for completeness of standardized information.

Global job posting works best for those jobs with relatively well-understood skill requirements. The more subtle or idiosyncratic the skill requirements, the more difficult the job description is to translate globally. As noted earlier, employees below a certain level are not likely to rotate internationally, so clarity about skill requirements also helps screen out certain types of postings for which the company reasonably wants to recruit only locally.

There are technological hurdles to implementing the virtual solutions model, and one should not expect instant results. Even when using established technologies like video broadcasting, learning will take on new forms and periods of adjustment will be required.

What Can Steve Do?

There is no instant solution to Steve's problem. The people he wants with the skills he needs are not going to convene in Singapore to work together for two years. But, by employing a combination of strategies, Steve can accomplish his goal. He can:

- Select a SWAT team to come in and set up the equipment, a clearly defined task that can be accomplished in a short time with minimal interpersonal contact. Technical people from Tokyo, just a few hours away by plane, could fly in three or four times to set up the equipment and conduct inspections once the facility is running.
- Virtually connect the talented engineer with the Singapore team using E-mail, the phone, and video conferencing, combining this with a short-term awareness-building assignment to foster personal relationships with the technical team and build cross-cultural understanding.
- Ask European, Asian, and South American regional heads to set up regular regional talent ID meetings to nominate potential people for both aspatial career and awareness-building assignments at their next regional conference. The list can be used to select people to conduct initial training sessions and handle early troubleshooting in Singapore as well as a few who

may be suited for a longer-term assignment to the new facility.

- Post jobs on an internal bulletin board or intranet web site with full details about the skills required, so that interested and qualified people can also volunteer for Singapore assignments.
- Set up a web page for the site and E-mail technically capable people throughout the organization to stay tuned for brainstorming sessions during the R&D process. Good ideas will win prizes.
- Start scouting for a local national to head up the R& D center, then begin the development with an awareness assignment to headquarters to teach about company culture.

This version of using the four strategies to manage a cross-national workforce differs from the traditional staffing mindset with which Steve initially approached the problem. These strategies allow firms operating on a global basis to make the best use of their widely dispersed internal resources and find innovative solutions to their HR problems.

Source: Academy of Management Executive: The Thinking Manager's Source by Roberts. Copyright © 1998 by the Society for Advancement of Management. Reprinted with permission of Society for Advancement of Management in the format Textbook via Copyright Clearance Center.

Endnotes

1. Adler, N. and Bartholomew, S. 1992. "Managing Globally Competent People," *Academy of Management Executive,* 6(3), 52.

2. The companies included: Amoco, Baxter, Dow (interviews at both U.S. and Canadian locations), General Motors, IBM, Merck, and Wyeth-Ayerst. Some information about distance learning as a knowledge dissemination/innovation transfer tool was also collected from Ford Motor Co.

3. See Taylor, S., Beechler, S., and Napier, N. 1996. "Toward an Integrative Model of Strategic International Human Resource Management," *Academy of Management Review,* 21(4), 959–985 for a description of the information flows in a globally integrated organization.

4. *Fortune.* 1995. "Retailers Go Global." February 20, 102–108.

5. *Fortune.* 1997. "Is Your Family Wrecking Your Career (And Vice Versa)?" March 3, 70–90.

6. This is consistent with the findings of a study by Brett, Stroh & Reilly of *Fortune* 500 company managers who were willing to relocate. They found that spouse willingness to move was the most significant factor in an employee's willingness to move. See Brett, J., Stroh, L., and Reilly, A. 1993. "Pulling Up Roots in the 1990s: Who's Willing to Relocate?" *Journal of Organizational Behavior,* 14(1), p. 49–60.

7. This total workforce number excludes employees of recent acquisitions by Merck.

8. Use of these assignments as a tool is still evolving and this aspect could easily change.

9. Schuler, R., Fulkerson, J., and Dowling, P. 1991. "Strategic Performance Measurement and Management in Multinational Corporations," *Human Resource Management,* 30(3), 365–392.

10. Loftin, R. B. 1996. "Hands Across the Atlantic," *Virtual Reality Special Report,* 3(2), 39–41.

11. See Kossek, E. E. 1993. "Globalization: What Every Human Resource Professional Should Know—Examples from Amoco Production Company," presented at the National Research Symposium of the Human Resource Planning Society, June.

12. Their list corresponds closely to that described in Tung, R. 1993. "Managing National and Intranational Diversity," *Human Resource Management,* 32(4), 461–477.

13. Ayree, S., Chay, Y. W., and Chew, J. 1996. "An Investigation of the Willingness of Managerial Employees to Accept an Expatriate Assignment," *Journal of Organizational Behavior,* 17(3), 267–283.

14. This strategy may not be for every organization, at least as it is implemented by Schlumberger. These paths require a move every three years. At the time of the move, employees are only permitted to move up to 2000 pounds of personal effects and are expected to take the next plane out once a new assignment has been made. As one employee commented, "they treat their people like cattle." See Kossek, E. E., cited above.

15. See Oddou, G. and Mendenhall, M. 1991. "Succession Planning for the 21st Century," *Business Horizons*, 34(1), 26–34 for a brief description of this problem.

16. See Arthur, W. and Bennett, W. 1995. "The International Assignee: The Relative Importance of Factors Perceived to Contribute to Success," *Personnel Psychology*, 48, 99–115, and Tung, R. 1981. "Selection and Training of Personnel for Overseas Assignments," *Columbia Journal of World Business*, Spring, 68–78.

17. Greenfield, C. 1996. *Work/Family Game.* Boston: Towers Perin.

18. An alternative way of expressing this is that companies producing overseas to sell overseas need to identify sources of customer value. See Bartness, A. and Cerny, K. 1991. "Building Competitive Advantage through a Global Network of Capabilities," *California Management Review*, 35(2), 78–103, for a full discussion of the identification process.

19. Grove, C. L. and Torbiorn, I. 1985. "A New Conceptualization of Intercultural Adjustment and the Goals of Training," *International Journal of Intercultural Relations*, 9(16), 205–233.

20. See Kossek, E. E., cited above.

21. After saying this, he noted that "more than one way to skin a cat" was precisely the type of phrase that needed to be eliminated from international communications.

Four Seasons Goes to Paris

Roger Hallowell, David Bowen, and Carin-Isabel Knoop, *Academy of Management Executive*

Europe is different from North America, and Paris is very different. I did not say difficult. I said different.

—A senior Four Seasons manager

The Linkage Between Service Culture and Competitive Advantage

The enduring success of service organizations such as Southwest Airlines. The Walt Disney Company, Wal-Mart, and USAA (among others) is frequently attributed in no small degree to their corporate cultures. These companies have built and maintained organizational cultures in which everyone is focused on delivering high customer value, including service, and individuals behave accordingly. The culture influences how employees behave, which in turn, shapes the value that customers receive, in part through the thousands of daily encounters between employees and customers.

Corporate culture has been linked to competitive advantage in companies, for better or worse,[1] and in service companies, in particular.[2] Culture is so important in service companies because of its effect on multiple factors affecting customer value, factors as critical as employee behavior and as mundane (but important) as facility cleanliness. These aspects are especially visible to customers, who often co-produce a service with employees. In many services employee and customer interactions take place continually, in many parts of the organization, so that no realistic amount of supervision can ever exercise sufficient control over employee behavior. Under these circumstances, culture becomes one of management's most effective, if unobtrusive, tools to influence employee thoughts, feelings, and, most important, behavior.

Understanding Corporate Culture

Our model of corporate culture, which uses Schein[3] as a point of departure, consists of the following four components: underlying assumptions, values, employee perceptions of management practices, and cultural artifacts.

UNDERLYING ASSUMPTIONS

These are basic assumptions regarding the workplace, such as the assumption that subordinates should fulfill their job requirements as a condition of employment.

VALUES

These are those things that are viewed as most important in an organizational setting, such as cost control, customer satisfaction, and teamwork.

Values exist in two forms in organizations. The first is what can be termed "espoused values," which are what senior managers or company publications *say* the values are.

The second form is "enacted values," which are what employees infer the values to be. Although enacted values, *per se*, are invisible, employees infer what they are by examining the evidence found in the next two components of culture: management practices and cultural artifacts. These two components are more readily observed than assumptions and values.

EMPLOYEE PERCEPTIONS OF MANAGEMENT PRACTICES (PARTICULARLY RELATING TO HUMAN RESOURCES): POLICIES AND BEHAVIORS

Employees' views of practices such as selection, training, performance appraisal, job design, reward systems, supervisory practices, and so on shape their perceptions of what values are actually being enacted in a setting. For example, although customer service may be an espoused value, if job applicants are not carefully screened on service attitude, or if employees who provide great service are not recognized and rewarded, then employees will not believe that management truly values service. In short: culture is what employees perceive that management believes.

CULTURAL ARTIFACTS

These include heroes, rituals, stories, jargon, and tangibles like the appearance of employees and facilities. Again, given the espoused value of customer service, if jargon used to characterize customers is usually derogatory, then a strong service culture is unlikely to emerge.

In contrast, if espoused values are enacted—and thus reflected in policies, management behaviors, and cultural artifacts—then a culture may emerge in which senior management and employees share similar service-relevant thoughts, feelings, and patterns of behavior. This behavior has the potential to enhance customer value and contribute to competitive advantage.

EXPORTING CORPORATE CULTURE: CAN CULTURE TRAVEL ACROSS BORDERS?

If a company succeeds in creating a corporate culture that contributes to competitive advantage in its home country can it successfully "export" that corporate culture to another country—particularly if that country's national culture is strongly distinct, as is the case in France?

THE ISSUE OF FLEXIBILITY VERSUS CONSISTENCY

Will an organization's *corporate* culture "clash" or "fit" with a different *national* culture? The key consideration here is what components of corporate culture link most tightly to competitive advantage and, as a consequence, must be managed *consistently* across country borders—even if they seem to clash with the culture of the new country. Alternatively, are there components of culture that are not critical to the linkage? If so, *flexibility* may enhance the competitiveness of the corporate culture given the different national culture.[4]

One way to frame this analysis is around whether the potential clash between corporate and national culture is over the corporate values themselves, i.e., *what* they are, or over the manner of their implementation, i.e., *how* they are enacted (specifically, management practices and cultural norms). Is there a clash between core corporate values and core country values? If so, and if those core values are critical to competitive advantage, then perhaps the company cannot be successful in that setting. If the clash is over how values are enacted, then some management practices or cultural forms can be modified in the new setting. However, this requires managers to ask which practices or forms can be modified, enhancing the competitive advantage of the corporate culture, and which practices, if modified, will undermine corporate culture.

In short, all of the elements of corporate culture can be thought of as the threads in a sweater: when a thread sticks out of a sweater, sometimes it is wisely removed, enhancing the overall appearance. However, sometimes removing a thread will unravel the entire sweater. Managers must determine which aspects of their corporate cultures will "stick out" in a new national environment and whether modifying or eliminating them will enhance the organization or weaken it.

Four Seasons Hotels and Resorts: Overview

In 2002, Four Seasons Hotels and Resorts was arguably the world's leading operator of luxury hotels, managing 53 properties in 24 countries. Being able to replicate "consistently exceptional service" around the world and across cultures was at the heart of the chain's international success and sustained advantage.

For Four Seasons, "consistently exceptional service" meant providing high-quality, truly personalized service to enable guests to *maximize the value of their time*, however guests defined doing so. Corporate culture contributed to the firm's success in two ways. First, through the values that the organization espoused. For Four Seasons, these were personified in the Golden Rule: "Treat others as you wish they would treat you." Second was the set of behaviors that employees and managers displayed, in effect the enactment of the firm's values. The organizational capability of translating core values into enacted behaviors created competitive advantage at Four Seasons. Doing so required managers to address a central question as they expanded into new countries: What do we need to keep consistent, and what should be flexible, i.e., what should we adapt to the local market?

PERFORMANCE

Four Seasons generally operated (as opposed to owned) mid-sized luxury hotels and resorts. From 1996 through 2000 (inclusive). Four Seasons increased revenues from $121 million to $347.5 million and earnings from $55.7 million to $125.8 million, a 22.6 percent compounded annual growth rate (CAGR). Operating margins increased from

58.8 percent to 67.9 percent during the same period. Four Seasons 2001 revenue per room (RevPAR), an important hospitality industry measure, was 32 percent above that of its primary United States competitors and 27 percent higher than that of its European competitors. Growth plans were to open five to seven new luxury properties per year, predominantly outside of North America.

Four Seasons entered the French market by renovating and operating the Hotel George V, a historic Parisian landmark. The hotel was renamed the Four Seasons Hotel George V Paris (hereafter, "F. S. George V").

INTERNATIONAL STRUCTURE

Each Four Seasons property was managed by a general manager responsible for supervising the day-to-day operations of a single property. Compensation was in part based on the property's performance. Hotel general managers had a target bonus of 30 percent of base compensation. Twenty-five percent of the bonus was based on people measures (employee attitudes), 25 percent on product (service quality), and 50 percent on profit.

Four Seasons' management believed that the firm's regional management structure was a key component of its ability to deliver and maintain the highest and most consistent service standards at each property in a cost effective manner. General Managers reported directly to one of the 13 Regional Vice Presidents or directly to one of the two Senior Vice Presidents, Operations. A Regional Marketing Director, an Area Director of Finance, and a Regional Human Resources Director completed each support team. The majority of these individuals were full-time employees of a Four Seasons–managed property, with a portion of their time devoted to regional matters including both routine management and deciding how to customize Four Seasons operating practice to the region.

MANAGEMENT

Four Seasons' top management team was noted for its longevity, many having been at the firm for over 25 years. Characteristics which executives attributed to their peers included an international flair, a respect for modesty and compassion, and a "no excuses" mentality.

Italian in Italy, French in France. The firm's top managers were very comfortable in a variety of international settings. Antoine Corinthios, President, Europe, Middle East and Africa, for example, was said to be "Italian in Italy, French in France." Born and educated in Cairo, Corinthios then spent 20 years in Chicago but described himself as a world citizen. He was as much of a cultural chameleon as he wanted Four Seasons hotels to be. "When I speak the language of the environment I am in, I start to think in the language I am in and adapt to that culture. If you are going global, you cannot be one way," he explained.

No bragging, no excuses. Modesty, compassion, and discipline were also important. A manager who stayed with Four Seasons from the prior management of the George V described the Four Seasons due diligence team that came to the property as "very professional and not pretentious; detail oriented; and interested in people. They did not come telling me that all I did was wrong," he remembered, "and showed a lot of compassion. The people are good, but still modest—many people in the industry can be very full of themselves." Importantly, excuses were not tolerated at Four Seasons. "Oh, but we have just been open a year" or "The people here do not understand" were not acceptable statements.

Strong allegiance to the firm. Both corporate and field managers often referred to the firm as a "family," complete with rules, traditions, and tough love. There was a strong "one-firm sentiment" on the part of managers in the field; they worked for the firm, not for the individual property to which they were assigned. For example, a general manager explained, "We are happy to let stars go to other properties to help them."

Service orientation. Customer service extended to all levels in the organization. Managers sometimes assisted in clearing restaurant tables in passing. "If I see that something needs to get done," a manager explained, "I do it."

Four Seasons' Approach to International Growth

Today, we have opened enough properties overseas that we can go into any city or town and pull people together to fulfill our mission.

—Isadore Sharp, Founder and CEO

DIVERSITY AND SINGULARITY

One of the things Four Seasons managers were wary about was being perceived as an "American" company. They found it useful in Europe to position Four Seasons as the Canadian company it was. One noted, "The daughter of a property owner once told us. 'I do not want you to be the way Americans are.' She assumed that Americans say 'Do it my way or take the highway.' Canadians are seen as more internationally minded and respectful of other value systems."

According to Corinthios, "Our strength is our diversity and our singularity. While the essence of the local culture may vary, the process for opening and operating a hotel is the same everywhere." He continued:

> My goal is to provide an international hotel to the business or luxury leisure traveler looking for comfort and service. The trick is to take it a couple of notches up, or sideways, to adapt to the market you are in. Our standards are universal, e.g., getting your message on time, clean room, good breakfast; being cared for by an engaging, anticipating and responding staff; being able to treat yourself to an exciting and innovative meal— these are global. This is the fundamental value. What changes is that people do it with their own style, grace, and personality; in some cultures you add the strong local temperament. For example, an Italian concierge has his own style and flair. In Turkey or Egypt you experience different hospitality.

As a result, "Each hotel is tailor made" and adapted to its national environment, noted David Crowl, Vice President Sales and Marketing, Europe, Middle East and Africa:

> Issy Sharp once told me that one of our key strengths is diversity. McDonald's is the same all over. We do not want to be that way. We are not a cookie cutter company. We try to make each property represent its location. In the rooms, we have 40 to 50 square meters to create a cultural destination without being offensive. When you wake up in our hotel in Istanbul, you know that you are in Turkey. People know that they will get 24-hour room service, a custom-made mattress, and a marble bathroom, but they also know that they are going to be part of a local community.

According to David Richey, president of Richey International, a firm Four Seasons and other hotel chains hired to audit service quality, "Four Seasons has done an exceptional job of adapting to local markets. From a design perspective, they are much more clever than other companies. When you sit in the Four Seasons in Bali, you feel that you are in Bali. It does not scream Four Seasons at you."

A manager explained Four Seasons' ability to be somewhat of a cultural chameleon with an analogy to Disney: "Unlike Disney, whose brand name is so strongly associated with the United States. Four Seasons' brand doesn't rigidly define what the product is. The Four Seasons brand is associated with intangibles. Our guests are not looking to stay in a Canadian hotel. Our product has to be 100 percent Four Seasons, but in a style that is appropriate for the country."

According to Crowl, Four Seasons learned from each country and property: "Because we are an international hotel company, we take our learning across borders. In Egypt, we are going to try to incorporate indigenous elements to the spa, but we will still be influenced by the best practices we have identified at our two spas in Bali."

GLOBALLY UNIFORM STANDARDS

The seven Four Seasons "service culture standards" expected of *all* staff *all* over the world at *all* times were:

1. **S**MILE: Employees will actively greet guests, smile, and speak clearly in a friendly manner.
2. **E**YE: Employees will make eye contact, even in passing, with an acknowledgment.
3. **R**ECOGNITION: All staff will create a sense of recognition by using the guest's name, when known, in a natural and discreet manner.
4. **V**OICE: Staff will speak to guests in an attentive, natural, and courteous manner, avoiding pretension and in a clear voice.
5. **I**NFORMED: All guest contact staff will be well informed about their hotel, their product, will take ownership of simple requests, and will not refer guests elsewhere.
6. **C**LEAN: Staff will always appear clean, crisp, well-groomed, and well-fitted.
7. **E**VERYONE: Everyone, everywhere, all the time, show their care for our guests.

In addition to its service culture standards, Four Seasons had 270 core worldwide operating standards (see Appendix 1 for sample standards). Arriving at these standards had not been easy; until 1998 there were 800. With the firm's international growth, this resulted in an overly complex set of rules and exceptions. The standards were set by the firm's senior vice presidents and Wolf Hengst, President, Worldwide Hotel Operations, who explained: "We had a rule about the number of different types of bread rolls to be served at dinner and number of bottles of wine to be opened at lounges. But in countries where no bread is eaten at dinner and no wine is consumed, that's pretty stupid."

"While 270 standards might seem extensive," Richey noted, "if there are only 270, there are thousands of things that are not covered over which the general manager and local management team have a lot of control."

In addition, exceptions to the standards were permitted if they made local sense. For example, one standard stated that the coffee pot should be left on the table at breakfast so that guests could choose to refill their cups. This was perceived as a lack of service in France, so it was amended there. Standards were often written to allow local flexibility. While the standards require an employee's uniform to be immaculate, they do not state what it should look like. In Bali, uniforms were completely different from uniforms in Chicago. Managers underlined the fact that standards set *minimum expectations*: "If you can do something for a client that goes beyond a standard," they told staff, "do it." As a result, stories about a concierge taking a client to the hospital and staying with that person overnight were part of Four Seasons lore, contributing to cultural artifacts.

To evaluate each property's performance against the standards. Four Seasons used both external and internal auditors in its measurement programs. "Our standards are the foundation for all our properties," a senior manager noted. "It is the base on which we build." "When you talk to a Four Seasons person," Richey concluded, "they are so familiar with each of the standards, it is astonishing. With many managers at other firms this is not the case."

"We have been obsessed by the service standards," Hengst concluded. "People who come from the outside are surprised that we take them and the role they play in our culture so seriously. But they are essential. Talk to me about standards and you talk to me about religion." Another manager added, "Over time, the standards help to shape relationships between people, and those relationships contribute to building our culture."

Delivering Intelligent, Anticipatory, and Enthusiastic Service Worldwide

A manager stated: "We decided many years ago that our distinguishing edge would be exceptional, personal service—that's where the value is. In all our research around the world, we have never seen anything that led us to believe that 'just for you' customized service was not the most important element of our success." Another manager added, "Service like this, what I think of as 'intelligent service,' can't be scripted. As a result, we need employees who are as distinguished as our guests—if employees are going to adapt, to be empathetic and anticipate guests' needs, the 'distance' between the employee and the guest has to be small."

There were also tangible elements to Four Seasons' service quality. The product was always comfortable—so much so that at guests' requests, the company made its pillows, bedspreads, and mattresses available for sale. Guests could also count on a spacious bathroom, which was appreciated by the world traveler, especially in Europe where bathrooms tended to be small. "However there are differences in the perception and definition of luxury," explained Barbara Talbott, Executive Vice President of Marketing. "In the U.S., our properties have public spaces with a luxurious, but intimate, feeling. In the Far East, our properties have large lobbies enabling guests to see and be seen. People around the world also have different ways of using a hotel—restaurants, for example, are more important in hotels in Asia, so we build space for more restaurants in each property there."

Human Resources and The Golden Rule

Four Seasons' managers believed that human resource management was key to the firm's success. According to one senior manager, "People make the strength of this company. Procedures are not very varied or special. What we do is fairly basic." Human resource management started and ended with "The Golden Rule," which stipulated that one should treat others as one would wish to be treated. Managers saw it as the foundation of the firm's values and thus its culture. "The golden rule is the key to the success of the firm, and it's appreciated in every village, town, and city around the world. Basic human needs are the same everywhere." Sharp emphasized. Appendix 2 summarizes the firm's goals, beliefs and principles.

Kathleen Taylor, President, Worldwide Business Operations, provided an example of how Four Seasons went about enacting the Golden Rule as a core value. "We give employees several uniforms so they can change when they become dirty. That goes to their dignity, but it is uncommon in the hospitality industry. People around the world want to be treated with dignity and respect, and in most organizational cultures that doesn't happen."

Managers acknowledged that many service organizations made similar statements on paper. What differentiated Four Seasons was how the chain operationalized those statements. Crowl noted. "A service culture is about putting what we all believe in into practice. We learn it, we nurture it, and most important, we do it."

In 2002, for the fifth year in a row. Four Seasons was among *Fortune* magazine's list of the top 100 best companies to work for in North America. While turnover in the hospitality industry averaged 55 percent. Four Seasons turnover was half that amount.

Going to Paris

However it developed its approach and philosophy. Four Seasons management knew that entering France would be a challenge.

THE GEORGE V OPPORTUNITY

The six hotels in Paris classified as "Palaces" were grand, historic, and luxurious. Standard room prices at the F. S. George V, for example, ranged from $400 to $700. Most palaces featured award-winning restaurants, private gardens, and expansive common areas. For example, the Hotel de Crillon, a competitor to the F. S. George V, was an 18th-century palace commissioned by King Louis XV. The nine-story George V was designed in the 1920s by two famous French art déco architects. The property was located in one of Paris' most fashionable districts. For comparative data on Parisian palaces, please refer to Appendix 3.

Observers of the Paris hotel scene noted that by the 1980s and 1990s, the George V, like some of its peers, was coasting on its reputation. In December 1996, H.R.H. Prince Al Waleed Bin Talal Bin Abdulaziz al Saud purchased the hotel for $170 million. In November 1997, Four Seasons signed a long-term agreement to manage the hotel. "We needed to be in Paris," John Young, Executive Vice President, Human Resources, explained. "We had looked at a new development, but gaining planning permission for a new building in Paris is very hard. Since we look for the highest possible quality assets in the best locations, the George V was perfect. It established us very powerfully in the French capital."

In order to transform the George V into a Four Seasons, however, an extensive amount of effort had to be placed into both the tangible and experiential service which the property and its people could deliver.

PHYSICAL RENOVATIONS

Four Seasons' challenge was to preserve the soul of the legendary, almost mythical, George V Hotel while rebuilding it for contemporary travelers. Four Seasons closed the hotel for what ended up being a two-year, $125 million total renovation. Because the building was a landmark, the façade had to be maintained. The interior of the hotel, however, was gutted. The 300 rooms and suites were reduced to 245 rooms of larger size (including 61 suites). Skilled craftsmen restored the façade's art déco windows and balconies, the extensive wood paneling on the first floor, and the artwork and 17th-century Flanders tapestries that had long adorned the hotel's public and private spaces.

The interior designer hired by Four Seasons, Pierre Rochon, noted: "My main objective was to marry functionality with guest comfort, to merge 21st-century technology with the hotel's 'French classique' heritage. I would like guests rediscovering the hotel to think that I had not changed a thing—and, at the same time, to notice how much better they feel within its walls."[5] The fact that the designer was French, Talbott pointed out, "signaled to the French that we understood what they meant by luxury."

While Four Seasons decided to build to American life-safety standards, it also had to adhere to local laws, which affected design and work patterns. For example, a hygiene law in 'France stipulates that food and garbage cannot travel the same routes: food and trash have to be carried down different corridors and up/down different elevators. Another law involved "right to light," stipulating that employees had the right to work near a window for a certain number of hours each day. As a result, employees in the basement spa also worked upstairs in a shop with a window for several hours a day, and as many windows as possible had to be programmed into the design.

The new Four Seasons Hotel George V opened on December 18, 1999 at 100 percent effective occupancy (occupancy of rooms ready for use). Managers credited extensive publicity, the millennium celebration, and the profile of the property for that success. The opening was particularly challenging because Four Seasons only took formal control of operations on December 1, in part due to French regulations. "The French are very particular about, for example, fire regulations, but the fire department would not come in and inspect until everything else was complete," a manager said.

Becoming a French Employer

Entering the French hospitality market meant becoming a French employer, which implied understanding French labor laws, business culture, and national idiosyncrasies.

RULES

France's leaders remained committed to a capitalism that maintained social equity with laws, tax policies, and social spending that reduced income disparity and the impact of free markets on public health and welfare.[6] France's tax burden, 45 percent of GDP in 1998, was three percentage points higher than the European average—and eight points higher than the OECD average. A further burden on employers was the 1999 reduction of the work week to 35 hours. Unemployment and retirement benefits were generous. Importantly, Four Seasons' management was not unfamiliar with labor-oriented government policy. "Canada has many attributes of a welfare state, so our Canadian roots made it easier to deal with such a context." Young explained.

The country was known for its strong unions.[7] "In France, one still finds a certain dose of antagonism between employees and management," a French manager underlined. The political party of the Force Ouvrière, the union that was strongest at the F. S. George V, garnered nearly 10 percent of the votes in the first round of the 2002 French presidential election with the rallying ary, "Employees fight the bosses!"

"If you look at the challenges of operating in France," noted Corinthios, "they have labor laws that are restrictive, but not prohibitive. The laws are not the same as, for example, in Chicago. You just need to be more informed about them." The law did give employers some flexibility, allowing them to work someone a little more during peak business periods and less during a lull. A housekeeper, for exam-

ple, might work 40-hour weeks in the summer in exchange for a few 30-hour weeks in the late fall. Furthermore, French employers could hire 10 percent to 15 percent of staff on a "temporary," seasonal basis.

A particularly tricky area of labor management in France involved terminations. "Wherever we operate in the world," a Four Seasons manager explained, "we do not fire at will. There is due process. There is no surprise. There is counseling. So, Paris isn't that different, except to have the termination stick is more challenging because you really need a very, *very* good cause and to document *everything* carefully. If you have one gap in the documentation, you will have to rehire the terminated employee."

NATIONAL AND ORGANIZATIONAL CULTURE

Geert Hofstede's seminal work, *Culture's Consequences*,[8] indicates a great disparity between North American (U.S. and Canadian) national culture and that of France. While Hofstede's work has been criticized for the construction of the dimensions along which cultures differ,[9] there is general agreement with the principle that cultures do differ. Further, Hofstede's work and that of other scholars indicate that the differences between North American and French organizational culture are large. Corinthios identified attitudes surrounding performance evaluation as one difference:

> European and Middle Eastern managers have a hard time sitting across from people they supervise and talking about their weaknesses. The culture is not confrontational. It is more congenial and positive. It is very important to save face and preserve the dignity of the person being reviewed. Some Four Seasons managers using standard forms might even delete certain sections or questions or reprogram them in different languages.

For Didier Le Calvez, General Manager of the F. S. George V and recently appointed Regional Vice President, another significant difference was the degree to which middle and front-line managers felt accountable. "The greatest challenge in France is to get managers to take accountability for decisions and policies," he said. "In the French hierarchical system there is a strong tendency to refer things to the boss."

Le Calvez was also surprised by managers' poor understanding of human resource issues. In France, when a manager has a problem with an employee, the issue generally gets referred to the human resources department. "We, at Four Seasons, on the other hand, require that operating managers be present, deal with the issue, and lead the discussion."

"SEEING IS BELIEVING"

When reflecting on their experiences with employees in France, several Four Seasons managers mentioned Saint Thomas ("doubting Thomas"). "They must see it to believe it," Le Calvez explained. "They do not take things at face value. They also tend to wait on the sidelines—once they see that something works, they come out of their shells and follow the movement." A Four Seasons manager continued: "Most of the workforce in France did not know what Four Seasons was all about. For example, they did not think we were serious about the Golden Rule. They thought it was way too American. Initially there were some eyebrows raised. Because of this skepticism, when we entered France, we came on our tip toes, without wanting to give anyone a lecture. I think *how* we came in was almost as important as *what* we did."

MORE DIFFERENCES

For several Four Seasons managers, working in France required a "bigger cultural adjustment" than had been necessary in other countries. "In France, I always knew that I would be a foreigner," a manager explained. "It took me a while to adjust to the French way." "There is simply an incredible pride in being French," added another. "The French have a very emotional way to do things," an F. S. George V manager explained. "This can be good and bad. The good side is that they can be very joyous and engaging. On the bad side, sometimes the French temper lashes out."

According to Four Seasons managers, what was referred to in the cultural research literature as the French "logic of honor"[10] was strong. While it would be degrading to be "in the service of" (*au service de*) anybody, especially the boss, it was honorable to "give service" (*rendre service*), with magnanimity, if asked to do so with due ceremony. In this context, management required a great deal of fact and judgment.

Managing differing perceptions of time could also be a challenge for North Americans in France. North Americans have been characterized as having a "monochronic" culture based on a high degree of scheduling and an elaborate code of behavior built around promptness in meeting obligations and appointments.[11] In contrast, the French were "polychronic" valuing human relationships and interactions over arbitrary schedules and appointments. These differences created predictable patterns summarized in Appendix 4.

Specific areas where Four Seasons and French national culture differed often related to either (French) guest expectations of a palace hotel, including its physical structure and tangible amenities, or manager-employee relationships. For example, in France, hotel guests expected a palace hotel to have a world-class gastronomic restaurant. They also expected exquisite floral arrangements and to be wowed by the décor. In contrast, Four Seasons hotels generally have excellent, although not necessarily world-class, restaurants and are known for their understated, subtly elegant look. An example of differences in employee-manager relationships can be found in the French managerial practice of being extremely cautious in providing employee feedback to the degree that, according to Four Seasons' managers, the practice is unusual. In contrast, Four Seasons management practice involved a great deal of communication, including feedback on an individual employee's performance, which managers believed critical to solving problems and delivering superior service.

CULTURAL RENOVATION AT THE F. S. GEORGE V

Awareness and management of French cultural patterns were especially important to Four Seasons managers in Paris because a significant portion of the former operator's management and staff remained. Young explained:

> When we explored options for refashioning the George V into a Four Seasons hotel, we realized that without being able to start from scratch, the task would be Herculean. The existing culture was inconsistent with ours. In a North American environment you can decide whom to keep after an acquisition at a cost you can determine in advance on the basis of case law. In France, the only certainty is that you cannot replace the employees. You are acquiring the entity as a going concern. Unless you do certain things, you simply inherit the employees, including their legal rights based on prior service.

To be able to reduce headcount, by law an enterprise had to plan to be closed for over 18 months. Because the F. S. George V owner wanted the renovation to be complete in 12 months, staff were- guaranteed a position with Four Seasons unless they chose to leave.[12] "Many of the best employees easily found other jobs, while the most disruptive were still there when the hotel reopened." Young said. "The number of people we really did not want was somewhere in the region of 40 out of 300 coming back on reopening."

Managers uniformly noted that the cultural renovation necessary to enable Four Seasons to be able to deliver its world-class service was on par with the extent of the physical renovation. Young provided an example. "During the due diligence process the former general manager went to lunch with one of our senior staff. Even though guests were waiting, the maitre d' immediately tried to escort the general manager and his party to the general manager's customary table. At Four Seasons this is seen as an abuse of privilege. For us, 'the guest always comes first.'"

Fortunately, in taking over The Pierre in New York, Four Seasons had been through a somewhat similar process. The scale of change necessary in each situation was enormous, as illustrated by this quotation from a senior Four Seasons manager: "Shortly after we bought The Pierre in 1981, a bell captain lamented that the times of the big steamer trunks were over. The staff had not adjusted to jet travel, despite its prevalence for two decades. This is the same kind of recalibration we had to do at the George V."

APPLES AND ORANGES

Young described the firm's approach to cultural transformation in acquired properties with existing staffing:

If we can achieve a critical mass of individuals among the workforce who are committed to doing things differently, to meeting our standards, that critical mass overcomes the resistance of what becomes a diminishing old guard. Progressively, that old guard loses some of its power. If one rotten apple can ruin the barrel, then you have to seed the organization with oranges that cannot be spoiled by the apples. As a result, a departing old-guard employee is *very* carefully replaced. Concurrently, individuals with the right culture and attitude are promoted. That creates a new

culture, bit by bit by bit. At the F. S. George V, we also appealed to the national pride of our staff to help us restore a French landmark— to restore the pride of France.

"UN BOSS FRANCO-FRANÇAIS"

To effect this cultural change, Four Seasons picked Le Calvez to be general manager. Le Calvez was described as both demanding and "Franco-Français,"[13] an expression used in France to describe someone or something "unequivocally French." At the same time, Le Calvez brought extensive Four Seasons and North American experience. Prior to opening the Regent Hotel in Singapore, he spent 25 years outside France, including 11 years at The Pierre. "He is very international, yet also very French, very attached to his country and its culture," an executive explained. "He knows everyone and has an unbelievable memory for names and events (what happened to so-and-so's mother in-law, etc.). He is very visible and accessible to the staff, eating in the staff cafeteria."

An F. S. George V manager noted, "The hotel's culture is embodied in the general manager—he shows a lot of love and respect for others and promotes social and cultural and ethnic integration." In a country where people typically referred to each other as Monsieur and Madame with their last name, Le Calvez encouraged the use of the first name. "It is more direct, relaxed, and straightforward. It represents the kind of relationship I want to have with my staff," he stated.

Young commented on the choice of Le Calvez: "The choice of senior leadership is absolutely critical. Adherence to our values and operational goals has to be extremely strong. Hotel openings require a lot of patience and tolerance because results are likely to be less positive as you manage through periods of major change."

THE TASK FORCE—"CULTURE CARRIERS"

To help Le Calvez and his team "Four Seasonize" the F. S. George V staff and ensure a smooth opening, Four Seasons assigned a 35-person task force, as it did to every new property. A manager noted:

The task force helps establish norms. We help people understand how Four Seasons does things. Members listen for problems and innuendoes and communicate the right information to all, and squash rumors, especially when there are cultural sensitivities. The task force also helps physically getting the property up and running. Finally, being part of the task force exposes managers who may one day become general managers to the process of opening a hotel.

The task force, composed of experienced Four Seasons managers and staff, reflected the operating needs of each property. For example, if an experienced room service manager had already transferred to the opening property, those skills would not be brought in via the task force.

"The task force is truly a human resource, as well as a strong symbol," a manager explained. "The approach supports allegiance to the firm and not just one property—because members of the task force are not associated with one hotel. We are excited to participate, even if it means working long hours for weeks away from home." Most task force members, who typically stayed three weeks for an opening, stayed seven to eight weeks at the F. S. George V.

STRONG TIDES

After working 25 years abroad, Le Calvez admitted that he was hesitant to return to work in France in light of the general tension he sensed between labor and management. However, he was encouraged by what he had seen at The Pierre, where Four Seasons managers noted that they had fostered a dialogue with the New York hospitality industry union. Le Calvez felt he could do the same in Paris. "When I arrived I told the unions that I did not think that we would need them, but since the law said we had to have them, I said 'Let's work together.' I do not want social tensions. Of course, this is not unique to me; it is Four Seasons' approach. We have to be pragmatic. So we signaled our commitment to a good environment."

Le Calvez communicated this commitment by openly discussing the 35-hour work week, the Four Seasons retirement plan, and the time and attendance system, designed to make sure that staff would not work more than required.

At the outset of negotiations, in preparation for the reopening, Le Calvez took the representatives of the various unions to lunch. As work progressed, he organized tours of the site so that union representatives could see what was being done and "become

excited" about the hotel. He noted that "Touring the property in hard hats and having to duck under electric wires builds bonds. Witnessing the birth of a hotel is exciting." Managers stated that the unions were not used to such an inclusive approach in France.

Young felt that dealing with unions in France was easier than in New York: "In France, you are dealing with an institution backed by stringent, but predictable, laws. In the United States you are dealing with individuals in leadership who can be much more volatile and egocentric."

Four Seasons' experience with The Pierre proved invaluable. According to Young:

In New York, we redesigned working spaces, and trained and trained, and trained staff. But we also burned out a couple of managers. The old culture either wears you down or you wear it down. In an environment with strong labor laws, management sometimes gives up the right to manage. At some point managers stop swimming against the tide. If that continues long enough, the ability to manage effectively is lost. The precedents in a hotel are those that the prior managers have permitted. If the right to manage has been given up, standards are depressed, productivity decreases, margins decrease, and eventually you have a bad business. Regulars are treated well, but many guests are not. Reversing this process requires enormous management energy. It is very wearing to swim against a strong tide. You are making decisions that you believe reasonable and facing reactions that you believe unreasonable.

THE 35-HOUR WORK WEEK

Managers believed that Four Seasons' decision to implement the 35-hour work week at the F. S. George V to meet the letter and spirit of French law was a major signal to the unions and workforce about the way the company approached human resource issues. "When we hire staff from other hotels, they are always surprised that we obey the law," an F. S. George V manager noted. "They were working longer hours elsewhere."

A 35-hour work week yielded 1,820 annual workable hours per full-time staff equivalent. But since the French had more holidays and vacation, an employee provided 1,500 to 1,600 workable hours. This compared to about 2,050 hours in the United States for a full-time equivalent. The manager added, "We did not really understand the impact of the 35-hour work week. Each of our 80 managers has to have two consecutive days off a week, and each of the staff can work 214 days a year. Not 215. Not 213, But 214."

In 2002, 620 staff covered 250 rooms, or 2.5 staff per room. On average, Four Seasons hotels had 1.6 employees per room. Depending on food and banquet operations, that average could rise or fall significantly. Table 1 shows employees-to-room ratios at selected Four Seasons properties.

Young felt that labor laws explained about 15 percent of the need for increased staff ratios in Paris; vacations and holidays, 10 percent; with the rest explained by other factors including some logistics of the operation, e.g., a historic building, all compared to U.S. norms. Corinthios elaborated:

> In Paris, you have six palaces competing for the same clients. It is a more formal operation. Guest expectations are very high, as is the level of leisure business (which requires higher staffing). People stay four to six days and use the concierge extensively. The concierge staffing at the F. S. George V is as big as anything we have in the chain. Then there is more emphasis on food and beverage. We have a fabulous chef and more staff in the kitchen for both the restaurant and room service—expectations of service in the gastronomic restaurant are very high.

Running the F. S. George V

RECRUITMENT AND SELECTION

Four Seasons wanted to be recognized as the best employer in each of its locations. In Paris, F. S. George V wages were among the top three for hotels. Salaries were advertised in help wanted ads, a first in the industry in Paris according to F. S. George V managers, who believed doing so would help them attract high quality staff.

At the F. S. George V, as across the firm, every potential employee was interviewed four times, the last interview with the General Manager. According to one executive, "In the selection process, we try to look deep inside the applicant. I learned about the importance of service from my parents—did this potential employee learn it from hers?" "What matters is attitude, attitude, attitude," Corinthios explained. "All around the world it is the same. Without the right attitude, they cannot adapt." Another manager added, "What we need is people who can adapt, either to guests from all over the world, or to operating in a variety of countries." One of his colleagues elaborated on the importance of hiring for attitude, and its challenges:

> You would think that you would have a lot of people with great experience because there are so many palace hotels in Paris. But because we hire for attitude, we rarely hire from the other palaces. We hire individuals who are still "open" and tend to be much younger than usual for palace hotels. Then we bet on training. Of course, it takes much longer to train for skills when people do not have them. We look for people persons, who

TABLE 1: EMPLOYEES-TO-ROOM RATIOS AT SELECTED FOUR SEASONS PROPERTIES

Property	Employees–to-Rooms Ratio
Four Seasons worldwide average	1.6
The Pierre New York	2.3
Four Seasons Hotel New York	1.6
Four Seasons Hotel George V Paris	2.5
Four Seasons Hotel Berlin	0.9
Four Seasons Hotel London	1.2
Four Seasons Hotel Canary Wharf, London	1.4
Four Seasons Hotel Milano	2.2

Source: Four Seasons.

are welcoming and put others at ease, who want to please, are professional and sincerely friendly, flexible, smiley, and positive. At the F. S. George V, people apply for jobs because they have friends who work here.

To spread the culture and "de-demonize" the United States, the new F. S. George V management recruited staff with prior Four Seasons and/or U.S. experience to serve as ambassadors. A manager noted, "Staff with U.S. experience share with other staff what the United States is about and that it is not the terrible place some French people make it out to be." Several managers had international experience. About 40 individuals had prior U.S. experience.

"Anglo-Saxon" Recognition, Measurement, and Benefits

Le Calvez and his team launched an employee-of-the-month and employee-of-the-year program. "This had been controversial at Disney. People said it could not be done in France, but we manage to do it quite successfully. It all depends how it is presented," Le Calvez noted. "We explained that the program would recognize those who perform. Colleagues can tell who is good at their job."

Le Calvez used the same spirit to introduce annual evaluations, uncommon in France:

> People said evaluations would be unpopular, but the system seems to work. We told the staff that it would be an opportunity for open and constructive dialogue so that employees can know at all times where they stand. This allows them to adapt when need be. We wanted to make clear that there would be no favoritism, but rather that this would be a meritocracy. Here your work speaks for itself. The idea that your work is what matters could be construed as very Anglo Saxon!

In another "Anglo Saxon" action, a *"Plan d'Epargne d'Entreprise"* was set up for George V employees. This was a combination tax-deferred savings account and 401(k) type retirement plan. "This is totally new in France," Le Calvez claimed. Employees could contribute up to 4 percent of their salary, and the hotel would match it with 2 percent, to be raised based on profitability. The unions signed the agreement,

although they were opposed to the principle of a non-government-sponsored retirement plan.

Implementing the Golden Rule

The Golden Rule was at work at the F. S. George V, as its human resource director illustrated: "Cooks, before joining Four Seasons, used to have very long days starting in the morning to prepare for lunch, having a break during the afternoon, and coming back to prepare dinner. Today they work on either the morning or afternoon shift, enabling a better organization of their personal lives."

"All these gestures take time to work," Le Calvez summarized. "At first employees do not think we mean it. Some new hires think it's artificial or fake, but after a few months they let their guard down when they realize we mean what we say."

Managers believed that the effect of Four Seasons' human resource practices was reflected in customer satisfaction. Indeed, Le Calvez proudly reported that guest cards often included comments on how friendly and attentive the staff were. "All the other palace hotels in Paris are beautiful, but we believe that we have a special focus on friendly and personable service." He continued, "We offer friendly, very personal service. We have a very young and dynamic brigade with an average age of 26, spanning 46 different nationalities."

COMMUNICATION

To promote communication and problem solving, the F. S. George V management implemented a "direct line." Once a month the general manager met with employees, supervisors, and managers in groups of 30. The groups met for three consecutive months so that issues raised could be addressed, with results reported to the group. Managers believed that the F. S. George V was the only palace hotel in France with such a communication process. It was important to note that the groups met separately—that is, employees met separately from supervisors—because subordinates in France did not feel comfortable speaking up in front of superiors.

French law mandated that a *comité d'entreprise* (a staff committee) be established in organizations with more than 50 employees. It represented employees to management on decisions that affected employees (e.g., salaries, work hours). At the F. S. George V, Le Calvez chaired the committee's monthly meeting, which included union representatives. "We would do these things anyway, so it is easy to adjust to these laws," Corinthios said. "We do it in France because it is required by law. But we do the same around the world; it just has a different name."

Every morning the top management team gathered to go over glitches—things that may have gone wrong the day before and the steps that had been, or were being, taken to address the problem. "Admitting what went wrong is not in the French culture," a French Four Seasons Manager explained. "But the meetings are usually very constructive."

Finally, about three times a year, Le Calvez and his team hosted an open-door event inviting employees and their families to spend some time at the hotel. "This is to break down barriers," he explained. "We take people around the hotel, into the back corridors. Try to remind people of a notion that is unfortunately being lost—that of the "*plaisir du travail*"—or enjoying one's work. Furthermore, we celebrate achievement. Good property rankings, for example, are recognized with special team celebrations."

The property also cultivated external communication with the press in a way that was culturally sensitive. Le Calvez and his team felt that they had been very open and responsive to the press (which they stated was unusual in France) and that as a result, "Not a single negative article had been written about Four Seasons Hotel George V since its opening." A colleague added, "The press appreciated that they were dealing with locals. It was not like Disney where everyone was American."

Culinary Coup d'Etat

In a significant diversion from typical Four Seasons practice, a non–Four Seasons executive chef was hired. "In France having a serious chef and serious food is important," the F. S. George V food and beverage director noted. "You cannot be a palace hotel without that." "We knew that what mattered in Paris was food and décor," Talbott added. Although only 7 percent of room guests were French, most restaurant patrons were French.

Chef Philippe Legendre from the world famous Parisian restaurant Taillevent was recruited. "Didier came to get me through a common friend," Legendre explained. Legendre accepted Four Seasons' offer because "there was something exciting about being part of opening a hotel." He also liked their language which he described as "optimistic" and "about creating possibilities."

Legendre felt that Four Seasons' real strength was around relationship management (with clients and among staff), which "is not something that we are that good at in France, or place particular emphasis on. We have a lot to learn in the social domain. Everything at Four Seasons is geared towards the needs of the guest. At first it was hard, especially the training. Perhaps because in France we think we know everything."

He continued: "After three years I might not talk the Four Seasons talk, I might not use the same words, but I have the same view and adhere to the same system."

Despite Legendre's success (earning two Michelin stars), a colleague added that "bringing in such an executive chef was problematic. The challenge is that with this chef you have someone with extraordinary talent, but who must still adjust to the way service is delivered at Four Seasons." Coexistence was not always easy. Legendre described a situation illustrating miscommunication and cultural differences that required tremendous patience on the part of the restaurant, guests, and management:

> Recently a man ordered an omelet and his wife ordered scrambled eggs. The man returned the omelet because he decided he wanted scrambled eggs. We made them. Then he sent them back because they did not meet his expectations. Of course, we realize that our oeufs brouillés are different from scrambled eggs, which don't contain cream. Because we are Four Seasons we cooked the eggs as he wanted them, like American scrambled eggs, and didn't charge for them. But cooking is about emotion—if you want to please someone, you have to do it with your heart. *We live differently in France.*

Results

A CULTURAL COCKTAIL

The F. S. George V was, in effect, a cultural cocktail. Le Calvez explained, "The F. S. George V is not *only* a French hotel—it is French, but it is also very international. We want to be different from the other palaces that are oh so very French. We want to project the image of a modern France, one that does not have to be dusty. We want to be a symbol of a France that is in movement, a European France, a France that stands for integration and equality."

The cultural cocktail also contained a number of elements unusual in France. At the time of the opening, journalists asked about the "American" smiling culture, which was referred to in France as "la culture Mickey Mouse." Le Calvez replied, "If you tell me that being American is being friendly and pleasant, that is fine by me. People tell me everyone smiles at the Four Seasons George V."

The spectacular flowers in the lobby of the F. S. George V (a single urn once contained 1,000 roses) were both very French and extremely international. "Paris is a city of fashion and culture, artistic and innovative," Le Calvez explained. "That is why, for example, we have the flowers we do. We can do that here." However, the flowers were designed by a young American. Another departure from French standard was the decision to hire women as concierges and men in housekeeping. These were viewed by managers as revolutionary steps in Paris.

SERVICE QUALITY

Richey summarized the results of the first F. S. George V service quality audit in October 2000, identifying some differences between French and North American business culture:

Keep in mind that this occurred less than one year after opening, and it takes at least a year to get things worked out. There were three things we talked to Four Seasons' executives about, mostly related to employee attitude. First, the staff had an inability to apologize or empathize. I think that could be construed as typically European, and especially French. Second, the team had a very tough time doing anything that could be described as selling. This is also typically European. For example: say your glass is empty at the bar. In Paris, they may not ask you if you want another drink. Third, the staff were rules and policy oriented. If something went wrong, they would refer to the manual instead of focusing on satisfying the guest.

Things had changed considerably by Richey's second audit in August 2001, when "they beat the competitive market set." The scores showed a significant improvement, raising the property to the Four Seasons system average.

More good news came in July 2002 with the results of an Employee Opinion Survey, in which 95 percent of employees participated. The survey yielded an overall rating of 4.02 out of 5. The questions that ranked the highest were: "I am proud to work for Four Seasons Hotels and Resorts" (4.65) and "I would want to work here again" (4.61).

The property also received several industry awards including Andrew Harper's Hideaway Report 2001 and 2002, World's Best Hotels and Resorts, Travel & Leisure Readers' Choice Awards 2001, #2 Best Hotel in Europe, and #5 World's Best Hotel Spa.

CONCLUSION: CULTURE, CONSISTENCY, AND FLEXIBILITY

The Four Seasons Hotel George V case illustrates how a service firm with a strong, successful organizational culture expanded internationally into a country with a distinct, intense national culture. When Four Seasons entered France, some elements of organizational culture were held constant, while others were treated flexibly. Managers never considered altering their *organizational values*, whether related to the service provided to guests which had to be engaging, anticipating, and responding; the property which had to be beautiful, luxurious, and functional; or how managers would treat employees, insisting that employees be treated as managers would like to be treated if they performed those jobs. While these values remained constant despite considerable differences in operating environments, the ways those values were enacted did sometimes change. This required changes in policies, management practices, and the use of cultural artifacts.

The tangible elements of service provide clear evidence of flexibility. Like all Four Seasons properties, the F. S. George V is luxurious. However, in France the first floor of the hotel is adorned with gilt and 17th century tapestries. No other Four Seasons property is decorated this way. The hotel elected to have a two-Michelin-star restaurant, despite the challenges of working with a famous chef in a country where there may be no more distinguished form of celebrity. More subtly, non-tangible elements of service quality changed, requiring changes in policies. For example, a coffee pot is never left on the table for guests to help themselves. This change enables the hotel to meet the standard for service set by a Four Seasons' organizational value ("anticipatory") as interpreted in France, where one should not have to pour coffee oneself.

Management practices also changed. In order to have an engaging, anticipating, and responding staff, managers relied upon employee selection even more heavily than at other properties. In this way management practice was intensified in response to a new national culture. However, the goal of those intensified selection efforts was to hire a less experienced staff than typical for other palace hotels and the chain. This was because of underlying, inflexible assumptions which many more experienced workers in France have about employment and how they should treat guests. Less experienced individuals are less set in attitudes and cultural stereotypes contrary to delivering the service for which Four Seasons is renowned. Management therefore focused more sharply on hiring based on attitudes rather than prior work experience. Thus this management practice changed in France to enable Four Seasons to remain true to its organizational values.

The use of cultural artifacts also changed. While a typical Four Seasons property opening would be accompanied by information to the press on the world-renowned service for which the chain is famous, including legendary service stories, in France this was an afterthought to the glory of the property and the appropriateness of the renovations for a *French* architectural landmark.

Many management practices did not change upon arrival in France. Employee of the month and year recognition programs, feedback practices, and meetings to discuss problems were implemented despite a general belief that they would be found incompatible with the French environment. Yet they were successful because of *how* they were implemented—using the words of one manager, "on tip toes." Their more awkward (from a French perspective) elements were amended, and their purpose was communicated gently, but repeatedly. The individuals carefully selected into Four Seasons' environment did not object to their use because they understood the intent of the practices, as well as their effect. The practices ultimately contributed to achieving the changes in organizational culture that Four Seasons managers believed were necessary, helping to ensure that the "oranges" (new employees) carefully selected into the property become the dominant culture carriers, overwhelming the leftover "apples" who refused to change, creating an environment in which those apples no longer fit comfortably.

Perhaps the most important element of management practice contributing to Four Seasons' success in France was management discipline. This took two forms, both of which can be viewed as contributing to the enactment of organizational values. First, discipline can be seen in the way Four Seasons managers lived the values they espoused: allowing guests to be seated first in the dining room; treating employees with dignity; adhering to local labor laws and internal policies designed to protect employees. Second, Four Seasons managers had the discipline to insist that employees deliver outstanding service to guests. This occurred through adherence to the core service-culture standards and 270 operating standards (as occasionally amended). Meeting these standards has resulted in customer loyalty. Thus discipline acts as a glue, ensuring that organizational values actually *drive* a culture, which in turn *contributes* to competitive advantage.

Managers in widely diverse service industries can benefit from Four Seasons' approach to global management when entering countries with distinct, intense national cultures. To do so they must understand their own organizational culture: What are their (1) underlying assumptions, (2) values, (3) employee perceptions of management practices (policies and behaviors), and (4) cultural artifacts? Managers must then ask what elements of their culture are essential to competitive advantage in existing environments, and how the new environment will change that linkage. When there is a change, does the element of culture itself need to change (coffee pot no longer left on the table), or does the way the element is implemented, the way a value is enacted, need to change, such as the implementation "on tip toes" of an employee-of-the-month recognition program. In general, *values core to the organization's "value proposition" (what customers receive from the firm relative to what they pay for it) will not change, but elements of how they are enacted may.*

While organizations eventually come to understand how to operate in a new national environment, successful organizations cannot afford the type of negative publicity and poor financial performance that accompany blundering into a new national culture, as Disney discovered after opening Euro Disney in France. The Four Seasons case study is a single case, based on a single organization. As such we do not claim that its findings are necessarily applicable to other firms. However, it illustrates an approach to global management that managers of other services may find useful, but which they must customize to their own organizational and cultural needs.

Appendix 1
Sample Core Standards

RESERVATIONS

Mission: To provide crisp, knowledgeable, and friendly service, sensitive to the guest's time, and dedication to finding the most suitable accommodation.

- Phone service will be highly efficient, including: answered before the fourth ring; no hold longer than 15 seconds; or, in case of longer holds, call-backs offered, then provided in less than three minutes.
- After establishing the reason for the guest visit, reservationist automatically describes the guest room colorfully, attempting to have the guests picture themselves in the room.

HOTEL ARRIVAL

Mission: To make all guests feel welcome as they approach, and assured that details are well tended; to provide a speedy, discreet, and hassle-free arrival for business travelers; to provide a comforting and luxurious arrival for leisure travelers.

- The doorman (or first contact employee) will actively greet guests, smile, make eye contact, and speak clearly in a friendly manner.
- The staff will be aware of arriving vehicles and will move toward them, opening doors within 30 seconds.
- Guests will be welcomed at the curbside with the words "welcome" and "Four Seasons" (or hotel name), and given directions to the reception desk.
- No guest will wait longer than 60 seconds in line at the reception desk.

HOTEL DEPARTURE

Mission: To provide a quick and discreet departure, while conveying appreciation and hope for return.

- No guest waits longer than five minutes for baggage assistance, once the bellman is called (eight minutes in resorts).
- No guest will wait longer than 60 seconds in line at the cashier desk.
- Staff will create a sense of recognition by using the guest's name, when known, in a natural and discreet manner.

MESSAGES AND PAGING

Mission: To make guests feel that their calls are important, urgent, and require complete accuracy.

- Phone service will be highly efficient, including: answered before the fourth ring; no longer than 15 seconds.
- Callers requesting guest room extensions between 1 A.M. and 6 A.M. will be advised of the local time and offered the option of leaving a message or putting the call through.
- Unanswered guest room phones will be picked up within five rings, or 20 seconds.
- Guests will be offered the option of voice mail: they will not automatically be routed to voice mail OR they will have a clear option to return to the operator.

INCOMING FAXES AND PACKAGES

Mission: To make guests feel that their communications are important, urgent, and require complete accuracy.

- Faxes and packages will be delivered to the guest room within 30 minutes of receipt.

WAKE-UP CALLS

Mission: To make certain that guests are awakened exactly on time in a manner which gently reassures them.

- When wake-up calls are requested, the operator will offer a second reminder call.
- Wake-up calls will occur within two minutes of the requested time.

GUEST ROOM EVENING SERVICE

Mission: To create a sense of maximum comfort and relaxation. When meeting guests, to provide a sense of respect and discretion.

- Guest clothing which is on the bed or floor will be neatly folded and placed on the bed or chair—guest clothing left on other furniture will be neatly folded and left in place; shoes will be paired.
- Newspapers and periodicals will be neatly stacked and left on a table or table shelf in plain view; guest personal papers will not be disturbed in any way.
- Guest toiletries will be neatly arranged on a clean, flat cloth.

LAUNDRY AND VALET

Mission: To provide excellent workmanship and make guests feel completely assured of the timing and quality of our service.

- Laundry service will include same-day service; express four-hour service; and overnight service (seven days per week).
- Dry cleaning service will include same-day service; express four-hour service (seven days per week).
- Pressing service will be available at any time, and returned within one hour; and can be processed on the normal laundry schedule.

ROOM SERVICE

Mission: To provide a calm, competent, and thorough dining experience, with accurate time estimates and quick delivery.

- Phone service will be highly efficient, including: answered before the fourth ring; no hold longer than 15 seconds; or, in the case of longer holds, call-backs offered, then provided in less than three minutes.
- Service will be prompt and convenient; an estimated delivery time (an hour and minute, such as "nine-fifteen PM") will be specifically mentioned; and the order will be serviced within five minutes (earlier or later) than that time.
- Continental breakfast will be delivered within 20 minutes, other meals within 30 minutes, and drinks-only within 15 minutes.
- Table/tray removal instructions will be provided by a printed card, and tables will be collected within twelve minutes of guest call.

Appendix 2
Four Seasons Goals, Beliefs, and Principles

Who We Are: We have chosen to specialize within the hospitality industry, by offering only experiences of exceptional quality. Our objective is to be recognized as the company that manages the finest hotels, resorts, residence clubs, and other residential projects wherever we locate. We create properties of enduring value using superior design and finishes, and support them with a deeply instilled ethic of personal service. Doing so allows Four Seasons to satisfy the needs and tastes of our discriminating customers, to maintain our position as the world's premier luxury hospitality company.

What We Believe: Our greatest asset, and the key to our success, is our people. We believe that each of us needs a sense of dignity, pride, and satisfaction in what we do. Because satisfying our guests depends on the united efforts of many, we are most effective when we work together cooperatively, respecting each other's contribution and importance.

How We Behave: We demonstrate our beliefs most meaningfully in the way we treat each other and by the example we set for one another. In all our interactions with our guests, business associates, and colleagues, we seek to deal with others as we would have them deal with us.

Appendix 2
Four Seasons Goals, Beliefs, and Principles

How We Succeed: We succeed when every decision is based on a clear understanding of and belief in what we do and when we couple this conviction with sound financial planning. We expect to achieve a fair and reasonable profit to ensure the prosperity of the company, and to offer long-term benefits to our hotel owners, our shareholders, our customers, and our employees.

Appendix 3
Comparative Data on Parisian Palaces

Property	Construction/ Style	Capacity (Rooms & Suites)	Amenities	Price (Dollar/ Single Room)	Owner	Lessee/ Operator
Bristol	Built in 1829 Louis XV–XVI style	180	1 restaurant: Le Bristol 1 interior garden 1 swimming pool 1 fitness center 1 beauty salon	480–600	Société Oetker[c] (1978)	Independent
Crillon	Built in the 18th century Louis XV–XVI style	152	2 restaurants: L'Ambassadeur and L'Obelix 1 fitness center Guerlain Beauty Institute	460–550	Groupe Hôtels Concorde[a] (1907)	Groupe Hôtels Concorde[a] (1907)
Four Seasons Hotel George V Paris	Built in 1928 Art Déco style	245	1 restaurant: Le Cinq 1 swimming pool 1 fitness center 1 beauty salon	670	Prince Al Waleed Bin Talal[d] (1996)	Four Seasons Hotels and Resorts (2000)
Meurice	Built in the 18th century Louis XV–XVI style	161	1 restaurant: Le Meurice 1 fitness center Caudalie Beauty Institute	470–550	The Sultan of Brunei (1997)	The Dorchester Group[b] (2001)
Plaza Athenée	Built in 1889 Belle Epoque style	144	2 restaurants: Le Relais Plaza	490–508	The Sultan of Brunei (1997)	The Dorchester Group[b] (2001)
Ritz	Built in 1898 Louis XV–XVI style	139	1 restaurant: L'Espadon Escoffier-Ritz cooking school 1 fitness center 1 beauty salon 1 swimming pool	From 580	Mohammed Al Fayed (1979)	Independent

Source: "Four Seasons Hotels and Resorts," Brian D. Egger, et al., Crédit Suisse First Boston, April 5, 2002, page 21. *http://meuricehotel.com, http://www.hotel-bristol.com, http://www.ritz.com, http://www.fourseasons.com/paris/vacations/index.html, http://www.plaza-athenee-paris.com, http://www.crillon.com.* Accessed June 2002.

^{a} Groupe Hôtels Concorde was created in 1973 to regroup the luxury hotels such as the Crillon, the Lutetia, and the Hotel Concorde Saint-Lazare (all in Paris) owned by La Societe du Louvre.

^{b} The Dorchester Group, a subsidiary of the Brunei Investment Agency, was established in 1996 as an independent United Kingdom registered company to manage luxury hotels, including The Dorchester in London, The Beverly Hills Hotel California and the Hotel Meurice in Paris.

^{c} The Oetker Group is a German agribusiness group which owns four luxury hotels in addition to the Bristol: the Cap Eden Roc in Antibes, France; the Park Hotel in Vitznau, Switzerland, the Brenner's Park Hotel in Baden Baden, Germany; and the Château du Domaine Saint-Martin in Vence, France.

^{d} Al Waleed Bin Talal owns 21.9% of Four Seasons' stocks. Investments by Prince Al Waleed in Four Seasons' properties include F. S. George V and Riyadh (100%); London (majority); Cairo, Amman, Alexandria, Sharm El Sheikh and Belrut (unspecified); and Aviara (minority).

Appendix 4
Predictable Patterns of Monochronic and Polychronic Cultures

Monochronic People (Americans)	Polychronic People (French)
Do one thing at a time	Do many things at once
Concentrate on the job	Can be easily distracted and manage interruptions well
Take time commitments (deadlines, schedules) seriously	Consider an objective to be achieved, if possible
Are low-context and need information	Are high-context and already have information
Are committed to the job	Are committed to people and human relationships
Adhere religiously to plans	Change plans often and easily
Are concerned about not disturbing others; follow rules of privacy and consideration	Are more concerned with those who are closely related (family, friends, close business associates) than with privacy
Show great respect for private property; seldom borrow or lend	Borrow and lend things often and easily
Emphasize promptness	Base promptness on the relationship
Are accustomed to short-term relationships	Have strong tendency to build lifetime relationships

Source: Academy of Management Executive: The Thinking Manager's Source by Hallowell. Copyright © 2002 by the Academy of Management. Reprinted with permission of Academy of Management in the format Textbook via Copyright Clearance Center.

Endnotes

1. Kotter, J. P. & Heskett, J. L. 1990. *Corporate culture and performance.* New York: The Free Press.
2. Heskett, J. L., Schlesinger, L. A., & Sasser, W. E., Jr. 1997. *The service profit chain.* New York: The Free Press; Schneider, B., & Bowen, D. E. 1995. *Winning the service game.* Boston: Harvard Business School Press; and Berry, L. L. 1995. *On great service.* New York: The Free Press.
3. Schein, E. H. 1990. American psychologist. *Organizational Culture,* 45(2): 109–119.
4. The theory behind this discussion finds its roots in the contingency work of scholars such as Lawrence and Lorch; see Lawrence, P., & Lorsch, J. 1967. *Organization and environment.* Boston: Harvard Business School Press. Other scholars, including James Heskett, have used the contingency perspective as a starting point for theories of internationalization of services; see Loveman, G. 1993. *The internationalization of services.* Harvard Business School Module Note No. 9-693-103. Boston: Harvard Business School Publishing. Heskett's views have influenced ours considerably. We are indebted to Professor Caren Siehl, Thunderbird, for much of the framework on managing the potential clash between organizational culture and country culture, which she developed for her organizational behavior MBA classes. In turn, Caren always acknowledges an intellectual debt to Professor Joanne Martin, Stanford University.
5. *Interior Design,* March 2000, p. S24.
6. For example maternity leave for a salaried employee's first child was six weeks of prenatal leave and 10 weeks of paid leave after birth; for a third child it was eight weeks off before and 18 weeks after birth.
7. Communist-controlled labor union (Confédération Générale du Travail) or CGT, nearly 2.4 million members (claimed); independent labor union or Force Ouvrière, 1 million

members (est.); independent white-collar union or Confédération Générale des Cadres, 340,000 members (claimed); Socialist-leaning labor union (Confédération Française Democratique du Travail) or CFDT, about 800,000 members (est.). Source: *http://www.cia.gov/publications/factbook/geos/fr.html*, accessed June 10, 2002.

8. Hotstede's work was based on a survey conducted by questionnaire with IBM employees in 50 different countries; see Hotstede, G. 1982. *Culture's consequences: International differences in work-related values*. Thousand Oaks, CA: Sage.

9. Hofstede's approach has not been without its critics but, as Hickson comments, Hofstede had "frail data, but robust concepts"; see Hickson, D. 1996. The ASQ years then and now through the eyes of a Euro-Brit. *Administrative Science Quarterly*, 41(2): 217–228.

10. See d'Iribarne, P. 1996/97. The usefulness of an ethnographic approach to the international comparison of organization. *International Studies of Management and Organization*, 18(4): 32.

11. Van der Horst, B. Edward T. Hall—A great-grandfather of NLP, *http://www.cs.ucr.edu/gnick/bvdh/print_edward_t_hall_great_.htm*, accessed April 20, 2002. The article reviews Hall, E. 1959. *The silent language*. New York: Doubleday.

12. One alternative was to give the staff a significant enough severance package to encourage them to go. However, as Young explained. "The government deplores that approach."

13. Usually used to describe a meal—say a first course of fromage de tête (pig's head set in jelly) or bouillabaisse (fish soup), followed by a main course of blanquette de veau (veal stew with white sauce) and rounded off with a plateau de fromage (cheese platter) or tarte aux pommes (apple tart).

Adapting to a Boundaryless World: A Developmental Expatriate Model

Juan I. Sanchez, Paul E. Spector, Cary L. Cooper, *Academy of Management Executive*

Adjusting to an international assignment can provoke feelings of helplessness in an unprepared executive, who may have difficulty sorting out appropriate from inappropriate behavior. In fact, learning to manage in and cope with a foreign environment involves such a profound personal transformation that it has an analog in the process of human development throughout the life-span. Expatriate executives are removed from the comfortable environment of their parental culture and placed in a less familiar culture. Indeed, a management style that works at home may fail to produce the desired response abroad, or it may be even counterproductive.[1] The sudden loss of control in one's environment that results from cultural shock abruptly disrupts one's equilibrium.[2] This uneven relationship between the executive and an environment that is perceived to exceed the executive's coping resources perfectly fits the definition of stress, which threatens well-being.[3] A recent comparison of expatriate executives with a similar group that did not relocate revealed an alarming increase in the stress-sensitive hormone prolactin, reduced mental health, and an increase in cigarette and alcohol consumption in the expatriate group during the first year abroad.[4]

Rivers of ink have been dedicated to the need to develop globally minded leaders. A better understanding of the stages involved in a successful adjustment to a foreign environment should help in the development of a global mindset. A profound personal transformation, involving the formation of a multicultural identity, is necessary to buffer the stress provoked by an international assignment.

Coping with stress can be seen as a process involving two steps—primary and secondary—in the evaluation of such adverse environmental conditions as having too much work and uncertain job responsibilities.[5] Adverse environmental conditions function as work stressors when an individual recognizes them as stressful through the mental process known as primary evaluation. Secondary evaluation involves the selection of a coping response to deal with the stressor. The same two steps can be distinguished in coping with stress during an international assignment. First, coping requires an understanding of the new environmental conditions or stressors that demand adaptive responses from the executive.[6] Second, leverage of the new stressors demands a revision of one's old repertoire of coping responses, which may no longer be effective in the new setting.[7] Our goals in this article parallel these two steps and are to shed light on the nature of the primary stressors faced by the expatriate executive, and formulate recommendations regarding strategies that facilitate the adjustment of expatriate executives. Our recommendations are divided into two categories—those directed at expatriate executives and those directed at their employers. To provide a framework or roadmap, our review draws a parallel with the process of human development, proceeding along the developmental stages experienced by expatriate executives as they struggle to adapt to their new world. This progression is summarized in Table 1, which presents each stage, its primary stressors, and the recommended coping strategies for both executives and their employers.

Expatriate Selection Stage

Technical skills, family situation, relational skills, and motivational state all play a crucial role in effective cross-cultural adjustment.[8] However, 90 percent of all companies base their international selections on technical expertise while ignoring the other areas.[9] Technically qualified candidates are not always capable of easily adjusting to critical cultural differences, such as those involving social status and group dependence.[10]

Openness to the profound personal transformation that awaits the expatriate executive is perhaps the most fundamental sign of expatriate readiness. It is not surprising that courage and risk taking are

TABLE 1: STRESSORS AND COPING RESPONSES IN THE DEVELOPMENTAL STAGES OF EXPATRIATE EXECUTIVES

Stage	Primary stressors	Executive coping response	Employer coping response
Expatriate selection	Cross-cultural unreadiness.	Engage in self-evaluation.	Encourage expatriate's self- and family evaluation. Perform an assessment of potential and interests.
Assignment acceptance	Unrealistic evaluation of stressors to come. Hurried time frame	Think of assignment as a growth opportunity rather than an instrument to vertical promotion	Do not make hard-to-keep promises. Clarify expectations.
Pre- and post-arrival training	Ignorance of cultural differences.	Do not make unwarranted assumptions of cultural competence and cultural rules.	Provide pre-, during, and post-assignment training. Encourage support-seeking behavior.
Arrival	Cultural shock. Stressor reevaluation. Feelings of lack of fit and differential treatment.	Do not construe identification with the host and parent cultures as mutually exclusive. Seek social support.	Provide post-arrival training. Facilitate integration in expatriate network.
Novice	Cultural blunders or inadequacy of coping responses. Ambiguity owing to inability to decipher meaning of situations.	Observe and study functional value of coping responses among locals. Do not simply replicate responses that worked at home.	Provide follow-up training. Seek advice from locals and expatriate network.
Transitional	Rejection of host or parent culture.	Form and maintain attachments with both cultures.	Promote culturally sensitive policies at host country. Provide Internet access to family and friends at home. Maintain constant communication and periodic visits to parent organization.
Mastery	Frustration with inability to perform boundary spanning role. Bothered by living with a cultural paradox.	Internalize and enjoy identification with both cultures and walking between two cultures.	Reinforce rather than punish dual identification by defining common goals.
Repatriation	Disappointment with unfulfilled expectations. Sense of isolation. Loss of autonomy.	Realistically reevaluate assignment as a personal and professional growth opportunity.	Arrange pre-repatriation briefings and interviews. Schedule post-repatriation support meetings.

among the core characteristics of successful expatriates who, knowing themselves, are willing to revisit their most deeply held assumptions.[11] Authoritarianism, rigidity, and ethnocentrism are personality aspects that impede adaptation to a foreign culture.[12] Because these are deeply ingrained personality traits that are not easily malleable, selection rather than training should be the strategy used to ensure that candidates possess these characteristics from the first day on the job. Although traditional personality inventories have not proven very effective at predicting expatriate success, available measures specifically designed to evaluate expatriate potential appear promising.[13]

A frequently reported explanation for expatriate failure has been poor adjustment of spouses.[14]

Despite the key role of family-related variables in successful expatriate management, assessing the family situation without violating privacy rights is a real challenge. A practical and potentially useful strategy involves providing a realistic preview of the assignment, then instigating a self-evaluation of readiness among family members. By reflecting on the results of this evaluation, the executives can appraise their family situation and can voluntarily withdraw if the prospect is not altogether favorable.

Assignment Acceptance Stage

The excessive emphasis on technical skills also seems to dominate the decision-making process that the expatriate executive and family go through before the offer is accepted. Typically, the candidate selected has technical expertise and experience related to the assignment. Therefore, the candidate does not envision being incapable of performing an assignment abroad that he or she has already done at home. Why are some managers and employers prone to overlook the cross-cultural demands of the assignment? The answer lies in the psychological perspective of work stress, which is driven by subjective appraisals of the executive's environment.[15] The objective reality of the situation does not directly provoke a stressful experience, but the subjective appraisal of the situation does. The subjective appraisal of stressors is, in essence, a judgment of person-environment fit.[16] Therefore, when an offer to take an international assignment is extended, candidates are probably unable to anticipate stressors they have not experienced before, unless they have had a prior international assignment. Ignorant of the alien environment to which they are about to be transplanted, executives might also overestimate the effectiveness of coping responses that work at home but may not work abroad. For instance, being outgoing, as it is normally understood in the U.S., may be perceived as being rude in other cultures, thereby provoking rather than preventing social isolation.

Consider the case of an executive with a demonstrated competence in launching start-ups who was selected to head the Asian operations of a U.S. corporation. When considering the transfer to Asia, the executive dismissed the possibility of feeling socially isolated because he considered himself and his family outgoing and friendly, and thought they would have no problems making friends and adjusting. Six months after his arrival in Japan, the executive expressed frustration at his inability to communicate effectively with others and at his feelings of social isolation.

When weighing the pros and cons of an international assignment, the stressors to be encountered are thought to be alleviated by the prospect of career advancement once the executive returns home. Promises of immediate promotion upon return are often the main driver of an executive's decision to accept relocation.

The executive may use these promises to convince a spouse who hesitates to give up local friends, family, and perhaps a good job. However, once the executive starts the international assignment, the management representatives who were involved in selecting the executive may very well move on to other posts or other corporations. Witnessing these departures from afar, the expatriate may feel that the expectations that motivated the transfer are vanishing too. In the absence of a future payoff, the new stressors will be reappraised and may appear more unbearable than when the prospect of a red-carpet return was alive.

The offer to take an international assignment frequently comes from out of the blue. For instance, an executive previously uninterested in living abroad was motivated by a hefty relocation bonus to accept an unexpectedly sudden but nevertheless career-enhancing assignment.[17] This kind of hurried decision may lead to an unrealistic appraisal of both the stressors awaiting abroad and one's cross-cultural skills.

How should executives and their employers cope with such unanticipated circumstances? One of the answers appears to lie in the clarification of expectancies beforehand. Executives who take on international assignments hoping that an immediate promotion will materialize upon return are oblivious to the pace of change in today's business environment, where vertical career paths are no longer the norm. Instead, executives should consider international transfers as an additional growth opportunity in their career development plans.

Rather than delivering hard-to-keep, long-term promises of promotion, employers should clarify expectations and highlight the developmental growth that will result from having completed the international assignment. For example, a U.S. executive who decided to take an assignment in Japan because it fit into his general career plan was not guaranteed a specific promotion upon repatriation.

Instead, he was made aware of what his general opportunities would be if he met his goals in Japan.[18]

Pre- and Post-Arrival Training Stages

Intercultural training can partly remedy cross-cultural insensitivity, but intercultural competence involves more than a series of country statistics and cultural gimmicks learned in a short, pre-departure training session. Making executives aware that they will face different business and social customs is not sufficient, because awareness does not necessarily bring competence in the host culture.[19]

The classic burnout symptoms of emotional exhaustion and a sense of reduced accomplishment of an American expatriate six months after he was put in charge of operations in Taiwan illustrate this point.[20] Because he was unable to obtain collaboration from local executives, he followed the recommendations of his California team. The implementation of such recommendations, however, worsened the situation he had been called to improve. Even though this executive was made aware of such cultural differences as Asians being more deferential and less straightforward in their business dealings than Americans, he had neither the interest nor the patience to participate in extended discussions of family and non-business matters with his new business acquaintances. He decided to cut his losses and gladly accepted his CEO's invitation to repatriate him.

Many corporations are becoming aware of the need to provide continued hands-on training rather than just pre-departure awareness training. An executive's pre-departure evaluation of the stressors experienced abroad may be unrealistic. Without some on-site experience in the culture, executives may overestimate their future ability to cope. In contrast to pre-departure training, post-arrival training gives expatriates a chance to evaluate their stressors after they have encountered them. A good example of this kind of on-site training is provided by the British trade giant Jardin Matheson.[21] The training format is project-based, with participants spending much of their time in their respective business areas. At regular intervals, they are brought together to discuss their experiences under the guidance of facilitators. Cultural differences are addressed when they surface in the context of working together, rather than as part of theoretical discussions regarding why Asians and Westerners behave differently.

Experiential training formats also provide an opportunity to react to cultural stressors and receive feedback about the adequacy of one's coping responses. One of these formats is the cultural assimilator, which employs descriptions of critical incidents involving stressful situations together with possible ways of coping with them.[22] With the help of a facilitator, participants discuss the consequences of their individual responses. The exchange helps reduce feelings of stress, because it reinforces the perception that they hold a reservoir of potentially effective coping responses. Foreigners trained using a Greek assimilator, for instance, felt significantly better adjusted to Greece than untrained individuals.[23]

From the employer's point of view, training is an opportunity to provide the social support that the expatriate executive needs.[24] Social support, however, can either reduce or alleviate the effects of stressors. Pre-departure training sessions, for instance, can significantly reduce stressors by providing basic information about housing, schools, foods, and transportation that may help the executives get by in the first few weeks of their assignments. Pre-departure training, however, is not likely to buffer or alleviate the cultural stressors to be faced by the expatriate executive, because cultural differences are best understood in post-arrival training sessions once they have been experienced. Although identifying the potential sources of social support is a difficult task for executives who are still unfamiliar with their host environment, training can provide the encouragement and motivation to seek the social network and activities that will make the new stressors more bearable.

Arrival Stage

Understandably, the prospect of an international assignment provokes quite a bit of excitement. However, the executive's arrival in an unfamiliar environment may soon bring almost as much frustration. Many of these frustrating times can be explained by feelings of inadequacy. In fact, the executive's sense of control, which plays a significant role in healthy adjustment, may be dramatically affected by the transfer.[25] Stressors like an excessive workload, which was not perceived as such because of the individual's sense of environmental control, suddenly turn worse because of what appears to be an uncontrollable new environment.

Feeling different, especially feeling that one is subject to differential treatment because of membership in a particular culture, can induce stress above and beyond that resulting from typical stressors such as conflict and ambiguity over perceived responsibilities.[26] If the expatriate executives attribute differential treatment to their membership in a different culture or group, their rejection of the host culture is likely to intensify. Thinking of the environment as beyond one's control induces a sense of helplessness.[27] For example, a U.S. expatriate executive in a Central American nation felt that his written requests for equipment maintenance were ignored because he was a foreigner. Later in his assignment, he learned that such written requests were routinely ignored, and that the way to get the work done was to drop by the maintenance shop or ask a maintenance employee for help at the beginning of the work day.

Social identity theory provides a vehicle to better understand and cope with feelings of cultural rejection. Individuals are likely to experience internal conflict when concurrent identification with two or more social entities is perceived as unacceptable. For instance, a U.S. expatriate in Mexico may feel that being an American and identifying with the Mexican culture are opposite poles of the same continuum and are therefore mutually exclusive. Feelings of frustration early in the international assignment may strengthen identification with the U.S. culture to the detriment of the host culture. When the executive construes his or her identification with the two cultures in this us vs. them manner, devastating psychological consequences may follow.

Expatriate executives who reject the host culture are destined to experience continuous frustration and negative feelings as they are forced to conduct business according to local usage. Figure 1 depicts the tortuous evolution of the internal struggle between executives' identification with the host versus the parent culture. The two identifications compete for the same space. Whereas identification with the parent culture dominates in the early phases of the assignment, identification with the host culture will dominate later on. A successful adjustment implies a final identification midway between the host and parent cultures.

Understanding that identification with both cultures is possible is the safest way to prevent acculturative stress.[28] The different degrees of identification with the host and the parent culture can be summarized in four quadrants (Figure 2). The upper right quadrant represents dual identification, which is indeed possible and least stressful. A U.S. executive on assignment in Japan indicated that his high allegiance to both the parent and the Japanese operation led him to try to bring their interests together rather than choose one over the other whenever he perceived discrepancies in their expectations and

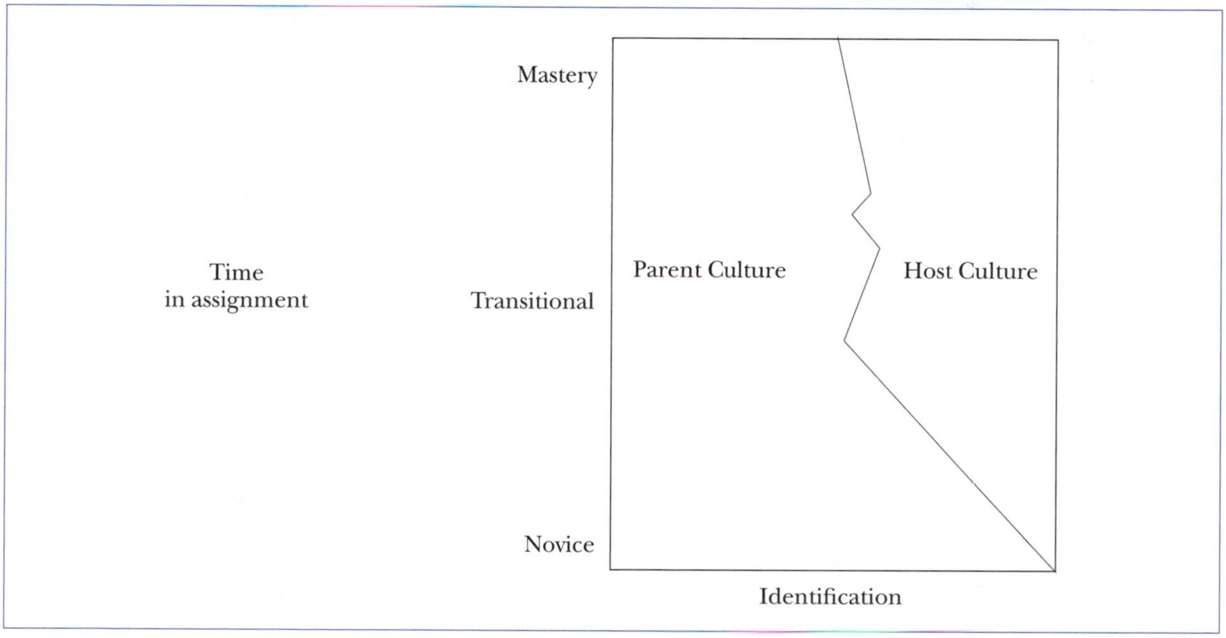

FIGURE 1: SUCCESSFUL EVOLUTION OF PARENT AND HOST CULTURE IDENTIFICATION

goals.[29] Reacculturation, as represented by the lower right quadrant, is significantly more stressful because one's parent culture is neglected rather than incorporated into the expatriate's new identity.

A better understanding of the host's ways should not necessarily be accompanied by a rejection of the parent culture. Executives run the risk of drifting in either direction by identifying too much with one of the cultures while rejecting the other. Rather than absorbing oneself in an internal battle for self-definition, the executive should learn to view identification with the host as compatible with identification with the parent culture.

Novice Stage

At the beginning of their international assignments, expatriates may make the mistake of ignoring culturally critical aspects. Why is it so difficult to make sense of and cope with the new stressors? Executives who feel stressed are likely to search their repertoire of coping responses for adequate ways to confront situations.[30] However, the choice of coping response would be determined by the effectiveness of responses used to cope with similar stressors in the past. Notions of response effectiveness are influenced by prior personal experience and culturally bound

notions of response adequacy and likelihood of success. In other words, the choices of coping responses have been shaped throughout the executives' personal and cultural experience. The problem is that such responses are no longer valid in a different culture characterized by different norms and values. Thus, the experience and knowledge of social norms that the expatriate executive used to select adequate coping responses at home have lost much of their informative value.

Expatriates need to become aware of the consequences that their old repertoire of coping responses has in the host culture. Ambiguity will be overwhelming at first. Uncertainty about what is demanded will be aggravated by one's inability to decipher the meaning of a situation. Blunders can be unwittingly committed by executives who misread culturally different situations.[31] An American expatriate in Beijing dared to challenge his Chinese colleague's idea by saying, "That's a very good point, but I don't agree with you." Although this observation was respectfully made in the eyes of the American, it offended the Chinese executive, thereby straining the business deal.[32] Another U.S. executive inadvertently offended his senior Mexican managers by asking for the junior manager's opinion in their presence.

Expatriate managers should pay attention to the functional value of the coping mechanisms employed by local executives, who make useful role models. Responses that imitate local uses can be successful, but expatriates should be sensitive to the true function of such responses, which can be rather subtle. Expatriate managers should think a bit like anthropologists trying to make sense of human behavior in a different cultural context.[33]

Coping styles have been classified as problem-solving (taking direct action to solve a problem) versus emotion-focused (taking action to make oneself feel better about a situation one cannot control).[34] Emotion-focused coping might be more characteristic of collectivistic societies, such as Asians or Hispanics, than of individualistic societies, like the U.S. or Australia, because members of collectivistic cultures are encouraged to subordinate their personal goals to those of stable groups. However, expatriate executives in collectivistic cultures may erroneously dismiss as mere emotion-focused coping some responses that are, in fact, culturally sensitive attempts to exert control over a situation. Showing deference to superiors, not questioning formal authority in public, aligning oneself with powerful others, and attending family functions provide not mere distraction or consolation, but also unquestionable power to influence one's environment in cultures where individual subordination to a powerful group is the norm to get ahead. Executives who understand these subtleties and choose to play the game stand the best chances of coping effectively with an unfamiliar situation.

An American executive who understood the importance of family and friendship in the Middle East made a point of reminding his business contacts there of his friendship by taking their picture together at every occasion and then mailing copies to them. This action may seem a bit manipulative to some, but we can attest to the sincerity of the American expatriate, who had already internalized some of the values and customs of his Middle Eastern partners.

More straightforward coping styles involving direct attempts to control situations of the kind expected in individualistic countries like the U.S. may be even counterproductive. A study of managerial stress in 24 countries revealed that exercising direct control over one's environment is associated with mental and physical well-being in the U.S., but not in many other countries.[35] Thus, expatriates who insist on employing the kind of direct control responses that have made them successful at home may only add to their stress level abroad.

Expatriates from individualistic societies should be reminded that the lengthy social interactions observed in collectivistic cultures are not a waste of time, but a necessary conduit to doing business. Executives from collectivistic cultures transplanted to an individualistic one may make the opposite mistake. For example, a southern European executive assigned to a financial institution in a U.S. territory was used to having decisions backed by social consensus, which are the norm in the world of European labor relations. He insisted on creating task forces representing every constituent before a decision was made on nearly every human resource issue. The local executives were in turn frustrated by the slow pace of these task forces, which they considered unnecessary.

The employer should facilitate integration into a local or regional network of other expatriates, who can be an extremely valuable source of tangible and informational support in the beginning off the assignment regarding schools, shopping, obtaining a driver's license, and the like. Whereas physically distant friends and family provide simply emotional support and consolation, other expatriates provide the kind of tangible support that directly reduces stressors.

Transitional Stage

Executives' continued frustration may lead to identity crises when they choose to reject the parent culture by fully embracing the host culture, or vice versa.

The ability to form and maintain attachments plays a significant role in executive health in general.[36] For example, keeping in touch with the expatriate community overseas allows executives to maintain their links with the parent culture. These links can be reinforced by Internet access to family, friends, and media from the parent culture. The employer's investment in such electronic communications should provide a significant return in the form of emotional support. Even though this support cannot reduce the stressors faced abroad, it should help alleviate the strain felt by the executive.[37]

Going native by becoming too identified with the host culture may elicit a negative reaction at headquarters, because the executive's allegiance may be questioned.[38] This reversed identification phenomenon may have the same kind of negative impact on the executive's well-being that the rejection of the host culture does, because a significant part of the self is being rejected.

Expatriate executives' conflicting feelings about identification with one culture to the exclusion of the other exacerbate the normally high levels of role conflict characteristic of executive positions. Successful expatriate executives cope with these conflicting roles through constant communication. Lags in communication provoke the kind of unhealthy us vs. them attribution mentioned earlier. An American expatriate in Holland negotiated for a trip to the U.S. every four months so he could bring the points of view of the Dutch operations to headquarters and also take headquarters' perceptions back to Holland. Physical separation and cultural differences made it difficult for the groups to understand each other's actions, and the tone of communications invariable deteriorated after three to four months.[39] The executive's trips back and forth kept negative feelings from getting too far out of hand. In essence, expatriates are forced to cope with conflicting demands imposed by their dual identification with the host and parent organizations by functioning as boundary spanners that walk the line separating the two cultures. The need to maintain this delicate equilibrium among multiple stakeholders calls for skills similar to those possessed by political diplomats.[40] The parent organization should not create additional role conflict for the expatriate with policies that are insensitive to cultural differences.

Mastery Stage

By the end of their assignments, successful expatriates have already developed the knowledge of cultural norms that allow them to understand their environment more fully. Over time, expats have also crafted a repertoire of coping responses adapted to their new stressors. Seasoned expatriates are capable of choosing among potential responses with a minimum of uncertainty because they have seen their choice succeed in the past. However, the developmental stages discussed here do not always follow a linear sequence, and making sense of a foreign culture will remain puzzling at times.[41] This ambiguity should not bother effective expatriates, who have already learned to cope with feelings of divided loyalty. They understand that feelings of identification with the host and the parent culture are not mutually exclusive. Instead of being frustrated, they enjoy their boundary-spanning roles of bicultural interpreters who walk between two or more cultures.

Accepting the profound personal transformation that comes with an international assignment is not easy. Fearing identity loss and unable to cope with a myriad of new stressors, nearly 40 percent of American expatriates return early.[42]

However, those who successfully complete their assignments become different people because they have experienced radically different events. Armed with the dual experience of having lived and worked both abroad and at home, expatriates are capable of seeing one culture through the eyes of the other. The ability to understand the cultural paradox that surrounds them and, most importantly, the fact that living with such a paradox does not bother them, represents the pinnacle of expatriate executive transformation. Not surprisingly, the healthiest expatriates are those who possess a strong sense of coherence and control.[43] These individuals have learned to live with and enjoy membership in more than one culture—the essence of being a global executive. A U.S. executive working in Holland described how he had learned over the course of his assignment that being conspicuous was often frowned on in that country. He learned to be more reserved in what he said and to wear more formal clothes even when grocery shopping, so that he would not stand out as much. He and other expatriates explained that these changes did not interfere with their identification with the U.S., which they still genuinely felt.[44]

Repatriation Stage: The Most Stressful Part of the Assignment?

Executives' repatriation can turn into the most stressful time of the entire international assignment. A survey of repatriated executives found that 33 percent were still holding temporary assignments three months after repatriation, more than 75 percent felt that their permanent post upon repatriation was a demotion from their international assignment, and 61 percent felt that they did not have opportunities to put their experience abroad to work. Perhaps the most dramatic finding was that 25 percent of the executives had quit their jobs within three months of repatriation.[45]

An expatriate banking executive working in Mexico returned to the U.S. to find an organization whose top management had radically changed and seemed unwilling to fulfill his previous bosses' promises of upward promotion. After lingering in support roles for about a year, the executive landed a job as vice president of international banking in another financial institution. Similarly, a Mexican executive was disappointed to learn that his employer planned to repatriate him to a relatively low-level management job back home. The executive had been known to share with his coworkers in the U.S. what he thought were his high chances of securing the general manager position in Mexico's operations. Dissatisfied with the repatriation offer, the executive quit his job and started an import-export partnership with one of the business acquaintances he had made during his assignment in the U.S.

Repatriation brings new stressors to executives. Feeling that others do not share their multicultural identification can create a sense of isolation. An expatriate who spent two years implementing a training program around the world characterized his repatriation as a much more traumatic event than going abroad. He complained about feelings of not belonging and about not having anyone to confide in.[46] Repatriated executives may also find themselves making an effort not to stand out by hiding the new interests and behaviors they acquired abroad. An expatriate who headed the Dutch operations of a U.S. firm admitted that he was afraid that others might label his new manners as snobbish.

How can expatriate executives cope with these feelings of lack of fit? In a way, the repatriated executives had already coped with the feeling of not fitting in when abroad. The essence of being bicultural is being proficient in both cultures, and that includes dealing with members of one culture who, unlike the repatriated executive, are unfamiliar with the other. In short, learning to live with and not be bothered by these multiple cultural identities continues to be necessary even when executives return home.

Another dramatic change confronted by repatriated executives is the frequent loss of autonomy, augmented by possibly unrealistic expectations about being promoted upon return.

The kind of bold management style that was accepted and even praised abroad may be unwelcome at headquarters. Insisting on this kind of bold style might provoke turf battles with executives from other functional areas. Employers can smooth this difficult transition by providing a sensible repatriation program that takes into account executives' interests and newly developed talents. In this sense, reentry training is at least as important as pre-departure training. Setting expectations about reentry well before it takes place is a fundamental component of this kind of training, which should begin when the expatriate is first selected and continue throughout the assignment prior to the return.[47] Pre-repatriation briefings and interviews with parent organization representatives to inform executives of available opportunities should help clarify how such opportunities fit into executive's post-repatriation career plans. After reentry, follow-up meetings are critical because they provide information regarding how executives are adjusting, whether they need additional support to cope with new stressors, and whether their coping strategies should be revised. When suitable openings are not immediately available at the parent organization, Swedish employers place expatriate executives in a multi-employer pool. Executives from this pool are loaned out to other employers who need them as a short-term solution.[48]

There are limitations to the recommendations presented here. First, the available research from which we drew is based primarily on the experiences of U.S. expatriates working abroad. Although many of our conclusions should apply to expatriates regardless of nationality, the unique aspects of every culture should not be ignored. Similarly, about 90 percent of all expatriate managers may be male, and the recommendations presented here are therefore based on primarily male samples.[49] However, contrary to stereotypical assumptions, the case of a female executive who received equal treatment during her assignment in Japan illustrates that female expatriates need not necessarily experience more frustration than their male counterparts, even if female executives are not common in the host country.[50]

A Survival Guide for Expatriate Executives and Their Employers

Employers need to actively support the adjustment process of their expatriate executives. Cross-cultural competence-oriented training should be provided before, during, and after the assignment. In addition, the parent firm should be sensitive to the delicate balance between the interest of the parent and the host firm that executives need to maintain, listening and working with them to define and achieve common goals.

Expatriation uproots executives from a familiar environment, thereby breaking the balance between the individual and his or her ability to cope with the environment. Feelings of internal conflict are likely to be aggravated by executives' inability to decipher the meaning of culturally different situations. Even though the strain associated with such negative feelings can be partly prevented by competence-oriented intercultural training, individual predisposition and courage to cross-cultural boundaries of both a physical and a psychological nature are necessary for healthy expatriate adjustment. Perhaps the

most challenging of all transformations is the ability to develop a dual identification.

Otherwise, the conflicting roles experienced by expatriate executives may be exacerbated by a divided sense of social identity that views identification with the host and the parent culture as mutually exclusive. In essence, an international assignment is not only a physical adventure in a more or less remote land, but also a psychological adventure that requires the willingness to revise deeply held beliefs concerning one's own identity.

Endnotes

1. Selmer, J. 1999. Effects of coping strategies on sociocultural and psychological adjustment of Western expatriate managers in the PRC. *Journal of World Business*, 34(1): 41–51.
2. Cummings, T. G., & Cooper, C. L. 1998. A cybernetic theory of work stress. In C. L. Cooper (Ed.), *Theories of organizational stress*: 101–121. Oxford, U.K.: Oxford University Press.
3. Lazarus, R. S., & Folkman, S. 1984. *Stress, appraisal, and coping.* New York: Springer, 19.
4. Anderzen, I., & Arnetz, B. B. 1997. Psychological reactions during the first year of a foreign assignment: Results of a controlled longitudinal study. *Work & Stress*, 11(4): 304–318.
5. Lazarus, R. S. 1966. *Psychological stress and the coping process.* New York: McGraw-Hill.
6. Beehr, T. A., & Newman, J. E. 1978. Job stress, employee health, and organizational effectiveness: A facet analysis, model and literature review. *Personnel Psychology*, 31: 665–699.
7. Shupe, E. I., & McGrath, J. E. 1998. Stress and the sojourner. In Cooper (Ed.), op. cit., 86–100.
8. Teagarden, M. B. & Gordon, G. D. 1995. Corporate selection strategies and expatriate manager success. In J. Selmer (Ed.), *Expatriate management. New ideas for international business*: 17–36. Westport CT: Quorum.
9. Earley, P. C. 1987. Intercultural training for managers: A comparison. *Academy of Management Journal*, 30(4): 685–698.
10. Spreitzer, G. M., McCall, Jr., M. W., & Mahoney, J. D. 1997. Early identification of international executive potential. *Journal of Applied Psychology*, 82(1): 6–29.
11. Ibid.
12. Locke, S. A., & Feinsod, F. 1982. Psychological preparation for young adults traveling abroad. *Adolescence*, 17: 815–819.
13. Spreitzer, et al., op. cit.
14. Teagarden & Gordon, op. cit.
15. Lazarus, op. cit.
16. Edwards, J. R., & Cooper, C. L. 1990. The person-environment fit approach to stress: Recurring problems and some suggested solutions. *Journal of Organizational Behavior*, 11: 293–307.
17. Schell, M. S., & Solomon, C. M. 1997. *Capitalizing on the global workforce.* Chicago: Irwin.
18. Black, J. S., Gregersen, H. B., Mendenhall, M. E., & Stroh, L. K. 1999. *Globalizing people through international assignments.* Reading MA: Addison Wesley.
19. Black, J. S., & Gregersen, H. B. 1999. The right way to manage expats. *Harvard Business Review*, March–April: 52–62.
20. Schell & Solomon, op. cit.
21. Williams, G., & Bent, R. 1996. Developing expatriate managers for Southeast Asia. In D. Landis & R. S. Bhagat (Eds.), *Handbook of intercultural training*, 2nd ed.: 383–399. Thousand Oaks, CA: Sage.
22. Brislin, R., Cusgner, K., Cherrie, C., & Yong, M. 1986. *Intercultural interactions: A practical guide.* Beverly Hills, CA: Sage.
23. Fiedler, R., Mitchell, T., & Triandis, H. 1971. The culture assimilator: An approach to cross-cultural training. *Journal of Applied Psychology*, 55: 95–102.
24. Fontaine, G. 1996. Social support and the challenges of international assignments. In D. Landis & R. S. Bhagat (Eds.), op. cit.: 264–281.
25. Spector, P. E. 1998. A control theory of the job stress process. In Cooper (Ed.), op. cit.: 153–169.
26. Sanchez, J. I., & Brock, P. 1996. Outcomes of perceived discrimination among Hispanic employees: Is diversity management a luxury or a necessity? *Academy of Management Journal*, 39: 704–719.
27. Spector, P. E. 1982. Behavior in organizations as a function of employee locus of control. *Psychological Bulletin*, 91: 482–497.
28. Sanchez, J. I., & Fernandez, D. M. 1993. Acculturative stress among Hispanics: A bidimensional model of ethnic identity. *Journal of Applied Social Psychology*, 23: 654–668.
29. Black, J. S., Gregersen, H. B., Mendenhall, M. E., & Stroh, L. K., op. cit.
30. Shupe & McGrath, op. cit.

31. Ricks, D. A. 1993. *Blunders in international business*. Cambridge, MA: Blackwell.

32. Schell & Solomon, op. cit., 7.

33. Osland, J. S., & Bird, A. 2000. Beyond sophisticated stereotyping: Cultural sensemaking in context. *The Academy of Management Executive*, 14(1): 65–77.

34. Bhagat, R. S., O'Driscoll, M. P., Babakus, E., Frey, L., Chokkar, J., Ninokumar, H., Pate, L. E., Ryder, P. A., Fernandez, M. J. G., Ford, D. L., & Mahanyele, M. 1994. Organizational stress and coping in seven national contexts: A cross-cultural investigation. In G. P. Keita and J. J. Hurrell, Jr. (Eds.). *Job stress in a changing workforce*. 93–105. Washington, DC: American Psychological Association.

35. Spector, P. E., Cooper, C. L., Sanchez, J. I., et al. 1999. A twenty-four nation study of work locus of control, well-being, and individualism: How generalizable are western work findings? Manuscript submitted for publication.

36. Quick, J. C., Nelson, D. L., & Quick, J. D. 1990. *Stress and challenge at the top. The paradox of the successful executive*. Chichester, U.K.: John Wiley.

37. Viswesvaran, C., Sanchez, J. I., & Fisher, J. 1999. The role of social support in the process of work stress: A meta-analysis. *Journal of Vocational Behavior*, 54: 314–334.

38. Adler, N. J. 1997. *International dimensions of organizational behavior*. Cincinnati, OH: South-Western.

39. Osland, op. cit., 118.

40. Saner, R., Yiu, L., & Sondergaard, M. 2000. Business diplomacy management: A core competency for global companies. *The Academy of Management Executive*, 14(1): 80–92.

41. Osland & Bird, op. cit.

42. Keally, D. J. 1996. The challenge of international personnel selection. In Landis & Bhagat (Eds.), op. cit., 81–105.

43. Anderzen & Arnet, op. cit.

44. Osland, J. S. 1995. *The adventure of working abroad*. San Francisco: Jossey-Bass.

45. Black & Gregersen, op. cit., 60.

46. Osland, op. cit., 171.

47. Martin, J. N., & Harrell, T. 1996. Reentry training for intercultural sojourners. In D. Landis & R. S. Bhagat (Eds.), op. cit.: 307–323.

48. *Sunday Telegraph*. Home truths await the returning executive. November 21, 1999.

49. Solomon, C. M. 1994. Success abroad depends on more than job skills. *Personnel Journal*, April: 51–60.

50. Black, et al., op. cit.

PART 3

HARVARD BUSINESS
SCHOOL CASES

Thomson Business & Professional Publishing is an authorized distributor of **Harvard Business School Publishing case studies** and, **Harvard Business Review article reprints**. This unique opportunity offers:

Convenience for You: Work with one source instead of multiple vendors, allowing your local Thomson representative to manage the prompt delivery of your teaching resources and student materials.

Convenience for Your Students: Students get everything they need in one afford-able package on the bookstore shelf-with less hassle for them and less concern for you that they get everything they need.

Affordable Resources: We are able to provide printed articles and cases at very affordable and competitive prices. If you package your coursepack with a Thomson textbook, you can be assured you are providing your students the best possible price. To learn more, contact your Thomson representative.

Access to our Business & Company Resource Center (BCRC): A complete business library at your fingertips, BCRC is an online business research tool that allows students to search thousands of periodicals, journals, references, financial infor-mation, industry reports, company histories and more. To learn more visit: http://bcrc.swlearning.com

If you are interested in ordering or learning more about Harvard Business School Publishing cases and articles–including those recommended in the case map pro-vided with this text—please contact your local Thomson sales representative.

Title/Info Link	Type	Length	Pub Date	Description
Best Buy Co., Inc. (A): An Innovator's Journey http://www.hbsp. harvard. edu/b02/ en/common/ item_detail.jhtml? id = 604043	Case	19 pp.	09/04/03	The CEO of Best Buy, a hugely successful retailing company, has hired consulting firm Strategos to imbue the company with an improved innovative capability. The six-month program of experimental learning yields new business ideas and also trains Best Buy employees as innovation coaches. However, this kind of learning is expensive and time consuming. Details the learning journey as experienced by Best Buy employees and raises the question of when such development programs are appropriate. Focuses on the learning process and stimulates debate about how people and organizations learn in general, as well as how an innovation capability can be fostered. Teaching Purpose: To address innovation from the perspective of senior management and to discuss various approaches toward creating and integrating a sustainable innovation capability within a large organization. Also, to highlight this kind of experiential learning.
Homestead Technologies: A Start-Up Built to Last http://www.hbsp. harvard.edu/b02/ en/common/ item_detail.jhtml? id = HR18	Case	19 pp.	01/31/01	Justin Kitch, CEO and co-founder of Homestead Technologies, an Internet communications company that offers a comprehensive resource for building web sites to individuals and businesses, wondered, in the midst of the dotcom boom in 2000, just how tight the connection was between building a company with a strong culture and high performance. Homestead Technologies' history, business model, competitive environment, culture, information-sharing procedures, and human resources management are described. Kitch asks whether companies built with a short-term mentality could create lasting value for customers, employees, and shareholders and wonders whether companies and their employees owe something to their surrounding communities. Although personally committed to to building an enduring organization that contributes to its employees as well as shareholders, Kitch asks whether this approach offers any long-term advantages over that of entrepreneurs who simply wanted to flip their companies. Teaching Purpose: To engage students in a discussion about whether companies built with a short-term mentality can create lasting value for customers, employees, and shareholders, or whether a company focused on building an enduring organization offers long-term advantages over "burgers"—companies built to flip.

Title/Info Link	Type	Length	Pub Date	Description
BRAC http://www.hbsp. harvard.edu/b02/ en/common/ item_detail.jhtml? id = 504012	Case	27 pp.	08/05/03	BRAC is the world's largest NGO and has over the past 20 years experienced tremendous rates of growth. The case looks at the diversity within the organization and the aspects of management that have made the organization so successful. Teaching Purpose: To discuss nonprofit management and managing growth and diversity.
General Mills and the Hawthorne Huddle http://www.hbsp. harvard.edu/b02/ en/common/ item_detail.jhtml? id = 303067	Case	21pp.	01/24/03	Examines the role of General Mills in the formation and leadership of the Hawthorne Huddle. The Huddle was in the Hawthorne neighborhood in Northern Minneapolis, which in 1997 was plagued with high crime and poverty. The Huddle served as a forum, held the first Thursday of every month. Its goal was to improve the livability of the Hawthorne neighborhood by pooling the resources, experiences, and perspectives of residents, educators, law enforcement, business and social service professionals, elected officials, and members of the faith community. It discussed, and focused on solving, problems affecting the community. In late 2002, it faced the retirement of its leader, Reatha King, former president and now chair of the General Mills Foundation, who was revered throughout the community. General Mills and the Huddle were focused on developing a transition plan and new leadership model for the Huddle. Teaching Purpose: To examine a corporation's role in community development and the critical need for leadership.

CHAPTER 3

Title/Info Link	Type	Length	Pub Date	Description
Lockheed Martin: The Employer of Choice Mission http://www.hbsp. harvard.edu/b02/ en/common/ item_detail.jhtml? id = 300032	Case	23 pp.	03/09/00	A Lockheed Martin manager is faced with the decision of where to focus the organization's resources in order to develop a world-class employee development system. The manager's recommendation will serve as the basis for the company's goal of becoming an Employer of Choice in the minds of its current and prospective employees. Compounding the difficulty of his decision is the pressure from the current financial, operational, and cultural challenges facing the business. With the defense industry becoming more cost competitive and contracts being awarded to non-traditional defense industry suppliers, Lockheed Martin is faced with a need to reduce its cost structure while developing employee talent and future leaders who can adapt quickly to change andeffectively lead in this new environment.

continued

Title/Info Link	Type	Length	Pub Date	Description
Siemen's Medical Solutions: Strategic Strategic Turnaround http://www.hbsp.harvard.edu/b01/en/common/item_detail.jhtml?id=703494	Case	18 pp.	06/24/03	Describes how Siemens Medical Solutions (MED) accomplished a remarkable turnaround from a money-losing operation to one of Siemens' most profitable divisions. By late 1966, a challenging market environment in the health-care industry as well as inefficiencies in the company's manufacturing, logistics, and sales/service processes had a negative impact on MED's profitability. Reacting to these challenges, CEO Reinhardt defined and implemented a comprehensive turnaround program centered around people, processes, and products. The case highlights the most important aspects of the company's turnaround and the following expansion and provides an outlook for the company's future challenges and opportunities. Teaching Purpose: To discuss how to accomplish a comprehensive turnaround of a large-scale global company.

CHAPTER 4

Title/Info Link	Type	Length	Pub Date	Description
Cirque du Soleil http://www.hbsp.harvard.edu/b02/en/common/item_detail.jhtml?id = 403006	Case	12 pp.	07/18/02	Cirque du Soleil must make strategic decisions regarding its artists (internal) and its strategy (external). How does Cirque du Soleil remain effective at attracting, retaining, and developing its people? Teaching Purpose: To highlight importance of seeing employees as customers.
Strategic Review at Egon Zehnder International http://www.hbsp.harvard.edu/b01/en/includes/search/search_results.jhtml?_requestid=12665	Case	23 pp.	08/02/04	Describes the history of the executive search firm Egon Zehnder International (EZI) from its inception through 2000. Internal and environmental changes lead EZI leaders to question whether the firm might be at an inflection point in its history. The EZI executive committee contemplates whether and how to engage in a strategy review process. Teaching Purpose: To illustrate how the leadership of a professional services firm can use an intensive strategy review process to build a shared understanding of firm values, market opportunities, changes in strategic direction, and employment of firm resources.

Title/Info Link	Type	Length	Pub Date	Description
Developing Professionals: The BCG Way (A) http://www.hbsp. harvard.edu/b02/ en/common/ item_detail.jhtml? id = 903113	Case	23 pp.	04/07/03	Provides a brief history of Boston Consulting Group (BCG) and the firm's approach to development and mentorship of its consultants and discusses the challenges facing three consultants who are nearing the two-year mark in working at BCG. Teaching Purpose: Provides a platform to discuss career development and mentorship in professional services firms in general and BCG's approach in particular.
De La Salle Academy http://www.hbsp. harvard.edu/b02/ en/common/ item_detail.jhtml? id = 404024	Case	14 pp.	07/21/03	Brother Brian Carty, headmaster and founder of De La Salle Academy, a private school for academically talented, economically disadvantaged children in grades six to eight in New York City, is scheduled to meet with the school's board of directors to discuss how the school and its education concept can be extended to more children. Over 750 children apply each year for the 50 spaces at De La Salle, and most of these have few other options if rejected but to enroll in the New York Public School system. The school relies on the financial support of the local community and charitable foundations to cover operating expenses, as most of the students are unable to pay the tuition of approximately $9,000 a year to attend the school. Not only do the school's graduates go on to elite preparatory and independent schools in the Northeast, but they also attend some of the most well-regarded colleges in the country, including Brown, Harvard, Stanford, and Yale. The case explores the school community and challenges students to consider why this organization has been so successful. Also challenges the reader to consider whether the concept can be duplicated elsewhere and, if so, how. Asks students to consider the degree to which Brother Brian is central to the community, and what action, if any, is needed to plan for his successor. Teaching Purpose: To think about corporate responsibility, replication of an organizational concept, and succession planning.

Title/Info Link	Type	Length	Pub Date	Description
Midwest Office Products http://www.hbsp. harvard.edu/b02/ en/common/ item_detail.jhtml? id = 104073	Case	4 pp.	03/02/04	Presents an easy introduction to time-driven activity-based costing (ABC) that allows students to build a simple ABC model of order profitability. Midwest's time-driven ABC approach is based on two categories of parameter estimates. The first is the cost per hour of employees performing diverse tasks, such as order-entry operators and delivery personnel performing desktop deliveries. The second is the estimated time required for employees to perform each type of task (manual vs. electronic orders, nearby vs. distant deliveries). Students apply the time-driven ABC model to five representative orders to estimate order profitability based on a far more accurate portrayal of the cost of processing and delivering orders. Stimulates a discussion about the actions, such as pricing and process improvements, to enhance the profitability of orders and also how to report and manage the cost of unused capacity. A rewritten version of an earlier case.
Offshoring at Global Information Systems, Inc. http://www.hbsp. harvard.edu/b02/ en/common/ item_detail.jhtml? id = 204144	Case	19 pp.	04/03/04	Presents an opportunity to explore the topic of offshoring high-tech jobs from several perspectives. Issues include: determining the stock price consequences of offshoring; examining the economic consequences of the offshore job to both the transferring and receiving countries; considering the competitive consequences of not offshoring; and thinking through the challenge of investing in a career that is vulnerable to future offshoring. Teaching Purpose: To shed light on the issues.

Title/Info Link	Type	Length	Pub Date	Description
Lonestar http://www.hbsp.harvard.edu/b02/en/common/item_detail.jhtml?id = 902006	Case	4 pp.	11/15/01	Explores the legal and ethical responsibilities of a manager who believes that he has heard of a serious instance of sexual harassment, but who has been implored by the victim not to report it. Discussion can focus on the immediate problem or be expanded to a broader analysis of the difficult choices involved in crafting organizational policies governing conduct, as well as effective procedures for reviewing apparent infractions.
Women and Power: Stories from Around the Globe http://www.hbsp.harvard.edu/b02/en/common/item_detail.jhtml?id=902203	Case	14 pp.	3/5/02	Uses vignettes and statistics of the broader issue discussed in each vignette to explore some of the ways in which gender is played out in the struggle for power and control. Disenfranchised groups—those not allowed access to critical resources—have little access to power. In many countries, women represent one of these disenfranchised groups. Women around the world are disproportionately denied access to employment, education, religious freedoms, many traditional routes to business funding, collective action, and social welfare. The vignettes explore ways in which inroads to equality are being made on new, innovative paths. Even mainstream approaches to accessing critical resources are becoming more gender neutral. The vignettes and statistics are meant to be illustrative rather than exhaustive. Teaching Purpose: To foster discussion of factors that lead to changes in the distributions of powers, rights, and resources across society.

CHAPTER 8

Title/Info Link	Type	Length	Pub Date	Description
SG Cowen: New Recruits http://www.hbsp.harvard.edu/b02/en/common/item_detail.jhtml?id = 402028	Case	15 pp.	5/13/02	Introduces the complexity of recruiting in professional services firms. Chip Rae must decide which recruits to keep after the final interview process. Asks managers and organizations fundamental questions about how they decide and the criteria used to make hiring decisions. Teaching Purpose: To teach the basics of recruiting processes and creating an excellent recruiting system.
JetBlue Airways: Starting From Scratch http://www.hbsp.harvard.edu/b02/en/common/item_detail.jhtml?id = 801354	Case	20 pp.	2/10/01	JetBlue Airways shows how an entrepreneurial venture can use human resource management, specifically a values-centered approach to managing people, as a source of competitive advantage. The major challenge faced by Ann Rhoades is to grow this people-centered organization at a rapid rate, while retaining high standards for employee selection and a small company culture. Teaching Purpose:To consider the role of human resource management, leadership, and values in a start-up venture, and to address the tension between a strong organizational culture and rapid growth.

Title/Info Link	Type	Length	Pub Date	Description
The Federal Reserve Bank of Chicago's Mentoring Program (A) http://www.hbsp. harvard.edu/b02/ en/common/ item_detail.jhtml? id = 403019	Case	15 pp.	7/19/02	Describes steps taken to implement and manage a successful employee mentoring program at the Federal Reserve Bank of Chicago. Begins by describing a cultural change at the bank that provided the context out of which the program grew. Goes on to describe the development of the program, highlighting design principles key to the program's success and its implementation and initial results after nine months. Program manager Amy Rubinstein and executive sponsor Jack Wixted considered how to expand the successful program to include more employees while maintaining the key aspects that contributed to the program's success. Teaching Purpose: 1) To demonstrate implementation of an effective human resources department program and 2) to demonstrate the key design principles in a successful mentoring initiative.
Microsoft's Vega Project: Developing People and Products http://www.hbsp. harvard.edu/b02/ en/common/ item_detail.jhtml? id = 300004	Case	19 pp.	3/27/00	Describes Microsoft's human resource philosophies and policies and illustrates how they work in practice to provide the company with a major source of competitive advantage. Summarizes the evolution of Microsoft's human resource philosophies and policies. Describes employee development, motivation, and retention efforts in one of Microsoft's product groups. Focuses on Matt MacLellan, a 26-year-old, 5-year Microsoft veteran, particularly on his careful development as a project manager under Jim Kaplan, his boss and mentor. Dissatisfied with his project management role, MacLellan decides to become a developer despite the fact that he had never written code professionally. Kaplan is faced with a difficult decision of whether to support his protege's radical career shift, and how to do it not only to MacLellan's satisfaction but also in the organization's best interest. Teaching Purpose: To illustrate the role of senior management as developer and coach of scarce human assets and the role of human resource policy in supporting an organization's development of competitive advantage. (A decision-oriented implementation case).

Title/Info Link	Type	Length	Pub Date	Description
The Firmwide 360-degree Performance Evaluation Process at Morgan Stanley http://www.hbsp. harvard.edu/b02/en/ common/item_detail. jhtml?id = 498053	Case	16 pp.	2/13/98	Describes Morgan Stanley's firmwide, 360-degree performance evaluation process. Evaluation forms are included as exhibits. Teaching Purpose: To introduce students to a 360-degree performance evaluation process.
AvantGo http://www.hbsp. harvard.edu/b01/ en/includes/search/ search_results.jhtml? _requestid=12604	Case	19 pp.	11/7/01	Richard Owen, CEO of AvantGo, is preparing for a meeting in which he will set the human resource policy for the firm going forward. It has been three months since the company's IPO, and given the tremendous cramp in hiring over the six months prior to the IPO, he knows that this meeting will set the expectations for the many annual evaluations that will follow. Uppermost in his mind is the decision over whether to implement a "forced-curve" grading scheme, and the implications of this decision on staff perceptions and notification. Teaching Purpose: To illustrate the challenges of a rapidly growing new technology venture, specifically with regard to the hiring, retention, and firing of new employees. Also examines the process of building a senior management team, including the decision of when to replace a CEO, how to do it, and with whom.

Title/Info Link	Type	Length	Pub Date	Description
The Excel Charter Academy Middle School http://www.hbsp. harvard.edu/b02/ en/common/item_ detail.jhtml?id = 804113	Case	24 pp.	1/5/04	This case is set in the summer of 2002 in a recently approved charter middle school in Boston. The school's founders face a choice of compensation plans as they finalize the initial teaching team in the school. In particular, the founders are actively considering two performance-based compensation plans as alternatives to the standard salary structure of public schools. These schemes vary in the degree to which they reward individual and school-wide performance, and both are controversial in principle and in practice. The protagonists' consideration of the topics range from specific implementation concerns about how to specify and gather performance data on teaching to the most general of inquiries about the nature of excellent teaching and teachers. Rich in biographical data on the schools' founders and on their educational and managerial philosophies. Exhibits include benchmarking data on performance compensation plans in selected charter schools in the northeast. Exhibits also profile compensation and promotion provisions in the Boston Public Schools. Teaching Purpose: To debate the merits of various compensation alternatives in public schools. To investigate the nature of high-performing school teams of teachers, an inquiry that involves consideration of, among other topics, how teachers learn and the nature of teaching.
The Ottawa Voyaguers http://www.hbsp. harvard.edu/b02/ en/common/item_ detail.jhtml?id = 404023	Case	12 pp.	7/23/03	Manuel Tertuliano, head coach of a professional soccer club, must make some difficult decisions about the compensation of six of his players. Specifically, he must decide how to allocate $850,000 among these six players in a way that will benefit his team, which has just finished second to last in the league and faces being eliminated from the league if team performance and game attendance don't improve. Tertuliano realizes that compensation is a key tool in motivating his players. In deciding on these six players' compensation, Tertuliano must ensure that he not only recognizes them, but also the other players on the team for the value each individual contributes to the team. Teaching Purpose: To consider the challenges in making compensation decisions.

CHAPTER 12

Title/Info Link	Type	Length	Pub Date	Description
Alaska Airlines and Flight 261 http://www.hbsp.harvard.edu/b02/en/common/item_detail.jhtml?id = 801113	Case	16 pp.	11/9/04	Weeks after the crash of Alaska Airlines Flight 261, 64 mechanics claim that they have been "pressured, threatened, and intimidated" into taking shortcuts. After briefly describing Alaska Airlines' history and CEO John Kelly, the case details how the airline responded to the crash and the resulting investigations. Also describes labor relations between management and its largest unions. At the end of the case CEO Kelly prepares for a news conference to respond to the mechanics allegations. Teaching Purpose: To address crisis management, corporate diplomacy diplomacy, labor relations, public relations, and transportation safety.
Cable Data Systems http://www.hbsp.harvard.edu/b02/en/common/item_detail.jhtml?id = 803132	Case	29 pp.	2/19/03	Describes the operating challenges of Cable Data Systems (CDS), a minority-owned cable installation company with a dual mission of maximizing profits and providing employment opportunities to minorities in urban markets. Following the merger of two cable installation companies in the Boston metro area, management at the combined entity (CDS) forecasts strong growth for its services. Accordingly, they build out the workforce and support infrastructure. But the company begins to lose cash in light of volatile customer demand and high labor costs. The latter is exacerbated by deteriorating and unresolved union issues. Examines the choices the CEO has to increase revenue and reduce labor costs. The decision is further complicated by outstanding issues with the previous owner, who has remained employed by the new company.

Title/Info Link	Type	Length	Pub Date	Description
Leaving http://www.hbsp.harvard.edu/b02/en/common/item_detail.jhtml?id = 400033	Case	1 pg.	8/6/99	A company supervisor listens to an employee, an African American woman, announce she is leaving the company and tries to understand the situation. Teaching Purpose: To assist managers/students in understanding the link between supervisor behavior, diversity, and employee retention.
Bradley Marquez: Reductions in Force http://www.hbsp.harvard.edu/b02/en/common/item_detail.jhtml?id = 403005	Case	8 pp.	7/15/02	Alberto Marquez has to make a decision how to initiate layoffs. He must struggle with how to achieve his numbers to please stockholders and also be loyal to his employees. There are a number of crucial decisions he must make moving forward. Teaching Purpose: To teach skills necessary to ensure a professional and ethical reduction in force.

CHAPTER 14

Title/Info Link	Type	Length	Pub Date	Description
Trend Micro (A) http://www.hbsp.harvard.edu/b02/en/common/item_detail.jhtml?id = 303065	Case	27 pp.	3/24/03	The founder and CEO of Trend Micro is seeking to develop an effective decision-making process for the company's multicultural executive team as part of his effort to develop a more cohesive and focused global organization. This case describes the company's growth and development, including the efforts made to develop an approach to decision making that melds the best of eastern and western cultures. Teaching Purpose: To explore approaches to decision making by a multicultural executive team.
Civil Service Pay in Hong Kong: Policies, System, Structure and Reform http://www.hbsp.harvard.edu/b02/en/common/item_detail.jhtml?id = HKU219	Case	21 pp.	8/12/02	In 2002, Hong Kong civil servants were the envy of many people. Their salaries, fringe benefits, and employment terms compared favorably with international standards. However, as civil servants staggered from one disaster and mistake to another, the public had an impression that their performance did not match their liberal remuneration. While private sectors were announcing massive layoffs, pay cuts, and reduced benefits in the sluggish economy, the Hong Kong government was under pressure to reduce civil service pay, and at the same time, to increase public accountability and improve performance. Teaching Purpose: To help students understand and appreciate the difficulty of establishing a civil service system that links pay to performance.

SUBJECT INDEX

E

e-HR, 51–52
Employee compensation. *See* Compensation
Employee performance evaluation. *See* Feedback sources
Employee performance incentives
"Super-measure" strategy, 472–481
Employee satisfaction, 94–102
age and, 95–96
company size and, 97
factors shared by most groups, 99
gender and, 96
immigration and, 97
security and, 100–101
Employee separation. *See* Separation (employee)
Employee skills, marketability of, 11
Employee stock ownership plans
at United Airlines, 527
Employee training. *See* Training (employee)
Employee value, sources of (exhibit), 4
Employment discrimination, 299–305. *See also* Employment law; Equal Employment Opportunity Commission (EEOC)
age-based, 301, 603–604
gender-based, 299–300
race-based, 301
under Title VII, 300–301
Employment law, 298, 315. *See also* Americans With Disabilities Act of 1990 (ADA); Equal Employment Opportunity Commission (EEOC); Sexual harassment
affirmative action, 309–310
enforcement under the EEOC, 305–308
executive orders, 308–309
federal antidiscrimination laws, 299–305
insurance and litigation trends (exhibit), 552
National Labor Relations Act (NLRA), 531–536 *See also* Unions
scope of laws, 298–299
sexual harassment, 310–314
workplace regulation compliance, 555–557
Employment litigation trends (exhibit), 551
Employment models, Lepak and Snell's (exhibit), 162
Employment practices compliance system (EPCS)
implementation of, 553–558
Employment practices liability insurance, 552–553
Equal Employment Opportunity Commission (EEOC), 297, 300–301, 305–308. *See also* Employment law
complaint process (exhibit), 306
strategic plan of, 308
voluntary mediation program, 308
Equal Pay Act, 299–300
Ethics, 53–54
Evaluation tools (employee performance). *See* Feedback sources, rating scales
Executive compensation
research in, 516–521
role of firm strategy in, 517–521
Executive search services, 351–352

F

Family and Medical Leave Act of 1992 (FMLA), 304–305. *See also* Employment law
Feedback sources (employee performance)
360-degree (multirater) systems, 448–449, 463–470
rating scales, 454–458
self-evaluation, 448
traditional, 447–448
Financial services industry
comparative employment practices within, 136–138
Firm performance
linkage to HRM practices, 184–187
Food and beverage industry
comparative employment practices in, 139–140
Fraud, reporting of, 82–87

G

Gender discrimination. *See* Employment discrimination
Global staffing systems
at Agilent Technologies, 390–391
design and implementation of, 390–400
at Dow Chemical, 392–394
at IBM
obstacles and benefits to, 400
at Proctor and Gamble, 397–398
at Shell Oil, 398–399
Government organizations
leadership development, 415–422
Griggs v. Duke Power (1971), 323

H

High performers
strategies for retention, 579–585
Hiring. *See also* Selection (from applicant pool)
for person-organization fit, 364–375
Human assets
characteristics of, 162–163
real value of, 20
understanding and measuring, 8–10
Human assets, characteristics of, 162–163
Human resource management system
strength of, 187–197
Human resource planning, 207–220
aggregate planning, 212–215
objectives of, 210–212
strategic and proactive, 244–248
succession planning, 215–219
Human resource practices
common misconceptions, 21–29
possible roles assumed (exhibit), 159
strategic *vs.* traditional focus, 159–166
Human resource value chain (exhibit), 8
Human resources, strategic reorganization of, 168–171. *See also* Outsourcing

Human resources culture. *See* Human resources philosophy
Human resources philosophy, 146–147

I

Industrial organization (I/O) model. *See* Strategic models
Intercultural effectiveness (exhibit), 418
International assignments
employee dissatisfaction, 380–388
Internet recruiting, 348, 349
Interviewing, 354–356
Investment orientation, degree of, 10–13
Investment perspective of human resource management, 5–6, 10–13

J

Job characteristics model (exhibit), 255
Job enrichment, 254
Job interfacing, 257
Job rotation, 253–254
Job satisfaction, 94–102

K

Knowledge management, 174–177
Kolstad v. ADA (1999), 555

L

Labor law. *See* Employment law
Labor relations
collective bargaining, 533–535
employment practices compliance, 553–558
failure of collective bargaining
mediation or arbitration, 536
strikes, 535–536
NLRB rulings under Bush appointments, 541–548
nontraditional strategies, 561, 562–563
organizing campaigns, 532–533
political appointments to NLRB, 541
types of bargaining items (exhibit), 534

union-management
cooperation
at Hathaway Shirt Co.,
559–560
Layoffs
Layoffs (RIF), 566–569
at Kodak, 568
strategies for avoiding
(exhibit), 568
Leadership development
international aspects,
415–422
Learning organizations. *See*
Organizational learning

M

Management training. *See*
Training (employee)
Management turnover rates
in overseas assignments,
378–388
Mergers and aquisitions,
human resource role in,
261–262
Meritor Savings Bank v.
Vinson, 310
Multirater feedback systems
(360-degree), 463–470.
See also Feedback sources
Murphy v. United Parcel Service,
Inc., 320

N

NASA leadership model
(exhibit), 416
National Labor Relations Act
(NLRA), 531–532,
531–536. See also Unions,
Employment law
National Labor Relations
Board (NLRB), 531–532
political appointments
to, 541
recent rulings
corporate campaigns,
548
discrimination, 545–546
employee free
choice, 541
employee involvement,
546
organizers' access to
property, 546–547
representation for
nonunion
employees, 544–545
secondary activity, 545
solicitation, 547–548
temporary employees,
543–544

withdrawal of
recogniton, 545
Noncompete clauses, 53

O

Offshoring, 260–261
Older workers, 575. *See also*
Diversity, generational
retirement of, 598–604
and training performance,
602
Oncale v. Sundowner Offshore
Services, Inc., 310
Organizational assets/capital
(exhibit), 7
Organizational culture,
201–206
defining and evaluating,
201, 204
poorly defined or
disfunctional, 205–206
in a software firm, 204–205
in a utility, 202–203
Organizational learning,
174–181
knowledge management in,
174–177
Organized Labor. *See* Unions,
Labor Relations
Outsourcing, 258–260,
277–287. *See also* Human
resources, strategic
reorganization of
by government, 259
of human resource
functions, 279–280,
281–282
guidelines for
(exhibit), 284
offshoring, 260–261
Outsourcing, availability of, 12

P

Package shipping industry
comparative employment
practices, 138–139
Parker, Horace
Pay systems. *See* Compensation
Performance assessments and
appraisals. *See* Feedback
sources (employee
performance)
Performance management
and downsizing, 289–293
failures and shortcomings
of, 458–460
feedback sources, 447–449
impact upon training
and development
(exhibit), 446

purposes of, 445–446
relationship with training
and development
(exhibit), 446
strategic choices in,
445–446, 458–461
"Super-measure" strategy,
472–481
timeline for (exhibit), 444
Person-organization fit (hiring
model), 365–375
benefits and problems from,
372–374
hiring process for
(exhibit), 366
steps in hiring process,
366–372
Philosophy, human
resources, 146
Planning, aggregate. *See*
Aggregate planning
Planning, succession, 215–218
Pregnancy Discrimination Act
of 1978, 302
Professional football (NFL)
comparative employment
practices in, 133–134
Promotion (employee)
from within, 39

R

Racial discrimination. *See*
Employment
discrimination.
Racial preference. *See*
Affirmative action
Recruiting, 344–353. *See also*
under Staffing
Recruiting methods, 348–353
executive search services,
351–352
Internet recruiting, 348, 349
on-campus recruiting,
352–353
staffing services, 350
Recruiting pyramid
(exhibit), 347
Reductions in the workforce
(RIF). *See* Downsizing
(employment); Layoffs
Regulations, workplace. *See*
Workplace regulation
compliance
Rehabilitation Act of 1973, 301
Religious discrimination. *See*
Employment
discrimination.
Resource-based view (RBV),
117–128. *See also* Strategic
models

Restructuring, responsible
defined, 590
downsizing strategies for,
592–594
international aspects,
588–589
strategies for, 586–595
at Charles Schwab &
Co., 592
at Cisco Systems,
Accenture, and
Motorola, 592–593
at Philips Electronics
Singapore, 593–594
suggestions for, 594–595
ten mistakes to avoid,
590–591
Retailing industry
comparative employment
practices within, 134–135
Retention (employee). *See*
Separation (employee)
Retirement, 574–576
of older workers, 598–606
strategic policy implications,
604–606
Retirement age
mandatory *vs.* flexible
598–604
Reward systems
strategic, 525–526
Risk, attitude toward, 11
Roberts v. County of Fairfax
(1996), 322
Rose v. Home Depot USA, Inc
(2002), 322

S

Salaries. *See* Compensation
Sarbanes-Oxley Act of 2002,
54, 82–89
policy changes required by,
89–90
and whistleblower
protections, 85–86
Screening. *See* Selection (from
applicant pool)
Selection (from applicant
pool), 353–359. *See also*
under Staffing new model
for, 364–375 (*See also*
under Hiring)
Self-evaluations. *See* Feedback
sources.
Self-managed teams, 36–37
Separation (employee)
international turnover,
378–388
layoffs (RIF), 566–569
retirement, 574–576

NAME INDEX

A

Agarwal, Naresh C., 516–521, 598–606
Alexander, Steve, 72
Alvares, Ken, 223
Anthony, W. P., 456
Argote, L., 117, 126
Argyris, C., 126
Arthur, J. B., 122, 184, 192
Arthur, M. M., 184
Ashforth, B. E., 186, 196
Ashkenas, R., 239, 243
Atwater, Leanne E., 463–470
Avolio, B. J., 600, 601

B

Bailey, Diane, 72
Baill, B., 251
Bain & Co., 586
Bales, R., 330
Balkin, D. B., 435, 439
Ballantyne, D., 247
Barnard, C. I., 189
Barney, J., 118, 122, 125, 128
Barney, J. B., 180, 184
Baron, J. N., 119
Barth, M. C., 602
Bartol, Kathryn M., 570–571
Bassi, L. J., 436
Bateson, G., 175

Beck, Robert, 36
Becker, B., 192, 196
Becker, B. E., 120, 122, 184, 185
Becker, Brian, 236
Becker, Gary, 436
Belkhodja, A., 602
Bem, D. J., 195
Bennett, N., 196
Berkson, H. M., 184
Berman, B., 240
Bethune, Gordon, 450, 472
Bierman, L., 124
Bingham, Charles, 149
Block, Peter, 272
Borucki, C. C., 186
Boswell, W., 120
Bowen, David E., 184–197, 186, 193, 364–375, 639–657
Boxall, P., 186
Boxall, P. F., 119, 121, 122
Bretz, R. D., 193
Brief, A. P., 186
Brockbank, Wayne, 236–248
Brower, Dana, 415–422
Brown, J. S., 126
Brown, Kenneth G., 21–29, 423–433
Brown, Wilfred, 604
Burack, Elmer, 451, 605
Burke, M. J., 186

Butler, J. E., 118
Bynham, William, 223

C

Cacioppo, J. T., 190
Cappelli, Peter, 118, 128, 132–143
Caproni, Paula, 73
Caray, R. L., 439
Cardy, R. L., 435
Carroll, Stephen J., 497
Cascio, W., 240
Cascio, W. R., 600
Cascio, Wayne F., 69, 71, 76, 586–595
Castro, Ida, 297
Cespedes, F., 246, 247
Chadwick, C., 128
Chaiken, S., 188, 190
Champagne, Paul J., 318–324
Charness, N., 602
Chatman, J. A., 195
Chaykowski, R., 600
Christopher, M., 247
Chuang, Alfred, 18
Cisco Systems, 592
Clark, M., 247
Clemente, M. N., 245
Colbert, Amy E., 21–29
Conference Board, 126
Conner, K. R., 125

Cool, K., 120, 175
Cooper, Gary L., 511, 659–668
Cosier, R. A., 601
Cotter, J. F., 245
Cox, Jr., T., 237
Crocker-Hefter, Anne, 132–143
Cropanzano, R., 193
Crowl, David, 642
Crown, W. H., 600

D

Dalton, D. R., 601
Dammerman, Dennis D., 227
Daniels, John D., 378–388
Davidson, E. J., 195
DeGroote, Michael G., 598–606
Delaney, J. T., 184
Delbecq, A., 186, 187
Delery, J. E., 123, 184, 187, 192, 196
Delp, N. D., 602
Denison, D. R., 185
Devanna, M. A., 117
Dierickx, Y., 120, 175
Doherty, J. L., 196
Doty, D. H., 184, 187, 192, 196
Doverspike, D., 602
Drazin, R., 187, 194
Drucker, P., 243

COMPANY INDEX

G

Gardner-Denver Co., 325
General Electric (GE), 157, 219, 453, 254
General Mills, 427, 429
General Motors (GM), 169, 242, 629–630, 634
Global Consulting Alliance, 161
Gourmet Awards Foods, 543, 544
Grand Union, 151–154
Great American Savings & Loan Association, 328

H

Harvard Business School, 136
Harvard University Center for Textile Research, 560
Hasbro, Inc., 60–61
Hathaway Shirt Co., 559–560
Healthy Companies International, 418
Hewlett-Packard (HP), 407, 429, 453, 491, 513
Hillhaven Highland House, 546
Home Depot USA, Inc., 322

I

IBM, 45, 303, 475, 488, 631
Intel, 63, 573, 581
International Brotherhood of Electrical Workers, Local 1229, 548
Interstate Warehousing of Ohio, 343
ITT, 242

J

Jamba Juice, 493
JCPenney, 581
Johnson & Johnson, 351, 431
Johnsonville Sausage Co., 268

K

K. Hovanian Enterprises, 216
KaiserPermanente Health Care System, 561
Kellogg Co., 352, 617
Kroger Co., 343

L

Lands' End, 474
Lee Hospital, 543
Levi Strauss, 41
Levitz Furniture Co. of the Pacific, 545
Lincoln Electric, 35, 39
Lincoln Financial, 351

M

Marriott Corp., 476
McDonald's, 610–611
McKinsey & Co., 135–136
Merck and Co., 569, 634–635
Merrill Lynch, 49–50
Microsoft Corp., 353, 453
MicroStrategy, 401
Motorola, Inc., 395–396, 425, 427, 430, 431, 510, 511, 513, 515, 592

N

Naomi Knitting Plant, 546
National Aeronautics and Space Administration (NASA), 415–416
Nike, 609
Nordstrom, 33, 36, 39, 134–135, 475–476, 477, 478, 479
Northern Telecom, 427, 428
NUMMI, 34, 38, 40

O

Oakland Raiders, 133–134

P

Pacific Bell, 506
Pall Corp, 548
Pepsi-Cola International (PCI), 139–141, 145–148
Pepsico, 453
Pet Inc., 514
Phelps Dodge, 504
Philips Broadband Networks, 292
Philips Electronics Singapore, 593–594
Phoenix Fire Dept., 271
Pixion, 557
Polaroid Corp., 546
Praxair Inc., 574
Price Waterhouse, 514
Private Industry Council (PIC), 351
Proctor and Gamble, 397–398, 425, 634

Q

Qsent, 556–557
QUALCOMM, 408
Qualex, Inc., 19–20
Quantum, 251
Qwest Communications, 477

R

Radio Shack, 505
Reebok, 609
Rite Aid, 506

S

Saab, 486
Sabre, Inc., 68–71, 73–79
San Francisco 49ers, 133–134
Sarasota Memorial Hospital, 105
SAS Institute, Inc., 444
Saturn Corp. (Division of General Motors), 426, 486, 561
Schlumberger, 633
Schuster-Zingheim and Associates, Inc., 511
Schwab, Charles & Co., 592
Sears Roebuck Co., 134–135, 228, 569
Service Employees International Union (SEIU), 561
Shell Oil Co., 398–399
Simmons Industries, 546
Social Security Administration (US), 415
Society for Human Resource Management (SHRM), 22, 161, 556
Sonoco, 226
Southwest Airlines, 32–33, 163–164, 476
Sprint PCS, 572
St. Elizabeth Manor, Inc., 542
St. Peter's Health Care, 351
Starbucks, 506
Stoody Co., 546
Sun Microsystems, 223, 453

T

Target Corporation, 428
Texas Instruments, 61, 242
Tompkins Associates, Inc., 513
Toyota Motor Co., 320
TRW Inc., 511, 512, 514

U

Unilever, 241, 242
Union For Needletrades, Industrial and Technical Employees (UNITE!), 559–560, 562
United Airlines, Inc., 319–320, 527, 572
United Auto Workers (UAW), 561, 562
United Food and Commercial Workers, 545
United Parcel Service, 5–6, 138–139, 320

University of Texas Law School, 334–337
UNUM, 224–225, 227
U.S. Customs Service, 415
U.S. Department of Agriculture, 415
U.S. Environmental Protection Agency (EPA), 415
U.S. Food and Drug Administration (FDA), 420
U.S. General Accounting Office (GAO), 416
U.S. Geological Survey (USGS), 415
U.S. Immigration and Naturalization Service (INS), 415
U.S. National Aeronautics and Space Administration (NASA), 415–416
U.S. Office of Personnel Management Federal Executive Institute (FEI), 415, 417
U.S. Postal Service, 210, 224
U.S. State Department Foreign Service Institute (FSI), 420–421
U.S. State Department Overseas Presence Advisory Panel (OPAP), 417
US West, 477
U.S.C. Center for Effective Organizations, 512
USX Corp., 435

V

Vic Koenig Chevrolet, 546
Virgin Atlantic, 474
Visiting Nurse Health System, 545
Vons Grocery, 546

W

Watson Wyatt Worldwide, 510
Webcor Packaging, 546
Wells Fargo Bank, 169
Wharton School, 136
Winn-Dixie Stores, 52–53
Wyndham Palmas Del Mar Resort and Villas, 543

X

Xerox, 427, 428, 431, 485, 486, 491

Z

Zytec, 426